# More Praise for Volume one of *An American Health Dilemma*

In this scholarly work, Doctors Byrd and Clayton have made an enormous contribution to all persons interested in understanding the historical roots and persistent effects of racism in health care.

M. ALFRED HAYNES, M.D.
Past President, Charles R. Drew Postgraduate Medical School

The authors have provided an invaluable service to the medical community by documenting the history of African American health from the beginnings to 1900. This painstakingly careful documentation of our history serves as an important source to dispel myths and "set the record straight." This is a must-read book for anyone involved in the delivery of health care in America and elsewhere. We are all deeply indebted to these two practitioners who have devoted so much of their lives to this much needed work.

JACKIE JENKINS-SCOTT
President and CEO, Dimock Community Health Center

Drs. W. Michael Byrd and Linda A. Clayton have embarked upon a monumental journey. These two outstanding physician-scientist-researchers are about the task of accurately chronicling the experience of the United States of America's African-American population in interaction with this nation's health care delivery system. This volume, the first of two, will not just reflect "problems." Nor will it simply present complaints. Rather these researchers will lay out for all to see the developmental history of African Americans as both recipients of and participants in the health care arena within both the history of the United States and before. Such an effort is long overdue.... These authors are to be commended for their product. It proceeds from their extensive research, their active interest in health policy and their commitment to appropriate health care for all persons. The data which they will provide should enhance the educational experience and knowledge base of us all.

LEONARD E. LAWRENCE, M.D.
The University of Texas Health Science Center at San Antonio

*An American Health Dilemma* is by far the most comprehensive historical and sociocultural analysis ever published on race and the African American medical experience. We are indebted to Drs. Byrd and Clayton for this groundbreaking volume. It is replete with information, covering all aspects of race and the American health care system, and will certainly become a standard and authoritative reference for scholars and laymen alike.

WILLIAM JULIUS WILSON
Lewis P. and Linda L. Geyser University Professor, Harvard University

*An American Health Dilemma* will serve as an authoritative guide and reference for anyone interested in the health of disadvantaged minority and poor populations in our nation. It will be a new standard.... For scholars in every discipline with an interest in the effect 'race' has on western culture, science, and medicine, *An American Health Dilemma* is a must read.

HENRY W. FOSTER, JR., M.D.
Professor Emeritus, Meharry Medical College
Senior Advisor to President Clinton on Teen Pregnancy Reduction and Youth Issues

We are grateful to the Lord and to the authors for this very extensive and carefully researched documentary clearly delineating the Dual Health Care System which impacts and often limits the quality of life for Black Americans. It is carefully researched from primary and historical records. Yet, it is tempered by years of private practice, teaching at two medical colleges, serving in South Africa, and helping the CBC and NMA shape Health Care Reform and found the African-American Health Care Summit.

This book clearly calls us to network throughout the Black Church and Community to be the Lord's channels to bring Healing and Wholeness to the Health Care System, and in turn, to our people and communities. Reading this book lifts the shout of acclamation as we reaffirm that it is only by His Grace and Mercy that we as African-Americans have survived as a people in this land amidst a Dual Health Care System!

> REV. CAROLYN COREY
> Executive Director, Black Churches and Black Colleges Network;
> Board Member & Secretary, National Black Pastors' Conference;
> Ordained Elder AMEZ Church

An *American Health Dilemma* documents for the first time, from medical and public health perspectives, the origins and evolution of race- and class-based health disparities in the United States.... This groundbreaking work will be an invaluable baseline for future exploration and amelioration of racial, ethnic, class, and gender bias in the American health system.... This unique and inordinately well-documented work is a milestone contribution to our national health care literature."

> AUGUSTUS A. WHITE, III, M.D., PH.D.
> Beth Israel Deaconess Medical Center, Boston

Drs. Byrd and Clayton once more provide a brilliant and illuminating analysis documenting the race- and class-based inequities that are endemic to the sociocultural fabric of the United States health system. An *American Health Dilemma Vol. 2* is a "must read" for its groundbreaking exploration and scholarly contribution to the historical analysis of race, medicine and health care in the U.S.

> LUCILLE C. NORVILLE PEREZ, M.D.
> President, National Medical Association

# An American Health Dilemma

## VOLUME II
### Race, Medicine, and Health Care in the United States 1900–2000

W. Michael Byrd, MD, MPH
Linda A. Clayton, MD, MPH

*With a Foreword by Dr. H. Jack Geiger*

Routledge
NEW YORK   LONDON

Published in 2002 by
Routledge
29 West 35th Street
New York, NY 10001

Published in Great Britain by
Routledge
11 New Fetter Lane
London EC4P 4EE

Copyright © 2002 by Routledge
Routledge is an imprint of the Taylor & Francis Group

Printed in the United States of America on acid-free paper.

Credits appear on page 809.

10   9   8   7   6   5   4   3   2   1

**Library of Congress Cataloging-in-Publication Data**

Byrd, W. Michael.
    An American health dilemma : Race, Medicine, and Health Care in the United
    States 1900-2000 and the problem of race / W. Michael Byrd and Linda A. Clayton.
      p.   cm.
  Includes bibliographical references and index.
    ISBN 0–415–92737–4 (v.2 : alk. paper)
    I. Afro-Americans—Health and hygiene—History. 2. Afro-Americans—
  Medical care—History. I. Clayton, Linda A.
  II. Title.

Full cataloging-in-publication data is available from the Library of Congress.

# ⋈ Contents

# )(( *List of Figures and Tables*

**Figures**

**Tables**

# ✕ Foreword

"Slavery is America's original sin," a political analyst once observed, "and racism is its chronic disease." It is a compelling description, and yet insufficient. Dispassionate terms such as chronicity are inadequate to convey the reality of more than three centuries of continuous violations of the American creed of equality—violations expressed, cumulatively, in millions of premature deaths, in uncounted episodes of human suffering both physical and emotional, and in repetitive assaults on human dignity. To think of racism as a disease, similarly, is a useful metaphor, but again, such a metaphor is inadequate to define the reality of a moral outrage that is still, sadly, built into the very fabric of American society. Race and class, deeply confounded from the beginning, have been among the most powerful structural determinants of the American social order.

It should be no surprise, then, that medicine—understood not merely as individual practice but as the vast institutional complex of physicians' offices, medical and dental clinics, hospitals, health insurance companies, medical and other health professional schools—is not immune. The practice of medicine is a treaty with society, a part of the social contract, and it operates on society's terms. If a special poignance attends preventable inequity in health status and discrimination in medical care, it is because these are dual violations, distorting both our social commitments and the ethical obligations of medicine. These are special, and often deadly, manifestations of a larger unfairness. On these grounds alone, they deserve the scrupulously detailed historical research and multidisciplinary analysis that Michael Byrd and Linda Clayton have brought to the task of documenting their origins, their evolution, and their current role in simultaneously reflecting and reinforcing the fundamental and still-unresolved conflict between our professed beliefs and the daily experiences of people of color.

The template for their effort is *An American Dilemma*, the classic 1944 study by Gunnar Myrdal and his colleagues that examined and documented racism in every major dimension of American society and focused on what was then called "the Negro problem" as a moral issue. Now, almost six decades later, it is instructive, and compellingly contemporary, to note what Myrdal said at the outset.

"The very presence of the Negro in America," he wrote, "his fate in this country through slavery, Civil War and Reconstruction; his recent career and his present status; his accomodation; his protest and his aspirations; in fact his entire biological and social existence as a participant American represent to the ordinary white man in the North as well as in the South an anomaly in the very structure of American society," and a "threat to moral integrity." And in observations on "controlling the death rate," Myrdal noted that "area for area, class for class, Negroes cannot get the same advantages in the way of prevention and cure of disease that whites can.... Discrimination increases Negro sickness and death both directly and indirectly and manifests itself both consciously and unconsciously."

Every word is still true today. We are more willing now to recognize that all this is not a "Negro problem"; it is primarily a white problem, a dominant-culture problem, and its effects in what is now a far more diverse society are felt not only by African Americans but also by Hispanics, Native Americans, Asian subgroups and Pacific Islanders, and ironically, as the following pages of this volume frequently attest, by poor and uninsured Whites as well. This is not to deny that there has been great and substantial progress since 1944. But as the historians Philip A. Klinkner and Rogers M. Smith have noted, it has been an unsteady march, with infrequent and relatively short bursts of social and racial change followed by long years of stagnation and regression. That, too, is convincingly documented in this second volume of a massive health-sector study.

Classic public health doctrine holds that the major determinants of the health of every population group lie in the social order: the physical, biological, social, economic and political environments in which its members, in the main, live. We will not finally eliminate the appalling disparities in the health status of African Americans and other people of color in the United States unless and until we have achieved a fundamental transformation of the racial and social class attitudes and policies that have so powerfully structured those environments and thus produced those disparities. Some goals, however, are much more readily achievable: universal health coverage; the elimination of racial and ethnic bias, both overt and unconscious, in the daily processes of health care through monitoring, enforcement of civil rights laws, and most of all through changes in the culture of medical and other health professional practice and education; and appropriate racial and ethnic diversity in the health care workforce.

To do these things will require us to overcome the dominant culture's resistance and its denial of social reality that have always characterized this struggle. In one recent national survey, for example, 58 percent of White respondents said African Americans had the same opportunities in life as Whites, 50 percent said African Americans were just about as well off as the average person in access to health care, and 11 percent said African Americans were better off. The truth — the social reality — is in the pages of this volume. This is a book, above all I hope, for White readers, as well as for health policy makers and health care workers at every level, for legislators and, finally, for patients of every race, ethnic group, and class. Once again, Myrdal had it right; he argued that the problem of racial inequity and discrimination "... is a problem in the heart of the American. It is there that the interracial tension has its focus. It is there that the decisive struggle goes on."

The struggle does, indeed, go on. *An American Health Dilemma* is a powerful and urgently needed contribution to its resolution.

H. Jack Geiger, M.D.
Arthur C. Logan Professor of Community Medicine, Emeritus
City University of New York Medical School

# ✖ Foreword to Volume One

This book represents an extraordinary achievement by the authors, who have brought together in two volumes the history of the African American health experience in the United States and its broader historical perspective.

In particular, *An American Health Dilemma: A Medical History of African Americans and the Problem of Race* documents in the most detailed manner how, from the nation's earliest period, the African American population suffered severely from years of slavery, racial discrimination, segregation of health care facilities, denial of health professional education opportunities and gross underfunding of those opportunities that existed, and neglect of the most elementary health needs of their community. It traces, through successive generations, the major barriers that prevented African Americans from receiving the most basic medical care and public health services, and examines the resulting high rates of death, disability, and human suffering.

Of additional importance, this book is the first to chronicle in such detail the courage, leadership, ingenuity, and scientific and professional skills of generations of individual African American physicians and other health professionals who struggled against great odds to build a responsive health system that would meet the needs of those living in a segregated society, often in great poverty.[1] It also highlights many of the important and heretofore unrecognized contributions made by a diverse group of African American pioneers to the broader world of medical treatment and biomedical science.

This series is of such significance because it seeks to explain and document the historical factors behind today's huge disparities in the level of health between Whites and African Americans.[2] The fact that African Americans today live substantially shorter lives than Whites; die more frequently from cancer, heart disease, stroke, and diabetes; and see their infants die at nearly twice the rate of Whites is in part a result of their unique and tragic historical experience in America. Growing from this, African Americans today also remain less likely than Whites to have health insurance coverage and less likely to be treated by a physician when they are ill.

The need for this book grows from the understanding that these health disparities and their historical antecedents are not well recognized by the majority of Americans, particularly White Americans. In fact, beliefs today are almost the opposite of the reality portrayed in this work. Surveys show that the majority of White Americans believe that discrimination, past and present, is not a major reason for the social and economic problems African Americans face today.[3] They also show that most Whites are not aware that African Americans have a shorter life expectancy, a higher rate of infant mortality, more problems with access to health care, and a higher rate of being uninsured than Whites.[4] It is my hope that these two volumes will become textbooks in classrooms across the country and will help bridge this wide gap in knowledge of the extent of African American health problems and their roots.[5] These volumes should also serve as important texts for minority students seeking greater understanding of the many contributions made by leaders of the African American medical community across many centuries. If not for the publication of these volumes, many of those extraordinary health care achievements would have remained unknown even to those most concerned with these issues.

The bringing together of this huge body of work about the history of the African American health care experience in the United States required years of dedicated research under difficult circumstances. We are all indebted to W. Michael Byrd, MD, and Linda A. Clayton, MD, for their devoted commitment to bringing this history to the broader health and medical community. I hope their effort will result in a movement in this nation to provide the African American population with a more responsive and caring health system in the new century.

I am very pleased and privileged that this important work was conducted under the auspices of the Department of Health Policy and Management and the Division of Public Health Practice of the Harvard School of Public Health.

ROBERT J. BLENDON, SC.D.
Professor of Health Policy and Political Analysis
Harvard School of Public Health and the Kennedy School of Government

# References

1. Cunningham RM Jr. Discrimination and the doctor. *Medical Economics* 1952; 29(1): 119–124.

2. U.S. Department of Health and Human Services, Centers for Disease Control and Prevention, National Center or Health Statistics. *Health, United States, 1999.* Hyattsville, MD, 1999; U.S. Department of Health and Human Services, Public Health Service, Agency for Health Care Policy and Research. *Health Statutes and Limitations: A Comparison of Hispanics, Blacks, Whites, 1996.* Rockville, MD, 1999; Collins KS et al. *U.S. Minority Health: A Chartbook.* New York: The Commonwealth Fund, 1999.

3. *The Washington Post,* Kaiser Family Foundation, Harvard University Survey Project. *The Four Americas: A Report on Government and Social Policy through the Eyes oif America's Multi-racial and Multi-ethnic Society.* Menlo Park, CA: Kaiser Family Foundation, 1999.

4. The Henry J. Kaiser Foundation. *Race, Ethnicity and Medical Care: A Survey of Public Perceptions and Experiences.* Menlo Park, CA, 1999.

5. Blendon RJ et al. How White and African Americans view their health and social problems: Different experiences, different expectations. *Journal of the American Medical Association* 1995; 273(4): 341–346.

# ⋊ Acknowledgments

This book is the culmination of many years of research, experience in academic medicine, and clinical practice. Without the aid and assistance of many individuals, institutions, and sponsors it could not have been completed. As foundation stones of intellect and inspiration we are all indebted to men like Drs. James McCune Smith, Martin Robison Delany, John Sweat Rock, George Whipple Hubbard, Robert F. Boyd, Charles Victor Roman, W. E. B. Du Bois, John A. Kenney, and General Oliver O. Howard, who laid the building blocks in the quest for justice and equity in health care for all people in the United States beginning in the nineteenth century. Often obscured by their high-profile abolitionist or academic careers, or buried behind the "veil" of racism, their accomplishments as health professionals deserve resurrection. Building upon these historical legacies and inspired contemporaneous leadership provided by scholars committed to progress in African American health, such as Drs. Hildrus Poindexter, W. Montague Cobb, Herbert Morais, Julian Lewis, William Darity, M. Alfred Haynes, and Paul Cornely, this book strives to continue their efforts. All of these often unacknowledged pioneers provided the energy and inspiration for this book.

Institutions that supported both authors as they worked on this project deserve recognition. Meharry Medical College in Nashville, the Harvard School of Public Health (HSPH) in Boston, the State University of New York Medical Center at Brooklyn, Boston's Beth Israel Deaconess Medical Center, and

Boston's Roxbury Comprehensive Community Health Center and Dimock Community Health Center hold permanent places in our hearts and souls. Other supportive institutions and organizations worthy of mention are the National Medical Association (NMA); the Congressional Black Caucus; the Summit Health Coalition in Washington; the Ennix-Jones Center of the First Baptist Church Capitol Hill in Nashville, Tennessee, while under the leadership of Reverend Ces' Cook; and the Black Churches and Black Colleges Network headquartered in Detroit, Michigan. Their assistance was critical in the realization of this project.

We will forever be indebted to AT&T, which funded our postdoctoral fellowships at Harvard. The Tennessee Managed Care Network and the Medical Care Management Company provided pivotal financial support, without which this project could not have been completed. The Harvard Pilgrim Health Care Foundation funded this project's bridge into multicultural medicine. The Robert Wood Johnson Foundation sponsored various projects on African American and disadvantaged minority health care that were indirectly related to the book. Without these corporate and institutional sponsors this work would not have been possible.

Special access to research resources was provided by Ms. Mattie McHollin and Ms. Cheryl Hamburg of the Kresge Learning Resource Center of Meharry Medical College; Ms. Beth Howse, Special Collections Librarian of the Fisk University Library; and Mr. and Mrs. Wolff and Ms. Madeline Mullin of the Rare Book Room of the Countway Library of Medicine of Harvard. The Widener, Lamont, and Tozzer libraries of Harvard provided rare and focused resources for the research. Special thanks are extended to Ms. Salena Abrams of the National Cancer Institute's (NCI) library and her colleagues at the National Library of Medicine who provided so much medical historical material. We will be forever indebted to these individuals and the professional staffs of these various institutions.

We are forever indebted to our editors. Mr. Ricardo Guthrie, our colleague during our Harvard training years, reemerged to become our "Maxwell Perkins" editorially on the entire book project. We cannot begin to articulate our sincere appreciation for Mr. Guthrie's overall role as consultant editor, researcher, and scholar in African American Studies during the latter phases of the project. A special note of appreciation is made for his exceptional ability to lend clarity and ease of reading to areas that were extremely complex, highly technical, or medically and scientifically oriented. We will be eternally grateful for his contribution. Mr. Kevin Ohe and Ms. Sylvia Miller at Routledge are advocates for the project who then orchestrated the book's progress through the complex publishing process.

Academicians who lent their expertise in preparing this manuscript include Dr. Lucius Outlaw, philosopher and international authority on race from Haverford College; Dr. Robert Robinson, Associate Director, Office of Smoking and Health of the Centers for Disease Control and Prevention in Atlanta;

Dr. Michael Blakey, chief anthropologist at Howard University and director of the New York African Burial Ground Project; and Dr. Cassandra Simmons, associate dean for students while at HSPH. Other scholars who heard, analyzed, and helped shape some of the content of the project were Dr. Deborah Prothrow-Stith of HSPH; Dr. Claudia Baquet of the University of Maryland School of Medicine; Dr. Ces' Cook, CEO of Faith-Based Centers of Excellence in Nashville; Dr. Leslie Falk, retired professor of family practice and nationally noted medical historian and health policy authority of Meharry; Dr. Charles Finch, of the Morehouse School of Medicine; Dr. Richard Allen Williams, author and founder of the Minority Health Institute in Los Angeles; Dr. B. Waine Kong, CEO of the Association of Black Cardiologists, Inc., in Atlanta; Mrs. Cheryl Hamburg, library director at Meharry; Dr. Robert Guthrie, noted academic psychologist and researcher; and Dr. Todd Savitt, medical historian of East Carolina University Medical School. Mrs. Joan Clayton-Davis, Program Manager of the Academy of Educational Development of Nashville, provided advice and encouragement, served as a sounding board, and read parts of our manuscript incisively and objectively. Her unwavering support and her comments and input were greatly appreciated. We thank Dr. Stephen Jay Gould, anthropologist at Harvard University, for sharing his library and expressing his interest and support for the project.

Many individuals have been sentinels of support and encouragement for this project. Some include Dr. Robert Jay Blendon and Dr. Deborah Prothrow-Stith of HSPH; Dr. Charles Johnson of Duke University, who was a bulwark of inspiration, encouragement, and support, serving in many ways as "father" of this project; Anthony Cebrun, J.D., M.P.H., whose indefatigable interest and support served as a spiritual beacon guiding this complex project to realization; the late Dr. Robert Hardy ("Bob"), our intellectual conscience, critic, policy analyst, and confidant—besides being a dear friend and spiritual support for both of us; Drs. Camara Jones and Bryan Gibbs of the Division of Public Health Practice at the HSPH; Drs. Eric Buffong, Richard Butcher, Ezra Davidson, Avis Pointer, Tracy Walton, Mike Lenoir, Yevonnecris Veal, Gary Dennis, Patricia Hart, Gilbert Parks, Anita Jackson, and Calvin Sampson, all of the NMA; Mrs. Rosemary Davis, Ms. Ruth Perot, Dr. Noma Roberson, and Dr. Ces' Cook, who provided spiritual, intellectual, and material support throughout the project; Ms. Sheree Bishop, videographer Chris Rogers, nurse Sandy Hamilton, Mrs. Linda Williams, and Mrs. Mary Lou Cornett, who provided vital academic, technical, and graphics support; Congressman John Conyers, Congresswoman Eva Clayton, Congressman Louis Stokes, Congresswoman Donna M. Christian-Christiansen, Congressman Earle Hilliard, and Congressman Bobbie Scott of the CBC; Drs. David Satcher, throughout his tenures as president of Meharry, director of the Centers for Disease Control and Prevention in Atlanta, and as sitting Surgeon General; Louis Bernard, chairman of the Department of Surgery at Meharry Medical College; Dr. Audreye Johnson, of the Department of Sociology of the University of North Carolina; Mrs. Joyce Clayton of the University of North Carolina; and Dr. Henry Foster, who will always be our mentor and chief. Health journalist and social scientist Dr. Kirk Johnson lent immeasurable aid in the editorial preparation and structuring of both volumes. Drs. John Boyce and Louis Camilian of SUNY-Downstate Medical Center lent unremitting support during the late stages of the project while my father was ill. Their loyalty and sensitivity will never be forgotten. Other lifelong supporters whose friendship and support blossomed around us in Brooklyn were Drs. Cathy Roans and Reba Williams and the staff of Kings County Hospital Center. Dr. Ruth Browne, Director of the Arthur Ashe Institute of Urban Health at SUNY-Downstate Medical Center, and her family provided pivotal support during our time in Brooklyn. We also thank Dr. Lemuel Evans of the National Career Institute, who always encouraged our work.

Providers of indirect, but critical, support were Mrs. Ruth Baker and members of our family in Fort Worth, without whom the lead author could not have survived the stresses in his life, and Mrs. Lois Henderson, a linchpin of our extended family, who served as a life-sustaining force for both authors. We will be forever indebted to our brothers (Larry, Burley, Walter, Douglas, and Donald), sisters (Joan, Maxine, Doris, Alice, and Judy), nieces, nephews, cousins, other family members, and friends who gave their encouragement and support—without which this project would have been impossible.

The authors also acknowledge the special support provided by Mr. Ziad Obeid and the staff of the Division of Public Health Practice of HSPH. Ms. Scarlett Bellamy and Ms. Knashawn Hodge, of the Department of Biostatistics at HSPH, provided irreplaceable biostatistical support and expertise. We thank the staff and personnel of the Department of Health Policy and Management at HSPH, especially Ms. Elizabeth Marshall, Marilyn, and Ms. Dawn Linehan Elliot. The Computer Lab at HSPH, especially Sydney and Phillipe, lent invaluable assistance. The resources of Harvard University's massive library and research infrastructure were freely utilized. Meharry Medical College Library, the National Library of Medicine, Fisk University Library, and several private libraries were also used. Without the support of these institutions and their staffs, preparing this book would have been much more difficult. The audiovisual departments at Meharry Medical College, the Beth Israel Deaconess Medical Center of Boston, and Chromatics of Nashville lent invaluable aid and assistance in preparing visual material for the book.

Others who provided valuable support include Dr. Ben Sachs, Dr. Susan P. Pauker, Dr. Lucille Norville Perez, Dr. Augustus White, III, Dr. Louis Sullivan, Dr. Herb Dreyer, Dr. Jack H. Geiger, Dr. Gabrielle Bercy-Roberson, Kerby Roberson, Esq., Ms. Sheila Thorne, George Heirston, Esq., Dr. Ken Edelin, Dr. David Harris, Ms. Seleste Harris, Mrs. Sylvia Watts-McKinney and the staff of the African Meeting House, Mr. Jim Scott, Mrs. Jackie Jenkins Scott, Rev. Ed Blackman, Mrs. Sandra Blackman, Rev. Ozzie Edwards, Rev. Carolyn Corey,

Mrs. Darlene Pope, Mrs. Ervina Jarrett, Mrs. Marilyn Thomas, Mrs. Carol Taylor, Mr. Monroe "Bud" Mosley, Ms. Dianne Kenney, Dr. John A. Kenney, Jr., Mrs. Sherry Pajari-Joseph, Mr. Randal Rucker, Mrs. Beatrice Riley, Mrs. Vina Fils-Amie, Mrs. Phyllis Cater, Mr. Elmer Freeman, Dr. Gillian Barkley, Ms. Anita Hamilton, Mr. Phillip Aquan, Mr. Briars Davis, Jr., Ms. Naima Roustoumi, Reverend Ozzie Edwards and his wife Lula Petty–Edwards, Mr. Raymond Offley, Mr. Luis Osorio, and our neighbors at the Bulfinch. We also thank our Boston and Fort Worth physicians—especially Drs. Jacques Carter, Clinton Battle, Mary King-Rankin, Kevin Dushay, Bruce Furie, Peter Gross, Walter Bagleman, Jerlin Dixon, Judy Ann Bigby, and Marie Francouer—as well as our University of California at San Diego heart and lung team, including Ms. Connie Watt, Maureen Cavanagh, R.N., David Garcia, N.P., and Drs. Stuart Jamieson, William Auger, Kim Kerr, Naohide Sakakibara, Israel Sarfov, and Mark Fuester, who kept both of us alive and well to complete this project. If other major contributors have been omitted we extend our heartfelt apologies.

# ✕ Preface

In the wake of a 1991 U.S. Senatorial election in Pennsylvania, an American public consensus evolved. Senator Harris Wofford's upset victory over heavily favored Republican candidate Richard Thornburgh crystallized the public mood that the country was in the throes of a national health crisis. Moreover, most Americans felt that this crisis required major reform of the health system.[1] Some characteristics of this health crisis, which we refer to as the "mainstream" health crisis, were runaway health care cost inflation;[2] a health system consuming 14 percent of the gross domestic product (GDP);[3] an $800 billion national health care budget—twice the per capita expenditure of other health systems by 1992 and exceeding $1 trillion by 1994;[4] 37 million uninsured Americans and 40 to 50 million more underinsured;[5] and insecurity among all Americans, including the middle and upper classes, about future access to basic health services.[6] This mainstream health system crisis was defined, and perceived, primarily as a crisis in costs, financing, and access.[7]

In response to this health crisis, between 1992 and 1994 newly elected President William Jefferson Clinton launched a campaign for the most comprehensive health system reform ever attempted in the United States. His attempt at reform not only failed but also became an epic political disaster.[8] After the fiasco, the mainstream crisis worsened, with the quality of care showing signs of deterioration and the ranks of the uninsured growing to at least 40 million, according to the American Hospital Association, with projections to top 45.5 million by the time of the next presidential election in 2000.[9]

But this mainstream health crisis is not the only problem. Forgotten in the national health crisis debate is an older, more ominous, culturally driven health crisis afflicting African American and other poor populations.[10] Its separateness and silence historically reflect both the nation's faulty approach toward racial problems and the current wave of polarization and denial that is distorting U.S. public policy dialogue regarding race and class.[11] Major aspects of the *African American health crisis* were forced into the health system establishment's consciousness with the mid-1980s release of the Malone-Heckler Report, which detailed the wide and deep racial health disparities plaguing the U.S. health system.[12]

Some characteristics of this African American health crisis include persistent segregation of the health system along race and class lines;[13] race- and class-based inequities and inequalities endemic to each structural component of the health system, the origin of which is over 375 years old;[14] significant race- and class-based health outcome and health status disparities—many of which are worsening;[15] and an African American health insurance crisis wherein 25 percent of African Americans are uninsured, at least 25 percent are underinsured, and another 25 percent depend solely on stigmatized and inferior government insurance (Medicaid or public aid) for basic health services. This contrasts with 12.4 percent of White Americans uninsured, with estimates of another 15 percent underinsured and 6.8 percent covered by Medicaid.[16]

The stubborn persistence of the race- and class-based health system conundrum can be explained on the basis of a medical-social culture hundreds of years old that is heavily laden and burdened by race and class problems compounding continued social and economic deprivation. These factors interactively impact and contribute to the adverse health status and outcomes of African American and poor populations.[17] Many manifestations of these health system cultural problems exist. First is a generalized assumption and projection that poor health status and outcomes for Blacks and the poor are "normal" and acceptable.[18] Second, Blacks and the poor are marginalized at all levels of the health system, from patients to providers.[19] Third, there is a "blind spot" among the general public as well as policy makers regarding the practical and symbolic significance of the alienation and segregation of Black and poor patients from the mainstream health system. Thus, it is seldom emphasized by health policy makers and health providers that the majority of African American and poor patients are forced to utilize city hospitals, community health centers, public health departments, and emergency rooms (ERs) instead of the mainstream system.[20] These institutions—many of which provide yeoman service against great fiscal and logistical odds—are traditionally underfunded, understaffed, and overutilized, with substandard physical plants and equipment. Fourth is the historical tradition of self-serving behavior by Eurocentric organized medicine, the health profession's education systems, and the hospital associations in the United States, which often ignore the special problems of Blacks and the poor in the health system.[21] Fifth is a refusal to address the inequitable representation of the nation's racial and ethnic minorities in the health professions in lieu of compelling evidence that Black and poor populations are more likely to be served—and in a higher quality manner—by such professionals.[22] Sixth is an ongoing resurgence of the application of scientific racist principles to Black and disadvantaged minority populations in the United States.[23] Finally, racially and ethnically divided health professions have factions that are often contentious, conflicting, and contemptuous of each other.*[24]

In the course of our professional development, we became deeply attuned to these problems. The formal beginning of this project at Meharry Medical College in Nashville, Tennessee, in 1988 was a product of a natural evolutionary process. After graduating from medical school, the lead author from Meharry (1968) and the coauthor from Duke University in Durham, North Carolina, (1975), both independently desired to know more about African American health. As medical students we learned about the medical, scientific, and technical aspects of the tremendous health deficits affecting Blacks on a disease-by-disease basis. What was missing from the curriculum was instruction on medical and public health remedies to understand and correct these inequitable health status, health system structural, and outcome deficits. As is the case with virtually all medical schools, Meharry and Duke lacked formal training in the structure or functioning of the health care delivery system with respect to various patient populations. They were far removed from explaining how race and class considerations and interactions impeded Black health from rising above levels that have long since disappeared in other developed countries.[25] Why African Americans were treated differently, often poorly, in this health system was a nagging question. Moreover, poor Black health status and outcome scarcely raised an eyebrow within the medical and health establishments.

After completing a military tour in Vietnam and a residency in obstetrics and gynecology in 1975, the lead author committed himself professionally to an inner-city, private, predominantly African American medical practice. Black physicians practicing in such settings are exposed to the naked health care system discrimination based on race and class experienced by their patients. As profit-driven "private" hospitals market their services to patients with financial means and formidable health insurance, they "cream skim" patient populations, often creating policies that automatically exclude Black, poor, and Hispanic patients.[26] These patients are automatically forced into publicly financed health facilities or into charity care. Because of the composition of their practices, minority physicians—who disproportionately practice in poor neighborhoods—have high numbers of Medicaid, uninsured, and poor patients. As a result, they

---

*The National Medical Association (NMA) and the American Medical Association (AMA), for example, are often diametrically opposed in philosophy and ideology regarding health needs, health care/services, and health rights of disadvantaged populations. Of numerous health professions that often divide along lines of "Black caucuses" or separate organizations, these are the most prominent examples.

are often excluded or purged from hospital staffs and health maintenance organization (HMO) provider lists as a form of economic credentialing and managed care's avoidance of indigent or severely ill patients. Unfair, discriminatory, often economically driven HMO and hospital staff peer review thwarts quality assurance mechanisms, transforming them into tools to decrease the number of non-paying, extremely sick, and poor patients (categories disproportionately overrepresented in Black and disadvantaged minority communities) utilizing the HMO and their affiliated hospitals.[27] On the professional level, Black, Hispanic, and dark-skinned foreign physicians, who Paul Starr referred to as the "medical profession's third world," are often subjected to these troubling scenarios in the course of caring for their patients.[28]

Confronting these realities led to heavy involvement in health policy issues at the local and regional levels, including the lead author serving as a consultant with the National NAACP and the Southern Christian Leadership Conference (SCLC) and as an advisor to health care crusader Edith Irby Jones, M.D., of Houston, Texas. During her tenure as first woman president of the NMA, the lead author's career moved in academic and health policy directions. Soon after testifying before the U.S. Congress about racial discrimination in the health professions in 1985, opportunities to move into health policy and academic medicine at the regional level and, later, at Meharry Medical College became available.[29]

Dr. Clayton was one of the early African American graduates of Duke University Medical School. Before joining Meharry's medical faculty in 1984 as the first director of Gynecologic Oncology, she had completed her ob-gyn and gynecologic oncology training at Duke, codirected the Southeastern Trophoblastic Disease Center, served as gynecologic oncologist at major teaching hospitals, and completed a Visiting Professorship at the University of Dundee in Scotland. She was providentially placed as the director of the Cancer Control Research Unit at Meharry between 1988 and 1991. Perplexed, regarding minority and disadvantaged patient health policy issues, until her collaborative work with the lead author in the Cancer Unit, she sought a deeper understanding of the African American health experience. During her training at Duke she observed that Black cancer patients seemed to be sicker, presented at later stages in their disease processes, and fared worse than White patients. Although the unique and progressive policies then in effect at the wealthy Duke University Medical Center shielded her from most of the blatant race- and class-based barriers and inequities rife in the U.S. health system, after leaving that protected and atypical environment these problems became apparent to her. She also had the good fortune of working in the universal British health delivery system for one year in Dundee, Scotland, where she observed that all patients, including her cancer patients (who are expensive to care for), received screening, early detection, and state-of-the-art therapeutic interventions without excessive delay regardless of the ability to pay. The vast differences in access to health care dictated by race, class, and the ability to pay in the U.S. health system became even clearer to her at Meharry.

The authors first worked together at Meharry's Ob-Gyn Department and Cancer Control Research Unit in 1988. The research, patient care protocols, and consultations initially focused on the cancer crisis in the Black community. Cooperative work with the director, and later coauthor of this book, who had broad, national experience in cancer research focusing primarily on the Black/White differences in cancer incidence and outcomes, deepened our mutual concerns about African American and disadvantaged health. Based on contacts and collaborations with the National Cancer Institute, our newly forged team launched innovative cancer projects building on the work of Drs. LaSalle D. Leffall and Jack White, which detailed Black/White differences in cancer.* One of our innovative and unprecedented projects focused on resurrecting the African American cancer experience from slavery to the present.[30] Moreover, as a team, in cooperation with the NMA and the Drew-Meharry-Morehouse Consortium Cancer Center, we developed the only extant video available, as well as accompanying documentary evidence and reports, about the African American experience in the health delivery system.[31] After creating and publishing several important scientific articles, projects, and lectures on African American health issues, we agreed that more knowledge and training was needed if we were to positively influence the struggle in national health policy.

Attracted by Dr. Robert Jay Blendon's pioneering and progressive work in health policy and management and following the counsel of our mentors Drs. William Darity and M. Alfred Haynes,** we attended the Harvard School of Public Health. While there our ideas, perspectives, and projects were highly praised and warmly received. After earning M.P.H. degrees in 1992 we were subsequently asked to remain at Harvard to complete our research and write two books focusing on the African American health experience.

This work is intended to continue the efforts begun by pioneer and contemporary scholars of African American health such as W. E. B. Du Bois, Hildrus Poindexter, Paul Cornely, Julian Herman Lewis, Herbert Morais, W. Montague Cobb, William Darity, M. Alfred Haynes, and Richard Allen Williams. Some of these giants are still active and assisted in the preparation of this book. We were blessed by their encouragement and oversight as the project unfolded. These

---

*Drs. LaSalle D. Leffall and the late Jack White are surgeons and mentors based at the Howard University Medical School whose research and careers focused on ameliorating the African American cancer crisis.
**Drs. William Darity and M. Alfred Haynes are trained public health researchers, consultant-managers, and educators whose careers focused on ameliorating health disparities suffered by African American and other deprived populations.

volumes may begin providing a basis for reexamination of the American health system and equitable reform, which is a goal dominating the careers and lives of three previous generations of African American health professionals and scholars. If this book sheds new light on the race and class dilemmas plaguing America's health delivery system, the struggle and sacrifice will have been worthwhile.

*Boston, Massachusetts*
*Winter, 2000*

# ✴ Introduction

## Race, Medicine, and Health Care: A Problematic American Relationship

*With a massive planned effort, it is possible to accomplish more than we have accomplished by chance in the past. Perhaps the wide gap in health status between Blacks and Whites can become part of our history, rather than something which we passively accept as a present reality.*

M. ALFRED HAYNES

*There is nothing mystical about the reasons why one group of people can easily become physically and mentally strong while another becomes physically weak and less mentally alert.... [W]hat should be stressed above everything else is that millions of babies may become both physically and mentally retarded by disease while in their mother's wombs—which is another way of saying that a people wholly ignorant or indifferent to basic health can themselves become inferior in fact.... [T]he system is so structured, worldwide, that Blacks are forced into conditions that can even lead to genetic [defects].... There must be a breakthrough or there will be gradual extinction.*

CHANCELLOR WILLIAMS

### On the Gap in Health Status between Black and White Americans

"Race" is the factor defining a major American health system dilemma. Its human consequences are pervasive, yet its effects throughout the health system are seldom acknowledged and are often downplayed. An article by Kevin A. Schulman in the February 25, 1999, *New England Journal of Medicine* unequivocally documenting racial and gender bias distorting clinical decision making[1] sent shock waves throughout the health system and reminded us how pervasive the race problem still is. Even the generalized call for efforts to understand, explain how and why, and, eventually, correct the deleterious effects racial and other forms of bias were having on American medicine and the health system was instructive, considering the fact that Black doctors have been attempting to call attention to and demanding corrective action in these areas for decades.

From the American health system's very beginnings, race has been a problem. Race remains a major determinant of American health and health care whether viewed from the perspective of majority indifference to the *African American health*

■ 1

*crisis*,\* White acceptance of racial differentials in health status and outcomes as "normal," continued racial bias in the health system, the repeated refusal of health researchers or the public to attribute racially differential or discriminatory results of scientific studies to race or racism, discriminatory barriers to African American entry into the influential health professions, or as a factor in the irrational resistance to the creation of a universal health system in the United States. Maintenance of the biological parity, competitiveness, and survival potential for Black and health-disadvantaged populations is still in question. Health may become another dimension of Douglas Massey's and Nancy Denton's chilling admonition that "more must be done to prevent the permanent bifurcation of the United States into black and white societies that are separate and unequal."[2]

The overarching goal of *An American Health Dilemma* is to come to grips with these problems in an objective and dispassionate manner: by expanding the knowledge base concerning the health experiences of African Americans and other health-disadvantaged groups; by critically examining, analyzing, and holding out alternate explanatory hypotheses for these medical-social and health system problems; and by offering new perspectives, policies, and interventions to correct them. Utilizing methods drawn from the biomedical and social sciences, history, epidemiology, and public health, both volumes of *An American Health Dilemma* provide a racial-historical and sociocultural analysis and account of medicine, health, public health, and the health delivery system, enabling an unprecedented juxtaposition of the mainstream health system experience and perspective to that of the poor and underserved. As in Volume 1, *A Medical History of African Americans and the Problem of Race: Beginnings to 1900*, the Black health experience proves to be the most illustrative surrogate for other health-disadvantaged groups in Volume 2, *Race, Medicine, and Health Care in the United States: 1900–2000*. The wide-ranging effects of race and racism on the U.S. medical profession, health delivery system, and health professions educational-research infrastructure, along with the resulting adverse health consequences on African Americans are explored in detail—often for the first time. Though much abbreviated in scope, this introductory chapter includes essential material from the introduction and the first chapter of Volume 1 such that individuals who have not read them would have the background necessary for Volume 2.[3]

## A Different Perspective

*An American Health Dilemma*, Volume 2, provides information addressing key questions about race, racism, scientific racism, class, ethnicity, culture, gender, and

---

\*The *African American health crisis* is described as the differentially poor health status and outcomes suffered by Blacks in virtually every measurable health status, outcome, and service indicator when compared to European Americans (see *An American Health Dilemma*, Vol. 1, Chapter 1, Table 1). This has been a nearly 400-year continuum.

the problems and biases they generate in the health system. To fully understand health and health care delivery as social processes it is necessary to present background information on the social, political, and economic environments in the United States. A brief chronological foray into past relationships between race, medicine, and health care contextualizes the 1900–2000 period. Volume 2 details the African American and disadvantaged-patient experience in the U.S. health system from the turn of the twentieth century to the dawn of the new millennium by tracking five major evolutionary health system currents. They include (1) the sociocultural milieu in which the U.S. health system evolved and developed as it grew into the $1.5 trillion megastructure of today—along with the major events surrounding race, racism, and scientific racism as they affected social aspects of health and health care delivery; (2) the twentieth-century evolution and development of a race- and class-based health system, including its structure, institutions, organization, and administration; (3) a public health–oriented assessment of health system performance and function, including comparative health status, outcomes, service utilization data, and provider participation regarding Black and White Americans; (4) the evolution of the White medical profession with special focus on its dominance of the health system, its history-based racism, public health posture, and medical-social impact; and (5) the evolution and development of the Black medical profession, focusing on its unique and rarely told story of African American health advocacy, its unique and singular commitment to the public health and service needs of Black and disadvantaged patients, its heroism and community leadership, as well as its struggles against professional discrimination and abuse.

Volume 2 of *An American Health Dilemma* is written in standard prose organized in chapters. Notes, the principal form of documentation, are cited in the text by numbers set as superior figures. Generous utilization of footnotes provides key information necessary to facilitate the reader's smooth journey through the text. Charts, graphs, tables, and illustrations are utilized to provide detail and lend clarity. These items are clearly labeled with necessary explanations and material at the base of tables or in captions and legends for illustrations to make them accessible to all readers. Appendices, a glossary, a select bibliography, and index are included. The book utilizes methodologies drawn from the disciplines of history, public health, medicine, medical history, biology, anthropology, sociology, history of science, epidemiology, psychology, political science, public policy, economics, Black studies, and medical ethics. Though history is utilized as a major organizational and analytic tool, the book is not written as pure history or medical history. Many *mainstream\** persons and institutions will be viewed in a new light.

---

\**Mainstream*—a term that is often used to describe the "general market," usually refers to a broad population that is primarily White and middle class. *Source:* U.S. Department of Health and Human Services. *Cultural Competence for Evaluators: A Guide for Alcohol and Other Drug Abuse Prevention Practitioners Working With Ethnic/Racial Communities.* Rockville, MD: Office for Substance Abuse Prevention, Alcohol, Drug Abuse, and Mental Health Administration, DHHS Publication No. (ADM)92-1884, 1992, vi.

In most instances their positive contributions are well known and beyond the scope of this inquiry; however, many have played major roles or greatly influenced African American health or health outcomes and/or the evolution of racial bias or scientific racism in Western and American society, medicine, and the other *life sciences*.* Through their actions, lectures, publications, policies and programs, and prestigious intellectual or social status, such persons and institutions have greatly affected the health system. Therefore, their entire contribution must be displayed, scrutinized, and analyzed objectively and without intellectual, scientific, ideological, or personal bias. It is not the intent of the authors to create any negative aspersions or impressions as a result of these examinations. For detailed discussions of specific methods and the innovative interdisciplinary approaches used throughout the work, refer to Volume 1. Brief review sections on race, racism, American scientific racism and its "blind spot," and their relationship to the life sciences as academic disciplines and sociopolitical subjects are included in this introduction to orient the reader and to provide background on these volatile and often misunderstood subjects. We strongly advise the reader to refer to the Introduction and Chapter 1 of the first volume for a more comprehensive treatment of these subjects.[4]

## Race as a Sociocultural Concept and Tool for Analysis

Ancient founders of science's precursors began a hierarchical and discriminatory cycle by suggesting that race might be a means of classifying mankind. Driven since ancient times by folk beliefs, religious teachings, and social customs based on differences in physical appearances of various geographic populations, by the eighteenth century race became the subject of formal theoretical speculation and scientific investigation. An extension of Western culture's intellectual pre-occupation with human inequality, race became a focus of empirical and scientific inquiry for the next three centuries. By the middle third of the twentieth century the traditional ideas of race and "races of man" that became dominant during the rise of science began breaking down, as more objective anthropological, pale-ontological, genetic, and DNA studies proved the unity of the human species, common African origins of all racial groups, and the biological insignificance of the old parameters of racial classification such as skin and eye color, hair texture, physical features, and skull size and shape. Yielding to a deluge of scientific evidence, race has come to be more objectively considered a sociocultural concept wherein groups of people sharing certain physical characteristics are treated differently — often on the basis of stereotypical thinking, discriminatory institutions and social structures, a shared worldview, and social myths.

---

*A *life science* is a branch of science (e.g., biology, medicine, anthropology, or sociology) that deals with living organisms and life processes.

There are many theories about race. Most of the credible and useful modern concepts emanate from the social or behavioral sciences. Three major paradigms about race, racism, and their mechanisms have proved most useful. They are Pierre L. van den Berghe's *paternalistic* and *competitive racism*, Robert Terry's sociologically oriented theories on race emphasizing interracial interaction and power relationships, and Joel Kovel's psychological archetypes of *dominative*, *aversive*, and *metaracism*. Their utility in no way diminishes the worth of other theoretical frameworks for examining race—we simply found them the most useful for examining and analyzing relationships between race, racism, and the U.S. health system.

The origins of the word "race" are disputed and may derive from Arabic, Latin, Spanish, or German sources, and predate the sixteenth- and seventeenth-century beginnings of modern Western science. Initial English use of the word may have been in a 1508 poem by William Dunbar in which he referred to "bakbyttaris of sindry racis" (backbiters of sundry races).[5] The word "race" appeared in the formal English literature in 1580, according to *Webster's Dictionary* and other sources. The *Webster's Dictionary* definitions of "race" are so broad and variegated they seem somewhat nebulous. *Webster's* first definition of "race" is "a breeding stock of animals" alluding to current biological definitions. It also defines "race" as "a family, tribe, people, or nation belonging to the same stock," and further describes "race" as "a class or kind of people unified by community of interests."

As recently as the early part of the twentieth century, laymen and some scientists used the word "race" to describe human groups that shared particular cultural characteristics such as religion or language (e.g., the "Jewish race" or the "French race"). Earlier, "[p]hysical anthropologists have called races the various sub-species of *Homo sapiens* characterized by certain phenotypical and genotypical traits (e.g., the 'Mongoloid race' or the 'Negroid race')."[6] Some modern zoologists refer to subspecies or varieties as synonymous with a race: a partially isolated breeding population with some differences in gene frequencies from other related populations. Recent conceptualizations of race have reinforced movement away from the biological to the sociological sphere. Audrey Smedley noted "of fifty-eight introductory textbooks in physical anthropology published between 1932 and 1979 there has been a progressive elimination of the term and concept of race from textbooks ... in the United States ... when either the term was no longer mentioned in the texts or the authors argued that races do not exist or are not 'real.'"[7] Such a paradigm shift has undermined the scientific standing of race as a biological or physical concept. Van den Berghe offers a precise and simple sociological definition of race, referring "to a group that is *socially* defined but on the basis of *physical* criteria."[8] Since there are virtually no biologically significant or inherent differences within the species *Homo sapiens*, what happens to people after van den Berghe's social selection takes place is paramount to understanding what is important about race.

After reviewing the broad range of ideas about *race, racism*—the nefarious by-product that produces negative results and outcomes for the persecuted race—requires definition.

> *Racism is any set of beliefs that organic, genetically transmitted differences (whether real of imagined) between human groups are intrinsically associated with the presence or the absence of certain socially relevant abilities or characteristics, hence that such differences are a legitimate basis of invidious distinctions between groups socially defined as races.*[9]

Race and racism are closely related and interdependent. As van den Berghe points out:

> *The existence of races in a given society presupposes the presence of racism, for without racism physical characteristics are devoid of social significance. It is not the presence of objective physical differences between groups that creates races, but the social recognition of such differences as socially significant or relevant.*[10]

If we are to understand how racism works (the mechanisms) and creates its outcomes (through mediators), the archetypes we have mentioned are important.[11]

Van den Berghe summarized some of the differences between the old-fashioned form of racism associated with slavery, *paternalistic racism*, and the more modern variety, *competitive racism*. In the former type Blacks were viewed as immature, irresponsible, improvident, fun-loving child-adults—inferior, but lovable as long as they did not deviate from clearly defined roles. This paternalistic racism allowed for extreme intimacy because it maintained social distance. The prejudiced White superior loved and was committed to the dependent Black, who was loyal and loved the master in return. Resistance or rebellion by the slave triggered extreme brutality. With the abolition of slavery, poor and working-class Whites, who were the majority (and demanded control) no longer accepted the slaveowner's paternalistic image of Blacks as good children or pets. To them Blacks were seen as clannish, uppity, insolent, aggressive, dishonest competitors for scarce resources. Therefore, *competitive racism* became the dominant racist mechanism of modern U.S. society.

Robert W. Terry's investigations of racism have evolved over the past three decades. His most recent efforts have crystallized on the concepts of *societal* and *individual* racism. Incorporating many of his original theories, Terry also focuses on social and institutional mediators of racism defined through power relationships. These mediators include (1) *power*, the unfair distribution or disproportionate capacity by the dominant White/Anglo group to make and enforce decisions; (2) differentially controlling *resources* such as money, education, information, and political influence by the dominant racial group; (3)

establishing societal *standards* according to dominant White/Anglo definitions, automatically marginalizing other group norms; and (4) incorrectly defining *problems* by the dominant White/Anglo group such that perceptions and solutions are distorted, inappropriate, manipulable, and dysfunctional. In the health arena, these principles can be applied in both historical and contemporary configurations, and also lend themselves to understanding the European American dominance of the health system.

Psychiatrist Joel Kovel devised a psychological archetype of racism focusing on European Americans as the source of the race problem. His *dominative racism* was based on direct physical oppression and sexual obsession, while his more modern *aversive racism* is characterized by avoidance by the dominant group (Whites) based on isolation of the subordinate group (Blacks). Grounded in complex and infantile psychological mechanisms, it explains the White flight to the suburbs and the creation of inner-city Black ghettos with all the attendant problems of segregation, isolation, and inequality. The most subtle, modern, and malignant form of racism is Kovel's *metaracism*. It pervasively represents pure racism because it is systematic and independent of individual factors, representing the last stage of racism that remains when racial passions have been washed away. *Metaracism* is "... the racism of technocracy, i.e., one without psychological mediation as such, in which racist oppression is carried out directly through economic and technocratic means."[12] It is the racism of differential taxation schemes wherein unequal, inner-city, public schools are produced; the racism wherein African Americans, who have more kidney and heart disease than any other population subgroup, receive fewer transplants and other highly desired invasive therapeutic procedures; the racism of discrimination and selection for education and jobs based on White culture–based "aptitude" and "achievement tests"; the racism of police profiling wherein African Americans are automatically criminal suspects; the racism of "reverse discrimination" wherein White males are "protected" by Civil Rights laws designed to help Blacks who were previously denied participation in American society; and the racism of computerized arrest-record files for job screening in neighborhoods where most of the Black adolescent males experience police encounters (whether convicted of crimes or not). Because it incorporates the most advanced forms of domination, mutates into multiple chameleon-like configurations (whatever forms are necessary to carry out its racist mission), and is the most detached from the older, hate-filled, odious forms of racism leading to discrimination and overt and covert violence, *metaracism* is the dominant mode of racism in postmodern,* late-capitalist, U.S. society.[13]

---

*Postmodern* is a "family resemblance" term used in a variety of contexts (politics, art, music) for things that are related to a desire to critique Enlightenment values and truth-claims mounted by liberal-communitarian and neo pragmatist persuasions, for a relaxation of the pretense of high-modernist culture, and for a laid-back pluralism of styles.

Has race always been this important in the realms of the Western and, later, U.S. life sciences and health care? Following is a short chronological foray into the ever changing relationships between race, science, medicine, and health care.

## Race, Society, and Health in America: A Background

Black intellectual and biological inferiority has been an incorrect assumption in Western scientific and lay cultures for more than a thousand years.[14] For people of African descent, Western and, later, American life sciences and health systems have helped spawn this ideology along with nihilistic and sometimes negative health policies. By the seventeenth-century English North American colonization, Western medicine and biology (then part of the natural sciences) had laid the foundation for the presumption of racial inferiority. Not fully appreciated until recently, racism, or its predecessor concept human inequality, tainted the ancient precursors of what we refer to as the biomedical sciences from their beginnings. By coincidence or design, in all the theoretical scientific and taxonomic efforts at racial and ethnic studies and categorization attempted since Greco-Roman times, dark-complexioned people—especially those of African descent—had been placed in the bottom ranks of the human family. This *history-based form of scientific racism** had profound and nefarious health and health care effects on enslaved Africans and, later, African Americans. Until now, these concepts have not been appropriately or adequately utilized as revisionist health or public policy history, as the basis of explanatory hypotheses or canons for the analysis of contemporary health system dysfunction or disparities, or as tools for building a culturally competent health system.

Even if the racist proclamations of legendary medical luminaries such as Galen (c. 130–c. 201 AD) or Avicenna (930–1037 AD) had little effect on the clinical practice of medicine over the 45 generations (1,500 years) their curriculums and ideology dominated Western academic medicine,** they certainly affected the minds of medical scholars and faculty members who dogmatically accepted and transmitted their teachings to European, and later American, medical students until well into the eighteenth century. The scien-

---

*Hereafter, the authors refer to *history-based scientific racism* as the concept promoting White superiority, Black or non-White inferiority, and what is known today as biological determinism created by Western scientists with its antecedents dating from natural sciences' very beginnings in Greco-Roman times. This contrasts with the more modern concept of *scientific racism* to be discussed later.

**Their contributions will be assessed below.

tific legitimization of the concept of "inferior races" of men by authoritative physicians and natural scientists not only appealed to ethnocentric European impulses and feelings of superiority, but justified and rationalized health care and health system stratification and thus contributed to medical and health status and outcome differences. Taking this state of affairs to its logical conclusion, the better trained an eighteenth-century European physician was, the more likely he could participate in activities such as the Atlantic slave trade without attacks of conscience. Trainees entering the profession with open minds about race were "trained" to become prejudiced. Moreover, such "scientifically proven" disparities and discrepancies could be looked upon by professional and lay observers as inevitable and uncorrectable. They could thus be viewed as events and outcomes determined by the natural order of things—or at the very least, fate.[15]

Long before the concepts of race and racial inferiority were mobilized as defenses and justifications for chattel slavery in the antebellum United States, they had profoundly affected the health and health care of enslaved Africans. English North America's preoccupation with health accentuated this dynamic as pragmatic Pilgrims and planters designated good health as a prerequisite to engaging in the competition so highly valued by Americans. As early as the 1830s Alexis De Tocqueville observed, "In America the taste for physical well-being is not always exclusive, but is general; and though all do not feel it in the same manner, yet it is felt by all. Everyone is preoccupied caring for the slightest needs of the body."[16] Therefore, legally sanctioned medical and environmental neglect of enslaved Africans and the institutionalization of an inconstant, often inferior, "slave health subsystem"—processes that began in the seventeenth century—had future implications and dire consequences for Black people. A "slave health deficit" transmitted from Africa by the Atlantic slave trade became institutionalized in English North America. Race in the embryonic health system became a marker almost as important as it was in the institution of slavery. A background summary on the relationship between race, the Western life sciences, and the evolution of the health system, with some medical-social implications, follows.[17]

## Race, Society, and the Life Sciences: The Evolution of Western Health Systems

### Ancient Scientific Precursors

Many feel that Greece was the birthplace of Western science. Besides the changes wrought by their gifts of empiricism, objectivity, and logic, the Greeks brought their cultural predispositions toward ethnocentricity and intolerance.

Greek scientific and medical forefathers such as Plato (428–348 BC) and Aristotle (384–322 BC) began arbitrarily assigning slaves of all races a lesser status within the human family. They speculated that slaves were inherently inferior and less intelligent.[18] They also created and promulgated the "Great Chain of Being,"* a major scheme of natural scientific classification. Implicit in such a system was the ranking of all species, including mankind. As Richard Milner noted in *The Encyclopedia of Evolution*: "Racism is embedded in the Chain of Being; the idea was used to rank the various races into 'higher' and 'lower.' Of course, the white Europeans who devised it were at the top."[19] It profoundly affected early taxonomic efforts, which represented an early and fundamental stage of scientific development. Some ancient philosophers and historians also displayed particular prejudices toward Blacks and Asians.[20] Thus, the ancients, including the Greeks through the Great Chain of Being, early philosophers and historians through their writings, and the early efforts at anthropological classification and ranking, provided the first social and scientific prototypes in Western culture for the future promotion of the biological concepts of Black and non-White inferiority and assumed White superiority.[21] Such hierarchical ranking by physicians and natural scientists may have resulted in the fact that slaves began receiving lesser medical treatment by lesser-trained "slave assistant" doctors by the Roman period.[22]

In the third century BC Greek physicians also established unfortunate precedents in scientific abuse at the medical school at Alexandria, Egypt, as Herophilus (fl. c. 280 BC) and Erasistratus (fl. c. 250 BC) are credited with performing live dissections on prisoners. Thus by 200 AD, as a social consequence of the slave system along with other scientific factors, Greco-Roman physicians had hierarchically ranked physical and psychological characteristics and suspended clinical ethics based on slave or prison status and race, with the traits of Blacks assigned to the bottom categories.[23] Galen, a second-century Roman physician of Greek origins whose teachings were accepted as dogma by both practitioners and teachers of Western medicine until at least 1700, had a great deal to do with promoting the concepts of Black physical and mental inferiority through his teaching and writings. Anointed a Western medical demigod, his teachings became a dominant force within Arabic medical teachings and thought that followed.[24]

Between the eighth and twelfth centuries Arabic culture added to Western civilization's burden of racial and color prejudice in medical, scientific, and lay circles during its period of dominance. Muslim physicians, including the great Avicenna,[25] added their own anti-Black prejudices to the racial biases inherited from Roman medical traditions dominated by Galen.[26] Moreover, Muslim societies began for the first time to limit slave status to Black Africans.[27]

---

*The *Chain of Being* is the concept that all of Nature, from unorganized nonliving matter to the most highly organized creatures, forms an unbroken physical and metaphysical series.

## The Renaissance, Race, and the Life Sciences

The Renaissance marked the separation of the natural sciences from philosophy. The Christian monks and the Arabs had preserved the Hippocratic (c. 460–377? or 359 BC), Galenic, and Arabic medical traditions during the Middle Ages. This medical corpus was used by the first Western European medical schools and hospitals founded between the eighth and twelfth centuries.[28] It contained some anti-Black, racist, and biological-determinist material. Though most of the scientific reawakening in the fifteenth and sixteenth centuries was concentrated in physics, astronomy, and mathematics, based on the discoveries and innovations of Nicolaus Copernicus (1473–1543), Galileo Galilei (1564–1642), and Sir Isaac Newton (1642–1727), progress was also made in medicine and biology.[29] Andreas Vesalius (1514–1564) almost single-handedly placed scientific medicine on a firm anatomical foundation, and Ambrose Pare (1517?–1590) revitalized the art of surgery, placing it on a scientific footing in the process. However, Paracelsus (1493–1541), a Swiss physician and philosopher who resurrected empiricism and pharmacology in Western medicine, also pioneered the notion of racially separate and unequal creations (an early version of "polygenesis"). David E. Stannard appreciated the significance of Paracelsus' prejudices, relating his argument "that Africans, Indians, and other non-Christian people of color were not even descended from Adam and Eve, but from separate and inferior progenitors."[30] Thus, like the rest of Western culture, medicine during the ages of Discovery and Reason when the North American English colonies were being founded had a firm core of anti-Black, racist, and biological determinist clinical and didactic teachings and practices that would be expanded upon for the next four centuries.[31]

## Race and the Ages of Science and Enlightenment

The eighteenth-century Enlightenment represented multiple paradoxes for Black and other non-White peoples. This was especially true for those in bondage. Philosophers such as Hobbes, Locke, Rousseau, Voltaire, Montesquieu, and Diderot infused Western culture with the ideals of freedom—freedom from superstition, freedom from intolerance, freedom to know (knowledge was held to be the ultimate power), freedom from arbitrary authority of Church or state, freedom to trade or work without feudal restrictions—though at the time these principles did not apply to Blacks or Native Americans. This philosophical movement ultimately led to the Age of Revolution, the American Bill of Rights, and the abolition of slavery throughout the Western world. Simultaneously, it was a cruel irony that in an age of rapid scientific advance borne of the Age of Reason, Blacks and other non-White persons would be categorized as subhuman compared to White Western Europeans.[32]

European physician-scientists such as Andreas Vesalius, William Harvey (1578–1657), and Giovanni Battista Morgagni (1682–1771) led the advances in biology and medicine. Other medical and scientific giants, such as Anton van Leeuwenhoek (1632–1723), the "Father of Microscopy," Marcello Malphighi (1628–1694), the "Father of Histology," and Carl Linnaeus (1707–1778), the "Father of Biological Classification," lent their names to speculations that established Blacks in both scientific and popular imagination as a separate, possibly deficient, species. For many, the writings of these scientific giants also served as pseudoscientific "proof" that Blacks were subhuman and inferior.[33] Thus succeeding generations of internationally respected Western natural scientists and physicians provided mounting "evidence" that supported the Western European cultural assumptions of White superiority and Black biological and intellectual inferiority. Some other well-known contributors to this unfortunate "scientific" movement were biological and medical icons such as Petrus Camper (1722–1789), Johann Friedrich Blumenbach (1752–1840), George Louis Leclerc de Buffon (1707–1788), and Georges Cuvier (1769–1832).[34] Their other contributions, at the cutting edge of scientific and medical advance, are too voluminous to recount here. A virtually universal assumption of Black inferiority at the social, religious, and scientific levels also served to rationalize, legitimize, and intensify medical participation in the highly profitable Colonial slave systems.[35]

Other than being a source of riches generated by the slave trade and remote colonies, Blacks were distant curiosities to most Western Europeans during the Age of Reason. This generalization also applied to the European natural scientists and physicians living in Europe. They were little concerned with Africa or Africans except as investment sources of profit or loss. This contrasted strongly with the situation in the colonies, in which both the medical profession and the health care systems were strongly affected by the institution of slavery. On the institutional level, especially in the American South, there was a *slave health subsystem* made up of slave healers, slave midwives, and overseers. The backup for this subsystem was provided by planters and their wives and, as a last resort, trained physicians who sometimes supervised complicated slave illnesses, provided contract care for slaves in some instances, and occasionally operated slave hospitals. All this was tempered by the fact that enslaved Africans received medical care only when it was clearly profitable (from their owner's perspective) to render it and were sometimes admitted as patients to the frequently dangerous almshouses, pesthouses, and poorhouse hospital facilities that were provided for the "unworthy poor."[36]

Public institutions were the dregs of the health system of that period. These circumstances, combined with the fact there were no requirements or standards for providing health care or living standards for Black slaves,* help explain African Americans' poorer health status and outcomes during and after that period. Being

---

*Over time, legal provisions for living standards, punishment limitations, and health provisions were established for White indentured servants or slaves. See Higginbotham AL Jr. *In the Matter of Color: Race and the American Legal Process, The Colonial Period.* New York: Oxford University Press, 1978, 53–54, 120–121.

outside the "mainstream" and slave health subsystem, in terms of health the few free Blacks did worse than the enslaved Africans. Therefore, based on the documentary evidence available, overall Black health status was the poorest of any group in the English colonies during the Colonial and Republican periods and was always based on the exigencies of the slave system.[37]

### Medicine, Biology, and Slavery in an Age of Scientific Dominance

By the nineteenth century racially oriented European pseudoscientific data, along with that produced by the "American School"* of anthropology, was being used in the United States to justify and defend Black slavery. The increasing cultural authority granted America's scientific and medical communities as a result of the nation's worship of the "new science" was being used to buttress America's commonly held racial ideology and mythology. When physicians and natural scientists such as Johann Friedreich Blumenbach, Louis Agassiz, Samuel George Morton, Josiah Clark Nott, and Ernst Haeckel (1834–1919) lent their internationally acknowledged credibility, prestige, and intellectual credentials to the ethnic notions of Black inferiority—some alleging that Blacks constituted the "missing link" between apes and man[38]—it was devastating to Black people.[39]

This assumption of animal-like racial inferiority also proved to be devastating to the health delivery status of Blacks.[40] European and American physicians, sworn to highly ethical humanitarian professional codes otherwise, had been prominent participants in the barbaric Atlantic slave trade and brutal New World slave health systems.[41] The professional assumption of poor health as "normal" for Blacks remained ingrained in the minds of White American physicians—who went so far as to create a lexicon of "Negro diseases" and alternate physiological mechanisms based on race—well into the twentieth century.[42] All these factors aggravated and perpetuated the pattern of inferior, inconstant, or unavailable health care for people of African descent in the United States. The health care provided for the enslaved Africans and the few free Blacks during this period was rarely, if ever, the

---

*The *American School* of anthropology was a scientific movement spearheaded by Samuel George Morton (1799–1851), internationally known University of Pennsylvania School of Medicine faculty member and naturalist. He was also president of the Academy of Sciences. A group of American scientists was internationally recognized for theories espousing separate creations of the races of mankind (polygeny) and the biological inferiority of Blacks and non-Whites, based on scientistic, numerical, and statistical evidence. Some members were physician and naturalist Louis Agassiz (1807–1873), the nation's academic leader of biology and paleontology residing at Harvard; Josiah Clark Nott (1804–1873), Penn medical school graduate and international authority on race and ethnology; Samuel Cartwright (1793–1863), Penn medical school graduate, faculty member at several Southern medical schools, scientific and lay writer, and lecturer on the medical separateness and inferiority of African Americans; and a cast of ancillary figures such as antiquarian George Gliddon (1809–1857) and naturalist Ephraim G. Squier (1821–1888). Prior to the early nineteenth century, all leading scientific movements had emanated from Europe.

best available and continued to be tempered by the exigencies of the slave system.[43] Throughout the Antebellum, Reconstruction, and Post- Reconstruction periods, the slave health deficit established early in America's Colonial and Republican eras continued.[44]

Persistent realities of absent or inadequate health facilities and services, medical exploitation for the sake of "science," and poverty that had begun in the Colonial and Republican eras dictated that the health status of free Blacks was as bad and often worse than that of the enslaved Africans.[45] When all populations and time periods are considered, overall Black health status remained the poorest of any racial or ethnic group in America from its Colonial beginnings to the Civil War.[46]

During the Civil War the health of African Americans was decidedly worse than that of European Americans. Black soldiers' receipt of inferior health care in the Union Army was related to an insufficient number of doctors being assigned to the Black units, untrained medical personnel being allowed to perform surgery on and provide health care for African American soldiers, reluctance of the War Department to commission available Black physicians, and grudging and deficient medical support provided by the Union Army's Medical Bureau. Black soldiers commonly died of war wounds from which White soldiers recovered. Slaves entering the Union lines, considered "contraband" by the government, received sporadic and limited health care in Union Army camps, while the majority of African Americans remaining in the slave South were victims of a collapsing Confederate health system.[47]

Caste, race, and class problems distorted the nation's hospital system from its beginnings. The nation's early hospitals discriminated against and sometimes medically abused Black patients.[48] Public hospitals, along with jails, almshouses, pesthouses, and the few public clinics where Blacks were sometimes admitted as patients, continued their roles as the dregs of the health system throughout the eighteenth and most of the nineteenth centuries. Though these facilities were provided specifically for the destitute and "unworthy poor," African Americans had only sporadic access to them.[49] Working- middle and upper-class White people of the time continued to receive their health care either in their physician's offices, a few private hospitals, or at home.[50] Clearly, the foundations of the American health delivery system were built on a class-stratified, racially segregated, and discriminatory basis.[51]

The late nineteenth century marked the belated professionalization of the American medical profession and the assumption of medicine's formal stewardship over the country's health delivery system. Medicine had evolved from a craft of variegated skill, training, and prestige levels early in the nineteenth century into what would become America's most respected, influential, monolithic, and highly paid profession. With a few notable exceptions, such as James McCune Smith (1811–1865), an 1837 graduate of the University of Glasgow medical school; John Sweat Rock (1825–1866), an 1852 American Medical College of Philadelphia graduate; and Martin Robison Delany (1812–1885), Daniel Laing, and Isaac H. Snowden, who attended Harvard University medical school in 1850, Black exclusion from the medical profession was a given.[52]

### Race, Medicine, Biology, and Education Reform: Late Nineteenth-Century and Early Twentieth-Century America

Fueled by misinterpretations, distortions, and misrepresentations of Charles Darwin's (1809–1882) evolutionary theories and Count Arthur de Gobineau's (1816–1882) influential racial treatise,* the pseudoscientific literature in both the social and natural sciences on Black biological, psychological, and intellectual inferiority grew in volume, intensity, and influence.[53] By the late nineteenth and early twentieth centuries American government and public policy documents, biological treatises, and medical journals were laced with pseudoscientific racist principles, derogatory racial character references, and pronouncements of impending Black racial extinction. The decline in already poor Black health was blamed on African Americans' self-destructive behavioral traits, immoral behavior, weak constitutions, inherent susceptibility to disease, distaste for labor, criminality, fondness for alcohol, disregard for personal hygiene, ignorance of laws of nutrition, and proclivity for sexual vices and immorality.[54] This climate of biological and scientific racism, along with the physical and legal atrocities being committed against Black citizens, served as the social setting and atmosphere in which the late nineteenth-century and early twentieth-century American hospital and medical education reform movements occurred.[55] Moreover, the American medical profession's *de facto* policy of Black exclusion and racial segregation became its official national policy in the 1870s[56] as the profession wrote African Americans off as a debauched, "syphilis soaked," unfit race.[57]

Johns Hopkins University, America's premier medical school, which would guide American medical education over the next 70 years, opened with rigidly segregated classes, hospitals, and medical staff in 1893. The school would remain racially segregated throughout its period of medical educational dominance until 1963.[58] Prior to the conclusion of Flexner medical educational reform, at least 14 Black medical schools had opened.[59] The only medical institutions in America where Blacks were even conceptualized as normal human beings were the post–Civil War Black medical schools and the few Black hospitals and clinics. Organized medicine's official policy of racial segregation in the health system continued until Court-ordered desegregation in the late 1960s.[60] Quietly,

---

*Count Arthur de Gobineau's two-volume *Essay on the Inequality of the Races* (1853–1855) was a defense of the French nobility against the modern ills of society. By explaining all historical and social arrangements on the basis of race, it came to be considered the seminal tract of modern racism. Any alterations of arrangements between the superior Aryan (White) race—purveyors of civilization and progress—and the lower races (Blacks, Yellows, and Finns) led to "racial mongrelization" and potential danger.

acknowledged by a tiny cadre of Black health professionals, the 300-year history of poor Black health status and outcome in America continued.[61]

By the 1920s the basic infrastructure of the American health delivery system was in place.[62] Having been structured on the basis of racial segregation and class exclusivity, it was very stratified and unequal.[63] Virtually all of America's medical and health professions schools remained segregated according to race, gender, and class. The growing population of Northern urban Blacks had varying access to an inferior tax-supported, segregated tier of the nation's dual, unequal, health system.[64] During the early decades of the twentieth century this system had come increasingly under White medical school control.[65] Hospital and health facilities continued to be rarities for the Southern Black majority.

Meharry Medical College and Howard University School of Medicine functioned as virtually the sole sources of trained Black medical and health care professionals between 1910 and 1970. Black underrepresentation in the medical profession rose to 2 percent levels around the turn of the century and remained there into the 1980s.[66] The Black medical schools were systematically excluded from the medical school stewardship movement over urban public hospitals and health facilities for most of the twentieth century.[67] Few realized this would generate future medical educational problems threatening Black representation within the medical profession and the very survival of the Black medical schools.

Black patients continued their traditional roles (the practice began during slavery with the rise of clinical training, anatomic dissection, and clinical research in medicine) as being overutilized for medical demonstration, dissection, and risky surgical and experimental purposes.[68] The Tuskegee experiment, an unethical, exploitive experiment in which treatment for syphilis was withheld from almost 500 rural illiterate, poverty-stricken Black men, was conducted for more than 40 years, beginning in the early 1930s. For more than 30 years it was clear that the experiment was subjecting the men to excess morbidity and mortality as the Tuskegee medical researchers deceptively told the men they were being treated.[69] It served as a marker for a common American research infrastructure problem.[70]

As a countervailing force against poor Black health status in the twentieth century, the African American medical profession became active in Black community and public health arenas. However the tiny, Black physician–led, well-intended but underfinanced Black hospital and public health movements could do little to stem the tide of poor Black health status and outcome.[71] Throughout the twentieth century African American health professionals and researchers such as W. E. B. Du Bois (1868–1963), Hildrus Poindexter (1901–1987), Paul Cornely (1906– ), and M. Alfred Haynes (1921– ) documented racial health differentials and poor Black health status.[72] Nevertheless, until the federal government and the federal courts forced the issue in the 1960s—spurred by Civil Rights organizations in concert with W. Montague Cobb leading the Black medical profession—the health delivery system remained racially segregated, overtly stratified on the basis of race and class, and patently unequal.[73] The mainstream medical profession continued to either reject or limit its contact with African American and poor Americans as patients or peers and support patterns of institutional racism, class bias, and professional racial discrimination in the health system through the 1990s.[74]

### Race, Medicine, Health Care, and Civil Rights

The 1964 Civil Rights Act, hospital desegregation rulings in the federal courts, passage of Medicare and Medicaid, passage of the Voting Rights Bill, and the community health center movement created a *Civil Rights Era* in health care for African Americans. The Black medical profession provided a dominant group of physicians* who unanimously supported activities that served to open the health system to all patients regardless of race, class, or socioeconomic status.[75] Nevertheless, the resulting health system changes were superficial and health care civil rights enforcement was virtually nonexistent,[76] but Black health status improved dramatically for a decade after 1965. These improvements were due to increased access for large blocks of the African American population to some health care, often for the first time, and the initiation of federal funding for health services.[77] Token efforts by White organized medicine at desegregating the medical profession and improving minority access to medical education were also made.[78]

Black health progress virtually stopped in 1975 as the commitment, political support, and funding for the special programs and shifts in health care financing and medical education that had been substituted for attacks on residential segregation, needed health delivery and education system structural changes, and equitable changes in health and public policies waned.[79] Black health status deteriorated relative to Whites after 1980, with African Americans continuing to suffer excess morbidity and mortality and having the highest death rates in 12 of the 15 leading causes of death. The Black population began losing longevity in the mid-1980s for the first time in the twentieth century.[80]

Moreover, at the beginning of the new millennium the majority of African Americans remain demographically, economically, and socially segregated and isolated within our nation's depressed inner cities.[81] These areas continue their history of being medically underserved and being provided substandard health care by the underfinanced, inferior public tier of the nation's dual, unequal health system.[82] Black health professionals, the only consistent spokespersons for African Americans and the poor in the health system, are threatened by cuts in medical educational financing, failures in support for the Black medical schools, and a shift away from minority health priorities and affirmative action by White medical schools.[83]

Thus, the growing Black *health and health care underclass* and other working and nonworking poor populations continue to be served by the inferior

---

*Other small, independent, integrated groups of physicians such as the Medical Committee for Human Rights also crusaded for quality health care for all citizens.

public health subsystem and largely ignored by private-sector medicine. The public institutional infrastructure, though serving a laudable purpose, has not adequately met the health needs of Black and poor populations for over three centuries—with resultant and understandable poor health outcomes.[84] Without major reforms it will continue its seemingly predetermined deficit-producing role. In the wake of failed health reform efforts, there are few indications that the present presidential administration intends to develop and implement public health, private, or government policies aimed at correcting these major health system structural deficiencies, ameliorate rampant residential segregation feeding the health disparities, rectify the institutional racism and class bias in the nation's health system, or remedy the long-standing, predictable, and now largely medically correctable race-based health deficits.[85] For a kaleidoscopic matrix of reasons, the "slave health deficit" has never been overcome. True to W.E.B. Du Bois's global prediction in 1903,[86] in America's health system the "color line" has clearly been, remains, and will continue to be a dominant factor in Black health outcome in the United States for the foreseeable future.

## Scientific Racism: The U.S. Archetype

To fully appreciate the effects of race on health and health care in the United States, a more detailed understanding of scientific racism is required. The elements that generate the peculiar U.S. form of scientific racism are complex and are deeply embedded within the health system and its *subculture*.* The reach, effect, and impress of *U.S. scientific racism* are shaped and augmented by certain peculiarities of this country's racial and scientific culture and by the American character. These elements include, but are not limited to the following:

- *scientific racism*, adhering to Allan Chase's classical mold, born of the Western biomedical and social science disciplines during the Industrial Revolution;
- the virulent strain of human inequality–based, anti-Black, biomedically oriented, deterministic scientific racism with ancient roots in the West's Greco-Roman scientific culture exacerbated by America's 246-year-long history of African slavery (the history-based form of scientific racism);

---

*A *subculture* is "a culture associated with social systems (including subgroups) and categories of people that are part of larger systems." The phenomenon occurs not only in large social units like the health system, but in smaller ones "such as large corporations, government bureaucracies, or military units, often forming around specialized interests or the bonds fostered by daily interaction and mutual interdependency." *Source:* Johnson AG. *The Blackwell Dictionary of Sociology: A User's Guide to Sociological Language.* Cambridge, MA: Basil Blackwell, 1995, 286–287.

- a Hippocratic-based Western medical ethical tradition that is not "sociologically friendly,"* strongly based on values and covenants rooted in individual doctor-patient contracts, elite medical professional protections and prerogatives, and the systematic deemphasis on and exclusion of social concerns;
- an elite, hierarchical, and socially insensitive bioethical scientific and intellectual tradition;
- persecutory, judgmental, and almost cruel streaks associated with some of the Protestant fundamentalist, Puritan ethic, and Calvinist religious traditions that shape the American character's posture toward the poor and/or unfortunate — which also commonly manifests as victim blaming;
- a dehumanizing alienation and cynicism grounded in the late-capitalist United States' quasi-religious devotion to material productivity, industrial capitalism, and the Industrial State — all promoted by communications media and advertising, grounded in cultural materialism, secularism, and relentless consumerism;
- the omnipresent manipulation of thought, style, and tastes (to stimulate demand, rationalize activity, and maintain material productivity) through cold, synthetic, public opinion and advertising campaigns dressed in the guise of objectivity and good cheer that create alienation, increase remoteness, potentiate violence, and distance people from each other while replacing human ties with a screen of cultural manipulation;
- and the absence of a sense of community, distrust in government, and the lack of compassion bred of the rugged individualism and "self-help" traditions ingrained in the American character; these attributes are exacerbated by and accentuated by an ersatz atmosphere generated by American cultural mendacity and falsehood pervading everything from shopping malls and television shows to the political process.

With roots stretching back into antiquity, the scientific racism born of this unique synthesis of elements has profoundly impacted the twentieth-century medical profession, the rapidly growing health system, and the societal interactions surrounding health and health delivery in the United States.[87]

---

*Sociologically friendly* is a humanistic, communitarian, egalitarian relationship category that contrasts with the Hippocratic tradition, which is built upon individualistic and not egalitarian and/or communitarian doctor-patient relationships, contracts, and covenants. Universality, or service to the entire society, is not a core Hippocratic objective.

Allan Chase's classic definition of *scientific racism* is "the perversion of scientific and historical facts to create the myth of two distinct races of humankind."[88] One group is defined as being traditionally composed of a small elite classified as healthy, wealthy (usually by inheritance), and educable. The lower group or "race" consists of a much larger portion of the population that is vulnerable, of low socioeconomic status (SES), and purportedly uneducable because of inherited inferior brains. Chase's definition casts a broad net but is an oversimplification if it is to account for the panoply of observed effects of scientific racism in the United States. The classical definition, which is grounded in the positivist philosophical* and popular notions of scientific racism as a scientific by-product of the Industrial Revolution, is undergirded but also transformed by the contemporaneous social, political, and economic elements such as the ones noted above.

Chase acknowledged that his restrictive definition of scientific racism originated in Thomas Malthus's (1766–1834) plea to stop providing relief for poor or underprivileged populations because doing so perpetuated inferior racial stock and undermined general social progress (Malthus was the first political economist and author of the oft-quoted *An Essay on the Principle of Population* [1798] ). Later developments led to the manipulation of science to preserve the status quo, justify social hierarchies, and decrease government and social spending on health and education for the poor. The proclamations of Malthus's disciples, Herbert Spencer (1820–1903), the founder of social Darwinism ("survival of the fittest"), and Sir Francis Galton (1822–1911), who applied the new science of statistics to determining who should be allowed to reproduce (the eugenics movement), added momentum to the classical scientific racism movement that persists today. These developments are discussed in great detail in Chase's *The Legacy of Malthus* (1980) and resurfaced in *The Bell Curve* (1994) as the subjects of a controversy and an ensuing debate. Though Chase was accurate, he was incomplete. He attempted to focus too intensely on recent history (from the nineteenth century forward) and negated the pernicious effects of many of the predecessor elements of America's racial-social culture, worldview, and national character. His conceptualization downplayed several major streams of racially and hierarchically loaded ideological, natural scientific and medical, and sociological thought that permeate Western and U.S. scientific history and culture.

Examples of these streams of *ideologies*** and thought abound. The world's

---

*Positivism*, until recently the dominant philosophy of Western science, holds that all phenomena are real, useful, certain, precise, organic, and relative, and that all knowledge consists in the description of the coexistence and succession of such phenomena. Its theories of the nature, omnicompetence, and unity of science vitiated the cognitive credentials of theory, metaphysics, ethics, aesthetics, religion, and nonnaturalist social science (e.g., history, sociology).

**Ideologies* hereafter refer to "sets of beliefs, values, and assumptions, held on faith alone and generally unrelated to empirical facts, that act as guidelines to or prescriptions for individual and group behavior." *Source:* Smedley A. *Race in North America: Origin and Evolution of a Worldview.* 2nd ed. Boulder, CO: Westview Press, 1999, 19.

four leading natural scientists of the nineteenth century, Georges Cuvier of France, Charles Darwin and Charles Lyell (1797–1875) of England, and Ernst Haeckel of Germany, were affected by contemporary beliefs about race and were participants, if not leaders, in the resulting scientific racism. Each believed in racial hierarchies, White superiority, and the inferiority of Blacks.[89] Leading nineteenth-century American biomedical scientists such as Samuel George Morton and Louis Agassiz expressed similarly biased opinions.[90] Internationally renowned icons and social and statistical scholars such as Herbert Spencer, William Graham Sumner (1840–1910), David Starr-Jordan, and Frederick Hoffman cleverly, sometimes disingenuously, twisted Darwin's evolutionary theories to rationalize and scientifically justify America's social and racial hierarchies.[91] What these men believed and wrote had far-reaching scientific and social impact throughout the twentieth century.

In the United States much of the material on scientific racism emanated from medical schools and universities and was included in core curricula of the nation's leading educational institutions. Influential Ivy League–trained gentleman scientists such as Madison Grant, author of *The Passing of the Great Race* (1916), and Lothrop Stoddard, author of *The Rising Tide of Color Against White World-Supremacy* (1920), produced a litany of popular best-sellers promoting racism backed up by "science." Thus, as Chase emphasized, at least five generations of well-educated Americans, including physicians, were brainwashed with this pseudoscientific, racist material. Influential early twentieth-century Americans such as Theodore Roosevelt, Oliver Wendell Holmes, Woodrow Wilson, Calvin Coolidge, and Warren G. Harding accepted this so-called "scientific" material at face value. Whether or not they had previously been racist, such materials undoubtedly influenced their policies in racialist directions.[92]

Rethinking the concept of scientific racism while reexamining and restructuring it in more constructionist* terms not only results in a more accurate definition of the term, but enhances its utility as an explanatory hypothesis of what has actually taken place in the United States. It then more accurately reflects the negative cumulative medical-social effects a largely nonscientific matrix of social, behavioral, and religious ideas, prejudices and practices have had on shaping the national character and *worldview on race*,** especially as they affected the nation's

---

*Constructionist* refers to the socially formed dimensions of an inquiry. This type of inquiry includes elements such as the history, social dimensions, and culture shaping an inquiry.

**Worldview* refers to "a culturally structured, systematic way of looking at, perceiving, and interpreting various world realities." In the United States, Australia, South Africa, and many other areas of the world "race is a cosmological ordering system that divides the world's peoples into what are thought to be biologically discrete and exclusive groups. The racial worldview holds that these groups are by nature unequal and can be ranked along a gradient of superiority–inferiority." *Source:* Smedley A. *Race in North America: Origin and Evolution of a Worldview.* 2nd ed. Boulder, CO: Westview Press, 1999, 19.

scientific and health systems—most prominently during their formative and early evolutionary stages—with regard to Black and poor people.

Though Chase conceded that "the much older forms of gut racism based on religious, racial, and ethnic bigotry" exacerbated the effects scientific racism had on certain ethnic and racial minorities throughout his book,[93] he underestimated the broad scope and virulent effect these factors, especially anti-Black racism exacerbated by the Western worldview on human inequality, exert on the U.S. paradigm of scientific racism. Perhaps in Western European countries where, until recently, persons of color have been distant, even minor concerns, his definitions would be more appropriate.[94]

### American Scientific Racism and the "Blind Spot"

The unique character of American scientific racism helps explain the "blind spot" about race plaguing the nation's health system and pointed out by James H. Jones in his book, *Bad Blood: The Tuskegee Syphilis Experiment* (1981) and alluded to by D. S. Greenberg in a 1990 *Lancet* article, "Black Health: Grim Statistics," and the authors' 1992 article in the *Journal of the National Medical Association*, "An American Health Dilemma: A History of Blacks in the Health System." American-style scientific racism, hereafter referred to as scientific racism, subsumes a myriad variety of health system and medical-social ideas, traditions, and practices such as the following:

- a presumption of poor health status and outcomes as "normal" for African Americans;
- unethical experimentation on African Americans;
- racial bias in clinical decision making;
- disproportionate levels of forced eugenic sterilization on Blacks;
- perpetuation of the traditional assignment of Black and disadvantaged minority populations to inferior tiers of the health delivery system;
- the perpetuation of the overutilization and exploitation of the Black population for medical teaching and demonstration purposes until recently (some recent reactions have been to exclude Blacks to avoid controversy, for researcher convenience, and purportedly to decrease costs);
- systematic underrepresentation (largely through socially imposed educational disadvantages) of Blacks and other disadvantaged minority groups in venues of higher education and the health professions;
- the pervasiveness and popularity of discriminatory culturally biased IQ and standardized testing;

- the current levels of exclusion of racial and ethnic minorities from mainstream medical research and clinical trials;
- the elite, discriminatory, nihilistic, and exclusionary health policies that had the effect of perpetuating inequities, disparities, and excess deaths among Blacks, the poor, and working-class Americans throughout the twentieth century;
- biased research practices that generated numerous unethical research studies such as the Tuskegee experiment;
- national health policies that produced effects such as closing down vital Black medical institutions such as Black hospitals and Black medical schools such as the Leonard Medical School at Shaw University;
- a tradition of eugenic sterilization and unethical hysterectomies being performed on Black women (laughingly referred to by White physicians as "Mississippi appendectomies");
- a U.S. medical establishment that sees the Nuremberg medical principles as having no relevance to its operations;
- and the evidence of Black scientific exploitation present every day in research laboratories throughout the world exemplified by the unauthorized use of Henrietta Lack's living cervical cancer tissue (HeLa cells) for research.

Nevertheless, it does not explain the generalized majority "unawareness," not framing these phenomena as problems, of being oblivious to the health and health system effects and consequences of racial bias and scientific racism, repeatedly refusing to seriously consider race and class issues as legitimate scientific or health concerns, and detaching these practices and behaviors from wrongdoing—which are characteristic of the "blind spot" phenomenon.

Understanding the potent mix and interactions between America's peculiar worldview on race, national character traits, postindustrial and neoliberal social and political mechanisms, and the classical concept of scientific racism helps explain both the pervasiveness and stubborn persistence of the U.S. health system's "blind spot," scientific racism, and its race and class dilemmas. Their complexity and depth are major reasons the U.S. health system has such difficulty purging itself of its scientific racist, race, and class problems.[95]

Factors such as these virtually guaranteed that the U.S. health and health policy environment throughout the Progressive era and the twentieth century would be poisoned by scientific racism. Imprecisely defined evolutionary and genetic theories, for example, were twisted by twentieth-century eugenicists and racial superiority advocates to manipulate the health system along with other major American institutions for their purposes (e.g., justifying eugenic sterilizations, defeating progressive education, health, and social programs). The U.S. Army's World War I mental examination process was distorted to scientific racist ends ("proving" the deterioration of U.S. racial stock due to an admixture with "inferior" groups), and the U.S. Congress was exploited to twist the immigration process in a prejudicial manner against Southern Europeans, Jews, Asians, and people of African descent (preserving U.S. racial "purity"). Even the Supreme Court was manipulated by the scientific racists to legalize unethical and eugenic sterilization policies by 1930. Clearly, the Western scientific legacy of racial typology and hierarchy was factor loaded against African American and ethnic American citizens as the U.S. health system structure and culture evolved throughout the twentieth century. Heightened awareness of the social and scientific dangers of racism generated by World War II, along with internationally accepted reform and legal measures, was largely rejected by the United States.[96] It is therefore unreasonable to speculate that such powerful forces contributing to American-based scientific racism, peculiar elements of America's racial–social and political culture, and the national character would have no effect on a U.S. health system already plagued by historical race and class problems.[97]

In addition to the health effects of racial bias, scientific racism, and the "blind spot" on patients, a toll has also been taken on Black doctors, Black health care professionals, and the institutional infrastructures to which African Americans have been restricted over time. Black physicians are victims to varying degrees of discrimination in the United States at both the personal and professional levels. Until the Civil Rights era, Black doctors were almost totally denied membership in professional organizations such as the AMA and specialty societies. For the most part, Black doctors were not permitted to have hospital privileges at White hospitals until the late 1960s. Since desegregation of the hospital system, Black hospitals— traditional African American health system oases and bulwarks against health discrimination—have been virtually eliminated. Racial discrimination against Black doctors has continued during the past three decades and has included the peer review process, obtaining and maintaining hospital staff privileges, obtaining appointments on key hospital committees, virtual exclusion from many vitally important postgraduate specialty and subspecialty training programs (e.g., neurosurgery), and obtaining faculty appointments at teaching hospitals. Discrimination continues against Black doctors and their patients in medical practice, often through managed care mechanisms: "economic credentialing" of their patients and practices; exclusion from managed care panels; exclusion from invitations to join or establish practices in lucrative settings; and virtual health system redlining of certain communities on the basis of race, class, ethnicity, SES, and administrative/economic profiling. It is therefore clear that racial bias, scientific racism, and the "blind spot" have had negative impacts on the health status, health outcome, and health service delivery for African Americans, as well as the professionals and institutions that serve them.[98]

## Tracing the Evolution of a Race-
## and Class-Based Health System

> *Insanity is when we keep doing the same thing and expecting*
> *a different result.*
> —ALBERT EINSTEIN

Racial bias in medicine and health care has paralleled racial bias and African American citizenship status in society (see Tables IA and IB). Volume 1 of *An American Health Dilemma* explored the origins of the present multitiered health system. Historical analyses reveal that since ancient times Western preoccupation with human inequality, certain turns in the evolutionary development of Western science (affected elements included reification, taxonomy, hierarchical ranking), and anti-Black racism and its antecedents have:

1. helped energize health system discrimination and deprivation against Blacks—facilitating, if not producing, poor health status and outcomes in the process;
2. produced racism, history-based and American-style scientific racism, and the "blind spot" in the biomedical sciences and health system; and
3. facilitated medical and scientific exploitation and abuse.

Factoring in the health-related influences of ancient precursor civilizations, Judeo-Christian and Eastern religions, and Greco-Roman and European medical and social structures and practices, all viewed through the prisms of race and scientific racism, Volume 1 chronicled historical and health system events that led to the racially segregated, caste-ridden health system of 1900. Viewed from this stance, the origins of the contemporary race- and class-based problems plaguing the American health system become clearer. Volume 1 and some other contemporary sources thus provide foundations for explanatory hypotheses and bases of policy analyses for understanding contemporary race and class health system problems that are logical, comprehensible, and thoroughly grounded in facts.[99]

By placing America's health system in balanced social and historical contexts, Volume 1 also revealed some other major historical themes and developments relevant to the race and class dimensions of Western, and later American, health and health care. Ancient precursor Egyptian, Mesopotamian, and Greco-Roman health and medical systems were highly varied in their approaches to racial and class differences, with Egyptian systems being more egalitarian and public health oriented and Mesopotamian and Greco-Roman systems being more biased and hierarchical. Before and during the Middle Ages, Classical, Judeo-Christian,

**Table IA African American Citizenship Status from 1619 to 2001**

| Time Span | Citizenship Status in Years | Percent (%) of U.S. Experience | Citizenship Status* | Comments |
|---|---|---|---|---|
| 1619–1865 | 246 | 64.40 | Chattel slavery | Abolition of Atlantic Slave Trade (1808)—Black influx stopped; Black immigration since: scant |
| 1865–1965 | 100 | 26.18 | Virtually no citizenship rights | Thirteenth, Fourteenth, and Fifteenth Amendments virtually nullified; legal segregation implemented 1896 |
| 1965–2001 | 36 | 9.42 | Most citizenship rights | School desegregation (1954), Civil Rights Act (1964), Voting Rights Act (1965) passed: apartheid, discrimination, institutional racism in effect |
| 1619–2001 | 382 | 100.00 | The struggle continues | Sum total |

*According to Thomas Marshall's criteria, citizenship carries three distinct kinds of rights relative to the State: (1) *civic rights*, including legal equality, free speech, free movement, free assembly, and organizational and informational rights; (2) *political rights*, including the right to vote and run for office in free elections; and (3) *socioeconomic rights*, including the right to have a job, collectively bargain, unionize, and access social security and welfare if necessary.

*Sources:* Brinkley A. *The Unfinished Nation: A Concise History of the American People.* New York: Alfred A. Knopf, 1993. Higginbotham AL. *In the Matter of Color: Race and the American Legal Process, The Colonial Period.* New York: Oxford University Press, 1978. Kluger R. *Simple Justice: The History of* Brown v. Board of Education *and Black America's Struggle for Equality.* New York: Alfred A. Knopf, Inc., 1976. Paperback Edition. New York: Vintage Books, 1977. Marable M. *Race, Reform, and Rebellion: The Second Reconstruction in Black America, 1945–1990.* Revised Second Edition. Jackson: University Press of Mississippi, 1991. Marshall TH. *Citizenship, Social Class, and Other Essays.* Cambridge, England: Cambridge University Press, 1950.

Table IB    African American Citizenship Status
            and Health Experience from 1619 to 2001

| Time Span | Citizenship Status in Years | Percent (%) of U.S. Experience | Citizenship Status* | Health and Health System Experience |
|---|---|---|---|---|
| 1619–1865 | 246 | 64.40 | Chattel slavery | Disparate/inequitable treatment; poor health status and outcomes; "Slave health deficit" and "Slave health subsystem" in effect |
| 1865–1965 | 100 | 26.18 | Virtually no citizenship rights | Absent or inferior treatment and facilities; *de jure* segregation/discrimination in South, *de facto* throughout most of the health system. "Slave health deficit" uncorrected |
| 1965–2001 | 36 | 9.42 | Most citizenship rights | Southern medical school desegregation (1948), Imhotep Hospital Integration Conferences (1957–1964), hospital desegregation in federal courts (1964); disparate health status, outcomes, and services with apartheid, discrimination, institutional racism, and bias in effect |
| 1619–2001 | 382 | 100.00 | The struggle continues | Health disparities/ inequities |

*According to Thomas Marshall's criteria, citizenship carries three distinct kinds of rights relative to the State: (1) *civic rights*, including legal equality, free speech, free movement, free assembly, and organizational and informational rights; (2) *political rights*, including the right to vote and run for office in free elections; and (3) *socioeconomic rights*, including the right to have a job, collectively bargain, unionize, and access social security and welfare if necessary.

*Sources*: Brinkley A. *The Unfinished Nation: A Concise History of the American People.* New York: Alfred A. Knopf, 1993. Byrd WM, Clayton LA. *An American Health Dilemma.* 2 vols. New York: Routledge, 2000, 2001. Higginbotham AL. *In the Matter of Color: Race and the American Legal Process, The Colonial Period.* New York: Oxford University Press, 1978. Kluger R. *Simple Justice: The History of* Brown v. Board of Education *and Black America's Struggle for Equality.* New York: Alfred A. Knopf, Inc., 1976. Paperback Edition. New York: Vintage Books, 1977. Marable M. *Race, Reform, and Rebellion: The Second Reconstruction in Black America, 1945–1990.* Revised Second Edition. Jackson: University Press of Mississippi, 1991. Marshall TH. *Citizenship, Social Class, and Other Essays.* Cambridge, England: Cambridge University Press, 1950.

Manichaean, and Arabic periods, color-based legends, scholarship, and ideologies injected color prejudice into social, medical, and scientific developments long before what most historians consider the dawn of modern science or racial slavery in America (when they contend race and racism were born). The scientific abuse and overutilization for medical teaching and demonstration purposes of disadvantaged groups is a Western medical tradition dating back to at least 300 BC in ancient Alexandria. The post–Civil War founding of Black medical and health profession schools and the beginnings of a "Negro medical ghetto" were new configurations of a "dual" and unequal American health system tradition and infrastructure that was already 250 years old. Compounded by the traditional American practice of separate and inferior treatment for Black, poor, and charity patients, these arrangements were codified, legalized, and institutionalized by 1900.[100]

Volume 2 takes up the story, examining how race- and class-based structuring of the U.S. health delivery system has combined with other factors, including physicians' attitudes—perhaps legacies conditioned by their participation in slavery and creation of the scientific myth of Black biological and intellectual inferiority—to create a medical-social, health system–cultural, and health delivery environment that contributes to the propagation of racial health disparities and, ultimately, the health system's race and class dilemma. It also details the paradox of how African Americans have had to rely upon these same providers and institutions for their health care. Results of the Georgetown study[101] remind us that, like other American institutions, the health system was "manufactured by whites through a series of self-conscious actions and purposeful institutional arrangements that continue today ... it ... was no historical accident; it was brought about by actions and practices that had the passive acceptance, if not the active support, of most whites in the United States."[102] Regarding the nation's health system attempts at racial redemption and reconciliation, H. Jack Geiger recalls that "Progress over the last 30 years has been substantial, but its course has been as erratic and fitful as the nation's overall commitment to racial justice and equal opportunity."[103] Another factor since the 1980s has been the co-option of the health system by business-oriented health managers who may be exaggerating the worst medical-social tendencies of an already "sick" American health system structure and subculture.

As Volume 2 chronicles the twentieth-century social, medical, and public health, economic-structural, and medical-social evolution of the American health system, factoring in the race and class dimensions at each juncture, the mother lode of facts, findings, and fresh perspectives suggest almost as many questions as answers. Will the health system also fall prey to what opinion researchers call White "racial resentment" and/or "belief in principle/policy-implementation disconnect"—possibly the latest widespread manifestations of America's anti-Black racism?[104] Such attitudes and beliefs may be driving U.S. society's cynical, harsh, intolerant, some consider unrealistic and socially irresponsible demands that African Americans—still being victimized by discrimination, institutional racism, and some forms of apartheid—overcome the effects of 246 years of chattel slavery (64.40 percent of the African American social experience), 100 years of legal segregation, discrimination, and brutal subjugation (26.18 percent of the African American social experience), in less than 40 years (9.42 percent of the African American social experience) (See Tables IA and IB). Until persistent institutional racism and racial bias in health policy, health system structure and processes, medical and health professions education, and health services delivery are eradicated—all of which play significant roles in access, availability, and quality of health care—African Americans will continue to experience poor health status and outcomes. Driven by an expanded data base and a host of explanatory and corrective hypotheses, new agendas and standards can be forged by the new challenges.

## New Challenges

At the beginning of the twenty-first century, as documented in Volume 2, the United States's health system is quietly undergoing its greatest transformation of the past 100 years. Almost by default, health care has been ceded as an entrepreneurial enterprise. Americans "are skeptical about the role of government in matters affecting [their] medical care and profess a faith in the ability of markets to shape the health care system."[105] The American capitalist manner of organizing and managing a business enterprise includes profit-taking, administration, and rationing by market forces, "cut-throat" competition, and aggressive advertising. Those with less to spend will automatically accrue less benefits, and the market shapes distribution and economic availability and viability. These principles are often in direct conflict with accepted principles of public health, humanitarianism, justice in distribution of health beneficence, health planning, and health and medical ethics. Moreover, they conflict with American value premises regarding social and economic inequality. In the new millennium, African Americans face either stagnant or widening racial health disparities for all major disease categories and health conditions compared to European Americans. Will the current transformation of the nation's health system into a privately owned, megacorporate, managed care–dominated, Wall Street–financed infrastructure solve the system's race and class problems? Are recent attempts to frame these health system defects in exclusively financial and SES terms leading to amelioration and solutions for these race and class problems? Will health care in the United States ever become universal and considered a human right available to all Americans, or is it to continue as a privilege, formally or informally means-tested, based on employment status, age, race, geographic location, ethnicity, or class? Whether universal, humane, quality health care can be provided by a system energized and organized by entrepreneurialism and the "market" is questionable (because with market competition there are always winners and losers, which dismantles the concept of universal). No hypotheses or theories relating health delivery and classical market capitalism have ever predicted success. The jury is out on the most massive ongoing health care and medical-social experiment in world history—currently underway in the United States.

Substantial measures such as the creation of a health policy institute dedicated to the study, assessment, and monitoring of the health of African Americans and other disadvantaged populations, along with the design and implementation of policies and programs for the production of a culturally competent health care workforce, represent realistic and significant first steps for dealing with these problems. Logic also dictates that the broader the dissemination of the message regarding the health system relationships among race, class, gender, ethnicity, culture, disability, age, sexual preference, and medicine and health care in the United States, along with the adverse outcomes these history-based problems and biases have produced, the more likely future health reform will follow a wholesome, fair, and equitable course inclusive of all Americans.[106]

---

## To Serve This Present Age?

Volume 2 corroborates the fact that disparate health care treatment and quality based on race and class are an American tradition that has been transmitted into the twenty-first century. The United States remains the sole Western democracy that is not committed to a universal health delivery system. Presently in violation of the Universal Declaration of Human Rights it signed in 1948, specifying medical care as a human right, the United States stands alone among its NATO and Organization of Economic Cooperation and Development (OECD) partners by not ensuring the provision of basic health services to most, if not all, of its citizens.*

The increasing distance between the haves and have-nots in America over the past three decades intensifies the disruptive potential of continued violation of the "American creed."** Continued or worsening twenty-first-century health disparities viewed across the chasm of the racial divide portend even worse scenarios. Therefore, history-based race and class problems lingering in the health system could pose a threat to the sanctity and future survival of the American

---

*Twenty-four of the 29 OECD countries ensured health services to at least 99 percent of their citizens (1997). Germany ensures 92.2 percent. Two OECD countries, Mexico and the Netherlands, made this assurance for 72.0 percent of their citizens, while Turkey ensures 66 percent. The U.S. figure was 33.3 percent. *Source:* Anderson GF, Poullier J-P. Health spending, access and outcomes: Trends in industrialized countries. *Health Affairs* 1999; 18:178–192, 181.

**Gunar Myrdal's concept of the *American creed* is a set of shared values and beliefs articulated by Thomas Jefferson in the Constitution and defended by Abraham Lincoln in his orchestration of "a new birth of freedom." These values include freedom, justice, and equal opportunity for all, buttressed by Judeo-Christian ideals of human brotherhood and the Golden Rule.

democratic system as we know it. As Kovel noted, "[T]o ... the Industrial State ... racism has become more threatening than useful as a regulator of culture. ... Just as racism has not been a simple matter of gratuitous evil, but rather has been an evil that has served a real use in maintaining the potency of American culture, so too may antiracism be directed both to the elimination of the evil and to the preservation of the potency of American culture."[107] Without rational approaches to reforming the health system, human capital or "Investment in Man" approaches* toward solving America's social problems which are grounded in improving education and health for disadvantaged populations will be permanently undermined and thwarted.

*An American Health Dilemma* lays the foundation for explaining major reasons why and how public attitudes toward race, class, and health leading to the acceptance, promotion, and perpetuation of patently unequal health status and outcomes for certain populations evolved. When such attitudes overwhelm and dominate American value premises espousing freedom, justice, egalitarianism, and equal opportunity for all, the "American creed" is violated. Repeated failure of the health system to live up to, or ideologically adopt, these ideals constitutes the new millennium's "American health dilemma."[108]

---

*These *human capital approaches* are based on the concept that workers are similar in many ways to machinery as forces of production. Therefore, enlightened societies should invest in education and health in order to enhance productivity.

## PART I

# Race, Medicine, and Health in Early Twentieth-Century America

# Black Americans and the Health System in the Early Twentieth Century, 1901–1929

## The Medical-Social Environment in the Early Twentieth Century, 1901–1929

Like other major components of society, the U.S. health system in the early twentieth century reflected the economic and social climate of the country. As America entered the new century, the U.S. health system was structurally and socially divided into a "mainstream" system serving the majority of Americans—largely White working, middle, and upper classes—and a smaller underfunded, segregated, and resource-poor health subsystem struggling to meet the needs of Blacks and the poor. Both of these general divisions of the system displayed startlingly variegated profiles based on ethnic, political, racial, and material resource considerations, all modulated by geography and demography. By the beginning of the Great Depression an identifiable health system with distinctive medical-social, ideological, and "dual" structural characteristics had been institutionalized. The changing U.S. political economy, social developments, and pace of biomedical scientific progress during the early twentieth century all strongly influenced these health system developments.

For American society the years between 1900 and 1930 were turbulent. Overall, it was an era of growing U.S. wealth and influence. During this period, America emerged as a dominant world power. However, for African Americans, according to many authorities and social critics, it was a social, economic, and political nadir. The period under scrutiny (1901–1929) and the preceding period (1861–1900) were dominated by wars. The social history of the preceding 40-year period began with the cataclysm of a bloody Civil War, while the 30-year period starting with 1900 was bisected by an equally gory world war. Both of these conflicts were the bloodiest and most massive of their kind up to the respective times they took place, and both were largely responsible, or at least served as catalysts, for the unprecedented levels and pace of social and economic change that affected the United States throughout this 68-year continuum. Thus they profoundly affected the health system.

Wartime advances were critically important as they served to promote progress in biomedical technology, health services development, and public health matters. As has been previously discussed, the Civil War and its aftermath forced dramatic technical and medical-social changes in the U.S. health system. It served as a preparatory phase for the American health system to come of age. In contrast, World War I marked large-scale destruction affecting Western European medicine, research, and health care—ending its dominance in the process. Almost serendipitously, the torch of medical progress passed to the United States. Only recently has this dominance in the biomedical sciences begun to be challenged. These physical facts, combined with European economic devastation caused by World War I, served to formally establish a new world order in medical and scientific relationships between the United States and previously dominant Europe. In retrospect, from a medical and scientific standpoint both these contiguous eras were revolutionary, variegated, and dynamic.

The period from 1900 to the Great Depression was also of tremendous importance to health care in that it represented the erection of the foundations and developing character of the current U.S. health system. The medical-social contours of today's health care infrastructure were also established. The cultural pervasiveness of health care and its delivery in the United States grew in importance. Moreover, the medical and health policy establishments' decision to ignore the U.S. health system's pervasive and florid race and class problems—causing these discriminatory conditions to become more entrenched in the health system's structure and subculture—was condoned by America's institutional and political power structure.[1]

The late nineteenth-century beginning of the Progressive Era (often cited as 1890–1920) was characterized by major increases in industrial growth and productivity; an increasing concentration of wealth and resources by a White, corporate infrastructure; an increasing demand for expanding markets for U.S. goods—often through imperialism and a jingoistic foreign policy; and a dramatic increase in the size and diversity of the American population, largely through immigration. Although interrupted by World War I (1914–1918), these trends, massive immigration excepted,* continued virtually unabated for the first three decades of the

---

*Changes in immigration laws such as those in 1921 and 1924 cut immigration dramatically.

twentieth century. Top-down corporate organization and management, complemented by impersonal and "machinelike" workforce techniques symbolized by the assembly line, were benchmarks of American efficiency. For a variety of reasons, only the health care system avoided these forms of social and political economic organization.

By the late nineteenth century the mainstream American economy became increasingly organized around mass production, corporate entities, and monopoly capitalism. The railroads and the Standard Oil Trust were prominent examples. Corporate takeover of virtually the entire economy threatened both the American worker and farmer prior to the twentieth century. Employers implemented techniques favoring increasing rationalization and depersonalization of the production process, applying the new "scientific management" approach of Frederick Winslow Taylor. This doctrine swept through corporate-dominated America. As Alan Brinkley described "Taylorism" in *The Unfinished Nation*:

> *Taylor urged employers to reorganize the production process by subdividing tasks. This would speed up production; it would also make workers more interchangeable (less skilled, less in need of training) and thus diminish a manager's dependence on any particular employee. If properly managed by trained experts ... workers using modern machines could perform simple tasks at much greater speed, greatly increasing productive efficiency.*[2]

These trends virtually eliminated the need for, and competitiveness of, skilled craftsmen. Individuality was questioned. It also irrevocably removed the workplace from the home—as had been the case with frontier and agricultural economic organizations. The down-skilling of production and the creation of interchangeable workplace workers combined with assembly line production techniques to produce unprecedented levels of industrial efficiency. Henry Ford's techniques in automobile production in 1914 represented the perfection of these methods. For America's workers these changes deemphasized the individual and were often adverse and devastating in both personal and human terms. Such developments led to profound social changes affecting the working, agricultural, and poorer classes. Many suggested applying these techniques to health care.

In contrast, the American health system, driven by preservation of primacy of the individual, physician autonomy, and the doctor-patient relationship, resisted most of these modern corporate approaches relative to health care delivery. Preservation of these values struck chords deeply woven in the American character. Just as the American public's stance on these issues was preserved and enshrined in the medical-social fabric of the health system until the dawn of the twenty-first century, the health system's attitudes and practices, which were questionable and tainted from moral and medical ethical standpoints relative to race and class issues, were also preserved. Pluralism, fee-for-service, racial discrimination, and class privilege remained. Thus the health care system, led by an autonomous White medical profession, remained invulnerable to the corporate takeover of its infrastructure until the last quarter of the twentieth century. Likewise, its medical-social practices relative to race and class also remained regressive in character.[3]

Other identifiable reactive phenomena to these corporate developments affecting American society in general were the formation of labor movements, the rise of the Socialist and Communist parties, farmers' cooperatives and political organizations, and anti-monopoly and anti-trust rulings and legislation. Most of this activity systematically discriminated against and/or excluded African Americans on political, social, or economic grounds. Simultaneously, the reorganization of the Southern agricultural plantation economy during the late nineteenth and early twentieth centuries around the share-cropping system virtually reinstituted bondage for large blocs of the Black population. These political and economic changes during the Gilded Age and Progressive eras—combined with the legalization of segregation and the systematic loss of Black suffrage—placed African Americans behind a racial "veil" and outside mainstream economic and social structures. The health system, spurred by the burgeoning acceptance of the ideology and methodology of mainstream science and gaining international prominence in the process, conformed to the era's pattern of being factor-loaded against African Americans.[4]

Progressive Movement politicians, social reformers, and community leaders espoused the reliance upon, and the application of, methods and data created by science to solve or ameliorate social problems. Major aspects of the Progressive Movement emphasized the dismantling of monopolies, increasing government oversight and regulation in many areas of American life, and the aggressive implementation of public policy based on scientific research by the so-called enlightened intelligentsia. Such thinking energized President Theodore Roosevelt to propose reforming the health delivery system in 1912. As Paul Starr noted:

> *Progressivism reached its peak in the election of 1912, when the Progressives bolted from the Republican Party and nominated former President Theodore Roosevelt as their candidate. Much like Lloyd George and Winston Churchill, Roosevelt supported social insurance, including health insurance, in the belief that no country could be strong whose people were sick and poor. But his defeat in 1912 by Woodrow Wilson postponed for another two decades the kind of leadership that might have involved the national government more extensively in ... compulsory health insurance....*[5]

Simultaneously, the vigorous labor movement—challenging rampant corporate and industrial domination—led to strikes and violence throughout the late nineteenth and early twentieth centuries. The rise in power and influence of the American Federation of Labor (AFL) and the founding in 1906 of the International Workers of the World (IWW) were both emblematic of the period. These developments led to policies throughout the Roosevelt, Taft, and Wilson administrations that dictated the growth and influence of the government both as a mediator and regulator in these areas—interventions that continue today. Unfortunately, much of this newfound, Whites-only social egalitarianism, confidence, and momentum gained by the creation and manipulation of public policy and social engineering was energized and undergirded by increasing levels of nativism, increasing reliance upon social Darwinism as an explanation and rationale for wide ranges of events and policies, and the growth of biomedically influenced racism built upon scientific foundations of eugenics,* psychometrics,** and anthropology.

The new Progressives did not question, but participated in and promoted, policies energized by these negative ideological and pseudoscientific trends. Leaders of social and public health policy as divergent as Yale professor and intellectual William Graham Sumner—in his famous and influential book *Folkways* (1906)—and Margaret Sanger, feminist birth control advocate and pioneer who founded Planned Parenthood, promoted race- and class-biased hereditarian and eugenic policies and programs. Presidents such as Theodore Roosevelt and Woodrow Wilson believed in and were influenced by these influential and popular doctrines. As historian Alan Brinkley noted about Roosevelt's concepts of civilization, "'Civilized' nations, as he defined them, were predominantly white and Anglo-Saxon or Teutonic; 'uncivilized' nations were generally non-white, Latin, or Slavic.... [R]acism was only partly the basis of the distinction."[6]

Contrary to his heroic and positive image, Wilson was a major reactionary leader as far as African Americans and women were concerned. As noted in Low and Clift, "As president of Princeton University, Wilson had barred Afro-American students from the school."[7] As president of the United States he refused to support women's suffrage and progressive health care legislation. In addition, Wilson, "[D]eferring to Southern Democrats, and reflecting his own Southern background, ... condoned the reimposition of segregation in the agencies of the federal government."[8]

Thus the dominant national, domestic, social, and public policy embodying racism and discrimination was once more reinforced by the federal government. Not since the Jacksonian period had government complicity in race-based discrimination been so blatant. Meanwhile, across the Atlantic similar ideologies and scientistic mechanisms energized and guided European social policies and colonial events. One such example that recently resurfaced in the *New York Times* in 1998 was the genocidal war (1904–1907) between Germany and the Hereros of

---

*The study of hereditary improvement by genetic control.

**That branch of psychology dealing with the measurement of psychological variables such as intelligence, aptitude, and personality traits.

Southwest Africa (Namibia),* which "later helped underwrite Nazi pseudoscience used to justify the Holocaust."[9] Pseudoscientific books based on studies performed on mixed-race children in that German colony during that period, supposedly "documenting" their inferiority, strongly influenced Adolf Hitler during the period he was writing about "subhuman races" in *Mein Kampf*. Such ideas and events defined nineteenth- and early twentieth-century contacts in both hemispheres between Western Europeans and non-White and indigenous peoples. These relationships would crystallize into the Holocaust, wars of liberation, and social strife later in the twentieth century.[10]

World War I, sometimes considered a failure of European progressivism, offered the United States an opportunity to demonstrate its Progressive Movement politics. Woodrow Wilson's brainchild, titled the Fourteen Points (an international paradigm that he hypothesized would prevent such conflicts in the future and establish a regulated world community), embodied Progressivism at the international level. The Fourteen Points dealt with the establishment of new boundaries and nations to replace the deposed Austro-Hungarian and Ottoman Empires, established general principles of international conduct such as free trade and freedom of the seas, and established a permanent international governing body—the League of Nations. Domestically, the United States war economy was mobilized by means of increased levels of planning and cooperation. Even the labor movement was officially recognized to further the output for the war effort. One glaring omission of Wilson's vision was the disposition and future status of the international colonial system. This largely involved emancipating the non-White majority of the world and mirrored Wilson's overtly segregationist policies involving race and White domination in the United States. In this country there was also a nasty undercurrent of paranoia, repression, and nativism in the guise of social unity and super-patriotism associated with the war. Though it was directed primarily at Germans, Socialists, and immigrants, Blacks bore the brunt of the outrages and excesses associated with this nationalistic movement, with an upsurge in lynchings and discrimination during and immediately following the war.

Much of the public policy that emerged in the early twentieth century under a banner of Progressivism led to discriminatory immigration policies against non-White peoples and Southern Europeans and the subjugation and exploitation of people of color in the United States and far-flung locations. Enactment of segregation and restrictive immigration laws was the primary mechanism, adding to the attenuating effects of the Great War itself, that

---

*The Hereros are a Black southern African tribe that, along with the Namas (their main nineteenth-century competitors, also known as Hottentots), once dominated central Namibia. After 20 years of German exploitation, oppression, and abuse, the Hereros rebelled, triggering a three-year-long genocidal war in which over 80 percent of the tribe was exterminated (German General Lothar von Trotha issued a *Vernichtungsbefehl*, or extermination order) and the remainder abused by policies such as imprisonment, forced labor, and sexual slavery to survive. They are now a minor tribe in the region.

effectively ended the massive wave of European immigration that had started in the late nineteenth century and implemented a legal racial caste system domestically. Certainly, non-Nordic, southern European, Russian, Asian, and non-White immigration would be virtually halted and the immigration of any other "undesirable" groups severely limited. Much of the justification for these policies was based on spurious scholarship and scientific racism. As Brinkley points out in *The Unfinished Nation*:

> *New scholarly theories, appealing to the progressive respect for expertise, argued that the introduction of immigrants into American society was diluting the purity of the nation's racial stock. The spurious "science" of eugenics spread the belief that human inequalities were hereditary and that immigration was contributing to the multiplication of the unfit.*[11]

Some of the energy driving these policies had imperialistic overtones. U.S. military and political actions such as the takeover and annexation of Hawaii, the occupations of Haiti and the Dominican Republic, and the acquisition of an international empire as a result of the Spanish-American War predicted America's colonial rule over and domination of non-White peoples and their territories. Native Americans were on the verge of extinction by the turn of the century and were systematically removed from the last of their Western lands. African Americans, as had become the national custom, absorbed the brunt of, and were relegated to the bottom, of all these policies, activities, and programs. As Howard Zinn said in *A Peoples's History of the United States*: "In the early part of the twentieth century, labeled by generations of white scholars as 'the Progressive period,' lynchings were reported every week; it was the low point for Negroes, North and South, 'the nadir,' as Rayford Logan, a black historian, put it."[12]

As a result of the resurgence of Black Codes,* elimination of Black suffrage, and legally enforced racial segregation, the small level of progress African Americans achieved during Reconstruction was eliminated. The process of subjugation that had started in the 1870s and was legally codified with Supreme Court–sanctioned segregation with the *Plessy v. Ferguson* decision of 1896 created a *de facto* environment of emancipation without freedom for African Americans that encompassed the Progressive Era and lasted through the Great Depression. The new wave of twentieth-century racial violence and social apartheid had already been justified and rationalized in the

---

*Black Codes were sets of laws modeled in many ways on the codes that had regulated free Blacks in the pre–Civil War South to guarantee White supremacy. For example, they authorized local officials to arrest unemployed Blacks, fine them for vagrancy, and hire them out to private employers to satisfy fines; forbade them to own or lease firearms; and restricted them to jobs such as domestic service and plantation work.

guise of social Darwinism and the rhetoric of Henry Grady's New South.* Early twentieth-century developments would simply be expansions on these same themes. Woodrow Wilson's expansion of racial segregation into both the District of Columbia and governmental departments went farther than the nation's positive response to Grady's request for the North to leave the racial problem alone and depend on the South to deal with the issue. It was the acknowledgment and spread of government-sanctioned apartheid, which was strongly reflected in the health system.[13]

Paradoxically, the 1920s decade earned the light-hearted sobriquet the "Roaring Twenties" largely as a result of its tumultuous sociocultural conflicts and transformations. This "new age," free-living ideology and approach to life were felt to be the nation's response to the war. They also permeated the nation's financial system—leading to a binge of expansion, speculation, and wealth that outstripped economic realities. The nation's economy, bloated and dependent upon artificial wealth and speculation, would collapse in 1929, leading to the Great Depression. The social manifestations reflected major conflicts between the modern, secular culture of the 1920s and the older, conservative, fundamentalist-based culture of the less affluent, less urban, more provincial Americans. These components were an explosive mix.

Many of these sweeping challenges and changes threatened and frightened traditional Americans. As Brinkley noted, "The result of their fears was a series of harsh cultural controversies."[14] Although African Americans began mounting increasingly active and effective programs of resistance between 1910 and 1930, Blacks continued to suffer as convenient scapegoats for U.S. society at large. Moreover, since 1890, oppressive racial and economic conditions in the South and hoped-for economic opportunity in the North helped fuel the first "Great Migration."** The Great War exaggerated this phenomenon that changed the nation's racial demographics, thus heightening racial tensions as Northern cities acquired significant Black populations—all looking for jobs. As Brinkley summarized:

> *No group suffered more from the inflamed climate of the postwar years than American blacks.... By 1919, the racial climate had become sav-*

---

*The "New South" was a post-Reconstruction mythological creation of Southern politicians and publicists emphasizing regional economic development, interregional cooperation, and leaving the region's race relations alone in the restoration of the South to full-fledged national participation. The statistical and social realities of poverty, anachronistic overdependence on agriculture, and Black racial abuse, segregation, and repression did little to undermine the myth.

**The Great Migrations refer to the movement of Southern Blacks off the farms and plantations where they had been concentrated since slavery to Northern and Southern cities. The first Great Migration of Southern Blacks, which was largely spurred on by World War I employment opportunities, occurred between 1890 and 1930. The second wave took place during and following World War II in response to war-related economic opportunities and the completion of the mechanization of Southern agriculture.

*age and murderous. In the South, there was a sudden increase in lynch-*
*ings: more than seventy blacks, some of them war veterans, died at the*
*hands of white mobs in 1919 alone. In the North, black factory workers*
*faced widespread layoffs as returning white veterans displaced them*
*from their jobs. . . . The result was a rash of urban disorders.*[15]

Between 1917 and 1921 race riots flared in Houston, Philadelphia, East St. Louis, Chicago, and Tulsa, for example. Hundreds of Blacks and a number of Whites were killed in Tulsa—including a Black physician, Dr. A. C. Jackson, whose murder was announced in a Black medical journal.[16] The NAACP and the militantly Black-nationalist United Negro Improvement Association (UNIA) advised Blacks to fight back. "In the end, however, most African-Americans had little choice but to acquiesce in the social and economic subjugation being forced on them,"[17] Brinkley observed.

Other major results of this tug-of-war between the values and practices of the old and the new in the United States were the prohibition of the sale of alcohol between 1920 and 1933, leading to generalized erosion of respect for law and the rise of organized crime; the passage and enactment of Restrictive Immigration Acts in 1921 and 1924, virtually eliminating Black, Asian, Southern European, and non-Aryan immigration into the United States; the post–*Birth of a Nation* resurgence of the Ku Klux Klan in 1915—the most prominent U.S. hate group, which specialized in terrorizing and brutalizing Negroes, Jews, Catholics, and immigrants, grew to a 1924 membership high of 4 million; and the reemergence of fundamentalist religion marked by religious revivals and events such as the Scopes trial.* Much of the philosophical and ideological underpinning and pseudoscientific justification of these events and activities were grounded in the beliefs and teachings emanating from the biological and biomedical sciences.

Based on informational and attitudinal interchange mechanisms of ingress and egress between a racist society and its biomedical system, a dynamic growth of scientific racism in the cultural fabric of both the health system and its social environment occured. Unquestioning acceptance of biologically, statistically, and psychologically determined principles of scientific racism generated, indeed popularized, scientific luminaries such as Sir Francis Galton, Herbert Spencer, William Graham Sumner, Karl Pearson, and Cyril Burt, whose works intensified the move toward biological determinism. During the early twentieth century these pseudoscientific principles, based on IQ testing, inborn criminality profiles, and "pauperism," were felt to be scientifically proven among U.S. protagonists. These

---

*In the 1925 Scopes trial a 24-year-old biology teacher was arrested and tried for teaching Charles Darwin's theory of evolution to his students in Dayton, Tennessee. The trial became a national media and cultural battle between religious fundamentalists and secular education. John Scopes was defended by the famed jurist Clarence Darrow, representing the American Civil Liberties Union; and William Jennings Bryan was the prosecuting attorney for the state.

principles were promoted and promulgated not only by the popular press and mass-circulation magazines but also by elite scientists and intellectuals such as C. B. Davenport, Lewis Terman, Henry H. Goddard, Harry Laughlin, Henry Fairfield Osborn, and Robert M. Yerkes. These activities created the United States fascination with and adoption of the "IQ myth" and a vigorous eugenics movement that remained unquestioned until the unsavory Nazi experience discredited them. Led by Justice Oliver Wendell Holmes and the United States Supreme Court, unethical and involuntary sterilization laws modeled on the *Buck v. Bell* decision of 1927 spread throughout the country. This allowed "defective" people* of virtually any type to be forcibly sterilized by the state. Blacks were victimized by these laws to a much greater extent than any other racial or ethnic group, especially in the South. This medicalization and biological justification for U.S. social hierarchies and problems spilled over into a family planning movement such that its leaders, Margaret Sanger being the most prominent example, proposed a bounty for the sterilization of poor women.[18] Despite the scientific debunking of the relationship between these conditions and biological determination by scientists such as Thomas Hunt Morgan, Joseph Goldberger, and Franz Boas by 1930, they continue to cloud and influence both public and health policy today.[19]

These events and developments interfaced with and intensified the complexity of the matrix of race and class problems plaguing the U.S. health system as it entered the twentieth century. During the next 30 years there were few signs of improvement, and many aspects of these medical-social problems worsened. Access to modern health care in the United States continued to be largely determined by a patient's race and class. As the health system transformed from a largely eleemosynary system into a capital-driven economy, Blacks and the poor suffered increasing exclusion for these "new" reasons. Clearly, in this emerging political economy of health care, well-to-do, native-born, Anglo-Saxon Whites were not only the middle-class majority, but were also the only subpopulation with free and complete access to the health system. This freedom and access encompassed everything from hospitalization and choice of physicians to obtaining health professions training. This was confirmed by the Committee on Costs of Medical Care (CCMC) Report, much of which was conducted in the late 1920s (1926–1932). Although the exact mechanisms changed with the increased utilization of both hospital and outpatient care, the new racial apartheid and class discrimination were actually part of a continuum of practices more than 200 years old. There were small subpopulations of poor Whites and Blacks who were "fortunate" enough to be located in areas where they could virtually trade their bodies in

---

*Some, but not all, of the people considered defective during this period included the retarded, the physically handicapped, the habitually poor (pauperism), repeat criminals, people of poor "racial stock," Negroes, chronic welfare recipients, and people with certain dread diseases such as tuberculosis. Many of these conditions, or predispositions toward contracting them, were falsely considered to be genetically transmitted.

exchange for up-to-date medical treatments in public or teaching hospitals or public health or hospital clinics. Even this avenue was largely confined to select groups of disadvantaged patients with rare and interesting disorders who presented themselves to medical teaching and training centers. However, others with mundane conditions were at risk for being used for surgical practice, risky experimental procedures, and eugenically oriented surgery.[20] In contrast, and for a variety of reasons, Western European countries opened up access to their country's health systems for their entire populations, spurred by the labor movements, unions, and actions of politicians such as Otto von Bismarck in Germany and Lloyd George and the Parliament in Great Britain. The French had begun the process during the Revolutionary and Republican eras of the late eighteenth and early nineteenth centuries.[21]

This matrix of medical-social difficulties heightened by issues of race and class in the United States health system, many of which stood in violation of both the American creed and the ethical foundation of the Western health subculture, blemished what grew to be the most dominant modern-era health delivery system on earth from the onset of the twentieth century. Acceptance of the premise of race- and class-based delivery of health care favoring the wealthy and Anglo-Saxon Whites contradicted the rhetoric of the American creed and the Constitution, which were egalitarian in nature. Moreover, since the Middle Ages, provision of health care to the poor was strongly entrenched and had become the ethical standard of Judeo-Christian Western culture. For more than 1,000 years the Western medical profession, by and large, had purported to complement and certainly not impede these policies. Nevertheless, remote slave and colonial systems, in which virtually all the European countries participated after the fifteenth century, had established a tradition of violating these principles. Thus strong and economically compelling precedents for deviance from these medical-ethical standards had been established and sometimes perpetuated. By the end of the early twentieth century, the U.S. health infrastructure, along with European colonial and the Republic of South Africa's health systems, would stand as examples of apartheid and health care discrimination. These health systems could be cited for institutionalizing policies and structures leading to race- and class-based health status and outcome differentials.[22]

In lieu of runaway health system progress, the environment for the perpetuation of the "slave health deficit" into the early twentieth century was created. The health care neglect of Blacks and their relegation to segregated and inferior facilities became institutionalized and acceptable. Paradoxically, as medical therapeutics, interventions, and technology became more effective, populations without access to the progress were placed at a growing disadvantage. Whether trickle-down benefits from the U.S. medical largess could maintain the race- and class-based health status and outcome differentials at socially acceptable levels was a question that remained unanswered. Virtually the only positive responses during the period between 1901 and 1929 to these medical, social, and physical atrocities were Black self-help and civil rights activities. One aspect of these activities was the formation and institutionalization of a racially separate medical profession and separate health and hospital systems. Because these efforts were handicapped by underfunding and spotty organization, they could not overpower the negative effects generated by the apartheid of a massive and generously funded mainstream health system. Although these separate self-help efforts improved African American health status and outcomes, they could not ameliorate the slave health deficit. Therefore, Blacks continued as victims of the greatest levels of racial violence, discrimination, segregation, and exploitation of any U.S. racial or ethnic group during the early twentieth century. Unfortunately, their health system experience also reflected these realities.[23]

## Health System Arise: 1901–1929

Compared to its major European counterparts, the United States had a late start in formal health system development. At the end of the nineteenth century, Western Europe's institutionalized health systems continued to set the standards for the world. Their established networks of hospitals, clinically based medical schools, public health agencies, and biomedical research institutes were the envy of the modern world. This comparative superiority to the United States system was especially prominent in certain health system constituent components. Some of the components of Western Europe's health systems that demonstrated their superiority included: (1) hospitals and other inpatient health delivery facilities that were already analogous to the future U.S. health institutional infrastructure; (2) the clinically and scientifically oriented health professions training and research infrastructure; (3) a public health infrastructure composed largely of massive public hospitals, public health agencies and departments, and clinics all allied with, and often administered by, their medical schools; (4) the growing network of German, French, and British biomedical research institutes, many of which were state sponsored; (5) advanced health care financing mechanisms that were already beginning to be universal, covering their entire populations; and (6) a much more specialized and technically trained health professions workforce.

European health care financing and funding mechanisms and infrastructures were not only more comprehensive and advanced, but they also developed along drastically different medical-social lines. In response to a different set of social and political realities, such as strong and influential labor unions and social movements, European politicians pushed to open up access to basic health care for all citizens. By the nineteenth century, the nexus between public health and social progress was established in Europe. British Prime Minister Benjamin Disraeli stated in an 1875 speech to Parliament, "The public health is the foundation on which repose the happiness of the people and the power of a country. The care of the public health is the first duty of a statesman."[24] As Paul Starr noted in *The Social Transformation of American Medicine* regarding Germany and other European nations:

> *In 1883 Germany established the first national system of compulsory sickness insurance. . . . Similar systems were set up in Austria in 1888 and in Hungary in 1891. . . . [I]n a second wave of reform, Norway adopted compulsory sickness insurance in 1909, Serbia in 1910, Britain in 1911, Russia in 1912, and the Netherlands in 1913.[25]*

These national public health and health insurance programs, largely independently funded by unions and worker alliances, provided for comprehensive health care with medical attendance and cash benefits to workers in order to make up for lost wages during illnesses. They also contained agencies that scientifically and statistically monitored and regulated the public's health. These agencies usually had state-authorized public health policy arms and enforcement capabilities. Europe entered the twentieth century with the beginnings of universal, mandatory funding and coverage financing its health systems, which were far superior to that of the United States. Its public health infrastructures were also much more advanced. Thus Britain and the Continent remained world leaders in medicine, public health, and medical financing until the devastation of Europe during World War I.[26]

This contrasted markedly with the evolving, almost rudimentary U.S. system, which was comparatively disorganized and almost totally reliant on private resources. All these traits accentuated the tendency toward access to high-quality health care being strongly based on race, class, and socioeconomic status. Access to health care and its beneficence was considered an individual rather than a societal concern. Social Darwinists, such as sociologist William Graham Sumner of Yale, biologist and president of Stanford David Starr Jordan, and MIT's Frances Amasa Walker, felt that health promotion–disease prevention and medical therapeutic interventions for the poor perpetuated "inferior" genetic lines. Such activities subverted the scientific mechanisms of "survival of the fittest." Therefore, working-class, immigrant, and minority populations' receipt of health care that could often be described as scant and inferior was logical, if not desirable. Inconsistent and often inadequate worker's compensation laws, which were implemented at the end of the nineteenth and the early twentieth century, were emblematic of the restrained approach to health services taken by the United States. These laws were very limited in scope and in coverage. They left the average working family at risk for economic calamity if most types of serious illness struck. Such laws were sometimes complemented by inadequate lodge, fraternal order, and benefit society coverage, which affected some 8 million American members. Instead of emphasizing their social and secret society functions, as a result of America's conservative social policies, these organizations began to function as "poor man's insurance companies" by the early 1900s in their roles of offering meager supplementary health benefits. J. Edward Perry noted that even in the Black community, besides offering health plans, "The lodges served as burial and mortgage insurance."[27] Often these were scant cash benefits of a few dollars a day covering a limited period of illness time. Even this highly porous fabric of health coverage, seldom offering hospital or more than episodic care, affected only 25 to 30 percent of U.S. families. These circumstances were reminiscent of past Puritan and Calvinist ethical standards of provision of charity medical care to the "unworthy poor." Defensible medical covenants providing decent health services for all, following the trends set by other Western European countries, were rejected. Clearly, such arrangements were tantamount to a rejection by the United States health system of the concept of leveling the playing field for all the nation's citizens as far as access and the provision of health care were concerned.

Acceptance of dual and unequal health facilities and outcomes based on race and class conformed to popular U.S. social attitudes and practices. Even in cities like Cleveland, Ohio, where racism in public accommodations was less evident preceding the Great Migration, by 1915 hospitals began discriminating against or excluding African American patients.[28] Dual and unequal medical facilities for Blacks and the formation of the "Negro medical ghetto" were natural by-products of Black ghetto formation in Northern and Southern cities, institutionalization of Black/White economic differentials during an industrial age, and codified legal practices separating the races and endorsing discrimination against African Americans.

Transformation of the health system into a private, money-based, economic system compounded African American health disadvantages caused by racism, prejudice, and segregation—largely exacerbated by public policy, social, and financial considerations. This worsened the absolute and relative health and outcome status of Black and other disadvantaged and identifiable minority groups in an early-twentieth-century health system already marred by inequalities based on class stratification and fundamental medical-social problems. Two of the most influential studies conducted on Blacks in the rural South of the 1920s, where more than two-thirds of Blacks lived, were Charles Johnson's *Shadow of the Plantation* and Carter G. Woodson's *The Rural Negro*. When Farley and Allen summed up these investigators' findings regarding the health care system in the rural South, they said:

> *Johnson and Woodson ... contend that medical and public health facilities provided no assistance for rural blacks. In many areas no doctors or nurses were willing to treat black patients, and blacks who needed hospitalization had to find an urban medical facility that had a Jim Crow ward.*[29]

The health system "could not help but reproduce the fundamental social relationships and values in microcosm,"[30] Charles Rosenberg observed.[31]

During the early days of the twentieth century, for the first time in the nation's history, health care itself came to be considered an essential need. The health care of this era could now be viewed as adhering to a standard similar to those defined in *A Dictionary of Epidemiology*: "Those services provided to individuals or communities by agents of the health services or professions, for the purpose of promoting, maintaining, monitoring or restoring health."[32]

Alexis de Tocqueville had noted early in the nineteenth century that not only did virtually all White Americans desire the "good life" but also that, "In America the taste for physical well-being ... is felt by all. Everybody is preoccupied caring for the slightest needs of the body."[33] However, until the early twentieth century, as we have seen, this American preoccupation with health and fitness remained largely an individual, not necessarily a medical or public health, concern. Moreover, these emerging standards applied only to the vast majority of Americans who were White.

Prior to the early twentieth century, the involvement of health professionals in the provision of health services was not considered essential. In fact, the distinct distrust most Americans demonstrated for regular physicians and their doctrinaire treatments was only gradually overcome. Earlier, Americans also displayed a distaste for the hospitals in which regular physicians practiced. Moreover, the American character favored the freedom to choose among a wide range of medical treatments—since no one was convinced they were effective. Such attitudes go a long way toward explaining the lack of public or political support for medical licensing laws, the persistence and general popularity of medical sects in the United States, the belated North American acceptance of hospitals and laboratory medicine, the continued success of traditional and spiritual healers in the United States, and the vigorous sales of herbal and patent medicines in America. Only after regular medicine had proven its scientific and technical superiority in the public mind was orthodox medicine permitted to rise to the forefront.

Changes in these long-lasting attitudes affecting American medical policies and practices were evidence of the dramatic transformations that took place in the relationship between the American public and the biomedical sciences and the health system between 1901 and 1929. They provide testimony to and reinforce the fact that the dominance and cultural authority ceded to the medical profession and the health care institutional infrastructure are largely early twentieth-century phenomena.[34]

Despite the less egalitarian race- and class-biased financing of U.S. health care, from an international perspective, other qualitative and quantitative health system differences emerged between 1901 and 1929. The U.S. health system entered the twentieth century with a shallow scientific base less developed and sophisticated than Europe's, but by the eve of the Great Depression the U.S.

system began its challenge for world leadership in the biomedical sciences. Much of the impetus for this transformation was supplied by World War I. During the early twentieth century America made revolutionary scientific and technical advances in areas such as medical diagnostics, surgery, and therapeutics; medical and health professions educational reform; medical and health care regulation; health policy development; health care infrastructure and hospital development; dental medicine and surgery; and health professions development, prestige, and authority. Major impediments in U.S. health system development from the standpoint of improving the health status and outcome of the entire U.S. population were its faulty health financing and failure to acknowledge or ameliorate its history-based, medical-social, race and class problems.[35]

The major impetus fueling the transformation of health care from a luxury into a necessity was the advance of scientific medical progress. As Richard Harrison Shryock points out in *The Development of Modern Medicine,* "The dramatic advances in medicine made it imperative that all people secure the services of regular medicine."[36] The fact that medicine was now effective at preventing certain diseases and poor outcomes led many Americans to conclude that the persistence of bad results meant that medicine was not doing its job or being utilized to its maximum effectiveness. The nineteenth century had birthed the sciences of microbiology, pharmacology, and immunology, but the twentieth century saw the implementation of large-scale vaccination programs against diphtheria, tuberculosis, and tetanus. Successful campaigns were mounted and undertaken worldwide against yellow fever, malaria, smallpox, and hookworm. Breakthroughs in the science of nutrition identified a lexicon of vitamin deficiency diseases, lending specificity to unprecedented empirical discoveries of the eighteenth century, such as Lind's discovery of scurvy in 1747. This provided a scientific basis for his recommendation for preventing and treating scurvy with citrus, which was equivalent to administering vitamin C. Goldberger's 1914 linkage of pellagra with vitamin B deficiency, the association of vitamin D with rickets, and George Richards Minot's 1926 discovery that raw liver consumption could effectively control pernicious anemia were examples of the new deficiency diseases discovered between 1901 and 1929. After Casimir Funk coined the term "vitamines" in 1912, a string of discoveries followed. Vitamin A was discovered in 1913, vitamin B in 1916, and vitamin D in 1922. Although much of the progress was American-based, most disadvantaged U.S. groups, such as African Americans, benefited little from the discoveries.[37]

Medical therapeutics also boomed with the elucidation and perfection of chemotherapy, radiology, and surgery. Syphilis was a major scourge of the nineteenth century and one of mankind's most dreaded diseases. Moreover, it seemingly proliferated with urbanization and population growth. Building on his basic science background in bacteriology and simultaneously laying the foundation of the new field of hematology, Paul Erlich (1854–1915) scientifically discovered the new anti-spirochete drug salvarsan in 1910. A less toxic derivative, neosalvarsan, was soon developed and became the drug of choice in the treatment of syphilis until the utilization of penicillin in the 1940s.[38] Ironically, Sir Alexander Fleming's chance discovery of penicillin in 1929 would not yield practical results until the late 1930s. Thus following Erlich's death in 1915, the "doldrum years" of chemotherapy ensued—punctuated by only two discoveries, atabrine and plasmochin for malaria—until the 1930s. From a therapeutic standpoint much progress also occurred in biochemistry and pharmacology, with the purification and formulation of medicines such as phenobarbital and insulin. Konrad Roentgen's discovery of X-rays in 1895 was immediately utilized diagnostically with sophisticated application to the gastrointestinal (GI) tract and urinary tract before the 1920s. Within a decade, X-rays, along with radium, were being utilized therapeutically for cancer. Because of Karl Landsteiner's discovery and elucidation of major blood groups in 1901, blood transfusion became a practical proposition by 1930. Such advances, along with improvements in asepsis, antisepsis, and surgical technique, complemented the benefits of surgical anesthesia. Through the efforts of physicians such as the Mayo brothers, William Halstead, and Harvey Cushing, surgery became both safe and effective by 1929.[39]

Medical diagnostics also came of age between 1901 and 1929. The infancy of a new branch of engineering, biomedical engineering, coincided with the appearance of the electrocardiograph (1903), the electroencephalograph (1929), and perfected blood pressure machines in the early twentieth century.[40]

By the early twentieth century, it became obvious that rampant medical progress had pushed state-of-the-art medical care and services out of reach of a growing portion of the population. The dominant reasons for the growing inaccessibility were largely economic, as the CCMC Report documented. However, there was also a medical-social component, including race and class segregation and exclusion. For example, mastery of the new medical advances required extensive education and specialized training for their application. Thus physicians were required to invest large resources in terms of both time and money into their education and training. Most of the advances, such as laboratory and X-ray facilities, were both capital and labor intensive—requiring special buildings and trained staffs for their implementation and application. This necessitated construction of hospitals capable of being disinfected and equipped with expensive laboratory, diagnostic, and therapeutic facilities. Both the structural economic and professional economic factors collided, compounding the effects of both. As a result, health care became very expensive. As Shryock observed in *The Development of Modern Medicine* regarding the increasing scarcity of medical care:

> *The most obvious explanation was to be found in the mounting costs of service. Here ... it is to be noted that it was the very progress which physicians had made in science, which involved them in new difficulties in the practice of their art. Technical improvement led to simultaneous increase in the demand for medical services and in the price that must*

> *be paid for them. And so the more that people trusted medical aid, the
> less they could afford it.*[41]

Since the medieval days, productive European workers had protected themselves against illness through guilds or benefit organizations. For the scant, relatively ineffective medical care available, such organizations met the needs of most people up to the nineteenth century in Europe and the United States. Most of the old home-centered care of previous eras was neither specialized nor expensive. The U.S. insurance structure did not change to meet contemporary needs. As Shryock observed, "The old tradition of voluntary insurance had not been expanded to meet their growing needs, and the still older tradition of charity did not meet their needs at all. A stigma was attached to charity hospitals, just as there had once been to charity schools."[42] Blacks, the most socioeconomically disadvantaged group in relative and absolute terms and the traditional victims of health system discrimination, were even more vulnerable to, and suspicious of, these same forces. Even in Northern cities such as Detroit, "availability and access to proper health facilities were still often denied to many," and "hospitals refused to admit African American patients,"[43] Eric J. Bailey observed. He further noted: "Fear of hospitals, a common occurrence in all groups, caused many African Americans to avoid using mainstream health facilities. This fear was based on a long-standing traditional belief that hospital physicians practiced experimental laboratory tests on patients."[44]

Thus their poorer health status, the barriers and abuses associated with the color line, and overreliance on traditional folk healers and remedies made Black's situation more acute. African Americans, who were largely excluded from the labor movements, large benevolent societies, and even many charity hospitals and health facilities, were generally abandoned by both the health and social welfare systems. The popularity and promotion of Booker T. Washington's enthusiastic ideology notwithstanding, for the few Blacks who could afford the new medical technology, exclusion and discriminatory treatment remained the rule. Thus tremendous medical-social and economic pressures contributed to a segregated Black health subsystem. African American physicians also required hospitals to engage in the new medical advances. Social pressures led to the formation and growth of racially separate health systems, hospitals, and health professions as Black doctors attempted to ameliorate the "slave health deficit." Meanwhile, virtually all of the European politicians and social systems by the late nineteenth century had begun to confront the issues of exploding medical costs and increasingly limited health system access. Factoring in explosive costs fostered by scientific advance and technology, the United States health system, with its archaic health financing and race and class prejudices, either failed to respond or responded inappropriately. Although these developments may have delayed it, they did not deter the maturation of the American health system.[45]

One of the hallmarks of the institutionalization of the United States health system was the growth of the hospital infrastructure. However, this growth assumed a peculiarly American profile. Instead of hospital distribution based on rational numerical requirements and specialized function based on the needs of the entire population, as in Europe, in America they were specialized social and public works of ethnic, religious, and racial communities. If Irish Catholic and Italian physicians were to be allowed hospital practices, Catholic and community hospitals were necessary as the facilitating vehicles. If a Jewish person desired a kosher diet and care administered by a Jewish physician—who was barred from many public and private hospital staffs—hospitals operated by the Jewish community were necessary. Therefore, much American hospital growth consisted of religious denominational and ethnic hospitals. There was also a significant number of specialty hospitals representing entrepreneurial ventures by specialty physicians or physician groups.

A tradition of fiercely independent, free-standing, provincial, and community-focused institutions arose. Such traditions, compounded by discrimination and strict racial segregation, spurred the opening of a network of Black hospitals to serve African American communities. This development also allowed the growing Black medical profession, which was almost universally excluded from White hospitals, a place to practice. As a result, there were more hospitals than were probably necessary, and they duplicated and overlapped services. Since they evolved largely out of medical-social rather than public health or scientific medical needs, they defied rational health delivery models of distribution or function. Moreover, they planted the seeds for a tradition of excess capacity, unnecessary institutional competition, and expensive duplication of services that still haunts the U.S. hospital system today. Regional coordination and economic planning beyond the institution's walls were outside the scope of the typical U.S. hospital. Therefore, one could argue, the rise of hospitals in the United States pandered directly to the American public's ethnic, religious, and social needs and biases. As Vanessa Northington Gamble noted about the origin of Black hospitals:

> *Racial discrimination, white self-interest, black professional concerns, divergent strategies for black social advancement, and changes in hospital care and medical practice all played major roles in the development of these institutions.... Regardless of motive, the goal behind the establishment of these hospitals was the same—to maintain and create a segregated hospital system.*[46]

True medical necessity based on rational health planning was secondary.

Besides social reasons, several biomedical and technical advances furthered the American acceptance of the hospital. Some were improvements in sanitation and hygiene due to the public's acceptance and the institutional application of the germ theory transforming hospitals into safe environments; improvements in modern surgery that required specialized environments (e.g., sterile operating rooms, specialized surgical anesthesia) available only in hospitals; the rise of laboratory medicine for diagnostic and therapeutic purposes that could only be made available in the hospital for logistical as well as economic reasons; the changing social environment wrought by urbanization and lack of traditional family supports that had favored home care; and the increased prestige and authority of modern science. These forces also increased African American acceptance of hospitals.[47]

The hospital infrastructure as we know it took its present shape during the first three decades of the twentieth century. In less than 40 years the number of U.S. hospitals increased almost twenty-five-fold. An 1873 survey identifyied only 178 hospitals in the United States—36 years later, by 1909, 4,359 were found. By 1920 the number had risen to 4,534, consisting of 4,013 general hospitals and 521 mental hospitals. Of these, approximately 202 were Black, according to 1923 estimates. Increasing numbers were not the only indicators of transformation affecting the hospital system. As the scientific character of hospitals changed, they emerged as essential institutions for medicine and its allied health professions. Between 1901 and 1929 hospitals underwent medicalization and specialization while simultaneously becoming the fiefdom of the medical profession. Many of these developments took place outside the boundaries and beyond the "veil" within which African American communities were allowed to function.[48]

Before the late nineteenth century the nature and acceptance of the U.S. hospital reflected the state of medicine and the social milieu in which it existed. Medical knowledge in the United States prior to that time was relatively nonspecialized, nontechnical, and purportedly available to any educated layman. Hospital care, largely confined to dependent, largely male populations without caretaker families, was predicated on poverty and dependence—requirements for admission to most of these institutions, which modulated their functions and prestige levels. Early hospitals, therefore, had distinct social and class characteristics that were identified with the poor, debauched, and disabled or infirm. As Charles E. Rosenberg, a leading authority on the evolution of U.S. health care institutions, observed about early hospitals, "Allied with medicine's limited technical resources, it produced a medical system minimally dependent on institutional care, in which dependence and social status, not diagnosis, determined the makeup of institutional populations."[49] Other major motivations behind hospital care, besides charitable stewardship, "grew out of the clinical and educational needs of an elite medical profession."[50] Rosenberg further articulated the rationale behind the 200-year-old American tradition of expecting the poor to sacrifice their bodies to medical progress:

> [B]oth lay and medical supporters of private hospitals contended that there could be no conflict between the hospital goals of laymen and physicians, for citizens of every rank would ultimately benefit from the clinical instruction that could be most effectively organized around the aggregated bodies of the poor.[51]

The Black experience in such institutions—when they were allowed entry—therefore was often characterized by heavy doses of discrimination, racism, and exploitation. Lacking the technical or specialized functions of later institutions, these hospitals often resembled large homes or dormitory facilities. "Until the twentieth century hospital expense budgets were dominated by the cost of food, heat, light, and labor—costs little different from those of an orphanage, boarding school, or rich man's mansion,"[52] Rosenberg observed.

By the 1920s, multiple scientific and social factors forced hospitals to undergo another set of changes. Rosenberg summarized these:

> *The hospital was no longer exclusively a resort for the dependent; diag nosis as well as social location had begun to determine hospital admissions. Technology had provided new tools and, equally important, a new rationale for centering acute care in the hospital. Medical men and medical skills had come to play an increasingly prominent part in the institution, gradually supplanting older patterns of lay control. Bureaucracy had reshaped the institution's internal order: a trained and disciplined nursing corps, a self-consciously professionalizing hospital administration, and an increasingly specialized profession had all played a role in transforming the . . . hospital.[53]*

All of these changes began to supersede and preclude even the consideration of the then-dominant mode of delivery—home care. The clinical laboratories, X-ray departments, and antiseptic and fully equipped operating rooms that the era's scientifically trained physicians needed were now headquartered in hospitals. Increasingly identified as quintessential twentieth-century institutions, hospitals began to be imbued with symbolic and social significance. They also became the focus of community pride. As Rosemary Stevens said of American hospital development of this era, "[B]etween 1870 and 1910, they assumed an unusually important function as the embodiment of social aspirations—of progress, science, efficiency, and humanitarianism."[54] An array of new facilities and materials was developed: special buildings for the particular care and isolation of diseases such as tuberculosis; facilities with lead-lined rooms for X-ray therapy; special plumbing, disposal devices, and chemistry hoods; new technological equipment for diagnosis and treatment; new and specialized categories of supplies ranging from pharmaceuticals, contrast media, and surgical appliances to photographic X-ray film; and specialized categories of health professions personnel varying from nurses and hospital administrators to laboratory technicians. These developments all drove the costs of providing hospital care through the roof. Moreover, by the end of the 1920s these new capital-intensive institutions could no longer be financed simply by charity and meager public funding.

Community-based capital investment, massive foundation and institutional financing, and patient fees were now necessary to finance the new emblem of medical progress—the modern hospital. Increasingly, not having full access to such institutions placed potential patients at a marked medical and social disadvantage. An already health and socioeconomic status disadvantaged Black population was placed at further risk by health institutional exclusion, discriminatory institutional segregation and disadvantage, and professional nonparticipation at the institutional level. Moreover, the entire dynamic countervailed the African American community's ability to scientifically keep pace with, or finance, adequate, separate facilities. Thus the health policy, medical-social, and health care financing seeds of the demise of the Black hospital were planted during the early twentieth century.[55]

American acceptance of hospitals had profound effects on health system standardization and quality assurance mechanisms. This was based on the fact that "hospital care … [was] so expensive and because hospitals [were] more amenable to organizational constraint."[56] Florence Nightingale's efforts from the early 1860s, suggesting a uniform format for collecting and reporting hospital statistics, laid the groundwork. Boston surgeon Ernest Codman furthered quality assurance efforts by devising a method of careful analysis of cases for which treatment was unsuccessful, called "end result analysis," in 1900. Early on, Codman's method failed to gain widespread acceptance. However the Joint Commission on Accreditation of Healthcare Organizations (JCAHO) traces its inception in 1951 to his original proposal. Between 1913 and 1917 the American College of Surgeons (ACS), with the support of the Carnegie Foundation and the American Hospital Association (AHA), became heavily involved in upgrading the nation's hospitals. Their publication of the *Minimum Standard for Hospitals* (1917) was precedent-setting and influential in health care quality assurance. The 1923 founding of the National Hospital Association (NHA), whose aim "was to ensure proper standards of education and efficiency in black hospitals"[57]—as part of the National Medical Association* (NMA)—was one response to these efforts.[58]

The first three decades of the twentieth century prepared the U.S. health care system ideologically, strategically, and materially for the expansion toward the costly, science- and technology-driven, and dominant health system of today. Based on the first systematic tallying of health care costs in 1946, retrospective estimates reveal that in 1929 the United States spent some $3.5 billion on health care, or 3.5 percent of the gross national product (GNP). Comparatively speaking, Great Britain would not reach comparable levels of GNP expenditures until 1954. United States health care expenditures declined to a low point of $2 billion in 1933 as a result of the Great Depression. Expenditures increased from that point, reaching a

---

*The National Medical Association is a professional society that represents at least three-quarters of the nation's approximately 25,000 African American physicians. Born of professional exclusion, segregation, and discrimination, this organization was founded November 18, 1895, in Atlanta, Georgia. Headquartered in Washington, D.C., the NMA publishes its own journal and has a proud history of advocacy for poor, underserved, and racial minority-patients.

$2.9 billion spending level and 4 percent of the GNP by 1935. Most significant was the fact that the prosperous 1920s supported the explosive expansion of the general hospital infrastructure while the Great Depression would threaten its very financial survival. The capital-intensive demands of the hospital, health professions educational and research infrastructures, as well as ambulatory care infrastructures demanded the transformation and restructuring of health care financing.

Most European systems had already moved toward government- or labor union–regulated collectives to finance health care. Simultaneously, the health care financing infrastructure in the United States stalled. Instead of rapidly maturing to meet the new demands generated by modern medicine and health care, the health professions, private health policy makers, and governmental functionaries failed to advise and exercise leadership in this area. The only available health insurers during the 1920s were the aforementioned small lodge, industrial, and fraternal networks that often underinsured small blocks of urban and corporate-dependent Americans.

By the late 1920s and early 1930s health care financing mechanisms in this country assumed characteristics that would continue to haunt the United States system into the twenty-first century. They remained individually based, nonstandardized, piecemeal, and ultimately inadequate. Fee-for-service payment prevailed in a demand-driven, pseudo-market, health care environment compounded by various mechanisms shielding real costs from individuals or policy makers. Despite the lowering of some of the real costs in delivering care secondary to efficiencies produced by the spread of telephone communication, mobility fostered by individual gas-powered automobiles, and the concentration of outpatient care in office locations instead of house calls, physician fees continued to increase. Concentrating inpatient services in centrally located hospitals and eliminating house calls automatically increased the efficiency of delivering services. Nevertheless, as third parties assumed an increased responsibility for paying for services, these costs also escalated rapidly. Moreover, hospitals began routinely billing above their true costs for their capital expansions, charity care, and inflated technology costs. Increasingly, only third-party payers dealt with the real dollar costs of health care services—helping facilitate both the real growth and cost inflation of these services.

Beginning in 1929, the Great Depression would force the issue. The economic downturn resulted in many hospitals, private clinics, and medical institutions facing bankruptcy. The ensuing environment became an ideal opportunity for rational reform of the entire system. Financing based on universal coverage, rational planning of the system, and capital investment in necessary, instead of luxury, services was a possibility. Instead, an artificial system propped up by increasing government involvement and funding of health care was chosen. This system was characterized by an overt dependence on patient fees instead of charity to cover the costs of services and by the acceptance of private health insurance as a dominant funding mechanism. This funding mechanism would explode in the 1940s. In order to provide a large "private" system for physicians and institutions, a piecemeal "public" sector was institutionalized without a structured funding mechanism to support it. Instead, tax-based public resources were increasingly earmarked to fund medical education, and tax breaks and artificial incentives were built into the "private" system to subsidize its expansion—rendering it an unofficial charity. However, all of these mechanisms were eventually shaped and tailored to meet the unique needs of the European American health providers and White middle-class consumers who constituted the upper half of the system. Most financing activity concentrated around mainstream, full-time, often trade union–based employment; most African Americans would not be able to meet these criteria because of unemployment, *de facto* underemployment (e.g., rural-agricultural-based and domestic employment with no health benefits), and trade union discrimination. All these major shifts in the health care political economy occurred as if African Americans were either absent, permanently disadvantaged pariahs undeserving of basic care, or placed in the U.S. system primarily for training or research purposes. Moreover, as the health financing mechanisms became more monetarized and commercially oriented, African Americans, because of their socioeconomic status and their arbitrary racial exclusion from the mainstream competitive economic and funding systems, would come to be almost permanently crippled in their efforts to obtain equitable health care. This period served as the preparatory phase for the health care financing infrastructures and mechanisms that would propel the system into the late twentieth century.[59]

As if in anticipation and preparation for stewardship over the increasingly influential and highly regarded U.S. health system, the health professions, led by physicians and the American Medical Association (AMA), organized during the early twentieth century. These events profoundly affected the medical professional, medical educational, and review and control infrastructures of the evolving health system. Indirectly, because of medical professional influence, the way governments at the local, state, and national levels interacted with the health system was also profoundly changed. For the first time in more than 200 years, the White organized medical profession was granted virtual stewardship over the nature and administration of the U.S. health system. By the 1930s its covenants with governments resulted in a relatively rigid structure of state licensing laws, state-imposed medical education and practice standards, the beginnings of some meaningful medical and public health regulation, and state-funded medical research. Through these physician-mediated regulatory and educational channels, governments were allowed entry to the administrative levels of the burgeoning health delivery system. African American physicians, although active in separate and circumscribed "unofficial" reform activities in their own racially segregated communities, which will be described later, were totally excluded from these important "official" processes.

In 1901 the AMA revised its constitution and created a new legislative body— the House of Delegates. This standardized body, based on predetermined state constituency representation and buttressed by representatives from the medical education infrastructure, encouraged official member participation, and enabled the body to wield both political and social power for the first time in America. As Paul Starr observed in *The Social Transformation of American Medicine,* "From a mere eight thousand members in 1900, the AMA shot up to seventy thousand in 1910, half the physicians in the country. By 1920 membership had reached sixty percent."[60] Barred from admission to local medical societies, African American physicians were forced to sit on the sidelines observing the phenomenal growth of both the profession and the health care industry. A more modern ethical code was also adopted in 1903. These events marked the beginning of a virtual hegemony exercised over the health system by White organized medicine that would go unchallenged into the 1960s. Neither the adoption of a new ethical code nor the administrative reorganization included Black physicians or socially oriented health policies. Official apartheid was the rule of the day in the medical profession until the late 1960s.

During the first three decades of the twentieth century the medical profession did more than just organize. White organized medicine also tightly regulated, while simultaneously reforming, the medical education system, imposing its influence on the legal regulation and standardization of health care provision and providers. As has been discussed earlier, based on a successful movement started in the 1870s and 1880s, physicians established a national network of state medical licensing laws by 1900. They overcame their sectarian divisions and were granted legitimate authority by politicians for the first time in the United States, creating a strict professional regulatory apparatus through accrediting and rating medical schools and requiring passage of examinations. Organized medicine as a power group dates from these beginnings.[61]

By the end of this era, in 1929, White organized medicine was a major political and social force. Not only had the medical profession regulated itself, but it had also gained control of all aspects of the health care system necessary to provide scientifically sound medical services to the populations it chose to serve. Moreover, it had gone a long way toward providing a substandard level of subsidized (usually public) funding and facilities, functioning for its own professional advantage and convenience (usually for training purposes) outside the mainstream health system for Blacks and the poor. This arrangement conformed to popular public attitudes and social practices. Remnants of this inferior subsystem remain today.

One of the major focuses of this reform, constituting the profession's center of power, was the medical education system. Reform of medical education was built upon the foundations of the graded, basic science–based curriculum and bedside teaching. The fundamentals of these methods had been applied successfully in the French and German medical schools beginning in the late eighteenth and early nineteenth centuries. Graded medical school curriculums and clinical clerkships based on clinical teaching and medical experience had quietly started in New Orleans and Chicago around the time of the Civil War. Beginning in the 1870s and 1880s, White organized medicine and physician-educators nurtured this movement with the establishment and widespread acceptance of the American Association of Medical Colleges' (AAMC) approach to medical education reform and adherence to the Johns Hopkins Medical School model by 1900. Acceptance grew for the graded curriculum, higher admission standards, bedside teaching of clinical medicine, and standardized examination and graduation standards similar to those in Europe.

African American admissions to mainstream medical schools during the first decades of the century were few and far between. About ten Black medical schools that had opened since the Civil War, and struggled with these expensive and privilege-based new standards, had survived. The power exerted by White organized medicine over Black institutions was greatly expanded during the first three decades of the twentieth century by regulatory, licensing, and medical education funding and reform routes.

Building upon the bold reforms of President Charles Eliot of Harvard and Daniel Coit Gilman of Johns Hopkins, the AMA—through its 1904 Council on Medical Education (CME) and the subsequent release of the Flexner Report in 1910—completely changed American medical education. Reversing the trend that had begun with the commercial medical schools in the eighteenth century (which by then had proliferated by 213 percent, from 75 to 160 between 1870 and 1910), the number of medical schools had dropped to 95 by 1915. By 1930, there were 76. Medical education reform also bred new confidence on the part of educational funding sources. Before then, medical education was viewed by foundations as a predominantly commercial rather than educational enterprise. Thus medical education was no longer excluded from educational funding. As a result of the new standards and the effects the Flexner report had on the educational establishment, Kenneth Ludmerer observed, "By 1930, American medical education was finally on a firm financial footing."[62] Between the turn of the century and the 1930s, $154 million poured into medical education from major foundations, more than any other educational area; individual gifts to medical education amounted to millions more than that; and between 1900 and 1923 states increased their contributions to medical education fifteen-fold. These were immense sums for the times. With the exception of Howard University Medical Department's tiny government subsidy, little of this funding was funneled through the Black medical schools. All the Black schools were threatened with closure during the first three decades of the twentieth century—only Meharry and Howard survived.

Although it was meager compared to the scale of funding obtained following World War II, the biomedical research infrastructure also began to obtain funding from foundations and individuals during the first three decades of the twentieth century. The AMA's CME ratings of the medical schools were the standards that state regulatory agencies and licensing boards utilized to govern the practice of medicine in their states. African American physicians' exclusion from White professional activities meant they had no influence on any of these activities. The only concession was that they were allowed to take medical licensing examinations. Seemingly, in some instances these were conducted in a racially discriminatory manner. As Dr. George Whipple Hubbard observed about the relatively high failure rates of African American medical school graduates, "It has been reported that in some states the examining boards are partial toward the white applicants."[63] However, considering the educational and socioeconomic status deprivations of the Black candidates, their success rates were surprisingly high.

By the end of this era the medical profession and the state regulatory apparatus had come to terms. For all intents and purposes, the medical profession had organized and gained control of major components of the United States health delivery system. These included the health profession's and allied health profession's administrative, regulatory, and licensing infrastructures; health profession's training and research infrastructures; the health care institutional infrastructure, made up overwhelmingly of hospitals; the pharmaceutical and medical supply industries; large segments of the local, state, and national governmental functions and institutions in public health and health care; and the health care financing infrastructure.[64]

Increasing specialization in most other areas of American life encouraged the corporate organization of the production of goods and services during the late nineteenth and early twentieth centuries. Many felt that as early as 1900 the reign of individualism in Western medicine had passed. The European experience suggested that the social role of medicine and the delivery of medical care were undergoing profound alterations relative to their covenants with increasingly industrialized Western societies. Contrary to the contemporary medical-social trends of the time, U.S. medicine was seemingly able to preserve traditional values and practices such as individual physician autonomy and decision making; to block third-party intrusion into the doctor-patient relationship; to prevent third-party intrusion into administrative, service delivery, or financial arrangements between the physician and his patient; and to preserve a freedom-of-choice marketplace of providers and institutions for patients. Considered triumphs by White organized medicine, these structural conventions were simply facts of life for Black physicians forced to practice on the fringes of the mainstream health system. White medicine's hegemony also presented potential threats to African American patients.

In a system already strongly grounded in the Puritan ethic and Calvinist traditions toward the provision of social services and health care to the underprivileged and the poor, the superimposition of this new ethic presented the possibility of unprecedented adverse consequences for Blacks and the poor. Preservation of individuality and local autonomy in the health system without generalizable service requirement standards or regulation invited racial discrimination and segregation. Rationalization and reorganization of the health system based on an artificial and medically mediated structure of market forces and entrepreneurialism—bolstered by and filtered through the existing foundation of social relationships—presented the potential for the permanent and predetermined perpetuation of adverse health status and outcome for Blacks and other disadvantaged groups. This, generally speaking, is what happened. For the tiny Black middle class, racial segregation and discrimination precluded their entry into the mainstream health system. Stories of hundreds-of-miles-long trips to obtain medical services in Nashville, Washington, Tuskegee, or Chicago, where Blacks owned or controlled formidable health facilities, were common. In urban Northeastern communities with established public health infrastructures, African Americans were sometimes served, often on a segregated basis, within those inferior subsystems. In most areas of the country, nonexistent or very inadequate provisions were made for the poor. Services for poor Blacks, in most areas, were out of the question.[65]

In a spontaneous and almost accidental way, the rational reorganization and function of the new health system of the first three decades of the twentieth century, driven by empirical methods and scientific objectivity, also pandered to the new corporate benefactors. Some authorities, such as E. Richard Brown, feel that these developments had even more profound and long-lasting effects on the health system; as Brown pointed out, "The crisis in today's health care system is deeply rooted in the interwoven history of modern medicine and corporate capitalism."[66] The new scientific objectivity and structuring of the system was suggestive of, and similar to, corporate organization in many ways. Paraphrasing Robert Alford, Brown went on to say, "[A]ll the groups seeking to systematize health care according to bureaucratic and business principles of organization 'are' corporate rationalizers"[67] who related well and resonated positively with businessmen. Thus as academic and specialist physicians and their functionaries attempted to organize the health system hierarchically and horizontally, giving more power to capital intensive services, they appealed ideologically and personally to their new corporate sponsors and supporters. White stewards usually presented Blacks' health care issues to these boards and conferences of White corporate executives as "problems." Of course, there was no Black participation in any of these activities.

Representatives of the corporate-based educational philanthropic hierarchy such as Frederick T. Gates, architect of the Rockefeller philanthropies, Henry S. Pritchett, first president of the Carnegie Foundation, and John D. Rockefeller, Jr., who took over the Rockefeller fortune and philanthropies in 1921, were favorably impressed with White physicians and their methods. As Gerald Jonas observed about Frederick Gates, probably the most influential figure in twentieth-century philanthropic giving, "Gates found himself drawn more and more to the science— especially the medical science—of the day."[68] Moreover, these leadership groups were relatively unconcerned with the medical-social aspects of the health system's transformation as they affected minorities. The shameful tradition of African American health being treated as a nonissue in modern health policy terms was thus established. It was assumed that improvements in medical science automatically benefitted the masses—whether the masses appreciated it or not. An aura of enlightened paternalism permeated many of the activities of the lay and professional reformers. In their estimation, the organization of the health system along individualistic, fee-for-service, market capitalist lines was also a most desirable development as far as their class was concerned. The corporate controllers felt that these developments ensured that the rationalization of the health system would not eliminate eventual corporate ownership or control of the system. As corporate and medical interests engaged and intertwined in mutually dependent relationships, eventual control by corporate capitalists became inevitable. The corporate development of the pharmaceutical and medical supply industries served as examples. Late twentieth-century evolution of the health insurance industry would also bear out their predictions.

Other medical-social considerations favored corporate development by the foundation establishment. As E. Richard Brown observed, mutual race and class ideologies and attitudes shared by the corporate executives meant that "[T]hey were drawn to the profession's formulation of medical theory and practice that exonerated capitalism's vast inequities and its reckless practices that shortened the lives of members of the working-class."[69] This included the continued failure of the United States health system to acknowledge and address its endemic race problems. Any deleterious effects segregation and discrimination had on Black health were deemed unworthy of consideration. Inexorably, due to this failure, these problems became deeply ingrained in the structure and culture of the nation's health system over the first three decades of the twentieth century.[70]

The shaping of the medical market by the White medical profession and its functionaries took many forms. Despite isolated instances of the corporate hiring of physicians by railroads, lumber companies, and mining concerns by the early twentieth century, the spread and acceptance of group medical practice was blocked by the White medical profession in the United States. Even highly respected doctor-run group practices such as the Mayo Clinic of Rochester, Minnesota, the Meninger Clinic of Topeka, Kansas, or the Palo Alto Clinic of Palo Alto, California, were frowned upon by the mainstream profession. White organized medicine imposed its own enforcement and sanctions for those transgressing the code. Physicians who participated in such arrangements risked being criticized by other physicians, sanctioned by White organized medicine, and being professionally ostracized. Paul Starr pointed out one example that occurred in 1919 when Chicago city fathers established a venereal disease clinic that served the poor at lower fee schedules:

> *Even though the patients were overwhelmingly poor, the Chicago Medical Society denounced the clinic as unethical, accusing it of unfair competition, and expelled its staff physicians. When it expelled Dr. Louis Schmidt, a medical professor at Northwestern and president of the Illinois Social Hygiene League, for having accepted on the league's behalf $12,000 out of the clinic's surplus, the controversy became a national issue, symbolizing the AMA's struggle to resist public health intervention in medical care.*[71]

These struggles in the changing political economy of the health system took place in arenas separate from, and what White physicians considered beyond the concern of, African American practitioners, whose burdens were hardly factored into these considerations. Racially segregated professional societies, medical practices, and hospitals ensured the nonparticipation and subsequent mainstream irrelevance of Black physicians.

Besides virtually outlawing group practice, White organized medicine also rejected some of the basic tenets of the corporate organization of health care delivery by strongly preserving professional autonomy and the doctor-patient relationship. Physicians also strictly defined the limitations of practice of allied health professionals who might be construed as practicing medicine. Doctors also prohibited lay profit-taking from medicine or health care delivery and the direct and rational financing of medical care and its institutions by the private or corporate sector. The intrusion of third-party payment and financing mechanisms were also avoided, along with the implied influence on administration and decision making that usually accompanied these mechanisms. Physicians successfully convinced their communities and politicians that the commercialization of medicine and lay intrusion into the doctor-patient relationship at virtually any level was "bad public policy" and, if allowed, would be detrimental to the American public and their health in the long term. Therefore, both the interprofessional organization and standards and the legal and regulatory boundaries of health care and practices reflected this unprecedented idealistic, professionally autonomous approach as far as the practice of medicine in the United States was concerned. The public was even advised and pressured to give financial support to medical institutions, schools, and facilities without the usual lay control or administration. White organized medicine demanded, and largely obtained, financing at all levels of the health system with "no strings attached." Even the physicians in the Army Medical Corps came to be treated deferentially for their rank, pay, and authority by other members of the officer corps. Some of this peculiar insulation of medical practice and institutions from the corporate world spilled over into the practices and experiences of some African American physicians.[72]

This granting of authority to the medical profession extended beyond direct patient care and hands-on clinical medicine to the profession's stewardship over education and training. Increasingly, in the United States only the medical profession, with its requisite scientific and patient care perspective, was deemed fit to make medically related decisions and administer medical affairs. White physician prestige levels rose even higher. This elevation of status and authority was not universal. Black physicians, by being barred from mainstream medicine for the most part, were excluded from many aspects of this quantum shift in status. Despite the medical and academic accomplishments of African American physicians such as Daniel Hale Williams (Northwestern University Medical School graduate), Harry Barnes (University of Pennsylvania Medical School graduate, certified American Board of Otolaryngology, 1927), and Nathan Frances Mossell

(University of Pennsylvania Medical School graduate), these practitioners were considered full-fledged physicians only by their patients and laymen who were exposed to their accomplishments. A few exceptional White doctors willing to accept a few African American physicians on an individual basis regarded and treated them as peers. Otherwise, only in their confined and segregated communities, behind the "veil," did African American physicians exert some influence. Moreover, most White professionals and the lay public attempted to undermine Blacks even in these domains. They planted seeds of doubt regarding the abilities of Black physicians in the minds of African American and White patients, who often failed to objectively evaluate these physicians' professional accomplishments. Imposition of these attitudes was so prevalent that despite the acknowledgment of medical abuse of Black patients at the hands of White physicians, African Americans often chose them over Black doctors for their medical care.[73]

The rapid growth in power and authority by the White medical profession over this 30-year period was unprecedented in the United States. In no other area of American life was the ceding of power so absolute or so rapid. At times, the process bordered on being irrational. Clearly, many of the health system policies and practices recommended by the White medical establishment did not meet the nation's medical or medical-social needs. Nevertheless, they were enacted and implemented. Policies promulgated by the medical profession and its functionaries were not forced to adhere to standards of either common sense or social utility. Contrary to their scientific pretenses, doctors often reflected the social and cultural biases and attitudes of the society at large—including racial practices. Moreover, despite these flaws the professional and cultural authority granted the biomedical sciences spilled over into areas other than health care and its delivery.

### The Health System as Arbiter of Racial, Reproductive, and Social Control

Physicians, reflected by the health system they erected, also became influential social and cultural leaders of a society increasingly enamored of, and hypnotized by, the power and prestige associated with the modern biomedical sciences. Even the orbits of some Black physicians were drawn into some of the lesser constellations illuminated by this prestige. Physicians continued their role as scientific authorities when called upon to categorize and rank groups of people on the basis of their biological and psychological characteristics. They became official, and sometimes unofficial, arbiters of legal, sociological, educational, and employment decisions. For example, during this period increasing numbers of physicians became advocates of eugenics and the *de facto* judges and perpetrators of involuntary incarcerations and forced legal sterilizations of inmates of state institutions—largely Blacks and the poor of both sexes. In this manner, physicians and the institutions they controlled became integral willing participants in the eugenics and nascent birth control movements during the early part of this century.

Many of the nation's attitudes and practices regarding reproductive rights, birth control, and society's role in the regulation of fertility were formed, or at the very least shaped, during this period. The eugenics movement appealed to the American psyche for many reasons. Some include, but are not limited to: allegedly being grounded in the objectivity of science; for expressing little sympathy for deviations from the "norm" (often considered failures or shortcomings); its emphasis on pragmatism; for offering easily understood and seemingly rational explanations for the existing social order; and coming down on the side of cutting public budgets.

Virtually all White physicians of the era approved of *positive eugenics*. This entailed society organizing itself for the selective mating of people born with endowments of "superior" genetic characters in order to better the human race. Another, more aggressive, approach articulated by birth control pioneer Margaret Sanger in her book *The Pivot of Civilization* (1922) criticized positive eugenics as the "'dangers of cradle competition' … explaining the advantages of birth control to lower the birthrate of the unfit."[74] Expanding on her vehemently feminist advocacy for birth control as an emancipatory mechanism for women, Sanger, who coined the phrase "birth control," also embraced the theory "that intelligence and other personality traits were genetically determined and therefore inherited."[75] By embracing the tenets of eugenics and aggressively applying them, Sanger shrewdly appreciated that:

> *Eugenics gave the birth control movement a national mission and the authority of a reputable science. By framing her campaign in eugenic terms, Sanger could demonstrate that birth control served the nation's interests. Birth control not only promoted women's health and freedom, it was also an essential element of America's quest for racial betterment.*[76]

Moreover, the eugenics "movement" was financed by the nation's wealthiest capitalists, including the Carnegie, Harriman, and Kellogg dynasties."[77] However, the racist overtones that came to be associated with *negative eugenics*, or the prevention of "bad breeding," would prove embarrassing to both the eugenics and birth control movements in later decades.

A brief discussion of the history of eugenics helps to explain its influence in the early years of the twentieth century. Sir Francis Galton (1822–1911), a gentleman scientist and the founder of eugenics—which he derived from the Greek word for "wellborn"—proposed selective breeding of human beings from the beginning. (See Figure 1.1.) Hereditarily predetermined, immutable, individual, and racial hierarchies permeated virtually all of Galton's work in eugenics. In his famous statistical and actuarial study, *Hereditary Genius* (1869), he noted:

> [P]rominent men in government, religion, commerce, and the arts …
> *proved, with redundant statistics and dozens of quaint notions about*

Figure 1.1  Sir Francis Galton (1822–1911)
Credited with being the founder of eugenics,
this English gentleman scientist made major
contributions to statistics as he attempted to
prove intelligence, success, and character
traits were hereditary.
Reproduced from Stigler SM. *The History
of Statistics: The Measurement of Uncertainty
before 1900.* Cambridge, MA: Belknap Press,
1986, 265.

*human development, what every adult has always known. To wit, that
the children of bankers and generals and cabinet ministers are statistically much more likely to find their way into the professions and the corridors of political and economic power than are the children of char
women, peasants, and ditch diggers.*[78]

Galton combined his findings with some of his distant cousin's, Charles Darwin of
*The Origin of Species* fame, to suggest that "affirmative state intervention in the
evolutionary process"[79] was needed if the human "stock" was to be improved.
Galton assumed individuals and groups were of different genetic stocks—traits that
were passed on to future generations. Racially privileged White Europeans of the
X class* were hereditarily endowed with superior traits of intelligence, character,
and noble qualities compared to "The Mongolians, Jews, Negroes, Gipsies [*sic*],
and American Indians."[80] He spoke disparagingly of Blacks:

*The Negro has strong impulsive passions, and neither patience, reti-
cence, nor dignity. He is warm-hearted, loving towards his master's children, and idolised by the children in return. He is eminently gregarious,
for he is always jabbering, quarreling, tom-tom-ing, or dancing. He is
remarkably domestic, and is endowed with such constitutional vigour,
and is so prolific, that his race is irrepressible.*[81]

---

*In Galton's mathematical scale men were graded by letters. The highest grade was X and the lowest
A, representing the range of noble and bad qualities of human beings. The higher the grade, the rarer
its incidence and higher its quality. C, somewhat more than average abilities, implied a selection of 1
in 16 births, whereas D (1 in 64 births) is sure of success in life. V class (1 in 300 births) is rare; while
X was so rare that Galton did not estimate its incidence.

Galton felt that "black people were as an entire race grossly inferior to even the lowliest of any white people."[82] He admonished society "in however remote a degree to give the more suitable races or strains of blood a better chance of prevailing speedily over the less suitable than they otherwise would have had."[83] Thus "[r]acism ... provided the theoretical framework for eugenic thinking,"[84] according to Dorothy Roberts.

From an African American perspective, the thrust of this societal interest in the selective control of reproductive rights reflected a new dimension of an old problem dating back to slavery. As Roberts notes in *Killing the Black Body: Race, Reproduction, and the Meaning of Liberty*, "While slave masters forced Black women to bear children for profit, more recent policies have sought to reduce Black women's fertility. Both share a common theme—that Black women's child-bearing should be regulated to achieve social objectives."[85] Although many physicians believed in its principles, few actively participated in negative eugenics. The negative eugenics movement was based upon the idea that by mandating and enforcing segregative and surgical strategies of preventing the further procreation of "beaten men from beaten races" with inferior unit characters in their bad bloods, society would arrive at the social benefits of *negative eugenics*, or the prevention of racial deterioration (now known as "genetic enslavement").[86]

Robert G. Weisbord also observed that "[r]acism was a frequent, almost a constant, companion of eugenics."[87] Roberts clarified the intimacy of the relationship in the United States:

> White Americans had for over two centuries developed an understand-
> ing of the races as biologically distinct groups, marked by inherited
> attributes of inferiority and superiority. Scientific racism predisposed
> Americans to accept the theory that social characteristics were heritable
> and deviant behavior was biologically determined. The use of steriliza-
> tion as a remedy for social problems was an extension of the brutality
> enforced against Black Americans.[88]

As a result, eugenics became a cornerstone of the Progressive Era. After the war and the immigration restriction campaign, it became more focused on African Americans.

Because of changing demographics and expansion of the public health sector to include Blacks (albeit under segregated and/or inferior conditions), the effects of the eugenics movement increasingly affected African Americans. "Disproportionately represented in the populations of public institutions, persons of African extraction were prime candidates for involuntary steriliza-tion."[89] Such acts were justified by authorities such as Paul Popenoe, editor of the *Journal of Heredity*, and Roswell Hill Johnson, co-author of the standard textbook *Applied Eugenics* (1918), who declared, "[I]n comparison with some other races the Negro race is germinally lacking in the higher developments of intelligence."[90] These authorities also alleged that Blacks were inherently predisposed to antisocial behavior, "had powerful, fluctuating emotions, and improvident character, and an inclination to immoral conduct."[91] Blacks were viewed as unfit from behavioral and intellectual viewpoints as well. In his book *Diseases of Society* (1906), whose title page displayed a large drawing of "a skull of a Negro murderer," Dr. G. Frank Lydston, one of the leading urologists in the Midwest and University of Illinois professor, recommended punitive and preventive sterilization, stating that "[i]ncurable criminals, epileptics, and the insane should invariably be submitted to the operation."[92]

He further postulated that "as blacks became more 'degraded' in their way to the inevitable, their criminal behavior would also increase, and he suggested 'penile mutilation' as one route to their improvement."[93] These were commonly held beliefs among early twentieth-century White physicians and behavioral scientists. This matrix of pseudoscience and dominant social attitudes also predicted and later dictated the differential and disproportionate effect the negative eugenics movement would have on African Americans during the Great Depression—a time of heightened social tensions. In both state and private institutions, Blacks became the most common involuntary victims of the eugenic gelder's knife.[94]

Near the turn of the century, without the benefit of enabling legislation, physicians began exercising their prerogatives to improve the racial stock through negative eugenics. Although a number of eugenic sterilizations purportedly took place in Kansas the year before, Dr. Harry Sharp independently began performing involuntary vasectomies at the Indiana State Reformatory at Jeffersonville, Indiana, in 1899. Basing his work on Sir Francis Galton's "scientific discoveries," Sharp went on to compile a series of 236 operations, which he reported in the medical literature and at the 1909 AMA convention in Atlantic City. As Allan Chase observed, he sterilized "those young inmates he deemed to be hereditary criminal or otherwise genetically defective types."[95] Lay, professional, and scientific support for eugenic ideologies and activities became so prevalent during the first three decades of the twentieth century in the United States that an infrastructure for eugenical research, propaganda, and politics developed. The result was that America adopted a eugenically oriented manner of viewing the control of reproductive processes as a substitute for solving, or a means of regulating, the nation's social problems. The health system became a major mediator of this agenda.

If Sir Francis Galton was the founder of eugenics, Charles Benedict Davenport (1866–1944), Harvard trained Ph.D. in biology (1902), was its "scientific pope" in the United States. Also a trained engineer (Brooklyn Polytech, 1886) and convert to eugenics after traveling to England to meet Galton and his disciple Karl Pearson around 1897, Davenport cultivated his academic and institutional contacts in the upper echelons of the nation's research and university infrastructure. In this rarified environment he parlayed his unique training in zoology, biostatistics, and genetics into a career as point-man for the scientific arm of the eugenics movement. Persuasive and politically astute, Davenport persuaded the newly established Carnegie Institution of Washington (1902) to provide him a laboratory and year-round biological farm at Cold Spring Harbor, Long Island, New York (1904). A temperamental, ideologically driven, somewhat myopic scientist, he served as director of the new Carnegie Institution Station for Experimental Evolution (SEE) until 1910. He then convinced Mrs. E. H. Harriman, widow of the railroad tycoon, to put up the money for 80 acres of land; a house with fireproof storage areas for records; salaries for a superintendent, stenographer, and two helpers; and six trained field-workers to be called the Eugenics Record Office (ERO) at Cold Spring Harbor. She poured in over a half million dollars until it was absorbed under the obscure rubric of the Carnegie Institution Department of Genetics in 1918.*

> Until the organization of the American Eugenics Society after World
> War I, the Eugenics Record Office, along with its subsidiary Eugenics
> Research Association, was the active center of all organized eugenical
> research, propaganda, and political activities in the United States.[96]

Under the leadership of Davenport and his fanatical second in command, superintendent Harry Hamilton Laughlin (1880–1943), Sc.D. from Princeton, the ERO produced a massive pseudoscientific data set still being used by eugenicists; coordinated and executed an immensely successful national political campaign to influence local and national politicians and implement eugenic policies; trained a corps of amateur field-workers who functioned as "scientific" researchers;** helped transform the pseudoscience of eugenics into a recognized academic discipline taught in major academic institutions throughout the United States, such as MIT, Harvard, Minnesota, Columbia, Brown, Northwestern, Clark, and Wisconsin; coordinated activities with the growing and increasingly influential birth control infrastructure; maintained a corps of Capitol Hill lobbyists and consultants; organized scattered eugenics activities and institutional programs (e.g., the Vineland, New Jersey, Training School for Feeble-minded Girls and

---

*Anxious to rid itself of the ERO by the late 1930s, the Carnegie Institution changed its name to the Genetic Record Office in 1939. Pressuring Davenport (1934) and Laughlin (1940) into early retirement, it closed the facility in 1940 and severed its ties to eugenics.

**These field-workers were women of good families, some with college training, but few with scientific research or postgraduate training in fields such as genetics, psychology, psychiatry, sociology, anthropology, neurology, or biology. They received several weeks of on-the-job training at ERO or Vineland, N.J. Thus equipped, they made medical and psychiatric diagnoses at a glance; compiled rumors, hearsay, old court and hospital records, and neighborhood gossip as databases on patients; diagnosed patients deceased for generations; and constructed genetic family trees based on such information. Chase describes these workers in detail in *The Legacy of Malthus*, pp. 120–124.

Boys) into a national movement; and disseminated eugenics propaganda through scientific and scientistic journals,* reports to the United States Congress, popular print media, and networks of eugenics and birth control meetings, programs, conferences, and organizations.[97] Although the racial hygiene** and eugenics movements had strong moorings in Germany, Robert N. Proctor observed its international scope in *Racial Hygiene: Medicine under the Nazis* as follows: "Eugenics movements flourished in England, Norway, Sweden, France, the Soviet Union, the United States, and many other countries."[98]

Three International Congress of Eugenics conferences were held, in 1912, 1921, and 1932. The first, held in London, was presided over by Charles Darwin's son, Major Leonard Darwin, and was attended by future Prime Minister Winston Churchill; the Lord Chief Justice, Lord Alverstone; the president of the College of Physicians, Sir Thomas Barlow; Gifford Pinchot, a future governor of Pennsylvania; Charles W. Eliot, president emeritus of Harvard University; Alexander Graham Bell; David Starr-Jordan, president of Stanford University; and Charles B. Davenport, director of the ERO and secretary of the American Breeders' Association (ABA). The next two were held in New York under the presidencies of Henry Fairfield Osborn, president of the American Museum of Natural History, and Davenport. The ERO was probably most successful and had the most long-term impact with its political agenda and efforts at influencing U.S. culture educationally. Proctor noted the growth of the movement: "In 1914 eugenics was taught in 44 American colleges and universities; by 1928 the number had grown to 376— 'racial hygiene' was thus taught in nearly three-quarters of all American colleges and universities."[99] Racial hygienists and biological determinists thus created a "eugenics conscience" through the nation's educational system, research institutions, and governing bodies.

The eugenicists had two major political goals. First, they wanted to restrict immigration of "undesirable" foreigners. Taking the lead from elite organizations such as the Immigration Restriction League (IRL, founded 1894), whose anti-immigrant, Aryan-oriented program was detailed in Prescott Farnsworth Hall's *Immigration and Its Effect upon the United States* (1906), Davenport formulated specious genetic theories he arbitrarily labeled "Mendelian,"*** providing a

---

*Scientistic—characteristic of, or having the attributes of, a scientist (used depreciatively). Hence scientistically (adv.) *Compact Edition of the Oxford English Dictionary*, p. 2668.

**Sometimes used interchangeably with the term eugenics, racial hygiene was often viewed as a legitimate concern of medicine that provided long-range preventive medicine for the germ plasm of humanity. This complemented both traditional curative medical care and concerns for the human social and physical environment provided by social medicine and public health.

***Gregor Johann Mendel's 1865 research in genetics, rediscovered in 1900, was highly respected and laid a foundation for modern genetics. "From around 1905 onward, Davenport used the lexicon and authority of Mendelian genetics to confirm the predictions and dogmas of Galtonian eugenics" (Chase, p. 117), virtually creating a new eugenically oriented biology in the process.

scientistic rationale of why this massive infusion of "inferior blood" posed a menace to American society:

> *To the early eugenicists who were also biologists, such as Davenport, each human trait or characteristic was produced by a specific gene for a specific unit character. These unitary traits of "unit characters" were discrete particles of hereditary information. In human beings, according to Davenport and the other self-styled "Mendelians," good blood consisted of a hereditary endowment brimming with excellent "unit characters" for physique, morality, intelligence, and specific skills such as music, mathematics, dancing, statesmanship, and moneymaking. The hereditary endowments of social classes and races, the eugenicists wrote, also included the unit characters that gave a person inborn constitutional immunity to tuberculosis, diphtheria, typhoid fever, measles, and all of the other infectious diseases that were far more prevalent in the overcrowded slums and sparsely populated hovels of rural poverty than among the affluent in their spacious town houses and gracious country estates.[100]*

The eugenicists' second political goal was to obtain legal approval for involuntary eugenic sterilization. This activist, negative eugenics was necessary to prevent society from being overrun by "bad blood":

> *Bad blood, according to the eugenicists, consisted of a hereditary endowment made up primarily of the unit character of pauperism—in the eugenic literature the major genetic defect of the poor—as well as the unit characters for insanity, epilepsy, criminalism, immorality, low Binet-Simon IQ test scores, graft (at least, wrote Davenport, in the Irish), nomadism, shiftlessness, pellagra, laziness, feeblemindedness, asthenia (general physical weakness), lack of ambition, and general paralysis of the insane. It was also a major postulate of eugenics that inferior heredity was, as well, a human genetic endowment in which the blood of an individual was lacking in any of the unit characters (genes) that were supposed to provide the body with inborn immunity or resistance to tuberculosis, pellagra, infant diarrhea, dysentery, measles, malaria, cholera, pneumonia, influenza, and all of the other deficiency and infectious or parasitic diseases associated with poverty.[101]*

Nurturing provided by schools, vaccinations, equality of opportunity, hospitals, clinics, better living conditions, and safer workplaces were, thus, a waste of taxpayer and private resources. These races and social classes were "doomed by their inferior genes to be ineducable, unhealthy, accident-prone, immoral, and unemployable,"[102] according to well-informed Progressives.

Grounded in these scientistic assumptions, the eugenicists' political campaign was a spectacular success. A systematic lobbying and disinformation campaign (1920–1924), conducted by the ERO and its eugenicist allies such as the IRL and the Eugenics Research Association, resulted in influencing Congress to pass the Immigration Act of 1924 (also known as the Johnson Act or the Johnson Restriction Act). This act reduced Italian, Jewish, Russian, Polish, and Hungarian immigration to a trickle. Allan Chase speculates that hundreds of thousands, if not millions, of Jews, Poles, and Russians exterminated by the Nazis between 1933 and 1945 might have been spared by immigration to the United States had this law not been enacted.[103] Sparked by Dr. Sharp's previously mentioned Indiana-based activities and lobbying, buttressed by a large contingent of physicians, on the virtues of the mass sterilization of "degenerate" men, in 1907 Indiana became the first state to pass an involuntary sterilization law. By 1913, 11 other states had followed suit. The highwater mark of the eugenicists' political campaign took place in the U.S. Supreme Court.

Allan Chase recapitulates the chronology and ERO influence in this landmark case in *The Legacy of Malthus*, stating, "In 1924, at the height of the eugenics-dysgenics hysteria in the nation, the state of Virginia passed a compulsory state eugenical sterilization law based on the model law proposed by ... [the] Eugenics Record Office."[104] The *Buck v. Bell* Supreme Court decision of May 1927, legalizing Virginia's compulsory sterilization law, was emblematic of the increasing social power exerted by the medical profession and of the influence of the eugenics movement by 1930. This law gave the state arbitrary power over the reproductive lives of so-called inferior Americans based on unproven genetic and scientific assumptions. This case is instructive in many ways. J. David Smith and K. Ray Nelson noted the significance of this decision in *The Sterilization of Carrie Buck*: "The majority opinion of the court held that Virginia's compulsory sterilization law was constitutional. Thus the precedent was established which gave state governments the right to become arbiters of the reproductive practices of citizens who were deemed to be defective in some way."[105]

The law's effects stretched far beyond the South and deeply into the nation's medical profession and scientific health establishment, redefining the nation's ethical landscape and the meaning of liberty for America's disabled, poor, underprivileged, and disadvantaged minorities. From the beginning of the process to sterilize Carrie Buck, the "test case" for the Virginia law, two physicians were called upon to verify the so-called immutable scientific facts justifying the sterilization. The officials supervising the state mental health facilities, where the "defectives" were incarcerated, were physicians responsible for informing Ms. Buck, a White woman who was later found not to be retarded, and approving the procedure. Physicians were called as expert witnesses during the trial proceedings. Doctors proved to be essential components involved in accomplishing eugenic goals. Moreover, their cooperation with the eugenics movement would be essential in that they were the only people legally authorized to perform the requisite surgical sterilization procedures on human beings.

The negative eugenics programs promoted by the ERO and the eugenics infrastructure emphasized segregation of the "unfit" from normal populations to preclude intercourse and involuntary sterilization to prevent subsequent off-spring. "Castration as the suitable punishment and preventive technique for sex criminals,"[106] as suggested by Dr. Thurman B. Rice, a teacher at the University of Indiana School of Medicine, in his book *Racial Hygiene* (1929), was considered somewhat extreme. In the next period under examination, Nazi Germany took negative eugenics a step further—exterminating whomever they considered mentally, physically, or racially unfit.

Between 1900 and 1930 most eugenic activities were built around segregation of the "unfit" from the "normal" population. This helps explain the proliferation of mental hospitals, colonies for "retarded" or "defective" children, and sanitariums for chronic illnesses such as tuberculosis and epilepsy during this era. Preexisting racial segregation serendipitously fit in quite well. Thus early in the period, White Southerners were little concerned with "defective" Blacks presenting a problem. As times changed, they could no longer ignore them. Paradoxically, during the 30 years that Blacks obtained more of their civil and public accommodations rights, necessitating more interaction between the races, eugenicists became alarmed and more aggressive toward African Americans. As the campaign against the impaired, the poor, and Blacks continued, Chase noted, "By World War II, thanks to the relentless campaign directed by Laughlin and Davenport out of the Eugenics Record Office, laws for the compulsory sterilization of the poor, the helpless, and the misdiagnosed were on the books of thirty states and Puerto Rico as well."[107] Eugenicists such as Thurman Rice reflected the increasing race-mixing anxiety sweeping through the movement in the 1920s, stating, "The colored races are pressing the white race most urgently, and this pressure may be expected to increase."[108] Roberts noted that by the 1920s:

> Eugenicists were ... worried that intermingling between Blacks and [W]hites would deteriorate the [W]hite race. Over half the papers presented at the Second International Congress of Eugenics in 1921 concerned the biological and social consequences of marriages between people from different ethnic groups.[109]

One response was, "By 1940, thirty states had passed statutes barring interracial marriage," and, "[a]ntimiscegenation laws were a eugenic measure."[110] Due to prevailing medical practices, cautions about undertaking major surgery, and the distance between the mainstream medical system and African Americans wrought by segregation and discrimination, a small number of Blacks were probably involuntarily sterilized during this era. As major surgery became commonplace and Blacks and the poor entered mainstream institutions, hundreds of thousands of such involuntary procedures began to be performed on Blacks, the poor, and disadvantaged in the United States.[111]

The mainstream biomedical sciences also promoted and promulgated societal beliefs in Black racial inferiority during this critical period of U.S. health system development. As an evolutionary component of the scientific subculture, James Reed noted in *The Encyclopedia of Southern Culture* that:

> *The history of "scientific racism" before the twentieth century is synonymous with the development of the modern scientific study of race. Scientific racism was not "pseudoscience" but an integral part of the intellectual world-view that nurtured the rise of modern biology and anthropology.[112]*

As James H. Jones points out, "Physicians did not dissent as a group from white society's pervasive belief in the physical and mental inferiority of blacks. On the contrary, they did a great deal to bolster and elaborate racist attitudes."[113] In the quasi-genocidal atmosphere the biomedical establishment was creating for African Americans, "the perpetrator's definition of the victims as economically useless and hopelessly primitive reinforced their exclusion from the universe of human obligation."[114] By the beginning of the twentieth century, most White physicians, many of whom were social Darwinists, declared that African Americans were totally unsuited for racial competition and predicted that Blacks would not survive in the United States.

Many in the health establishment blamed poor Black health status and outcomes on Blacks themselves due to their allegedly self-destructive behavioral traits. These professional pronouncements were devastating to African Americans, as Jones went on to say:

> *The effect of these views was to isolate blacks even further within American society—to remove them from the world of health and to lock them within a prison of sickness. . . . [A]s sickness replaced health as the normal condition of the race, something was lost from the sense of horror and urgency with which physicians had defined disease. The result was a powerful rationale for inactivity in the face of disease, which by their own estimates, physicians believed to be endemic.[115]*

These negative attitudes promoted by the White medical profession, their intermediaries, and the health system they supervised explain many of the nihilistic health policies of that period that include, but were not confined to, the erection and perpetuation of racially segregated health care facilities and institutions; the virtual uniform and systematic relegation of African Americans to inferior health care and services access, except in instances of their own marginally financed and sometimes "heroic" self-help efforts; the virtual total exclusion of African Americans from the mainstream medical profession; the continuation of the United States tradition of unethical experimentation, surgery, and sterilization on Blacks; and a boom in the eugenics movement.

As medical sciences, health care, and health services became more effective and efficacious, disparate access to the health system itself became an increasingly important factor in the subpar Black health status and outcome in the United States. Not only was health policy affected at all levels by these medical-social forces, but new foundations were laid for the perpetuation of the dysfunctional relationship between Black and poor people and the professional education and research infrastructures. Thus as James H. Jones, Allan Brandt, James Reed, Henry K. Beecher, and others have hypothesized, unethical experimentation on disadvantaged groups—as exemplified by the Tuskegee experiment—were not isolated incidents, but were true reflections of the ideology, policies, and practices of the mainstream U.S. health system. Therefore, not only did the system neglect and demonstrate disdain for disadvantaged groups in the provision of health services, but these groups were also expected to surrender their bodies for whatever experimentation and research the system desired. Services provided to the unfortunates and poor would thus be "paid for" with the currency of "scientific advance." This unhealthy relationship between the African American community and the United States health system would not be substantively challenged or altered until the Civil Rights era of the 1950s and 1960s.[116]

In summary, one of the major reasons for the fundamental change in the way the United States approached health care between 1900 and 1930 was the rise of modern science. Moreover, the medical profession, largely based on prestige and cultural authority acquired through biomedical-scientific progress and through various other mechanisms, attained credibility with both the public and the politicians. By the end of the 1920s, medicine was the darling of the educational foundation and corporate educational funding system. Full-fledged and well-financed medical and health professions educational reform based on the Johns Hopkins model elevated American medical, dental, and health professions education levels to the best in the world. Despite scientific medical progress, the medical-social milieu deteriorated as a result of resurgent scientific racism in the forms of vigorous eugenics, psychological testing, and eugenically oriented birth control movements. Shaped by social Darwinist influences of the times, the United States health system's race and class problems persisted, if not worsened, during the first three decades of the twentieth century.[117]

## The Evidence of Things Not Seen: Black Health in the Early Twentieth Century

> *Faith is the substance of things hoped for, the evidence of things not seen.*
>
> —St. Paul

The Black experience in the U.S. has been one forged in a crucible of hope. The anticipated incorporation of African Americans into the mainstream of American life envisioned after the Civil War clearly failed to happen. This assessment, an expected result of continued racial discrimination and exclusion, extended to the United States health care system. Both physicians and biostatisticians, such as Frederick L. Hoffman,* made dire social Darwinist predictions of Black racial extinction.[118] (See Figure 1.2.) These were largely framed in epidemiological and *health risk appraisal* (HRA)** terms. Despite the first large-scale post–Civil War analysis suggesting Black population growth was outstripping that of Whites,[119] Hoffman assured the social Darwinists and health establishment that "in spite of their fecundity ... 'in the struggle for race supremacy the black race is not holding its own,' and eventual extinction was inevitable."[120] Factoring in the Great Migration to "unsanitized" cities that Hoffman and other scientists felt accounted for "their deathrate ... becoming ever greater than that for whites,"[121] "Even under the same conditions," wrote Hoffman, Blacks were "still subject to a higher death rate"; it was a matter of "racial inferiority."[122] Some physicians and social Darwinist scholars reinterpreted subpar Black health status and outcomes since slavery: "The data on blacks' health and longevity now became evidence of the unfair advantage that slavery had granted them.... From this point of view ... the purpose of attaining freedom for blacks was to allow for their elimination."[123] From their viewpoint, Black elimination through poor health outcome was evidence that slavery had artificially ensured Black survival and that Blacks were failing in open racial competition with Whites. Excess health-related deaths became a remedy to the American Negro question:

---

*Hoffman was a nationally renowned statistician with the Prudential Life Insurance Company. His book, *Race Traits and Tendencies of the American Negro* (1896), an exhaustive study based on over 50 years of demographic, medical, and anthropometric data, was considered definitive on the American Negro question. Hoffman was an influential consultant with the American Association of Labor Legislation (AALL) study evaluating the health system before World War I.

**Health risk appraisal (HRA). A generic term applied to methods for describing an individual's chance of becoming ill or dying from selected causes. Source: Last JM, ed. A Dictionary of Epidemilogy. 2nd ed. New York: Oxford University Press, 1988, 58.

> *This "ultimate solution" may not have been planned with the same effi-*
> *cient brutality as that "final solution" to be implemented a few decades*
> *later, but the two were close relatives in the Social Darwinist family,*
> *sharing a common goal of genocide and justified by a similar scientific*
> *rationale.*[124]

Physician Charles S. Bacon in a medical journal article suggested assisting the process of extinction.[125] He "did not doubt the 'eventual elimination' of blacks in the United States, but since the latest census data indicated that the 'race is not doomed ... in the immediate future,' he suggested 'helping along the process of extinction....'"[126] The danger was that "policies of racial oppression had previously been rationalized as an implication of science, now they *were* science, part of the organic process of evolutionary improvement,"[127] William H. Tucker observed.

Despite this negative racial and medical-social environment, African American physician Henry Butler, one of the founders of the NMA, observed a generation after the Civil War at an 1896 Atlanta University Conference on Black health that: "It was then announced that the Negroes were dying out and that soon the race would be gone. But only one generation has passed, and from four millions they number to-day nearly eight millions. It is therefore evident to us all that this proposition, too, has collapsed."[128]

Significantly, well-intentioned Whites such as George G. Bradford and Horace Bumstead, an early president of Atlanta University, were beginning to realize the truth and impact of the connections between health and social performance perceived earlier by European leaders such as Benjamin Disraeli and Otto von Bismarck and American health pioneers such as Oliver O. Howard and George Whipple Hubbard. Referring to the health condition of African Americans

**Figure 1.2    Frederick L. Hoffman (1865–1946)**
German-born insurance statistician whose racist predispositions coupled with his mastery of the statistical approach to social problems reinforced scientific predictions of Black extinction and to the refusal of insurance companies to insure African Americans.

Reproduced from Numbers RL. *Almost Persuaded: American Physicians and Compulsory Health Insurance, 1912–1920.* Baltimore: The Johns Hopkins University Press, 1978, 16.

in the first Atlanta University Study, Bumstead noted, "Important as is the industrial education of a state, it is evident that no rapid economic advance can be made by a race physically ... weak."[129] At no time since their arrival in the Americas have African Americans shared equal health status or outcome with other Americans. While the sanitation, nutritional, and environmental health conditions African Americans were forced to live under were responsible for much of their health condition, an ever growing responsibility for their unfavorable health picture based on race can be laid squarely at the feet of the health system. As health care treatments, procedures, and interventions became more effective, the proportion of the race-based health deficit due to structural and functional defects in the system could be expected to increase.

Mortality rates are one of the "gold standard" measures of a population's health status and outcome as well as an index of a health system's performance regarding any group. They are also a reliable indicator of the standard of living reflecting not only the aforementioned quality of available medical care but other parameters such as income, nutritional status, environmental quality (which includes the quality of water and air along with pollution levels), and cultural habits. Although this is a relatively insensitive indicator and poor reflector of population morbidity, its availability as a health indicator over time makes it indispensable to health historians tracking trends in the health status and outcomes of various populations.[130]

It is difficult to describe mortality trends for any U.S. group before 1940. The reason is that a national system of registering deaths did not exist before 1933, when all states registered at least 90 percent of their deaths and thus were qualified for inclusion in the Death Registration Area (DRA).* Nevertheless, investigators have utilized census data to estimate death rates among Blacks during the decades following the Civil War. As Du Bois pointed out in 1906, in *The Health and Physique of the Negro American,* other useful sources of information on Black health could be obtained from "reports of the life insurance companies; vital records of various cities and towns; reports of the United States Surgeon General; reports from Negro hospitals and drug stores; reports from medical schools; [and] letters from physicians."[131] Moreover, Du Bois mobilized an unprecedented and growing network of Black social scientists and graduate student researchers headquartered in Atlanta; Washington, DC; and at other Black colleges. They conducted surveys, scoured available public health records, and compiled a database on Black health in both urban and rural areas for Du Bois's Atlanta University Studies.

The situation regarding Black mortality data and health conditions leading up to this period was summarized by Reynolds Farley and Walter R. Allen: "Although there are ambiguities in using these ... procedures, there is a consensus that health

---

*Death Registration Area.* A geographic area for which mortality deata are published. *Source:* Last JM, ed. *A Dictionary of Epidemiology.* 2nd. ed. New York: Oxford University Press, 1988, 35.

conditions improved very little among blacks in the late nineteenth century."[132] Douglas C. Ewbank, more recently, utilized plantation records on slave health in the most successful attempt thus far to objectify the early Black health experience. Utilizing various methods, several authoritative investigators noted a decline in Black life span between the Civil War and 1900, while a few noted little change. Virtually all authorities agree that, at best, around the turn of the century Black life span was no more than 30 to 32 years, compared to 49.6 years for Whites. As far as Black mortality rates during the early twentieth century, as Farley and Allen summarized, "mortality rates declined in the twentieth century in the DRAs of 1900 or 1910, with the greatest gains during the 1930s."[133] However, with early DRAs consisting of such unrepresentative samples of the Black population, whether or not these slight improvements in the early data applied to the entire African American population is debatable. There is also controversy over whether improvements in Black health status or mortality continued during the 1920s. Thompson and Whelpton found in their demographic monograph written for President Herbert Hoover's Committee on Social Trends (1933) that "not only was the age-standardized death rate for blacks about 80 percent higher than that for whites, but it also increased by about 7 percent during the 1920s, while that for whites fell by 10 percent, implying that black mortality rates were actually increasing for some part of this century."[134] Ewbank leaves room for that possibility, noting, "It is certain adult mortality decreased between 1900 and 1940, but it is possible that there were periods when mortality rates remained constant or even increased."[135] Virtually all agree that Black mortality declined somewhat during the 1930s and fell more rapidly in the following decade. Perhaps the 1920s set the precedent for the spurt in declining longevity for the Black population that repeated itself during the decade beginning in 1984.[136]

There are several factors that explain and complicate the pursuit of statistical accuracy regarding Black mortality in the early twentieth century. Explaining Black/White differences in mortality during this period is thereby rendered more difficult. This includes sampling errors regarding the Black population; urban/rural mortality discrepancies and trends; poor and disparate reporting of deaths and causes of death among the Black population; disproportionate, possibly preventable, deaths associated with the reproductive process compounded by lack of access to hospital facilities and health services; disproportionate death rates in childhood among Blacks; and excess, possibly preventable, deaths due to tuberculosis, other infectious diseases, and sanitation-related diseases such as typhoid fever and diarrheal diseases.

The 1900 DRA data represented only 26 percent of the total national population's registered deaths, because the data set was obtained from the Northeastern United States. These data were usually interpreted to represent all U.S. deaths. This was a dangerous assumption. For Blacks, the sample represented only 4.4 percent of African American deaths. Moreover, it was a distorted representation of the African American population. Ninety percent of the sampled American Blacks were urban dwellers in an era when only 23 percent of African Americans lived in cities. This sampling bias was exaggerated by the excess mortality associated with city life at the same time that rural Black mortality probably was increasing. By 1930, some of this discrepancy would have been erased due to improved public health programs, sanitation, and living conditions in most cities, followed by plunging death rates. Another factor rendering the mortality trends more confusing and less accurate was the admittedly poorer reporting of Black deaths and cause of deaths. Much of this inaccuracy was bred by the lack of medical attendance due to discrimination and the paucity of trained Black physicians and the lack of access to hospital facilities where terminal events were accurately recorded. Chronic Black population undercounts compounded these problems.

Another factor to be considered when interpreting these mortality trends is the limitation of the Black usage of health services. This disproportionately affected reproductive outcomes, thereby differentially shortening longevity statistics, worsening reproductive health statistics, increasing Black years-of-life-lost-figures, and distorting gender-related mortality statistics.

Black maternal mortality rates three to four times the White rates were related to the fact that by 1921 in rural Mississippi 79 percent of White women had deliveries by physicians compared to only 8 percent of Blacks. Care provided by Black granny midwives, some of whom were poorly trained, could not equalize the outcomes. Similar results were reported in 1918 from lowland North Carolina. Dramatic and preventable deaths in otherwise young, healthy women due to hemorrhage, infection, and obstetrical accidents were common throughout the South. This resulted in increased mortality and decreased Black fertility, which were also affected by soaring levels of tuberculosis and syphilis. Black poverty and the high cost of medical care were not the only reasons for lack of utilization of health services by Blacks. As Ewbank pointed out: "The second possible factor was social custom. Given the shortage of black doctors and nurses and the prevailing racial attitudes, black women did not have equal access to physician care. They may also have felt more comfortable with black midwives."[137] The racial differences in mortality and other health care outcomes were less dramatic in Southern cities like Baltimore, where there were public clinics that Blacks could attend.[138]

Antedating the era of U.S. slavery Blacks had suffered excessive infant and childhood mortality compared to Whites. This trend was prominent between 1901 and 1929 and has continued throughout the twentieth century. In 1906 Du Bois estimated that "black infant mortality rates were at least twice the white rates."[139] Ewbank found in his comprehensive historical and statistical investigation of Black/White health differences of the early twentieth century "that even after controlling for region and urban-rural residence, occupational status, and literacy, the single largest determinant of the proportion deceased was race."[140] Lack of physician attendance, home care, and midwife deliveries probably contributed to an undercount of the figures emanating from the earlier decades under investigation. As access to hospital deliveries and basic health services increased and sanitation conditions improved in the Black living areas of most cities, these figures improved. During this 30-year period most cities also improved the quality of their milk supplies with the implementation of pasteurization and refrigeration. Improvements in all these areas translated into 50 to 70 percent improvements in Black childhood mortality between 1910 and 1920.[141]

As has been stated, Black mortality probably began improving, although later and at slower rates than White mortality, between 1900 and 1910. Unless new information surfaces, this may have been the first objective improvement in mortality, and presumptively in health status and outcome, since before the end of slavery. During the early twentieth century Blacks generally died of the same diseases as Whites. However, the epidemiological and health risk appraisal profiles were different and more severe. Du Bois explained the higher death rates of African Americans, stating, "The Negro death rate is, however, undoubtedly considerably higher than the white. . . . [T]he excess is due principally to mortality from consumption, pneumonia, heart disease and dropsy, diseases of the nervous system, malaria and diarrheal diseases."[142] He also found that the "black infant mortality rates were at least twice the white rates" and "again the Southern cities are in excess of the Northern cities."[143] In urban Black populations, which at the time constituted no more than 25 percent of the total, the profile demonstrated near 1900 was different from the more prevalent rural experience. Du Bois recorded the health experience of Blacks in cities in the following manner:

> The causes of death of which Negroes form more than their part are in the following order: Syphilis leads with 20.5 per cent of the total deaths;* then come marasmus, whooping cough, consumption, inanition, pneumonia, inflammation of the brain, child birth, typhoid fever, epilepsy, cholera infantum, still births, premature births, inflammation of the kidneys, dysentery, heart disease and Bright's disease.[144]

Although the terminology is imprecise according to today's definitions, the over-representation of disease and deaths related to the reproductive processes and childhood is obvious and goes a long way toward explaining Ewbank's much more recent and statistically rigorous findings that Black women during this period had shorter life spans than Black men.[145] Based on the statistical information, Du Bois found that the six leading causes of death taking a disproportionate toll on the Black population consisted of "consumption and pneumonia, infantile marasmus, cholera infantum, inanition, [and] heart disease," which "each year . . . constituted over half of the deaths."[146] Du Bois and his cadre of investigators went on to state their findings regarding the overall leading cause of death in the Black community,

---

*Then, as is appropriate now, Du Bois cautioned taking this figure at face value for comparative purposes. He noted, "The comparison is not valid here as few physicians of better class patients would report syphilis as a cause of death. Hence the small white rate in part."

revealing, "Consumption is the chief cause of excessive death rate. . . . It attacks the young men and women just as they are entering a life of economic benefit and takes them away. This disease is probably the greatest drawback to the Negro race in this country."[147]

All of these findings corroborate and explain how the "slave health deficit" and excessive mortality affected African Americans as they entered the twentieth century.[148]

During the first 30 years of the twentieth century the health status of Americans improved. For White Americans, already experiencing much better health status and outcome than Blacks, this improvement had begun around 1880. For African Americans measurable health improvement as reflected in declining mortality rates, increased longevity, and improved infant mortality rates was not definitely discernable until at least 1910. J. W. Leavitt and Ronald Numbers recognized this in *Sickness and Health in America*, stating, "[N]ot all Americans have benefitted equally from these changes. . . . [W]hites continue to outlive nonwhites."[149] The etiology for these racially disparate improvements in health status and outcome is not completely clear to either historians or epidemiologists. In pursuit of the reasons for this health improvement Leavett and Numbers concluded, " [T]he three most likely candidates are medical practice, public health measures, and improvements in diet, housing, and personal hygiene."[150] Of these major factors, most authorities agree that medical practice had the least effect on the observed improvements in health status and outcome during the first three decades of the twentieth century. Medicine was armed therapeutically during this period with diphtheria antitoxin, insulin, and tedious and somewhat effective antiluetic* therapy. These were significant additions to their limited nineteenth-century therapeutic armamentarium. However, these measures had limited abilities to alter epidemiologic disease profiles of entire populations (especially if the therapies were unavailable to large subsets of these populations).

If Blacks had experienced universal access to antiluetic therapy, in light of this disease's catastrophic mortality and morbidity toll on African Americans, measurable progress may have been discernable. Definitely more significant was the fact that the germ theory had proved itself and transformed many aspects of American life, becoming a major factor in controlling infectious diseases. This had profound effects on sanitation standards and practices, which had a lot to do with the control and conquest of life-shortening infectious diseases. There were also new and effective surgical and obstetrical interventions that could transform outcomes for individual patients and ensure the utility of trained professionals. Built upon nineteenth-century technological improvements in agriculture, food preservation, and nutrition, the distribution of food in the United States improved dramatically. Such advances may have improved

---

*Lues* is a plague or pestilence, specifically, syphilis.

the nation's general health more than any other factor. Perhaps more significant for the future was the fact that health care had become wholeheartedly accepted and regarded as a social good by the end of this period. In America medicine represented the triumph of twentieth-century rationality and science to everyone from corporate nabobs to the average man or woman in the street. Health care and its allied services joined food, clothing, shelter, and education as a basic need in modern, industrialized U.S. society.

Nevertheless, the old medical-social dogmas and practices regarding Blacks and other disadvantaged groups were dredged up out of the past and perpetuated. Physicians were major perpetrators of racialist dogma. The profession's menu of stereotypical and prejudicial racial ideologies about Blacks spilled over into the nation's prestigious medical journals, such as the *Journal of the American Medical Association*. One 1910 example read:

> *Whatever the motive that guided the pen which decreed absolute suffering, it stands as one of the world's greatest tragedies, for now the Negro was free, not to live but to die, and he took advantage of his freedom. He was free indeed—free as the birds of the air—free to get drunk with cheap political whiskey and to shiver in the cold because his scanty savings went to purchase flashy and flimsy garments, free never to bathe, and to sleep in hovels where God's sunlight and air could not penetrate—absolutely free to gratify his every sexual impulse; to be infected with every loathsome disease and to infect his ready and willing companions, and he did it—he did it all. The result is the Negro of 1909, the Negro of today.*[151]

This is one citation from this bias-loaded article. The fact that "medical articles" containing material of this nature could appear in one of the nation's most authoritative, peer-reviewed medical journals speaks to how some White physicians developed and perpetuated derogatory and stereotypical views of Black patients. Policies and practices based on draconian classifications of "worthy" and "unworthy" poor intensified, and racial barriers to quality health care loomed higher than ever. Thus the practice of stigmatizing, segregating, and isolating Black and poor patients from the mainstream majority continued, if not intensified, throughout the era. The efforts to deny access to and discriminate against Black patients in the health system were more blatant than they had been in the Reconstruction era. As noted historian Barbara Fields said about glossing over past White racist attitudes by not viewing them in a *constructionist** context, "I lose patience with the argument that because of some one's 'time,' his limitations are, therefore, excusable or even praiseworthy. It is not true that it was impossible in

---

*\*Constructionist* refers to the socially formed dimensions of an inquiry. Such an inquiry includes elements such as the history, social dimensions, and culture shaping a subject.

that time and place to look any higher."[152] This statement holds special moral relevance to health and health care in that it affects an individual's share of the range of opportunities normal for his society. However, as James H. Jones describes early twentieth-century medical and public health attitudes:

> [W]hen race relations had sunk to their nadir, physicians became harsher in their published views. While continuing to assert the inherent susceptibility of blacks to disease, they emphasized environment and life-style as the principal factors behind the crisis in black health. They criticized blacks for living in ignorant neglect of the simple rules of personal and community hygiene, noting with disgust the absence of pure water supplies and proper facilities for the disposal of human waste in black homes. Only rarely was there a hint of compassion or sympathy in their comments for the plight of the people whom they discussed. Writing as though blacks were solely responsible for the socioeconomic conditions in which they lived, some even suggested that disease held the ultimate solution to the race problem.[153]

Absence of justice in a medical-social sense made the failure to equitably include Blacks and the poor in the evolving health system more visible, paradoxical, and even unethical. Similar to other U.S. failures and shortcomings across the racial divide, the conflict of American ideals with its health system practices and realities created a dilemma with which the U.S. health system still wrestles. Paradoxically, as medical progress speeded up, the consequences of the dilemma for African Americans increased exponentially. Moreover, superimposed professional and cultural dimensions of the U.S. health system's race and class problems rendered the American health dilemma even more gut-wrenching and difficult to correct.[154]

## A Golden Age of Medical Suzerainty: The European American Experience

The medical professional movements that started during the late nineteenth century bore fruit during the first three decades of the twentieth. The White medical profession, led by the AMA, consolidated its control over the medical licensing process, the medical education process, postgraduate medical training, the hospital industry, and the biomedical research infrastructure. Based on these multiple mechanisms, White physicians regulated both entry into the profession and the way health care was delivered in the country. By the end of this period they also exerted a great deal of influence over the progress of specialization in medicine and the pharmaceutical industry, while consciously and unconsciously imposing many of their social beliefs and practices on the health system. Much of this so-called professional progress and dominance was illusory—more perception than reality. Influential Black physician-leaders in the NMA mistakenly thought the White medical profession had been highly organized for a century or more.[155] The detailed investigations of the profession by authorities such as Rosemary Stevens, Herbert Morais, E. Richard Brown, and Paul Starr reveal the public impression of what was transpiring was not actually as smooth nor as coordinated as it appeared.

Regulatory functions that were assigned to governmental agencies or centuries-old professional guilds closely allied to national governments in Europe and other nations were hurriedly and sometimes haphazardly assumed by a poorly organized and imperfectly formed U.S. medical profession. Close scrutiny also revealed that in both style and substance, the White U.S. medical profession was much more disorganized, with heterogenous, contentious factions. Moreover, while much of this authority was being assumed, overt and often volatile conflict between medical, political, and institutional factions was occurring. The profession, largely through the AMA and its spin-off bodies, was granted quasi-official legal and legislative authority that was wielded and administered in autocratic and often discriminatory fashions. No attempt to institute democratic processes permeated these events or policies. These are some of the reasons the system's race and class problems have never been addressed and why the covenant between the health system and U.S. society has never been sensitively crafted. This may help explain why the medical profession in the United States has habitually defined the public good according to its own needs. These early ethical and medical-social formulations of both the profession's and health system's goals and objectives, along with their strict limitation of the boundaries of public health, may be largely responsible for some of the health system dysfunctions we presently experience.[156]

By 1900, the American medical profession was coming to power and coming of age. Its efforts at reorganization facilitated its political and professional mobilization to influence national medical organization and development. As Rosemary Stevens observed, the organization followed the recommendations of the special committee on reorganization in 1901, whereby "[m]embership in the county society carried a membership in the state association; the state associations in turn appointed delegates to the national association."[157] AMA secretary and editor of its journal George Simmons "defended this plan as being the only one on which the AMA could be organized if it were to represent the profession of the whole country."[158] The fact that African Americans were denied membership at the county level was not considered an issue.

All of the areas mentioned above, state medical licensing being only one, were thus dominated by White organized medicine. Notwithstanding the founding and growing influence of organizations such as the National Confederation of State Medical Examining and Licensing Boards (founded in 1891) and the National Confederation of State Medical Boards, state medical associations were politically unwilling to surrender to mandates of a national authority for state licensing. Continued efforts at national standards of medical licensing, as suggested by respected physicians such as William Rodman in 1902 and the voluntary National Board of Medical Examiners in 1915, were thwarted by White medical power politics. Avoidance of national medical licensing standards and authority was institutionalized by state interests in reciprocal licensing arrangements represented by the founding of the American Confederation of Reciprocal Examining and Licensing Boards in 1902. Even with the fusion of two confederations of state boards in 1912 to form the Federation of State Medical Boards of the United States, national licensing standards were never established. The AMA, through its committees, its prestigious and widely distributed *Journal of the American Medical Association* (JAMA), and its house of delegates, remained the only mediator and stabilizing factor. These activities, along with White organized medicine's growing stranglehold on medical educational reform, were tantamount to controlling entry into the profession. This matrix of events had monumental negative effects on the Black medical profession, cutting the licensing potential of African American physicians through raised requirements and closing Black medical schools in the process.[159] In these variegated areas the governmental and legal apparatus at all levels came to the European American medical profession for recommendations and policies that would be transformed into the laws and practices governing the nation's health care system.

As interactions and relationships between the AMA and White medical specialty societies progressed throughout the early twentieth century, even the levels, prestige, and progress within the profession after obtaining a degree and license would fall under White organized medicine's control. Buttressed by JAMA, AMA membership of 8,400 in 1900 climbed to over 83,000 by 1920. As mentioned previously, this constituted more than 60 percent of the United States medical profession.

Few, if any, African Americans—who constituted approximately 2 percent of the medical profession during this period—were AMA members. Despite their serving as the medical representation of one-tenth of the population, none participated in these revolutionary health policy or health system developments. As this socially and legally authorized professional hegemony was achieved, White organized medicine's policy of racial exclusion assumed increasingly ominous and dire dimensions of professional disadvantage for African American practitioners, who could only respond to rules established by exclusionary others. Moreover, White organized medicine had proven itself hostile to the interests of the African American community. By the end of this wave of standardization of the profession, African American physicians would be almost exclusively relegated to two medical schools (Howard and Meharry) for training, virtually excluded from organized professional and specialty societies, and purposely exiled to the periphery of the U.S. medical world.

By 1930 the trends toward specialization in medicine, spurred by the World

War I experience, were unavoidable. The medical sciences' expanded didactic and technical knowledge bases required such a division of labor. Medical political wars between the general practitioners (GPs), the numerically dominant group largely trained in the pre-Flexner reform era, and the specialists, which had smoldered during the late nineteenth century, flared up again during the early decades of the twentieth century. The formal establishment of specialty societies and boards began with the founding of the American College of Surgeons in 1913. The AMA, through its committee structure, cooperative efforts with the American Association of Medical Colleges (AAMC), and its relationships with other bodies such as the National Board of Medical Examiners and the state licensing boards, strongly facilitated specialty organization. As Stevens noted, "Of 145,000 active physicians in 1931, nearly 25,000 (17 percent) were in full- time specialty practice, the majority being surgeons."[160] In these organizational efforts the AMA largely represented and was influenced by White GPs, although much of the leadership came from the ranks of academic and specialty physicians. Despite these interprofessional antagonisms, which the AMA attempted to mediate, as was the case in the past, specialists were the elite of the profession—often from privileged social backgrounds, with more academic training, and possessors of highly sought-after hospital and medical school appointments. The AMA walked the tightrope accommodating these opposing forces as it transformed itself from a primarily reform organization (i.e., medical licensing and medical education) in the early part of the century to a political one (i.e., defining medicine's role in a democratic society) by 1930.

The AMA's role as the agency leading the institutionalization of specialization in the United States rendered it an autocratic, quasi-governmental body with professional considerations always primary. Public needs did not dictate the number or types of specialists, where they fit into the delivery of care, or how they were credentialed. The specialty colleges and boards flagrantly excluded and discriminated against Blacks and women, usually operating like exclusive, private, White men's clubs. Many of the distorted relationships between the specialty boards and colleges and the public established during this period persist today.

Despite the AMA and the specialty colleges' racial bar, White organized medicine disingenuously put on a public face of egalitarianism within medicine while compromise arrangements between the organization and the specialty societies reflected this loosely applied ideology—for White males only. By 1930 only the surgeons, ophthalmologists, pediatricians, otolaryngologists, and obstetrician-gynecologists had established official boards and credentialing standards. Most of the other specialties would formally organize during the 1930s and 1940s. By 1931, of the 25,000 acknowledged specialists in the United States, Dr. Daniel Hale Williams, a charter member of the American College of Surgery (1913), and Philadelphia otolaryngologist Dr. Harry Barnes, the first Black board-certified specialist (the American Board of Otolaryngology, 1927), were the only African Americans allowed to receive specialty credentials. In lieu of the African American physician's vital role of health care provision to the Black community, the direction that the organization and structuring of the United States medical profession was taking became increasingly devastating to Black physicians. Remnants of this systematic professional deprivation and isolation would haunt the Black medical profession into the twenty-first century.[161]

Medical specialization and licensing were not the only hot-button issues facing White organized medicine in the first three decades of the twentieth century. Medical educational reform—in process since the Civil War—had accelerated in pace during the 1870s and 1880s and became the crowning achievement that consolidated U.S. medicine's suzerainty over the health system. White physicians convinced both the public and the corporate-based educational foundation world that upgrading and standardizing medical education were a pressing need that would serve the public good.

Momentum was generated by the practicing profession represented by the AMA, by the state licensing boards and by the medical educational establishment of leading medical schools spearheaded by the AAMC, all buttressed by the increasingly powerful and influential *JAMA*. The Johns Hopkins Medical School system was the model. It emphasized higher entrance requirements, including a college degree; a four-year medical course with two years of basic science and two years of hospital-based, bedside clinical medicine; contiguous hospital and research laboratory facilities all utilized in the training process (where medicine "could be studied as well as learned," according to William Welch, a Johns Hopkins medical leader); the application of German clinical and departmental principles of organization, including the establishment of full-time teaching clinical professorships; and the inclusion of postgraduate training residencies in the teaching hospital as part of the total educational process. Clearly, implementation of these new standards would be terribly expensive. It would also serve to virtually eliminate diversity among the people entering the medical profession. Only the privileged need apply.

A profession with historically elite tendencies became even more homogeneous. Impoverished, largely immigrant populations, racial and religious minorities, and women suffered nearly automatic elimination in the process of the new standardization requirements. There were 160 medical schools in 1900. Many of these were proprietary diploma mills. As Kenneth Ludmerer said in *Learning to Heal: The Development of American Medical Education*, "By 1930, there were only seventy-six medical schools, all of which were of acceptable quality."[162] The process by which this took place is emblematic and instructive regarding the rise of a sovereign profession. Of the ten Black medical schools present at the turn of the century, only Howard and Meharry survived.[163]

Most of the nineteenth-century medical educational reform efforts had been internal affairs among small elite groups of European American medical leaders and medical school deans. The public was scarcely aware of these developments. The Illinois State Board of Health had fired the opening volley, making an overt move toward standard-setting by compiling a list of approved medical educational institutions in 1894. The list was published in *JAMA*. In 1896 the AMA had followed this with the first report on medical colleges, detailing their fees, courses, and officers. The *JAMA* published its first medical number* in 1901, including a compilation of medical practice laws. The following year reports from medical examining boards in thirty-two states were published in *JAMA*, showing which candidates from specific colleges passed or failed the examinations. This was unprecedented. However, the *JAMA's* role as an instrument of public exposure did not stop here. The first state board number compared the various medical schools, pointing out state boards that facilitated passing "favorite sons." Interestingly, there is written evidence suggesting that special considerations and "set-asides" in the licensing process took the form of discrimination against African American physicians.[164] This was not publicized. Public disclosures upped the ante in educational reform and forced immediate changes so that public confidence in the profession could be maintained.[165]

In the late nineteenth century the AMA had established cordial and intimate relationships with the state licensing boards and the AAMC. All of these bodies had been actively recommending elevated standards of medical school entry, improving the quality of medical graduates, and ensuring that candidates for licensing were qualified to practice medicine. With an eye toward the future, the AMA had integrated organizations such as the AAMC and state licensing board consortiums into its national reorganization in 1901. After the massive reorganization in 1890, the following year the AAMC, in conjunction with the Confederation of State Boards, had endorsed a three-year medical course. Based on observations of Johns Hopkins's success, the AAMC recommended a four-year course of study by 1894. High school graduation became an official AAMC admission policy by 1900. As Anne Stoline and Jonathan P. Weiner noted, these new requirements "made it much harder for a relatively poor person to obtain a medical education and thus altered the social structure of the profession."[166] This generalization also applied to disadvantaged minority group members and women, who encountered greater difficulties on the road toward becoming physicians.[167]

Significantly, after its 1901 reorganization "the American Medical Association made reform of the medical schools its top priority," according to Paul Starr, who noted, "Since there was no chance of intervention by the federal government, any national action would have to be undertaken by the association itself, via the state licensing boards, which its members controlled."[168] One of the AMA's first acts was to form a committee to engage the United States Congress on the subject of national medical licensing. The AMA subsequently published a recommendation in 1902 that the president of the United States form a national board to set standards for any physician hired by the federal government. This national standard would be recognized and transferable to the various states. Individual state

---

*A *number* is an issue of a scholarly journal dedicated to a particular topic (e.g., subject, institution, person).

licensing boards and their consortium agencies rejected this transfer of medical licensing power and felt that such measures were constitutionally questionable.

There was an AMA response to this impasse:

> The earlier failure of the licensing agencies to provide an integrated national leadership strengthened the role of the AMA as a national agency working through the individual states. Its vehicle, derived from an educational committee appointed by the AMA in 1902, was a new, permanent, and largely self-sustaining council, the AMA Council on Medical Education.[169]

The Council on Medical Education (CME) was established in 1904. Its goals and objectives were to make an annual report on medical education to the AMA House of Delegates; to make suggestions for educational improvement, and to act as the AMA's principal agent in raising standards. The CME was symptomatic of how White organized medicine took control of official governmental, quasi-governmental, and legal functions regarding the standards and regulation of health care and the health care system. Black medical schools fared poorly from the very beginnings of this process.[170] As Stevens observed regarding the CME, "In its design as a central regulating body for medical education, the council filled a function which under other conditions might have been regarded as the role of national government."[171] Such unprecedented circumstances geometrically increased the power of the AMA. Stevens went on to say, "The council found itself with the power to present suggestions as if they were legally required."[172] Thus the CME became a quasi-public agency. This presented few problems, as far as White Americans were concerned, before World War I when the public will and organized medicine's wishes coalesced on upgrading medical education.

After the war, when the wishes of these factions diverged as physicians serving the public decreased, doctor/patient ratios plateaued, and the new quasi-experimental medical care bred by the scientific-based reform became prohibitively expensive, health system dysfunction and friction between the profession and the public quickly surfaced. The newly empowered, organized medical, quasi-public agencies such as the CME did not respond well to these problems because, as Stevens observed, "[T]he council carried the long-term disadvantage of prescribing standards, an autocratic function which in other countries was the function of government or of professional guilds, while at the same time having to submit to democratic control."[173] However, as Bullough and Bullough, Herbert Morais, W. Montague Cobb, E. Richard Brown and others documented, the mechanisms for democratic lay control or influence in this autocratic process were absent in the United States. Had that not been the case, racial segregation and exclusion vitiated many of the potential advantages of governmental appointed representation and authority, and government deference to the private sector conflicted with democratic approaches toward equitable representation. As a result, health policies and practices in all components of the U.S. health system that were strongly influenced by the medical educational and research systems often failed to meet, or even consider, the nation's important medical-social needs. Issues such as ensuring access to all Americans regardless of race, religion, or ability to pay or democratic participation at all levels of health care delivery by all U.S. citizens were not addressed. Few appreciated that the seeds of long-term health system dysfunction were being sowed.[174]

After an initial conference in 1905 to which the state licensing boards were invited, the CME sprang into action. The council, under the leadership of Arthur Dean Bevan, the prominent Chicago surgeon affiliated with Rush Medical College, set an "ideal" standard including a university degree for admission, a five-year medical course, and a sixth year of internship. It then established a set of minimum standards including 4 years of high school for admission, a four-year medical course, followed by passage of a state licensing examination.* The CME also targeted "especially rotten spots" among medical education institutions in Illinois, Missouri, Maryland, Kentucky, and Tennessee. These states had a total of 54 medical schools; only six of these institutions conformed to standards. For the first time, as Stevens observed, "the existing movements of publicity and regulation were combined."[175] The concept of ranking schools—which had been initiated by the Illinois Board of Health—on the basis of failure rates on state licensing exams was adopted nationally by the CME. This movement appeared very threatening to Black medical education with its financial handicaps, deficiencies in clinical facilities and laboratories, and educationally deprived student population.[176]

The CME decided to survey the medical schools in 1906 and 1907. The council, in Dr. Bevan's words, was "exceedingly lenient" in the evaluation. Nevertheless, of the 160 schools inspected, 82 were categorized as class A (acceptable), 46 in class B (doubtful), and 32 in class C (unacceptable). The ratings compiled by the inspection teams led by Dr. N. P. Colwell were forwarded to medical school deans and state licensing agencies. The results, other than the board failure rates that were already being published in *JAMA*, were not made public. State medical societies and boards, most of which by then were AMA affiliates or functionaries, were also informed of the results and encouraged to push for further reform by doing things such as appointing "the right sort of men" to the licensing boards. As E. Richard Brown observed, "Within two years the state medical societies, under the guidance of the Council on Medical Education, dominated the state boards."[177] All this activity generated a tremendous amount of internal and external pressure to upgrade the system. As had been the original intent, the council immediately began to exert "a national influence and control of medical education."[178] Political economic undercurrents were implicit in these activities, as E. Richard Brown pointed out: "The cost of a scientific medical education was shattering the

---

*This would be documented by the lists of state board results already being published annually in *JAMA*.

financial arrangements of proprietary medical schools. The council could not order schools closed, but it rallied political allies in the state boards and the forces of the marketplace to wreck the *ancien regime*."[179] Marketplace influences included the educational foundation infrastructure, the largest funder of higher education in late nineteenth- and early twentieth-century America. Between 1900 and 1910, Brown observed, physicians led the conversion of "[c]orporation heads, presidents of elite universities, and philanthropists" as they "all joined in the support of the new religion of science."[180] The AMA's 1905 action creating a national physician directory and card index also complemented and further facilitated professional cohesion among White physicians while promoting the profession's increasingly positive public image.[181]

Even these revolutionary changes were meager predictors of the medical educational reform explosion that would follow. Bevan's relentless pursuit led to a complete dismemberment of the old educational system. The vehicle for this event was the report *Medical Education in the United States and Canada: A Report to the Carnegie Foundation for the Advancement of Teaching*, better known as the "Flexner Report." It originated from the Carnegie Foundation for the Advancement of Teaching, founded in 1905 to improve the status of college and university teachers and establish a uniform system of higher education. Bevan met with Henry S. Pritchett, president of the foundation, at the Chicago Club in 1907, seeking support for a Carnegie-sponsored study of medical education. He shared the materials obtained in the recent AMA survey with Pritchett. As E. Richard Brown observed, "Bevan's request for a study of medical schools fit well with the foundation's general program and provided an opportunity for the foundation to move into reforming professional education."[182] After consulting with Charles Eliot, Harvard University president and trustee of the Carnegie Foundation, General Education Board, and the Rockefeller Institute for Medical Research, and Simon Flexner, M.D., Director of the Rockefeller Institute, Pritchett decided to fund the study. Flexner suggested that his brother, Abraham, serve as what would now be termed the principal investigator.[183]

Abraham Flexner was a professional educator born in Louisville, Kentucky, in 1866 and educated at Johns Hopkins (A.B., 1886), Harvard (M.A., 1906), and the University of Berlin (M.A., 1907). After teaching and running a private school, Flexner matriculated to earn graduate degrees in the United States and Europe. Returning unemployed from Europe in 1908, "prepared to do almost anything," he unsuccessfully sought employment with Henry S. Pritchett at the Carnegie Foundation for the Advancement of Teaching. In the interim, decisions favoring this study had been made in the boardrooms of major medical and educational institutions, at lily-White* professional organization headquarters, educational foundations, and European American exclusive private men's clubs. Abraham

---

*Lily-White refers to its unique informal usage, "Excluding or seeking to exclude Black people."
*Source: The American Heritage Dictionary*, 3rd ed., s.v. "lily-white."

Flexner was subsequently engaged by this same agency to conduct the study of the medical profession as an "objective," nonphysician educator. At their November 1908 meeting the Carnegie Foundation trustees appropriated the necessary funds to begin the study. "Bevan directed the reform campaign, Pritchett financed it with Carnegie's money, and Abraham Flexner implemented it,"[184] as E. Richard Brown succinctly summarized the American medical education reform process.[185]

The Flexner Report, also referred to as "Bulletin Number Four," "has been called the single most important document in the history of American health care."[186] Other health policy experts such as Rosemary Stevens labeled the report as the triumph of standardization in medical education. Medical historians such as Ervin Ackerknecht and Richard Shryock viewed the report as a major transformation of American medicine into scientific directions backed up, for the first time, by the financial and political resources of major educational foundations such as Rockefeller and the General Education Board (GEB). Specialist historians on medical education such as Ludmerer viewed the report as a public acknowledgment that modern medicine had entered the scientific era and that the scientific method should dominate both the practice and training processes of medicine. The fact that the reform failed to address the health system's medical-social shortcomings was hardly mentioned. Students of medical history and health policy as they affected African American and disadvantaged persons viewed the report as a watershed event of consciousness-raising in regards to previously ignored Black medical and health professions schools; the report painted a derogatory and critical picture of them. Morais, Cobb, Epps, and Savitt noted that the report categorized all these institutions as inferior and all Black physicians as limited, and assigned the products of these Black health professions schools to a caste designated as "sanitarian" and "public health" professionals rather than as participants in the biomedical scientific and surgical revolution. It codified a new institutional caste system in the health professions.[187]

Abraham Flexner was an excellent scholarly technician. After being engaged by the Carnegie Foundation for the Advancement of Teaching, Flexner voraciously researched the history of medical education in the United States and Europe. He then did extensive and lengthy site visits at his alma mater, Johns Hopkins. He met with and was strongly influenced by its prestigious medical school faculty, including Drs. William Welch, William Halsted, Franklin Mall, John Abel, and William H. Howell. Hopkins's medical school represented "a small but ideal medical school embodying in a novel way, education in England, France, and Germany," according to Flexner.[188] After the Hopkins site visits and meetings he went on to say, "The rest of my study of medical education was little more than an amplification of what I had learned during my initial visit to Baltimore."[189] Using Johns Hopkins as his model, he then visited every one of the 155 medical schools in the United States and Canada. Colwell, the secretary of the AMA, went with him on most of the visits. They inspected the schools and wrote the report in 18 months.[190]

The AMA had evaluated schools, even if on an indirect basis, at least three times previously. The CME had site-visited and rated most schools once and conducted at least two surveys of the schools and the state licensing boards. Results of the surveys and some of the findings were published in *JAMA*. The Flexner Report was to be much more extensive and thorough. The inspection process for Bulletin Number Four was reflected by the later composition of the report. First, general comparisons of the "ideal" of medical education were compared to what actually existed in the United States and Canada. All schools were inspected with site visits and evaluated based on their own records, files, and operational procedures. Descriptions of each U.S. and Canadian medical school were undertaken based on the following criteria: "entrance requirements; size and training of faculty; financial resources; laboratories and clinical facilities."[191] Anticipating future funding, most deans and administrators of the various schools revealed everything to the inspection team. As Brown observed:

> *In nearly all cases, the school administrators and faculty laid bare the facts of their existence—facilities, laboratory equipment, numbers of faculty and their qualifications, numbers of students and their preparation, the curriculum, patients available as teaching material, income from student fees, and endowments.*[192]

Abraham Flexner proved to be a strict, if sometimes impulsive, critic. Virtually all agreed that although he was passionate, he was basically objective.

As the profile of medical education changed—including the tremendous expenses associated with scientific medical training—proprietary and poorly funded medical schools were pressured out of the market. The wave of raised standards by the state licensing boards that swept the country by the 1890s and early twentieth century forced many of these institutions to close before the Flexner Report. Nevertheless, Flexner is often utilized as the focal point of American medical school reform. Virtually everyone agrees that the report served as the culmination of a five-decade-long movement. Its effects were immediate, profound, and long-lasting. The most dramatic and popularly recounted effect of the report was the closure and numerical reduction of American medical schools. As Rosemary Stevens summarized:

> *Twenty colleges were said to have closed in order that their conditions would not be described in the Flexner report. Between 1904 and 1915, ninety-two schools merged or closed their doors in the face of higher state board requirements, financial difficulties, or the adverse publicity of the Flexner report. By 1915, the number of schools had been reduced to ninety-five, and there were only eighty-five in 1920.*[193]

Only 76 remained by 1930. Flexner, the foundations, and White organized medicine intended to reform medical education in patterns of strictly scientific, research-oriented medicine; reduce the number of health professionals produced; produce academically qualified, "higher-quality" health professionals; and solicit adequate funding for medical education.

As a reflection of American pragmatism, some influential health policy makers contended, the emphasis on pure medical science and research at the expense of technical and treatment advances directly benefiting patients in the Flexner "movement" went too far. By 1927 William Pusey, a leading physician and medical educator, recognized extremism in this emphasis on research-oriented medicine. He called these scientists "'an ultrascientific group' for whom research and scholarship [were] the ends of medicine."[194] He explained:

> *Back of this ultrascientific group whose influence I am now considering—largely responsible for it, in fact—is a certain sort of influence in the great philanthropic foundations.... [T]his influence will have it that medicine must be all science, and it is using its enormous weight to bring this about. It has been able to get overemphasis on this point even outside strictly academic circles in medicine.... [T]here has been too much insistence on one policy in medicine; on one pattern in the organization of medical education and research; on one sort of man, on one sort of training.*[195]

Amelioration of the health system's race and class problems was never entertained. Clearly, this reform produced greater professional unity. It also produced greater homogeneity and fostered the imposition of an autocratic upper-class referendum on the United States health system. Whether this ideologically driven reification of science by the profession and allies at the expense of social utility was best for the country's health system remained an unresolved issue. It certainly did not bode well for the African American population.[196]

Prior to the Flexner reform, predominantly economic and regulatory forces were already limiting the number and character of U.S. and Canadian medical schools. Formal adoption of this new "ideal" of scientific, research-oriented medicine (with access to teaching resources to be restricted to highly qualified and credentialed students) exponentially compounded the problems of proprietary, minority group (e.g., women, Blacks, and sects), and poor medical schools. Acknowledging the potential limiting effects of his recommendations, Flexner predicted: "no more than one (university-affiliated) medical school per city, the selection of schools for survival according to population criteria, and the drastic reduction in the number of schools from 155 to 31, each giving a four-year course and each with no more than seventy graduating students."[197] Implementation of such criteria was much more expensive in terms of time, tuition, and institutions. Huge amounts of funding would be required for the new network of medical school–controlled hospitals, contiguous research laboratories, and full-time medical school, house staff, and research faculties. New levels and mechanisms of funding would be required. In contrast to Western Europe, private and corporate sectors in the United States through newly established educational foundations were the chosen stewards of scientific medicine. Rosemary Stevens observed, "Foundations were thus the most vital outside force in effecting changes in medical education after 1910, and for a long time they took the place of government support."[198] It is no wonder that inherent flaws were injected into the new medical education system. Neither the United States corporate culture (which was providing the funding), nor the nation's medical profession (which was guiding and supervising the reform) had enlightened views on race, class, or gender problems—nor were they concerned about medical ethics or social equity.[199]

Quantitative and qualitative changes in African American medical education, however, had begun before the Flexner Report. In 1900 there were ten Black medical schools. By the eve of Flexner reform in 1908, only seven had survived the tightening matrix of financing, regulatory, and academic standards. As educational reform progressed, educational foundation leaders realized by 1918 that "the AMA would wreck all medical education for blacks if left to its own devices."[200] Believing in the social importance of Black doctors and nurses practicing in their own communities, the foundations protected several germinal institutions for minority health professions education. By 1923, of the 14 Black medical schools brought into existence in the United States, only Meharry Medical College and Howard University survived. These institutions remained virtually the sole sources of medical training for African Americans between 1910 and the 1970s. Black doctor/patient ratios, already five to six times as high as those for Whites, plateaued and rose slightly in the 1940s to levels that would not decline until after World War II. Access to health care for African Americans, which persisted at continuous crisis levels, had demonstrated some improvement beginning in the late nineteenth century. This component also began to be undermined as a result of the developing national medical educational policy.

Representation in medicine for women was also slashed as a result of Flexner reform. Only one of 17 women's medical schools survived.[201] As Ludmerer said, "[T]he representation of women in the medical profession remained very low ... until the feminist movement of the early 1970s finally facilitated the entry of women into the profession in larger numbers."[202] As a result, the U.S. medical profession assumed its present image and status as being an elite race-, gender-, and class-exclusive profession. Intentionally and inevitably, based on the effects produced by the policies implemented, the U.S. medical profession became an almost exclusively European American male, middle- to upper-class enterprise.[203]

Not only was entry into the medical profession further restricted institutionally by these quantitative reductions in educational opportunity as far as Blacks were concerned, but recognizable predetermined and profound qualitative changes in the system were also placed in much greater relief after medical educational and professional policies had been formally outlined by Flexner. Thus the possibility of Blacks, or to a slightly lesser degree of poor or working-class youth, receiving medical training looked slimmer than at any time since the Civil War. As far as African Americans were concerned, the title of the significant article by Susan Hunt, "The Flexner Report and Black Academic Medicine: An Assignment of Place," delivers a stinging message.[204] Before the push for reform beginning with the post-1900 activities of the CME and the Flexner Report, Blacks, women, and other disadvantaged groups had been largely ignored by the profession. The new reformers and their reforms officially assigned African American physicians a subservient and inferior "place" administratively and ideologically in the new and scientific health system. Instead of remaining a professional nuisance of low priority, African American and women physicians now became a "problem." Even though the opinion of most White physicians was articulated by Abraham Flexner when he stated, "The medical care of the Negro race will never be wholly left to [N]egro physicians,"[205] complete professional and social separation could not be accomplished if African American physicians were included in the new regulatory and standardized system. Where, how, and in what capacity they would function was the question. Moreover, these questions would have to be answered immediately if the new privately controlled reform network was to remain credible to its corporate and general publics. Therefore, in many ways, the official acknowledgment and preservation of the two remaining Black schools presented a problem to the White medical establishment and its corporate-based suitors.

Even though Flexner was perceptive enough to recognize the need for African American health professionals, he was not progressive enough to force European American schools to train Blacks. Even the "ideal," Johns Hopkins University, was strictly segregated along racial lines (its first African American medical school graduate was in 1967). While he pushed for the survival of Meharry and Howard and continued existence of the Negro physician, he proffered survival in exchange for establishment of official racial caste status. Flexner's Chapter XIV, "The Medical Education of the Negro," drips with racism, condescension, and self-interested paternalism. Hunt, in the *Journal of the National Medical Association* (*JNMA*), took selected statements from the chapter (see Table 1.1), presenting them and discussing the "implications for black academic medicine."[206]

Flexner agreed that Black physicians were necessary to the "mental and moral improvement"[207] of their race; Black physicians and nurses were needed to promote public health and instruct principles of hygiene in their community, thus negating the African American population as a "potential source of infection and contagion."[208] This self-serving policy accommodated the universal and racist assumption of the period that Hunt articulates when she states, "[T]he black population ... at the time, was considered to be a major source of infectious disease."[209] Since in Flexner's view Blacks "were a permanent factor in the nation,"[210] such a policy was needed to protect the White population. As Flexner said, "Self-protection not less than humanity offers weighty counsel in this matter;

Table 1.1   Key Statements Excerpted from "The Medical Education
of the Negro," Chapter 14 of *The Flexner Report on*
*Medical Education in the United States and Canada.*

- The medical care of the negro race will never be wholly left to negro physicians.

- The negro must be educated not only for his sake, but for ours.

- The negro is perhaps more easily "taken in" than the white; and as his means of extricating himself from a blunder are limited, it is all the more cruel to abuse his ignorance through any sort of pretense.

- Make-believe in the matter of negro medical schools is therefore intolerable.

- If at the same time these men can be imbued with the missionary spirit so that they will look upon the diploma as a commission to serve their people humbly and devotedly, they may play an important part in the sanitation and civilization of the whole nation.

- Their duty calls them away from large cities to the village and the plantation, upon which light has hardly as yet begun to break.

- It is greatly to be hoped that the government may display a liberal and progressive spirit in adapting the administration of this institution to the requirements of medical education.

*Source*: Hunt S. The Flexner report and Black academic medicine: An assignment of place. *Journal of the National Medical Association* 1993; 85:151–155.

self-interest seconds philanthropy."[211] To meet these goals and objectives, Black physicians trained in a special type of second-class medicine were needed. Howard and Meharry were to provide "a substantial education in which hygiene rather than surgery ... is strongly accentuated."[212] "A well-taught [N]egro sanitarian will be immensely useful; an essentially untrained [N]egro wearing an M.D. degree is dangerous,"[213] Flexner declared.

Retreating to his racist assumption that Blacks were intellectually deficient and automatically more naïve and less perceptive than Whites, Flexner stated, "The [N]egro is perhaps more easily 'taken in' than the white; and as his means of extricating himself from a blunder are limited, it is all the more cruel to abuse his ignorance through any sort of pretense."[214] Even though White medical leaders involved in the standard-setting* were almost totally ignorant of the African

---

*As has been stated on numerous occasions, Whites such as Oliver O. Howard, George Whipple Hubbard, and Charles F. Meserve knew as much about Black education as anyone living. However, Whites such as these who were actually involved in Black education during these periods were automatically excluded, if not totally ostracized, from high policy-making positions.

American's externally imposed educational deprivation, they were charged with overseeing the medical standardization process. Despite their ignorance about Black primary, secondary, or higher education, they "presumed to know what was best" for the Black schools. On this paternalistic basis, Flexner pleaded for uniform standards for both White and Black schools, stating, "Make-believe in the matter of [N]egro medical schools is therefore intolerable. Even good intention helps but little to change their aspect. The [N]egro needs good schools rather than many schools."[215]

Flexner's medical educational reform policy recommended that caste status be conferred on these schools by their educational missions and their professional products. This policy limited the type of practice that Blacks would be allowed and pigeonholed them into what most physicians considered mundane career paths. Continued racial segregation was a given. Hunt remarks, "As a result, [B]lack physicians would have little chance to engage in advanced medicine."[216] Surgery and the subspecialties were considered the most advanced medical disciplines, with research ranked closely behind. In comparison, hygiene was an unglamourous medical cousin often delegated to nurses and medical volunteers. As Hunt notes about African American physicians' subservient role in the profession:

> [W]hite physicians would always supply the skills required by complicated conditions. . . . By systematically limiting the extent of practice, notions of inferior [B]lack intellectual ability grew as [B]lacks faced medical conditions they were unable to treat. Flexner's attitude of helping [B]lacks prepare themselves adequately from a restricted form of practice reinforced a concept of limited [B]lack ability.[217]

Although Meharry and Howard ignored the racist mandate to create only an inferior caste of health professionals, in actual practice they were often required to frame their pleas for funding in terms that seemingly reinforced their mission to train "second-class physicians." In some ways this racial-professional gap has never been bridged.

The assignment of place for women was also reinforced by the Flexner Report, which "also recommended closing the three women's medical colleges."[218] The egregious gender discrimination created by Bulletin Number Four and its long-lasting effects on the medical profession are more thoroughly covered by other specialist scholars.[219]

Flexner reform had generated much more than reductions in the number and variety of U.S. and Canadian medical schools and medical students. For example, as Ludmerer observed, "the Flexner report certainly stimulated the teaching hospital movement nationwide."[220] During this process, much of which occurred during the first three decades of the twentieth century, it permanently changed the profile of the U.S. hospital industry and infrastructure. As Rothstein observed, "Early in the century few medical schools [had] formal affiliations with hospitals."[221] Although Rosenberg documents and describes long-standing teaching hospital affiliations in medical education centers such as Philadelphia and New York City, Rothstein quantifies the phenomenon after the turn of the century:

> When the AMA carried out its inspection of medical schools in 1906–1907, only 6 medical schools had hospital privileges where medical students could examine patients and write histories (i.e., clerkships) and 5 other schools could engage in ward walks at hospitals. Another 88 had clinics in hospital amphitheaters either regularly or occasionally, and 55 had no hospital connections.[222]

His quantitative analysis also included results of the early Flexner reform period, stating:

> During the next two decades, medical schools greatly increased the number of their hospital affiliations. In 1927, 317 hospitals were affiliated in varying degrees with medical schools. . . . Forty-nine of the hospitals were owned and operated by medical schools, and 77 others gave medical schools total or substantial authority to use patients for educational purposes.[223]

He went on to observe, "Public hospitals, which were understaffed and underfunded, were more likely than private hospitals to affiliate with medical schools."[224] Thus this transformation was not just numerical. Reform also had a major imprint on shaping and defining the function of the nation's hospitals and how they interacted with patients.

Influenced by the Johns Hopkins model, the medical education reform movement also helped transform the nation's medical-social culture surrounding the hospital infrastructure. Instead of being objects of dependency and tight-fisted charity administered by the upper-class stewards of the community, poor, identifiable minority, and disadvantaged patients were adopted by early twentieth-century medical reform as "teaching material" for medical school and postgraduate trainees. This new symbiotic relationship between medical schools, public and tax-supported hospitals, and the public health sector infrastructure largely composed of public clinics and dispensaries was reflected in the fact that much of the costs of the medical schools' indigent teaching patients was borne by cities, states, and philanthropic sources. African American physicians and other health professionals were almost totally excluded from these training institutions and programs.[225] Continuing an old tradition, African American, indigent, and low-income working-class patients were still required to virtually sacrifice their bodies in exchange for treatment. These patient groups were transformed from one under-class status to another. Paradoxically, as these categories of patients obtained increased access to such training institutions, they may have put themselves at more risk for medical abuse and unethical experimentation—all in the name of scientific advancement.[226]

Accentuating the need for these new forms of organization of health care was an explosion in costs for medical and surgical care. Technical developments in medicine were making health care and health services more expensive and less accessible to the general public. Institutional organization emphasizing ever-larger hospitals marked a new level of complexity and dependency on hospitals in the delivery of health care for the average practitioner. Huge capital-intensive investments such as modern hospitals or research institutions were beyond the means of physicians or their traditional supporters (charities, religious organizations, lodges, and women's clubs). Such funding had to come from tax-supported public or wealthy private institutional coffers. Moreover, these lay community resource allocations came without strings attached. Physicians were permitted to maintain their autonomy and define their own roles within this technological infrastructure while the community provided the resources. Moreover, doctors provided the expertise that drove policy decisions on how resources were to be expended and allocated. In terms of organization, hospital-based medicine was definitely the wave of the future. In these hospitals, physicians performed their newly developed and safe surgery; treated their interesting and complicated cases; obtained convenient specialty consultations; and sharpened their medical-technical skills as a function of continuing education and medical research. The profession's reaction to this changing environment was to affiliate, and "[B]y 1929, seven of ten physicians had some kind of hospital attachment."[227] Thus the profession's color bar regarding hospital privileges became an increasing burden and handicap to Black physicians as medical progress evolved.

As a countermeasure, African American physicians established small hospitals of their own. Du Bois identified nearly 50 Black hospitals by 1906, and the NMA identified almost 75 by the 1920s. In light of the aforementioned capital-intensive requirements for modern hospitals that absorbed virtually all of the various mainstream community support, Black hospitals became increasingly risky and economically fragile endeavors. One dramatic example of the economic pinch already felt in hospital construction by the Black community was Frederick Douglass Memorial Hospital of Philadelphia, which erected a new building in 1908.

Frederick Douglass Memorial Hospital, founded in 1895, was one of the premier African American hospitals in the United States for the first three decades of its existence. Its founder, Nathan Frances Mossell, M.D., and this flagship institution represented the pinnacle of African American hospital-based medicine in the United States. Mossell's comments in a health services article on hospital standards reveal the level of meager funding for African American institutions compared to that received by White institutions and how resigned Blacks were to their subordinate status. Mossell, seemingly oblivious to what the Black/White funding differentials meant to his project, stated:

> A building, the Frederick Douglass Memorial Hospital, now in course
> of erection at Philadelphia, five stories high, 54 by 78 feet, for the
> accommodation of one hundred patients, is costing $100,000 including
> furnishings and equipment, or $1,000 per bed; the most recently con-
> structed hospital in New York City, with four hundred fifty beds, costing
> $2,400 per bed; the Belgrave Hospital for children, the costliest hospital
> in England, built for the accommodation of seventy-eight patients at a
> cost of $3,500 per bed.[228]

Clearly, as early as 1908 the Black medical establishment encountered financial
difficulty in "keeping up" with the technologically driven race to build modern and
up to-date health institutions. If the highly regarded Frederick Douglass Memorial
Hospital, which had received institutional funding from the state of Pennsylvania,
was financially disadvantaged compared to its White competitors, one can imagine
the dire financial circumstances of the other 50 or so Black hospitals in existence at
this time. Clearly, the new scientific medical technology had become so expensive
that total community support was required to meet the new institutional and organizational standards. Such funding was beyond the capability of impoverished
African American communities. Therefore, contradicting the 1896 *Plessy v.
Ferguson* ruling, due to emerging financial realities in U.S. health care—just as in
education—there could be no "separate but equal" facilities or services.[229]

The other organizational response to this shockingly expensive health care
landscape focused on the health care financing infrastructure. Prior to the twentieth century, a significant portion of individual health care was financed on a
fee-for-service basis. Individual practitioners diversified their service capabilities to
compete in a highly competitive professional environment overpopulated with
physicians. African American medical leader Robert F. Boyd (see Figure 1.3) and
other physicians obtained accessory degrees in dentistry and pharmacy. Technical
advances requiring specialization and postgraduate training were countervailing
trends against these old ways of delivering health care. Elaborate and specialized
hospitals with laboratory, diagnostic, and ancillary support services were required.
How were patients going to continue to pay their bills and financially stabilize an
increasingly expensive health care system?[230]

Two surges of reform in the United States occurred within thirty years of the
Great Depression to grapple with the broad issue of relieving the economic problems associated with sickness and health. The medical profession made pivotal and
long-lasting decisions that affected how the U.S. health system would deal with
these problems. Large prospective studies on the health care system were
conducted during the early twentieth century at the instigation of the labor movement organizations and the government in the midst of Progressive reforms. In the
early decades of the century, research indicated that sickness had become the
leading cause of immediate poverty, that the proportion of families unable to
"make ends meet" increased from 4.7 to 16.6 percent, and that poor health was

**Figure 1.3   Robert F. Boyd (1858–1912)**
Physician and founder of the National Medical
Association, Boyd became the twentieth-century
model of the successful Black medical practitioner.
   Courtesy of Meharry Medical College, Black
Medical History Archive Collection, Meharry
Medical College Library, Kresge Learning Re-
sources Center, Nashville, Tennessee.

responsible for at least one-third of the charity cases in some industrialized states.
Reformers in medicine, labor, and politics agreed that some form of compulsory
health insurance might need to be enacted.

   An early movement for health system reform reached its peak between 1912
and 1915 and was led by academicians and labor union officials—largely through
the American Association of Labor Legislation (AALL). Recommendations for
compulsory health insurance for industrial workers and their families were brought
to center stage. Such actions would serve as income and social stabilization for
working families, but could also deliver health care in more efficient and less
expensive ways. The reorganization necessary to carry out reform emphasized
public health goals instead of individual illnesses; changed payment mechanisms
from fee-for-service to capitation; promulgated the formation of large, centralized,
multispecialty group practices of physicians; and placed most branches of the
health system under the administrative control of health departments. These possibilities created a firestorm of resistance first from the insurance industry, which
would lose substantial portions of profitable insurance markets, and later by the
medical profession. Even the labor unions under Samuel Gompers and the American Federation of Labor (AFL) were against it. Finally, corporations, many of
which initially favored the reform, fought against the movement when experts
admitted that health care costs would not fall, but would probably increase. African
Americans, who were already either excluded or on the periphery of the health
system, were not union laborers. Largely relegated to rural serfdom and domestic
service, the Black population was now in the throes of the struggle against racial
discrimination, violence, and legal segregation heralded by the Jim Crow era.

Racial conflicts bred by the demographic shifts generated by the first Great Migration of Blacks from the South (1890–1920) flared up in both Northern and Southern cities. These social factors, compounded by poverty, rendered Blacks invisible as patients involved in early twentieth-century health reform. Discrimination and caste considerations within the medical profession itself robbed African Americans of what could have been their most effective health policy spokesman—the Black medical profession. By 1918, battered by White organized medicine, the first wave of health system reform was dead.[231]

Publicly, the reform movement for compulsory health insurance seemed to have been placed on the back burner during the prosperous 1920s. This silence was deceptive. Even though the public debate about health reform would not resurface until the 1930s, several momentous events took place in the intervening decade that changed the ground upon which the health reform battles were fought. Factors controlling and influencing the debate on relieving the economic burden of illness changed dramatically. Also noteworthy was the fact that during the 1920s White organized medicine consolidated its control of the U.S. health care system. One symptom of its growing power and influence was the 1927 AMA defeat of the extension of the popular and efficacious Sheppard-Towner Act. The Sheppard-Towner Act, a federal program providing matching funds to the states for the establishment of prenatal and child health centers, had been enacted over AMA protests in 1921. Its passage had been hailed as a victory for women reformers and as evidence of the power of the new female franchise. Virtually all agreed this popular program was positive and successful as far as women and children were concerned. Thus its recision represented the consolidation of the beginnings of a "Golden Age" of White organized medicine's power. Its ability to squelch programs regardless of their public health appropriateness or excellence was unequaled. Popularity with the public at large did not seem to matter. Paradoxically, in the flush of such health policy victories, events and data piled up during the 1920s that would loosen White organized medicine's grip on the U.S. health system forever.

Issues surrounding financial problems associated with illness changed during the 1920s. Chastened by the previous decade's defeat through controversies raised by various interest groups, the continued rise in health care costs, and the growing cultural authority and political influence of the medical profession, lay and health professional reformers had to reframe their pro–health insurance arguments to meet new needs. Paul Starr summarized what happened during the 1920s: "Though the broad objective of health insurance continued to be relieving the economic problems of sickness, the focus of reform shifted from stabilizing income and increasing efficiency to financing and expanding access to medical care."[232] The dramatic changes in health financing that took place during the 1920s were revealed by studies performed and analyzed during that decade. Startling increases in costs of physician's services and hospital care emerged. Not only could physicians do more thanks to technical and logistical advances (e.g., cars, good roads, telephones, fewer house calls), but they also dramatically increased their fees over general inflation rates due to their increasing monopoly power secondary to the effects of restrictive professional entry and licensing. Increases in hospital charges grew from 7.6 percent of a $48.41 total medical bill in 1918 to 13 percent of a $108 medical bill in 1929 to 40 percent of a family's total medical expenditures by 1934. These trends were devastating to African American access to the system at patient and professional levels. As Stoline and Weiner observed about another changing trend in hospital financing, "As more affluent people used the hospital and were able to pay for their care, hospitals began to operate from a patient revenue base instead of relying chiefly on philanthropy."[233] Thus Paul Starr concludes about rising hospital costs that "not until the twenties did the middle class feel the impact and reformers appreciate change."[234] The greatest catalyst to the changed health policy landscape of the 1930s was the Committee on the Costs of Medical Care (CCMC) study conducted between 1926 and 1931.

The final CCMC reports were released in November 1932. Chaired by AMA stalwart Ray Lyman Wilbur, M.D., the CCMC was originally composed of some 15 economists, physicians, and public health specialists. It later expanded to 50 members in various health-related fields. Neither women, Blacks, disadvantaged nor ethnic minority groups were represented, for as Rosen noted: "Women, blacks, Jews, Italians, and members of other ethnic groups did enter the medical profession, but for the most part in small numbers, and they generally remained peripheral to the centers of professional power."[235] Funded by more than $1 million from eight private foundations, CCMC released some 27 research reports and provided more objective information on medical care in America over the five years of its existence than had previously been released. Its findings, though biased by the committee's composition and determination process of medical need, reflected the new health care financing problems. However, 1920s policy makers refused to accept its portrayal of proposed solutions and shocking prescience of future health system trends. This roadblock did not diminish the report's utility as a barometer of then-current professional and establishment health policy opinion. The CCMC report found that virtually everyone was cheated relative to their health care needs; that health care was financially out of the reach of many Americans, especially the poor and working classes; that health care provision should be driven by medical needs and not by demand based on the ability to pay; that the medical establishment should be the determinants of the populations' health needs; and that the present health system was totally disorganized, especially in an era of spectacular health care efficacy and specialism. As solutions, the CCMC "favored reducing economic barriers to medical care, turning over power to professionals, and rationally organizing medical care on a bureaucratic model."[236] Surprisingly, the report proposed that a greater portion of the national budget than 4 percent should be expended on health care. The new voluntary, prepaid health insurance system should expand the health system and health services utilization.

Black organized medicine, reeling from the effects of the Flexner Report, had little connection to, and was not considered by, the CCMC report. Blacks as patients, many of whom were medically indigent, were part of the impoverished and uninsurable segments of the population the report chose to ignore. The harshness of the exclusion of such patients was epitomized by the minority report of the CCMC, the position ultimately adopted by the AMA, which stated: "The minority ... was only too happy ... to recognize the duty of the state to give complete and adequate care to the indigent, thus freeing private physicians from responsibility for an unprofitable part of their practice."[237] After the system was better organized according to CCMC recommendations, such populations would be dealt with "later." Thus the *de facto* expulsion of the Black population from the mainstream health system (on health policy, financial, and racial grounds) was officially endorsed and became integral to national health policy.

Although favoring the promotion of group practice and group payment for medical care, the CCMC report opposed compulsory health insurance. Despite the later adoption of some of its recommendations in the Social Security Act of 1935 and the resurrection of many of its predictions decades later, it was not a popular report. Rosemary Stevens observed that the AMA editorialized and propagandized that the CCMC final report was some sort of socialist dogma: "There is the question of Americanism versus sovietism for the American people."[238] The savaging of the report in both the *JAMA* and the *New York Times* as a "radical" document convinced President Franklin Delano Roosevelt, who was just entering office, that his administration should avoid the health insurance issue. Unfortunately, as a result of developments that occurred in the 1920s, White organized medicine, as Stevens recounted, saw "[i]ts political line hardened in a stubborn, conservative defense of a system of practice which was already, scientifically, if not socially, outmoded."[239] She went on to observe, "It was unfortunate that the types of practice arrangements being condemned by organized medicine were not economic devices alone; they were also organizational adjustments to functional specialism."[240] White organized medicine had, once more, proved its suzerainty— some felt to its own disadvantage.[241]

One phase of professional control that affected the health status and outcome of the United States population, especially Blacks, the poor, and the underserved, was to restrict the limits of public health. "[T]he United States did not establish government health agencies as rapidly as European countries did."[242] Though Louisiana established an ineffective state board of health in 1855, most health departments were institutionalized after the Civil War. New York's Metropolitan Board of Health, established in 1866, developed into one of the most progressive health departments in the world. Massachusetts established the first effective state board of health in 1869. Building on eighteenth-century roots, in 1870 the federal government placed its network of marine hospitals under a Surgeon General in the Marine Hospital Service. In response to new cholera and yellow fever epidemics, the 1878 Congress gave the service the authority to quarantine vessels that risked transmitting contagions. Recurrent epidemics led to the establishment of a short-lived National

Board of Health in 1879. Due to political resistance and mechanizations, the board was abolished four years later. "Thereafter, public health remained almost entirely a state and local responsibility," Starr recounted. [243]

Although small cadres of U.S. physicians joined in the leadership and functioning of these scattered progressive public health activities, the profession as a whole or as a political pressure group fought against them vehemently. Characteristically, individual White American physicians projected themselves to the public as an ethical professional group of selfless, humane, "family doctors"; however, their group actions revealed instead that they were a cold, reactionary, mean cabal as far as the entire U.S. population was concerned. This "states' rights" approach to public health in the United States would have profound implications for, and adverse effects on, African American and other health-disadvantaged populations. It would lead to the establishment of a pattern of underdevelopment in public health as the norm for most of the United States.[244]

The foundations of public health were fluid and shifted dramatically between the nineteenth and twentieth centuries. After the Civil War, public health was largely focused on sanitation and environmental concerns and was closely allied with engineering. With the revolutionary late nineteenth-century breakthroughs in bacteriology and immunology, public health refocused on the individual, making the reliance on the techniques of medicine and personal hygiene paramount. Progressive health departments such as New York City's, taking advantage of and pragmatically applying the new scientific advances, proved that it was possible to control diphtheria, tetanus, and some communicable childhood infectious diseases by the late nineteenth century. New York pioneered publicly accessible, free diagnostic laboratories and vaccine production and immunization programs by the early twentieth century. International acclaim followed. Moreover, by 1880 the utilization of reporting, isolation, and the control of sputum made major inroads on the dread "white plague," tuberculosis. Cutting-edge school health programs in cities such as Boston and New York City established internationally respected standards of effectiveness. Utilizing regular examinations and screenings, school nurse programs, and occasionally—when allowed to—immunizations, they proved that schoolchildren of all races and classes, could largely be protected from the ravages of myriad diseases that could permanently impair their hearing, sight, and intellectual capabilities.

The other arm of public health, actually by way of increasing access to medical care for Blacks, the poor, and working classes, was the dispensary movement. Dispensaries were actually free outpatient clinics and affiliated pharmacies run by volunteer physicians and medical students and trainees. They were strongly entrenched in urban population centers in the Northeast and Midwest. By 1900 there were approximately 100 in the country. In their attempts to control the nature and availability of medical care, physicians politically demonized dispensaries and public health clinics by blocking the erection of new facilities and ostracizing or professionally destroying the physicians who staffed them. One of the oldest and most venomous medical crusades adversely affecting public health was the White medical establishment war against dispensaries.[245]

Physicians had fought against the dispensary movement throughout the nineteenth century, accusing them of representing unfair competition and serving as a refuge for economically privileged patients seeking to avoid paying for medical services. Although the studies conducted to evaluate these allegations scientifically never proved their validation, the propagandistic cabal from the organized White profession continued. These institutions' presence not only ideologically represented "state medicine" to physicians, but also, they alleged, hurt them financially. These assertions impressed many in the United States public, especially influential Progressive reformers, as false issues born of an extremely conservative ideology. Thus decimation of dispensaries and hospital clinics in the early twentieth century was accomplished largely by the medical profession itself. This policy had a devastating effect, further limiting access to care for working-class, indigent, and Black patients.

The effect of the White medical profession on all of these progressive and salutary public health activities was strongly negative. American physicians, with few exceptions, fought against and eventually succeeded in undermining or virtually ending these programs. Physician activity against these public health activities peaked during the first 30 years of the new century. Those programs the White medical establishment did not eliminate, they severely vitiated, and they limited the effectiveness of the programs they allowed to survive. This was especially devastating for Blacks and the poor. Most of these groups, including their children, were systematically locked out of the burgeoning mainstream health system developed for most Americans. These public programs were often the only health care they received.

The White profession's internal problems with the production of excess numbers of physicians, commercial medical schools, and slipshod standards and sectarian wars were never publicly projected as responsible for U.S. physicians' fragile financial position. Nevertheless, these ideological factors came back to haunt them even as they wrested control of these internal professional problems. Some of the major factors foiling physician's early efforts to close dispensaries and hospital clinics had been the profession's political weakness, and low prestige, and overpopulation of both practitioners and schools. This would change as medicine's cultural authority and political power increased dramatically at the dawn of the twentieth century and as the White medical establishment reorganized the health system administratively. As students of the dispensary movement noted: "[T]he chief question discussed in articles about dispensaries, as well as their annual reports, had not been the needs of patients and how they might be met most efficiently, but instead, 'How shall we keep people from getting treatment.'"[246] This was especially devastating to Black patients who often could not obtain treatment at other outlets.

Eventually, through the multiple effects of the enactment of professional sanctioning, exclusion, and ostracizing measures; decreasing the number of medical schools and their student populations by the White profession; and establishing alternative teaching institutions as competition, most dispensaries disappeared by 1930. Other progressive public health measures had limited effect. Innovative and standard-setting programs such as the one initiated in New York City by Hermann M. Biggs and William H. Park—establishing the nation's first publicly accessible diagnostic bacteriological laboratory in the late nineteenth century—were limited and circumscribed. This program, supplemented by immunization and antitoxin production and administration programs, had tremendously cut the death rate for diphtheria and "pseudo diphtheria" in New York City. Nevertheless:

> *despite international acclaim these achievements soon excited protests from local manufacturing chemists and doctors, who denounced the health department's activities as "municipal socialism" and unfair competition with private business. [I]n April 1902, over a thousand physicians and druggists signed a petition urging the mayor to root out this continued "commercialism" in the health department.*[247]

Yielding to political pressure, city politicians drastically curtailed the health department programs and activities, to the detriment of the city. Black and poor populations who had benefited greatly from these programs were hardest hit.

After Koch's isolation of the tubercle bacillus, city health departments attempted to control tuberculosis. Based on scientific data, public health experts felt the disease was contagious and controllable through voluntary and mandatory reporting and proper sanitary care of the victims. Blacks had the highest prevalence and mortality rates from tuberculosis and were often poor besides. Thus they stood to benefit greatly from the new programs. Physicians protested, alleging that health department policies violated their doctor-patient relationships and invaded patient rights to confidentiality. Thus protection of rights (never extended or relevant to Black patients) restricted public health policy. Even public health programs benefitting children were not spared the wrath of the medical profession. As Starr observed: "Like other public health programs, health services for school children shifted from environmental to individual concerns in the late nineteenth century and then ran into barriers imposed by private practitioners."[248] Health department officials bowed under the pressure, making specific rules to render no treatment to children discovered with health problems. This "no-treatment" proviso has lingered and remains in many health departments policies to the present day. For many Black and poor children, this translated into denial of the only medical or dental care they might receive. During the early twentieth century, to suppress and prevent any active treatment in school-based health programs, authority for school health programs was often switched from the health departments to the school boards. In many disparate ways private, physician-led interests created barriers to effective and coordinated public health programs. This adversely affected Black and poor populations to much greater degrees than it did the general population. One questions why the early twentieth-century medical profession, which was granted unprecedented social and cultural authority while overseeing the growth and transformation of the U.S. health system, intensified its promotion and promulgation of race and class segregation and discrimination at the professional, institutional, and patient levels.[249]

These heavy-handed and callous public health policies with regard to Blacks and the poor revealed a dark side of the U.S. medical profession and the health establishment it guided. The authors agree with Stephen J. Gould, John S. Haller Jr., Allan Chase, William Stanton, and James H. Jones that the late nineteenth and early twentieth centuries were the most intensely scientific racist periods in U.S. history. Investigators such as Rosemary Stevens and Paul Starr have covered these other forces, including, but not confined to, the ascendancy of the medical profession as the stewards of health system growth, maturation, and change; the necessity of creating a hospital system to accommodate new medical-scientific advances; the overhaul of the medical education system to conform to modern scientific standards; the realignment of the system to facilitate specialization in medicine; and the struggle to institute modern public health measures based on scientific breakthroughs in an excellent manner. The deleterious effects of the eugenics movement, psychological testing movement, social Darwinism, the growth of biological determinism, and the orientation of the nascent birth control movement in eugenic directions on the burgeoning health system are only hinted at or implied in most accounts. Superimposition of these scientific racist components on the health system's centuries-old race and class problems created a serious medical-social "mix" indeed.

In some ways the first three decades of the twentieth century could certainly be viewed as a Golden Age for the White medical profession. Tentative organizational movements begun during the late nineteenth century became the foci of medical professional dominance during the twentieth. The White medical profession, led by the AMA, consolidated its control over the medical licensing process, the medical education process, postgraduate medical training, the hospital industry, and the biomedical research infrastructure. The majority of medical, social, and scientific historians agree that most of these were positive developments. However, the health system continued to be plagued by its history-based problems of class and race. Moreover, the peculiarly American version of scientific racism concerning ethnic Americans, Native Americans, and African Americans grew prominent and flowed over into several public policy areas. Racial ranking and hierarchies based largely on the theories and practices of IQ testing and intellectually fashionable biological-determinist and genetic theories were pervasive. Eugenics transported from Britain and Germany flourished and tainted the United States medical profession and the nascent birth control movement. Augmented by the White medical profession, the peculiar U.S. dream-myth of creating some form of "meritocracy," automatically creating a "natural aristocracy," seemed within reach, utilizing negative eugenics and psychometric testing mechanisms. This might have worked out if the scientific premises these tools (e.g., IQ testing, unit character genetic inheritance, biologic determinism) were based upon had been correct, and if U.S. social conditions had represented an even playing field to Americans of all races, socioeconomic backgrounds, and creeds. Due to the specious science upon which mental testing was based, Henry Goddard and Carl C. Brigham later publicly recanted and apologized by the 1930s; however, by then they had done millions of Americans and the behavioral and related health sciences great harm. For example, by the time Goddard recanted in 1928 and Brigham in 1930, due to exposure of the scathing spotlight of good science, they had helped chart the United States on a seemingly irreversible course away from its ideals of nondiscrimination and equality of opportunity.

There were other areas where health-related progress was modulated not only by the force of scientific racism hanging over the system but by fiscally conservative policies regarding social or community welfare programs as well. These new "sciences" complemented the old aristocratic perogatives and practices. Real scientific progress tainted by scientific racism was unable to override this centuries-old American tradition of inadequate social programs. Grudging implementation of hookworm programs, sanitation improvements, and maternal and child health programs, especially in the South, was due to political resistance and medical professional neglect or noncooperation. European American organized medicine rescinded the Sheppard-Towner Act by the late 1920s. Doctors, backed by insurance companies and special interests groups, rejected the findings and recommendations of the progressive AALL and CCMC reports on the health system. Public health, which in the South had traditionally lagged behind the national norms, slowly improved, but deficiencies created the environment in which the Tuskegee experiment could occur.

It would require massive federal intervention during the Great Depression, often overriding physicians' and organized medicine's protests, to begin substantive corrective actions of massive public health problems born of previous deficits. Therefore, this early twentieth-century period of U.S. health history, from the White medical professional standpoint, can be characterized as the best of times and the worst of times. However, the entire society—especially African Americans, of all the disadvantaged groups still suffering the heaviest disease and death burdens of any population group—benefited very little. For many reasons reflected in the American character, political process, backward public and health policies, and the proliferation of both gut-level and scientific racism, Black and poor people died unnecessarily, their children were labeled as "slow learners" for many preventable health-related reasons, they suffered unnecessary morbidity, and they were subjected to unnecessary abuse at the hands of the criminal justice and health systems. These sad occurrences could be only partially attributed to U.S. public health failures. Moreover, perpetuation of the tradition of overutilization and, often, unethical medical experimentation on Blacks and the poor would create the environment for the infamous Tuskegee experiment, which commenced in 1932.

Blacks continued to face naked discrimination in the health professions. The era of the Great Depression that followed would expose many within the medical establishment and their system's deficiencies and lower the threshold of public tolerance. Franklin Delano Roosevelt and others would take advantage of these circumstances and attempt to push U.S. health and its health system into the twentieth century.[250]

## Another Golden Age of Medical Suzerainty: The African American Experience

Despite the overwhelming adversity experienced by African Americans in the health system during first three decades of the twentieth century, the era could be looked upon as a Golden Age for the African American medical profession. African American physicians entered the new century disorganized and virtually invisible. By 1930 they were the most organized, intellectually sophisticated, and highly respected professional group in Black America. As Carter G. Woodson noted in *The Negro Professional Man and the Community*: "The physician or dentist, then, easily became the outstanding man in the community.... [I]n fact, he became the man of the hour.... Whether he would or not ... the Negro in this sphere becomes as much a business man or community leader as he does a professional figure."[251] During this period Black doctors organized professionally; developed enough technical sophistication and competency to launch a Black hospital movement; spearheaded and staffed African American training movements in medicine, dentistry, pharmacy, and nursing; and became advocates and ombudsmen for Black health and civil rights activists fighting against segregation and discrimination in health.

After decades of frustrated attempts at gaining acceptance by White organized medicine throughout the 1870s and 1880s, Black doctors grudgingly realized they would not be admitted into the White profession. As Benjamin Brawley observed about African Americans in the early twentieth century, "As never before the Negro began to realize that the ultimate burden of his salvation rested upon himself, and he learned to respect and to depend upon himself accordingly."[252] By 1880 Black physicians were forming local organizations such as the Tennessee Colored Medical Association (founded 1880); The Medico-Chirurgical Society of the District of Columbia (founded April 24, 1884); the Lone Star State Medical Association (founded August, 1886); the Old North State Medical Society of North

Carolina (founded 1887); the Association of Physicians, Dentists, and Pharmacists in Georgia (founded 1893); and the Alabama Medical, Dental and Pharmaceutical Association (founded 1896). The first formal call for a national organization emanated from the premier issue of America's first Black medical journal, *The Medical and Surgical Observer*,[253] in 1892. From an obscure beginning on November 18, 1895, at the First Congregational Church in Atlanta, Georgia, the NMA was formed[254] during the Atlanta Cotton States Exposition.[255]

After a shaky beginning between 1895 and 1904—operating with less than 50 members— the NMA boasted a membership of 500 by 1912. Early conventions in 1897 (Nashville) and 1899 (St. Louis) were small affairs, but the 1903 convention in Nashville seemed to breathe new life into the NMA. However, many agree that the 1908 New York meeting was the breakthrough that permanently established the NMA as a national organization.[256] Although the virtues of professionalization in medicine as a social good were appreciated by African American physicians of the early twentieth century, they encountered a special set of obstacles. They wanted what other groups sought from professionalization, such as the institutionalization and advancement of a specialized and exclusive body of knowledge; the development of educational institutions to promulgate this knowledge; the development and enforcement of an ethical code; the setting and enforcement of standards of practice among members; as well as with the comradeship, security, and fellowship highly valued by all members of any profession. They also wanted their organization to serve as an avenue for professional improvement and guild-like protection. However, the color line not only produced an almost implacable division of the profession in America, but also distorted the Black groups' maturation by extinguishing vital external stimulants of professional development. W. Montague Cobb described the effects of racism on minority professional societies' maturation and acquisition of legitimacy:

> *Minority professional societies lacking compelling power and responsibility, thus can ... develop a lethargy toward public health matters of general community import.... [E]fforts of the minority society to discharge their due share of duty ... are actively thwarted by exclusion of their members from significant participation.... [M]inority professional societies are deprived of valuable experience in organizational function and suffer the general disadvantages of isolation.*[257]

All regulatory and standard-setting functions were exercised by White physicians and their organizations. Moreover, African American physicians were barred from important community functions such as health policy setting, public health consulting, and actually administering the health system. "This situation renders the vitality and potency of the medical society of the minority group more dependent on the idealistically determined drives of the individual members than is true for the dominant society."[258] The professional subjugation went further; as Cobb pointed out, "In matters of dispute the majority society can overrule the minority."[259] Without external inputs, feedback, and legitimacy so vital for professional societies to thrive, it is amazing that Black organized medicine survived.[260]

Despite such disadvantages, the African American medical profession had acquired a sense of both place and identity by the onset of the Great Depression. As J. Edward Perry noted, leadership physicians such as C. V. Roman, John Kenney, Daniel Hale Williams, Austin Maurice Curtis, Nathan Francis Mossell, and George Cleveland Hall provided the inspiration and leadership to put Black medicine on a solid footing. This spirit was manifested in several ways. The most important was the rising confidence based on the success and acceptance of a Black medical profession. As Dr. Hubbard noted in a 1909 medical journal, the experiment he and General Howard undertook to tackle the African American health crisis by training Black health professionals had been an overwhelming success. Referring to Meharry Medical College, he stated: "[T]here are now about 2,000 living medical graduates. It is probable that about 1,600 or 1,700 [85 percent] of these are residing in the South and Southwestern States ... 1,500 of these are practicing medicine."[261] Moreover, building upon the gaslight era exploits and examples of Daniel Hale Williams, R. F. Boyd, John Wesley Anderson, and Nathan Frances Mossell (see Volume 1), African American physicians had carved out a niche for themselves by 1930. Using a practice model laid out by R. F. Boyd, they accomplished this by focusing their private practices within their own communities—thereby lessening the chances of interracial competition or conflict; by becoming African American community resources and advocates for public health, health promotion, and disease prevention activities for Black people locally and in the community at large; by living conservatively and practicing by the highest professional and ethical standards—including positive interactions, where possible, with their White colleagues; by serving their communities, often voluntarily, in what were sometimes considered undesirable public service roles such as jail or school physicians; and by thwarting the impact of institutional segregation and discrimination by spearheading Black hospital and nurse training movements. Although largely confined to the Black community in their efforts, this may have ensured the survival and enhanced the positive impact of these pioneer African American physicians.[262]

Another major, externally imposed crisis facing the African American medical profession during the first three decades of the twentieth century was the reform of medical education. Educational reform efforts, oblivious to African American needs, hurt Black medical education at almost every level. Medical school admission criteria were raised based on rigidly enforced White standards. Moreover, even when African Americans earned outstanding academic records, as was the case with Louis Tompkins Wright and Aubre de Lambert Maynard, strained relationships with White medical schools and institutions often resulted. Graduating as valedictorian of his class at Clark University in Atlanta (1911), Louis T. Wright was mistakenly accepted to Harvard Medical School on the basis of his graduating from the prestigious university of the same name in Worcester, Massachusetts. Dismayed when he arrived for classes, Harvard faculty members examined Wright verbally in the field of chemistry on short notice. His performance was so impressive that he was admitted into the class of 1911. In his third year an assistant professor of obstetrics informed him "that he could not perform deliveries at Boston Lying-In Hospital because he was 'colored.'"[263] Louis Wright responded: "[H]e had paid his tuition and insisted on being treated like any other student. His classmates supported him, and he uneventfully participated in the obstetrical rotation."[264] Wright subsequently graduated with his M.D. (cum laude) in 1915, ranking fourth in his class. Professionally, he went on to become the first Black physician admitted to the staff of any New York hospital (1919), the first Black police surgeon in New York City (1929), the second African American elected to a fellowship in the American College of Surgeons (1934), a diplomate of the American Board of Surgery by examination (1938), and the first African American Director of Surgery at Harlem Hospital (1943–1952). Despite his overwhelming successes, Wright's encounters with racial discrimination in both American society and medicine outraged him. Discriminatory treatment when he registered his medical license in Georgia, in the Army Medical Corps, and when he applied for hospital staff privileges in New York City, and barriers and delays in obtaining his surgical credentialing and promotions despite his brilliant academic* and clinical performance reinforced his determination to fight against racial discrimination and often pitted Wright against the White medical establishment. Regarding the AMA: "Wright felt that it had grown from a mild, academic body to a trade association of vast power. He opposed it, and held the association responsible for the inequalities in medical care. He condemned the association's silence on discrimination and the practice of it."[265] As far as Black people were concerned, he opined: "The American Medical Association has demonstrated as much interest in the health of the Negro as Hitler has in the health of the Jew.... Some day the nation will wake up to the fact that disease germs are not color conscious."[266] His fundamental fairness and egalitarian ideals were reflected in his health care civil rights activities, but did little to endear him to the White medical establishment.

Aubre de Lambert Maynard, legendary New York physician and director of surgery at Harlem Hospital (1952–1967), was the surgeon who performed the emergency thoracotomy that saved Dr. Martin Luther King Jr.'s life from a stab wound to his chest on September 20, 1958. Accepted in 1922 at all four medical schools to which he applied on the basis of a stellar academic record, his first choice was College of Physicians and Surgeons of Columbia University:

---

*Wright received 94 percent, the highest mark, on the Maryland medical licensing examination; 95.7 percent, the highest mark that year and one of the highest marks ever made, on the Georgia medical licensing exam; in New York on the medical licensing exam he got a mark of 92.4 percent; and on the competitive civil service examination for police surgeon in New York City he placed second, four-tenths of one percent behind the first man on the list.

*In a preliminary interview with the dean, Maynard was informed that after the first two years at Columbia it would be best for him to transfer to Howard University for his clinical years because of the "embarrassment" that might arise if he carried out certain examinations on white patients. Maynard informed the dean he would not accept this form of bigotry, and subsequently withdrew his acceptance to Columbia University and re established his acceptance to the New York University Medical School.[267]*

Despite their outstanding academic credentials, both Wright and Maynard were limited in their options for postgraduate training.* For most Blacks, educationally underserved during their preparatory phases due to segregation and discrimination, this was a major barrier.

Events between 1905 and 1930, when the Flexner reform era was in full swing, had adverse effects on Black medical education, and indirectly on Black health. The nation would not begin addressing these issues until the 1950s. Medical education reform brought Black medical education to the attention of the White medical establishment for the first time, often reinforcing its biases and deprecation. Educational reform raised the educational and laboratory standards for medical schools. Capital-intensive improvements in faculty, physical plant, and laboratory technology were beyond each Black school's financial means. Of the seven Black schools in operation in 1905, only the two chosen by the Flexner Report for survival, Meharry and Howard, survived beyond 1923. Of the three schools surviving by 1914, Leonard and Meharry would be downgraded to class "B" ratings. Leonard was forced to close its doors in 1918, and Meharry would not recapture its class "A" rating until 1922. Howard hung on by a thread, barely surviving and maintaining its class "A" rating. Todd Savitt described the net effect of Flexner reform, noting: "The number of black practitioners in the United States dropped five percent between 1932 and 1942, while the number of white physicians increased 12 percent."[268] Black access to medical care, as reflected by doctor/patient ratios, physician visits, and other measures, also deteriorated. Barriers to Black medical education were exacerbated by declining African American admissions and graduations from White universities and professional schools nationwide.[269]

The longer and more intensive course work required for graduation imposed impossible financial burdens on already strapped African American students and institutions. The internships required by many states to take licensing examinations were impossible for most African American graduates to fulfill because they were usually barred from hospital training programs because of their race. As noted

---

*Rejected as a candidate for internship at Boston City, Peter Bent Brigham, and the Massachusetts General Hospitals due to his race, Wright completed his internship at Freedmen's Hospital of Howard University in 1916. Dr. Maynard completed his internship and his basic surgical training at Harlem Hospital between 1926 and 1928.

earlier, the few Black graduates of White medical schools were routinely denied post-graduate professional training slots in White hospitals. For example, when African Americans successfully agitated and parlayed their growing political power in St. Louis into the opening of City Hospital No. 2 (a separate Black city hospital) in 1919:

> there were very few other institutions in the United States where black physicians could receive formal accredited postgraduate training, i.e., Howard University in Washington, D.C.; Meharry Medical College in Nashville; Provident Hospital in Chicago; and Harlem Hospital in New York.... [I]t was one of only five institutions in the United States that offered hospital training to black physicians.[270]

There were not enough training slots to accommodate half the meager physician output of the Black medical schools. Ten years later the situation had improved slightly, in that three large non-Negro hospitals accepted an occasional Black intern. They were Cook County in Chicago and Harlem and Bellevue in New York City. As Morais noted: "Of the Negro hospitals, only twelve were at that time approved for 68 internships; and Freedmen's Hospital in Washington, D.C., had as many as 24. Since there were more than a hundred Negro graduates each year, this meant a deficit of 30 or more internships annually."[271] Graduates of schools not meeting the AMA, CME, and state medical board's new standards, which increasingly required postgraduate training, were not permitted to sit for licensing examinations. All of these edicts increased the difficulty of obtaining a well-rounded medical education for poor or disadvantaged students, especially African Americans.[272]

A corollary of the threatening environment for Black medical education was the plight of the African American nursing profession. From the beginning, Southern nurse training programs were closed to Blacks. After hopeful beginnings, the New England Hospital for Women and Children in Boston, where Mary Eliza Mahony, the first African American graduate nurse, had trained (1879), allowed five other Black nurses to complete their training by 1900. Other schools, such as Women's Hospital and Blockley of Philadelphia, Women's Infirmary in New York, and Jefferson Park Polyclinic in Chicago, had trained a few African American nurses in the late nineteenth century. But the increasingly rigid color line closed these opportunities and generated more pressure for Black nurse training schools between 1901 and 1930.

More than 90 percent of the Black nurse training programs were spearheaded by African American physicians who knew trained nurses were prerequisites for first-rate clinical care. Pioneer efforts such as Spelman College's nursing program in Atlanta (1886), Provident Hospital of Chicago (1891), Dixie Hospital Training School at Hampton Institute (1891), and Tuskegee Institute's nursing training course (1892) were followed by scores of twentieth-century institutions such as Mercy Hospital School in Philadelphia (1907), Good Samaritan Hospital of Columbia, South Carolina (1910), and Hubbard Hospital's Nursing School affiliated with Meharry (1910). The post–World War I survey conducted by the NMA's Dr. John A. Kenney presented very favorable data regarding the status and competency of Black nurses by 1919. He stated:

> The Negro nurse through the efficiency of the nurse training schools scattered all over the country, has come to take her place in the world's work, as we regard the future so far as the health and mortality of the race is concerned.... [I]t will be much improved ... through its physicians and nurses ... [who] will meet the demands of the communities where we are located, either in large or small numbers.[273]

As Darlene Clark Hine noted, "By 1928 these schools had produced 2,238 graduates, accounting for 80.3 percent of the total of 2,784 black graduate nurses."[274] Therefore, pushed by the countervailing forces of improvements in the scientific quality of medical care and the tightening noose of exclusion and segregation by White training institutions—the crushing demands of African American public health and clinical needs juxtaposed against White exclusion and discriminatory segregation from these services—the Black nursing profession was forced to meet new levels and demands of competence, professional organization, and cooperation with African American physicians. There were several results. As Darlene Clark Hine noted, "By 1920, there were approximately ... thirty-six black nurse-training-schools."[275] However sterling these accomplishments, they were met by suffocating discrimination. Besides professional competence, determination and heroism were also required. For example, when Meharry Hubbard graduated its first nursing class in 1912:

> That same year, Hubbard nurses attempted to take the examination required for a license from the State of Tennessee. When they arrived at the prescribed time and place, the secretary of the licensing board refused to administer the test to them. Protests by black citizens and the Rock City Academy of Medicine led state officials to reconsider the prohibition.[276]

Despite the protests of Black medical societies and citizens, there was an impasse until 1914, when the two Hubbard Training School graduates for that year were "[c]alled from their work one afternoon [and] presented an examination over ten nursing subjects. Although allowed no time for review, they both earned passing grades. Thereafter, Meharry's nursing graduates were admitted to the state examination without opposition."[277] There was a third response to the professional exclusion, segregation, and degradation displayed by the White nursing profession and the American Nurses Association (ANA): Martha Franklin, an African American graduate of the Women's Hospital program in Philadelphia, and Adah Bell Thoms, president of the Lincoln Hospital Nursing Alumnae Association, convened a meeting in 1908 at St. Mark's Episcopal Church in New York City. That convention resulted in the founding of the National Association of Colored Graduate Nurses (NACGN). Membership grew from 125 in 1912 to 500 by 1920. By 1928 the NACGN began publishing its own organ, the *National News Bulletin*.[278]

Before they could consolidate their organizational and professional gains, the African American health professions were faced with several monumental issues. There was a major rebirth of scientific racism disseminated in both the medical and scientific literature and the popular press. The editor of *JNMA* observed: "Current literature fairly teems with the discussions of the Negro question.... [T]hey seem [to make] arguments to establish preconceived notions, rather than inquiries after truth. Spectacular rhetoric, rather than sound conclusion seems to be their goal."[279] Racist White physicians openly declared:

1. The Negro is to blame for his own susceptibility to disease (Tuberculosis).
2. The Negro is to blame for the white man's susceptibility to disease (Uncinariasis).
3. The Negro is responsible for typhoid fever. Yet typhoid fever is due more to defective sanitation than anything else; and the white man is in absolute control of the legislative, judicial and executive departments of our government—local, state and national.
4. The Negro is responsible for Uncinariasis (hookworm), yet it flourishes most where there are few or no Negroes; namely, among factory hands and in the mountain districts.
5. He makes the impression that the poor and ignorant Negro is more dangerous to the public health than the poor and ignorant white man.
6. He completely ignores the efforts of intelligent Negroes, lawyers, doctors, teachers, preachers, etc., to improve the health of their people and the community in general.
7. He implies that the South is more unhealthy than other semi-tropical regions of the earth.
8. He ridicules the South for trying to get rid of the saloons, and yet declares it will perish if it doesn't.
9. ... the address ... smacked more of the cheap politician seeking notoriety and office by playing to passion and prejudice than a doctor discussing, philosophically, a scientific subject for the diffusion of knowledge.[280]

African Americans were falsely labeled by White doctors and intellectuals as disease incubators and transmitters for hookworm, tuberculosis, and typhoid fever. As Black physician C. W. Birnie stated:

> *Almost daily, we find newspapers, and magazines teeming with articles endeavoring to prove that the Negro race stands as a menace to the white men socially, morally and physically.... [S]yphilis and gonorrhea which of all in the list have been used most to the Negro's detriment by both medical and lay writers; newspapers and magazines have been made to*

> *circulate the idea that its prevalence should be laid at the door of the Negro race.*[281]

Medical references as varied as *JAMA* and the *Medical Record*, along with influential popular magazines such as *Hampton's*, *Scribner's*, and *McClure's* labeled the Negro as "syphilis soaked" and directly responsible for a panoply of diseases including pellagra. These influences not only were embedded in medical school curricula but were also utilized to justify racial segregation and nullification as public health and public policies. Resulting racialist approaches to individual and institutional patient care proved detrimental to the health status of both races.

The new surge of scientific racism took many forms. African American physicians were aware of how this movement adversely affected Black health and health care. This placed new demands on Black doctors, as C.V. Roman noted:

> *Ethnography, Ethnogeny, Ethnology, Ethography, Ethology and Ethno-psychology are cognate medical studies, and their discussion not only interests, but affects the medical profession. A knowledge of these subjects is necessary for the physician who would understand his profession fully, and maintain his proper ... position.*[282]

Dorothy Roberts chronicled a potent new component of scientific racism that grew dominant during the early decades of the twentieth century:

> *Paralleling the development of eugenic theory was the acceptance of intelligence as the primary indicator of human value. Eugenicists claimed that the IQ test could quantify innate intellectual ability in a single measurement. ... The introduction of "mental tests" at the turn of the century to measure intelligence replaced physical measurements, such as cranial capacity, as the means of determining human inferiority and superiority.*[283]

The IQ testing movement, which continues to have racist overtones today, began innocently enough in France. In an effort to improve institutional child care, the French government commissioned behavioral scientists to devise tests to measure and facilitate the education of mentally disadvantaged youngsters. The first widely accepted mental tests were published by one of the founders of experimental psychology, Alfred Binet, Ph.D., and his physician colleague, Theophile Simon, between 1905 and 1911. Growing out of Galton's "reaction tests"* —which evolved into more elaborate "mental tests" pioneered by his American graduate

---

*Galton founded his anthropometric laboratory for the measurement of man hoping he could develop physical and mental criteria by which he could make eugenical selections on who should survive to reproduce. Physiological "reaction tests" were part of his early efforts.

student, James Cattel, and other behavioral scientists such as R. Meade Bache, K. T. Waugh, and later Oxford and Harvard professor of psychology William McDougall—Binet tests "were designed to appraise the mental or learning capacities of *individual* students."[284] However, Binet warned, strict criteria had to be applied: "[T]he individuals tested must have had the same, or approximately the same, environmental and educational opportunities. Furthermore, Binet's test, unlike the later revisions, employed simple everyday problems unrelated to formal classroom instruction."[285] German psychologist William Stern expanded the concept, suggesting that the mental age (MA) be divided by the chronological age (CA) of the person tested, then multiplied by 100 to express the findings in mathematical terms (the "intelligence quotient," or IQ):

$$IQ = \frac{\text{Mental Age (MA)} \times 100}{\text{Chronological Age (CA)}}$$

Stern warned others of the shortcomings of his 1912 creation when used alone or to compare or catagorize people: "The IQ may be regarded only as a first approximation; it takes on significant value only when the bare quantitative statement is completed by a qualitative diagnosis. To base any pedagogical estimate upon the IQ alone for practical purposes (e.g., assignment to opportunity classes) is indefensible."[286]

Ignoring these scientific caveats, American psychologists and eugenicists Henry Herbert Goddard, Ph.D., of the Vineland, New Jersey, Training School for Feeble-minded Girls and Boys, and Lewis Terman, Ph.D., of Stanford University, had no doubts about what intelligence was* or how to measure it—when armed with this psychomedical model instrument. They admired Binet, but:

> it often happens that the devoted disciple transforms the ideas of the prophet in the very process of transmitting them ... [I]n this case ... [a]ccepting Binet's empirical method [they] substituted Binet's idea of intelligence as a shifting complex of interrelated functions, the concept of a single, underlying function (faculty) of intelligence. Further, [they] believed that this unitary function was largely determined by heredity, a view much at variance with Binet's optimistic proposals for mental orthopedics.[287]

That their attribution of intelligence to heredity might be a function of their both receiving doctoral training from G. Stanley Hall at Clark University of Worcester, MA, "a disciple of Galton and Spencer ... the foremost American exponent of the concept of genetically predetermined behavioral traits,"[288] is a possibility. As they applied "science" to society, they popularized intelligence testing, realizing its

---

*Intelligence has yet to be precisely defined.

staggering potential as a tool for eugenics. The health care system was an irreplaceable and critical participant.

Concomitant with the quiet, almost covert, assumption of power by physicians over the health care system, intelligence testing joined eugenics as major mechanisms of hereditarian policy and social control. These developments differentially affected African American and other disadvantaged populations. Doctors and other biomedical scientists determined not only who was legally sane or insane but who was to be eugenically sterilized and, ultimately, who was "fit" or "unfit." Their highly respected opinions and practices became components of a *racial hygiene movement** which shaped and distorted the health care system while also strongly influencing educators and educational practices.

Physicians or other biomedical scientists became commissioners of state health boards (with ultimate responsibility for states' mental health services), superintendents and principals of state mental hospitals and colonies, and expert witnesses in legal incarceration and insanity proceedings. Their legitimization of psychometric testing and eugenics in the administration and policies of these health systems, mental and educational institutions, and legal channels strongly influenced U.S. society. Physician participation and endorsement of these methods for classifying, ranking, and disposing of "fit" and "unfit" Americans strongly influenced judges, educators, psychologists, social workers, educational institutions, and nationally accepted standards and processes. Moreover, the medical profession eventually adopted related tests and techniques as admission criteria for entry into medical schools and postgraduate training programs. Finally, physicians were the sole group legally authorized to perform the eugenic sterilizations or psychosurgeries (e.g., frontal lobotomies) commonly performed in the United States as the result of these practices.[289]

A series of studies of degenerate American clans, beginning with Richard Dugdale's *The Jukes: A Study in Crime, Pauperism and Heredity* (1874)** and culminating in *The Kallikak Family* (1912), succeeded in injecting the myth of hereditary feeble-mindedness and degeneracy into the American psyche. The latter book, written by Goddard, compared two family lines descended from a New Jersey Revolutionary War soldier, Martin Kallikak: one from a marriage to a proper Quaker woman and the other from a feeble-minded barmaid. Based on con-

---

*Racial hygiene* was a movement turning the attention of physicians away from the individual or environment, toward human "germ plasm." It was supposed to complement personal and social hygiene, providing long-run preventive medicine for U.S. germ plasm by combating the disproportionate breeding of "inferiors," celibacy of the upper classes, and the threat posed by feminists to the reproductive performance of the family.

**Highly praised by Sir Francis Galton, Dugdale described how, between 1730 and 1874, 709 descendants of a frontiersman named Max cost New York taxpayers $1,308,000 in welfare, prison, health, and other institutional care. Other books described the Nams and the Nats of New York (C. B. Davenport); the Ishamael tribe of Indiana; the Happy Hickory family and Hill Folk of Ohio; the Dacks, a degenerate Irish family from Pennsylvania; and the Forkemites of Virginia.

clusions drawn from unconventional research and scientific methodology,* Goddard found that offspring from the former union allegedly produced successful,
productive citizens while spawn from the second mating purportedly produced
paupers, prostitutes, and criminals. Riding the tide of his popular book, Goddard
popularized IQ testing on Ellis Island immigrants for the federal government,[290]
while "documenting" the existence of "inferior" populations and the inheritability
of mental deficiency and antisocial behavior.

Meanwhile, Lewis Terman's revisions of the Binet scales in 1916 were "put to
use in a manner of which the professor from the Sorbonne had never dreamed."[291]
After violating Binet's principles by adding "questions . . . based much more directly
on the amount of formal and informal education (that is, school plus family
libraries and cultural activities, peer group and community experiences) the children had received prior to taking the new American IQ tests,"[292] Terman, future
president of the American Psychological Association (APA), led American behavioral scientists in emphasizing racial and "the blood lineage theme to explain
differing scores along the continuum."[293] He posited elaborate schemes extending
Binet's description of gross mental deficiencies and idiocy "to a vague notion of
genius—with various classifications along the way."[294] Moreover, his standardization of methods for employing the "new IQ tests to certify the children of less
suitable strains of native-born American Nordics as hereditarily 'uneducable'"[295]
had profound sociopolitical implications. Terman extended his findings to other
groups, stating:

> [Mental retardation] represents the level of intelligence which is very, very
> common among Spanish-Indians and Mexican families of the Southwest
> and also among negroes. Their dullness seems to be racial. . . . [T]here will
> be discovered enormously significant racial differences which cannot be
> wiped out by any scheme of mental culture.[296]

His recommendations for Spanish-Indian, Mexican, and Negro children were
draconian: "Children of this group should be segregated in special classes and be
given instruction which is concrete and practical. They cannot master abstractions,
but they can often be made efficient workers, able to look out for themselves."[297]
Terman went on to recommend "an IQ test score scale, based on the Stanford
Revision of the Binet-Simon scale, for the *clinical* diagnosis of human mental-

---

*Behavioral scientific peers criticized early eugenic-oriented psychometricians such as Henry God-
dard, C. B. Davenport, and, later, the U.S. Army for allowing nonscientifically trained amateurs to
administer tests, collect data, construct genetic trees, and make clinical psychological diagnoses without scientific or medical training. These fieldworkers and various categories of testers were seldom
qualified by college or postgraduate training in biology, psychiatry, psychology, sociology, anthropology, or medicine; instead, they received on the job training lasting six, or more weeks. The entire early
psychometric database rests on the efforts of these "scientists." See earlier note on ERO fieldworkers.
Chase describes these workers in detail in *The Legacy of Malthus* (pp. 120–124).

ity,"[298] with the potential to widely extend the use of this tool into the general health system and practice of clinical medicine.

Binet, who was never quite satisfied with his tests, was the first of a long line of critics of using solely mental tests to make clinical psychological diagnoses. Other agnostics included researchers such as Dr. J. E. Wallace Wallin, a prominent clinical psychologist; Ms. Mary Campbell of Chicago's municipal psychologic laboratory; and, initially, Robert M. Yerkes, Ph.D., then an assistant professor of comparative psychology at Harvard. They "pointed to the basic weaknesses of the American versions, and interpretations of the test scores, of the Binet tests: the IQ tests measured not that still mysterious quality called 'intelligence,' but the amount and the quality of classroom learning the people tested had had *recently*."[299] They also researched, documented, and criticized the use of amateurs to administer these new Goddard and Terman versions of Binet's tests. Revisionist tests allegedly made, clinical psychological diagnoses with the power to incarcerate people or limit their opportunities for life. Nevertheless:

> The 1916 Stanford-Binet scales maintained their dominance in the test-ing world for 20 years—until the 1937 version. This revision retained the majority of the old test items but was extended downward to the 2-year-old level and upward to the 22-year-old level. In repetition of the original revision, this version failed to include Black children in its nor-malization data.[300]

Academic controversies raged at APA meetings between 1915 and 1917 but had little effect on future events affecting eugenically oriented psychometric testing.

At the onset of U.S. entry into World War I, the army commissioned Robert M. Yerkes, then-president of the APA, to preside over the administration of intelligence tests to 1.7 million recruits. Expectations were that the results would be useful for duty assignment and training purposes. The army group intelligence tests were hastily written up by a committee selected by Yerkes, who was also chairman of the Eugenics Section of the American Breeders' Association's Committee on the Inheritance of Mental Traits. Goddard and Terman were the key members selected. The committee developed the World War I IQ* tests in six weeks, recruited several thousand enlisted men (who knew nothing about psychology) to administer them, and began testing nearly two million men.[301] Not surprisingly, "The Army Alpha test for literate draftees attempted to measure abilities 'independent of prior education,' and was quickly regarded as a bona fide measure of innate mental capacity—even though the test contained general information items that were most certainly culturally laden."[302] White, middle-

---

*The IQ tests consisted of an Alpha version for large groups of literate test takers and a Beta version for large groups of the illiterate, those who could not read English, or those who failed the Alpha test. Those failing the Beta test were given Goddard or Terman modifications of the Binet test on an individual basis.

class culture also pervaded the Army Beta test for illiterates and non–English speakers; its shortcomings were compounded by being "extremely difficult to administer."[303] The astounding results of the Army IQ tests "left most of the 1.7 million young men who took these tests branded as having the minds of 10- to 14-year-old children. The miracle was that, in 1917–18, 95 percent of the recruits tested did not do as badly as did the mayor of Chicago, who in 1915 'could not pass the 10-year-old test.'"[304] The IQ test debacle, whose skewed results the army then refused to use for assignment and training purposes, labeled almost half the U.S. draft age population as retardates (47.3 percent qualified as morons) with African Americans faring worse than any other group.[305] Racial and ethnic implications of the tests were summarized best in Princeton psychology professor Carl C. Brigham's book *A Study of American Intelligence* (1923), "which analyzed the Alpha and Beta results by race and came to the grim conclusion—based, Brigham insisted, on a dispassionate scientific examination of the evidence and not on prejudice"[306] that "Northern Europeans scored higher than Blacks and immigrants from Italy, Poland, Greece, and Russia: 'At one extreme we have the American negro. Between the Nordic and the negro, but closer to the negro than the Nordic, we find the Alpine and Mediterranean type.'"[307] Basing the degeneration of the American population "through 'racial admixture' with Negroes and inferior immigrants" on lax immigration and racial segregation policies,[308] Brigham concluded, "American intelligence is declining, and will proceed with an accelerating rate as the racial admixture becomes more and more extensive."[309]

After assisting Yerkes, Goddard, Terman, and the others throughout the World War I testing process, Brigham rose to eminence and was regarded as one of the nation's leading psychometricians. Soon, however, Brigham began having second thoughts about the uses and abuses fostered by IQ testing. He later wrote, in 1929: "The more I work in this field, the more I am convinced that psychologists have sinned greatly in sliding easily from the name of the test to the function or trait measured. Tests have encouraged an enormous series of hypostatized 'traits.'"[310] Nevertheless, he had been chosen by the College Board to chair a committee to develop a general "aptitude" test for college admission: "Brigham called this test, which was clearly modeled on the Army Alpha, the Scholastic Aptitude Test. On June 23, 1926, the SAT was experimentally administered for the first time, to 8,000 high school students."[311] The rise of White culture–based IQ testing as a eugenic tool for racial classifications and ranking; for justification of legal sanctions, segregation, and incarceration; for a scientistic rationale for nihilistic public health and health services delivery policies and programs; for dysfunctional educational policies, especially at the primary and secondary levels; and, increasingly, as the "gatekeeper" of a new American "meritocracy" is history.

The new eugenics-based IQ testing movement appealed to the American character in many ways. It validated the nation's traditional race and class prejudices, its rising Nativist tendencies, the Progressive movement ideology of utilizing science to solve society's problems, and its traditional impatience with the poor. The lingering problem of scientific racism, mediated by new IQ testing, birth control, and the biological determinist, genetic inheritance, and eugenics movements, infiltrated the health system at every level—including prestigious educational and policy institutions, medical and health professions schools, public (e.g., mental hospitals, "colonies" for epileptic and disabled children, tuberculosis facilities) and private health services institutions, and medically oriented branches of the birth control movement. Before World War I:

> *Although blacks were considered intellectually inferior, the intelligence of the recent immigrants was a much more pressing practical concern. Unlike the blacks, most of whom were still living in segregated conditions at the time and hence posed little threat of any kind, the "immigration issue" was widely regarded as the nation's major social problem.*[312]

The combination of the war's accentuation of the first Great Migration of the Black population from the South, changing demographics in the nation's cities, and an emerging civil rights struggle made African Americans much more of a "problem" as the 1920s drew to a close. Thus African American physicians perceptively appreciated that scientific racism posed a threat to their patients, provider and training institutions, and public health efforts to solve Black communities' immense health problems. Scientific racism, in all its "modern" configurations, grew so forcefully that it permanently altered U.S. policies on health, race, government, the military, industry, the legal system, immigration, education, birth control, and public perceptions.

Cognizant of these facts, Black leaders such as Dr. C. V. Roman, editor of the *JNMA*, sounded warnings about the Black profession's need to respond appropriately to the threat of scientific racism, stating: [T]oday . . . the persistent agitation of the race question is slowly, but surely, undermining the foundations of our success."[313] As Roman, often referred to as the sage of the NMA, exhorted Black doctors, "The race question is up to the Medical Profession, and a crisis is impending. It is up to the colored medical men."[314] African American physicians and health care providers fought doggedly to counteract the negative health-related forces being inflicted upon their people.[315]

World War I strained the U.S. health care system in many ways. Besides demanding huge levels of professional manpower and logistical and technical support, it also tore off the genial scab of U.S. government racial policy and exposed unvarnished anti-Black racism. This racism not only resulted in the army IQ test debacle; Black troops were also almost exclusively assigned to stevedore and labor duties instead of combat. The War Department also engaged in overt racial discrimination in the treatment and assignment of African American physicians, nurses, and dentists. As physician I. H. Roberts summed up: "The medical profession did not require draft or conscription to answer the call to duty. When the armistice was signed, there were 35,000 medical officers in the army and 3,000 in the navy—26 per cent of the entire profession. Of the above number there were only *one hundred colored.*"[316] Dr. Roberts goes on to explain the reason for the Black underrepresentation:

> *We view with regret and with a keen feeling the injustice done us by the discriminatory action of the War Department: color, race prejudice, not professional qualifications or loyalty or devotion to one's country, was the basis of the unjust action.... [T]he department had the power to make provision for the colored medical men, but the department failed to put into execution that fair play of which America boasts.*[317]

As Arthur E. Barbeau and Florette Henri pointed out in *The Unknown Soldiers: Black American Troops in World War I,* "At a time when the Army was seeking doctors and dentists, black men in these professions were being turned down for commissions; later they were drafted as privates."[318] In other instances, as George E. Cannon, M.D., pointed out in the NMA study "The Negro Medical Profession and the United States Army," "Negro medical men, who were drafted, were assigned as privates with no apparent chance of being transferred to the Medical Reserve Corps. On the other hand, white physicians and dentists were transferred to the Medical Reserve Corps."[319] Regarding the nursing situation, "it was a very white Red Cross; the organization did not welcome black volunteers and was most reluctant to use black nurses,"[320] Barbeau and Henri observed.

African American troops were the victims of discrimination that also affected their health status and outcomes. At the start of the process, "draft boards accepted blacks with disabilities which would have disqualified whites."[321] Barbeau and Henri noted, " [M]ore significant in relation to health differences between black and white soldiers were the poor clothing, housing, feeding, and working conditions of black troops, especially in the South."[322] Although the American Red Cross practiced racial segregation and discrimination in many of its programs and activities, it "generally treated black soldiers fairly in its hospitals."[323] This contrasted with the army, where: "Sick men, including venereals, were often forced to work without medical treatment."[324] In some army hospitals racial animosity was so intense that "white patients attacked black patients with knives and forks for not yielding their places in the mess lines."[325] U.S. Army medical reports showed "that in treatment ... blacks got from 10 to 30 percent fewer days of hospitalization,"[326] when proper hospitalization was instituted.

The overall situation created an uproar at the August 27, 1918, NMA convention held in Richmond, Virginia. A strong "Declaration" protesting racial discrimination at all levels resulted from intense discussions at the meeting, which was eventually transmitted to the Secretary of War. An NMA subcommittee representing 5,000 Black physicians and thousands of Black dentists and nurses finally met with a representative of the Secretary of War. The war's end and the Armistice defused the issue before the meeting took place. However, a circuitous and ineffective apology was offered by the government. Soon after the incident, as a minor step forward, the NMA was called upon by the Surgeon General to screen a list of consultants for health promotion–disease prevention activities at some army camps. However, the emergence of the most professionally and intellectually trained Black group on earth to protest the unfair treatment by their government represented a new era in race relations in the United States.

Before this period ended in 1930, protests against racial segregation and discrimination in health by the Black medical establishment had extended to the federal and presidential levels. When the Harding administration decided to build a VA hospital for Black veterans at Tuskegee Institute, another firestorm was precipitated. The $2.5 million predominately neuropsychiatric facility with 600 beds and 27 buildings was dedicated on February 12, 1923, Lincoln's birthday. However, it was established under a White physician-superintendent's supervision with plans to open "with a full staff of white doctors and white nurses with colored nursemaids for each white nurse, in order to save them from contact with colored patients!"[327] African American physicians, led by Dr. John A. Kenney, *JNMA* editor and Tuskegee Institute's medical director, fought for Black staffing of the facility. J. Edward Perry, physician-author and 1923 NMA president, described him in this struggle: "John Kenney, as a tall oak in the forest, stood unswervingly in defense of the ability of Negroes to command the situation."[328] The White community was outraged as "[T]he Ku Klux or Hooded Knights with torches of flames marched over the premises ... installing Negroes[;] it created a great furor."[329] The NMA met with President Harding and the head of the VA. Despite the cross burnings, Klan parades, and threats on Dr. Kenney's life, African Americans were victorious in obtaining a Black medical staff. The NMA, NAACP, and Robert Russa Moten, president of Tuskegee Institute, had united, influencing health policy in the process. It was a sign of things to come. These and other indicators registered that the influence and prestige of the NMA was rising exponentially. The organization felt confident enough to publish and successfully enforce membership requirements in the organization after 1919—membership requirements similar to those of the AMA 15 years earlier.[330]

Adherence to the new education reform and regulatory dictates implemented by the White medical establishment was not accompanied by commitments ensuring the provision of medical care or services for African Americans. Therefore, "slave health deficits" persisted into the twentieth century. Black health did not demonstrate definite signs of improvement until the second decade of the century. Some data indicate that Black health status deteriorated during the 1920s. In fact, the few public health programs that opened up to Blacks after World War I, especially those directed at maternal and infant care (e.g., the Sheppard-Towner Act), by 1930 began contracting and closing down the few opportunities proffered Blacks. Southern efforts at controlling tuberculosis and venereal diseases were directed almost exclusively at the White population. With the growing awareness of public health matters during the first decade of the new century triggered by the

American Public Health Association (founded in 1872, with its new journal emerging in 1904) and the Atlanta University Studies, the White medical establishment was forced to acknowledge Black health problems. Observing medical establishment hostility and neglect, African American physicians began taking organized action by 1910.[331]

African American physicians and social scientists began studying disease and public health problems affecting Blacks for themselves. The NMA formed hookworm, pellagra, and tuberculosis commissions. Accepting the fact that most of their White colleagues were unconcerned, Black organized medicine initiated and supported formal health promotion and disease prevention (HP/DP) programs independent of the White establishment. These programs and information emanated from organizations such as the Bay State Medical Society of Boston, the North Jersey Medical Society, and Tuskegee Institute. The latter published health bulletins on topics such as "Tuberculosis," "Typhoid Fever," and "The Danger of Flies." Special attention was focused on tuberculosis: "In Nashville, Tennessee, Dr. Robert F. Boyd, head of the Anti-Tuberculosis League, held meetings in churches to instruct people in the cause prevention and cure of 'the Great White Plague.'"[332] Institutions were established to combat this special problem in the Black community: "Special tuberculosis sanatoria were established for Negroes, and anti-tuberculosis leagues were organized from 1907 to 1909 by Negro medical societies in Louisiana, Alabama, Virginia and the District of Columbia."[333] Free clinics and public clinics for tuberculosis staffed by African American physicians sprang up throughout the country.

A burgeoning Black hospital movement initiated near the turn of the century gained momentum and flourished by 1930. Largely barred from internships and specialty training, African Americans established, against great odds, teaching hospitals and postgraduate training programs such as the John Andrew Clinics and programs affiliated with Meharry, Howard, and Southern Black hospitals to train themselves. Prohibited by custom and law from practicing in White hospitals with White nursing assistance, Black physicians opened nurse training schools over the entire country, establishing a competent Black nursing profession.

Black physicians began studying the hospital situation affecting their people and established hospital commissions within the NMA and the National Hospital Association by 1923. In their earnest attempts to upgrade Black hospitals and meet hospital accreditation standards, Black doctors began consulting with the AMA, the American College of Surgeons (which led the hospital accreditation movement), and the health foundations to erect an accrediting body similar to the White profession's by the early 1920s. In a wave of professionalism and idealism, they also wanted to establish a set of minimum standards to ensure that Black hospitals adhered to "adequate clinical and laboratory facilities to insure correct diagnoses, a thorough study and diagnosis of each case in writing, and a monthly audit of the medical and surgical work of the hospital,"[334] as they assumed White hospitals were

doing. Such credentialing would facilitate Black institutions' implementing accredited postgraduate, medical specialty, and allied health professions training programs sorely needed by African Americans—otherwise locked out of the
mainstreamhealth system. There is no evidence that African American physicians
were told—they never seemed to be aware of nor mentioned the "White hospital
crisis" in the literature—how poorly the White hospitals had recently performed
on surveys and inspections based upon the standards their White consultants were
recommending. As Harry Dowling revealed about the White hospitals:

> *The results of the first survey in 1918 were devastating: 692 hospitals of*
> *one-hundred-bed capacity or more were surveyed; only eighty-nine, or 13*
> *percent, met the limited requirements of the American College of Sur-*
> *geons. To avoid embarrassment, "the secretary was instructed to take the*
> *reports of the other 87 percent to the basement and burn them. The board*
> *feared the consequences of letting the true conditions in hospitals be*
> *known."*[335]

By 1920, 58 percent (407) of 697 White hospitals became accredited—
although 43 percent (175) of these were approved provisionally and given time
to correct their deficiencies.[336] Nevertheless, both Black and White branches
of the profession enthusiastically embraced and aggressively tried to implement hospital standards.

As part of their struggle against scientific racism, African American physicians also began debunking old medical myths, such as that Blacks did not
suffer with cancer or were genetically predisposed to pellagra. Black physicians
throughout America mobilized to combat segregation and discrimination in the
health arena at all levels.[337]

Despite the salutary and sometimes heroic efforts of African American
physicians in all these areas, White judgments were unforgiving. Nineteenth-
century professional disdain and prejudice toward African American physicians
seemed to intensify. As C. V. Roman pointed out:

> *[T]he recent declaration of a Harvard professor that the Northern Negro*
> *medical man is a failure; the resolution of a Louisiana Medical Society*
> *declaring it a menace to the public welfare to permit Negroes to practice*
> *medicine, and the agitation in Mississippi for the enactment of a statute*
> *absolutely excluding the Negro from the practice of law, medicine, phar-*
> *macy or dentistry.... are but ... signboards....*[338]

The White medical establishment and its spheres of influence, which had been
restrained in their attempt to close down Black medical education after the war,
were mean-spirited and judgmental and had already made up their minds about
Black health professionals. A population's destiny was hanging in the balance, with
the Black medical profession standing on the parapet.[339]

# Black Americans and the Health System during the Great Depression and World War II, 1930–1945

Between 1930 and 1945 economic and military events overshadowed health care and racial issues in the United States. The Great Depression and World War II had momentous effects on the nation, African Americans, and the health care system. All would be different after the war.

The Great Depression displayed the weaknesses in America's economic and social systems. The October 1929 stock market crash, which brought the curtain down on the economic boom of the "Roaring Twenties," exposed long-standing weaknesses in both the American economy and health system. Some of the economic weaknesses included, but were not limited to, U.S. business and corporate involvement in risky economic speculation and investments during the previous decade; maldistribution of wealth, with more than half America's families living at or below subsistence levels; a lack of diversity and overdependence of the economy on construction and automobiles; and the international debt structure, which led strapped European governments to default on U.S. loans that financed World War I. In *The Unfinished Nation* Alan Brinkley alludes to how African Americans were differentially affected: "Most African-Americans had not shared very much in the prosperity of the previous decade; they now experienced more unemployment, homelessness, malnutrition, and disease than they had in the past, and more than most whites experienced."[1] The stock market collapse initiated a long economic decline for the entire U.S. society that by 1931 had accelerated into a worldwide catastrophe. America would not fully recover until the end of World War II.[2]

By 1933, 14 million Americans were unemployed, industrial production was down to one-third of its 1929 levels, and national income had dropped by more than half. The American gross national product (GNP) plummeted 25 percent in three years—from $104 billion in 1929 to $76.4 billion in 1932. Gross farm income, which differentially impacted African Americans (37 percent of whom were involved in agriculture), dropped from $12 billion to $5 billion in four years. By 1932 unemployment reached at least 25 percent and never dropped below 15 percent until 1940. Furthermore, "African-American organizations estimated that the percentage of unemployed black workers was at least twice the rate of the country as a whole."[3]

The 1927–1932 Committee on the Cost of Medical Care (CCMC) study, one of the largest and most detailed health system studies of all time, revealed that levels of medical care were directly related to income. Adverse economic changes thus had profound effects on both health status and health care in general. Racial differentials in virtually all measurable health status and service parameters painted an extremely grim picture for African Americans in the market-based health system of that time. An example in the CCMC study focusing specifically on African Americans, virtually all of whom were in the poorest economic rank, cited "a sample of five hundred Negroes in Tipton County, Tennessee, who were suffering from syphilis. When investigated, only three per cent of them had been given both neoarsphenamine and mercury, and only fourteen per cent had received any professional medical treatment whatever."[4] Continuance of the few public health programs that had begun to provide Blacks some treatment, especially in the South where most Blacks lived, was placed in question. Therefore, for Black and poor Americans, the Depression lessened their already seriously compromised ability to obtain medical care.[5]

Franklin Delano Roosevelt's Democratic landslide election victory over Republican Herbert Hoover in 1932 was the commencement of a new era in American history. Roosevelt's New Deal, a matrix of policies and programs designed to deal with the socioeconomic Depression (see Table 2.1), has been labeled a revolution by some and a major reform effort by others. Roosevelt's reforms had significant health system effects: broadening access to the system, establishing precedents of government responsibility for providing health care for certain groups (the disabled, poor children, certain elderly poor), and institutionalizing health insurance as a financing mechanism for hospital and health care. Most credit the New Deal with preserving economic capitalism in America. By extending federal regulation over new areas of the economy, including banking, the stock markets, and agriculture, it represented the beginning of a social-democratic order similar to that of Western European countries. New Deal programs also erected the beginnings of a modern social welfare system. It could also be compared to a midwife overseeing the birth of a significant U.S. labor movement, including the 1936 founding of the Congress of Industrial Organizations (CIO). Politically, the New Deal established a Democrat-led political

## Table 2.1 Leading New Deal Agencies

AAA    Agricultural Adjustment Administration. Founded in 1933 to provide advice and assistance to farmers, and to regulate farm production.

CAB    Civil Aeronautics Board. Founded in 1940 to regulate private and commercial flying activities and to promote safe flying conditions.

CCC    Civilian Conservation Corps.

CCC    Commodity Credit Corporation. Founded in 1933 as a financial agency to support the activities of the Department of Agriculture.

CSB    Central Statistical Board. Founded in 1933 to coordinate federal and other statistical services.

EHFA   Electric Home and Farm Authority. Founded in 1935 to aid in the electrification of American homes.

EIB    Export-Import Bank of Washington. Founded in 1934 to aid in financing exports and imports, and to assist foreign trade.

FAA    Federal Alcohol Administration. Founded in 1935 to supervise the marketing of alcohol.

FCA    Farm Credit Administration. Founded in 1933 to provide a complete credit system for farmers by making both long-term and short-term credit available to them.

FCC    Federal Communications Commission.

FCIC   Federal Crop Insurance Corporation. Founded in 1938 to provide insurance protection against unavoidable loss in the yield of certain crops.

FDIC   Federal Deposit Insurance Corporation. Founded in 1933 to insure the deposits in the nation's banks.

FERA   Federal Emergency Relief Administration. Founded in 1933 to cooperate with the states in relieving hardships caused by unemployment and drought.

FHA    Federal Housing Administration. Founded in 1934 to insure private lending companies against loss on home-mortgage loans, and on loans for improving and repairing small properties.

FLA    Federal Loan Agency. Founded in 1939 to supervise federal loan activities.

FSA    Farm Security Administration. Founded in 1937 to help farmers purchase needed equipment.

FSA    Federal Security Agency.

FSCC   Federal Surplus Commodities Corporation. Founded in 1935 as a marketing agency to dispose of government surpluses.

FWA    Federal Works Agency. Founded in 1939 to bring federal construction and public-works activities under one agency.

HOLC   Home Owners' Loan Corporation. Founded in 1933 to grant long-term mortgage loans at low cost to home owners in financial difficulties.

MLB    Maritime Labor Board. Founded in 1936 to secure better relations between labor and management in the shipping industry.

NEC    National Emergency Council. Founded in 1933 to coordinate the various field agencies of the Federal Government.

NLRB   National Labor Relations Board.

NRA    National Recovery Administration. Founded in 1933 to carry out the plans of the National Industrial Recovery Act to fight the Depression.

NRPB   National Resources Planning Board. Founded in 1939 to provide the president with information useful to planned development and use of national resources.

NYA    National Youth Administration. Founded in 1935 to provide job training for unemployed youths and part-time work for needy students.

PWA    Public Works Administration. Founded in 1933 to increase employment and purchasing power through the construction of useful public works such as bridges in the various states. the Federal government lent state and local governments the money for these projects.

RA     Resettlement Administration. Founded in 1935 to resettle families with a low income on more productive land.

REA    Rural Electrification Administration. Founded in 1935 to aid farmers in the electrification of their homes.

SEC    Securities and Exchange Commission. Founded in 1934 to protect the public from investing in unsafe securities and to regulate stock market practices.

SMA    Surplus Marketing Administration. Founded in 1940 to handle various duties of the Department of Agriculture.

SSB    Social Security Board. Founded in 1935 to secure a sound social security system.

TVA    Tennessee Valley Authority.

USHA   United States Housing Authority. Founded in 1937 to aid in the development of adequate housing throughout the nation.

USMC   United States Maritime Commission. Founded in 1936 to help secure a powerful United States merchant marine.

WPA    Works Progress Administration. Founded in 1935 to provide work for needy persons on public works projects.

*Source: World Book Encyclopedia*, 1957 edition., s.v. "new deal," 5550.

coalition made up of labor unions, liberal Northern reformers, working-class progressives, Jews, conservative Southern Democrats, and Blacks that would dominate U.S. politics for the next half century.[6]

Although the Roosevelt administration was not hostile to Black aspirations, as Brinkley said, "One group the New Deal did relatively little to assist was African Americans."[7] A major example is the Social Security Act, which Brinkley described as "the most important single piece of social welfare legislation in American history."[8] Based on the way it was structured,* most of the pension and health benefits through its disability and aid to dependent children programs were closed off to Blacks. As pioneer Black sociologist George Edmund Haynes pointed out in *The Crisis*, there were no antidiscrimination provisions in the bill.[9] Many Americans are unaware of the conservatism of the New Deal's racial policies and programs.

A general misconception persists that Blacks were favored by the Roosevelt administration. As Manning Marable points out in *Race, Reform, and Rebellion: The Second Reconstruction in Black America, 1945–1990,* "Government agencies in the 'New Deal' administration of Roosevelt were organized along strictly segregated lines."[10] As Howard Zinn further noted, "For black people, the New Deal was psychologically encouraging (Mrs. Roosevelt was sympathetic; some blacks got posts in the administration), but most blacks were ignored by the New Deal programs."[11]

Other discriminatory examples abound: Civilian Conservations Corps (CCC) camps were racially segregated, the Works Progress Administration (WPA) relegated Black and Hispanic workers to the least-skilled and lowest-paying jobs, and federal housing projects were racially segregated. Nevertheless, internal pressure from the first lady and external pressure from Black leaders like A. Philip Randolph to force the administration to adopt antidiscrimination rules and regulations were unrelenting and highly publicized.** Nevertheless, "New Deal relief agencies did not challenge, and indeed reinforced, existing patterns of discrimination."[12] Despite the limited commitment and checkered record of the Roosevelt administration on African American rights, the Black transfer of political allegiance from the Republican to the Democratic Party by 1936 was built upon the fact that by 1935 some 30 percent of African Americans were receiving some form of government assistance. Despite the mixed messages emanating from the Roosevelt administration, "[t]raditional patterns of segregation and disfranchisement in the South survived the Depression largely unchallenged,"[13] triggering the second Great Migration of Blacks to the North.[14]

---

*Because the act excluded domestic servants and agricultural laborers and targeting the elderly (because of their shorter average life span, Blacks were underrepresented in this group) up to two-thirds of African Americans were excluded from Social Security benefits. Administration of the program, often in Southern hands, added another barrier to Black participation.

** Executive Order 8802, the first presidential directive on race since Reconstruction, prohibited racial discrimination in defense industries and established the Fair Employment Practices Committee (FEPC). In response to a threat of the first Black "March on Washington," Roosevelt signed the order on June 25, 1941.

By the 1930s it was also becoming clear that American post–World War I foreign policy was failing. Limited American internationalism, the policy eschewing collaborations and treaties with foreign nations in the years between the wars, did not project or protect American international interests, failed to produce global stability, and failed to keep the United States out of another catastrophic world war. Some hypothesize it was linked in many ways to the economic Depression. Moreover, it kept the United States militarily and economically involved in the affairs of its immediate neighbors such as Nicaragua, Panama, Haiti, Columbia, and the Dominican Republic (some labeled this imperialism). Economically, it failed to preserve international free trade or open markets. Such developments repeatedly highlighted, somewhat cynically, the conflict between America's rhetorical commitment to "freedom and justice for all" and its flawed policies toward African American, Jewish, Latino, Asian, and other non-White groups. This racially and ethnically discriminatory foreign policy, including the virtual colonization of the Philippines, Hawaii, Puerto Rico, and the Virgin Islands, mirrored U.S. social, political, and public policy. It was also reflected in the U.S. health system, as America refused to provide any form of collective or universal health coverage. U.S. refusal to come to grips with modern international, social (including medical-social), and racial policies left windows of opportunity for the rise of socialist (e.g., Stalinist Russia 1925–1953) and fascist, totalitarian, and racist regimes such as those founded by Mussolini (1922), Hitler (1933), and Franco (1936). By the end of 1941 President Roosevelt and the American people finally concluded that the United States could not survive as a nation, nor could Western civilization endure, if Hitler and fascism gained dominance over Europe and Asia. At that time few realized these ideological shifts in the United States would have profound social and health care consequences and that events would soon force social-political realignment in America.[15]

By September 1940, Congress established the first peacetime military draft in American history. Six months later it authorized Roosevelt to transfer munitions to Great Britain—now standing practically alone against Hitler—through a procedure called lend-lease. The Japanese reacted to stiffening American diplomacy against its expansion into Southeast Asia by attacking the U.S. fleet at Pearl Harbor in the Hawaiian Islands on December 7, 1941.

The military history of World War II is well known. The most striking domestic wartime effect may have been its ending the Great Depression. The effects of the Great Depression opened some doors of employment opportunity for African Americans; however, health care remained segregated and stratified, so that most Blacks were still cordoned off from professional participation or high-quality health services. The U.S. economy turned around; the 1939 federal budget of $9 billion ballooned to $100 billion by 1945. The GNP soared from $91 billion in 1939 to $166 billion in 1945. The 15 million men and women taken out of the labor pool by the military led to a labor shortage. By necessity, jobs were made available for women and minorities, including African Americans. Union membership boomed. However, despite exuberant Black expectations, segregation and discrimination in both the military and civilian sectors continued unabated. In response to a great deal of official and unofficial pressure, there was some desegregation of small segments of the military, which allowed some Black physicians and nurses into the army, permitted Blacks to join the Marine Corps (1942), mandated some desegregated army officer training (1941), allowed Blacks into general navy service (1942), and established some African American pilot training schools (established at Tuskegee in 1942). Integration of some ground army troops did not occur until 1945.

On the home front, attempts to provide equity in employment and living accommodations led to corporate, union, and civilian resistance varying from administrative and regulatory discrimination to race riots in cities such as Detroit, New York, Mobile, and Beaumont, Texas. Obviously, the increased wartime government interest and investment in fitness and public health, some of which benefitted African Americans, could not compensate for or override this negative atmosphere overall.[16]

Although it was the largest war, from the standpoint of the proportion of the total population involved, since the Civil War and the most popular war in U.S. history, African Americans had only mixed feelings about World War II.[17] Blacks had been tragically disappointed after the First World War, and the race issue had been submerged by the larger issues surrounding the Depression and the war itself. The overall effects of the negative racial environment made African American interest in the war lukewarm. As Zinn observed, "There seemed to be widespread indifference, even hostility, on the part of the Negro community to the war despite the attempts of Negro newspapers and Negro leaders to mobilize black sentiment."[18] A "Draftee's Prayer," which appeared in a Black newspaper in January 1943, captures much of the sentiment:

> *Dear Lord, today*
> *I go to war: To fight, to die,*
> *Tell me what for?*
>
> *Dear Lord, I'll fight, I*
> *do not fear,*
> *Germans or Japs;*
> *My fears are here.*
> *America!*[19]

Nevertheless, being exposed overseas to nonsegregated environments, seeing an interdependent international world, and proving themselves to be vital to the U.S. military effort had salutary and positive effects on both African Americans and European Americans. As Manning Marable stated:

> *Blacks and an increasing sector of liberal white America came out of the war with a fresh determination to uproot racist ideologies and institutions at home.... [B]y 1945, a growing number of white Americans in the North had concluded that the system of racial segregation would have to be modified, if not entirely overthrown.*[20]

This pervasive feeling influenced the U.S. Congress to ponder whether returning African American U.S. service men would tolerate overt and covert segregation, oppression, and discrimination. The same concerns could apply to the shoddy and deficient health services to which their families and the majority of their friends and neighbors were exposed.[21]

## A Health System Stressed: The Years of the Great Depression, 1930–1941

The 1920s health system that preceded the Great Depression demonstrated several fundamental problems. The definitive report on U.S. health care in the 1920s, the CCMC report, reinforced and documented these findings. The most prominent systemic flaws were the severe maldistribution of health care based on socioeconomic status, poor geographic distribution of health services and facilities, the inability of many individuals to purchase adequate health care privately, escalating capital needs and training requirements for the health care system, inadequate resource allocation to public health measures, and serious qualitative and quantitative divisions of the health system along race and class lines. Health reform advocates contended that massive reform and restructuring of the health system were necessary to solve these problems. Social Progressives from early in the century and health reformers* in the post–World War I period felt that America needed to follow Europe's lead in providing a universal, compulsory, national health system. The Great Depression of 1929, representing an almost total collapse of the U.S. financial and social systems, exaggerated health system and medical-social defects that were already present. Daniel S. Hirshfield's assessment in *The Lost Reform*, "The American system of medical care underwent a period of prolonged and widespread crisis during the 1930s, since at bottom it was only the system of the 1920s immeasurably exacerbated by the economic chaos of the Great Depression,"[22] is accurate.[23]

As the proportion of families with low incomes increased from 10 to 43

---

*Health reformers were a diverse group of American physicians, social scientists, interest groups, private foundations (e.g., the Milbank Fund), labor unions (and their representatives), and corporate executives who felt that the United States deserved some type of universal, compulsory, national health insurance or, better still, a universal health system. Europe had been engaged in such activities since the nineteenth century. Reformers were usually pitted against the American Medical Association.

percent between 1929 and 1933, their use of physician and hospital services plummeted, and those forced to use health services because of acute or emergency conditions could not pay for them. Alarms were sounded about plunging health indicators and access to health services. As Ed Cray noted, "In rural Pennsylvania there were 216,000 cases of undernourishment among the 800,000 children examined in 1931; at the same time, tuberculosis clinics reported double the pre-Depression case load."[24]

The situation was worse in the South, where government-run health facilities and public health clinics were more rudimentary than the rest of the country. Studies conducted in the South during the Depression revealed the health effects of diets insufficient to produce normal body weights and to fight off diseases in children. In certain towns typhoid fever and dysentery were epidemic. The Depression experience for Blacks, still suffering under a continuum of health status and outcome differentials that could still be described as a "slave health deficit," was worse. Disturbingly, "the health status of Southern blacks would take a downturn, if such were imaginable,"[25] Beardsley noted in *A History of Neglect: Health Care for Blacks and Mill Workers in the Twentieth-Century South.*[26]

Hospitals, doctor's offices, and academic health centers were all on the verge of collapse due to the Depression. This generated tremendous pressure for the government to step in. Both public and private solutions were proposed to stabilize the health care system. Despite White medical establishment protests, the government and the private sectors, acting in the interests of hospitals and patients, implemented emergency programs. The Roosevelt administration, in response to the Depression, enacted some crisis health care legislation for the elderly and the poor.

After focusing on economic and agricultural recovery measures for most of his first year in office, Roosevelt turned to social welfare. The nation was in the throes of a deepening crisis. On June 8, 1934, Roosevelt established the cabinet-level Committee on Economic Security (CES) to "study problems related to the economic security of individuals."[27] Initially, the CES had a strong emphasis on reforming the health care system. Its goals and objectives consisted of preparing expert reports on the economic, social, and health needs the Depression was imposing on the American people. From the beginning the report was to be submitted to the president and Congress in 1935 as the basis for legislation emphasizing the need for unemployment insurance, old-age pensions, and health care. Due to anticipated political resistance led by the AMA, the medical societies, and their political allies, the first two items assumed first priority. The report from the Technical Committee on Medical Care, the medical portion of the CES, was delayed twice, then never released. The resulting 1935 Social Security Act, a fundamentally conservative piece of social legislation, therefore abandoned compulsory health insurance completely.[28]

The Social Security Act, absent a compulsory health insurance plan, did have some significant health provisions. Roosevelt slipped these past the AMA despite

## Joe "King" Oliver: A Casualty in the Depression South's Health System

If there was a "famous" African American during the 1920s and 1930s Joe "King" Oliver (1885–1938) fit the description. One of the most significant jazz cornetists of all time, his classic compositions such as "Dipper Mouth Blues," "Canal Street Blues," and "Dr. Jazz" enjoy continued popularity by New Orleans style jazz lovers—some who are probably unfamiliar with Joseph Oliver.

Born on a plantation near Donaldsonville, Louisiana on May 11, 1885, Oliver was raised and artistically nurtured in New Orleans. A veteran of the rough-and-tumble musical world of that city's red-light district, Oliver—then "King" of jazz trumpeters—migrated to Chicago in 1918 and changed the American musical scene forever. His Creole Jazz Band (1922–1925), Dixie Syncopators (1925–1927), and scores of other bands he led throughout his career introduced and popularized New Orleans jazz to the world. Oliver's musical impact on Chicago, New York, and the nation was so extensive, jazz historian James Lincoln Collier wrote, "In 1927 it seemed . . . that the New Orleans music of Oliver . . . was coming to fruition and would move out to capture the world." He was billed as "The World's Greatest Jazz Cornetist," and served as Louis "Satchmo" Armstrong's lifelong musical and professional mentor. By 1930 fickle musical tastes had shifted to big-band music of the "sweet" and "jazz" oriented varieties. Though no longer a headliner, Oliver remained well known, led successful commercial bands, and enjoyed a stellar reputation based on his past fame and recordings.

During the early 1930s Oliver was reduced to touring with bands, often to rural Southern areas. They were always paid much less than their White peers, and the Great Depression cut fees earned by Black performers, even of Oliver's stature, to the bone. By 1935 a combination of bad luck, broken booking engagements, and health problems began to hound "King" Oliver's career. Great cornet or trumpet players require the physical assets of ideal lip size, relaxed and open throat muscles and vocal chords, good strong teeth, a broad and powerful diaphragm, and a robust, strong, body. Louis Armstrong recalls, "King Oliver was so powerful, he used to blow a cornet out of tune every two or three months" (Williams; 79). Oliver began having trouble with his teeth in 1927, which manifested as sore gums. This interfered with his playing on his last classic recording dates (1927–1931).

By 1935, the gum condition evolved into pyorrhea. Unable to afford dental care, often touring as a "front" for various bands, and seldom able to play, he soon lost his teeth. As Frederic Ramsey, Jr. said, "A cornetist can't play without teeth." Oliver wrote to his niece:

> I receive your card, you don't know how much I appreciate your thinking about the old man. . . . Thank God I only need one thing and that is clothes. I am not making enough money to buy clothes as I can't play any more. I get

a little money from an agent for the use of my name and after I pay room rent an [*sic*] eat I don't have much left. . . . I've only got one suit and that's the one sent me while I was in Wichita, Kansas. . . . But I don't feel downhearted. I still feel like I will snap out of the rut some day. (Ramsey; 87–88)

By 1937 unprincipled agents had so misused "King" Oliver's name by booking bands under his name in his absence, breaking engagements, accepting fees under false pretenses, and rendering unsatisfactory service—ruining his reputation in the process—that his touring days as a "front" man were over. He was reduced to running a fruit stand and, later, working as a pool hall attendant in Savannah, Georgia. As his health problems mounted, he began to feel trapped. Writing his half-sister, Victoria Davis:

I am feeling pretty good, but just can't get rid of this cough. Don't like that sticking on me so long. I just can't get rid of it. I've tried most everything. My heart don't bother me just a little at times. But my breath is still short, and I'm not at all fat. . . . I would like to live long as I can, but. . . . Don't think I will ever raise enough money to buy a ticket to New York (Ramsey; 90).

He finally alluded to how the health system seemed to be preventing him from overcoming his problems. He wrote, "I got teeth waiting for me at the dentist now. . . . I've started a little dime bank saving. Got $1.60 in it and won't touch it" (Ramsey; 90).

Having been exposed to public-sector health services systems in the Midwest and Northeast, Oliver appreciated how cut off from health care Blacks in the South really were. Sharing his experiences in the Southern health system with Victoria, who had cared for him as a child and often served as a surrogate mother figure, he wrote:

It's not like New York or Chicago here. You've got to go through a lot of red tape to get any kind of treatment from the city here. I may never see New York again in life. (Ramsey; 91)

When Louis Armstrong, then on a Southern tour, encountered his tired but cheerful mentor tending a small vegetable stand, "The younger man broke down and cried, gave him money to buy some clothes and said he was going to send him money regularly" (Williams; 79). The last opportunity for Oliver to escape his medical "trap" had passed. Always a proud man, evidently he never mentioned his health plight to his friend, who could have afforded his escape to New York where some care would have been available. His sense of rejection by the health system and resignation to dying unattended was clear in the last letter to Victoria:

. . . before I go further with my letter I'm going to tell you something but don't be alarmed. I've got high blood pressure. Was taking treatment but I had to discontinue. My blood was 85 above normal. Now my blood has started again and I am unable to take treatments because it cost $3.00 per treatment and I don't make enough money to continue my treatments. Now it begins to work on my heart. I am weak in my limbs at times and my breath but I can not asking you for any money or anything. A stitch in time save nine. Should anything happen to me will you want my body? Let me know because I won't last forever and the longer I go the worst I'll get unless I take treatments. (Ramsey; 90)

Two months later, on April 10, 1938, Joseph Oliver died of a cerebral hemorrhage in Savannah. Using her rent money, Victoria retrieved his body from Georgia and buried him in her plot at Woodlawn Cemetery in the Bronx, New York City. Though his name has almost disappeared, Joe "King" Oliver's music deriving from his Creole Jazz Band is still played today—representing part of the classic repertoire of jazz, one of America's native art forms. Oliver's plight at the hands of the health system was typical for a Black person of his time.

**Notes**

Beardsley EH. *A History of Neglect: Health Care for Blacks and Mill Workers in the Twentieth-Century South.* Knoxville: The University of Tennessee Press, 1987.

Charters SB, Kunstadt L. *Jazz: A History of the New York Scene.* Garden City, NY: Doubleday, 1962. Reprint Paperback Edition. New York: Da Capo, 1981.

Chilton J. *Who's Who of Jazz: Storyville to Swing Street.* Philadelphia: Chilton Book Company, 1972.

Collier JL. *The Making of Jazz: A Comprehensive History.* New York: Dell, 1978.

Cray E. *In Failing Health: The Medical Crisis and the A.M.A.* Indianapolis, IN: Bobbs-Merrill, 1970.

Hadlock R. *Jazz Masters of the Twenties.* New York: Collier, 1965.

Hirshfield DS. *The Lost Reform: The Campaign for Compulsory Health Insurance in the United States 1932 to 1943.* Cambridge, MA: Harvard University Press, 1970.

Morais HM. *The History of the Negro in Medicine.* New York: Publishers Company, Inc., 1967.

Ramsey Jr. F. King Oliver and his Creole Jazz Band. 59–91. In: Ramsey Jr. F, Smith CE, eds. *Jazzmen.* New York: Harcourt Brace, 1939. Reprint Paperback Edition. New York: A Harvest/HBJ Book, 1967.

Williams M. Papa Joe. 79–120. In: Williams M. *Jazz Masters of New Orleans.* New York: Macmillan, 1967. Reprint Paperback Edition. New York: Da Capo, 1979.

---

medical establishment resistance. Health programs were contained in Titles IV, V, VI, and X of the act. As Paul Starr observed, "the act extended the government's role in public health in several provisions unrelated to social insurance. It gave the states funds on a matching basis for maternal and infant care, rehabilitation of crippled children, general public health work, and aid for dependent children under age sixteen."[29] Title X also provided some state medical assistance for the blind. However, none of these health programs contained antidiscrimination provisions. This legislation, based on a regressive tax, preserved racial segregation and discrimination, excluded farm and domestic workers from benefits (thereby excluding two-thirds of Blacks), and avoided major health system reform. As senator and economist Paul Douglas pointed out, Southern politicians lowered the Social

Security old-age pension provisions so that they would not be forced to pay Black pensioners higher amounts than they thought desirable.

Largely unnoticed and unacknowledged by the medical establishment, health crises caused by the Depression triggered almost inadvertent government involvement in health care at local levels. Beneficence for African Americans was serendipitous and spotty. Local charities found themselves unable to provide the volume of public aid health care when large blocks of previously self-sufficient citizens became medically indigent; at this time discrete, crisis-oriented, supposedly short-term government health programs kicked in. They were affiliated with the Federal Emergency Relief Administration (FERA), the Civil Works Administration (CWA), the Works Progress Administration (WPA), and the Farm Security Administration (FSA).[30]

The largest and most diffuse federal program was the $500 million FERA program initiated during the president's first 100 days in office. Supervised by Roosevelt's aggressive troubleshooter Harry Hopkins and operating in at least 26 states, this "direct relief" program focused on propping up the overstressed state and local government poor relief and charity networks. Some of these agencies provided health care for the indigent. As Hirshfield observed, "The existence of millions of 'decent' unemployed" Americans "forced many states and localities to re-examine and change their system of providing care to the needy."[31] This early New Deal program was so massive and chaotic that abuse plagued its operation. Hirshfield noted that racial discrimination was also a problem: "Negro physicians complained about being excluded from participation in certain southern states."[32] Although "Rules and Regulations No. 7" was issued to solve these major operational problems, as Cray observed, the FERA program "could not cope with the deepening crisis."[33] Overall, "[d]uring its hectic existence the FERA program achieved both positive and negative results in its attempt to provide medical care to a large fraction of the population."[34] Nevertheless, it left large populations of physicians and patients with the impression that government-run programs were not all bad and could preserve the doctor-patient relationship. It expanded medical care into previously underserved urban and rural areas. However, the quality of medical care provided and the administrative soundness of the programs were highly variable depending on personnel and location.[35]

Other federal programs that provided medical care to particular population groups as one facet of a different area of concern were the CWA, WPA, and FSA programs. These programs also improved the distribution of health care to the urban poor, some Blacks, and certain rural poverty areas. WPA programs not only provided labor to build and improve hospitals, clinics, medical centers, and diagnostic laboratories but also conducted mass immunizations, dental health projects, school examinations for children, and medical and public health research for the needy. The FSA enlarged its health programs drastically in 1937 when it took over the Resettlement Administration. Agents observed that loan defaults skyrocketed when illness struck poor farm families. Therefore, the FSA helped finance and implement health cooperatives in poor rural communities for the hundreds of thousands of farm families no longer able to afford medical care. As Hirshfield points out, "Eventually they existed in eighty-eight different counties in forty-three separate states."[36] By 1943 over 600,000 persons were covered by the cooperatives. Faced with underfinancing and resistance by the medical profession and other providers, the program grudgingly went out of existence by 1947.

Physicians, also going bankrupt in the early 1930s, requested government intervention. However, while the AMA and the county medical societies cooperated reluctantly with sorely needed government programs such as those run by the FERA and FSA, which were often tailored to meet doctor and hospital needs, they complained on official and national levels about "third-party interference." By 1938 a second attempt at comprehensive health system reform, including compulsory health insurance, was made. As will be discussed, White medical establishment resistance combined with public apathy to defeat this new National Health Program.[37]

Alongside these government efforts at shoring up the U.S. health system were important private efforts. Hirshfield identified three basic types of voluntary, private approaches:

> cooperative medical care plans established and administered by lay groups; plans for budgeting of medical expenses under the control of the organized medical profession and limited to specific income groups; and private nonprofit hospitalization insurance plans covering certain broad groups of the population.[38]

In contrast to the government programs, which proved to be discrete and temporary health crises solutions borne of the Depression, these private efforts left permanent imprints and reshaped the American health system. Since the Great Depression, health reformers have never been able to marshal enough medical establishment, political, or popular support to displace these approaches and implement a universal, compulsory, national health system in the United States.[39]

Moves toward forming the first medical cooperative group were probably begun in 1929 by Dr. Michael Shadid in Elk City, Oklahoma. From a health policy perspective:

> Under cooperative plans participating members paid annual fees into funds which were controlled by membership-elected boards of directors. The fees were used by the boards to hire physicians and other professional personnel, build or rent medical facilities, and administer the plans. In return for their fee prepayments, the participating members were eligible to receive as much of the specified categories of medical care as they needed from the cooperatives during the current year.[40]

In allegiance with the Oklahoma Farmer's Union, and against much medical opposition, Dr. Shadid organized a clinic and hospital, hired salaried doctors, and provided general and preventive medical services to members for a preset fee. In response to the Depression health crisis Shadid's cooperative was operational by 1932. By 1936 the health cooperative was expanding. Los Angeles doctors Donald Ross and H. Clifford Loos began a similar cooperative to provide medical care and hospitalization for 400 employees of the city's Department of Water and Power. This successful effort also took place in 1929. The quintessential effort at "cooperative medicine" was the Group Health Association (GHA), organized on a nonprofit basis in 1937 to provide medical and hospital care through salaried physicians to federal employees in Washington, DC. The AMA's attempt to sabotage this effort was so blatant that it lost an anti-trust suit filed by the GHA in 1939. The AMA's conviction was upheld by the Supreme Court in 1943. Although the cooperative form of health care delivery was allowed to survive, its role was limited:

> The general opposition of the medical societies to cooperative plans, even when legal, remained a significant handicap to cooperatives, such as the Health Insurance Plan of Greater New York.... [A]lso, the exclusion of all nongroup individuals and of those unable to pay the annual fees made the cooperative of limited, but important, usefulness.[41]

Cooperative health plans thus continued to emerge. Largely for financial and social reasons they were of limited utility to Black and poor Americans, however. For African Americans, the "race problem" overrode virtually any mechanisms or policies designed to limit exclusion.[42]

The other type of health care delivery experiment was the voluntary organized medical society program. Plans like the Detroit Medical Service Bureau were based on payment arrangement and credit extensions mediated by county medical societies. Such plans were called *budget plans* and offered no protections from the group purchase of medical care nor professional fee escalation. A few of these plans, like the Oregon County Medical Society Plan (1932), were *medical indemnity insurance plans*. However, they were run by physicians and thus did not interfere with medical decision-making or fee determination. However, "[t]he primary weaknesses of the indemnity plans was their lack of administrative control of fees and utilization and their failure to cover most of the low-income population."[43] With these inherent flaws, by the 1940s problems such as reductions in covered services, fee escalations, and rising deductibles appeared. These natural results of overutilization of services by patients and maximization of fees by physicians led to the competitive demise of such plans. Interestingly, after the AMA adjusted its national policies allowing prepaid health insurance and hospital plans in the late 1930s, a new flurry of state medical society prepaid plans covering home, office, and hospital doctor visits began in California (California Physicians

Service started in 1939), New York, and Pennsylvania. They would eventually evolve into the Blue Shield plans covering physicians fees.[44]

The third private approach to the Depression health crisis was a response to the hospital fiscal emergency described by one authority on American hospitals: "As more individuals became impoverished, more patients flocked to hospitals as ward rather than private patients and to government rather than nongovernmental institutions. Hospitals were caught in a double bind. The demand for free care rose, while hospital income declined."[45]

And although city hospitals were "burdened by the sudden increase in patients," their primary problem "was that demand increased without increased tax budgets."[46] Paul Starr, focusing on the voluntary hospital's plummeting income bind, observed, "Beds were empty as utilization fell, bills were unpaid, and contributions to hospital fund-raising efforts tumbled"[47]:

> In just one year after the crash, average hospital receipts per person fell from $263.12 to $59.26, and average hospital deficits rose from 15.2 to 20.6 percent disbursements. In 1931, according to AMA data, only 62 percent of beds in voluntary hospitals were occupied on the average day compared to 89 percent in government hospitals.[48]

Voluntary and private hospitals fended off their demise by turning to insurance. The history of the establishment of the Blue Cross in Dallas, Texas, late in 1929 (when Baylor University Hospital agreed to provide up to 21 days of hospital care to 1,500 school teachers for $6 per person) is well documented. The idea spread immediately throughout the Dallas hospital community and then became a national movement. By 1934 there were similar citywide prepaid hospital plans in Sacramento, California; Essex County, New Jersey; St. Paul, Minnesota; and Cleveland, Ohio. The American Hospital Association (AHA) soon took over the promotion of group hospitalization. Utilizing foundation monies from the Rosenwald Fund, the AHA established guidelines for prepaid hospital plans (1933), standardized hospital control of the process (1934), avoided cut-throat competition by outlawing single hospital prepaid plans, and established a network of standard Blue Cross plans by 1938. Commercial carriers began experimenting with a similar product in 1934: "By 1940 the insurance companies had about 3.7 million subscribers, while the thirty-nine Blue Cross plans in operation had a total enrollment of more than 6 million."[49] This approach to the hospital crisis stabilized the White U.S. hospital industry through voluntary and cooperative means.

Though the Black health care infrastructure was not included in the new financing arrangements, the White private sector was preserved, while compulsory health insurance and a national health program had been avoided. Strong divisions along race and class lines prevented this biased health care financing activity from bolstering the 200 or more African American hospitals that were struggling for survival during the Great Depression. As Beardsley noted about Depression stressors on Black hospitals, "when hospital facilities were available to blacks, they were strained to the point of collapse."[50] The half-way measures of a group hospitilization did not solve the problem of health care provision to Blacks and the poor on several counts: it failed to pay for doctor fees or medical services, had no portability, had no preventive or health promotion components, and, by not adhering to a sliding fee scale (there was a single fee for participation), was aimed strictly at middle-class incomes. By combining these faults with overt redlining of high-risk, low-income, and farm families, Blue Cross plans made no pretense of addressing the health system's race, maldistribution, or class problems.[51]

Many of the health system faults displayed and exaggerated by the Great Depression were concealed by governmental and private solutions and programs that were marshaled to avert a total collapse of the system. The basic reasons for the faults, however, remained unaddressed. Despite the government efforts, as Hirshfield pointed out, "[t]oo many of the unemployed or underemployed were not receiving adequate care; too many farmers were finding doctors and medical facilities harder and harder to locate and pay for; and too many middle-class people were still facing individual financial and social disaster because of serious illness."[52] The series of private and governmental programs had modified the health system's problems and offered some short-term solutions—but not long-term cures. Comprehensive and fundamental changes in the health system had not been addressed. For health programs to work in the United States, cooperation was needed between the physicians, patients, hospitals, government public health agencies, politicians, and private corporations (e.g., insurance companies, medical supply companies, pharmaceutical houses). If proposed solutions worked, affected patients were pleased, and no one's ideologies or ethics were breached, they were accepted. No one, including patients, desired radical change unless it was necessary. The racial beliefs of the European American majority would also be respected. Overseas, European patients seemed to be motivated by ideology while American patients, except on racial matters, were motivated by pragmatism.

Physicians, the medical societies, and their supporters (pharmaceutical companies, insurance companies, etc.) believed these superficial changes would permanently solve the system's problems. Furthermore the solutions proposed were to be framed in terms of traditional medicine grounded in the doctor-patient relationship, free competition, individual responsibility and initiative, and fee-for-service. Understanding this ideology is necessary to comprehend some of White organized medicine's responses to the Depression health crisis. Despite the plethora of physicians' practices collapsing due to the drop in practice income, the AMA openly fought, and only sometimes grudgingly cooperated with, governmental aid programs and health insurance schemes to help patients pay their doctor bills. As Starr elaborated on White organized medicine's response to declining national health and Depression health policies, "The AMA's response to the economic crisis . . . emphasized restricting the supply of doctors rather than amplifying the demand for their services."[53] Moreover, "Each of the five years prior to 1934 had shown an increase in applicants accepted by medical schools; each of the next six years showed a drop."[54] The number of first-year medical students declined from 7,578 to 6,211 from 1933 to 1934, and 25 states eventually prohibited the licensing of foreign doctors. Such negative approaches to the maldistribution crisis were emblematic of the White profession's insensitive, and some would say inappropriate, approach to America's medical-social needs. Nevertheless, certain aspects of these nihilistic policies were reversed in response to the extra stresses produced by World War II. The war forced the health system to confront new challenges.[55]

## World War II: The Health System, 1942–1945

World War II, much like the Great Depression, did not change the fundamental contours of the U.S. health system. It did have some major effects that persisted in the postwar health system. Some of the effects included, but were not limited to, dramatically increasing the government funding of medical research, education, and numbers of medical school trainees; raising the priority and funding levels of public health, especially as it affected sexually transmitted diseases (STDs) and other infectious diseases such as tuberculosis; increasing government participation in funding indigent health care in some areas; serving as a catalyst for the indemnity health insurance and prepaid hospitalization movement; acquainting millions of servicemen and their families, often for the first time, with access to quality medical and health care in a unitary (military-based) system; and raising funding levels and standards for the hospital care of servicemen's families in the United States. These events had multiple direct and indirect effects on Black and poor people. For African Americans, in terms of health care, the world would never be the same.[56]

In response to the wartime demand for physicians, U.S. medical and health professions schools were mobilized to increase production. Programs such as the Army Specialty Training Program (ASTP) were implemented at Black and White medical and dental schools. As Timothy Jacobson noted, "The year 1942 saw the institution . . . of the national accelerated program of physician education whereby new first-year classes were admitted every nine months (June 1942, March 1943, December 1943, September 1944, and June 1945); the school operated on a year-round basis."[57] Special abbreviated postgraduate medical training programs such as the "9-9-9 Plan," which allowed draft-deferred residency training, were also implemented. All medical schools and academic health centers (AHCs), including African American health centers, were included.[58]

The war also raised awareness and funding levels for public health. Large federal subsidies to Southern states for public health had begun in 1935 with Social Security. Wartime insistence on fitness and health raised federal funding levels for anti–venereal disease (VD) programs in some states by 40–80 percent. Later in the war, penicillin usage was encouraged through federally funded programs. As Edward Beardsley pointed out, "For the first time states could contemplate compulsory treatment of all cases, for with penicillin a complete syphilis cure was possible after only a few days of hospitalization."[59] Although these efforts were often concentrated around military bases, programs combating malaria and tuberculosis were generally well funded and wide-ranging. These efforts, buttressing those initiated by federal Social Security programs initiated during the Depression, included many Blacks and poor Whites.[60]

As noted earlier, World War II served as a catalyst for the indemnity health insurance and prepaid hospitalization movement. The wartime freezing of wages artificially elevated the importance of fringe benefits in collective bargaining agreements. Health benefits thus became important bargaining chips for largely White union members, and labor unions moved aggressively in these areas:

> [T]he movement toward voluntary hospital insurance was stimulated ... through the wage stabilization policies which were put into effect during World War II. Before the war there had been both labor and employer interest in health services, but benefits rarely appeared as part of the process of collective bargaining. During and immediately after the war wage increases were restricted, but as a result, fringe benefits acquired a new importance.... [B]y the end of 1949, voluntary health insurance through collective bargaining was surging through the vast steel and automobile industries; already 3 million workers were covered, and the tide was barely under way.[61]

In 1940 only 9 percent of the civilian population was covered by hospital benefits, 4 percent for surgical benefits, and 2 percent for in-hospital medical benefits. By 1950 these figures were 51 percent, 36 percent, and 14 percent, respectively. However, because of prerequisite employment, required premium levels, and uncovered medical expenses, these remained largely middle-class approaches to health care financing. For these reasons, by 1941 statistics from the Social Security Board's Division of Health Studies "showed that the poor were not benefiting from voluntary hospitalization insurance."[62] Because of persistent racial discrimination in employment, labor unions, and pay scales, the African American experience was even worse and continued to be differentially impacted.[63]

In response to a crisis generated around military bases early in the war, the Emergency Maternal and Infant Care (EMIC) program was created in early 1943. Pregnant military wives moving to communities around military bases could not afford the medical or hospital care in those areas. Hospitals, many of which were substandard, were overcrowded and expensive. The problem was especially acute in the South, where many military bases were located. The Children's Bureau created the EMIC program, providing free hospital, maternal, and infant care for the dependents of servicemen. It was also charged with upgrading hospital OB-GYN services. This generated a tremendous demand for hospital care by the families of millions of servicemen often unaccustomed to access to quality medical services and health care. Families of Black servicemen, because of segregated facilities, presented an extra menu of problems requiring various measures such as upgrading segregated facilities, changing hospital policies, and authorizing services in Black institutions. Nevertheless, this demand would persist after the war.[64]

Government efforts improved the health of underprivileged groups during the war. The military health system, although racially segregated, was a universal-access, relatively high-quality system. The thousand-bed, all-Black hospital established at Fort Huachuca in southern Arizona for the all-Black 93rd Division represented the best of a flawed, racially segregated system. This facility was commanded by Lieutenant-Colonel Midian O. Bousefield, who was Black, and was staffed by 40 African American physicians and more than 100 Black nurses. By the end of the war scant and spotty desegregation had occurred in a few military health facilities. Federally funded anti-STD, anti-malarial, and anti-tuberculosis (TB) measures, public health, and guaranteed prenatal, perinatal, infant care, and hospitalization through the EMIC program positively affected patients who had never had health care. This was especially so in the South. Blacks benefited directly (GIs and their families) and indirectly (Blacks living around military bases) from the military health system, even though it was almost totally segregated. As Beardsley noted, "For the first time in memory, millions of young Southerners of both races received medical and dental care, housing, clothing, and food of first quality."[65] Just as in World War I, this increased awareness levels of these populations and raised their expectations after the war.[66]

## African American Health: 1930–1945

*Our death rate is without the slightest doubt a death rate due to poverty and discrimination.*

W. E. B. Du Bois, "Postscript: Our Health,"
*The Crisis*, February 1933.

*[The Black health problem] has . . . been due . . . to the attitude of indifference that the white people have assumed toward the welfare of the Negro people. The health problems of the Negroes have not been a matter of serious social interest.*

Edward Byron Reuter, *The American Race Problem*

Although the health status of all Americans was generally not good during the Great Depression, the Black/White continuum of health status and outcome differentials (by now an American tradition we refer to as the "slave health deficit") persisted. Poor health for African Americans was an expected norm as they entered the 1930s: "Up to 1930 the status of Negro mortality in the United States stood out when it was compared with the rates of different European countries. It was not only higher than that of the general population of the United States but also higher than that of most European populations."[67] By the 1930–1945 period it had become clear that the health of African Americans was so poor it had prevented their enjoying the expected health, fertility, and population demographic transitions experienced by other Western developed countries. Farley and Allen describe the normal health-related pattern of Western demographic progress:

> At a first stage, rates of birth and death are high and the population grows slowly. At a second stage, improvements in the standard of living and, perhaps, the introduction of public health measures lead to a fall in death rates, but the birthrates remain high so the population grows rapidly. At a third stage, couples control their fertility, birthrates decline, and the population moves toward a lower growth rate.[68]

European Americans, living beside and often in the midst of African Americans, experienced the characteristic demographic pattern early in the century. African Americans, for a variety of health and policy-related reasons, did not. The same researchers describe the aberrant Black health and demographic pattern that had become obvious by the 1940s:

> We can be certain that the black population of the United States did not go through the demographic transition that characterized many Western nations. The fall in fertility preceded rather than followed the decline in mortality and was not attributable so much to the intentional control of fertility as it was to an increase in health problems: more tuberculosis and venereal diseases. During the era of fertility decline, death rates among blacks remained quite high, and the transition to low rates of growth occurred without the elimination of infectious disease. The transition to low rates of birth and mortality took place after 1940.[69]

Documenting these racial health status and outcome deficiencies and understanding how they adversely influenced and impacted the African American population's historical health experience become a major focus of this inquiry.[70]

As previously noted, longevity and mortality rates, infant and child mortality, and low birth-weight statistics are the "Gold Standards" of health status and health system performance. According to the World Health Organization (WHO) and the *Oxford Textbook of Public Health*, these health status indicators (see Table 2.2) answer questions "about equity and inequity, because they refer to conditions known to occur at very different rates in rich and poor populations."[71] Moreover, with a series of caveats in mind, by utilizing U.S. census data on deaths and births one is able to approximate some of the major direct and indirect indicators of

**Table 2.2  Indicators of Health-Status and Mortality Frequently Used to Identify Inequities in Health (based on WHO 1981a)**

| Indicator | Definition | Range | |
|---|---|---|---|
| | | Least-developed countries | Most-developed countries |
| Infant mortality rate* | $\dfrac{\text{No. of deaths during a period of time}}{\text{No. of live births during same period}} \times 1000$ | 200 | 10 |
| Child mortality rate | $\dfrac{\text{No. of deaths of children aged 1–4 years during a year}}{\text{Total no. of children aged 1–4 years at the middle of the year}} \times 1000$ | 100 | 0.4 |
| Life expectancy at birth | Average no. of years which a person is expected to live under the prevalent morality pattern | <40 | >70 |
| Low birth-weight | $\dfrac{\text{Live-born babies with birth-weight less than 2500g}}{\text{Total no. of live-born babies}} \times 100$ | 50% | 4% |

*More correctly called "Infant mortality ratio."

*Source:* Abelin T. Health promotion. 557–589. In: Detels R, Holland WW, McEwen J, Omenn GS, eds. *Oxford Textbook of Public Health.* Volume 3. *The Practice of Public Health.* Third Edition. New York: Oxford University Press, 1991, 577.

health status as early as the nineteenth century. As was previously mentioned, before the 1940s mortality trends are relatively difficult to discern in that there was no national system for registering U.S. deaths before 1933; data on Blacks were artificially concentrated on the approximately 4.4 percent of Blacks living in Northern cities (when more than three-fourths of Blacks lived in Southern rural areas). Meanwhile, the 1900 Death Registration Area (DRA) comprised a sample of 26 percent of the entire U.S. population. Addition of the Birth Registration Area in 1915 also helped in mortality computations. Data-gathering on African Americans was further hampered by both inaccurate death and birth registration (often due to lack of medical attendance) and undercounts in the census. Comparative mortality statistics for different populations based on crude death rates have been noted to be treacherous. This is especially so when groups such as African Americans and Hispanic/Latino Americans, who are younger populations, are compared to European Americans. Direct comparisons between such groups is not accurate. Such populations must be grouped in age-specific categories and statistically adjusted for age such that race or ethnicity is the only variable being measured—hence age-adjusted death rates. However, these reservations have not deterred detailed study of historical Black death rates by credible scholars such as Edward Byron Reuter, Jitsuichi Masuoka, Reynolds Farley, Walter Allen, and Douglas Ewbank.[72]

Despite the adverse social effects created by the Great Depression, Black mortality rates and longevity projections improved dramatically throughout the first half of the twentieth century. Although the Black mortality rate decline probably did not begin in earnest until after 1910, Farley and Allen noted that "data from the DRA imply that the life span of blacks increased by 20 years between 1900 and 1940"[73] (see Table 2.3). Despite the deficiencies in the DRA* and the stagnant to declining socioeconomic status, this increased Black life span was probably real, being strongly related to substantial reductions in infant mortality and infectious diseases in the African American population. A nascent federally sponsored public health movement, expanded during the Great Depression, probably had some positive effects. Nevertheless, comparative Black/White death rates revealed Black age-adjusted death rates approximately 58 percent higher than Whites in 1900, based on the limited 1900 DRA. The age-standardized death rate showed a little improvement by 1910 to 27.4 per 1,000 population, while rising to a rate 70 percent higher than the White population on a relative basis. According to the new 1910 DRA, Black mortality rates were 60 percent higher than those for Whites in 1910, tracking the same trends in Black mortality decline over the next three decades. Therefore, though the data confirm a 20-year increase in life span for Blacks between 1900 and 1940, "the age-standardized death rate for blacks was

### Table 2.3 Life Expectancy by Sex and Race: US 1900–1945

|      | Black males | | | Black females | | |
|------|-------|------|------|-------|------|------|
|      | Birth | 10   | 60   | Birth | 10   | 60   |
| 1900 | 32.5  | 41.9 | 12.6 | 35.0  | 43.0 | 13.6 |
| 1920 | 46.9  | 44.9 | 13.7 | 48.0  | 44.9 | 14.0 |
| 1930 | 50.1  | 46.6 | 14.1 | 52.6  | 49.0 | 15.3 |
| 1945 | 56.1  | 50.1 | 14.7 | 59.6  | 53.8 | 16.5 |
|      | White males | | | White females | | |
| 1900 | 48.2  | 48.0 | 14.4 | 51.1  | 52.2 | 15.1 |
| 1920 | 57.9  | 54.6 | 14.8 | 60.0  | 56.4 | 15.7 |
| 1930 | 60.6  | 55.9 | 14.9 | 64.5  | 60.0 | 16.4 |
| 1945 | 64.4  | 57.9 | 15.4 | 69.5  | 62.4 | 17.8 |

*Source:* Hart N. The social and economic environment and human health. 150–180. In: Holland WW, Detels R, Knox G, eds. *Oxford Textbook of Public Health*. Volume 1. *Applications in Public Health*. Second Edition. Oxford: Oxford University Press 1991, 165.

*The DRA in 1900 included only ten states (Connecticut, District of Columbia, Indiana, Maine, Massachusetts, Michigan, New Hampshire, New Jersey, New York, Rhode Island, and Vermont); only New York and the District of Columbia harbored significant Black populations. Moreover, initial findings could have been confounded by 1910 DRA additions (California, Colorado, Maryland, Minnesota, Montana, Ohio, Pennsylvania, Utah, Washington, and Wisconsin) and the inclusion of the entire nation to the DRA in 1933.

**Table 2.4  Death Rates, Standardized for Age, in the Death Registration States of 1900 and 1910**

| Year | Non-Whites of Both Sexes | Whites of Both Sexes |
|---|---|---|
| **Death Registration Area, 1900** | | |
| 1900 | 27.8 | 17.6 |
| 1905 | 27.5 | 16.4 |
| 1910 | 27.4 | 16.1 |
| 1915 | 25.0 | 15.2 |
| 1920 | 24.5 | 14.6 |
| 1925 | 22.1 | 13.1 |
| 1930 | 21.8 | 12.1 |
| 1935 | 18.9 | 11.2 |
| 1940 | 16.6 | 10.2 |
| **Death Registration Area, 1910** | | |
| 1910 | 24.0 | 15.0 |
| 1915 | 23.2 | 14.4 |
| 1920 | 23.7 | 14.1 |
| 1925 | 22.4 | 12.8 |
| 1930 | 21.0 | 12.1 |
| 1935 | 19.0 | 10.8 |
| 1940 | 16.7 | 9.3 |
| Total U.S.A., 1985 | 6.9 | 5.2 |

*Note:* DRA states of 1900 are Connecticut, District of Columbia, Indiana, Maine, Massachusetts, Michigan, New Hampshire, New Jersey, New York, Rhode Island, and Vermont.

The following states were added to the DRA of 1910: California, Colorado, Maryland, Minnesota, Montana, Ohio, Pennsylvama, Utah, Washingon, and Wisconsin.

*Source:* Farley R, Allen WR. *The Color Line and the Quality of Life in America.* New York: Oxford University Press 1989, 27.

about 60 percent greater than that for whites."[74] As can be seen in the Table 2.4, if the comparative figures are calculated as Black/White ratios, despite African American improvement, the racial gap does not close between 1900 and 1940 (See Table 2.4). "The Negro death rate in the 1930s was higher than that of any other large group in the population,"[75] Reuter concluded.[76]

These improved mortality rates and longevity projections are difficult to comprehend in light of the adverse socioeconomic effects the Great Depression had on African Americans and the sporadic increases in Southern mortality noted by 1933. This is especially relevant when it is combined with Reuter's observation that at the time, "[t]here [was] a very general indifference to Negro health."[77] Nevertheless, the previously mentioned aberrant relationships between demographic patterns, mortality and morbidity indicators, and fertility trends characteristic of evolving Black health and population growth in the United States compared to other Western industrialized societies further distort most attempts at analysis or explanatory hypotheses.

Observed improvements in African American mortality and longevity could have been the result of one or more of these factors:

> (1) the virulence of disease decreases; (2) medical advances eliminate some diseases or reduce mortality from others; (3) public health measures lessen the prevalence or impact of contagious diseases; (4) increases in the standard of living improve the health of the population, enabling them to withstand diseases.[78]

Hypothesizing that disease virulence would suddenly decline in a particular population to lengthen life span within less than a generation is scientifically unsound. Because of racial segregation, discrimination, and socioeconomic status, Blacks had very little access to the dominant, private, fee-for-service medical and health care system. Thus, "Medical advances probably had limited effects on the health of blacks until well into the twentieth century since most blacks lived in rural areas where they had little access to physicians or hospitals."[79] Declining economic fortunes during the Great Depression made Black access to medical advances offered by the mainstream system even less. As Beardsley noted about public health services, "from 1930 to 1933, health work in the South followed the same path to stagnation and bankruptcy as American business."[80] As early as 1936 the government-funded National Health Survey of 1935 and 1936, published by the Public Health Service in 1938, and the 1941 Social Security Board's Division of Health Studies were statistically documenting that the emergency New Deal government health programs, the limited Social Security health programs, and the voluntary, private hospitalization movement sweeping the country were not benefiting the poor as significantly as they should have. Concerning poor African American health, Reuter discussed the ramifications of poverty and deprivation on health and the effects inexpensive corrective actions could have. This helps explain why sympathetic health promotion and disease prevention efforts from Black physicians and nurses were so critical:

> Poverty is the greatest enemy.... [D]eaths occur in families where the father's wage is low, where the mother goes out to work, where poverty compels the group to live in alley houses or rear tenements. The causes are ... ignorance ... and the inability to provide adequate care which go with poverty rather than the poverty itself; mortality and morbidity rates may be greatly reduced without great change in wages or housing accommodations.[81]

Farley's and Allen's analysis attributes much of this improvement in mortality and longevity to the increasing impact of public health measures such as sanitation and malaria prevention, combined with some qualitative, if not always quantitative, improvements in the African American standard of living.

Although Black access to the embryonic public health care sector in the South, where most Blacks lived, did not improve until the 1920s through funding of public health programs by private foundations like the Rosenwald Fund, increased government funding for health care during the Depression made major progress against infant deaths, venereal diseases, and tuberculosis. The influence of the energetic but segregated African American hospital network and health subsystem was positive but hard to measure objectively. However, as private and government interest in Black health rose in the 1920s and 1930s, both Beardsley and Gunnar Myrdal felt that the improved African American health status and outcome observed during the Depression could be explained by private and government interventions. Inferring that the Black health environment, health services, and medical-social milieu were so deplorable, as Myrdal stated, "Any intelligent efforts to reduce Negro morbidity and mortality will result in striking success."[82] Reuter reinforced this conclusion, observing, "Their death rate has declined and their health improved in spite of the partial and inadequate community facilities. It may be further reduced as the community desires its reduction."[83] Interestingly, both of these scholars felt that more consideration would be given to Black health by U.S. Whites if some program for controlling the African American birth rate were forthcoming. A decline in Black death rates would continue until the 1950s.[84]

Disease-specific reasons for the excessive Black mortality and abbreviated longevity are legion (see Figure 2.1). As Reuter noted, "The death rate of infants and young children is an important item in the explanation of the excessively high death rate of the Negro people."[85] Nevertheless, African American child mortality rates* improved markedly during the first half of the twentieth century. As Ewbank pointed out:

> Between 1900 and 1940, q(5) declined from 264 per 1,000 to 90 in 1940, a decline of 66 percent. During this same period the rate for whites continued the decline experienced between 1880 and 1900, dropping 67 percent from 161 in 1900 to 53 in 1940.... [T]herefore, between 1900 and 1940 the child mortality rate among blacks remained about 70 percent above that of whites.[86]

---

*The child mortality rate is the proportion of all live births that survive to their fifth birthday. It is expressed as:

$$\frac{\text{No. of deaths of children ages 1–4 years during a year}}{\text{Total no. of children ages 1–4 at the middle of the year}} \times 1000$$

This rate is often referred to as q(5).

## Figure 2.1 Ratio of Non-White to White Mortality Rates for Selected Causes of Death, United States: 1929–1931

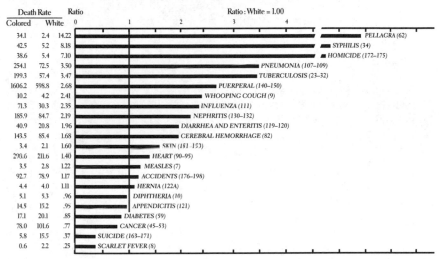

| Death Rate Colored | White | Ratio | | | | |
|---|---|---|---|---|---|---|
| 34.1 | 2.4 | 14.22 | | | | PELLAGRA (62) |
| 42.5 | 5.2 | 8.18 | | | | SYPHILIS (34) |
| 38.6 | 5.4 | 7.10 | | | | HOMICIDE (172–175) |
| 254.1 | 72.5 | 3.50 | | | | PNEUMONIA (107–109) |
| 199.3 | 57.4 | 3.47 | | | | TUBERCULOSIS (23–32) |
| 1606.2 | 598.8 | 2.68 | | | | PUERPERAL (140–150) |
| 10.2 | 4.2 | 2.41 | | | | WHOOPING COUGH (9) |
| 71.3 | 30.3 | 2.35 | | | | INFLUENZA (111) |
| 185.9 | 84.7 | 2.19 | | | | NEPHRITIS (130–132) |
| 40.9 | 20.8 | 1.96 | | | | DIARRHEA AND ENTERITIS (119–120) |
| 143.5 | 85.4 | 1.68 | | | | CEREBRAL HEMORRHAGE (82) |
| 3.4 | 2.1 | 1.60 | | | | SKIN (151–153) |
| 290.6 | 211.6 | 1.40 | | | | HEART (90–95) |
| 3.5 | 2.8 | 1.22 | | | | MEASLES (7) |
| 92.7 | 78.9 | 1.17 | | | | ACCIDENTS (176–198) |
| 4.4 | 4.0 | 1.11 | | | | HERNIA (122A) |
| 5.1 | 5.3 | .96 | | | | DIPHTHERIA (10) |
| 14.5 | 15.2 | .95 | | | | APPENDICITIS (121) |
| 17.1 | 20.1 | .85 | | | | DIABETES (59) |
| 78.0 | 101.6 | .77 | | | | CANCER (45–53) |
| 5.8 | 15.5 | .37 | | | | SUICIDE (163–171) |
| 0.6 | 2.2 | .25 | | | | SCARLET FEVER (8) |

*Source:* Harold F. Dorn, "The Health of the Negro," unpublished manuscript prepared for this study (1940), figure 7.

*Note:* The figure "1" indicates that the two races have the same death rate, the figure (2) indicates that the non-White rate is twice the White rate, and so on. Texas is not included in the computations, since data were not available for it. Non-White rates were standardized on the total White population of death registration states of 1930. The rate for puerperal causes is per 100,00 births, including stillbirths.

*From:* Myrdal G. *An American Dilemma: The Negro Problem and Modern Democracy.* New York: Harper and Row, 1944, 173.

Instead of one Black child in four dying by his or her fifth birthday, as was the case in 1900, less than one in ten died by age 5 in 1940. "Nationally, the average rate of decline in q(5) between these two dates was 2.7 percent."[87] Despite the improvement, Blacks did not reduce their risks relative to Whites. Infant mortality also showed marked improvements from a 1910 infant morality rate* (IMR) over twice the White rate—261.6 per 1,000 for Blacks and 129.7 per 1,000 for Whites. By 1933 the Black rate was 85.4 compared to 52.8 for Whites. The 1944 figures were 67.2 and 39.2 respectively (see Table 2.5). Nevertheless, between 1915 and 1944 the ratio of Black to White infant mortality rates (the disparity between the Black and White infant mortality rates) did not decline appreciably.

---

\* The infant mortality rate is the number of infants dying during the first year of life per 1,000 live births. It can be expressed as:

$$\frac{\text{No. of deaths during a period of time} \times 1000}{\text{No. of live births during the same period}} \times 1000$$

Table 2.5  Infant Mortality Rates, by Color, Birth-Registration
States or United States, 1915–1966* †

| Year | Total | White | Non-White |
|------|-------|-------|-----------|
| 1915–19 | 95.7 | 92.8 | 149.7 |
| 1920–24 | 76.7 | 73.3 | 115.3 |
| 1925–29 | 69.0 | 65.0 | 105.4 |
| 1930–34 | 60.4 | 55.2 | 98.6 |
| 1935–39 | 53.2 | 49.2 | 81.3 |
| 1940–44 | 42.6 | 39.2 | 67.2 |
| 1945–49 | 33.5 | 31.3 | 49.8 |
| 1950–54 | 28.1 | 25.4 | 44.8 |
| 1955–59 | 26.4 | 23.4 | 43.7 |
| 1960 | 26.0 | 22.9 | 43.2 |
| 1961 | 25.3 | 22.4 | 40.7 |
| 1962 | 25.3 | 22.3 | 41.4 |
| 1963 | 25.2 | 22.2 | 41.5 |
| 1964 | 24.8 | 21.6 | 41.1 |
| 1965 | 24.7 | 21.5 | 40.3 |
| 1966 | 23.7 | 20.6 | 38.8 |

* *Source:* Dept. of Health, Education, and Welfare, *Vital Statistics of the United States, 1964*, Vol. II, *Mortality*, Part A, Table 2–1; and U.S. Bureau of the Census, *Pocket Data Book U.S.A. 1969*, Table 30.

†Rate per 1,000 live births.

*From:* Reuter EB. *The American Race Problem*. Revised Third Edition. Revision and Preface by Masuoka J. New York: Thomas Y. Crowell, 1970, 166.

The specific diseases causing excess infant deaths were the same killers plaguing infants of all races in that age group. Respiratory diseases such as pulmonary tuberculosis and pneumonia were prominent, and whooping cough seemed to be particularly dangerous. Epidemic diarrhea and typhoid fever were also problematic. Some of the effect on child, and especially infant, mortality is related to Black exclusion from professional attendance and hospital facilities. In 1937, 35 percent of Southern Black babies were delivered by a physician, compared to 90 percent of Southern White babies. By the end of the period the majority of Northern White and Black babies had physician attendance at delivery either in-hospital or at home. The disparate racial infant mortality rates were also related to low hospital delivery rates. In 1940, when 52 percent of all U.S. infants were delivered in hospitals, the White proportion at (56 percent) was more than twice the Black proportion (22 percent).[88]

A predominance of infectious and chronic diseases accounted for the excessive mortality in the adult African American population during the 1930s and early 1940s (see Table 2.6). As Ewbank points out, "[B]lacks suffered higher mortality

Table 2.6  Negro Deaths by Important Causes, Registration Area
1931 and 1964*

| | Number of Deaths | |
| --- | --- | --- |
| Cause of Death | 1931 | 1964 |
| Total deaths | 174,023 | 209,065 |
| Tuberculosis, all forms | 20,683 | 14,358 |
| Pneumonia | 15,040 | 9,495 |
| Chronic nephritis | 11,246 | 2,404† |
| Cerebral hemorrhage | 10,263 | 15,164 |
| Cancer and other malignant tumors | 6,528 | 26,839 |
| Influenza | 5,558 | 264 |
| Syphilis | 4,657 | 707 |
| Pellagra | 2,832 | 8 |
| Diabetes mellitus | 1,465 | 4,312 |
| Malaria | 1,195 | . . . . . |

*Source: 1964 data Dept. of Health, Education, and Welfare. *Vital Statistics of the United States, 1964*, Vol. II, *Mortality*, Part A, Table 1–25.

†Includes unspecified nephritis and other renal sclerosis.

From: Reuter E.B. *The American Race Problem*. Revised Third Edition. Revision and Preface by Masuoka J. New York: Thomas Y. Crowell, 1970, 170.

from virtually all causes, with relative risks for most causes being in the range of 1.3 to 1.5. The few causes for which whites showed higher rates . . . were probably underreported for blacks."[89]

Tuberculosis and pneumonia caused one-fifth of the African American deaths during the 1930s. For example, in New York City in 1931, tuberculosis killed five times as many Blacks as Whites. Nevertheless, the 1910–1920 decade began with a drop in mortality from tuberculosis and typhoid in both Blacks and Whites, a trend that continued throughout the Depression. This accounted for as much as one-half of the decline in Black mortality. As can be seen in Table 2.6, cancer became a prominent cause of Black mortality between 1931 and 1964. African American males and females shared in the health distress, but the gender-specific exposure to the hazards of reproduction and childbirth took a heavy, albeit peculiar, toll. Exposures such as maternal mortality rates between two and three-and-a-half times White rates over the first four decades of the twentieth century pushed African American female mortality rates above male rates until the onset of World War II (see Table 2.7). A 1940 U.S. government report citing official 1936–1938 statistics concluded that the death rates for African American mothers and babies were "far higher than those for the United States as a whole,"[90] Morais noted.

Venereal diseases were another set of problems differentially affecting African American health. Although overreported in Black populations and hidden in

**Table 2.7 Maternal Mortality Rates in Selected Years by Color, Birth Registration States or United States, 1915–1966*a**

| Year | Total | White | Non-White |
|------|-------|-------|-----------|
| 1915–19 | 727.9 | 700.3 | 1,253.5 |
| 1930–34b | 636.0 | 575.0 | 1,080.7 |
| 1945 | 207.2 | 172.1 | 454.8 |
| 1950 | 83.3 | 61.1 | 221.6 |
| 1955 | 47.0 | 32.8 | 130.3 |
| 1960 | 37.1 | 26.0 | 97.9 |
| 1961 | 36.9 | 24.9 | 101.3 |
| 1962c | 35.2 | 23.8 | 95.9 |
| 1963 c | 35.8 | 24.0 | 96.9 |
| 1965 | 33.3 | 22.3 | 89.9 |
| 1966 | 29.1 | 20.2 | 72.4 |

*Source: Dept. of Health, Education, and Welfare. *Vital Statistics of the United States, 1964*, Vol. II, *Mortality*, Part A, Table 1–16.

aRate per 100,000 live births.

bFor 1932–34 Mexicans are included in Non-White category.

cFigures by color exclude data for residents of New Jersey.

From: Reuter EB. *The American Race Problem*. Revised Third Edition. Revision and Preface by Masuoka J. New York: Thomas Y. Crowell, 1970, 174.

White populations by medical-social and reporting mechanisms,* VDs represented a growing menace of major importance. As Farley and Allen noted:

> Among blacks, the death rates from syphilis increased between 1910 and 1930.... [T]he overall death rates from syphilis tripled from 30 per 100,000 in 1910 to 90 in 1935. At this time syphilis was a common cause of infant deaths. In the mid-1930s, there were about 3 infant deaths from syphilis per 1,000 Black births, which is a rise from the rates reported for previous decades.[91]

Related to the spread of STDs among Blacks was the reduction in African American fertility. This was another marker with profound health status implications. The 1930s represented the tail end of a 75-year period of declining fertility in the Black population. The sharp reduction from 7.7 to 2.6 in total fertility rate of African Americans between the Civil War and the Great Depression cannot be explained by changes in marriage or cohabitation patterns or contraceptive

---

*Whites with venereal diseases and venereal disease-related deaths are overwhelmingly treated in the private system and, for social reasons, have diagnoses altered or unreported to official agencies. Statistics showing overwhelming numbers of Blacks receiving any treatment for VD come from public clinics or hospitals, which report every case. STD and VD are now used interchangeably.

usage. Epidemiologic patterns of prevalence rates and trends, correlated with demographic data, suggest the decline may have been due to fertility-reducing diseases such as tuberculosis, gonorrhea, and syphilis. There is strong evidence that these patterns are correlated with the reduced birth rates in the 1920s and 1930s. This is one area where inadequate preventive, public health, and therapeutic programs resulted in excess mortality, morbidity, and poor reproductive performance for the African American population. As the prevalence of these diseases was reduced and effective STD control programs were initiated, the ground was laid for the fertility explosion that gripped the entire population following World War II. Overall, as far as the improvements in African American health between 1930 and 1945 were concerned, Myrdal said: "The greatest progress seems to be made in reducing deaths among Negroes due to tuberculosis, syphilis, diphtheria, whooping cough, diarrhea, and enteritis."[92] Nevertheless, the huge deficits in health care between Blacks and Whites in the United States remained.[93]

Scholars concentrating on the Black population throughout the 1920s and 1930s, such as Charles S. Johnson and Carter G. Woodson, contend that to comprehend why improvements in health status and outcome failed to close the race-based health disparities, an appreciation is required of the oppressive socioeconomic conditions and health care segregation and discrimination suffered by African Americans. As Morais noted in a 1939 article in *The Crisis*: "It is shocking to note that a race which has a much higher percentage of the disease [tuberculosis, syphilis, diphtheria, whooping cough, diarrhea, enteritis, etc.] is held to an economic level favoring its incidence, and that this people is largely denied the benefit of all modern methods that science has given humanity with which to fight it."[94] This articulates the seeming indifference, if not cynicism and outright hostility, demonstrated by controlling elements in American society, including the medical profession and its infrastructure, regarding African America's health plight. As private health experiments supported by the AMA and its cabal spread throughout the country like wildfire during the World War II era, government statistical data demonstrated by 1938 and 1941 that Blacks and the poor were not being equitably served. The same policies and programs continued without pause.

In the South, where two-thirds of the Black population was concentrated through World War II, African Americans were mired in the semifeudal tenant-sharecropper system that had substituted for slavery. With the exception of a small class of Negro professional and middle-class businessmen, the vast majority of Southern city-dwellers were unskilled workers or domestic servants. Their poverty compounded their health plight, where public hospitals and clinics were either nonexistent or shockingly deprived. Similar to the West in the nineteenth century, the North in the twentieth century served as a safety valve for escape from seemingly hopeless oppression: "Almost a half-million Negroes, responding to the siren call of economic security and freedom, left the eleven states of the old Confederacy from 1910 to 1920. Nearly 800,000 more moved away during the twenties and were followed by another 400,000 during the thirties."[95] These 1.7 million persons, however, found themselves living in or near poverty, serving as Northern strike-breakers, trade union outcasts, and unskilled and domestic workers. For all African Americans, both Northern and Southern, "[i]mpoverishment and deprivation were formidable barriers to good health."[96] As Myrdal said of the health plight of the Negro masses:

> Area for area, class for class, Negroes cannot get the same advantages in the way of prevention and cure of disease that whites can. There is discrimination against the Negro in the availability to him of medical facilities.... [I]t is hard to separate the effects of discrimination from those of concentration of Negroes in areas where medical facilities are not easily available and in those income brackets which do not permit the purchase of medical facilities in the competitive market. Discrimination increases Negro sickness and death both directly and indirectly and manifests itself both consciously and unconsciously.[97]

One Northern manifestation of the gut-wrenching Black health care needs was the overwhelming inundation by Black patients of the public facilities in Northern cities, as exemplified by the Harlem Hospital Center in New York City:

> The demands made on Harlem's out-patient clinic were staggering. From 1920 to 1932, dispensary visits increased by more than 300 per cent, from roughly 80,000 to 250,000.... [S]o overcrowded were its facilities that the syphilis clinic was forced to exclude new patients and limit old ones to no more than 300 per session. Similarly, the bed capacity of Harlem Hospital was inadequate to meet even the barest needs of the neighborhood.[98]

During the 1930s, with health foundation prodding and increasing federal support, health departments began providing some basic health services to indigent populations, with the inclusion of some Blacks, in cities such as New York, Louisville, Detroit, Baltimore, Boston, Philadelphia, Chicago, and Birmingham.

Coupled with the growth of public sector provision of health services to Blacks, the growth of what W. Montague Cobb described as the "Negro medical ghetto" proceeded. According to Black medical leader John A. Kenney, there were 225 Black hospitals by 1931. This may have been the high point, according to Cobb, for the Depression decreased these numbers to 112 by 1947. Besides providing up-to-date care to individual Black patients, African American physicians continued their strong public and community health traditions. This Black professional and hospital movement had salutary effects on the health of the African American population. As has been noted, all of these developments were associated with improved Black health status and outcomes in lieu of the Great Depression.[99]

Other legacies from the eighteenth- and nineteenth-century health systems that were reinforced in the early twentieth century were racial and medical-social attitudes. By the 1920s these negative trends, reinforced by the strong eugenics, social Darwinist, biological-determinist, IQ testing, and eugenically oriented birth control movements, threatened to dominate and ideologically distort the system's policies and practices. Poor health outcomes afflicting Blacks and the poor were thus "scientifically" rationalized as being genetically and hereditarily predetermined. Psychometric testing was projected as a "weapon" capable of sorting out the worthy (high IQ test scorers) from the unworthy. Segregation, involuntary sterilization, nihilistic public health and educational policies, and incarceration were considered "solutions" for the nation's poor, disabled, mentally challenged, or racially "inferior" populations and the problems they generated. Equitable and positive public health and health delivery programs for the entire population were viewed with suspicion and were projected as "bad things" by influential zealots spearheading these scientific racist movements. The Great Depression, however, and the rise of Hitler and Nazi Germany, which espoused similar ideologies and policies, helped mitigate the rise of these phenomena. By the end of World War II many of these activities either had gone underground or had been thoroughly discredited.[100]

Such a health system environment also helped perpetuate the U.S. tradition of misusing Black, poor, socially disadvantaged (e.g., prisoners), and disabled (e.g., mentally challenged children) patients for medical experimentation, eugenics, or demonstration purposes. These practices came to be justified and defended on the grounds of "scientific research," health professions "teaching purposes," or limiting defective genes (and shortening the welfare rolls in the process). Their medical-social or ethical implications are seldom mentioned or discussed. As late as the mid-1920s highly respected African American social scientists such as E. Franklin Frazier contended that White physicians regarded their people "simply as experimental material."[101] This gap between medical ethics and U.S. health system practices occurred on several levels, including but not limited to utilizing uninformed or poorly informed patient populations for research that could injure or, at the very least, compromise their health outcomes; performing excessive or unnecessary surgery on patients, often under coercion or without their consent, especially for eugenic purposes; overutilizing patients and tailoring their care and treatment on the basis of the professional training or research needs of the personnel or institution (i.e., for surgical, demonstration, or "teaching and training material") instead of the purely medical indications dictated by their individual case; and denying, inadequately treating, or abusing patients in need of basic care or services because they fail to have rare diseases ("uninteresting" or routine cases) or do not meet criteria for research protocols.

In the period between 1930 and 1945, the profile of this misuse and abuse changed as the research aspects of these practices became more prominent. The latter was largely a result of the Flexner/Johns Hopkins model for medical education and biomedical research that had been enacted at a network of major

American medical centers. The infamous Tuskegee sysphilis experiment, initiated in the early 1930s,* is illustrative. Not only academic physicians, such as those at prestigious academic health centers, but also government physicians at federal and state levels were more interested, and became heavily involved, in the new wave of institution-based formal scientific research. The old eighteenth- and nineteenth-century models of individual physicians conducting limited studies on small groups of patients (often their own) after office hours and publishing their results was passé. However, the ethical issues, and the tradition of overusing African American patients for these inhumane and unethical purposes, remained. Dr. John A. Kenney, one of the most influential and highly respected physicians in the United States, lent perspective to the enormity of the problem during that era. In his 1941 plea "that a monument be raised and dedicated to the nameless Negroes who have contributed so much to surgery by the 'guinea pig' route,"[102] he said:

> In our discussion of the Negro's contribution to surgery, there is one phase not to be overlooked. That is what I may vulgarly, but at the same time seriously, term the "guinea pig" phase ... one of that practically endless list of "guinea pigs." ... [U]ntold thousands of ... Negroes have been used to promote the cause of science. Many an heroic operation performed for the first time on a nameless Negro, is today classical. Even Negro physicians, surgeons and nurses, at times wince at the scenes ... of Negroes used for experimental and teaching surgery.[103]

These practices probably had more discrete rather than widespread or general adverse effects on Black health. It would become much more of a problem after World War II.[104]

The war obscured, diverted, or deemphasized most of these trends by focusing most of the national energy on winning the largest military conflict in history. Despite wartime stresses, racial segregation and discrimination remained in place in both the military and civilian health care sectors. Nevertheless, it was clear that fundamental structural and medical-social changes were needed for the African American population to achieve justice and equity in health care. Thus the "slave health deficit" continued throughout the Great Depression and World War II.[105]

---

*Initially implemented as part of a U.S. Public Health Service/Rosenwald Fund rural syphilis public health and treatment program in the late 1920s, the nontreatment phase of approximately 400 syphilitic Black men with 200 uninfected controls began in 1932 in Macon County, Alabama (Tuskegee, the county seat, is home of the famous Tuskegee Institute). The purpose was to study the effects of syphilis on untreated African American men. Fueled by patient deception, professional paternalism, blocking patients from receiving penicillin after WWII, and coming to view the patients as laboratory animals, the experiment continued for forty years. It resulted in 100 deaths from untreated syphilis, scores of blind and demented participants from the ravages of syphilis, numerous presentations at medical meetings, and more than 13 scientific papers. It was scientifically flawed from its beginnings, and most of the subjects received some treatment in order to render them noninfectious early in the study.

## Hegemony Denied: The Seeds Are Planted for White Medicine's Descent

When the Great Depression struck in 1929, White physicians and medical societies, represented by the AMA, were flushed and reinvigorated with power-enhancing constitutional and leadership changes and were waging what they considered a successful war to upgrade medical education, medical practice, and medical ethics. Just when the White medical profession could contemplate complete health system hegemony in the United States, economic and social forces generated by the Great Depression and World War II nudged this goal beyond its grasp. These two cataclysmic events shifted the nation's health agenda beyond the boundaries of what the White medical profession most wanted to preserve—traditional medical practice. In their efforts to preserve the ideological, financial, and medical-social matrix represented by "traditional medical practice," White organized medicine's concerns would shift away from medical into political matters. Organized medicine's reaction and resistance to health reform and its total rejection of universal health and hospital coverage, through compulsory health insurance or any other mechanism, would plant the seeds of its eventual capitulation to corporate control.

The Great Depression vividly demonstrated how financial and industrial collapse could endanger the personal security of the average American. Attitudes changed as most Americans who had been predisposed to libertarian-like autonomy before the Great Depression were willing to accept some government assistance in providing those personal security measures necessary to preserve "life, decency, and freedom of the individual."[106] Nevertheless, as Hirshfield pointed out, "while the reformers and their programs seemed to triumph in most areas during the . . . New Deal, one important reform was defeated. Government insurance against sickness (health insurance) was not achieved despite the best and most determined efforts of the reformers."[107] He went on to say, "During 1933 one in twenty Americans was admitted to a general hospital, the total cost of medical care to the nation was two and a third billion dollars, and fewer than 6 percent of the population had any kind of insurance to pay its medical bills."[108] Regardless of the debates about traditional medicine and individual freedom, the 1930s reality indicated that: "the public knew that medical bills were rising, that good doctors were harder to find. [W]ith the coming of the Great Depression these problems grew constantly worse, until millions began to feel . . . something extensive and immediate had to be done."[109] Physicians, represented by the AMA and the medical societies, knew the U.S. health system under the stress of the Great Depression was not working effectively. However, their commitment was to traditional medical practice built upon the conventional doctor-patient relationship, personal responsibility, individualism, and financial arrangements determined by the provider. By the 1920s medical care was already unaffordable and inaccessible to many Americans. This was due to capital-intensive technological advances in medical practice, laboratory advance, and medical specialization; the rise of impersonal institutional relationships in medicine; the maldistribution of services based on race, class, and geography; and expenses generated by highly technological, selective, and prolonged training. Responding to these pressures, physicians, the medical societies, and their representative national voice, the AMA, also knew that effective remedies had to be forthcoming.[110]

The American medical profession was also transformed by America's change from an agricultural to an industrial economy during the early twentieth century. Physicians became members of an urban industrial society dependent upon their professional competence and income. Survival depended on their becoming both professional students, to ensure their specialized knowledge, and businessmen, to thrive economically. These changes were both threatening and frightening to physicians who emotionally wanted to be viewed as rural general practitioners (GPs). This traditional medicine image was firmly grounded in the long-revered and highly valued concept of American individualism. Hirshfield described the solo GP ideal: "[H]e, despite the fact that he carried almost all his tools in his little black bag and kept his accounts in his head, supplied the best . . . of medical care to his patients. . . . [B]y fulfilling his role of family doctor, by preserving the doctor-patient relationship, and by caring for the poor and unfortunate without payment or complaint, [he] upheld the finest traditions of professional service."[111] This intimate doctor-patient relationship was an individual, personal, and reciprocal relationship built upon trust, caring, and responsibility. However, as James H. Jones later pointed out, race, and some aspects of class, constituted a "scientific blind spot" not included in most White physician's concept of the traditional medicine model.

Despite the fact that by 1930 the biomedical, behavioral, and anthropological sciences had undermined the basic tenets upon which scientific racism was based, most American physicians were still influenced by beliefs grounded in social Darwinism, theories of genetic inferiority of certain ethnic groups and races, eugenics, biological determinism, and the validity of psychometric testing. As far as Blacks were concerned, Jones observed, "Most physicians . . . continued to echo racial explanations for the high mortality rates among blacks," despite the fact that "[r]acial inferiority and moral depravity as catchall explanations had become incongruous with scientific laws upon which modern medicine rested."[112] Although a small cadre of public health and academic physicians attempted to be objective by separating their scientific opinions regarding Black and poor patients from their social prejudices, the medical-social landscape of the U.S. health system was fertile ground for future ethical breakdowns. The negative racial animus was accentuated during the Great Depression: "Because . . . physicians worked on a fee-for-service basis . . . the poverty of most blacks made them unprofitable patients. Racial prejudice also excluded many blacks from medical care, closing the doors of many private offices and hospitals alike."[113] Most Blacks fortunate enough to enter the health system at all were forced to be clients of tax-supported or privately supported public or charity clinics.

Although most doctors, motivated by their economic self-interests and pseudoscientific biases, refused to voluntarily provide adequate health care for Blacks and the poor, most physicians believed internal reform of the profession was the answer to all problems. As Jones noted:

> By the 1930s, medicine had emerged as an autonomous, self-regulating profession whose members were in firm control of the terms, conditions, content, and goal of their work. Indeed, from a sociological standpoint, medicine had emerged as the quintessential profession.... Resistance to lay control was the cornerstone of medicine.[114]

Virtually all White doctors believed that external problems based on the high demand, high costs, and maldistribution of medical services would respond to discrete, temporary reforms and rearrangements of the present system. Comprehensive health system overhaul, as proposed by the health reformers, embodying compulsory health insurance and universal access to care and hospitalization was not viewed as necessary. They preached and promoted this ideology throughout their professional and nonprofessional confederacy, which at times included the American Public Health Association, some organized hospital associations, and elements of the U.S. Public Health Service. Changing the health system's structural and medical-social defects relative to its history-based race and class problems was never an issue on their agenda.[115]

Medical reformers viewed the threatened collapse of the health system generated by the Great Depression as an opportunity to overhaul the system. On the other hand, the medical profession, shaken and made insecure by the Depression, felt it had to fight to preserve their control and the ideals of traditional medicine. Both sides hardened their positions. Beginning in 1912, swept up in the Progressive movement, White organized medicine had resigned itself to the implementation of some form of compulsory, or what they sometimes called social or government-guaranteed, insurance. By 1917, even the American Hospital Association, twenty state medical societies, and the National Organization for Public Health Nurses endorsed the American Association of Labor Legislation's (AALL) model bill. These proposals would entitle virtually every American to health care, hospital coverage, and some type of sickness benefit. Due to a combination of public apathy (intensified by World War I), interest group resistance, and increasing opposition rising from the White medical establishment, all efforts to implement compulsory health insurance or progressive health legislation were defeated (see Appendix 2-A). The medical profession led the fight for this resistance, especially after 1917.[116]

The CCMC report was released by 1932. This massive 28-volume report, the largest analysis ever of health care in America, revealed that the U.S. health system was in a shambles. The study, in process since 1927, revealed that health care was prohibitively expensive, maldistributed, and unavailable on both financial and demographic grounds to large segments of the population. It created an uproar. The expert panelists drawn from the medical, public health, and economic communities disagreed sharply on recommendations for corrective action.

Early in the 1920s, physicians, the medical societies, and the AMA had focused on articulating that organized medicine "opposes . . . state treatment of disease, except (a) in the institutional care of the delinquent, diseased, and defective; (b) the treatment of those diseases whose treatment is essential to prevention; (c) the recognition and securing the correction of common defects of school-children."[117] Such a limited program essentially ignored Blacks, the poor, underemployed or unemployed Americans, or even middle-class citizens faced with catastrophic illness. The AMA-led campaign went so far as to criticize and denigrate the highly prestigious CCMC health study, a product of five years of work by 45 nationally respected experts in finance, medicine, and public health funded with over $1 million dollars provided by eight private foundations. Dr. Morris Fishbein editorialized on the largest scientific study of the health care system up to that time: "One must review the expenditure of almost a million dollars by the committee . . . with mingled amusement and regret. A colored boy spent a dollar taking twenty rides on the merry-go-round. When he got off, his mammy said, 'Boy, you spent yo' money but where you been?'"[118] (See Figure 2.2.) The use of derogatory racial stereotypes

**Figure 2.2 Morris Fishbein (1889–1976)**
(Right) Physician and editor of *JAMA*, for almost three decades, vigorously opposed government aid in medical care and prepaid, group practice, which he denounced as "socialized medicine."
Reproduced from Campion Frank D. *The AMA and U.S. Health Policy Since 1940.* Chicago: Chicago Review Press for the American Medical Association, 1984, 110.

and Negro dialect in an important health policy article in one of America's most prestigious medical journals indicates a great deal about the racial attitudes of the leadership of White organized medicine in the mid-1930s. By the end of the 1920s the AMA and its medical establishment had fought and defeated the Sheppard-Towner Act, an effective program for poor mothers and children, and had limited the health program for veterans. Thus, the 1935 defeat of the health care component of the President's Committee on Economic Security, which originally favored some form of national health insurance, was the culmination of a trend.

Disagreement on the CCMC report was so sharp that majority and minority reports had to be issued in 1932. As Hirshfield described: "The Majority Report, an essentially weak and conciliatory document, proposed that voluntary health insurance experiments be tried and stated that: 'The costs of medical care should be distributed over groups of people and over periods of time, through the use of insurance, taxation, or both.'"[119] The Minority Report (See Summaries of Majority and Minority CCMC Reports in Appendix 2-B), which was dominated by the views of the White medical professional establishment,

> *bitterly criticized the majority recommendations on health insurance. It condemned both voluntary and compulsory insurance and warned of the dangers of group practice and professional reorganization. The Minority Report also criticized and called for an end to the limited governmental programs that had been started in the 1920s to help veterans and children and called for the restoration of the general practitioner "to the central place in medical practice."*[120]

Morris Fishbein, the volatile editor of *JAMA*, brought the conflict to a flash point with an emotional, attack-laden article on the signers of the Majority Report, and irresponsibly linked them with communism:

> *These two reports represent . . . the difference between incitement to revolution and a desire for gradual evolution based on analysis. . . . [T]he alignment is clear—on one side the forces representing the great foundations, public health officialdom, social theory—even socialism and communism—inciting to revolution; on the other side, the organized medical profession . . . urging an orderly evolution guided by controlled experimentation which will observe the principles which have been found through the centuries to be necessary to the sound practice of medicine.*[121]

This muckraking article had been approved by the AMA's board. Fishbein also branded the majority report as "incitement to revolution" and the group practice prepayment plans as being "medical soviets." He made these statements without acknowledging the 28 studies upon which the recommendations for the final report were based.[122] This explosive rhetoric completely ruptured most illusions of cooperation that had previously existed between the reformer and medical society factions for the previous two decades, and represented White organized medicine's rightward reactionary shift over the last decade.[123]

Social Security, which was based on CES research and recommendations, was passed with the limited health care components alluded to earlier. This was the Roosevelt administration's response to the health establishment's backlash. However, the alarm created by the government push for compulsory health insurance within the CES triggered an unprecedented emergency meeting of the AMA house of delegates in 1934. The "Ten Principles" (see Appendix 2-B) formulated "were guidelines for the establishment of group payment indemnity plans to be controlled in all respects by the local medical societies."[124] These principles, which would shape AMA policy in the long term, demanded complete physician control of any medical services program, preservation of traditional doctor-patient relationships, and freedom of choice for patients and providers. This was tantamount to the government sanctioning the continued lockout of African American patients and providers from the mainstream health system. To accomplish their goals, Dr. John A. Kingsbury, ex-commissioner of charities of New York City, pointed out that the AMA and its constituent bodies "sought to use personal influence on those in high places, have spent thousands of dollars in publicity campaigns of misinformation, have spread false rumors, and have resorted to scurvy attack on personalities."[125] Government programs and private group practices were still considered unacceptable in the United States health system. There is no evidence that these developments factored in the rampant race and class segregation and discrimination plaguing the system.[126]

Meanwhile, critically needed medical relief programs were being implemented through FERA, CWA, WPA, and FSA. Although a veneer of cooperation with the AMA was obtained, the local and state medical societies complained about, sabotaged, and openly fought many of these programs at the local level. This stance was not exclusive to physicians, as Clifton O. Dummett pointed out: "The American Dental Association, by official action, opposed compulsory health insurance and insisted that American dentistry was against any form of compulsory dental services."[127] The fact that the Depression meant that these programs were now serving not only the poor but also millions of their previously middle-class patients modulated their resistance. Even though the AMA had kept national health insurance out of the Social Security Act: "[P]assage of the act without the national health-insurance section pleased the A.M.A., but the organization was distraught with the provision for federal aid to the states to support dependent children and to provide medical care for mothers and newborn infants."[128] The most impassioned outcry was against the rural medical cooperatives established for poor farm families in cooperation with the FSA. Physicians who cooperated with any prepaid group or cooperative practices were harassed professionally, denied AMA membership, and threatened with being stripped of their medical licenses. Physician, medical society, and AMA behavior was so egregious in many of these instances that White organized medicine lost a series of criminal lawsuits, beginning with the Group Health Association (GHA) case* in 1941, which was upheld by the U.S. Supreme Court in 1943. Nevertheless, the Depression had revealed cracks in White organized medicine's united front against compulsory health insurance. Movements in California (1935), New York (1936), and Rhode Island (1936), all with some medical society support, had to be quelled by the AMA.[129]

Although the racial problems in the health system had not been appropriately considered or addressed, the host of public and private programs had permanently altered the economic and social dimensions of the Depression health crisis by 1935. Nevertheless, the programs failed to address the underlying causes of the failure to provide adequate care to the poor, the unemployed, African Americans, the underemployed, poor farmers, and growing numbers of middle-class families. This was part of the reason for the formation of President Roosevelt's Interdepartmental Committee to Coordinate Health and Welfare Activities late in 1935. Created to coordinate the expanded health and welfare activities of various federal agencies, it represented a second effort at establishing a national health program. After a successful year of interagency coordinating, early in 1937 the interdepartmental committee began surveying the nation's health needs and developing a national health program based on these findings. Building upon Social Security health programs already in place, the Committee formulated programs for public health, maternal and infant hygiene, aid to disabled and blind children, hospital construction, compulsory health insurance, tax-supported medical care, and temporary disability insurance. Buoyed by the effects of the Depression on the national medical crisis and the widespread acceptance of the Social Security and emergency government-sponsored health measures, the reformers felt the time was, once more, ripe for reform.

The new political strategy was based upon anticipated public readiness to accept government health insurance, uniting government agencies into a pro-insurance alliance, and educating and influencing public opinion about the virtues of a nationalized, unitary, compulsory health system. Reformers felt that proper unity and mobilization would ensure passage. However, due to the strategic naïveté and political timidity of the Technical Committee on Medical Care subcommittee of the interdepartmental committee, in the plan presented at the National Health Conference at Washington's Mayflower Hotel on July 18, 1938, the health insurance proposals (compulsory health insurance, tax-supported medical care, and temporary disability insurance) and aid to the medically indigent (Recommendation III) had been deemphasized to the point of oblivion.[130]

At odds were the reformers versus the White medical establishment and American public's views on the role of government in national health policy. Physicians,

---

*GHA was harassed by the local medical society to such an extent that it encountered difficulty in hiring and maintaining its salaried medical staff. GHA sued the District of Columbia Medical Society and won on anti-trust grounds.

the medical and most of the health professions societies, and the AMA felt that the federal government should serve as no more than brokers and facilitators of health reform proposals presented by private interests, individuals, or professional groups. The White medical establishment felt that the government should never be involved in health policy formulation, promotion, implementation, or direct administration. It was felt that such activism on the government's part could lead to totalitarianism. The public's views were not so extreme. Chastened by the Depression experience, the American public still felt that a government "takeover" of the health system was extreme and that the discrete, stop-gap measures and conservative government programs like Social Security should be given a chance to solve the nation's health crisis. In contrast to Europeans, Americans held on to the belief that health care provision was a personal, not social, responsibility. It was not until the post–New Deal, post–World War II era that the average American began accepting the idea of individual security as an essential element of individual freedom.

The reformers' concept of freedom included the sacrifice of small amounts of personal freedom, such as compulsory participation in a health plan, in exchange for the social good of high-quality health care for all. This belief system was ahead of that of most Americans. This contrasted strongly with anti-insurance forces' contention that absolute freedom was the only mechanism allowing for progress and problem-solving in a democratic society. Blacks, based on their harsh experiences as victims of *de jure* and *de facto* racial segregation and discrimination for over three centuries, were always on the sidelines during these White ideological personal freedom, radical individualism, and states' rights arguments. This four-year round (1935–1939) of conflict between the reformers and White organized medicine regarding another effort to introduce compulsory health insurance, led by the president's advisors, government agencies, and a cadre of progressive health and public policy foundations and their progressive leaders and adherents, was also doomed to fail. African American professional groups had been invited to health policy conferences for appearance's sake as early as 1931 by the Hoover administration. However, for the first time African American physicians and their professional associations would be invited by the Roosevelt administration actively to participate in conferences that significantly impacted the health system.[131]

Resistance measures by the anti-insurance foes were effective. Despite President Roosevelt's lukewarm support for extending the health provisions of Social Security, by December 1939 the National Health Program, which had been taken up by New York Senator Robert F. Wagner as a *cause célèbre*, was killed. The reformers' acceptance of the feigned negotiation efforts of the AMA and its functionaries as genuine cooperation proved politically naïve. Applying political pressure through letter-writing campaigns and backdoor meetings on Capitol Hill had proved effective for the medical lobby. The health reformers had learned a lesson. Instead of compromising with the AMA, hospital associations, and professional groups, as they had done with the Wagner Bill, the next effort should be a comprehensive, federally administered health care program. Weak and permissive health legislation with federal-state approaches and heavy overlays of professional supervision would never pass. The battle would resume, after a pause, as the Wagner-Murray-Dingell Bill, a comprehensive government-run compulsory health program. It was introduced initially in 1943 and biannually throughout the decade.[132]

Beginning in 1937 the AMA fought the second round of Roosevelt administration efforts at national health reform with a panoply of methods. In the process, White organized medicine helped define the art of political lobbying for the future. Some of the techniques employed by the medical profession and its cabal included, but were not limited to, hiring advertising agencies to coordinate their political and public relations campaigns; creating and utilizing propaganda and disinformation in their campaigns; regularly practicing political persecution, intimidation, and repression of those who disagreed; performing and promoting false and inaccurate research and disseminating the results; compromising the AMA membership's medical judgments for political ends; displaying overtly racist metaphors in their writings; establishing questionable political front groups to perform unsavory political functions such as propaganda dissemination; and regularly practicing demagoguery by identifying and associating health reform with subversion of the government and soviet-style communism. One example was the propaganda campaign attempting to discredit the National Health Survey released in 1938. Under the Public Health Service this carefully conducted 740,000-home survey involving 2.3 million persons documented the health deprivation of 40 million Americans. Disingenuously refuting the results, the AMA's Bureau of Medical Economics released a 1939 report based on questionnaires submitted by local medical associations and physicians. This report purportedly proved that only 40,000, not 40 million, persons, were denied medical service (African Americans alone represented more than 10 million!). This was not the only propaganda measure. To protect its tax-exempt status as a nonpolitical organization, the AMA set up a "front group," the National Physicians Committee (NPC). Financed by the AMA and pharmaceutical houses, the NPC engaged in frank propaganda, exaggerations, and scare tactics. NPC behavior was so egregious that the New York public relations firm Raymond Rich Associates refused to represent the AMA after a 17-month stint unless it severed its ties with the NPC. The firm's resignation letter stated:

> The very integrity and sincerity of the association are at stake.... [S]tated simply, the association has yet to take unequivocal and effective action on the policies which it adopted on our recommendations last year [1948]: to seek the truth on economic and social aspect of medicine, to put the public first, and to become adequate to its responsibilities.[133]

White organized medicine had entered the 1930s with wide-ranging political and social influence largely grounded in public trust. By 1945, as the nation entertained the adoption of some type of national health plan, physicians, medical societies, and the AMA were viewed with growing distrust by the public, who felt the profession had evolved into a self-promoting interest group. In the process, it had become the model of effective political lobbying on Capitol Hill and the nation's state capitols and statehouses.[134]

---

## Black Doctors Come of Age: Fighting Back for Black Patients during the Depression and the War, 1930–1945

> *Black physicians ... not only helped deliver the babies in their communities; they also assisted at the birth of the civil rights struggle in the United States. Without their help the civil rights struggle would have been stillborn.*
>
> DAVID BARTON SMITH, *HEALTH CARE DIVIDED*

African American physicians constituted between 2 and 3 percent (they reached 2.5 percent in 1910) of the U.S. medical profession between 1930 and 1945. By the third decade of the century the effects of Flexner reform were strongly felt by the African American community. There were fewer African American physicians, a growing Black population, and escalating Black physician–to–Black patient ratios. By 1930 the number of Black doctors had declined from 3,855 in 1920 to 3,770 in 1930. The slight numerical increase to 3,810 by 1942 represented a relative decline to 2.1 percent of 180,496 U.S. physicians. Black physician–to–Black patient ratios, which had been 1:3,194 in 1925, climbed to 1:3,770 in 1930 and 1:3,810 in 1942. These trends, demonstrating the greater adverse impact of Flexner reform and the Great Depression on the health circumstance of the African American population, forced some government and foundation support for Meharry and Howard, the remaining Black medical schools.[135]

This era could be viewed as a preparatory or threshold era for the Civil Rights era and for African American entry into the mainstream health system. Such a view proved overly optimistic as the effects of racism and classism on the U.S. health system's culture and medical-social structure proved much more intransigent and resistant to change than those in the educational or legal systems. However, as will become obvious as the story unfolds, the health system's institutional progress for Black American patients produced a paradoxically precarious position for African American physicians and health professionals. As Myrdal pointed out about the era:

> *The prospects of the Negro physician are becoming increasingly uncertain because of the present growth of all kinds of public health facilities. This trend cannot fail to take the low income clientele away from the private practitioner, and this, of course, means that the Negro doctor may lose all his patients unless he is given a place in the new public health system.*[136]

Thus the potential proffered by an open health system in the services sector might also prove to be a threat eliminating Black health providers (physicians, dentists, nurses, hospitals).

If the traditional African American health professional and provider exclusion and discrimination from participation were perpetuated, all Black patients who had previously been forced to utilize the segregated and discriminatory health services and "Negro medical ghetto" sectors would be taken away by White professionals and their institutions. For a culturally competent and inclusive transformation to occur, a place had to be made in the system for African American heath providers. Social scientists noted:

> *Many Negro doctors, particularly in the South, are quite pessimistic about their chances of getting such a place, and, for this reason one sometimes finds the most ardent opponents of any program of "socialized medicine" among Negro doctors. They are undoubtedly right in assuming that an extension of the public health services to low income families would constitute a tremendous risk from their point of view.*[137]

Thus the strain of Black opposition to progressive health policy that persisted throughout the period from 1930 through 1945 is comprehensible. Nevertheless, despite personal and professional risks, African American physicians and allied health professionals responded to positive, and sometimes heroic, leadership in their ranks and advocated for the needs of their people and through organizations such as the National Medical Association (NMA), National Dental Association (NDA), and National Association of Colored Graduate Nurses (NACGN), allied with the National Association for the Advancement of Colored People (NAACP), the NAACP Legal Defense and Educational Fund (LDF, or "Inc. Fund," incorporated 1939),* and the National Urban League (NUL). This largely untold story of Black health professionals' crusade for justice and equity in health and health care constituted a vital part of African American health professional organization's maturation and transformation into vital forces for change in the United States.[138]

African American medical professionals underwent other important changes between 1930 and 1945. Although at lower levels than at White schools, the effects of foundation support on the two remaining Black medical schools began to be felt. Some evidences of this were the dedication of Howard University's new $500,000 medical school building in 1928 and the opening of Meharry's completely new $2 million plant in 1933. Such logistical support, along with faculty education upgrading under the leadership of Dean Numa P. G. Adams, the

---

*LDF was incorporated in 1939 to receive tax-deductible contributions for those areas of the NAACP's work that met the Internal Revenue Service's guidelines. It was tied to the parent body by interlocking boards.

new Black dean at Howard, and presidents John J. Mullowney and Edward Lewis Turner at Meharry, buttressed by Meharry's first Black dean, Dr. Michael J. Bent, led to marked improvements in the overall quality of Black physicians. Over the years these programs were financed and promoted by the National Research Council (NRC), General Education Board (GEB), and the Carnegie Foundation for the Advancement of Teachers (CFAT). One-fourth of Howard's and nearly one-half of Meharry's graduates had to retake their state licensing examinations before the 1930s. This proved that medical education could not fully compensate for the fundamental educational deprivation to which African Americans were subjected. By 1935, Meharry and Howard graduates showed consistently lower than 10 percent failures.[139] Harvard's and Washington University's state medical examination failure rates averaged 6 to 7 percent, while Southern White medical schools averaged 13 percent during this era. Factoring in systematic Black educational disadvantage, these academic feats were remarkable. Such improvements in scientific competency and educational performance undoubtedly had a great deal to do with the rising confidence of the African American medical profession between 1930 and 1945.[140]

Other qualities such as political activism and civil rights advocacy, which began with abolitionist physicians such as James McCune Smith, Martin Robison Delany, and Sarah Parker Remond, became prominent again. Not since the 1840s debates between James McCune Smith and then–Secretary of State John C. Calhoun regarding alleged Black biological inferiority had African American physicians assumed such a strong public posture in defense of their people. Borne of the peculiar American reality of a racially separate medical profession, the quiet resistance and organizing of the Reconstruction, post-Reconstruction, and early twentieth century gave way to the resurgence of open criticism of health discrimination and proselytizing for health care as a human right in the 1930s. As early as the turn of the century, advocacy by African American physicians such as Henry Butler of Atlanta had begun focusing on the structural inequalities of the health system, discriminatory medical treatment, and making recommendations for correction. Quietly, the scientific and public health–oriented thrust of the Black profession continued as the NMA organized pellagra, tuberculosis, and hookworm commissions; founded a Black hospital movement; and emphasized public health throughout the World War I years and the 1920s. Subdued and subtle approaches to the Black health crisis yielded to more confrontational and strident measures in the 1930s and 1940s.[141]

The typical African American physician between 1930 and 1945 was a Meharry graduate practicing in the largely rural South or a Howard graduate practicing in the urban North. Molded in a professional tradition of serving the underserved and spurred on by activists such as Mordecai Johnson, Howard University's first African American president, Black doctor's applied their already eleemosynary and missionary tendencies to the Depression. Beardsley remarks about Black physicians of the era:

> To black Southern doctors' credit, many did considerable charity and
> public health work. In the period before World War II half the patients of
> rural black doctors were charity cases.... [P]hysicians contributed
> substantially to preventive medicine, vaccination of children and running
> prenatal and adult clinics—nearly always for free.[142]

African American physicians continued to present a distinct profile even after the wartime economic boom and increasing government pressures against racial discrimination had set in. As Dr. Paul Cornely pointed out in the *JNMA*, the post–World War II African American physician had an annual gross income of $10,267 and spent longer hours in his office and saw more patients than his White colleague. Nevertheless, his income was 25–30 percent lower because of the predominance of poor patients in his practice (see Figure 2.3). As the era progressed, Black doctors became involved in far more than rendering otherwise unavailable health services to their communities.

Spurred by dynamic national leaders such as Drs. C. V. Roman, John A. Kenney, Paul Cornely, Peter M. Murray, and Midian O. Bousefield, African American physicians shed their low-profile and sometimes obsequious postures to attack the structural and medical-social problems plaguing the health system—including segregation. Often during this process, they inadvertently emerged as community leaders. They began to feel a sense of confidence and responsibility regarding health and medical-social matters affecting the African American community. Although they were systematically excluded from local White medical societies, hospital staffs, and most postgraduate training programs, many Black doctors overcame some effects of their professional isolation and carved out singular niches in their communities.

**Figure 2.3 Paul Cornely (1906– )**
Physician and epidemiologist based at Howard University Medical School, Cornely led in documenting the poor health status and outcomes of African Americans from the 1940s through the 1970s and subsequently became the first Black president of the American Public Health Association.

Reproduced from Morais HM. *The History of the Negro in Medicine.* New York: Publishers Company, Inc., 1967, 100.

## John Andrew Kenney, M.D., 1874–1950: The National Medical Association's Twentieth-Century Man

Born on June 11, 1874, in Albermarle County, Virginia, the son of John and Caroline Kenney, John Andrew Kenney served two generations of patients and physicians in the health system. Although he was able in both mind and body, his greatest gifts were of the spirit. Dr. Kenney had a compelling sense of duty; a tremendous capacity for work; a long- and short-term vision for both the Black and White medical professions and the patients they cared for; indefatigability coupled with flexibility, a brilliant and eclectic intellect, and a capacity for tremendous self-sacrifice. Utilizing his gifts, he facilitated African American health and medical progress in the early twentieth century that would not have occurred without his leadership, and allowed Black organized medicine (still the chief avenue for people of color and the underserved in regards to the U.S. health system) to remodel itself into a modern, survivable entity that could represent these constituencies into the twenty-first century.

Graduated as valedictorian at Hampton Institute in 1897, Kenney earned his M.D. degree from Leonard Medical School at Shaw University in Raleigh, North Carolina, in 1901. Between 1901 and 1902 Kenney completed an internship at Freedmen's Hospital of Howard University. Responding to Booker T. Washington's invitation, Kenney accepted the positions as medical director, chief surgeon, and school physician for Tuskegee Institute Hospital and its affiliated institutions and

**Figure 2.4 John A. Kenney (1874–1950)**
Physician and editor of the *Journal of the National Medical Association* for over thirty years, Kenney led the crusade for justice and equity in health and health care for all Americans in the first half of the twentieth century.

Courtesy of Meharry Medical College, Black Medical History Archive Collection, Meharry Medical College Library, Kresge Learning Resources Center, Nashville, Tennessee.

nursing program in 1902. An energetic administrator, he reorganized the school of nursing and established the John A. Andrew Clinic (1912) and the John A. Andrew Clinical Society (1918) to perpetuate the clinic. Until well into the 1960s these bodies served patients within hundreds of miles of Tuskegee Institute; the clinic was one of the few institutions where Black physicians could acquire new knowledge and experience in their fields. His efforts led to the building in 1912 of the John A. Andrew Memorial Hospital at Tuskegee, a modern multistory facility with up-to-date wards, classrooms, and operating rooms.

Meanwhile, during his tenure as general secretary (1904–1912) for the NMA, he and Dr. Henry F. Gamble of Charleston, West Virginia, drew up plans for the publication of a medical journal (1908) for the NMA board. For 39 years, Dr. Kenney served as either associate editor (1909–1916), editor (1916–1948), or business manager for the *Journal of the National Medical Association* (*JNMA*), the oldest continuously published African American periodical. (See Figure 2.4.) At Tuskegee he published one of the first monographs detailing early Black participation in the medical profession, *The Negro in Medicine* (1912). After heading the NMA's Hookworm Commission (1910), Dr. Kenney was elected fourteenth president of the organization (1912).

Everything Kenney did was focused in some way on improving the health of all Americans and upgrading the quality of Black performance in the medical profession. Improved preparation and equipment meant better patient outcomes, so he felt African American physicians were obligated to become well trained and cognizant of the latest medical practices. He influenced Booker T. Washington to initiate National Negro Health Week (1915), an observance everyone agrees had salutary effects on the nation's health for decades. During his tenure with *JNMA*, Kenney kept the journal afloat financially, sometimes making national tours to raise contributions and generate subscriptions himself. Moreover, he made contact at the nation's leading medical institutions with White medical leaders such as Drs. George Crile and Howard A. Kelley of Cleveland's Lakeside Hospital and Johns Hopkins Hospital in Baltimore, respectively, sharing professional and collegial concerns. His ability to win over friends to his cause of Black patients and doctors was irreplaceable in the hostile social and professional environments in which African Americans functioned. However, Dr. Kenney occasionally paid a dear price for adherence to his idealism and high principles.

When arrangements between Tuskegee Institute and the federal government for the construction of a Veteran's Administration (VA) hospital for blacks on institute land were completed in 1922, Dr. Kenney advocated for an African American staff. Local White leaders, some openly affiliated with the Ku Klux Klan, insisted the staff be White. A series of meetings with Tuskegee's administration and local leaders led to confrontations and Klan parades at the institute and, finally, a cross-burning in Dr. Kenney's front yard. Kenney sent his family north after one of his White patients warned him that the Klan intended to kill him. Invited to live with NMA Executive Board Chairman Dr. George Cannon, Kenney led outraged NMA members in meetings with President Warren G. Harding. After several conferences with the president,

VA head General Hines, and an NMA committee, Black personnel staffing the hospital was agreed upon. Dr. Kenney returned to Tuskegee two months later, resigned after a year, and moved to Newark, New Jersey, on September 1, 1924, where he established a private practice.

Unaccustomed to being denied hospital privileges because of his race, the indefatigable Dr. Kenney opened the thirty-bed Kenney Memorial Hospital (1927) in Newark, named in honor of his parents. He ran the institution virtually by himself until 1934, after which he turned it over to the Black community of northern New Jersey, represented by the Booker T. Washington Community Hospital Association. It was renamed Community Hospital, and he served as its medical director until 1939, when he returned to Tuskegee. The hospital he founded survived into the 1950s, providing a practice and training base for several board-certified surgeons. Serving Tuskegee as medical director for five more years, Dr. Kenney went into semi-retirement in Montclair, New Jersey, in 1944. He resigned suddenly as editor of his beloved *JNMA* in 1948, two years before his death from a cerebral hemorrhage.

Strongly influenced by Booker T. Washington, George Washington Carver, and Daniel Hale Williams, Kenney placed Black community health interests first. When segregation was in full swing he pushed for excellent Black hospitals capable of providing training slots to African American medical graduates. When his own medical school alma mater, Leonard, was closed by Flexner educational reform, he pushed harder for support of Howard and Meharry. Because continuing medical education and postgraduate training were virtually closed to Black physicians while he lived, he founded the John Andrew clinics to compensate for professional educational discrimination. When the federal government made efforts to implement a national health system in the 1930s and 1940s, Kenney saw it as beneficial to Black patients and supported it. His courageous defiance of the Ku Klux Klan and founding of Black self-help organizations and institutions was inspirational. But his spirit and character were deeper than that. Dr. Kenney was an innately quiet "doer" driven by an enduring devotion to his ideals, pragmatism, and the community good. The world was unquestionably a different and better place because he lived. Some might say he had been chosen by a higher power to be Black medicine's leader in troubled times—truly serving as the NMA's "Twentieth-Century Man."

### Notes

Alexander PN. Kenney, John Andrew. In: Salzman J, Smith DL, West C., eds. *Encyclopedia of African-American Culture and History* (5 Vols). New York: Macmillan Library Reference USA, Simon and Schuster Macmillan, 1996, p. 153.

Announcement. The John A. Andrew Memorial Hospital, Tuskegee Institute, Alabama. *Journal of the National Medical Association* 1918; 10:xx.

Announcement. The Annual Clinic of the John A. Andrew Memorial Hospital, Tuskegee Institute, Alabama. *Journal of the National Medical Association* 1918; 10:43.

Cobb WM. John Andrew Kenney, M.D., 1874–1950. *Journal of the National Medical Association* 1950; 42:175–177.

Du Bois WEB. Opinion: The Tuskegee hospital. *The Crisis* 1923; 26:106–107.

Du Bois WEB. Opinion: Tuskegee and Moton. *The Crisis* 1924; 28:200–202.

Hospital for ex-service men to be at Tuskegee. *Journal of the National Medical Association* 1922; 14:208.

Items of interest: Item 7, Medical School of Shaw University. *Journal of the National Medical Association* 1912; 4:96–97.

Kenney JA. *The Negro in Medicine*. Tuskegee: Tuskegee Institute Press, 1912.

Kenney JA. The passing of the Leonard Medical School. *Journal of the National Medical Association* 1918; 10:126.

Kenney JA. Some facts concerning Negro nurse training schools and their graduates. *Journal of the National Medical Association* 1919; 11:53–68.

Kenney JA. The editor afield. *Journal of the National Medical Association* 1920; 12:24–27.

Kenney JA. Howard University School of Medicine. *Journal of the National Medical Association* 1920; 12:30–31.

Kenney JA. Hospital symposium: The Negro hospital renaissance. *Journal of the National Medical Association* 1930; 22:109–157.

Kenney JA. A brief history of the origin of the John A. Andrew Clinics by the founder. *Journal of the National Medical Association* 1934; 26:65–68.

Kenney JA. The National Health Act of 1939. *Journal of the National Medical Association* 1939; 31:154–160.

Kenney JA. Senator Wagner says non-governmental hospitals are eligible for support under his bill. Negroes are protected. *Journal of the National Medical Association* 1939; 31:173–177.

McBride D. Inequality in the availability of Black physicians. *New York State Journal of Medicine* 1985; 85:139–142.

Morais HM. *The History of the Negro in Medicine*. New York: Publishers Company, 1967.

Sixth annual clinic: John A. Andrew Memorial Hospital, Tuskegee Institute, Alabama. *Journal of the National Medical Association* 1917; 9:109–112.

To counteract the effects of their patients being excluded from or relegated to overtly inferior health facilities, Black physicians led a movement to erect Black hospitals, especially in the South. Nevertheless, marked discrepancies in hospital and health services availability for African Americans remained. As P. Preston Reynolds pointed out, even highly regarded Blacks were placed at risk in the United States health system:

> *Near Dalton, Georgia, a woman was injured in a car crash. The closest hospital advertised "no Negroes," so an ambulance was summoned from 66 miles away to take her to the closest hospital that treated black persons. The woman, Juliette Dericotte, died. She had been a national YWCA executive and Dean of Women at Hampton and Fisk College.*[143]

Walter White's father-in-law, a Black person with nearly White physical features, died at Atlanta's Grady Municipal Hospital under suspicious circumstances following an automobile accident. He had been "wheeled across the street through the rain to the black ward in the old building"[144] after hospital officials discovered his racial origins. The White physician's response upon making the discovery: "What! Have we put a nigger in the white ward?"[145] Walter White later became the executive director of the NAACP and worked alongside Black physicians such as

Louis T. Wright and W. Montague Cobb to dismantle racial segregation and discrimination in the health system. If African Americans of privileged circumstances were experiencing such maltreatment in the health system, one can imagine what the majority of the Black population endured.

Black physicians such as Dr. Matilda Evans of South Carolina opened pioneer hospitals and free maternal and child-care clinics (1930) that laid the groundwork for Depression-triggered public health programs in South Carolina. Dr. L. W. Long, a Meharry graduate, established a sorely needed Black hospital in Union, South Carolina, in 1931. By 1932 he had reinvigorated the state NMA constituent body, providing annual clinics for Black physicians that endured into the 1970s. He also served as a liaison with the White medical establishment at the medical school, legislative, and medical society levels, leading to eventual integration and increased African American participation in that state. Another Meharry graduate, Dr. Pierce Moten, had a leadership role in the opening of a vitally needed Black hospital in Birmingham, Alabama, in the 1920s. In response to a Black mother giving birth on a Birmingham sidewalk, he established the Southside Clinic for maternal and infant care in 1937. It would receive national recognition and foundation support.

Meanwhile, in St. Louis, Missouri, despite the Great Depression and a conundrum of local politics, Black hospital movement events were afoot that would not only improve African American access to quality health care throughout the Midwest, but would also elevate the profile of Black and disadvantaged people's health nationally. In the wake of a successful campaign the previous decade to establish a city hospital for treating indigent Black patients, training Black nurses, and allowing African American physicians a site for training and practice, City Hospital No. 2 had opened in 1919. Patient overcrowding, technical inadequacies, and the national attraction generated by postgraduate and specialty training programs* for Black physicians quickly overwhelmed the secondhand facility,** leading to agitation for a new physical plant. A movement beginning in 1921 that became associated with a prominent young Black lawyer named Homer G. Phillips culminated in the opening of a modern 685-bed hospital facility in 1937 that established a new era of medical care for St. Louis's African American patient and professional communities and became a national resource for Black postgraduate medical training. Its contribution surpassed the indefatigable Phillips's dream of upgrading Black patient care and producing stellar African American specialist physicians and health professionals (tragically, Phillips was the

---

*There is evidence that City Hospital No. 2 had an accredited surgical residency program as early as 1927. Some of the first Black radiologists in America received their initial training in this facility. By 1930 St. Louis was one of less than half a dozen sites in the United States where African American physicians could receive recognized specialty training.

**The "new" Black facility occupied buildings formerly used by Barnes Medical College at the corner of Lawton and Garrison avenues.

victim of an unsolved assassination on June 18, 1931). Strongly affiliated with Washington University School of Medicine, with some early associations with St. Louis University, Homer G. Phillips Hospital (1937–1979) became one of the largest sites of postgraduate professional training for African Americans for more than 40 years. It is questionable whether its production of excellently trained African American surgeons, orthopedic surgeons, urologists, ophthalmologists, internists, dermatologists, pediatricians, dental surgeons, nurses, and allied health professions has ever been replaced since its closure in 1979. Certainly, the output of these valuable health professionals in St. Louis and surrounding areas has slowed to a trickle.[146]

Several aspects of this transformation of Black medicine fed into, and indeed may have been triggered by, changes taking place at the national level. Much of this transformation was related to and promoted by the evolution of the NMA into a vehicle for progressive medical and medical-social change. "Although there was no evidence that Association appeals had any direct impact on health policy in the early twentieth-century South, criticism was valuable at least in raising the sights of black professionals and in challenging the smug contention of whites that blacks created their own problems."[147] African American national medical leaders, always affiliated with the NMA, became prominent at the ideological, political, policy, and programmatic levels. They began to objectively criticize and mobilize to change the dual and discriminatory health system.[148]

During the 1920s and 1930s, the NMA received a harsh message based on the White medical establishment's response to its World War I protests against racial discrimination and the repeated efforts of Black doctors to desegregate local medical societies and to cooperate with White organized medicine in hospital and medical school standardization efforts. Traditionally, the AMA ignored Black physicians, overtly discriminated against them, or thwarted their efforts at professional participation at any level. An embarrassing 1939 rebuff to NMA efforts at professional fairness and participation through cooperative national health planning in 1939 "revealed that when the test came the AMA would choose racial separatism over medical advance."[149] By 1939 even the Nazis had noted the disparate treatment meted out to Black physicians by the AMA when "Germany's foremost racial hygiene journal reported on the refusal of the American Medical Association to admit black physicians,"[150] Proctor observed.

Seemingly, during this era the AMA attempted to lure Black doctors to its side in the fight against any national health plan. Failing to accomplish this, it forgot its promises to negotiate the desegregation of county medical societies, to consider removing the "col." designation (an abbreviation denoting African American physicians) from the names of the few Black physicians on AMA rosters, or to contemplate ensuring African American representation in the AMA house of delegates.

This kind of internecine professional warfare was especially tragic for African American patients, who had only Black physicians to represent them in the system.

However, by the 1930s the nature of this unhealthy relationship between Black and White medicine changed for the better. As Beardsley pointed out, "Had the NMA not spoken out, Southern blacks would have had no one to voice their health needs, for local medical organizations were hardly free to offer that kind of sustained criticism. And if Southern officials were unwilling to listen, there were those in the North who would."[151] As late medical leader Dr. W. Montague Cobb articulated in an interview, Black doctors had decided they had to "raise Hell" to get what they and their patients wanted. This ideological shift manifested in many different ways.[152]

Over the years two competing strategies emerged within the Black medical and civil rights leadership. "One was a strategy of accommodation whereby black leaders would request through well-established patterns of civility, from the white business elite, monies for black institutions, such as hospitals. . . . The other strategy was one of integration."[153] Both strategies furthered the cause of improving Black health. The former was spearheaded by Drs. Peter Marshall Murray and Midian O. Bousefield and their coterie of foundations, government agencies, think tanks, and collaborations with civil rights organizations. The latter, which would have more long-term impact, was led by Drs. Louis T. Wright, W. Montague Cobb, and Paul Cornely. It was built around collaborative efforts of the NAACP, the NUL, and, whenever possible, the American Public Health Association (APHA).

Of equal importance to the ideological shift was the political one. Although the AMA snubbed the NMA whenever possible, the federal government had begun to acknowledge the African American professional body at some level during and after the World War I and Tuskegee VA hospital controversies. Meanwhile, as the private foundations such as CFAT, the GEB, the Rockefeller Foundation, the Duke Endowment, and the Rosenwald Fund shifted their emphasis to health and health-related projects during the 1920s and 1930s, African American physicians such as the aforementioned Dr. Peter Marshall Murray and Dr. Midian O. Bousefield became nationally recognized health policy advisors. They were called upon to supply data, conduct inspections, and make programmatic and policy recommendations about Blacks in the health system. Dr. Paul Cornely, University of Michigan-trained physician public health expert, and Dr. Hildrus Poindexter, Harvard-trained physician-researcher, supplied much of the data about Blacks in the health system. These two physician-researchers hailed from Howard University's Department of Preventive Medicine. Not since Du Bois's epochal Atlanta University Studies from the early twentieth century and a few dry statistical government monographs had the disparate Black health data been so effectively laid out. The stark disparities and poor outcomes had a profound effect on the foundations and the public health infrastructure. This was the modern version of "missionary" work that Black physicians such as Dr. Daniel Hale Williams, Dr. George Cleveland Hall, and Dr. Robert F. Boyd had promoted in the turn-of-the-century South, where three-fourths of African Americans lived and the bulk of Black doctors lived and practiced.

Drs. Murray's and Bousefield's elections to presidency of the NMA in 1933 and 1934, respectively, facilitated the coordination of their consulting work between the foundations and Black organized medicine. Their work resulted in programs to improve Black nurse training, improve physician training, upgrade hospitals, and improve TB and STD outcomes. As a result of their efforts, by the 1940s African American physicians and public health nurses were participating, although not at the policy level, in Southern health departments. Their earlier direction and influence spilled over into government programs during the Depression. Observers noted: "In response to pressure from black medical leaders, including Peter Murray and M.O. Bousefield, Hopkins told his state directors that black doctors were to be given an equal chance to participate in medical relief work."[154] Through the Duke Endowment and the other medical foundations, Murray and Bousefield detailed coherent programs for improving Black health in both Southern and Northern cities. Toward the end of the era, the NMA was invited and sent representatives to participate in the National Health Conference held in Washington July 18–20, 1938. The conference was designed to highlight findings and reports of the Roosevelt administration's Technical Committee on Medical Care. This was followed by a closed conference later that year: "On Nov. 21, a National Medical Association committee met with U.S. government officials representing the President's national health program to present the Negro viewpoint in the government's plans for medical care of the nation."[155] Led by the NMA, African American organizations such as the National Advisory Council, the NAACP, and the NACGN actively supported progressive health care legislation such as the National Health Act of 1939. This health policy pattern would continue into the postwar years. Invariably, they were the sole health professions organizations taking such bold positions on health reform.[156]

In an almost backhand manner, ideological and institutional underpinnings vital to the health care civil rights struggle that followed were begun between 1930 and 1945. Paradoxically, this development was manifested by a competition between the two strategies for change leading to justice and equity in health care. The accommodation approach spearheaded by Drs. Bousefield and Murray, not challenging the racially segregated status quo in the health system and preserving the compliant and sometimes obsequious professional etiquette that existed between Black and White doctors, was felt to be more pragmatic and undoubtedly led to health progress for African Americans in the 15 years before the end of World War II. The opposing view, antisegregationist to the core, led by Drs. Louis T. Wright and W. Montague Cobb, would dominate the field by the late 1940s.[157]

As has been noted, Black physicians had been close to the African American civil rights struggle since the abolition movement. Many advocated resistance to segregation and discrimination rather than accommodation. Physicians such as

Dr. James McCune Smith not only were abolitionist and civil rights leaders, but also participated in movements against organizations like the African Colonization Society and the New York Colonization Society, which proposed moving the Black population out of the United States. After the Civil War, African American physicians had been integral participants in Black liberation groups such as the Afro-American League, the Afro-American Council, the NAACP, and the National Urban League. Groups like the Niagara Movement, the United Negro Improvement Association (UNIA), and—by the 1940s—the NAACP had traditionally incorporated health agendas in their activities. Collaborative efforts between the NMA and Black civil rights and service organizations had resulted in successful campaigns to desegregate the staffs of Harlem Hospital (1919) and the Tuskegee VA (1926) and for the erection of Black hospitals like Homer G. Phillips Hospital (1937) in St. Louis. Men such as Homer Phillips, a prominent community leader and physician John A. Kenney, the victim of cross burnings and Ku Klux Klan activity in Alabama, had made tremendous sacrifices and had faced the threat of loss of life in the process.[158]

For one wing of the Black health care civil rights movement, caste status for African American patients and physicians and the conversion or erection of racially segregated institutions were not acceptable. The influence of this wing grew as World War II approached. Led by Northern and border-state physicians such as Louis T. Wright and W. Montague Cobb and organizations they were affiliated with, some Black groups rejected such accommodations outright. For example, as early as 1931 a report issued by the Manhattan Central Medical Society, *Equal Opportunity: No More, No Less*, sharply criticized the Julius Rosenwald Fund for promoting racial-medical segregation through its hospital and medical education programs. The report refers specifically to the University of Chicago–Provident Hospital of Chicago joint venture for the separate training of Black medical students and interns and to fund participation in the erection of a Black hospital in Harlem. By 1932 this group of physicians and their affiliated organizations also took on the VA system, fighting against construction of more segregated VA hospitals. There were proposals circulating to build Black VAs in Northern areas such as New York City where officially segregated governmental hospital facilities did not exist. The so-called "radicals" were successful in blocking these projects. Physician-activists such as Wright, in the tradition of Dr. Nathan Frances Mossell, who led similar fights in the late nineteenth century, were so uncompromising in their pursuit of idealism and excellence that they were opposed by many of their own race. Nevertheless, this group would eventually win out. Although accommodation to racial segregation and caste status for African American patients and physicians was the dominant approach throughout the 1930 to 1945 epoch, the ideological groundwork had been laid for the upcoming confrontational health care civil rights struggle.[159]

African American physicians and their professional institutions fought to empower their people in other ways. As early as the end of World War I it was clear that Meharry and Howard had to upgrade both their physical plants and teaching faculties to remain academically competitive and to train highly qualified physicians. Without these actions both of these African American survivors of Flexner reform would lose their accreditation. What could be viewed as a success for African American physicians was the mustering of support from the Rosenwald Fund, General Education Board of the Rockefeller Foundation, and National Research Foundation for faculty improvement, physical plant upgrading, and endowment procurement during the 1930s and 1940s. Initially providing shoe-string funding for plant improvement during the late 1920s, the foundations ultimately enabled Howard to erect its critically needed medical building and afforded Meharry a completely new physical plant. Perhaps more important were the initial successes of President John J. Mullowney at Meharry and Dr. Ernest Everett Just, world-renowned professor of zoology at Howard University, in obtaining medical school faculty training funds from the Rosenwald Foundation (1919) and the National Research Council (1923), respectively. This established a pattern wherein a total of 34 projected Meharry faculty and 28 projected Howard faculty received awards between 1919 and 1940 for advanced study at Eastern and Midwestern universities in their respective fields. The improvement of academic standards and facilities at the Black medical schools not only secured their Class A ratings but also insured their survival into the post–World War II era.[160]

During the Depression era these improvements in the Black medical schools served as evidence of equalizing educational opportunity at that level. However, other educational and competency problems remained for African American physicians. Social scientist Ira De A. Reid articulated the problem during the Depression and World War II eras:

> When the Negro physician receives his degree in medicine and is licensed to practice there is little distinction between his training and that of any other American physician—but the equality ends there, for race proscription then begins. Opportunities for internships and residences are circumscribed, hospital and clinical facilities are denied, membership in county medical and other professional and scientific societies is refused (in the South). Hence the Negro physician becomes the general practitioner par excellence—isolated and serving a low income group.[161]

Thus these automatic professional limitations were imposed by the educational process, which was largely controlled by White medical schools. Examples that Reid pointed out in his economic study revealed that "[e]ven in cities like Atlanta and Richmond where white medical colleges have control over large public wards of local hospitals, Negro physicians are not permitted to participate in their programs."[162] However, despite these limitations, the stubborn area of discriminatory access to postgraduate training and specialization showed signs of improvement. Though Blacks continued to be barred entry to medical schools in the South, between 1930 and 1945 possibilities of obtaining postgraduate training improved dramatically. As Morais noted, this was especially important regarding internships as they "gradually became a prerequisite for a license to practice."[163] By the mid-1940s the number of internship slots for Blacks had increased to at least 158. Of these openings, 109 were in Black institutions. For the first time, internships were available for virtually every African American medical school graduate. Access to specialty training was much slower in developing.[164]

Medical advance demanded specialization wherein physicians required two or more years of approved training beyond internship in a special field such as surgery or radiology. In the 1920s there were no specialty training slots (referred to as residencies) available to African American physicians. This situation was particularly grave for a Black population burdened with more severe and complex illnesses in a health system where they were often denied access to specialty services on the basis of racial and medical-social criteria. Morais notes, "in the 1930s they [specialty training programs] began to appear increasingly at accredited Negro hospitals."[165] By 1939 at least 31 specialty programs were established at Black hospitals, and by 1947 there were a total of 116 opportunities available. Eighty-five of these residencies were found in Black hospitals. The largest teaching loads were carried at Freedmen's Hospital, with 17 internships and 27 residencies; Homer G. Phillips Hospital in St. Louis, with 36 internships and 30 residencies; and Harlem Hospital in New York, a mixed hospital, with 35 internships and 13 residencies. Small patient loads and limited resources meant that Meharry's Hubbard Hospital could afford only 12 approved internships and eight residency slots; however, its programs were included among those of high quality and were configured according to the Johns Hopkins model.[166]

The tumultuous relationship between African American physicians and the specialty boards began to show signs of improvement between 1930 and 1945. Black participation in this area was agonizingly slow. The reasons were multiple; many of the roots of the problem were educational.

As noted by Henry Allen Bullock, in *A History of Negro Education in the South,* and James D. Anderson, in *The Education of Blacks in the South, 1860–1935,* the initial efforts of the ex-slaves to create an educational system that would extend and support their emancipation failed. Instead, Northern industrial philanthropists, some Black educators, and Southern White school officials who guided educational policy for African Americans pushed Black children into a system of industrial education that presupposed permanent Black political and economic subordination. Educational deprivation was structured into the system. Although this conflicted with the aspirations of ex-slaves and their descendants, their lack of economic and political power meant that White elites exerted absolute control over the structure and content of Black education for the first half of the twentieth century. This helped explain the substandard premedical education due to discriminatory and inadequate educational resources allocated for Black children at the primary, secondary, and college levels. Most Black colleges were underequipped from both facility and faculty standpoints. Deficiencies were especially glaring in the sciences. Thus Black medical schools, often collaborating with their African American feeder institutions, did remarkably well in preparing competent African American physicians.

These educational disadvantages were exacerbated by the paucity of specialty training available to Black medical school graduates. The discriminatory educational system covertly reinforced the segregation and discrimination policies of the specialty boards by severely limiting the number of qualified Black physician candidates. The first African American physician to be professionally acknowledged as a specialist was the legendary surgeon Daniel Hale Williams. He was a charter member of the American College of Surgeons (ACS) in 1913. No other Black would be accepted into the ACS until Louis T. Wright was admitted in 1934. By the 1920s, specialty boards had usually developed rigid training requirements followed by the passage of a competency examination. Dr. W. Harry Barnes of Philadelphia was the first board-certified Black specialist. Otolaryngology (head, eyes, ear, nose, and throat) was his specialty. Although he received some training at his alma mater, the University of Pennsylvania, he negated the color bar by obtaining specialty training at the Universities of Paris and Bordeaux. He became a Diplomate of the American Board of Otolaryngology in 1927. By 1947 a total of 93 Black physicians had met the requirements of specialty certification. Nearly half were Black medical school graduates (43), and they were almost evenly divided between medical (49) and surgical (44) specialties.[167]

Board certification was a mechanism open to virtually anyone completing a designated course of specialty training and willing to take, and able to pass, a set of examinations. Various "colleges" of specialists were more social and exclusive by design. That made the admission of African American physicians more difficult. There were only two African Americans who had been made fellows of the ACS by 1945. One of them was deceased by that year. Dr. Algernon B. Jackson of Philadelphia was the only inductee into the American College of Physicians as of the mid-1940s, and there were two Black fellows in the American College of Radiology. A short list of approximately twenty Blacks had been admitted to Alpha Omega Alpha, the physician's honor society, by the end of World War II. No chapters were allowed at Meharry or Howard and no graduates of these schools were members. This reflected the elite and exclusionary policies of the American medical education system and its coterie of specialty boards, organizations, and colleges.[168]

Meanwhile, the Black nursing profession, which had been nurtured through the late nineteenth and early twentieth century by the African American medical profession, became more independent and ventured on the aggressive pursuit of professional integration. In some ways its break from the traces of medical stewardship between 1930 and 1945 was a more radical departure in the struggle against health segregation and discrimination than that of the Black physicians. Having grown in numbers from 2,433 in 1910; 3,331 in 1920; and 5,589 in 1930 to an estimated 9,000 in 1945, Black nurses were especially hard hit by the Great

Depression. Denied most hospital, public health, and institutional positions because of race, most Black nurses struggled to remain professionally active, working private duty and within the confines of the well-defined Negro medical ghetto. Token numbers of Black nurses were hired in the 1930s in a few Northern public and private hospitals; however, evidence furnished by the NACGN revealed limited progress in the hiring of Black nurses in the public health arena during the 1930s, despite the Rosenwald Fund's stop-gap efforts to pay the salaries of African American public health nurses in several states. By the end of the war, a majority of Black nurses were working in institutional settings. Meanwhile, the General Education Board of the Rockefeller Foundation and the Rosenwald Fund allowed the NACGN to remain active nationally with a headquarters housed adjacent to White organized nursing organizations at the Rockefeller Center. Black organized nursing waged a crucial campaign against the health care professional racial discrimination within the War Department. The NACGN campaign successfully overthrew the initial War Department quota of 56 Black nurses, opening up recruitment based on qualifications, not race. By 1945, through eroding entrenched beliefs about the alleged inferiority of Black health care professionals, NACGN paved the way for the desegregation of the American Nurses Association (ANA). Under the direction of creative and dedicated leaders like Mabel K. Staupers, RN, NACGN's executive director, and Estelle Massey Riddle, RN, later an ANA board member, and forging professional and civil rights campaigns, Black nurses would become the first U.S. health profession to be desegregated (1949) and NACGN members would be accepted in many areas of the nursing profession.[169]

By 1945 there were approximately 1,533 African American dentists, with Meharry and Howard remaining the principal institutions for training. Black dentists had tried to form a national professional society beginning in 1901. They spent several decades ensconced within the NMA along with the Black pharmacists. Although two dentists served as president of the NMA, dentists felt overshadowed and ignored. Between 1932 and 1940, the African American dental profession formally established an independent dental professional association built upon a foundation of a fledgling National Dental Association (originally named the Tri-State Dental Society and, later, the Inter-state Dental Association) which had originated on July 19, 1913. Permanently adopting the National Dental Association (NDA) title in 1933, it began publication of its own journal, *The Bulletin*, in 1941. It formally severed ties with the NMA in 1940. Discrimination was still rife in the profession, with a 1945 survey revealing that only 20, or 55.5 percent of, American dental schools freely accepted Negroes. Many Northern and all Southern components of the White American Dental Association (ADA) refused to accept Black dentists as members. Besides being cut off from continuing education, they were precluded from being officially designated as dental specialists by many state boards and barred from holding many responsible administrative positions.

Of the six African American schools of pharmacy, only Xavier University in New Orleans and Howard University survived through the Great Depression. Meharry's School of Pharmacy, which was established in 1889, closed in 1938. Based on the American Council of Education Pharmaceutical Survey released in 1947, only 45 of 65 schools of pharmacy admitted African American students. Cobb concluded that the major problems facing Black dentists and pharmacists as of 1945 were racial discrimination within the profession, especially relative to training facilities, and securing adequate numbers of well-qualified students to fill the expanding number of academic openings.[170]

Although the Great Depression and World War II tested the mettle of the U.S. health system to the greatest extent since the Civil War, justice and equity in health care for Blacks and other disadvantaged minority groups remained an elusive goal. Contrary to many popular beliefs about the New Deal, when it came to caste, class, or race issues, the government did the least to challenge or change the existing order. The health care system did not escape these influences. Despite medical establishment and institutional resistance against progressive change in most instances, African American health continued to improve during this period. Morais observed, "Evidence of 'some narrowing of the health gap between the two races' served as 'unmistakable proof of the steady advance of modern medicine and the indomitable will of the Negro people to survive.'"[171] The broadening effects of international exposure due to the war and the demonstrated health needs of the majority of the American population during the Depression failed to obliterate race and class discrimination in the health system. In many ways it hardened the AMA and its White medical establishment into bastions of reaction and conservatism. They were sometimes driven to unethical and embarrassing extremes to sabotage progressive health policies that would have benefited Blacks and the poor. As one Urban League spokesman told African American doctors, the AMA attitude "is not only reactionary but indicative of an amazing indifference to one of the gravest health problems that America faces."[172] Nevertheless, the struggle against such resistance strengthened and matured Black medicine and its allied health professions and set the stage for the ensuing struggle during the "Civil Rights Era in health care."[173]

## PART II

# Race, Medicine, and Health before, during, and after the Black Civil Rights Era

# Black Americans and the Health System from World War II through the Civil Rights Era, 1945–1965

## Peace Be Still

*Now are our brows bound with victorious wreaths;*
*Our bruised arms hung up for monuments;*
*Our stern alarums chang'd to merry meetings,*
*Our dreadful marches to delightful measures.*
*Grim-visag'd war hath smooth'd his wrinkled front.*
WILLIAM SHAKESPEARE, *RICHARD III*

World War II was over. The sociocultural milieu that followed—the Cold War, the Red Scare, and the Eisenhower Years—affected all Americans and profoundly influenced the evolution and functioning of the health system. African Americans and other disadvantaged minority groups, made keenly aware by their wartime experiences of their victimization through racial discrimination and socioeconomic oppression, began agitating for justice and equity in all arenas of American life. The curtain rose on the African American civil rights era. Health care was no exception.

Flushed with victory over fascism, the United States entered the post–World War II era with a variegated agenda. Wartime changes in health and health care had reflected military goals and objectives. Similarly, postwar health care developments were dominated by the major economic, political, and social issues of the time. Nevertheless, the period from 1945 to 1965 proved that patience was running thin relative to America's handling of its race problem. To fully comprehend health care developments during this era, especially as they affected African Americans, an appreciation of the sociopolitical and economic environment is necessary.

The dominant geopolitical agenda of the period revolved around the ideological and political conflict between the Soviet Union and its Western allies — the United States, Britain, and France. As early as the Teheran (1943) and Yalta (1944) conferences it became clear that Stalin's Soviet Union rejected the Atlantic Charter's (1941)* principles advocating an end to colonialism and emphasizing self-determination. The Union of Soviet Socialist Republics (USSR) intended to dominate a buffer-zone of vassal states in postwar Central and Eastern Europe. Moreover, this ideological conflict, later resulting in a Cold War, was undergirded by communist belief in the inevitable expansion of their political system to dominate the globe. To counter this threat, and to secure what some considered its own imperialist interests and borders,** the United States adopted a policy of "containment."[1]

The containment policy initiated and perpetuated by presidents Truman, Eisenhower, Kennedy, and Johnson dominated and shaped virtually everything in post–World War II America, including sociopolitical, economic, health care, and racial issues. Containment entailed instituting and maintaining a large, long-term U.S. military establishment; creating a worldwide network of political and military mechanisms and alliances such as the United Nations (UN), founded April 25, 1945, the Organization of American States (OAS), founded in 1948, and the North Atlantic Treaty Organization (NATO), founded April 4, 1949; and massive, politically motivated, financial arrangements such as the $400 million expenditure by the United States for the postwar defense of Turkey and Greece (1947) against communist aggression and the $12 billion Marshall Plan (1947–1950) for European economic development. Although there were many other effects of containment policy that affected day-to-day American life, these major factors defined and shaped everything. The new role of the United States as leader of the Western democracies also required domestic tranquillity and concrete evidence of commitment to democratic principles. The nation's policies regarding the "race question" became increasingly untenable and epitomized America's foreign policy vulnerability.[2]

Responses to the realities of the dropping of the atomic bomb on Japan (1945) and successful Russian espionage leading to Soviet development of nuclear capa-

---

*The Atlantic Charter envisioned a world wherein nations abandoned their traditional reliance on military alliances and spheres of influence. Instead, they governed their relations with one another through democratic processes, international arbiter organizations, and overarching protection of the right of self-determination.

**Some of the United States's actions in Mexico, the Caribbean, the Pacific Rim, Central America, and South America over the preceding century could be viewed in such a manner.

bility (1949) brought on a new stage of Cold War strategy. The Cold War expanded beyond postwar Europe into Asia with the expulsion of U.S. ally Chiang Kai-shek from the Chinese mainland (1949) by communist armies and the partitioning of Korea into a communist North and procapitalist South (1948–1950).[3] These international conflicts between pro- and anticapitalist forces reflected the instability of global affairs and had serious repercussions in the United States. The most important nonpolitical effects were economic. Economic consequences of Cold War foreign policies and the reconversion from a full-time war economy affected the U.S. standard of living, public policy, and domestic politics. Despite a series of labor disputes, there was an unexpected wave of sustained affluence, largely confined to the White population, from the late 1940s into the 1960s. This was fueled by government spending on the military, public schools, veterans' benefits, and interstate highways. The "mainstream" health care system was also a major beneficiary.

There was unprecedented corporate growth, especially during the 1950s. Over 4,000 corporate mergers occurred in that decade alone. A 47 percent expansion of the suburbs—which, due to financial, social, and real estate practices fostering racial separation, were almost exclusively White—fueled the building trades, auto manufacturing, appliance and furniture industries, and oil companies. Patterns of residential segregation, combined with the Northern migration of African Americans (almost one-half of the Black population lived in the North by the 1960s), created physically deprived and threatening urban ghettos in the nation's metropolitan centers. Government policies promoting racial discrimination in housing, as established and practiced in the Home Owners' Loan Corporation (HOLC, 1933) and the Federal Housing Administration (FHA, 1937), were perpetuated in the postwar years.[4] The GI Bill subsidized housing, education, and job training. Real estate, educational, and occupational segregation and discrimination meant that Whites were the disproportionate beneficiaries of these programs. These new housing trends and developments perpetuated traditional race and class segregation, thus accentuating quality-tiering of the U.S. health system, and created a unique set of health problems.*[5] Side-by-side technical and structural expansion of the private and public health care sectors fostered expanded government roles in health care but did not ameliorate their separate and unequal development.

This accelerated economic landscape resulted in a growth of the gross domestic product (GDP) by 250 percent between 1945 and 1960—from $200 billion to over $500 billion. By 1960, though it was inequitably distributed, Americans had the highest living standard in the world, with twice the purchasing power of the vaunted 1920s. Moreover, buying power increased 20 percent between 1945 and 1960.[6]

---

*As Morais and others noted about the postwar era, and subsequent studies have further documented, rat and roach infestation, environmental pollution, and underserved health zones have combined to create unique unhealthy environments grudgingly populated by African American and other poor populations. Recent revelations have also exposed the fact that Black and poor communities have been differentially targeted as toxic waste and dump sites as functions of corporate and governmental policies.

Besides creating a materialistic, consumer-oriented society, these unantici-pated economic events generated a wave of conservative public attitudes and political outcomes. This profoundly affected African America's optimistic, some-times unrealistic, postwar mind-set and sociopolitical agenda. Initially, the Truman administration felt the World War II experience had prepared the American public for a progressive social agenda regarding government health insurance, prepaid medical care, federally funded public education, expanded Social Security bene-fits, long-range environmental and public works planning, an end to racial segregation and discrimination, and governmental promotion of scientific research. This overreaching progressive social agenda, especially Truman's campaign for racial justice and civil rights, almost permanently split the Democ-ratic Party during the 1948 presidential elections because of interparty conflict and Southern Democratic Party resistance. It also planted the seeds for the present conservative renaissance and the Republican Party's now familiar "Southern strategy" of the 1960s through the 1990s.

During the 1948 presidential election, the nation's ambivalence emerged about implementing a forward-looking social milieu emphasizing workers, social justice, and common people. This milieu, which emerged during the New Deal and the war years, returned to cutthroat laissez-faire capitalism and reduced govern-ment spending policies as recommended by conservative Republicans. After Truman's surprise victory and the return of a Democratic Congress to Capitol Hill, only a small expansion of Social Security, a slight increase in the minimum wage, and a weak National Housing Act (1949) were approved. Truman's attempts to combat discrimination through the Fair Employment Practices Act (1949) and the first major civil rights bill of the century (1948) were defeated.[7] Not only were most of President Truman's social reform proposals rejected out of hand by the conserva-tive public and both Republican (1946) and Democratic party–dominated (1948) Congresses, but also, on the labor front, the Wagner Act of 1935* was attacked and largely reversed. New labor legislation, the Taft-Hartley Act, "which limited the powers of unions, declaring certain of their tactics 'unfair labor practices' and giving the President power to secure 80-day 'cooling off periods' by court injunction,"[8] was enacted. It did not destroy the labor movement, but weakened it, making it harder to organize workers in nonunion industries.[9]

Perhaps just as ominous as the conservative political climate from an African American perspective were the side effects of the extremist national crusade against communist subversion. Energy for this movement, which some describe as a near-hysteria against the communist threat, was generated by a series of previously noted international events, U.S. determination never to be caught off guard again as it

---

*The National Labor Relations Act of 1935 limited the tactic employers often used to resist unions—failing to recognize or bargain with them. This was accomplished largely by providing workers with more federal protection, creating an enforcement mechanism (the National Labor Relations Board) that could compel employers to recognize and bargain with legitimate unions.

was by the Japanese at Pearl Harbor, and a sometimes unhealthy and intense conservative paranoia. The result was a suppression of any views not promoted by the government, suspicion of any liberal or left-leaning activities, and a growing fear of internal communist subversion. Progressive social reform efforts such as the Civil Rights Movement were also held suspect. Prominent Republican politicians of the period, such as Richard Nixon, who would later be elected president in 1968, and Joseph McCarthy, the first-term Republican senator from Wisconsin whose intimidating presence loomed over America far longer than the four years (1950–1954) of his ascendancy, misused anticommunism as a partisan issue. The federal government itself was also involved in virtual anticommunist witch hunts. Eminent African American scholars such as W. E. B. Du Bois were harassed, had their passports voided, and had their books banned from libraries. Similar actions were taken against Black artists and intellectuals such as Langston Hughes and Paul Robeson, whose Black Liberation writings and activities led to interaction with socialists, communists, and political activists of every political persuasion. African American leaders like these had spoken out and supported efforts to obtain justice and equity in health care for Blacks.

The House Un-American Activities Committee (HUAC) was formed in 1947, and government employees such as Alger Hiss (1948) whetted the public appetite for spy hunts and sent chills of fear throughout government and private sectors. Presidents beginning with Harry Truman launched federal loyalty programs and internal security investigations, resulting in thousands of resignations and hundreds of dismissals. Federal Bureau of Investigation (FBI) anticommunist activities under J. Edgar Hoover intensified, leading to more abuses of individual and civil rights by that agency. Punishments meted out ranged from incarceration, as in the Hiss trial, to executions, as in the case of the Rosenbergs (1953), who were convicted as Russian atomic spies. Black civil rights leaders and organizations were forced to abandon many of their progressive platforms and allegiances, sometimes spy on each other, and denounce anything tainted with communist or even socialist social agendas. As Columbia University social scientist Manning Marable pointed out, "The impact of the Cold War, the anti-communist purges and near-totalitarian social environment, had a devastating effect upon the cause of blacks' civil rights and civil liberties.... [T]he paranoid mood of anti-communist America made it difficult for any other reasonable reform movement to exist."[10] Corporations utilized this hysteria to keep unions and workers in line at home and to encourage foreign investment abroad. Even some within the labor union movement felt compelled to purge socialists, communists, and antiracist advocates.* The period from 1945 to 1954 was an overwhelmingly nihilistic and negative one for the Black Civil Rights Movement. This also had an oppressive effect on medical-social advances in health care.[11]

---

*Because many of the antiracist advocates also demanded elimination of class divisions in American society, the Black-White coalitions were easy targets of Red-baiting by the federal government as well as the general public—which was still unconvinced of the necessity of civil rights for Blacks.

Central to the expansion of affluent, suburban, middle-class culture was the rise of television. In 1946, after World War II, there were 17,000 television sets in America. By 1957 there were 40 million—almost as many sets as there were families. Television was a totally new and unique American phenomenon. This quantum leap in communications and technology fueled profound changes in consumerism and corporate mind control as TV replaced newspapers, magazines, and radios as the leading information source. It created vast markets for new fashions and products. As a diversion and entertainment medium, television's uniform images of American life—one that was overwhelmingly White, middle-class, and suburban, as depicted by TV shows like *Ozzie and Harriet* and *Leave It to Beaver*—challenged the dominance of movies and radio. Despite their artificial, homogenized images of American life, which served to domesticate and negate cultural and racial diversity and conflict, they nevertheless had the potential to produce social unrest. As Brinkley observed in *The Unfinished Nation*, "At the same time that television was reinforcing the homogeneity of the white middle class, therefore, it was also contributing to the sense of alienation and powerlessness among groups excluded from the world it portrayed."[12] In African American and other disadvantaged minority communities the insensitive and cynical use of this powerful new medium had the unrealized potential for triggering the release of centuries-long pent-up frustration and anger.[13]

Science and technology became darlings of the television-ruled media. Atomic weapons, the exploration of space, and medicine were prominent interests. The series of announcements about Russian and American satellite launches into space, starting in 1957, generated fierce competition between the two superpowers' science and space establishments. However, medical discoveries like Dr. Jonas Salk's discovery of an effective polio vaccine in 1955 generated equal excitement. The virtual elimination of dread diseases like diphtheria and tuberculosis, improvements in longevity, and improved health indicators (e.g., infant mortality) influenced the heightened expectations and near-worship of medicine and health care in the United States. Many contended that media manipulation of these events, along with the commercial exploitation through advertising, would lead to the public's developing false and unrealistic expectations of the capabilities of modern medicine. These messages were not lost on African Americans. Moreover, the maldistribution of this medical progress became more obvious as Blacks and the poor were denied access. By the late 1950s, through the media and other sources, America also became aware of widespread poverty and exclusion of large blocs of the population from the mainstream of U.S. social and economic life. With improvements in communications and information technology in a free society, the plight of Blacks, Hispanics, and residents of Appalachia, representing at least 15 percent of the population, became increasingly hard to hide or ignore. Exposés such as Michael Harrington's *The Other America* (1962) raised general awareness levels concerning poverty and other issues African Americans had focused on for decades. The postwar years, for Blacks, represented the preparatory and initial stages for the greatest era of social change since the Civil War.[14]

Despite the social conservatism of the American public, World War II had changed the world and raised Black expectations. The United State's anticommunist mood, combined with the political reactions to the Cold War, muzzled virtually all overt signs of progressive social reform, public ideological debate, or political movements for ten years. This included the Black Civil Rights Movement. Accommodation, anticommunism, and tacit allegiance to White liberals and labor bureaucrats became the almost silent strategies of Black middle-class leadership and politics from 1945 to 1955. However, the quiet struggle in legislative corridors and the courts had not abated. In fact, presidential actions such as Truman's endorsement of his Civil Rights Committee report, *To Secure These Rights*, in 1946; his desegregation of the army with Executive Order 9981 in 1948; and his addition of a civil rights plank to the Democratic Party agenda in the 1948 election fueled overblown expectations in the Black community. Meanwhile, the NAACP intensified its legal assault on segregation in the courts. The 1944 *Smith v. Allwright* case struck down the White primary, a device used by Southern Democrats to bar registered Blacks from voting in the only important election in the one-party South. *Sweatt v. Painter* in 1950 forced Texas to admit Heman Marion Sweatt to the University of Texas Law School after finding the Texas Jim Crow school* to be inferior. Oklahoma State University was also forced open to African Americans in 1950 with *McLaurin v. Oklahoma*. After struggling to desegregate the army and end discrimination in the defense industries during the war, the National Urban League (NUL) continued its quiet approach of influencing public policy through social welfare programs and scientific investigation. It would not become identified with an activist commitment to the Civil Rights Movement until the 1960s.[15]

By adhering to a meticulously planned twenty-year program of incremental legal struggle against segregation, with public education as the main area of challenge, formulated by chief NAACP counsel Charles Hamilton Houston (1895–1950), racially segregated schools were outlawed. The May 17, 1954, Supreme Court ruling in *Brown v. Board of Education*, outlawing racially segregated public schools, was a landmark case overturning *Plessy v. Ferguson*, the 1896 case legalizing racial segregation on the basis of "separate but equal" accommodations. Seemingly, this watershed ruling offered limitless possibilities for justice and equity to African Americans in all areas of American life—including health care.[16] Fruits of this breakthrough would not be realized immediately.[17]

Triggered by Southern resistance to court-ordered school desegregation, Ku Klux Klan violence, and atrocities such as the Emmett Till lynching (1955), a grassroots Black Civil Rights Movement emerged from places as unlikely as Baton Rouge, Louisiana (1953), Montgomery, Alabama (1956), and Greensboro,

---

*In response to Sweatt's 1946 law school application, Texas hurriedly threw together a "Black" law school, which was inferior in every way to the law school of the University of Texas.

North Carolina (1961). The famed Montgomery movement was a year-long city bus boycott; the Greensboro protest was the first of a new wave of lunch counter sit-ins. Direct-action protests against segregation soon spread over the entire nation. By the 1960s the traditional civil rights infrastructure (e.g., NAACP, CORE, NUL), despite being falsely accused and identified with communist activities, joined in this new direct action phase of the Civil Rights Movement, and new organizations such as the Southern Christian Leadership Conference (SCLC, founded 1957) and the Student Non-Violent Coordinating Committee (SNCC, founded 1960) were formed. The decade of 1955 to 1965 represented the largest national wave of resistance and protest against racial segregation and discrimination by the African American population in the nation's history. It profoundly affected, and forced the reexamination of, America's democratic institutions—including the health care system.[18]

The pinnacle of the nonviolent phase of the Black Civil Rights Movement occurred in the early 1960s. This was also a period of ferment and significant progress in health care for African Americans. Efforts in health care civil rights were coordinated by medical organizations such as the National Medical Association (NMA) and the Medical Committee for Human Rights (MCHR) and were joined by civil rights organizations such as the NAACP, NUL, and SCLC. Health care policy and civil rights activities by these organizations were largely ignored on an official level by White U.S. health care leaders and institutions.[19] Lunch counter protests, which had sporadically taken place in the 1940s and 1950s, became a sustainable tactic after African American college students from North Carolina A&T adopted the practice on February 1, 1961, in Greensboro, North Carolina. This official beginning of the country's "Second Reconstruction" spread across the nation like wildfire. As a result, by 1970 desegregated lunch counters were the rule rather than the exception nationwide. The 1961 Freedom Rides, sponsored by CORE, highlighted racial segregation in interstate commerce and galvanized the nation's attention on civil rights. The March on Washington on August 23, 1963, was a tour de force in gaining support and disseminating the message of Black civil rights. According to Brinkley, "The march was the high-water mark of the peaceful, interracial civil-rights movement—and one of the last moments of real harmony within it."[20] Clearly, the pursuit of Black civil rights was now a national, albeit loosely organized, movement. The SCLC's Project "C" ("C" stood for confrontation) campaign in Birmingham, Alabama (1963), successfully desegregated many aspects of America's most segregated city. It riveted worldwide attention on both the movement and the brutality of racial segregation in the United States. The Mississippi Freedom Summer project, conducted by SNCC in 1964, focused on voting rights and education for African Americans. The killings and violence precipitated by the effort exposed the ugly and sinister political and public policy roots of systematic racial segregation, oppression, and discrimination in the Deep South.[21]

There were official responses to this wave of nonviolent protests, confrontations, and demonstrations. Although the federal court system continued the legal dismantling of segregation and discrimination, civil rights legislation more dramatically reflected the nation's response between 1955 and 1965. Congress, led by presidents Truman, Eisenhower, Kennedy, and Johnson, teamed up to pass the Civil Rights Act of 1957, the Civil Rights Act of 1960, the Civil Rights Act of 1964, and the Voting Rights Act of 1965. These significant pieces of legislation transformed the mood of the country while legally addressing the problems of school segregation, voting rights, employment discrimination, and access to public accommodations. Unfortunately, fervor, impatience, and the perception of lax enforcement of the new laws and policies drove the Civil Rights Movement into new and more violent directions after the Watts riots and the White backlash of 1965.[22]

The fervor of the Civil Rights Movement spilled over into health care. The founding of the Medical Committee for Human Rights, a formal organization of Black and White physicians and health workers in 1964, was emblematic of some changes in the health subculture. The organization, along with the NMA, gave medical aid to civil rights workers, provided a "medical presence" at demonstrations to minimize attacks and violence, mobilized health professionals to be more supportive of the Civil Rights Movement, and raised funds for civil rights activities. Litigation, direct action protests, and demonstrations, based on the African American tradition of viewing health care as a civil rights issue, generated pressures forcing the health care system to change its policies, structure, and politics. Massive liberal peace, environmental, and women's movements emanating from the nation's youth also shook up and began to change the American character by 1965. The health system, and the American body politic, would never be the same.[23]

## Health Reform Resisted: Accommodation in the U.S. Health System, 1945–1965

Explosive postwar expansion of the United States health system was at hand. At issue was whether to redistribute resources to benefit the entire population (as medical reformers, some politicians, and disadvantaged minority groups proposed) or to channel resources to benefit physicians, providers, and corporations (including insurance companies). Although the postwar U.S. health system faced increasing medical-social pressure for change between 1945 and 1965, it maintained most of its "market-like" characteristics, its tiered structure of race- and class-based inequities and inequalities, and its middle- and upper-class leadership, ideology, and orientation. Throughout the late 1940s and 1950s the medical establishment was preoccupied with tailoring the expanding role of government in medical education and research to meet its needs. Reorganizing medicine's and the health system's political stances and structural organization was also necessary to withstand lay challenges grounded in egalitarian considerations from labor unions and citizens' and workers' cooperatives within the health system. Throughout this period, all components of the health system grew by leaps and bounds and became America's third largest industry in terms of manpower, with a workforce of 2.5 million people and a significant portion of the nation's economy.

This quantum leap in the scale of American medicine and health care produced chaos. The growth in health care expenditures between 1950 and 1970 from $12.7 billion to $71.6 billion, representing a growth from 4.5 to 7.3 percent of the GNP, was as much a product of historical accident as planning. Energized by capitalist and competitive—not public health—mechanisms, distribution problems ballooned. This was especially prominent during the early part of the period. As Paul Starr pointed out:

> The postwar expansion did not remedy the acknowledged deficiencies in the distribution of medical services. . . . [T]he first phase of postwar policy, favoring growth without redistribution, gave way by the mid-1960s to policies that tried to improve distribution yet without any fundamental reorganization of the system.[24]

Such growth without targeted corrective actions accentuated, not ameliorated, the maldistribution of health care services. Rich and poor populations encountered higher barriers as "the market" tailored the health system, often ignoring patient needs. As Professor Milton Roemer of the UCLA School of Public Health noted in 1967, inefficiencies and barriers were growing exponentially as problems and "were . . . a consequence of the crazy quilt of a fragmented nonsystem of health-service delivery in our country."[25] Accentuation and institutionalization of the race- and class-based maldistribution and inequality problems were especially devastating for Black and poor patients. Untrammeled growth without public accountability maintained and institutionalized these populations' separate and inferior health environments, accommodations (inside and outside hospitals), and facilities.

Underrepresentation in the health professions for African Americans, disadvantaged ethnic minorities, and women continued to be a problem. Attempts were made to bridge the disadvantaged populations' health gap through poorly planned, sometimes serendipitous mechanisms such as traditional medicine, informally obtained medical advice from pharmacists, growing networks of government-sponsored hospitals (e.g., VA hospitals, state hospitals), and growing networks of structurally restricted* health department facilities. These efforts focused on providing health care and services for "have-not" and identifiable ethnic minority populations. Despite the technical and fiscal characteristics of these so-called compensatory mechanisms or programs, previously structured race and class

---

*In most areas of the country, White organized medicine and its lobby restricted the public health care sector to preventive (e.g., immunizations), instead of therapeutic, medicine. This "defining the boundaries of public health" meant that detected disease problems, even among children, were referred into the private system for treatment. Most of these patients went untreated.

health system arrangements (separation, segregation, and disparate quality) were maintained. African Americans received the worst of the lot in all areas and continued to lag in both health status and outcomes.[26]

The major component of the health system demonstrating the most vigorous, and what some would classify as dysfunctional, growth was health care institutions—mostly hospitals. Strongly rooted in the medical model and largely ignoring the benefits of preventive and outpatient care, hospital care was expensive and inefficient. Straitjacketed by the hospital-based medical model, increased postwar demands for health services dictated that the United States build up its fragile and spotty hospital infrastructure. Because of the Depression, wartime neglect, and scant economic resources dictated by market factors in some areas, many needy communities had deficient or absent hospital facilities at the end of World War II. This was especially true in the South. Another demand for hospital services arose from returning veterans. The Hill-Burton Act, which between 1947 and 1971 provided $3.7 billion of government funding, was one response to this structural and institutional maldistribution of mainstream health resources. Eventually these government sources were matched by $9.1 billion of private funding—which virtually rebuilt America's private hospital system. A construction program to expand and upgrade the VA hospitals was also passed after the war.

Although the Hill-Burton Act pumped billions of dollars into the nation's nearly 6,000 short-term, nongovernmental hospitals between 1947 and 1965, it did not stabilize the private hospital system for disadvantaged Americans. Inherent flaws grew more prominent, such as persistent race- and class-based admissions and access to accommodations and services policies; previously mentioned built-in public health and fiscal inefficiencies inherent in the model; fierce and fragmenting institutional autonomy; burgeoning residential racial segregation; perpetuation of small, chronically understaffed institutions; the emergence of academic health centers (AHC)–dominated medical empires whose emphases were on prestige, research, and training instead of delivering primary health services to needy populations; failure to rationalize and coordinate health planning or services on a regional basis; a generalized substitution of institutional prestige for strategic planning; emphasis on hospital and medical center competition instead of cooperation relative to the acquisition of charity resources and technological upgrading; and the virtual disappearance of charity as the dominant institution-sustaining resource. Moreover, Hill-Burton did little to ameliorate racial segregation and inequalities. In fact, the government's allowable "separate but equal" Hill-Burton provisions institutionalized segregation where it had not existed and often accentuated the plight of the racially excluded African American patients and doctors throughout the South for the first two decades of its existence. Not until 1964 and 1965, near the end of the Hill-Burton program,* would the federal courts finally outlaw segregation in government-funded health programs and their provider institutions.

---

*The Hill-Burton program lasted from 1947 to 1971.

Regulations in the program itself accentuated the hospital reconstruction program's failure to address the system's race and class distribution problems. The Hill-Burton Act meticulously removed the federal government from decision-making relative to funding. Thus, local authorities, for whom racial segregation and discrimination were *de facto* and *de jure* realities, were encouraged to perpetuate apartheid using government resources. Moreover, formulas favoring hospital financing in low-income states (which the program did) often favored middle-income communities within those states. Regulations requiring communities to raise two-thirds of their hospital's costs before approval and proving the hospital's financial viability in effect cut off poor communities. Concessions that institutions provide a "reasonable volume" of services to persons unable to pay were unspecified and unenforced—and, therefore, ignored and ineffective.

In the North, where Blacks obtained increasing access to public hospitals in the postwar era, growth of the public sector was accentuated and exaggerated by increasing residential and class segregation, White flight from central cities, and White suburbanization. Expanding health empires centered around AHCs capitalized on these problems as center-city communities were rendered more vulnerable to institutional manipulation due to their increasing deficits in education, community leadership, and political influence. This exacerbated the inequitable race- and class-based tiering of the health system. The AHCs gratified their institutional, financial, research, educational, and prestige needs while ignoring community health priorities. Many of these phenomena, driven by AHC priorities, increasingly resembled nineteenth-century Western European–based colonial models for delivering social services. In the process, large, increasingly Black, public aid populations became "training material" for the medical school and research infrastructure, which continued its tradition of being dysfunctional ombudsmen for poor, often non-White, populations. As Barbara and John Ehrenreich observed about the disturbing cultural and social distancing between Black patients and White doctors-in-training in big city hospitals of the era:

> As interns and residents, young doctors get their training by practicing on the hospital ward and clinic patients—generally non-white. Later they make their money by practicing for a paying clientele—generally white. White patients are "customers"; black patients are "teaching material." White patients pay for care with their money; black patients pay with their dignity and comfort.[27]

John Kosa, Aaron Antonovsky, and Irving Kenneth Zola elaborated further on the unhealthy relationship between public clinics and hospitals and their clientele in *Poverty and Health: A Sociological Analysis*:

> House officers tend to dislike the kind of people they come to meet in clinics. The clientele is often seen as desirable only insofar as the doctors-

> *in-training can learn more about medicine by treating them. . . . One may assume that the alienation from private-practice medicine has its origin in the usages of the public outpatient clinic. Here the neophyte doctor learns that these people are unwanted as private clientele. His later decisions about where to practice and what kind of practice to establish are affected by what he learns in this setting.*[28]

Moreover, official discriminatory AHC mechanisms wherein Black physicians practicing in the underserved communities had historically been denied hospital and medical school staff appointments would become clear with the enactment of Title 19.*[29] Ed Cray observed that a major effect of these policies was growing health services disparities between the mainstream and public care sectors, noting the low quality of care documented in New York City's public hospital system, the nation's largest and most elaborate, near the end of the Hill-Burton era: "The city's 20 municipal hospitals are so inadequately staffed, overcrowded and underfinanced that a New York State investigation commission determined in 1968 that patients were being denied minimally sufficient care."[30] Moreover, as governmental efforts through Medicare/Medicaid and Hill-Burton to stabilize the health institutional infrastructure through massive public subsidy got mixed reviews, the performance of other branches of this massive infrastructure grew even more inconsistent.

The nation's 20,000 nursing homes, which were in a shambles before 1965, flourished financially after Medicare/Medicaid passage. However, the infusion by 1968 of more than $1 billion of annual funding from Title 18 did not translate into improved standards, regulations, or racial justice in the system. The 124 Black hospitals in existence at the end of the war did not fare well in the competition subsidized and promoted by the White-dominated government, business, and philanthropic interests dominating the postwar health system. By 1965 African American patients and physicians began abandoning the Black hospital infrastructure by choice and circumstance. Within twenty years, these institutions virtually disappeared.[31]

Despite mixed responses from the AMA and the White medical establishment, the health education and research infrastructure burgeoned between 1945 and 1965. As medical technology advanced, medical education became more expensive and biomedical research more costly. With private resources dwindling, the federal government became more involved in the U.S. health education and research infrastructure. During the decade of the 1940s, the average income of medical schools tripled from $500,000 to $1.5 million a year. The average school's income had grown to $3.7 million by 1958 and $15 million by the late 1960s.[32] As William G. Rothstein noted regarding the sources of the growth of medical school finances from $69.5 million in 1947 to $884 million in 1965 (see Table 3.1):

---

*Title 19 (Medicaid) is an amendment to the Social Security Act which provides health care for the poor and medically indigent (including those in nursing homes). It was passed along with Title 18 (Medicare) which provides care for the elderly and disabled.

## Table 3.1 Medical School Expenditures by Sources of Income, 1947–1982

| Income Source | Private Schools | | | | | Public Schools | | | | |
|---|---|---|---|---|---|---|---|---|---|---|
| | 1947 | 1960 | 1965 | 1970 | 1982 | 1947 | 1960 | 1965 | 1970 | 1982 |
| All sources[a] | $42.7 | 247 | 478 | 881 | 3,647 | 26.8 | 192 | 406 | 818 | 4,531 |
| Tuition fees | 19.47 | 8.1 | 6.0 | 5.1 | 9.2 | 13.6 | 4.3 | 3.0 | 2.1 | 3.2 |
| State appropriations | 1.4 | 3.5 | 2.4 | 3.6 | 3.0 | 62.2 | 31.3 | 26.6 | 30.2 | 33.0 |
| Indirect cost recovery | [b] | 4.7 | 7.4 | 7.5 | 9.0 | [b] | 3.6 | 5.8 | 4.3 | 4.5 |
| Professional fee income | [b] | 2.7 | 2.5 | 5.4 | 22.6 | [b] | 3.2 | 3.3 | 8.2 | 17.0 |
| Hospital reimbursement | [b] | [b] | [b] | [b] | 13.2 | [b] | [b] | [b] | [b] | 7.5 |
| Sponsored research | 26.0 | 43.1 | 47.2 | 32.8 | 21.4 | 16.5 | 31.8 | 36.9 | 22.4 | 17.0 |
| Sponsored training and multipurpose | [b] | 13.3 | 16.8 | 30.1 | 10.8 | [b] | 11.3 | 14.8 | 22.2 | 8.6 |
| Other operating income | 53.2 | 24.6 | 17.6 | 15.5 | 10.8 | 7.7 | 14.4 | 9.6 | 10.5 | 9.2 |
| Total | 100 | 100 | 99.9 | 100 | 100 | 100 | 99.9 | 100 | 99.9 | 100 |

[a]Income in millions of dollars.
[b]None or not broken out separately.
*Sources:* U.S. Surgeon General's Committee on Medical School Grants and Finances, *Part II: Financial Status and Needs of Medical Schools* (Washington, D.C.: U.S. G.P.O., 1951), 34–35; John A. Cooper, "Undergraduate Medical Education," in *Advances in American Medicine*, eds. John Z. Bowers and Elizabeth F. Purcell (New York: Josiah Macy, Jr., Foundation, 1976), 1:296–97; H. Paul Jolly, et al., "U.S. Medical School Finances," *Journal of the American Medical Association* 252 (1984): 1539.
*From:* Rothstein WG. *American Medical Schools and the Practice of Medicine.* New York: Oxford University Press, 1987, 234.

> *The major new sources of medical school income have been research, state and federal aid for educating physicians.... [I]ncome from sponsored research and indirect cost recovery (research overhead), primarily from the federal government, reached 54.6 percent of the income for expenditures of private medical schools and 42.7 percent of that of public medical schools in 1965.*[33]

Ginzberg noted the decline in philanthropy and the relative government takeover of biomedical research in *The Financing of Biomedical Research* (see Figure 3.1): "The outstanding features of this period of rapid growth were the decline in private sources of funds from 54 percent of the total in 1950 to 32 percent in 1965 and the corresponding increase in the share of public, largely federal, sources from 46 to 68 percent."[34] This unprecedented financial reallocation promoting health research and education as big-ticket items was even more important in that "Americans now gave science unprecedented recognition as a national asset."[35] As a national advisory board reported at the end of the war:

> *Penicillin and the sulfonamides, the insecticide DDT, better vaccines, and improved hygienic measures have all but conquered yellow fever, dysentery, typhus, tetanus, pneumonia, meningitis. Malaria has been controlled. Disability from venereal disease has been radically reduced by new methods of treatment. Dramatic progress in surgery has been aided by the increased availability of blood plasma for transfusions.*[36]

Moreover, Americans wanted more of this scientific beneficence. The medical profession—always resistant to government control of any aspect of the profession—and the medical education and research infrastructures had to make adjustments

**Figure 3.1  Sources of National Funds for Biomedical R&D as Percentages of Total, 1940–1987**

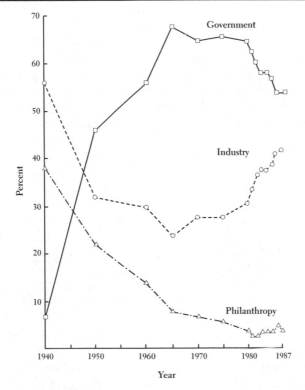

*From:* Ginzberg E, Dutka AB. *The Financing of Biomedical Research.* Baltimore: Johns Hopkins University Press, 1989, 18.

to the new realities. The former had to figure out how to channel the new resources and national demands to fit the needs of the profession as it presented a favorable public image, while medical academicians and researchers, already the darlings of the corporate foundation infrastructure, had to further mold their ideologies and reshape their agendas to coalesce with those of their government and corporate benefactors. However, the Black medical schools benefited little from these trends. For example, Meharry's financial plight became so desperate by 1948 that the institution was almost forced to trade its autonomy in exchange for segregationist Southern state government support. As James Summerville pointed out:

> *Were Meharry to close, the victim of its own financial difficulties, these states would not only lose a continuous flow of black physicians, dentists, and nurses but they would also have to open the doors of their own all-white medical schools to black students in order to make up the difference. The former possibility was acceptable to a few Southern politicians who were indifferent to the continued high mortality and morbidity rates among black people. The latter course they were determined to resist.*[37]

Strategically, the institution was to be utilized by Southern states as the regional site for Black medical, dental, and nursing training so that their health professions schools could maintain racial segregation.[38]

Not only did the federal government influence the contours of the medical education and research infrastructure scattered throughout the nation, but it also erected a monumental biomedical research consortium of its own, headquartered in Bethesda, Maryland. Building upon the National Institutes of Health (NIH) and National Cancer Institute (NCI) which had been formed despite AMA opposition in 1937, the NIH grew to 19 institutes, including the institutes of Mental Health (1946), Heart Disease (1948), Dental Care (1948), Arthritis and Metabolic Diseases (1950), and Blindness and Neurological Diseases (1950) as examples. The budget increased from $3 million in 1940 to $500 million in 1960 and $1.5 billion by 1967. This amounted to 40 percent of the total research monies granted nationally and made the NIH and NCI big health system players by 1965.[39]

A major cause of the 1960s' medical-social problems in the U.S. health system was rooted in postwar changes in the health care financing industry. For millions of working-class Americans (still 75 percent of the population in the 1990s) these policies resulted in inadequate and limited health coverage; failure of the system to insure high-risk groups like the elderly, Blacks, the chronically ill, the disabled, and the poor; and continued financial vulnerability of many Americans because of escalating health costs. In contrast to European systems, American health insurance was never designed to protect the financial stability of average families. It was designed to give the middle class access to hospitals and other providers in the system. High-risk groups were not a consideration. Labor unions smarting from a postwar conservative backlash aggressively bargained for the compromised U.S.

version of health benefits after the Inland Steel decision in 1948.* As a result, according to Paul Starr:

> *Between 1948 and 1950 the number of workers covered by negotiated health plans jumped from 2.7 to more than 7 million. By the end of 1954, 12 million workers and 17 million dependents were enrolled in collectively bargained health plans. Unions were now negotiating the purchase of a fourth of the health insurance in America.*[40]

As Starr went on to observe, "By the end of 1954, over 60 percent of the population had some type of hospital insurance, 50 percent some type of surgical insurance, and 25 percent medical insurance (though often only for in-hospital services)."[41] The health financing industry grew by leaps and bounds between 1945 and 1965. Although America's Western European allies had chosen to provide social insurance and income protection from illness for their populations through comprehensive, nationally run health systems, the United States provided only an "illusion" of such protection. Although the number of Americans with health insurance increased dramatically (see Figure 3.2), benefits and coverages offered by the United States health insurance industry were limited and offered only a small amount of financial security for an average family. These private insurance plans never paid more than 30 percent of the nation's total health bill.

Even these limited, usually employer–labor union negotiated benefits excluded most Blacks and the poor because of labor union and job discrimination. The growth of comprehensive health coverage offered by direct-service and cooperative plans such as Kaiser in California and Health Insurance Plan (HIP) of New York had been successfully contained by the AMA and its functionaries. Studies by the Commonwealth Fund (1950s), the Commission on Civil Rights (1966), and the National Advisory Commission on Civil Disorders (1963 and 1968) all documented that hospital discrimination was rampant and that Blacks with health insurance in many instances were blocked from receiving the health services to which they were entitled. This reinforced the results documenting racial discrimination in the hospitals by the NUL studies (1959) conducted by Dr. Paul Cornely. These reports applied to cities as varied as Memphis, Detroit, Chicago, and New York.

Guided by the medical establishment, conservative politicians, their own labor unions, and businessmen, Americans had chosen a market-dominated health system after the war. By the 1960s, the physician– and medical society–controlled Blue Cross and Blue Shield hegemony had been challenged by 1,000 or more commercial insurance carriers who controlled more than half the insurance business by the mid-1960s. The deleterious effects of competition and a commercial

---

*The 1948 Inland Steel case codified the acceptance of fringe benefits as part of welfare bargaining in labor contract negotiations. These benefits, including health insurance, were covered under the phrase "other conditions of employment." *Source:* Stevens R. *American Medicine in the Public Interest.* New Haven, CT: Yale University Press, 1971, 271n.

**Figure 3.2 Proportion of Americans Covered by Some Type of Health Insurance, 1940–1985**

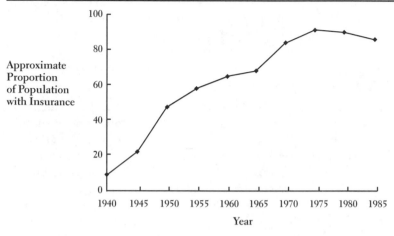

Approximate Proportion of Population with Insurance

Year

*Sources:* Health Insurance Association of America, Blue Cross and Blue Shield Association, Health Care Financing Administration.

*From:* Stoline A, Weiner JP. *The New Medical Marketplace: A Physician's Guide to the Health Care Revolution.* Baltimore: Johns Hopkins University Press, 1988, 29.

market had pushed the new health insurance market away from financial innovation or effective quality review toward the more profitable experience rating instead of the more economical and equitable community rating, away from efficiencies and comprehensiveness of direct service plans, and away from insuring poor, chronically ill, disabled, and "high-risk" populations like Blacks and the elderly. Intensification of residential and social segregation, continued health professions segregation, and legal protections for health system racial segregation and discrimination represented by the status quo made the situation worse. Expansion of White access to the health system through factors such as the Hill-Burton Act and the explosion of the health insurance industry did change the U.S. health system from one excluding the majority (all but the wealthy) early in the century to one inadvertently focused on excluding minorities (Blacks, the elderly, the disabled, and the poor).[42]

Paradoxically, the same factors that pushed the health care financing components of the health system purportedly to protect private voluntary financing mechanisms ensured future government intervention. By the1960s public opinion and historical forces dictated that health care be considered a basic necessity. Bullough and Bullough articulated enlightened contemporary attitudes of the era: "Before the 20th century, medical intervention was not necessarily a significant factor determining life expectancy; diet, sanitation, and other aspects of the environment were far more important in explaining the differential life expectancies between rich and poor."[43] By the mid-twentieth century, health care emerged as an important quality of life and longevity factor. The exclusion of large blocs of the population from the mainstream health system based on age, race, ethnicity, disability status, and socioeconomic status would not be tolerated indefinitely in a representative democracy. By 1965, this segmentation of the health system—secondary to outmoded financing mechanisms and social customs and spurred by the Black Civil Rights Movement—had gone unchallenged as long as it could.[44]

Between 1945 and 1965 White organized medicine (dominated by general practitioners and primary care specialists) and its establishment worked to reap the benefits of a rapidly expanding economic market generated by Blue Cross–Blue Shield and the commercial insurance industry and to marshal the growth of expanding AHC-based medical empires (which controlled 25 percent of community hospital beds by 1972). These agendas served as dampers preventing the medical and most other health professions from rationally fulfilling America's major medical-social needs. This was reflected in their continued policies of fighting progressive health care legislation enabling access of Black and poor populations to "mainstream" health care and limiting the numbers of medical school graduates. This was, in fact, a continuation of White organized medicine's nineteenth-century campaign against dispensary abuse and contract practice, which helped shape primary care services in the private sector.

Shortages and maldistribution of physicians continued. Although there was a slight increase in absolute numbers, specialization (up to 75 percent of the new physicians), academic medical requirements (30 percent working as salaried physicians), and dramatic increases in the demand for medical care forced the AMA to agree to increased physician output by the 1960s. Expansion of the training segments of the profession (interns, residents, and fellows) to provide some services to underserved populations and broadening licensing laws to allow foreign medical graduates (FMGs) to gain entry into the system palliated some of the personnel shortfalls. Shortages and maldistribution pressures were so great in the health professions that one can speculate on their importance in the desegregation of the nursing profession in 1946. Moreover, African American medical school graduates had gained entry into postgraduate training programs in largely White hospitals by 1965. These events and measures, accentuated by the hierarchical growth of AHC-connected power-broker physicians, contributed to the modern configuration of the fragmented U.S. medical profession. This evolved into competitive "town and gown" divisions of the White medical profession and the creation of a medical profession "third world" composed of African American physicians, dark-skinned foreign physicians, and inner-city practitioners who failed to follow the White patients into the suburbs.

Despite these unfavorable professional trends, the White medical establishment fought against expansion in the numbers of health professionals, equal opportunity for all groups for training, and ending gender discrimination in medicine until cajoled by popular and political interests and forced by financial circumstances* and government and legal coercion to implement some reforms. After a series of NAACP court victories against racial discrimination in graduate education, the University of Arkansas admitted the first African American, Edith Mae Irby, to a Southern medical school in 1948. (See Figure 3.3.) By the 1960s, 14 of the 26 Southern medical schools had admitted Black students, albeit on a token basis. Nevertheless, African American doctor/patient ratios remained much lower than those in the White population. Physician-led national health system policy and suzerainty over allied health professions training led to continued shortages of nurses, dentists, and allied health professionals in both relative and absolute terms.

Following World War II increasing pressure forced the AMA and its medical establishment to end blatant racial segregation and discrimination. The posture assumed by White organized medicine and its allies was resistance. Other than a few token acknowledgments at its 1950 and 1952 conventions and individual representatives in local and national organizations, the AMA ignored its racial discrimination problem. Taking a cue from national White organized medicine, progress moved at a snail's pace in the desegregation of county and state medical societies, medical specialty organizations, and hospital facilities. Between 1945 and 1965 there was a great deal more racial progress in the areas of nursing and health professions education than in the massive medical practice and services infrastructures themselves.[45]

**Figure 3.3 Edith Irby Jones (1927– )**
Edith Mae Irby integrates the University of Arkansas medical school in 1949.
Reproduced from *Ebony* (Pix Inc.), November, 1995, 231.

---

*Physicians openly acknowledged at AMA meetings that the funds they and private donors provided were inadequate to finance the medical school and research expansion they knew was necessary.

The federal government became a pervasive force in the United States health care system after the war through its financial influence on the institutional health care, health education, and research infrastructures. Before the mid-1960s it proved to be poorly coordinated and liable to easy outside control by interest groups (e.g., corporations, lobbyists, and educational institutions). A prime example is Mary Lasker's and Mary Mahoney's* private, lay lobby for scientific research—the American Society for the Control of Cancer (ASCC, later the American Cancer Society [ACS]). The ACS became so powerful that it not only determined NCI policy but also manipulated presidents, Congress, and surgeon generals in the interests of its causes. Agenda-setting by elite organizations such as these and the institutions they represented had little to do with massive unmet health service needs of the United States population. As Paul Starr observed:

> *Gleaming palaces of modern science, replete with the most advanced specialty services, now stood next to neighborhoods that had been medically abandoned, that had no doctors for everyday needs, and where the most elementary public health and preventive care was frequently unavailable. In the 1960s many began to observe that abundance and scarcity in medicine were side by side.*[46]

The postwar growth of the Columbia-Presbyterian AHC complex in upper Manhattan next to Harlem is an excellent example. As the period being examined ended, these trends intensified. For disadvantaged minorities socially, geographically, and politically segregated and isolated from mainstream social and medical systems, the situation grew even worse.

Another reason for the government's paucity of socially focused goals and objectives relative to the health system's race and class inequities and inequalities was that its massive involvement was divided through a matrix of competing agencies and institutions. Federal health programs included, but were not limited to, 64 United States Public Health Service (USPHS) agencies; three Food and Drug Administration (FDA) agencies; a VA consisting of 166 hospitals, a $1.5 billion budget, 5,000 full-time and 2,000 part-time physicians treating 86,000 patients daily; a Department of Defense (DOD) health service; Office of Economic Opportunity (OEO) health programs and clinics; Department of Agriculture meat inspection programs, Atomic Energy Commission (AEC) health programs; and health programs administered through the Bureau of Indian Affairs. Compounding this fragmentation into discrete programs, no powerful lobbies or interest groups represented the government's biggest health constituencies: the people. Even conferral of cabinet status with the formation of the Department of

---

*These wealthy women came from families that were heavily involved in health care lobbying and utilized modern advertising techniques. Their fortunes had been made in the newspaper and advertising industries.

Health, Education and Welfare (DHEW or HEW) in 1953 did not correct the power imbalance. Groups such as underrepresented minorities, senior citizens, children, welfare recipients, and social workers had no powerful lobbying or political groups representing them on Capitol Hill before 1965. Moreover, powerful, monied interest groups such as the AMA, the hospital industry, the insurance industry, and the tobacco industry were lined up against these groups and their health interests. Problems generated by these imbalances remain today.[47]

The post–World War II health policy approach of expanding the health system without redistribution of services or beneficence, accentuated by rampant race and class discrimination, inevitably generated pressure for federal intervention into the U.S. health system and service delivery. This was an unanticipated effect generated by policies set by the health system's dominant professional, health insurance, and policy-making bodies. Following a plethora of commissions and reports documenting hospital and health care segregation and discrimination between 1945 and 1960, slow but effective frontal legal assaults on health care apartheid were begun. The Greensboro (1962–1963) and Wilmington (1954–1964), North Carolina, cases outlawing hospital segregation and discrimination set the stage for legal reforms. Government agencies began applying the law, though resistance by the health establishment was pervasive and government enforcement lackluster.

Despite AMA and medical establishment resistance, by the 1960s African Americans and the poor enjoyed improved access to a selective and impersonalized version of medical care through government-sponsored health programs such as the Kerr-Mills program (1960), providing government health funding for the elderly poor, passage of Medicare and Medicaid (1965), and improved postwar government-sponsored programs at AHCs and their affiliated public and teaching hospitals. Despite the positive intentions of some public health and health reform advocates, medical-social assessment of this care revealed that it had not lost the overriding characteristics of health care for inner-city or poor people in America: "[T]he whole history of medical care of the poor in this country indicates that there has not ever been any well-thought-out plan but rather health programs have taken the path of least resistance."[48] And the myth of "good care for the poor"* was perpetuated: "In the process we have disguised this kind of medical care by saying that charity patients receive outstanding medical care.... This, like most folk sayings, is only half true because the poor do not receive adequate care—as can be demonstrated statistically or by actual observation of the kind of health care offered."[49]

Simultaneously, also in a characteristic manner, huge blocks of these "new" funds disappeared as they were siphoned from government into private, AHC-

---

*The nature and content of care in public hospitals and clinics varied widely and deviated from the personalized, uncompromising, consistent, and continuous medical model idealized by the AMA. As detailed by Kosa and Zola, Bullough and Bullough, and others, public care was modified by budgetary considerations and social distancing, shaped by the teaching or research needs of the institutions delivering the care, and occurred in institutions that were often strapped for funding, overcrowded, and viewed in a deprecatory manner.

dominated "health empires,"* the voluntary hospital system, and private corporate coffers. Aggressive moves toward community-based mental health services emanated from the liberal, academic mental health establishment. Initiatives begun under the Kennedy administration were bolstered by President Lyndon Johnson and led to the erection of community mental health centers, often alongside neighborhood health centers (NHCs), throughout the nation. After preliminary studies and pilot programs, Regional Medical Programs (1964) and, later, a Comprehensive Health Planning Program (1969) were government attempts to introduce regional and interinstitutional health planning to foster rationalization, efficiency, and equitable distribution of health care within the system.

An NHC movement began in 1965. The Office of Economic Opportunity (OEO) sponsored 100 centers, and HEW sponsored 50 more. Old programs such as the Hill-Burton Act were tailored to meet new needs and to subsidize community health centers. Federal court rulings, public pressure, and Black civil rights activism forced token desegregation of most of the nation's medical and nursing schools. Although stark race- and class-based disparities remained, government-induced changes by the late 1960s were responsible for gradual improvements in access and utilization in health services by the elderly poor, the indigent, and African Americans. By the 1970s Bullough and Bullough acknowledged that these policies laid the groundwork for the creation of another generation of a second-class tier of dual and inferior medical care for Blacks and the poor: "Americans, perhaps uncomfortably conscious of the fact not all people can afford medical care, have developed a second system of charity care, which is somewhat less than second class."[50] In most instances, for a panoply of reasons, these measures, with their serendipitous, sometimes positive, effects on long-standing maldistribution and public health problems exacerbated by race and class segregation and discrimination, proved to be too little and too late. It would take the passage of Titles 18 and 19 (Medicare and Medicaid) to make a significant dent in the problem.

In contrast to the defeat of the Wagner-Murray-Dingell Bill (the National Health Bill) of 1946 by the AMA and its establishment, the Kerr-Mills program was passed in 1960, providing government-funded health care for the aged poor. Regional Medical Programs were enacted to knit together AHCs, the nation's massive scientific research agenda, and medical care. Toward the end of the era, despite massive multimillion-dollar campaigns launched by the AMA, the pharmaceutical, and the insurance industries to defeat them, Medicare and Medicaid were passed as Great Society programs in 1965. Medicare Part A was a compulsory,

---

*These "health empires" were conglomerates of independent hospitals, health care centers, mental health centers, and state and federal government programs, centered around AHCs. These empires emphasized prestige, profits, teaching, and research and downplayed the provision of primary health services. Headed largely by social or academic elites and staffed by professional and working-class Whites, these infrastructures considered African American, ethnic American, and poor populations to be the least desirable elements, useful only for "teaching" purposes.

categorical,* hospital insurance program administered by the Social Security Administration, while Medicare Part B was a voluntary insurance covering physicians' bills. Medicaid was a voluntary, means-tested assistance program, linked to the welfare system and to states to provide medical care for the poor. Despite the shortcomings of the NHC movement, the AHC primary health care programs, the community mental health center movement, and the absent-to-lackluster health care civil rights enforcement of the new rulings by the courts, these programs represented health, health care, and medical-social progress for African Americans.[51]

Although not as prominent an influence bolstering the dominant high-tech medicine as compared to previously discussed health system components, the pharmaceutical and medical instrument and supply industries rose to prominence between 1945 and 1965. The pharmaceutical industry expanded after World War I, but "its period of explosive growth came in the aftermath of the second World War, fueled by the accelerated national expenditures for health care and biomedical research."[52] Growing to almost 800 companies by 1965, pharmaceuticals topped $1 billion in annual sales by 1950 and nearly doubled to $2 billion in sales by 1965. Morever, they contributed a significant amount of the national biomedical research budget, providing $40 million annually by the mid-1960s. With corporate profit margins hovering between 15 percent and 20 percent (the highest corporate profits on record) throughout the postwar period, pharmaceuticals contributed significantly to rising health care cost inflation.

The medical instrument and supply industries came of age with America's commitment to high-tech medicine. Expensive pieces of medical technology, such as X-ray and laboratory equipment, could now be purchased by hospitals and medical institutions with incomes virtually guaranteed by government programs, the Blue Cross–Blue Shield system, and the private health insurance industry. Now financially secure, voluntary and not-for-profit health delivery entities were allowed to go to the private bond market for capital, and for-profit entities began tapping equity markets. Medical instrument and supply companies' annual sales began approaching half the levels of the pharmaceutical industry.[53]

Ambulatory care facilities also underwent great changes in function and configuration by the 1960s. Ambulatory care is defined as "health care service given to a person who is not a bed patient in a health care institution."[54] Throughout U.S. history most ambulatory care has been delivered in noninstitutional settings such as private physicians' offices or private homes. Institutions providing ambulatory care date back to at least 1786 with the founding of the Philadelphia Dispensary, the first free dispensary in the United States. American traditions of institutional ambulatory care centered on the poor and were based upon assumptions of society's genteel stewardship and responsibility for provision of charity health services. Consistent with this role was the expectation that

---

*Categorical means that everyone designated to a particular category (i.e., over 65 years old) is eligible despite demographic characteristics or socioeconomic status.

indigent sick patients accept roles as experimental and "clinical material" for privileged medical trainees in dispensaries, hospital clinics, and public health facilities. In some areas outside the South, where most African Americans lived, the few people of color allowed any formal medical care were clients of these public and charity institutions.

Late nineteenth- and early twentieth-century efforts at changing these relationships toward normal doctor-patient relationships grounded in medical needs and professional services rendered under conditions of mutual respect were repeatedly thwarted by an implicit bargain struck between public health and the American medical profession. Avoidance of competition by ambulatory facilities for fee-for-service patients able to afford noninstitutional care continued to be the aim. The traditional covenant was epitomized by the published promise of the George White Health Units in Boston, the most famous public outpatient facilities of the 1920–1940 era: "no prescription given; no sickness treated."[55] American physicians, in essence, continued their proscription on eleemosynary and public health facilities engaging in diagnosis and treatment of diseases. Only preventive and public health programs such as immunizations, venereal disease, sanitation, and contagion treatment (e.g., tuberculosis) were permitted. This profoundly affected most ambulatory facilities. For many African Americans this served as yet another impediment that, along with extant racial policies, blocked their access to needed medical services.[56]

In response to heightened postwar awareness of the United States health system's maldistribution flaws (often linked to marked health disparities, inequities, and inequalities based on race and class), between 1945 and 1965 an alternative model of health delivery emerged from the War on Poverty movement. It was a predominantly ambulatory care model expropriated from Europe. As 1960s federal policy-makers endeavored to "reform" the American health care system along more egalitarian lines, the Office of Economic Opportunity funded pilot NHCs in low-income areas. This new model embodied traditional health care reform concepts such as comprehensive health care, *social medicine*,* preventive medicine, and community participation. With over 876 community health centers (most NHCs were renamed CHCs by 1975) serving 6 million persons between 1965 and 1975, a paradigm for national health reform emerged that resonated positively with widely held American values and goals in health care. For reasons to be discussed later, this was not to be.[57]

The other mode of health delivery that could technically be considered ambulatory was home nursing care programs. Despite being more cost-effective than in-hospital care, "In 1964 the United States Public Health Service found there were fewer than 100 cities with home-care programs in which visiting nurses

---

*Social medicine* is the practice of medicine concerned with health and disease as a function of group living. The health of people as members of families, significant groups, and communities dominates this discipline.

provided nursing care in the patient's home."[58] Besides competing with dominant hospital and medical models, the effectiveness of these programs was eviscerated by organizational and financing flaws in the United States health system. These negative effects on visiting-nurse programs led to sporadic nurses' visits and the implementation of the nurses' recommendations being dependent on the patients having someone at home to provide care. Prescriptions and therapeutic regimens often went unfilled due to financial considerations. African Americans were especially burdened by these deficiencies. Because of the lack of establishment legitimization and support, this category of ambulatory care could be viewed as a lost cause during this era. It would be resurrected in later decades of the twentieth century as home health care.[59]

### The Last Best Chance for Poor Americans: State and Charity Efforts

State and local governments have been involved in providing for "children, idiots, distracted persons, and all that are strangers, or new comers to our plantation" since at least 1641 in English North America.[60] The health care dimensions of providing for the poor became more defined as eighteenth-century almshouses, workhouses, poorhouses, and pesthouses assumed increasing hospital functions. This helps explain why in-hospital care was defined in public rather than private, poor instead of self-sufficient, and dependent instead of independent terms in this country. Hospitals would not shed this stigma in America until the twentieth century. Contagion control, quarantines, provision of charity health care, and care for the mentally ill—historically public health functions—were traditionally left to state and local governments. Public health,* the other health-related arm of growing government responsibility in complex societies, remains saddled with moral and class aspersions today.[61]

The founding of effective state health departments such as that in Massachusetts in 1869 was emblematic of the firm bureaucratic organization of public health that occurred in some places after the Civil War. Though retarded by European standards, public health advocates such as the American Public Health Association (founded 1872) made significant strides between 1890 and 1910. This "Golden Age" of public health, characterized by free immunization programs, founding of health centers, mandatory tuberculosis registration, free dissemination of laboratory and antitoxin services, and school-based health clinics in some Eastern cities such as New York and Boston, was rolled back or terminated by 1920. Viewing public health on an individualistic rather than population or societal basis was also inherent in the scientific progress in fields such as bacteriology,

---

*Public health* is one of the efforts organized by society to protect, promote, and restore the peoples' health. It is a combination of sciences, skills, and beliefs that are directed to the maintenance and improvement of the health of all the people through collective or social actions.

microscopy, and pathology. Prior to the 1880s specific disease causes were unknown and associated generally with sanitary conditions such as garbage, unpleasant odors, lack of cleanliness, and dilapidated surroundings. Sanitary reform involved neighborhood cleanups, isolating sick individuals from the larger population, and draining swamps. Many public health functions and concepts resided inside the realm of engineering. After scientific progress refocused public health on specific diseased individuals and disease prevention practices (e.g., hand washing, personal hygiene), local and state governments, boards of education, public health departments, and sanitation reformers were more easily defeated in their public health efforts by organized medical and health system forces preoccupied with the question: "How shall we keep people from getting treatment?"[62] By 1930 the boundaries of public health had been clearly defined:

> *The artificial separation of diagnosis from treatment, and more generally of preventive from curative medicine, was part of what later critics would describe as the "fragmentation" of the medical system. The defense of private interests set one of the limits to the rational organization of medical care in America. Wherever public health overreached the boundaries the professions saw as defining its sphere, the doctors tried to push it back.... [T]his was not just true of medicine. It was a cardinal principle in America that the state should not compete with private business. The physicians' view of the boundaries of public health was consistent with prevailing beliefs held by public officials regarding the boundaries of state action.[63]*

This dichotomy determined local and state government roles in the system that remain deeply ingrained in the culture of the United States health system.

Despite the medical profession and its establishment edict—in place since the 1920s—dictating the separation of personal health care provision from public health, by the 1960s service maldistribution forced local and state health agency participation in challenging the model. Traditional public health provider functions proved insufficient:

> *The first [function] was to provide environmental, health-related services such as inspection of food and water and the maintenance of public health laboratories. The second was to collect vital statistics. Third, local health departments generally provided preventive personal health services (especially those that would help control communicable diseases) such as the inoculation of infants and adult screening for tuberculosis and venereal disease.[64]*

Between 1945 and 1965 a massive in-migration of low-income Caribbean and African American populations to the nation's urban centers combined with the out-migration of more affluent, largely White, populations to the suburbs intensified health services maldistribution problems. The crisis was exacerbated by the out-migration of most private practice physicians, who followed their patients to the suburbs, while an aging, shrinking core of office-based practitioners remained to work in underserved innercities. What public health practitioners refer to as acute sickness services in inner-city hospital emergency rooms, health department clinics, and public hospitals increased dramatically. Another result of this health care demographic shift, as Barbara and John Ehrenreich observed, was that by the 1960s: "[m]ajor centers of medical research and education, such as Harvard Medical Center, Johns Hopkins, and Columbia, abut on urban slums, which are some of the nation's most disgraceful backwaters of medical neglect."[65] This triggered new challenges to the health delivery system. Some evidences were a renewed demand for increased physician output, the aforementioned NHC movement, and another round of attempts to rationalize and equalize health delivery. Increased federal funding and resources resulted in some superficial changes promoted by local and state health agencies, but the basic health system structure, grounded in fee-for-service and the private delivery of health services, remained—battered but unchanged.[66]

Of the voluntary health agencies and organizations, two of the five categories, made up of hundreds of local and national bodies concerned with specific diseases or problems and self-help (mutual aid) associations, are of concern here. Professional associations (e.g., AMA, AAMC, AHA, and the medical specialty societies), philanthropic foundations (e.g., the Rockefeller, Carnegie, and Robert Wood Johnson foundations), and public interest groups (e.g., the Health Research Group) are discussed along with the components of the health system with which they are most closely connected.

Following the lead of the National Foundation for Infantile Paralysis, the most successful voluntary organization of the postwar period, by the 1960s ACS became the most influential health lobbying group. Such organizations raised billions of dollars annually to support programs ranging from supporting single hospitals or neighborhood clinics to eradicating a particular disease (March of Dimes) or treating a single organ (American Heart Association). These organizations proved in different ways that money and scientific research can combine to make dramatic progress at ameliorating (e.g., polio) or making significant progress against (e.g., cancer) targeted diseases. But for underserved, especially minority, populations, these developments did not deviate from the principle that the privations and diseases that receive public and governmental support are the ones dictated by the needs of the middle and upper classes.[67] Moreover, as James T. Bennett and Thomas J. DiLorenzo, authorities on the economics of nonprofit organizations, pointed out in *Unhealthy Charities*:

> *Health charities plead for money for programs to aid those in need while*
> *at the same time holding millions of dollars in cash, stocks, bonds, real*

> *estate, and automobiles. . . . Many implicitly allude to helping disease*
> *victims while admitting that they do absolutely nothing in terms of direct*
> *assistance. Instead, tens of millions of dollars are spent annually to*
> *educate high-income health professionals about disease while the poor*
> *are largely ignored.*[68]

The March of Dimes, raising more money than any other health campaign, funded research that produced a successful vaccine. The ACS, utilizing mass advertising and lobbying techniques, became the darling of the U.S. Congress and the executive branch of government—placing the NIH, particularly the NCI, on a new and elevated level. Despite their medical-social and programmatic shortfalls regarding the poor and underserved, voluntary health agencies—which assumed large parts of the responsibility for patient and professional education on particular diseases and occasionally provided specialized disease-specific support services at the patient level—became major players in the nation's health system during this period. They also proved that the American public was fascinated with and would pay to fund scientific research.[69]

---

## Prelude to Progress: Black Health, 1945–1965

From a public health perspective, socioeconomic status and health tend to parallel one another. Comprehending the unfavorable epidemiologic state of disadvantaged groups in the United States such as African Americans is difficult when it is shorn of its demographic and vital statistics variables. Moreover, as Nicolette Hart reiterates in the last two editions of the *Oxford Textbook of Public Health,* race is a determinant of health and disease: "Though a genetic attribute, fixed at conception and generally irreversible, racial inheritance is also a sociopolitical-economic and cultural variable and a fundamental source of social and health stratification."[70] Although there is evidence of slight improvement in African American health status around the time of World War I, as has been mentioned there are conflicting data regarding improvements in Black health or mortality during the 1920s.[71] With Depression-induced government involvement in both public and personal health services, despite the nation's economic hard times there may have been some slight improvements in Black health starting in the mid-1930s. During the 1940s mortality rates and other health indicators improved dramatically for Blacks, but substantial racial differentials remained. Between 1950 and 1970 there was little improvement. Regarding Black male death rates, for example, Reynolds Farley and Walter R. Allen observed that: "from 1950 to 1970 there was very little improvement. Indeed, the age-adjusted death rates of black men in the late 1960s were at the same level they had been 20 years earlier."[72] Improvements in longevity and other indicators for African American women throughout the period after 1940 were more substantial, for reasons to be discussed later.[73]

Between 1945 and 1965 the African American population grew 43.7 percent from 14,662,000 to 21,064,000. Postwar prosperity and economic growth lifted living standards. African Americans were big beneficiaries. Although economic gains for African Americans had been erratic, by 1964 Black poverty rates had declined below 50 percent (compared to 1939 rates of 93 percent). Nevertheless, "[d]uring the affluent 1950s, Negro Americans were disproportionately represented in the one-fifth of the population classified as the hard-core poor and the one-fourth above them who lived on the verge of poverty."[74] In a Black population undergoing rapid urbanization and industrialization, the National Research Council found that two decades after Myrdal's *An American Dilemma* (1944), "36 percent of black families and 9 percent of white families received incomes below poverty thresholds."[75] Black unemployment (5.9 percent) after the war was 1.69 times the White rate (3.5 percent), and rose erratically to 1.98 times the White rate by 1965 (8.1 and 4.1 percent Black and White rates, respectively). Meanwhile, Black youth unemployment throughout the 1950s was consistently almost twice that of White youth unemployment. African American family income fluctuated dizzily, rising to 56.8 percent of White family income during the Korean War in 1952, only to drop to 51.7 percent of White income by 1959.

Education is an important criterion for obtaining a privileged niche in the competitive and unequal occupational structure in the United States. Moreover, education, employment, and occupation are strongly correlated with health status and outcomes. Between 1945 and 1965 there was a substantial reduction in Black/White inequality in the basic amount of schooling received. However, large gaps remained, as Richard Kluger noted in *Simple Justice*: "In 1945, the South was spending twice as much to educate each white child as it was per black child. It was investing four times as much in white school plants, paying white teachers salaries 30 percent higher, and virtually ignoring the critical logistics of transporting rural Negroes to their schoolhouses."[76] When comparing racial outcomes related to high school attainment, "The percentage of whites finishing high school was four times that of blacks."[77] Racial differences in achievement test scores and college entry and completion were just as stark. Even though colleges "were flooded with returning veterans able to pay tuition with their GI Bill benefits ... college-starved Negroes were hit hard by segregation."[78] The possibilities for graduate, postgraduate, or professional education for Southern Blacks (75 percent of the Black population) after World War II were circumscribed by segregation and discrimination:

> [T]here was still no institution in the South where a Negro could pursue studies for a doctorate. Excluding Howard University, there was one accredited medical school in the South for Negroes, but twenty-nine for whites. There was one accredited school of pharmacy for Negroes, but twenty for whites. There was one provisionally accredited law school for Negroes, but thirty-six for whites. There was no accredited engineering school for Negroes, but thirty-six for whites.[79]

Ambrose Caliver, the senior specialist in Negro education in the United States Office of Education, probably the leading national authority on the subject, noted: "Poor health and family disorganization continued to cause low school-attendance and high pupil-dropout rates ... and almost all those young blacks who did advance intellectually had to work while studying, to the detriment of their school-work or their health or both."[80] The end result of all these factors was that at the end of World War II about one-fourth of the entire Negro population entered the new era functionally illiterate. Clearly, much remained to be done from an educational standpoint.[81]

Although the *Brown v. Board of Education* decision had outlawed segregation in public education in 1954, progress along educational lines was slow: "In 1954 about 2.2 million black students attended all-black schools. By 1960 barely 235,000 black students attended formerly all-white schools."[82] When Black children were allowed to attend integrated schools, their academic performance and standardized test results seemingly improved. But resistance such as the Little Rock, Arkansas, school crisis in 1957, which threatened the constitutional system of government when a state government refused to obey a Supreme Court order, as well as the Atlanta public school system efforts to maintain segregation between 1958 and 1962 were the rule rather than the exception. In fact, it appeared that the South would simply adopt tactics successfully used in the North to perpetuate racially segregated education. On the collegiate, graduate, postgraduate, and professional levels, more African Americans were admitted into mainstream educational institutions under pressure generated by the legal and civil rights communities.

Other sources fueled Black economic progress throughout the period. As a National Research Council report recounted, "The major sources of black gains in earnings and occupation status from 1939 to 1965 were South-to-North migration and concurrent movement from agricultural employment to nonagricultural industries. These shifts were facilitated by high rates of employment, job creation, and output growth."[83] Nevertheless, throughout the prosperous postwar period, Blacks continued to occupy the lowest rung of the employment and economic ladder. Therefore, "[d]uring the post–World War II period, the millions of poor Negroes living in city ghettos or in rural slums lacked money to command private care and received precious little public medical assistance. Their low-income status helped swell the death rate among them."[84] Compounding an already bad situation was the fact that although Black physician numbers rose 10.5 percent, from 3,800 to 4,200 nationally between 1940 and 1960, the Black doctor/patient ratio dropped from 1:3,753 in 1948 to 1:4,500 in 1960. Another factor often correlated with health status and outcome, marital status, began to show a gradual decline in marriage rates, slow increases in divorce rates, and an increase in Black out-of-wedlock births from 16.8 to 23.6 percent between 1940 and 1963.

African Americans seemed to be making progress despite the system. Health and public policy shortfalls related to the nation's race and class problems, including those afflicting the health system, bedeviled signs of progressive change. For example, Black migrants to the urban North were beneficiaries of those region's public health progress relative to reliable sanitation, clean water supplies, waste disposal, and mandated immunization programs. Moreover, many public acute sickness service health facilities such as city hospitals, public health departments, and hospital outpatient services were opening up to Black clientele. However, authoritative sources, including Carter G. Woodson's *The Rural Negro* (1930) and Charles S. Johnson's *Shadow of the Plantation* (1934), provided substantial evidence that conditions for rural African Americans deteriorated throughout the 1920s and Great Depression. Earnings, housing, nutrition, and clothing were worse for rural Blacks than they were in 1900. Breakdown of the share-cropping system and the mechanization of agriculture eliminated the need for unlettered, Black tenant farmers and farm workers. Therefore, statistical gains projected from Northern health progress was countervailed by Southern health decline. Despite its shortcomings, the Northern migration represented improved housing and health environments for a large percentage of African Americans. However, once more, other factors blunted the expected social and health-related improvements. As Massey and Denton related in *American Apartheid,* "Throughout the United States—both in southern and northern cities—ghettos had become an enduring, permanent feature of the residential structure of black community life by 1940, and over the next thirty years the spatial isolation of African Americans only increased."[85] The intensification of this process in the postwar years:

> rests on a foundation of long-standing white racial prejudice ... and to the widespread translation of this sentiment into systematic, institutionalized racial discrimination within urban housing markets.... What was new about the postwar era was the extent to which the federal government became involved in perpetuating racial segregation.[86]

The relationship between residential segregation and racial discrimination in health and health care led David Barton Smith to observe that:

> At a structural level, it is shaped by residential segregation and the limitations of the health-related resources in predominantly minority communities as opposed to more affluent, predominantly white communities.[87]

Residential segregation emerged as one of the major factors promoting permanent bifurcation of the United States health system into Black and White entities. Residential segregation, and the apartheid it produces, adversely affects the "economic institutions to produce and distribute the material livelihood of the people, ideological beliefs (religion, morality, and political culture) to uphold shared values, linguistic codes to facilitate communication, and social institutions (marriage, family, education, law, and so on) regulating relationships and protecting rights of every citizen."[88] It destroys the social and economic environment African Americans depend upon to "make stable and harmonious coexistence possible for a large number of people sharing the same territory and cooperating together in producing their livelihood"[89]—namely, the very fabric of their society. Despite signs of material and statistical progress, the National Research Council reported: "In the 1960s Blacks deeply resented their continuing second-class status. Despite their gains ... blacks in general did not share the affluent life styles of the white majority."[90] This frustration—another postwar dream deferred—spilled over into the health system and was reflected in the persistence of disparate African American health status and outcome.[91]

The health system itself, adding to burden imposed by socioeconomic and demographic factors, had adverse affects on Black health throughout this period. As the National Research Council noted: "During much of the period covered ... there was open segregation of medical facilities in the United States. In the 25-year period before 1965, persistent barriers to access to preventive, primary, and hospital care influenced the quality of life and the patterns of illness observed among blacks."[92] African Americans, burdened with historically driven health disadvantages, did not need a racially discriminatory and hostile health system compounding their health shortfalls. Improvements in Black access to public and personal health care, to quality hospitalization, to quality preventive health services, and to culturally competent and sensitive health providers (more common in the next period of inquiry) were the fruits of a health care Civil Rights Movement that had its roots in the 1945 to 1965 period. This evolutionary process will be taken up in detail later.

Mortality continued to be employed as the principal indicator of a population's health status.* The huge 14.6 year (31 percent) gap in life expectancy between Whites and Blacks in 1900 continued to close. Comparisons of 1945 death rates reveal an age-adjusted rate** of 9.5 per 1,000 population for Whites and 13.1 per 1,000 for Blacks, a 37.9 percent higher rate. By 1965 Black age-adjusted mortality had declined 21.4 percent to 10.3 per 1,000, while the White rate had declined 22.1 percent to 7.4 per 1,000. However, the Black/White differential in death rates increased from 37.9 percent in 1945 to 39.2 percent in 1965. Most of this erratic reduction in age-adjusted mortality was generated

---

*Mortality remains the most precise method to measure the distribution of health in a population. It is the only indicator that can be used confidently to study health trends over time between and within societies.

**Since differences in the age composition of a population (e.g., the Black population has traditionally been younger than the White population) influence total mortality rates, it is preferable to use age-specific mortality rates when comparing population groups. This is accomplished by a computational process known as "age adjustment."

by the female segment of the population, with the males, especially African American males, making no progress from the late 1940s until the 1960s. Meanwhile, between 1945 and 1965 the expectation of life at birth increased for Blacks 6.4 years (from 57.7 years to 64.1 years) while increasing 4.2 years (from 66.8 years to 71 years) for Whites. This reduced the Black/White disparity in expectation of life from 9.1 years (a 15.8 percent difference) in 1945 to 6.9 years (a 10.8 percent difference) in 1965. How much of this improvement was due to improved living conditions for the African American population or improvements in access to quality preventive and therapeutic health care services is difficult to determine.[93]

African Americans have consistently suffered poor pregnancy and infancy-related health outcomes compared to European Americans since slavery in English North America to the present-day United States. The rate at which children die before their first birthday, infant mortality, is an indicator, used both nationally and internationally, of the overall health status of a community or nation. Despite impressive improvements in reducing overall infant mortality in the United States, for African Americans infant mortality rates have remained approximately twice the rate for Whites over the course of the twentieth century. (See Figure 3.4.) After a rapid decline for both races between 1940 and 1945, progress was slow until after the 1960s. Between 1945 and 1965 the infant mortality rate (IMR) in the United States decreased from 38.3 per 1,000 live births to 24.7, a 35.6 percent decrease. A racial comparison of the data reveals a picture that was not so bright. Beginning the period with a 1945 IMR of 56.2 per 1,000 live births, a figure more than 1.5 times (precisely 1.58) the White rate, the African American IMR dropped to 41.7 per 1,000 live births by 1965. As Farley noted, "Since 1950, the decline among whites has been faster than the decline among non-whites."[94] As a result, by 1965 the Black/White differential in IMRs had climbed so that the Black rate was 1.94 times the White rate, and the Black IMR, which was 58 percent higher than the White rate in 1945, had climbed to 94 percent higher than the White rate.

For the first five decades of the twentieth century most infant mortality* took place between the 28th day and first year (the postneonatal period) of life. Infant demise within this period was usually related to low standards of living and infectious diseases. With advances in living standards and control of infections by the 1960s, most infant mortality occurred between birth and 28 days (the neonatal period). During the two decades between 1945 and 1965 U.S. neonatal mortality declined from 24.3 deaths per 1,000 live births to 17.7 deaths per 1,000 live births. The Black rate in 1945, 32.0 per 1,000 live births, was 1.37 times higher, or 37.3 percent, than the White rate (23.3 per 1,000 live births). Despite the overall decline in neonatal mortality rates by 1965, the Black rate, 25.4 per 1,000 live births, climbed to 1.58 times higher than the White rate of 16.1 per 1,000 live

---

*Usually stated as the infant mortality rate, which is the number of deaths of live-born infants from birth to the first year of life per 1,000 live births.

## Figure 3.4 Infant Mortality Rates by Race, 1940–1984

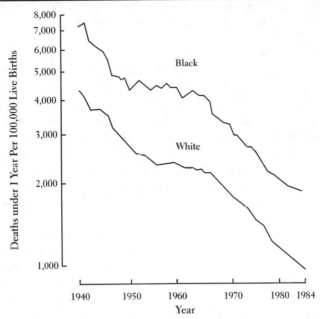

Note: Data for 1950, 1955, 1960, 1965, and 1970–1984 refer to Blacks and Whites. For other years, data refer to non-Whites and Whites.

Sources: Robert D. Grove and Alice M. Hetzel, *Vital Statistics Rates in the United States: 1940–1960* (Washington, DC: U.S. Government Printing Office, 1968), Table 38; National Center for Health Statistics, *Health, United States, 1983*, Table 11; *Vital Statistics of the United States: 1981*, vol. 11, Part A, Table 2–1; *Monthly Vital Statistics Report*, vol. 34, no. 13 (September 19, 1986), Table 10.

From: Farley R, Allen WR. *The Color Line and Quality of Life in America*. New York: Oxford University Press, 1989, 48.

births. Moreover, the Black/White percentage difference in the rates also climbed from 37.3 to 58 percent. Postneonatal mortality is largely a reflection of living conditions and preventive infant care received after birth. Black/White ratios of postneonatal mortality did not show any signs of improving for decades, hovering above 2.18 until 1975. The 1950 Black postneonatal mortality rate, 16.1 per 1,000 live births (218 percent higher, or 2.18 times the White rate), declined slightly to 15.2 (281 percent higher, or 2.81 times the White rate) by 1965, demonstrating that the Black/White odds ratio had increased.

Both IMRs and neonatal mortality rates are directly related to low birth weight.* As Farley observed, "Women in the United States bear lightweight infants compared with women in Japan or in prosperous Western European nations.

---

*Low birth weight (LBW) is below 2,500 grams at birth, while very low birth weight (VLBW) is below 1500 grams at birth.

However, black women are about twice as likely as white women to deliver children weighing less than 5.5 pounds."[95] Although the National Center for Health Statistics (NCHS) began reporting low birth weight by race in 1969, data recorded as "non-White" before then reflected the rates of the African American population. As early as 1950 non-Whites experienced a LBW rate (10.2 percent) suggestive of a Black/White ratio almost 1.5 times the White rate (7.1 percent). The Black/White ratio increased to 2.01 in the late 1960s and the Black rate remained at least twice the White rate into the late 1980s.

Maternal mortality is defined as the number of deaths of women per 100,000 live births from complications of pregnancy, childbirth, or within 90 days after giving birth. Black/White differences in maternal mortality are greater than infant mortality differences, and although the rates fell for both groups between 1945 and 1965, racial disparities barely changed. The Black maternal mortality rate in 1945, 456.7 per 100,000 live births, was 2.7 times the White rate of 172.1 per 100,000 live births. By 1965 the Black rate had dropped to 88.3 per 100,000 live births compared to the White rate of 21.0 per 100,000 live births, but the Black/White odds ratio had increased to 4.2. Some of the same factors that influence infant mortality, such as late or absent prenatal care, inadequate prenatal care, high teen pregnancy rates, and high unintended pregnancy rates, affect maternal mortality rates. Between one-third and one-half of maternal deaths are preventable if efforts are made to ensure early and adequate prenatal care.[96]

As we have seen, the health of children of African descent has always been poor compared to that of European American children for the 325 years before the year 1945 in English North America and, later, the United States. Although the 1945 to 1965 period perpetuated that tradition, Black children began to benefit from some of the impressive health gains for all American children after 1950. According to the NCHS, the death rate from all causes for children aged 1 to 4 years in 1950, 139.4 per 100,000 resident population, improved to 84.5 by 1970. For children aged 5 to 14 years, comparable rates were 60.1 in 1950 and 41.3 in 1970. But as the National Research Council (NRC) pointed out, "black children have not shared equally in the overall health gains, and their death rates are much higher than those for white children."[97] Black male childhood death rates in 1960, 1.43 to 1.99 times the White male rates in the 5 to 14 and 1 to 4 age groups, respectively, are representative. Despite the fact that nearly all of the childhood mortality decline after 1950 was due to reduction in infectious diseases and deaths from other natural causes, Black children did not benefit equitably. As a 1959 National Office of Vital Statistics report pointed out:

> Communicable childhood diseases are very important to Negro American health. Compared to white mortality rates, Negro mortality rates are particularly high during early life. This is in part due to diseases, such as whooping cough, meningitis, measles, diphtheria, and scarlet fever, for which there are no known racial susceptibilities. Though fatal complica-

*tions of these disorders can be drastically reduced by modern medicine,*
*Negroes have death rates from them at least twice those of whites.*[98]

Whooping cough, so highly fatal during the first two years of life, but which can be prevented by immunization, claimed a Negro death rate nationwide six times that of White from 1949 to 1951. These data dramatized the continuing need for improved medical services for Black children throughout the 1945 to 1965 period.[99]

The aberrant profile of excess adult Black mortality and morbidity compared to Whites that emerged after the late nineteenth century began a trend toward "normalcy" between 1945 and 1965. The disproportionate prevalence of Black deaths from tuberculosis, syphilis, pellagra, and "ill-defined" (or "unknown")* causes began declining toward White rates — especially in the South, where most Blacks lived. Cancer and accidents became prominent causes of death among African Americans for the first time. Whatever the etiologies — gains in quality of life, economic progress, access to medical services, or alterations in disease patterns and exposures — Black health profiles, although still markedly less favorable than Whites, began to resemble those of other Americans for the first time.

Although hunger and starvation among Blacks were "rediscovered" by the American public in 1967 following a Senate investigation, deaths from pellagra — the skin, gastrointestinal tract, and central nervous system disease linked to the dietary deficiency of nicotinic acid — virtually disappeared by 1965. The cause of this lethal nutritional disease, a major scourge on the Black population since emancipation that was endemic in 2 to 25 percent of the Southern population until the 1930s, was discovered by Public Health Service epidemiologist Joseph Goldberger, who began researching the problem in 1914. Differentially affecting Blacks, by the 1920s pellagra was found to be related to the nutritionally deficient diet composed of corn meal, sorghum, and salt pork that most African Americans were forced to survive on in the South. The addition of more expensive dietary items such as fresh meat, poultry, fresh vegetables, milk, and eggs prevented the disease. In lieu of continued Black Southern poverty throughout the 1930s, government programs strategically provided some of these food items along with yeast to Southern health programs and practically eliminated the disease. By the 1940s pellagra deaths per 100,000 of the non-White population in Southern states declined below 20. (See Figure 3.5.) Improvements in nutrition for African Americans, as with any other group, translated into better health outcomes.

Tuberculosis, the scourge of the Black community since the nineteenth century, along with venereal diseases such as syphilis and gonorrhea, came under a modicum of control with the introduction of penicillin, heavier funding of government clinics and venereal disease prevention programs, and medical breakthroughs. As Beardsley observed, "Mortality from TB, the particular scourge of black Americans, had been falling since the century's turn with little help from

---

*This designation on a death certificate usually indicated an absence of medical attendance at death.

Figure 3.5  Pellagra Deaths per 100,000 Population,
Non-Whites in Southern States

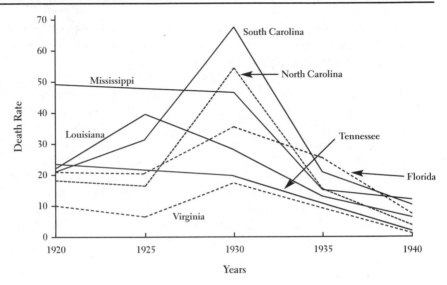

*Source:* Farley R. *Growth of the Black Population: A Study of Demographic Trends.* Chicago: Markham, 1970, 220.

medical science. But it was only after the war that it finally lost its terror, owing to the provision of more sanitarium space and the introduction of effective chemotherapy."[100] Because of improved White health status, the virtual disappearance of the disease in that population, and TB control programs, "[b]y the late 1960s that program and the sanitariums were mostly benefitting black tuberculars."[101] In 1945 Black tuberculosis mortality rates in cities of over a million people were almost twice that of Negroes in cities with populations between 100,000 and 200,000. However, between 1910 and 1950 in Manhattan the non-White death rate from tuberculosis dropped from 445.5 to 62 per 100,000 population. Despite these improvements, by the 1960s TB death rates for Blacks remained four times higher than those for Whites. TB is a contagious disease, but an excellent screening test was available and effective chemotherapy was becoming accessible; it was the type of malady that organized public health forces battled best. By 1970 the war against tuberculosis was thought to be largely won.

Syphilis and gonorrhea were the two most common venereal diseases affecting the Black population. Although gonorrhea, which is two to four times as common as syphilis, seldom kills, it causes pelvic infections and a great deal of painful disability, scarring of internal genital organs, and sterility. Untreated syphilis can cause terminal illness and death in a small percentage of its victims, while "investigations suggest that 30 to 50 percent of the pregnancies occurring in syphilitic women who receive no care end in fetal deaths; upwards of 20 percent of the infants born to such women die from congenital syphilis shortly after birth."[102] Early in the century African American hospital patients given Wasserman tests for syphilis suggested prevalence rates of 25 percent to 30 percent among certain Black populations. Despite the detection of similar rates in certain White populations, syphilis was labeled a "Black disease" by the White medical profession.[103] By the 1920s, officials of the Julius Rosenwald Fund felt that pregnancy wastage caused by syphilis combined with high maternal mortality rates caused by lack of obstetrical care or attendance kept Black death rates high. In order to determine the prevalence rates and eventually launch treatment programs for venereal diseases, the Rosenwald Fund, the USPHS, and state health agencies launched cooperative pilot programs at various sites in the late 1920s. Monies for treatment quickly ran out and the Great Depression eliminated hope for finding other funding sources. Nevertheless, some of the research continued. The infamous Tuskegee study was born of these efforts. Due to the fact "that for every southern black who received any treatment for syphilis, there were twenty-five who had the disease but were not treated,"[104] the 1930s prevalence rate for syphilis among Southern Blacks was estimated at 20 percent and syphilitic death rates peaked in the mid-1930s. (See Figure 3.6.) With

**Figure 3.6  Deaths from Syphilis per 100,000 Non-whites, Death Registration States of 1910 and All Death Registration States**

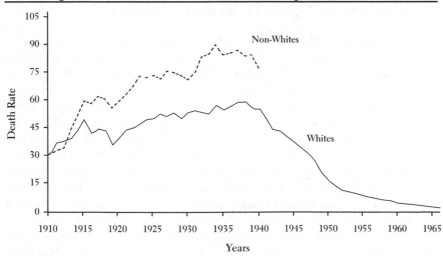

*Source:* Lindner and Grove, op. cit., Tables 16 and 18. Robert D. Grove and Alice M. Hetzel. *Vital Statistics Rates in the United States: 1949–1960*, Washington, D.C.: U.S. Government Printing Office, 1968, Table 63. U.S., National Center for Health Statistics, *Vital Statistics Rates of the United States: 1961 through 1966*, Vol. II, Part A, Tables 1–9 or 1–10. Deaths of Mexicans were included with deaths of non-Whites for years 1932 to 1934.

*From:* Farley R. *Growth of the Black Population: A Study of Demographic Trends.* Chicago: Markham, 1970, 224.

the federal push for public health programs during the Depression combined with the improved Black access to treatment and hospital care (see Table 3.2) afforded by World War II, syphilitic death rates in African Americans plunged during the 1940s through the 1960s.[105]

**Table 3.2  Proportions of Non-White Births Occurring in Hospitals, 1935–1965**

| Date | Percent of Hospital Births |
|------|----------------------------|
| 1935 | 17.3 |
| 1940 | 26.7 |
| 1945 | 40.2 |
| 1950 | 57.9 |
| 1955 | 76.0 |
| 1960 | 85.0 |
| 1965 | 89.8 |

*Source:* Farley R. *Growth of the Black Population: A Study of Demographic Trends.* Chicago: Markham, 1970, 229.

## A Profession under Siege: White Medicine, 1945–1965

The social influences of World War II and a changing American society exerted unrelenting pressure on the White medical profession for health system change. The war and postwar social devastation in Western Europe had heightened international acceptance of medical care as a "need right" that should be made available to all citizens. Moreover, millions of veteran GIs returned from the war having had positive experiences with social medicine as practiced by the U.S. military services and foreign allies. Most of these veterans wanted such services available for their families. African Americans harbored similar feelings along with a newfound determination to end racial segregation and discrimination. However, by then "the AMA was building roadblocks to hold back every effort to extend medical care.... The AMA had made medical care a superbusiness and turned scalpels into swords to defend it from those who envisioned it as something more."[106] White organized medicine's desperate efforts to promote its self-interests and thwart these powerful social forces weakened the political hold of physicians on the American public and toppled them collectively from their high moral ground.

Within the ranks of White organized medicine, internecine warfare continued and even intensified. Much of the conflict was grounded in increased medical specialization, competition for prestige and economic success, and control of burgeoning scientific and medical knowledge. A major influx of foreign medical school graduates was the nidus of another set of problems. Medical school budgets increased, shifting significant blocks of physician manpower toward academic medicine. Thus, "full-time positions doubled nationally, increasing from 4,212 in 1950–51 to 11,319 by 1959–60."[107] The clash in medical-social viewpoints between "town," private practice physicians, and "gown," medical academicians, is reflected in Martin L. Gross's 1966 evaluation: "Only an estimated one third of the university physicians are members of the AMA, and many do not even belong to the county medical society."[108] Moreover, the new medical educational empires extended their power through the control of more hospital beds (up to 25 percent by the end of the era) and mobilized more medical manpower engaged in the training process. Residency positions increased from 5,000 in 1940 to 12,000 by 1947 to 25,000 by 1955. This had the indirect effect of allowing African American medical school graduates postgraduate training slots in some White hospitals for the first time, because:[109]

> Between 1940 and 1950 the proportion of approved house staff positions that hospitals were unable to fill rose from 10 to 30 percent. The house staff shortage ... resulted directly from the decision to expand hospitals without expanding medical school enrollments. By 1957 hospitals were looking for more than 12,000 interns annually, but American medical schools were graduating fewer than 7,000 students a year.[110]

Simultaneously, "Congress and state legislatures cooperated by making it easier for foreign-trained doctors to enter and work in the United States," fostering "the peculiar slant of American health policy (expanding hospitals, but keeping down medical enrollments)" that "was producing a new lower tier in the medical profession drawn from the Third World."[111] Starr noted, "During the 1950s foreign medical graduates increased from 10 to 26 percent of all house staff."[112] The foreign influx, initially from Europe, but by the 1960s mostly from Korea, India, and the Philippines, "often took jobs that Americans did not want (for example, in state mental institutions)."[113] At the other end of the spectrum, White American medical specialists not only were guaranteed more income but also marshaled more prestige and authority within the profession. Twenty-four percent of active practitioners represented themselves as full-time specialists in 1940; 69 percent claimed that status by 1966. Private practitioners viewed moves such as expending AHC influences and FMG increases as incursions into their clinical practices and community authority.

Interprofessional distancing was manifested in many other ways. For example, in the 1920s and 1930s medical school science departments often performed diagnostic tests for the clinical faculty. Thus, basic sciences in medical schools were often taught by scientists, though sometimes not physicians, whose interests focused on clinical medicine. They made efforts to relate their instruction to clinical problems. However, as medical science moved toward molecular levels:

> The anatomists lost interest in gross anatomy and became electron micro-
> scopists and cellular biologists; the biochemists turned from nutrition and
> intermediary metabolism to molecular structure and enzymology, and the
> physiologists from the function of mammalian organ systems to cells; the
> bacteriologists became microbiologists concerned with microbial physi-
> ology and genetics; and the pharmacologists turned from studying the
> effect of drugs on intact animals to chemistry and the effect of chemical
> agents at the cellular level.[114]

The increases in physician income registered during the era did little to soften the interprofessional squabbling: "Between 1945 and 1969, while the consumer price index rose at an annual rate of 2.8 percent, physician's fees rose 3.8 percent and their annual incomes at 5.9 percent a year. The average net profit from medical practice rose from just over $8,000 in 1945 to $32,000 in 1969."[115] Much smaller, less intense versions of these interprofessional conflicts took place at the Black medical schools. The postwar leadership offered by the White medical profession seemed ill-suited to presenting a unified front for or against any public policy affecting the nation's health or health system.[116]

Although the AMA and its coterie of health professions associations, hospital industry representatives, health insurance interests, and pharmaceutical industry supporters had been largely successful before the war, politically thwarting President Franklin Roosevelt's efforts to liberalize the health system, the shock of Harry S. Truman's election to the presidency in 1948 threatened to disrupt medical establishment plans. Before the 1948 elections, expecting a turn away from the leftward trends associated with the Great Depression and World War II, AMA strategists noted that "the politically moderate *Time* magazine described the federal government as a 'modern, bureaucratic Great White Father,' protecting the helpless, regulating business, guaranteeing full employment, and bringing security to the farmer and the old and the sick."[117] Faced with "a president elected to office after committing himself to a compulsory national health insurance plan,"[118] the AMA was stunned.[119]

Before this new challenge, the AMA had led effective campaigns defeating recent efforts at progressive health care legislation on Capitol Hill. Beginning in 1943 the AMA led in defeating the biannually introduced Wagner-Murray-Dingell Bill, which legislated a universal, comprehensive, federally administered health care program. First introduced in 1943, the bill languished in a Congress preoccupied with World War II. Reintroduced in 1945, "the bill had the substantial boost of President Truman's endorsement and a tide of public sentiment which seemed to favor the measure."[120] Truman went on record in a message to Congress on November 19, 1945, declaring that every American citizen had "the right to adequate medical care and the opportunity to achieve and enjoy good health" and "the right to adequate protection from the economic fears of sickness."[121] Passage of such a bill into law would have represented a landmark health system breakthrough for African Americans with the potential to desegregate large blocs of the health system and go a long way toward equalizing health services for both races. The AMA and its conservative political allies like Republican Senator Robert A. Taft campaigned against the bill and were eventually joined by the American Hospital Association (AHA), the American Bar Association (ABA), the American Dental Association (ADA), the Protestant and Catholic Hospital Associations, the Chamber of Commerce, and the American Grange. The election of a conservative Republican Congress in 1946 had as much to do with killing the bill before reporting it out of committee as did AMA resistance. The 1947 version of the bill never reported out of congressional committee.

Since the turn of the century, punctuated by a short interval of Progressive influence between 1912 and 1920, the AMA had a stellar record of defeating progressive health care legislation at local, state, and national levels. This included everything from programs for the elderly to programs for expectant mothers, infants, and children. For example, long after defeating the Sheppard-Towner Act of the 1920s* and child health care programs during the Depression, "the AMA was still fighting government-funded health care for children":[122] "In 1945 its lobbyists appeared to oppose a bill introduced by Florida Senator Claude Pepper which would have increased the authorization under the ten-year-old Social Security Act to spend $50 million on maternal, child health and crippled children's care, as well as another $20 million on child welfare."[123] AMA lobbying killed the bill in Congress, contending it would relieve parents of their obligations to care for their children and open the door to government-sponsored medical care for all—the dreaded "socialized medicine." Three years later "the association was back on Capitol Hill to oppose a grant-in-aid proposal for the federal government to help underwrite the cost of medical examinations for schoolchildren."[124] Despite support for the legislation from the Parent-Teacher Association (PTA), the AMA prevailed, alleging the bill would upset traditional patterns of medical practice and project the schools into the field of curative medicine.[125]

To fight against the Truman plan—another form of "socialized medicine"—the AMA took several steps. The 1949 assistant secretary-general manager of the AMA, Ernest B. Howard, M.D., recalled: "That was the year we went to war with Truman."[126] The AMA House of Delegates voted to assess each member $25 in 1949; to engage the services of an outside public relations firm to devise and execute a political strategy; and to expand its Washington, DC, offices, where its legislative apparatus was headquartered. In a flurry of extremist politics, accusations and cross-accusations, embarrassment, and unfavorable publicity, the AMA was also forced to distance itself from the National Physician's Committee (NPC). Of these actions, engaging an outside public relations firm to design and supervise its public relations and political campaign against the government and its health

---

*The Sheppard-Towner Act established the Board of Maternal and Infant Hygiene and led to strengthened federal and state child health programs.

reformer allies was the most significant. Another factor having practical consequences for physicians after 1949, for the first time since 1911 when dues were required, the $25 membership charge became an annual fee whose failure to pay could have threatening consequences:* "Those who refused to pay were rather crudely warned their names would be passed on to local medical societies, organizations with the power formally to discipline or informally censure members."[127] These actions changed the face of political lobbying on Capitol Hill for all time, setting new standards and making the AMA the prime model of effective political action in the future.

The public relations firm hired by the AMA was a natural. The firm had recently led the California Medical Association's campaign to defeat Governor Earl Warren's proposal for statewide compulsory health insurance in 1945. This firm had orchestrated Warren's previous election to governor in 1942 and started the ascendency of Richard M. Nixon. Moreover, the San Francisco–based company, led by Clem Whitaker and his wife, Leona Baxter, had an unmatched 15-year track record of 58 wins and five losses in California politics. It approached political campaigning with unconventional but prescient strategies. Regarding Whitaker and Baxter's strategies, political expert Theodore H. White and others observed: "[I]t would be cheaper to influence politics by mobilization at the grass roots than by buying votes retail, one by one, as was then the practice.... [A] campaign won as a public issue will stay won—for some years at least."[128] According to their principles, courting individual legislators: "is a waste of time and money because it is inconclusive. Not only is the composition of the legislature always changing, but legislatures are like women—you have to keep buying them candy and flowers."[129] This strategy also represented the coming of a new age of issue-oriented campaigning, heavy reliance on political education and propaganda, interest group influence and endorsements, and pragmatic politics instead of traditional one-on-one political lobbying. Ideologically oriented political campaigning, "which hewed not too closely to the truth,"[130] became acceptable and, indeed, mainstream.

For the AMA this represented an immense change in its strategy to defeat "socialized medicine." Previously, Morris Fishbein, M.D., editor of *JAMA* between 1924 and 1949, had placed the issues surrounding government-sponsored compulsory national health insurance on ideological and crusading bases instead of a politically pragmatic footing. Over the years, "Dr. Fishbein gave organized medicine its 'voice'; he opened up to it the real sources of power, money, legislative action, and public assent. Astonishingly, he managed to hold back the twentieth century for 50 years for the benefit of organized medicine."[131] A man of words and more of a "salesman rather than scientist by talent,"[132] he continuously made anti-"socialism" arguments, pitting the "justice" of the physician's cause against that of

---

*County medical societies had the power to terminate or deny hospital privileges, cut off referrals, launch professional and character assassinations, and call for investigations into medical licensing. African American physicians suffered these penalties routinely based on color.

a monolithic government and its allies in his books, speeches, articles, and features in periodicals. He won over laymen with his medical advice newspaper columns. This overall approach produced fiery editorials and righteous crusades but was politically unsound. Nevertheless, "President Truman's request for health insurance created such consternation at the AMA headquarters that it was decided that Dr. Fishbein and the committee working with him needed help."[133] Although there were numerous underlying reasons, Fishbein's inability to change and adapt to the new political environment may have helped lead to his retirement during this period.

Buttressed by millions of AMA dollars, Whitaker and Baxter moved their offices to 1 South LaSalle Street in Chicago, close to AMA headquarters. From there they launched massive political and propaganda campaigns between 1949 and the 1960s. They mobilized the organization's entire county-state-national structure and stressed that: "People are more interested in politics than ever before, but their interest is an after hours interest. . . . To attract their attention you must put on a fight or a show or both."[134] They developed hard-hitting campaign literature that AMA historians concede sometimes contained exaggerations, pompous overstatement, and hyperbole:

> *Whitaker and Baxter had no gift of humor, little appreciation for subtlety. As a matter of professional conviction, they dealt in hammer blows, repeated hammer blows. Hard-sell marked their ads, the pamphlets they prepared, the speeches they wrote. They simplified issues; they emotionalized them; often they exaggerated and overstated them.*[135]

Besides obtaining endorsements, executing massive mail campaigns, contributing editorials, making public AMA statements, and distributing news releases, "the . . . 1949 . . . Whitaker and Baxter campaign utilized press, radio, television, magazines, billboards, and posters to convey to the American people the message that national health insurance was bad medicine."[136] From monies raised on the physician tax, $1.1 million was spent on newspaper and magazine ads and radio commercials. Over 100 businesses spent $2 million of their own resources running AMA advertisements in newspapers. Between October 8 and October 22, 1949, "every daily and weekly paper in the nation carried a five-column by 14-inch ad paid for by the A.M.A."[137] More than thirty national magazines and 1,600 radio stations shared in the advertising bonanza. Local newspapers sold "boilerplate" ads by the AMA to local merchants, generating an estimated $19 million dollars. As Ruth Harmer noted in *American Medical Avarice*, "In 1949 and 1950, the AMA achieved the dubious distinction of being the biggest spender among Washington lobbies. It provided almost double the budget of the second largest lobby."[138] Putting aside the question of whether the nation's largest professional organization entrusted with the nation's health should be engaged in such activities, no saturation campaign up to that point had been so comprehensive.

The "working from the top down" advertising approach created the appearance of a reality wherein a majority favored a voluntary (which would never make health care available to everybody) rather than mandatory (wherein everyone automatically became a member of the health system through some mechanism) system of health insurance. Whitaker and Baxter publicists failed to compare the coverage offered by the insurance companies with the compulsory plan proposed in the pending federal bill.* Even though the numbers covered by voluntary insurance were increasing:

> *Less than 2.5 percent of all those with voluntary insurance had coverage equal to that which the federal government proposed as minimal, and voluntary health insurance covered less than nine percent of the national health bill. Even if every person in the country were under some sort of voluntary insurance plan, only a fraction more than one-quarter of the nation's medical bill would be met.*[139]

The Whitaker and Baxter campaign failed to explain the relationship between the purchase of voluntary insurance and income. This explains why the richer, industrial states of the East, which contained one-third of the nation's population, had 60 percent of the voluntary health insurance policies written by Blue Cross, the major insurer. The 43 percent of the population living in the poorer South and West represented only 17 percent of the Blue Cross policies. Ignoring the survey data indicating that Americans wanted a universal, government-operated health system, brochures keyed to the "voluntary way" theme, asking: "Who is for Compulsory Health Insurance?" and answering: "The Federal Security Administration. The President. All who seriously believe in a Socialistic State. Every left-wing organization.... The Communist Party."[140]

One Whitaker and Baxter pamphlet asked and answered: "Would socialized medicine lead to socialization of other phases of American life?.... Lenin thought so. He declared: 'Socialized medicine is the keystone to the arch of the Socialist State.'" (The Library of Congress could not locate this quotation in Lenin's writings.)[141] Both Harmer and James Howard Means of Harvard reiterated that "[t]he Communist Party was held to be the chief promoter of national health insurance"[142] in AMA campaigns. Further creating a climate of unreality and appealing to a growing anticommunist hysteria, the AMA campaign denied that the Truman plan gave participants freedom of choice. In reality, "the Truman bill specifically guaranteed that for both doctor and patient."[143] Even with the Truman-endorsed bill buried, the association spent more than $500,000 the next year and $250,000 in 1952 to prevent its resurrection. Nevertheless, the Whitaker and Baxter–led AMA campaigns were devastatingly effective.

---

*The federal coverage was much more inclusive and comprehensive than the AMA private proposals.

By the end of October 1949, everyone conceded that President Truman's health plan was dead. In June of that year the AMA House of Delegates gave Whitaker and Baxter a standing ovation, and Morris Fishbein, the man who had enshrined the term "socialized medicine" into a household epithet, was restricted to editing the *JAMA*. His retirement six months later represented the end of an era. Reeling from public relations and electoral defeats, the few remaining congressional supporters of national health insurance silently buried the 1951 version of the Truman health bill in committee and adjourned. The AMA and Whitaker and Baxter had other items on their agenda.[144]

When the Korean War call-up started in 1950 and Congress and the War Department attempted to reinstate medical care for the dependents of military personnel by extending the Emergency Maternal and Infant Care (EMIC) program (which had provided services for 1.5 million dependents of GIs in the four lowest ranks at a cost of $127 million dollars during World War II), an AMA spokesman alleged in the *New York Times* that a new "opening wedge on socialization" of medicine loomed.[145] Another AMA spokesman testifying before a House of Representatives subcommittee said that extending medical care to the wives and children of enlisted U.S. soldiers:

> was "impractical," "harmful to national defense" and would overload
> military hospitals with dependent wives and children. Off-post care
> provided by private physicians interfered with the doctor's right to charge
> whatever he felt the traffic would bear; care within military hospitals
> would be even worse . . . since the private practitioner would be eliminated
> entirely.[146]

Despite subsequent Department of Defense (DOD) surveys indicating that 80 percent of those who would use any form of the aid-to-dependents medical program would have annual incomes of less than $4,300 and without such a program would go without medical care, the AMA prevailed. As the health care problems of military dependents intensified, AMA opposition in 1950, 1951, 1952, and 1953 drastically modified the Dependent Medical Care Act of 1956, the bill that eventually passed, adding many repressive barriers and copayments for military dependents.

Determined to introduce some kind of health insurance bill, the Democrats unveiled the Falk-Cohen compromise in 1951, which "provided for 60 days of free hospital care each year for people sixty-five years or older who were already covered by Social Security."[147] To "build a record" for the legislation, the president sought to justify the future Medicare bill with another study documenting the need for national health insurance. In 1952 he appointed Dr. Paul Magnuson, former head of the VA Department of Medicine and Surgery to chair a panel on the health needs of the nation. Despite the withdrawal of the AMA representative, the effort obtained favorable comment from the prestigious *New England Journal of Medicine*: "The appointment of a well balanced, unprejudiced commission to study the health needs of the nation is a logical way of bringing further emphasis to bear on the problem. The President is to be congratulated on his determination to seek expert advice, and he should receive the fullest cooperation from organized medicine."[148] The report's conservative recommendations, geared to complement the Falk-Cohen legislation, urged federal funds to underwrite health care for low-income groups—the poor, the aged on fixed incomes, migrant workers, and the unemployed. Statistics indicated that medical costs were rising about 5 percent annually while the incomes of Social Security recipients and the poor failed to keep pace with inflation. The gap between the ability to pay and need was widening each year. The AMA opposed the report and the bill, labeling them "Creeping Socialism."

The eight years of the Eisenhower administration (1952–1960) were relatively quiet ones for the AMA relative to national health insurance. Even the Democrats had dropped the issue from their platform by 1952. Nevertheless, the AMA's Washington lobby was busy opposing aid to medical schools, scholarships for students, medical care for military dependents, and school health proposals. Despite AMA opposition a few Social Security amendments had been passed in 1950 to broaden coverage under old-age and survivors' insurance to raise payments to recipients and to include an additional 10 million Americans. Nevertheless, "[t]he opposition of the AMA and the Chamber of Commerce . . . still blocked the addition of coverage for those permanently and totally disabled before age sixty-five. The AMA denounced disability insurance as 'another step toward wholesale nationalization of medical care and the socialization of the practice of medicine.'"[149] Most progressive health measures throughout the 1950s were either defeated outright or emasculated to such an extent they were rendered virtually useless for the populations they were designed to serve. Even federally funded medical school building programs and medical research were trimmed to conform to AMA control and conditions. Much of the AMA opposition was never allowed to surface publically.

The AMA's long-standing opposition to medical care for veterans is well known. Unable to completely defeat the implementation and much of the growth of the VA system, by the 1950s the AMA routinely curtailed its expansion. Attacking necessary postwar expansion of the VA system in 1952 the AMA held that "[t]he situation [of veterans' medical care] may almost be stigmatized as communistic medicine in its most militant form, endeavoring to edge its way into American life under the cloak of patriotism."[150] By 1954 with 20 bills dealing with veteran's medical care pending before the U.S. Congress, the AMA favored only one. This legislation authorized the investigation of the system. In the postwar years the AMA forced the government to give private practitioners a piece of the $1.5 billion VA pie. Along with its 5,000 full-time doctors seeing 86,000 patients daily in 166 VA hospitals, 2,000 doctor beneficiaries of AMA lobbying efforts served as consultants.

Rhode Island Representative Aime J. Forand resurrected the Falk-Cohen plan for medical care for the aged in 1957. Frank D. Campion noted, "the AMA sensed a new threat in the form of the Forand bill, which proposed hospitalization insurance for the retired population through Social Security. It seemed like the 1940s all over again."[151] The AMA sent up peals of "socialized medicine" and "the beginning of the end of the private practice of medicine." Again, "the AMA undertook a massive campaign to portray a government insurance plan as a threat to the doctor-patient relationship."[152] Scuttled in both the 85th and 86th Congresses, the bill at least got hearings in the latter. Moreover, health reformers and Democrats began framing health care reform as a problem of the aged. They thereby gained a growing constituency who felt the problem of hospital costs, which had doubled in the 1950s, with unusual directness. A staff member of the 1959 Senate subcommittee on aging recalled: "The old folks lined up by the dozen everyplace we went.... And they didn't talk much about housing or recreational centers or part-time work. They talked about medical care."[153]

Significantly: "[o]pinion polls had shown support before, but in the entire history of the campaign for national health insurance, this was the first time that a groundswell of grassroots support forced the issue onto the national agenda."[154] This led to organized labor fighting for the bill. Moreover, a traditional AMA ally, the American Nurses Association, broke ranks with the medical and health care establishments and supported the bill. Although it didn't go as far in its support, the American Hospital Association publicly stated that some kind of national health insurance might be required to relieve the plight of the elderly poor. In retrospect, these were the birth pangs of Medicare.[155]

The 1960 Congress responded to the demands for Medicare, passing a halfway measure called the Kerr-Mills program. As Cray observed "Kerr-Mills was another poor law; one first had to qualify either for state welfare rolls—often swearing a pauper's oath—or meet state imposed standards of medical indigency. Its limitations were greater than its assistance."[156] The AMA approved it. Introduced by two of Congress's most powerful members, Senator Robert Kerr of Oklahoma and Representative Wilbur Mills of Arkansas, chairman of the House Ways and Means Committee, the bill extended federal support to the states for welfare medical care for the elderly. The program had the stigmata of being a form of welfare and "means tested," wherein the elderly recipients were forced to prove their impoverishment. Moreover, state participation was elective. Even some AMA members such as Russell B. Roth, vice chairman of the Council on Medical Service in the early 1960s, considered Kerr-Mills inadequate, stating, "When the AMA selected Kerr-Mills as the vehicle of its deliverance, it picked a woefully creaky, sputtery and undependable glory-wagon."[157] Later, comparing it to the King-Anderson bill, Medicare's predecessor, which was introduced in 1961, Roth felt "Kerr-Mills was a totally inadequate alternative."[158] Although the federal government promised to provide 50 percent to 80 percent of the funds (depending upon the financial status of the state) with the Kerr-Mills bill, state participation in the program three years after its inception proved to be low. Only 19 states were participating, and two of the states, New York and California, were dispensing about half of all funds disbursed by the program. Thirty-one states failed to launch programs or put up the funds necessary to participate. The conservative program in effect from 1961 to 1965 was a political, health policy, and medical-social fiasco.[159]

John F. Kennedy had used the medical-care-for-the-aged bill (later renamed Medicare), mired hopelessly in committee, as a major domestic platform plank for his successful 1960 presidential election. Campaign polls indicated public approval margins of two to one. Building upon many of the principles contained in previous Wagner-Murray-Dingell bills, and named the King-Anderson bill (after Clinton P. Anderson [D-NM] and Cecil R. King [D-CA]), it provided 90 days of free hospital care and some nursing home care, but almost no physician services as an earned right to retirees (65 years or older) on Social Security. It was to be financed by a 7 percent increase on the Social Security portion of payroll taxes. The AMA House of Delegates responded: "the King-Anderson bill did not meet the needs of the situation and would lead inevitably to further government encroachments on medical care."[160] Then it threatened to withdraw patient care: "The medical profession is the only group which can render medical care under any system.... [I]t will not be a willing party to implementing any system which we believe to be detrimental to the public welfare."[161] By February 1961 a bitter propaganda war had begun—the AMA versus organized labor, the progressive wing of the Democratic party, the Senior Citizens lobby, and the health reformers.

To defeat this legislation White organized medicine relied on paid network television speeches, grassroots state and county medical society campaigns, seven-column ads in 31 major newspapers, radio spots on stations in 34 cities, a 91-page position paper, thousands of pamphlets stating the AMA position, public service announcements, speaker's bureaus, sponsored teas by the Women's Auxiliary to the AMA, and canned radio talks. The AMA's Washington lobby stayed on duty when Congress was in session and provided speech-writing services for congressmen willing to speak against the King-Anderson bill. For two years the opposing groups warred with each other, climaxing in nationally televised speeches for and against the legislation—pitting President Kennedy in support of the bill against Dr. Edward Annis, the AMA spokesman—on May 20 and 21, 1962. The AMA officially admitted that the campaign cost hundreds of thousands of dollars. Two months later, on July 17, despite popular and presidential support, the health bill, which had passed the House, was defeated in the Senate by a vote of 52-48.

Between 1962 and 1965 the King-Anderson health bill was waylaid in the House Ways and Means committee by Wilbur Mills and a coterie of conservative legislators. However, a combination of events by 1964—including President Kennedy's assassination; a sense of national remorse surrounding the country's failure to fulfill Kennedy's egalitarian social agenda; worsening of health access experienced by America's elderly and poor citizens; the nation's rejection of extreme right-wing politics embodied by Barry Goldwater; the rise of President Lyndon Johnson, a man who believed in Medicare; and a Democratic sweep of the Congress in 1964—ensured an imminent AMA defeat and passage of some type of progressive health care legislation.

The ever-pragmatic Wilbur Mills, resigned to the fact that some legislation would pass, combined the administration's bill with a proposed Republican measure covering doctors' bills and a third program to aid services for the poor. The Democratic compulsory hospital insurance program under Social Security became Medicare Part A. The revised Republican program of government-subsidized voluntary insurance to cover physicians' bills became Medicare Part B, and the program for the poor became Medicaid. President Johnson signed the programs into law on July 30, 1965, as Title 18 and Title 19 amendments to the Social Security Act. Despite the millions of dollars it expended, the AMA had suffered its first major legislative defeat. Smarting with defeat and threatening to revolt against both plans and patients, the AMA was called in to help write the administrative and operating guidelines authorized by the legislation. Another Johnson administration appeasement was to make over 20 changes to, in effect gutting, the recommendations made by the 1964 Presidential Commission on Heart Disease, Cancer, and Stroke (the DeBakey Commission), appointed at the behest of the Lasker lobby. Its recommendations to establish at government expense "a national network of regional centers, local diagnostic and treatment stations, and medical complexes designed to unite the worlds of scientific research, medical education, and medical care"[162]—measures that would have rationalized, regionalized, and rendered efficient large segments of the health system—were virtually killed by the AMA.[163]

Between 1945 and 1965, under siege for internal and external social change, White organized medicine forever changed its character. Originally formed under a rubric of professionalization, medical educational reform, and protection of the public, the American medical profession had always operated with a hidden agenda. Bedeviled historically by unbridled competition from legitimate (e.g., midwives) and illegitimate (e.g., faith healers, root doctors) contenders and disdain from populist-oriented politicians, doctors had always made jealous, low-profile attempts to regulate and restrict rights to practice medicine. Moreover, financial survival had always been a high priority. After World War II all this was exacerbated by a growing cacophony of public criticism about lack of access to care, the spiraling costs of health care, too few doctors, and perpetuation of the tradition of low-quality care for poor and minority Americans. Responding during the postwar period, the profession mobilized the most potent and successful political influence campaign ever conceived. Physician-leaders made modernizing organizational changes within the AMA, girding the organization for public relations and political battle; openly formed political action arms—something traditional physicians would never have been identified with; allocated millions of dollars for public and professional education campaigns to openly influence public opinion and the political process about the health system and health care delivery issues; and cut ties with rogue political elements within the profession itself who were fighting medicine's political battles through clumsy and embarrassing methods.[164]

A creature of White organized medicine's 1930s battles against compulsory, government-sponsored health insurance, the National Physicians' Committee for the Extension of Medical Service* (NPC) was formed in 1938. Theoretically a "nonprofit, nonpolitical organization for maintaining ethical standards and extending medical service to all the people,"[165] between 1938 and 1951 it quickly became the AMA's antireform political action and public campaign arm. Led by two former AMA presidents and several former trustees, it was officially acknowledged by Morris Fishbein and the AMA's board in 1939 for its "public relations activities."[166] The NPC was a reflection of former AMA president (1932) Dr. Edward H. Cray's personality—a Dallas ophthalmologist with a fiercely individualistic, pioneer spirit who did not feel it was beneath a professional medical society's dignity to "stoop" to political campaigning and techniques to influence public opinion and policy. Although it also served as a safety valve siphoning off some overzealous AMA members from the politically ultraconservative Physicians' Committee for Free Enterprise in Medicine,** the NPC played political hardball.

The NPC raised 90 percent of its funds from the pharmaceutical industry; the rest came from 22,000 physicians.[167] Morever, although it was the official spokesman for AMA causes, it shielded the medical organization's tax-exempt corporate entity from accusations of engaging in political campaigning. The NPC fought vociferously against the Wagner-Murray-Dingell bills spending $905,359 on pamphlets, speeches, print advertisements, and radio talks between 1940 and 1945 alone. However, as AMA historians were forced to admit, "[t]he National Physicians' Committee favored blunt, even crude, material, reflecting the anger that surged through some segments of medicine. But the harsh tone offended many others; the press and parts of the public."[168] Although the NPC was endorsed by the AMA House of Delegates in 1942 and again in 1945, its rhetoric and tactics began to rankle with AMA officials.

As early as 1943 the NPC released posters and pamphlets that were cavalier with the facts. One poster designed for display in doctors' waiting rooms showed an elderly woman timidly facing an angry doctor saying: "Make it snappy sister.... The doctor can't sit listening to your tale of woe. He's not a private physician. He works for the government, not you. You're just one of the people assigned to him by the political overseer.... So snap into it, comrade!"[169] Hyperbole and exaggeration were standard operating procedures for the NPC as it alleged that a national

---

*The organization is usually referred to as the National Physicians' Committee (NPC).

**Frank Gannett, a man with an extremely bad history with the press, had formed a physicians' branch of the notoriously ultraconservative Committee to Uphold Constitutional Government, which attracted some AMA members.

health insurance bill was: "designed to act as the catalyst in transforming a rapidly expanding federal bureaucracy into an all-powerful totalitarian state control. Human rights as opposed to slavery is the issue."[170]

Such metaphors struck chords of special irony to African Americans being denied access to health care and being denied their citizenship rights. Criticism rained down on the AMA and its members, who perceived that the NPC was causing them to lose credibility. The AMA brought in the prominent public relations firm Raymond Rich Associates as consultants. After a 17-month evaluation in 1948, Raymond Rich recommended that:

> *the A.M.A. disassociate itself from the National Physicians Committee, that the committee's overzealous activities be curbed in any event, that the[y] document the statistics it had ... glibly used over the years to support the A.M.A. case against the need for a national health insurance program, and that the national organization provide a forum for dissenting physicians who could no longer argue the merits of positions contrary to A.M.A. policy in the pages of the "scientific" journal of American medicine.[171]*

When the AMA trustees declined to accept its recommendations in 1949, Raymond Rich Associates resigned, stating:

> *The very integrity and sincerity of the association are at stake.... Stated simply, the association has yet to take an unequivocal and effective action on the policies which it adopted on our recommendation last year [1948]: to seek the truth on the economic and social aspects of medicine, to put the public first, and to become adequate to its responsibilities.[172]*

Raymond Rich included this paragraph in a letter sent to all AMA officers and members of Congress. "The A.M.A. had nurtured a viper in its bosom,"[173] Cray graphically stated.

After a series of embarrassing incidents, the NPC outrage constituted "the straw that broke the camel's back" in December, 1949. In a letter sent to all AMA members and thousands of Protestant clergymen, the AMA had paid the "Reverend" Dan Gilbert $3,000 to include information on health care in his clergy-oriented newsletter. In the letter to AMA members and selected Protestants clergymen, Gilbert alleged national health insurance was a: "real threat to religious liberty.... [T]his monster of anti-Christ ... this monstrosity of Bolshevik bureaucracy ... would establish quotas for the baby crop in the same way that the Agriculture Department set quotas for farm production."[174] Known for spotting "communist plots," being "careless of facts, and given to savage language,"[175] the ultra-right-wing, conservative, extremist preacher's salutation, "Dear Christian American," struck most people as anti-Semitic.[176] In the ensuing uproar, it was discovered that the "reverend" had no degree from any recognized divinity school, had worked with right-wing extremists during the 1930s, and had consorted with the American-born-and-bred fascist organization, the Silver Shirts. The AMA disavowed the letter but then praised the NPC for defending the AMA against national health insurance. The letter alienated thousands of physicians and the State Medical Society of the State of New York from the AMA and hastened the NPC's demise. By 1951 the NPC had been dissolved, Whitaker and Baxter assumed its functions, and its remaining assets were given to the American Medical Education Foundation.[177]

Besides disassociating itself from rogue political elements, the AMA made fundamental changes in its organization, structure, and ideology between 1945 and 1965. The experiences gained fighting off the Wagner-Murray-Dingell bills, the Truman plan, and the Forand bill led White organized medicine away from old-fashioned crusades toward modern management and political action. Even before the Medicare/Medicaid defeats of 1965, the AMA virtually placed itself on a wartime footing, deciding it must intervene in the public policy decisions affecting its future.

Of the three broad strategies available for public policy activity—directly engaging in the legislative process by lobbying; taking the organization's case to the public, or undertaking a program of political action—the AMA emphasized the second and expanded its role in the first. Whitaker's and Baxter's public relations campaign took the organization's viewpoint to the public and was a smashing success. However, by the 1960s the AMA was becoming involved in too many political issues for repeat campaigns alone to be effective. Direct organizational involvement in undertaking a direct program of political action, the third option, risked the AMA's tax-exempt status and could have violated the Federal Corrupt Practices Act. It skirted these limitations by other mechanisms.

After much soul-searching, the AMA formed the American Political Action Committee (AMPAC) in 1961. It was separate from the AMA, although the organization nominated its board of directors. Instead of making repeated ideological pleas in legislators' offices, AMPAC became adept at monitoring congressperson's voting records, endorsing candidates, targeting others for defeat, buying pre-election media time, and coordinating the work of local political organizations that rang the doorbells, furnished campaign workers, and got "right-minded" people to the polls.

Some of the other activities the AMA engaged in between 1945 and 1965 included streamlining its headquarters operation from over 800 employees in 1950 to 650 in 1960. More than 230 were let go when the association shut down its antiquated printing plant and began subcontracting for such services. However, much of that reduction was counteracted by increases in public relations staff, economic researchers, and legislative staffs. Support staffs for the new Student American Medical Association, the Joint Commission on Accreditation of Hospitals (JCAH), and the expanded number of councils and committees were also provided. During this period the AMA established the American Medical Education Fund (AMEF) to raise funds from the medical society and business and physician sources to support medical schools. All this new staffing and reorganization were restructured under the new office of Executive Vice President Francis James Levi Blasingame, M.D., a surgeon from Wharton, Texas, who reported directly to the board of trustees. The prominence and importance of the state-county grassroots organizations increased exponentially with the creation of a field service division. Although their causes and ideology remained conservative, dominated by European American interests, and reactionary from a medical-social perspective, White physician-leaders made modernizing organizational changes within the AMA, girding the organization for public relations and political battle; successfully formed political action arms — something previous generations of physicians would never have been identified with; and allocated millions of dollars for public and professional education campaigns about health care system and delivery issues to openly influence public opinion and the political process.[178]

The medical profession, led by the AMA, remained one of the most segregated professions in America. Little official effort was made between 1945 and 1965 to correct the situation. Other than scattered efforts by local and county medical societies, such as the New York County Medical Society's submission of an antidiscrimination resolution at the 1948 AMA convention, and a few medical societies admitting Blacks throughout the 1950s, little was done to combat professional segregation and discrimination. The AMA formally acknowledged racial discrimination in its ranks for the first time at its San Francisco convention in June 1950, advising its membership to "study" the situation. In 1952, at its Chicago convention, it reaffirmed that resolution. The AMA, and the White medical profession generally, in regard to African American health, continued to have "blind spots," which allowed them to ignore the devastating effects of their traditional policies of racial exclusion and discrimination in the health professions, maintenance of race and class barriers in health delivery, and proscription of universal coverage or government involvement in health and health care.[179]

---

## Wade in the Water: Blacks in Medicine and Health, 1945–1965

African Americans, led predominantly by physicians, dentists, and nurses of color, were major participants in the legislative, legal, and conciliatory efforts to end racial discrimination in the U.S. health care system between 1945 and 1965. Transmutation of their efforts in health care civil rights into the overall African American Civil Rights Movement helped set the stage for the most dramatic improvements in Black health since the Civil War.

A review of the post–World War II situation in the U.S. health system clarifies why Black physicians, dentists, and nurses continued their traditional roles as health care civil rights workers, both on formal and informal levels.* As W. Montague Cobb observed about the persistence of the detrimental effects produced by the hospital system's race problem, "In 1946 . . . the 'Negro medical ghetto' as described was intact. There were no plans for abandoning it, though it was bursting at the seams. . . . But 'organized medicine' was blind to this as to other realities."[180] (See Figure 3.7.)

Moreover, "[a]t the mid-1940s . . . only the supreme optimist could have found any reason to be encouraged about medical desegregation. Even among black physicians (North and South) there were scarcely any signs of a willingness to challenge the segregationist status quo."[181] African American health personnel had participated in World War II, served in Jim Crow units, and experienced segregation and discrimination in the armed forces. These professionally trained African Americans were sensitized to the acquisition of their God-given human, citizenship, and professional rights. Nearly one in six (16 percent) Black practitioners served in the

**Figure 3.7 W. Montague Cobb (1904–1990)**
Academic physician, editor of the *Journal of the National Medical Association* for over thirty years, and leader of the Health Care Civil Rights Movement, Cobb was also a pioneer anatomist, physical anthropologist, and eclectic scholar.
From Morais HM. *The History of the Negro in Medicine.* New York: Publishers Company, 1967, 143.

---

*Physicians such as Louis T. Wright and W. Montague Cobb were prominent members, serving on committees and boards, of civil rights organizations. Practicing physicians such as Hubert Eaton, a litigant in a landmark hospital desegregation case, was initially involved in his case at an informal level that later evolved into a complex lawsuit.

war, and African American nurses were forced to engage in a civil rights struggle to be allowed to serve their country as trained nurses. Therefore, in contrast to the highly publicized postwar courtroom and street corner struggles for racial integration in education, voting rights, and public transportation and accommodations in buses, hotels, and restaurants, a quieter struggle took place in health care. Its focus "was the fight aimed at discriminatory practices in American medicine and health care, and it had as principal targets the all-white medical society and school and the rigidly segregated Southern hospital."[182] Postwar surveys and studies of racial segregation and discrimination in the health system portrayed a grim picture of the U.S. health system—not just in the South, but throughout the entire nation.

Hospital segregation and discrimination were almost universal throughout the South in the postwar period and well into the 1960s. However, as Beardsley observed: "After passage of Hill-Burton in 1946 Southerners of both races, but blacks particularly, began to enjoy an access to modern hospital care that they had never known before. Although segregation itself set limits on quality of care, all hospitals receiving federal aid had to make some provision for black patients."[183] Given that Black accommodations were often segregated and inferior in some hospitals, "getting into previously all-white facilities at least moved blacks in position to strike for full equality."[184] As a Black doctor in Florida said, "it will be easier for us to come from the basement to the other floors than it will be for us to come from across town."[185] Nevertheless, progress throughout the health system was agonizingly slow, as P. Preston Reynolds noted:

> *In the 1960s, the legacy of discrimination still existed for black persons seeking admission to medical schools, appointments to the medical staff of hospitals, membership in medical societies, and access to hospital care. Hospitals that cared solely for black persons were inferior to those that cared for white persons, and facilities that were designated for black person in mixed-race hospitals included and were sometimes limited to a basement, attic, or separate building behind the main hospital. Consequently, equality in health care remained an elusive dream for black persons.*[186]

For African American physicians seeking postgraduate professional training or hospital staff privileges in the 1960s, Cornely portrayed a grim picture.[187] Reynolds summarized the findings in these areas:

> *Discrimination also existed in postgraduate residency training. In the North, only 10% of the total number of hospitals surveyed accepted African Americans as interns and residents, and only 20% had African-American physicians as members of the medical staff. In the South, only 6% of hospitals offered internships and residencies, and 25 percent provided medical staff privileges to African-American physicians.*[188]

The larger percentages of Black doctors on Southern hospital staffs represented privileges on segregated wards in "mixed-race" hospitals.[189] As late as the 1960s there is abundant evidence that Black physicians were being denied hospital privileges in Northern cities such as New York City, Chicago, and Detroit.[190] Although on the surface segregation and discrimination in American medicine and the health system appeared intact, unseen forces were building that, given proper direction, threatened to overthrow the old order.

Reports from the health and medical fields detailed the burden of health care segregation and discrimination. In a 1952 poll by *The Southern Patriot*, the official organ of the Southern Conference Educational Fund, of 2,414 ballots to hospital administrators in 18 Southern states and the District of Columbia to measure support for segregated, integrated, or separate hospitals:

> *The results of the poll showed that 71 per cent of those replying voted for hospitals with segregation. In the eleven states of the old Confederacy ... 335 ... or 74.9 per cent, favored segregated hospitals: 51, or 11.4 per cent, desegregated; and 61, or 13.7 per cent, separate hospitals. In Georgia, Louisiana and Mississippi, there was not a single ballot cast for non-segregated hospitals.*[191]

Another survey of 2,400 Southern hospital administrators gathered by the Southern Conference of Methodists on accepting desegregation revealed as late as 1956: "Of these, 17 per cent were willing to accept it; 62 per cent were adamantly opposed to it; and 11 per cent felt that the most practicable way to solve the problem was by having separate hospitals. Eleven per cent were unwilling to indicate their positions."[192] Despite hopeful intentions, these attitudes were reflected in the massive buildup of segregated and discriminatory hospital facilities throughout the South, promoted by the Hill-Burton Act and compounded by the status of the Southern Black health infrastructure. Morais recorded:

> *Hospital segregation was widespread throughout the South. The "separate-but-equal" Negro hospitals were usually small and antiquated. Adequate facilities and personnel were lacking. Some white hospitals admitted Negroes to designated "colored" floors or wards. In these hospitals, there were few beds available, and waiting lists for admission were long. In other white hospitals, Negroes were unable to gain admittance, even in emergency cases.*[193]

A 1959 study on racial integration of medical schools, medical societies, Blue Cross–Blue Shield plans, hospitals, and health agencies conducted by Dr. Paul Cornely, professor of preventive medicine at Howard University, reflected predictable results. Out of 60 cities, 45 in the North and 15 in the South: "Cornely concluded that discrimination in access to hospital care and appointments to the

medical staffs of hospitals was widespread throughout the United States."[194] Therefore, things were not much better in other parts of the country.

Political expediency dictated by heavy Negro votes in cities affected by the
explosive Northern and Western migration of Southern Blacks forced grudging
improvement in access to public and private hospital facilities: "despite the favorable trend, surveys throughout the 1950s showed that hospitals in the North were
still resorting to ingenious devices to separate Negro from white patients and to
exclude Negro physicians and nurses from hospital staffs."[195] To perpetuate the
discriminatory policies and practices of private hospitals, protect White fee-for-
service physicians' private offices from being inundated by Black and poor patients,
and negate the ill effects generated by the shortage of Black physicians and health
professionals in the Washington, DC, area, as late as 1956, Harry Dowling pointed
out, "the city hospital was being called on to furnish 47 percent of outpatient
services for the indigent population of the District of Columbia."[196] Similar
circumstances and occurrences were taking place in Western cities. A 1950 survey
of hospital discrimination in Los Angeles County by a Southern California chapter
of the National Council of Arts, Sciences and the Professions found that "discriminatory hospital practices fell into two categories: discrimination against patients of
minority groups and discrimination against physicians, nurses and technicians of
minority groups. It was found that some hospitals practiced one type of discrimination; some, another; and some, both."[197] The questionnaire was sent to 32
hospitals; 17 responded. In the study, "Eleven hospitals in the Los Angeles area,
including those in Burbank, Pasadena and Long Beach, had racial segregation of
patients, while six treated patients without discrimination."[198] Eight hospitals had
"poor" records on hospital staff integration, while five were making definite
progress on the problem.

The Detroit Commission on Community Relations released a report on racial
factors in hospital policies and practices in 1956. The report revealed that of 47
hospitals, 43 had African American patients. Of the 13 admitting them on emergency and accident bases and the 30 that experienced significant numbers of Black
admissions: "twenty hospitals assigned beds on the basis of a discriminatory policy,
with groupings of all-white, segregated or partially segregated; and twenty-seven on
the basis of a policy with groupings of integrated and partially integrated."[199] In
areas including eastern and southwestern Detroit where there were significant
numbers of Black residents, "the bed-assignment policy was uniform segregation
except in government hospitals."[200] Concerning the complexity and subtlety
surrounding health discrimination in Detroit, which is applicable to America
generally, the commission deduced:

> *In view of the distribution of Negro population in each of the five divi-*
> *sions of the Detroit study area ... the Medical and Hospital Study*
> *Committee concludes that it is not the simple factor of geographic loca-*
> *tion of the hospital or other chance circumstance which accounts for the*

> fact that 17 hospitals do not normally admit Negro patients and that 30
> hospitals do admit significant numbers of Negroes.[201]

The report concluded by soundly condemning Detroit's hospital system and extolling Black citizens' legal, moral, and financial right to equal hospital accommodations despite previous customs, practices, or expedient patterns of service.

The 1955 Committee to End Discrimination in Chicago Medical Institutions study, "What Color Are Your Germs?" revealed rampant racial segregation and discrimination in that city, which by then had a Black population of 590,000. In a city with 65 hospitals and 6,000 doctors, almost 50 percent of all sick or injured Black Chicagoans utilized Cook County Hospital, the overcrowded public facility: "[A] large percentage—patients with paid-up hospitalization policies and enough money to engage their own physicians and surgeons—go there because it's the only hospital that will accept them."[202] Some private hospitals admitted, "Negroes were accepted only when enough 'Negro beds' were available."[203] The study cited recent deaths of African American children and adolescents due to delayed treatment of accidents and illnesses caused by inappropriate, discriminatory referrals.

Black physicians were also the victims of discrimination in Chicago and other cities. In 1956, an Urban League study of Chicago noted, "Of its 226 Negro physicians, only 16, or 7.1 per cent, served at predominantly white hospitals."[204] With a few exceptions, the pattern of discrimination prevailed nationally: "Ahead of Chicago were Gary (82.4 per cent), Brooklyn, New York (70.6), Philadelphia (28.2), Los Angeles (24.8), Indianapolis (23.1), Boston (21.1), Detroit (15.6), and St. Louis (10.6). Below Chicago were Kansas City (5.4), Washington, D.C. (3.6), Atlanta, Nashville and New Orleans."[205] Some Southern cities did not have a single Black physician serving on the staff of a predominantly White hospital. "From the health and medical field ... for the first time medical segregation itself began to come under attack from respected individuals and groups,"[206] under this fusillade of health data and reports. Even the Commission on Hospital Care, a joint venture of the conservative AHA and the Commonwealth Fund, condemned the denial of service on "religious, economic, or racial" grounds. Although commission members did not challenge the legal sanctity of racial segregation, they felt that Black quality of care should not suffer.[207]

Since the nineteenth-century contributions of African American physicians such as James McCune Smith, Martin Robison Delany, John Sweat Rock, and Alexander T. Augusta, Black health concerns had been inextricably linked to African American abolition of slavery, emancipation, and civil rights. Until the end of that century Black physicians invariably became so involved in emancipation and civil rights activities that their medical careers often suffered. Although this trend moderated, twentieth-century Black medical leaders continued the tradition, becoming heavily involved in civil rights activities throughout the 1945 to 1965 period. Following the lead of predecessor physicians such as John A. Kenney,

Nathan Frances Mossell, Midian O. Bousfield, Peter Marshall Murray, and Louis T. Wright, many of whom were still active during the early part of this period, a new generation of civil rights physicians emerged to continue the activist tradition.

After the NMA's formation in 1895, much of this advocacy and health care civil rights work became identified with it. The organization's heavy medical-social mission had never been confined exclusively to the race issue because "[t]he NMA has always been keenly alert to its responsibility for seeing to it that the poor circumstanced get adequate medical care."[208] Even after World War II, race and class remained major health system problems. As can be discerned from the survey just cited, there was still a pressing need for these kinds of activities in the modern era.

One of the most significant leaders to emerge during this period was W. Montague Cobb, M.D., Ph.D. (1904–1990). Long a stalwart on Howard University's top-flight medical school faculty, Cobb emerged as associate editor of the *Journal of the National Medical Association (JNMA)* in 1948 in the wake of the unexpected resignation of its previous editor and medical leader, John A. Kenney, M.D., who had served in that capacity since 1916. Cobb became editor from 1949 to 1977 after the brief tenure of Ulysses Grant Daily, M.D., of Chicago.

As Lesley Rankin-Hill and Michael Blakey noted, "Cobb's life and work reflect a profound integration of science and social activism."[209] Born in Washington, DC, on October 12, 1904, of a modest entrepreneurial family of African American and Native American ancestry, Cobb attended the prestigious Dunbar High School and graduated from Amherst College in 1925. Cobb received the Blodgett Scholarship for proficiency in biology at the world-renowned Woods Hole Marine Laboratory in Massachusetts in 1925 before attending and graduating from Howard University Medical School in 1929. Selected by Howard's first Black Dean, Numa P.G. Adams, M.D., to upgrade Howard's Department of Anatomy, Cobb was sent to Case Western Reserve University with a General Education Board (GEB) fellowship for postdoctoral training under Dr. T. Wingate Todd in gross anatomy and physical anthropology. After completing his Ph.D. in 1932, he headed Howard's Anatomy Department (1947–1969); held visiting professorships at Harvard, Stanford, and Maryland, and was president of the American Association of Physical Anthropologists (1957–1959), president of the Anthropological Society of Washington (1949–1951), president of the NAACP (1976–1982), and president of the NMA (1964–1965). "As the leading activist scholar in the Afro-American community and the only Afro-American physical anthropologist Ph.D. before the Korean War," Cobb wrote over 1,100 publications and taught over 6,000 anatomy students.[210] As a reflection of Cobb's social responsibility amid the racial turmoil of his time:

> *Cobb's applied anthropology involved the accumulation of extensive data on the one hand and the formation of organizations for social activism on the other. It was directed toward solving problems of health*

*care and racism. His work thereby served to balance the widespread*
*distortion and neglect of medical and racial problems facing Afro-*
*America between 1930 and the present day.*[211]

"It was that task—building pressure against medical segregation in North and South—that Montague Cobb set for himself."[212] His accomplishments and the health care Civil Rights Movement of the 1960s and 1970s are inextricably linked.[213]

Cobb's initial interest in America's "race" problem was scientific. He and Julian H. Lewis, M.D., Ph.D. (1891–1989), the physician-pathologist-physiologist and first African American to hold a regular academic appointment at the University of Chicago, were interested in counteracting the myths and theories—then prevalent among White physicians, anthropologists, and biologists—that had evolved concerning the biological inferiority of Blacks. In Lewis's most prominent work, *The Biology of the Negro* (1942), "he sought to present a thorough, objective treatment of a subject that white anthropologists, biologists, and others had often used to buttress prevailing theories of black racial inferiority."[214] What distinguished these men, including Dr. Paul Cornely, whom we discuss later, from previous Black physicians who had taken on the "race" issue were their eminent, variegated, and specialized scientific qualifications—equivalent to any White scientists in the debate at that time.

Cobb became interested in civil rights after developing his singular expertise and authority regarding the materials and methods of documentation, processing, and preservation of anthropological material (1932); the ontogenetic, phylogenetic, structural, and functional aspects of cranio-facial anatomy (1930s–1940s); comprehensive studies of cranial suture closure (1930s–1950s); establishing a Laboratory of Anatomy and Physical Anthropology at Howard University documenting the health ravages that racism inflicted on African Americans (1930s–1969); and the biological diversity of the African American population. Between 1946, when he joined the NAACP, and 1949, when he assumed editorship of the *JNMA*, a personal civil rights transformation occurred and, as Cobb himself stated, "we started raising Hell."[215] Carrying on in the tradition of African American surgeon Louis T. Wright (1891–1952), who had "combined his profession and his civic activities to promote better health assurance and expand equal opportunities for Negroes,"[216] Cobb testified before the U.S. Senate in support of national health insurance on April 16, 1946.[217] Wright, who as previously noted had become disenchanted with White organized medicine and its policies early in his career, had favored national health insurance from the beginning. As part of Cobb's role representing the NAACP, "he prepared two seminal monographs, *Medical Care and the Plight of the Negro* (1947) and *Progress and Portents for the Negro in Medicine* (1948), which helped raise public awareness of how discriminatory practices had adversely influenced the access of blacks to health care services and professional opportunities."[218]

Between 1945 and 1949, "because of flagrant, widespread clinical discrimination, a long, relentless, bitter fight with the Department of Public Health and Gallinger Hospital was spearheaded by Dr. W. Montague Cobb ... Howard University College of Medicine anatomy professor and president of the Medico-Chirurgical Society."[219] Cobb protested against an inadequate number of hospital beds for African Americans in the district—of which half were Jim Crow and excluded Black physicians as attendants; the exclusion of physicians of color from Gallinger Hospital, the District's public hospital, despite its heavy Black patient load; that institution's being exclusively controlled by lily-White Georgetown and George Washington medical schools while Howard, the oldest historically Black medical school in the country, was excluded; and the exclusionary and discriminatory delivery of health care at patient and professional levels in Washington. By 1948 Gallinger's staff was desegregated and staff appointments and teaching services for African American physicians at Howard were secured. Cobb's activities in the NAACP also mirrored those of his mentor Louis T. Wright, who had created the organization's medical committees, spearheaded "a dozen investigations into discriminatory medical training and care,"[220] and chaired the board from 1935 to 1952. Cobb chaired the NAACP's National Medical Committee from 1955 to 1956 and its National Health Committee from 1957 to 1968, and served as its president from 1976 to 1982.

Cobb placed the "race agenda" at the forefront of organized medicine during his academic-medical and social activist careers. Expanding his role beyond professor of anatomy at Howard, during his tenure as editor of *JNMA* he meticulously documented Black medical history— becoming "Dean" of the discipline in the process. With students and colleagues he shared his famous quotation, "If we do not tell our own story, no one will."[221] He increased the size and broadened the scope of the *Journal*, including "The Integration Battlefront"—a section consisting of items of interest relating to the evolving struggle for equal rights in medicine and health. The action for which Cobb may be most widely remembered—beyond his titanic medical and medical-social accomplishments—was his formation and leadership, along with Dr. Paul Cornely, of the Imhotep National Conferences on Hospital Integration. The organization's purpose was "the elimination of segregation in the fields of hospitalization and health."[222] Fortuitously, in 1964 and 1965, at the height of the Civil Rights Movement, Cobb also served as NMA President.[223]

Cobb, Cornely, and Wright were joined by scores of other African American physicians in the civil rights struggle between 1945 and 1965. At the end of World War II NMA president Emory I. Robinson, M.D., pushed the VA to desegregate its facilities: "Despite the fact that veterans were legally entitled to medical care without discrimination, 24 of the 127 veterans hospitals operating in the beginning of 1947 had separate wards for Negro patients. Nineteen of them, all located in the South, refused to admit Negroes except in cases of medical emergencies."[224] Yielding to health care civil rights pressures, "in October, 1954, the agency ordered the end of segregation in all of its hospitals."[225] Beginning as early as 1950, Southern capitulation to a series of desegregation directives and orders was complete. According to Beardsley: "One group of hospitals in the region ... had accepted patient integration.... They were the South's Veterans' Administration hospitals, which in 1950 had opened their wards to black patients under pressure of a directive from the VA's chief medical administrator."[226]

On a variety of levels, the brilliant surgeon Charles Richard Drew had been leading several revolutions in the health system—many of which came to fruition or culminated during this period. They included, but were not limited to, Drew qualifying himself scientifically and professionally to participate in the vanguard of the Allies' health struggle against fascism during World War II through the blood bank movement; raising the esteem of African Americans in medicine, through his achievements, to the highest levels since Daniel Hale Williams's successful operation on the human heart on July 9, 1893; elevating the surgical training and specialization of Black surgeons, especially at Howard University Medical School, to unprecedented levels—equivalent to any in the world; quietly challenging, resisting, and reforming racist practices at the professional, policy, and training levels in the health system; and making what many considered the supreme sacrifice in an act of furthering African American medical-surgical education.

His magnificent contributions have been belatedly recognized beyond the confines of academic medicine, rendering him an American icon and legendary Black role model in the process. Meanwhile, the brilliant and multifaceted surgeon Matthew Walker (1906–1978), chairman of the Department of Surgery at Meharry (1944–1973), led the school to the forefront of community health and health care for the poor while upgrading his department and the medical school scientifically in the years encompassing World War II to the civil rights era. As a pioneer in the rekindled national movement to serve the poor and underserved (Meharry had adopted this mission since its inception), he established and maintained a clinical and training affiliation with the Taborian Hospital (1942–1970s) in the Mississippi Delta in service of that state's drastically underserved Black population. Dr.Walker also worked with the OEO, Dr. Harold D. West, the institution's first African American president, and Meharry social scientist Dr. Ralph Hines in the early 1960s to establish a modern, 30,000-square-foot neighborhood health center that served an underserved urban Black population in North Nashville from 1969 and eventually bore his name.

During the immediate postwar period other African American physicians also responded to the desperate health care needs of Black patients in the oppressive atmosphere of the rural South. During the war, Dr. Theodore R. M. Howard, a Meharry surgeon trained at the Mayo Clinic, served as chief surgeon for a short

## Surgeon Charles Richard Drew: The Man and the Myths

> Glory is nothing more than Oblivion postponed.
> —RAMON Y. CAJAL, NOBEL LAUREATE

Charles Richard Drew (1904–1950) was one of America's premier clinical research scientists as well as superb surgeon, teacher, and athlete. Dubbed *the* legendary African American medical scientist, he is credited with a primary role in developing the technology responsible for establishing effective blood banks and the mass collection of whole blood, is held largely responsible for the mass production of blood plasma during World War II, and supervised and administered the "Plasma for France" and "Blood for Britain" programs, which saved tens if not hundreds of thousands of lives during the war. He led another quiet revolution, of which he was most proud, as a pioneer surgical teacher upgrading the quality and sophistication of African American surgical training and practice. Moreover, Drew elevated the esteem in which African Americans in medicine were held, through his personal accomplishments, to the highest levels since Daniel Hale Williams's successful operation on the human heart during the gaslight era. He also quietly challenged, resisted, and sometimes triggered reforms of the medical profession's comfortable but unjust racial policies and practices—especially in the medical education and research arenas. He is now trumpeted as an American medical icon and a demigod in the African American community, and many have difficulty disentangling myth from reality regarding Dr. Drew's struggle as an educational pioneer and indefatigable fighter against racial discrimination.

Delivered at home on June 3, 1904, in Washington, D.C., Drew was born to privileged working-class parents. Blessed by instruction at some of the finest African American primary and secondary schools then available, Drew entered Amherst College (1922) after graduating from Dunbar High School, Black Washington's elite college preparatory school, with academic and athletic honors. Drew's Amherst experience was marked by athletic achievement (honorable mention All-American football player and more than a dozen letters in athletics), aptitude for biomedical sciences, and an awakened interest in pursuing medicine. Financially unable* to enter medical school upon graduation (B.A. degree, 1926), Drew accepted a position as athletic director-coach and biology and chemistry teacher at Morgan State College in Baltimore, elevating that institution's previously mediocre athletic programs to championship caliber during his two-year tenure (1926–1928).

Rejected at Howard Medical School for lacking two credits in English required for admission, Drew entered McGill University Medical School (1928) in Canada. While at McGill he achieved high academic honors, was elected to the National Medical Honor Society and Alpha Omega Alpha (the medical honor society), and

---

*There was nothing equivalent to "student loans" during that era, and government grants were extremely rare. Blacks had little access to these meager financial resources for education.

continued to be a star track athlete.* Through his work with Dr. John Beattie, the British anatomy professor and research scientist on McGill's faculty, Drew's interest in research on blood transfusion was piqued. Despite his meticulous savings from the previous three years, loans from Amherst classmates (which he repaid in full), and working as a student, Drew's funds ran out in the Depression year 1931. His matriculation and career were saved by a Julius Rosenwald Fellowship, which allowed him to graduate second in his class of 137 and earn his M.D., C.M. (Master's of Surgery) degree (1933). He completed both his internship (1934) and a residency in Internal Medicine (1935) at Montreal General Hospital while continuing to work with Beattie.

Encouraged by his friend and colleague Dr. W. Montague Cobb, Drew returned to Howard University Medical School as an instructor in pathology (1936), a routine preparatory step for surgical training, followed by a surgical residency (1937). In 1938 he was chosen as Howard's General Education Board Fellow in Surgery to be trained at Columbia University College of Physicians and Surgeons at Presbyterian Hospital, New York City (1938–1940). His work was so outstanding that he was allowed by Dr. Allen O. Whipple, chief of the Department of Surgery at Columbia, and Dr. John Scudder, assistant professor of clinical surgery, to work simultaneously towards a M.D.Sc. (Doctor of Science in Medicine). Fortuitously, Scudder's research interests were fluid balance, especially during surgery; blood chemistry; and blood transfusion—areas that overlapped Drew's previous research in Canada.

While working an around-the-clock schedule of clinical responsibilities and research activities in Presbyterian's wards, clinics, blood bank, and laboratory, Drew earned Dr. Scudder's praise as not only "my most brilliant student, but one of the greatest clinical scientists of the first half of the twentieth century" (Wynes 1988, 55). Drew's doctoral dissertation (Drew 1940):

> "Banked Blood," was to bring together not only the results of his own research and knowledge gained through the Presbyterian Hospital's blood bank, but all that was known on the subject at that time, whatever the source of that knowledge. Dr. Scudder, ten years after Drew's death, said that "Banked Blood" was considered a masterpiece. Strangely . . . it was never published (Wynes 1988, 56).

Drew completed the second residency and M.D.Sc. degree and passed Part I of the American Board of Surgery (ABS) exam during1940, but war clouds swirling over Europe forced Drs. Scudder, Alexis Carrel (winner of the Nobel prize for blood vessel surgery), and Karl Landsteiner (winner of the Nobel prize for elucidating the basic blood groupings), and Drew to plan the nation's wartime blood bank needs and initiate the "Plasma for France" program (1940). As a brilliant trainee, Drew was drawn into this elite planning team before he was technically a peer. Health care

---

*During that period in Canada, graduate and professional students were allowed to compete in intercollegiate athletics. More than a decade later, when Drew visited his alma mater, the entire football stadium crowd remembered and cheered his athletic accomplishments at McGill.

emergencies created by the fall of France and the Battle of Britain brought him back to New York City three months after returning to Howard's surgery department. Dr. Beattie, who was now chief of research for the Royal College of Surgery and chief of the transfusion service for the Royal Air Force in Great Britain, Dr. Scudder, and the Board of Medical Control of the Blood Transfusion Betterment Association had decided Drew was the biomedical scientist to head up the "Blood for Britain" program. This was a quasi-experimental effort to mass-produce useful blood and blood products, especially plasma, for transfusion under wartime and battlefield conditions. Accepting the fact that Drew was probably the most knowledgeable physician-scientist in the world to tackle this unprecedented problem, Howard granted him leave for these duties. Drew's report (Drew et al. 1941) on the early program, which lasted five months, verified his leadership in the field. Nevertheless, he resigned his position early leading the follow-up blood bank programs and returned immediately to Howard.

Drew's early departure from the program at the end of March 1941, soon after completing his ABS certification with flying colors,* raises a question obscured by the mythology surrounding his life. This act may have been related to the U.S. armed forces policy stipulating that "colored" blood would not be acceptable. As protests poured in from all over the country, Albert Deutsch's newspaper article summed up the situation in which Drew was trapped:

> At the very time Drew was setting up this Red Cross blood bank, helping to save thousands of American lives through his brilliant scientific and administrative work, his blood would have been rejected by the Red Cross had he offered to donate it. Later, when the Red Cross modified its policy and accepted Negro blood on a Jim Crow basis, his blood would have been segregated with that of other Negroes (Deutsch 1944).

Historians disagree over whether Drew actually held a press conference denouncing both the exclusionary and Jim Crow blood policies as unscientific and degrading to African Americans (Logan 1982, 191; Wynes 1988, 69–70; Haber 1970, 163–164). It is unclear whether his abrupt departure was totally voluntary to secure his position as Howard's chief of surgery, under pressure, or symbolized a strong protest against an unscientific and egregious policy (Logan 1982, 190–191; Wynes 1988, 65–71; Hayden 1986, 803; Cobb 1950, 243)

Early in life Drew attended racially segregated primary and secondary schools. At Amherst he suffered racial discrimination during travel with the college's athletic teams, was excluded from the campus's fraternity system, and was denied the position of captain of the football team despite being its acknowledged star.

---

*During his oral ABS examination, his Johns Hopkins surgical examiner queried Drew on the use of blood and plasma for the treatment of secondary shock. Drew's reply was so laden with detailed knowledge that the examiner retired and recruited other examiners to be exposed to this candidate's knowledge. He was soon recruited as the first Black surgeon to become an examiner for the ABS.

Nevertheless, having experienced Canada's more progressive racial policies during his early professional training, upon returning to the United States, despite his achievements and professional excellence (National Board of Medical Examiners certification, internal medicine residency, two surgical residencies, sole African American with M.D.Sc. degree, diplomat of the ABS, and fellow of the International College of Surgery [1946]), he was denied AMA membership and fellowship in the American College of Surgery, driving him to both public and private protests (Drew 1947, 222–224; Wynes 1988, 91–92). Moreover, other than Howard and Meharry, few U.S. medical schools admitted African Americans, and, due to the racially segregated and discriminatory health professions education and research infrastructure, there were few places where Blacks could receive first-rate postgraduate professional training. These were not myths. Nevertheless, Drew was idealistic in his optimism, as Dr. Asa Yancy Sr., one of Drew's eminent trainees and, later, associate dean of Emory University Medical School, recounts: "Dr. Drew had strong faith in the concept that if an individual performed exceedingly well in life's endeavors, such as surgery or other professional or vocational pursuits, that the excellence of performance would transcend barriers of racial segregation and discrimination" (Yancy 1987, 90). Thus Drew was continuously struggling, usually in his quiet but determined manner, to overcome the hurdles of racial segregation and discrimination. Even his death, despite being directly related to his first love—educating Black doctors—had freedom-fighting implications. In April 1950, instead of flying or taking the train from Washington to the John Andrew Clinic at Tuskegee, Alabama, one of the few places where America's Black physicians could receive continuing medical education, he drove—sacrificing his comfort so that two of his residents who could not afford travel expenses could attend the meeting. His demise on April 1, on Route 49 near Haw River, North Carolina, as the result of a terrible automobile accident, reflected a spirit of sacrifice, innate generosity, and struggle to assist other Black physicians educationally denied by mainstream American medicine.

Another myth with racial overtones was that Dr. Drew bled to death after being refused admission to a segregated White hospital. This myth has been perpetuated by reputable sources, according to Drew biographer Charles E. Wynes:

> *Time* magazine . . . in its March 29, 1968, issue, eighteen years after Drew's death, recalled how he "bled to death" after "he was turned away by an all-white hospital" . . . even *The New York Times*, as recently as June 14, 1981, said in a philately column commemorating the issuance of a postage stamp in honor of Drew, that "the segregated hospital to which he was taken had no blood plasma that might have saved his life" (Wynes 1988, 106).

Although the hospital was segregated, it is documented that it had both blood and plasma. In fact, Drew was transfused in the process of receiving the best available surgical care in a timely and dignified manner (Wynes 1988, 104–106; Sampson 1984; Yancy 1987, 86–88).

When Drew, one of the best trained and most knowledgeable surgeons on earth, returned to Howard in 1941, "he was made professor and chairman of the Department of Surgery at Howard University, and chief surgeon at Freedmen's Hospital" (Yancy 1987, 83). The surgery program quickly grew in size, subspecialty sophistication, and esteem. While chairman, his excellent organizational and teaching skills upgraded Howard's medical training and resulted in Drew's training more than half the Black board-certified surgeons in the country between 1941 and 1950.

He received the prestigious Spingarn Medal (1944) and honorary doctorates from West Virginia State College (1945) and Amherst (1947), published voluminously, served Howard as Freedmen's Hospital chief of staff (1944–1946) and medical director (1946–1948), served as a surgical leader and stalwart for the National Medical Association (NMA), and was appointed physician consultant to the surgeon general of the U.S. (1949) on European hospitals. Posthumously he has become an American medical scientific icon and role model to African Americans and others interested in scientific careers. A medical school, several blood banks, numerous schools, streets, organizations, and awards bear his name. His portrait hangs at American Red Cross headquarters and at the NIH, and he is one of the few surgeons appearing on a U.S. postage stamp. Drew was made a fellow of the American College of Surgery more than a year and a half after his death. No mention is made as to whether he was ever allowed membership in the AMA. Charles Richard Drew—an uncompromisingly generous African American who made major contributions to modern blood banking, which has saved millions of lives, and conformed to the Greek ideals of superior mind and body—truly belongs to the ages.

## Notes

Cobb WM. Charles Richard Drew, M.D., 1904–1950. *Journal of the National Medical Association* 1950;42:239–245.

Deutsch A. *PM*, March 30, 1944.

Drew CR. Banked blood: A study in blood preservation. Ph.D. dissertation, Columbia University, June, 1940.

Drew CR, et al. *Report Concerning the Project for Supplying Blood Plasma to England.* New York: Blood Transfusion Association, June, 1941.

Drew CR, Scudder J. Studies in blood preservation; fate of cellular elements and prothrombin in citrated blood. *Journal of Laboratory and Clinical Medicine* 1941;26:1473–1478.

Drew CR. The early recognition and treatment of shock. *Anesthesiology* 1942;3:176–194.

Drew CR. Letters to the Editor of J.A.M.A., January 13 and January 30, 1947. *Journal of the National Medical Association* 1947; 39:222–224.

Haber L. *Black Pioneers of Science and Invention.* San Diego: Harcourt Brace Jovanovich, 1970, 151–167.

Hayden RC. Drew, CR. 802–803. In: Salzman J, Smith DL, West C. eds. *Encyclopedia of African-American Culture and History.* 5 vols. New York: Macmillan Library Reference USA, Simon and Schuster Macmillan, 1996, 802–803.

Logan RW. Drew, CR. 190–192. In: Logan RW, Winston MR, eds. *Dictionary of American Negro Biography.* New York: W.W. Norton, 1982, 190–192.

Morais HM. *The History of the Negro in Medicine.* New York: Publishers Company, 1967, 107–109.

Negro surgeon, world plasma expert, derides Red Cross blood segregation. *Chicago Defender,*
   September 26, 1942, 6.
Organ CH, Kosiba MM, eds. *A Century of Black Surgeons: The U.S.A. Experience.* 2 vols.
   Norman, OK: Transcript Press, 1987, 15–17.
Sampson CC. Dispelling the myth surrounding Drew's death. *Journal of the National Medical Asso-
   ciation* 1984;76:415–416.
Starr D. *Blood: An Epic History of Medicine and Commerce.* New York: Knopf, 1998 (pbk. ed.
   New York: Quill, 2000).
The nation . . . races . . . Black vacuum. *Time,* March 29, 1968, No. 13, 91:26.
Wynes CE. *Charles Richard Drew: The Man and the Myth.* Urbana: University of Illinois Press,
   1988.
Yancy AG. The life of Charles R. Drew, M.D., M.D.Sc. and perspectives of a former resident in
   general surgery. In: Organ CH, Kosiba MM, eds. *A Century of Black Surgeons: The U.S.A.
   Experience.* 2 vols. Norman, OK: Transcript Press, 1987, 63–102.

time at Taborian Hospital in the all-Black town of Mound Bayou, Mississippi,
after which he established the Friendship Clinic in the same vicinity. By 1946 Dr.
Howard's efforts were so sucessful at providing hospital services to Mississippi's one
million Blacks—who suffered medical deprivation reminiscent of underdeveloped
countries—that he gained national attention in the February 23, 1946, issue of
the *Saturday Evening Post.* His work catapulted him to national fame, to the presidency of the NMA (1956), and into the health care civil rights struggle alongside
the NMA and NAACP. When he questioned, in 1955, why the assailants in the
Mississippi killings of George W. Lee, Lamar Smith, and Emmett Till went
unapprehended despite FBI intervention, Dr. Howard was publically attacked by
J. Edgar Hoover. Repudiating Hoover's allegations that his statements were false
and irresponsible, Howard declared he would continue to "cry out against injustice
and against that kind of administration of justice which permits murderers to go
free to boast of their crimes."[227]

The mood was indeed changing in the NMA: "With Cobb in the vanguard
and his colleagues joining increasingly behind him, the black medical profession
began about 1949 to move onto the offensive."[228] Cobb had shifted strategy:
"[u]nlike earlier black doctors like Murray and Bousfield, he argued that it was
naive to believe that segregated institutions could be improved. Segregation was
inherently discriminatory."[229] Perceptive about the changing attitudes about
discrimination:

> Cobb recognized a growing disaffection with segregation in the white
> profession, but to capitalize on it he believed that he must first change the
> thinking of his own colleagues. Unless he could bring them to see that
> institutionalized discrimination was the greatest obstacle to black health
> and medical progress—and stir them to act on that belief—little would
> change.[230]

For Black doctors the resulting changes in attitudes sometimes transformed professional activities into civil rights causes. For example, eight NMA physicians staged

a sit-in at the restaurant in the Biltmore Hotel in Atlanta, Georgia, where they were attending a Fulton County Medical Society meeting on February 20, 1961. They were arrested, booked, fingerprinted, and released on bail. Although much of this health care civil rights activity was spontaneous, leaders such as physicians W. Montague Cobb and Paul Cornely were major catalysts.

Paul Bertau Cornely, M.D., Ph.D. (1906– ), the other major protagonist triggering this movement, was born in Pointe-à-Pitre, Guadeloupe; received his early schooling in Santurce, Puerto Rico; and emigrated with his family to the United States in 1920. Receiving his early education in New York and Detroit, he transferred to the University of Michigan and received A.B. (1928), M.D. (1931), and Ph.D. (1934) degrees. The first African American to earn a doctorate in public health, Cornely was a Howard University faculty member throughout his career (1934–1973), developing highly acclaimed programs in preventive medicine, public health, and physical medicine and rehabilitation. His application of scientific survey, epidemiologic, and biostatistical techniques to Black health status and outcomes; examining access of African American and other disadvantaged minorities to health services; and evaluating the distribution and supply of health personnel laid the groundwork and supplied the objective public health database undergirding the health care Civil Rights Movement. He received accolades for a string of scientific research and articles from the 1930s through the 1980s, highlighted by his studies of the Southern health system for the Rosenwald Fund* and NUL (1944–1947) through General Education Board** (GEB) funding and his series of public health studies and articles on the presence and effects of racial segregation and discrimination on the nation's health system. As a result of the acknowledgment he received for his research, he became the first Black president of the American Public Health Association (APHA) in November 1969. His influence in the NMA and friendship and advocacy with Cobb during the late 1940s helped push Black doctors into the civil rights arena.

Cobb and Cornely, collaborating with their friend, mentor, and colleague Louis T. Wright—whose activism in civil rights dated back several decades—established clear linkages between the Black Civil Rights Movement trumpeted by the NAACP and NUL and the African American patients Black physicians were

---

*The Rosenwald Fund (1917–1948) was a private philanthropic foundation founded to promote the welfare of African Americans. Based in Chicago, it was endowed by a Jewish immigrant (Julius Rosenwald) who helped build Sears, Roebuck and Company. Emphasizing education (the fund built some 5,000 schools for Blacks), it reorganized and expanded in 1928, developing programs in health, medical economics, fellowships for the professions, library service, social studies, general education, and race relations.

**The General Education Board was an educational philanthropic foundation founded to further African American public school, and later, higher education. Founded in 1902 by White, Northern, largely corporate reformers, its mission was shaped by the industrial education movement for Blacks emanating from Hampton and Tuskegee institutes. The foundation, originally funded by John D. Rockefeller, supported many educational enrichment, buildings, and endowment projects for the Black medical schools.

serving: "In challenging Southern hospital segregation Cobb said that, just as in the fight against all-white societies and schools, he must heighten black doctors' awareness in order to make them an instrument of change."[231] Cobb assailed and inspired others, writing in one editorial: "what were needed were 'pioneer spirits,' who rather than yield to the allure of 'fundamentally insulting placebos' would 'tighten their belts and continue the struggle for principle.'"[232] The atmosphere of racial struggle reminiscent of earlier decades in Black organized medicine generated by the Cobb-Cornely leadership saw both individual and local groups of African American physicians throughout the nation challenging and resisting segregation and discrimination in both health care and the profession by the late 1950s. For example, Black physician Carr McFall of Charleston, a leader associated with South Carolina's Palmetto Association, through pressure and negotiation successfully broke down the walls of segregation in the White medical societies in Charleston and Greenville, South Carolina, by 1952. Physicians such as Albert C. Perry, Jr., of Monroe, North Carolina, were victimized for engaging in civil rights and NAACP activities. After being attacked by the Ku Klux Klan in 1957 and being forced to serve prison time on trumped-up abortion charges, Perry's medical license was revoked in 1960. Beardsley noted: "By 1953 the NAACP was urging state chapters to form local physician health committees to survey and report on the extent of hospital segregation."[233] Projecting the NAACP as the action arm of the NMA, Black doctors responded to Cobb's pleas for financial support. By 1954 the NMA was able to give thousands of dollars to the NAACP.[234]

Heightened awareness and coordinated civil rights activity orchestrated by Cobb's multifaceted campaign and the 1954 *Brown v. Board of Education* decision set the stage for the successful attack on segregated Southern hospitals. The cause was buttressed when Paul Cornely, who was then a member of the APHA's committee on medical care, drafted a 1954 resolution repudiating discrimination and segregation in health delivery. It was adopted by the APHA in 1955. At the association's 1956 meeting Cornely contended that segregation and discrimination "are environmental factors and are just as damaging to health as water pollution, unpasteurized milk, or smog"; therefore: "Every public health worker, whether in the North or South ought not to accept the patterns of his community as sacrosanct."[235] He went further, suggesting financial sanctions by the "addition of nondiscriminatory clauses to all federal and state health laws, denying public money to any hospital or health center maintaining separate facilities for blacks."[236] In the heady atmosphere created by the Cobb-Cornely team, legal action against racist health care was inevitable.

The march of medical science dictated that modern health care become more intimately tied to state-of-the-art hospital care. Segregation and discrimination against Black patients and physicians thus grew more debilitating from both health and professional perspectives. African American physicians such as Daniel Webster Davis, in actions against the Medical College of Virginia (1957) hospitals, and George R. Watts, battling Gastonia Memorial Hospital in Gastonia, North

Carolina, that same year, began legal challenges to *de jure* segregation and discrimination in hospitals at both patient and staff levels. General practitioner Hubert Arthur Eaton, M.D. (1916–1998), a University of Michigan Medical School graduate (1942), was a veteran civil rights activist in Wilmington, North Carolina, who initiated a series of lawsuits in 1956 against a publicly funded hospital that discriminated against Black patients and refused Black physicians staff privileges. After a series of defeated and dismissed court actions which came to be known as *Dr. Hubert A Eaton, et al., v. the James Walker Memorial Hospital in Wilmington, North Carolina*, a federal appeals court upheld Eaton's lawsuit in 1964, establishing a legal precedent for the elimination of discrimination in publicly funded hospitals. "[I]f you don't know what to do, go to court; that is the only way we know of in Wilmington, North Carolina,"[237] Eaton, leader of the "Wilmington three," advised previously timid Southern physicians.

Another 1964 federal court decision, *Simkins v. Moses H. Cone Memorial Hospital*, struck at the very heart of government-sanctioned and government-funded health care segregation and discrimination—the Hill-Burton Act. Ten years after its inception (1946), 3,047 projects had been approved by the Hill-Burton Act. By March 1964, 104 segregated hospitals and health facilities had been built with Hill-Burton money—84 for "Whites only" and 20 for Blacks. After the expenditure of over $2 billion in federal funds, the 1963 *Report of the United States Commission on Civil Rights* found that:

> the evidence clearly shows that Negroes do not share equally with white citizens in the use of such facilities. As patients and medical professionals, they are discriminated against in their access to publicly supported health facilities. Commission investigation also shows that the federal government, by statute and administration, supports racial discrimination in the provision of health facilities.[238]

In February 1962, 11 African Americans, led by dentist George Simkins, Jr., and including physicians, dentists, and laymen, filed a suit charging racial discrimination against two Greensboro, North Carolina hospitals that had benefited from Hill-Burton funds. The case became known as *Simkins v. Moses H. Cone Memorial Hospital*. Legal arguments focused on the "separate-but-equal" provision of the act. Guided by Thurgood Marshall and Jack Greenberg and the staff of the Legal Defense and Education Fund of the NAACP, the U.S. Court of Appeals in Richmond, Virginia, ruled "racial discrimination for both patient and staff was illegal in Federally aided hospitals and held the 'separate-but-equal' provision of the Hill-Burton Act unconstitutional,"[239] on November 1, 1963. By refusing to review the decision, the U.S. Supreme Court sustained the decision on March 2, 1964. Meanwhile, as early as 1962, with congressional support from Senator Jacob Javits of New York and Representative John Dingell of Michigan, who had joined Cobb-Cornely, the NMA, and their allies against the "separate-but-equal" clause of

Hill-Burton and its promulgation of racial segregation and discrimination with federal funds, an antidiscrimination amendment to the act was introduced on Capitol Hill. Despite the NMA's representatives meeting with President Kennedy and eliciting his support, the Javits amendment was rejected by a roll-call vote of 44 to 37. Possibly in response to the 1964 court decisions, by August of that year the American Hospital Association recommended deletion of the "separate-but-equal" provision from the Hill-Burton Act. For the first time since the Civil War era, the federal courts and Congress had taken halting steps* toward making illegal racial segregation and discrimination in health care, protected since 1896 by "separate-but-equal" provisions of *Plessey v. Ferguson*.[240]

In what might have been the most important series of actions forcing the desegregation of hospitals and other health care institutions in the country, Cobb organized and led, with Cornely's help, the Imhotep National Conferences on Hospital Integration between March 8, 1957, and May 18, 1963. Named after the ancient physician and god of healing Imhotep (from the Greek for "he who comes in peace"), these annual national meetings sought to assemble White and Black physicians and hospital administrators to discuss hospital segregation and discrimination face to face. Cobb hoped integration could be achieved voluntarily, without divisive court and legislative battles. If the White medical establishment remained unmoved, Black victims could at least air their grievances and feel morally that the Whites had turned their backs on peaceful solutions.

The organization proposed to make a three-pronged attack on the problem: "the enactment of laws to render segregated practices illegal; the filing of court suits to end the use of public funds for the construction and/or maintenance of segregated projects; and the use of persuasion on the administrative front to achieve the elimination of discriminatory patterns."[241] Late in 1956, the newly formed organization invited the AMA, AHA, and other leading hospital agencies to send representatives to the first meeting in Washington, D.C., on March 8–9, 1957. The NMA, an organization dealing with the health system's race and class problems on a daily basis, felt that "The Imhotep Conference [on Hospital Integration] will afford a golden opportunity to broaden understanding of the problem and unify action in respect to the elimination of one of the present major barriers to making the best in medical facilities available to all of the people of the nation."[242] The organizers, the Council on Medical Education and Hospitals of the NMA, the NAACP, and the Medico-Chirurgical Society of the District of Columbia, encountered difficulty finding a site willing to host the meeting in Washington, D.C. Cobb relied on his own minister, Reverend Robert Pierre Johnson, for providing a site. The Fifteenth Street Presbyterian Church, Cobb's place of worship, which was founded in

---

*These actions applied exclusively to publicly funded health segregation and discrimination. Segregation resulting from "state action" was held to be violative of the "equal protection clause." Private entities were covered by a different aspect of the law.

the wake of the infamous Snow Riots* and previously pastored by Reverends John Francis Cook, Henry Highland Garnet, and Francis J. Grimke, hosted the initial and several subsequent conferences (1959–1962).

Although there were 175 official attendees at the first conference, not a single White medical, nursing, or hospital association sent official representatives. Some 32 organizations sent unofficial observers. Thus the conference in lieu of 21 states and 49 localities being represented, including 26 chapters of the NAACP, 16 NMA affiliates, and 4 NUL branches, was to provide only a forum for a largely Black audience. Without Whites to address, Cobb, Cornely, and the other conveners preached to the converted. The annual conferences continued, but so did the White boycott by organizations such as the AMA, AHA, ANA, the National Health Council, USPHS, the American Protestant Hospital Association, and the Catholic Hospital Association. Seemingly, as conference attendance dwindled (by 1960 conference attendance had shrunk to 30 registrants), the conferences yielded few visible results. Nevertheless, they had raised awareness levels about the evils of hospital segregation and discrimination and exerted political pressures on Capitol Hill and throughout the nation about health care civil rights whose influence would be harvested later.

The final Imhotep National Conference convened in Atlanta in 1963 at the Union Baptist Church. Cobb and Cornely had by then resorted to implementing NAACP-led local, regional, and national campaigns on health issues, augmented by mass mailings and letter-writings. A confluence of nonhealth events, the Black Civil Rights Movement, and shifting political fortunes revealed the value of keeping the issue alive:

> *An eighth Imhotep Conference became unnecessary because in 1964 the Civil Rights Act was passed. At the insistence of President Lyndon B. Johnson, the Department of Health Education and Welfare convened a Conference on the Elimination of Hospital Discrimination on July 27, 1964, at which all the organizations which had declined invitations to the Imhotep Conferences were represented in depth: the Federal Hospital Council, the American Hospital Association, the American Medical Association, the American Dental Association, and the American Nurses Association.*[243]

Amazingly, at this White House conference, Mr. Hobart Taylor, associate special counsel to the president (an African American) delivered the president's greetings. Referring to the future of hospital segregation and discrimination, HEW Secretary Anthony J. Celebreeze announced:

---

*The Snow Riot was a racially motivated riot occurring in 1835 in the District of Columbia in which White mobs destroyed homes, businesses, churches, and virtually all the Black schoolhouses in an attempt to intimidate the city's Blacks and abolitionists.

> *[T]he President felt that, to promote compliance with the new law as it pertained to hospitals, it would be helpful if all concerned knew just what this law was and meant; thus, needless controversy and litigation might be avoided. Therefore, there were present all the officials who would explain their particular areas and answer any pertinent questions. The Secretary expressed the President's belief that understanding the impact of the law would stimulate voluntary compliance for the common ideal.*[244]

For the first time since Reconstruction, the federal government became directly involved in the health and health care of African Americans. This "Second Reconstruction" would soon make its presence felt in the case of Black health.[245]

### An Era of Liberation Accompanies Health and Health Care Advance

The late 1950s and early 1960s were a time of liberation for oppressed peoples worldwide. After World War II, national liberation movements had erupted in Asia and Africa, bringing the curtain down on colonialism. In Africa, Libyan independence dawned in 1952 and Morocco and Sudan broke their chains of colonialism in 1956. Tunisia and Ghana became independent in 1957, followed by Guinea in 1958. In Asia the British Raj ended in 1948 and French Indochina expelled the French in 1954. Meanwhile, European influence in China ended in 1949. By the mid-1960s: "the Assembly of the United Nations had 56 African and Asian member states, 50.4 per cent of the total membership, as compared to only 11, or 21.6 per cent in 1945, when the organization was founded."[246] Inspired by this flood of independence and self-determination by people of color throughout the world, the Black Civil Rights Movement in America, led by Reverend Martin Luther King, Jr., gained momentum. African American physicians were at the forefront.

A new militancy entranced Black physicians as it had transformed African Americans in general. As Morais observed:

> *With the deadline for social justice long overdue, Negroes in the medical and allied professions threw themselves into the battle to close the citizenship gap in the health field. As marches, sit-ins and other forms of direct action for equal rights rocked the nation, an ever growing number of the country's over five thousand Negro doctors became part of the irresistible ground swell.*[247]

They staged sit-in demonstrations, manned picket lines, and marched on government institutions—including the Capitol. Kenneth W. Clement, M.D., 1963 NMA president, captured the spirit:

> *In this hour of the Negro's greatest struggle for his civil rights and his civil freedom, we need do well to remember that the cause of the Negro physician and his patient is one and inseparable. Not only must we redouble our efforts in the traditional areas, litigation, legislation and conciliatory conferences; we must also join in the direct action program assault on every form of social evil based on race. For this is the era of mass involvement and direct action. This we recognize, approve and applaud. But, my fellow-physicians! We must do more than approve, we must participate.*[248]

A biracial group of physicians picketed the AMA convention in Atlantic City on June 12, 1963, appealing to White organized medicine "to speak out immediately and unequivocally against racial segregation and discrimination ... wherever [they] exist in medicine and health services."[249] The physicians represented the newly formed Medical Committee for Civil Rights, and their program had the support of the American Jewish Congress, CORE, the NAACP, the National Catholic Conference for Interracial Justice, the Physician's Forum, the SCLC, and SNCC. At the same convention, John L. S. Holloman, M.D., of New York City and one other leader of the Medical Committee for Civil Rights, handed Dr. Edward Annis, president of the AMA, a letter reiterating the committee's appeal to the AMA to speak out against racial segregation and discrimination in local and state medical societies and health care facilities. Two weeks later Black physicians picketed the AMA's Chicago headquarters in conjunction with the NAACP convention, which criticized the AMA's regressive racial policies.

Direct action protests against White organized medicine continued. Pickets numbering in the hundreds greeted AMA conventions in New York City in 1965 and Chicago in 1966. They were organized by the renamed Medical Committee for Human Rights (MCHR); this biracial organization had grown in numbers and influence and included White medical luminaries such as Nobel Laureate Albert Szent-Gyorgyi, Paul Dudley White, Leslie A. Falk, Leo Davidoff, Benjamin Spock, Albert B. Sabin, Howard A. Rusk, Leo Mayer, Louis C. Lasagna, and Samuel Z. Levine. Outstanding Black physicians such as Leonidis H. Berry, Paul Cornely, and Albert B. Britton, Jr., were also members. By 1965 the committee's activities expanded to:

> *(1) give medical aid to civil rights workers; (2) provide a "medical presence" at demonstrations and marches to minimize physical attacks against marchers; (3) mobilize health professionals to become more supportive of the Civil Rights Movement; and (4) raise financial contributions for civil rights activities and organizations.*[250]

The committee provided medical support such as immunizations, first aid, and medical treatments for local communities and civil rights groups involved in the

Freedom Summer project in Mississippi in 1964; sponsored the autopsies of the slain civil rights workers Michael Schwerner, Andrew Goodman, and James Chaney in August 1964; led by Alvin F. Poussant, provided care for indigent Blacks in Holmes County, Mississippi, and for civil rights marchers in that state; and provided medical support for the Selma to Montgomery, Alabama, demonstration in March, 1965. The NMA, NUL, and NAACP were heavily involved in these activities. The committee, along with the NMA, provided these services by sending volunteer teams of doctors, medical students, and nurses to staff the various sites of civil rights activities; purchasing and equipping mobile medical vans where necessary; purchasing and transporting medical supplies to different sites where they were needed; and coordinating medical activities, where cooperation was possible, with local and state medical agencies and authorities. Nationwide, other African American and some White physicians were rendering similar services to people involved in the Civil Rights Movement on local and less formal levels.

Mature enough by April 1965 to hold its first national convention, by the summer of that year the committee had expanded its program. Now included were:

> protection and care of student civil rights workers; development of rural health centers and mobile health units; health education; aid to community workers in developing health and medical programs; surveying medical needs and documenting discriminatory patterns in health services in the North and South, to provide a basis for change.[251]

Under the national chairmanship of Dr. John L. S. Holloman, Jr., MCHR membership increased to 3,000 and chapters to 17. At its next annual convention in Chicago, March 1966, the committee drew up plans to initiate pressure for better medical care in poverty-stricken Appalachia.[252]

The Civil Rights Movement of the 1960s also spurred the NMA into direct and official action. The son of the previous editor, president, and leader of the NMA, John A. Kenney, Dr. John A. Kenney, Jr., 1963 NMA president, summed up Black medicine's posture: "The time has come in the problems that confront physicians, especially ... Negro physicians, that something more than talk is absolutely necessary."[253] Instead of succumbing to impatience or despondency regarding White organized medicine and its cabal's resistance to desegregating and integrating the health system, Cobb warned prophetically in 1963:

> For seven years we have invited them [representatives of the American Medical Association and other major hospital organizations] to sit down with us and solve the problem. The high professional and economic levels of these bodies and the altruistic religious principles according to which they are supposed to operate seem to have meant nothing. By their refusal to confer they force action by crisis. And now events have passed beyond them. The initiative offered is no longer theirs to accept.[254]

Figure 3.8
John L. S. Holloman, Jr.
leads African American
physicians and civil rights
protesters picketing the
AMA convention in New
York City in 1965 for the
desegregation of orga-
nized medicine and the
health system.
  From Morais HM.
*The History of the Negro
in Medicine.* New York:
Publishers Company,
1967, 164.

On the civil rights front, the organization adopted a resolution at its 69th annual convention in Washington on August 2–6, 1964, directing its "component and constituent societies to recruit volunteers to render medical care in areas of the South where events determine the need."[255] Volunteers were recruited to go to Mississippi in support of the Freedom Summer project after the organization appointed an ad hoc committee headed by Dr. Albert B. Britton, Jr., for the task.

Just as the March on Washington on August 28, 1963, marked the high point of the nonviolent, interracial phase of the 1960s Black Civil Rights Movement, "Bloody Sunday," March 7, 1965, marked the apogee of medical participation in the direct-action phase of a King-dominated, peaceful crusade. (See Figure 3.8.) Black and sympathetic White physicians had been organizing groups protesting against racial injustice for almost 20 years, but the thoroughness, logistical sophis-tication, and professionalism of the medical support provided at the civil rights activities at Selma, Alabama, were unprecedented. The planned march of demon-strators from Selma to Montgomery, Alabama, was a high point of a months-long voter registration campaign led by SNCC and, in its latter stages, the SCLC. Anticipating trouble in Selma, the Medical Committee for Human Rights trans-ferred its small medical truck, originally furnished by the National Council of Churches, in February. Upon attempting to cross the Edmund Pettus Bridge en route to Montgomery, the marchers were brutally attacked, gassed, and clubbed by policemen and Alabama State troopers. Injured marchers were attended by physi-cians representing the Medical Committee for Human Rights and the NMA. This nationally televised outrage intensified the marchers' determination to complete the march. Both medical organizations beefed up their manpower to support future activities: the MCHR* sent Drs. John L.S. Holloman and David M. French

---

*By 1965 the Medical Committee for Civil Rights had been succeeded by the Medical Committee for Human Rights.

(associate professor of surgery at Howard) with funds for logistical and organizational purposes; the NMA sent Dr. Cobb for the same reasons; three mobile first-aid stations were provided by the Dallas County Voters League; Black undertakers provided ambulances; a large medical van with complete X-ray and lab facilities was supplied by the International Ladies Garment Workers Union; arrangements were made with hospitals along the entire route of the march; and NMA and MCHR physicians accompanied the protesters at all activities. Four thousand people marched the 50 miles to Montgomery, starting on Sunday, March 21, 1965. On the March 25 arrival in Montgomery, it was clear the medical matters had been well handled. Physicians and activists were unable to prevent the brutal murder of civil rights worker Mrs. Viola Liuozzo by marauding gunmen late that night; however, over 120 physicians served throughout the campaign.

As Cobb predicted, the NMA's three-year-old campaign to enact a Medicare bill for the aged under the Social Security Act succeeded on July 27–28, 1965, when Titles 18 and 19 passed the House and Senate. President Lyndon B. Johnson immediately flew to Independence, Missouri, to sign the bill into law as Harry S. Truman, who had fought so hard for national health insurance for the American people, watched. The NMA first placed itself on record favoring Medicare in August, 1962, becoming "a dissenter from the dominant organization of American medicine."[256] It reaffirmed its position in March 1963 and testified on behalf of the legislation on Capitol Hill on January 22, 1964. Both the NMA's past president Dr. Kenneth W. Clement and the indefatigable Dr. W. Montague Cobb, who was the current NMA president, testified in favor of the bill. The NMA's traditional role as the sole medical supporter of progressive health legislation evidenced earlier in the era, such as with Emory I. Robinson's (then NMA president) support of President Truman's Senate Bill 1606 in 1946, was vindicated.[257]

Between 1945 and 1965, much of the health care civil rights struggle "took place ... in pages of medical journals, at professional meetings, and in firm but generally friendly talks between black and white physicians and hospital administrators."[258] Although cacophonous legal and social pressures emanated from the courtrooms and the streets, much progress was made against segregated and discriminatory education, hospital staff appointments, and medical societies in this manner. Regarding the latter two problems: "In 1950, at the urging of Cobb, Murray, and the NAACP, the AMA finally reversed its sixty-year-old policy of accepting exclusion among member societies."[259] The resolution expressed the AMA's "deep concern" about the problem and advised member bodies to "study this question in the light of prevailing conditions with a view to taking such steps as they may elect to eliminate such restrictive provisions."[260] The AMA went no further than this lukewarm approach at its 1952 Chicago convention. The New York State Medical Society's 1949 election of Dr. Peter Marshall Murray to its national House of Delegates, the first African American member of that policy-making body, and dropping the designation "colored" after the names of the few Black doctors listed in the 1950 edition of the *American Medical Directory* were considered great progress.

Agitation for racial equality within the AMA overtook the national organization. County and state affiliates desegregated in Baltimore, Maryland (1948); the state of Missouri (1950); Arlington County, Virginia (1951); the District of Columbia (1951); Bibb County, Georgia (1952); Pulaski County, Arkansas (1953); and the Alabama Medical Association (1953). In 1954 North Carolina and Virginia removed racially restrictive membership bars. By 1955 Dr. Peter M. Murray could summarize in the *New York State Medical Journal*: "Negro physicians are now admitted to membership in some county societies in every state with the exception of two."[261] Even Cobb noted progress in professional discrimination, reporting: "Of southern state medical societies (including the medical society of the District of Columbia) 53 percent (9 of 17) offered memberships to African-American physicians."[262] When the Clarksdale and Six Counties Medical Society in Mississippi accepted its first Black physician-member in 1956, Louisiana was the sole Southern state of the seventeen with racially exclusive medical society membership requirements intact. However, Morais observed by 1960, "Despite these successes, most county medical societies in the South continued to exclude Negro physicians from membership."[263] Moreover, patterns of resistance such as North Carolina's making Blacks eligible for "scientific membership"*[264] only, suggested to Beardsley "that beneath the surface of white professional acceptance lay a wide stratum of prejudice."[265] This caste status was rejected by most members of the Old North State Medical Society (the NMA-affiliated state organization), who censured two of their members for accepting the arrangement. Nationally, many Northern, Midwestern, and Western medical societies had "quotas" or more stringent requirements for Black physicians.

The struggle physicians of both races had been engaged in against the racially discriminatory policies of medical specialty boards broke out publically after World War II. In April 1945, Dr. George D. Thorne, a Black surgeon on the staffs of Sydenham and Lincoln Hospitals in New York City, requested an application for membership in the American College of Surgeons (ACS). He was refused an application form and told in writing, "fellowship in the college is not being conferred on members of the Negro race at the present time."[266] This action raised a public outcry involving physicians of both races; New York State Assemblyman Philip D. Schupler and State Senator Lazarus Joseph, who suggested that Governor Thomas E. Dewey intervene; and the medical and news media. Dr. Louis T. Wright, sole African American member of the ACS since 1934, opined the action "cannot be justified," stating "it is a wrong thing."[267] Mounting public pressure on the ACS led to a pause in its discriminatory policy and the admission of distinguished Philadelphia surgeon, Dr. F. D. Stubbs, into its ranks. He was soon followed by four others.** Progress in desegregating specialty societies proceeded:

---

*"Scientific membership" meant that Blacks could attend technical and business sessions of the society but were excluded from strictly social functions.

**Peter Marshall Murray of New York and Ulysses G. Daily, Roscoe C. Giles, and Carl G. Roberts of Chicago.

"In 1947, there were 93 board-certified Negro specialists in the country; in 1952, 190; and in the summer of 1958, about 350."[268] A trend having been established, other specialty societies began opening their doors to qualified Blacks.

Gaining entry into Southern and White medical schools was a much more public, and much more important, fight. Not only did it take longer, but "the opening of white colleges was critical to the black profession—and its patients."[269] Alarmingly, "[b]y the late 1940s the supply of new Negro doctors and dentists was estimated to be insufficient even to replace the number lost each year to deaths and retirement. As a result the black patient-to-physician ratio always too high, was mounting upward."[270] By 1949 the U.S. Surgeon General estimated that it would take 5,000 additional Black doctors just to get the ratio down to 1,500:1, which was twice the national average. Northern schools could help with liberalizing their admissions policies, "but it was more important to open the twenty-six colleges in the South (one-third of the nation's total) . . . where 75 percent of blacks lived, and as of 1948 not one had accepted a black applicant."[271] Cobb observed: "Just as the military academies train officers for the armed forces without regional distinction, so the nation's medical schools collectively train health personnel . . . for the care of the health of the American people. The policy of racial discrimination was a flagrant misuse of a national resource."[272] Cobb's efforts at reconciliation and amelioration of the problem revealed that it would take more than polite persuasion and bargaining to open the doors of Southern medical schools.

Southerners were not unconcerned about the need for more Black doctors: "[t]he problem was that integration was outside all imaginable solutions."[273] As was previously mentioned, the Southern Governors' Conference hatched a scheme (some say Meharry's board suggested it) to persuade Congress to assist them in providing Meharry with a 70 percent subsidy to train its Black students in 1948 and 1949. The governors felt this would put the Southern medical schools outside the reach of the *Murray* (1935),* *Gaines* (1938),** and *Sipuel* (1947)*** decisions. Besides criticizing Meharry "for being a willing dupe," Cobb alleged:

> We do not find the Southern Governors' Conference recognizing the long-time injustice to their Negro population. . . . Instead, we see the deplorable

---

*Black Amherst graduate Donald Gaines Murray applied for admission to the University of Maryland Law School. After he was denied admission and after an ensuing court battle, the judge ordered he be admitted. The state's appeal the next year was denied.

**Lloyd Gaines sought admission to Missouri's all-White law school. Denied admission, he was referred to the state's Lincoln University (which had no law school) or to apply out of state. In that he was entitled to equal protection of the law, the court ruled he be admitted to the University of Missouri's school of law.

***Although Ada Lois Sipuel's rejection by the University of Oklahoma Law School was upheld by all the Oklahoma courts, the U.S. Supreme Court ruled the state had to provide her with a legal education "in conformity with the equal protection clause of the Fourteenth Amendment and provide it as soon as it does for applicants of any other group."

> spectacle, on the one hand, of an offer to keep Meharry alive by ...
> [using it] to take the South's responsibility for training Negro medical
> professionals off its hands and to perpetuate traditional discrimination;
> and on the other the Meharry Trustees offer the school as an outright
> gift.[274]

The NAACP joined the fight against the Southern Governors' Conference plan,
alleging it was a dodge to maintain segregation with inadequate facilities for
Blacks—circumstances previous court rulings in the *Gaines* and *Sipuel* cases
would no longer let stand. Congress defeated the measure in committee by a one-
vote margin.

In response to coordinated efforts of the NMA and NAACP during the late
1940s and 1950s, medical schools in Southern and border states where Blacks had
been barred slowly did a turnaround:

> To eliminate racially discriminatory admission policies, the National
> Association for the Advancement of Colored People instituted a series of
> legal proceedings which resulted in a number of favorable Supreme Court
> decisions. Following these decisions, the University of Arkansas permitted
> the registration in 1948 of Edith Mae Irby, the first Negro admitted to a
> Southern all-white medical school.[275]

In 1947 and 1948 in the South, her enrollment raised the Southern total to 235
(Meharry had 234) Black medical students out of a total medical enrollment of
5,533. Of 1,268 Southern medical school graduates in 1947 and 1948, only 58
were Black; all graduated from Meharry. Although 25 percent of the region's total
population was African American, this represented only 4.5 percent of Southern
medical school graduates.

Progress was spotty in Southern and border states. In 1949 St. Louis University
and the University of Texas admitted Black medical students. Washington University in St. Louis, the University of Louisville, the Medical College of Virginia, the
University of Maryland, and the University of North Carolina followed suit in
1951. By 1960 six more had broken the racial barrier. Thus:

> within a decade or so, more than half of all Southern medical schools,
> fourteen out of twenty-six, were admitting Negro students, albeit on a
> token basis.... [A]s a result of these victories, the number and percentage
> of Negroes enrolled in predominantly white medical schools increased
> steadily during the post–World War II period.[276]

Despite the fact as late as 1955 and 1956 Howard and Meharry had 525 of the 761
(69 percent) African American medical students enrolled, "[b]y the late 1950s, 42
percent (11 of 26) of southern medical schools admitted African-American

students,"[277] Cobb reported in the *JNMA*. Enrollment of Black students in White medical schools increased from 15.8 percent of the Black total nationally in 1947 and 1948 to 31.0 percent in 1955 and 1956. By 1966 all 26 Southern and border-state medical schools, including Duke (1963), Emory (1963), Johns Hopkins (1963), Baylor (1966), LSU (1966), Vanderbilt (1966), and the Medical College of Alabama (1966), admitted African American students.

Responding to the exploding costs of medical education in the postwar period, a group of African American physicians founded Provident Medical Associates, Inc., in 1946. The organization focused on the medical education of Negroes and the conditions under which they practiced. Growing in size and influence, by 1952 it changed its name to National Medical Fellowships, Incorporated, and began awarding millions of dollars of fellowship grants to deserving Black students in medicine to continue their studies and training. Following advice "which had first been suggested by President Emory I. Robinson in 1946 and later by President Matthew Walker in 1954,"[278] the NMA officially established the Student National Medical Association in 1965.[279]

During the twentieth century, White organized medicine became accustomed to professional unanimity within its ranks. On regulatory, health policy, and medical-social matters, the AMA spoke for what it considered "the profession," and with a single voice. Nevertheless, dissident physician groups began cropping up after World War I. In the four and one-half decades between 1940 and 1984 the AMA formally recognized physician organizations to the left such as the Physicians Forum, the Medical Committee for Human Rights, and Physicians for Social Responsibility. Other groups officially recognized as politically to the right of the AMA were the Private Doctors of America (formerly the Council of Medical Staffs), the Congress of County Medical Societies, and the Association of American Physicians. Although the NPC embarrassed the AMA to such a degree through its reactionary leanings and extremist actions that the AMA was eventually forced to discontinue its activities, the AMA never publically condemned the NPC's actions or ideologies. Throughout the 1945-to-1965 period, the AMA never acknowledged the existence of the NMA in its official history.

Of the non-AMA professional groups documented to have affected the American health system the most in the postwar period, the NMA and the MCHR would rank highest. Traditionally, the AMA strove to keep all physicians in line. During the defeat of the Wagner-Murray-Dingell bills and the Truman plan, NMA support for these progressive health bills broke ranks with White organized medicine's recommendations. Even though it refused to acknowledge the NMA publically, "the AMA did not want the NMA on record as opposing its position."[280] Moreover, "[e]arlier, AMA leaders had approached their black counterparts with a vague offer of recognizing black medical societies as AMA affiliates if the NMA would join against Truman's 'socialized medicine' scheme. Cobb and others who believed strongly in the plan rejected the offer, and the projected bargain collapsed."[281] In 1949 the AMA took stronger, directed actions. Headquartered at a downtown Detroit hotel, the Book-Cadillac, the general manager of the AMA parlayed with NMA representatives housed at the Negro hotel Gotham.* After wining and dining select NMA members at the Book-Cadillac, General George F. Lull, the AMA general manager, had them prepare a motion to rescind the NMA approval of S. 1606, the national health plan. Presenting the motion in the final section at the end of a grueling legislative session, Dr. C. Herbert Marshall of Washington, D.C., who had just been installed as the 49th president of the organization, stood up and said, "If you pass this motion, you'll get a pat on the back from the AMA and a kick in the pants from 11 million Negroes and the NAACP."[282] The AMA made a final attempt to get the NMA to rescind its endorsement at its Hampton convention in 1950.[283] It also failed.

Meanwhile, in 1946 the ANA's House of Delegates passed a resolution calling for the admission of all qualified nurses regardless of race, creed, or national origin. The ANA had made halting attempts to desegregate the nursing profession as early as 1926.** The recommendation was accepted by the 1948 ANA convention. The ANA and the National Association of Colored Graduate Nurses (NACGN) established an intergroup relations program anticipating amalgamation. Josepha Bacote noted in the *Journal of the National Black Nurses Association*: "[i]n 1949, ANA suggested that NACGN's functioning and responsibility be absorbed by the ANA." At its 1949 convention the NACGN felt its organization was obsolete and voted to dissolve. On January 26, 1951, under the stewardship of Mabel K. Staupers, then president of the ANA (1949–1951), the NACGN dissolved to integrate with the ANA. Ten years later, one state and several districts still denied Black nurses membership in the national organization. Moreover, by 1961, "[t]here were still problems of salary differentials based on race, inequities in job opportunities and advancement, segregated nursing schools, and often only token or no representation of Negro nurses in policy-making areas."[284] Despite lofty plans and platitudes, a great deal remained to be done to bridge the racial divide in the nursing profession.[285]

Clearly, after 1945 the AMA could not keep all White physicians or health providers in line on its discriminatory racial policies or its backward health policies. Progressive desegregation of medical societies, medical schools, hospitals, and specialty societies occurred throughout the era despite AMA resistance. The nursing profession began desegregating by 1951. Although a great deal of progress was made, much more remained to be done. African American physicians remained virtually the sole advocates for the Black population's interests in the public health, health policy, and political arenas. Moreover, they disproportionately cared for Black and underserved populations and

---

*Detroit was not then an open city as it is now. The White downtown hotels made only a tiny number of rooms available to African American clients.

**The 1939 ANA president stated that a polling letter would be sent out to constituent bodies querying them about integration of the profession. Nothing else was heard of this effort.

worked for less pay—seeing more patients than their White colleagues, as documented in Paul Cornely's 1951 *JNMA* study.[286] Paradoxically, African American communities interested in their health status, outcomes, and facilities, often led by "Jim-Crowed" NMA physicians, were expected to financially support White institutions that systematically excluded or discriminated against them through their taxes, fees, and political acquiescence. This was part of the battle facing Black hospitals, training institutions, and medical schools. The era demonstrated a new level of maturity for Black organized medicine. Black physicians could define African American health policies, mobilize public opinion to support them, and influence the political process to achieve some positive outcomes. Although the newly honed partnership between the Black medical establishment and the federal government remained distorted through White condescension and paternalism, as evidenced by the Johnson administration's turning to the AMA for its sole medical advice on drawing up the Medicare/Medicaid legislation, it offered the African American population more health possibilities then ever before.[287]

## Persistent Old Problems: Universal Access and Scientific Racism

The period from 1945 to 1965 was one of explosive growth and expansion for the health system. Health institutions such as hospitals, medical schools, and research facilities grew by leaps and bounds. This exponential growth led health care to expand to consume from 4.5 percent of GNP in 1945 to 7 percent in 1965. The health insurance industry grew just as impressively. Passage of Medicare and Medicaid in 1965 would mean undreamed-of growth in the future.

The major problem generated by the health system's explosive growth and improved technology was the sharp rise in costs. Health care grew beyond the reach of many Americans—especially the elderly. The response to this crisis, the passage of Medicare and Medicaid in 1965, represented a partial and short-term solution to the problem and the first health policy defeat for the AMA and its medical establishment. It also represented the emergence of the NMA and its allies who publically supported progressive health care legislation and change, convincing Congress that these vital health care reforms did not represent health system Armageddon medically or structurally. This nonviolent crusade for justice and equity in health care dovetailed perfectly into the civil rights struggle to dismantle segregation and discrimination in America's institutions. However, there were troubling signs of conflagration and conflict ahead as forces of impatience and confrontation not committed to Gandhian concepts of nonviolence began to occupy center stage of the Black Civil Rights Movement.

Meanwhile, an oppressive side of the U.S. health system survived the postwar decades. Nurtured by history-based defects and "blind spots" in U.S. scientific culture, unethical experimentation, race- and class-biased eugenically oriented surgery, and medical exploitation of the underprivileged for the sake of "science" and training continued. Little was gained from the World War II Nazi experiences gleaned from the Nuremberg and Buchenwald, Germany, Doctors' Trials—the most famous being known as the "Medical Case," which took place between December 9, 1946, and August 19, 1947, at Nuremberg. Twenty Nazi doctors and three of their accomplices were tried. Fifteen were found guilty* and seven were executed on August 20, 1947. The 10-point code of human experimentation ethics known as the Nuremberg Code (see Appendix 3A) that resulted from the trial "was conducted by U.S. judges under the authority of the U.S. military, U.S. procedures were followed, and U.S. lawyers acted as the prosecutors.... [I]f any country should feel itself bound by the legal precepts of the Nuremberg Code, it is the United States."[288] It has seldom been utilized or referred to in the U.S. jurisprudence system, despite the fact that it "set the general agenda for all future ethical and legal questions pertaining to the conduct of human experimentation."[289] As health lawyer and bioethicist George J. Annas noted in *The Nazi Doctors and the Nuremberg Code*:

> *Although courts in the United States may use the Nuremberg Code to set criminal and civil standards of conduct, none have used it in a criminal case and only a handful have even cited it in the civil context. Even where the Nuremberg Code has been cited as authoritative, it has usually been in dissent, and no U.S. court has ever awarded damages to an injured experimental subject, or punished an experimenter, on the basis of a violation of the Code.*[290]

Historian Robert Proctor and influential German physician Christian Pross concur: "Most leading German physicians supported the Nazis. Why? Physicians commonly boasted that their profession had shown its allegiance earlier, and in greater strength, than any other professional group ... and ... the majority of physicians had actively or passively participated in medical crimes."[291] Tens of thousands of German physicians who had participated in Nazi Germany's unethical, sometimes barbaric, health policy were never tried. Since 1980 German organized medicine has been confronting its Nazi past; in 1997, President Clinton apologized to the remaining victims of the Tuskegee syphilis experiment. The question is raised why such a commendable code of ethics has had so little impact in two countries with long histories of unethical therapeutic and nontherapeutic experimentation, unethical eugenically oriented surgery, and medical abuse and exploitation involving Blacks and other disadvantaged groups.

---

*One additional defendant was acquitted of medical crimes but was found guilty of SS membership.

America and Germany had strong Teutonic (later rechristened Nordic)* scientific cults dating from the nineteenth century. Many American academics and scientists "stood in awe of Spencer and Galton, Freeman and Lapouge, Gobineau and Ripley."**[292] As Christian Pross points out:

> Long before ... physicians and anthropologists had tried to prove that certain human beings were less worthy of living than others. In the nineteenth century, the theory of the inequality of the human races, of the differentiation of the "superiors" and "inferiors," was an attack of the declining European gentry on the demands for equality, freedom, and brotherhood and the declaration of human rights during the French Revolution. It provided the ideological tools for a biological solution to the social question. Despite the fact that in the period of industrialization poverty, venereal disease, tuberculosis, and alcoholism spread in the slums of the big cities, their social causes were simply denied, and it was suggested that it was the individual's fault if he was poor and sick. Poverty was understood as a sign of degeneration and hereditary inferiority.[293]

Both nations became infatuated with the concept of *racial hygiene*, a concept invented by medical scientists in the first place. As Proctor explains:

> At the end of the nineteenth century, German social Darwinists, fearing a general "degeneration" of the human race, set about to establish a new kind of hygiene–a racial hygiene (Rassenhygiene) that would turn the attention of physicians away from the individual or the environment and toward the human germ plasm. In the eyes of its founders (Alfred Ploetz and Wilhelm Schallmayer), racial hygiene was supposed to complement personal and social hygiene; racial hygiene would provide long-run preventive medicine ... by combating the disproportionate breeding of "inferiors," the celibacy of the upper classes, and the threat posed by feminists to the reproductive performance of the family.[294]

---

*Frances Amasa Walker, president of MIT (1891–1897) and previously chief of the Bureau of Statistics and Superintendent of the Census (1830–1860), alleged that large numbers of non-Nordic, low-class, degraded peasantry of grossly inferior types were "degrading" the quality of the U.S. population during the nineteenth-century process of immigration and population expansion. Blacks faced extinction because of their inferiority.

**Edward Freeman was a nineteenth-century professor of history at Oxford and leader of the Teutonic cult that burgeoned in Europe and America following the release of Frenchman Joseph Arthur de Gobineau's *Inequality of the Races* (1853–1855). Count Georges Vacher de Lapouge, another disciple of de Gobineau who dabbled in history and craniology, published *L'Aryen: son rôle social* (1899), predicting adverse racial changes in the shape of Frenchmen's skulls as a sign of degeneration. American economist and self-styled "raciologist" William Z. Ripley, in his book *Races of Europe*, attempted to make the cephalic index the successor to phrenology.

Moreover:

> *Racial hygienists followed Eugen Fischer's claim that the science of ge-*
> *netics had shown that "all human traits—normal or pathological, physi-*
> *cal or mental—are shaped by hereditary factors." They argued that the*
> *environment—whether climate, nutrition, or education—played a rela-*
> *tively minor role in the development of human character, and that mod-*
> *ern science had "destroyed the theory of the equality of men."*[295]

The lives of African Americans had been placed particularly at risk due to this kind of thinking for 250 years.

Adolf Hitler was strongly influenced by the racial hygiene movement through the discipline's literature, such as Fritz Lenz's and Eugen Fischer's* book *The Principles of Human Heredity and Race Hygiene*, which Hitler read in Landsberg prison in 1923 while writing *Mein Kampf* (1925).[296] By the 1930s this prominent engine of health policy in Nazi Germany, which had roots stretching back before and through the Weimar Republic, was scientifically labeled as "hereditary and race hygiene."[297] Under Hitler a regime had come to power willing to put these policies in action. As Chase repeatedly pointed out, Americans and Germans supported "the utopian view of a society cleansed of everything sick, alien, and disturbing."[298] With doctors as the co–change agents of these biological solutions to society's problems, "medicine turned into destruction. It abandoned its purpose of healing the sick individual, of alleviating his suffering, and abandoned the Hippocratic *nil nocere* when experimentation was done for its own sake, for 'superior' aims."[299] When biomedical scientists and physicians recommended "medical solutions" to such "problems," it represented "only part of a larger attempt by the German medical profession to medicalize or biologize various forms of social, sexual, political, or racial deviance; Jews, homosexuals, Gypsies, Marxists, and other groups were typecast as 'health hazards' to the German population."[300] Between the Weimar Republic and the end of the war, periodic economic stresses on the German health system and overall economy coalesced with policies of "sterilization of the 'inferior' and the elimination of 'unnecessary eaters.'"[301] In the areas of the Nuremberg Laws,** the Marital Health Laws,*** and the Sterilization Law, German physicians used American physicians as their models:

---

*Physician, medical scholar, and geneticist Eugen Fischer performed racial research "documenting" superior and inferior "races" while at the University of Freiburg and throughout his career. Later director of the Kaiser Wilhelm Institute for Anthropology, Human Genetics, and Eugenics (1926–1942), under Hitler he was named rector of the University of Berlin (1933) and served as a judge in Berlin's Appellate Genetic Health Court.

**The Nuremberg Laws, enacted in 1935, excluded Jews from German citizenship and outlawed marriage or sexual relations between Jews and non-Jews.

***The Marital Health Laws required couples to submit to medical examinations before marriage to prevent "racial pollution."

*Nazi physicians on more than one occasion argued that German racial policies were relatively "liberal" compared with the treatment of blacks in the United States. Evidence of this was usually taken from the fact that, in several southern states, a person with ½nd black ancestry was legally black, whereas if someone were ⅛th Jewish in Germany (and, for many purposes, ¼th Jewish), that person was legally Aryan (a ¼ Jew for example, could marry a full-blooded German). Nazi physicians spent a great deal of time discussing American miscegenation legislation; German medical journals reproduced charts showing the states in which blacks could or could not marry whites, could or could not vote, and so forth.[302]*

There were other specific areas where Nazi physicians advised Hitler to follow their American scientific colleagues: "As soon as Hitler took power, one of the first things he did was to replace the mild Weimer Republic law permitting voluntary sterilization for medically certified reasons with a national law styled directly on the Eugenics Record Office's Model Eugenical Sterilization Law published by H. H. Laughlin in 1922."[303] The Eugenics Record Office, headed since its 1910 inception by Harvard Ph.D. Charles B. Davenport, was located at Cold Spring Harbor, Long Island, New York.

Meanwhile, as publicly funded health institutions such as city and county hospitals, state mental hospitals, and family planning clinics proliferated, African American, Latino American, and poor citizens became victims of increasing numbers of unethical forced sterilizations, unnecessary surgery, and medical abuse for so-called eugenical and "scientific" reasons. For example, at the Whitten's State Training School in South Carolina, a mental health hospital that admitted African Americans: "[d]uring the ten years between 1949 and 1960 for which the state mental hospital published records, 102 out of 104 surgical sterilizations were performed on African Americans ... despite the fact that, throughout the period, the hospital admitted more than twice as many Whites as Blacks."[304] Though the eugenics movement was waning in the United States after the first four decades of the twentieth century, "[d]isproportionately represented in the populations of public institutions, persons of African extraction were prime candidates for involuntary sterilization."[305] State courts in California and state legislatures in states such as Oklahoma, Maryland, and Mississippi began rendering punitive and coercive sterilization rulings and legislation in the 1945 to 1965 period. Much of this legal activity was directed against disadvantaged minority groups such as Latinos and Blacks. Performance of sterilizations on Black women became so common in some areas of the South that the phrase "'Mississippi appendectomy' ... [became] a euphemism for a tubal ligation or hysterectomy performed on southern black women without their consent and for no good health reason."[306] Although no one will ever know exactly how many of these clandestine procedures were performed in an era of medical secrecy and sloppy record keeping, Fannie Lou Hamer, a leader of the biracial Mississippi Freedom Democratic Party, shocked a 1965 audience on Capitol Hill by stating "that 60 percent of the black women taken to Sunflower (Mississippi) City Hospital were sterilized there without any valid medical reason. Frequently they were not informed that they had been made infertile until they were discharged from the hospital."[307] Although motivated by theological reasons, Catholic clergy such as the Most Reverend Patrick O'Boyle, Archbishop of Washington, began speaking out in sermons such as "Sterilization and the Medically Indigent" by 1962. "The Catholic divine implied that sterilization programs for the medically indigent had a special impact on black people, a negative impact to be sure,"[308] according to Robert G. Weisbord. Excessive surgery, especially on disadvantaged minority women, for the sake of training, experience, and experimentation was also an American tradition that seemed to be proliferating. These growing problems would trigger a firestorm of controversy during the next period as women's rights groups such as the Committee to End Sterilization Abuse, *Ms.* magazine, and the National Organization for Women (NOW) directly confronted the medical profession on the issues of unethical sterilization and unnecessary and excessive genital surgery on women.[309]

Meanwhile, utilitarianism and expediency instead of ethics guided both therapeutic and nontherapeutic research in the United States. Despite the British Medical Association's efforts beginning in 1946 to find a code that was less legalistic and applicable to therapeutic experiments instead of the outrageous German nontherapeutic ones, the release of the World Medical Association's Declaration of Helsinki in 1964 (see Appendix 3B), offered little practical patient protection. Although the Declaration of Helsinki was an ethical as opposed to a legalistic document such as the Nuremberg Code, it provided only guidelines and depended upon the physician-researcher's conscience to protect patients. Both have seldom been used in U.S. courts. For African American, Latino American, poor, and other disadvantaged patient groups often considered "inferior" by U.S. physicians, little protection was offered. Despite what was happening in the United States, as Annas observed: "almost no experiments resulted in lawsuits in the 1940s, 1950s, and 1960s."[310] The U.S. tradition of overutilizing prisoners, the institutionalized retarded, the mentally ill, and disadvantaged minorities continued.

When Henrietta Lacks walked through the doors of Johns Hopkins Hospital in February, 1951, complaining of ceaseless vaginal bleeding, she could not realize that her death 10 months later at age 31 would make her a symbol of the experimental medical abuse sustained by African Americans. Lacks's cervical cancer cells possessed a singular ability to multiply aggressively outside her body and flourish under laboratory conditions, instead of having to be delicately coddled by laboratory technicians like other cells without assurance of survival; her cells were sold to laboratories and utilized throughout the world as HeLa* cells. Their use

---

*Of the thousands of laboratory scientists using HeLa cells throughout the world, few recognize Lacks's name.

fueled hundreds of research advances and thousands of scientific publications in cancer, molecular biology, and viral research and the conquest of polio. She was also a contemporaneous symbol of the U.S. medical system's research and medical exploitation of Blacks and other disadvantaged populations. White Johns Hopkins researcher Dr. George Gey, who died in 1970, became famous for recognizing and capitalizing on her cells' peculiar properties, virtually creating the medical specialty of cell-line culture. Had the medical community simply utilized Henrietta Lacks's cells clandestinely, in obscurity, it would have been insult enough. Instead: "[h]er cells were taken without her husband's permission. And although HeLa distribution has become an industry worth billions, her family has received nothing, not even the courtesy of a few answers."[311] Even her hospital record was destroyed.[312] Her husband, Mr. David Lacks, Sr., in a 1994 interview said: "As far as them selling my wife's cells without my knowledge and making a profit—I don't like that at all.... They are exploiting both of us."[313] Henrietta Lacks represents a generations-long tradition of experimental and medical abuse heaped on African American and poor people in the United States.[314]

Meanwhile, the Tuskegee syphilis experiment took another ominous turn during this period. Shorn of the last vestiges of the positive motives that had energized the original syphilis control programs initiated collaboratively by the U.S. Public Health Service (USPHS) and the Rosenwald Fund in the late 1920s, between 1942 and 1965 the Tuskegee Study of Untreated Syphilis in the Negro Male—the longest nontherapeutic experiment on human beings in medical history—crossed new thresholds in distancing itself from conventional ethical or scientific standards.

The Rosenwald Fund withdrew from the project in 1931 due to the financial effects of the Great Depression. The fund, the USPHS, and the states that were required to provide portions of the funding also felt overwhelmed by the enormity and scope of the health problems they had discovered in rural, poor, largely Black populations between the late 1920s and 1931.* Before the programmatic dissolution and breakdown occurred late in 1931, the unprecedented syphilis control program possessed some salutary properties. These included but were not limited to the identification and quantification, often for the first time, of the prevalence, incidence, and public health and economic significance (e.g., syphilis definitely lowered workforce efficiency) of syphilis in rural, usually poor, Black populations;

---

*Butressed by the adjunct sociological study funded by the Rosenwald Fund, Charles S. Johnson's *Shadow of the Plantation* (1934), and two early medical reports (1930) expressing deep scientific and medical-social concerns by a Black physician, Dr. H. L. Harris, who had been sent by the fund as a consultant, the six pilot studies, Tuskegee being the prime example, demonstrated that most rural Black communities suffered ill health not only because of syphilis but due to tuberculosis, malnutrition, pellagra, hookworms, rickets, unhealthy lifestyles, systematic exclusion from access to basic health care, and deprivation caused by socioeconomic status. Treating syphilis without providing comprehensive health and social welfare programs would be futile. None of the lead agencies were committed or felt equipped to tackle such a problem.

the provision of diagnosis and treatment for poor, Black, rural populations hitherto denied such medical care for financial,* racial, or social reasons; and the provision of some basic medical services and health promotion/disease prevention programs, emphasizing venereal diseases, tuberculosis, hygiene, and nutrition, to these underserved populations for the first time. When the USPHS returned to Macon County with no funds for continuing ongoing or initiating new antisyphilis treatment in 1932, led by influential USPHS physicians Drs. Taliaferro Clark and Oliver Clarence Wenger, the agenda had changed.[315] Nontherapeutic experimentation, curiosity born of American "racial medicine" traditions,**[316] and the rationale that "proving" and documenting racial susceptibilities to syphilis might pressure Southern legislatures into funding syphilis control and public health programs for Blacks attained primacy. As far as USPHS doctors were concerned, "[t]he fate of syphilitic blacks in Macon County was sealed (at least for the immediate future) regardless of whether an experiment went forward. Increasing the store of knowledge seemed the only way to profit from the human suffering there. Indeed, the PHS had only to place a de facto situation under a microscope to convert the region into a scientific laboratory."[317] To lead investigator Dr. Clark, "Macon County offered thousands of infected Negroes who lived outside the world of modern medicine yet close to a well-equipped teaching hospital that could easily double as a scientific laboratory."[318] Several factors changed everything about how the program would be viewed. They included the facts that Drs. Clark and Wenger misrepresented the new program, identifying it with the Rosenwald/ USPHS treatment program of the late 1920s, bartering the goodwill that program had generated in Macon County and at Tuskegee Institute's John Andrew Hospital; investigators would have to deceive the patients throughout the experiment to assure their cooperation; a program intended to last one year lasted 40; and, with the advance of medical science, the patient/participants were denied, even "walled off" from, increasingly effective, life-saving, and curative therapies for four decades.

The USPHS launched the Tuskegee Study of Untreated Syphilis in the Negro Male with approximately 400 infected Black males and 200 nonsyphilitic Black males to serve as controls in 1932, deceptively telling "local residents that they had

---

*Dr. Michael Davis, the nationally renowned medical director of the Rosenwald Fund's health programs, discovered that the average cost of syphilis therapy on a fee-for-service basis was $300 per year. Since curative therapy required approximately 20 treatments with arsenicals and/or other available agents, one to two years to complete treatment was average. Based on these figures, he pointed out that 80 percent of the American public could not afford syphilis therapy on a fee-for-service basis and would have been categorized as "medically indigent" by the medical profession's usual definitions.

**"Racial medicine" charts "the influence racial attitudes have exerted on the perception and response of white physicians to disease in blacks.... A rare point of agreement ... was that the health of blacks had to be considered separately from the health of whites.... Advocates of racial medicine argued that differences in natural immunity, degree of susceptibility, and relative severity of reaction to various diseases often separated the races" (Jones 1982, 16, 17).

returned to Macon County to treat people who were ill."[319] Significantly, James H. Jones noted, "The PHS did not inform them that they had syphilis. Instead the men were told they had 'bad blood,' a catchall phrase rural blacks used to describe a host of ailments."[320]

Moreover:

> While the PHS had not intended to treat the men, state health officials demanded, as the price of their cooperation, that the men be given at least enough medication to render them noninfectious. Consequently, all of the men received a little treatment. No one worried much about the glaring contradiction of offering treatment in a study of untreated syphilis because the men had not received enough treatment to cure them. Thus, the experiment was scientifically flawed from the outset.[321]

The study would continue until 1972.

The period during and following World War II was an ethical, scientific, and legal turning point for the Tuskegee study. Although it was "known as early as 1932 that 85 percent of patients treated in late latent syphilis would enjoy prolonged maintenance of good health and freedom from disease as opposed to 35 percent if left untreated"[*][322] and "[s]cientists in this study reported in 1936 that morbidity in male Negroes with untreated syphilis far exceeds that in a comparable nonsyphilitic group and that cardiovascular and central nervous system involvements were two to three times as common,"[323] continued denial of treatment to the infected men took on a more sinister ambiance during the 1940s. For example, the available therapeutic agents in 1932, including mercury, bismuth, arsphenamine, neoarsphenamine, iodides, and various combinations thereof, were toxic, sometimes did not work (15 percent to 20 percent of the time), and required prolonged therapy (up to two years). The documented efficacy of penicillin for treating syphilis by the late 1940s and mounting scientific evidence of its effectiveness in this disease throughout the 1960s (to include treatment of neurosyphilis) was revolutionary. Its appearance should have changed, if not terminated, the study if scientific and ethical considerations had been prioritized.

Awareness of ethical culpability seemed to surface as Dr. Wenger, one of the principal investigators, reported at a medical seminar in 1950: "We know now, where we could only surmise before, that we have contributed to their ailments and shortened their lives. I think the least we can say is that we have a high moral obligation to those that have died to make this the best study possible."[324] Moreover, the USPHS, local health department, and state health department colluded during and after the war to block study participants, who

---

*Most of the infected subjects entered into the Tuskegee study would have been classified as having the latent stage of the disease.

by then were being manipulated as if they were captives, from being treated. There were written communications between USPHS doctors and Alabama health officials between February 1941 and August 1942 stating that:

> *known seropositive, untreated males under 45 years of age from the Tuskegee Study had been called for Army duty and rejected on account of a positive blood. The local board was furnished with a list of 256 names of men under 45 years of age and asked that these men be excluded from the list of draftees needing treatment! ... [T]he board agreed with this arrangement in order to make it possible to continue this study on an effective basis.*[325]

This was a continuation of USPHS's "walling off" the study subjects from treatment by local physicians, Tuskegee Institute's hospital, the VA hospital, and local and state public health agencies, begun in 1933, which lasted until at least 1969.[326] Besides violating Alabama's public health statutes requiring public reporting and prompt treatment of venereal disease cases, the stringent, federally sponsored Henderson Act (1943) requiring the treatment of tuberculosis and venereal diseases, inspired by the wartime emergency, was also violated to perpetuate the study.[327] Periodic reviews from within the medical infrastructure elected to continue the study.

Between 1945 and 1970 four reviews—three formal (1948, 1952–1953, 1968–1970) and one informal (1951)—of the Tuskegee Study took place. During the previous 15 years the USPHS doctors "had kept it going through the national syphilis campaign, World War II, the development of penicillin, and public reaction to the Nuremberg trials.... [T]he experiment had evolved into something of a 'sacred cow' within the USPHS."[328] Its longevity was further assured by Jones's observation that:

> *Administratively, the Tuskegee Study was an easy project to run, making few demands on PHS officials. The mechanism for following the subjects and securing autopsies functioned reasonably well, with most of the work done by health professionals in Macon County. The experiment was also cheap to maintain. Nurse Rivers was the only staff member assigned full time to the study, and her salary was never high. The Milbank Fund paid the burial stipends. Other expenses were easily absorbed by the PHS as routine operating costs.*[329]

Familiarity with the study and inbreeding within the USPHS muzzled criticisms about its scientific merits, its morality, and a series of procedural and conceptual weaknesses in the study's protocol voiced in 1948. An invitation to the Norwegian director of the Oslo syphilis study for a visit (1951) and informal audits complemented internal recommendations for upgrading recordkeeping and reviewing the clinical criteria for syphilis. These measures also led to the reorganization of the files, the transfer of the autopsy reports to punch cards, and a single set of diagnostic standards in 1952. In 1969 an ad hoc committee reviewed the 37-year-old Tuskegee Study in three hours and ten minutes and barely approved it. Prophetically, the committee's first observation was: "1. This type of study would never be repeated."[330] Drs. Anne Yobs, Arnold Schroeder, and James Lucas, highly placed officials in the USPHS, made separate recommendations for terminating the study on the basis of ethics, scientific irrelevance (e.g., "largely of *historical* interest"), and absence of credible informed consent criteria during 1970.[331] Evidently, no one listened. The study would not be terminated until a public firestorm engulfed the agency and all institutions and parties involved with the Tuskegee study as they underwent public scrutiny in 1972.[332]

For a plethora of reasons African Americans were, and continue to be, over-represented in prison populations and institutionalized populations for the mentally ill. Blacks also utilized public hospitals and clinics to a greater degree than Whites. These factors increased their vulnerability to overutilization for experimentation, training purposes, and medical abuse. Black, socially disadvantaged, handicapped, and poor populations were unethically utilized for radiation experiments by institutions as varied as MIT, Harvard, and the Oregon State Prison during the 1945 to 1965 period.[333] Consent for these studies, ranging from the ingestion of radioactive breakfast cereal to the administration of high doses of testicular radiation, was either absent or deficient. That these studies were being conducted in public institutions such as city and county hospitals; the Fernald State School in Waltham, Massachusetts, for the retarded; and the Washington State Prison makes the occurrences more shocking.[334]

The 1945 to 1965 health care era represented the best and worst of times in the United States. As far as African Americans were concerned, their nonviolent crusade for justice and equity in health care dovetailed perfectly with the civil rights struggle to dismantle segregation and discrimination in America's institutions. It seemed to have a disturbingly sluggish effect on the health care system. However, there were troubling signs of conflagration and conflict ahead as forces of resistance to change confronted impatience and aggressiveness in the struggle for civil rights. A tumultuous period loomed ahead.[335]

## CHAPTER FOUR

# Civil Rights Gains, Conservative Retrenchment, and Black Health, 1965–1980

## On the Cusp of Equality: Justice Denied

*If we — and now I mean the relatively conscious whites and the relatively conscious blacks, who must ... insist on, or create, the consciousness of the others — do not falter in our duty now, we may be able, handful that we are ... [to] end the racial nightmare, and achieve our country, and change the history of the world. If we do not now dare everything, the fulfillment of that prophecy, recreated from the Bible in song by a slave, is upon us: "God gave Noah the rainbow sign, No more water, the fire next time!"*

—JAMES BALDWIN, *THE FIRE NEXT TIME*

The troika of assassinations that occurred from the 1960s to 1980 — President John Kennedy on November 22, 1963, in Dallas; the Reverend Martin Luther King, Jr. in Memphis on April 4, 1968; and Senator Robert Kennedy in Los Angeles on June 6, 1968 — were emblematic of the end of an era of promise and hope and the beginning of a new Post-Liberal Age. African Americans were becoming impatient with President Kennedy's, and later President Johnson's, national commitment to racial justice. America's extremist, profoundly racist, and violent tendencies were exposed, and many contended that fascist-inspired conspiracies allied with clandestine foci of governmental power were responsible for fueling these events and their aftermath. This turbulence was accompanied by a "generation gap" embodied in the mostly White, New Left political (e.g., the Students for Democratic Society [SDS] founded in 1962), and counterculture movements. Youth's rejection of American society's banality, hollowness, alienation from nature, artificiality, and growing technocracy fueled antiwar protests; triggered a reassessment and redefinition of the American value system governing sex, behavior, art, and politics; fostered a burgeoning feminist movement; reawakened concerns about the deteriorating environment; and launched anticapitalist freedom movements "from the political left, to create a great new community of 'the people,' which would rise up to break the power of elites."[1] Nevertheless, the violence and disruption characterizing the first third of this period were followed by repression and retrenchment overlaying the social and political environment, which changed with alarming speed throughout the era. After a blush of initial prominence, the race issue was forced into the background.

The dramatic contrast between the revolutionary first five years of this period (1965–1970) and its conservative ending became identifiable by 1968. Evidence of a definite right-wing retrenchment was discernable with the election of Richard Nixon. Despite the national turmoil wrought later by Watergate and the Republican Southern strategy, the right wing would be ideologically and politically dominant by 1975. By emphasizing ending the Vietnam War, muzzling and controlling the counterculture, deemphasizing individual civil liberties, downsizing the federal government, slowing down or obstructing the implementation of civil rights measures, focusing on a new and diverse international order superimposed on the Cold War, and shifting the judicial system toward the Right, Richard Nixon in 1968—leading the new Republican, conservative, and Christian Right—forever altered America's political landscape.

The decade before 1965 had been the most revolutionary for African Americans and the poor since the Civil War. Despite disappointments bred by White America's shock and resistance to the Supreme Court's outlawing racially segregated public schools in 1954, the period was marked by the nonviolent phase of the Black Civil Rights Movement; the Civil Rights Acts of 1960 and 1964; the Voting Rights Act of 1965; initiation of President Lyndon Johnson's multifaceted Great Society and War on Poverty programs; the formation of a predominantly White student-led counterculture protesting against the Vietnam War; a Native American civil rights movement; Hispanic American activism; seeds of a gay liberation movement; and a soon-to-become-prominent feminist movement. From a health care standpoint, the desegregation of most of the nation's hospitals, the enactment of Medicare/Medicaid, and the beginning of the neighborhood health center (NHC) movement by 1967 represented the first national efforts in a century to open the health care system to Blacks and the poor. As Karen Davis and Cathy Schoen observed in *Health and the War on Poverty: A Ten Year Appraisal*, "Of all the programs arising from the War on Poverty and the Great Society, those devoted to health care receive[d] the largest and most rapidly growing share of budgetary resources."[2] These events represented an upward surge by the dispossessed in America, catalyzed by a youth-led uprising against an increasingly unpopular war. By 1965 the newly sensitized nation had embarked on solving its problems through political reform, social legislation, and public policy shifts in what was projected by many as an orgy of liberalism. Despite the adverse foreign policy imagery generated by racial and social conflict in the world's greatest democracy, these lofty, often clumsy, efforts were soon replaced by a period of national retrenchment, turmoil, and self-doubt.

The domestic programs emphasized by the Kennedy and Johnson administrations focused on two things: maintaining America's economic strength and expanding the federal government's role in social welfare. For the first time, many of the nation's problems affecting Blacks and the poor—such as unequal education, race- and class-based poverty, discrimination in employment, denial of political and voting rights, and race- and class-based health disparities—were placed on the government's agenda. President Johnson named his corrective programs the Great Society. Simply having the government involved in setting standards and demonstrating concerns through programs like Medicare and Medicaid, the Office of Economic Opportunity (OEO), and Community Action Agencies (CAA) not only provided benefits but also upgraded the quality of life for disadvantaged Americans. The goal of Johnson's creation of the new cabinet agency, the Department of Housing and Urban Development (headed by the first African American cabinet officer, Robert Weaver), in 1966 and the Model Cities program was to improve inner-city housing and provide federal subsidies for urban redevelopment. President Johnson was also able to pass legislation to upgrade schools educating poor children.[3]

The Vietnam War undercut Lyndon Johnson's Great Society dream and destroyed his presidency. U.S. involvement in French Indochina evolved from a failed effort to support an ally preserving its colonial empire after World War II. After the French defeat at Dien Bien Phu in 1954, followed by the partition of Vietnam into the communist North and pro-Western South, the poorly understood, but slowly escalating war was presented by President Eisenhower as American support of an anticommunist crusade initiated by previous presidential administrations. Following President Kennedy's assassination, a program of financial aid and military support consisting of approximately 15,500 Americans and $1 billion in military aid annually to resist a North Vietnamese Communist invasion and takeover escalated during the Johnson Administration into a U.S. military intervention costing over $100 billion annually and supporting over 536,000 troops on duty in Vietnam by January 1969. The military buildup from an African American perspective was inequitable:

> [B]lacks were poorly represented in the officers' ranks, and grossly over-represented among enlisted personnel.... [A]nd because blacks tended to be placed in "combat units" more often than middle class whites, they also bore unfairly higher risks of being killed and wounded. From January to November 1966, 22.4 percent of all army casualties were black.[4]

Economically, Johnson's promises of "guns and butter" proved untenable. As Dr. Martin Luther King, Jr., summarized: "The promises of the Great Society have been shot down on the battlefields of Vietnam—making the poor ... White and Negro ... bear the heaviest burden both at the front and at home."[5] Because of the war, the U.S. economy destabilized, forcing substantial tax increases and an inflation rate escalating from 2 percent in the early 1960s to 6 percent by 1969. Congressional conservatives demanded and received a $6 billion reduction in funding for Great Society programs. Moreover, as the war completed its 7-year course with no victory in sight, between 1965 and 1967 American students protesting the war became a significant political force and, by 1968, drove Johnson out of office.

Meanwhile, racial tensions were escalating. By 1965, racially motivated civil unrest became a true political problem. Even before Malcolm X's assassination on February 21, 1965, many social critics felt that nonviolent direct action, an effective tactic of protest against segregation used in the South, would have little appeal in the Northern ghettos: "Dead at the age of 39, Malcolm quickly became the fountainhead of the modern renaissance of black nationalism in the late 1960s."[6] James Baldwin predicted as early as 1963 that race riots would soon "spread to every metropolitan center in the nation which has a significant Negro population."[7] Sixteen days after the Civil Rights Act of 1964 passed, urban rioting ensued. The Watts riot in Los Angeles "followed the Voting Rights Act of 1965 by five days."[8] As Marable noted in *Race, Reform, and Rebellion,* "In the spring and summer months of 1964, 1965, 1966, 1967, and 1968, massive black rebellions swept across almost every major U.S. city in the Northeast, Middle West and California."[9] Urban rebellions numbering in the hundreds indicated that the mood and thrust of the Black Civil Rights Movement had changed.

Some African Americans made material progress during the 1960s. But the decline in percentage of Black families in poverty from 48.1 percent in 1959 to 27.9 percent in 1969, the ratio between family incomes of Blacks and Whites rising from 54 percent to 61 percent, and unemployment rates for non-White married males declining from 7.2 percent in 1962 to 4.3 percent in 1965 did not keep pace with the expectations of freedom and equality awakened in the Black masses during the decade. Moreover, "[n]on-white youth unemployment actually increased in these years, from 24.4 percent in 1960 to 29.1 percent in 1970. The quality of black urban life—poor housing, rat infestation, crime, high infant mortality rates, disease, poor public education—continued to deteriorate."[10] Led by a young generation of secular civil rights leaders such as Stokely Carmichael, H. Rap Brown, Floyd McKissick, Huey Newton, Eldridge Cleaver, Fred Hampton, and Bobby Seale, the Black masses, 69 percent of whom now lived in cities and 45 percent outside the South by 1966, rallied to the cry of "Black Power."

"Black Power," an ambiguous term, meant different things to various people. To many it harkened back to militarily armed Black separatism, while to others it implied anticapitalism. Others used it as a peal to participate in capitalism (Black real estate ownership, political power, and Black-owned corporations). Many referred to it in purely Afrocentric cultural terms. Because the movement had no coherent ideology, White conservatives from the corporate sector, including President Nixon, adopted one wing of the Black Power Movement as a "new" form of Black capitalism. Nevertheless, "[w]ithin two weeks, 'Black Power' sparked a national debate, dividing old friends and bringing to an abrupt halt the last vestiges of unity between the left and right wings of the desegregation movement."[11] Particularly alarming to Whites, many who were allies or were in sympathy with the Civil Rights Movement, was the formation of overtly revolutionary organizations such as the Black Panthers (1966) and the Deacons of Defense, the adoption of revolutionary stances by organizations such as the Student Non-Violent Coordinating Committee (SNCC), and the growth in influence of separatist groups such as the Nation of Islam. White government and private responses to these developments were often repressive, sometimes illegal, and too often violent. This revival of Black Nationalist energy culminated in the Gary Convention, a national Black political convention held in Gary, Indiana on March 10–11, 1972, and the founding of the National Black Political Assembly.* These developments also phased different aspects of the Black health care movement, imbuing some programs with a nationalist edge reminiscent of Marcus Garvey's Universal Negro Improvement Association (UNIA).** The Black Civil Rights Movement was forever changed.[12]

Suddenly, old guard integrationists such as Reverend Martin Luther King, Jr., Roy Wilkins, Bayard Rustin, Reverend Andrew Young, A. Philip Randolph, Dorothy Height, Whitney Young, and James Farmer were on the "fringes" of the movement. The militants took the 1960s murders of civil rights activists such as Medgar Evers, Michael Schwerner, James Chaney, Andrew Goodman, Viola Liuzzo, and Malcolm X as evidence that the nonviolent approach was not being respected by their opponents. Furthermore, "King's assassination was only one more indication to black nationalists that white capitalist America had no intention of resolving racial conflicts 'non-violently.'"[13] Moreover, as Dr. King discovered prior to his death, "the Civil Rights Movement's old goals of voter education, registration, and desegregated public facilities were only a beginning step down the long road towards biracial democracy":[14]

> *Quietly, King was beginning to articulate a democratic socialist vision for American society: the nationalization of basic industries; massive federal expenditures to revive central cities and to provide jobs for ghetto residents; a guaranteed income for every adult American. King had concluded ... that America's political economy of capitalism had to be transformed....*[15]

With a redefined set of goals and objectives, mainstream America was far less comfortable with the new demands Blacks were making. The right wing of the fragmented Civil Rights Movement ventured into electoral strategies. Political activities such as formation of the Mississippi Freedom Democratic Party and, later, Jesse Jackson's 1980s abortive presidential candidacies, took place within, and

---

*This organization was founded to formulate and implement a Black political agenda, elect African Americans to political office, and mobilize the Black community politically.

**The UNIA is a political and social organization founded in 1914 by Marcus Garvey to promote Black self-help, Black nationalism, and repatriation to Africa as mechanisms of Black uplift and self-determination. At its height in the mid-1920s, it is reputed to have been the largest political organization in African American history.

further fragmented, the Democratic Party. Meanwhile, the Nixon administration systematically went about destroying the still-powerful radical wing of the Black Power Movement while implementing a program to co-opt the conservative South for the Republican Party—the Southern Strategy.[16]

After three decades of postwar economic prosperity, America suffered economic problems between 1965 and 1980. The foundations of U.S. economic prosperity—cheap raw materials from the Third World and an absence of competition—crumbled during the 1970s. Moreover, Lyndon Johnson had triggered an inflationary spiral in the late 1960s by financing both his war and Great Society without raising taxes. A fatal combination resulted when raw material prices rose, especially for oil, and Japan, the Pacific Rim, and Western Europe became manufacturing competitors. The Organization of Petroleum Exporting Countries (OPEC), especially those in the Middle East, hiked their prices 500 percent and used petroleum as a political bargaining chip in regard to Arab-Israeli relations. Fuel embargoes and shortages, OPEC aggression and political sanctions, and the changing economic conditions produced soaring inflation that Nixon tried to cure with government controls, a tight money policy at the Federal Reserve, periodic tax hikes, and relentless government program cuts. "The Nixon pattern—of lurching from a tight money policy to curb inflation at one moment to a spending policy to cure recession at the next—repeated itself during the two administrations that followed,"[17] Allen Brinkley observed.

Against the dismal backdrop of the Vietnam War, President Nixon, in partnership with his chief foreign policy advisor Henry Kissinger, had a great deal to do with constructing a new international order. Instead of the traditional Cold War's "bipolar" world—the United States and the Soviet Union being the only great powers—America adapted to a new "multipolar" international order, wherein Western Europe, Japan, China, and the Pacific Rim were also major players. Nixon visited China in February 1972 and produced the first Strategic Arms Limitation Treaty (SALT I) with Russia, freezing growth for some nuclear missiles that same year. In May 1972 Nixon consulted with Soviet leaders in Moscow for the first time, establishing trade, cultural exchange, and space technology agreements. He and Henry Kissinger seemed to be bringing the Vietnam War to an end through negotiations in Paris. Though these momentous accomplishments deflected world attention somewhat, Nixon's Vietnam policy threatened his presidency domestically. Any popularity he may have had with Black voters dissipated, as:

> [h]e tried, unsuccessfully, to persuade Congress to pass legislation
> prohibiting school desegregation through the use of forced busing. He
> forbade the Department of Health, Education, and Welfare to cut off
> federal funds from school districts that had failed to comply with court
> orders to integrate. At the same time, he began to reduce or dismantle

> *many of the social programs of the Great Society and New Frontier. In 1973, he abolished the Office of Economic Opportunity, the centerpiece of the antipoverty program of the Johnson years.*[18]

Although his "Vietnamization" policy,* invasion of Cambodia in April 1970, and the 1972 "Christmas bombing" of Hanoi in North Vietnam were unpopular and did not prevent the deaths of 15,000 more Americans between 1969 and 1971, they resulted in a cease-fire and prisoner exchange by January 1973. In 1972, Nixon had won a landslide victory over Democrat candidate George McGovern, a liberal South Dakotan, whose pro-Black, feminist, and youth-power views were out of touch with the conservative mood of the country. Having achieved historical diplomatic accomplishments and obtained an overwhelming conservative electoral mandate, Nixon committed errors that tainted, then ended, his presidency.

By March 1974 the Watergate scandal resulted in the resignation of over a dozen high officials—even the vice president, Spiro Agnew, faced scrutiny and resigned for accepting graft during his previous term as governor of Maryland—on charges including burglary, illegal use of federal agencies against private citizens, forgery, illegal wiretapping and electronic surveillance, perjury, obstruction of justice, and bribery, among others. Nixon seemingly confirmed Plutarch's observation that character is fate. As Sitkoff observed:

> *At least from 1969, Nixon operated on the principle that, at his direction, federal officials could violate the law. On June 17, 1972, members of his Special Investigations Unit (created without congressional authorization) were arrested while burglarizing the national offices of the Democratic party in the Watergate office-and-apartment complex in Washington, D.C.*[19]

The resulting investigation of this act, and revelations of presidential crimes by Congress, the popular media, and the Supreme Court, led to Nixon's threatened impeachment. He resigned from the presidency on August 9, 1974.[20]

The dismal outcomes of the 1970s—America's first military defeat in Vietnam, the "failed" Great Society programs, the Watergate scandal, and the declining U.S. economy—shook the confidence of the American people and their faith in government. Although Gerald Ford's custodial presidency (1974–1977) proved that the system worked by quietly removing a corrupt and criminal president's administration, little else was accomplished during his term. His attempt to restore the political integrity of the government was smashed "when he granted Richard Nixon 'a full, free, and absolute pardon' for any crimes he may have committed during his presidency."[21] Ford's popularity subsequently declined and

---

*This consisted of a slow withdrawal of American troops and a heavy build-up of South Vietnam's army to continue the war.

never recovered. He continued Nixon's policies of not enforcing civil rights laws and publically opposed the Supreme Court's efforts to integrate schools on repeated occasions. Not only did he give the anti-busing forces hope, "Ford [also] had the Justice Department look for 'a proper record in a case that would justify . . . a proceeding before the Supreme Court to see if the court would review its decision in the Brown case and several that followed thereafter.'"[22] Ford's civil rights positions further alienated him and the Republicans from African Americans. His failure to address and correct the economic "stagflation" (high inflation, high unemployment, sluggish markets, rising prices) displeased the entire populace, and his version of extending Nixon's and now–Secretary of State Henry Kissinger's foreign policy (e.g., completing SALT II and communicating with Russia and China) alienated his party's right wing for being soft on communism. After barely edging out California governor Ronald Reagan for the Republican nomination, he lost a close 1976 election to self-proclaimed Washington "outsider," Georgia Governor Jimmy Carter, who seized upon Ford's shortcomings and capitalized on the public's skepticism regarding the federal government.

Jimmy Carter assumed the presidency (1977–1981) facing problems of staggering complexity and difficulty. Facing his task with an image of honesty and piety, and a management style some considered self-righteous and inflexible, Carter manipulated the economy with various strategies to fix it. At various times his strategies included raising public spending, cutting federal taxes, tightening the money supply, and calls for voluntary restraint. None of them worked. Compounding another major OPEC-iniated fuel shortage in 1979 were interest rates that soared to the highest levels in American history (at times over 20 percent). Internationally, the symbiotic relationship the United States had established over the years (beginning in the early 1950s) with the Shah of Iran fell apart. With the Shah driven into exile by a rebellious Moslem clergy leading a fiercely religious fundamentalist society that rejected his repressive, authoritarian autocracy, Iranians stormed the American embassy in Teheran on November 4, 1979. Inspired by religious leader Ayatollah Ruhollah Khomeini, they seized diplomats, CIA operatives, and military personnel as hostages and demanded the United States return to Iran the Shah, who was then undergoing cancer treatment in New York City. Refusing to surrender the Shah, Carter unsuccessfully attempted to release the 53 American hostages for the balance of his term. Capitalizing on the international disarray, the Soviet Union invaded Afghanistan on December 27, 1979. Carter fumed, imposed economic sanctions on the USSR, and led an American boycott of the 1980 Olympic Games. None of his foreign policies seemed to work. After he had turned over control of the Panama Canal to the government of Panama amid much popular and Congressional resistance, the public became even more distressed and depressed about America's status in the world.

President Carter seemed much more effective as a mediator. His brokering of a peace treaty between Egypt and Israel between 1977 and 1979 at Camp David may stand as the crowning achievement of his presidency. However, his preachings on human rights rang hollow. Carter preached human rights abroad but failed to practice them at home. Raised in a racially caste-ridden environment in a segregationist Southern state, Carter, who considered himself a racial liberal, began sending mixed racial messages during his campaign. Not only was he against forced busing for desegregating schools, but he also responded poorly when queried about neighborhood segregation:

> [Q]uestions in South Bend and Pittsburgh led to additional warnings from the candidate about "alien groups" and "black intrusion." "Interjecting into [a community] a member of another race" or "diametrically opposite kind of family" or a "different kind of person" threatened what Carter called the admirable value of "ethnic purity."[23]

In the view of Reverend Andrew Young, a Carter supporter: "[It was] a disaster for the campaign. I don't think he understood how loaded it [was] with Hitlerian connotations."[24] Despite his appointment of a few token Blacks to his administration, Carter, whose election had depended heavily on Black support, distanced himself from the racial issue or Civil Rights enforcement. His disappointing performance was highlighted by his appearance following the Miami race riots wherein he seemed self-righteously to blame the community itself for the area's long-standing racial problems and implied that Washington would provide only reluctant support. The largely Black crowd assembled outside City Hall splattered his car with eggs upon his departure. Realistically, Miami, in the throes of Cuban, Haitian, and Central American mass migrations, was undergoing some of the most traumatic and dramatic racial and cultural transformations, clashes, and power struggles of any American city. The struggles of Miami, in truth, predicted America's troubled racial landscape and cultural diversity problems for the coming decades.

Neither Ford nor Carter reestablished the credibility of the American presidency, and neither solved America's complex economic, international, domestic, or racial problems. "Inflation threatened to erode the buying power of all citizens."[25] Despite early civil rights gains, at the end of the period African Americans "still lagged far behind the whites in income and opportunity; unemployment ... [was] fixed at ... 6 percent, which for minorities and the young, translated into much higher figures."[26] The promise of Blacks achieving justice and equity in health care was also thwarted. An America accustomed to rapid change now seemed overwhelmed by the dizzying new pace of events that planted seeds of national doubt and "defeatism." Between 1960 and 1980 the optimism dictating dramatic social change and confidence that the federal government could effect the changes America needed came to an end. Failures abroad and at home established the environment for America to go through three distinct phases: (1) A period of agitation and reform in the first 10 years (1960–1970), when broader entitlements to social welfare (including health care) and the regulation of industry gained currency in public opinion and law; (2) a period of stalemate, beginning in 1967, when inflation and doubts about national solutions (including the Great Society and incremental reforms of the health system) became dominant; and (3) a growing reaction against liberalism and government solutions resulting in the election of President Reagan in 1980 and the subsequent reversal of many earlier efforts at redistributive and regulatory programs. America was willing to try something new to repudiate the doubts and "defeatism." The stage was set for a radical new type of leadership.[27]

---

## Health System Accommodation, "Crisis," and Separate Development

> *Health of mind and body is so fundamental to the good life that, if we believe men have any personal rights at all as human beings, they have an absolute moral right to such a measure of good health as society, and society alone, is able to give them.*
>
> —ARISTOTLE, 333 BC

> *[T]here are no health care needs of the disadvantaged that should be treated as special. In fact, there are undoubtedly many problems of health for the disadvantaged which were brought about because medical care for this group has been handled in a special way, separate [and] different from the care of the privileged. Added to this we have the tradition of separating the separated along racial lines, overtly or covertly, which further complicates the special problems of health care.*
>
> —LEONIDAS H. BERRY, M.D., 1966

### A Conflagration of Costs and Failed Government Control

The U.S. health delivery system underwent drastic transformations between 1965 and 1980. The major stabilizing factors that had sustained the health system since Flexner reform (1910), "the dominance of the medical profession; local sponsorship of community hospitals; and the practice of cross-subsidization, which enabled physicians and hospitals to care for many of the poor by overcharging the affluent,"[28] were battered and buffeted by change during this period. Although the health system maintained, and in many ways expanded, its "market-like" characteristics, much of the status quo relative to its structural race and class relationships, and its middle- to upper-class orientation, it also demonstrated enough flexibility to accommodate the "expanded role of federal and state governments in financing and delivering health care services."[29] However, Bruce McLaury, the president of the Brookings Institution in 1978, made a declaration that revealed cracks in the foundation of the old system:

*Many of the federal health programs and policies begun in the 1960s reflected a desire to redeem the American promise of equal opportunity by improving access to services that help people lead healthy, productive lives. Medicare and Medicaid began in 1966 to pay the medical bills of the elderly and the poor; comprehensive community health centers opened their doors in many underserved and poor communities; and the maternal and child health program started new projects designed to serve the health care needs of disadvantaged mothers and children.[30]*

These publicly financed health programs broached medical-social customs and practices, shattered conventional public health boundaries, violated health financing practices, and espoused egalitarian ideologies that had been assiduously avoided by the health establishment.

These programs, along with a powerful matrix of destabilizing forces, grew to challenge the integrity and stability of the traditional health system order throughout this period. However, the health system's responses to its menu of problems, including the nagging race and class issues plaguing the system, disappointed health reformers, social activists, feminists, and supporters of the Civil Rights Movement. This led to an extraordinary loss of confidence among health system and medical proponents, who, like most other American institutional leaders, suffered in the public's eyes during the 1970s. The system was ripe for revolutionary change by 1980.

The basic premises that had guided government health policy since World War II were declared bankrupt. The premises were "first, that Americans needed more medical care—more than the market alone would provide; and second, that medical professionals and private voluntary institutions were best equipped to decide how to organize these services."[31] Despite the fact that "[t]he reduction of financial barriers increased the use of such services by lower income groups and contributed to improved health,"[32] U.S. health care cost increases, distribution defects, medical-social shortcomings, and lack of proven efficacy proved to be such intractable problems that "[t]he economic and moral problems of medicine displaced scientific progress at the center of public attention."[33] Simultaneously, health politics shifted from a redistributive to a regulatory focus. Paul Starr, in *The Social Transformation of American Medicine*, observed that the politics of health care during the 1970s mimicked American politics and public policy in general—transitioning through three phases:

1. *A period of agitation and reform in the first half of the decade, when broader entitlements to social welfare and stricter regulation of industry gained ground in public opinion and law;*

2. *A prolonged stalemate, beginning around 1975, when the preoccupation increasingly became coping with inflation, doubts arose about the value of medical care, and initiatives such as national health insurance were set aside;*

> 3. *A growing reaction against liberalism and government, culminating in the election of President Reagan in 1980 and the reversal of many earlier redistributive and regulatory programs.*[34]

As the combined federal, state, and local funds for health care ballooned from $8 billion in 1966 to $57 billion by 1977,[35] cost containment became paramount. By 1980 America's carte blanche health system and unrestricted mandate to medicine and its health establishment had ended.

During the late 1960s and 1970s, a perception emerged that the health system was in the throes of another "crisis." Cumulative effects of many destabilizing factors became discernable. They included a doctor glut that had been growing since World War II, the adverse effects of which were exacerbated by unregulated specialization; a generalized community loss of ties and commitment to local voluntary hospitals; continued violation of the "American creed" in health care relative to African Americans and many of the poor; health financing changes such as eliminating cross-subsidy for providing health services for the poor and creating a "cost-of-care disconnect" between patients and the health system through health insurance mechanisms; an increasing reliance on market forces instead of health planning for the distribution of health care and providers; and an erosion of credibility of the medical profession. Medicare and Medicaid enactment in 1966—which transformed millions of medically indigent into paying patients and facilitated health system access to large blocs of previously excluded segments of the American population*—instead of producing unmitigated good was the straw that took the health system to the edge of the abyss of fiscal meltdown and structural disarray. How this major event was handled—wherein health care was granted entry into the money economy subsidized by government funds and questions arose as to whether future health policy would be determined by financiers and bankers or physicians—proved critical.

The "crisis" was brought to the public's attention by influential elements within the mainstream establishment. For example, Walter P. Reuther, President of the United Auto Workers (UAW), speaking for the labor unions before the American Public Health Association (APHA) in 1968, "declared the nation's health care system to be in a state of 'crisis' and announced the formation of a group, with himself as chairman, to promote the urgently needed remedy: a federally financed, federally administered program of 'universal' national health insurance."[36] The organization Reuther referred to was the Committee of One Hundred for National Health Insurance. The "lead" vice chairman was Mary D. Lasker, who had provided fiscal and executive support for previous national health insurance proposals, successfully applied modern marketing techniques to voluntary health

---

*Despite the programs' well-documented shortcomings, they represented unprecedented African American entry and access to the "mainstream" health system and had disproportionate salutary effects on the Black population.

campaigns and agencies (e.g., the American Cancer Society), and persuaded Congress to expand the National Institutes of Health (NIH) into the international health megaforce it is today. Other vice chairmen were Michael DeBakey, M.D., the internationally renowned cardiac surgeon, and Whitney Young, executive director of the National Urban League. Isidore S. Falk, veteran of the Federal Security Agency, served as the committee's technical consultant.

Within four years of what were considered the Medicare/Medicaid "break-throughs," President Nixon announced in 1969, "We face a massive crisis in the area.... [U]nless action is taken within the next two or three years ... we will have a breakdown in our medical system which could have consequences affecting millions of people throughout this country."[37] Responding to liberal pressures and government costs for Medicaid rising to $4.3 billion in 1969, the Nixon administration released a report criticizing the program as being "badly conceived and badly organized" and overdependent upon technology, acute care, and inpatient care rather than preventive medicine. *Business Week* magazine ran a January 1970 cover story on a "$60 billion crisis" perceived by the middle and upper classes, noting how poor health status and outcomes in America were compared to Western Europe.[38] Declaring that American medicine stood "on the brink of chaos," *Fortune* summed up the situation:

> *Much of U.S. medical care, particularly the everyday business of preventing and treating routine illnesses, is inferior in quality, wastefully dispensed, and inequitably financed. Medical manpower and facilities are so maldistributed that large segments of the population, especially the urban poor and those in rural areas, get virtually no care at all—even though their illnesses are most numerous and, in a medical sense, often easy to cure.*
>
> *Whether poor or not, most Americans are badly served by the obsolete, over-strained medical system that has grown up around them helter-skelter.... [T]he time has come for radical change.[39]*

Academics such as Jerome B. Weisner, president of the Massachusetts Institute of Technology, described the effects the health system "crisis" had on average Americans in 1973:

> *The shortcomings in our medical care system become dramatically evident to the average citizen when illness strikes close to home. He is stymied by unbelievable disorganization with lack of clear-cut entry points to care, particularly at night, on weekends, and on holidays. He is overwhelmed by the skyrocketing costs of illness, especially when admission to a hospital becomes necessary. He is appalled by the obstructions to care due to such factors as his geographic location, the per capita income and urbanization of his neighborhood, and his accessibility to a medical center.[40]*

Contemporary surveys revealed 75 percent of male heads of families agreed. Paul Starr described political dimensions of the "crisis": "[I]n a political sense, the medical system was very much in crisis, not because it was really about to break down, as the president and the business press suggested, but because it had lost their confidence. Medicine had overdrawn its credit. It also aroused a variety of new social movements to much bolder opposition."[41]

The "crisis" affected the health system and its various components in many different ways, often destabilizing them in the process. Ed Cray, commenting in *In Failing Health: The Medical Crisis and the A.M.A.*, noted the negative effects on the poor due to worsening physician maldistribution and overreliance on market forces: "The better markets attract doctors; the poorer languish. The City of Beverly Hills, one of the wealthier in the nation ... had one doctor for every 225 people. Meanwhile, the Negro ghetto of Watts, 20 miles away, had but one doctor for every 2,700 people. Nor is Watts exceptional."[42] Simultaneously, suburban doctors were opening slum offices that served as Medicaid mills. Seeing 150 patients per day, such officers missed diagnoses, and patients were mismanaged. Anything requiring more than three minutes of the physician's time or that was not treatable by a vitamin cocktail or penicillin shot was sent to the closest charity hospital emergency room or clinic. As Starr noted, "In the 1960s many began to observe that abundance and scarcity in medicine were side by side. After World War II, medicine had been a metaphor for progress, but to many it was now becoming a symbol of the continuing inequities and irrationalities of American life."[43] Simultaneously, African Americans were still perceived by health reformers as victims in the health system, and Black doctors were expressing both hope and concerns about inequities, exclusion from health planning, and perpetuation of socioeconomic and racial tiers in their reorganized Great Society health system. Despite the "crisis" and the deficiencies in Medicaid and Medicare that were being revealed daily, African Americans were charting health status and outcome improvements.[44] Moreover, by 1980 influential health policy-makers such as Arnold Relman, editor of the *New England Journal of Medicine*, sounded warnings about the power and influence of an emerging corporate-funded, commercially oriented, medical-industrial complex.[45] This eclectic "crisis" thus had varying effects on different races, subsets of the population, ethnic groups, neighborhoods, and health care institutions.[46]

For the middle class, private health costs were skyrocketing such that medical care was climbing beyond the economic reach of many average families. Availability of family doctors or physicians on weekends or holidays largely disappeared. As Starr observed, "[A]rticles announcing the health crisis typically pointed out that Americans—even excluding Blacks—had higher infant mortality rates and lower life expectancy than most Europeans."[47] At its root, the "crisis" was a child of unresolved conflicts between a health system geared toward expansion and meeting a society's needs while failing to establish and maintain some control over health care expenditures. No system could sustain cost explosions such as those between 1970 and 1980, when health care expenditures rose from $69 billion to $230 billion (a jump from 7.2 to 9.4 percent of GNP). Starr noted:

> *Growth of this kind cannot be indefinitely sustained regardless of the administration in Washington; other sectors of the economy cannot and will not support it. Yet controlling expansion means redrawing the "contract" between the medical profession and society, subjecting medical care to the discipline of politics . . . or reorganizing its basic institutional structure.*[48]

The accommodation to reform crafted by the White medical establishment after the passage of Medicare and Medicaid, the initiation of the NHC movement, and the enactment of the Great Society and War on Poverty health programs did not meet any of these requirements. For most mainstream health system providers and financiers, the reforms dreaded by the medical establishment produced windfall profits and expansion but also further destabilized the system, sowing the seeds for their loss of public trust. An almost apartheid-like "separate development" for segments of the health system serving Blacks and the poor apart from mainstream America was not only maintained, but grew. Although the public was amenable to it, neither American medical nor lay leadership were willing to take the health system out of the marketplace, minimize health system inefficiencies bred by cutthroat competition, or compromise individual-oriented, doctor-patient social and economic relationships needed to produce a universal, cost-effective, and coordinated health system. Thus, European Americans led a chorus of complaints. Many of the facts were not new, but the furor they created was.

In 1970 Senator Edward Kennedy and Representative Martha W. Griffiths of Michigan introduced the Health Security Program, the liberal and health reformer's answer to the health "crisis":

> *Health Security called for a comprehensive program of free medical care, replacing all public and private health plans in a single, federally operated health insurance system. Though it did not involve any nationalization of facilities nor require physicians to work on salary, it would have set a national budget, allocated funds to regions, provided incentives for prepaid group practice, and obliged private hospitals and physicians to operate within budget constraints. There were to be no copayments by consumers.*[49]

Nixon responded to Kennedy's political challenge by pushing for a massive reform of the health system built upon a foundation of managed care. He was convinced by his policy advisors and by Minneapolis physician Paul Ellwood that health maintenance organizations (HMOs) would maintain medical quality and cut costs. Moreover, Nixon's and the Republicans' conservative ideology resonated positively with Ellwood's conception on many levels. Ellwood:

> described his vision of a system based on market forces. Care would be provided by groups of doctors, which he named Health Maintenance Organizations, or H.M.O.'s. These groups would compete for patients seeking to provide the best care at the lowest price. Although none of the building blocks of the plan were new, the integrated concept was, and it became the cornerstone of President Nixon's health policy.[50]

The Nixon administration supported HMO hegemony in the health system's future. Nevertheless, a consensus was building—after a 20-year hiatus—that some type of national health insurance characterized by rationality, systematic planning, and built-in cost control mechanisms was necessary. In his first message to Congress on August 12, 1974, President Ford had asked for passage of national health insurance.[51] Heeding the warning of Treasury Secretary William Simon, who said health insurance would be "an unmitigated disaster and could bankrupt the country,"[52] he withdrew the proposal.

In 1976, with the health system's inflation rate continuing to run about three points ahead of the economy's whopping 6.8 percent rate, the health sector was creating "serious repercussions throughout the economy,"[53] President Carter's Council on Wage and Price Stability warned. The community health center movement was threatened by cost inflation pressures as early as 1971. Even the insurance industry wavered in its support of the medical establishment. Moreover, big labor, corporate health insurers, and the government openly agreed with the public that something radical might be needed.[54]

Although the Medicare/Medicaid reforms were not comprehensive and excluded large blocks of the population from various services, most of the alarms expressed by presidents and the business community, which echoed the concerns of the common man, were about money. As Louise Lander pointed out in *Defective Medicine*, "the steadily increasing proportion of the gross national product eaten up by expenditures on medical care (rising from 4.6 percent of GNP in fiscal 1950 to 8.6 percent in fiscal 1976) . . . caused something approaching panic in both government and industrial circles."[55] Gone were the days when efficiency and redistribution had been equal concerns in health politics. Cost containment now ruled the roost. Meanwhile, African American physicians and policy-makers were preoccupied with eliminating three centuries-old racial health disparities. The rate of growth in the cost of medical services in the five years after Medicare was 7.9 percent annually compared to only 3.2 percent a year in the seven preceding years. At the same time the rate of inflation for all other services rose from 2.0 to 5.8 percent annually. Per capita national health expenditures, previously at a level between $142 and $198 from 1960 to 1965, rose to $336 by 1970. Government health expenditures of $10.8 billion (26 percent of the nation's health bill) in 1965 exploded to $27.8 billion by 1970 (37 percent of the nation's health bill). The annual rate of increase in health expenditures for federal and state governments was 20.8 percent in the same period. There were many valid reasons for the fiscal explosion. Some of the reasons included increasing access of large blocs of the population (i.e., many African Americans and some of the poor) to medical services in the health system; expanding welfare roles with America's backlog of eligible recipients (one criteria for Medicaid participation); previously underpaid hospital employees demanding wages equivalent to those in the rest of the economy; and increasingly expensive and complex medical equipment and procedures. Moreover, sharply increased demand for medical services without concomitant increases in productivity automatically drove prices upward. But these factors only accentuated the inflationary effects of overuse of hospitalization and surgery, the windfall profits being experienced by the medical profession, and excessive profits being extracted by health care suppliers and institutions. This public debate and its revelations had cowered the traditional foes of national health insurance such as physicians, the health insurance industry, and hospitals into unaccustomed acquiescence and silence. Had Medicare and Medicaid, themselves, triggered this "crisis"?[56]

Although not solely responsible, Titles 18 and 19 certainly helped precipitate the "crisis." After their mid-1960s defeats in the legislative battles, doctors and the hospitals won the political endgame by writing the rules and regulations for the new laws and government programs.[57] Paradoxically, the Medicare and Medicaid regulations so favored physicians and other providers—the government's accommodation to the private medical sector—that they sowed the seeds of the medical establishment's losing its mandate to supervise the health system. Generally, physicians' fees were billed on the old fee-for-service, usual and customary charge basis with patients sustaining balances for unpaid bills. This reinforced incentives to see more patients, perform more surgical procedures, and generate more fees. Prevailing charges were established by doctors practicing in wealthy neighborhoods and "silk stocking" hospitals; thus, doctors flocked to those areas and institutions at the medical peril of poor and working-class areas and health institutions usually located in central cities. Preventing illnesses or managing clinical problems conservatively cut income. The more services doctors provided, the more they were paid. If one doctor charged less than his or her colleagues, he or she was not only paid less but also generated a billing profile that automatically lowered his fee scale in the future. Young physicians fresh out of training billed more for the same procedure than their older peers, thus establishing the trend for the future. And new, technologically advanced procedures—especially surgical ones, which often took less time to perform and required expensive new equipment, extra technicians and technical assistance—yielded higher fees. Moreover, hospital fees for operating rooms, use of the new equipment, and the assistants for these newer procedures were all billed separately. Medicaid reimbursement, although it was based on usual and customary charges, outlawed overbilling, which drastically decreased Medicaid patients' appeal to doctors and hospitals and their ability to find providers willing to care for them. Hospitals billed the government, as they had billed Blue Cross–Blue Shield and private insurers, based on charges in many instances and occasionally on costs. Hospitals were even paid in advance for antic-ipated services rendered to government-insured patients for several years.[58] Institutions that reduced costs, with lesser charges as a result, reduced their income. Hospitals could solve their financial problems by maximizing reimbursements, not by minimizing costs. Moreover, institutions customarily received bonuses from both government and private insurance systems for depreciation, capital improve-ments and expansion, equity on investments, and maintaining training programs. These are isolated examples of the new rules and regulations that favored this type of "gaming" of the entire health system. Economic dysfunction because of the government's accommodation with the medical establishment was inevitable.

By the 1970s people in developed Western societies were defining access to health care as a right instead of a privilege. Americans were no different, although the creation of statutory rights in the United States have proved elusive. As James G. Haughton, first deputy administrator of the New York City Health Services Ad-ministration, stated, "The status quo with its dual standards of health care is no longer acceptable."[59] However, the nation's social structure and culture helped de-fine the health system response to this changing attitude. Having no strong socialist tradition or labor movement, the American system favored the formation of social protest groups outside the traditional political parties to generate pressure and claims under the Bill of Rights. These tactics, although much more effective in other areas,* were tailored to "fit" health concerns. The Black Civil Rights Move-ment, which was losing influence in the 1970s for a plethora of reasons, set the standard for rights movements focusing on women, children, gays, students, Chi-canos, Native Americans, prisoners, and welfare recipients. Not only was the health rights movement for *access to health care* (entitlement), it also involved *rights in health care*. Patient rights to informed consent, courteous treatment by providers, information sharing in medical decision making, and equitable treatment of women and minorities in all levels of the health system became cutting-edge is-sues. However, this extension of rights in the health arena generated tremendous expenses that politicians and the medical establishment were forced to confront, and demands for radical medical-social changes within the health subculture grew.

---

*Health care is a peculiar activity in its relationship to society. Unstable or disruptive environments automatically undercut effective delivery of health care with the expected results (unnecessary deaths and disability). Forces that disrupt health services lose the moral high ground almost immediately, becoming targets of condemnation—regardless of the issues involved. Unmet health care needs are usually silent. The gaps between the providers (i.e., physicians, nurses, technicians, hospitals) and needs are too wide to be substantively bridged (i.e., first aid is no substitute for life- or limb-saving surgery), even on a temporary basis. Social function without health care has increasingly proven to be untenable—even modern armies perform better when they are provided assurances of health services.

The end result of these complex interactions was, as has been emphasized before, the loss of confidence in the medical establishment, politicians, and federal government to deal with society's health care issues. One writer in *Fortune* magazine near the beginning of the era said: "The doctors created the system. They run it. And they are the most formidable obstacle to its improvement."[60] Health rights advocates and reformers agreed with this assessment, and developments during the 1970s seemingly vindicated their position. A generalized resurgence of conservatism and lack of faith in change pushed the nation backward socially toward self-reliance, radical individualism, and fear of government involvement in day-to-day life. Weak promises and/or attempts at universal health systems by Presidents Kennedy, Johnson, Nixon, Ford, and Carter were quashed during the period, and an inappropriate overreliance on the market in health was reaffirmed.[61]

## Hospitals and Health Care Institutions: A Part of the "Crisis"

The end of World War II and the postwar years marked the end of a medical era in the United States. Quentin Young alluded to major changes in the system relative to health care institutions:

> *The transformation of the medical care system was heralded by two "casualties": by the decline of the general practitioner and the rise of specialization; and ... the shift of medical service from the physician's office to the hospital. These changes had irreversible effects on hospitals, which underwent more thoroughgoing changes than any other portion of the health care system.*[62]

Karl Hammond of the Imhotep Society Research Committee of Princeton University, citing a 1971 Department of Health, Education, and Welfare (HEW) report, noted: "The percentage of primary care physicians to total physicians has dropped from 75 percent in 1931 to 39 percent in 1967."[63] And the number of short-stay hospitals* increased from 5,768 in 1960 to the all-time high of 6,229 in 1980. These quantitative changes in manpower and the health institutions infrastructure were accompanied by qualitative changes associated with "the recent, relatively unheralded rise of a huge new industry that supplies health-care services for profit."[64] In 1980 Arnold Relman described the changing character of health institutions in more detail: "There are now about 1,000 proprietary hospitals in this country. [T]hese hospitals constitute more than 15 percent of nongovernmental acute general-care hospitals," while "about 300 voluntary nonprofit hospitals are managed on a contractual basis by one or another ... profit-making hospital corporations."[65] The proportion of the nation's hospital beds under the control of

---

*These figures exclude psychiatric, tuberculosis and other respiratory disease hospitals.

for-profit firms was, thus, approaching 20 percent. These changes in the hospital system, one of the major stabilizing factors in the health system, had profound future effects and implications. Similar changes were affecting the nursing home industry. As early as 1970 the Ehrenriechs had noted, "Nursing homes are the ideal way to cash in on Medicare and Medicaid. Every oldster is at least partially covered and every oldster is a potential customer."[66] Relman noted that by "1977 there were nearly 19,000 nursing home facilities of all types, and about 77 per cent were proprietary."[67] Although profound health financing changes, a shift to managed care, and the implementation of review and control measures led to declining hospital numbers in the 1980s, the 1965 to 1980 era was a boom time for health care institutions (predominantly hospitals and nursing homes).

Medical education financed by the GI Bill of Rights, government-supported educational grants and loans, and indirect government sources (e.g., medical school research and faculty grants) increased physician output and promoted medical specialization. The hospital changed into "the physician's workplace," where complex procedures deliverable only in specialized surroundings complemented by technically trained health workers and capital-intensive high-tech equipment sent costs spiraling upward. Postwar health care financing mechanisms and economics, emphasizing prepaid hospital insurance, encouraged the process. The passage of Medicare and Medicaid in 1965, unlocking federal and state government treasuries to the health care market, was a windfall for health care institutions that fueled the potential for destabilizing the old system.

Moreover, the financing system encouraged inflation and waste. Prepaid hospital insurance shielded the consumer from real medical costs and was handled as a "benefit" from the workplace. Therefore, consumer demands for the "best" were unmodulated by cost considerations. As mentioned earlier, incentives were based on the principle that the more services delivered the more could be billed; thus more fees were paid to professional and institutional providers. Surgical fees, being much higher than other charges, encouraged excess surgeries in hospital settings. The expansion of the health workforce—nurses, dietitians, social workers, radiology and research technicians, physical and occupational therapists, and venipuncturists—was unprecedented and expensive. Nursing, for example, driven by scientific, professional, and financial incentives, divided into specialties such as neonatology, intensive care, emergency care, and nurse practitioners. With precedents already established by the Hill-Burton Act of 1947, government subsidy for hospital renovation and expansion was built into the financing system. For all these reasons, health care institutions and the expenses of hospitalization were considered the leading causes of health care costs inflation.

From 1965 to 1975, hospital "third-party payments rose from 77 to 91 percent of total costs."[68] As Eli Ginzberg observed, such strong cash flows enabled nonprofit hospitals to break away from the philanthropic sources that previously underwrote their expenses and enter the conventional capital markets. This undermined hospitals' dependency on charity and community resources and weakened the influence of hospital boards and community institutions. Hospital administrators could now finance capital improvements and expansions demanded by scientific advance and their staffs independent of their communities. Or, as Richard Roberts noted, hospitals could also "venture into the community not seeking donations, but rather seeking investment money through the issuance of tax-free hospital bonds."[69] Weakened community concern and commitments to the voluntary, largely nonprofit hospitals and the abundant new revenue streams also encouraged a new growth spurt in the for-profit hospital sector, which by 1980 had become a major industry.

Despite these changes, "[t]he large voluntary hospitals continued to be dominant providers of inpatient care for the majority of citizens, with the municipal hospitals attending to large numbers of the poor."[70] The separate development of the nation's hospital system along public and private lines continued. Regarding the care of poor patients, Young noted that, "[i]n 1974, in 600 of the 3,400 counties of this nation the public general hospital, typically run by the county government, served as the only hospital resource for private and public sectors alike."[71] Assisted by poorly planned "urban renewal" projects, privileged and well-positioned hospital boards (made up of bankers, real estate developers, and merchants), and the absence of substantive health planning, these largely urban institutions built upon their long service and teaching hospital traditions to capture billions of public and private dollars to evolve into brave new hospital complexes. Most were dominated, or became components of, academic health center (AHC) empires. This carefully orchestrated shift in inner-city land use, facilitated by new monies, building technology, and human resources, developed under private aegis. Unanticipated were the sociological and medical-social problems created by this displacement of lower-class dwellings and communities, which by the postwar years dominated the nation's Eastern and Central inner cities.

The new business ethos injected into the health system subculture by the health corporations even came to influence the voluntary hospital sector—the larger sector of the hospital movement. They were becoming more like investor-owned hospitals, emphasizing:

> *profit by concentrating on providing the most profitable services to the best-paying patients ... skimming the cream off the market for acute hospital care ... elimination of low-frequency and unprofitable (though necessary) services, and exclusion of unprofitable patients (e.g., uninsured patients, welfare patients, and those with complex and chronic illesses).*[72]

Health policy authorities discerned that

> *more than simple imitation may contribute to the similarity of for-profit and nonprofit facilities. Both regulatory constraints and economic pressures reduce degrees of freedom, and declining surpluses brought about by*

*competitive pressures may reduce the ability of nonprofit hospitals to engage in such forms of discretionary behavior as providing care to patients who lack the means to pay.*[73]

Therefore, the public perception was that many nonprofit hospitals were "failing to live up to their charitable mission" and were "not justifying their tax exemptions,"[74] according to a Twentieth Century Fund Report on the effects of the profit motive on patient care.

Meanwhile, as Starr observed, "Hospital costs had become especially troublesome. From 1950 to 1965 per capita expenditures on community hospitals rose 8 percent annually; after 1965 the rate of growth jumped to 14 percent a year."[75] Nevertheless, Republicans allowed hospitals a 6 percent annual price increase when President Nixon imposed his 1971 wage-price freeze. However, the price controls for hospital costs remained in place after they were lifted in 1973 for all other segments of the economy. Virtually everything having to do with health care institutions during this era revolved around their highly criticized expansion and escalating costs. External, governmental regulation of the hospital industry became a major factor destabilizing the health system.

On the economic front, as early as 1964 New York became the first state to regulate capital expenditures of both hospitals and nursing homes. By 1972, "certificate of need" programs in 20 states required health care institutions to get state approval for construction projects and large capital investments. Some states began controlling the rates hospitals could charge. At first it was applied to Medicaid patients only. The regulation soon expanded to all patients. New York in 1971 and other states such as Connecticut and New Jersey began mandatory controls of hospitals after 1976. Congress, after 1972, gave HEW the power to deny full Medicare reimbursements to institutions that had expanded or invested without proper approval. Ensconced in this new wave of regulation was the final step* necessary to desegregate the health care system,

*securing legislative language that would apply to all federal programs, not just the Hospital Survey and Construction Act (Hill-Burton). This was accomplished through Title VI of the 1964 Civil Rights Act, which stipulated that all federal funds must support only those programs and institutions that provide services to all Americans regardless of race, creed, or national origin.*[76]

As P. Preston Reynolds observed, the "passage of Medicare ... would provide financial support to hospitals for medical care to elderly patients, a cost that previously had gone uncompensated. With one stroke, more than 7,000 hospitals were

---

*The first step was a series of legal victories culminating in the 1963 *Simkins v. Moses H. Cone Memorial Hospital*, which declared the "separate but equal" clause of the Hill-Burton Act unconstitutional.

subject to civil rights regulations set forth in Title VI of the Civil Rights Act."[77] A detailed analysis of the act, published in the 1965 *Journal of the National Medical Association,* raised the possibility of even wider health impact:

> Four titles of the Civil Rights Act of 1964 may have an impact on the practices of health facilities in general and of Hill-Burton projects in particular. Title II prohibits discrimination in restaurants and may include restaurants within hospitals. Title III would require public hospitals to provide "equal utilization" of their facilities without discrimination. Title VI prohibits discrimination by hospitals which have received Federal financial assistance. Title VII, which does not apply to public hospitals, may prohibit employment discrimination by private hospitals and by labor unions for hospital employees.... The full impact of the Civil Rights Act for health facilities will be revealed by administrative regulations and judicial interpretations.[78]

Within two years of the enactment of the Medicare legislation most hospitals were beginning to comply with the new racial desegregation laws:

> In June of 1968, some 8,000 hospitals were cleared for participation in Medicare. Of these, more than 3,000 had revised traditional practices in the past two years in order to obtain Medicare clearance. There were approximately 250 hospitals, most of them in the South, which have refused to comply with Title 6 of the Civil Rights Act and hence cannot receive Federal assistance.[79]

These massive qualitative and quantitative changes in the United States health institutional infrastructure between 1965 and 1980 meant that the health system would never be the same.[80]

### Big Government Health Care, Regulatory Failure, and Emerging Health Care Financial Markets

Federal government involvement in health care had become significant in the post–World War II era through Hill-Burton funding and expansion of the NIH and U.S. Public Health Service. Between 1965 and 1980, with the passage of Medicare and Medicaid, government funding of health professions education, and a burgeoning NHC movement, the federal government became not only a larger structural component of the U.S. health system, but a major power center as well.\*

---

\*Health economist Eli Ginzberg defines ten principal centers of power that influence the structure and operations of the health system through the 1990s: the federal government, state governments, the business community, the hospital system, insurance companies, the legal system, organized consumer groups, for-profit medical and hospital organizations, U.S. citizens studying medicine abroad, and the national political arena.

"States and the federal government were the principal sectors responsible for the large-scale expansion of medical schools, which doubled the nation's output of physicians between 1965 and 1980"[81] and increased their portion to half the nation's health system expenditures by the end of the period.* Therefore, federal and state government health programs, the still-dominant not-for-profit community hospitals, all but four of the nation's medical schools, and, until 1986,** Blue Cross/Blue Shield systems comprised the "service" rather than for-profit sector of the health system. This nonprofit sector still comprised over 90 percent of the health system with federal and state governments making up an ever larger share.

Depending upon one's perspective and/or the revelation of contrary comprehensive financial data sets—which are often difficult to obtain—these institutions were not delivering health care primarily to make money. However, as Ginzberg delicately defines the preponderance of the financial arrangements in the health system, the lion's share of the funds and programs remained "in private hands," with institutions and agencies serving as conduits and managers for public and private funds and resources. Despite lusty growth of the for-profit sector during the 1970s and early 1980s, "privatization" of the health system had not progressed very far.

The Medicaid and Medicare programs became so large that they threatened to burst the federal and state governments' budgets. Regulatory reaction by the federal government to this development was so swift and severe that it fulfilled all the detractors' fears that government intervention in health could destabilize the system. Moreover, the financial impact of Medicare/Medicaid on the health system had been exploited by the Johnson administration and combined with Title VI of the 1964 Civil Rights Act to trigger

> steps ... by the federal government to eliminate explicit discrimination in access to hospital care for minorities and, in doing so, illustrates the use of health and program legislation to effect institutional and social change.... Furthermore, the Medicare certification program was essential in implementing a federal policy of equity in health care and thus was a critical tool in exposing and eliminating racism in medicine.[82]

Fiscal problems proved to be major destabilizing factors leading to far-reaching and permanent changes. The attempts to eliminate racism in medicine, however, followed the pattern of public school desegregation with gradual incremental

---

*By 1980 public funds accounted for 42 percent of national health expenditures. When this is added to the subsidy provided health care through tax exemptions for employers and employees, over half the nation's health bill is paid by government. See National Center for Health Statistics. *Prevention Profile. Health United States, 1991.* Hyattsville, MD: Public Health Service, 1992, 274.

**By 1986 the Blue Cross/Blue Shield system had adopted so many characteristics in common with the commercial health insurance carriers such as experience rating and for-profit activities and enterprises, they lost their special tax-exempt status.

changes spiced up by a few discrete, sometimes spectacular, demonstration programs with a *de facto* result of maintaining a multi-tiered system based on quality, race, and class. The majority of African American, Latino, welfare, medically indigent, chronically disabled poor, and immigrant patients continued to use the same publically funded city and county hospitals, public health departments, inner-city stressed hospitals, neighborhood and community health centers, and university training and teaching hospitals, while the majority of European Americans continued to use private doctors' offices and private hospitals (both of which were now often located in suburbs), a growing number of free-standing surgical and laboratory facilities, free-standing or AHC-based consulting facilities, and prestigious AHC private hospitals, pavilions, and wards.

In the late 1960s and early 1970s the government established a nationwide review and control infrastructure aimed at controlling health care costs through rationing use of hospitals and surgery through peer review mechanisms. When it appeared these mechanisms would be insufficient to control the cost inflation problem, during the early 1970s the Nixon administration promoted and implemented the use of HMOs as devices to control costs. The difference between these organizations and previous prepaid plans such as Kaiser Permanente, the Group Health Cooperative of Puget Sound, and the Health Insurance Plan of New York (HIP) was the latters' emphasis on preventive care and the maintenance of "wellness." Although hard to prove because of confounding factors such as overrepresentation of young, well populations and particular personality profiles, if HMOs saved money it was through lower hospitalization rates augmented by fewer specialists and procedures.

Sold on the concept by Dr. Paul M. Ellwood, Jr., "a Minneapolis physician who concentrated on the study of alternative delivery systems rather than clinical practice,"[83] President Nixon began funding federally sponsored HMOs. Planning to have over 1,200 HMOs by 1980 so that they could be "everywhere available so that families will have a choice,"[84] 110 were in existence by 1972. He committed $375 million over five years in support of the HMO concept with the Health Maintenance Act of 1973. Despite the federal government's funding 106 HMOs during the 1970s, their success and the public's response to them were disappointing. By 1974 Congress tried to get a grip on rising medical costs by passing the National Planning and Resources Development Act. It was an attempt to federalize the planning process, heretofore a local responsibility, of the U.S. health system. It had very little effect on spiraling hospital costs, and emphasis shifted to other measures. Thus, the optimistic early predictions of improvements as a result of government involvement in health financing, health education, health services delivery to civilian populations, health planning, and social engineering in the health system produced mixed results, at best, by 1980. In lieu of dramatic and documented improvements in health status, outcomes, and access for Black and poor populations and the first systematic steps toward desegregating the health system— although the majority of the system remained *de facto* segregated along racial, class, socioeconomic, and ethnic lines—critics felt the new reliance on government had done more harm than good to the health system.[85]

No component of the health system was placed under more pressure throughout this period than the health care financing infrastructure. Critics often cited inappropriate financing as the principal flaw in the U.S. health system and alleged it was heavily responsible for the destabilization and runaway cost inflation between 1965 and 1980. Of the formal accountability criteria, financial matters, quality of care, and provision of needed services—to be discussed in more detail later—health financing became increasingly dominant. Moreover, health care financing presented more avenues for destabilizing public trust–based, informal accountability mechanisms. These mechanisms had been built upon a historical foundation of nonprofit, community-based, "voluntary" hospitals; local control of such institutions by volunteer trustees on hospital boards, although not publically accountable, which exercised an oversight function in the community's interests; and the public's presumption of high levels of health professionalism and ethical behavior in their community institutions. A Twentieth Century Fund Report on the profit motive and health care revealed that at both institutional and individual levels, "[P]roviders of care have traditionally been expected to behave in ways that do not serve their short-term economic interests. . . . [T]here has been a heavy societal reliance in health care on assumptions about and trust in these elements. Trust has in many ways substituted for more formal mechanisms of accountability."[86] Besides the introduction of for-profit institutions and their ethos into the health system— whose actions often undermined the public's trust—health care financing mechanisms also reinforced and perpetuated two-centuries-old race and class hierarchies and discrimination that had plagued the U.S. health system.

By 1970, five years after the enactment of Medicare/Medicaid, 86.4 percent of the American population had some type of hospitalization insurance. Moreover, the third-party share of health expenditures paid increased from 45 to 67 percent between 1960 and 1975, which facilitated runaway health care cost inflation. "The commonly perceived villain was the health care system itself. Because so many patients were so protected by insurance, it was argued, there were few incentives for them to hold down costs."[87] This set up a vicious cycle, "Hospitals demanded the biggest, the best, and the latest in buildings and equipment. Doctors developed ever more costly procedures. To many, the health care system was operating without response to other societal needs."[88] Several other confounding mechanisms fed into the health care cost inflation. Tax breaks encouraging health spending were variegated and potent in their effects. By 1979, "Because the law allow[ed] them to subtract many health-insurance premiums and medical expenses from their taxable income, U.S. taxpayers . . . paid $17 billion less in taxes then they otherwise would have."[89] The $17 billion tax reduction was equivalent to 14 percent of gross medical expenses. Thus, health care was 14 percent cheaper than its true 1979 costs to the average consumer—a subsidy by definition. Dollars spent on health insurance are "excluded" from taxable income (not counted as income) and thus are not subject to local or state income taxes or Social Security taxes. To Americans covered by employment-based health insurance, according to elaborate calculations by health economists such as Alain Enthoven, Ronald Hoffman, and Eugene Steuerle, "the final saving from an extra dollar spent on health care in the form of employer-paid premiums is 35 percent."[90] However, the arrangements, which were incrementally enacted by Congress between 1942 and 1954, triggered two concerns: "(a) It contributes to escalating health care costs by subsidizing noncostworthy care, and (b) it unjustly benefits the rich more than the poor."[91] Both phenomena inflict differential adverse effects on socioeconomically disadvantaged populations such as African Americans:

> *Because they lower the net price of insurance and increase the use of care, they increase demand for it and thereby raise its price. But poorer persons already benefit less from the subsidies. If they also end up paying higher prices for what care they do get, poorer people may finally actually lose from the subsidies, not merely gain less than the rich.*[92]

Paul T. Menzel describes another group of tax breaks that increased inflationary pressures in *Medical Costs, Moral Choices*: "There are other tax breaks for medical care. Contributions to hospitals are 'charitable' and therefore deductible. Non-profit hospitals can sell bonds whose interest to their holders is tax-free, and these hospitals themselves are tax-exempt."[93] Clearly, tax-deductible contributions and the purchase of tax-exempt bonds financially benefit wealthy, not poor, Americans. Alain Enthoven described how federal tax subsidies for employer and employee health insurance "further reduced incentives to economize in buying health insurance and in using health services."[94] This provides further evidence that the net effect of tax policies regarding health is that they encourage excessive and noncostworthy insurance helping generate health care cost inflations, and that they subsidize the rich to a much greater extent than the poor.

Moreover, until the 1980s, governmental and private insurers reimbursed hospitals on the basis of charges and provided extra funding for depreciation, plant development, and a return on equity. For instance:

> *In California in 1979 … Blue Cross and the commercial insurance companies reimbursed hospitals 12 percent more than their "full financial requirements" (which includes the actual costs of providing care, working capital, and capital replacement costs). … Medicare reimbursed hospitals 4 percent less than their full financial requirements, and Medi-Cal paid them 18 percent less.*[95]

It must be remembered that these basic inflated hospital rates were built upon a foundation of charge-based, plant subsidy, and investment-depreciated billing practices that had been in effect since the 1930s and 1940s Blue Cross/Blue Shield hospital insurance revolution. Such costly billing practices were further exaggerated after the 1965 passage of Medicare/Medicaid, as demonstrated by the explosion in hospital bed daily rates.

Many contended the profit motive and new "Wall Street" mentality sweeping the health system were the reasons both voluntary community and for-profit hospitals began implementing strategies during the late 1970s and 1980s to tailor their patient bases and fill their beds with "full-fledged" private insurance patients instead of "naked Medicare" patients (Medicare patients without supplementary insurance policies covering deductibles, copayments, and overbilling usual and customary charges) and Medicaid patients (e.g., Medi-Cal in the example above). Such strategies included, but were not limited to patient "dumping";* misusing the "quality assurance" process (physicians with high percentages of Medicaid, "naked Medicare," or other categories of "undesirable" patients were either excluded from or pressured off hospital staffs); economically profiling their medical staffs by discouraging physicians practicing in poor, barrio, or ghetto neighborhoods from joining hospital staffs; and monitoring the percentages of no-pay, bad debt, or financially burdened patients (e.g., patients or families having difficulty paying deductibles or co-payments) in a physician's practice and utilizing such data as overt, or in some instances covert, "quality assurance" parameters. These practices evolved in an environment wherein admitted patients (who were incapable of paying the hospitals' already inflated prices, puffed up by decades of government and insurance company reimbursement policies, and their expected "bonuses") were considered "empty beds" by hospital administrators. Civil Rights laws made such patient screening practices illegal, but patient flow could be more subtly controlled by hospital staff practices and procedures. Nevertheless, hospital "dumping" became such a problem that laws were implemented in most states barring the practice, although they often proved ineffective.**

Such practices became widespread and were often energized by the commercialization of the health system. The system's oversight and accountability processes, since their maturation beginning in the 1940s, have been linked to the government and private insurers' roles as financiers of health care. Of the major areas of health system accountability in the United States—the technical, through regulatory, licensure, and inspection mechanisms; the financial, through auditing and business management mechanisms; and the medical-social, through standard-

---

*Patient "dumping" is the process wherein "undesirable" patients (usually indigent, uninsured, underinsured, or patients without a designated private physician on their staffs) are turned away from the hospital emergency room to be rerouted to public or alternative facilities.

**In 1993 Congress enacted the EMTALA (Emergency Medical Treatment and Active Labor Act, 42 U.S.C.A. § 1395dd) in response to "its concern that hospitals were 'dumping' patients [who were] unable to pay, by either refusing to provide emergency medical treatment or transferring patients before their emergency conditions were stabilized." See Areen J, King PA, Goldberg S, Gostin L, Capron AM. *Law, Science and Medicine.* Westbury, NY: The Foundation Press, Inc., 1996, 1216.

izing, monitoring, and ensuring that the system was serving all its people in an equitable and quality manner—the financial received the most attention. As noted by Bradford H. Gray, lead investigator of the Twentieth Century Fund Report *The Profit Motive and Patient Care:*

> *Payers have systems for monitoring and auditing to ensure that services being filed for are in fact provided and are necessary. Mechanisms to ensure quality include regulatory requirements built into conditions of participation, certification and accreditation requirements and some activities of peer review organizations. These all have significant short-comings.... By contrast, procedures for monitoring access to care are much more rudimentary.*[96]

Other than giving "certain categories of patients the financial means to purchase care, mechanisms by which the government has held providers accountable for caring for patients who lack the means to pay are quite limited."[97] Thus, antecedent systematic financial oversight policies extended to health institutions based upon traditions of community service, trust, and professionalism compounded by history-based medical-social flaws put the system and, especially, disadvantaged patients at risk. One glaring example epitomizing this overweening "trust" in market forces guiding health care was the financial disadvantage encountered by public hospitals or urban hospitals utilized by high percentages of Medicaid, "naked Medicare," or medically indigent patients.* Their noncompetitive patient mix, eleemosynary missions, and dependency on charitable and tax-based funding threatened these vital institutions' survival in this commercial environment. And when public hospitals and clinics succumbed or were absorbed into the for-profit sector, few institutional arrangements were created to handle their dependent—now displaced—patient populations. It is difficult to measure the degree of fraud, abuse, and failures to exercise accountability in the public interests that occurred throughout the health system during this era, according to Gray. Based on the available oversight data,

> *the evidence suggests that a variety of types of difficult-to-detect malfeasance can result from excessive zeal in the pursuit of economic goals, and that the corporate transformation of health care and the growing presence of profit-oriented providers have created new challenges and complexities for the parties with oversight responsibility.*[98]

---

*Medical indigency* usually denotes not being covered by major medical insurance—based on "mainstream," full-time employment. It has little to do with income (some wealthy Americans are uninsured), employment status (most service jobs do not offer health insurance plans and most of the uninsured work), or socioeconomic status (unemployed professional or management types are often uninsured).

In "The Monetarization of Medical Care," Ginzberg articulated the system's vulnerability to financial exploitation by allowing "opportunities created by faulty public policy, primarily through reimbursement, for those with money making proclivities to establish a strong niche in what was a formerly a quasi-eleemosynary sector."[99] Building upon their background of business practices and the weaknesses of the regulatory system, this cash flow "gold mine" proved irresistible to the for-profit sector and led to a flurry of new for-profit hospitals and buy-outs of old not-for-profit facilities.

That health system market forces sometimes had socially undesirable results was a major conclusion reached by the National Commission on the Cost of Medical Care (1975–1977). By 1971, HMOs were being promoted as the panacea for the system's ills. Despite legislation favoring HMOs, millions of dollars of government-sponsored funding was expended for this model of delivery, and high levels of presidential publicity and support were generated during the early 1970s. It was not nearly enough, however:

> By mid-1979, there were 217 HMOs, far less than the 1,700 the Nixon administration originally foresaw … the total enrollment of 7.9 million people was twice as many as in 1970. … But HMO enrollment was still only 4 percent of the nation's population, and the administration projections gave them less than 10 percent by 1990.[100]

Clearly, indemnity health insurance financing and the fee-for-service model of delivery were still dominant as the country entered the 1980s. However, for the first time in U.S. history, fed by Medicare and Medicaid funds, the for-profit system, with its free access to equity markets, emerged as a major player in the health system.

Health care financing changes during this period were charged with curing some of America's long standing medical-social ills. As E. Richard Brown noted, "When President Johnson signed the Medicare and Medicaid legislation into law on July 30, 1965, a great many Americans believed that the elderly would no longer be impoverished by medical care costs and that the poor would get the care they needed from essentially the same sources as the middle class."[101] Although the programs were only partially successful, Davis and Schoen point out "that the poor's access to medical services greatly improved between 1965 and 1975."[102] Nevertheless, the changes in health care financing represented by Medicare and Medicaid created unintended flaws in access to mainstream health delivery systems for the elderly poor, indigent populations, and underserved ethnic minorities such as African Americans. These changes also created new, and perpetuated 200-year-old, forms of health system race and class hierarchies and discrimination.

The programs reflected the traditional class and race arrangements and groupings that had divided the American health system from its colonial beginnings. Moreover, they also mirrored the medical profession's and health establishment's history-based social insecurities and race and class biases.[103] Medicare was "primarily a social insurance program administered by the federal government as an earned right to 'entitled' persons," while "Medicaid is a public assistance program following the well-established pattern of other welfare measures."[104] Intentionally or not, the American biases against indigency, disability, and not being well-born were incorporated into the original and subsequent alterations in the legislation. Despite noble intentions: "While Medicare covers almost all people over sixty-five (all who receive any kind of Social Security), it pays less for the poor than for the relatively rich. The poor cannot afford its ungraduated coinsurance as easily as others, and they more often live in underserved areas."[105]

And: "Medicaid does not cover many of the near poor at all. In the mid-1970s, half of those under sixty-five with less than $5,000 family income had no hospital or surgical coverage whatsoever. Ironically, sometimes those who are covered by Medicaid were initially made poor by inadequate earlier insurance."[106] Moreover, while Medicare was burdened with problems of daunting deductibles, copayments, and patient responsibility for unreimbursed charges, reimbursement rates to physicians and institutions for Medicaid patients were the lowest in the system. They could not be billed for cost overruns like Medicare recipients; reimbursement rates were lower to hospitals for Medicaid patients; and reimbursement rates were lowered to nursing homes accepting Medicaid beneficiaries. These were major barriers to populations already saddled with race and socioeconomic burdens in a market-based, capitalist health system. As a result, most physicians refused to accept Medicaid recipients as patients and health provider institutions grew reluctant to admit them. Moreover, the first peer review and cost-benefit analyses and rationing were initially implemented on Medicare and Medicaid populations and with more severity, placing providers who served them under scrutiny and liable to financial, legal, and professional sanctions. These practices, which were hidden from the public, had profound and differential effects on physicians and other health professionals who served low socioeconomic or disadvantaged minority populations.[107]

### The Health Care Work Force and Attempts at Regulation

Another aspect of the perceived health "crisis" was the shortage of physician personnel. Doctor/patient ratios, which hovered between 125 and 133 per 100,000 population (between one physician per 800 and one per 752 patients) in the 1930s, stabilized at those levels throughout the 1940s into the 1950s. They began climbing gradually after the war to a level of 153 per 100,000 (one physician per 654 patients) by 1960. For African Americans, post-Flexner figures deteriorated below 1900 levels to 1 Black physician per 3,377 Black patients during the 1940s. However, despite the overall numerical increase, specialization, practice patterns, and institution-based physicians cut the number and availability of primary care doctors. There were other factors involved, as Fitzhugh Mullin pointed out:

*By 1960, medicine had a great deal more to offer the average patient than it had in the time of Flexner. The population responded by calling on the medical system far more than it had previously. Whereas in 1930 the average American saw a physician little more than twice a year, annual doctor visits had reached 4.5 per person by 1964. During the same period, hospital admissions rose from 56 to 145 per 1,000 population, and average hospital days from .9 to 1.3 per person per year.[108]*

The demands for service in the health system had changed. Compounding these real qualitative and quantitative needs, the popular quest for equality, freedom, and social change embodied in ongoing Black civil rights, feminist, and medical student movements were demanding equitable representation for disadvantaged minorities* in the medical and health professions.

Expanding on the initial government involvement in medical education and research embodied in amendments to the Public Health Service Act during the 1940s and 1950s, "The first major interest the federal government showed in directly supporting health professional education came in 1963, with the Health Professions Education Assistance Act."[109] Building upon this foundation, grants for increased enrollment and subsidizing tuition for low-income students were added in 1965. In 1968 the Health Manpower Act granted medical schools funding for increased enrollments and was extended as the Health Training Improvement Act in 1970. The Carnegie Commission on Higher Education's 1970 report, called *Higher Education and the Nation's Health: Policies for Medical and Dental Education*, is what actually placed reform of the health professions manpower pool on the health professions education agenda. It called for a 50 percent expansion in medical school enrollment, dramatic increases in nonphysician providers, an increase in general medical (as opposed to specialty) training, and the creation of a National Health Service Corps.

The National Health Service Corps, referred to as the "most specific federal program designed to deal with the doctor shortage in underserved areas"[110] was enacted in 1970 as part of the Emergency Health Personnel Act. It was soon followed by the Comprehensive Health Manpower Training Act of 1971, which gave medical schools "capitation" for each enrollee, provided funds to initiate family medicine departments and training programs, and gave financial incentives

---

*Of the four racial/ethnic minority categories at that time, Black Americans, Hispanic Americans, Native Americans, and Asian Americans, the latter were neither underrepresented nor deprived in many facets of American life. Although historically they were victims of non-White and cultural prejudice, discrimination, and exclusionary legislation, Asian Americans were not considered "disadvantaged" or "underrepresented" minorities in many tabulations. See: Strelnick H, Younge R. Affirmative action in medicine: Money becomes the admissions criteria of the 1980s. 151–175. In: Sidel VW, Sidel R, eds. *Reforming Medicine: Lessons of the Last Quarter Century*. New York: Pantheon, 1984, 154; U.S. Department of Health and Human Services. *Health Status of Minorities and Low Income Groups*. Washington, DC: U.S. Government Printing Office, 1985, 19–21.

for accepting and enrolling higher numbers of minority students (traditionally 2–3 percent of medical students). In the flurry of equal rights legislation and medical education funding, in 1970 "the American Association of Medical Colleges (AAMC) committed itself to increase the representation of blacks (and other minorities—as yet a relatively small number) in the first-year entering classes to 12 percent of the total by 1975, a goal endorsed by the American Medical Association."[111] Although the 12 percent goal was never reached, the highest proportion of African American enrollment, 7.5 percent, was reached in 1974–1975, with 10 percent of that first-year medical school class being disadvantaged minorities. Despite the fact "[b]y 1972 virtually all of America's medical schools had some type of program for increasing black student enrollment,"[112] disturbing trends clouded the picture by 1980. As David McBride reported on minority enrollment in medical schools less than a decade after the 1978 Supreme Court decision, *Regents of University of California v. Bakke*, in the *New York State Journal of Medicine*:

> [T]he longer view presented in this analysis as well as recent trends should suggest cause for concern. Developments stemming from the Bakke decision (in which the Supreme Court ruled to prohibit quotas based solely on race in the selection of students for admission to universities) and the weakening of governmental policies to enforce integration in the education and employment of minority health professionals are turning back the clock of progress.[113]

Meanwhile, due to the effects of social movements and anti-discrimination legislation, female medical school enrollment rose "from less than 9 percent in the sixties to approximately 25 percent in 1980."[114]

Residency programs in primary care were subsidized by the Health Professions Education Assistance Act of 1976. The Health Manpower Education Initiative Awards (1972), offering federal dollars for Area Health Education Centers (AHEC), was an effort to better distribute health care providers geographically through educational interventions. The infusion of federal and private funding increased the number of medical schools from 86 in 1960 to 103 by 1970 and 126 by the 1980s. Between 1965 and 1973, "$295.3 million was allocated for loans and scholarships to the health professions schools for students with 'exceptional financial need.'"[115] Between 1960 and 1978 medical school enrollment jumped from 30,000 to 60,000. Due to federal grants for training nonphysician providers, by the early 1980s 1,800 nurse practitioners, 12,500 physician's assistants, and 2,300 nurse-midwives were practicing—many in underserved areas. These programs had profound, albeit temporary, effects. They were never institutionalized to levels beyond the reach of the whims of Congress or presidential administrations. Overall, they did increase the health profession's human resource pool by 1980, but they failed to solve many professional inequities in health delivery, and the system's work force distribution problems, or implement equitable minority representation in the health professions.

Inflation in health care costs was also a concern throughout the period. When President Nixon imposed a general wage-price freeze between August 1971 and January 1973, he gave doctors special dispensation. He limited doctors' annual fee increases to 2.5 percent. However, when controls were lifted for all other sectors, doctor's fees and hospital charges remained under price controls more than a year longer than the rest of the economy: "As expected, the controls did work temporarily, holding price increases in medical care to 4.7 percent in 1972 and 3.1 percent in 1973. But in 1975, after the controls in the health care field were lifted … the medical care total of the Consumer Price Index promptly spurted ahead at a 12.5 percent annual clip."[116] Just as in other areas of the health system, the health profession's problems were studied, refinanced, and reformed with little end result. The system either resisted and rejected the reform, as it did in the instance of achieving parity in minority representation in the health professions; absorbed the reform without fundamentally changing the system, as it did with producing more doctors and nonphysician providers; or successfully incorporated the reform until it was destroyed through underfunding and/or lack of institutional or government commitment, as exemplified by affirmative action in medicine.[117]

With government coffers now open to the health system, state and local government involvement in health increased and Medicaid grew to account "for a third or more of many state health expenditures."[118] As the health system opened up through entitlement and social service programs to underserved populations, there was rapid growth in traditional state health functions such as public health activities; personal health and medical care services; the regulation of health institutions, organizations, and occupations; education and training programs, federal-state programs; and other regulatory programs. The heavy state expenditures on personal health services for the poor—often as prerequisites for participation in government programs*—were unprecedented. Traditionally, health planning had been a local responsibility "performed on a volunteer basis and often accomplished with commendable cooperation between local government agencies and local medical organizations."[119] As health care costs began escalating in the 1960s, more than 20 states enacted certificate-of-need legislation (1964) to control duplication and overexpansion of facilities and services. Some federal participation in state and local health activities went along with the Hill-Burton Act, Regional Medical Programs, and the Comprehensive Health Planning Act of 1966. The latter, being largely ineffective, assumed new powers in 1972 when Medicare/Medicaid expanded its regulatory and punitive functions (i.e., lowering reimbursements to institutions or programs out of compliance with certificate-of-need regulations).

---

*For example, the Medicaid program was a joint federal-state program wherein the federal government picked up 50 to 83 percent of the tab, depending on the state's financial status. However, voluntary state participation was required.

When Congress enacted the National Planning and Resources Development Act of 1974, the country was divided into 204 local planning groups under the authority of the secretary of HEW and his hierarchy. It consisted of a national advisory counsel, state planning agencies, and state coordinating councils sitting atop the planning groups cooperatively formed by the secretary and state governors. The 204 local bodies, Health System Agencies (HSAs), were to "develop plans for future needs, and, through the administration of certificate-of-need laws now required of all states by the new planning act, passing judgment on plans to expand or construct facilities or to broaden services."[120] The HSAs represented jurisdictions of population clusters of 500,000 to 3 million people and were to consist of a minimum of one-third providers (i.e., physicians, hospital administrators, pharmacists, paramedics, etc.) and a maximum of one-third public officials. Consumers, some of whom made solid contributions to the HSAs but lacked health training, qualifications, or backgrounds, were the majority. The program, representing in many ways a government attempt to administer health care under a public utility model (i.e., power through rate setting, licensing, and certification) ruled by a health "czar," failed. By 1977, hospital costs continued rising so catastrophically that "the Carter administration proposed putting a cap on hospital prices."[121] Congress opted instead for a cooperative effort to control hospital costs between the American Hospital Association (AHA), the Federation of American Hospitals (representing the for-profit hospitals), and the AMA. Between 1981 and 1983 the HSA planning act was phased out.

Despite these measures, the fiscal pressures exerted on state and local governments by the health programs were unprecedented. The growth in federal spending from $4 billion to $65.7 billion for health services between 1965 and 1980 was accompanied by state outlays exploding from $4.8 billion to $31.3 billion, respectively. For state and local governments such a commitment "represented an even greater burden on the more limited taxable resources at these levels of government."[122] Moreover, as E. Richard Brown pointed out: "Because welfare, Medicaid, and other programs intended to sustain the poor are supported at the local level by even more regressive sales taxes and somewhat progressive income taxes, they tend to redistribute income from the working class and lower-middle class to the poor."[123] Thus, unpopular tax bases and the fact that they served mainly poor people who did not pay for them made these health programs and institutions politically vulnerable. As last resorts, various states such as California and Illinois dealt with this "crisis" by restricting Medicaid benefits, stiffening the eligibility requirements for health coverage, implementing stringent prior authorization programs, and closing Medicaid enrollment. This is why the Medicaid program has never served more than two-thirds (typically one-half or less) of the nation's poor. As these cost pressures mounted, other sectors of the public health care sector suffered. For example, by the early 1980s, "[M]any California counties . . . closed their public hospitals. California's once extensive county hospital system . . . shrunk from sixty-five hospitals operated by forty-nine of the state's fifty-eight counties in

1964, to thirty-three hospitals in twenty-six counties in 1982."[124] Many other tax-supported health facilities nationwide suffered similar fates. Unexpected results secondary to the health reforms led to actions at the state and local levels that were detrimental to the populations many of the programs were designed to protect—the poor. The improvements in health status, outcomes, and access to services disadvantaged populations such as African Americans experienced during the era were placed at risk by the 1980s.[125]

Due to runaway health care cost inflation produced by health system changes, emphasis shifted to cost control instead of expanded redistribution of care by the late 1960s. As has been alluded to, 20 states between 1964 and 1972 had begun cost-compelled regulation of the health system, including hospitals. This was evidenced by the appearance of formal health planning and cost-containment programs. Certificate-of-Need (CON) programs were started in the 1960s. Based on the principle that costs would be controlled if health institutions were required to obtain preapproval for expansions and major expenditures by regulatory agencies, as these fell under the control of the medical and hospital establishments, they quickly became failures. By the late 1970s "A study of the effects of CON programs found that they slowed construction of hospital beds, but that other capital expenditures increased and the net effect was negligible."[126] Other reviews were more pessimistic, pointing out different defects in CON activities: "Special circumstances of a hospital, instead of real community bed needs, have usually dominated CON decision[s]. CON legislation may actually have escalated hospital costs by driving capital expansion away from beds and into advances in technology."[127]

Due to the unexpectedly vigorous inflationary pressures generated by Medicare and Medicaid, Professional Standards Review Organizations (PSROs) had cropped up in 20 states by 1970. By March of that same year Congress, compelled by inflationary health care costs, started exploring a formal peer review program. This effort would contrast strongly with the voluntary peer review programs the medical profession had been engaged in at the hospital level for more than 50 years. For example, traditional hospital tissue committees that compared preoperative diagnoses with pathology reports on excised tissues were not designed to penalize the surgeon but to sharpen his diagnostic skills. The medical profession looked to peer review as a teaching method emphasizing quality-of-care factors; Congress wanted to use the process as an internal audit stressing cost surveillance, identifying "problem" physicians and having punitive overtones.

The initial PSRO legislation stressed "norms" of treatment and "profiles" of physicians that reinforced organized medicine's fear of "cookbook medicine." The legislation's final wording—"to promote effective, efficient and economical delivery of health services of proper quality"[128]—prioritized costs over quality. Despite AMA resistance, the Bennett PSRO amendment was enacted on October 30, 1972. Immediately after its enactment the AMA participated in developing the regulations. PSROs were then established throughout the country, most with the cooperation and supervision of county and state medical societies. When local or regional medical institutions failed to comply, the government then stepped in and formed PSROs of its own. However, Starr noted, "[b]y 1979 the reputation of health care regulation was none too good. Some early evaluations of the PSRO program suggested that it cost more than it saved."[129] Besides their ambiguous goals and objectives, others posited reasons for PSROs' shortcomings: "Made up entirely of physicians, whose orientation is naturally toward improving the quality of care regardless of price, PSROs, ironically, may have actually contributed to cost escalation."[130]

As previously noted, the National Health Planning and Resource Development Act (1974) was one of the later attempts to establish formal health planning in the United States. The HSAs failed to regulate the health system or correct its economic distresses and were phased out in the 1980s. HMOs proved to be another variety of "programs" tried by the government "which ... were ... evaluated on the narrow grounds of cost control—and found wanting."[131] HMOs, having disappointed their supporters and failing to interest the American public, paradoxically underwent a round of strict regulation by the federal government. The Health Maintenance Organization Act (1973) rendered HMOs the most regulated components of the reformed health system for the purported interests of quality and cost containment. Requirements were so high, and the mandate that the plans accept all the health system's sickest patients placed HMOs in noncompetitive positions compared to other types of health insurances that could pick and choose whom they insured ("cherry picking"). For most of the plans, the 20–40 percent savings generated by the Kaiser HMOs never materialized.[132]

## Pharmaceutical, Medical Supply, Medical Education, and Research Infrastructures: Adjusting to Market Forces

While major efforts at controlling costs were exerted on many components of the health delivery system, little energy was directed at cost containment affecting the pharmaceutical, medical supply, and equipment industries. Having experienced phenomenal growth after World War II, with profits hovering between 15 and 20 percent, the pharmaceutical industry began leveling off between 1965 and 1980. Since the 1950s the drug industry had ranked first or second in profitability with profits during this era of approximately 10 percent on sales. "Based on investment, drug profits after taxes have been averaging about 18 percent per year since 1960, compared with about 11 percent for all major manufacturing corporations,"[133] as Milton Silverman and Philip R. Lee noted.

Although pharmaceutical use and prescriptions increased with the aging of the population, with expansion of access to pharmacologic breakthroughs through Title 18 and 19, and with scientific progress, access to modern medications such as sulfa drugs and penicillin, antihypertensives (e.g., hexamethonium, hydralazine, rauwolfia), oral antidiabetic drugs (e.g., tolbutamide, chlorpropamide), the polio vaccines, or major tranquilizers (e.g., chlorpromazine, reserpine)—all of which drastically changed mortality rates for their respective diseases and/or altered the way large blocs of patients with particular diseases were managed (e.g., the deinstitutionalization of mental patients)—was severely limited or not forthcoming.* Nevertheless, despite industry claims that pharmaceuticals constituted 8 percent of the nation's health care costs, a full accounting including costs of prescriptions dispensed by hospital pharmacies and government institutions and over-the-counter medications shows that: "the real annual drug bill to the public was at least $17.0 billion, or approximately 20 percent of all health care expenditures."[134] Considering the problems of runaway health care cost inflation throughout this period, the pharmaceutical industry did very well.

Pharmaceutical industry diversification noted during the preceding period intensified. The menace posed by government regulation seemingly hastened the process. Recognizing drug company diversification into "anything … their technology and marketing skills prepare them," the Ehrenreichs noted that "drug companies have been turning to cosmetics, chemicals, hospital supplies, and electronic equipment for hospitals."[135] Beneficiaries of the health care boom themselves, giants in the medical supply industry such as Baxter, Becton-Dickinson, and Johnson and Johnson all began investing in the drug industry. Companies in other industries such as Dow Chemical, 3M, Bristol-Myers, Colgate-Palmolive, Union Carbide, and DuPont joined the rush toward pharmaceutical and hospital supply manufacturing. When American Home Products, Inc., manufacturer of Boyardee Foods, Gulden's Mustard, and Preparation H, purchased Wyeth, the ethical drug firm,** a situation developed wherein: "Anybody who makes anything which can be swallowed, inhaled, absorbed, or applied would like to make drugs—and vice versa."[136]

As the hospital grew in its dominance, the medical supply industry grew explosively. By 1969, 3 years after Medicare, hospital expenditures were running at $20 billion a year. Approximately $7.5 billion went for goods and services—food, bed linen, dust mops, and cleaning supplies—"but billions went for more specifically medical equipment, from scalpels, syringes, and catheters to X-ray equipment, electronic blood cell counters, and artificial kidneys."[137] Giants in this seemingly recession-proof industry Bristol-Myers and Johnson & Johnson "had total revenues of $8.9 billion (BM: $3.5 billon; J&J: $5.4 billion) and profits of $774 million (split roughly fifty-fifty)," by 1981.[138] Moreover, by then both had

---

*Prescription services for Medicare recipients have never been enacted, and pharmacy services for Medicaid patients have always been severely limited. Policy and financing changes in these areas would have dramatically increased patient access to vital pharmaceuticals.

**Ethical drugs are drugs sold only by physicians' prescription and whose advertising is directed only to physicians. Because the manufacturers follow this self-imposed ban on advertising to the public, these are often called *ethical drugs* and their manufacturers, the *ethical drug industry*. This has been, until recently, a traditional and basic distinction between prescription and nonprescription drugs.

established historic growth rates of 13 percent annually. By 1980, IBM, General Electric, and Hewlett-Packard had become major suppliers of both computers and health care technology. As Stanley Whol observed in *The Medical Industrial Complex,* "Expensive medical gadgetry is one of the prime reasons for escalating health care costs."[139] Medical electronic equipment was responsible for generating 8 percent of Hewlett-Packard's $2.25 billion in revenues by the early 1980s, for example. American Hospital Supply, American Sterilizer, C.R. Bard, and Baxter Travenol provided everything from sterilizing equipment, disposable hospital supplies, and scalpels to the burgeoning health system. All generated billions in revenues and double-digit profit rates between 1965 and 1980. The pharmaceutical and medical supply components of the health care system contributed heavily to its assuming the characteristics of a "medical-industrial complex."[140]

As postwar government support increased to support medical education and biomedical research, AHCs burgeoned. As Ginzberg noted, "For the first fifteen years of enlarged appropriations 1950–1965, the universities and medical schools were often in a catch-up game; the federal government had more money to distribute than the medical centers were capable of absorbing effectively."[141] This helps explain why—of the three sectors of the medical profession* and sectors of the health system they dominated—the AHCs grew at least twice as fast as 1950s predictions, becoming what many referred to as "health empires" in the process. Following precedents established by Johns Hopkins (1893) and Columbia-Presbyterian (1910–1928) in New York City, hubs were created around university-affiliated medical schools and their network of hospitals that were supplemented after World War II by series of research institutes. During the 1960s and 1970s, responding to pressures generated by academic medicine, accrediting agencies, and research agendas, networks radiating from the AHCs** were created by absorption or affiliations with community hospitals, especially those with residency programs. By 1974, as Hammonds observed:

> *Medical schools, medical centers, and large hospitals control the resources for a wide geographical area through networks of affiliations. For example, Einstein Medical College and Montefiore Hospital control 2000 of the 2700 practicing doctors in the Bronx, New York, as well as neighborhood health clinics and experimental projects for its ghetto areas. Similar situations exist in Boston, Cleveland, Baltimore, and Seattle.*[142]

---

*The medical profession informally evolved into three major segments following World War II: institution-based, often academic, physicians; the majority of practicing physicians who followed their patients into the suburbs; and the medical "third world"—consisting of Black physicians, dark-skinned foreign physicians, and older physicians who maintained their practices in deteriorating, demographically changing, inner cities often surrounded by, but apart from, AHCs. See Chapter 3 for details.

**There were seven such networks in New York City, six in Chicago, and five in Philadelphia.

By the 1970s urban health empires controlled 32 percent of the general hospital beds in Detroit and 79 percent in Philadelphia.

As the medical-industrial complex grew in the urban areas, these institutions, whose agendas emphasized profits, research, and teaching instead of patient care, developed symbiotic, but flawed, relationships with the inner-city, heavily minority communities that had grown up around them. As Barbara and John Ehrenrich noted in *The American Health Empire: Power, Profit, and Politics,*

> *Profits, research, and teaching ... are independent functions of the medical system, not just adjuncts to patient care. Patients are the indispensable ingredient of medical profit-making, research, and education. In order that the medical industry serve these functions, patient care must be twisted to meet the needs of these other "medical" enterprises.*[143]

Patterns of care established then are recognizable today. Rich patients became profitable because "They can afford luxury ... [and] for them, the medical system produces a luxury commodity—the most painstaking, super technological treatment possible; special cosmetic care to preserve youth, or to add or subtract fatty tissue; even sumptuous private hospital rooms with carpeting and a selection of wines at meals."[144] As the Ehrenriechs observed about New York City of the 1970s, "The poor, on the other hand, serve chiefly to subsidize medical research and education—with their bodies."[145] Alonzo Yerby, former commissioner of hospitals in New York City, stated at a 1967 White House Conference on Health:

> *The pervasive stigma of charity permeates our arrangements for health care for the disadvantaged, and whether the program is based upon the private practice of medicine or upon public or non-profit clinics and hospitals, it tends to be piecemeal, poorly supervised, and uncoordinated.... In most of our larger cities, the hospital outpatient department, together with the emergency [room], provide the basic sources of care for the poor. Today's outpatient department[s] still retain some of the attributes of their predecessors, the 18th century free dispensaries. They are crowded, uncomfortable, lacking in concern for human dignity and, to make it worse, no longer free.*[146]

Dr. Yerby "called on physicians of the country to help bring about equal access to health services ... in such a way ... [that] 'the poor will no longer be forced to barter their dignity for their health.'"[147] The middle class was caught in the middle: "The majority of Americans have enough money to buy their way out of being used for research, but not enough to buy luxury care. Medical care for the middle class is, like any other commodity, aimed at a mass market: the profits are based on volume, not on high quality."[148] Expansion of AHC laboratories, erection of private patient pavilions, and provision of housing for faculty and staff were not enough.

"As teaching and research programs have expanded, these institutions have sought greater access to 'teaching material' (poor patients) through control of outposts such as public hospitals and neighborhood health centers."[149] This ongoing monopolization of health care resources, urban real estate (which is rendered nontaxable when purchased by academic institutions), and public funding predicted the fall of AHC empires as they became more identifiable and culpable as the source of many health system and neighborhood problems. Conflicts generated when patient care became secondary to economic considerations during the 1965 to 1980 era helped create the "crisis" perceived by poor and middle-class patients. These conflicts contributed to the erosion of confidence in physicians and the medical establishment.

Simultaneously, America's biomedical research infrastructure experienced spectacular growth, largely from government largesse, between 1965 and 1980. Although the huge overall annual growth rates in total funds of 16 percent per year, with a growth of 18 percent per year in federal funding between 1950 and 1965, were things of the past, the 1966 to 1982 period experienced a 3.2 percent annual increase in total funds and a 2.1 percent annual increase in federal funding. The rise in biomedical research spending from $1.9 to $9.5 billion in current dollars, a fivefold increase between 1966 and 1982, was still impressive.

The federal government took its cue from its wartime experience, public expectations, and Vannevar Bush's influential 1945 report, *Science: The Endless Frontier*, which predicted "the excellent prospects for achieving striking advances in the health of the American people if the government would continue and expand its funding of biomedical research."[150] Prior to 1965, the federal government "made huge sums available for construction and equipment and training grants to increase the supply of future investigators, as well as clinical center grants to enable selected medical schools to explore specialty areas or to strengthen their general clinical research base."[151] However, this funding was concentrated at a select group of major research-oriented universities on the East and West Coasts, which utilized the period to "set about expanding staff and facilities to be better positioned to compete for the ever-growing pool of federal dollars."[152] However, as Ruth Hanft, Linda Fishman, and Wendy Evans pointed out in the Association of Minority Health Professions Schools (AMHPS) report, *Blacks and the Health Professions in the 80s: A National Crisis and a Time for Action*: "[T]he financing of the minority health professions schools differs substantially from the majority schools. Sources of revenue are less diverse and some minority schools derive little revenue from biomedical research."[153] Thus, very little of this funding above vital necessities filtered down to Meharry, Howard, or the other African American health professions institutions.

By 1965 government was funding 65 percent of biomedical research. For the first time state and local governments, whose participation had previously been too small to be measured, contributed 2 percent to that total. The nonprofit sector reached an all-time high of 53 percent, while the for-profit sector (industry) declined

7 percentage points from 1960 levels to 27 percent, although it must be remembered "[i]ndustry for the most part, then as now, uses its research and development (R&D) funds for applied research and development aimed at improving existing products and bringing new products to market."[154] Foreign performers contributed 3 percent. Institutions of higher education such as research-oriented universities, medical schools and hospitals, and specialized nonprofit institutions continued to perform most of the basic biomedical research in the United States. This contrasted with European "models of government-sponsored research institutions, under ministerial direction and oversight, as the principal recipients of R&D funds."[155] Despite the admonitions of medical school deans, university presidents, and organizations such as the American Association of Medical Colleges, biomedical research funding dwindled to a stream during the late 1960s.

In reality, the biomedical research funding stream was divided into several smaller tributaries. In response to a changing social and political climate:

> *President Johnson ... noted that the federal government had supplied about two out of every three dollars for research in the past decade and a half in the hope of achieving significant breakthroughs in medical knowledge and techniques, and that it was time to bring such discoveries as had been made to Americans wherever they lived, even those distant from the centers of medical excellence.[156]*

In the spirit of Medicare/Medicaid and the Great Society programs, the president noted: "[I]f significant breakthroughs from research were not yet imminent, it might be ... advisable to redirect federal funds to expanding and improving programs that could improve access to health care for the uninsured and underinsured."[157] The 1966 Regional Medical Program (RMP) was one effort to speed up the diffusion of recent medical advances from the major educational and research centers to the rest of America. However, in less than four years RMPs had "given up on their original missions of planning and regionalization and become little more than funding sources for medical school's pet projects."[158] Thus, by alternative methods, funding for research and teaching in AHCs was sustained:

> *By the late 1960s and early 1970s, with the expanded research infrastructure largely in place, federal appropriations in constant dollars had begun to level off. The financial position of the AHCs was shored up in part by the new dollars that began to flow from ... Medicare and Medicaid, which compensated ... for the decrease in funding from the NIH and other federal agencies. Between 1963 and 1976 the flow of federal funds for the expansion of medical school facilities and for increased student enrollments provided yet additional sources of support for medical schools.[159]*

For minority health professions training and research institutions, even these funding sources did not ameliorate their fiscal problems. The Association of Minority Health Professions Schools' (AMHPS) report detailed some of the revenue shortages in minority schools:

> *Patient care revenue is a lesser source of revenue in all minority health professions schools. Clinical revenues remain a problem in two of the three medical schools, the dental and pharmacy schools. Hospital and clinic revenues, a substantial source of revenue for majority schools, currently contribute few funds to minority schools. The low socioeconomic status of patients cared for by faculty of minority medical schools make practice plan revenue a smaller potential source of revenue for these schools.[160]*

The report goes on to point out how these schools' restricted affiliations (often due to discrimination) with public institutions (e.g., public hospitals and VA facilities),* to which majority institutions have easy access, compromise their missions of training minority health professionals. Moreover, the report implies, and authorities such as James Summerville, W. Montague Cobb, and Mark L. Walker corroborate, the negative political environments in which Black health professions schools must function and the strained, often hostile, relationships these institutions endure with contiguous, powerful, White medical institutions.[161] These forces negatively affect them financially and educationally, thwart their research efforts, and impair their ability to attract stellar faculty.

Another source of research funding bloomed in the early 1970s. After President Nixon's declaration of a "war on cancer," the allocation of funds to the National Cancer Institute increased from $170 million in 1971 to almost $400 million in 1976—over one-third of the NIH appropriation. Moreover, as Ginzberg noted, "In 1976 and 1977 the NIH was still able to make about $23 million a year available for the construction of research facilities at universities and medical schools."[162] Although more restrictive funding practices for biomedical research and training lay ahead, the 1965 to 1980 period was one of prosperity for the White biomedical education and research infrastructure.[163]

### The Ascendency of Ambulatory Care and Voluntary Health Agencies: Separate Development and Moral Ambiguity

In 1930, four in ten encounters between physicians and patients took place in a patient's home, and only one in 16 physicians worked in a hospital full-time. By the

---

*Although both Meharry and Vanderbilt are private medical schools located in Nashville, Tennessee, Meharry and its training programs were locked out of the Nashville VA hospital and the public bond–funded children's hospital.

1950s only one in ten doctor-patient encounters took place in patient's homes and one in six doctors worked in hospitals full-time. Despite a great deal of medical work being shifted to hospitals by the 1960s, the majority of doctor-patient encounters—those that occurred with non-bed patients outside institutions—were categorized as ambulatory care. Between 1965 and 1980 most ambulatory care—which by definition is personal health care provided to an individual through other than community or public health services—took place in physicians' offices. These encounters were grounded in the traditions of individual doctor-patient relationships, fee-for-service financing arrangements, individual and professional autonomy, and vertical relationships between physicians and their lay clientele. Ambulatory care also epitomized many of the health system's fundamental problems—lack of universal access, perverse incentives for service delivery, maldistribution of medical care and health services, overemphasis on individual doctor-patient relationships, inadequate financing mechanisms, and prevalent race and class discrimination. As if to confirm David Rutstein's allegation, "our major gap in medical care, ambulatory services" waited to "be repaired by a new system."[164] He discerned that the dysfunction in the ambulatory care sector reflected the fact that overall community health status and outcome were minor considerations in our health system.

A major liberal agenda item left over from the postwar years was increasing access to health services to remaining underserved populations such as the medically indigent, African Americans, the disabled, and the increasing ranks of the elderly poor. This second round* of extending health services to the poor and underserved required another expansion of outpatient facilities in urban and rural poverty areas. Based on the evidence, the race and class dimensions and implications of this process were unanticipated and largely unplanned for.

Between 1965 and 1980 important qualitative and quantitative changes took place in ambulatory care and the facilities required for its delivery. This was a response to the fact that despite previous concerns and programs, "The evidence grew that health care was still essentially a privilege with a price tag and that for the poor it was unavailable, inaccessible, inappropriate in its organization and focus, and ineffective in its delivery."[165] Early in the period, primary ambulatory care services became more accessible to large blocs of the population, especially among disadvantaged minorities and the poor. Later in the period, fueled by the astronomical cost inflation and government augmented cash flows associated with inpatient services, traditional emergency rooms, and hospital-based clinics, the nature of outpatient care diversified into surgery (surgicenters) and the provision of care for minor emergencies and primary care with the emergence of freestanding

---

*The first round of the federal government extending health services to underserved U.S. populations arbitrarily spanned from the New Deal initiatives in the 1930s to the postwar health system expansion throughout the South promulgated by Hill-Burton funding. Medicare/Medicaid could be considered part of the second round. All were basically Democratic Party initiatives.

"emergi-centers."* For some of the same health financing, but predominantly for medical-social, demographic, and often racial reasons,**[166] another important new kind of ambulatory care facility, the neighborhood or, later, community health centers (NHCs and CHCs), designed to help the poor and underserved, were created and soon became permanent fixtures in American health care delivery.

Through President Johnson's War on Poverty, "health care was a part of the Great Society package—but not in terms of structural change in the health care system."[167] H. Jack Geiger's analysis of this round of reforms was crystalline:

> *The centerpieces of the liberal reform effort, Medicaid for the poor and Medicare for the elderly (poor and nonpoor alike), were limited to the financing of health care. They reimbursed physicians and hospitals ... on their own terms and without significant change in the location, organization, or control of their services ... delivered in their usual and customary ways. A third component, the maternal- and child-health program, offered inducements to existing medical care providers to extend and organize services to these high-need groups more coherently, and did establish minimum standards as criteria for funding.... But, in early 1965 a fourth component—the neighborhood health center program—was proposed to the Office of Economic Opportunity.[168]*

The new ambulatory delivery model was also designed to remove financial barriers to access to health care, but had much broader goals:

> *These included (1) providing care, not merely assuring its funding; (2) creating a new kind of institution in the health care delivery system— neighborhood or community health centers, serving defined communities and populations, and combining curative and preventive services; (3) shifting the locus of services from hospital to local community, and the emphasis from complex tertiary care to primary care; (4) establishing new patterns of professional organization, with emphasis on multidisciplinary teams that included paraprofessionals recruited from the target communities; (5) broadening the scope of "medical" services to include health-related environmental and social concerns; and (6) giving the poor an assured role in the design and control of their own health services.[169]*

---

*The first freestanding "emergi-centers" were established in Delaware and Rhode Island in 1973. These facilities, which spread nationwide, provide care for minor emergencies and nonurgent patients—some for 24 hours per day, seven days a week. Other, "urgi-centers" or "Doc in the Box," facilities provide less comprehensive services with more limited hours.

**Authorities as varied as Andrew Hacker, Douglas Massey and Nancy Denton, Nicholas Lemann, David Barton Smith, and William Julius Wilson have noted that American public and economic policies have consciously or unconsciously promoted physical separation of the races in the United States.

This new form of health delivery, built around ambulatory service models, broke medical-social barriers in American health care. It was the provision of holistic health care for the individual as a member of the broader community. Improving health status and outcomes of previously shunned communities was envisioned as a tool for social empowerment and full participation in a wholesome democratic society. Thus, this was not just an extension of the old public clinic, settlement house movement present since the 1900s. It went beyond the menu of preventive, social welfare, and nutritional services, and was not bound by covenants to carefully "avoid even the threat of competition with fee-for-service private practice or hospital 'charity wards' and dispensaries."[170] That these new institutions were grounded in the concept of the right to health care as an entitlement, along with these other characteristics, probably doomed them to the fringes of the mainstream health system. They were plagued by the vagaries of separate development for the 4 to 5 million primarily minority and disadvantaged Americans they eventually served.

The origins of these new ambulatory care facilities stretched back to overseas models such as the Peckham Health Center in England, John Grant's work at Peking Union Medical College in China and, later, Puerto Rico, and Sidney Kark's work with health centers serving African and Indian populations in South Africa. These centers' missions were mirrored in the U.S. models by their epidemiological orientation and service to underprivileged populations that exhibited extreme poverty, high birth and death rates, heavy burdens of infectious and chronic diseases, high unemployment levels, low literacy rates, substandard housing and nutrition, and limited medical care resources. For the first time Blacks in the rural South and Northern urban ghettos, poor Appalachian Whites, Puerto Ricans in cities, Mexican Americans in the West and Southwest, and Native Americans on reservations and certain urban areas were targeted for comprehensive health services delivery. From the initial effort—the Columbia Point Health Center of Boston (June 1965)—to over 150 centers by 1971, the OEO provided $308 million and HEW another $110 million in funds. Most early start-up funding (1965–1966) went through hospitals, medical schools, and health departments, but by the early 1970s shifted to new health corporations (59 percent) composed of community groups in partnership with health providers. As Geiger noted:

> By 1982 there were 872 centers ... serving 4.2 million people. Of these, according to a 1976 survey, 71 percent were poor, 80 percent belonged to a minority, 49 percent had no employed family member, and 41 percent were under eighteen—in sum, the population that has the highest health risks, the greatest burden of illness, disability, and preventable death, the least access to primary care, and the highest rates of hospitalization.[171]

Documentation accrued suggesting these ambulatory centers improved all these parameters in the populations they served and also provided socioeconomic development (e.g., employment, job training) in their communities.

The health centers provided valuable health and social services to their communities. Karen Davis, at that time a deputy assistant secretary of HEW, evaluated the institutions' performance in 1981, noting that the

> health centers have been highly effective in increasing access to primary care, have reduced hospitalization and reduced costs, have maintained quality of care, have achieved good "market penetration" and continuous coverage of their target communities, and have made measurable (and sometimes striking) improvements in the health status of populations at very high risk of illness.[172]

Despite their constant struggles with community control—wherein health professionals were often in conflict with community representatives; a "scarcity of physical facilities adequate to house high-quality health services in poverty areas"[173]; and professional staffing shortages born of a training system wherein specialization and serving privileged populations were the ideals, the Achilles heel of this new system lay in the areas of politics and health financing.

By the 1970s health centers were under assault. Direct health center funding was cut, Medicaid and other reimbursement sources were reduced, categorical funding for preventive programs that the health centers were effective at implementing was terminated, and the management (and eventually the funding) of the health centers was largely turned over to the states whose historical failures and inabilities had created the needs for these institutions in the first place. Moreover, Congress limited health center enrollee eligibility requirements, subsidies for nonpaying patients, and fiscal administration in ways that kept them dependent on public funding. Initial estimates that Medicare and Medicaid reimbursements would pay up to 80 percent of their overhead were inflated—reimbursements never covered more than 10 to 20 percent. CHCs and NHCs were forced to mobilize community and political support to stave off closure and ensure their survival during the 1970s. Nevertheless, they suffered 200 closures by 1984. Moreover, when the Nixon and Ford administrations began dismantling OEO, the centers were turned over to HEW (1970–1973), which grouped them under the new Bureau of Community Health Services and, in the interest of cost-cutting, changed their mode of operating.

The emphasis shifted from the proven successes evidenced by improved health status of served communities and a decreased need for hospitalization (accomplished by providing comprehensive medical care and health services) to aggressively pursuing physician productivity; intensive third-party billing;

rigid administrative and fiscal controls; reduction in outreach, transportation, and other nontraditional health services; and defunding and deemphasizing community boards. Around the mid-1970s health centers were encouraged to "market" themselves to middle-class populations and engage in the competitive health marketplace.

Between 1964 and 1982, despite these impediments, the percentage of the population with no physician visits in the past two years declined from 19.1 to 13.2 percent. Among African Americans, the improvement was even more dramatic, declining from 26.6 percent to 12.7 percent in the same years. Health parameters such as infant mortality, maternal mortality, incidences of and mortality from many chronic diseases, and hospitalization rates, which will be discussed later, improved dramatically in populations served by health centers. A marginalized model of health care had proved so successful that some factions of the mainstream patient population demanded it be made available to them. Some components of the health center approach such as health care (multidisciplinary) teams, formal health promotion and disease prevention activities, and provision of ancillary services where indicated were incorporated into many "high-grade" health plans. Despite the system's overall isolation and the "mainstream" health system's rejection of the health center model, their effects were pervasive, and the system would never be the same.[174]

By this time, thousands of voluntary health agencies and organizations had been established both locally and nationally that were concerned with specific diseases and the constellation of problems associated with them. Others emphasized medical self-help (mutual aid associations). As prominent members of the nonprofit sector, they were supported wholly or in part by private contributions and efforts proffered by volunteers. The only quasi-official voluntary organization, designated as such by Congress, was the American National Red Cross, the "official" agency in national and international disaster relief situations. Other not-for-profit, often voluntary, sometimes charitable entities ("nonprofits") such as professional associations (the AMA, AAMC, AHA) and the medical specialty societies; philanthropic foundations such as the Rockefeller, Carnegie, and Robert Wood Johnson Foundations; not-for-profit hospitals, health institutions, and nursing homes; and public interest groups such as the Health Research Group, part of Public Citizen, Ralph Nader's organization, are considered within the components of the health system in which they are most intimately connected.

The thousands of voluntary health agencies (VHAs) that had arisen in the United States by 1965, such as the American Cancer Society (ACS), the American Heart Association (AHA), the National Foundation for Infantile Paralysis (NFIP), and the American Lung Association (ALA), were charitable organizations. One might think, then, that these charitable health agencies' primary foci, by definition, would be poor, disadvantaged, and health-needy populations. African Americans, the least healthy and poorest population subgroup, along with other health-disadvantaged Americans, should have been disproportionate beneficiaries. However, this was often not the case, for as James T. Bennett and Thomas J. DiLorenzo, authorities on the political economy of the nonprofit sector and authors of the sole objective and evaluative report on VHAs since the 1980s, observed, "To a large extent some health charities seem to benefit primarily the medical establishment rather than disease victims, their families, or the public."[175] This helped explain Bakal's observation regarding the deviation of many health charities from their primary missions: "All too frequently, the offer of help to medically indigent patients is nothing more than a referral to community agencies (which, in turn, are often unable to help).... Where care actually is provided, it may duplicate that already available from other resources in the community or be of questionable quality."[176] Seemingly, as VHAs succeeded in their pursuit of fund-raising, public education, political lobbying, professional education, and scientific research throughout the 1970s, becoming major political players in the biomedical research funding process on Capitol Hill, their commitment and linkages to the poor, their primary mission, seemingly wavered, then waned.

Major problems emerged during the 1965 to 1980 era with regard to charitable health agencies, as in other sectors of the nonprofit community, that could be grouped around accountability and performance evaluation. Not held to the same incentive-based standards as for-profit enterprises (pleasing consumers, withstanding the rigor of competitive markets, satisfying investors and stockholders, and dealing with the regulatory apparatus) or government agencies (subject to taxpayer scrutiny, being publically accountable, liable to the electoral and political process), nonprofit entities, especially charities, "tend to be judged more by their self-professed good intentions than by their performance, they typically escape the close public scrutiny that private businesses (and even government entities) receive."[177] What the public knew about nonprofit entities such as charities and hospitals was self-reported and, all too often, self-serving. As Bennett and DiLorenzo noted, "most charities—both large and small—suffer from bureaucratic inertia and diminished effectiveness."[178] Moreover, as the founders with their missionary zeal was replaced by professionals who considered the organization as a source of economic security and livelihood, fund-raising and wealth accumulation often replaced charitable services as prime motivators. Ostensibly founded to serve the public good, nonprofits and health charities, unlike for-profit businesses or government enterprises, were:

> viewed as motivated by neither profit nor political advancement. Supposedly, their only concern is "doing good." Therefore, criticisms of charities are often construed as criticisms of charitable activities themselves, and only a hard-hearted Scrooge or a dyed-in-the-wool Grinch with highly questionable motives would criticize charity. Charities have thus become

*sacred cows, even in the eyes of the media; nonprofits are therefore spared the public and media scrutiny that businesses and government routinely receive—at least until a scandal ... breaks.*[179]

Therefore, health charities, and nonprofits in general, were not controlled by or accountable to consumers, contributors, shareholders, voters, the media, or public opinion. An enormous potential for mischief emerged during this period.

By 1965 signs of trouble loomed ahead in the voluntary nonprofit sector of the health system. VHAs were prone to some of the same problems plaguing other nonprofit sectors of the health system (e.g., hospitals and nursing homes) at the organizational and managerial levels. The nonprofits' structural and organizational defects of self-perpetuating, no-risk, voluntary boards answerable to no one; virtually independent upper-level management whose survival was not judged by conventional performance criteria; the absence of the usual incentives (the bottom line, competition, public accountability) for meticulous board or administrative oversight; overreliance on volunteers in key management and administrative positions; a presumption of, and overreliance on, trust and goodwill; year-end spending binges; and voluntary, selective, public reporting were laid bare. These potential problems were exacerbated for the health charities, especially VHAs, by overreliance on medical professionals for board-level and administrative leadership, which tended to sway the organizational agenda and the organizations' medical-social roles and engender nonbusinesslike traits in their organization and management. For example, the NFIP board's discovery in 1972 that its "'unpaid volunteer' president ... was actually paying himself a salary of $100,000 (more than $300,000 in current dollars), plus an expense account of over $70,000 for his 'part-time volunteer' job,"[180] sent shock waves throughout the nonprofit infrastructure. A 1975 report on nonprofit hospitals by the United States General Accounting Office: "found 'overlapping interests' (a euphemism for conflicts of interest) at seventeen of the nineteen nonprofit hospitals it investigated. In six of the nineteen hospitals, 25 percent or more of the board members had conflicts of interest."[181] The report disclosed overlapping interest involving banks serving the hospitals, providers of legal services to hospitals, and health providers connected with the hospitals. These findings substantiated sociologists Amatai Etzioni and Pamela Doty's arguments that: "omissions, ambiguities, and loopholes in the laws make it possible for the trustees and staff of not-for-profit corporations to engage in a variety of financial practices which bring them personal profits."[182] Nonprofit nursing homes were also found to be culpable. Mary Mendelson in her 1974 exposé *Tender Loving Greed* concluded that:

*the term "nonprofit" does not mean what it would seem to mean: there are plenty of opportunities for profit in a nonprofit operation. All it*

> *means is that the [nursing] home by law does not produce profits for tax purposes: it does not return cash dividends to its owners.... Once having achieved nonprofit status, the home enjoys some important advantages. It does not pay income taxes, in some states it does not pay the local property tax, and in various places it is exempt from water taxes. It also enjoys official favor. The federal government and foundations prefer nonprofit operations in giving grants for special projects.[183]*

Since health charities shared the same structures and incentives as nonprofit hospitals and nursing homes, the same risks for conflicts of interest and exploitation existed.

Health charities ranked at least fourth in contributions from all sources, receiving $1.6 billion in revenues in 1965 and $2.4 billion in 1970, an increase of 50 percent. These organizations gained the respect of the American public over the years and "have been granted many special privileges by government to encourage their activities and to provide subsidies that lower their operating costs."[184] With their growing emphasis on research and professional education, the major health charities fulfilled their needs for organizational survival and expansion while straying farther from their implicit missions of service and resource provision for the needy. As Bakal revealed:

> A "surprising, little-known fact" about the health charities ... is that their expenditures on research "represent only a small fraction of all dollars spent on research in this country.... Most ... now comes from the government, usually for programs to battle the same ailments as the health agencies." Nevertheless, "some health agencies tend to emphasize research in their fund-raising appeals because this come-on has been found to attract the most money, although many [health charities] actually devote larger portions of their budgets to other activities."[185]

Nevertheless, the voluntary health sector is credited with lobbying successfully for the meteoric expansion of the national research budget from $1.884 billion in 1965 to $7.969 billion in 1980, a four-fold expansion—$1.174 billion (61 percent) in 1965 and $4.723 billion (69 percent) in 1980 being federal funding.[186] Tailored by AMA and VHA recommendations, much of this largesse was channeled through the NIH and its various institutes and through AHCs and their functionaries. Through mechanisms of controlling the national research, research publishing, and research funding agendas, major health charities, the medical profession— which founded, headed, and administered the AHCs, the VHAs, and much of the

NIH—and the federal government almost became another iron triangle* for biomedical research funding on Capitol Hill during this era.

As early as 1921 the Rockefeller Foundation expressed concerns about the plethora of health charities engaging in behavior that was "unscientific, wasteful, and misleading."[187] Unimpressed by this admonishment, the voluntary health infrastructure was indicted by another Rockefeller Foundation–sponsored report conducted in 1945 by Selskar M. Gunn and Philip S. Platt, health experts of the first rank, who presented: "a devastating and carefully documented picture of useless activities, of failure to take up new problems and serve developing needs, of waste of contributors' money, and failure to achieve health-protection goals that should long since have been reached and passed."[188] The study's recommendations to correct the unscientific, wasteful, and misleading behaviors of health charities were ignored. Another study funded by the same foundation in 1961 recommended uniform accounting procedures and a national commission to oversee the activities of health charities. After some 15 years, uniform accounting procedures were adopted by most major health charities, but they were "uniformly confusing and uninformative—as much is hidden as is revealed."[189] The second "recommendation was ... ignored by the executives and members of health-charity boards of directors, who apparently were convinced that they were above well-meaning and constructive criticism."[190] Although the voluntary health infrastructure continued to do a great deal of good, especially in generating public and political pressure for biomedical research, informing the public of the importance of particular diseases, and marshaling America's strong voluntary spirit toward health causes, storm clouds loomed ahead. Questions were raised about whether a trusting and well-meaning public would continue to support a voluntary health care infrastructure that increasingly distanced itself from its eleemosynary roots; spent the public's charity resources on research and educational agendas and projects primarily benefiting privileged individuals and elite institutions; and engaged in poorly documented, sometimes misleading, occasionally downright inaccurate, if not dangerous, advertising. The health charity infrastructure's future did not seem secure if it maintained a "business as usual" posture.[191]

## The Health "Crisis" Endgame: Government as the Culprit and Enemy

Although some improvements in health care outcomes, access, and utilization secondary to the redistributive and regulatory reforms in the health system occurred during the 1960s and 1970s—especially for Blacks and the poor—

---

*Iron triangle* is a widely used public policy term referring to "the symbiotic partnership of military services, defense contractors, and members of Congress from states and districts where military spending is heavy and visible" (Smith). Eli Ginzberg and others have alluded to the close relationships between health system players (e.g., doctors, patients, and hospitals), interest groups and increased government involvement in health care proved to be a double-edged sword. A covenant was struck between the medical establishment and President Johnson's victorious political team that had won the Medicare and Medicaid "wars"—a covenant that tilted legal and health financing changes resulting after 1965 toward perpetuating the doctor-patient relationship (preserving fee-for-service and freedom of choice for doctor and patient) and not threatening traditional health system institutions or practices. Subsequent turmoil was inevitable. Thus, major health system defects remained and new problems were generated. Besides triggering a cascade of economic and regulatory activity in response to subsequent health care cost inflation, "the ... long-term acceleration of health care costs ... came to play the dominant role in shifting the power center of American medicine away from physicians."[192] Financially, things got so bad that by the late 1970s, health care came to be viewed as another liberal reform measure that had spun out of control.

By 1980 there was a generalized public perception, especially among the European American majority, that "big government" was the problem. Such perceptions were generated by lingering effects of counterculture and social movements and changes from the "wild" 1960s; the economic and foreign policy turmoil of the 1970s; the perceived failure of the welfare state to solve U.S. social problems; unpleasant (school integration, forced busing, affirmative action) and sometimes violent (urban race riots) confrontations generated by the Civil Rights Movement; and an unbridled growth of government spending and activism (the federal courts, social programs, regulatory activities). Critics felt "the welfare state has become 'overloaded' and Western democracies have become 'ungovernable.'"[193] Conservatives alleged that the politically mediated role of the state in resource allocation and income distribution raised unrealistic expectations and highlighted the inherent conflict between the political process and efficiency. As Paul Starr observed, "This combination of circumstances gave conservatives an opportunity to carry out broad cutbacks not only in government expenditures but also in government functions."[194] Downsizing, reprivatization, program terminations and funding cuts, block grants to states at lower funding levels, and competition were some of the conservative strategies that gained in popularity as solutions to the nation's problems.

The new conservative mood also affected the health system between 1965 and 1980. Conservatives, physicians, and the medical establishment had resisted post–World War II health system reforms on the basis of "voluntarism" (voluntary health insurance, voluntary patient choice of provider, providers voluntarily rendering services to patients they chose under the charitable circumstances they

---

contractors (e.g., insurance companies, HMOs, the pharmaceutical industry), and the Congress as another "iron triangle" or "medical triangle." Sources: Smith H. *The Power Game: How Washington Works.* New York: Ballantine Books, 1988, 173–78, 173; Ginzberg E. *The Medical Triangle: Physicians, Politicians, and the Public.* Cambridge, MA: Harvard University Press, 1990.

chose), potent political lobbying, and massive public advertising campaigns. The conservative shift to "competition" in the early 1970s manifested initially as government endorsements and funding of managed care projects and HMOs. When these competitive models failed to reign in health care cost inflation, broader-based competitive strategies appeared. By 1975 Duke University law professor Clark Havighurst "formulated proposals for expanding antitrust activity in the health care field, which the Federal Trade Commission entered in 1975"[195] to foster competition. The most sophisticated and influential statement of a "market" approach to health policy was developed by Stanford economist Alain Enthoven, who formulated a competitive model for national health insurance. This laid the foundation for the last adaptation of conservative strategy, which proposed that: "The problems of health care in America could be cured by relying on competition and incentives, if only government's role were reduced to a minimum."[196] Concurrently, almost silently, the health system emerged as a major macroeconomic entity in the United States economy.

Instead of a unitary, universal health system designed to serve the public, rational health planning, and organization—to be held accountable for efficiency and delivering quality care as solutions to the nation's health system financing, organizational, maldistribution, and medical-social problems—early government interventions into expanding medical care and health services fueled a transformation of the health care political landscape and created a jumble of corporate, for-profit health institutions and organizations alongside new forms of medical and health services delivery for the poor and underserved. More disturbing was the fact, intended or not, that the system remained truncated along race and class lines, as the poor were seldom included in the heavily funded mainstream health system expansion. Although never articulated or openly implemented as a policy, "separate development" of the health system for different populations seemed to apply.

Despite marked improvements in access and a proliferation of delivery models, race-, socioeconomic-, and class-based health disparities remained in virtually every measurable health parameter. Race and class barriers and geographic and social separation in the health system were maintained, often by new and innovative mechanisms. What began early in the period as a "first step" in a hopeful and progressive transformation from a provincial, eleemosynary, autonomous health nonsystem that excluded blocs of Americans based on race, social custom, and socioeconomic status toward a universal health system, evolved into an emerging and variegated corporate giant with increasing market-like characteristics with caste-like delivery tracts for Blacks and the poor.

Within a decade after enactment, Medicare was covering less than one-half of the health expenditures of the nation's elderly, and the Medicaid program covered less than half of the U.S. poor. Moreover, a new type of medical indigency was created by the "Medicaid–private insurance corridor"—a purgatory of the categorical social welfare system wherein the very poor were eligible for Medicaid and millions of poor, near-poor, and working poor Americans, excluded from private health insurance for a plethora of workplace and political-economic reasons, were left in limbo. As E. Richard Brown pointed out, being poor was not enough: "The poor who do not wear a 'label' that qualifies them for Medicaid are left far behind the Medicaid-eligible poor and nonpoor groups."[197] Categories of people completely outside both the "mainstream" and indigency systems were part-time workers, recently unemployed workers, the working poor unable to afford individual insurance, and those too well-off to require public assistance. Although most of these Americans, many of whom were Black, were in the work force, due to their lack of health insurance they were outside the mainstream health system. The problem is a persistent and growing one today.

Due to poor enforcement, a lack of commitment by most of the institutions, and inadequate funding and institutionalization of equal opportunity, only token desegregation of the nation's medical education and training programs occurred. The vitally needed Black medical schools, Meharry and Howard, which were still producing more than 80 percent of African American physicians (2.1 percent of American physicians in 1970) at the beginning of the era, were eventually joined by several other institutions in California (Charles R. Drew University of Medicine and Science, founded 1978), Georgia (Morehouse School of Medicine, founded 1975), New Jersey (University of Medicine and Dentistry of New Jersey at Newark [UMDNJ]), and New York (the Sophie Davis School)* to help ameliorate the problems of health deprivation in underserved areas. Again, commitment varied, funding was uncertain, and these institutions survived as best they could. Some were threatened with closure during the period in lieu of the federally primed expansion of all components of the U.S. health system. By 1980 there were almost five times as many Black medical school graduates (768, or 5.1 percent of the total graduates), 23.2 percent of whom graduated from minority medical schools. Despite the efforts, which by 1980 were waning, African Americans constituted 2.6 percent of the nation's physicians.

The overall mix of health system changes provided fertile soil for the "competitive strategy" implemented by the Reagan administration after 1980. These changes included the naïve attempts to expand access to medical services and health care without fundamentally changing the system; the explosive growth of government expenditures on health, which generated cost inflation, exploitation, and waste; unsuccessful attempts to control health care costs inflation; the perceived failure of health programs to eliminate disease and improve health in lieu of astronomical costs by both liberal and conservative leadership; a stepwise shift toward conservative, ideologically driven, com-

---

*The Sophie Davis School was an affiliate of the City College of New York established to provide preclinical training to many minority students pursuing a medical education.

petitive "market" solutions to the health system's problems; the meteoric rise of the for-profit, corporate sector in the health system; the silent, often unacknowledged improvements in health status and outcomes for African American and poor citizens despite pervasive health system flaws; the half-hearted attempts at desegregating the health and medical education/research systems; the perceived doctor glut (despite glaring minority underrepresentation in the health professions); clumsy attempts at government regulation of health care; and the failed attempts at comprehensive health planning. The competitive strategy, plus Reagan's policies of cutting "public regulation, public health services, and public financing for the personal health services for the poor,"[198] predicted troubled times for African American patients and the United States health system. Events were taking place that favored the rise of corporate medicine and health care.[199]

---

## Sun Pierces the Shadows: One Step Forward, Two Steps Backward—Black Health, 1965–1980

> *[T]he unlettered Negro elder statesman of the south ... was asked,*
> *"What do your people want?" He answered, "nothing specially. They*
> *don't want no special schools, no special place to live, no special jobs, no*
> *special hospitals or wards, no special drinking fountains. They just want*
> *each child to go to the best school he can, each man to get the best job*
> *he can, go to the best hospital he can, to be a good laborer, a good*
> *soldier, a good doctor, and dream of being President like anybody else in*
> *the country—if he can."*
> —Leonidas H. Berry, M.D., 1966

The 1965 to 1980 period was a watershed in the health of African Americans. Amazing health progress was tempered by history-based racial health deficit legacies; a health system torn between a population that was doing better, according to objective health indicators, while metaphorically "feeling worse," according to a cabal of public and health policy makers; and a health system burdened by lingering race and class problems. Although improvements in health status and outcomes were noted for all groups throughout the period, Blacks never came close to achieving parity with Whites. This helps explain why M. Alfred Haynes's classic 1975 study, "The Gap in Health Status Between Black and White Americans," documenting the racial health gap early in the period based on the latest available health indicator and services data,[200] struck like a thunderbolt piercing any complacency surrounding Black health or the struggle that lay ahead. (See Figure 4.1.)

By 1980 African Americans numbered 26.5 million or 11.7 percent of the

**Figure 4.1**
**M. Alfred Haynes (1921– )**
First to document the halt in health
progress in 1975 and to predict the
Black Health Crisis of the 1980s
and 1990s, Haynes served as presi-
dent of the Charles R. Drew Post-
graduate Medical School in 1979
and leads in efforts to ameliorate
the African American cancer crisis.
   Courtesy of W. Michael
Byrd/Linda A. Clayton, *African
American Public Health and
Medical History Slide Collection*,
Harvard School of Public Health,
Boston, MA.

U.S. population. The age distribution of the Black population was markedly
different than Whites. Only 7.9 percent of the Black population was over 65
years old, 58.8 percent under 30, and 33.4 percent between 30 and 64 years of
age, compared to 12.1 percent, 48 percent, and 40 percent, respectively, for
Whites. In spite of a younger population (which logic dictates should be healthier) with a higher fertility rate than European Americans, the Department of
Health and Human Services, based on 1980 statistics, noted: "With regard to
disease-specific mortality, blacks have higher age-adjusted death rate for 13 of
the 15 leading causes of death."[201] Blacks also experienced higher overall mortality rates and shorter lifespans than any other population group—a 361-year-
continuum by 1980. The causes of the African American's profound and
history-based health deficits were, and continue to be, multiple. Explanations
and causes for the nation's legacy of poor Black health status and outcomes rest
somewhere within the realm of the determinants of health itself. These determinants, according to John M. Last, can be classified as *hereditary* or *acquired*
or, alternatively, can be classified under headings such as *physical, biological,
behavioral, social, cultural,* or *spiritual.*[202] Nevertheless, by the 1980s health
analyst–epidemiologist Antonio René observed, "In recent years there has been
increased interest in the role of the U.S. health care delivery system in
accounting for health status differences."[203] Haynes also documented that the

racial health status and outcome differences were strongly related to health system access problems: "it is shown that many of the differences are related to the accessibility of medical care, which in turn is largely influenced by socioeconomic factors."[204] Of the 15 groups listed on the race item of the 1980 U.S. census—White, Black, American Indian, Eskimo, Aleut, Chinese, Filipino, Japanese, Asian Indian, Korean, Vietnamese, Hawaiian, Samoan, Guamanian, and "Other"—Blacks continued to be the largest minority group. African Americans were also burdened with the lowest median income, the highest levels of poverty (34.2 percent versus 11.2 percent for Whites), low educational levels, and, as has been stated, the worst health status and outcome of any other racial or ethnic group. Over 50 percent of Blacks still lived in the South. Tracking the health of African Americans throughout this tumultuous and conflicted period is a daunting and complex challenge.

The "Great Equation," that "Medical Care Equals Health,"[205] is one of the great American commonsense myths about health and has exerted much influence in health policy circles. Aaron Wildavsky's perceptive 1977 analysis of the concept in "Doing Better and Feeling Worse: The Political Pathology of Health Policy"—although based on some assumptions not readily applicable to most African Americans—revealed that:

> the Great Equation is wrong. More available medical care does not equal better health. The best estimates are that the medical system (doctors, drugs, hospitals) affect about 10 per cent of the usual indices for measuring health: whether you live at all (infant mortality), how well you live (days lost due to sickness), how long you live (adult mortality). The remaining 90 per cent are determined by factors over which doctors have little or no control, from individual life style (smoking, exercise, worry), to social conditions (income, eating habits, physiological inheritance), to the physical environment (air and water quality).[206]

Nevertheless, partially due to his assuming a nonexistent homogeneity of circumstance, place, and treatment of America's various patient populations in the health system, Wildavsky's rational analysis does not explain the tremendous leap forward in health status and outcome experienced by African Americans during the Civil Rights Era in Health Care between 1965 and 1975. Other evidence suggests his 10 percent estimate may not be applicable to all underserved racial or ethnic groups in the U.S. health system. As Karen Davis noted about another health-disadvantaged group, "Statistics on American Indians suggest that, during a period of greatly increased expenditures for Indian health care, there have been quite astonishing drops in mortality rates from a number of causes amenable to better medical care."[207] Despite the perceived health system "crisis" and retrospective projections of failure of government medical and social programs, groups such as African Americans and Native Americans benefited mightily from these efforts.

Such findings suggest that the 1965–1975 decade is comparable in many ways to the 7-year period between 1865 and 1872 (some would argue the period lasted 12 years until 1877), when the federal government actively intervened in the health system for the first time, providing health services to the African American population along with well-known rations, education, and civil rights programs afforded by the Freedmen's Bureau legislation. (See Chapter 6, Volume 1.) These were federal responses to the abrupt dismantling of the "slave health subsystem," the socioeconomic and political collapse of the South and its plantation and slave systems, and the abandoning of uneducated, untrained, previously medically dependent slave populations into a depressed but competitive postwar economy. The resulting freefall in Black health status leading to the deaths of from one-fourth to one-third of the freedmen during the early years of the Reconstruction[208] goaded the post–Civil War Congress into passing what was equivalent to disaster relief (which included health care) legislation today.[209] Although this first Reconstruction was a laudable attempt to correct and equalize the poor status and outcomes of destitute Black and White citizens, the American public grew impatient with the active government intervention (i.e., Freedmen's Bureau programs, public schools, land grant colleges, egalitarian state constitutions) that benefited underprivileged populations until well into the twentieth century. Thus, the accompanying health programs, which were remarkably successful at improving Black mortality and stemming rampant epidemics decimating that community, were underfunded, never incorporated into the mainstream health system, and discontinued too soon to have permanent salutary effects on Black health.[210]

This hitherto scarcely acknowledged historical legacy could serve as a barometer for the often countervailing complexities surrounding the deep core of social consciousness contained in the American character. Further confounding our ability to discern factors positively influencing African American health between the 1960s and 1980 are several other difficult-to-evaluate history-based and contemporary factors obscuring the assessment of Black health status and outcome trends during the period. A major proof of the difficulties created by this conundrum is the paradox of a period generally perceived by the mainstream health system as a "crisis," but which resulted in the most rapid and dramatic improvements in Black health in the nation's history.* For example, prior to the 1950s–1965 Black Civil Rights Movement—which was

---

*Arguments could be made that the Reconstruction era yielded the most dramatic health improvements for African Americans. However, comprehensive and quantitative proofs supporting this view would be sparse. (See Chapter 6, Volume 1.)

quietly paralleled by a health care Civil Rights Movement led by Drs. W. Montague Cobb and Paul Cornely, the NMA, and its presidents and boards, allied with civil rights organizations (NAACP, NUL, NAACP-LDF)—Black exclusion or relegation to the periphery of the mainstream health system (i.e., city and public hospitals, health departments, government institutions) was so complete as to render health policies and events affecting African Americans virtual non sequiturs.

The mainstream health system establishment only became directly concerned with Black health and the forced interaction between the races when there was court-ordered and government agency–pressured desegregation of health institutions or governmental budgetary considerations resulting from health system expansion and capacity building to include African Americans. Such a radical and official opening of the mainstream health system to the majority of African Americans (i.e., desegregating most of the nation's hospitals, health departments, and nursing homes in the late 1960s and 1970s) by force of law and regulations was a tremendous (but difficult to measure) agent of change positively affecting Black health. The production of more Black physicians was also implemented during this period.[211] This proven method of improving the quality of health care for the Black community was reaffirmed

**Figure 4.2**
**The Morehouse**
**School of Medicine**
**in Atlanta, Georgia**
Reproduced from
the *Journal of the*
*National Medical*
*Association* 1989
(May) volume 81,
no. 5, cover.

Figure 4.3
Charles R. Drew
University School of
Medicine, Los Angeles,
California
Reproduced from the
*Journal of the National
Medical Association* 1989
(April) volume 81, no. 4,
cover.

while simultaneously extending health care access and professional opportunity to African Americans. The opening of two predominantly Black medical schools (Morehouse School of Medicine in Atlanta and the Charles R. Drew Health Science Center in Los Angeles; see Figures 4.2 and 4.3) and a systemwide, programmatic effort to increase the output of Black physicians by the medical education system resulted. Other legislative and policy measures whose effects on Black health are easier to measure also took place.

The decade from 1965 to 1975 thus represented the second major period reflecting the core values of a multicultural democracy and a striving toward human equality in health for African American and poor people in the United States — comparable to a "Second Reconstruction" in the health system.[212] The government commitment, through the enactment of Medicare and Medicaid, to paying the health bills of almost 50 million elderly, disabled, and low-income people and erecting a substantial primary care network for an additional 6 million people through some 876 health centers by the early 1980s was a major enabling force for African Americans and the poor in the health system. For the first time, large blocs of previously medically indigent populations became paying customers with access in some instances to quality comprehensive health care in a commercially driven health system. Programs enacted between 1957 and the late 1970s expanded the capacity of the health system and differentially affected poor and underserved groups such as African Americans, Hispanic/Latino Americans, Native Americans, and other people of color. Some included the Indian Health Assistance Act; the Maternal and Infant Care (M&I) program; the Children and Youth (C&Y) program, designed to meet the comprehensive needs of mothers and children in poor communities; and the Migrant Health Act, which provided grants establishing special clinics for migrant and seasonal workers. The National Health Services Corps (1970) and National Health Service Corps Scholarship Program (1972) were enacted specifically to secure an expanded health care work-force capacity in underserved urban and rural areas by providing financial and educational incentives for physicians to practice in these settings — which were essential parts of the new "poverty" health infrastructure. Although most of these laudable, and necessary, enabling, expansive, and capacity-building programs for African American and underserved populations were erected on the fringes of, and never fully incorporated into, the mainstream health system, an effort had begun to attain the public health goals of accessible, affordable, available, acceptable, adaptable, accountable health care with adequate capacity to include previously excluded Americans. Some health system pundits seemed nonplussed when the health status and outcomes of previously underserved Americans improved so dramatically, while others ignored the phenomenon almost entirely.[213]

The length of life, or life expectancy, continues to be the gold standard of measuring vitality and the distribution of good health. Life expectancy at birth reflects infant mortality and cumulative mortality from all causes throughout life. As Nicolette Hart notes in the *Oxford Textbook of Public Health*: "Among indicators used to measure the distribution of health in a population, only one, mortality, can be used with any degree of precision to study trends over time between and within societies."[214] This takes on added significance if meaningful comparisons are to be made between the health of groups within a society. In 1970, near the beginning of the period, Haynes reports: "According to the latest available data, the Black in the United States lives, on the average 6½ years less than the White. At birth, the life expectancy for Whites is 71.7 years; for Blacks, it is 65.3 years."[215] Based on his calculations of the median age at death for the Black and White populations he further observed: "Although they pay Social Security, Blacks *on the average* (especially males) hardly survive to receive it."[216] (See Tables 4.1 and 4.2.) Between 1965 and 1980 American life expectancy increased 3.5 years (5%), with Whites gaining 3.4 years (4.8%) while Blacks, gaining longevity at a more rapid rate, accrued 4.0 years (6.2%). Black males, with a life expectancy of 63.8 years — a life span last experienced by White men in 1943 and the shortest of any U.S. racial or ethnic group in 1980 — gained the least life expectancy (2.7 years or 4.4%) since 1965, while African American women made the largest gains (5.1 years or 7.6%). The U.S. Department of Health and Human Services found in 1980 that:

**Table 4.1   Differences in Life Expectancy, by Sex and Color,
United States, 1970**

|                   | Both Sexes | Male | Female | Sex Differences |
|-------------------|------------|------|--------|-----------------|
| White             | 71.7       | 68.0 | 75.6   | 7.6             |
| Non-White         | 65.3       | 61.3 | 69.4   | 8.1             |
| Color differences | 6.4        | 6.7  | 6.2    |                 |

*Source*: National Center for Health Statistics, *Vital Statistics of the United States*, vol. II, sec. 5, Life Tables, U.S. Department of Health, Education and Welfare Publication (HRA) 74–1104.

*From*: Haynes MA. The gap in health status between black and white Americans. In: Williams RA, ed. *Textbook of Black-Related Diseases*. New York: McGraw-Hill, 1975, 2.

**Table 4.2   Median Age at Death, by Sex and Color,
United States, 1970**

| Sex    | White | Non-White |
|--------|-------|-----------|
| Male   | 71.5  | 64.9      |
| Female | 79.4  | 72.9      |
| Median age at death for total population ...... | | 74.9 |

*Source*: National Center for Health Statistics, *Vital Statistics of the United States*, vol. II, sec. 5, Life Tables, U.S. Department of Health, Education, and Welfare Publication (HRA) 74–1104.

*From*: Haynes MA. The gap in health status between black and white Americans. In: Williams RA, ed. *Textbook of Black-Related Diseases*. New York: McGraw-Hill, 1975, 2.

"While nonwhites have experienced considerably greater declines in mortality than have whites in the past 10 years, they still experienced a mortality rate 37.5 percent higher than that of whites in 1980, compared with a mortality rate 44.1 percent higher than that of whites in 1970."[217] In lieu of the progress, White Americans lived 6.3 years longer than Black Americans in 1980 compared to 6.4 years longer in 1970. White males lived 6.9 years longer than Black males (70.7 versus 63.8) and White women lived 5.6 years longer than Black women (78.1 versus 72.5).

Improved health status indicated by the gains in life expectancy between 1965 and 1980 was reflected by declining death rates. As Haynes pointed out, in 1972 (based on the latest data then available) the overall racial differences in death rates appear insignificant at first glance, the White rate being 9.3 deaths per 1,000 population compared to a non-White rate of 9.4 per 1,000. The real differences emerge when the rates at different ages are compared. As Haynes found, "The significant fact is that Blacks are dying at an earlier age."[218] (See Table 4.3.) The mortality rate differentials between Whites and Blacks were large during infancy (+ 12.5 deaths per 1,000), very small during childhood, then increased throughout

Table 4.3   Mortality Rate (Per Thousand) by Color at Selected Ages,
United States, 1972

| Age, yr | Non-White | White | Differences |
|---------|-----------|-------|-------------|
| All ages | 9.3 | 9.4 | −0.1 |
| Under 1 | 28.3 | 15.8 | +12.5 |
| 1–4 | 1.2 | 0.7 | +0.5 |
| 5–14 | 0.5 | 0.4 | +0.1 |
| 15–24 | 2.1 | 1.2 | +0.9 |
| 25–34 | 3.6 | 1.3 | +2.3 |
| 35–44 | 6.6 | 2.5 | +4.1 |
| 45–54 | 12.9 | 6.5 | +6.4 |
| 55–59 | 20.5 | 12.3 | +8.2 |
| 60–64 | 29.2 | 18.6 | +10.6 |
| 65–69 | 38.5 | 28.8 | +9.7 |
| 70–74 | 50.1 | 42.3 | +7.8 |
| 75–79 | 67.6 | 65.3 | +2.3 |
| 80–84 | 88.4 | 102.5 | −14.1 |
| 85+ | 109.6 | 167.0 | −57.4 |

*Source:* National Center for Health Statistics, *Vital Statistics Report, Monthly Vital Statistics Report,* vol. 20, no. 13, suppl. 2, U.S. Public Health Service, Aug. 30, 1972.

*From:* Haynes MA. The gap in health status between black and white Americans. In: Williams RA, ed., *Textbook of Black-Related Diseases.* New York: McGraw-Hill, 1975, 3.

life until age 80, at which time the death rate of Whites surpassed that of Blacks. Haynes popularized another more interesting way of expressing the mortality differential between the races—this was in terms of excess deaths. Assuming that the death rate of Blacks was the same as Whites at specific ages, a certain number of deaths could be expected. These were the *expected deaths*. The number of deaths that actually occurred in the Black population that year (1970) was far in excess of the deaths expected on the basis of White mortality rates. The difference between the *expected deaths* and the deaths that actually occurred is called the *excess deaths*. The total number of *excess deaths* Haynes computed in all age groups in the non-White population up to age 75 in 1970 was 84,532. In other words, almost 45 percent of the total non-White deaths (190,888 observed deaths) in 1970 were excess deaths: "These deaths would not have occurred if the population had been White."[219] (See Table 4.4.) Another interesting way of expressing the mortality difference in 1970 was in terms of person-years lost (now called years of potential life lost, YPLL) because of premature death. If one assumed that were it not for premature death, Black persons would have lived a period of time equal to the average life expectancy of the non-White population, one can make the conversion to person-years lost by multiplying the number of persons dying prematurely by the average number of years of life remaining at the age of death. Therefore, if a Black

**Table 4.4   Excess Deaths in Non-White Population at Specific Ages, United States, 1970**

| Age, yr | Expected Deaths | Observed Deaths | Excess Deaths |
|---------|-----------------|-----------------|---------------|
| Under 1 | 10,445 | 19,791 | 9,346 |
| 1–4 | 1,928 | 3,179 | 1,251 |
| 5–9 | 1,103 | 1,799 | 696 |
| 10–14 | 1,127 | 1,712 | 609 |
| 15–19 | 2,673 | 4,174 | 1,501 |
| 20–24 | 2,281 | 5,094 | 2,813 |
| 25–29 | 1,692 | 4,958 | 3,266 |
| 30–34 | 1,747 | 5,750 | 4,003 |
| 35–39 | 2,527 | 7,831 | 5,304 |
| 40–44 | 3,957 | 10,944 | 6,987 |
| 45–49 | 5,795 | 13,928 | 8,133 |
| 50–54 | 8,115 | 16,530 | 8,415 |
| 55–59 | 11,286 | 20,596 | 9,310 |
| 60–64 | 14,475 | 22,914 | 8,439 |
| 65–69 | 18,316 | 27,670 | 9,354 |
| 70–74 | 18,913 | 24,018 | 5,105 |
| Total to age 74 | 106,380 | 190,888 | 84,532 |

*Source:* Derived from data from National Vital Statistics Division: *Vital Statistics Report of the United States*, vol. 22. no. 8, Table 2, U.S. Public Health Service, 1970.

*From:* Haynes MA. The gap in health status between black and white Americans. In: Williams RA, ed. *Textbook of Black-Related Diseases.* New York: McGraw-Hill, 1975, 4.

person died at age 5, and the average number of years of life remaining at that age of death is 64 years, this premature death represents the loss of 64 person-years. Two such persons facing similar circumstances would amount to 128 person-years lost. (See Table 4.5.) Table 4.5 shows how the number of excess deaths in the non-White population affect the person-years lost. It clearly demonstrates that the greatest impact could have been made on the life expectancy of the Black population in 1970 by preventing the 620,574 person-years lost during the first year of life.

Between 1965 and 1980, overall age-adjusted death rates declined 20.3 percent. By 1980 age-adjusted death rates had fallen 25.2 percent for Blacks and 21.1 percent for Whites, but Blacks continued to have substantially higher death rates than Whites. Nevertheless, the Black/White gap in death rates narrowed somewhat from the 1965 differential of 45 percent. These health gains were most notable for causes of illness and death affected by medical care intervention, such as infant deaths, influenza and pneumonia, tuberculosis, cerebrovascular disease, heart diseases, and diabetes. Conditions not expected to be significantly affected by availability of improved health services, such as suicide, homicide, and cirrhosis, showed upward trends in Blacks. Cancer, a group of conditions demonstrating increasing susceptibilities to improvements with modern techniques for screening,

**Table 4.5   Person-Years Lost in Non-White Population by Age, United States, 1970**

| Age, yr | Excess Deaths* | Person-Years Lost** |
|---|---|---|
| Under 1 | 9,346 | 620,574 |
| 1–4 | 1,251 | 90,072 |
| 5–9 | 696 | 47,467 |
| 10–14 | 609 | 38,610 |
| 15–19 | 1,501 | 87,808 |
| 20–24 | 2,813 | 151,339 |
| 25–29 | 3,266 | 160,360 |
| 30–34 | 4,003 | 177,733 |
| 35–39 | 5,304 | 210,568 |
| 40–44 | 6,987 | 245,243 |
| 45–49 | 8,133 | 248,869 |
| 50–54 | 8,415 | 221,314 |
| 55–59 | 9,310 | 207,613 |
| 60–64 | 8,439 | 156,965 |
| 65–69 | 9,354 | 142,180 |
| 70–74 | 5,105 | 62,281 |
| Total to age 74 | 84,532 | |

*Transferred from Table 4.4.

**Calculated using life tables for 1970.

*From:* Haynes MA. The gap in health status between black and white Americans. In: Williams RA, ed. *Textbook of Black-Related Diseases.* New York: McGraw-Hill, 1975, 5.

early detection, and treatments, also demonstrated increasing mortality among African Americans.[220] As Reynolds Farley noted, despite the 1970s increases in mortality among both races attributable to respiratory cancer: "Death rates for cancer of other sites have been rising among blacks, but constant or declining among whites."[221] Comparisons between Blacks and Whites of the percentage change in death rates—probably the most commonly used operational measurement of health*—for selected causes from 1960 to 1980 and the preceding years of 1950 to 1960 are illuminating. (See Table 4.6.)

---

*Operational measurements of health, commonly utilized in the literature, employ a single or composite health index, such as life expectancy or expected disability-free days over the remaining life span. These overall measurements, however, are relatively insensitive to changes resulting from specific health programs or increased access to health services. Disaggregated measurements of health such as infant and general mortality by specific disease causes of death; incidence and severity of acute conditions by type (e.g., ear, nose, and throat infections; respiratory, digestive, and urinary conditions; dietary deficiencies; skin infections); the incidence and degree of deterioration from chronic conditions (e.g., hypertension, diabetes, kidney disease, heart conditions, arthritis, asthma, obesity); pregnancy outcomes (e.g., prematurity, low birth weight, stillbirth, and abortions [miscarriages]);

**Table 4.6   Percentage Change in Death Rates from Selected Causes by Race and Years, United States, 1950–1980**

|  | Percentage Change 1950–1960 | Percentage Change 1960–1980 |
|---|---|---|
| Infant deaths* | | |
| White | –14.6% | –52.% |
| Black | 1.0 | –51.7 |
| Influenza & pneumonia | | |
| White | 7.4 | –50.4 |
| Black & other | –3.0 | –67.4 |
| Tuberculosis** | | |
| White | N/A | –64.4 |
| Black & other | N/A | –50.8 |
| Cerebrovascular disease | | |
| White | –10.8 | –48.8 |
| Black & other | –9.4 | –53.3 |
| Arteriosclerosis | | |
| White | –19.1 | –57.3 |
| Black & other | –12.7 | –57.2 |
| Diseases of the heart | | |
| White | –6.3 | –29.8 |
| Black & other | –13.6 | –27.8 |
| Diabetes | | |
| White | –7.9 | –28.9 |
| Black & other | 25.6 | –13.0 |

* Change in deaths per 1,000 live births. All others are change in deaths per 100,000 population.
**Data not available by race for 1950–1961; percentage change is for 1962–1980.
*Source:* Computed from death rates in U.S. Department of Health and Human Services, 1985b.

*From:* Davis K, Lillie-Blanton M, Lyons B, Mullan F, Powe N, Rowland D. Health care for Black Americans: The public sector role. In: Willis DP, ed. *Health Policies and Black Americans.* New Brunswick, NJ: Transaction Publishers, 1989, 215.

It seemed as if the rate of health status, outcomes, and utilization improvements had changed to a higher gear during the 1965 to 1980 era—especially for African Americans. As shown in Table 4.6, the infant mortality rate, another gold standard of health status, declined by over 50 percent between 1960 and 1980 for Blacks and Whites. This was a drop from 44.3 deaths per 1,000 live births to 21.4 per 1,000 live births. Although White Americans experienced a rapidly increased rate of decline in infant mortality, from a –14.6 percentage change in the decade

accidental deaths and injuries; deviations from desired family sizes and spacing of children; functional capacity (e.g., disability, handicap, limitation of activity or mobility, inability to go to work or school or to care for oneself, loss of teeth, hearing, or vision); unremedied health defects in children (e.g., hearing, visual, dental, growth and development); and levels of preventive services (as indicators and predictors of the probability of future impairment or death) are more useful for these purposes. See Davis K, Schoen C. *Health and the War on Poverty: A Ten-Year Appraisal.* Washington, DC: Brookings Institution, 1978, 20–21.

of 1950 to 1960 to a −52.0 percentage change between 1960 and 1980, the rate of improvement for African Americans was phenomenal compared to previous trends. The dramatic −51.7 percentage change in Black infant mortality during the latter era, following a typical 1.0 percentage change between 1950 and 1960, was unprecedented. Improvements in reproductive health were not confined to infants during the era. As Davis and Schoen noted, "Maternal deaths resulting from complications of childbirth—much rarer than infant deaths—declined by two-thirds between 1965 and 1974 and by almost 90 percent between 1950 and 1974."[222] All of these improvements were probably enhanced by the effects on the nation's maternal and child health system of the new age of government involvement in health financing for the poor, the racial desegregation of the health system, and the enhanced health institutional infrastructure for previously underserved populations. Along with the rest of the population, African Americans experienced dramatic declines in age-adjusted mortality rates in other leading causes of death in the United States. These included deaths from influenza and pneumonia, which dropped 67 percent, compared to a 3 percent improvement among Blacks between 1950 and 1960. Even the mortality from Black America's traditional scourge, tuberculosis, declined 51 percent between 1960 and 1980. During the decades of 1960 to 1980, Black mortality rates from cerebrovascular diseases and arteriosclerosis declined by more than 50 percent compared to less than 10 percent and 13 percent, respectively, between 1950 and 1960 (see Table 4.6). As Karen Davis stated in "Health Care for Black Americans: The Public Sector Role": "This dramatic decline in mortality represents both the lower rate of uncontrolled hypertension in the population and improved access to health services."[223] Deaths from diabetes and heart disease dropped 13 and 28 percent, respectively. Although the gains in mortality from diabetes in the 1960 to 1980 period seem modest, they represented a sharp departure from the 26 percent increase in Black diabetic mortality observed between 1950 and 1960. (See Table 4.6.)[224]

Infant mortality rate (IMR) is the second most widely used method of measuring the health status of a population. This prominent disaggregated measurement of health status is defined as the number of babies alive at birth who die within the first year. Haynes's study had begun defining the racial aspects of this health index, revealing: "Except for congenital malformations and hemolytic disease of the newborn, in which the mortality is greater for the White than for the Black, for most causes of infant death, the rate is higher for the Black."[225] Further detailing the relationship between IMR and the Black population, his landmark study also revealed: "The four leading causes of death among Black infants are (1) immaturity unqualified, (2) influenza and pneumonia, (3) postnatal asphyxia and atelectasis, and (4) neonatal disorders arising from disease of the mother during pregnancy."[226] The death rate from influenza and pneumonia in Black infants was three times the White rate; for immaturity, two times the White rate; and for the latter two conditions, 1⅔ times the rate for Whites. Although not ranked in the top four killers of Black infants, the rate of infant death because of gastritis and duodenitis was six times the White rate. (See Table 4.7.) Scientific examination and analysis of the racial dimensions of health parameters were unprecedented during this period, harkening back to Du Bois's Atlanta University Studies and the pioneer work of Hildrus Poindexter and Paul Cornely.

The IMR's popularity as a method of measuring health status is based on its having been recorded over long periods of time for many U.S. subpopulations and the belief that it is especially sensitive to the adequacy of medical care—rendering it a good indicator of the health and welfare of a society and the influence of improved medical care on health. These characteristics and the fact that "disaggregated measurements are expected to be particularly sensitive to improved access to medical care"[227] make the IMR and other disaggregated measurements especially important in the evaluation of African American and disadvantaged minority health. Haynes noted that: near the beginning of the era, "Eighteen of 1,000 White babies born will die during the first year, but 33 of 1,000 Black babies will die (1969)."[228] Statistical indices gathered during infancy had a disproportionate importance in the African American population "because deaths at this age contribute most highly to decreasing life expectancy, and because the probability of dying is greater at this age than at any other single age until one reaches the age of 65,"[229] Haynes reiterated.

**Table 4.7  Average Annual Infant Mortality Rates\* for Selected Causes, by Color, United States, 1965–1967**

| Cause of Death | ICD Code | White | Non-White |
|---|---|---|---|
| All causes | | 2,062.9 | 3,838.2 |
| Infective and parasitic diseases | 001–138 | 24.4 | 58.1 |
| Influenza and pneumonia | 480–493, 763 | 188.0 | 605.1 |
| All other diseases of respiratory system | 470–475, 500, 527 | 48.1 | 126.1 |
| Gastritis and duodenitis | 543, 571, 572, 764 | 24.0 | 149.4 |
| All other diseases of digestive system | 530–542, 544–570, 573–587 | 28.1 | 40.2 |
| Congenital malformations | 750–759 | 350.3 | 303.3 |
| Birth injuries | 760–761 | 188.2 | 235.6 |
| Intracranial and spinal injury at birth | 760 | 55.7 | 99.4 |
| Other birth injury | 761 | 132.5 | 136.3 |
| Postnatal asphyxia and atelectasis | 762 | 348.0 | 579.5 |
| Immaturity unqualified | 776 | 302.6 | 660.9 |
| Neonatal disorders arising from certain diseases of mother during pregnancy | 765–769, 771–774 | 330.5 | 541.8 |
| Symptoms and ill-defined conditions | 780–793, 795 | 40.0 | 217.4 |
| Accidents | E800–E962 | 68.8 | 159.5 |
| Residual | 140–468, 590–749, E963–E965 | 81.4 | 145.4 |

\*Mortality rate per 100,000 live births.

*Source:* National Vital Statistics Division: *Vital Statistics of the United States*, for the years 1965–1967, vols. I and II-part A, U.S. Public Health Service.

*From:* Haynes MA. The gap in health status between black and white Americans. In: Williams RA, ed. *Textbook of Black-Related Diseases*. New York: McGraw-Hill, 1975, 8.

After a period of relative stability between 1950 and 1965, Black IMR declined from 41.7 per 1,000 live births in 1965 to 21.4 per 1,000 live births in 1980—a 48.7 percent decrease. (See Table 4.8.) Nevertheless, the Black/White odds ratio for IMRs climbed slightly from 1.94 in 1965 to 1.95 in 1980, reflecting the more rapid improvement in White (49 percent decrease) versus Black IMRs (48.7 percent decrease). Throughout the 15 years under study, Black IMRs remained 1 ½ to 2 times higher than the White rates. However, excess Black infant deaths* declined from 11,729 to 6,118 (a 48 percent decrease) during the same period, and Black fetal death rates (stillbirth rate)** declined markedly from 27.2 to 13.1 stillborn infants per 1,000 infants born. Despite this 52 percent decrease, the Black fetal death rate remained 63.8 percent higher than the White rate (8.0 stillborn infants per 1,000 infants born in 1980).[230] Between 1965 and 1980 the Black postneonatal mortality rates*** fell slightly more rapidly than neonatal mortality rates****—52 percent and 46.8 percent, respectively. Meanwhile, the Black/White ratio of neonatal death rates climbed from 1.65 to 1.88, reflecting a widening differential between the races. Although the Black postneonatal death rates declined from 15.2 per 1,000 live births to 7.3 per 1,000 live births during the period, Black rates remained at least twice as high as White rates. Meanwhile, maternal death rates for Blacks improved dramatically in the 15 years between 1965 and 1980, declining from 88.3 to 21.5 deaths per 100,000 live births. This 75.6 percent decrease should not mask René's findings:

> Although in 1980 the black mortality rate for this category was 3 percent of what it was in 1940, the difference in rates between white mothers and black mothers had increased from 2.4 times as high in 1940 to 3.2 times as high in 1980. In the years 1977 to 1979 the maternal mortality rate stood four times higher than that of the white population in the United States.[231]

This was especially disconcerting considering that ratios for maternal mortality between Blacks and Whites had become four times as high as early as 1955 and remained at that level for most of the 1960s.[232] For some maternal and child health parameters such as low birth weight (LBW, birth weight less than 2500 grams) and very low birth weight (VLBW; birth weight less than 1500 grams), progress was not as dramatic. This is usually the obstetrical end point, or result, of a fetus being born

---

*Excess Black infant deaths* is defined as the number of Black infants who would not have died if the Black infant mortality rate were the same as the rate among Whites.

**Fetal death rate (stillbirth rate) is the number of stillborn infants per 1,000 infants born, including live births and stillbirths.

***Deaths between 28 days and one year after birth per 1,000 live births.

*****Deaths within 28 days after birth per 1,000 live births.

**Table 4.8  Infant, Neonatal, Fetal, and Maternal Mortality Rates, by Race, 1940–1980**

| Year | 1940 | 1950 | 1960 | 1965 | 1970 | 1973 | 1974 | 1975 | 1976 | 1977 | 1978 | 1979 | 1980 |
|---|---|---|---|---|---|---|---|---|---|---|---|---|---|
| Infant deaths | 47.0 | 29.2 | 26.0 | 24.7 | 20.0 | 17.7 | 16.7 | 16.1 | 15.2 | 14.1 | 13.8 | 13.1 | 12.6 |
| White | 43.2 | 26.8 | 22.9 | 21.5 | 17.8 | 15.8 | 14.8 | 14.2 | 13.3 | 12.3 | 12.0 | 11.4 | 11.0 |
| Black and other | 73.8 | 44.5 | 43.2 | 40.3 | 30.9 | 26.2 | 24.9 | 24.2 | 23.5 | 21.7 | 21.1 | 19.8 | 19.1 |
| Black | 72.9 | 43.9 | 44.3 | 41.7 | 32.6 | 28.1 | 26.8 | 26.2 | 25.5 | 23.6 | 23.1 | 21.8 | 21.4 |
| Ratio Black/White | 1.7 | 1.6 | 1.9 | 1.9 | 1.8 | 1.8 | 1.8 | 1.8 | 1.9 | 1.9 | 1.9 | 1.9 | 1.9 |
| Percent difference | 68.8% | 63.8% | 93.4% | 94.0% | 83.1% | 77.8% | 81.1% | 84.5% | 91.7% | 91.9% | 92.5% | 91.2% | 94.5% |
| Fetal deaths |  |  |  |  |  |  |  |  |  |  |  |  |  |
| White | — | 19.2 | 16.1 | 16.2 | 14.2 | 12.2 | 11.5 | 10.7 | 10.5 | 9.9 | 9.7 | 9.4 | 9.0 |
| Black and other | — | 17.1 | 14.1 | 13.9 | 12.4 | 10.8 | 10.2 | 9.5 | 9.3 | 8.7 | 8.5 | 8.4 | 8.0 |
| Black | — | 32.5 | 25.8 | 27.2 | 22.6 | 18.6 | 17.0 | 16.0 | 15.2 | 14.5 | 14.7 | 13.8 | 13.1 |
| Ratio Black/White | — | 1.9 | 1.8 | 2.0 | 1.8 | 1.7 | 1.7 | 1.7 | 1.6 | 1.7 | 1.7 | 1.6 | 1.6 |
| Percent difference | — | 90.1% | 83.0% | 95.7% | 82.3% | 72.2% | 66.7% | 68.4% | 63.4% | 67.8% | 72.9% | 64.3% | 63.8% |
| Neonatal deaths | 28.8 | 20.5 | 18.7 | 17.7 | 15.1 | 13.0 | 12.3 | 11.6 | 10.9 | 9.9 | 9.5 | 8.9 | 8.5 |
| White | 27.2 | 19.4 | 17.2 | 16.1 | 13.8 | 11.8 | 11.1 | 10.4 | 9.7 | 8.7 | 8.4 | 7.9 | 7.5 |
| Black and other | 39.7 | 27.5 | 25.9 | 25.4 | 21.4 | 17.9 | 17.2 | 16.8 | 16.3 | 14.7 | 14.0 | 12.9 | 12.5 |
| Black | 39.9 | 27.8 | 27.8 | 26.5 | 22.8 | 19.3 | 18.7 | 18.3 | 17.9 | 16.1 | 15.5 | 14.3 | 14.1 |
| Ratio Black/White | 1.5 | 1.4 | 1.6 | 1.6 | 1.7 | 1.6 | 1.7 | 1.8 | 1.8 | 1.9 | 1.8 | 1.8 | 1.9 |
| Percent difference | 46.7% | 43.3% | 61.6% | 64.6% | 65.2% | 63.6% | 68.5% | 76.0% | 84.5% | 85.1% | 84.5% | 81.0% | 88.0% |
| Maternal deaths | 376.0 | 83.3 | 37.1 | 31.5 | 21.5 | 15.2 | 14.6 | 12.8 | 12.3 | 11.2 | 9.6 | 9.6 | 9.2 |
| White | 319.8 | 61.1 | 28.0 | 21.0 | 14.4 | 10.7 | 10.0 | 9.1 | 9.0 | 7.7 | 6.4 | 6.4 | 6.7 |
| Black and other | 773.5 | 221.6 | 97.9 | 83.7 | 55.9 | 34.6 | 35.1 | 29.0 | 26.5 | 26.0 | 23.0 | 22.7 | 19.8 |
| Black | 781.7 | 223.0 | 103.6 | 88.3 | 59.8 | 38.4 | 38.3 | 31.3 | 29.5 | 29.2 | 25.0 | 25.1 | 21.5 |
| Ratio Black/White | 2.4 | 3.6 | 3.7 | 4.2 | 4.2 | 3.6 | 3.8 | 3.4 | 3.3 | 3.8 | 3.9 | 3.9 | 3.2 |
| Percent difference | 144.4% | 265.0% | 270.0% | 320.5% | 315.3% | 258.9% | 283.0% | 244.0% | 227.8% | 279.2% | 290.6% | 292.2% | 220.9% |

*Source:* National Center for Health Statistics: *Vital Statistics of the United States, 1983,* Public Health Service, DHHS, Hyattsville, MD.

*From:* René AA. Racial differences in mortality: Blacks and Whites. In: Jones Jr W, Rice MF, eds. *Health Care Issues in Black America: Policies, Problems, and Prospects.* New York: Greenwood Press, 1987, 25.

early (prematurity or preterm birth) or growing subnormally in the uterus (intrauterine growth restriction). Between 1970 and 1980 the percentage of LBW infants decreased gradually from 7.94 to 6.84 percent of live births (a 13.8% decrease). (See Table 4.9.) LBW is the principal cause of death in the first week of life,* and obstetricians have learned that "appreciable compromise, both physical and intellectual, afflicts many such children."[233] During the decade of 1970 to

*During the 1970s LBW infants were 20 times as likely to die as heavier infants, and almost two-thirds of all infants that died were LBW.

**Table 4.9  Live Births, According to Race and Beginning of Prenatal Care, Selected Years, 1970–1980**

| Race and Characteristic | Year | | | | | | |
|---|---|---|---|---|---|---|---|
| | 1970 | 1975 | 1976 | 1977 | 1978 | 1979 | 1980 |
| Total* | Percent of Live Births | | | | | | |
| Birth weight: | | | | | | | |
| 2500 grams or less | 7.94 | 7.39 | 7.26 | 7.07 | 7.11 | 6.94 | 6.84 |
| 1500 grams or less | 1.17 | 1.16 | 1.15 | 1.13 | 1.17 | 1.15 | 1.15 |
| Prenatal care began: | | | | | | | |
| First trimester | 68.0 | 72.4 | 73.5 | 74.1 | 74.9 | 75.9 | 76.3 |
| Third trimester | 7.9 | 6.0 | 5.7 | 5.6 | 5.4 | 5.1 | 5.1 |
| White | | | | | | | |
| Birth weight: | | | | | | | |
| 2500 grams or less | 6.84 | 6.26 | 6.13 | 5.93 | 5.94 | 5.80 | 5.70 |
| 1500 grams or less | 0.95 | 0.92 | 0.91 | 0.89 | 0.91 | 0.90 | 0.90 |
| Prenatal care began: | | | | | | | |
| First trimester | 73.4 | 75.9 | 76.8 | 77.3 | 78.2 | 79.1 | 79.3 |
| Third trimester | 6.2 | 5.0 | 4.8 | 4.7 | 4.5 | 4.3 | 4.3 |
| Black | | | | | | | |
| Birth weight: | | | | | | | |
| 2500 grams or less | 13.86 | 13.09 | 12.97 | 12.79 | 12.85 | 12.55 | 12.49 |
| 1500 grams or less | 2.4 | 2.37 | 2.4 | 2.38 | 2.43 | 2.37 | 2.44 |
| Prenatal care began: | | | | | | | |
| First trimester | 44.4 | 55.8 | 57.7 | 59.0 | 60.2 | 61.6 | 62.7 |
| Third trimester | 16.6 | 10.5 | 9.9 | 9.6 | 9.3 | 8.9 | 8.8 |
| Racial Difference | | | | | | | |
| Birth weight: | | | | | | | |
| 2500 grams or less | 7.02 | 6.83 | 6.84 | 6.86 | 6.91 | 6.75 | 6.79 |
| 1500 grams or less | 1.45 | 1.45 | 1.49 | 1.49 | 1.52 | 1.47 | 1.54 |
| Prenatal care began: | | | | | | | |
| First trimester | −29.0 | −20.1 | −19.1 | −18.3 | −18.0 | −17.5 | −16.6 |
| Third trimester | 10.4 | 5.5 | 5.1 | 4.9 | 4.8 | 4.6 | 4.5 |

*Includes all other races not shown separately.
Source: United States Department of Health, Education, and Welfare, *Health United States: 1979*.
From: René AA. Racial differences in mortality: Blacks and Whites. In: Jones Jr W, Rice MF, eds. *Health Care Issues in Black America: Policies, Problems, and Prospects.* New York: Greenwood Press, 1987, 28–29.

1980, Black LBW percentages decreased only 9.9 percent. Thus, in 1980, 12.49 percent of Black babies born were LBW compared to 5.70 percent of White babies—a risk more than twice (119 percent higher) the White rate. Despite medical progress, percentages of VLBW infants—where the highest death rates and percentages of mentally and physically challenged infants are concentrated— in Blacks increased from 2.40 percent (2.5 times the White rate in 1970) to 2.44 percent (2.7 times the White rate in 1980)—an increase of 1.7 percent. Nevertheless, by 1981 the weight of the evidence supported the positive effects of government health programs—which were under attack by conservatives and some political and academic factions in the mainstream health system because of the perceived system "crisis" and costs. The positive effect of these programs on the reproductive health of the poor was so convincing that the normally ultraconservative Institute of Medicine took a position in their favor, stating:

> *The women at high risk of having low birthweight infants make least use of the health care system during pregnancy. Are these women at high risk because they do not have early and complete prenatal care and advice, or are the very conditions that interfere with the mothers' willingness and ability to use health care services the same conditions that place infants at high risk? Regardless of this distinction, prenatal care has beneficial effects.*[234]

As the ideological and policy battles raged over whether health care itself, government health programs, and prenatal care were efficacious or cost-effective throughout the 1970s, Black health progress in these areas began abating.

Infant, maternal, and neonatal mortality rates usually reflect the quality of prenatal care, hospital care during delivery, and newborn nursery care, while post-neonatal mortality is more closely related to the infant's home environment and quality of preventive pediatric care. Improvements in maternal and infant health care are usually shared by small children. Thus, between 1960 and 1980 death rates for Black children 1 to 4 years old dropped 47.0 percent for males and 51.3 percent for females. Nevertheless, 1980 age-adjusted death rates for Black male toddlers (110.5 deaths per 100,000 population), remained 67.2 percent higher than those for their White peers (66.1 deaths per 100,000 population) while Black female children in the 1 to 4 age group (84.4 deaths per 100,000 population) suffered death rates 71.2 percent higher than White girls (49.3 deaths per 100,000 population).[235] Despite the progress in some areas of children's health, the overall vaccination rates for U.S. children remained abysmal compared to those in other Western industrialized nations. (See Table 4.10.) For example, the vaccination status of children 1–4 years old during 1976 and 1981 reveal that over this five-year period the percentage of children vaccinated for rubella and mumps increased, while statistics for measles, diphtheria-tetanus-pertussis (DPT), and polio vaccinations showed a slight reduction. For all categories except DPT, the percentage of

Table 4.10  Vaccination Status of Children 1–4 Years
of Age, According to Race: United States, 1976 and 1981

|  | Measles | Rubella | DPT | Polio | Mumps |
|---|---|---|---|---|---|
| **1976** | | | | | |
| Total | 65.9 | 61.7 | 71.4 | 61.6 | 48.3 |
| Race | | | | | |
| White | 68.3 | 63.8 | 75.3 | 66.2 | 50.3 |
| All other | 54.8 | 51.5 | 53.2 | 39.9 | 38.7 |
| **1981** | | | | | |
| Total | 63.8 | 64.5 | 67.5 | 60.0 | 58.4 |
| Race | | | | | |
| White | 65.7 | 66.6 | 71.0 | 63.8 | 60.5 |
| All other | 55.3 | 55.2 | 52.0 | 42.7 | 49.1 |

Source: U. S. Department of Health, Education, and Welfare, Health United States: 1983.

From: René AA. Racial differences in mortality: Blacks and Whites. In: Jones Jr W, Rice MF, eds. Health Care Issues in Black America: Policies, Problems, and Prospects. New York: Greenwood Press, 1987, 30.

non-White children receiving vaccinations increased. The percentage of White children vaccinated increased for measles, rubella, and mumps, but declined for polio and DPT. Significantly, these data indicate that less than 50 percent of non-White children were receiving vaccinations for polio and mumps, with the greatest racial differences occurring for DPT (19 percent) and polio (21 percent). René summarized the situation: "Because the percentage of nonwhite children vaccinated is lower for each disease, one might expect that, should an epidemic occur, the nonwhite population would pay a higher price in disability and death than the white population."[236] A number of factors contribute to these poor immunization patterns, "among them the lack of a public campaign on the ill-effects which these diseases can cause and, more probably, the availability of medical care,"[237] René reasoned.[238]

Heart disease continued to be the leading cause of death in the United States between 1960 and 1980. At the beginning of the period the National Center for Health Statistics indicated that some 13 percent of U.S. adults had definite heart disease. An almost equal number were suspected of having heart disease.[239] Hypertensive heart disease was the leading cause of death, followed by coronary heart disease. Exploring the racial differences in prevalence and types early in the period, Haynes found (see Table 4.11) that:

> Black adults are twice as likely as White adults to have heart disease—
> 24.4 per 100 Black adults have definite heart disease, compared to 12.0
> per 100 White adults. For suspected heart disease, the respective preva-

*lence rates are 14.8 and 11.3 per 100.... [T]he difference between the races is largely due to the marked difference in rates for hypertensive heart disease.*[240]

Black men had prevalence rates for definite heart disease more than two times as high as those for White men ages 18 to 79, and Black women's prevalence rates were nearly twice those for White women in the same age range. Black men had higher prevalence rates for definite heart disease for every age group except ages 75 to 79, and Black women had higher rates throughout the entire age range. Table 4.12 shows that the greatest gap between the races occurred in the age groups of 65 to 74 for men and 55 to 64 for women. Racial differences in the prevalence of hypertensive heart disease were apparent in every age group for both men and women. Table 4.13 shows that the prevalence rate for hypertensive heart disease was three times as high for Black men as for White men and more than twice as high for Black women compared to White women. These heart disease findings were directly related to the higher prevalence rates for hypertension in the Black population compared to Whites in all age groups. (See Table 4.14.)

Although there was a decrease in overall mortality (by 23 percent) and Black male mortality from heart disease during the 1960 to 1980 period (by 14 percent), the mortality rate differential for Black males rose to become approximately 18 percent higher than that for White males by 1980 (327.3 deaths per 100,000 population for Black men versus 277.5 deaths per 100,000 population for White men). (See Table 4.15.) The latter differential had widened from a 1.5 percent racial differential in 1960 (381.2 deaths per 100,000 population for Black men versus 375.4 deaths per 100,000 population for White men). Moreover, the Black/White ratio for

**Table 4.11  Prevalence of Types of Heart Disease in White and Black Adults, United States, 1960–1962**

| Types of Heart Disease | Prevalence, percent | |
|---|---|---|
| | White | Black |
| Total | 12.0 | 24.4 |
| Hypertensive | 8.2 | 20.8 |
| Coronary | 2.9 | 2.6 |
| Rheumatic | 1.1 | 1.7 |
| Congenital | 0.2 | 0.2 |
| Syphilitic | 0.1 | 0.7 |
| Other | 0.3 | 0.2 |

*Source:* National Center for Health Statistics, Heart disease in adults, United States, 1960–1962, *Vital and Health Statistics,* U.S. Public Health Service Publication 1,000, ser. 11, no. 6, September 1964.

*From:* Haynes MA. The gap in health status between black and white Americans. In: Williams RA, ed. *Textbook of Black-Related Diseases.* New York: McGraw-Hill, 1975, 15.

Table 4.12   Prevalence of Heart Disease among White and Black
Adults, by Age and Sex, United States, 1960–1962

| Age, yr | Prevalence, percent | | | |
| | Men | | Women | |
| | White | Black | White | Black |
|---|---|---|---|---|
| Total 18–79 | 11.5 | 23.8 | 12.5 | 24.8 |
| 18–24 | 1.4 | 1.9 | 0.8 | 3.2 |
| 25–34 | 2.5 | 7.9 | 1.4 | 6.8 |
| 35–44 | 6.1 | 18.1 | 4.9 | 14.0 |
| 45–54 | 11.3 | 33.0 | 9.6 | 36.6 |
| 55–64 | 22.5 | 41.6 | 23.7 | 52.2 |
| 65–74 | 31.3 | 56.9 | 43.5 | 70.1 |
| 75–79 | 39.3 | 32.2 | 44.8 | 69.5 |

*Source:* National Center for Health Statistics, Heart disease in adults, United States, 1960–1962. *Vital and Health Statistics,* U.S. Public Health Service Publication 1,000, ser. 11, no. 6, September 1964.

*From:* Haynes MA. The gap in health status between black and white Americans. In: Williams RA, ed. *Textbook of Black-Related Diseases.* New York: McGraw-Hill, 1975, 15.

Table 4.13   Hypertensive Heart Disease among White and Black
Adults, by Age and Sex, United States, 1960–1962

| Age, yr | Prevalence, percent | | | |
| | Men | | Women | |
| | White | Black | White | Black |
|---|---|---|---|---|
| Total 18–79 | 6.5 | 19.1 | 9.8 | 22.2 |
| 18–24 | 0.2 | 1.9 | | 1.6 |
| 25–34 | 1.1 | 5.2 | 0.7 | 4.7 |
| 35–44 | 4.0 | 15.2 | 2.7 | 14.0 |
| 45–54 | 7.7 | 24.4 | 6.8 | 31.5 |
| 55–64 | 11.7 | 33.1 | 19.5 | 46.4 |
| 65–74 | 16.3 | 50.2 | 37.5 | 66.4 |
| 75–79 | 24.0 | 32.2 | 37.1 | 69.5 |

*Source:* National Center for Health Statistics, Hypertension and hypertensive heart disease in adults, United States, 1960–1962. *Vital and Health Statistics,* U.S. Public Health Service Publication 1,000, ser. 11, no. 13, September 1964.

*From:* Haynes MA. The gap in health status between black and white Americans. In: Williams RA, ed. *Textbook of Black-Related Diseases.* New York: McGraw-Hill, 1975, 16.

**Table 4.14  Prevalence Rates of Hypertension for White and Black Adults, by Age And Sex, United States, 1960–1962**

| | Prevalence, percent | | | |
| | Men | | Women | |
| Age, yr | White | Black | White | Black |
|---|---|---|---|---|
| Total 18–79 | 12.8 | 26.7 | 15.3 | 26.6 |
| 18–24 | 1.7 | 1.9 | 0.9 | 3.4 |
| 25–34 | 3.6 | 12.5 | 2.3 | 8.6 |
| 35–44 | 11.8 | 26.5 | 6.2 | 25.7 |
| 45–54 | 16.5 | 30.9 | 15.5 | 41.3 |
| 55–64 | 20.2 | 44.6 | 30.6 | 37.9 |
| 65–74 | 25.0 | 52.7 | 46.6 | 64.1 |
| 75–79 | 30.3 | 59.8 | 44.1 | 69.5 |

*Source:* National Center for Health Statistics, *Hypertension and hypertensive heart disease in adults, United States, 1960–1962. Vital and Health Statistics,* U.S. Public Health Service Publication 1,000, ser. 11, no. 13, September 1964.

*From:* Haynes MA. The gap in health status between black and white Americans. In: Williams RA, ed. *Textbook of Black-Related Diseases.* New York: McGraw-Hill, 1975, 16.

male heart disease deaths deteriorated from 1.0 in 1960 to 1.2 in 1980, further demonstrating a disturbing and seemingly growing racial divergence. Black women fared somewhat better. The 31 percent decrease in heart disease mortality that Black women experienced kept pace with the general decline. However, the 48.5 percent higher mortality from heart disease that Black women suffered compared to White women in 1960 rose slightly to 49 percent by 1980. (See Table 4.15.) The Black/White ratio for females remained stable at 1.5. Later in the period other epidemiologists confirmed Haynes's observation that: "In part because they have higher blood pressure levels, black people experienced substantially higher cardiovascular mortality than whites for all age groups."[241] René revealed other disturbing race-based heart disease trends that emerged during the period under study:

> *Racial differences in heart disease mortality, especially for men at younger ages, are large. For each five-year age group, 25 to 39 years of age, heart disease mortality for black men was more than twice as high as for white men in 1980.... Racial differences in heart disease mortality were greater for women than for men, especially at younger ages.*[242]

Notwithstanding the higher prevalence of and death rates from heart disease on a comparative basis with Whites, African Americans experienced lower hospitalization rates for cardiovascular conditions. Upon closer analysis, "Whatever the causes

## Table 4.15  Age-Adjusted Rates for Selected Causes of Death, According to Race and Sex, United States, 1960, 1970, 1980

| Year/Cause of Death | 1960 | 1970 | 1980 | Percent Difference 1960 to 1980 |
| --- | --- | --- | --- | --- |
| **All causes** | 760.9 | 714.3 | 585.8 | −23.0% |
| Diseases of the heart | 286.2 | 253.6 | 202.0 | −29.4 |
| Cerebrovascular diseases | 79.7 | 66.3 | 40.8 | −48.8 |
| Malignant neoplasms | 125.8 | 129.9 | 132.8 | 5.6 |
| Respiratory system | 19.2 | 28.4 | 36.4 | 89.6 |
| Digestive system | 41.1 | 35.2 | 33.0 | −19.7 |
| Breast | 22.3 | 23.1 | 22.7 | 1.8 |
| Pneumonia and influenza | 28.0 | 22.1 | 12.9 | −53.9 |
| Chronic liver disease and cirrhosis | 10.5 | 14.7 | 12.2 | 16.2 |
| Diabetes mellitus | 13.6 | 14.1 | 10.1 | −25.7 |
| Accidents and adverse effects | 49.9 | 53.7 | 42.3 | −15.2 |
| Motor vehicle accidents | 22.5 | 27.4 | 22.9 | 1.8 |
| Suicide | 10.6 | 11.8 | 11.4 | 7.5 |
| Homicide and legal intervention | 5.2 | 9.1 | 10.8 | 107.7 |

| Race | White | | | Black | | | Ratio Black/White | | | Percent Difference | | |
| --- | --- | --- | --- | --- | --- | --- | --- | --- | --- | --- | --- | --- |
| Year/Cause of Death | 1960 | 1970 | 1980 | 1960 | 1970 | 1980 | 1960 | 1970 | 1980 | 1960 | 1970 | 1980 |
| **All causes** | 760.9 | 714.3 | 585.8 | 1246.1 | 1318.6 | 1112.8 | 1.4 | 1.5 | 1.5 | 35.8% | 47.6% | 49% |
| Diseases of the heart | 286.2 | 253.6 | 202.0 | 381.2 | 375.9 | 327.3 | 1.3 | 1.5 | 1.6 | −1.5 | 8.1 | 17 |
| Cerebrovascular diseases | 79.7 | 66.3 | 40.8 | 141.2 | 122.5 | 77.5 | 1.8 | 1.8 | 1.8 | 75.8 | 78.1 | 85 |
| Malignant neoplasms | 125.8 | 129.9 | 132.8 | 158.5 | 198.0 | 229.9 | 1.1 | 1.3 | 1.3 | 11.9 | 28.3 | 43 |
| Respiratory system | 19.2 | 28.4 | 36.4 | 36.6 | 60.8 | 82.0 | 1.1 | 1.1 | 1.4 | 5.8 | 21.8 | 41 |
| Digestive system | 41.1 | 35.2 | 33.0 | 60.4 | 58.9 | 62.1 | 1.3 | 1.4 | 1.6 | 27.2 | 40.6 | 56 |
| Breast | 22.3 | 23.1 | 22.7 | 53.8 | 53.1 | 30.6 | 2.3 | 2.1 | 1.7 | 126.5 | 106.9 | 72 |
| Pneumonia and influenza | 28.0 | 22.1 | 12.9 | 70.2 | 70.2 | 28.0 | 2.1 | 1.8 | 1.9 | 2.8 | 76.1 | 94 |
| Chronic liver disease and cirrhosis | 10.5 | 14.7 | 12.2 | 16.2 | 33.1 | 30.6 | 1.0 | 1.9 | 1.9 | −4.9 | 66.9 | 86 |
| Diabetes mellitus | 13.6 | 14.1 | 10.1 | 21.1 | 33.3 | 17.7 | 1.4 | 1.7 | 1.6 | 56.8 | 56.8 | 31 |
| Accidents and adverse effects | 49.9 | 53.7 | 42.3 | 82.0 | 82.0 | 41.8 | 1.0 | 1.3 | 0.9 | 43.4 | 43.4 | 35 |
| Motor vehicle accidents | 22.5 | 27.4 | 22.9 | 38.2 | 32.9 | 21.4 | 0.9 | 0.9 | 0.9 | 24.9 | 24.9 | 31 |
| Suicide | 10.6 | 11.8 | 11.4 | 50.1 | 32.9 | 11.4 | 1.2 | 1.2 | 0.7 | −45.6 | −45.6 | −5 |
| Homicide and legal intervention | 5.2 | 9.1 | 10.8 | 44.9 | 82.1 | 71.9 | 0.5 | 0.6 | 6.6 | 1051.3 | 1024.7 | 559 |

| Race | White | | | Black | | | Ratio Black/White | | | Percent Difference | | |
| --- | --- | --- | --- | --- | --- | --- | --- | --- | --- | --- | --- | --- |
| Year/Cause of Death | 1960 | 1970 | 1980 | 1960 | 1970 | 1980 | 1960 | 1970 | 1980 | 1960 | 1970 | 1980 |
| **All causes, male** | 917.7 | 893.4 | 745.3 | 1246.1 | 1318.6 | 1112.8 | 1.5 | 1.6 | 1.5 | 65.2 | 62.3 | 29 |
| Diseases of the heart | 375.4 | 347.6 | 277.5 | 381.2 | 375.9 | 327.3 | 1.1 | 1.6 | 1.5 | 48.5 | 50.0 | 49 |
| Cerebrovascular diseases | 80.3 | 68.8 | 41.9 | 141.2 | 122.5 | 77.5 | 1.8 | 1.9 | 1.8 | 103.1 | 92.0 | 75 |
| Malignant neoplasms | 141.6 | 154.3 | 160.5 | 158.5 | 198.0 | 229.9 | 1.1 | 1.1 | 1.2 | 16.7 | 14.8 | 20 |
| Respiratory system | 34.6 | 49.9 | 58.0 | 36.6 | 60.8 | 82.0 | 1.1 | 1.1 | 1.1 | 7.8 | 7.9 | 7 |
| Digestive system | 47.5 | 41.9 | 39.8 | 60.4 | 70.2 | 60.4 | 1.3 | 1.4 | 1.4 | 10.6 | 21.4 | 39 |
| Pneumonia and influenza | 31.0 | 26.0 | 16.2 | 70.2 | 53.8 | 33.1 | 2.1 | 2.1 | 2.0 | −4.9 | −8.1 | 2 |
| Chronic liver disease and cirrhosis | 14.4 | 20.0 | 15.7 | 14.8 | 33.1 | 30.6 | 1.0 | 1.7 | 1.9 | 131.1 | 94.7 | 35 |
| Diabetes mellitus | 11.3 | 12.7 | 9.5 | 16.2 | 21.0 | 17.7 | 1.4 | 1.9 | 1.8 | 41.3 | 29.8 | 17 |
| Accidents and adverse effects | 70.5 | 76.2 | 62.3 | 119.5 | 82.0 | 62.3 | 1.7 | 1.6 | 1.3 | −9.9 | −4.2 | −31 |
| Motor vehicle accidents | 34.0 | 40.1 | 34.8 | 38.2 | 32.9 | 32.9 | 1.1 | 1.3 | 1.2 | −64.2 | −59.7 | −57 |
| Suicide | 17.5 | 18.2 | 18.9 | 100.0 | 50.1 | 11.4 | 0.5 | 0.5 | 0.6 | −55.4 | −45.6 | −39 |
| Homicide and legal intervention | 3.9 | 7.3 | 10.9 | 44.9 | 82.1 | 71.9 | 11.5 | 11.2 | 6.6 | 686.7 | 581.8 | 328 |

| Race | White | | | Black | | | Ratio Black/White | | | Percent Difference | | |
| --- | --- | --- | --- | --- | --- | --- | --- | --- | --- | --- | --- | --- |
| Year/Cause of Death | 1960 | 1970 | 1980 | 1960 | 1970 | 1980 | 1960 | 1970 | 1980 | 1960 | 1970 | 1980 |
| **All causes, female** | 555.0 | 501.7 | 411.1 | 916.9 | 814.4 | 531.1 | 1.7 | 1.6 | 1.3 | 65.2 | 62.3 | 29 |
| Diseases of the heart | 197.1 | 167.8 | 134.6 | 292.6 | 251.7 | 201.1 | 1.5 | 1.5 | 1.5 | 48.5 | 50.0 | 49 |
| Cerebrovascular disease | 68.7 | 56.2 | 35.2 | 139.5 | 107.9 | 61.7 | 2.0 | 1.9 | 1.8 | 103.1 | 92.0 | 75 |
| Malignant neoplasms | 109.5 | 107.6 | 107.7 | 127.8 | 123.5 | 129.7 | 1.2 | 1.1 | 1.2 | 16.7 | 14.8 | 20 |
| Respiratory system | 5.1 | 10.1 | 18.2 | 10.9 | 10.9 | 19.5 | 1.1 | 1.1 | 1.1 | 7.8 | 7.9 | 7 |
| Digestive system | 33.9 | 28.1 | 25.4 | 37.5 | 34.1 | 35.4 | 1.1 | 1.2 | 1.4 | 10.6 | 21.4 | 39 |
| Breast | 22.4 | 23.4 | 22.8 | 21.3 | 21.5 | 23.3 | 1.0 | 0.9 | 1.0 | −4.9 | −8.1 | 2 |
| Pneumonia and influenza | 19.0 | 15.0 | 9.4 | 43.9 | 29.2 | 12.7 | 2.3 | 1.9 | 1.4 | 131.1 | 94.7 | 35 |
| Accidents and adverse effects | 25.4 | 27.2 | 21.4 | 35.9 | 35.3 | 25.1 | 1.2 | 1.3 | 1.2 | 41.3 | 29.8 | 17 |
| Motor vehicle accidents | 11.1 | 14.4 | 12.3 | 10.0 | 13.8 | 8.4 | 0.9 | 1.0 | 0.7 | −9.9 | −4.2 | −31 |
| Suicide | 5.3 | 7.2 | 5.7 | 1.9 | 2.9 | 2.4 | 0.4 | 0.4 | 0.4 | −64.2 | −59.7 | −57 |
| Homicide and legal intervention | 1.5 | 2.2 | 3.2 | 11.8 | 15.0 | 13.7 | 7.9 | 6.8 | 4.3 | 686.7 | 581.8 | 328 |

*Source:* United States Department of Health, Education, and Welfare, *Health United States, 1983.*

*From:* René AA. Racial differences in mortality: Blacks and Whites. In: Jones Jr W, Rice MF, eds. *Health Care Issues in Black America: Policies, Problems, and Prospects.* New York: Greenwood Press, 1987, 36–37.

of the higher prevalence, the higher death rate may be due to inadequate health care. That some of this inadequate health care has stemmed from lack of access, owing to financial limitations, is hinted by the downward step function in death rate, which occurred a few years after the inception of Medicaid."[243] Heart disease mortality rates for both races were declining, but White rates were declining more rapidly than Black rates; thus there was a relative worsening of the mortality experience for African Americans. However, the overall picture regarding African Americans and cerebrovascular disease during this period was one of progress.

The third leading cause of death in the United States in 1980 was cerebrovascular disease or stroke. Cerebrovascular mortality rates declined for both Black and Whites after 1960. René noted: "For both sexes combined, blacks' rates have decreased slightly, from a level 89 percent higher than whites in 1960 to 80 percent higher in 1980."[244] However, despite Black male decrease in cerebrovascular mortality, Black male rates were 85 percent higher than those for White males in 1980, compared to the 75.8 percent Black/White gap in 1960 (see Table 4.15). Despite the seeming increase in racial disparity for males, disparate mortality rates caused by cerebrovascular disease for females seemed to be decreasing. Black women's rates declined from 103 percent higher than White women's rates in 1960 to 75 percent higher in 1980. Women generally have lower rates than men. Possible factors related to the declines in both cerebrovascular and cardiovascular mortality were suggested by results from physical examinations performed on nationwide samples of adults during the years 1960 to 1962, 1971 to 1975, and 1976 to 1980. (See Tables 4.16 and 4.17.) These examinations revealed a decline of 17 percent in the proportion of the U.S. population with elevated blood pressures, with Blacks experiencing the greatest decline (25 percent). As Davis reported, "The proportion of the adult black population with elevated blood pressure levels dropped from 33 percent in 1960 to 1962 to 25 percent in 1976 to 1980."[245] Moreover, as was stated about the National Center for Health Statistics (NCHS) samples and surveys in the *Health Status of Minorities and Low Income Groups* (1985):

> *From 1960–1962 to 1976–1980, among white men, white women, and black women, roughly twice as many were on medication and controlled in 1976–1980 compared with 1960–1962. Among black men, three times as many were medicated and controlled in the latest time period compared with the earliest time period. However, black men still have the lowest rate of hypertension control.*[246]

Therefore, improvements in cardiovascular and cerebrovascular mortality and morbidity statistics can be attributed, at least in part, to lowered incidence, improved management and rehabilitation of stroke victims, and effective hypertension therapy (since hypertension is a major risk factor for strokes and heart attacks).[247]

Table 4.16   Prevalence Rates* of Adults 25–74 Years
with Definite Hypertension,** by Race, Age, and Sex,
United States, 1960–1962, 1971–1975, 1976–1980

| Age | White | | | Black | | |
|---|---|---|---|---|---|---|
| | 1960–1962 | 1971–1975 | 1976–1980 | 1960–1962 | 1971–1975 | 1976–1980 |
| **Males** | | | | | | |
| 25–34 | 3.6 | 7.5 | 8.4 | 12.5 | 16.4 | 11.7 |
| 35–44 | 11.8 | 14.0 | 10.6 | 26.5 | 36.3 | 22.3 |
| 45–54 | 16.5 | 22.6 | 21.2 | 30.9 | 36.7 | 23.0 |
| 55–64 | 20.2 | 25.2 | 22.3 | 44.6 | 58.6 | 39.2 |
| 65–74 | 25.0 | 30.8 | 24.5 | 52.7 | 43.3 | 27.5 |
| **Females** | | | | | | |
| 25–34 | 2.3 | 2.2 | 2.3 | 8.6 | 12.4 | 4.3 |
| 35–44 | 6.2 | 6.6 | 6.5 | 25.7 | 23.8 | 17.6 |
| 45–54 | 15.5 | 13.9 | 12.1 | 41.3 | 39.7 | 37.3 |
| 55–64 | 30.6 | 27.6 | 18.3 | 37.9 | 45.6 | 36.4 |
| 65–74 | 46.6 | 34.9 | 26.3 | 64.1 | 46.3 | 3.4 |

*Rate per 100 population.
**Systolic blood pressure of at least 160 mmHg and/or diastolic blood pressure of at least 95 mmHG.

*Sources:* Abstracted and compiled by CHESS from (1) Hypertension and Hypertensive Heart Disease in Adults, United States, 1960–62. National Center for Health Statistics. DHEW Publication No. (HRA) 74–1282. *Vital and Health Statistics.* Series 11. No. 13. November 1973. Table 2. (2) Hypertension in Adults 25–74 years of age. United States, 1971–1975. National Center for Health Statistics, DHHS Publication No. (PHS) 81–1671. *Vital and Health Statistics.* Series 11. No. 221. April 1981. Table 21. (3) Blood Pressure Levels and Hypertension in Persons ages 6–74 years: United States, 1976–1980. National Center for Health Statistics. DHHS Publication No. (PHS) 82–1250. Advance Data No. 84, October 1982. Table 5.

*From:* U.S. Department of Health and Human Services. *Health Status of Minorities and Low Income Groups.* Washington, DC: U.S. Government Printing Office, 1985, 125.

Between 1965 and 1980, mortality from malignant neoplasms was the second leading cause of death in the United States. By 1980 the age-adjusted mortality rate for cancer was 132.8 deaths per 100,000 population—almost a 6 percent increase since 1960. For White Americans this represented a 4.3 percent increase since 1960 and a 3.9 percent increase since 1950. For "all other"* Americans the increase in cancer mortality was 13.5 percent since 1960 and a 23 percent increase since 1950. During the 1970s a group of oncologists, surgeons, and medical

---

*The "All Other" designation lumps the health indices of Blacks and other non-White groups under one category. The designation traditionally includes Blacks, Hispanic Americans, Native Americans, and Asian Americans. Other terms used have been non-Whites and racial minorities. In 1950, 93 percent (92 percent in 1960) of nonwhites were African Americans; Blacks represented only 84 percent by 1980. Thus, the term has diverged from the Black experience. This practice increasingly tends to mask true Black health status and outcomes, since Black indices are consistently worse than those for any other racial or ethnic group.

Table 4.17 Prevalence Rates of Hypertension for Persons 25–74 Years of Age by Treatment History, Race, and Sex with Standard Errors of Percent: United States, 1960–1962, 1974–1975, 1976–1980

| | Percent of Population[4] | | | Percent of Total with Hypertension[1,4] | | | | | | | | |
| | Hypertensive[1] | | | Never diagnosed[2] | | | On medication | | | On medication and controlled[3] | | |
| Race and Sex | 1960–62 | 1974–75 | 1976–80 | 1960–62 | 1974–75 | 1976–80 | 1960–62 | 1974–75 | 1976–80 | 1960–62 | 1974–75 | 1976–80 |
|---|---|---|---|---|---|---|---|---|---|---|---|---|
| **All people** | | | | | | | | | | | | |
| 25–74 years[5] | 20.3 | 22.1 | 22.0 | 51.1 | 36.4 | 26.6 | 31.3 | 34.2 | 56.2 | 16.0 | 19.6 | 34.1 |
| White men | 16.3 | 21.4 | 21.2 | 57.6 | 42.3 | 40.6 | 22.4 | 25.9 | 38.3 | 11.8 | 15.1 | 20.9 |
| White women | 20.4 | 19.6 | 20.0 | 43.9 | 29.7 | 25.2 | 38.2 | 48.5 | 58.6 | 21.9 | 28.1 | 40.3 |
| Black men | 31.8 | 37.1 | 28.3 | 70.5 | 41.0 | 35.7 | 18.5 | 24.0 | 40.9 | 5.0 | 12.3 | 16.1 |
| Black women | 39.8 | 35.5 | 39.8 | 35.1 | 28.9 | 14.5 | 48.1 | 36.4 | 60.6 | 20.2 | 22.3 | 38.3 |
| | | | | | *Standard error of percent* | | | | | | | |
| **All people** | | | | | | | | | | | | |
| 25–74 years[5] | 0.83 | 1.26 | 0.68 | 1.66 | 1.70 | 1.53 | 1.62 | 2.21 | 1.99 | 1.65 | 1.49 | 2.02 |
| White men | 0.95 | 2.19 | 1.04 | 3.75 | 2.63 | 1.80 | 3.07 | 3.22 | 2.47 | 2.59 | 2.56 | 2.01 |
| White women | 1.07 | 1.14 | 0.66 | 2.77 | 2.08 | 1.97 | 2.24 | 3.61 | 2.40 | 2.24 | 2.93 | 2.99 |
| Black men | 3.37 | 5.94 | 1.86 | 7.07 | 10.38 | 4.27 | 5.53 | 10.79 | 4.52 | 2.18 | 6.69 | 3.72 |
| Black women | 3.73 | 3.60 | 1.96 | 3.72 | 7.42 | 2.73 | 3.87 | 8.30 | 3.22 | 3.21 | 7.93 | 4.35 |

[1]Elevated blood pressure (that is, a systolic measurement of at least 160 mmHg or a diastolic measurement of at least 95 mmHg) or taking antihypertensive medication.

[2]Reported never told by physician that he or she had high blood pressure or hypertension.

[3]Subset of "On Medication" group; those taking antihypertensive medication whose blood pressure was not elevated at the time of the examination.

[4]Age adjusted by direct method to the population at midpoint of the 1976–1980 National Health and Nutrition Examination Series.

[5]Includes all other races not shown separately.

*Source:* National Center for Health Statistics. *Blood Pressure Level and Hypertension in Persons Aged 6–74 years; United States, 1976–80.* DHHS Publication No. (PHS) 82–1250. Advance Data Number 84. U.S. Government Printing Office, Washington, DC. October 8, 1982, Table 7, 10.

*From:* U.S. Department of Health and Human Services. *Health Status of Minorities and Low Income Groups.* Washington, DC: U.S. Government Printing Office, 1985, 125.

researchers based at Howard University, utilizing statistical methods and following trends in large groups of common cancers, documented an alarming rise in cancer mortality among African Americans between 1950 and 1967[248] (see Table 4.18). As a result of, or perhaps due to, their efforts, during the 1979 American Cancer Society (ACS) presidency of Howard surgeon LaSalle D. Leffall, M.D., the first African American physician to fill that position, the "African American Cancer Crisis" became a significant health policy agenda item for the first time.

Their revelation of an "African American Cancer Crisis," which was later corroborrated by Claudia Baquet, Linda A. Clayton, the U.S. Department of Health and Human Services (DHHS), the ACS, and others,[249] showed that: "[i]n white Americans, cancer incidence between 1950 and 1967 for all sites combined increased by 12 percent. In blacks, however, it increased by 27 percent. Cancer mortality increased by 10 percent in Whites and 50 percent in Blacks during this period."[250] The growing racial differential was exemplified by the age-adjusted cancer mortality rates, which increased 23 percent for White men and 82 percent for Black men between 1960 and 1980. Although the rates for all women declined during the same period, for White women they declined 10 percent compared to a 2 percent decline for Black women. As René noted, "For all malignant neoplasms, the racial differential in the mortality rates increased from 15 percent in 1960 to 33 percent in 1980."[251] For Black males, this growing differential represented a difference of 11.9 percent in 1960 and 43.2 percent in 1980. The change was less dramatic in women, with the difference in rates between Black and White females growing from 16.7 percent in 1960 to 20.4 percent in 1980. Especially problematic were the Black increases in mortality for cancers of the lung, digestive system,* breast, and prostate and multiple myeloma. For example, "Malignant neoplasms of the respiratory system, the leading cancer problem, increased from a 5.8 percent difference in 1960 to a 41.2 percent difference in 1980."[252] Malignancies of the digestive system followed a similar pattern. Black women, who experienced less overall cancer morbidity and mortality, charted a racial percentage difference increase in digestive system mortality from 10.6 percent in 1960 to nearly 40 percent in 1980. Moreover, "Breast cancer mortality for black females was below that of white females in 1960 and 1970; in 1980 breast cancer mortality rates for black females surpassed those of white females."[253] By 1980 data from the National Cancer Institute (NCI) indicated that for most cancer sites, White Americans were more likely to have localized (rather than systemic) cancers at diagnosis. Based on such findings,[254] René, Clayton, Baquet, Haynes, Leffall, Byrd, and others have postulated that Blacks do not receive medical attention as early as Whites, that Blacks may not have access to appropriate cancer screening compared to Whites, and/or that cancer diagnoses are not made in early evaluations of Blacks.[255]

---

*This includes cancers of the colon, pancreas, stomach, and esophagus.

## Table 4.18 Trend of Non-White and White Mortality Rates for the Most Frequent Cancers, 1950–1967

| Trend | ICD Numbers | Cancer Type | Sex | Death in 1967 | Average Yearly Change per 100,000 Non-Whites | Whites | Confidence Level |
|---|---|---|---|---|---|---|---|
| Group I Increase significantly slower in Whites | 170 | Breast | F | 27,985 | 0.188 | 0.012 | |
| | 153 | Colon | F | 17,877 | 0.215 | –0.092 | |
| | 177 | Prostate | M | 16,345 | 0.451 | –0.090 | |
| | 153 | Colon | M | 15,205 | 0.289 | 0.088 | |
| | 157 | Pancreas | M | 9,696 | 0.340 | 0.157 | |
| | 175 | Ovary | F | 9,168 | 0.108 | 0.043 | |
| | 157 | Pancreas | F | 7,190 | 0.215 | 0.059 | |
| | 181 | Bladder | M | 6,019 | 0.048 | –0.016 | |
| | 150 | Esophagus | M | 4,306 | 0.294 | –0.013 | |
| | 155 | Biliary + liver | F | 3,790 | 0.037 | –0.047 | P ≤ 0.001 |
| | 155 | Biliary + liver | M | 2,955 | 0.155 | 0.031 | |
| | 181 | Bladder | F | 2,743 | 0.018 | –0.043 | |
| | 161 | Larynx | M | 2,468 | 0.085 | 0.008 | |
| | 145–148 | Pharynx | M | 2,270 | 0.068 | 0.009 | |
| | 203 | Multiple myeloma | M | 2,081 | 0.134 | 0.059 | |
| | 203 | Multiple myeloma | F | 1,798 | 0.090 | 0.042 | |
| | 172 | Corpus uteri | F | 1,743 | 0.065 | 0.006 | |
| | 150 | Esophagus | F | 1,321 | 0.063 | –0.003 | |
| | 144 | Mouth unspec. | M | 702 | 0.021 | –0.005 | |
| | 163 | Lung | M | 27,089 | 1.306 | 0.956 | |
| | 162 | Lung | M | 18,294 | 0.882 | 0.652 | |
| | 199* | "Other" | M | 12,290 | 0.191 | 0.009 | P ≤ 0.01 |
| | 180 | Kidney | M | 3,693 | 0.076 | 0.050 | |
| | 141 | Tongue | M | 1,186 | 0.025 | –0.007 | |
| | 204 | Leukemia | M | 8,222 | 0.144 | 0.016 | |
| | 163 | Lung | F | 5,839 | 0.183 | 0.116 | |
| | 180 | Kidney | F | 2,201 | 0.018 | 0.004 | P ≤ 0.05 |
| | 145–148 | Pharynx | F | 640 | 0.010 | 0.004 | |
| | 197 | Conn. tissue | F | 605 | 0.025 | 0.015 | |
| Group II Decrease significantly faster in Whites | 199* | "Other" | F | 11,180 | –0.009 | –0.167 | |
| | 151 | Stomach | M | 10,396 | –0.498 | –0.688 | |
| | 151 | Stomach | F | 6,654 | –0.303 | –0.393 | P ≤ 0.001 |
| | 154 | Rectum | M | 5,836 | –0.054 | –0.143 | |
| | 191 | Skin | M | 1,169 | –0.000 | –0.039 | |
| | 191 | Skin | F | 683 | –0.005 | –0.033 | |
| | 196 | Bone | M | 1,031 | –0.024 | –0.049 | |
| | 194 | Thyroid | F | 681 | –0.000 | –0.015 | P ≤ 0.01 |
| | 154 | Rectum | F | 4,595 | –0.092 | –0.128 | P ≤ 0.05 |
| Group III No statistically significant difference | 204 | Leukemia | F | 6,114 | 0.019 | –0.004 | |
| | 193 | Nervous system | M | 4,165 | 0.068 | 0.060 | |
| | 162 | Lung | F | 3,185 | 0.073 | 0.078 | |
| | 193 | Nervous system | F | 2,988 | 0.030 | 0.039 | |
| | 200.1 | Lymphosarcoma | M | 2,277 | 0.030 | 0.019 | |
| | 201 | Hodgkin's disease | M | 2,062 | 0.010 | 0.003 | |
| | 200.1 | Lymphosarcoma | F | 1,796 | 0.006 | 0.015 | |
| | 201 | Hodgkin's disease | F | 1,384 | –0.003 | 0.006 | P > 0.05 |
| | 176 | "Other" gyn. | F | 805 | –0.007 | –0.014 | |
| | 197 | Conn. tissue | M | 769 | 0.026 | 0.021 | |
| | 178 | Testis | M | 682 | 0.001 | –0.004 | |
| | 202 | Reticuloses | M | 717 | 0.010 | 0.016 | |
| | 202 | Reticuloses | F | 559 | 0.008 | 0.011 | |
| | 194 | Thyroid | M | 298 | –0.001 | –0.006 | |

*Includes ICD numbers 156, 165, 195, 198, and 199
*Source:* Henschke et al. Cancer mortality in Negroes. *Cancer* 1973; 31: 765.
Data from Report 33 of the National Cancer Institute.

*From:* Leffall Jr LD. Cancer mortality in blacks. CA 1974; 24: 44–45.

Although accidents and other adverse effects are not readily amenable to health system interventions, they were the third-leading cause of death in the United States between 1965 and 1980. By the end of this era, it was noted: "More than 153,000 Americans die annually as a result of accidental injuries.... [I]n 1979, 70 million people suffered nonfatal accidental injuries requiring medical treatment.[256] Thus trauma, accidents, and violence also affected African American health. This category was the leading cause of death for persons between 1 and 34 years of age, with a mortality rate of 57.5 deaths per 100,000 persons. Motor vehicle accidents accounted for 50 percent of the total, although racial differentials dictated that "deaths from motor vehicle accidents represent[ed] proportionately more deaths for the total population (50 percent) than for non-Whites (40 percent) or blacks (38 percent)"[257] by 1980. In 1970 the age-adjusted accident mortality rate of non-Whites was 43 percent higher than that of Whites; by 1980 the differential mortality among non-Whites was only 19 percent higher than Whites—demonstrating a decade-long decreasing disparity between Blacks and Whites. Black female motor vehicle accident mortality decreased from 10 deaths per 100,000 in 1960 to 8.4 deaths per 100,000 in 1980. And after experiencing higher motor vehicle death rates in the 1960s and 1970s, "By 1980, the motor vehicle accident death rate of black males (31.1 deaths per 100,000 population) was 13.4 percent lower than the rate for white males (35.9 deaths per 100,000 population)."[258] Nevertheless, after steadily increasing from the early 1960s, the overall accident and adverse effect mortality rates for Black males remained 31 percent higher than for White males by 1980. The Black female overall accident and adverse effect rate was 17 percent higher than that for White females by 1980. (See Table 4.15.) Mortality from homicides and legal intervention was seven times higher for Black men than White men, even though Black male homicide rates decreased slightly (1.5 percent) between 1970 and 1980. The huge Black/White differential in homicide rates in females in 1970 (6.33) decreased by 1980 (4.22) "due to the larger increase in deaths from this source among white females (52.4 percent) than among black females (1.5 percent)."[259] Although accidental deaths constitute accurate measurements, the relative impact of *non-fatal* accidents is made difficult by the paucity of published data by race in this area. Moreover, disadvantaged minorities tend to use health facilities less often. However, based on the sketchy data available, Black patients seemingly had a slightly higher percentage (9 percent) of physician visits related to accidents, poisonings, and violence than all patients (7.3 percent). Hospitalizations for Blacks and Whites in both 1971 (10.3 percent and 10.5 percent, respectively) and 1981 (9.3 percent and 9.7 percent, respectively) related to accidents, poisonings, and violence seemed to be equal.[260]

Despite their tendency to be cyclical, probably due the cyclical nature of influenza, the combined categories of pneumonia and influenza ranked as the fifth leading cause of death in the United States as of 1980. (See Table 4.19.) Over the past 30 years, the mortality rate from this acute cause of death has decreased by almost 51 percent (from 26.2 deaths per 100,000 population to 12.9 deaths per

**Table 4.19   Age-Adjusted Death Rates for Influenza and Pneumonia, by Race and Sex, United States, Selected Years from 1950 to 1980**

| Year | Total Both Sexes | Total Male | Total Female | White Both Sexes | White Male | White Female | All other Both Sexes | All other Male | All other Female |
|---|---|---|---|---|---|---|---|---|---|
| | | | | Rate per 100,000 Population | | | | | |
| 1950* | 26.2 | 30.6 | 22.0 | 22.9 | 27.1 | 18.9 | 56.9 | 63.4 | 50.6 |
| 1960 | 28.0 | 35.8 | 21.8 | 24.6 | 31.0 | 19.0 | 55.2 | 68.0 | 43.3 |
| 1970 | 22.1 | 28.8 | 16.7 | 19.8 | 26.0 | 15.0 | 38.1 | 50.1 | 27.9 |
| 1980 | 12.9 | 17.4 | 9.8 | 12.2 | 16.2 | 9.4 | 18.0 | 26.1 | 11.9 |
| Decrease 1950–1980 | 50.8 | 43.1 | 55.5 | 46.7 | 40.2 | 50.3 | 68.4 | 58.8 | 76.5 |
| % total** decrease occurring in 1970–1980 | 69.2 | 86.4 | 56.6 | 71.0 | 89.9 | 58.9 | 51.7 | 64.3 | 41.3 |

*Based on enumerated population adjusted for age bias in the population of races other than White.

**There was a substantial decrease in death rates between 1970 and 1980. This now contains the percentage of that decrease that occurred during the last of these three decades (i.e. 1970, 1980: 1950–1980).

*Source:* Compiled by CHESS from (1) Department of Health, Education and Welfare. *Mortality Trends for Leading Causes of Death, U.S. 1950–69.* Rockville, MD. Series 20, No. 16. Table K, 30. (2) Department of Health, Education, and Welfare. *Monthly Vital Statistics Report.* Summary report. Final Mortality Statistics 1970, vol. 22, no. 8; 1980, vol. 32, no. 4.

*From:* U.S. Department of Health and Human Services. *Health Status of Minorities and Low Income Groups.* Washington, DC: U.S. Government Printing Office, 1985, 103.

100,000 population). Non-White mortality and female mortality declined the most (68.4 percent and 55.5 percent declines, respectively). (See Table 4.19.) As reported in the *Health Status of Minorities and Low Income Groups:* "In 1950, the non-white-to-white ratio was 2.34 for males and by 1980 that ratio had dropped to 1.61; for females, the 1950 nonwhite-to-white ratio was 2.68, and it dropped to 1.27 by 1980."[261] Nevertheless, "in 1980 there remained a 72 percent difference in mortality between black males and white males and a 35 percent difference in mortality between black females and white females."[262] (See Table 4.19.) Progress on these conditions seemed so promising in 1980 that the DHHS predicted: "At these rates of convergence, the female differential could disappear by the end of this decade, and the male differential could disappear by the end of the century."[263]

Cirrhosis of the liver was the sixth leading cause of death in the United States in 1979. Confusion abounded on whether to classify this entity as an acute or chronic condition. It was being recorded on the Health Interview Survey as an acute condition, and although it develops over a long period of time, it goes through acute phases. Most deaths attributed to it probably occur during the acute episodes, and, unlike most chronic conditions, it has prominent reversible characteristics. The death rate from cirrhosis of the liver increased steadily from 1950 to 1973—a rise of approximately 60 percent for Whites and 242 percent for non-Whites. (See Table 4.20.) The increases were greater for males than females with male-to-female ratios for Whites of 1.18 and 1.28 for non-Whites. After 1973 there was a steady decrease of approximately 20 percent in cirrhotic death rates. (See Table 4.20.) The etiology of the decline is unknown, but DHHS speculated it may have been caused by several factors: the extension of health insurance coverage to treat alcoholism and its complications; the implementation of strict drunk driver statutes requiring treatment and rehabilitation for retention of drivers' licenses; U.S. physicians becoming more knowledgeable, receiving better training, becoming less judgmental toward alcoholism, and incorporating rehabilitation into their treatment; participation in Alcoholics Anonymous becoming more socially acceptable; political figures, sports stars, and celebrities becoming more open with their struggles with the disease; and the health community adopting a new holistic therapeutic model consisting of psychotherapy and medical treatment. Despite this enigma, the overall mortality of the disease increased 43.5 percent over three decades (1950–1980), with non-White percentage mortality rates skyrocketing 170.3 percent in that same time period. The overall percentage increase among Whites was 27.9 percent, while non-White males topped all race-sex groupings, increasing 212.2 percent (non-White women charted a 128.8 percent rise). More evidence that all races did not progress equally, as far as cirrhosis was concerned, suggested, "The difference in mortality rates for blacks and whites in 1960 was negligible (2.8 percent), but by 1980 the racial difference in mortality rates had risen to 94 percent."[264] In addition, "The non-white-to-white ratio inverted from 0.86 to 1.82 during the 30 year period,"[265] the DHHS observed.[266]

### Table 4.20  Age-Adjusted Death Rates for Cirrhosis of the Liver, by Race and Sex, United States, Selected Years from 1950 to 1980

| Year | Total | | | White | | | All Other | | |
|---|---|---|---|---|---|---|---|---|---|
| | Both Sexes | Male | Female | Both Sexes | Male | Female | Both Sexes | Male | Female |
| | Rate per 100,000 Population | | | | | | | | |
| 1950* | 8.5 | 11.4 | 5.8 | 8.6 | 11.6 | 5.8 | 7.4 | 9.0 | 5.9 |
| 1960 | 10.5 | 14.5 | 6.9 | 10.3 | 14.4 | 6.6 | 11.9 | 14.9 | 9.1 |
| 1970 | 14.7 | 20.2 | 9.8 | 13.4 | 18.8 | 8.7 | 23.8 | 31.3 | 17.4 |
| 1980 | 12.2 | 17.1 | 7.9 | 11.0 | 15.7 | 7.0 | 20.0 | 28.1 | 13.5 |
| % Increase 1950–1973 | 76.5 | 83.3 | 70.7 | 59.3 | 66.4 | 50.0 | 241.9 | 267.7 | 205.1 |
| % Decrease 1973–1980 | 18.7 | 18.2 | 20.2 | 19.7 | 18.6 | 19.5 | 20.9 | 17.1 | 25.0 |
| % Increase 1950–1980 | 43.5 | 50.0 | 36.2 | 27.9 | 35.3 | 20.7 | 170.3 | 212.2 | 128.8 |

*Based on enumerated population adjusted for age bias in the population of races other than white.
*Source:* Compiled by CHESS from (1) Department of Health, Education and Welfare: *Mortality Trends for Leading Causes of Death, U.S. 1950–69.* Rockville, MD. Series 20, No. 16. Table K, 30. (2) Department of Health, Education, and Welfare. *Monthly Vital Statistics Report.* Summary Report. Final Mortality Statistics 1970, vol. 22, no. 8; 1980, vol. 32, no. 4. (3) Department of Health, Education, and Welfare. *Monthly Vital Statistics Report.* Advance Report of Final Mortality Statistics 1980, vol. 32, no. 4.

*From:* U.S. Department of Health and Human Services. *Health Status of Minorities and Low Income Groups.* Washington, DC: U.S. Government Printing Office, 1985, 103.

Diabetes accounted for 2 percent of all deaths and was the seventh leading cause of death in the United States in 1980. Most diabetics died of complications of the disease related to deterioration of the kidneys and arteries or changes in the nervous system. This contrasts with 48 percent of diabetic deaths being related to diabetic acidosis or coma precipitated by severe water depletion and electrolyte changes in the pre-insulin era. Such deaths constituted only 1.2 percent of the mortality by 1980. As the DHHS noted, "Diabetics have more severe atherosclerosis, twice as many heart attacks and about twice as many strokes as nondiabetics of the same age."[267] Moreover, by 1980 epidemiologists had observed that diabetes "is associated with 50 percent of all amputations among adults, 20 percent of all cases of kidney failure, and 15 percent of all cases of blindness."[268] Approximately 600,000 new cases of diabetes were being diagnosed annually, and the disease was disproportionately affecting the non-White population. In 1973, "the reported prevalence rate per 1,000 population among whites was 19.9 and among all other races 23.9."[269] Later prevalence rates (1976) for type II diabetes in the four race/gender groups confirmed these impressions, with age-adjusted prevalence rates for non-White males computed at 27.9 per 1,000 population compared to 20.0 per 1,000 population for White males—a 39.5 percent higher rate. For non-White females, the 36.9 per 1,000 population prevalence rate was 76 percent higher than the White female rate of 20.8 per 1,000 population. The non-White/White ratio of disease prevalence for males was 1.29, while the non-White/White risk ratio for women was 1.69. (See Table 4.21.)

African Americans' overall age-adjusted mortality rates from diabetes declined 13 percent from 1960 to 1980, resulting in "modest gains in reductions of deaths from diabetes."[270] Age-adjusted Black male diabetic mortality rates vacillated

**Table 4.21  Crude and Age-Standardized Type II Diabetes Prevalence Rates, United States, 1976**

|  | Prevalence per 1,000 Persons | | |
|  | Crude Rate | Age-Standardized Rate* | Ratio |
|---|---|---|---|
| All | 21.6 | 21.6 | 1.0 |
| White Males | 19.3 | 20.0 | 0.92 |
| White Females | 22.7 | 20.8 | 0.96 |
| Non-White Males | 21.1 | 27.9 | 1.29 |
| Non-White Females | 30.7 | 36.6 | 1.69 |

*Age-standardized to the U.S. 1976 population.

*Source:* The public health impact of diabetes. In: *Advance in Diabetes Epidemiology*, ed. Eveline Eschwege. INSERM Symposium No. 22. Institut Nationale de la Santé et de la Recherche Medicale, Elsevier Biomedical Press, Amsterdam, New York, Oxford, 1982, Table 2.

*Source:* U.S. Department of Health and Human Services. *Health Status of Minorities and Low Income Groups*. Washington, DC: U.S. Government Printing Office, 1985, 127.

between 16.2 deaths per 100,000 population in 1960, 21.2 deaths per 100,000 population in 1970, and 17.7 deaths per 100,000 population in 1980. This was a net increase of 1.5 deaths per 100,000 population (a 9.3 percent rise in mortality rate) during the period. Although this slight increase seemed troubling at the time, African American diabetic mortality levels viewed retrospectively continued to climb throughout the 1980s and early 1990s.[271] Meanwhile, White male diabetic mortality rates declined erratically from 11.3 deaths per 100,000 population in 1960 to 9.5 deaths per 100,000 population in 1980. In Black females, age-adjusted diabetic mortality rates declined sporadically from a rate of 27.3 deaths per 100,000 population to 22.1 deaths per 100,000 population—a 23.5 percent decrease. The racial differential in diabetic mortality between Whites and Blacks climbed steadily between 1960 and 1980. Although overall Black diabetic mortality declined erratically from 22.0 deaths per 100,000 population in 1960 to 20.3 deaths per 100,000 population in 1980, the percentage differences between Black and White mortality climbed steadily from 71.9 percent in 1960 to 123.1 percent in 1980. The ratio between overall Black/White mortality rates also increased steadily from 1.72 to 2.23 during the same period.[272] Further indications of the growing racial differential in diabetic mortality were changes in the Black female rates. Despite the sporadic decline mentioned here, the percentage difference in the Black and White diabetic mortality rates climbed steadily from a 99.3 percent difference in 1960 to a 141 percent difference in 1970 to a 154 percent difference in 1980. The Black/White ratio of diabetic mortality exhibited a similar trend, consistently increasing from 2.0 in 1960, 2.4 in 1970, and 2.5 in 1980.[273] However, these small increases could only be viewed favorably in light of dramatic increases in diabetic mortality among Blacks during preceding decades.[274]

Another often overlooked health status indicator worthy of examination is dental health. At least six categories of dental health indicators were being utilized by 1980: (1) utilization of dental health services; (2) dental caries; (3) periodontal disease; (4) filled teeth; (5) standardized dental examinations and surveys; and (6) missing teeth. Despite the plethora of disaggregated measures, or indicators, of dental health, gauging the dental health status of a nation or a subpopulation within a nation is a difficult undertaking. Nevertheless, whether indicators were clustered together into indexes such as the DMF index,* the PI index (periodontal index), or hygiene indexes,** all indicate that there were striking racial differences in dental health and that there was poor dental health among disadvantaged

---

*The DMF index is a composite score of decayed, missing, or filled teeth. The first two categories reflect morbidity (decayed teeth [D] and missing teeth [T]) while the last category reflects restorative dental care (filled teeth). Since the latter reflects healthy teeth (although not as healthy as unfilled teeth without decay, such teeth do not require health care at the time of examination), this brings into question the utility of the DMF index as a health status measure.

**The Simplified Oral Hygiene Index (OHI-S), Simplified Debris Index (DI-S), and the Simplified Calculus Index (CI-S) are three measures based on the judgment of dental examiners.

minorities, those of lower income, those of lower educational levels, and those living in rural areas. Of the trends showing signs of closing the Black/White dental health gap, the utilization measures, which will be discussed with other health utilization data, showed the most progress between 1960 and 1980.

Several clinical indicators displayed the dental health differences in the White and Black populations: the comparative condition of teeth, the prevalence and severity of gum disease, oral hygiene, and the total absence of teeth (edentulism). Despite the fact that "as has been concluded many times elsewhere in the literature … blacks appear to have naturally healthier teeth from the standpoint of dental decay,"[275] Blacks experience worse DMF indexes than Whites. In the 1960–1962 NCHS data Haynes noted 21.2 DMF teeth per person in White adults compared to 14.5 in Black adults. While the overall DMF count in the White population was almost 50 percent higher than in Blacks, in a major component of the count—the average number of decayed teeth per person—the situation was reversed. The largest racial difference he found was in the number of filled teeth, "with White adults having an average of five times as many filled teeth as Black adults"[276] (see Figure 4.4). In both races DMF counts were higher for women than for men, with more pronounced gender differences in the Black population. The racial differences persisted in the 1971–1974 NCHS studies, although there were overall declines in the number of decayed teeth (17 percent), with women continuing to have slightly lower decayed tooth rates. For both sexes "and for all age groups above 5 years, blacks had a higher average number of decayed teeth and a higher average number of missing teeth."[277] For filled teeth, the sole representative of the use of dental care and services within the index, there were striking comparisons between the sexes, with White females having 9 percent more restorative dental care than White males and Black females having 27 percent more than Black males. But the DHHS noted: "The comparisons within sex but between the races are even more startling. White women average 3.84 times more filled teeth than black women, and white males average 4.7 times more filled teeth than black males."[278] These ratios and the resulting index seem to be due to, and were distorted by, the fact that both male and female Blacks had decayed teeth in need of fillings and were not getting needed dental services. Adding together the decayed and filled teeth to get a measure of total dental caries restored and unrestored, Blacks had about half the dental caries rates for Whites (8.0 for White males, 8.4 for White females, 3.7 for Black males, and 4.3 for Black females). Comparing the number of filled teeth (F) to the combined number, we obtain a measure of dental health needs met (i.e., F/D + F).* The DHHS noted: "This measure demonstrates that whites have 'dental health needs met' scores (for dental caries) that are twice those of blacks (0.8375 for white males, 0.8690 for white

---

*The ratio of filled/decayed teeth (F/D) added to filled teeth (F) comprises a "dental health needs met" score. *Source:* U.S. Department of Health and Human Services. *Health Status of Minorities and Low Income Groups.* Washington, DC: U.S. Government Printing Office, 1985, 189.

**Figure 4.4  Average DMF (Number of Decayed, Missing, and Filled Teeth) and Components for White and Black Adults, United States, 1960–1962**

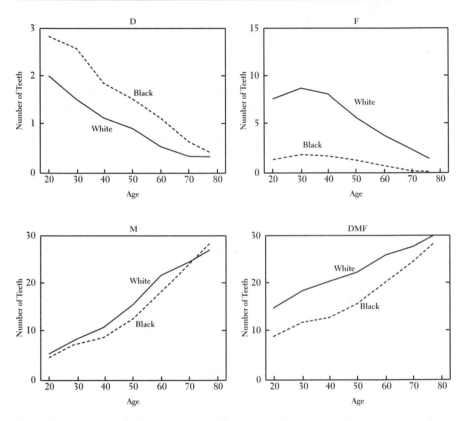

*Source:* National Center for Health Statistics: Selected dental findings in adults by age, race, and sex, United States, 1960–1962, *Vital and Health Statistics*. U.S. Public Health Service Publication 1,000, ser. 11, no. 7, February 1965.

*From:* Haynes MA. The gap in health status between black and white Americans. In: Williams RA, ed. *Textbook of Black-Related Diseases*. New York: McGraw-Hill, 1975, 16.

females, 0.4054 for black males, and 0.4419 for black females)."[279] The lack of access and receipt of dental services seemed to be the dominant factor, rather than genetics or nutrition, accounting for racial differences in teeth.

By 1980 periodontal disease was thought to be the most significant factor in the loss of teeth in adults over 35 years of age. This cluster of diseases is associated with the deterioration of the tissues that anchor the teeth—from mild inflammation of the gums and connective tissues to generalized destruction of foundation materials, including bone. Tooth loss is inevitable in advanced stages of periodontal disease. It was suspected at that time—which was supported by scientific studies associating diminished periodontal pathology with cleanliness, tooth-brushing, decreasing mouth bacteria, and the absence of plaque and calculus—that oral hygiene and preventive care played significant roles.

In the 1960–1962 studies, Haynes found the prevalence and severity of gum disease measured by the Periodontal Index (PI), a classification of individuals based on a visual appraisal of the condition of the tissues supporting each tooth in the mouth: "Black adults have a mean PI higher than White adults—1.60 compared to 1.06."[280] Blacks had higher PIs than Whites for both sexes except for the oldest males (75 to 79 age range). During the 1960–1962 NCHS study, "Only 15.8 percent of Black persons have no gum disease, compared with 27.8 percent of White persons. In addition, the percentage of Black adults with a more severe form of the disease [was] higher than for Whites."[281] The frequency of destructive periodontal disease to the point of pocket formation was 50 percent higher in Blacks than Whites—36.0 compared to 23.9 percent. The 1971–1974 NCHS study revealed improvements for both races. The overall Black PI declined to 1.28, with a pattern of increasing racial differentials in all age groupings. However, the White decline (28 percent) was more pronounced than the Black decline (20 percent), and the Black/White ratio, or risk of periodontal disease, increased from 1.51 in 1960 to 1962 to 1.68 in 1971 to 1974. In those years Black males had almost 1¼ times the risk of gum disease as White males, and Black women experienced almost 1⅔ the risk of having peridontal disease as White women. More hopeful were the findings in 1971–1974 studies that preventive measures such as toothbrushing, oral cleanliness, and stopping smoking had positive effects on the risks for periodontal disease and could serve as supplements to dental services in combating racial disparities in this area.

Rates of edentulous persons differed greatly by race. In the NCHS 1960–1962 data, Haynes found: "In the White population, 19.2 percent are edentulous, while only 11.3 percent of the Black population have lost all their teeth."[282] For males this racial differential held true for every age grouping (ages 17 to 89), while Black women had higher rates of edentulism in the 25 to 34 and 65 to 74 age groupings. The 1960–1962 racial differential between Whites and Blacks (White rates 70 percent higher than Blacks) did not change appreciably in the 1971 to 1974 data set (White rates 69 percent higher than Blacks). Over a 13-to-14-year period followed by the National Health Survey between July 1957 to June 1958 and 1971, edentulism rates dropped rapidly.[283] How Blacks continued to have lower rates of edentulism despite the association of edentulism with low income, low educational levels, high levels of severe periodontal disease, and low levels of utilization of dental health services presented a paradox. This was further complicated by the fact that based on 1971–1974 NCHS data, African Americans had consistently higher scores (fared poorly) on virtually all the indices of oral hygiene—the OHI-S, the DI-S, and the CI-S—which increased their risks for periodontal disease and edentulism.[284]

While examination of indices of medical and dental health are critical in evaluating and comparing health status and outcomes of different populations, assessing how the health system responds to health needs is also warranted. Prior to

1965, utilization of physician and hospital services differed dramatically on the basis of race and class. For African Americans this situation was compounded by René's observation: "Blacks receive considerably fewer preventive services, on the average, than do white people."[285] Clearly, the operational and disaggregated measures of health status, especially mortality statistics, gave some indication of the health status of African Americans and the amount of health care they needed. Since World War II, despite racial discrimination, oppression, and segregation, the United States began providing African Americans an unprecedented and singular "second-tier" health care infrastructure and environment that served as a virtual launching pad for "Second Reconstruction" health improvements. But although equality, even equity, remained just beyond Blacks' grasp, Butch Lewis, the well-known African American sports and entertainment promoter and philanthropist, provided a contemporaneous appraisal through contrasting what was happening to African Americans compared to their South African counterparts. In his words, African Americans should not "forget just how blessed we are. Things we take for granted—indoor toilets, plumbing and electricity—were nowhere to be found [in South Africa]. Public housing developments that are looked down on here would be considered castles in South Africa's shanties."[286] Despite the fact that Black excess deaths hovered between 60,000 and 85,000 annually and millions of years of potential life were lost over the period, Blacks made significant improvements in their health status and outcomes between 1965 and 1980. Nevertheless, wide, deep, race-based health disparities remained. And by 1980, although the causes of poor health are complex and difficult to explain—ranging from harmful environments, biological and genetic determinants, socioeconomic status, cultural and spiritual determinants, and unhealthy lifestyles—with improvements in health interventions and therapies and modern medicine's ability to prolong life and selectively delay death, the health system discrimination and access to health services grew ever more important.

The increased use of health services and access to the health system afforded by Medicare/Medicaid, the community health center movement, and programs to increase involvement of minority and disadvantaged populations in the delivery of health care proved to be tremendously important factors positively influencing health indicators and beginning, if not a racial convergence, at least a trend toward improving the health of U.S. populations. In fact, study of health services utilization coupled with "[c]omparisons of rates over time or between population groups may suggest changes in health status and health needs over time."[287] A brief examination of health services utilization as related to African American and disadvantaged patient health status and outcomes during this pivotal era follows.[288]

Examining utilization data provides unique insights into the functioning of the nation's health system during any period. Understanding which part of the system gets used, to what extent, by whom, for what, and why, "is a topic in itself when assessing the health status of subpopulations of our society."[289] After the 1970s, the DHHS cited Wilson's and White's 1977 article in *Medical Care* about changing relationships in utilization between the poor and nonpoor: "[F]or hospital and physician care, where more program efforts have taken place, there have been reductions or eliminations of differences in utilization between the poor and nonpoor."[290] Despite the esoteric debate between health economists over whether increased utilization leads to open-ended improvements in health status or whether health status improves up to a point beyond which further utilization yields no results, as of 1980, the DHHS concluded: "[I]t is obvious that, at least for racial/ethnic minorities and the disadvantaged, we have not as yet reached that part of the curve for many health problems where increased utilization has no effect."[291] Along with acknowledging that factors such as socioeconomic status, cultural patterns and behavior, and problems in health care delivery contribute to the poor health status of the Black population compared to Whites, Haynes acknowledged: "The difference in the availability of health care to the two groups reflects an essentially dual system of health care."[292] Despite the fact that health services utilization for African American and other disadvantaged minorities improved dramatically between 1965 and 1980 with concomitant improvements in their health status and outcomes, the higher levels of mortality and morbidity in these populations, their huge history-based deficit of unmet health care needs, shortfalls in dismantling the dual and unequal health system, and the fact that wide, deep disparities in their health status and outcomes remained compared to the White population suggested a great deal more needed to be done. Brief discussions of the three major categories of medical care utilization follow: (1) ambulatory care, (2) inpatient care, and (3) extended or long-term.

In spite of reporting their health as poor or fair and suffering from more chronic conditions than Whites in the early 1960s, African Americans saw physicians less often than European Americans. As Karen Davis noted, "In 1964 poor blacks and other minorities saw physicians an average of 3.1 times per year compared to an average of 4.7 times for whites."[293] In 1963 to 1964, Haynes noted a −11 percent Black/White difference for seeing a physician during the past year, based on NCHS data, compared to a −12 percent Black/White difference, according to the Center of Health Administration Studies of the Health Services and Mental Health Administration (HSM), in 1970. During the 1970s, the number of physician visits per year for the White population declined, while the number of physician visits per person per year for the Black population increased. By 1978, the average number of visits for poor Blacks and Whites, although unadjusted for health status,* were similar. Even when income was not a consideration, prior to 1964 Blacks were less likely than Whites to have seen a physician in two years or more. (See Table 4.22.) "By 1976 the proportion of the population seeing a physician over a two-year period did not vary substantially by race or income,"[294] according to Davis.

---

*One principle of public health is that all things being equal, sicker populations should utilize more health services if equal, or at the very least equitable, health outcomes are to be obtained. One major health services utilization indicator is physician visits per unit time.

Table 4.22   Use of Health Services by Selected Indices

|  | Poor | | | Nonpoor | | |
|---|---|---|---|---|---|---|
|  | White | Black and Other | Ratio White:Black | White | Black and Other | Ratio White:Black |
| Average no. of MD visits per person per year* | | | | | | |
| 1964 | 4.7 | 3.1 | 1.5 | 4.7 | 3.6 | 1.3 |
| 1976–1978 | 5.7 | 5.0 | 1.1 | 4.9 | 4.4 | 1.1 |
| Percentage with no MD visits in past two years* | | | | | | |
| 1964 | 25.7% | 33.2% | 0.8 | 17.1% | 24.7% | 0.7 |
| 1976 | 15.1 | 14.9 | 1.0 | 12.9 | 13.4 | 1.0 |
| Hospital discharges per 100 persons** | | | | | | |
| 1964 | 15.0 | 10.0 | 1.5 | 13.0 | 10.0 | 1.3 |
| 1979 | 21.0 | 17.0 | 1.2 | 13.0 | 12.0 | 1.1 |

*U.S. Department of Health and Human Services, 1980.

**President's Commission for the Study of Ethical Problems in Medical and Biomedical and Behavioral Research 1983.

*From:* Davis K, Lillie-Blanton M, Lyons B, Mullan F, Powe N, Rowland D. Health care for Black Americans: The public sector role. In: Willis DP, ed. *Health Policies and Black Americans.* New Brunswick, NJ: Transaction Publishers, 1989, 218.

Increasing proportions of American women received early and adequate prenatal care between 1965 and 1980. Early, continuous, and comprehensive prenatal care is one of the most important factors associated with healthy births and low infant mortality. The overall percentage of women receiving early prenatal care* increased from 68.0 percent in 1969 to 76.3 percent by 1980. For Black women, the percentage receiving early prenatal care rose from 42.7 percent (the non-White total was 44.5 percent) in 1969 to 62.7 percent (the non-White total was 63.8 percent) in 1980—a 47 percent increase. Nevertheless, a 26.4 percent Black/White gap remained, as 79.3 percent of White mothers received early prenatal care in 1980. For African Americans, these were remarkable improvements in ambulatory health care utilization.

These figures did not obscure the dual health experiences of Blacks and the poor compared to Whites in their utilization of the health system. This duality extended to where these populations received their services—often overcrowded, underfunded, public hospital clinics, public health department clinics, hospital emergency rooms, and charity facilities—and to the quality of the services themselves. Physician visit utilization data reveal higher numbers of visits later in the

*Early prenatal care* is defined as care starting in the first trimester.

period for low-income groups, except the 0 to 17 age group, where the occurrence of visits varied widely. For Whites between 1963 and 1970, Haynes and Anderson found that 73 percent of White patient visits took place in private physicians' office compared to 60 percent for Blacks. Moreover, "the proportion of the Black population who sees physicians in hospital clinics is more than three times that for White[s]."[295] Telephone consultations between White patients and their physicians were three times more common than for Blacks. And these trends and differences persisted for every income level and in both sexes. Following utilization trends early in the period, Anderson "has shown that the Black population is the group least likely to have any regular source of care and is most likely to use a clinic."[296] In 1970, 30 percent of Blacks and 16 percent of Whites reported having a clinic as their source of regular care. The term "clinic" referred to outpatient departments of hospitals, hospital emergency rooms, or large prepaid group practices. When queried as to whether they were usually seen by the same doctor, about two-thirds of Whites reported "Yes," while about two-thirds of Blacks reported "No." These basic patterns persisted for all Americans through 1980, with slightly more physician encounters occurring in hospital outpatient departments (12.2 percent in 1964 and 13.1 percent in 1980); greater percentages of Whites seeing physicians in doctors' offices compared to Blacks (68.4 percent of Whites compared to 57 percent of Blacks); far more Blacks (26.2 percent) and low-income patients seeing physicians in hospital outpatient departments compared to Whites (11.3 percent); most physician encounters (over 80 percent) being for diagnosis and treatment of conditions; and far fewer Blacks, proportionately, contacting physicians by telephone. (See Table 4.23.) The quality of the services rendered also varied. Davis found that in indicators of good medical practice such as periodic physical examinations, the poor lagged behind others in the 1970s, with 31 percent of high-income adults not receiving such an exam in the past two years compared to 45 percent of low-income adults. She noted that 34 percent of high-income women did not have Pap smear examinations between 1971 and 1973 compared to 57 percent of low-income women; similar differences occurred for breast examinations.

Physician visits suggest variations in access to ambulatory services, while "hospitalization data reflect who makes the greatest demand upon the more intensive (and expensive) inpatient care services."[297] By the 1965 to 1980 period, it was becoming obvious that ambulatory care offered the greater prospects for prevention, cost savings, and earlier detection. By 1980, avoiding inpatient services for the groups with the most severe morbidity—the elderly and the poor—was expected to reduce overall health care costs. Both the total number of hospital discharges and length of stay within short-stay hospitals declined slightly, according to NCHS data between 1975 and 1980. Along with the hospitalization rate for the poor increasing 40 percent between 1964 and 1974, the previous 50 percent gap in hospitalization rates for poor Whites compared to poor Blacks was cut. "By 1979 the poor were hospitalized at a higher rate than the nonpoor, reflecting their poorer health status

## Table 4.23 Physician Visits, According to Source or Place of Care and Selected Patient Characteristics, United States, 1964, 1975, and 1980

| Selected Characteristic | All Sources or Places[1] | | | Doctor's Office or Clinic or Group Practice | | | Hospital Outpatient Department[2] | | | Telephone | | |
|---|---|---|---|---|---|---|---|---|---|---|---|---|
| | 1964 | 1975 | 1980 | 1964 | 1975 | 1980 | 1964 | 1975 | 1980 | 1964 | 1975 | 1980 |
| | Number per person | | | Percent of visits | | | | | | | | |
| Total[3,4,5] | 4.6 | 5.0 | 4.7 | 69.7 | 67.1 | 67.1 | 12.2 | 13.2 | 13.1 | 11.0 | 13.1 | 12.8 |
| **Age** | | | | | | | | | | | | |
| Under 17 years | 3.7 | 4.2 | 4.4 | 62.2 | 62.2 | 63.1 | 13.7 | 14.6 | 13.1 | 18.3 | 17.7 | 17.3 |
| 17–44 years | 4.6 | 5.0 | 4.4 | 73.8 | 66.1 | 66.4 | 13.0 | 13.7 | 14.2 | 8.1 | 12.2 | 11.3 |
| 45–64 years | 5.0 | 5.6 | 5.1 | 76.8 | 72.6 | 70.7 | 10.0 | 12.1 | 12.3 | 6.1 | 9.7 | 10.2 |
| 65 years and over | 6.7 | 6.6 | 6.4 | 64.2 | 76.2 | 75.7 | 8.5 | 9.0 | 10.2 | 8.2 | 8.5 | 8.9 |
| **Sex[3]** | | | | | | | | | | | | |
| Male | 4.0 | 4.4 | 4.1 | 69.9 | 65.4 | 65.7 | 13.2 | 15.0 | 15.4 | 9.3 | 11.5 | 11.3 |
| Female | 5.1 | 5.6 | 5.3 | 69.5 | 68.1 | 68.0 | 11.4 | 12.0 | 11.6 | 12.2 | 14.1 | 13.8 |
| **Race[3–6]** | | | | | | | | | | | | |
| White | 4.7 | 5.1 | 4.8 | 71.0 | 68.1 | 68.4 | 10.2 | 11.9 | 11.3 | 11.7 | 14.0 | 13.8 |
| Black[7] | 3.6 | 4.9 | 4.6 | 56.2 | 58.5 | 57.0 | 32.7 | 23.5 | 26.2 | 4.2 | 7.0 | 5.5 |
| **Family Income[3–8]** | | | | | | | | | | | | |
| Less than $7,000 | 3.9 | 5.9 | 5.5 | 62.0 | 60.1 | 58.8 | 25.9 | 19.7 | 20.7 | 4.8 | 10.0 | 9.1 |
| $7,000–$9,999 | 4.2 | 5.2 | 4.4 | 65.2 | 64.0 | 61.7 | 22.3 | 17.9 | 16.0 | 6.6 | 9.8 | 13.8 |
| $10,000–$14,999 | 4.7 | 5.0 | 4.9 | 69.5 | 64.5 | 66.1 | 11.1 | 16.1 | 14.0 | 11.7 | 12.9 | 13.2 |
| $15,000–$24,999 | 4.8 | 4.9 | 4.7 | 71.5 | 68.6 | 70.5 | 7.4 | 12.4 | 10.8 | 13.8 | 13.7 | 12.9 |
| $25,000 or more | 5.2 | 5.0 | 4.6 | 72.9 | 70.2 | 70.6 | 6.7 | 8.9 | 9.0 | 12.9 | 15.7 | 14.5 |
| **Geographic Region[3]** | | | | | | | | | | | | |
| Northeast | 4.5 | 5.3 | 4.7 | 67.2 | 63.4 | 63.0 | 10.1 | 15.5 | 15.7 | 11.5 | 14.0 | 13.6 |
| North Central | 4.4 | 4.7 | 4.7 | 72.2 | 68.4 | 69.4 | 10.6 | 11.7 | 10.7 | 11.7 | 14.7 | 14.9 |
| South | 4.3 | 4.6 | 4.6 | 68.9 | 67.7 | 66.8 | 14.0 | 13.1 | 13.2 | 11.0 | 11.2 | 11.3 |
| West | 5.5 | 5.9 | 4.9 | 70.9 | 69.1 | 69.2 | 14.3 | 12.7 | 13.0 | 9.5 | 12.9 | 11.4 |
| **Location of Residence[3]** | | | | | | | | | | | | |
| Within SMSA | 4.8 | 5.3 | 4.9 | 68.2 | 65.6 | 66.1 | 12.3 | 14.0 | 13.8 | 12.1 | 13.6 | 13.1 |
| Outside SMSA | 4.1 | 4.4 | 4.4 | 72.9 | 71.0 | 69.5 | 11.9 | 11.4 | 11.3 | 8.8 | 11.9 | 12.0 |

[1]Does not add to 100 percent because it does not include all sources or places (e.g., house calls).

[2]Includes hospital outpatient clinic or emergency room.

[3]Age adjusted by the direct method to the 1970 civilian noninstitionalized population, using four age intervals.

[4]Includes all other races not shown separately.

[5]Includes unknown family income.

[6]In 1964 and 1975, the racial classification of persons in the National Health Interview Survey was determined by interviewer observation. In 1980, race was determined by asking the household respondent.

[7]1964 data are for all other races.

[8]Family income categories for 1980. Adjusting for inflation, corresponding income categories in 1964 were: less than $2,000; $2,000–$3,999; $4,000–$6,999; $7,000–$9,999; and $10,000 or more; and in 1975 were: less than $5,000; $5,000–$6,999; $7,000–$9,999; $10,000–$14,999; and $15,000 or more.

*Source:* National Center for Health Statistics; Data from the National Health Interview Survey, Division of Health Interview Statistics. In *Health United States, 1982.* DHHS Publication No. (PHS) 83–1232. Hyattsville, MD, 1982.

*From:* U.S. Department of Health and Human Services. *Health Status of Minorities and Low Income Groups.* Washington, DC: U.S. Government Printing Office, 1985, 239.

and greater need of care," according to Davis, Lillie-Blanton, and their group of investigators.[298] Although the hospital discharge rates between Blacks and Whites doubled (from 0.5 to 1.0 percent) during the 1975 to 1980 period, by then they were so similar, differences remained slight.

The utilization of dental services continued its 50-year rise between 1965 and 1980. Although Blacks and the poor benefited in a relative sense, progress in utilization was slow, and levels of the American population with no dental visits remained high. (See Table 4.24.) As the DHHS summarized in its monograph, *Health Status of Minorities and Low Income Groups,* covering the period to 1980· "[I]n the dental area, where there have been only minimal efforts to increase access to care, there have been no major changes between the poor and the nonpoor in the amount of dental care received."[299] With the exception of certain Great Society and some Medicaid programs that included subsidies for some dental care, most of these access changes were energized by attitudinal (or at least behavioral) changes and a perceived need for dental care and were, thus, extremely sensitive to factors such as public service announcements, ad campaigns (especially toothpaste and flossing), economic trends, income, and educational levels. As an example of the "shockingly bad" dental health among the poor in the mid-sixties, Davis found that: "among children between six and eleven, those whose family's income was less than $3,000 had an average of 3.4 decayed, unfilled teeth, but children in families with incomes of $15,000 or more had an average of only 0.7."[300] Over the 17-year period (1964 to 1981) there was a 12 percent decrease in Whites who had no dental visits in the past two years and a 7 percent drop among the nonpoor (38.4 percent in 1964, to 31.5 percent in 1981) accompanied by virtually no changes in the number of visits in these populations. Among non-Whites, the change was much more dramatic, with a drop of 21.6 percent in the proportion of poor people who had not had a dental visit in the past two years—the figures being 74.7 percent in 1964 compared to 53.1 percent in 1981. (See Table 4.24.) The biggest drop was in the lowest age bracket (under age 17). The White/Black ratio with respect to dental visits dropped from 1.89 in 1964 and 1975 to 1.64 in 1981—reflecting unpredictable surface changes in utilization floating upon a large bedrock of nonutilization of the dental system by almost one-half of the American population. If this rate of racial change persisted without fundamental changes in the dental health care delivery system (i.e., financing, general access, manpower), the ratio would drop to 1.0 by the end of the century,[301] the DHHS predicted.

Another major component of medical care utilization requiring measurement is a population's use of extended or long-term care. Extended care is usually long-term inpatient, continuing, or convalescent care provided for patients who are not expected to improve mentally or physically—the largest example being the growing population of functionally disabled elderly Americans. A smaller segment of extended or long-term care can be considered services provided for patients who can return home but still need some nursing or therapeutic services on a regular basis. Although by 1980 extended or long-term care facilities included long-stay

## Table 4.24 Percent of the Population with No Dental Visits in the Past 2 Years, by Poor and Nonpoor Status, Color, and Age, United States, Selected Years 1964–1981

(Data are based on household interviews of the civilian, noninstitutionalized population).

| | Total | | White | | All Other | |
|---|---|---|---|---|---|---|
| Age and Year | Poor | Nonpoor | Poor | Nonpoor | Poor | Nonpoor |
| | Percent of persons with no dental visits | | | | | |
| **All ages** | | | | | | |
| 1964 | 65.8 | 40.0 | 62.5 | 38.4 | 74.7 | 58.6 |
| 1973 | 56.5 | 34.6 | 55.3 | 33.2 | 60.3 | 48.8 |
| 1976 | 52.8 | 32.6 | 52.3 | 31.4 | 54.6 | 44.9 |
| 1978 | 52.2 | 32.1 | 51.0 | 31.0 | 55.6 | 42.5 |
| 1979 | 52.7 | 32.5 | 52.6 | 31.2 | 53.1 | 44.0 |
| 1980 | 51.2 | 32.7 | 50.6 | 31.5 | 53.0 | 42.6 |
| 1981 | 51.4 | 32.8 | 50.8 | 31.5 | 53.1 | 42.7 |
| **Under 17 years** | | | | | | |
| 1964 | 73.2 | 44.7 | 66.6 | 42.5 | 82.9 | 66.3 |
| 1973 | 58.3 | 37.2 | 55.8 | 35.2 | 62.2 | 55.6 |
| 1976 | 52.9 | 35.0 | 52.5 | 33.5 | 53.6 | 47.6 |
| 1978 | 51.6 | 35.2 | 49.9 | 33.7 | 54.3 | 47.3 |
| 1979 | 50.4 | 36.0 | 50.0 | 34.4 | 50.8 | 47.6 |
| 1980 | 51.9 | 36.4 | 51.1 | 35.1 | 53.2 | 45.2 |
| 1981 | 52.6 | 36.6 | 52.1 | 35.0 | 53.5 | 47.1 |
| **17–44 years** | | | | | | |
| 1964 | 46.3 | 30.1 | 40.2 | 28.5 | 61.3 | 48.1 |
| 1973 | 38.9 | 28.1 | 35.9 | 26.8 | 48.5 | 40.6 |
| 1976 | 37.4 | 27.0 | 35.1 | 25.7 | 45.1 | 39.3 |
| 1978 | 36.3 | 26.6 | 33.0 | 25.4 | 45.8 | 37.1 |
| 1979 | 36.6 | 26.8 | 34.9 | 25.5 | 41.5 | 37.9 |
| 1980 | 34.9 | 26.5 | 32.3 | 25.3 | 42.3 | 36.8 |
| 1981 | 35.6 | 26.8 | 32.8 | 25.4 | 43.1 | 37.1 |
| **45–64 years** | | | | | | |
| 1964 | 66.7 | 43.6 | 65.0 | 42.6 | 72.6 | 59.7 |
| 1973 | 61.5 | 38.3 | 60.5 | 37.4 | 65.1 | 51.1 |
| 1976 | 60.2 | 35.8 | 59.2 | 34.7 | 64.0 | 49.6 |
| 1978 | 59.7 | 34.3 | 58.9 | 33.5 | 62.3 | 43.8 |
| 1979 | 60.6 | 34.7 | 58.9 | 33.4 | 66.2 | 49.5 |
| 1980 | 57.5 | 34.4 | 56.6 | 33.2 | 60.2 | 47.5 |
| 1981 | 59.7 | 34.5 | 60.2 | 33.5 | 58.1 | 45.0 |
| **65 years and over** | | | | | | |
| 1964 | 78.5 | 63.5 | 78.0 | 62.9 | 83.0 | 76.6 |
| 1973 | 72.8 | 55.9 | 72.0 | 54.7 | 79.2 | 76.8 |
| 1976 | 69.8 | 51.8 | 69.4 | 50.6 | 73.3 | 73.1 |
| 1978 | 69.4 | 50.6 | 68.1 | 49.8 | 78.1 | 64.2 |
| 1979 | 70.7 | 49.3 | 70.1 | 48.5 | 74.7 | 62.0 |
| 1980 | 70.4 | 50.9 | 69.8 | 49.8 | 74.3 | 68.3 |
| 1981 | 70.0 | 49.9 | 69.3 | 48.9 | 73.7 | 65.3 |

Note: Definitions of poor and nonpoor are based on family income:

| | Poor | Nonpoor |
|---|---|---|
| 1964 | under $3,000 | $3.000 and over |
| 1973 | under $6,000 | $6.000 and over |
| 1976 | under $7,000 | $7,000 and over |
| 1978 | under $7,000 | $7,000 and over |
| 1979 | under $7,000 | $7,000 and over |
| 1980 | under $7,000 | $7,000 and over |
| 1981 | under $7,000 | $7,000 and over |

*Source:* Unpublished data from the National Heath Interview Survey, National Center for Health Statistics. In: Changes in morbidity, disability, and utilization differentials between the poor and nonpoor: Data from Health Interview Survey: 1964 and 1973. Ronald W. Wilson and Elijah L. White. Reprinted from *Medical Care*, August 1977, vol. XV, no. 8.

*From:* U.S. Department of Health and Human Services. *Health Status of Minorities and Low Income Groups.* Washington, DC: U.S. Government Printing Office, 1985, 194.

psychiatric and other hospitals (e.g., hospitals with average length of stay of 30 days or more), homes for the mentally retarded, homes for dependent children, homes or resident schools for the emotionally disturbed, resident institutions for drug abuse or alcoholic patients, and various other institutions, the overwhelming majority of such facilities were nursing homes. They provided less intensive nursing and medical services than acute care hospitals, and demand for them was growing explosively as the population aged,* government and third-party payers applied increasing pressure on short-stay hospitals to discharge patients no longer needing acute care services, the government began paying for these services, and families and relatives became increasingly reluctant and unable to care for their own elderly.

In the 1960s, Haynes's racial comparisons of the use of nursing and personal care homes found that "the utilization rate of the White is about 2½ times that for the Black."[302] This higher utilization gap favoring Whites held for almost every age group, especially for White females. At the time, although 10 percent of the total population was non-White, only 4 percent of nursing home residents were non-White. For other long-term care institutions—utilized at much lower rates than nursing homes—such as geriatric and chronic disease hospitals, mental hospitals, chronic disease wards, and nursing home units of general hospitals, Haynes found "no great racial differences in the utilization of these hospitals."[303] Profound shifts in utilization created by the "rediscovery of community" movement and the discovery and introduction of major tranquilizers in the mental health services, for example, resulted in a decline in the national census of mental hospitals from a 1954 high of 634,000 to 579,000 by 1963. As Starr noted, 1960s legislation further buttressed "the adoption by Congress in 1956 of amendments to Social Security that provided greater aid to states to support the aged in nursing homes.... By transferring such patients from mental hospitals to nursing homes, the states could transfer part of the cost of upkeep to the federal government."[304] Further reactions to the liberalized eligibility requirements for public payments for nursing home care in the mid-1960s, and again in 1972 under the Medicaid program, resulted in the number of nursing home residents increasing 153 percent in the 14 years during the 1963–1969, 1973–1974, and 1977 utilization data collection periods. The increase in the over-65 population was 36 percent during the same period. The persistence of racial disparities in nursing home utilization triggered a statement by the Institute of Medicine of the National Academy of Science in their 1981 report, *Health Care in a Context of Civil Rights*:

> *(1) Racial differences in life expectancy do not account for lower use by Blacks because the disparities in use of nursing homes exist above 75*

---

*Americans 65 years of age and older grew from 4 percent of the U.S. population in 1900 to 11.2 percent in 1980. Moreover, the Black elderly population was projected to grow at a faster rate than the White elderly population for at least the next 20 years.

> *where survivorship by Blacks is high, (2) superior health status of Blacks*
> *does not account for lower use since elderly Blacks have more disabilities*
> *than elderly whites, (3) it is possible that Blacks living as part of the*
> *extended family is a result rather than a reason for less use of nursing*
> *homes, (4) some persons believe that Blacks reside proportionately higher*
> *in unlicenced boarding facilities, [and] (5) nursing homes discriminate*
> *against Medicaid patients, a disproportionate number of whom are*
> *Black.*[305]

Regarding discrimination against Medicaid recipients, the report noted that in some Southern states, such as Mississippi, Alabama, and South Carolina, White Medicaid recipients resided in nursing homes in excess of their proportion among the states' elderly poor. Blame has also been leveled at the ambiguity of the guidelines directing the implementation of Title VI of the Civil Rights Act, poor definitions in the regulatory guidelines against institutional discrimination directing providers, and government nonenforcement of the civil rights laws by the Office of Civil Rights (OCR) and others.[306]

Taking into account these statistics, indices, and data sets, the overall progress African Americans made in health status, outcomes, and utilization between 1965 and 1980 was unprecedented. Certainly, some of the *acquired determinants* of health, including a spectrum of variables from health environments, socioeconomic status, infections, trauma, and cultural characteristics, were improving. Nevertheless, the legacy of need was so great and the health status, outcome, and utilization disparities based on race were so wide that Black health did not approach that of White Americans at the end of the period. Moreover, as Davis, Haynes, and others pointed out, overt, institutional, "statistical," and covert discriminations were still prevalent in the health system. For example, some Southern towns maintained segregated waiting rooms and kept Black patients waiting until all White patients had been served,* waiting times for Black patients averaged between four and six hours according to some contemporary studies,[307] and in some locales the quality of care rendered by local physicians was poor (Black patients were not asked to undress for physical examinations in some instances).[308] Some of these overtly discriminatory practices persisted until the late 1980s in some communities. Institutional discrimination was frequent, often:

> *arising from segregated housing or past discriminatory practices that have*
> *led to current patterns of the location of physicians, hospital staffing,*
> *referral practices, and patient preferences. Some of the causes cited are*
> *the distance of hospitals and other facilities from black communities,*

---

*The lead author personally experienced these phenomena in some Southern cities well into the 1980s.

*familiarity with certain hospitals from past association, lack of private physicians causing patients to turn to charity hospitals, scarcity of physicians in minority neighborhoods, and patients' lack of information or awareness that Medicaid benefits are available in private hospitals.*[309]

Such discriminatory practices and situations were not overt, making them even more difficult to overcome. Another group of practices, "such as ambulance drivers taking black accident victims to charity hospitals and the restriction of hospital staffs to specialists (black physicians tend to be general practitioners),"[310] could have been categorized as overt or "statistical" discrimination, "depending on whether the rules governing these decisions are devised for the express purpose of excluding blacks from certain facilities or simply work on balance to exclude blacks."[311] Despite these caveats, the first two-thirds of this period (1965 to 1975), when virtually all health status, outcome, and utilization parameters for Blacks were improving, has been viewed as the Civil Rights Era in Health Care for African Americans. As the 1970s ended, the political landscape and public will changed—which helps explain why funding, participation levels in government-funded health programs, and Black health progress slowed, then began stagnating, by 1980.[312]

Therefore, although great health progress for African Americans was evident between 1965 and 1980, much remained the same. The "Negro medical ghetto," whose infrastructure remained basically intact at the beginning of the period, with scores of Black hospitals, a few Black medical and health professions schools, and pervasive *de jure* or *de facto* segregation throughout the health and biomedical education systems, began to be replaced by a new set of institutional arrangements. Token numbers of Blacks were admitted to many predominantly White institutions and programs, overt legal segregation was outlawed in health institutions, and a few middle-class African Americans fulfilled their aspirations of the American dream in their encounters with the health system at both the clinical and professional levels. Nevertheless, for most African Americans huge racial disparities in health remained, and most of the nation's racial health apartheid was maintained in a new, *separate* health system. Most Blacks continued using newly configured city and county hospitals and the old hospital, public health, and charity clinics—now spruced up with government funds. With increased demand for direct health services and little allocation of the expanded health manpower pool into urban or rural poor areas, reliance increased on emerging new networks in inner-city urban and rural poor locations, on alternative health providers (e.g., PAs and nurse practitioners), and hospital emergency rooms. As urban flight proceeded apace, White middle- and working-class populations abandoned old neighborhoods and institutions. Rather than channel the publicly financed health care dollars into the mainstream system, networks of alternative systems with widely divergent characteristics and outcomes such as "clinic patient" branches of AHCs, NHCs, CHCs,

Medicaid mills, and migrant health centers were constructed to serve the newly empowered Blacks, Latinos, and poor.* Urban hospital clientele and fiscal profiles changed with a new generation of usage. Reformers' zeal did not make poverty-threatened rural areas or populations economically lucrative or popular practice sites for New Age physicians or health entrepreneurs, so rural health care deprivation continued. Race- and class-based health quality gaps persisted as extensions of the alterations in the nation's urban economy, patterns of residential segregation, and new political configurations and outcomes regarding issues of race, representation, and class. By 1980, despite material and sometimes expensive health and programmatic interventions, new semantics, civil rights terminology, rules of racial etiquette, and token participation or gestures, it became clear that only small dents had been made in the edifice of the nation's centuries-old racial health dilemma.[313]

---

*Most of these institutions obtained very high marks relative to their effectiveness at improving the health status and outcomes of the difficult populations they served, effectively penetrating their various markets and fostering overall community good. Their shortfalls were usually related to being underfunded, burdened by overly restrictive fiscal regulation, and subject to the government's bureaucratic administration. Medicaid mills were not positive health care institutions for an entirely different set of reasons related to low-quality, assembly-line care; provision of fragmented care; and their design to "game" the system to maximize profits.

# The Medical Profession during an Era of Civil Rights Gains and Conservative Retrenchment, 1965–1980

## Bloody, but Unbowed: The White Medical Profession, 1965–1980

After absorbing a legislative defeat with the passage of Medicare/Medicaid in 1965, the White medical profession began moving to reassert its dominance over the U.S. health care system. No infrastructure like organized medicine's, led by the AMA, could undergo what it did between 1960 and 1965 and remain the same. From the public's viewpoint, the White medical establishment had fought all efforts at progressive health care legislation, from the Wagner-Murray-Dingell bill in the 1940s through its Falk-Cohen-Ewing-Ball-Cruikshank-Biemiller-Forand permutations throughout the 1950s and 1960s, not only with strength, unity, and intransigence, but with a vitriolic intensity and animosity that tainted the healer image of American doctors and threatened to undermine the profession's cultural authority. There was little public awareness of what African American physicians were doing.

In an attempt to comprehend the depth and animus of organized medicine's resistance to health reform, Wilbur J. Cohen, a secretary of HEW who was considered an arch-enemy of the AMA during the 1940s, 1950s, and 1960s, said:

> I can't say that I understand it completely, but I can give you three hypotheses. First, I think the most single, long-range factor was Dr. Fishbein's famous 1932 editorial, the one where he called the Committee

*on the Costs of Medical Care report inciting to revolution and to socialism and communism. His use of that incendiary language set the tone of the discussion for years to come. Then there was the note developed by people like Marjorie Shearon\* in the 1950s and 1960s that national health insurance was some kind of socialist or communist plot. She got out a newsletter in Washington called Challenge to Socialism. I'd go on to what I call the devil theory of history. Doctors ... were not particularly sympathetic to national health insurance, and they could not explain to themselves or anybody else why all these other people were in favor of it. They really couldn't understand why other people wanted national health insurance, and they preferred to believe in this conspiratorial and devil theory, that somebody was trying to do something to them that was unjustified ... They couldn't imagine anyone being for national health insurance the way I was, simply because I thought it was the right thing to do.[1]*

The AMA and allies such as Blue Cross–Blue Shield, the American Hospital Association (AHA), the American Dental Association (ADA), the health insurance industry, and the rest of the health establishment vehemently fought against passage of Medicare and Medicaid. They utilized politics largely emphasizing nihilism; began massively funded public relations and "education" campaigns such as the Women's Auxiliary to the AMA's Operation Coffee Cup, FM radio spots, and newspaper ads; were supporters of alternative plans such as Kerr-Mills, the Byrnes bill, and Eldercare; and spent millions of dollars through AMPAC, the AMA's political action committee. The White medical and health care establishment waged a pitched battle against what they considered a hostile press, labor unions, two U.S. presidents, and three U.S. Congresses—and they lost.[2] Marginalized and largely segregated—and with very little to lose in the political currency of the day—Black health professionals supported the progressive health bills.

The magnitude of the defeat sent a message to White organized medicine: "The size of the final vote on Medicare, almost three to one in the House of Representatives, underscored a disjunction that had opened between the AMA and society."[3] As a result, attitudes began changing and policies shifting among physicians. Moreover, rapprochement loomed after the passage of Titles 18 and 19, as "two presidential meetings and the events of the following months established a new relationship between organized medicine and the federal government,"[4] according to Campion. This new, almost silent relationship, forged on the superior political organization and veiled threats of noncooperation of the AMA and the hospital industry, took advantage of the Johnson administration's obsession with a

---

\*Marjorie Shearon, Ph.D., was a former employee in the Public Health Service and the Federal Security Agency who became a health consultant to the Republicans and conservatives.

smooth takeoff of Medicare/Medicaid programs rather than the consequences of budgetary concessions yielded—denying the government any leverage to control costs—to the medical and health establishments. The government, liberal reformers, doctors, and the health care industry would all pay dearly for the resultant massive transfer of public monies into the health system. They would lose public and congressional confidence over the next decade as effects of the concessions on the system evolved.

Signs of White organized medicine's corroded powers began cropping up everywhere. As Paul Starr observed: "For the first time in a century, American physicians faced a serious challenge simultaneously to their political influence, their economic power, and their cultural authority."[5] The AMA was often relegated to the role of participant rather than the "authority" or opinion leader. Because of internal stresses and external pummeling, the organization, along with the profession itself, also began experiencing more internal dissent. Organized medicine's resignation, voiced by the AMA's Council on Medical Service in 1968 that "society is moving inexorably and rapidly in the direction of a system of financing health care for all persons,"[6] was emblematic. The profession's reactions to the 10 to 15 health reform proposals introduced during the early 1970s were half-hearted, often disorganized, sometimes vacillating, and could be viewed as weak. The AMA's own alternative Medicredit plan, based on the retention of Medicare, voluntary participation, and reliance on the existing health system, although promoted by an expensive public relations campaign, was presented as if efforts at its passage were doomed to fail. Although its intent to "use ... federal income tax dollars to subsidize private health insurance policies for everyone except the Medicare population—100 percent subsidization for the poor, and the subsidization on a graduated scale and tax credit incentives for everyone else,"[7] was a quantum leap ideologically and medical-socially for the AMA, neither the public nor Congress seemed to notice. The battles over the major plans, the Health Security Act of 1970 (sometimes referred to as the Kennedy-Griffiths Bill), President Nixon's Comprehensive Health Care Insurance Program (CHIP),* and the Long-Ribicoff catastrophic health bill** were, seemingly, fought over the heads of the AMA and defeated on the horns of the health-cost inflation dilemma (medical costs were 40 percent higher in 1975 than in 1970).

In the wake of the Nixon resignation, the single attempt during the 1970s to pass a national health insurance bill failed in August 1974. Initially, it was a bipartisan attempt to craft a national health insurance plan from several current proposals, utilizing Chairman of the Ways and Means Committee Wilbur Mills's

---

*The CHIP called for mandated employer-employee insurance, improvements in Medicare for the elderly, and state-assisted plans for high-risk and low-income populations.

**The Long-Ribicoff Bill called for catastrophic health insurance coverage for victims of exceptionally long and/or expensive medical episodes.

proven skills and leadership. When Republican President Ford and HEW Secretary Caspar Weinberger proposed national health insurance, passage seemed imminent. Built upon foundations of the administration's CHIP proposal, Russell Long's catastrophic insurance, and a federalized Medicaid system, consensus began foundering upon complex financing issues. Sensitive to the hot-button issue of health care cost inflation, Congressional consensus fell apart. Members with labor ties refused to compromise, holding out for a sweeping approach similar to the Kennedy Bill—while others wanted either no legislation or legislation minimizing government involvement. Policy expert Wilbur Cohen speculated that Congress was afraid of a health bill that would transfer between $40 and $80 billion from the public to the private sector during that politically charged economic moment. As usual, "The medical profession, in wide agreement with the AMA position, was overwhelmingly opposed to national health insurance."[8] Learning from the past and "[a]voiding the mistakes of earlier campaigns, the AMA this time made good use of a skillfully developed political base, an effective legislative strategy, and believable public relations"[9] to help defeat the bill, according to Campion.[10]

Symptomatic of the compromised power of White organized medicine was their response to the government's blizzard of regulations between 1970 and 1975 and their outright attacks later in the decade. For example, by 1970 cost overruns generated by the Medicare program (1965 cost projections for Part A Medicare were $3.1 billion by 1970, compared to real costs of $5.8 billion) and reports by the Senate Finance Committee—which concluded, "The Medicare and Medicaid programs are in serious financial trouble"—revealed that the cost-control mechanisms built into the programs were not working. Initially, with AMA consultation, the Congress established a formal Peer Review Organizations (PRO) program attached to other health legislation in 1970. The secretary of HEW would contract with state medical societies or organizations they designated to conduct review programs. Not satisfied with the thrust of the professionally governed review emphasizing quality of care and education of physicians and institutions, Congress overrode the AMA and established a program stressing cost surveillance—which also served as an internal audit. Legislation for this Professional Standards Review Organization (PSRO)—named the Bennett Amendment after Senator Wallace Bennett (R.-UT)—enacted in 1972 despite AMA resistance, established arbitrary "norms" of treatment along with physician treatment and cost "profiles." These indices would set off alarm bells and red lights when "limits" of so-called "accepted practice" were violated. Originally the government wanted "national norms of health care, government ownership of records, and mandatory advance approval by PSROs for elective surgery."[11] These measures were successfully resisted. Computerization was emphasized, and many of the concepts "drew heavily from developments in the private sector."[12] Physicians, the AMA, and concerned observers derided the initiative as "cookbook medicine." The fact that the AMA accommodated and later became involved in the implementation of these programs outraged many physicians and further fragmented the medical profession.

The medical profession in general, and the AMA specifically, had reservations about the Nixon administration's aggressive approach endorsing and implementing HMOs. As Campion noted:

> *Careful to avoid a break with the Nixon administration despite policy differences, the AMA showed restraint in voicing its reservations. These echoed the old objections to contract practice. Didn't an HMO set itself up in such a way as to skew the participating physician's loyalty from the medical needs of the patient toward the financial, corporate interests of the HMO? Wasn't that basically the sort of thing that the lumber and mining companies did back in 1905? Nevertheless, the House of Delegates did not adopt a policy of objection; the AMA fell back instead on the pluralistic policy it adopted in 1959—that a physician should be free to practice under any system of health care delivery that suited them.*[13]

As previously noted, the Nixon administration gave HMOs government financial aid for start-up and maintenance and in December 1973 passed a law requiring "businesses with more than twenty-five employees to offer at least one qualifying HMO as an alternative to conventional insurance in their health benefit plan, if there was a qualifying HMO in the vicinity."[14] The profession did virtually nothing to block these actions. The previously mentioned National Health Planning and Resources Development Act (93–641), passed in 1974, was intended to consolidate health planning and regulatory functions contained in three previous programs into one overarching regulatory, oversight, and planning bureaucracy that could provide the framework for a future national health service. The act was charged with drawing up three-year plans, reviewing proposals for new projects, guiding state certificate-of-need programs, and regulating the uses of federal funds. Federally funded bureaucracies provided oversight for the required state agencies, and nonmedical or health-related personnel wielded majority control of the 204 regional HSA boards. This regulatory web, combined with PSRO legislation, "threatened to limit doctors' discretion in institutions" and "indirectly encouraged hospitals to regulate physicians."[15] As Russell Roth, an AMA president, complained, "[D]octors and administrators had been 'pointedly relegated to a minor role' and spoke of the 'general resentment in the professional community' that it wasn't entrusted with leadership of the effort."[16] Discriminatory misuse of these new powers by the controlling White health infrastructure would have devastating effects on Black physicians.[17]

During the period of 1965 to 1980, the White medical profession's flagship organization, the AMA, went through both leadership and financial crises. This further compounded the profession's growing lack of internal and external cohesion. Between 1970 and 1975 the organization operated on the basis of deficit financing, liquidating its assets in the process. Prior to this era, the AMA's publishing ventures, led by the prestigious *Journal of the American Medical*

Association (weekly circulation 240,000), had been profitable enough to support the organization between 1912 and 1949. Slowly, with changing costs of publication, mailing overhead, declining advertising revenues (largely from the prescription pharmaceutical industry), changing standards and markets in medical publication, and membership fluctuations, revenues from the organization's 14 major publications began to decline.* Many of the AMA's publishing activities, such as some of the specialty journals and public information pamphlets, were money-losing operations either distributed free with membership or disseminated for scientific, health policy, public health, public informational, or opinion leader purposes. All these publications were not-for-profit activities. For example, *Today's Health*, whose purpose was the health education of the public, the *American Medical News*, a medical newspaper, and *Prism* (which lost $2 million in 1973), the organization's magazine for the discussion of social, ethical, and political issues, were often money-losing ventures. The latter publications, and part of *JAMA*'s distribution, were mailed free of charge (as controlled-circulation publications). The lost publications revenue, failure to implement adequate membership dues increases, a bulky semi-autonomous department, committee, council, and organizational structure, and a lack of emphasis on recruitment and retention all proved financially counterproductive to the organization. After much rancorous infighting, an almost complete leadership turnover, a substantial raise in membership dues, and a dramatic reorganization—including modernizing the AMA's publishing empire—the organization entered the 1980s in stable condition.

These developments, compounded by President Nixon's health "strategy," the highly publicized "health crisis," new left social movements, and organized medicine's accommodations with the federal and state governments' regulatory juggernaut led to the formation of physician interest groups on the right and the left. The AMA reluctantly went along with Nixon's endorsement of HMOs, a political move "which it publicly regretted and privately tried to reverse."[18] The AMA professed a concern for the poor, implored the profession to shift its emphasis to family practice, had its presidents (e.g., Dr. Walter Bornemeir 1971) endorse neighborhood health centers, and expressed concern with social issues such as sex education, alcoholism, and air pollution. However, "these concessions to public opinion alienated die-hard conservatives who argued that the AMA had sold out its membership."[19] Complicity with PSRO regulation was seemingly the final straw. By 1973, rigidly conservative physician groups such as the Association of American Physicians and Surgeons and the Council of Medical Staffs (later the Private Doctors of America), led by Jose L. Garcia Oller, M.D., a New Orleans neurosurgeon, systematically attacked the AMA's policies and accused the organization

---

*The AMA published the *Archives of Dermatology, Archives of Environmental Health, Archives of General Psychiatry, Archives of Internal Medicine, Archives of Neurology, Archives of Ophthalmology, Archives of Otolaryngology, Archives of Pathology, Archives of Surgery,* and *American Journal of Diseases of Children.*

of a "sell-out." Garcia Oller also leveled personal attacks on high-ranking AMA officials during speeches at medical meetings throughout the country. The
Association of American Physicians and Surgeons eventually "sued the government over the constitutionality of PSROs."[20] Within White organized medicine,
national AMA conventions became emotion-laden, confrontational, highly
charged affairs by the mid-1970s. Moreover, the AMA was in the throes of this
turmoil while simultaneously trying to improve its "negative" public image. These
political battles, social forces, and rights movements affected White-organized
medicine early in the period under study. As Starr noted, "In 1971 for the first time
in a half century, AMA membership fell to 50 percent of the profession as young
doctors refused to join."[21] What many in the profession perceived as a radical
group, the Medical Committee for Human Rights, had formed on the left. As
mentioned earlier, it had become heavily involved in the Black Civil Rights Movement, human rights issues, and medical ethical campaigns. Moreover, its
membership had grown to at least 7,000 by 1971.[22]

Justifiably proud of its efforts in upgrading standards of American medical education, beginning in the nineteenth century, the White medical profession had assumed more of a low-profile role in the field by the postwar years. Instead of its
traditional dominant role in health professions education policy, White organized
medicine was, in fact, under assault and felt the brunt of public criticism for artificially rationing the supply of physicians. Spurred by national reports such as those
by Ewing (1948) and Bane (1959),* neither of which suggested objective methods
of projecting future numbers of needed physicians, an almost blindly charging 40-
year campaign to increase physician output peaked in intensity during the era. The
Bane report emphasized population growth and the impact of specialization on
physician manpower needs, while tracking trends in the number of physicians
since 1930 and tabulating annual additions to the physician supply represented by
foreign medical graduates (FMGs). The report "recommended that by 1975 the
United States should have twenty to twenty-four additional four-year medical
schools and an overall production of 11,000 medical school graduates annually."[23]
None of the reports factored in the tremendous growth in grassroots health care demand documented since the 1930s, much less the explosive pressures for medical
care generated by the Medicare/Medicaid programs. Nor did they rationalize
physician distribution by specialty needs assessment, social demographics, or geography. Bolstered by legislation and programs such as the Health Professions Educational Assistance Act of 1963, the expanded Health Professions Educational
Assistance Amendments in 1965, educational capacity building aspects of
Medicare and Medicaid (1965), and various Great Society programs, medical

---

*The Ewing Report, released during President Truman's whistle-stop campaign in 1948, included
health manpower projections. It was considered a partisan document in some circles. The Bane
Report, released in 1959, was a nonpartisan, Surgeon General–initiated report that focused on health
manpower projections.

schools sprouted across the country. As Campion noted, "During the twelve years after 1968, the number of medical schools rose from ninety-four to 126, the size of the graduating class from 7,973 to 15,135, and the physician/population ratio from 161 per 100,000 to 219."[24] This exceeded all projected goals. Nevertheless, despite these seeming numerical successes and a plethora of aforementioned special programs to increase the pool of disadvantaged minority health professionals, minority populations continued to be underserved and, "[a]s general practitioners became a rapidly dwindling species, many people," largely representing average Americans, "were frustrated that they no longer seemed to have any access to medical care even in areas where doctors and hospitals were numerically abundant,"[25] Starr noted.

The demand for family doctors escalated. Campion framed the issue and captured the mood of the time, noting: "Whatever happened to the family doc of revered memory? To many people, especially those in large urban communities, he had almost vanished. Around 1910 there had been one general practitioner for every 600 people; now, fifty years later, there was only one for every 3,000."[26]

These pressures generated demand for a new specialty—family practice. Strongly influenced by prestigious commission reports and the public mood, the American Board of Family Practice was incorporated in 1969. The most influential report on graduate medical education was the Citizens Commission on Graduate Medical Education, often called the Millis Report.* Besides endorsing the creation of the new specialty, it proposed dropping the internship, incorporating all postgraduate training into a standardized, clinical, three-to-four-year training exposure in one of the specialties; deepening ties between postgraduate medical training and the university; and the creation of a powerful new commission of graduate medical education.[27] Fearing some agency outside medicine would take the lead in the residency program accreditation process, C. H. William Ruhe, M.D., AMA staff secretary to the Council on Medical Education, led the charge and eventually formed an expanded Liaison Committee on Medical Education that included not only the AMA and AAMC, but also the other influential players in graduate medical education, the American Board of Medical Specialties, the Council of Medical Specialty Societies, the American Hospital Association (AHA), and, now, public representation. Provisionally approved by all participating bodies on January 25, 1972, pending ratification by all parent bodies, it would oversee both undergraduate and graduate medical education. White organized medicine was eventually forced to share oversight responsibility for continuing medical education with six other organizations: the AAMC, the AHA, the American Board of Medical Specialties, the Council of Medical Specialty Societies, the Association

---

*The Citizens Commission on Graduate Medical Education was convened in 1963 to provide an *external* and objective examination of postgraduate training in medicine with the public's interest in mind. It was chaired by John S. Millis, Ph.D., president of Western Reserve, and included three physicians, five Ph.D.s, a retired Supreme Court Justice, the executive director of the American Association for the Advancement of Science, and one other university president.

for Hospital Medical Education, and the Federation of State Medical Boards. After at least five years of infighting, the Liaison Committee for Continuing Medical Education (LCME) was finally formed in 1977. Acrimony did not abate. Multiple accrediting bodies resulted until the Accreditation Council for Continuing Medical Education was formed after a rapprochement among the constituent organizations in 1981. The pattern wherein White organized medicine seemed to be responding to, rather than initiating, health education policy and regulation — once its bailiwick — was established.

The AMA, through its Council on Medical Education (CME), had controlled training and accreditation standards for allied health professions since 1933, when the American Society of Clinical Pathologists (ASCP) sought assistance in establishing training standards for its laboratory assistants. Previously the ASCP had established "[a] registry of medical technologists ... in 1928, administered by the society in conjunction with the American College of Surgeons; and continuous study was made of the curricula of schools for laboratory technicians."[28] This unprecedented request for assistance, along with similar requests by other allied health professions groups such as the American Occupational Therapy Association and the American Physical Therapy Association, resulted in the CME's collaboration with the allied health groups, the concerned medical specialty societies, and educators in various fields to create the Essentials* for approved training in these various fields by 1935 and 1936. Growth was slow between 1937 and 1967, with the AMA's CME providing Essentials, oversight, and accreditation for a total of eight allied health professions. However, passage of federal health manpower legislation, beginning in 1963, and passage of Medicare and Medicaid in 1965 signaled a massive expansion of the health system along with huge escalations in demand for health services. As a result, there were 26 accredited allied health professions by 1983, and the number of individual training programs requiring inspection and regulation jumped from less than 200 in the 1940s to over 3,000 by 1983. For many reasons, regulatory power was diffused to the allied health professions organizations themselves and the educational institutions involved in their training (hospitals conducted nearly half, junior/community colleges over a quarter, and four-year colleges and universities around 15 percent of the training programs) with the formation of the AMA's Committee on Allied Health Education and Accreditation in 1976. Although it remained a committee of the AMA and was staffed and financed by that organization, it was no longer the sole arbiter — through its 17 program review committees — of inspecting, granting, denying, conferring probationary status, or renewing accreditations in these young disciplines. Input from a variety of sources was demanded and granted. Through drastic increases in physician out-

---

*The Essentials were reports from expert committees in various health fields detailing standards, curriculums, admissions policies, faculty qualifications, library standards, and educational administration guidelines published by the AMA for various health professions. The tradition was established with the first "Essentials of an Acceptable Medical College," published in 1910.

put, changes in the immigration laws, and newer and more stringent licensing requirements, the American medical profession acquiesced in stemming the tide of foreign medical graduates (FMGs) by the late 1970s. As the official history of the AMA noted, "[T]he presence of FMGs unquestionably prevented a serious manpower crisis in the 1950s, 1960s, and early 1970s ... and ... thousands of FMGs have successfully blended into the American medical system."[29] Though tending not to enter private practice as often, and with a predilection for institutional practice academically, FMGs have acquitted themselves well: "During the years of 1966–80, eighteen American physicians were awarded the Nobel prize in medicine and physiology. Of that group, ten were graduates of American medical schools, one was a graduate of a Canadian school, and seven were FMGs."[30] The National Medical Association, Black medicine's national voice throughout the era, was not allowed to participate in any of these critical policy or educational activities. They were never mentioned in the AMA's official history.[31]

More than a decade after the 1954 Supreme Court decision outlawing segregated schools, neither the medical profession nor the medical education system had responded enthusiastically to the call for racial integration. As Todd Savitt noted, "With just two schools regularly accepting African Americans for medical training from the 1920s through the 1970s ... [t]he percentage of African-American physicians remained at between 2.5 and 3 percent of all physicians during that period."[32] With a background of having barred Blacks throughout most of its 118-year history up to 1965, the AMA "had its first Black delegate in 1949 and changed its bylaws to ban racial discrimination in 1968,"[33] according to Wolinsky. Although the Civil Rights Movement and the coming of integration opened most predominantly White medical schools to Black students, it also generated pressures responsible for the opening of the Morehouse School of Medicine in Atlanta and the Charles R. Drew University of Medicine and Science in Los Angeles. While civil rights pressures led to the desegregation of most local, state, and national medical societies and opened some White hospitals to Black house officers between 1965 and 1980, "the percentage of black physicians in the United States registered no significant change during this period from the sub-3 percent that had existed in 1920,"[34] according to Savitt. Although affirmative action programs produced gains in minority medical student admissions, which reached a peak of 8.2 percent minority enrollment in 1974–1975, any allusion to the parity goal of 12 percent "representative" minority enrollment set by the AAMC/AHA/AMA/NMA consortium in 1970 was undermined by the Bakke and DeFunis reverse-discrimination cases. As Hal Strelnick and Richard Younge observed, "In 1974–75, only 17.6 percent of all black medical students attended predominantly black schools, compared with 30 percent as recently as 1968–69. By 1979–80, the predominantly black schools (including Morehouse) were again enrolling almost 30 percent of all the new black students."[35] This sudden reversal in trends was emblematic of the faltering commitment to and halting progress of desegregating America's largest and most powerful physician trade group.[36]

### Black Doctors Defending Poor and Underserved Health Battlements: Struggling to Maintain Hard-Won Gains, 1965–1980

*The medical profession must show genuine concern for the black man,*
*the poor man, the old man, not because it is the law of the land but*
*because it is the right thing to do.*
— JOHN L.S. HOLLOMAN JR., M.D., NMA PRESIDENT 1966–1967

In 1965 approximately 2.1 percent of America's 305,115 physicians were Black (approximately 6,407 physicians). This percentage had risen slightly to 2.6 percent by 1980 and 2.7 percent by 1983. Nevertheless, this tiny professional group, usually led by the NMA, had exerted a tremendous influence on establishing new health system and professional priorities and desegregating the U.S. health delivery system despite White organized medicine's attempt to relegate them to the fringes of medical power and authority.

Due to the nature of their professions and barriers to their work, Black physicians and health professionals had been uniquely preoccupied with some of American democracy's major shortcomings. Constitutional paradoxes resulting in not only the denial of equal justice but also the denial of equal educational and work opportunities differentially affected Blacks in the healing arts. Broadus N. Butler, director of the Office of Leadership Development in Higher Education of the American Council on Education, recognized the significance of African American health professional participation in the civil rights struggle, including the movement's educational dimensions, stating in the *Journal of the National Medical Association (JNMA)*:

> It is no accident ... that the NAACP and the ... coalition of non-violent
> Civil Rights groups and human relations organizations produced so
> much toward the advancement in the total quality of life and prosperity
> in this nation by holding out education and the full utilization of our
> human resources as the sine qua non of national realization.[37]

Therefore, it seemed logical that during the 1960s and 1970s efforts to increase the representation of Blacks and other minorities in the health professions—a prominent item on Black organized medicine's agenda since its beginnings—were made on a national level. This policy shift was predicated on both reason and the assumption that increasing the numbers of disadvantaged minority health professionals would improve access to health services for Blacks and other poor people based on their connectedness with these populations and willingness to serve in underserved communities. As Gerald D. Jaynes and Robin M. Williams, Jr., pointed out regarding Black physicians in a 1980s National Research Council report, *A Common Destiny: Blacks and American Society*, "Although more than 80 percent of black patients report having a white physician as their primary provider, the assumption is supported by the fact that more than 80 percent of the clients of black physicians are black."[38] The veracity of these assumptions was corroborated by facts compiled by authorities such as Hanft, McKinney, Gray, and Keith in minority health manpower reports, the health policy literature, and medical and public health journals,[39] noting that the "location and practice patterns of minority health professionals are significantly different from those of majority health professionals" because "Black practitioners are more likely than whites to locate in areas with high percentages of poverty and in urban areas with significant black populations."[40] These facts, compounded by the huge race-based mortality, morbidity, health status, and health services gaps and the disparities represented by general American doctor-patient ratios of 1:700 compared to ranges of 1:3,000 and 1:10,000 in Black communities, especially in the nation's inner cities, represented gross medical education and health system failures. Black health professions' manpower shortages were even worse in other areas such as dentistry (e.g., there was one Black dentist per 11,500 Blacks, and Blacks were only 2.31 percent of the nation's dentists in 1970),* pharmacy (e.g., 2.28 percent of the nation's pharmacists in 1970), veterinary medicine (e.g., 1.3 percent of veterinarians in 1970), psychiatry (e.g., 1 percent of the nation's psychiatrists), optometry (less than 1 percent of the nation's optometrists in 1970) and health services administration. Underrepresentation in nursing, although not as severe at 5.7 percent, was problematic, and was certainly not proportionately representative of the African American population. Clearly, training Black and disadvantaged minority health professionals was the most direct method of confronting and correcting this aspect of the health manpower maldistribution problem. And as Leonidis H. Berry, M.D., 1965 to 1966 NMA president, stated, "The time has come when most citizens will no longer accept discrepancies in mortality and morbidity rates in population groups as a fact of race."[41] Moreover, African Americans remained the largest and one of the fastest-growing U.S. minority groups, representing 11.1 percent of the population, 22.6 million people, in 1970, and growing to 26.7 million, 11.8 percent of the U.S. population, by 1980. Black health professionals had innovative proposals to supplement their 97-year pedagogic track record and hard-won, community-based, hands-on experience regarding recruiting, mentoring, and successfully training disadvantaged minorities for health careers. Thus strident calls emanated from the Black health professions throughout the 1970s for corrective action.

As a result of attempts between 1965 and 1970 to correct minority underrepresentation in the health professions (e.g., Blacks represented 2.39 percent of U.S. medical students in 1968–1969 and approximately 7,663, or 2.2 percent, of U.S. physicians in 1970), 75 percent of Blacks applying to medical school were

---

*At the time, the American Dental Association classified any area served by less than one dentist per 3,000 as a dental emergency area.

accepted in 1969. This high acceptance rate quickly plummeted to 43.9 percent in 1973–1974 and 39.4 percent in 1979–1980, while nonminority acceptance rates rose from 34.7 percent in 1973–1974 to 47.9 percent in 1980–1981. The aforementioned AAMC goal of 12 percent minority enrollment in the freshman class beginning in 1976 seemed out of the question in the wake of waning medical school commitment to increasing minority medical school enrollment by 1975[42] and the *deFunis v. Odegaard* (1974) and *The Regents of the University of California v. Bakke* (1978) U.S. Supreme Court decisions.[43] Black enrollment peaked at 7.5 percent in 1974–1975 and declined the next year to 6.7 percent—a level that remained relatively stable until the decline in the 1990s. Despite government-mandated increases in enrollment of minorities and women in health professions training programs between 1960 and 1980: "[g]eographic maldistribution of health care providers and lack of access for needy populations . . . continued in the last two decades despite increased numbers of physicians and family practitioners."[44] Moreover, in contrast to the sizable increases in medical school enrollment of women from 9 percent to 25 percent of the student body—with further growth anticipated—Black enrollment rose from less than 3 percent and leveled off at approximately 7 percent, with decreases expected. The proportional number of Black physicians rose approximately one-half of one percentage point between 1965 and 1980.[45]

African American physicians and health professionals compiled a commendable, sometimes heroic, record of active participation in the Black Civil Rights Movement. At the beginning of the era in 1965, their role expanded as Black physicians staunchly supported and were applauded by the federal government and other progressive groups for their vital, but impermanent, role in the passage of legislation for Medicare/Medicaid, government aid to professional education that mandated inclusion of minorities and women, and governmental programs creating and implementing the delivery of health services to poor and underserved Americans. African American physicians and health professionals had an important and worthy policy agenda in the wake of the Civil Rights Era. However, after the long-fought battles for justice and equity in health care, they were not given leadership authority at the national health policy level. The following health policy and political trends were noted in a 1966 editorial in *JNMA*:

> *The N.M.A. . . . is not being given the recognition it has earned, for two reasons. First, a new power grab is on in shaping the course of health care for the future, and in the jockeying for position, the N.M.A. is not considered; and second, even our liberal friends do not want to see a strong N.M.A., unless they can control it. . . . Organized medicine as represented by both the American Medical Association and the Association of Medical Colleges has been notoriously conservative in recognition of problems relating to the Negro.[46]*

406 ■ *Race, Medicine, and Health before, during, and after the Black Civil Rights Era*

Consistent with the health system's pervasive racial discrimination early in the period and residual problems that persist today, as early as 1966 the Congress began taking action to nullify enforcement of Title 6 of the Civil Rights Act of 1964 in the health system. Despite their firsthand experience with these and other race- and class-oriented health system problems, African American physicians were virtually excluded from the design or implementation of Medicare/Medicaid and the medical educational reforms to meet the new demands of the health system and ensure minority health professions representation.[47]

By 1968 it was clear that Black physicians and health professionals would be permitted only a limited role in shaping and administering potentially progressive health policies and programs as the AMA and its medical establishment coterie stepped forward to co-opt the administrative and financial power and influence implicit in the assumption of such leadership. The AMA and its functionaries designed and implemented health delivery system templates for government financing, administering, and regulating health care, and as far as educational goals were concerned: "The Establishment . . . seems determined to preempt the field of aid to medical education of Negroes, even to the extent of pushing out independent and Negro sponsored efforts in this area,"[48] Cobb noted in 1968. By 1978 this "inadequate input from the black perspective"[49] was being cited by 1978–1979 NMA president Jesse B. Barber, M.D., as a major determinant accounting for the fact that: "[t]he evidence that effective health care is not being attained by the black community as a whole is overwhelming and incontrovertible."[50] Relegated to sideline positions by the medical establishment, African American doctors also began documenting and articulating their frustrations and reactions to continued inequities. They compiled evidence throughout the period of systematic health system resistance to fully dismantling racial discrimination, affirmative action, a truly unitary health delivery system, and the delivery of equitable and culturally sensitive health care.[51]

John L. S. Holloman, M.D., 1966–1967 NMA president, observed that:

> *forward looking legislation for medical progress with provisions for better quality and more widely available health care has, for the most part, been vigorously opposed by organized medicine. It is most ironic that the responsibility for the implementation of this legislation, in large part, is now being placed in the hands of those same individuals who have opposed it in the recent past.*[52]

Black doctors recognized that even the NHC movement was being coopted by AHCs and the medical establishment, as: "We see a mad scramble for federal funds from the Office of Economic Opportunity as plans for Neighborhood Health Centers around the country are developed."[53] African American doctors and health professionals were also frustrated in their efforts to increase minority representation and participation in the critical area of health professions educational finance:

> *It would seem crystal clear that insofar as the Macy Foundation and National Medical Fellowships, Inc. are concerned, the National Medical Association does not exist. The further inference is obvious that the white power structure is intent upon dominating what financial aid is to be given to the recruitment of Negroes for medicine and does not desire either competition or attempts at collaboration from Negro organizations, large or small.[54]*

Other actions by African American health professionals, often on the fringes of mainstream activities in these areas, seemed necessary.

Consistent with their historical traditions, Black health professionals remodeled these adversities and setbacks into opportunities. As Leonidis H. Berry, M.D., viewed the mid-1960s landscape, "The climate would seem to be right as never before for progress against second and third-class medical care for millions of Negroes purely on account of race."[55] Lionel F. Swann, M.D., 1967–1968 NMA president, was just as positive and defiant regarding what some would consider a hopeless situation, stating: "We stand on the threshold of history. Never before has a national medical organization attempted comprehensive health care on a private basis. We have been given a golden and unprecedented opportunity. Victory is within our grasp! ... We have accepted the challenge. We have become totally involved. Let us become totally committed."[56] Such attitudes and opinions, which led to subsequent actions taken by Black organized medicine, led Dr. Paul Cornely to remark in 1970: "The black doctor has been excluded from many of the ghetto programs; only recently, by virtue of the stimulus given by the National Medical Association ... , is the black doctor getting part of the action."[57] Recognizing that the NMA was their principal resource and that they had few mechanisms for identifying and researching their policies and problems, for analyzing the problems and agenda items they identified, for proposing solutions or implementing new policies and programs for ameliorating identified problems or concerns, or for designing long- and short-term evaluation mechanisms to determine the efficacy of their corrective policies and programs, African American physicians, turning once again to their NMA, took positive action.

In a collaborative effort with the Johnson administration, HEW, HUD, the FHA, Mayor Walter Washington's city administration for the District of Columbia, and the Equitable Life Assurance Society, starting in 1968, the NMA embarked on a private, comprehensive health care program for the inner city—the National Medical Association Foundation. Having been excluded from the massive government health program and educational efforts because of racial and power politics, Black physicians launched a privately funded and staffed effort focusing on improving health care systems for the urban poor through the establishment of a nationwide network of multiservice health facilities and, building upon their singular expertise and experience in this area, a community-based series of talent recruitment and motivation programs to steer Black and underprivileged youth

into health careers. The foundation, which was incorporated and officially organized by the NMA in 1967, broke ground for a nursing home and comprehensive
health center in Washington, D.C., in late 1969 and eventually had active
programs in Detroit, Los Angeles, and Montgomery County, Maryland. What the
NMA attempted with its unique effort was:

> to bring the poor into the mainstream of medicine by treating them in the
> same place at the same time and by the same doctors and health
> personnel as their more affluent neighbors. . . . The NMA thus became the
> first national organization of health professionals to promote the concept
> of a single system of quality health care for both poor and nonpoor in the
> same physical setting.[58]

The concept was unprecedented, even revolutionary, in the United States. Its initiation by health professionals—represented in the public mind by powerful White
groups who traditionally fought against progressive health care policies and
programs—almost defied contemporary reality. Besides living up to the egalitarian
public health ideals articulated by Dr. Alonzo Yerby of the Harvard School of
Public Health, NMA Foundation programs attempted to address bridging the gaps
between rich and poor, Blacks and Whites, Anglo-Saxons and disadvantaged
minorities. They also served as a countervailing force to the grudging recognition
that "[t]he much touted neighborhood health clinics are an extension of the
hospital clinics. . . . In spite of the other attributes of the neighborhood health
center, it is still segregated and differentiated treatment."[59] Efforts to ensure continuity and parity in funding for institutions serving Blacks and the underserved
were also implicit. Almost predictably, these grandiose plans and programs were
short-lived. Most of these well-intended efforts eventually foundered in head-to-
head competition for support against massively funded, White-controlled,
government programs by: (1) being vulnerable to White medical establishment
inattention and retribution (e.g., control of hospital staff privileges, laborious
"justification for funding" processes, and, later, "peer review" mechanisms); (2)
being under constant threat of government-controlled patients being forced to
enroll in large (the Nixon HMO plan recommended at least 10,000 enrollees),
White-controlled, federally sponsored HMOs or prepaid plans that might discriminate against, or, due to size and demographics alone, economically exclude Black
physicians*; and (3) lacking the political connections or influence to tap mainstream government and private funding sources, relying on the limited fiscal

---

*Most groups of White physicians starting such an HMO or prepaid plan would not have staffed it
with Black physicians in significant numbers. The start-up costs of such large, complex delivery systems conforming to the staffing and required regulatory rigor would be beyond the fiscal capabilities
(e.g., obtaining such a loan or possessing the venture capital) of either a single Black physician or a
group of Black physicians.

resources of the "progressive" private sector, charitable organizations, and a poverty-ridden Black community.[60]

Since the NMA could not directly affect national health policy, it gradually shifted its emphasis to components of the Black health crisis. During the same period, the mainstream system redirected its efforts toward cost-cutting, competition, commercialism, and entrepreneurialism. Simultaneously, it shifted the terrain undergirding the attack on race- and class-based health discrimination and disparities from increasing resources and equalization toward self-help, self-improvement, health promotion/disease prevention programs, and ultimately, old-fashioned victim-blaming. While the NMA analyzed and rejected many of the policies recommended by the AMA and its cabal, it continued its vigilance in addressing critical health challenges facing African American and underserved communities, such as disease-specific and manpower shortage issues and elements of the Black health crisis as exemplified by the racial health disparities in virtually all leading health indicators. Meanwhile, the previous efforts by mainstream organizations to address these issues waned.[61]

Although the new federal guidelines and programs improved the overall condition of African Americans in the health system between 1965 and 1980, Black physicians, the Negro medical ghetto, Black patients, and health professionals were forced to make drastic adaptations. These dislocations included, but were not limited to, a threatened change in the nature, characteristics, and commitment of African American doctors and health professionals who were largely educated in White institutions; the medical and mainstream health system abandonment and "health colonization" of inner-city and largely Black communities; and shifting profiles of the health institutions serving African American and underserved communities to include more White-controlled AHCs and government agencies in direct competition with Black hospitals and private clinics. Instead of collaborating with and strengthening the Black community's traditional health institutions, the new White decision-makers implemented policies to destroy them. The results, such as the virtual elimination of Black hospitals — previous sites of medical care provision and professional training in a segregated America — were sometimes devastating to access to care and Black traditions of community pride, self-sufficiency, and institutional viability.

Throughout their 200-year history, the few Black health providers able to obtain formal training displayed a commitment to and concern for promoting the health of the African American community. Empathy and orientation among African American health workers sympathetic to the Black community was further established during the last century with the opening of the Black medical, health professions schools, and training programs and establishment of the Negro medical ghetto. Black doctors have traditionally borne themselves in a way that "reflects the NMA's philosophy ... as the world's first and only socioeconomically oriented medical organization,"[62] according to 1971–1972 NMA president Emerson C. Walden, M.D. Thus the desegregation of the nation's White medical and health education infrastructures under the pressures of social and legal forces, especially in the South, represented both an opportunity and a threat to both the Black profession and patients. Early efforts in desegregated training promoted individuals such as Drs. Edith Irby Jones, the first Black graduate of a Southern medical school (University of Arkansas 1952); Henry W. Foster, dean of America's Black obstetrician-gynecologists, founder of the influential pregnancy prevention and uplift "I Have A Future" program, and Surgeon General candidate; Samuel L. Kountz, surgical transplant pioneer and chief surgeon at a major AHC (SUNY Downstate Medical Center 1972); and Robert L. Gamble, the first African American graduate of Johns Hopkins Medical School (1967). Although stressed by professional isolation and discriminatory barriers, they were forced to survive in White institutional training settings and made significant and lasting contributions to Black health and life in America.[63] Would Black health pundits' predictions questioning the orientation and commitment to the African American community by Black health professionals trained in White institutions become a real problem? As the education of Black medical students was transferred to faculties at predominantly White institutions, Frierson warned: "[T]he education and professional socialization of black physicians are conducted primarily by those who are not black and have few ties to the black community. Because black physicians are the primary medical resource to the black community, this situation demands concern."[64] Confusing trends became discernable between 1965 and 1980. The result of the Black community's growing dependency on White health professions institutions (what contemporaneous studies were documenting as overwhelmingly negative toward Blacks and other disadvantaged minorities) deserves further study.[65]

Throughout the late 1960s and 1970s, Black physicians and health professionals were forced to change. Increasingly coerced to interact with the mainstream health system at the institutional, professional, and pedagogic levels, African American health professionals were compelled to abandon or at least modify their Negro medical ghetto and the comforts proffered by their separate professional lives. Initially, most of these changes were more potential than real, portending future attitudes and characteristics. They occurred as by-products of the increased numbers of young African Americans admitted into traditional health professions training programs (e.g., medicine, dentistry, nursing), results of the appearance of new allied health professions with their minority representation, and outgrowths of grudging mainstream compliance with new desegregation laws and regulations. Moreover, what this new generation of minority health professionals trained throughout the nation's health institutions were going to do in relation to the African American community was speculative at best. The nature of the changes were difficult to discern, but greater efforts to study Black physicians and health professionals emerged as their recruitment and participation in the nation's health system became priorities.[66] Haynes's 1969 study revealed that as of 1967 (the latest data then available), 83 percent of Black physicians were graduates of Howard University or Meharry Medical College. They were concentrated in New York, California, and Washington, D.C., and were less likely to practice in groups (2 percent of Black doctors compared to 9.5 percent of Whites). His study also revealed that 39 percent of African American physicians were general practitioners, compared to 23 percent of all U.S. physicians. Haynes's finding that Black board certification rates (22 percent) were somewhat lower than the national average (31 percent) conflicted with Schwarz's 1970 study (41.5 percent Black board certification rate), but was probably more accurate, reflecting both a much higher and representative response rate in Haynes's study and the discriminatory financial and training-access problems still impeding Black attainment of medical specialty boards.[67]

Claude H. Organ, M.D., U.S. surgical leader and first African American chairman of the American Board of Surgery—himself a Black graduate of a White medical school (Creighton 1952)—reported to the 1970 NMA convention "that 73 percent of black medical students in the United States were enrolled in white medical schools in 1969–70, as against 46 percent from the previous year."[68] Total medical school enrollment for Black students charted a 33 percent increase (from 782 in 1968–1969 to 1,042 in 1969–1970), and first-year enrollment increased an astounding 65 percent (from 266 in 1968–1969 to 440 in 1969–1970). Although these rate increases were not sustained, maintaining these levels of African American trainee representation in 84 of the nation's 101 medical schools represented not only tremendous progress but also an almost certain likelihood that the Black physician profile would change. As the Association of Minority Health Professions Schools (AMHPS) reported, "In 1970–1971 there were 180 black graduates from U.S. medical schools; 94, or 52.2 percent were graduated from Howard University and Meharry Medical College. By 1972–1973 minority schools accounted for 36.7 percent of black graduates."[69] Between 1969 and 1973, first-year enrollment for all medical schools increased 31.2 percent while Black enrollment more than doubled. Even though Black enrollment increased 15.8 percent between 1973 and 1982, this failed to keep pace with the overall 22 percent medical school enrollment increase. Thus, although the proportion of Black medical students in minority medical schools dropped to 17.6 percent in 1974–1975, the proportion increased to 23.7 percent by 1981–1982 as Bakke decision effects proliferated and the commitment to proportional representation waned. "The experience of black student enrollment in the majority schools of dentistry, pharmacy and veterinary medicine has been less successful,"[70] the 1983 AMHPS report noted. Would these profound educational changes alter what behavioral and social scientists documented as a surprisingly liberal arm of a very conservative profession?[71]

Carter G. Woodson performed the first comprehensive and detailed social scientific study of Black professionals in *The Negro Professional Man and the Community* (1934). (See Figure 5.1 on next page.) Focusing on Black physicians, dentists, nurses, and lawyers for various scientific reasons, he documented that health professionals, especially physicians and dentists, had become the leading figures in most Black communities by the 1930s. A brief survey of his findings on Black physicians revealed, that:

> [T]*he Negro physician has done much for the promotion of health. In fact, he has been the missionary of health among people who prior to his time had no one to take special interest in such preachments and in the dissemination of information of this kind.... In spite of all the shortcomings of the physicians herein pointed out this professional class has done something for the uplift of the masses.... Negro physicians have contributed to educational and uplift causes in their communities, engaged in civil rights struggles, and pressured communities into positive public health practices affecting the African American and community at large.*[72]

Although the observations of E. Franklin Frazier, in works such as *The Negro in the United States* (1957) and *Black Bourgeoisie: The Rise of a New Middle Class in the United States* (1957), could lead one to think the Black physician was "somewhat more conservative in his politico-economic views than white doctors," later studies found "that Negro doctors are in fact much more liberal ... not only more liberal than white Protestant and Catholic doctors, but also more liberal than Jewish doctors."[73] The reasons hypothesized for this greater liberalism and progressivism among Black doctors included, but were not limited to, their experiencing greater difficulties in gaining access to medical training; the majority being trained in the

**Figure 5.1**
**Carter G. Woodson (1875–1950)**
Considered the "father of African American history," Woodson documented the impact and importance of Black health professionals within their communities and the world.

Reproduced from Books Inc. *In Black America.* Los Angeles: Presidential Publishers, 1970, 51.

unique medical-social milieu of Howard University and Meharry Medical Colleges; encountering difficulties in obtaining, and being limited in their options for, postgraduate training; encountering difficulties in gaining, and being relegated to the lower levels of, hospital staff appointments; being restricted from medical specialties compared to Whites due to the additional costs of and difficulty being accepted for training and making a living practicing a specialty in the ghetto; resentment about the much lower incomes Black doctors generated compared to White doctors (approximately 50 percent of White doctors' income); being recipients of undesirable referrals from White colleagues, when there were referrals at all; being trapped in solo practices on the basis of their circumstances despite admiring group practice as a concept; a sense of being victimized by the medical profession's loss of prestige due to the actions of the AMA; and strongly supporting what many of them consider the organizational rival of the AMA, the NMA.[74] Some of these studies revealed that "Negro doctors ... are presently disposed to support progressive changes in the organization of health services in the United States, and to press for changes in community relations."[75] Thus, "while Frazier may have been justified in branding some Negro doctors black Babbits on the basis of their life-styles ... they may constitute a potential source of revolutionary leadership,"[76] according to Lenski, Richard, Schwarz, and others.[77]

As African American medical and other health professions withstood drastic transformations in their educational, training, and professional environments, they were also forced to adapt to a rapidly changing and threatening landscape where they practiced. African American physicians, and other minority health providers, had continued their concentration in cities after World War II. The aforementioned abandonment of the urban centers by many components of the mainstream health system created virtual health system wastelands in the nation's inner cities, where Black doctors and a thin and underfunded veneer of public health and charity programs were the sole health resources. Previously mentioned out-migrations of White doctors, most White not-for-profit and proprietary hospitals, and service sectors of the health system worsened the health profiles and prospects of already underserved areas, rendering them more vulnerable to a fusillade of "corrective" government health programs during the 1960s and 1970s. As J. Alfred Cannon, M.D., of the Charles R. Drew Postgraduate Medical School observed, "Health providers and organizations never before interested in the health needs of the black community began attempting to come into the black community with hastily conceived and often inept health programs."[78] Swann thought it was "ironic that Federally sponsored health programs, aimed largely at improving the health status of 'Inner City' citizens are directed by 'Suburban Oriented Physicians,' either in advisory or administrative capacities."[79] Although some of these efforts were genuine and the programs worthy: "The health establishment (medical schools, public health departments, health speculators, etc.) now wished to be the major providers of health services to poor and black communities because in a word that's where the money was."[80] Consequences of this "health colonialism," borrowing Cannon's term, was a major factor leading to the eventual demise of the Black hospital. By 1990 "of the more than 400 black hospitals that have existed at one time or another,"[81] Travella in a 1990s *Washington Post* article observed, "[t]oday, there are only eight."[82] Moreover, the viability of Black health professionals was threatened as "black physicians and other black health providers are now shoved aside under the guise that large and efficient health delivery machinery is available from outside the community."[83] The mechanisms utilized to facilitate this "takeover" may have been more devastating to Black communities than the acts themselves: "The local health leaders and local black technical resources are viewed as competitors by the health colonists and discredited. . . . [L]ocal black health resources who in the early days manned the health battlements in poor and black communities virtually alone are now depicted as ineffective, parochial and inept."[84] Inner-city Black doctors who through the Medicare and Medicaid programs finally realized "after long hours and low fees, that adequate compensation for his services can be rewarding and fulfilling,"[85] were undercut not only by their elite and often hostile White peers but also by a new panoply of federal and local government-funded institutions and programs invading their neighborhoods.[86]

During this period African American physicians, like many others, were threatened by the economic (e.g., declining fee-for-service financing) and structural reorganization (e.g., HMOs, independent practice associations [IPAs], and preferred provider organizations [PPOs]—virtually all under White and outside of Black community control) of health care delivery. Besides having to compete in this new environment, African American physicians also had to cope with disturbing new professional, interprofessional, and medical-social problems generated by direct interaction with previously segregated and White-run institutions and organizations. As Charles Epps, M.D., dean of Howard's medical school said, "Black physicians cannot depend on their blackness to attract patients; they must offer services and conveniences as efficiently as the competition."[87] The economic survival of African American physicians was in question not only because of their poor business practices but also because of their public image, which was not always favorable,[88] and to new criteria for participation in insurance programs (e.g., HMOs, IPAs, and PPOs) and for attaining and maintaining hospital privileges such as board certification in various specialties. Whether Black doctors could survive under the traditional practice patterns Richard referred to as "monochromatic" (all-Black clientele) general and nonspecialty practices and the "garbage referral system"* was also in question.

By the 1980s it was becoming obvious that the Black medical profession was

---

*The few referrals Black doctors obtained from their White colleagues were when White doctors wanted to rid themselves of their, or their patients', cooks or domestics or indigent patients, or for treatment of socially marginal conditions such as venereal diseases or unwanted pregnancies that White patients wanted to conceal from their families or friends.

under attack at many levels.[89] Moreover, as the health system became obsessed with cost-cutting, it became "difficult for black physicians to get privileges at some hospitals because it is a belief that we tend to attract high-risk, high demand patients who are a liability to the profit-making plan"; thus, "Often minority physicians are penalized financially and socially for trying to serve poor inner-city people,"[90] according to Edith Irby Jones, the first female NMA president from 1985 to 1986. Not only was the Black health professional subject to the overt and covert racism African Americans live with daily, but the less violent forms that racism takes, such as institutional racism, "mini-insults," and "microaggressions," which Black physicians, until now, had largely avoided in their practices, constituted a new range of racial stressors. Psychiatrist Carl C. Bell, M.D., described the dangers of such Black professionals becoming "marginal men" in such new desegregated environments and increasing their risks for becoming impaired professionals or being "at risk for egoistic and anomic suicide."[91] Thus, during this era, with the advent and abuse of the peer review laws and "quality assurance" programs supplementing White organized medicine's already racist views and practices:

> *black doctors ... practice in hospitals where they are harried by day and haunted by night by the fact they are black and their patients are poor— where physicians live constantly at tiptoe stance, never quite knowing what to expect next, plagued with inner fears and outer resentments, forever fighting a degenerating sense of "nobodiness," and grimly preparing for the next inquisition by a "committee" of their cold, insensitive, authoritarian, intolerant, white "peers."*[92]

By the 1980s, purges of Black physicians from White hospital staffs had surfaced in Detroit, Chicago, and Houston, for example.[93] The Lone Star State Medical Association revealed a professional pogrom in Fort Worth, Texas, that labeled over 90 percent of black doctors there as deficient; one third had their positions eliminated, another one third were forced to practice outside major hospitals, and the rest were harassed."[94] As early as 1973, R.F. Gilum, M.D., had predicted in the *JNMA*, "If the PSRO program is without significant input from blacks and other minorities in the medical professions, it is quite likely that it will operate in a way that is insensitive and neglectful of the needs of black patients and professionals."[95] By the mid-1980s, the problem of peer review abuse and race-based hospital staff purging under the guise of "quality assurance" became so prevalent and pernicious that it was revealed by the lead author of this book at hearings before the U.S. Congress at the behest of the sitting NMA president, Edith Irby Jones.[96]

Despite the abuse, many well-intended African American physicians such as Drs. Clyde W. Phillips, Agnes Lattimer, and Edward Cross attempted to transform often decrepit, underfunded, public, and not-for-profit institutions into decent, up-to-date facilities sensitive to community needs—usually with little long-term results. These belated Black appointments heading hospitals, clinics, or health centers were often made when these institutions were swirling in controversy or on their last legs functionally or fiscally. Without unprecedented community support and major health policy shifts, no leader or administrator could have succeeded in these endeavors. Other establishment health reform and medical efforts in the Black inner cities were actually part of the Civil Rights Movement. They were, in fact, the result of attempts to placate desperation and urban unrest with health care—with all the attendant hostility, confrontation, and trouble such too-long-unattended-to problems usually carry with them. Neither Black physicians nor health care *per se* had much to offer to correct the long-standing effects of such massive dysfunctional social forces and advanced societal disorganization and collapse.[97]

Blacks in the medical and other health professions, having reached the apogee of their power between 1965 and 1970, reeled under the barrage of professional, health policy, psychological, and self-identity blows inflicted by a health system blinded by commercialization, deprofessionalization, cost-cutting, competition, political power, and budget overruns. Black health providers' power lever on medical-social issues, especially those concerning equity, medical ethics, race, and class, became less fashionable and was engulfed in an increasingly conservative health system ripe for commercial takeover by 1980.

# Western Science's Deep, Dark Secret and the U.S. Health System's Mendacious Legacy

On medical testing and treatments that have overstepped their bounds:

> [W]hen one hears that those who were in the hands of the government, and apparently mistreated, were less empowered, because they were poor, they were prisoners, or they were minorities, or in the case of the youngsters at the Fernald School, they were retarded[, s]omething in all of us just shrinks back and we find that repugnant.
>
> HAZEL R. O'LEARY, SECRETARY OF ENERGY, 1992–1997

## Questioning Scientific Traditions in the United States

When journalist Jean Hellar broke the story on the Tuskegee syphilis experiment on July 25, 1972, in the *Washington Star*, few realized that the subsequent events would send shock waves through the American scientific and biomedical establishments. The resultant conflagration would take on a life of its own and help define the disturbing relationship between the African American, biomedical, and scientific communities into the twenty-first century. Since its public disclosure and transformation from an event in American research history into a powerful metaphor for scientific exploitation, "[t]he Tuskegee Syphilis Study is frequently described as the singular reason behind African-American distrust of the institutions of medicine and public health."[1] While this and James H. Jones's observation—"No scientific experiment inflicted more damage on the collective psyche of black Americans than the Tuskegee study"[2]—are true, Vanessa Northington Gamble critiques such appraisals of the Tuskegee study as overly simplistic. For African Americans, she says, "Such an interpretation neglects a critical historical point: . . . mistrust predated public revelations about the Tuskegee study. Furthermore, the narrowness of such a representation places emphasis on a single historical event to explain deeply entrenched and complex attitudes within the Black community."[3] H. Jack Geiger agrees that its deeper significance in the Black community is that it represented the scientific racism that pervades American health institutions, historically and contemporaneously, and reflects the devaluation of Black human rights and lives in the health system.[4] Tuskegee directed attention to generalized defects plaguing the entire U.S. biomedical research and health system beyond the confines of the Black community. In the wake of the public outrage and demands for institutional reform to protect human subjects involved in biomedical research, U.S. physicians and scientists no longer exercised free reign over the design and conduct of scientific experiments performed on human beings. Rules were also established to protect Black and poor women from unethical surgeries and sterilizations at the hands of personnel and institutions representing the medical and health establishments. In retrospect, a wide range of fundamental and history-based medical-social and ethical flaws pervasive in American medical and life sciences and its health system were exposed. Debridement of the "scab" covering the wound of the Tuskegee experiment can barely be appreciated—even today.

As has been noted earlier, U.S. attitudes and practices within the medical and scientific communities seemingly condoned scientific research on vulnerable populations:

> [I]t was not uncommon in the 1940s for physicians to use patients as subjects in experiments without their knowledge or consent. This occurred frequently in research involving potential new therapies, where there was at least a chance that the patient-subjects might benefit medically from being in an experiment. But it also occurred even in experiments . . . where there was never any expectation and no chance that the experiment might be of benefit to the subjects.[5]

Despite the drastically altered bioethical environment wrought by Nazi medical atrocities, American human experimentation at the beginning of the 1965 to 1980 era was problematic. As medical historian David Rothman observed: [A] utilitarian ethic continued to govern human experimentation—partly because the benefits seemed so much greater than the costs, and partly, too, because there were no groups or individuals prominently opposing such an ethic."[6] This overriding *utilitarian* ethic—with some *consequentialist** overtones from medical and scientific perspectives—spilled over into other areas of the health system and affected the care meted out to, treatment of, and vulnerability for scientific exploitation of African American, socially and economically disadvantaged patients, disabled patients, wards of tax-supported institutions, and incarcerated populations. Moreover, this ethic was reflected through a prism of more than three generations of pseudoscientific eugenic and biological determinist education and public propaganda. Nevertheless, Allen M. Hornblum, author of *Acres of Skin: Human Experiments at Holmesburg Prison: A True Story of Abuse and Exploitation in the Name of Medical Science*, observed that American physicians of the time felt the recent precedent of "Nazi medicine was a horrible but distant medical aberration that could never happen here."[7] Indeed:

> the moral superiority of American research was the perceived norm by which Nazi doctors were judged. In addition, the reasoning continued, because scientific progress was best achieved through independence and autonomy, and since Nazi science had flourished under governmental intrusion and control, American doctors deserved deference and encouragement, not oversight and outside management.[8]

During this period, "prestigious medical journals published articles reporting and recommending the use of vulnerable, institutionalized children or prisoners as 'ideal' test subjects."[9] In the medical ethics field, James H. Jones noted that the United States lagged far behind other Western industrialized countries by the 1960s:

> An NIH report in 1964 further strengthened the case for action. The result of years of inquiry, the paper revealed that within the American medical profession there were no generally accepted codes on clinical research. The legal status of studies involving human subjects remained ambiguous at best, and wide variations existed in official attitudes toward human experimentation. The potential for abuse became clear.[10]

---

*Utilitarianism* is the moral theory that an action is morally right if it produces at least as much good (utility) for all people affected by the action as any alternative action the person could do instead. Debates surrounding utilitarianism as a moral theory concern whether and how utilitarianism can be clearly and precisely defined, formulated, and applied and whether the moral implications of utilitarianism in particular cases are acceptable or instead constitute objections to it. *Consequentialism* is the broader view that morally right action is action that maximizes the good, however the good is understood. Source: Audi R, ed. *The Cambridge Dictionary of Philosophy*. Cambridge, U.K.: Cambridge University Press, 1995, 824, 825.

The Nuremberg Principles, which outlined universal guidelines for protecting human rights—based on harsh lessons from World War II—were adopted by the United Nations in 1946 and, by the 1960s, had gone a long way toward changing the human rights and moral standards of the world. Moreover, the Nuremberg Code, formulated at the German Doctors Trial (October 25, 1946—July 19, 1947)*—at a predominantly U.S. legal preceding** conducted under the aegis of U.S. judges and military authority, based on U.S. procedures, and tried largely by U.S. prosecuting attorneys***—became the most complete and authoritative legal statement on informed consent to human experimentation. It represented a new starting point in this area, according to the *Encyclopedia of Bioethics* and other sources—especially regarding nontherapeutic and/or nonbeneficial experimentation.

Paradoxically, America virtually ignored the Nuremberg Code, which, as of 1992, "has almost never been cited by U.S. courts in its more than four decades of existence."[11] Simultaneously, throughout the 1960s and 1970s, "civil protests raised America's concerns for the rights of black people, and the ethical standards of the medical profession regarding the treatment of nonwhite patients changed dramatically."[12] For the first time, questions had been publically raised about the American medical profession's ethical "blind spot" regarding "race"[13] and "a host of unanswered questions about the social and racial attitudes of the medical establishment in the United States."[14]

Unlike Nazi Germany, the U.S. government had not mobilized its resources and authority to impose scientific racism and exploitation as an arm of *general* public policy in the United States. Except for *isolated* exceptions, government-funded promotion of policies or projects with overt or covert scientific racist or unethical research overtones has been sporadic and/or under private control. Some of the exceptions include the previously mentioned U.S. Sanitary Commission Anthropometric Studies during the Civil War; the World War I army IQ tests; state and government-funded psychometric studies**** and sterilizations in state and federal institutions; the 1924 Immigration Restriction Act; unethical surgeries, experiments, and sterilizations performed in public hospitals; the rash of government-funded unethical sterilizations per-

---

*The hearing itself began on December 9, 1946, consuming 139 trial days, including six days for final arguments and the personal statements of the defendants.

**There is definite evidence that representatives from the United Kingdom and France participated in the Doctors Trial. However, participation by the Soviet Union, the other "great power," cannot be excluded.

***The Nuremberg Doctors Trial resulted in four German physicians being hung for having violated the Nuremberg Code in administering drugs and performing surgical operations on Jews, Catholics, and other political prisoners. Nine others received life terms; three others, who were not physicians, were also hanged.

****Results of these studies were utilized to justify everything from incarcerations, retention in institutions, sterilizations, denial of remedial education or psychological therapies, to adverse legal decisions.

formed throughout the health system in the 1960s and 1970s[15]; and the United States Public Health Service (USPHS)–sponsored Tuskegee syphilis study. Even when abuse has been widespread—as in the case of the forced sterilizations—effects have generally been quiet and hidden, or at least spared public scrutiny. Thus resultant ill effects in areas including, but not limited to, eugenics, public health, clinical and surgical ethics, clinical research codes, genetics and heredity, psychometric testing, infection control, and reproductive control tended to seem isolated and difficult to discern and quantify—as they are often disguised under a self-righteous veneer of scientific and social beneficence. Moreover, until after World War II, most influential Whites felt that African Americans were shielded away from mainstream society by Jim Crow and antimiscegenation laws; were politically docile, demonstrating little affinity for movements such as communism or anarchy; were less intellectually capable than Whites and thus were automatically shunned by most Americans; and, in contrast to the European immigrants, were a slowly growing population numerically. Though the overall history-based pattern of Black health exploitation and abuse was not abated, during the early part of the century, depending upon local practices or Jim Crow laws, certain pockets of the Black population were somewhat protected from malfeasance by White attitudinal barriers and denial of access to health services and institutions. This was conflated by the fact that "there was no campaign of antiblack propaganda anything like the systematic and relentless barrage directed against the immigrants."[16] Although "[t]he eugenicists judged blacks even more biologically undesirable than immigrants," they "paid them much less political attention,"[17] as William H. Tucker noted in *The Science and Politics of Racial Research*. Ironically, as Black's contact with Whites and the "mainstream" health system increased, so did incidents of exploitation and abuse.

The misuse of science by the Nazis as a foundation of political ideology, as *the* rationale for public policy, and as a tool of nationalistic and foreign policy, although carried to extremes, was not new. Nineteenth- and early twentieth-century German social Darwinists such as Alfred Ploetz, Fritz Lenz, and Eugen Fischer—who helped structure the scientific racist rationale "[t]o clean the body of the *Volk* of everything sick, alien, and disturbing,"[18] such as Jews, Slavs, Gypsies, and disabled persons—were analogous in many ways to antebellum American scientists such as Samuel Cartwright, Josiah Clark Nott, and Samuel George Morton, who utilized "science" to justify rationally Black slavery and buttress the proslavery arguments of Southern politicians and zealots such as John C. Calhoun, Jefferson Davis, and Alexander H. Stephens. Both movements attempted to justify and succeeded in fostering the imposition of negative social, medical, and scientific policies on large, discrete groups of people—leading to adverse outcomes ranging from racial discrimination and segregation and systematic denial of quality health care to scientific abuse, exploitation, and death.

Other historical continua undergirding the U.S. biomedical sciences and exposed by the Tuskegee syphilis experiment bear examination. Initial reactions from the medical community when the Tuskegee story broke were strident, defensive, and out of sync with the public attitudes of the times:

> *Their letters defending the study appeared in editorial pages across the country, but their most heated counterattacks were delivered in professional journals. The most spirited example was an editorial in the* Southern Medical Journal *by Dr. R.H. Kampmeir of Vanderbilt University's School of Medicine. No admirer of the press, he blasted reporters for their "complete disregard for their abysmal ignorance," and accused them of banging out "anything on their typewriters which will make headlines."*[19]

In addition to accusing the media of sensationalism, Kampmeir recapitulated the results of the groundbreaking Oslo untreated syphilis study (1891–1910, with a follow-up in 1929), never explaining why it needed to be repeated, and reasserted the hotly contested clinical and scientific argument that penicillin would not have benefited the men.* By failing "to discuss the social mandate of physicians to prevent harm and to heal the sick whenever possible [Kampmeir] seemed to reduce the Hippocratic oath to a solemn obligation not to deny treatment upon demand,"[20] thus suspending most medical ethical considerations surrounding the Tuskegee experiment. Then Kampmeir implicitly blamed the men for contracting the disease, demonstrating no compassion or sensitivity to the ethically normative and human need for treatment of a serious disease and cynically explaining the higher death rates in the untreated syphilitics by stating: "This is not surprising. No one has ever implied that syphilis is a benign infection."[21] This defense reaffirms Martin S. Pernick's contention about American public health, using it as a totem for the U.S. health system: "Racism and other social prejudices became part of ... public health in the past, not just because these values were prevalent among health professionals, but because health professionals convinced themselves that their sciences were purely objective."[22] Such thinking was traditional in America concerning experimentation on Blacks and the disadvantaged and the medical aspects of the problem—which Jones labeled a "scientific blindspot to ethical issues" and the *Atlanta Constitution* called "a *moral astigmatism* that saw these black sufferers simply as 'subjects' in a study, not as human beings [italics added]."[23] As the *Washington Post* observed, "There is always a lofty goal in the research work of medicine but too often in the past it has been the bodies of the poor ... on whom the unholy testing is done."[24] But the shielding of scientific practices, pronouncements, and outcomes from the usual rigors of public scrutiny was

---

*Most physicians at that time and virtually all physicians now would disagree with Dr. Kampmeir's position.

not new in Western culture. The social costs of scientific racism, along with the political overtones implicit in Western life sciences, also became apparent during this period.[25]

Western science and medicine have been cloaked in images of "objectivity" for centuries, if not millennia. Pernick observed, "This widely shared faith in objectivity did not succeed in eliminating subjective values from medicine, but it did serve to delegitimate the openly political and ethical debate that is necessary if a culture is to assess its value judgements intelligently."[26] As Stephen Jay Gould noted, certain scientists: "have often invoked the traditional prestige of science as objective knowledge, free from social and political taint. They portray themselves as purveyors of harsh truth and their opponents as sentimentalists, ideologues, and wishful thinkers."[27] An example of this centuries-old tradition is Charles White's 1799 scientific defense of polygeny, White racial superiority, and the "Great Chain of Being,"* *Account of the Regular Gradation of Man*, wherein:

> *he tried to raise the status of apes while lowering the worth of supposedly inferior people ... [and] elevated orangutans by arguing that they willingly submit to that most enlightened of contemporary medical practices—bloodletting.... Then in a double whammy designed to raise apes and debase black humans, he portrayed the simians as both slavers and sexual abusers (ever so human, if not particularly admirable).*[28]

William H. Tucker noted:

> *Setting an example followed by scores of researchers during the next two centuries, White declared his lack of malice toward blacks; his only purpose was "to investigate the truth, and to discover what are the established laws of nature." He fervently proclaimed no desire to see blacks oppressed just because they were a separate species, of greater biological proximity to anthropoids than to Europeans, and hoped that nothing he said would "give the smallest countenance to the pernicious practice of enslaving mankind."*[29]

Louis Agassiz, the world-renowned Harvard physician-biologist who harbored a personal racist bias toward African Americans,[30]** wrote in 1850 defending his "objective" assignment of Blacks to a separate species: "Naturalists have a right to consider the questions growing out of men's physical relations as merely scientific questions."[31] Harvard geneticist Edward M. East was intolerant of oppression or discrimination on the basis of color in the 1920s; "[n]evertheless, as a scientist, he concluded that blacks were physically as well as mentally inferior and had little of

---

*See chapters 1 and 4, Volume 1.

**See also chapter 5, Volume 1.

value to contribute to the higher white race," stating: "'Gene packets of African origin are not valuable supplements to the gene packets of European origin.... [I]t is the white germ plasm that counts.'"[32] The renowned psychometrician and later secretary of the College Entrance Examination Board [CEEB], who designed the SAT, Carl C. Brigham, placed the "American negro" at the lower end of his racial intelligence scale,[33] argued that "the most sinister development in the history of this continent, [was] the importation of the negro,"[34] and lobbied for the exclusion of southern and eastern European immigrants because they scored poorly on supposed tests of innate intelligence. He wrote in 1923: "The steps that should be taken to preserve or increase our present intellectual capacity must of course be dictated by science and not by political expediency."[35] Impressions of Blacks by United States physicians and society have been negatively influenced, if not distorted, by this train of "scientific" thought.

Although some scientists such as Gunnar Myrdal began explicitly questioning the objectivity of the medical, psychological, and biological allegations about human nature as early as 1944, only by the end of the era in question (1965–1980) did scientists such as Robert V. Guthrie, a research and academic psychologist at the University of Pittsburgh and author of *Even the Rat Was White* (1976); George Albee, a professor of psychology at the University of Vermont; and Stephen Jay Gould, the eminent Harvard biologist, speak out publically and in writing on the subject.[36] Guthrie stated in 1976:

> *Some of the dubious research of the 1920s has lingered nearly fifty years as a phantomlike apparition of pseudointellectualism. Present-day proclamations purporting to present evidence of limited intellectual capacities in black Americans resemble the claims of biased 1920 educational psychologists; race-betterment policies and recommendations for genetic control of the "socially unacceptable" reemerge with the same bigotry of a half-century ago. These theories recur with an appearance of "newness" enough to obscure the cobwebs of antiquity and actually encourage a repeat of the same defenses utilized decades ago. This is occurring today in the arguments against the continued use of IQ tests and allegations of inherited mental deficits in black and brown children.*[37]

Albee, as the recipient of the Award for the Distinguished Contribution to Community Psychology at an American Psychological Association conference in 1982, stated:

> *I have come to believe that I have had the whole "scientific" process reversed. Instead of facts being useful as the objective building blocks of theories, rather it is more accurate to say that people ... select*

*theories that are consistent with their personal values, attitudes, and prejudices and then go out into the world or into the laboratory, to seek the facts that validate their beliefs about the world and about human nature, neglecting or denying observations that contradict their personal prejudices.*[38]

"I criticize the myth that science is an objective enterprise, done properly only when scientists can shuck the constraints of their culture and view the world as it really is,"[39] Gould declared in 1981.[40]

As has been discussed previously, Western science, especially the life sciences, has been preoccupied with human inequality and burdened with the task of answering questions surrounding this subject. Aristotle, Plato, and Socrates began the inquiry. As Tucker pointed out:

*The truth is that though waged with scientific weapons, the goal in this controversy has always been political; indeed, the debate has no strictly scientific purpose or value. The question of genetic differences between races has arisen not out of purely scientific curiosity or the desire to find some important scientific truth or to solve some significant scientific problem but only because of the belief, explicit or unstated, that the answer has political consequences.*[41]

Both Gould and Tucker, assessing efforts to claim one group genetically less desirable or capable than the other, reaffirmed the thinking of French mathematician-scientist Marquis de Condorcet (1743–1794), who called such endeavors attempts "to make nature herself an accomplice of political inequality."[42] While tainting and distorting, if not poisoning, Western science's action agenda over the centuries, this phenomenon, more importantly, has bred a prejudicial and biased scientific culture among Western biomedical scientists and physicians—despite their allusions and rhetorical commitment to objectivity and fairness—wherein certain races and ethnic groups have been ranked higher, treated deferentially, and valued more than others. In such an environment, Tuskegee was no aberration—it was part of the norm.

After the Great Depression and World War II, it seemed that many scientists were determined to be on the "right" side of social and political issues. In the early parts of the century, scientific participation negatively influenced the eugenics movement, psychometric testing, infection control, social welfare (e.g., school health programs, free immunization programs, health programs for the poor, broadening health care entitlements for disabled Americans), individual freedom movements (e.g., women's rights, Black civil rights), and the immigration movements. As Gunnar Myrdal observed about the biological sciences and medicine:

> *They have been associated in America, as in the rest of the world, with conservative and even reactionary ideologies. Under their long hegemony, there has been a tendency to assume biological causation without question, and to accept social explanations only under the duress of a siege of irresistible evidence. In political questions, this tendency favored a do-nothing policy. This tendency also, in the main, for a century and more, determined people's attitudes toward the racial traits of the Negro.*[43]

Furthermore, as Tucker noted:

> *In addition to this altered political context, a different kind of scientific transition was taking place during the 1930s and 1940s, catching the whole field of "racial science" in a paradigm shift that replaced evolutionary development with cultural differences as the preferred explanatory construct for the diversity of human behavior. With this change in emphasis from Charles Darwin to Franz Boas, from the dominance of instincts to the importance of learning, human beings were now viewed as the creatures as well as the creators of culture.*[44]

Moreover, recent World War II "historical experience had indicated that the linkage between biological and political equality was popular in principle and devastating in practice."[45] A consensus was building that future prospects of the misuse of science toward scientific racist political ends were frightening and could not be allowed to occur again. During the same period, politically oriented statements on human equality, such as the UNESCO statement on "race,"* were being drafted and pressures were mounting for Black civil rights in the United States. Major scientific spokespersons, such as Otto Klineberg, professor of psychology at Columbia University, realized that a major obstacle to human rights was "the belief, widely and stubbornly held, that some races and peoples are inferior."[46] Thus much of the new generation of scientists, "Instead of dismissing the question of racial differences as scientifically meaningless and politically irrelevant, ... insisted that there were no significant differences in intelligence between blacks and whites."[47] Many scientists also alleged that racial segregation should be struck down because it produced demonstrable psychological harm, especially to the personality development and the motivation to learn among Black children. Thus, when scientific testimony was needed for *Brown v. Board of Education of Topeka, Kansas*, eminent scientists such as psychologists Kenneth and Mamie Clark of Columbia University and the City College of New York, Otto Klineberg, Swedish social scientist Gunnar Myrdal, Jerome S. Bruner from Harvard, social scientists

---

*The UNESCO Statement on Race (1950) asserted that all men [sic] belong to the same species, *Homo sapiens*, and although there exist populations within that species that differ from each other in their gene frequencies, which might be called biological races, "race" is not so much a biological phenomenon as a social myth.

Floyd and Gordon Allport, David Krech from Berkeley, M. Brewster Smith from Vassar, and many others emphasized these points. However, these attempts to shift the paradigm opened the door for segregationists to shift the terms of the battle away from inherent constitutional rights to debates about the empirical evidence presented by the scientists.[48]

---

## Science and the Right-Wing Defense of Segregation

In the wake of *Brown v. Board of Education of Topeka, Kansas*, a small—some considered misdirected—movement by conservative scientists occurred. Working under the mistaken assumption that the Supreme Court decision had been based primarily on egalitarian-oriented scientific evidence emanating from social and biomedical scientists under the influence of recent UNESCO pronouncements on race and public reaction to the Nazi Holocaust, prominent adherents promoting opposing viewpoints mobilized. Intentionally or not, they instigated a new wave of scientific racism in the United States. Participants included, but were not limited to, such scientific luminaries as Wesley Critz George, former head of the Department of Anatomy at the University of North Carolina Medical School, distinguished scientist, and president of the North Carolina Academy of Science, who authored the report, *The Biology of the Race Problem*,* commissioned by Alabama's segregationist governor John Patterson, which refuted the UNESCO documents and the scientific evidence presented to the U.S. Supreme Court in *Brown*; Frank C. McGurk, a professor of psychology at Villanova University and author of the controversial September 21, 1956, *U.S. News and World Report* article, "A Scientist's Report on Race Differences"; Henry E. Garrett, the leading scientific spokesman for segregation and chair of the Psychology Department at Columbia University for 16 years, then-professor at the University of Virginia, past president of the American Psychological Association and the Eastern Psychological Association, fellow of the American Association for the Advancement of Science, and member of the National Research Council and the Psychometric Society; Robert E. Kuttner, a trained researcher in zoology and biochemistry and a prominent member of the Liberty Lobby**; Dwight J. Ingle, chair of the Department of Physiology at the University of Chicago, editor of the prestigious journal *Perspectives in Biology and Medicine* and author of *Who Should Have Children?*, who played the role as mediator and disseminator of the

---

*The report was reprinted in book form by the Patrick Henry Press and was a best-seller on the Citizens Council book list.

**The Liberty Lobby, an umbrella organization for neo-Nazi politics, was founded in 1955 by Willis A. Carto, one of the most influential figures in far right politics. It adopted Francis Parker Yockey's view of Jews as "culture distorters" and projected Hitler's defeat as the defeat of Europe and America.

scientific racist work of Garrett and others until his personal anti-Black, racist views were published in *U.S. News and World Report* and other forums; Robert Gayre of Gayre, Scottish physical anthropologist and International Association for the Advancement of Ethnology and Eugenics Executive Committee member, who served as editor-in-chief of *Mankind Quarterly*; Ernest van den Haag, New York University professor and behavioral scientist who provided expert testimony at school integration trials and at World Court hearings in support of continued U.S. racial segregation, South African apartheid, and the denial of the ballot to Blacks; and A. James Gregor, professor of social and political philosophy at the University of Hawaii and, later, at Berkeley and the Hoover Institute, who praised Hitler's racial and political policies early in his career, was integral in institutionalizing the scientific Right, and proposed protecting Blacks from the "dominant" group who would demoralize, exploit, and eventually eliminate the weaker race if allowed to interact with them.

One other noted scientist devoid of a consciously political agenda was drawn into this scientific and political maelstrom—largely because of his scientific bloodlines and co-optation of his work by the political Right. Carlton Coon, a Harvard-trained physical anthropologist based at the University of Pennsylvania, was the last of a long line of prestigious, typologically oriented scientists in this field whose work could be traced back to scientists such as Aleš Hrdlička and his mentor and giant in the discipline, Earnest A. Hooton, who represented the "measuring school" of anthropology.* Coon was a participant in the prestigious Wenner-Gren Foundation for Anthropological Research conferences** and served a term as president of the American Association of Physical Anthropologists (1962–1963). Coon's long-anticipated book based on his life's work, *The Origin of Races* (1962), claimed "that different portions of *homo erectus*, the immediate ancestor of *homo sapiens*, had evolved into the latter state at different times, as each of the five main subspecies or races crossed the genetic threshold separately."[49] Coon further theorized that Caucausoids, the White race's ancestors, passed this critical point 200,000 years earlier than the ancestors of modern Blacks, the Congoids, who became *Homo sapiens* only 40,000 to 50,000 years ago. He then "suggested a correlation between the amount of time a subspecies had actually existed as *Homo sapiens* and the level of civilization attained by its members."[50] From the beginning, the book was

---

*Hooton was also known for arguing that criminality was inherited. Based on the analysis of his measurements of height, weight, noses, ears, and bodies, he identified "old American," "Alpines," Irish-American, "East Baltic," and "Negro and Negroid Criminals."

**Founded in New York in 1941, the Wenner-Gren Foundation for Anthropological Research was one of the many institutions for scientific research funded by this Swedish benefactor. Axel Leonard Wenner-Gren (1881–1961) was an immensely wealthy financier and industrialist with holdings in Europe, the Bahamas, and Mexico. However, he had strong pro-Nazi leanings and was closely linked with German espionage networks—including the exploitation of his close friendship with Edward VIII of England.

controversial, served as a blemish on the end of a laudable academic career, and was immediately mobilized by Southern and segregationist sympathizers, including many physicians, as "scientific" ammunition.

A distant relative of Coon, business executive and part-time author Carleton Putnam — with whom he has often been confused — was a nonscientist who published the racist book *Race and Reason*. Putnam posited that "blacks were genetically inferior to whites and should be separated from whites if not actually returned to the African continent. Perpetuation and even strengthening of the segregation laws ... was the only hope for mankind."[51] *Race and Reason* was considered by most an offensive and misguided book that misinterpreted accurate data in a biased way and placed a scientific veneer on racist and biological-determinist ideas. The book sold 60,000 copies in six months; was adopted by the Louisiana State Board of Education as required reading for all university deans, faculty, and students of anthropology, sociology, and psychology; inspired the Virginia legislature to pass a resolution supporting segregation on the basis of the "scientific evidence" of Black inferiority; led to the endorsement of the book by a block of Southern senators such as Strom Thurmond of South Carolina, Richard B. Russell of Georgia, and Harry F. Byrd of Virginia; and led to Mississippi governor Ross Barnett's declaring "Race and Reason Day" on October 26, 1961. A growing New Right infrastructure emerged during the post-*Brown* era, typified by the aforementioned Liberty Lobby, the blatantly Hitlerian *American Mercury* magazine, Willis Carto's Noontide Press; Noontide Press's publication of Francis Parker Yockey's book *Imperium** and other right-wing "classics," and *Mankind Quarterly*, a new professional journal in the field of anthropology, specializing in race and ethnology, founded in 1960 at Edinburgh. Conservative scientists also founded the International Association for the Advancement of Ethnology and Eugenics (IAAEE) in 1959. This organization's influence reached into the U.S. House and Senate, into the nation's foundation infrastructure (e.g., the Pioneer Fund),** and into some of the nation's institutions of higher education (including medical schools), and provided respectable academic platforms for dialogues on "race" and related problems that had previously been confined to Ku Klux Klan or neo-Nazi literature.[52] The IAAEE's heavily promoted *Mankind Quarterly*:

> *churned out a steady stream of scientific racism. The largest number of articles ... concerned blacks in the United States. One complained of the "Negrophile ... perversion of history and the social sciences," which*

---

*\*Imperium* is dedicated to the "Hero of the Second World War" (i.e., Hitler) and is often cited as the neo-*Mein Kampf* for neo-Nazis.

\*\*The Pioneer Fund was established in 1937 by Massachusetts textile millionaire Wycliffe Preston Draper to promote "race betterment" by funding research and the education of children descended from White persons who settled in the original 13 states. Later, Draper offered grant money to leading geneticists for studies that would prove the inferiority of Blacks and promote their repatriation to Africa.

> *"palm[s] off colored mediocrities as statesman and geniuses"; another proposed restricting the participation of blacks in the polity because it was "obvious that the Negro in the United States is ... inferior" and "even if ... of adequate intelligence he may be temperamentally unsuited for citizenship"; yet another contrasted the Western commitment to exploration and the pursuit of knowledge with the essence of "Negritude," expressed in a "cry" from Martinique: "Hurray for those who have never invented anything, Hurray for those who have never explored anything, Hurray for those who have never conquered anything."[53]*

The organization also published monographs and reprints of articles, some of which eventually appeared as a 1967 book, *Race and Modern Science.*[54]

As the Civil Rights Movement ran aground on ideological conflict and fragmentation in the mid-1960s, losing much moral authority in the process, and as Lyndon Johnson's War on Poverty foundered, scientific racists and segregationists began raising new questions about the national policy of improving the living conditions of Blacks and the poor. As Robert Kuttner wrote to the editor of *Perspectives in Biology and Medicine*, "The feasibility of producing any significant change in the position of minority racial groups rests on the assumption that genetic capacity is approximately the same for all groups."[55] Therefore, programs for medical care, improved nutrition, and educational assistance for African Americans were justified only if Blacks were genetically equal to Whites. By the 1960s such social-Darwinist thought was resurrected, along with the old eugenics principles, by scientists other than IAAEE members, such as Henry E. Garrett, A. James Gregor, Robert E. Kuttner, and Ernest van den Haag. By 1964, Dwight Ingle, the University of Chicago physiologist, was publishing articles such as "Racial Differences and the Future" in *Science*, wherein he predicted Black racial suicide because of high birth rates "among indolent incompetent Negroes" and recommended sterilization or some other method of "conception control ... for all who, either because of genetic limitations or because of poor cultural heritage, are unable to endow children with a reasonable chance to achieve happiness, self-sufficiency, and good citizenship."[56] In 1965 he would be joined by Dr. Shockley, a scientist from an unexpected sector of the scientific world.

---

## Science as Racialism

Though science has contributed to Western progress, intelligence testing is a prime example of how scientific methods employed by behavioral scientists, physicians, and other scientists have been utilized to assign "place" in society based on "meritocracy." This has far-reaching implications in many areas, including medicine and health care.

Seldom do scientists who specialize in one scientific discipline attempt to become authoritative in another, unrelated discipline. This is precisely what William Bradford Shockley, Nobel Laureate and occupant of a named chair in engineering at Stanford University, attempted to do. Having earned the ultimate scientific credential along with two colleagues for inventing the transistor, Shockley, who admitted he had no biomedical or genetics training, in a 1965 speech for a Nobel conference titled "Genetics and the Future of Man" laid out the foundation of a eugenics program designed to "solve" the nation's social problems. Building upon a student paper on population control he had written 35 years earlier, Shockley presented what "was largely an unimproved reprise of earlier eugenical thought."[57] *U.S. News and World Report* took this seriously, publishing a four-page interview with Shockley in its November 22, 1965, issue. "In this interview, Shockley averred that the quality of the human race is declining in this country because society was not doing enough research into the genetic factors that make people what they are."[58] Because of the increasing reproduction of the "inferior strains," the "government should change sides in the War on Poverty; the rich should receive larger income tax exemptions for their children than the poor," said Shockley, who "also disclosed his fear that, especially among blacks, the genetically least capable were producing the largest number of offspring."[59] The interview was reprinted in Stanford University Medical School's alumni magazine, *Stanford M.D.* This triggered an angry response from all seven members of Stanford's Department of Genetics, which included another Nobel Laureate, Joshua Lederberg:

> The geneticists called Shockley's statements the "kind of pseudo scientific justification for class and race prejudice [that] is so hackneyed that we would not ordinarily have cared to react to it. However, Professor Shockley's standing as a Nobel Laureate and as a colleague at Stanford, and now the appearance of this article with a label of Stanford medicine, creates a situation where our silence could leave the false impression that we share or acquiesce in this outlook which we certainly do not."[60]

Stanford University later turned down Shockley's 1972 proposal to teach a course he called "Dysgenic Question: New Research Methodology on Human Behavior Genetics and Racial Differences" on the recommendation of biology professor Colin S. Pittendrigh and the faculty committee, who stated:

> [N]o geneticist of stature—indeed, none that I know of—regards Professor Shockley as adequately familiar with the complexities of the genetic problems to which he addresses himself.... [T]he essentially geno-cidal policies [Shockley] has seemed to propose are not only painful for black people to hear but are abhorrent to all decent people whatever their skin color.[61]

Despite the rejections and repudiation by his peers and colleagues, Shockley embarked on an aggressive campaign to disseminate his views and seek vindication from others. He engaged in many activities, including but not limited to, becoming a one-man public relations and lobbying voice to utilize the media to disseminate and popularize his views; launching (in 1966) an annual campaign to convince the National Academy of Sciences of the need "for the study of the racial aspects of the 'heredity-poverty-crime nexus'"[62]; creating the Foundation for Research and Education on Eugenics and Dysgenics (FREED), whose original board included Sir Cyril Burt,* to spearhead his crusade against "genetic enslavement"; formulating the "Voluntary Sterilization Bonus Plan," a bounty incentive sterilization plan endorsed by then–Vice President Spiro Agnew that was reminiscent of those proposed earlier by birth control pioneer Mrs. Margaret Sanger (1926) and columnist and social critic H. L. Mencken (1937)[63]; introducing his "White gene" hypothesis, loosely based on geneticist T. E. Reed's work and Shockley's own calculations and speculations, wherein "White genes" were touted as adding IQ points to Black scores; and promoting genetic improvement by personal donations to the Repository for Germinal Choice, a sperm bank designed to produce gifted children through artificial insemination of intelligent women with genetically superior sperm.

Meanwhile, his corpus of racial theories and thought became increasingly bizarre, as did his associations. Initially suffused with the enthusiasm of fresh discovery, after his ideas and theories were attacked by geneticists and biologists, Shockley, now on the defensive, found it necessary to defend the ethics of his proposals. Opponents of eugenics, the basis of policies in the Third Reich, were portrayed as totalitarians. Nazis were to be defended. "The lesson to be learned from Nazi history," Shockley lectured to his colleagues, was "the value of free speech, not that eugenics is intolerable."[64] When he took up race, he offered "statistical evidence for an 'orderly relationship' in which whites achieved comparatively greater 'eminence' than blacks, while blacks were disproportionately represented in the statistics on illegitimacy and crime."[65] Blacks were entering "genetic enslavement," according to Shockley, because the Negroes with the fewest Caucasian genes were the most prolific and the least intelligent. He considered this to be *dysgenic* — retrogressive evolution through the disproportionate reproduction of the genetically disadvantaged. Any remedy dictated that the relatively "pure" Black population would have to be prevented from reproducing. Resulting genetic improvement would help overcome "*unreasonable* prejudice" (emphasis added). Tucker noted: "This was not an idle adjective that the physicist had chosen; if blacks were indeed genetically disadvantaged, he saw nothing unreasonable about prejudice against them. As he had pointed out to the Stanford

---

*Sir Cyril Burt (1883–1971) was a British educational psychologist and psychometrician of the first rank. His mentor was Charles Spearman, the "father of factor analysis." Until Burt's fabrications of his data on intelligence and twins was discovered, it served as the foundation evidence of the heritability of IQ. Nevertheless, its influence was widespread and served as the core data for Arthur Jensen's notorious *Harvard Educational Review* article (1969) on the supposedly inherited and ineradicable differences in Black and White intelligence in the United States.

geneticists, Shockley saw nothing wonderful about inferior human beings."[66] Between 1967 and 1969, Shockley became embroiled in a controversy by repeatedly referring to an aggressive eugenics program that he alleged had been in place in Denmark for 30 years. This program purportedly sterilized persons who were categorized as "unfit," including citizens who were disabled or scored below a cutoff IQ point of 70. He also alleged that prisoners in Denmark were offered early release in exchange for sterilization. Citing a long March 7, 1966, *U.S. News and World Report* article, "The Unfit: Denmark's Solution," as his source, an investigation led by Erik Olaf-Hansen, medical editor of the Copenhagen *Politikken*, revealed that the jointly run sterilization program — by the Danish Health Ministry Mothers' Aid Centers and the national University Institute of Medical Genetics — in Denmark was not eugenic in intent or practice. Denmark's abortion and sterilization laws, similar to most civilized nations and states such as England, New York State, and Switzerland, were designed primarily for the protection of mothers, children, and families from the medical, economic, or social consequences of unwanted or medically inadvisable pregnancies. Comparing the Danish program with Nazi-type eugenic programs seemed to be a distortion and misrepresentation by *U.S. News and World Report*.

Moreover, Shockley was increasingly attacked for basing part of his defense of Black intellectual inferiority on the Armed Forces Qualification Test (AFQT) mental test scores, which most psychologists by then considered totally unreliable. He increasingly stated: "Nature has color-coded groups of individuals so that statistically reliable predictions of their adaptability to intellectually rewarding and effective lives can easily be made and profitably be used by the pragmatic man in the street."[67] His crude correlation of skin color with native ability and intrinsic worth and its utilization to judge and dispose of "defective" parts (human beings) may have been a reflection of Shockley's engineering background. Accordingly, Shockley and his right-wing supporters concluded that opening the doors to equal citizenship for all U.S. citizens (including the right to vote), Medicare and Medicaid to extend health care, compensatory education programs such as Head Start, affirmative action programs designed to ensure the participation of all groups in American institutions, and social programs for the disabled and needy were all wrong for the country because they were dysgenic. As Chase repeatedly pointed out, these views held much weight in conservative medical circles as well as popular opinion.

With the Nazi overtones that permeated his work, Shockley became a celebrity to the neo-Nazi movement. Moreover, the Ku Klux Klan, White Citizens Council, and other racist groups welcomed his commentary and considered him an ally. His associations and collaborative activities with the IAAEE increased over the years, and he eventually endorsed book covers of works by nonscientists such as Carleton Putnam and extreme far right theoretician Wilmot Robertson. However, he remained somewhat self-conscious about praise and endorsements in publications such as *Mankind Quarterly* and George Lincoln Rockwell's neo-Nazi paper, *White Power*. His highly publicized campaigns, which regularly reached mainstream media outlets such as the *Wall Street Journal* (whose editor agreed that programs to aid the disadvantaged were "futile or even self-defeating" because they could not "repair genetic damage"),[68] produced little public support. The fact that most of his programs and proposals were unappealing, combined with the condescending and pugnacious persona he assumed when presenting his eugenics programs, may help account for this.[69]

The most important feat Shockley may have executed for his "movement" was helping convert educational psychologist Arthur Jensen to his cause during 1966 and 1967. Unlike Shockley or Ingle, men with outstanding scientific credentials in other fields, Jensen could not be considered an outsider driven by political motives into fields in which he had no proven expertise. Moreover, unlike men such as Putnam, or even Garret, his research and writings were sophisticated, elegant, and nonpolemical. Earlier, in 1963, Jensen seemed quite enthusiastic about the educability and hidden IQ potential of Black and other culturally disadvantaged children.[70] Although Jensen embraced Sir Cyril Burt's hereditarian* views regarding intelligence earlier in his career, stating at one point that: "in Caucasian populations ... some 80 to 90 per cent of the variability in measured intelligence can be attributable to genetic factors and about 5 to 10 percent to social environmental factors,"[71] he did not seem to harbor Burt's eugenic views regarding race, class, and intelligence. Jensen stated in a 1967 article in *Educational Research*, a British journal:

> [T]he fact that Negroes and Mexicans are disproportionately represented in the lower end of the socio-economic-status scale cannot be interpreted as evidence of poor genetic potential. For we know that there have been, and are still, powerful racial barriers to social mobility. Innate potential should be much more highly correlated with socio-economic-status among whites than among Negroes or other easily distinguishable minorities, who are discriminated against on the basis of intellectually irrelevant characteristics.[72]

In the same article he wrote on Black intelligence: "Since we know that the Negro population for the most part has suffered socio-economic and cultural disadvantages for generations past, it seems a reasonable hypothesis that their low-average IQ [test score] is due to environmental rather than to genetic factors."[73] Jensen claimed his conversion to genetic explanations for racial differences in intellectual and social performance was an evolutionary, empirical process.

Interested in a scientific career, Jensen grew disenchanted with conventional clinical psychology and sought the more rigorous quantitative approaches being

---

*The heritability of a trait is defined as the proportion of observed differences between persons that is caused by genetic differences.

practiced by English psychologist Hans J. Eysenck. From Eysenck's world-renowned research department in the University of London's Institute of Psychiatry at Maudsley Hospital emanated dozens of books and hundreds of articles critical of environmentalism and championing hereditarian explanations. However, it was noted, "In Britain, promoted by ... academic psychologist Hans Eysenck, the claim of biological differences in IQ between races has become an integral part of the campaign against Asian and black immigration."[74] The fascist National Front was using the data to legitimize its racist claims "that modern biology has proven the genetic inferiority of Asians, Africans, and Jews."[75] Nevertheless, Jensen obtained a postdoctoral fellowship at Maudsley in the late 1950s, where he stood in awe of Eysenck, his world-renowned professor, and Eysenck's mentor, Sir Cyril Burt. While in England, Jensen attended the Walter van Dyke Bingham Memorial Lecture, "The Inheritance of Mental Ability," wherein Burt summed up his 50-plus years of research on inheritance and mental ability. Burt's lecture, which Jensen considered "the best lecture I have ever heard,"[76] allegedly demonstrated that heredity was the predominant cause of individual and class differences in intelligence. Much of the data on which the lecture was based was later found to be fraudulent.[77] Upon returning to the United States, the focus of Jensen's own learning research shifted to ethnic minorities and the poor and the genetics of intelligence.[78]

Temporarily absent from his post as an educational psychologist at the University of California at Berkeley, Jensen spent a year (1966–1967) as a fellow at the Center for Advanced Study in the Behavioral Sciences on the Stanford campus. Although by now he was convinced that individual and class differences in ability were largely genetic in origin, Jensen still opposed the view that "culturally disadvantaged children" with low IQs were:

> destined for intellectual and occupational mediocrity. This wide-spread belief gives rise to various plans for watered-down, less intellectual, and less academic educational programmes tailored to the apparent limitations of a large proportion ... of low socioeconomic status children.... This is a harmful and unjust set of beliefs.... Failure to distinguish between hereditary retardation and cultural retardation, as well as being a social injustice, results in a waste of educational potential and talent. The consequences are especially damaging to the social progress of minority groups and the costs are borne by our whole society.[79]

A dramatic shift in his views occurred during that year on Stanford's campus. His belief in genetic explanations for racial differences increased dramatically, and "he also suddenly expanded his interests from intelligence and educability—his area of professional expertise—to the problem of eugenic decline caused by the proliferation of poor blacks."[80] His review of "the total world literature" on the genetics of intelligence, with special emphasis on the work of his intellectual hero, Sir Cyril

Burt, certainly influenced his thinking, but some observers felt "it was ... not coincidental that his pronouncements suddenly became a more finely nuanced version of Shockley's."[81] Jensen's adoption of Shockley's "simplest possible hypothesis" scientific strategy; his discovery of the "official decision" justifying the Great Society programs and downplaying the importance of hereditarian and biological-determinist views for social policy in two obscure government documents—which Shockley and other right wing zealots routinely used in their presentations*[82]; and his adoption of a paternalistic and condescending warning (based on Shockley's reasoning and presentations that acceptance of "egalitarian dogma" dismissing genetic explanations could "unwittingly harm" living and unborn Black children) were too suggestive to overlook. Jensen claimed that the inverse relationship between socioeconomic class—largely genetically determined according to him—and family size was exaggerated in Blacks, leading to a greater increase in the racial gap in ability, and that the policy of ignoring this "might well be viewed by future generations as our society's greatest injustice to Negro Americans."[83] He predicted that if present policies continued, "future generations of Negroes ... could suffer the most well-meaning but misguided and ineffective attempts to improve their lot in life."[84] Although delicately and vaguely phrased, Jensen's point was clear:

> [A]ntipoverty programs, *"misguided and ineffective attempts"* to improve *the quality of life, were providing the inferior black poor greater opportunity to reproduce their kind. Instead of well-baby clinics and child-development programs, the real need was for a different kind of government assistance, one that would give priority to sterilization and conception control.*[85]

Not since the late nineteenth- and early twentieth-century pronouncements of scientists such as Sir Francis Galton, Charles B. Davenport, Lewis Terman, Carl Brigham, and Robert W. Shufeldt, M.D. had prominent members of the biomedical-scientific-research establishment railed so directly against socially progressive health and educational programs for Blacks and the poor. These were ominous social and political predictions with strong scientific racist and negative eugenic overtones.

Jensen went from being a well-published scholar known only to a small coterie of experts and institutions engaged in research in educational psychology to a focus of national attention in short order. In the 1969 winter issue of the *Harvard Educational Review (HER)*, "Jensen produced the most explosive article in the history of

---

*A 1965 U.S. Department of Labor's Office of Policy Planning and Research report, *The Negro Family*, stated "there is absolutely no question of any genetic differential: Intelligence potential is distributed among Negro infants in the same proportion and pattern as among Icelanders or Chinese or any other group." In 1966 an Office of Education journal, writing about the AFQT, asserted it was "a demonstrable fact that the talent pool in any one ethnic group is substantially the same as that in any other ethnic group."

American psychology, triggering one of the most bitter scientific controversies since Darwin and catapulting him from relative obscurity to national prominence and, in some quarters, notoriety."[86] His article, "How Much Can We Boost IQ and Scholastic Achievement?," was the longest in the journal's history, filling virtually every page in the issue. It was an invited article—reflecting the intimacy between Jensen and the nation's core intellectual and educational establishment. Jensen's ideas on Black racial inferiority, the failure of socially oriented compensatory education programs, heredity and intelligence, and biological determinism found resonance. Such a development suggested that the editorial staff of one of the nation's premier educational journals, headquartered at one of America's top-rung institutions of higher learning, had been monitoring and assessing Jensen's work on heredity and intelligence from afar. Inviting such a lead article, as well as suggesting the topics that *HER* wanted to cover in a proposed outline and arranging commentaries from a group of psychologists with differing perspectives, suggests the weight this menu of ideas held in the United States scientific community.[87]

The article has been the subject of library shelves of criticism and controversy from scientists, expert analysts, serious journalists, and polemicists in the popular media. Jensen argued that most of the difference in performance on IQ tests between Blacks and Whites was genetic. Thus, Jensen posited, compensatory education must fail because the Black children it was designed to help were, on average, genetically inferior in intelligence to White children.[88] From a social action standpoint, "no program of education could equalize the social status of blacks and whites, and . . . blacks ought better to be educated for the more mechanical tasks to which their genes predisposed them."[89] A broad range of authorities alleged that Jensen's "new and uncomfortable" scientific information—science had to speak the truth—was not new. Gould stated: "again, I shall argue, Jensen had no new data; and what he did present was flawed beyond repair by inconsistencies and illogical claims."[90] Professors Mark Golden and Wagner Bridger, in the October 1969 issue of *Mental Hygiene*, declared that: "Jensen does not offer any startling new evidence to support his point of view, but instead dredges up old data and the same sterile arguments from the past."[91] Scientific writer Allan Chase contextualized the *HER* article, referring to it as "Jensenism," the term coined by *New York Times Magazine* science writer Lee Edson:

> *Intellectually, Jensenism was a throwback to the Terman and Goddard IQ testing concepts of the pre-World War I era, and the biology and genetics of even earlier periods—but it was now presented with mathematical pyrotechnics far more esoteric than the simple pedigree charts, tables, and curves of the Davenports, the Shueys, and the Garrets. . . . Separated only by the dimensions of time and lexicon, Jensen's conclusions . . . that society has to "develop the techniques by which school learning can be most effectively achieved in accordance with different patterns of ability" . . . are . . . modern hand-wringing liberal variations of*

> *Terman's 1916 lament that the poor and non-Nordic school-children of California had inherited so few genes for intelligence that, while they did have the mentality to make "an excellent laborer" or a good servant girl, they were "uneducable beyond the merest rudiments of training."[92]*

The fact that Jensen's proposals were reminiscent of the dual and unequal educational policies Blacks had been victims of since the Civil War, and that justification for such arrangements had often emanated from the scientific community, was virtually ignored. Moreover, Chase and others observed that although Jensen's *HER* article and his later books and articles on the same themes were packed with scholarly references and citations, upon close observation they often referred readers to the tainted Armed Forces Qualification Test (AFQT) data, Sir Cyril Burt's artificial data sets compiled by imaginary research assistants, overtly racist scientists and Liberty Lobby members such as Robert E. Kuttner, or the writings such as those of Audrey Shuey,* a protegé of Henry E. Garrett.[93]

Criticism of Jensen's *HER* article went beyond its prejudices, ranging from shortcomings of its database to its science, its methodology, its conclusions, and its flawed sociopolitical implications. For example, Jensen's opening salvo was an abrupt dismissal: "Compensatory education has been tried and it apparently has failed."[94] This rush to judgment** was based on unquestioning belief in Jensen's unsubstantiated correlations of heredity and race with intelligence and ability, along with acceptance of his speculative theories about "Level I" and "Level II"*** learning abilities. The data backing up this conclusion, reached in the first five pages of his 123-page article, were contained in several reports: the Commission on Civil Rights report, a commission report on the Higher Horizons Program in New York City, and evaluations of the Head Start program. In the former government report on the evaluation of what appeared to be the longest-lived project (eight years):

---

*Professor Audrey M. Shuey, of the Randolph-Macon College of Virginia, was the author of *The Testing of Negro Intelligence* (1958)—a review of 380 "original investigations of Negro intelligence." She had taken her doctorate in psychology under Professor Henry E. Garrett at Columbia; the purpose of her book seemingly "was to interpret the Army intelligence test scores of World War I, the civilian intelligence test scores of the twentieth century, and the contemporary AFQT mental test scores, to reach her conclusion that these mental test scores, 'all taken together, inevitably point to the presence of native [genetic] differences between Negroes and whites as determined by intelligence tests.'" Source: Chase A. *The Legacy of Malthus: The Social Costs of the New Scientific Racism.* New York: Knopf, 1980, 451–453.

**Most of the compensatory education programs cited by Jensen, such as Head Start—which many psychologists felt would take a generation to affect outcomes in populations that had suffered centuries of discrimination and deprivation—had not been in effect more than five years.

***"Level I" learning abilities are based on rote memory and are found in abundance among disadvantaged children. "Level II" learning abilities are grounded in conceptualization and abstract reasoning, in which disadvantaged children are "genetically" deficient.

> *Its description of the Banneker Project in St. Louis clearly stated that the*
> *program had not involved the expenditure of federal money and that it*
> *had attempted to raise motivation rather than provide instructional assis-*
> *tance for students. Banneker was thus completely irrelevant to the model*
> *that Jensen had claimed was unsuccessful.*[95]

In his other example, the Higher Horizons Program, "[t]he commission's description ... suggested the opposite of Jensen's conclusion: an apparently successful compensatory model had failed because of improper implementation on a larger scale."[96] Moreover, by the time Jensen's *HER* article appeared, there was mounting evidence that millions of dollars in funds being appropriated to school districts for compensatory education were being misappropriated for items such as swimming pools and radio stations. His use of Head Start to prove the worthlessness of compensatory education seemed strange. As Tucker reminds us:

> *Head Start ... had never been designed as a solution for the educational*
> *problems of the disadvantaged; it was intended as the first payment on a*
> *long-overdue moral debt to the poor, a humanitarian response to the*
> *plight of children in the richest country in the world who had never seen*
> *a dentist or doctor, never enjoyed a balanced diet, or never played with art*
> *materials and children's books. Though the opportunity for educational*
> *enrichment was one purpose, comprehensive health examinations,*
> *improved nutrition, other support services for the pre-schoolers' families,*
> *and the "maximum feasible participation" of parents were all goals of*
> *equal importance.*[97]

Moreover, the hastily thrown together programs were not uniform, varying greatly from region to region. The early modest gains in IQ with a drop-off when the child entered elementary school were, thus, understandable. Jensen himself had said: "pre-school intervention without adequate follow-up in the first years of elementary school is inadequate, because the culturally disadvantaged child does not go home after school, as does the middle-class child, to what is essentially a tutorial situation."[98] However, now the child rather than the lack of sustained follow-up, was at fault. Longitudinal studies of Head Start would later prove that it was one of the Great Society's most successful programs. If it failed to produce higher IQ scores in all instances, it certainly improved school performance and led to more productive and satisfying lives. Interestingly, after critiquing Head Start's failure to increase IQ scores, Jensen stated: "it seems likely that if compensatory education programs are to have a beneficial effect on achievement, it will be through their influence on motivation, values, and other environmentally conditioned habits that play an important part in scholastic performance, rather than through any marked direct influence on intelligence per se."[99]

Falling victim to a major scientific fallacy, *reification*—"our tendency to convert abstract concepts into entities (from the Latin *res*, or thing)"—and recognizing the importance of mentality and mental ability in our lives and culture, Jensen assigns the word "intelligence" "to this wondrously complex and multifaceted set of human capabilities."[100] He falls back on Harvard psychologist E. G. Boring's method of avoiding having to identify what this complex matrix of interrelated functions really is "by defining intelligence as whatever the tests test."[101] Thus test scores came to represent a single, scalable thing in the head called general intelligence (or *g*). Jensen left out the fact that Binet, inventor of "[t]he first really useful test of intelligence and the progenitor of nearly all present-day intelligence tests," according to Jensen,[102] would never have accepted applying his empirical *methods* while substituting his *"idea* of intelligence as a shifting complex of interrelated functions" for "the concept of a single, underlying (faculty) of intelligence."[103] While pointing out IQ tests' origins in "educational settings" such as the Paris schools of 1900, being shaped by "instructional methods" evolved within "an upper-class segment of the European population" and educational traditions of Europe and North America, Jensen later negates IQ tests' cultural and elite scholastic attainment overlay.[104] Jensen then reinforces his error by committing a second major scientific fallacy characteristic of most biological determinists—*ranking*: "our propensity for ordering complex variation as a gradual ascending scale."[105] He uses a well-known 1905 Edward L. Thorndike (1874–1949)* quote, "In the actual race of life, which is not to get ahead, but to get ahead of somebody, the chief determining factor is heredity," to introduce his discussion of the inheritance of intelligence—an exposition of his herditarian beliefs.[106] Jensen's *HER* article incorporates "the common style embodying both fallacies of thought . . . quantification, or the measurement of intelligence as a single number for each person," and expounds upon "the abstraction of intelligence as a single entity, its location within the brain, its quantification as one number for each individual, and the use of these numbers to rank people in a single series of worthiness, invariably to find that oppressed and disadvantaged groups—races, classes, or sexes—are innately inferior and deserve their status,"[107] when evaluated according to Gould's criteria.[108]

Jensen's entire theoretical framework rests on the assumption that IQ and other valid tests of mental attributes measure something we can legitimately call "intelligence." If we disregard the scientific controversy surrounding the transformation of

---

*E. L. Thorndike, a Columbia University professor of psychology, authored some 50 books and was the most influential educational psychologist of the early twentieth century. However, his hereditarian beliefs and advocacy of the pseudobiology of eugenics, strongly grounded in those of Sir Francis Galton, injected elitist and antidemocratic values into the eugenics movement. A charter member of the Galton Society, he crusaded for eugenical sterilization of low IQ achievers, epileptics, habitual criminals, and moral degenerates. His crowning achievement, *Human Nature and the Social Order* (1940), further buttressed the privileged few's fitness to rule and decried equal treatment of "unequal" persons, efforts to decrease economic inequalities, and uplift for the disadvantaged. He felt reproductive capacity should be regulated by the state and guided by "impartial scientific truth."

Dr. Binet's complex entity into an innate objective attribute, located in the head, measurable by tests, a unitary quantity that can be assigned a single number, after which "People may then be ranked on an ascending ladder from Ape to Einstein—a single scale that captures the most important aspect of their potential,"[109] this long-lived psychometric "science" of IQ-heritability-racial differences in intelligence might have some basis. Stephen Jay Gould observed "The only important theoretical justification that psychometricians have ever offered for viewing intelligence as a real attribute that can be measured by a single number (IQ) arises from an arcane subject called 'factor analysis.'"[110] Sir Cyril Burt, doyen of the mental testers, noted that age scale methods (Binet IQ testing) and correlational methods (factor analysis)* were the important factors in the history of mental testing.[111] Gould's books *The Mismeasure of Man* and *An Urchin in the Storm* decipher these abstrusely mathematical, ethereal, psychometric techniques in a way that is comprehensible to nonscientists.**

"Factor analysis" was a concept developed in 1904 by British psychologist Charles Spearman to explain his observation that people who do well on one mental test tend to do well on others (evidence of a positive correlation).[112] Wondering whether there might be a common factor underlying this tendency, he compiled series of measured associations between two tests given to several people (correlation coefficients). Correlation coefficient values range from −1.0 (a good score on one test implies an equally bad score on the other) through 0.0 (the score on one test allows no prediction about scores on the other) to 1.0 (a good score on one implies an equally good score on the other). Spearman then extracted a single number, or what statisticians call the "first principal component," from them. He reified this number into an "entity," tried to give it an unambiguous causal interpretation, called it *g* or general intelligence, and concluded: "All examination in the different sensory, school, and other specific faculties may be considered as so many independently obtained estimates of the one great common Intellective Function."[113] Spearman believed his *g* (one great common Intellective Function) was a heritable physical entity, identifying it with a general inborn "cerebral energy." He also "argued that blacks and poor people had less of this energy than whites and upper-class people."[114] Burt, Spearman's protegé who succeeded him as professor of psychology at University College, London, devoted his career and went to extremes (even scientific dishonesty and fraud) to defend his two-factor theory of intelligence*** and hereditary interpretation of *g*. As Gould observed:

---

*Factor analysis* is rooted in abstract statistical theory and based on the attempt to discover "underlying" structure in large matrices of data.

**The authors strongly suggest utilizing Gould's books as references to introduce this very complex subject. Moreover, Jensen has written several subsequent books (e.g., *Bias in Mental Testing*) that contain relevant references in the field.

***Spearman's controversial two-factor theory of intelligence led to the belief that every mental test measured two components: a *general* (*g*) factor and a *specific* (*s*) factor. The *g* assessed the test's measure of general intelligence, while *s* accounted for its content of specific information (i.e., math skills, language skills, or spatial aptitudes).

> From 1904, when Spearman's seminal article appeared, through the
> 1930s, factor analysis became an industry in psychology; it was invariably
> done in the principal components orientation.... The g identified as the
> first principal component was reified into an entity and both people and
> groups were ranked according to the amount of g they supposedly
> contained.[115]

For anyone believing in the hereditarian theory of IQ, "the theoretical justification
for using a unilinear scale of IQ resides in factor analysis itself,"[116] Spearman
continuously emphasized. After decades of scientific and sociopolitical conflict:

> Spearman's doubts began to grow until he finally recanted in his last ...
> book of 1950. He seemed to pass off the theory of energy ... as a folly of
> youth (though he had defended it staunchly in middle age). He even
> abandoned the attempt to reify factors, recognizing belatedly that a
> mathematical abstraction need not correspond with a physical reality.
> The great theorist had entered the camp of his enemies and recast himself
> as a cautious empiricist.[117]

Nevertheless, from the World War I IQ tests, to serving as the foundation of
Jensenism as first elucidated in the *HER* article, to helping create the myth of
psychometric testing as the basis of a coming meritocracy, change came too late.
While recanting is usually redemptive, Spearman's work had already harmed and
stunted the lives of millions of people—and planted a seed in the American version
of democratic society that is still harmful.

What Jensen, who "resurrected the original form of Charles Spearman's argument for factor analysis"[118] in the *HER* article, and other hereditarian
psychometricians failed to mention is that "the principal component orientation
for axes had no theoretical, mathematical, or psychological necessity. It merely
represented one of a literally infinite number of possible positions for the place-
ment of axes through a swarm of vectors."[119] In other words, there were other
legitimate methods for analyzing the intelligence data. Despite the fact these other
methods would not appeal to what Gould refers to as our "deep and subtle prejudices for unilinear ranking and notions of progress, and our not so subtle
preferences for ordering people by inferred 'value' (with one's own group invariably most worthy), it is not surprising that principal components seemed the most
'natural,' indeed the only proper way to perform factor analysis," the other ways
were just as valid.[120] American statistician and psychologist L. L. Thurstone virtually destroyed the psychometric edifice in the 1930s by presenting an alternative
argument.[121] Focusing upon locating clusters of more specialized abilities instead
of some inchoate common variance, placing axes near the clusters of vectors themselves produced what he called "simple structure." He used these simple structure
axes to identify what he called "primary mental abilities," or PMAs (e.g., verbal

skills as distinguished from math skills). However, he, too, committed the fallacy of reification, calling his simple structure axes—presented as the title of his major book—*Vectors of the Mind* (1935). Nevertheless, Gould's description of Thurstone's model is instructive:

> *Simple structure axes are every bit as good, mathematically, as principal components. They resolve the same amount of information and can be massaged to yield equally cogent psychological interpretations. But note what has happened to g, the supposedly ineluctable and innate quantity of general intelligence. It has disappeared; it just isn't there anymore.*[122]

He elaborates: "Instead of a pervading and dominating general intelligence and some secondary factors, we now have a set of PMAs. The data have not changed one whit. If the same data can yield either a dominant *g* with subsidiary factors, or a set of PMAs and no *g* at all, then what claim can either solution have to necessary reality?"[123] Seemingly, some of the more modern concepts of intelligence are more closely related to Thurstone's PMAs.[124]

The decade following the *HER* article was not kind to Arthur Jensen on a scientific level—although he gained public fame and notoriety. His oft-repeated estimated heritability of 0.8 *within* the White population, using his arbitrary system and largely based on Burt's faked data,[125] was too high. Even more important from reputable geneticists' standpoint, "the value of heritability *within* either the white or the black population carries no implication whatever about the causes for different average values of IQ *between* the two populations."[126] For example, a population of very short people may demonstrate heritabilities above 0.9 for height, but owe their relative stature to poor nutrition. This is why geneticists, who teach this early in any basic course, treat variation *within* and *between* groups as entirely different phenomena. According to noted authorities such as Stephen Gould and R. C. Lewontin, Jensen's conflation of these two concepts in his *HER* article, the founding document of Jensenism, marked a fundamental error.[127] He seemingly responded to the professional criticism, for his 800-page manifesto, *Bias in Mental Testing*, claimed triumph for his hereditarian psychometric viewpoints published 10 years earlier—but bypasses the issue of heritability in two paragraphs, referring the reader to other sources for elucidation on this "highly technical and complex" topic.[128]

Following his circuitous and technical defense of the heritability of intelligence, Jensen made a liberal racial disclaimer regarding the primacy of individuality in the selecting process for positions such as college, graduate or professional schools, employment, or promotion:

> *The variables of social class, race, and national origin are correlated so imperfectly with any of the valid criteria on which the above decisions should depend, or, for that matter, with any behavioral characteristic,*

> that these background factors are irrelevant as a basis for dealing with
> individuals—as students, as employees, as neighbors. Furthermore, since,
> as far as we know, the full range of human talents is represented in all the
> major races of man and in all socioeconomic levels, it is unjust to allow
> the fact of an individual's racial or social background to affect the treat-
> ment accorded him.[129]

Having said this, Jensen then politely expounds, always using cautious, scientific language, on the fact that Blacks test 15 points (or 1 standard deviation)
lower than Whites on IQ tests and perform less well scholastically. After citing
authorities such as Kuttner, Shuey, and the Coleman report* to establish the
last points, he articulates the "increasing realization among students of psychology of the disadvantaged that the discrepancy in their average performance
cannot be completely or directly attributed to discrimination or inequalities in
education"; thus these investigators are "left with ... various lines of evidence,
no one which is definitive alone, but which, viewed all together, make it a not
unreasonable hypothesis that genetic factors are strongly implicated in the average Negro-white intelligence difference."[130] He then cynically cites the scientific conditions under which his hypothesis could be tested: "No one has yet
produced any evidence based on a properly controlled study to show that representative samples of Negro and white children can be equalized in intellectual ability through statistical control of environment and education."[131] In the
United States, such an experiment would require the creation of idealized
neighborhoods not reflective of current reality (not shaped by racial discrimination, residential segregation, and apartheid—products of discriminatory real
estate practices and residential financing) and peopled by artificial Americans
(uninfluenced by the nation's racial culture). It would also require the creation
of artificial schools (where race was not a pedagogic consideration), with artificial economic conditions (where participating Blacks were truly on an equal
financial footing with Whites), artificial health conditions (where the participating African Americans received the same quality, comprehensiveness, and
intensity of health services from birth as Whites), and where the children were

---

*The Coleman report, *Equality of Educational Opportunity* (1966), was commissioned by the
Congress and generated by a task force led by Johns Hopkins sociologist James S. Coleman. Educational Testing Service (ETS) administered tests and questionaires and collected, collated, and generated
the data. It reiterated many of Moynihan's findings, alleging that the principal sources of Black children's scholastic failure stemmed from their home environments and family backgrounds and not from
the schools. Reservations about the conclusion, "schools bring little influence to bear on the child's
achievement that is independent of his background and general social context," rested in the fact that a
number of the schools sampled failed to return the lengthy questionnaires (raising issues of sampling
bias) and that questionnaire items reflected a strong middle-class bias. Moreover, nine years of so-called
educational equality could not be expected to compensate for 235 years of educational deprivation for
any group.

isolated from the U.S. cultural and media milieu (where evidence of racial stereotyping, persistent discrimination, and conflict are everyday events).

Despite the improbability of these hypotheses ever being scientifically tested, and the possible damage to millions of people his scientific speculation could cause, Jensen continued his socially devastating speculation. Jensen's conjecture on "Possible Dysgenic Trends," a subheading beginning on page 91 of the *HER* article,* includes data from legitimate behavioral scientists alongside those from Sheldon (a geneticist) and Elizabeth (a plant physiologist) Reed of the Dight Institute for Human Genetics of the University of Minnesota. Despite their lack of clinical training or experience in studying the pathology or treatment of mentally retarded patients, the Reeds's 719-page book on that subject, *Mental Retardation: A Family Study* (1965), is cited by Jensen as authoritative. The book contained data collected by amateur "eugenics field workers"** Sadie Deavitt and Marie Curial, who interviewed family members, collected court records, made subjective psychiatric diagnoses, recorded neighborhood gossip, and constructed family trees for 549 inmates of the State School and Hospital for the Feebleminded and Epileptics at Faribault, Minnesota between 1911 and 1918, and by mailed questionnaires to the descendents of 289 probands***—eventually totaling 80,000 persons—whose confidential files, including their IQ test scores, were opened to the Reeds by state, county, and educational agencies without their permission. The Reeds made diagnoses, ranked mental ability, and conjectured "that bad genes were involved in at least five out of every six retardates in these 80,000 white Americans,"**** whom they had never seen, examined, or evaluated except for covertly and at times illegally obtained slips of paper.[132] The Reed's definition of mentally retarded included: "those who scored below 70 on standard intelligence [IQ] tests, or those so classified by careful subjective judgement."[133] Such a definition—not including social performance, standard medical history and physical examination, family history, personal or developmental history, school progress reports and school work, evaluation of practical knowledge or general information, reasonable social history, economic efficiency evaluation, assessment of moral reactions, and mental examinations—ran counter to accepted psychiatric and psychological professional practices of the time. Chase's overall assessment of the work reads: "The Reeds's massive 'study of

---

*There are several other sections in the *HER* article that cite the Reeds.

**See Chapter 1, Volume 2. Chase also describes this category of workers in great detail in *The Legacy of Malthus*, 120–24.

***A *proband*, or propositus, is the original person diagnosed as having a mental or physical disorder whose descendants and relatives are studied in genetic investigations.

****Standard medical and research review texts of the period, such as Stevens and Heber's *Mental Retardation*, found it possible to make precise identification of the cause of mental retardation in only 15 percent to 20 percent of all cases.

mental retardation,' then, turns out to be just another eugenic sterilization tract, in the stereotyped tradition of all eugenic writings of this century, from Davenport and Madison Grant to Lena Sadler and Theodore Russell Robie."*[134] Jensen also discussed and assessed patterns of intelligence, learning, and scholastic achievement between different races, ethnic groups, and social classes in the *HER* article.[135]

After carrying the reader through elaborate discussions of early learning research, compensatory education programs and their results, and the relationship between race, ethnicity, class, SES, and IQ testing, accompanied by impressive scatter diagrams, normal distribution curves, and growth curves, Jensen hypothesizes his aforementioned Level I (associative ability) and Level II (conceptual ability) learning models. The conclusion an unbiased observer could reach about this exposition superimposed upon the content of the entire *HER* article, factoring in Jensen's own admission about scholastic performance relative to IQ tests—"The child's performance does not depend primarily, as it would in conventional IQ tests, upon what he has already learned at home or elsewhere before he comes to take the test"[136]—is that the ability to perform well on European, scholarly-based, culture-laden IQ tests depends upon being raised and nurtured in that environment. There is no short cut. For American children to perform equally well on European-derived IQ tests and in Jensen's admittedly "upper-class shaped European scholastic environments," if those goals are of national importance (which many feel they are not),[137] all children will have to be afforded the opportunity to grow up in similar milieu. The economic, social, cultural, and educational playing fields will have to be leveled for all Americans, including African Americans, Hispanic/Latino Americans, working-class and poor Americans—something liberal reformers have been postulating for years. Tailoring the educational system into two tiers (echoes of the Industrial Education Movement for Blacks) overseen by a psychometrically chosen "meritocracy," one for the underclass and one for the privileged 20 percent based on hypotheses such as Jensen's and/or applying negative eugenics programs to prevent the disadvantaged from proliferating, presents a much more sinister course for American democracy.

Another troubling issue raised by the Jensen *HER* article was the fact that at least 29 (18.23 percent) of the 159 direct citations and several other implicit citations (e.g., Charles Spearman, Lewis Terman) emanated from scientists, institutions, or publications that had demonstrated well-documented racial, ethnic, or class bias. Is it possible that their simple inclusion in a "reputable"

---

*Dr. Lena Sadler, an irascible Chicago surgeon, was a prominent participant in the 1932 Third International Congress of Eugenics in New York City. She called for the compulsory sterilization of millions of Americans whom the Great Depression had thrown out of work since the Wall Street crash of 1929. In 1932 Dr. Theodore Russell Robie, of the Essex County Mental Hygiene Clinic in New Jersey, called for the sterilization of, at the very minimum, 14,000,000 Americans who had made low IQ test scores since World War I. This was a major theme of his presentation, "Selective Sterilization for Race Culture," at the 1932 Third International Congress of Eugenics held in New York City.

publication such as the *HER* could either obscure or legitimize their scientific methods (e.g., the Reeds) or negate their declarations of racial or class bias (numerous examples cited above), thus, elevating such attitudes or biases into credible scientific discourse to be inflicted on an unsuspecting public? Their inclusion in such scientific discourse, especially on subjects as explosive and influential as Jensen's 1969 *HER* article, calls, perhaps, for a long overdue reevaluation of American scientific institutions, scientific culture, financing and funding mechanisms, scientists, peer review processes, and scientific products (e.g., reports, journals, position papers, funded research, government consultations) with the goals of objectivity and fairness in mind.[138]

Disciples of Jensen helped advance his hereditarian and eugenic concepts. As R. C. Lewontin, Steven Rose, and Leon Kamin noted: "Quite soon the claim of the genetic inferiority of blacks was extended to the working class in general and given wide popular currency by another professor of psychology, Richard Herrnstein of Harvard."[139] Herrnstein's influence lingered far beyond his tenure as professor and chairman of that institution's Department of Psychology, with the sensation created by the posthumous publication of a book he coauthored with Charles Murray, *The Bell Curve: Intelligence and Class Structure in American Life* (1994). This "book argues that I.Q. scores—and their large genetic component—are the key to understanding who gets ahead in America and who languishes in crime, poverty and dependency."[140] Herrnstein was an open admirer of Shockley, who by 1970 was in the midst of his campaign to place race, genetics, and inheritance of intelligence on the National Academy of Science's research agenda. Shockley even sent reprints of Jensen's *HER* article to each academy member.

Herrnstein's most famous dissertation of his hereditarian ideas appeared in his famous "IQ" article in the September 1971 *The Atlantic Monthly*, which was derived from Jensen's *HER* article.[141] It was later expanded into a book titled *I.Q. in the Meritocracy* (1973). Herrnstein expressed fears in a 1973 *Science* interview that if people continued breeding as they presently were, there was a danger of large portions of the population becoming "genetically enslaved." He later expressed his shared beliefs with Shockley about the inherited capacity for high or low IQ test scores and that psychometric test results should be utilized by U.S. census takers as a database for lawmakers to observe eugenic or dysgenic social trends. Subsequently, they could utilize these data to limit or tailor the U.S. population on an "objective" basis.[142] The momentum of this new biological-determinist, hereditarian, Black intellectual-racial inferiority-based scientific racist movement continued and gained strength throughout the 1970s. The end of the Civil Rights Movement, President Johnson's Great Society, and affirmative action programs that had begun channeling Black rights beyond public accommodations and voting rights (which cost nothing economically) into compensatory education, social welfare, health care, and equal employment opportunity programs that required White taxpayer participation, Whites sharing institutions with previously excluded Americans, and Whites competing with disadvantaged minorities for jobs and educational advancement seemingly heightened interest in "scientific" rationales for preserving the old order and the racial hierarchy. The atmosphere generated by the Tuskegee revelations, intentionally or not, exposed many of these phenomena not only to extrascientific scrutiny but also to inspection from novel and more egalitarian perspectives, heightening public awareness of the seamy side of U.S. science and how it was being manipulated for political purposes.[143]

## America's Attempt at Reproductive Control as Social Policy

Another burgeoning area of the dark underbelly of the American biomedical and health care system during the 1965 to 1980 period was the epidemic of forced sterilizations and unethical surgery. Though few have previously related the exposure of this biomedically mediated malfeasance to the Tuskegee revelations, both triggered far-reaching reforms within the health system while eliciting drastically different public responses. Why Tuskegee triggered a tempest while the forced sterilizations raised hardly a whimper will be discussed later. Most of the victims of this new sterilization–unethical surgery epidemic were the expected, and in many ways traditional, targets of the scientific racist, Galton-oriented, hereditarian, social Darwinist, biological-determinist influenced U.S. scientific and health system — African Americans, Hispanic/Latino Americans, lower-middle-class and working-class families unable to afford the costs of proper medical care, the mentally challenged, the disabled, the incarcerated, the indigent, institutionalized children, and the unemployed.

By 1980 the United States had had compulsory sterilization laws on the books for more than 70 years (the first law was enacted in Indiana in 1907). Spurred by Sir Francis Galton's international eugenics movement, 30 states and one colony (Puerto Rico) eventually enacted similar draconian forced-sterilization laws. Most were based on the Model Eugenical Sterilization Law drafted sometime before 1922 by Harry H. Laughlin, superintendent of the Eugenics Record Office (ERO) and coeditor of the *Eugenical News*, who published it in his book *Eugenical Sterilization in the United States*. The Model Law called for each state to appoint a state eugenicist responsible for enforcing compulsory sterilization laws. Besides being directed at the "feebleminded," insane, criminalistic (including the delinquent and wayward); epileptic; inebriate (including drug addicts); diseased (including those with tuberculosis, the syphilitic, the leprous, and others with chronic infectious and legally segregable diseases), blind (including those with seriously impaired vision), deaf (including those with seriously impaired hearing), deformed (including the physically disabled), and dependent (including orphans, "ne'er-do-wells," the homeless, tramps, and paupers), the state eugenicist's jurisdiction included all the above people he judged to be members of "socially inadequate classes." Of the 63,678 people sterilized under these laws between 1907 and 1964, 33,374 (52.4 percent) "were sterilized against their will for being adjudged feebleminded or mentally retarded, which in most of these states was defined as having an IQ test score of 70 or lower."[144] Beginning with the Great Depression and World War II, "involuntary sterilizations in the South had increasingly been performed on institutionalized Blacks."[145] As Dorothy Roberts observed: "The demise of Jim Crow had ironically opened the doors of state institutions to Blacks, who took the place of poor whites as the main target of the eugenicist's scalpel."[146] By 1955 South Carolina's State Hospital reported that all 23 persons sterilized over the previous year were Black women. Of the nearly 8,000 "mentally deficient persons" sterilized by the North Carolina Eugenics Commission between the 1930s and 1940s, 5,000 were Black. The State Hospital for Negroes in Goldsboro, where all of the doctors and most of the staff were White, seemingly operated on Black patients confined there for being criminally insane, feebleminded, or epileptic. Before the war, Black men there were castrated or given vasectomies (at much higher rates than White men at other institutions) for being convicted of attempted rape, for being considered "unruly" by hospital authorities, or to make them "easier to handle." None were asked for their consent.[147] Nevertheless, even after factoring in the racist intent involved in the Black/White differences in many of these adverse outcomes, "[t]hese victims of Galton's obsessive fantasies represented ... the smallest part of the actual number of Americans who have in this century been subjected to forced eugenic sterilization operations by state and federal agencies,"[148] according to Chase. Ironically, by the 1960s, when the first generation of mandatory sterilization laws were repealed, a wave of new laws assaulting reproductive rights and a massive and unprecedented wave of forced sterilizations—many of them paid for by the government and facilitated by new health financing mechanisms, often obscured under the guise of expanded health services for the poor (especially the pervasive family planning programs), and carried out by health delivery system components already in place—swept the country. They differentially affected and were executed on African American women.

In the atmosphere created by a new generation of eugenicists such as Jensen, Shockley, and Herrnstein and a reemerging environment of scientific racism hovering over the health system, a contemporary wave of legislation was launched whose goals and objectives were compulsory sterilization and punitive control of reproduction. New books set the tone in the early 1970s: "Edgar R. Chasteen published *The Case for Compulsory Birth Control* and the well-known biologist Garrett Hardin argued in *Exploring New Ethics for Survival* that supporting children gave the government the right to strip their parents of the capacity to produce more."[149] Such efforts at social and reproductive control were not new in America and in fact represented a "renaissance" during the period under investigation. As Robert G. Weisbord reminded us in *Genocide? Birth Control and the Black American*, in the United States "[p]rocreation was not declared to be a basic civil right and liberty until 1942."[150] In that year the U.S. Supreme Court overturned Oklahoma's Habitual Criminal Statute, which provided for the sterilization of certain recidivists convicted of "felonies involving moral turpitude," because it ran afoul of the equal protection clause of the Constitution by exempting some criminals (e.g., embezzlers) while applying its penalties to others (e.g., Jack T. Skinner, the chicken thief and twice-convicted armed robber who challenged the law).[151] Moreover, punitive sterilization bills had been introduced in Mississippi since 1958, ostensibly to solve the Black "illegitimacy problem." First introduced to the Mississippi Legislature by Representative David H. Glass, "An act to Discourage Immorality of Unmarried Females by Providing for Sterilization of the Unwed Mother under Conditions of the Act" "provided for the chancery court to order the sterilization of single mothers, most of whom were Black."[152] Although the bill passed the House by a 72-to-37 vote, it was dropped by the Senate after a national protest, including the release of a Student Nonviolent Coordinating Committee (SNCC) pamphlet titled *Genocide in Mississippi*. By 1964, after much public outcry and legislative hand-wringing:

> *a measure passed the Mississippi house stipulat[ing] that any person who became the parent of a second out of wedlock child would be guilty of a felony punishable by a sentence of one to three years in the state peniten-tiary. A subsequent conviction would be punishable by three to five years in prison. However, a convicted parent had the option of submitting to sterilization in lieu of imprisonment.*[153]

The bill was sharply denounced by Dr. Alan F. Guttmacher, president of Planned Parenthood; by the Association for Voluntary Sterilization; and by SNCC, which quickly recognized the bill's racist overtones. In 1971 Representative Lucius N. Porth, a Republican in the South Carolina legislature, directed a compulsory ster-ilization bill at public assistance recipients who had already borne two children. Such welfare mothers would be sterilized or forfeit their welfare payments. While receiving applause in the National States Rights Party's (NSRP)* voice, *The Thun-derbolt*, the bill was decried by civil libertarians and civil rights groups. The American Friends Service Committee spokesman called it "ridiculous and author-itarian," while a leader of the NAACP in South Carolina alleged the bill was "an attempt to employ Hitler type tactics upon the poor."[154] Both Larry Bates, a Tennessee state representative, and Webber Borcher, a Republican in the Illinois General Assembly, authored bills in 1973 to limit, by coercion, the fertility of welfare recipients. Both, in essence, limited welfare births to two; the Tennessee bill refused to supply benefits beyond the second child unless the mother agreed to and submitted to a sterilization operation, while the Illinois bill required steriliza-tion upon the second birth to maintain eligibility for public assistance. A mother refusing sterilization under the Tennessee statute would have each subsequent ille-

---

*The NSRP enthusiastically endorsed involuntary sterilization of Blacks and also favored stripping African Americans of their U.S. citizenship and deporting them to Africa.

gitimate child beyond the second declared a dependent, destitute, or orphan child by the state. The revolutionary bills offered by Gene Damschroder, state representative in Ohio, in 1973 involved both parents: "One required the sterilization of welfare mother[s] if they received public assistance for more than two out of wedlock children," and a "companion measure provided for the sterilization of fathers who failed to support their minor children."[155] His sterilization suggestions were labeled "Neanderthal," "outrageous," and "unconstitutional"[156] by the American Civil Liberties Union (ACLU).

As a reflection of the American sociocultural, political, and medical social milieu, by the mid-1960s records of overzealous courts throughout the country were "studded with cases of black and brown minority group members who were pressured to undergo sterilization operations or to limit their fecundity by some other means."[157] In 1965 a California court pressured Miguel Andrada, a Hispanic/Latino American, who had pleaded guilty to a charge of nonsupport, to undergo sterilization rather than serve a prison term. In 1966 California Judge Frank P. Kearney pressured Nancy Hernandez, a 21-year-old Hispanic/Latina American woman to accept sterilization after she pleaded guilty to a misdemeanor for being present when her common-law husband was smoking marijauna. Because she was the mother of two and a welfare recipient at the time, the judge thought Mrs. Hernandez was "in danger of continuing to live a dissolute life endangering the health, safety and lives of her minor children."[158] In concert with the ACLU, the ruling was overturned. Another California court ruled in *People v. Dominguez* (1967) that the defendant's probation on a second-degree robbery charge was contingent on her not having more illegitimate offspring. When she unintentionally became pregnant, her probation ruling was overturned by an appellate court ruling that said that contraceptive failure was not an indication of criminality and thus the ban on pregnancy was unreasonable and invalid. These were not isolated cases.

The problem was a national one. For example, in Prince George's County, Maryland, three young women seeking public assistance in 1967 were promptly arrested for child neglect solely because their children were born out of wedlock. During the proceedings the judge threatened the mothers that they must study and understand contraceptive methods, and practice these methods or be at risk of losing their children. The intimidation was real, with the judge ruling neglect on the basis that the "youngsters (two of the women involved had three out of wedlock children, one woman had four) [were] found to be living in an unstable moral environment."[159] The court ordered the children taken from their mothers and placed in foster homes. Planned Parenthood filed a Friend of the Court brief, with the appeal pleading that involuntary imposition of family planning on persons unwilling to accept it was an infringement on a person's constitutional right to privacy. The appeal court ruled against the lower court, ruling that what had been done was not in the children's interests but that they had been used as pawns to punish the mothers. The children were returned to their parents.[160]

Despite the feigned legitimacy of the eugenically driven government, institutional, and legal health system mediated assault on the reproductive rights and potential of America's disadvantaged populations, it was exposed in 1974 before Federal District Judge Gerhard Gesell, in a case brought on behalf of poor victims of involuntary sterilizations performed in hospitals and clinics participating in federally funded family-planning programs, that: "[o]ver the last few years, an estimated 100,000 to 150,000 low-income persons have been sterilized annually under federally funded programs."[161] "A study discovered that nearly half of the women sterilized were Black."[162] In a significant percentage of these forced sterilizations, patients were pressured to comply by physicians' using their professional services (e.g., obstetrical care and delivery, abortion services) as bargaining tools. If the women did not agree to undergo sterilization, physicians refused to provide medical services. Although denounced by the federal judge, these cases did not begin to reflect the volume of involuntary gonadal surgery being committed against equally poor people by nonfederal state and voluntary agencies. This confirmed Roberts's observation about the 1970s: "[M]ost sterilizations of Black women were not performed under the auspices of eugenic laws. The violence was committed by doctors paid by the government to provide health care for these women."[163] This was occurring at the same time that sterilization became the fastest growing form of birth control in the United States, reaching a peak of 1,102,000 in 1972 and dropping off to 936,000 in 1974, according to the Association for Voluntary Sterilization. However, according to Chase, as far as the disproportionate impact on poor Americans was concerned:

> This ... equals the rates at which poor people were subjected to compulsory sterilization in Nazi Germany, where two million Germans were sterilized as social inadequates during the twelve years of the Third Reich. The German Sterilization Act of 1933 was derived quite openly from Laughlin's Model Eugenical Sterilization Law.[164]

High government officials estimated that possibly another 250,000 sterilizations annually, hidden in hospital records as hysterectomies, could be added to the total previously cited. A significant proportion of this sterilization abuse, disguised as hysterectomies, which are major surgeries, were medically needless overkills whose results could have been accomplished by much simpler procedures such as tubal ligations or clipping. As Chase noted about the epidemic, "The chief victims of medically needless hysterectomies are, predictably, Galton's original targets: the lower-middle-class and working-class families who cannot afford the costs of proper medical care, and the unemployed."[165] Blacks were disproportionately represented in these populations, and a new dimension compounded the system's potential for abuse: "Teaching hospitals performed unnecessary hysterectomies on poor Black women as practice for their medical residents. This sort of abuse was so widespread in the South that these operations came to be known as 'Mississippi appendectomies.'"[166] The government's Medicaid reimbursement policies seemed to encourage the practice. Physicians were paid $800 for performing a hysterectomy, compared to $250, for a tubal ligation and, under the 1975 revision of the Medicaid law, "the national government would now provide a flat 90 percent of the medical costs of surgical sterilizations suffered by poor or medically indigent people under Medicaid ... but would, henceforth, provide only matching funds of the costs of abortions,"*[167] despite the more extensive operation's 20 or more times greater risk of mortality. Moreover, hospital fees for extended operating room time, prolonged anesthesia, extra bed days, and necessary preparatory and postoperative laboratory evaluations also made major surgeries such as hysterectomy more attractive to hospitals.

Such practices were not confined to the South: "In April 1972, the *Boston Globe* ran a front-page story reporting the complaint by a group of medical students that Boston City Hospital was performing excessive and medically unnecessary hysterectomies on Black patients."[168] There were clear-cut racial and medical safety implications in the accusation: "[T]he medical students were upset over the possibility that Afro-Americans and Spanish-speaking women might be sterilized more frequently by hysterectomy while white women were more likely to be sterilized by tubal ligation, a less drastic procedure."[169] The egregiousness of Boston City's policies was compounded by charges alleging that surgeries were performed for "training purposes" rather than for medical indications; that radical and dangerous procedures were often used when simpler, less dangerous alternatives were available; that medical records failed to record what had actually been done to patients; that patients were pressured into signing consent forms under duress and without adequate explanation; and that doctors treated patients callously, which added clinically to the women's distress.[170] When queried about the situation, the chairman of the obstetrics and gynecology department at the Boston University School of Medicine, which exercised oversight responsibility, replied: "[O]ne should not condemn the entire service 'because of one bad apple.'"[171] A director of obstetrics and gynecology at a municipal hospital in New York City reported similar outrageous practices: "In most major teaching hospitals in New York City, it is unwritten policy to do elective hysterectomies on poor black and Puerto Rican women, with minimal indications to train residents."[172]

Weisbord noted that although such practices were not recommended, and even frowned upon, in standard patient care practice, "At the Baltimore City Hospital, a dozen women were asked to consent to sterilization only minutes before a Caesarian section and the sterilization procedure were to be performed."[173] Dr. Bernard Rosenfeld of Los Angeles County Hospital and the Health Research Group noted in a 1973 study that: "doctors in some cities are cavalierly subjecting women, most of them poor and Black, to surgical sterilization without explaining

---

*Depending upon the current rate of assistance to their citizens, the individual states would be reimbursed from 50 to 81 percent of the costs of hospital abortions.

either potential hazards or alternate methods of birth control."[174] These included procedures performed at that hospital, where 75 percent of the patients were Chicanos and 10 percent African Americans. One little-known corollary of the unwholesome Tuskegee and Macon County African American health experiences is the fact even before the Tuskegee experiment began, USPHS physicians, operating syphilis treatment clinics throughout the rural South, allegedly sterilized any and all Black women with syphilis. "One investigator has guessed that as many as a thousand such women were neutered in Macon County alone," many of whom "were perfectly capable of giving birth to normal, healthy babies after being cured," according to Weisbord.[175] A joint American Public Health Association and American College of Obstetricians and Gynecology study done in 1967, examining the abortion, contraceptive, and sterilization services of teaching hospitals, found that 53.6 percent of teaching hospitals nationwide made sterilization a requirement for obtaining an abortion.[176] The fact these coercive "package deals" did not lead to litigation charging infringement of constitutional rights may be more astounding than the revelation. Perhaps the fact during that era teaching hospitals served disproportionately poor and minority-group patient populations, who had less tendency to sue, might account for that circumstance.[177]

These case studies involving direct clinical care in hospitals and provider institutions—where the panache of sacrificing all for science, research protocols, and advancing scientific careers and publications was less prominent than in the Tuskegee syphilis experiment—raise the issue more directly: "How could doctors who had taken the Hippocratic oath treat their patients so brutally?"[178] However, as Chase observed, "Of all the noble professions, that of medicine seemed to be particularly susceptible to the punitive dogmas of eugenical sterilization of the poor."[179] Physicians in powerful positions, as the chief of surgery at a Northeastern hospital confided to author Gena Corea, believed that "a girl with lots of kids, on welfare, and not intelligent enough to use birth control, is better off being sterilized."[180] "Not intelligent enough to use birth control" was often the code phrase for "Black" or "poor," Corea observed while collecting data for her book during the 1970s. Another physician rationalized his violation of his patient's autonomy and his medical ethics, conferring upon himself the mantles of prosecutor, judge, and jury based on his social valuations, stating: "As physicians we have obligations to our individual patients, but we also have obligations to the society of which we are a part.... The welfare mess ... cries out for solutions, one of which is fertility control."[181] In a 1972 Planned Parenthood–World Population Society study, in various urban and rural areas of the United States, 30 to 52 percent of all doctors polled advocated that welfare mothers who became pregnant should be forced to accept sterilization for being allowed to continue receiving benefits. In lieu of their training and purported professional obligations to their patients, physicians of the era were in sync with popular opinion. Thus, recruiting members of the medical profession to perform the vital functions necessary to carry out scientific racist policies—eugenics-based surgery on human beings; provision of diagnoses and signatures to incarcerate patients; acting as researchers on racist, classist, or sexist research; providing expert testimony to rationalize and legitimize, on the basis of "science" or "biology," liberty-violating legal acts (e.g., *Buck* v. *Bell*, which involved the forced sterilization of a White woman incarcerated in an institution for the "feeble-minded" in 1927)—has never been a problem in America.[182]

One case that broke into the media in July 1973 was triggered by the refusal of two indigent Black patients in South Carolina, Marietta Williams and Dorothy Waters, to be sterilized. Dr. Clovis H. Pierce, the only obstetrician in Aiken County, South Carolina, who accepted Medicaid patients, demanded they be sterilized if they were to receive his prenatal, obstetrical, and postnatal services. This was confirmation of the findings in the aforementioned 1974 case in the federal district court in Washington, wherein:

> [t]he District court found that an estimated 100,000 to 150,000 poor women were sterilized annually in federally funded programs, and that physicians sometimes coerced women to be sterilized by conditioning their provision of abortion and obstetrical services to poor women on the requirement that the women be sterilized.[183]

Williams, a 20-year-old woman, "charged Dr. Pierce with refusing to deliver her third child unless she allowed him to sterilize her."[184] He had threatened to take her to court unless she signed the consent form. When Waters did not sign sterilization papers during her last prenatal visit, Dr. Pierce threatened her: "Listen here, young lady, this is my tax money paying for this baby and I'm tired of paying for illegitimate children. If you don't want this sterilization, find another doctor."[185] This physician had sterilized 18 welfare mothers, 16 of whom were Black, the previous year, telling the local press that his policy was to require sterilization after delivery of a welfare mother's third baby to reduce the welfare rolls. Despite his actions, previous court rulings, and unethical behavior toward his patients, the U.S. Court of Appeals ruled against the two patients, who sued Dr. Pierce for violation of their civil rights in 1978, finding that he had secured adequate consents and was not acting under any legal coercion by the state.[186] Moreover, both the Aiken County Medical Society and the South Carolina Medical Association rallied to Dr. Pierce's cause during the dispute.[187] Despite Tuskegee, there was a long way to go in securing Black or poor patients' health care civil rights.

The Welfare Department in North Carolina coerced Nial Ruth Cox, who became pregnant at age 17 in 1964, into being sterilized. Threatening to cut her entire family (her mother and eight brothers and sisters) off welfare because of her "immorality," the agency advised her she would have to be sterilized temporarily* when she turned 18, or the family would lose their benefits. The physician advised her "that the effect of the procedure 'would wear off.'"[188] Cox's mother consented

---

*At that time, from a practical, clinical standpoint, there was no "temporary" form of surgical sterilization available to women.

to her daughter's sterilization under a North Carolina law allowing mental defectives under age 21 to be sterilized with parental consent. Although there was no evidence of her being mentally defective, Cox underwent the operation, which left her permanently infertile.

As Angela Davis reported in her classic work, *Women, Race and Class* (1981), "It was not until the media decided that the casual sterilization of two Black girls in Montgomery, Alabama, was a scandal worth reporting that the Pandora's box of sterilization abuse was finally flung open."[189] This 1973 case involved the Relfs— Minnie Lee, age 14, and Mary Alice, age 12, the youngest of six children of an uneducated couple of Black farmhands (Lonnie and Minnie Relf)—living in Montgomery on relief payments totaling $156 a month. "Apparently believing that their race and poverty made these young girls candidates for birth control, the nurse had been giving them regular shots,"[190] Roberts noted. Although the monthly Depo Provera injections the girls had been receiving had to be discontinued,* nurses from the federally funded Montgomery County Community Action Agency "asked the Relfs for permission to admit the youngest Relf sisters to a hospital for injections of the long-acting experimental contraceptive Depo Provera,"[191] in June 1973. Weisbord noted: "A third daughter, Katie, age eighteen, who had previously been fitted with an intrauterine device after a miscarriage, supposedly averted sterilization by locking herself in a bedroom when the nurses came to fetch her."[192] Minnie Relf, unable to read or write, signed the consent form with an "X." In later congressional testimony: Mrs. Relf "told the committee that she did not learn that Minnie Lee and Mary Alice had actually had surgery until she went to visit her daughters in the hospital. By then the sterilizations were a fait accompli."[193] Confused, angry, and feeling deceived, the Relfs turned to the Southern Poverty Law Center for help in July 1973. The resulting lawsuit exposed the widespread sterilization abuse taking place nationally and led to Judge Gerhard Gesell's aforementioned decision (March 1974). Evidence of sterilization abuse and the profile of its victims mounted as Carl W. Tyler, Jr., M.D., chief of the Family Planning Evaluation Branch of the Centers for Disease Control, in a 1974 report titled "Preliminary Data on Sterilization of Minors and Others Legally Incapable of Consenting" prepared for the DHEW, revealed that: "Blacks younger than age 21 underwent sterilization with greater frequency than did whites in the same age group.... Welfare recipients under age 21 underwent sterilization more often than did those not receiving welfare, regardless of race."[194] Litigation and such reports also led to federal regulations prohibiting the use of federal funds for the sterilization of institutionalized persons and those declared incompetent by a state or federal court and required the informed consent of the patient to be steril-

---

*That spring, after the hormone was linked to cancer in laboratory animals, the federal government in Washington had ordered an end to injections of Depo Provera for contraception. After decades of heated debate about the drug Depo Provera was approved by the FDA for use in the United States in 1992.

ized and that such patients be at least 21 years old.[195] Although the protections against sterilization abuse triggered by this decision were not as comprehensive or thorough as they could have been, they were a step in the right direction.

Meanwhile, "[o]ther women of color were also sterilized at startling rates."[196] For example, in Puerto Rico a decades-long crusade incorporating the efforts of the International Planned Parenthood Federation, the Puerto Rican government, the federal government, and research projects such as Dr. Clarence Gamble's "experiment in population control" in Turjillo Alto from 1950 to 1958 resulted in an "island-wide sterilization campaign ... so successful that by 1968 more than one-third of the women of childbearing age in Puerto Rico had been sterilized, the highest percentage in the world at that time."[197] During the 1970s similar systematic efforts on Indian reservations left more than 25 percent of Native American women infertile.[198] A physician testified to the effectiveness of these policies, reporting that: "[a]ll the pureblood women of the Kaw tribe of Oklahoma have now been sterilized. At the end of the generation the tribe will cease to exist."[199] Thus, for some small Indian tribes, this policy was literally genocidal. One authority on race, ethnicity, and reproductive rights wrote: "It is amazing how effective governments—especially our own—are at making sterilization and contraceptives available to women of color, despite their inability to reach these women with prenatal care, drug treatment, and other health services."[200] While Black, Puerto Rican, Chicana, and Indian women were being forcibly sterilized and herded into government birth control programs, White middle-class women found it nearly impossible to find doctors who would sterilize them.[201]

Between 1965 and 1980, especially in the wake of the Tuskegee revelations, federal courts were being overtaken by events that forced them to protect the health and human rights of Black and poor patients, especially against sterilization abuse. Moreover, women received the last component of their reproductive rights in 1973—legalized abortions. Of the three components of birth control prerequisite for the emancipation of women—individual choice,* safe contraception, and abortion when necessary—after the Hyde Amendment in 1977,** poor women and many women of color were denied federally funded abortions except in cases involving rape or risk of death or severe illness. Not only were poor women pressured into dangerous, sometimes fatal, illegal abortions, but there were also: "many more victims—women for whom sterilization has become the only alternative to the abortions, which are ... beyond their reach. Sterilizations continue to be federally funded and free, to poor women, on demand."[202] Nevertheless, in the late 1970s women activists from the Committee to End Sterilization Abuse introduced guidelines to the New York City Council to prevent coercive sterilization. These guidelines would later set the stage for federal sterilization reform. The key

---

*This is consistent with the older concept of "Voluntary Motherhood."

**This legislation was named after Congressman Henry Hyde who chaired the Clinton impeachment hearings.

provisions were required informed consent in the preferred language of the patient; a 30-day waiting period between the signing of the consent form and the sterilization procedure; and prevention of obtaining consent during labor, immediately after childbirth or an abortion, or under the threat of losing welfare benefits. Amid the growing Women's Health Movement protesting dominance of women's health care by male professionals, exploitation and experimentation upon women in the areas of contraception and potentially dangerous drugs and procedures, and the medicalization of normal reproductive events into medical conditions, White women crusaded *for* their *sterilization rights*. As Davis observed:

> While women of color are urged, at every turn, to become permanently infertile, white women enjoying prosperous economic conditions are urged, by the same forces, to reproduce themselves. They therefore sometimes consider the "waiting period" and other details of the demand for "informed consent" to sterilization as further inconveniences for women like themselves.[203]

Linda Gordon pointed out the historical roots of the fragmentation of the feminist movement along race and class lines over reproductive rights, some of which originated during the early twentieth-century race-suicide allegations that were leveled at privileged White women by eugenicists who they felt were not reproducing enough. The schism grew wider and deeper:

> This happened in two ways. First, the feminists were increasingly emphasizing birth control as a route to careers and higher education—goals out of reach of the poor with or without birth control. In the context of the whole feminist movement, the race-suicide episode was an additional factor identifying feminism almost exclusively with the aspirations of the more privileged women of the society. Second, the pro-birth control feminists began to popularize the idea that poor people had a moral obligation to restrict the size of their families, because large families create a drain on the taxes and charity expenditures of the wealthy and because poor children were less likely to be "superior."[204]

More evidence of the race and class breach in the women's health movement was noted by Rodriguez-Trias and Gordon, who observed that White women focused their energies on *health care*, while women of color and working-class women emphasized *health status*:[205] "The focus on the interests of white privileged women led to a myopic vision of reproductive rights."[206] In a move considered insensitive by some, groups articulating the reproductive rights concerns of middle-class White women, such as the National Abortion Rights Action League, Planned Parenthood, the Association for Voluntary Sterilization, Zero Population Growth, and the ACLU, fought against the New York as well as national guidelines. Although some of these groups had old, hardline bloodlines running back to the eugenics movement or were allied with the right wing, their opposition to sterilization reform seemingly had no eugenic motive:

> [T]hey simply failed to understand the concerns of the poor minority women. Focusing on the obstacle the regulations would pose to middle-class white women, they ignored the ravages on minority women's bodies the new law would help to prevent. They wrongly believed that any criticism of sterilization would give support to the enemies of women's reproductive choice.[207]

Nevertheless, in 1978 HEW issued rules incorporating the New York guidelines that also prohibited hysterectomies for sterilization purposes or the use of federal funds to sterilize minors, the mentally incompetent, or institutionalized persons.

One major reason White women were unable to find physicians willing to sterilize them was the "120 formula," prescribed and promoted by the American College of Obstetrics and Gynecology (ACOG). If a woman's age multiplied by the number of children she had did not total 120, she was not a candidate for sterilization. Additionally, she then needed the endorsement of two physicians and a psychiatrist. Few White women with fewer than three children or who were less than 40 years old met the criteria. This reluctance to sterilize middle-class White women continues today, according to many authorities. Nevertheless, the disparate experiences of White women and women of color led to an understandable clash of agendas surrounding sterilization and reproductive rights.[208]

## Experimental Abuse and Exploitation in the Name of Medical Science

In the midst of the clamor over the Tuskegee revelations, the Relf case, and the women's health movement, a sinister but silent new wave of scientific racism in the form of unethical experimentation peaked during the first half of the 1965 to 1980 period. Confirming and conforming to what appears to be the usual pattern in the United States, the disproportionate victims were African Americans, the disadvantaged, and other people of color. World War II seemingly established precedents wherein government charges, including soldiers, prisoners of war, and inmates of penal institutions became prime candidates for medical experimentation. Despite the diminished sense of urgency with the war's end, between the 1950s and 1970 human experimentation programs took place in hundreds of American institutions, affecting thousands, if not scores of thousands, of U.S. citizens. As Allen M. Hornblum described the period after the war in *Acres of Skin: Human Experiments at Holmesburg Prison: A True Story of Abuse and Exploitation in the Name of Medical Science*: "Over the next two decades, the number of American medical research programs ... rapidly expanded as zealous doctors and researchers, grant-seeking universities, and a burgeoning pharmaceutical industry raced for greater market share."[209]

Eileen Welsome, in *The Plutonium Files: America's Secret Medical Experiments in the Cold War*, revealed that: "Cold War scientists had used American citizens as guinea pigs" under the aegis of the Department of Energy and U.S. Army.[210] They "had conducted several hundred radiation experiments on American citizens, including one in which eighteen people were injected with plutonium.... They exposed over 200,000 [soldiers, sailors, and Marines] in over 200 atmospheric atomic and hydrogen bomb tests...."[211] Most of this experimentation, which involved all categories of vulnerable institutionalized Americans as well as military personnel, did not conform to either Hippocratic principals or the Nuremberg Code. Having already been granted professional sovereignty bordering on omniscience[212] but lacking a moral compass, "the best and brightest in America's medical community put scientific interests and benefit to future patients above the health of their subject-patients"[213]:

> *Domestically, the well-being of research subjects was viewed as important, but, in the eyes of medical practitioners, not as important as scientific advancement. Many in the medical community believed the vigorous protection of research subjects, combined with the Hippocratic ideal of* primum non nocere *("first of all, to do no harm") was too restrictive a code of professional ethics, especially for physicians who had not committed the pseudo-scientific outrages of the concentration camps. The result was a marginalization of the Code and the creation of an ethical loophole that allowed physicians to pursue a pragmatic and utilitarian course while de-emphasizing the Code's critical provisions of informed consent by autonomous subjects. Since research was seen to have social importance, doctors could easily avoid the Nuremberg Code's prescriptive safeguards and aggressively pursue their individual goals.[214]*

American doctors and the biomedical establishment had seemingly forgotten the declaration by Claude Bernard, the famous French physician and founder of modern experimental medicine:

> *It is our duty and our right to perform an experiment on a man whenever it can save his life, cure him or gain him some personal benefit. The principle of medical and surgical morality, therefore, consists in never*

*performing on man an experiment which might be harmful to him to any*
*extent, even though the result may be highly advantageous to science, i.e.,*
*to the health of others.*[215]

By the 1960s many American physicians and biomedical researchers were injecting their subject-patients with polio, hepatitis, tuberculosis, typhoid, malaria, and cancer cells; performing burn and radiation studies on subject-patients' body parts, testicles, and, occasionally, their entire bodies; feeding them radioactive and other toxic substances; applying and smearing poisons, infectious agents, and irritants to their body surfaces; and subjecting volunteers to various powerful hallucinogenic and psychotropic drugs.[216] Not only were these acts performed with questionable, or totally absent, informed consent, they were often Phase I tests,* which were the riskiest, concentrating on the toxicity rather than efficacy of an agent, and usually categorized as nonbeneficial, *nontherapeutic* experimentation. Balancing the risks versus benefits to the subject-patient was difficult. It was a struggle to define legally, ethically, and pragmatically such terms as *therapeutic research*—"research designed to improve the health condition of the research subject by prophylactic, diagnostic or treatment methods that depart from standard medical practice but hold out a reasonable expectation of success"—versus *nontherapeutic research*—"research not designed to improve the health condition of the research subject by prophylactic, diagnostic or treatment methods."[217] Marcia Angell, past executive editor of the *New England Journal of Medicine* describes the balancing act:

> In a therapeutic trial, particularly one in which subjects stand to gain
> greatly, they may be willing to take proportionately greater risks, and this
> may be ethically permitted. In a nontherapeutic trial, however, where no
> benefit is expected for the subjects themselves, the risks should be vanish-
> ingly small, or "minimal," in the words of the federal regulations.[218]

Modern standards cast a harsh light on what took place throughout U.S. scientific research history, especially during the 1965 to 1980 era.[219]

Documented evidence of U.S. malfeasance in unethical experimental research occurred with Philippine prisoners as early as 1906 (the Phillipines was then an American territory). Dr. Richard P. Strong, director of the Biolog-

---

*In FDA Phase I tests, the new compound or IND (investigational new drug) is tested on small groups of healthy persons to determine the drug's effects on the body's metabolism and to detect toxicities. In Phase II tests, substantial groups of normal subjects are tested with gradually increasing dosages of the IND until limits of safety have been determined. Phase III tests assess the drug's efficacy as a disease fighter and evaluate its market potential. The FDA created these new requirements in response to the 1962 thalidomide (a tranquilizer drug causing major congenital deformities in the offspring of pregnant women who ingested the drug) disaster.

ical Laboratory of the Philippine Bureau of Science, experimentally administered the cholera bacterium to 24 inmates of Bilibid penitentiary, resulting in
13 deaths. Six years later he used more Philippine prisoners to study beriberi,
a dietary deficiency disease characterized by mental disturbances, heart failure,
and paralysis, which resulted in several deaths. Dr. Strong, a Yale graduate and
alumnus of Johns Hopkins Medical School, later became professor of tropical
medicine at Harvard.[220] Prison inmates were utilized for sometimes dangerous
medical experiments involving dietary deficiency diseases throughout the first
two decades of the the twentieth century—including an experiment by Dr.
Joseph Goldberger of pellagra fame. At the behest of Mississippi governor Earl
Brewer, Goldberger supervised an experiment inducing pellagra in adult
White males, the group with the least likelihood of contracting the disease,
through dietary manipulation. Although suffering was extreme, no one died in
what was described as "a hellish experiment."An untroubled Dr. Goldberger
commented in a public ceremony that "science and humanity were forever in
[the governor's] debt,"[221] seemingly ignoring the prisoner-subjects. Responding
to the few rare protests about prisoner abuse from members of America's scientific and university community early in the century, one writer commented:
"The most curious misconception [is] that the aim of science is for the cure of
disease—the saving of human life. Quite the contrary, the aim of science is the
advancement of human knowledge at any sacrifice of human life."[222] As if to
advance that viewpoint, between 1919 and 1922 hundreds of San Quentin
inmates were subjected to a bizarre testicular transplant experiment wherein
glands of rams, goats, and boars were transplanted into their scrotums. Dr. L.
L. Stanley, whose staff conducted the experiment (they eventually performed
over 10,000 procedures between 1918 and 1940),[223] praised the availability of
prison populations for conducting such experiments.

Seemingly, the use of prison inmates and soldiers for medical experimentation during the 1920s and 1930s was relatively rare—albeit beyond the realm
of research ethics and public concern. Even government-funded research such
as the USPHS's Tuskegee experiment was poorly funded and a low priority outside scientific circles. However, with the outbreak of World War II, the situation
changed. Fueled by President Roosevelt's Committee on Medical Research—
charged with discovering antidotes or at least control measures for diseases that
devastated troops at war, such as influenza, malaria, and dysentery—and $25
million in congressional appropriations, a new biomedical-industrial complex
was founded. Over four years, not only were the coffers of hospitals, colleges,
universities, medical schools, corporate institutions, and the nascent medical-
pharmaceutical industry filled, but the demand for research sites where dozens
of "volunteers" could be tested also simultaneously increased exponentially.
Prisoners in Massachusetts, New York, New Jersey, Illinois, and Georgia, for
example, patriotically volunteered during the war for dangerous blood plasma,
malaria, sleeping sickness, sand-fly fever, and dengue fever experiments. Many

articles favorably describing the experiments were published in prestigious scientific journals such as the *Journal of Infectious Diseases* and in the popular press, but there were also deaths. Even juvenile penal facilities such as the National Training School for Boys were mobilized to test the effect of ultraviolet irradiation on airborne germs. After the fervor of winning the war dissipated with victory, the research infrastructure, centered around the nation's universities, medical schools, pharmaceutical houses, and governmental institutions, remained.[224]

This was a pivotal period. Despite the establishment at the end of the war of the Nuremberg Code governing human experimentation, U.S. doctors thought that it applied only to German physicians: "American exceptionalism and our victory in the war worked against any call for a special code of medical ethics — particularly one that presented potential obstacles to America's rapidly emerging scientific dominance. U.S. postwar research wished to be unfettered by a code of medical conduct."[225] At that critical juncture, Hornblum noted: "The confluence of self-interest, utilitarianism, and the ideologies of science and medicine militated against the American medical community's immediate embrace of the Nuremberg Code. Prisoners were too valuable as research subjects to be jettisoned. They needed to be used, not protected."[226] The decision-making in these heavily financed, corporate-influenced areas determined the laissez-faire attitudes and led to what David Rothman called "the gilded age of research."[227] Dr. Andrew C. Ivy, eminent researcher and vice president of the University of Illinois Medical School, was the AMA's chosen expert on medical ethics and one of America's medical representatives on the witness stand at the Nuremberg trials. He extolled the virtues of research on prisoners in the United States, emphasizing the acquisition of "voluntary" consent. This viewpoint, although failing to deal with the issues of *informed consent* and coercion, was publicly endorsed in *JAMA*,[228] along with the findings of the Green Committee, which explored the medical practices used in Illinois prisons during the war.

Throughout the 1950s, human experimentation expanded, especially in federal and state prisons. Highly publicized experiments included those performed on Sing Sing prisoner Louis Boy, who volunteered for a scientifically specious exchange transfusion (it was estimated they exchanged some 18 quarts of blood) with an eight-year-old leukemia victim to act as a "blood cleaning agent." The leukemia patient died, but as a reward for Boy's heroism, Governor Dewey of New York released him from his life term. When Dr. Albert B. Sabin, the polio hero, produced new "highly attenuated strains of live polio virus" that he felt were not quite ready for the general public, he tested them on 133 inmates at the federal Ohio facility at Chillicothe. Such experiments shed a favorable public light on the practice—prisoners were perceived to be giving back to society. Moreover, "The public felt if famous doctors like Albert Sabin could perform experiments on prisoners, then 'it must be valuable' and all right."[229] Despite the fact that "[d]octors and university hospitals recognized their good fortune at the availability of a regular supply of human guinea pigs and did not want a skittish public or curious media interrupting the pipeline,"[230] the variety and gravity of the experiments increased.

As the biomedical research movement burgeoned during the 1950s and 1960s, prisoners, various categories of institutionalized patients,* and enlisted U.S. Army personnel were involved in experiments including but not limited to exposure to dioxin, the potent carcinogen; being ordered to stand in a field without protection against radiation while a nuclear device was exploded; being injected with live cancer cells; being innoculated with ectodermotropic viruses such as wart virus, vaccinia, herpes simplex, and herpes zoster; submitting skin for skin grafting; undergoing mind-control experiments with marijauna and LSD; being infected with bacteria such as *Staphylococcus aureus* and fungi such as *Candida albicans*; having testosterone applied to their scalps;**[231] being injected with tularemia, an infectious disease usually transmitted by fly, tick, flea, and lice bites that if untreated can result in death; undergoing widescale drug tests; undergoing shoddy mass plasmapheresis operations leading to hepatitis epidemics and deaths; being infected with viral hepatitis; being infected with malaria that was then treated with experimental drugs for malaria; being infected with diseases transmitted by "airborne particles"; being subjected to vaccine experiments; having Phase I tests performed on them with new anticoagulants, analgesics, steroids, tranquilizers, and deodorants; undergoing, according to the research physician, "pain tolerance studies"; allegedly being forcibly injected with experimental drugs; undergoing risky radiation exposure experiments to their testicles; being exposed to potentially life-threatening central nervous system rubella infections; and being exposed experimentally to cholera, typhoid fever, and smallpox. They virtually traded their bodies, and in some instances their future well-being, in exchange for better treatment (e.g., medical care, food, and housing) in their respective institutions, honorary certificates, favorable media coverage, and, for some, what have been described as "slave wages."*** The academic, research, and

---

*This included mentally retarded orphan children, senile elderly patients, and other institutionalized, often disabled, populations.

**The topical application of testosterone was considered so controversial at the time that the editors of *JAMA*, where the "modest investigative report" appeared, published a disclaimer in an editorial in the same issue.

***Prison "volunteers" were often given tiny stipends for participating in experiments. Others, such as retarded or disabled children, earned nothing more than what the researchers alleged was "being paid attention to" and "better care." Twenty dollars to several hundred dollars annually or five dollars for a blood study or biopsy were typical fees earned by prisoners. Prisoners and other "volunteers" were much less discerning—some considered prisoners "reckless" and "desperate economically"—than civilian volunteers. All acknowledged they were paid far less than students or noninmate volunteers.

governmental institutions involved in this wide range of experimental medical abuse were impressive.[232]

Institutional participants in this movement read like a "Who's Who" in the medical, research, scientific, and defense firmament. While there is no attempt to pass judgment, a partial list of active institutional participants, institutions whose previous activities were documented or investigated or whose participation spilled over into the public media between 1965 and 1980, sheds light on the perceived legitimacy and pervasiveness of the problem. Some included the University of Pennsylvania Medical School; Temple University Medical School;* Northwestern University School of Medicine; University of Florida College of Medicine; Medical College of Virginia; University of Cincinnati Medical Center; Tufts University Medical School; New York University Medical Center; the Manhattan Project; Oak Ridge National Laboratory; the Universities of Rochester, California at Berkeley, and Chicago; Los Alamos Laboratory's Health Division; National Institute of Allergy and Infectious Diseases in Bethesda, Maryland; National Heart Institute; Communicable Disease Center; National Institutes of Health (NIH); Atomic Energy Commission (AEC); National Aeronautics and Space Administration (NASA); U.S. Public Health Service Hospital in San Francisco; the Central Intelligence Agency (CIA); the National Foundation for Infantile Paralysis;** Sloan-Kettering Institute for Cancer Research; Ohio State University Research Foundation; U.S. Army Chemical Corps; Massachusetts Institute of Technology; the University of Washington; Baylor, Tulane, and Johns Hopkins; New York universities; and the Universities of Maryland, Colorado, Utah, and Indiana.[233] This list is by no means complete; it is a partial compilation of scientific investigators and their affiliated institutions whose activities in this area were documented, investigated, or recorded in the media between 1965 and 1980. Again, the participants resemble a hall of fame of U.S. biomedical research. They include but are in no way limited to Dr. Albert M. Kligman, professor of dermatology at the University of Pennsylvania School of Medicine, who ran the Holmesburg Prison research program from 1951 through 1974; Drs. Albert B. Sabin and Dr. Jonas E. Salk of polio vaccine fame; Dr. Victor Hass, head of the Microbiology Institute; Dr. Joseph Stokes, Jr., of Children's Hospital of Philadelphia and the University of Pennsylvania Medical School; Dr. Charles A. Doan, director of medical research of the Ohio State University College of Medicine; Drs. Chester M. Southam and Alice E. Moore of Manhattan's Sloan-Kettering Institute; Dr. Austin R. Stough, an Oklahoma physician;

---

*Temple University Medical School may not have been directly involved in the human research cited, but it did provide medical personnel to work on studies under the supervision of the University of Pennsylvania.

**The National Foundation for Infantile Paralysis may have been an involuntary participant in that it funded Dr. Sabin but never gave him clearance to conduct human field trials on his vaccines.

Dr. Joseph Boggs, director of laboratories at Children's Memorial Hospital in Chicago and associate professor of pathology at the Northwestern University School of Medicine; Dr. G. Robert Coatney of the NIH; and Dr. William L. Epstein, chairman of the dermatology department at the University of California. Some of this assemblage committed regrettable acts, while others were guilty of simply not screening their professional associations or affiliations carefully enough.[234] Efforts to weigh the gravity of their actions are better confined to reference works in this area.

Although Hornblum has clearly documented that a significant portion of the nation's unethical human research occurred in the nations's penal institutions, such as Holmesburg Prison in Philadelphia, Atlanta Federal Penitentiary, Sing Sing Prison in New York, Stateville Penitentiary in Illinois, Oklahoma State Penitentiary, Colorado State Penitentiary, and prisons in Washington and Oregon, for example, some of the experimental abuse took place in other types of institutions. Some examples of institutions that participated in such research, whose prior participation was documented or investigated, or whose participation was revealed in the public media during the 1965 to 1980 era included, but were not limited to, Iona State Hospital in Michigan; Johns Hopkins Hospital; Jewish Chronic Disease Hospital; Oak Ridge Army Hospital; the Billings Hospital of the University of Chicago; University of Rochester Hospital (now Strong Memorial Hospital); Massachusetts General Hospital; DC's Lorton Reformatory; Arkansas Children's Colony, a school for the mentally retarded; Dooley and St. Philip Hospitals in Virginia; the University of Chicago's Lying-In Hospital; Cincinnati General Hospital; Sunland Center at Fort Myers, where retarded children were experimented upon; Army facilities near Edgewood Arsenal, Maryland; Fernald and Wrentham State Schools in Massachusetts; Willowbrook State School and Hospital in Staten Island, New York; Woodbine (boys) and Vineland (girls), New Jersey, institutions for the retarded and developmentally disabled; Riverview Home for the Aged;[235] and some of the "leading medical schools, university hospitals, private hospitals, governmental military departments (the Army, the Navy and the Air Force), governmental institutes (the National Institutes of Health), Veterans Administration hospitals and industry"[236] that Dr. Henry K. Beecher referred to in his landmark article, "Ethics and Clinical Research."* Thus, as reflected by this partial compilation and by Dr. Beecher's estimate of the scope of unethical experimentation, "The basis for the charges is broad."[237]

The transition to preserve America's biomedical technology edge, usually hidden from public view or contemporary bioethical standards, seemed inevitable. This transition was led by the medical profession and the pharmaceutical industry, both of which had scientific, professional, and entrepreneurial interests in human experimentation, and the biomedical-industrial and military-industrial complexes, which were spoiled by short-term wartime experimental arrangements that were

---

*Some of these institutions and agencies were previously mentioned in this chapter.

still in place and by an ongoing cold war being waged largely by covert, espionage, and psychological warfare methods. Further accentuating U.S. research's ethical move toward pragmatism and utilitarianism, which led to a laissez-faire attitude toward human research in the biomedical and scientific communities, was the explosive growth in research funding epitomized by the 624-fold growth in the NIH research budget between World War II and 1965. This was further buttressed by huge expenditures pouring into the system from the pharmaceutical, chemical, defense, and personal products industries, which included but were not limited to pharmaceutical houses such as Pfizer; Hoffman-Larouche; Parke-Davis; Abbot; Smith, Kline and French; Lederle; Wyeth Laboratories; Merck, Sharp and Dohme; Shearing Plough; Cutter Labs; Eli Lilly and Company; and Squibb. Medical supply, personal products, and other firms, including R.J. Reynolds Tobacco Company, Johnson and Johnson, the Chocolate Manufacturers Association of the USA, Helena Rubenstein, DuPont, American Home Products, Bristol-Myers, Dow Chemical, and Proctor and Gamble, also actively participated.

Efforts to impugn or pass judgment are counterproductive. Revealing the facts may preclude future errors in judgment and increase the sensitivity of the U.S.'s medical and biomedical research communities and the institutions they guide and influence. As Allen Hornblum and Jessica Mitford observed, retrospective investigations have been hindered because of a conspiracy of silence surrounding the unethical experimentation issue, embarrassment, and fears of legal culpability by individuals and institutions involved. Such a climate makes it even more difficult objectively to evaluate the range of activities—spanning the entire spectrum from good to bad—in which participants engaged before most questionable human experimentation was discontinued by 1980. Detailed evaluations and judgments, with assignment of overt or covert gravity or culpability regarding these complex and variegated experiments, are better left to specialty studies in scientific abuse and bioethics such as those of Allen M. Hornblum, Henry K. Beecher, Jay Katz, Eileen Welsome, Linda Marsa, Jessica Mitford, George J. Annas and Michael A. Grodin, Arthur L. Caplan, William H. Tucker, and Bradford H. Gray.[238]

## Public and Official Responses to U.S. Medicine's and the Health System's Deep Secrets

The reactions to the revelations of scientific racism and abuse that took place in the United States health system between 1965 and 1980 were instructive. The Tuskegee experiment ended in 1972 "because a whistle blower in the PHS, Peter Buxton, leaked the story to the press. At first health officials tried to defend their actions, but public outrage quickly silenced them, and they agreed to end the experiment."[239]

As a result, the government made a $10 million out-of-court settlement in 1974, the survivors were finally treated, and the deceased men's families and remaining participants received small cash payments. Government and official responses for the protection of experimental subjects such as the Belmont Report were issued.[240] Nevertheless, the deep distrust bred of their historical health experience, compounded by the Tuskegee experiment and other health and scientific abuse, is part of the burden members of the Black community carry into the twenty-first century as they confront the AIDS epidemic and their history-based health deficit.[241] In contrast, when Judge Gesell made his historic denunciation on March 15, 1974, about the fact that thousands of poor people had been coerced into permanent sterilizations upon the threat of losing all or part of their federally supported welfare benefits, it was not followed "by national cries of shame and outrage but, instead, by a national shrug and yawn."[242] This duplicated in many ways the German public's reaction to the daily newspaper accounts of the Nazi Eugenics Courts.

There was a public outcry when one case was publicized that violated the principals of the Nuremberg Code. Between 1956 and 1970 at the Willowbrook State School and Hospital in Staten Island, New York, scores of children were enrolled annually to a total of between 700 and 800 and into a "hepatitis study, in which hepatitis was studied by deliberately infecting institutionalized retarded children with the virus."[243] Dr. Cyril Wecht, coroner of Allegheny County in Pennsylvania and past president of the American College of Legal Medicine, explains the case in the book *Legal Medicine*: "They took retarded youngsters, with no informed consent and most probably without any kind of consent, and gave them orally a fecal extract containing hepatitis virus to see what the medical results would be."[244] Many of the patients contracted hepatitis, which for a certain percentage of such patients is a fatal disease. Revelations from another human experimentation study that became one of the most notorious and controversial cases of the mid-1960s took place at the Jewish Chronic Disease Hospital in Brooklyn, wherein 22 elderly patients, without their knowledge or consent, were injected with live cancer cells by researchers from the Sloan-Kettering Institute for Cancer Research to determine whether people suffering advanced stages of other diseases could reject externally administered doses of cancer. Despite resistance by the hospital, medical institutions, medical organizations, and the cancer researchers, William A. Hymen—representing the patients—persisted in the case, winning a victory in the Court of Appeals of the state of New York. It took 14 months, but the court rendered a judgment that there was "fraud and deceit" in the cancer experiment. As a result, "the New York State Board of Regents put the two doctors on probation for a year, with the warning that their medical licenses could be suspended if further transgressions of professional ethics occurred."[245] Interestingly, the researchers, along with the NIH, conducted a similar experiment on a much larger cohort of inmates (at least 396 inmates—almost half of them Black) at the Ohio State Penitentiary in 1952 without any fanfare,[246] according to health journalist Harriet Washington.

When the *Philadelphia Sunday Bulletin* broke the July 31, 1966, story, "FDA

Ban on Drug Tests by U. of P. Specialist Imperils Research Program at Holmesburg Prison," announcing that all further drug tests at the prison were banned — followed by a related story in *Time* a week later,[247] Dr. Albert M. Kligman, a professor of dermatology at the University of Pennsylvania School of Medicine, and his ethically compromised experimental empire were exposed. Expanding exponentially since the 1950s, exploiting the pharmaceutical and defense industries' growing needs for untrammeled human experimentation, Kligman established a massive experimental research facility at Holmesburg Prison capable of multiple Phase I, II, and III drug tests, studying radioactive isotopes, unprecedented dioxin testing, dangerous dimethyl sulfoxide (DMSO) testing,[*] climate chamber testing, testing of mind-altering drugs, and scores of mundane product tests. By the 1960s, the volume and quality of the work being produced in the facility raised suspicions in official and scientific circles. Dr. Frances O. Kelsey,[**] FDA chief of the Investigational New Drug (IND) branch of the division of new drugs, studied Kligman's operation, and found: "[b]etween 1962 and 1966, the Holmesburg research program had conducted 193 studies. 'Used in the studies were 153 experimental drugs, including 26 drugs for which firms were seeking marketing permission and 14 others whose makers wished to market them for new uses.'"[248] Investigations revealed that the facility was built upon Dr. Kligman's virtually unlimited experimental access to uninformed and/or poorly informed inmates in the Pennsylvania prison system. As peers noted about the internationally renowned dermatologist, he was "[c]onsidered at once a genius, a medical pioneer, and the archetypical entrepreneur ... credited with both 'unilaterally [raising] dermatology to its high status today'" while "[pandering] to the worst instincts in medicine."[249] As early as 1951 Kligman displayed disturbing attitudes toward human experimentation when he conducted a "controlled experiment" wherein he "experimentally infected" retarded children with ringworm (tinea capitis) in order to test various fungistatic agents (a class of therapeutic drugs). In his medical school lectures he cavalierly joked about the retarded children's responses as he rubbed infectious organisms into their abraded scalps during such experiments, quipping: "These kids want attention so bad, if you hit them over the head with a hammer they would love you for it."[250] His presentations and publications regarding this work received stellar reviews and commendations from his colleagues at the annual meeting of the Society for Investigative Dermatologists.[251] Seemingly, the ethics of his experimental practices were never mentioned.

Nevertheless, Kligman's scientific sloppiness, conducting experiments beyond

---

[*]DMSO, a by-product of the timber industry, had become a universal solvent facilitating the absorption of other drugs into a person's bloodstream. Eventually banned from human testing by the FDA for its disturbing psychological and toxic effects, it was being used in veterinary and human medicine for a variety of ailments ranging from daily "aches and pains" to "painful bladder conditions."

[**]Dr. Kelsey is credited with preventing thalidomide (it later proved to cause major birth defects if taken by pregnant women) from being marketed in the United States.

his range of expertise or training, failing to employ the technically trained or qualified personnel necessary to conduct the experiments (using cheap inmate labor instead), poor to absent record-keeping, and experimental recklessness such as his highly publicized (in the scientific literature) DMSO and testosterone experiments led to the withdrawal of his drug-testing privileges by the FDA in 1966. The FDA action effectively marked the beginning of the end for his lucrative prison research program. Dr. Frances O. Kelsey reported findings that led to the FDA action:

> *Dr. Kligman reported tests on three groups of prison volunteers. But when the FDA checked, prison records turned up only two groups, who were studied for a much shorter time than the researcher had claimed. Moreover, it was charged by the agency, one prisoner had had a severe reaction to the controversial drug solvent that was being tested. That was not acknowledged in the report. The physician was also charged with allowing comparison subjects to take other investigational drugs instead of a placebo, thus rendering the conclusions meaningless. And he is said to have reported blood tests on patients who were not even in the hospital at the time claimed.[252]*

Despite the overwhelming evidence of malfeasance and public shock and concern, Kligman's prestigious professional colleagues Dr. Luther L. Terry, former U.S. surgeon general and vice president of medical affairs at the University of Pennsylvania, and Dr. Donald M. Pillsbury, emeritus professor, former chair of Penn's dermatology department and one of the great names in the field, rallied to his defense, helped orchestrate his appeal, and facilitated his rapid reinstatement. According to FDA physicians Drs. Kelsey and Alan Lisook, his reinstatement was unprecedented and represented a "singular case." Nevertheless, Dr. Kligman's scientific and professional luster would never be the same, and he eventually closed down his Holmesburg Prison experimental program in 1974. He promptly destroyed all the records.

When the *New York Times* broke the story "Prison Drug and Plasma Projects Leave Fatal Trail" on July 29, 1969, a long-smoldering example of deadly experimental and biomedical scientific abuse was exposed.[253] Dr. Austin R. Stough, an Oklahoma general practitioner and part-time prison physician at the Oklahoma State Penitentiary at McAlester, began testing drugs and undertook a major experimental project on the technique of plasmapheresis* in 1962. As Hornblum noted: "Pharmaceutical companies sought out private or university-affiliated physicians who had access to the stockpile of human material isolated behind high prison walls and living in highly regimented conditions that were rare, if not impossible, to find outside prison walls."[254] Within a few years, Stough had practically cornered the market, overseeing 130 investigational experiments for 37 pharmaceutical companies—leading some to estimate he may "have conducted between 25

---

*\*Plasmapheresis* is the process wherein after extracting whole blood from the subject, the plasma, fluid constituting approximately 55 percent of the blood, is removed and the remaining cells are reinjected.

percent and 50 percent of the initial drug tests in the United States and a quarter of the tests done on a blood process that created an important plasma by-product used to protect people exposed to infectious diseases."[255] This mass production of hyperimmune gamma globulin, which commands premium prices, along with the fees accrued for supervising drug tests, netted Dr. Stough millions of dollars. Despite several isolated clinical disasters that befell prisoner-subjects due to poorly trained staff and shoddy operations, Stough's plasmapheresis and drug-testing programs expanded into the Alabama and Arkansas prison systems. "By mid-1963, 'the incidence of viral hepatitis, an often fatal disease of the liver, was climbing sharply' in the prisons in which Dr. Stough had instituted his plasmapheresis program," leading an inmate to proclaim, "They're dropping like flies out here,"[256] according to Hornblum. Despite federal investigations concluding that both the technique and apparatus utilized by Dr. Stough were at fault, there is no evidence that a single pharmaceutical company severed relationships with him. By 1969, when the institutional, corporate, scientific, ethical, and medical malfeasance became public, despite the secretive nature of events occurring behind prison walls and sloppy record-keeping, at least 544 illnesses and deaths could be fixed and attributed to the experimental operations—the CDC estimated more than 800. Oklahoma took over Stough's plasma and drug operations, Alabama halted the plasma program but continued his drug-testing experiments, and Arkansas authorities permitted him to continue the plasma operation without interruption.

Another notorious case during the era was the aforementioned Relf sisters sterilization case. Amid much public clamor, the $1 million lawsuit filed by the girls' father against the federal government and a Montgomery, Alabama, clinic resulted in the 1974 Gesell decision in the federal court system against sterilization abuse.[257]

In the wake of, or perhaps because of, repeated repugnant revelations of scientific and scientific racist abuse in the system, efforts were begun to reform health system research, and measures were initiated to protect all patients, Black, Brown, White, and poor. Many of the patient-protective efforts targeted the legal system. In the research arena, the most significant postwar efforts were at the federal level, starting in the mid-1950s, although some states enacted some research guidelines to deal with local concerns and pressures. The Clinical Center of the NIH adopted guidelines that applied to the use of normal volunteers. The Nuremberg Code was referred to as the "ten commandments" of human medical research and was characterized as a powerful set of *ethical* principles rather than *legal* requirements that had to be followed. In the wake of the thalidomide experience, the FDA's Drug Amendments Act of 1962, a law aimed at keeping unsafe or useless drugs off the market by requiring proof of safety and efficacy from the drug companies, required that experts utilizing experimental drugs on patients inform them of the investigational nature of such use and, with certain exceptions, obtain their consent. It was the FDA's first venture into regulating research. Recognizing the widespread failure of the drug industry to obtain patient consent despite the guidelines, the FDA enacted patient consent regulations in 1966. In December 1965, the NIH, an agency directly involved in the research business—and, therefore, more reluctant to regulate it—decided to prepare guidelines that required "'prior review' of the judgement of principal investigators concerning the welfare of human beings used in clinical and behavioral studies."[258] It marked the beginning of the Investigational Review Board (IRB) system:

> In 1966, the NIH promulgated the policy of not approving new or continuing grants involving research with human beings unless the grantee institution provides prior review of the judgement of the principal investigator by a committee of his institutional associates regarding the "rights and welfare [of subjects], the appropriateness of the methods used to secure informed consent, and the risks and potential medical benefits of the investigation."[259]

Both sets of rules attempted to view research in a positive light and attempted to protect subjects, "but not at the expense of hindering research."[260] Significantly, the regulations were not directed at researchers, but at institutions—be they drug companies, universities, or research institutions. And violations could lead to a lack or withdrawal of funding or nonacceptance of the research data—but there were no other penalties.

In the wake of the 1973 Congressional Hearing on Human Experimentation, which was: "[o]stensibly designed to hear testimony about providing enhanced training on the ethical and legal implications of advances in bioethical research, the forum was really intended to address issues related to shocking revelations about the Tuskegee Syphilis Study,"[261] the federal government became more involved in the regulation of human research. Created on July 12, 1974, by the National Research Act, the National Commission for the Protection of Human Subjects of Biomedical and Behavioral Research was charged with identifying "the basic ethical principles which should underlie the conduct of biomedical and behavioral research involving human subjects,"[262] studying the nature of fetal research, and developing HEW guidelines and recommendations to regulate these activities. Comprehensive federal regulations governing government-conducted or -sponsored research with human subjects and special regulations governing fetal research, research on pregnant women, and *in vitro* fertilization resulted by August 8, 1975. However, there were glaring limitations: these rules applied only to grants and contracts involving human subjects under HEW jurisdiction and were not applicable to research funded by other sources; like previous federal rules and regulations, compliance was the responsibility of the *institution* and not the *investigator*; and sanctions for noncompliance were limited to a loss of funding, not criminal penalties. Moreover, while the Nuremberg Code was seemingly designed to govern nonbeneficial research, the new regulations applied to any "research, development, or related activity which departs from those accepted methods necessary to meet [the subject's] needs,"[263] thus broadening and lengthening their reach far beyond the Code's. However:

*the Code's detailed rules for protecting subjects, such as requiring prior animal experimentation, requiring that the beneficial results be "improcurable by other methods or means of study," requiring that the experiment should be conducted so "as to avoid all unnecessary physical and mental suffering," and prohibiting experiments "where there is reason to believe that death or disabling injury will occur," [we]re absent.[264]*

Interestingly, due to social and political considerations surrounding the 1973 *Roe v. Wade* decision legalizing abortions in the United States and heightened concerns about fetal protection from decisions by uncaring women about to undergo abortion and overzealous researchers, these protections were included in the rules and regulations governing *in utero* and *ex utero* fetal research.[265]

What accounted for the varied U.S. reactions to the revelations of overt scientific racism such as sterilization abuse, experimental exploitation, and broaches of medical ethics? Dividing the episodes into basic categories may facilitate analysis and bring clarity to a complex set of issues. For convenience, the episodes revealed during the 1965 to 1980 era can be categorized as purely unethical experimentation, unethical experimentation compounded by entrepreneurial considerations, unethical sterilizations, unethical medical treatments, and psychometric abuse and discrimination.

Public reaction to the purely unethical experimentation episodes, such as the Jewish Chronic Disease Hospital episode in Brooklyn and the Willowbrook experiments, elicited vigorous public outcries despite the indifference of the hospitals, the researchers, the affiliated institutions, and professional organizations. These episodes may have appealed to the public's generalized empathy bred of perceived, and real, vulnerability of the sick, elderly and disabled, or mentally or physically challenged. Such victims, especially children, are held blameless, and virtually everyone finds their abuse repugnant. There was a brisk public response to the Holmesburg Prison experiments, wherein the doctor-researchers were heavily involved financially in their unethical research activities. But the widespread unethical research/entrepreneurial activities of Dr. Stough, which probably resulted in more deaths and serious disability than those in Holmesburg, seemingly triggered a muted response—if the sanctions against Stough and Kligman personally and the state and official limitations of their activities are benchmarks. These responses probably measure ethical thresholds and reinforce the American tendency to wash away many sins of those engaged in healthy competitive capitalism. The helplessness and vulnerability of the elderly victims in New York and the disabled children at Willowbrook epitomized the public's perception of victimization we all face when ill or compromised. Unperceived and little-spoken-of were the implicit disadvantage and ultimate vulnerability for abuse, wherein this society places virtually all of its disabled citizens—both young and old—in harm's way. In a callous comparison, similar to used cars, if you are not fully functioning in America, you are automatically at risk. In contrast, the marginalization of incarcerated criminals placed them somehow outside the sphere, or at least on the margins, of human concern and caring. This seemed to apply, muzzling any response, even when researchers such as Kligman and Stough were strongly motivated in their abuse by monetary and career goals. Even Tuskegee, wherein the unethical research was clouded by the "race factor" (which automatically devalues Black patients in America), uninformed, poorly educated, poverty-stricken African American patients subjected to experimental abuse by sophisticated White professionals triggered a vigorous public outrage.

Due to an environment clouded by 100 years of the eugenics movement there was a muted response to the huge numbers of unethical sterilizations cited in Judge Gesell's federal court decision, and it aroused little public interest. The fact that a large percentage of the abused were welfare recipients and Black further clouded the issue. The Relf sisters' age and lack of children or sophistication may have been sole reasons their case elicited some advocacy response. As Weisbord and Roberts have documented, "race" and poverty have repeatedly elicited negative responses in the United States when juxtaposed to reproductive rights.[266] The public, then as now, seemed almost oblivious to the abuse inflicted on disadvantaged minorities and underprivileged Americans by the psychometric testing movement. By 1980, the rise of IQ and standardized testing was seemingly accepted as a fact of American life and a means of playing out the competitive ethos and myth of a U.S. meritocracy.[267] Their overt racial, cultural, and class biases and basic unfairness are largely unquestioned.

A common thread, even if only implicit, seemed to be an evolving cultural mechanism for devaluing certain groups or categories of human beings. Blacks, Hispanic/Latino Americans, and other identifiable minority groups, incarcerated criminals, the disabled, the less intelligent or scholastically limited, the mentally challenged of all types, the socially abandoned (e.g., orphans and homeless persons), and the destitute were walled off from public concern for various reasons by the American public and thus rendered more vulnerable to abuse in the process. Valuations were strongly influenced by race, socioeconomic status, class, and stereotypes. Cultural history and social customs are also important factors. Another common thread in all these phenomena was the active presence of social Darwinism and Galtonian eugenic principles undergirding American public attitudes and modulating responses to nefarious health system, educational, and scientific practices. Eugenical sterilization served as an excellent metaphor for the pathology in the system. For example, "polls taken in this nation in 1965 and 1971 showed that between 20 and 70 percent of the respondents are convinced that forced surgical sterilization is the only feasible solution to some of our most pressing problems."[268] These perceived problems included the nation's welfare expansion, large poverty and underclass populations, the large corps of physiologically and mentally compromised individuals, homelessness, increasing crime rates, and unwanted racial and ethnic minorities. Chase posited that three generations of solemnly teaching Galtonian eugenics as a legitimate science had "borne fruit" by the 1960s. Concentrating this dogma on the educated classes, the nation's future politicians, scholars, researchers, and even religious leaders made its effects more pervasive. Ominously, as revealed earlier, physicians were generally in agreement with the lay public.

This devaluation of certain groups and stratification of humanity on a "natural," even false "biological," basis assumed many guises and raises many questions about their inconsistency with America's democratic ideals. Questions were raised whether certain compromised groups, especially "deficient" racial or ethnic categories, should be allowed to proliferate or reproduce. Eugenics posited that mentally or physically compromised groups were not viewed as worthy of protection from experimentation that might benefit society as a whole. Society might benefit if criminals were eugenically eliminated, and—based on their existence outside the realm of social safeguards—shouldn't they be "fair game" for experimentation? Perhaps groups with low IQ scores and limited inherited potential represented waste and squandering when they received society's full educational and cultural benefits, and wouldn't they be better off when channeled into limited occupational and training pursuits? And eugenics raised the question that perhaps financially dependent classes do not deserve to reproduce, nor do they merit the minimum amounts of food, medical care, decent housing, or cultural amenities prerequisite for the proper development of their inherited or genetic potentials.

Disturbingly, medicine, the biomedical scientific research system, the clinical behavioral sciences, and the health system itself were increasingly used as the mediators of these policies and ideologies. Using racist, eugenic birth control policies as her example, Roberts stated: "the chief danger of these policies is the legitimation of an oppressive social structure. Proposals to solve social problems" in this manner makes social and "racial inequality appear to be the product of nature rather than power."[269] Just as mobilizing eugenic social theory is "a way of reading the structure of social classes onto nature,"[270] according to Donald McKenzie, as far as Blacks are concerned—which helps explain their reaction to Tuskegee—the threat "is not the actual elimination of the Black race; it is the biological justification of white supremacy."[271] Perhaps most important was the fact that this way of thinking "affected the way Americans valued each other and thought about social problems."[272] As World War II had proven, eugenic and scientific racist ideology, embodied in acts such as compulsory sterilization laws, creation of educational and occupational "tracking," culture-based IQ testing, withdrawal of social necessities (e.g., food, clothing, housing, health care, education) from the needy, and abusive experimentation, facilitates and often precedes truly genocidal policies and actions.[273]

---

## Disturbing Conclusions: The Best and Worst of Times

Despite the perpetuation of a medical and scientific environment wherein abuse and exploitation were pervasive for Blacks and disadvantaged populations, the overall thrust of the 1965 to 1980 period was health system and medical-social reform. For the first time in the nation's history it was conceded, though not legally mandated, that Black and other disadvantaged groups had a "right" to health care. Discriminatory treatment in the United States health system was not deemed an inevitable, even justifiable, result of race, financial, or class disadvantage. The 1965 passage of Medicare and Medicaid drastically expanded government responsibility—unapproached in scope and breadth since the Civil War and Reconstruction periods—for the provision of health services to specific population groups. Quietly, Blacks and the poor experienced their greatest health improvements since the First Reconstruction (1865–1877). The enactment of these programs in 1966 for the nation's older citizens (over age 65) and its poor and/or disabled represented political defeats for the AMA and its medical establishment, which had successfully blocked virtually all progressive health care legislation for the previous seven decades.

For the first time civil rights, women's rights, student's rights, and human rights became legitimate health system concerns. Included in the panoply of "rights" movements of the era was a professed government commitment to non-discrimination in health care, and minority and disadvantaged group representation in the previously elite health professions. The decade from 1965 to 1975 represented a "Civil Rights Era" in health care, as Blacks and other disadvantaged minorities charted unprecedented gains in virtually all indicators measuring health status, health outcomes, health services, and representation and participation in the health professions. By 1975, public, governmental, and White medical establishment enthusiasm for righting long-term wrongs and inadequacies in the health system began slowing down and progress began to grind to a halt.

In spite of the well-intended reforms, the health system power-brokers refused to implement the fundamental reorganization and restructuring necessary to foster true and long-lasting efficiency, equity, and economy. Buffeting by exposure of the system's ethical abuses and medical-social shortcomings lowered the health establishment's prestige and authority in the public eye, rendering it more vulnerable to radical change. Profit-taking, duplication, and health technology warfare encouraged by "competition" remained paramount, despite the runaway cost inflation bred by the new infusion of capital into the system. This development led to heavy-handed, expensive, often insensitive and discriminatory governmental regulation, especially from Black and poor people's perspectives, that failed to reign in costs and generated new sets of problems. The health care financing industry, organized labor, and business interests lost confidence in the old order built upon remnants of the traditional eleemosynary health system for the poor and some Blacks, supervised by the White medical profession and a largely voluntary hospital industry. A vibrant proprietary health service sector rushed in to fill the power vacuum and capitalize on both the cash flow stream and the disarray. By 1980 the ideological and organizational direction of the U.S. health system hung in the balance.

## PART III

# The Coming of the Corporation

# Retrenchment and a Dream Deferred: The Black Health Crisis of the 1980s and 1990s

### Failed Liberalism: "Friendly" Authoritarian Conservatism Triumphant

By 1980 the liberal reform years in the United States were over, and the dream of justice and equity in health care and most other areas of American life had proved elusive for Blacks and the poor. The rightward shift in ideology, politics, and public policy that took place between 1980 and 1993, the Reagan-Bush years, greatly facilitated these failed expectations.

Following a decade and a half of heightened possibilities, a perception of repeated domestic social and economic policy failures, dramatic international power and economic shifts, and variegated foreign policy failures—with the self-doubts and insecurities inherent in these events—most Americans entered the 1980s with a loss of confidence in liberal politics, cynical if not jaded attitudes toward social activism, and damaged faith in the Keynesian economics that had dominated since the Great Depression. Thus the promise by Ronald Reagan, "a man whom, not many years before, many Americans had considered a frightening reactionary," to make "a change in government more profound than any since the New Deal of fifty years before"[1] was delivered to receptive ears.

One of the common predictions made about the Reagan administration (1981–1989) was that there would be an assault on the civil rights gains of the

1960s. Political pundits, prestigious media outlets, law journals, and respected columnists agreed that the assault was in motion by the end of his first term. While declaring himself a racial and civil rights crusader with 40-year-old anecdotes and "some of my best friends were Black" stories on the rare occasions that African Americans gained his attention, Reagan's "friendly racism" (borrowing Kenneth O'Reilly's term)* objected to the civil rights establishment and its agenda philosophically and politically, even to the extent of opposing the Civil Rights Act of 1964 and questioning the value of the *Brown* decision. A professional actor and an articulate campaigner who rhetorically advocated racial justice, Reagan cleverly appropriated and distorted Martin Luther King Jr.'s morally and constitutionally correct advocacy of a color-blind society (where one's skin color truly did not matter) and the achievements of the Civil Rights Movement. He then tried to reverse the hard-won accomplishments of Black Americans. Turning these concepts and fulfillments on their heads, in Reagan's hands "color-blind" became the right-wing code word for the attack on affirmative action, and "civil rights" came to mean: "If you happen to belong to an ethnic group not recognized by the federal government as entitled to special treatment ... you are the victim of reverse discrimination."[2] This finely tuned racial and social agenda animus staining the administration's self-named movement, the "Reagan Revolution," affected virtually all executive branch activities during this period. It became a facet of Reagan's continuation of "Nixon's southern strategy of pitting white Americans against the 'special interests' and pleadings of African Americans," and playing the "race card," which included "heavy-handed claims that the Democrats catered to blacks, in the process demanding that white middle America pay taxes to support programs to help welfare queens and street criminals."[3] Moreover, these strategies shaped and influenced events—the subsequent Bush administration's negative election campaigns and policies; the rightward shift in the public mood; destruction of much of the civil rights infrastructure, such as the Civil Rights Division of the Justice Department and Civil Rights Commission; and loading the Supreme Court and federal judiciary with ultraconservative judges, for example—long after Reagan's term in office. Deep cutbacks in health policy objectives and health care delivery to Black and other medically disadvantaged and/or indigent persons or groups, targeted and disapprovingly labeled by the president as victims of "'a new kind of bondage' fostered by welfare programs and other government handouts,"[4] were justified by a threatening new wave of therapeutic nihilism in medical care,[5] usually led by conservatives. Reagan's administration "called for major cutbacks in entitlement to health care for the poor and elderly,"[6] according to authorities

---

*Kenneth O'Reilly is an academic political scientist and writer who has published widely on racial dimensions of American politics and civil rights. He used the term in O'Reilly K. *Nixon's Piano: Presidents and Racial Politics from Washington to Clinton.* New York: The Free Press, 1995, 355.

in social medicine* such as Karen Davis. Fiscally and politically powerless groups, such as African Americans, were victims of these socially regressive health policies.[7]

The Reagan Revolution fostered a menu of conservative policies and programmatic changes intended to "solve" the nation's problems. Based on the arbitrary assumption that the woes of the U.S. economy were largely the result of excessive taxation and overregulation of the free market, Reagan implemented a bold experiment called "supply-side" economics (some called it "Reaganomics"). Based on these theories, in his first months in office he made the largest tax cuts in the nation's history, with particularly generous benefits to wealthy individuals and corporations, and began to deregulate private enterprise. As a counterpoint to the expected reduction in government revenues from the tax cuts, dramatic $40 billion cuts in the federal budget were hastily made. The cuts were largely to social programs, which disproportionately affected Blacks and the poor, especially expenditures for their health care. Simultaneously, he implemented massive increases in military spending: "In the ten years from 1980 to 1990 the government spent $2 *trillion* on the military, more than was spent during the thirty previous years."[8] "And, by early 1982 ... the nation had sunk into the most severe recession since the 1930s," Brinkley noted.[9] Despite a mixed economic recovery, a new economic pattern was established as "Reagan presided over record budget deficits and accumulated more debt in his eight years in office than the American government had accumulated in its entire history."[10] As Davidson and Oleszek noted, "Never before had the nation seen such huge deficits during an economic expansion."[11] During the Reagan-Bush years the national debt rose from $907 billion in 1980 to nearly $3 trillion in 1990. The deficits, despite continued cuts to social programs, continued to be fueled by the tax cuts for the well-to-do, a huge defense budget, the increasing fixed costs of "entitlement" programs such as Social Security and Medicare, and interest payments on the enormous federal debt. Disbursements for entitlement programs were exacerbated by an aging population (8 percent over age 65 in 1970 versus 12 percent in 1990) and the increasing costs of health care.

Inflation at the beginning of the period threatened to erode the buying power of all citizens and undermine the fiscal stability of the nation's cities.[12] This adversely impacted the health of Blacks and the poor by decreasing city tax bases, revenues, and funding sources for the nation's already fragile public health infrastructure composed of public and charity clinics and city and county hospitals. The aforementioned recession was followed several years later by an economic

---

*Social medicine refers to the progressive public health movement initiated in the 1940s and 1950s which extended the boundaries of public health as they concerned all health problems, including chronic diseases and "the whole of the economic, nutritional, occupational, educational, and psychological opportunity or experience of the individual or of the community." Some contended this extended outlook beyond environmental and communicable diseases posed public health's challenge of the future. *Source:* Fee E. History and development of public health. In: Sutchfield FD, Keck CW. *Principles of Public Health Practice.* Albany, NY: Delmar Publishers, 1997, 21–22.

recovery largely confined to the wealthiest 20 percent of Americans. For example, the 1994 *Economic Report of the President* referred to the fall in real income between 1979 and 1990 for men with only 4 years of high school—a 21 percent decline—as "stunning."[13] Regarding African Americans:

> *Relative income of African American households held steady at about 60 percent of white income in the 1980s, but the relative wealth position of most black families deteriorated. Historically, black wealth always has been much lower than that of whites, the legacy of slavery, discrimination, and low incomes. Between 1983 and 1989, a bad situation grew worse. In 1983, the median white family had eleven times the wealth of the median nonwhite family. By 1989 this ratio had grown to twenty.[14]*

During the uneven economic recovery favoring the rich and upper middle class, the economy created 11 million new jobs (mostly in the low-wage service sector without health insurance), and the consumer price index dropped from 13.1 percent in 1979 to just 4.1 percent in 1986. Moreover, the Dow Jones industrial average of stocks reached an all-time high. However, unemployment rose from 7 to 11 percent and 8.4 million people sank below the poverty line, an increase of 40 percent. The African American unemployment rate, 14 percent when Reagan entered office, continued the pattern of being twice that of Whites, which seemingly stabilized at over 6 percent throughout the Reagan-Bush era. And the Black poverty rate hovered around 36 percent. Moreover, as O'Reilley noted, "While Reagan offered corporate America cash (through tax-rate cuts, depreciation allowances, etc.), he offered the rest of White America little more than antiblack rhetoric and Meese/Reynolds sideshow campaigns that did nothing to stop the slide of working—and middle—class living standards."[15] As Edward Wolff documented in *Top Heavy: A Study of the Increasing Inequality of Wealth in America*, a 1995 Twentieth Century Fund report, "The increase in wealth inequality recorded over the 1983–89 period in the United States is almost unprecedented. The only other period in the twentieth century during which concentration of household wealth rose comparably was from 1922 to 1929."[16] Despite the deficits and social malaise in rural areas and the nation's cities, the Reagan administration refused to raise income taxes or reduce military spending (which was 29 percent of the budget). It could do little to reduce entitlements (legislated entitlements were 20 percent of the budget) or interest payments on the national debt (15 percent of the budget), so further cuts were made in the remaining 35 percent of the budget, largely confined to "discretionary" domestic spending targeting programs aiding the poorest and politically weakest Americans:

> *There were reductions in funding for food stamps; a major cut in federal subsidies for low-income housing (which contributed to the radical increase in homelessness that by the late 1980s was plaguing virtually all*

*American cities); strict new limitations on Medicare and Medicaid payments; reductions in student loans, school lunches, and other educational programs; and an end to many forms of federal assistance to the states and cities—which helped precipitate years of local fiscal crises as well.*[17]

As a result, the plight of Black, working-class, and poor people worsened, their previous health progress was threatened, and the United States, because of persistent trade and budget deficits, became a debtor nation for the first time since 1914.[18] Nevertheless, despite Reaganomics "promoting prosperity at the expense of the poor"; increasing the number of Americans with no health insurance to 37 million, most of whom were employed working-class people or children, and making "homelessness" part of the national lexicon; the administration's "borrowing rather than taxing to re-arm" and thus mortgaging the nation's financial future; and generating malaise for Black, working-class, and poor Americans, the GOP boasted of creating 16.5 million new jobs, bringing down the unemployment rate to a 17-year low, raising the GNP by one-third, and cutting double-digit inflation down to about 4 percent,[19] according to Harvard Sitkoff.[20]

With the electorate seemingly oblivious to a "series of scandals that might well have destroyed another administration,"*[21] George Bush, Reagan's vice president, won the presidency (1989–1993) in 1988 on the premise of continuing the Reagan Revolution. Having "identified himself clearly with no major issue and . . . [taking] credit for no major accomplishments,"[22] Bush capitalized on his ties with a still-popular Reagan's pervasive aura of personal appeal and charisma; new-found national confidence built upon Reagan's nationalistic rhetoric, patriotism, and often bellicose foreign policy, which nevertheless was instinctively restrained and usually more talk than deeds; and fear of another round of Democratic social experiments and permissiveness stoked up by a presidential campaign described as "almost certainly the most negative, and many believed among the most discreditable, of the twentieth century."[23] Following the dictates of political advisors such as Roger Ailes and Lee Atwater, and exploiting the Democratic Party image of being soft on crime and pro-

---

*Top EPA officials resigned when it was disclosed they were flouting laws they had been appointed to enforce; CIA and Defense Department officials resigned after revelations of questionable stock transactions; Reagan's secretary of labor resigned after being indicted for racketeering (although he was later acquitted); White House counsel and, later, attorney general Edwin Meese resigned in 1988 after being attacked for controversial financial arrangements many believed compromised his office; massive misuse of funds by the Department of Housing and Urban Development—channeling them away from low-income housing into "sweetheart" contracts with GOP political cronies; and the development of something like a "secret government," unknown to the State Department, DOD, and parts of the CIA, dedicated to advancing the administration's foreign policy goals and objectives through secret, sometimes illegal, means (later known as the Iran-Contra Affair). *Source*: Brinkley A. *The Unfinished Nation: A Concise History of the American People*. New York: Knopf, 1993, 887–888.

Black, the 1988 Bush campaign inflamed the nation's deep-seated racial and "psycho-sexual fears," using a Democratic candidate's terminology, demonizing, distorting, and propagandizing quota queens and Willie Horton, a convicted African American robber and murderer incarcerated in Massachusetts. Horton, who had been uneventfully furloughed (a program in effect in many states) on nine previous occasions, escaped and committed assault and rape in 1987. Bush and the GOP sensationalized and blamed these crimes on his Democratic opponent Michael Dukakis, Massachusetts's governor. The successful campaign, largely built on racial division and discrediting Dukakis, served as the culmination of an effort to divide Southern Blacks away from the populists while appealing to Northern blue collar workers and suburbanites. Dividing the traditional, but shaky, Democrat coalition and adding the disaffected elements to the wealthy and relatively well-to-do, which the GOP already dominated, completed the Southern strategy begun in the 1960s by Barry Goldwater and Richard Nixon.[24]

Despite an ever-tightening recession gripping the U.S. economy, the Bush administration seemed unable to define a domestic policy agenda. Although burdened by a staggering national debt and federal deficits, a Democratic Congress that was not very cooperative with the White House, and accommodations to the right wing of the GOP, the Bush administration seemed to be uninterested in fundamental, cutting-edge issues, including the greying of America; Hispanic and Asian immigration; the role and place of non-Whites in the United States and Bush's "New World Order"; problems emanating from skyrocketing drug abuse, AIDS, and homelessness; defining the role of the New Right and Religious Right; intense New Right and Religious Right assaults on feminism and abortion; the changing Left and the new environmentalism; and the culture wars being fought over all aspects of the concept "multiculturalism." Any of these important issues had the potential to explode and fracture the body politic; his inattention to them would reemerge to haunt President Bush.

Meanwhile, between 1989 and 1991 a tumultuous series of international events, led by the 1989 political collapse of the Soviet bloc in Central and Eastern Europe—Poland, Hungary, Czechoslovakia, Bulgaria, Romania, and East Germany—resulted in the United States emerging as the sole world superpower. Following declarations of independence of every republic in the Soviet Union and the outlawing of the Communist Party, nearly 75 years after its birth the U.S.S.R. itself disintegrated on December 25, 1991. These events enhanced both Reagan and Bush's popularity, since both were identified as avid anti-communists. President Bush's popularity also benefitted as a result of his aggressive foreign policy when he dispatched troops to Panama in 1989 to overthrow and capture that nation's military leader Manuel Noriega and for check-mating and reversing Iraqi dictator Saddam Hussein's military annexation of the emirate of Kuwait in August 1990. His approval ratings soared over 90 percent, the highest in the history of polling, for several months following his leadership of an international United

Nations coalition (authorized November 29, 1990) and subsequent expulsion from Kuwait and military defeat of Saddam Hussein's forces during the Persian Gulf War (January 16, 1991–February 28, 1991). However, Bush's foreign exploits failed to maintain his presidential popularity by the eve of the 1992 elections. Despite his impressive international record, economic recession and domestic social issues combined to raise frustration levels among middle-class Americans, forcing them to demand that the government "address such problems as the rising cost of health care"[25] and sociocultural issues threatening to tear American democracy apart.[26]

The presidential election of 1992 represented a surprising referendum for change. For the first time in recent history, the health policies of the previous 12 years of the Reagan and Bush administrations "led to such an enormous demand for change that health care reform became the second most important issue (after jobs) in the 1992 election."[27] William Jefferson Clinton, a young, five-term Democrat governor from Arkansas not frightened off by Bush's early popularity in the polls, won a decisive victory (receiving 43 percent of the vote) over Bush (who received 38 percent of the vote) and independent Texas billionaire Ross Perot (who received 19 percent of the vote) by emphasizing broad economic issues, many of the aforementioned agenda items Americans were concerned with, and promises to reform the health system.[28]

---

## Health Markets and the Facade of Public Health

Between 1980 and the mid-1990s, the health system expanded to 14 percent of the GDP, becoming the largest industry in the country. It was also the largest employer, with approximately 2.1 million nurses, over 600,000 doctors, and more than 11 million other employees (10 percent of the nation's total workforce) working in over 6,250 hospitals or health-related settings. The health status and outcomes of the American population displayed gradual, but slowing, rates of improvement. African Americans shared little of the favorable aspects of either trend.

Throughout the health system's financial growth and transformation process, gradual improvements in health status and outcomes were largely confined to White, middle-class populations.[29] Despite the initiation and perpetuation of policies that were counterproductive to the public's health; the emergence of unwholesome health system trends, policies, and practices; and the misuse and occasional abuse of publically funded health resources, the public health community was virtually starved of essential funding and rendered almost silent. As the nation increasingly fell behind other industrialized countries according to standard health indicators, U.S. public health goals and objectives appeared in various reports and publications. The goals and objectives, framed in the popular rhetoric of increasing the span of healthy life, reducing the health disparities among Americans, and achieving generalized access to health promotion and disease prevention (HP/DP) services, appeared first in *Healthy People: The Surgeon General's Report on Health Promotion and Disease Prevention* (1979), the U.S. Public Health Service's (USPHS) 1980 publication *Promoting Health/Preventing Disease: Objectives for the Nation*, and, finally, the USPHS's 1986 *The 1990 Health Objectives for the Nation: A Midcourse Review*.[30] Despite the absence of comprehensive health planning, an increasing reliance on market forces in health care, a decaying public health infrastructure, few specific programs aimed at improving the entire population's health, or significant funding allocated to reach the stated 1990 or 2000 goals, these lofty and idealistic goals and projections were trumpeted and framed in the reassuring language and panache of public health and taught in schools of public health for the next 20 years.

During this period, when America's relative health status and outcome indicators deteriorated in comparison to other developed countries, Elizabeth Fee observed: "In the Reagan revolution of the 1980s, federal funding for public health programs was cut. Through the mechanism of the block grants, power was returned to state health agencies, but in the context of funding cuts, this was the unpopular power to cut existing programs."[31] Nicolette Hart observed that the policy shift had health consequences for African Americans:

> *Race mortality differentials narrowed between 1950 and 1980, though . . . recent evidence (1985 to 1990) indicates a slowing down of the process with some demographic reversal in the Black population. This almost certainly reflects the increase of poverty sponsored by "Reaganite" policies in the 1980s, demonstrating the sensitivity of longevity as a barometer of social and economic inequality.*[32]

Such actions, after a decline in public health from the 1950s—coming on the heels of an era when "the new health and social programs of the 1960s bypassed the structure of the public health agencies and set up new agencies to mediate between the federal government and local communities"[33]—left public health, using the Institute of Medicine's terminology and assessment, in "disarray" and "a threat to the health of the public."[34] Public health practice and the nation's schools of public health had become so detached from their grounding in population-based approaches to improving health, "in the concepts of social justice," and in their professional mission as "strong proponents of the ethical distribution of resources,"[35] that some felt only a "facade" of public health remained in America. This added to the impetus for "the 1988 report on *The Future of Public Health* by the Institute of Medicine (IOM)," which "focused attention on the discipline."[36] The report not only concentrated on public health's contemporary difficulties but also made clear recommendations about reaffirming and improving the profession's national role and mission of service to *all* people. It also predicted Krieger and Birn's 1998 contention and rallying call based on the "belief that social justice should be the foundation of public health"[37] and signaled a 1990s rebirth of public health practice.

As the nation continued its uneasy silence behind the facade of public health generated by politicians, the medical establishment, academics, policy-makers, and the media, the corporate transformation of the health care system, which actually began with the passage of Medicare and Medicaid in 1965, continued. This development constituted the most important change in health care's institutional structure since the rise of professional sovereignty at the dawn of the twentieth century. It had been facilitated by the increasingly lucrative provision of medical care through public financing; the dominance of the idea since the 1970s "that medical care is a market good, not a public good"[38]; the mid-1970s conservative appropriation of liberal reform, using managed care and HMOs as the vehicles for business investment; enabling the entry of for-profit corporate enterprises into mainstream health delivery by their purchasing chains of hospitals and nursing homes throughout the late 1960s and 1970s, which served as a beachhead of for-profit corporations and Wall Street in the delivery of medical care; and government-augmented pressures for efficient, business-like management of health care as tools to control costs. These changes broke down traditional barriers and voluntary public service–oriented health delivery mechanisms, often encouraging corporate control of health services. Significantly, rhetoric aside, very little funding for HP/DP or public health–oriented programs was included in this structural transformation. As a result, two of the four traditional power centers,*[39] physicians and voluntary hospitals—preoccupied with preserving community trust, maintaining professionalism and its prerogatives, and coping with government regulation during the 1980s and early 1990s—almost unconsciously and silently lost their autonomy.[40]

The original early 1970s allusions to a medical-industrial complex by Harold Meyers and Barbara and John Ehrenreich referred to the close "linkages between the doctors, hospitals, and medical schools and the health insurance companies, drug manufacturers, medical equipment suppliers, and other profit-making firms"[41] that had arisen after World War II. These entities were seemingly interlocked in a "seamless web of influence" representing "a common front for a particular style, structure, and distribution of medical care," and the label simultaneously "emphasized the hidden connections between industry and a medical system that was still made up almost entirely of independent practitioners and local, nonprofit institutions."[42] The medical-industrial complex had been forged and, until the Black Civil Rights Move-

---

*In 1977 Eli Ginzberg identified four power centers in the health care system that influence the nature of U.S. health care and the role of government in it: (1) physicians, (2) large insurance organizations, (3) hospitals, and (4) a highly diversified group of participants in the profit-making activities within the health system.

ment, was legally and socioculturally grounded in a centuries-old American tradition of separate and discriminatory race- and class-based health care and medical and health professions training.[43] As previously noted, until the 1965 passage of Medicare/Medicaid, linkages between the Congress and the medical-industrial complex's spokesman—the AMA and its coterie—constituted another "Iron Triangle" of influence on Capitol Hill.

The medical-industrial complex's new configuration, largely in place by the early 1980s, revealed huge health care corporations with Wall Street connections as central elements of the system. Arnold S. Relman, editor of the *New England Journal of Medicine*, alerted his readers about the overarching importance of the emerging, newly configured medical-industrial complex. According to Starr: "Relman wanted to distinguish the growing businesses that sell health services to patients for a profit, such as chain hospitals, walk-in clinics, dialysis centers, and home care companies, from the 'old' complex of firms that sell drugs, equipment, and insurance."[44] He also implicitly demonstrated "how the capitalist class (and its different components) has an enormous influence on the way in which health care is financed and delivered."[45] Managed care led the way:

> When the managed-care movement got started in the 1930s and '40s, it was run by doctors and health reformers who were filled with ideas about delivering good care to the masses at a modest price. They weren't good businessmen and they didn't want to be. Their politics tended toward socialism; getting rich was seen as loathsome. Even in the 1960s and 1970s, most HMOs were nonprofit and proud of it. They paid administrators small salaries and plowed back 90 percent or more of premiums into direct patient care.[46]

By the mid-1990s, when almost half the managed-care industry was for-profit, less than 75 percent of premium dollars went to direct patient care in proprietary HMOs.[47] As George Anders observed about this new version of American managed care, "those who got managed care contracts, made sure that frugal medicine was practical—and pocketed the difference."[48]

Stanley Whol, a physician and health entrepreneur himself, writing in *The Medical Industrial Complex*, warned of the adverse effects that this commercialization and Wall Street intrusion phenomenon were having on American medicine and health care.[49] Thus this went beyond the increased penetration of profit-making firms into medicine, but represented drastic changes in not only the health system's ideology, bending toward a "bottom line" mentality, but also "the organization and behavior of nonprofit hospitals and a general movement throughout the health care industry toward higher levels of integrated control."[50] Starr was prescient, outlining most of the structural elements involved in the transformation: (1) a change in the type of ownership and control, previously dominated by nonprofit and governmental organizations, to for-profit health care companies; (2) horizontal organization embodied in a decline of freestanding institutions and the rise of multi-institutional systems—accompanied by a shift in control from community boards to regional and national health corporations; (3) a shift from single-unit organizations operating in single markets to "polycorporate" and conglomerate enterprises, often organized under holding companies, with both nonprofit and for-profit subsidiaries, involved in a variety of health care markets; (4) a shift from single-level-of-care organizations (e.g., acute care hospitals) to organizations embracing multiple phases and levels of care (e.g., HMOs); and (5) industry concentration—the increasing concentration of control and ownership of health services in regional and, sometimes, national markets[51]—by the early 1990s. Intentionally or not, the appropriation of the health system by capitalist market and corporate forces posed a clear and present danger to economically disadvantaged populations such as African Americans.

Equally important to Blacks, working-class, and poor Americans, as has been previously alluded to, may have been the changes such a transformation wrought on the medical-social environment, medical ethics, public trust and accountability, and ideology governing the health system. As Bradford H. Gray reminds us in *The Profit Motive and Patient Care*:

> *The system in which these economic transformations . . . occurred was not one in which cost-effective, high-quality care was being provided to everyone who needed it. The question is not whether a satisfactory system is threatened but whether persistent shortcomings of the system are being mitigated or exacerbated by the economic and organizational changes that are sweeping over health care and replacing traditional forms of responsibility with new structures of accountability.*[52]

More troubling are the results:

> *Unless changes are made, important aspects of the health-care system may be in peril. Parts of the HMO industry operate under their own version of Gresham's law, in which bad plans drive out the good. Cost cutting predominates, even if it means denying care and trying to keep sick people off membership rolls. Profiteering becomes the norm; quality-improvement programs are scrapped if they don't yield quick financial payoffs. Meanwhile the people writing checks for this coverage—corporate employers and government administrators overseeing Medicare and Medicaid—often don't seem to care. They channel workers and beneficiaries into the cheapest managed-care programs they can find, with little regard for medical quality.*[53]

Most of these developments seemed negative and begged the questions raised by health policy authorities as varied as Paul Starr and Vincente Navarro. Starr queried: "The recent debate over medicine has failed to address a central issue. Is it the purpose of national medical policy to maximize the health of the country?"[54] Meanwhile, Navarro, professor of health policy, sociology, and policy studies at Johns Hopkins University, identified other factors as he examined the motives driving the U.S. health system: "[C]ontrary to official rhetoric, the moving force in health care delivery is not responding to people's needs but satisfying the greed of those who control key institutions in our society, including health care."[55] He contends that: "The economic and political order—capitalism—governs the financing and delivery of health services."[56] His allegation that "it is business 'entrepreneurship' that is the moving force behind our medical institutions,"[57] is chilling and reinforces the findings of highly regarded health system think tanks such as The Center for National Health Program Studies and health policy analysts such as David U. Himmelstein and Steffie Woolhandler at Harvard Medical School.[58] Thus the new system has also retained a facade of public health and no longer overtly focuses on legally or socially sanctioned racial or class discrimination or distinctions. Nevertheless, for African Americans, Hispanic/Latino Americans, and other disadvantaged ethnic groups, the working class (almost 75 percent of the population),[59] those with chronic illnesses who do not have adequate public or third-party coverage, and the poor in the health system, such a transformed medical-industrial complex represents a threatening and potentially hostile new health care environment.[60] (See Figure 7.1.)

### Health Financing: The "Market" Becomes Dominant

A key factor shaping the delivery of health care is the system for financing those services. As Navarro, editor of the *International Journal of Health Services*, noted, "The insurance companies and the large corporate employers are the major forces that shape this financing. Their economic and political influence is enormous, limiting considerably the government's ability to respond to popular demands."[61] Although health care financing is decentralized in the United States, by the early 1990s the insurance industry may have become the most powerful financial component in the health system. (See Figure 7.2.) Insurance companies exert power not simply by collecting the nation's health insurance premiums; by often serving as a conduit for government funds entering the system; but also by administering, and financing through distributing almost 80 percent of the nation's health care dollars (approximately 20–25 percent of American health care costs are borne by patients). They also exert their influence on the political process affecting healthcare itself. In the last 20 years they have also expanded their boundaries and influence beyond financing of care into the provision of services and/or tightly managing the delivery of the care for which they pay. These patterns have become

Figure 7.1 Occupational Distribution by Social Class and Gender, 1990

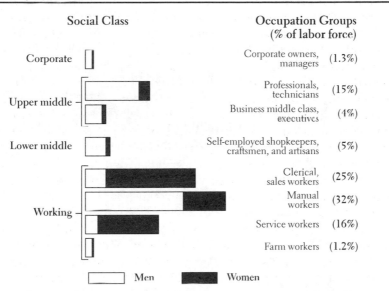

| Social Class | Occupation Groups (% of labor force) | |
| --- | --- | --- |
| Corporate | Corporate owners, managers | (1.3%) |
| Upper middle | Professionals, technicians | (15%) |
| | Business middle class, executives | (4%) |
| Lower middle | Self-employed shopkeepers, craftsmen, and artisans | (5%) |
| Working | Clerical, sales workers | (25%) |
| | Manual workers | (32%) |
| | Service workers | (16%) |
| | Farm workers | (1.2%) |

☐ Men   ■ Women

*Source:* Navarro V. *Dangerous to Your Health: Capitalism in Health Care.* New York: Monthly Review Press, 1993, 20.

---

## Figure 7.2   Decentralized Health Care Financing in the United States

- More than 1,000 private health insurance companies
- 50 state Medicaid programs (supported by federal, state, and, in some states, local government funds)
- The federal Medicare program
- Thousands of large companies that self-insure
- The Department of Veterans Affairs, the Army, Navy, and Air Force
- The Public Health Service (the Indian Health Service)
- State governments providing inpatient hospital psychiatric care for the indigent mentally ill
- Federal, state, and local government programs for the mentally retarded and mentally ill, as well as for alcoholics and drug abusers
- Local government (county or municipal) programs providing or paying for care of the indigent
- Private foundations, voluntary organizations, and charities
- Millions of individuals who pay directly out-of-pocket for all or a portion of their health care.

*Source:* Lee Pr, Benjamin AE, Weber MA. Policies and strategies for health in the United States. 297–321. In: Detels R, Holland WW, McEwen J, Omenn GS, eds. *Oxford Textbook of Public Health.* Vol. 1. *The Scope of Public Health.* 3rd ed. New York: Oxford University Press, 1997, 301–302.

so pervasive that if they continue, this HMO or managed care movement will represent a private sector appropriation of regulatory functions once exercised by the government.* It is a real threat that accountability and public responsibility—once vested in the American political process, Washington, 50 state capitols, local governments, and the medical establishment—will be transferred to corporate interests and Wall Street.

By the end of the 12 years of the Reagan-Bush era, Americans were profoundly dissatisfied with the health care system. As Navarro noted, "According to a Harris poll taken on January 5, 1993, 49 percent of Americans felt that 'the American health care system has so much wrong that it needs to be completely rebuilt,' while another 32 percent wanted to see profound changes in the health care sector."[62] Much of this discontent focused on health care financing or on factors closely related to it such as managed care. Regarding the growing influence of market forces on the financing configuration of the U.S. health care system, Philip R. Lee, A. E. Benjamin, and Mark A. Weber summed up:

> The most dramatic changes have been in the shift away from indemnity, fee-for-service plans to managed care plans in an attempt by employers to control their health-care expenditures. In many cases, benefits have been reduced, costs shifted to employees, and choice of plans and providers [were] limited. Insurance companies have become less and less willing to accept individuals with pre-existing conditions, and for many small employers, the costs have grown to levels where they no longer can afford to insure their employees. For those who have health insurance, there is great uncertainty about being able to keep it, particularly if moving from one employer to another.[63]

As a result, during the period in which the proportion of Americans not covered by insurance increased 22 percent, direct out-of-pocket expenses for health care increased 42 percent, the mode of funding health services became more regressive than in the past, and administrative costs for health care quadrupled.[64] Moreover, while the costs of care increased and health benefits declined for the majority of Americans, the profits enjoyed by the health insurance and pharmaceutical industries, along with the incomes of physicians,** increased. By 1993, "The top twenty drug companies saw their profits increase 15 percent per year over the past ten years (compared with an average increase of 3.2 percent for the top Fortune 500 companies)."[65] Executive compensation of the 26 most important health care corporations, already 54 times the salary of a nurse in 1985, increased to 85 times

---

*In virtually all other Western industrialized countries these functions are either assumed or closely regulated by national governments and are held to high accountability standards.

**The average earnings of physicians climbed from $89,900 in 1981 to $164,300 in 1992—well above inflation rates or increases in income for American families.

that salary in 1992. In 1993 the CEO of the Hospital Corporation of America, one of the largest for-profit health care companies, was the nation's highest paid person in the United States, with a salary of $127 million a year.[66] This was but one of several gargantuan managed-care executive salaries which by 1996 included Leonard Ahramson, "who appears each year on the Forbes 400 list of the richest people in America (estimated wealth: nearly $1 billion),"[67] according to Anders.

In spite of the tremendous wealth and profits being generated by the health system, major flaws in health care insurance coverage and services delivery affect average Americans, and many of these defects are getting worse. Some U.S. health system's characteristics that reveal its insurance coverage and delivery flaws in the 1990s and new millennium include:

(1) *It is not universal*. Seventeen percent of all Americans, 28 percent of African Americans, and 32 percent of Hispanics do not have any form of health insurance.

(2) *It is not comprehensive*. Americans spend more in out-of-pocket expenses than the citizens of any other advanced capitalist country.... Moreover, the overwhelming majority do not have coverage for long-term care.

(3) *It is not secure*. Sixty-two percent of working people — those whose employers self-insure their employees — can have their health insurance dropped if their condition requires treatment that is considered too expensive.

(4) *It is not fair*. The head of General Motors, who makes $1.8 million a year, pays the same premium for his health care as an unskilled assembly line worker in a General Motors plant.

(5) *It is inefficient*. Twenty-five cents out of every health dollar are spent on administration and paper shuffling.... [N]o other country spends this much on the administration of its health services.[68]

They help explain the two major concerns driving public dissatisfaction with the U.S. health system, cutting across virtually all demographic, class, race, and ethnic groups: the dramatic increases in health care costs and the fear of losing all or part of their health benefits in our largely employment-based health insurance system.[69] The fact that "[i]n 1990, 35.7 million people did not have health insurance, an increase of roughly 25 percent since 1980,"[70] proved that these were not idle concerns. Moreover, Jennifer Edwards, Robert Blendon, and Robert Leitman, reaffirming that certain basic health delivery principles still applied, made some sobering predictions: "The uninsured receive substantially less health care and have worse health outcomes once care is sought. This problem is expected to get worse as health care providers who in the past provided discounted or free care to the medically indigent are less able to do so because of greater costs constraints."[71] For African Americans and other ethnic minorities the situation was even more alarming, according to Llewellyn Cornelius's findings in the National Medical

Expenditure Survey: "Between 1977 and 1987, the percent of uninsured African Americans grew from 18% to 25%. During the same period, the percent of uninsured Hispanic Americans increased from 20% to 35%, while the percent of uninsured whites grew from only 12% to 15%."[72] Other data from the National Medical Expenditure Survey[73] indicated that minority populations' health access gains during the 1970s were being threatened and racial health disparities in insurance coverage were increasing once again, and suggested that "interventions to solve the insurance problem would have a positive effect on health care access for minorities,"[74] according to Cornelius.

This—what pundits and the public alike have described as a "nonsystem"— has been promulgated largely through the economic and political power wielded by insurance companies. For example, "From 1981 to the first half of 1991 ... the insurance industry's political action committees (or PACs) contributed $60 million to members of Congress, with much of the money going to the chairs and key members of health-related committees."[75] Not only conservative politicians were beneficiaries, but also many who were considered liberals, centrists, or progressives. Recipients of AMA, insurance company, and medical industry PAC money were often influential members of Congress overseeing and regulating the nation's health system. Although the complex interactions between the insurance and medical industries, interest group politics, the politicians involved in the process, and political financing are outside the scope of this book, they undoubtedly exert and produced immense effects on the agenda-setting and political processes affecting health care. There was little wonder the level of public discontent had reached an all-time high and was strong enough to influence major political elections by 1992 and 1993.[76]

Notwithstanding the rising tide of public discontent with the U.S. health system, especially its financing and politics, dramatic changes took place in how health care was paid for during the 12 years of the Reagan-Bush era. By the 1990s commercial health insurance companies such as Prudential and John Hancock wrote more than 50 percent of the health insurance policies in the United States. The market share of voluntary health insurance companies, Blue Cross and Blue Shield, dropped from over 50 percent before the 1960s to 45 percent in 1965 to 33 percent in 1986. The decline continues today. Despite the "Blues's" long history of enjoying state-mandated organizational privileges in exchange for their public service image, accepting everyone despite their health status and attempting to preserve community rating, the competitive disadvantages they suffered against commercial insurance carriers engaged in "cherry picking," experience rating, commercial marketing, and targeting younger, healthier, populations combined with a spate of recent managerial scandals threatens their survival.[77] Their reflexive imitation of the strategies, policies, and tactics of their for-profit competitors was so effective that the "Blues," as was previously mentioned, lost their tax-exempt status in 1986.

A major structural change in health care financing was the growth of self-insured or self-funded health plans. Companies, as employers, began this process as a means of controlling their health care costs: "Self-insurance refers to the assumption of claim risk by an employer, union, or other group, whereas self-funding refers to the payment of insurance claims from an established bank or trust account."[78] Potential savings accrue from such plans, as they are exempt from most premium taxes and companies retain the interest on reserves. Moreover, these plans have been exempt from much state insurance regulation and state laws mandating minimum benefits under the Employee Retirement Income Security Act of 1974 (ERISA). Characterizing the law, Howard Berliner, a professor of health policy at the New School for Social Research in New York, noted: "federal laws like ERISA barred states from regulating existing company health plans."[79] In many states this allows them to disenroll employees or their covered family members with high-cost medical conditions, for example. Extending ERISA's protection for those "administering an employee benefit plan" beyond self-insurance situations, "H.M.O.s like U.S. Healthcare, Kaiser Permanente, Prudential and Pacificare have asserted in court that malpractice claims against them are pre-empted by the 1974 law,"[80] Robert Pear noted in the November 17, 1996, *New York Times*. This controversial application of the law has been upheld in courts even when the HMOs have set the guidelines for treatment, economically intimidated the physicians' practices participating in the plan,* and limited access to medical specialists. In regard to self-insured plans, Anthony R. Kovner also noted: "One common operational mode of self-insured plans is the administrative services only (ASO) plan. Under an ASO plan, the insurance carrier handles the claims and benefits paperwork for the self-insured group. Insurance claims are normally paid from an employer bank account."[81] By 1986, 46 percent of companies were at least partially self-insured. This grew to 67 percent by 1992. Over the past two decades these developments have greatly enhanced the power and authority of major corporations and employers as major health care players—sometimes pitting them politically, for the first time, against the AMA and other components of the medical-industrial complex.

Between 1980 and 1993, all three major private, nongovernment, structural financing mechanisms, commercial insurance, Blue Cross/Blue Shield, and self-insured plans engaged in a range of new insurance approaches and the establishment of new relationships between insurers and providers. Although fee-for-service insurance still accounted for 62 percent of the health insurance market in 1992, only 12 percent was the classical unmanaged type. Fifty percent of private fee-for-service policies used some "managed" care approaches to limit utilization. HMOs, integrating a wide range of health services delivery with insurance for health care, often on a capitated basis, grew to capture 9 percent of the market.

---

*AMA lawyers have alleged that "H.M.O.'s can force doctors to change their clinical decisions by threatening to terminate their contracts." *Source:* Pear R. HMO's using federal law to deflect malpractice suits. *The New York Times,* Sunday, November 17, 1996, 24.

This "managed" care form of health insurance is reshaping the way Americans relate to the health sector—if not by the numbers directly enrolled, then by the pervasive influence of its concepts and methodologies. One HMO-influenced approach, preferred provider organizations (PPOs), "which either limit beneficiaries to a set list of physicians and other providers or provide economic incentives to use physicians who have offered discounts to the insurer,"[82] expanded rapidly to capture 13 percent of the market. One variant of this arrangement is "independent practice associations" (IPAs), which "charge capitation rates to subscribers (or their employers) but provide care through doctors in private practice, whom they generally pay by fee-for-service, though at a discount from their usual rates."[83] Another variant of the managed care/HMO theme, point-of-service (POS) plans—which usually require members to go to providers within their networks while also allowing them to go to nonnetwork providers at much higher costs—accounted for 16 percent of the market. In all, the definition of "managed" care has grown beyond the classic capitated, closed, internally controlled and staffed health financing and delivery entity exemplified by Kaiser and Puget Sound of 25 years ago to encompass a variety of management arrangements and schemes to control health care costs and utilization. Lee, Benjamin, and Weber summed up the growth of relatively classic HMOs, stating: "Between 1980 and June 1995, enrollment in health maintenance organizations and other managed care organizations more than quintupled, from 9 million to 51.5 million people."[84] Thus at least one in five Americans now receives health care from some type of formally designated HMO—which number 630, according to recent Group Health Association of America figures.*

Based on a growing body of evidence, the health care financing system and its coterie of conservative politicians and health policy experts seem staunchly determined to preserve capitalist health "markets"[85] even at the risk of raising the public's ire. As Jane Bryant Quinn observed in a *Newsweek* column in 1997, many health care researchers and academics seemed to be reluctant about criticizing the competitive "market" ideology. She recalled one response to her queries on how HMOs are working: "'The free market doesn't reward high quality; it rewards lower costs,' one prominent health-care researcher lamented to me. 'But don't quote me,' he said, 'or I'll lose my job.'"[86] The reputable public media demonstrate no such reluctance. In fact, there is evidence of a growing public dissatisfaction with managed care and HMOs.[87] Indicators of this growing public mood include, but are not limited to: (1) increasing litigation against and regulation of the managed care/HMO industry as means of "defending" patients and providers in response to managed care/HMO's draconian cost-cutting measures;[88] (2) decisions made by diversified groups of participants in profit-making activities within the health arena, HMOs, and managed care entities in pursuit of profits—instead of providing a vital

---

*These are 1996 figures. *Source:* Kovner AR, Jones S. *Health Care Delivery in the United States.* 6th ed. New York: Springer Publishing, 1999.

public service—have increasingly priced health care out of the reach of average Americans and have soaked the system to benefit the rich, further limited access to quality basic services, pushed more working Americans out of the system, and raised public enmity;[89] (3) economic stresses produced by health "markets" and public distrust of government shred the health care "safety net" crucial to growing populations of uninsured and underinsured Americans;[90] (4) growing evidence that HMO–managed care entities misrepresent what they do in the name of "cost containment" and under the ERISA guise of "administering employment benefit plans"—placing a positive spin on their performance;[91] and (5) a growing adversarial relationship between patients and the health system as a result of the managed care/HMO phenomenon and the corporate takeover of health care.[92]

Other effects and results of corporatization and alterations in health financing toward a "market"-like health system include, but are not limited to: (1) deterioration in overall access and suggestions of adverse effects on the health status and outcomes of particular disadvantaged populations;[93] (2) a perception of declining quality of care;[94] and (3) the potential for creating a permanent "health and health-care underclass" by disproportionately affecting disadvantaged groups, especially African Americans; low-wage, working Americans; and the elderly poor, whose health status, outcomes, and utilization are not improving at acceptable rates.[95] Moreover, there is abundant evidence that the increasingly commercially based health system is becoming contaminated with overt and covert signs of fraud, unethical management, and corruption.[96] Despite these concerns, the decentralized and variegated paradigms of U.S. health care financing have been projected as holding the promise of efficiency, controlling costs, and prudent resource allocation through "market" and competitive forces.[97]

Health care costs continued to escalate despite the intensification of cost-control measures throughout the era. Some of these variegated cost-control measures included health planning, which in the United States was primarily used to control capital investments in health care; entrepreneurial-oriented "managed care" devices such as capitation,* price negotiation and discounting, provider bonuses for cost savings, and selective providers; regulatory control through pre-certification, rigid treatment guidelines, restrictive pharmacy lists, and utilization review (UR) seeking to achieve efficiency in the basic unit of service and the patient-practitioner encounter and alternative retrospective quality assurance (QA) driven reimbursement measures—compared to open-ended, classical, fee-for-service, cost-plus, and retrospective reimbursement; entry into "competitive" commercial alternate health delivery models such as outpatient surgical centers, ambulatory primary health centers ("doc in the box"), and commercial emergency medical services (e.g., staffing and administering ERs, ambulance and emergency and non-emergency transfer services); encouragement of the public to join HMOs—a highly touted cost-modulating measure that Americans seemingly

---

*See Glossary of Commonly Used Managed Care, Health Policy, and Health Reform Terms.

never trusted; and prospective payment systems (PPS) to providers such as capitation and diagnosis related group (DRG) reimbursement. Throughout this period of partial regulation (e.g., DRGs, managed care/HMO measures, and PPS), government cutbacks on socially based medical programs, and implementation of "market competition" and entrepreneurialism throughout the 1980s, the basic incentives for increasingly costly health services remained.

Determinants of how much it costs to operate the health care system are what Starr labeled "upstream" choices: "investment decisions in the physical capacity of the system, its technological complexity, and the specialized training of its key decision-makers, doctors."[98] Federal policies in place since the 1960s were now producing more than twice as many physicians, the overwhelming majority of whom chose specialty practice in high-income areas and billed in a fee-for-service mode. Additionally, as Starr noted: "Investment in hospitals and high-tech services grew rapidly, stimulated in part by generous provisions in Medicare for reimbursing hospitals' capital costs. Whatever might have been accomplished by regulation was undone by these developments."[99] Efforts to alter the financial incentives, the organization of medical practice, the pharmaceutical and medical supply infrastructure, and the hospitals—in other words, a fundamental restructuring and reorganization of the U.S. health system—while enforcing halfway attempts to control costs, were doomed.

Therefore, despite the fact that managed care/HMO and cost control principles became dominant factors in the health system, by 1993 advocates of these strategies, such as Alain Enthoven, admitted in health policy journals such as *Health Affairs* "that managed care plans ... apparently have not helped to slow national health expenditures."[100] Seemingly, the only souls required to sacrifice as a result of stringent cost-control measures in the United States' variant of "managed" care and HMOs were large subsets of typical American patients such as the elderly and poor, the chronically ill, Black and other disadvantaged minorities, the working class, and medically indigent Americans (MIAs),[101] while the beneficiaries of the increasingly market-oriented health system were the providers (e.g., doctors and hospitals) and insurance companies. By 1999, at a Harvard University conference it was reported that Paul Ellwood, "[t]he father of the HMO movement, had given up on the ability of doctors and health plans to guarantee safe medical care and ... call[ed] on strong government regulation to improve the 'unacceptable' quality of American medicine."[102] Much of the angst vented in the 1992–1993 election cycle represented the public's realization that it had been misled by its health establishment, academic and health education institutions, media, and politicians, who had portrayed "managed care" and the "market" as panaceas for America's health system dilemmas. But "managed care"—whose cost saving performance as of 1992 led John K. Iglehart to state in the *New England Journal of Medicine*, "The evidence regarding whether managed care plans saves money is mixed"[103]—and the "market," often cast in the rubric of public health, could not touch the depths of the problems. American distrust of government, and overreliance on "market" forces to solve social problems and political machinations have led to muddled thinking and policies on the financing and organization of health care for the poor and disadvantaged minorities. Medicaid managed care and other HMO settings are proving to be unreliable for many vulnerable populations and financially threatening to the "safety net" providers they depend on for their health care.

The basis for the "dilemmas" actually lay in the realms of unaddressed ideological, structural, "process," "outcome," class, political economy, medical-social, and race problems. By 1999, conceding that competition had "temporarily tamed" 1980s double-digit medical care inflation, "Ellwood conclude[d] that market forces will never work to improve quality, nor will voluntary efforts by doctors and health plans."[104] And evidence still mounts that the long-dreamed-of managed care and "market" system promise of true cost-containment and savings through "competition" has not borne fruit,[105] according to many observers and experts.[106]

### Hospitals and Nursing Homes: Changing Roles, Changing Masters

As Kovner has noted, "The hospital remains the institutional center of the U.S. health care system despite the enormous pressure in recent years to move the focus of care to the ambulatory setting."[107] Arising between the eighteenth and early twentieth centuries as public institutions for the poor and, later, as socioculturally sensitive health service providers to various discrete communities at both the patient and professional levels,* at least three-fourths of the nation's hospitals remain private and predominantly voluntary in the 1990s. Notwithstanding their race and class flaws, previously discussed in great detail, these predecessor institutions had a largely eleemosynary and service orientation. During the mid-twentieth century these characteristics changed as hospitals joined the money economy and became businesses.[108] The health system's ongoing corporate transformation encouraged this process, and hospital care grew from 9.2 percent (1980) to become 40 percent of the nation's health expenditures and from 3.8 percent (1980) to 4.4 percent of the nation's GNP by 1986—declining slightly to 38 percent ($256 billion) and 4.1 percent GDP by 1990, probably due to managed care measures (e.g., discouraging hospitalization, shortening length of stay). Community hospitals' employment grew from 3,025,000 full-time equivalent staff in 1986 to 3,535,000 in 1991, pouring $225 billion, of which $102 billion was for labor, into the economy. This was up from $140.6 billion, of which $75.8 billion was for labor, in 1986.

Since the twentieth-century institutionalization of the American hospital and the rise of the nursing home after the 1930s, hospitals and nursing homes have remained the dominant American health care institutions. The number of acute

---

*Based on the long-term racial and class discrimination practiced by American hospitals, an argument could be made they did not meet the needs of the *entire* U.S. population.

care community general hospitals peaked in 1980 (6,229)—at the crest of a major hospital growth era between 1945 and 1980 energized by the private insurance revolution (1930s–1950s), the Hill-Burton Act (1946–1974), and the enactment of Medicare/Medicaid (1966)—and gradually declined by 1993 (5,579). By the early 1990s there were also some 880 specialty hospitals and 300 or so federal facilities (including VA and military hospitals). According to Marc Roberts at the Harvard School of Public Health (HSPH), "60 percent are not-for-profit entities, 26 percent are operated by local governments and 14 percent are owned by for-profit corporations."[109] Varying in size from 20 to more than 1,000 beds, they vary enormously in structure, activities, financing, and other features.

In response to cost-control efforts, the influences of diagnosis related groups (DRGs) and managed care, and the "managerial imperative," Iglehart's health care industry mantra and motivating force of the 1980s,[110] hospital occupancy rates decreased with regard to mean discharge rates (the ratio of total discharges in a year to number of beds) and average length of stay (LOS). Farley calculated the average occupancy rate of community hospitals in the United States as declining nearly 20 percent during the late 1980s,[111] a trend that prevailed into the 1990s. Simultaneously, as a result of the emergence of investor-owned and not-for-profit multihospital corporations in the industry, there were fewer independent hospitals. Kovner noted that, according to the American Hospital Association, "In 1991 multihospital systems owned, leased, or sponsored 2,368 hospitals and managed under contract 505 hospitals, putting more than 43 percent of U.S. hospitals under multihospital systems."[112] Despite a rise in ownership to nearly 15 percent of the nation's acute care hospital capacity by the mid-1980s, followed by a decline to less than 10 percent by the mid-1990s, the most important long-term impact the proprietary hospital industry had "may have been the transformation of the ethos and ideology of the health delivery system into a for-profit industry with a 'Wall Street' mentality and market orientation."[113]

Although some hospitals did well fiscally—despite their being hampered by suburban out-migration of their patients and professional staffs, vertical integration* problems, excess capacity, declining reimbursements for services, and inefficient technology wars to compete with other hospitals for patients and professional staffs—according to Robert J. Blendon at HSPH a significant portion of hospitals feared failure (43–46 percent between 1986–1990), were operating under distressed conditions (12 percent in 1990), or closed (4 percent between 1986–1989).[114] Most endangered by the "competitive strategy" encouraged by the Reagan-Bush administrations were rural hospitals, Black hospitals, inner-city hospitals, public and city hospitals, and teaching hospitals. These institutions, traditional "safety net" providers, were threatened by their lack of competitiveness

---

*Vertical integration—organizing a health system with various capabilities that can provide all levels of care (e.g., ambulatory centers → primary care hospitals → tertiary care [specialty] hospitals → long-term care facilities).

bred of their patient profiles of sicker, often MIAs; their unfamiliarity with managed care delivery and financing models; their need for substantial administrative system development; chronic provider and personnel shortages; for the Black hospitals, traditional discriminatory financing and administrative arrangements compounded by low esteem in most communities; and the shifts of service delivery from an acute, inpatient care focus to primary and clinic-based care.

Some teaching hospitals succumbed to the "competitive strategy" developed during this era while others made dramatic though unproven, adjustments. Represented by the Council of Teaching Hospitals (COTH), they declined in number from 358 to 285 between 1986 and 1991. Typically, these facilities "are larger and are located in large urban areas" and "offer more specialized services and provide more uncompensated care than non-COTH hospitals"[115] and traditionally serve as oases of up-to-date care for African American, poor, and inner-city populations. Although their missions of education, research, and patient care contribute to their strengths, "COTH members care for a disproportionate number of the poor."[116] Their representation of 6 percent of the nation's short-term nonfederal hospitals between 1990 and 1994 they "claimed between 45–50% of the total deductions for charity care ($2.98–5.6 billion respectively) and 27–28% of the deductions for bad debt (approximately $3.1–3.8 billion respectively)."[117] Despite their decreased numbers, the charity care and bad debt burdens borne by these inner city institutions increased from 1984 levels of $1.2 billion and $2.5 billion, respectively as they continued to care for more uninsured patients and underwrote more uncompensated care.[118] Their fragile position in the "competitive" commercial environment threatens the already limited access to quality care for African American and other underserved, inner-city populations. The health system's medical-social and medical educational integrity—which clouds America's future as the world leader in biomedical science and technology—is threatened as well.

As demographic disadvantage and patient profiles became major factors, "turfing" and "dumping" became prominent patient management strategies,* cost-shifting was curbed or ended, reimbursement rates dropped, and tax-supported public and charity financing dried up, some rural, inner-city, teaching (e.g., Hubbard Hospital of Meharry Medical College), and public hospitals closed (e.g., Philadelphia General Hospital) or were "spun off" into freestanding corporations (e.g., Regional Center of Memphis [MED]).[119] Despite the fact that 5 percent of all U.S. hospital beds in the public hospitals of America's 100 largest cities dispensed 40.3 percent of the nation's computed charity care and 19.3 percent of the system's bad debt in their efforts to serve some of the nation's most underserved and least healthy populations, many of the remaining Black, inner-city, and public

---

*Turfing* and *dumping* are strategies wherein private hospitals, after ascertaining that a patient cannot pay (by performing a means test, or "billfold biopsy"), "consult with" or "transfer" such "undesirable" patients to public or charitable facilities for care. These practices became so prominent in the 1980s that laws were created to curtail these often unethical and occasionally dangerous acts.

hospitals—the bulwark of America's "safety net" health institutions that disproportionately served African American, Hispanic/Latino American, and other disadvantaged clientele—closed. As Emily Freidman's 1987 comprehensive *JAMA* series on public hospitals conveyed, neither the medical establishment, the hospital industry, nor health care planners had any regrets about the state of America's race- and class-biased and segregated health delivery system as they continued to plea for maintenance of the status quo.[120] Ironically, as these essential community providers (ECPs) closed due to "market" forces, much of the hospital expansion occurred in the already overbedded, underutilized, urban hospital markets remote from the underserved rural or inner-city populations. All these factors combined to create and accentuate tremendous access problems for already underserved Black, urban working-class and poor, and rural populations. The overt and implicit cynicism and denial were bad portents for the future of these populations in the commercialized health system. The onslaught of the HIV/AIDS epidemic, with its tremendous medical-social and fiscal outlay, which began to epidemiologically affect these same disadvantaged populations differentially during this period, may make health care institutions the flash points for breaking the back of the health system. The other major health care institution, the nursing home, does not present a more reassuring picture.[121]

Based on 1991 population projections, it is predicted that the United States needs 600,000 more nursing home beds by 2010. Despite there being 19,100 nursing homes and related care homes housing 1,624,200 beds by the late 1980s, "there is a recognized shortage of nursing home beds because the growth of the elderly population has outpaced the growth of beds."[122] Because of the national decline in hospital occupancy, 15 percent of 3,000 hospitals in an AHA survey planned to add long-term care beds in the future in spite of the fact that at least 24 percent of hospitals already owned skilled nursing facilities (SNFs), 12 percent owned intermediate care facilities (ICFs), 33 percent provided home health services, and 14 percent provided homemaker services. Over 75 percent of nursing homes are owned by proprietary organizations, 20 percent are owned by voluntary groups or hospitals, and 5 percent are government-owned. Although over 50 percent of nursing homes are operated independently, 28 percent were affiliated with chains (e.g., Beverly Enterprises, ARA, and Hillhaven) in 1977, growing to 41 percent by 1985. Bed and facilities shortages and crazy-quilt financing have created new and perpetuated old access problems for certain populations in need of long-term care. African American underrepresentation in nursing home populations in spite of their being sicker, surviving longer than Whites beyond age 75, and having fewer social supports in their homes has been a persistent, sometimes embarrassing, phenomenon plaguing the industry.

Some 16,000 nursing homes, about 86 percent of the industry in 1995, were certified by the Health Care Financing Administration (HCFA), the agency charged with inspecting and regulating them. Approximately 12 percent of nursing home revenues are paid by Medicare, and 52 percent are paid by Medicaid, "widely thought of as the Government's health insurance program for the needy," while "it is in fact the primary payer of nursing home bills for the elderly after they have exhausted their savings."[123] According to the Kaiser Foundation, the government assists over two-thirds of the people in nursing homes. In 1993 Medicare/Medicaid spent some $42 billion in nursing home bills for 1.4 million elderly Americans. Despite such massive expenditures, 36 percent of nursing home revenues came primarily from out-of-pocket patient resources in 1995 — from patients over two-thirds of whom are indigent within 1 year of nursing home admission. Typically, as Harrington, Himmelstein, and Woolhandler from the Working Group on Long-Term Care Program Design of the Physicians for a National Health Program describe the process: "To qualify for Medicaid, families must either be destitute or 'spend down' their personal funds until they are impoverished."[124] Most of these elderly people were "tax-paying, middle-class people until they got sick," according to Robin Toner of the *New York Times*.[125] With a cruel system fraught with a financing crisis wrought by the $38,000 average cost per year's care; questionable to poor quality of care being widespread throughout the industry, according to HCFA and *Consumer Reports*;[126] persistent allegations and evidence of discriminating against Medicaid recipients, less well-to-do candidates for admission, expensive-to-care-for sicker patients, and African Americans;[127] and a growing bed shortage, the industry seems predestined for harder times, more rounds of recrimination, and harsher castigations. As institutional health care costs escalate and the aging population creates more demand for long-term care, a diverse mix of health care (e.g., Medicare-certified Home Health Agencies [CHHAs], community-based services, hospice services, and adult day care and respite services) and housing services (e.g., assisted living, Continuing Care Retirement Communities [CCRCs], congregate living arrangements, and board-and-care homes) for the elderly will proliferate.[128]

### Government's Changing Role in Health Care

Between 1980 and 1993 the government's role in health care underwent dramatic changes. Riding a rising tide of public cynicism and anti-government sentiment, the Reagan administration implemented a third adaptation of conservative thought on the burgeoning health system. Previous conservative appeals to, and reliance upon, voluntarism and charity to achieve the health system's societal obligations — gored and buried during the liberal 1960s — followed by Nixon's Tory-like reformism embodied in government ideological and fiscal investments in managed care, HMOs, and regulation, gave way to a new conservative fundamentalism in health politics and economics. The health care cost inflation and hospital-cost containment battles raging since the late 1970s mobilized the anti-regulatory, reprivatization reliance on "market" competition and incentives and forces set on "reducing the government's role to a minimum." According to the *Oxford Textbook of Public Health*, the three major federal policy shifts advanced by the Reagan administration that directly affected health care were:

> (1) *significant reduction in federal expenditures for domestic social pro-grammes; (2) decentralization of programme authority and responsibility to the states, particularly through block grants; and (3) deregulation and greater emphasis on market forces and competition to address the problem of continuing increases in the costs of medical care.*[129]

Built upon traditional American political, economic, and social values and practices emphasizing private sector dominance, federalism, the American character, and pluralism, the governmental system extended its role of expanding the private health care system through public subsidy during the Reagan-Bush era.

Although the structure, diversity, and roles of the government units affecting the health system at the federal (1 unit), state (50 units), and local (84,955 units) levels changed little since the preceding period, their effects changed dramatically. (See Figure 7.3.) By 1993, of the total national health expenditure of $884 billion, the federal government spent $281 billion (32%), while state and local governments spent $107 billion (12%). Health care comprised almost 19 percent of federal government expenditures (up from 12% in 1980) and 12 percent of state and local government expenditures (down from 13% in 1990). The federal government continued to be the largest and most diverse governmental participant in the health system. "The stability and latest modest increase in *share* of funding has occurred in the context of rapid increases in total spending, causing the absolute amount of public spending to rise dramatically,"[130] as Anthony R. Kovner and Steven Jonas observed. The federal government controlled or participated in: the Medicare program, still the largest and most expensive program to finance hospital and physician services for elderly and disabled Social Security beneficiaries; the Medicaid program, now transformed* into the joint federal-state program to pay for medical care and long-term care of the aged, blind, and disabled (27% of recipients and 69% of expenditures) and poor families and their children (49% of recipients and 16% of expenditures); Department of Defense health expenditures for direct health care for military personnel and health insurance for military dependents; Department of Veteran's Affairs and Office of Personnel Management programs (federal employees health benefits); Department of Labor programs

---

*Medicaid was originally conceived of as a program for MIAs, especially poor children and their families; in 1976 it covered up to 65 percent of the poor. Through influences of the political process and powerful interest groups, the program now poorly finances artificially impoverished (by "spend down" mechanisms), largely White middle-class Americans (paying 52 percent of their nursing home bills), to whom it disburses almost 7 of 10 program dollars.

**Figure 7.3 Summary of Governments' Major Health Care Roles**

|  | Financing | Delivery | Regulation |
|---|---|---|---|
| **Federal** | Large role through Medicare and Medicaid; other categorical programs. | Operates facilities for veterans and Indians | Sets standards for Medicare providers; prohibits discrimination by providers; determines what drugs and devices may be sold. |
| **State** | Funds Medicaid, mental health, medical education, and public health programs. | Operates mental hospitals, health departments, and medical schools. | Regulates insurance industry; licenses facilities and personnel; establishes health codes. |
| **Local** | Subsidizes public hospitals; funds local health departments. | Operates county and municipal hospitals; operates local health departments. | Establishes local health codes. |

*Source*: Fig. 12.1. Summary of Governments' Major Health Care Roles. 325. In: Kovner AR. *Jonas's Health Care Delivery in the United States*. 5th ed. New York: Springer Publishing Company, 1995.

(occupational health and safety); Department of Transportation programs (highway and vehicle safety); Department of Justice programs (Bureau of Prisons); Environmental Protection Agency programs ; Department of Housing and Urban Development programs; and some 200 separate federal programs administered by U.S. Department of Health and Human Services (USDHHS), including the programs by NIH and the FDA, research and training services (e.g., mental health, substance abuse), construction of health facilities, categorical public health programs (e.g., childhood lead poisoning, maternal child health, STD programs, HIV/AIDS programs), and public health and health care services for American Indians and Alaska Natives.

Most significant during the period were the economic fluctuations producing a recession followed by a recovery with slow, but top-heavy, growth and an exploding federal deficit combined with tax cuts and regulations in The Equity and Fiscal Responsibility Act (TEFRA) of 1982—all of which "severely limited the fiscal capacity of the federal government to fund programmes" and "by requiring the development of a prospective payment system for hospitals ... initiated a major reform of the Medicare programme."[131] Despite Reagan's rhetorical commitment to deregulation and stimulation of pro-competition market forces, government "regulations to limit hospital reimbursement and physicians' fees ... increased dramatically"[132] during his administration.[133]

As the government's function as a public subsidizer and financier of the private system and competitive market grew and "market" mechanisms increasingly yielded distributional advantages for particular influential groups, certain mechanisms evolved to produce predictable patterns and results:

> *(1) A more costly health care system yields higher prices and incomes for suppliers—physicians, drug companies, and private insurers. (2) Private payment distributes overall system costs according to use (or expected use) of services, costing wealthier and healthier people less than finance from (income-related) taxation. (3) Wealthy and unhealthy people can purchase (real or perceived) better access or quality for themselves, without having to support a similar standard for others. Thus there is, and always has been, a natural alliance of economic interest between service providers and upper-income citizens to support shifting health financing from public to private sources.*[134]

These and other developments and actions seem to bear out Robert G. Evan's analysis of the resurgent interest in the respective roles of the state and "market" in health care during the Reagan-Bush era: "In practice, advocates have never wanted a truly competitive market, but rather one managed by and for particular private interests."[135] Overall U.S. health system performance throughout the era, especially with regard to Blacks and other disadvantaged minorities, the poor, and the working class, reinforces the "international experience over the last forty years," which "demonstrated that greater reliance on the market is associated with inferior system performance—inequity, inefficiency, high cost, and public dissatisfaction."[136] "The United States is the leading example,"[137] Evans noted in 1995. Alarmingly, "[W]hen Republicans announced their plans to reform Medicare, they renewed with a vengeance a long-languishing commitment to promote market principles as the basis for allocating health care resources,"[138] Iglehart observed.

Just as government policy had increased access and equity in the health system throughout the era of 1965 to 1980, its policies, or the absence of same in many instances, served to erode those parameters in the Reagan-Bush era. Despite public expenditures increasing from 26.2 percent of national health expenditures ($41.9 billion) in 1965 to 46.2 percent in 1995, and public spending for health jumping from $105.2 billion to $456.4 billion or 434 percent between 1980 and 1995, several striking observations were noted: (1) Medicaid coverage of the poor dropped from its high point of 65 percent in 1976 to 38 percent by 1988, recovering to 58 percent (especially between 1989 and 1993 in last-ditch efforts to include indigent pregnant women and their children and some of the working poor); (2) the uninsured population grew from 12.5 percent of the population in 1980 to 17.3 percent in 1993, most of whom were working Americans; (3) access to health care for the poor and minorities diminished, and adverse impacts on their health status and outcomes were confirmed; (4) consumer cost sharing increased; (5) the government failed to address the issues of uncompensated care or long-term care; and (6) there was an inadequate government response to the HIV/AIDS epidemic.[139] Throughout the era, the nation's public health system, traditionally federal, state, and local governmental functions, deteriorated.

Formal public health systems in existence since the nineteenth century, whose origins stretch back to the original American colonies, traditionally focused on concerns such as clean water and safe food supplies. A USDHHS report, *For a Healthy Nation: Returns on Investment in Public Health* (1995), revealed that the public health system was challenged by outbreaks of new infectious diseases such as HIV/AIDS, the Hanta virus in the American Southwest, the Ebola virus in Zaire, and familiar diseases with new patterns of resistance, such as tuberculosis. The system revealed weak points in its readiness, but rose to combat the problems. However, while "increasingly being asked to provide medical care for the indigent and uninsured,"[140] public health officials were also charged with applying their expertise to a range of new, often troublesome, social issues with health implications that have recently been framed in public health terms such as violence, unintended teenage pregnancies, substance abuse, and a host of conditions associated with high-risk health behaviors. Therefore:

> At the same time priorities and funds were being shifted among and to new public health challenges, increasing numbers of uninsured Americans were adding responsibilities to public health agencies. More are becoming dependent on public hospitals, health departments, and community health clinics to meet their needs for medical care and mental health services.[141]

The result was that while public institutions such as city hospitals were being stripped of resources because of tax revolts and anti-government sentiment politically, "national, state, and local health agencies have become increasingly involved in providing basic direct health-care services to those shut out of the private health insurance system."[142] Concurrent with the public sector being forced to prop up the market-based, "mainstream," private health system, the dominant and increasingly commercial system is astronomically driving up the price of providing personal health services and is forcing more people out of all systems, making it impossible for many Americans to receive even basic health services.

This nightmarish merry-go-round within the health system—itself decreasing the numbers of medically insured Americans, increasing the numbers of MIAs, with shrinking support to provide care for them—questions the viability of the U.S. system of private competitive insurance as a financing mechanism and the commerical "market" as a delivery system. Henry J. Aaron of the Brookings Institution described the problem in 1991:

> First, insurance creates incentives for patients to demand and for physicians to provide health care that is expensive relative to benefits. Second, powerful forces are reducing the capacity of insurance to serve as many people in the future as it has in the past. Third, any system of health insurance that involves multiple channels of payment to providers for

> *each patient will have major advantages, but those advantages will be*
> *purchased at enormous administrative costs. Fourth, multiple channels of*
> *payment inherent in the current U.S. financing system make it difficult or*
> *impossible to reduce the amount of low-benefit, high-cost care....These*
> *propositions add up to a dilemma. The United States can continue its*
> *current financing system without major change. But if it does so, strong*
> *forces will act to reduce the number of people with health insurance and*
> *to continue driving up the amount spent on ... care.*[143]

This complex and virtually automatic mechanism for increasing the numbers and proportion of MIAs, a problem with deep political and ideological roots, not only translates into some of the unassailable health system inefficiencies that Woolhandler and Himmelstein referred to in their 1991 *New England Journal of Medicine* article[144] but also portends fewer resources for essential public health services.

The ten *essential elements** necessary for the promotion and preservation of the public's health, which include population-based services upon which the "goals of reducing preventable death and disease and increasing the span of health life for all Americans at an affordable price depend,"[145] include:

> *Conducting a community diagnosis*—collecting, managing, and moni-
> toring health status and analyzing health-related data to identify
> community health problems and forming a basis for information-based
> decision making.
> *Preventing and controlling epidemics*—diagnosing, investigating, and
> containing diseases, injuries, health problems, and health hazards in
> the community.
> *Promoting healthy lifestyles*—informing, educating, and empowering
> people about health issues.
> *Providing targeted outreach and forming partnerships*—ensuring access to
> services for all vulnerable populations and developing culturally appro-
> priate care while developing and implementing policies and plans that
> support individual and community health efforts.
> *Mobilizing the community for action*—mobilizing community partnerships
> to identify and solve health problems.
> *Providing a safe and healthy environment*—maintaining clean and safe air,
> water, food, and facilities by enforcing laws and regulations that protect
> health and ensure safety.
> *Providing personal health care services*— linking people to needed personal
> health services and ensuring the provision of health care when other-
> wise unavailable.

---

*The ten essential elements for any community striving for the highest level of health possible were developed by the National Association of County Health Officials (NACHO) in 1994 in response to the 1988 IOM report, *The Future of Public Health*.

*Providing laboratory testing*—identifying disease agents.

*Measuring performance, effectiveness, and outcomes of health services*—evaluating and monitoring health care providers and the health care system.

*Promoting research and innovation*—conducting research for new insights and innovative solutions to health problems.[146]

The substantial shift of public health resources into provision of personal health services means that most of the ten are being neglected in the United States. Violation of the public health principle and ideal "access to a personal health-care delivery system that is supported by a strong public health system"[147] which maximizes the public's health, displays another American entrepreneurial health systems'*[148] dilemma.

This imbalance between the private and public sectors—which some view as a manipulation and even obstruction of the latter's mission as the government stands aside observing—resulted in only 1.6 percent of the total health budget being expended on vital public health services, according to 1994 and 1995 Public Health Foundation and CDC documents. As Lee, Benjamin, and Weber noted:

> *Between 1981 and 1993, estimated national health expenditure increased more than 210 per cent. During that same period, funds for population-based activities by state and local health agencies grew by only about two-thirds of that rate. States and localities have decreased their support for disease and injury surveillance, health education, and children's programmes. At the federal level, growth in spending for public health was limited largely to HIV/AIDS and immunization, often at the expense of public health needs.[149]*

These trends, compounded by the aforementioned pressures and diversion of scant resources to provide medical care to the indigent, have "eroded the capacity of state and local public health agencies to fulfill their basic community-wide responsibilities."[150] This erosion of the public health infrastructure helps explain why "old health problems are re-emerging, avoidable epidemics of waterborne and foodborne illnesses are occurring with more frequency, and unhealthy personal behaviours that contribute to the morbidity associated with numerous chronic diseases are also on the rise."[151] The new outbreaks of *Cryptosporidium* in Wisconsin's water supply and recent multistate outbreaks of *Escherichia coli*, with resulting deaths, morbidity, and enormous, if not incalculable, costs, may predict the health future of the United States if no corrective actions are taken by both the government and private sectors.[152]

---

*Milton Roemer contends that the United States is the sole health system in a highly industrialized country that can be categorized as an "entrepreneurial health system" as of 1997.

### The Changing Health Care Work Force

For the past 50 years health care employment has grown faster than overall employment in the American economy. Between 1983 and 1994 the total U.S. work force grew by 24 percent while the total health industry work force grew by 42 percent, to nearly 12 million people. The slowing in growth of the hospital work force to 17 percent during this period may indicate that current health system changes are slowing the growth in jobs in some components of the health sector. Health care system changes are dictating the numbers and types of workers and where and how they will practice and work. As Christine Kovner and Edward S. Salsberg noted: "The transformation of health care is disrupting historic roles for physicians, nurses, and other health care professionals. Increasing corporatization of health care, competition, the expansion of managed care, the development of integrated delivery systems, and new technologies—all have an impact on the workforce."[153] Major factors affect the work force, including some of the following:

- As competition expands, health care facilities and organizations are far more concerned with costs, productivity, and outcomes than in the past, leading to a reassessment of how many workers are needed and how they are used.

- Hospitals, the largest source of employment in the health field, are under pressure to reduce costs. Many are reducing staff and redesigning their operations.

- Care is shifting from inpatient to ambulatory care settings.

- HMOs, other managed care arrangements, and other purchasers of service are constraining and limiting the roles of physicians, reducing their autonomy.

- Many settings are substituting lower-cost workers.

- All settings are concerned with customer relations and patient satisfaction, and most sites want workers who are flexible, computer-literate, and customer-oriented.[154]

Little appreciated is the fact that the health care work force is one of the new labor categories in which African Americans and other disadvantaged minorities are overrepresented (previous labor categories in which Blacks were prominent were agricultural workers and domestics). (See Table 7.1.) Moreover, the class, race, and gender characteristics of, and problems facing, the American health sector labor force resemble those of Western Europe in many ways.

Most scientific bibliographies referring to the health care work force emphasize physicians. Although the number of allopathic patient care physicians nearly doubled and the physician-to-population ratio increased from 135:100,000 to

Table 7.1 Occupational Structure of the U.S. Labor Force in the Health Sector (by percent)

| | Percentage of Health Sector Labor Force | | Percentage of Jobs in Category Held by Women | | Percentage of Jobs in Category Held by African-Americans | |
|---|---|---|---|---|---|---|
| | 1970 | 1987 | 1970 | 1987 | 1970 | 1987 |
| Physicians | 7.3 | 6.9 | 6.9 | 18.2 | 3.0 | 4.0 |
| Dentists, pharmacists | 6.5 | 5.0 | 7.9 | 9.2 | 2.5 | 3.0 |
| Administrators, scientists | 3.5 | 9.0 | 30.0 | 42.0 | 5.0 | 6.0 |
| Therapists | 3.4 | 3.0 | 76.0 | 80.0 | 7.0 | 8.0 |
| Technologists, technicians | 8.0 | 9.0 | 69.0 | 72.0 | 18.0 | 19.0 |
| Registered nurses | 17.1 | 11.1 | 97.0 | 97.0 | 6.0 | 9.0 |
| Clerical workers | 8.0 | 14.0 | 93.0 | 94.0 | 19.0 | 20.0 |
| Nonclerical workers | 46.0 | 44.0 | 82.0 | 84.0 | 22.0 | 23.0 |
| Total | 100.0 | 100.0 | 72.0 | 78.0 | 18.0 | 22.0 |

*Source:* Navarro V. *Dangerous to Your Health: Capitalism in Health Care.* New York: Monthly Review Press, 1993, 101.

216:100,000 people between 1975 and 1995(a 60 percent increase), the overall percentage of physicians in the health care labor force appears to be declining. (See Table 7.1.). Increasingly important in the agenda-setting, policy-making, and program implementation roles for the health labor force are senior administrators and corporate executives. Despite their lack of medical training or clinical perspective, they are rapidly displacing physicians, senior nurses, pharmacists, dentists, and other health professionals in these important roles. However, this highly paid upper echelon of the health care work force (approximately 15 percent), predominantly White male executives and physicians, contrasts strongly with the middle group, the 32 percent of the health care work force, made up of registered nurses, administrators, accountants, therapists, technologists, and technicians, which is predominantly female, with substantial minority representation, and lower middle class. The bulk of the health care work force, comprising almost 60 percent, is "the army of blue-collar workers in lower-paid occupations, who are disproportionately members of minority groups."[155] This heterogenous group also includes clerical and nonclerical workers, most of whom are women and many of whom are working poor. (See Table 7.1.)

The U.S. health care work force displays the highest income differentials among all developed countries. Average net incomes (i.e., income after taxes) range from $890,000 annually (32 times a nurse's salary) for chief executives of the large insurance companies, $850,000 annually (30 times a nurse's salary) for the average physician specialist, and $150,000 annually (5 times a nurse's salary) for a generalist physician to $28,000 a year for the average nurse and $16,000 annually for the average cleaning person in the hospital. By any standard, most of the workers in the health sector are poorly paid. One health analyst pointed out (see Figure 7.4):

> *If we compare the standard of living of the labor force in the health sector with that of the labor force as a whole in 1990, we find that the standard of living was much lower for health workers: while 30 percent of the overall labor force was considered "poor," 50 percent of the health sector labor force fell into this category.*[156]

"'Poor' is defined here as a family that has just enough income to buy the minimum required food, has no money for recreation, lives in low-quality and low-rent housing, has no savings, drives a used car or uses public transportation, and purchases new clothes only every three years."[157] Health care workers are also poorly organized, with less than 18 percent belonging to unions. This mirrors the health care work forces in Great Britain, where 43 percent of kitchen workers in the National Health Service are immigrants from the British Commonwealth, and in Germany, Switzerland, and France, where 40 percent, 60 percent, and 38 percent, respectively, of all hospital workers are immigrants. Critical to the economies and health systems of these countries, they provide a "docile" working class without full citizenship or voting rights, thus representing a "third world within the first world."[158] Employer associations, their political functionaries and instruments, and the media divide the working class through racism, multiculturalism, and perpetuating interest group politics.[159]

Despite the previously mentioned and variegated efforts to solve the U.S. health system's physician maldistribution problem since 1980, only one-third of practicing physicians are generalists, compared to two-thirds practicing as specialists. Active generalist physicians per 100,000 population increased only 13 percent

**Figure 7.4  Standard of Living of the U.S. Labor Force and the Health Sector Labor Force (by percent)**

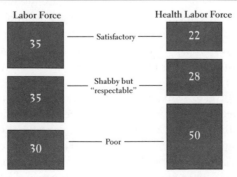

*Source:* Navarro V. *Dangerous to Your Health: Capitalism in Health Care.* New York: Monthly Review Press, 1993, 103.

compared to 24 percent for specialists; and between 1980 and 1993 the number of active generalist doctors per 100,000 population increased 20 percent, compared to 29 percent for specialist doctors. Moreover, while one-third of physicians' assistants practiced in communities of less than 50,000 population, only 12 percent of nonfederal physicians practiced in nonmetropolitan areas as of 1993. "[T]he Public Health Foundation's Bureau of Health Professions projects a year 2000 shortage of 35,000 generalist physicians and a surplus of 115,000 specialist physicians if current patterns of specialty choice and numbers of graduates persist,"[160] according to the Council on Graduate Medical Education's (CGME) 1995 projections. The massive increases in numbers of medical school graduates over the past 3 decades have done little to correct the shortage of providers in underserved inner city and rural areas. The recent attacks on affirmative action by the courts may further limit the production of African American, Hispanic-Latino, Native American, and other disadvantaged minority physicians with proven track records of serving in their own underserved communities.

The number of actively practicing registered nurses (RNs) increased from 1.9 million in 1992 to 2.1 million in 1997—which included 53,799 clinical nurse specialists, 63,191 nurse practitioners (NPs), 30,386 nurse anesthetists, and 6,534 nurse midwives (which declined in number since 1992). With the rapid changes wrought by managed care regarding professional roles, responsibilities, and functions, in nursing care, "The issues for the twenty-first century will likely focus on scope of practice, prescriptive authority, and reimbursement."[161] Expansion of authority and utilization of advanced practice nurses (e.g., NPs and nurse midwives) will be likely, especially if financial barriers to health care are removed.

There are also dramatic changes in the health industry work force based on relative growth of labor sectors and the settings in which they work. The fastest-growing setting is other health services (including home care), with an annual growth rate of 10.6 percent from 1983 to 1994. Running a distant second is the work force employed in offices of physicians, dentists, and other health practitioners, growing at a 4.9 percent clip during the same period, probably a reflection of the strong trend toward ambulatory setting for health care delivery. Hospital employment, still 40 percent of the work force, has stabilized and may begin to drop due to the major organizational changes, competition, and challenges posed by managed care. Any changes will have profound effects on job opportunities in the Black community. Employment in long-term care facilities, currently employing at least 1.3 million full-time equivalents (FTEs), and home health care agencies is expected to grow—with increasing needs associated with managed care pressures for out-of-hospital care and the aging of the population. However, there is a ubiquitous, silent, almost predatory segment of the work force expanding and threatening to overwhelm the entire U.S. health system if it is not recognized, regulated, and controlled.

The rapidly growing work force that is extremely hard to track is the administrative and clerical work force. The administrative and clerical work force, which constituted 18 percent of U.S. health employment in 1968, accounted for 27 percent in 1996, and this is an undercount. Because their ubiquity in doctors' offices and ambulatory facilities, where they are often not catagorized as such, administrative and clerical workers are difficult to count. As Woolhandler, Himmelstein, and Lewontin noted in the February 1996, *American Journal of Public Health* and the *Center for National Health Program Studies Chartbook*:

> Over the past 30 years there has been a steep increase in administrative and clerical employment in U.S. health care, and a much smaller increase in clinical personnel. The number of health care managers grew from 129,000 in 1968 to more than 1 million by 1996. The number of clerical and administrative support personnel rose from 590,000 in 1968 to more than 2 million by 1996.[162]

Kovner and Salsberg recognized the trend, noting that "there has been a significant growth in employment ... in support services for health maintenance organizations ... and other managed care organizations"; however, they noted the niche's diversity and observed that it "includes nurses, physicians, and clerical staff for utilization review, quality monitoring, case management, customer relations, and other functions."[163] Little appreciated is the fact that the bureaucratic costs and burdens this sector consumed amounted to between 19.3 and 24.1 percent, according to how it was calculated, of U.S. health spending as early as 1987. The trend has continued, if not worsened, as private carrier waste, costs of fragmentation (more payers to bill), lack of comprehensiveness in coverage (administering the multiple levels of "coverage," pre-approval, billing-denial cycles), and emphasis on micromanagement have proliferated under the American version of "managed" care. This shift of health care dollars to administration instead of clinical care is beginning to adversely affect quality of care, as nurses and physicians report more and sicker patients with less time to care for them, doctors are urged to shun the sick, dissatisfaction with care and caring levels rise, and "market competition" chills medical and clinical research.[164] Health care system deficiencies of this magnitude are now affecting the majority of the U.S. patient population, not just African Americans, working-class Americans, MIAs, and the disadvantaged.[165]

### Health Care Sectors in Flux: Education-Research and Ambulatory Care

With the changes wrought by managed care and the world's only "market"-driven entrepreneurial health system, the health professions education and research infrastructures plateaued in girth and production between 1980 and the early 1990s, but displayed alarming inabilities to adapt to a threatening new environment. Enrollments in the nation's 125 allopathic and 17 osteopathic medical schools had been relatively stable since the 1980s, with graduations ranging between 15,300 and 16,300 per year. The most striking change in medical school graduates was the increase of women graduates from 16.2 percent in 1975 to 40.9 percent by 1995–1996. Despite the decrease in demand for upper-level, expensive-to-train clinical personnel such as physicians and nurses, production of these health professionals continued to increase or remain stable. Although the number of physicians approximately doubled and the number of nurses roughly tripled between 1968 and 1996, physician representation in the health care work force declined from 11 percent to 6 percent, and the employment of nurses in the work force decreased from 41 percent to 38 percent.

The medical education system has been openly criticized "for not encouraging primary care, for overemphasizing high-tech tertiary care, for emphasizing organ systems rather than the whole patient, for not educating more underrepresented minorities, and for not preparing physicians to work in the managed care environment."[166] These problems have been accentuated by a postgraduate training system some consider "out of control." Kovner and Salsberg noted:

> *Throughout the 1980s and early 1990s there has been a sharp increase in the total number of residents and specialty areas in which physicians could train. The number of residents increased by 42% from 1982 to 1995. During this same period, the number of first-year residents rose ... 13%, from 18,972 in 1982 to 21,372 in 1995. The rapid growth in the total number of residents reflects the sharp increase in the number of residents going on to subspecialty training.*[167]

Compounding this physician surplus, 33 percent of the excess first-year residency slots* were filled by international medical school graduates (IMGs). Despite more physicians' and nurses' functions being appropriated by physicians assistants, advanced training nurses (e.g., nurse practitioners, nurse midwives), and lay-allied health personnel as dictated by the demands of managed care, the number of residency, specialty, and subspecialty training programs has continued to grow. Despited special efforts to support the Black medical schools by the Congresional Black Caucus (CBC) led by Congressman Louis Stokes (D-OH) these excesses have never effectively addressed the deficient number of generalist or specialty physicians of African American or other underrepresented minority persuasion.

For each resident in training in 1993, hospitals received approximately $184,000 annually, embedded in complex hospital reimbursement formulas used by Medicare and Medicaid for graduate medical education (GME).[168] With these facts in mind, this high level of public financing for GME, totaling $8.6 billion in 1995, has been hard to justify and is being reconsidered. "Congress has considered

---

*In 1995 there were 16,072 U.S. medical school graduates to fill 21,372 first-year residency slots.

legislation to decrease this financing, but efforts have been blocked by concerns with the impact on teaching hospitals and care for the poor in inner cities that are served by residents,"[169] according to Iglehart. The Pew Health Professions Commission (1995) also recommended that U.S. medical schools reduce graduates by 20 percent in anticipation of a physician surplus and increasing influence of managed care.[170] Moreover, evidence is accumulating that total reliance on the "market" is not producing appropriate numbers of trained public health, dental, nursing, or allied health professional personnel to provide rational staffing patterns while maintaining quality personal and public health care.

There is also growing evidence suggesting that the shift of more health funding into profits, overhead, and personal health care by managed care and HMOs is threatening clinical research.[171] As John S. Sergent, M.D., chairman of the Department of Medicine at St. Thomas Hospital in Nashville, Tennessee, noted, "The simple fact is that large university-based hospitals and their teaching and research programs are much more difficult to streamline to be competitive," based on standards set by "an insurance company concerned only with patient care and the bottom line."[172] Another dimension of the research problem was unearthed by a *Boston Globe* report on public research and private profit: "Tracking government-funded research to develop new treatments, a Spotlight team investigation revealed a billion-dollar taxpayers' subsidy for pharmaceutical companies already awash in profits. The investigation also documented a pattern of scientists and universities cashing in on government-funded inventions."[173] This recent pattern of misuse of public research funds for private profit is another disturbing trend emerging in the U.S. "market"-based health system.[174] Another dimension of commercialization's effects on the health system's research infrastructure has been unfolding since the last half of 1998 on television programs such as Emily Rooney's *Greater Boston*. Her investigative team focusing on the media has uncovered close relationships between university and laboratory-based medical researchers, the pharmaceutical industry, and media outlets. These relationships have financial and agenda-setting roots that are seldom revealed to the public when sometimes sensationalized health and medical research news stories break. The question is whether biomedical researchers, the media, or the public are well served by these developments. The HMO–managed care movement seems to be having more positive effects on the ambulatory care sector.

The shift from inpatient to outpatient care was one of the major phenomena shaping the 1990s health system. In 1980 there were about seven outpatient visits for every inpatient admission. By 1992 there were 409 million outpatient visits and 33 million inpatient admissions, for a ratio of 12.5 outpatient visits per inpatient admission. In 1993 the American Hospital Association noted: "Factors related to the shift from inpatient to outpatient care include changing reimbursement policies, technological innovations, and growth in the number of outpatient departments."[175] All these factors were promoted, promulgated, and sometimes imposed by the HMO–managed care industry.

Even surgery was shifted outside hospitals. Approximately 24 million surgical operations were performed in short-stay hospitals. Over half (54%) were performed as outpatient procedures. As Lee, Benjamin, and Weber observed, "Between 1980 and 1990 the percentage of surgical operations performed in short-stay hospitals on an outpatient basis tripled from 16 to 51 percent."[176] Augmenting the growth in outpatient operations in short-stay hospitals was a substantial increase in surgical procedures performed in free-standing ambulatory surgical centers. "Between 1984 and 1993 the number of free-standing ambulatory surgical centers increased from 330 to 1862, and the number of procedures performed increased from 518,000 to 3.2 million."[177] Advances in surgical techniques fostering less invasive procedures and anesthesiology and pain control advances also played major roles.

Financial disequilibriums created by the HMO–managed care movement— namely, increasing numbers of MIAs through noninsured, underinsured, and coverage denial mechanisms—caused distortions in utilization patterns, effectively neutralizing the overall health system cost savings generated by newly established outpatient delivery patterns. John Billings summed up some of these complex and interactive, sometimes dysfunctional, trends:

> While lack of insurance promotes underutilization, it also has the effect of steering uninsured patients to providers who are willing to provide care regardless of ability to pay. These providers tend to be institution-based providers, such as hospital outpatient departments, emergency rooms, and community-based clinics. . . . Medicaid patients also tend to be heavy utilizers of care in these settings, partially due to low rates of participation by office-based physicians.[178]

Costs in these institution-based training settings are usually higher for reasons previously discussed, and these providers' (e.g., public hospitals, NHCs, CHCs, health department clinics) efficiency and viability in the new competitive environment, emphasizing outpatient care and noninvasive surgical procedures, is questionable:

> Although the failure of some hospitals in this competitive environment is viewed by some as an effective means of reducing the huge oversupply of hospital beds in many communities, the impact of hospital closures and provider failures on access to care for low-income patients may be serious. The providers most at risk are those with the highest levels of care to vulnerable populations. With the loss of these traditional safety net providers, it is not clear that these patients will be assured access to

> *needed care from the remaining providers, who may be located further*
> *away and who have previously avoided provision of care to these*
> *patients.*[179]

The close relationship between health system movement toward ambulatory care and the destabilization of health care provision for African Americans, the poor (including the elderly poor), and MIAs is embodied in pressures to enroll Medicare (which is already paying less than 50 percent of elderly Americans' health care costs) and Medicaid populations into HMOs. There is some evidence that these health delivery and financing institutions may intend to discourage inpatient utilization and further limit use of services through outpatient overuse (relative to the severity of illness for sicker low-socioeconomic-status patients), limiting services (e.g., the number of office visits and use of expensive pharmaceuticals), and outright service denials as cost-cutting measures. Imposing such strategies on populations already suffering health disparities, access problems, and underutilization of services from barriers already built into the health system seems unwise at best and cruel at worst.[180]

## Myths and Managed Care

Between 1980 and the mid-1990s, the U.S. health system fell completely under the influence of the HMO–managed care movement. Despite the fact that this movement was transforming a vital, often compassionately delivered, public service into a pseudo-commodity; was relentlessly, almost inevitably, driving more working-class and disadvantaged Americans (including significant proportions of the nation's children) out of the health system; was starving, distorting, and crippling population-based public health and its functions and responsibilities; was slowly eroding and undermining America's hard-won and heavily financed medical education and research infrastructure; and was systematically dismantling the already fragile safety-net health system that African Americans and the poor depended upon for basic health services, the myth of "market reform" held sway. Accordingly, results of the Robert Wood Johnson Foundation–supported studies on access to care in 1976, 1982, and 1986 and their studies on racial and sociocultural barriers revealed that:

> *overall use of medical care declined. Access to physicians' services for indi-*
> *viduals who were poor, Black, and uninsured decreased between 1982*
> *and 1986. While hospital care declined for these groups, the decline in*
> *hospital use was comparable to that for the general population, but the*
> *uninsured, Black, and Hispanic populations received less hospital care*
> *than what might be appropriate given their burden of illness. Underuse of*
> *services was found among key population groups. . . . [R]ecent studies and*

*an initiative by the Robert Wood Johnson Foundation have identified
sociocultural barriers to care as some of the most subtle and difficult to
deal with.[181]*

After posing a scenario, "Let's assume that the economy goes south really rapidly
and really badly," New York health policy professor Berliner predicts, "I think we
could be facing very drastic times ahead."[182] If these assessments represent the
results proffered by an entrepreneurial health system to average Americans and
Black and other underserved populations during plush economic times, what does
the future hold for them and the nation's health and health system?

## Black Health and the Threat of a Permanent "Health and Health Care Underclass"?

### An Opening Health System Gambit

*The founding fathers of this country cited life, liberty, and the pursuit of
happiness as inalienable rights for each citizen. Yet the quality of life —
a healthy life — is, in the 1990s, still not assured for far too many black
Americans.*

LOUIS W. SULLIVAN, M.D., SECRETARY, U.S. DEPARTMENT
OF HEALTH AND HUMAN SERVICES, 1989–1993

In August 1985 the Secretary of Health and Human Services, Margaret M.
Heckler, submitted a report to the Reagan administration that sent shock waves
throughout the health establishment. Much like the annual report cards on health
status of the American people, *Health, United States, The Report of the Secretary's
Task Force on Black and Minority Health* (also known as the Malone-Heckler
report) documented significant health progress in the United States. However,
unlike its predecessors, which always emphasized the fact that Americans were
living longer, that health indicators such as infant mortality were declining, and
that *overall* health showed uniform improvements, it highlighted "a sad and significant fact; *there was a continuing disparity in the burden of death and illness
experienced by Blacks and other minority Americans as compared with our nation's
population as a whole.* [Heckler's emphasis]."[183] Noting that this health disparity
has existed "ever since accurate federal record keeping began — more than a generation ago"[184] (as this study documents, the Black health deficit has actually existed
more than 380 years in America), Heckler stated that "although our health charts
do itemize steady gains in the health status of minority Americans, the stubborn
disparity remained — an affront both to our ideals and to the ongoing genius of
American medicine.... I felt — passionately — that it was time to decipher the
message inherent in that disparity."[185] Despite DHHS and the federal government

having scores of programs with a significant impact on improving the health status of African Americans and other minorities, *The Report of the Secretary's Task Force on Black and Minority Health* "was ... a common effort to carry out a comprehensive and coordinated study to investigate the longstanding disparity in the health status of Blacks, Hispanics, Asian/Pacific Islanders, and Native Americans compared to the nonminority population."[186] Although Secretary Heckler probably did not realize it at the time, while observing the drastic health system changes and events that occurred in the immediate future, she may have harbored forebodings, shared by the authors.[187] Intentionally or not, if the nation did not acknowledge and take specific actions toward ameliorating African American and disadvantaged populations' health disparities, America was on a course that would establish a permanent "health and health care underclass"—mediated through its health care system with Blacks and other disadvantaged minorities serving as the foundation.

The creation of the Secretary's Task Force in 1984 and release of the report over the following two years were emblematic of an awareness of the significance of the racial health disparities, even during a conservative political administration. The National Research Council (NRC) appreciated the growing weight of the health issue as part of the nation's overall racial problem, devoting to it an entire chapter, "Black Americans' Health," of their report, *A Common Destiny: Blacks and American Society* (1989), stating:

> *Who will live and who will die and how much handicap and disability will burden their lives depend in large part on conditions of education, environment, and employment as well as on access to adequate medical services. Health is not only an important "good" in itself, it is also a determinant of life options during the entire life.[188]*

Ronald L. Braithwaite and Sandra E. Taylor reinforced this concern:

> *Health is of crucial importance to people in all walks of life. Factors such as income, education, occupation, environment, and access to services impact health status. The disparity between black and white health has been linked to these factors, both individually and collectively. Perhaps the most common link is that the disadvantage in health for blacks is largely due to their overrepresentation in lower income groups. The combination of factors accounting for this disparity cannot exclude racial bias.... [B]eing black in America has significant costs.[189]*

The observation of Ivor Livingston, editor of *Handbook of Black American Health*—"The plight of Blacks is particularly devastating and urgent because, as a group, they experience a disproportionate burden of poverty, sickness, and death"[190]—adds even more weight to these concerns.

Relying heavily on mortality data, the Malone-Heckler report captured a snapshot of the historical continuum of America's racial health disparities. Relying on sound public health principles, USDHHS and its consultants reaffirmed that mortality measures the distribution of vitality and health in a population, not only reflecting advancements in medical care and therapeutic interventions, but reflecting social contributors such as improved nutrition, sanitation, housing, and education to declining mortality as well.[191] The Task Force "identified six medical conditions for which the gaps in mortality between whites and blacks are the greatest."[192] Taken together, these six causes of death accounted for nearly 86 percent of the excess Black mortality when compared to the White population. They included "accidents and homicides (35.1 percent), infant mortality (26.9 percent), heart disease and stroke (14.4 percent), cirrhosis (4.9 percent), cancer (3.8 percent), and diabetes (1.0 percent)."[193] The statistical technique that captured the real-life or pragmatic effect—best defining the health disparity in terms comprehensible to the average person—is excess deaths. The Task Force defined it as: " ... the difference between the number of deaths observed in minority populations and the number of deaths which would have been expected if the minority population had the same age and sex-specific death rate as the nonminority population," and "quantified the number of deaths that would not have occurred had mortality rates for minorities equaled those of nonminorities."[194] The Task Force revealed that some 42.5 percent of Black deaths up to age 70 (58,942 of 138,635 total deaths) were "excess deaths." In other words, if one attended ten Black funerals in a given year, four of them, based on statistical probability, would not have taken place had these people all enjoyed the health and health system advantages of America's White citizens.

However, as the NRC noted about the USDHHS's Task Force report:

> *The report did not attempt to encompass the full dimensions of disparities in health status; while the mortality for these six conditions are important, they do not capture the full personal and societal costs of deaths from other causes and of chronic or acute illness. In particular, this methodology has omitted important health problems of black children.*[195]

In addition: "The USDHHS report glibly prescribed more healthful diets, 'life style changes,' exercise promotion, and health education to reverse mounting black mortality and suffering from cancer, brain-damaged babies, maternal deaths, and untreated high blood pressure and diabetes mellitus."[196] African Americans were seemingly "blamed for being murder victims, for having to live in ghetto neighborhoods, for being born poor, for having matriarchal families, for having to work in toxin-exposed jobs, and for being victims of poor diets and too much environmental stress."[197]

Despite the report's shortcomings, it served as a wake-up call alerting the health establishment that the reforms implemented during the 1960s, analogous to the health system's opening gambit to solve a history-based problem, had not ameliorated America's race- and class-based health problems and disparities. The observation of Dr. Louis Sullivan, the first African American secretary of the USDHHS, after the release of the report—"The number of excess deaths has continued to increase, reaching 80,000 in 1988"—was emblematic of "this sobering depiction of black health in America."[198] Moreover, stagnant or deteriorating health indicators along with the establishment by the federal government of racially "separate and unequal objectives"[199] for the nation's *Healthy People 2000: National Health Promotion and Disease Prevention Objectives* in 1990 suggested that race-based health disparities might be accepted as "normal" in the future and were subtly being institutionalized.[200] An encapsulated, comparative review of Black health through the 1980s and early 1990s follows.[201]

### *Health System* en passant: *Black and Disadvantaged Health*

*We use the disparities to get attention, but we don't want them to last forever.*
SHIRIKI K. KUMANYIKA, PH.D., M.P.H., R.D., CO-CHAIR, FOURTH
NATIONAL MINORITY FORUM, NHLBI, WASHINGTON, DC, 1992

By 1990 the African American population numbered nearly 31 million people, approximately 12 percent (estimated 12.7% in 1997) of the population—constituting the leading edge of the nation's emerging majority minority population. Although Hispanic/Latinos and Asian/Pacific Islanders are the fastest-growing ethnic minority groups, Blacks remain the nation's oldest, nonindigenous racial or ethnic group.*[202] The Black population remains younger than the White population, with a median age of 28 years compared to 33.9 years for Whites. Socioeconomically, White median family income ($36,915) is 1.7 times (72.3 percent) greater than the median Black family income ($21,423). While Black poverty levels increased from 31 percent of the population being below the poverty level in 1979 (compared to 9 percent of Whites) to 31.9 percent in 1990 (compared to 10.7 percent of Whites), between 1994 and 1996 Black rates declined, to 28.4 percent in 1996 (compared to 11.2 percent of Whites). Educationally, African Americans have fewer high school graduates (66.7 percent) compared to Whites (79.9 percent).

In 1996, American life expectancy at 76.1 years surpassed by 0.3 years the previous all-time high reached in 1992 and 1995. After reaching the 75-year threshold in 1989, U.S. life expectancy fluctuated over the next five years while

---

*Of the nonindigenous groups populating the United States, over half the ancestors of African Americans were here by 1780. The similar median arrival date for European American ancestors is about 1890. Not until the 1840s did Europeans constitute more American arrivals than Africans.

dropping in international rankings for life expectancy at birth from 22nd to 23rd for males and 18th to 19th for females between 1988 and 1995. Disturbingly, *The Nation's Health*, the American Public Health Association's (APHA) newspaper, reported in 1993: "Life expectancy at birth for the average American rose from 73.7 years in 1980 to 75.4 in 1990, but a gap of almost 15 years separates life expectancies for black males (64.5 years) and white females (79.4 years). And the gap is widening."[203] Overall gains in U.S. life expectancy slowed down in the 15-year period from 1980–1995 compared to the preceding 1965 to 1980 period—the 15 years encompassing what the authors have often referred to as the "Civil Rights era" in health care. Instead of the overall 3.5-year (5 percent) gain charted between 1965 and 1980 with Blacks gaining longevity at a more rapid rate (6.2 percent) than Whites (4.8 percent), overall life expectancy between 1980 and 1995 increased only 2.1 years (2.8 percent), with Whites gaining at a 2.8 percent rate compared to a Black rate of 2.2 percent.

The already wide Black/White disparity in life expectancy increased in the decade and a half encompassing the Reagan-Bush era. The 15-year increase from 1980's 6.3-year Black/White disparity—with fluctuations between 6.8 and 7.1 years from 1989 to 1995—to 1995's 6.9- and 1996's 6.6-year Black/White differences represented a worsening trend in Black/White life expectancy disparities. The increase amounted to almost 10 percent by 1995, declining slightly to an almost 5 percent increase the next year (1996)—the final years of tabulated data available for an already 361-year-old health disparity (1619 to 1980) for African Americans. Between 1980 and 1995 Whites gained 2.1 years of longevity, increasing from 74.4 years to 76.5 years (2.82%). Black life expectancy climbed from 68.1 years in 1980 to 69.6 years in 1995 (1.5 years or 2.20%). Most of the overall White gains in life expectancy at birth occurred between 1985 and 1995 (1.2 years or a 1.59 percent increase). Of the life expectancy gains for Blacks during the 15-year period, the greatest progress was between 1980 and 1984—an increase from 68.1 to 69.7 years (1.6 years or a 2.35 percent increase). Between 1985 and 1995, Black life expectancy for both sexes climbed only 0.1 years (from 69.5 to 69.6 years), or 0.14 percent, and actually declined 0.1 years, from 69.7 to 69.6 years of longevity, if 1984 is taken as the starting point.

During the 1985–1995 decade, a period of minimal life expectancy increases for African Americans, Black males (BM) lost 0.1 years (–0.1 years) of life expectancy, a –0.153 percent decrease. Meanwhile, White male life expectancy increased 1.5 years, or 2.08 percent. During the same decade, Black female life expectancy increased 0.9 years, or 1.14 percent. The same modest gains were charted by White females. Black men, who lived 6.9 years (9.8 percent) less than White men in 1980, lived 8.2 fewer years (11.2 percent) than White men in 1995 and 7.8 years (10.6 percent) less in 1996. Black women, who suffered a 5.6-year race- and gender-based longevity disparity (7.2 percent less longevity) in 1980 compared to White women, closed their race and gender life expectancy disparity to 5.0 years (6.3 percent fewer years) in 1984. Then, after fluctuating between 5.0 and 5.9 years (1992) for a decade, Black female longevity deteriorated once more, creating a 5.7-year Black/White life expectancy disparity (6.9 percent fewer years) by 1995—resulting in a 0.1 year (1.8%) gain over 15 years in comparative gender-based longevity. Based on any measurement technique, the race-based longevity disparity had widened and deepened, seemingly becoming institutionalized in the process, over the 1980–1995 period, with some hopeful fluctuations present beginning in 1996.[204]

Between 1980 and 1996 the annual number of deaths in the White population increased from 1,738,607 to 1,992,966, or almost 15 percent. Meanwhile, the annual number of deaths in the Black population increased from 233,135 in 1980 to 282,089 in 1996, almost 21 percent.[205] The age-adjusted 1996 death rate of 491.6 deaths per 100,000 U.S. standard population was a record low, 2.4 percent lower than the rate of 503.9 in 1995. The age-adjusted death rate for the White population was 466.8 deaths per 100,000 U.S. standard population compared to 738.3 deaths per 100,000 U.S. standard population for Blacks (58 percent higher than the White rate)—both all-time lows. Despite these values being the lowest recorded rates for both races, Black death rates were 51 percent higher than White death rates in 1980 and 1985—thus, over the long term, the racial disparity in death rates was increasing. Moreover, since the release of the Secretary's Task Force findings, the differentials in death rates between Blacks and Whites for most medical conditions and chronic diseases have either stagnated (e.g., cancer, diabetes) or increased (e.g., heart disease, diseases of the perinatal period). As Peters, Kochanek, and Murphy of the Division of Vital Statistics noted, "In 1996 the age-adjusted death rate for the black population was 1.6 times that for the white population, unchanged since 1987."[206] This represented an initial rise—and then a stubbornly persistent increase—in the racial health disparity over the past decade: "For 1960–86 the race ratio was 1.5."[207] Despite the fact that "[a]ge-adjusted death rates decreased almost every year between 1980 and 1996 for white males and females," for Black males and females:

> *age-adjusted death rates fluctuated between 1980 and 1985. For black males age-adjusted death rates increased from 1985 to 1988, while for black females age-adjusted death rates declined between 1985 and 1987, then rose in 1988. Except for 1993, age-adjusted death rates for black males and females have followed a general downward trend since 1988.*[208]

Moreover, since 1985 for Native Americans and 1992 for Hispanic Americans, death rates have been rising slowly and erratically. The Native American death rate, 468.2 in 1985, was 468.5 in 1995, while the Hispanic death rate, 380.2, in 1992 rose to 386.8 in 1995. Therefore, in marked contrast with the White population's steady health progress implicit in declining death rates, there was erratic, slower, and sometimes negative progress in death rate decline of age-adjusted death rates for Blacks and other minorities. Nevertheless, the 1996 figures, 976.0 deaths per 100,000 population for Black males and 561.0 deaths per 100,000 population for Black females, were also record lows.*

### Leading Causes of Death

Significant Black/White health status and outcome disparities are also embodied in disaggregated health indicators such as the leading causes of death. Blacks led in 13 of the 15 leading causes of death in 1989. Age-adjusted death rates for the Black population were lower than those of the White population for two leading causes of death—Chronic obstructive pulmonary diseases and allied conditions and Suicide. The largest racial differentials wherein the Black population fared worse than Whites were Homicide and legal intervention (6.6 times the White rate); HIV infection (3.3 times the White rate); Nephritis, nephrotic syndrome, and nephrosis (3.1 times the White rate); Septicemia (2.7 times the White rate); and Diabetes mellitus (2.3 times the White rate).[209] The largest increases in age-adjusted mortality rates noted for the Black population in 1989 were HIV infection (28% increase), Diabetes mellitus (12% increase), Homicide and legal intervention (5% increase), and Suicide (4% increase). Death rates for Malignant neoplasms, including neoplasms of lymphatic and hematopoietic tissues, increased slightly for both Black and White populations (less than 1 percent).[210] The National Center for Health Statistics (NCHS) noted: "Major causes contributing to the widening differential in mortality between the black and white populations between 1988 and 1989 were HIV infection; Homicide and legal intervention; Diabetes mellitus; and Malignant neoplasms."[211] An increasingly popular operational measure of health utilized in descriptive epidemiology is the 10 leading causes of death, of which Blacks led in 9 in 1989.

In 1996 African Americans led in 12 of the 15 leading causes of death and 8 of the top 10 leading causes of death. Between 1989 and 1996, Alzheimer's disease—an illness strongly correlated with longevity, thus differentially affecting the White population—had displaced the category, "Certain conditions originating in the perinatal period," from the top 10 or 15 leading causes of death in both the general and White populations. Despite the White pattern of disease divergence away from that of Blacks, and the alterations in importance and priorities these changes signaled, Diseases originating in pregnancy, the perinatal period, and early childhood remained the 10th leading cause of death, a monumental health problem, in the African American community in 1996.[212] Understandably, Blacks, still suffering huge longevity, elderly insurance, and health services disparities, were

---

*The bundled endnote for the mortality section remains #214.

not as affected as others on official levels by the ravages of Alzheimer's disease. Nevertheless, for Whites, age-adjusted death rates were 1.2 times higher for Chronic obstructive pulmonary diseases and allied conditions (COPD), 1.8 times higher for Suicide, and 1.5 times higher for Alzheimer's disease compared to the Black population in 1996. And although there were differences in ranking, 7 of the 10 leading causes were the same for the White and Black populations.

> *Suicide, chronic liver disease, and Alzheimer's disease were among the 10 leading causes for the white population but not for the black population. HIV infection, [H]omicide, and Certain conditions originating in the perinatal period (perinatal conditions) were among the 10 leading causes for the black population but not the white population.*[213]

This pattern of racial divergence in disease profiles might have important implications in the future and is certain to affect the nation's health agenda, health policy-setting, and health resource allocations. Historically, as exemplified by the persistence of the nation's wide, deep, race-based health disparities, attention and dollars of the U.S. public, scientists and politicians have traditionally followed the concerns of the White majority population—not necessarily public health problems, logically dictated unfavorable population-based health trends, or focusing on the correction of disparate objective health status or outcome indicators for various populations.

Ratios comparing the Black population to the White population were at least 1.5 times greater for eight of the leading causes of death (see Table 7.2). Black/White mortality rate ratios declined between 1989 and 1996 in some areas, suggesting improvement, or closing of, the Black/White health status and outcome disparities. Some of these include, Homicide and legal intervention which declined from the 1989 level of 6.6 times the White rate to 6.2 times the White rate in 1996—a parameter, until recently, only loosely connected to health interventions; Nephritis, nephrotic syndrome, and nephrosis (i.e., kidney diseases), which declined from 3.1 times the White age-adjusted mortality rate to 2.6 times the White rate in 1996; Chronic liver disease and cirrhosis, a constellation of diseases whose age-adjusted Black/White mortality ratios declined from 1.7 in 1989 to 1.3 in 1996; and, Cerebrovascular diseases (e.g., stroke), which declined from a Black/White age-adjusted death rate ratio of 1.89 in 1989 to 1.8 in 1996—which may be of questionable significance statistically.

Leading causes of death that showed no improvement in the Black/White age-adjusted death rate disparities between 1989 and 1996 include: Malignant neoplasms, including neoplasms of lymphatic and hematopoietic tissues (i.e., cancer)—the Black/White ratio of age-adjusted death rates remained stable at 1.3 between 1989 and 1996; and, Pneumonia and influenza, diseases whose mortality is strongly influenced by age and affected by medical intervention, Black/White mortality ratios seemingly stabilized at 1.5. There were also death rate ratios for the

**Table 7.2   Percent of Total Deaths, Death Rates, Age-Adjusted Death Rates for 1996, Percent Change in Age-Adjusted Death Rates from 1995 to 1996 and 1979 to 1996, and Ratio of Age-Adjusted Death Rates by Race and Sex for the 15 Leading Causes of Death for the Total Population in 1996: United States**

| | | | | Age-Adjusted Death Rate | | | | |
| | | | | | Percent Change | | Ratio | |
| Rank[1] | Cause of Death (Based on the Ninth Revision, International Classification of Diseases, 1975) | Percent of Total Deaths | Death Rate | 1996 | 1995 to 1996 | 1979 to 1996 | Male to Female | Black to White |
|---|---|---|---|---|---|---|---|---|
| ... | All causes | 100.0 | 872.5 | 491.6 | −2.4 | −14.8 | 1.6 | 1.6 |
| 1 | Diseases of heart | 31.7 | 276.4 | 134.5 | −2.7 | −32.6 | 1.8 | 1.5 |
| 2 | Malignant neoplasms, including neoplasms of lymphatic and hematopoietic tissues | 23.3 | 203.4 | 127.9 | −1.5 | −2.2 | 1.4 | 1.3 |
| 3 | Cerebrovascular diseases | 6.9 | 60.3 | 26.4 | −1.1 | −36.5 | 1.2 | 1.8 |
| 4 | Chronic obstructive pulmonary diseases and allied conditions | 4.6 | 40.0 | 21.0 | 1.0 | 43.8 | 1.5 | 0.8 |
| 5 | Accidents and adverse effects | 4.1 | 35.8 | 30.4 | −0.3 | −29.1 | 2.4 | 1.2 |
| | Motor vehicle accidents | 1.9 | 16.5 | 16.2 | −0.6 | −30.2 | 2.2 | 1.0 |
| ... | All other accidents and adverse effects | 2.2 | 19.3 | 14.2 | − | −27.6 | 2.7 | 1.5 |
| 6 | Pneumonia and influenza | 3.6 | 31.6 | 12.8 | −0.8 | 14.3 | 1.6 | 1.5 |
| 7 | Diabetes mellitus | 2.7 | 23.3 | 13.6 | 2.3 | 38.8 | 1.2 | 2.4 |
| 8 | Human immunodeficiency virus infection | 1.3 | 11.7 | 11.1 | −28.8 | ... | −4.3 | 5.8 |
| 9 | Suicide | 1.3 | 11.6 | 10.8 | −3.6 | −7.7 | 4.5 | 0.6 |
| 10 | Chronic live disease and cirrhosis | 1.1 | 9.4 | 7.5 | −1.3 | −37.5 | 2.4 | 1.3 |
| 11 | Nephritis, nephrotic syndrome, and nephrosis | 1.0 | 9.2 | 4.3 | − | − | 1.5 | 2.6 |
| 12 | Septicemia | 0.9 | 8.1 | 4.1 | − | 78.3 | 1.3 | 2.8 |
| 13 | Alzheimer's disease | 0.9 | 8.1 | 2.7 | − | 1,250.0 | 0.9 | 0.7 |
| 14 | Homicide and legal intervention | 0.9 | 7.9 | 8.5 | −9.6 | −16.7 | 3.7 | 6.2 |
| 15 | Atherosclerosis | 0.7 | 6.3 | 2.2 | −4.3 | −61.4 | 1.3 | 1.1 |
| ... | All other causes | 14.8 | 129.5 | ... | ... | ... | ... | ... |

− Quantity zero.
... Category not applicable.
− − − Data not available.
[1]Rank based on number of deaths.

*Source:* Table B. National Center for Health Statistics. Deaths: Final Data for 1996. *National Vital Statistics Reports: 1998;* 47(9). Hyattsville, MD: U.S. Department of Health and Human Services, 5.

Black population compared to the White population whose values deteriorated, suggesting widening racial health status and outcome disparities. They included, but were not limited to: Human immunodeficiency virus infection (i.e., HIV-AIDS) — Black/White ratios for age-adjusted death rates increased from 3.3 in 1989 to 5.8 in 1996; Septicemia, a parameter closely related to aging — Black/White ratios for age-adjusted mortality rates increased from 2.7 to 2.8 between 1989 and 1996; Diabetes mellitus's Black/White age-adjusted death rate ratios increased from 2.3 in 1989 to 2.4 in 1996; Diseases of the heart — Black/White ratios for age-adjusted death rates increased from 1.4 in 1989 to 1.5 in 1996; Certain conditions originating in the perinatal period, whose Black/White ratios* increased from 2.3 in 1989 to 2.4 in 1996; and Atherosclerosis's Black/White ratios of age-adjusted death rates which rose from 1.0 in 1989 to 1.1 in 1996 (which may not be significant statistically). What is significant is that the age-adjusted death rate for the leading cause of death, heart disease, declined overall by 2.7 percent in 1996, and the age-adjusted death rate for cancer, the second-leading cause of death, declined by 1.5 percent the same year. These disease categories combined accounted for 55 percent of all U.S. deaths in 1996. Unfortunately, African Americans displayed stable or widening racial disparities according to age-adjusted death rates in both indices. Although the White population has experienced progress in infant mortality and other conditions associated with the perinatal period, so that these causes no longer rank among their leading causes of death, that laudatory circumstance does not apply to the Black community.[214]

### Poor Pregnancy Outcomes

Long utilized as the basis for public health benchmarks "because death rates among infants are a particularly sensitive indicator of health standing of populations,"[215] as well as a measuring standard of health system performance, the USDHHS stated: "The birth of a healthy infant to a healthy woman is the most important goal of our nation."[216] Infant mortality and indices related to the perinatal period and reproductive health loom as major issues in the health of our nation, charting the population's most vulnerable health period until it reaches the age of 65. Moreover, these outcomes inordinately influence other important health indices such as death rates, length of expected life at birth, excess death measurements, and years of potential life lost. As measures of health system performance they are extremely sensitive barometers recording the effects of medical interventions, and these measures respond chronologically more rapidly than any other available measures to targeted health system programs, innovations, interventions, or changes.

In 1996, 28,093 U.S. babies died before reaching the age of one, leading to an

---

*Inasmuch as deaths from these causes occur mainly among infants, ratios are based on infant mortality rates rather than age-adjusted death rates.

infant mortality rate (IMR) of 7.3 deaths in the first year of life per 1,000 live births—the lowest rate ever recorded in the United States. Of those deaths, Blacks, constituting 12.6 percent of the population, contributed 8,404, or 30 percent, to that total. Historically, as Singh and Yu documented:

> *The rate of decline in infant mortality during 1950 through 1991 differed significantly for Black and White infants. The infant mortality rate for White infants during this period declined by 3.23 percent per year, while the rate for Black infants dropped by 2.89 percent annually. As a result, the racial disparity in the infant mortality rate increased between 1950 and 1991.*[217]

While the Black/White racial disparity in IMR in 1965 yielded a ratio of 1.94, it never increased beyond 1.95 through 1980. Since then it has increased erratically and approached 2.5 times the White rate. Despite the long-standing racial disparity in infant deaths, wherein Black rates have traditionally been higher than White rates for generations,[218] the NCHS noted for some of the most recent available data: "[t]he mortality rate for white infants declined 3.2 percent (6.1 in 1996 compared to 6.3 in 1995). Although not statistically significant, the rate for black infants declined 2.6 percent (14.7 in 1996 compared with 15.1 in 1995)."[219] This record-breaking 1996 IMR for Black infants ranked somewhere between the 1974 (14.8 per 1,000 live births) and 1975 (14.2 per 1,000 live births) IMRs recorded for White infants. The disturbing widening of the Black/White disparity has been accompanied by a slowing down of improvements in IMR during the 1980–1995 period (a 39.68 percent overall improvement) compared to the preceding 1965–1980 period (a 49.98 percent overall improvement). Rapidly improving Black IMR figures in the 1965–1980 period (48.68%) were less than one percentage point behind White improvements (48.38%). However, recent rates of improvement in IMRs between Blacks (29.43 percent improvement) and Whites (42.72 percent improvement) between 1980 and 1995 diverged sharply to more than a 13 point difference. At these rates, as Singh and Yu also predicted, convergence of the racial disparities in IMRs seems unlikely in the foreseeable future.

Although the U.S. neonatal mortality rate (NMR) declined by 2 percent from 4.9 to 4.8 deaths for infants under 28 days of age per 1,000 live births, "the rate did not change significantly from 1995,"[220] according to the NCHS. The Black rate, at 9.6 deaths under 28 days per 1,000 live births, was nearly 2½ times the White rate of 4.0 deaths under 28 days per 1,000 live births. Between 1995 and 1996 the overall postneonatal mortality rate (PMR)—deaths to infants ages 28 days to 11 months per 1,000 live births—declined 7.4 percent to 2.5 deaths per 1,000 live births. The White rate decline was from 2.2 to 2.1 deaths per 1,000 live births, while the rate decline for Blacks from 5.3 in 1995 to 5.1 in 1996 was not statistically significant, according to the NCHS. In 1993 the U.S. ranked 25th internationally in the perinatal health parameters (e.g., IMR, NMR, and PMR), with Black rates ranking in the mid-30s, exceeding those of Costa Rica, Puerto Rico, Poland, Cuba, and other developing or Eastern bloc nations.

An understanding of risk factors determining poor pregnancy outcomes and reflected in high infant mortality can be derived from studies of low birth weight (LBW). Feroz Ahmed, an authority on infant mortality in African Americans, noted:

> *From the standpoint of prevention of infant mortality, it is important to differentiate between the roles of birth weight distribution and birth weight–specific mortality rates, that is, death rates for each narrow birth weight category. If in a given population the latter are too high as compared to the rates in another population, there may be a deficiency in neonatal intensive care or other neonatal or pediatric care. However, if the birth weight–specific rates are fairly low and the infant or neonatal mortality are still high, the IMR is due to a poor birth weight distribution.[221]*

Poor birth weight distribution, which "may be due to a variety of obstetrical, medical, health care, behavioral, cultural, environmental, socioeconomic, or even biological factors ... stands out as the principal proximate determinant of the relatively high infant mortality rate in the United States."[222] The decline in U.S. IMRs over the last three decades has mainly been achieved through dramatic improvements in neonatal care.

The incidence of LBW infants (weighing less than 2,500 grams) for Blacks has hovered between 12 and 14 percent, compared to White rates vacillating between 5 and 7 percent for 25 years. Neither has improved. All races, Black, and White very low birth weight rates (VLBW, or infants weighing less than 1,500 grams) have increased from 1.17 to 1.35 percent for all races (a 15 percent increase), 2.40 percent to 2.97 percent for Blacks (a 24% increase), and 0.95 percent to 1.06 percent for Whites (a 12 percent increase) between 1970 and 1995:

> *Black American infants have the highest incidence ... of low birth weight among all ethnic groups, more than twice as high as the rate for White Americans.... This high incidence of low birth weight is mainly, but not entirely, responsible for the very high infant mortality rates among Black Americans. Blacks also have higher mortality rates among normal-weight neonates as well as higher postneonatal mortality rates.[223]*

Maternal mortality figures also display disturbing racial disparities. According to the NCHS, the nation's maternal mortality figures continue to be an undercount because "the number does not include all deaths occurring to pregnant women, but only to those deaths reported on the death certificate and assigned to the cause of death, Complications of pregnancy, childbirth, and the puerperium.... It excludes, for example, deaths occurring more than 42 days after the termination of pregnancy and deaths of pregnant women due to external causes (accidents, homicides, and suicides)."[224] Nevertheless, Rosenbaum, Layton, and Liu noted in the 1991 edition of the Children's Defense Fund's *The Health of America's Children*: "In the United States, maternal mortality, like infant mortality, continues to be a stark and basic reminder of the enormous variation in living standards among Americans."[225] Of the six annual increases in maternal deaths recorded since national data first became available in 1940, the 21 percent increase in the overall maternal death rate between 1995 and 1996 is the second-largest annual increase, behind the 27 percent increase between 1987–1988. Two of the rate increases occurred in the 1980s and two in the 1990s (1993–1994's 18 percent increase). Alarmingly, maternal death rates, which declined 71 percent between 1965 and 1980, declined only 32 percent between 1980 and 1995. Black improvements, which had been spectacular (76% decline) between 1965–1980, outpacing White improvements (68% decline), declined only 2.8 percent between 1980 and 1995. White maternal mortality rates declined 46 percent during the same interval. Perhaps this is reflected in the lower racial disparity levels of the 1970s and early1980s—Black rates in the 1950s and 1960s, over four times White rates, began improving in the late 1960s—climbing erratically to those same 1960s levels in the 1990s, setting a record-breaking 5.8 Black/White ratio in 1995. Moreover, "In 1996 a total of 294 women were reported to have died of maternal causes ... compared to 277 in 1995,"[226] according to the NCHS. At least 41 percent of those deaths were African Americans.*

Sociodemographic factors such as maternal age, parity, birth interval, marital status, and socioeconomic status and maternal risk factors such as inadequate health care, nutrition, drug abuse, smoking, alcohol abuse, sexually transmitted diseases, and other medical factors detailed in the scientific literature on LBW and adverse pregnancy outcomes disproportionately affect African Americans. However, they do not operate among Blacks in the same way as they do among Whites or other ethnic groups. For example, as researchers at Howard University noted, "There is growing evidence that the impact of teenage motherhood, of being unmarried, or of not having a high school education is not as great among Blacks, especially inner-city poor Blacks, as in other groups."[227] Because the evidence suggests that Black teenage mothers contribute small numbers of all births and infant deaths and their risk of poor pregnancy outcome may be only marginally higher than mothers in their early and mid-20s, "equating teenage pregnancy with

---

*Fourteen of the other deaths were recorded as "All other," an official nonracial designation often including African Americans who are not recorded as such. Much of the National Hospital Discharge Survey (NHDS) data, classified as Whites, non-Whites, and "race not stated," contains no racial designation, serving as an impediment to accurately recording vital health data, defining the nation's health problems, and designing effective population-based approaches to ameliorating racial health disparities.

high infant mortality is not empirically valid."[228] Even though the relative risk for LBW or infant death is not as high for unmarried Black women as for unmarried White women, unmarried status remains a risk factor more important than age, as nearly two-thirds of Black births occur outside marriage. Such unmarried mothers are more likely to be unemployed, poor, and dependent on public assistance. Moreover, substance abuse, high-risk sexual behavior, and crime are often the defining features of their environments. Despite the fact that the lack or inadequacy of prenatal care is a lesser factor affecting pregnancy outcomes of Black compared to White women, "the proportion of Black women not receiving adequate prenatal care is so high that, by providing adequate prenatal care to the more than 50 percent of the Black pregnant women who do not receive it, a major dent can be made into the infant mortality rate among Blacks."[229] As Ahmed noted, "The lack of adequate prenatal care, however, is only part of the lack of adequate health care in general for a large section of the American population. Blacks suffer disproportionately from the absence of this basic human right."[230] For Black women, compared to White or Asian women, high birth rate, reflected in high parity and short birth intervals, remains a risk factor for unfavorable pregnancy outcomes. Provision of adequate health services in the form of prenatal, pediatric, postpartum, substance abuse prevention and therapy, and family planning services, including abortions, would automatically, in some high-risk groups, address the problems of prenatal and postpartum substance abuse, a major factor in the high incidence of infant mortality among Blacks, postneonatal mortality, and unwanted subsequent pregnancies.

For African Americans the major risk factors mentioned here often operate in an environment of poverty, social disadvantage, and hopelessness. This may explain why socioeconomic status measures alone used in risk factor analysis fail to capture the full impact of socioeconomic status on Black pregnancy outcomes. Moreover: "Dependency on drugs and irresponsible sexual behavior—products of an environment of hopelessness, alienation, and loss of self-esteem—seem to have emerged as mega confounders that drastically offset the normal effect of many favorable factors."[231] For such reasons and because of the overriding realities of a nihilistic, draconian, and punitive U.S. social environment, one cannot predict or assume that "macro-level social programs aimed at alleviating poverty and creating jobs and adequate incomes will automatically change the environment so radically as to cause a major decline in ... infant mortality in the short run."[232] Thus, in many Black populations, maternal age, marital status, educational attainment, and even the adequacy of prenatal care—which, as we have stated, often show anomalous patterns among many African Americans—"may only be the variables through which the effects of the potent variables of substance abuse, risky behaviors, and dangerous environments are mediated."[233] Therefore, "the health care focus, including prenatal care and substance abuse prevention programs, will remain an important stratagem in the fight against high infant mortality among Black Americans"[234] in the near future. Realistically, the root causes of this aspect of the health problem are deeply imbedded in the long and devastating history of racism in the United States. Until a national commitment to reverse the hounding legacy of racial injustice in America is made, no major reduction of Black IMRs or closing of the Black/White disparities is likely.[235] For African Americans the news is no less troubling for the health of Black children.

### Children's Health

It is widely accepted that a healthy childhood is the foundation for health and productivity later in life. There is also widespread agreement that access to basic health care and preventable services—which in this country are strongly tied to health insurance—is vital to children's well-being and future success. Untreated visual and hearing deficits, malnutrition, and preventable childhood diseases may lead to poor academic performance and in some cases permanent disabilities or death. Poor children are noted to suffer disproportionately from health problems and lack of health insurance. According to the Children's Defense Fund (CDF), "more than 20% of all children and 46% of African American children in the United States were living below the poverty level in 1991."[236] The poverty rate for all children in America has continued to grow despite rising national prosperity. The 1996 poverty rate for children was 20.5 percent, accounting for 40.3% of Hispanic children, 39.9% of Black children, and 16.3% of White children—the first year child poverty rates among Hispanics outpaced Blacks.[237] According to the CDF's calculation of census bureau data: "children in the 1960s were, on average, 34 percent more likely to be poor than persons 18 or older. In 1996 children were 81 percent more likely than adults to be poor (20.5 percent of children lived in poverty versus 11.3 percent of adults)."[238] In 1991, 12.6 percent of children of all races, younger than 18, were without health insurance throughout the year. For uninsured Black and Latino children (under 18 years of age), the percentages were 15.1 percent and 26.7 percent respectively.[239] In 1996 there were 11.3 million children through age 18 who had no health insurance. This, according to the CDF, was the highest number of uninsured children ever recorded by the Census Bureau, representing 14.8 percent of America's children,[240] based on census data.

Black and low-income children in the United States are noted to have poorer overall health status in comparison to Whites: "Despite their worse health status, black children and low-income children receive the fewest health services."[241] In 1990 Black children received an average of 3.2 physician contacts per year (30.4 percent fewer contacts), compared to 4.6 contacts for Whites. Also in 1990, the percentages of Black and White children with no physician contact in the past year were 21.5 percent and 17.4 percent, respectively. In 1995, the number of physician contacts per year for Black and White children under 5 were noted to be 5.8 and 6.7 (13.4 percent fewer contacts), and for children 5–14 years old the number of contacts were 2.5 and 3.6 (30.6 percent fewer contacts for Black children), respectively.[242]

Black children are more likely than Whites to experience health-related difficulties that negatively affect their physical, emotional, and educational development. Some include but are not limited to anemia, malnutrition, lead poisoning, and diseases preventable by immunization. Children who suffer from malnutrition have adverse health and learning affects, including iron deficiency anemia, which is associated with poor cognitive development, fatigue, trouble concentrating in school, and stunted growth. Jones and Roberts reported that "iron deficiency anemia interferes with mental processes, especially those involved with visual attention and learning concepts."[243] Because of their poor health status, Black children are more likely to be hospitalized and experience longer hospital stays compared to Whites—largely because, compounding their baseline nutritional deficits, they suffer more serious conditions which are often due to inadequate primary health care and delay in seeking proper medical attention.

It was noted in *Health United States 1998* that hospitalization for asthma is an indicator for adequacy of preventive care. Black children suffer disproportionately from asthma, which is one of the most common chronic diseases of childhood. Usually treated in an outpatient setting, hospitalization for asthma indicates severe disease. The National Cooperative Inner City Asthma Study performed a comprehensive analysis of factors associated with the severity of asthma in inner-city children. As causes of excess morbidity, the study's researchers cited exposure to allergens including dust-mites and cockroaches, poor air quality, and inadequate access to medical care.[244] The *Healthy People 2000* goal for asthma was set for no more than 2.25 asthma hospitalizations per 1,000 population for children 0–14 years old. According to data reported in *Health United States 1998*, "White, but not Black, children in each socioeconomic group attained the goal by 1989–91."[245] They further reported that Black children had an asthma hospitalization rate 3.3 times that of Whites and that the Black rates were higher for each income category.[246]

Another serious health hazard for children is lead poisoning—which occurs in epidemic proportions in the Black community. It has been documented that metabolic effects of lead poisoning in children occur at blood level concentrations as low as 7–12 µg/dl, and that at subclinical levels of lead intoxication "children sustain permanent cognitive and behavioral damage that manifests itself in poor school performance and a variety of learning disabilities."[247] Moderate blood levels (13–25µg/dl) have significant effects on central nervous system functions to include "intelligence, behavior control, fine motor coordination, neurological dysfunction and motor impairment."[248] The most severe effects of lead poisoning occur at very high levels and are manifested as acute encephalopathy, seizures, coma, and death, but most cases of lead poisoning are largely asymptomatic. In 1992 Reed noted: "In affluent and middle-class suburbs, only 3 percent of white children have dangerous levels of lead in their blood, compared to 30 percent of inner city black children."[249] It was reported in *Health United States 1998* that, among populations with similar demographic profiles that 22% of Black children in families below poverty had an elevated blood level, compared with only 6% in high-income families, and that in each income group, Black children were more likely than other races and ethnic groups to have elevated blood lead levels.[250]

In addition to these facts, immunization rates for preventable infectious diseases of childhood—which have the potential to cause blindness, hearing deficits, developmental delay, and death—grew slowly and in some instances fell during the late 1970s and early 1980s. In 1976 only 65.9 percent of children ages 1 to 4 years old were vaccinated for measles. The rate dropped to 63.8 percent by 1981, with 65.7 percent of Whites and 55.3 percent of "All other" children receiving measles vaccinations. There was a rise in the number of reported cases of measles from 1,497 in 1983 to 2,704 cases in 1985. By 1989 and 1990 the incidence of measles had increased dramatically among preschool children in inner cities, with "the largest outbreaks occurring primarily among unvaccinated Black and Hispanic children in large cities such as Chicago, Dallas, Houston, Los Angeles, Milwaukee and New York."[251] These data, along with those reported in *Morbidity and Mortality Weekly Report*,[252] demonstrate that non-White children payed a higher price in suffering, disability, and death from the epidemics.

As a result of the Clinton administration's immunization initiative, begun in 1993, immunization rates have improved dramatically and, as expected, rates of vaccine-preventable childhood illnesses have fallen significantly. In 1996, the rates of vaccination of Black and White children 19 to 35 months of age for combined series, DPT, polio, and measles were 74, 79, 90, 89 and 79, 83, 92, 92 percent, respectively. While the rates have improved significantly for both races, they still reflect a disparity for Black children. The 1996 rates were lower for both Black and White children below the poverty level, with combined series rates of 70 and 68 percent, respectively—indicating even lower rates for White children below the poverty level. While overall childhood immunization rates have improved, they still do not compare favorably with those of other Western industrialized countries. One can only hope these rates will remain stable or continue to improve under subsequent presidential administrations.

As with adult mortality, childhood mortality is a gold standard for health status and outcome reflecting quality of life, extreme states of ill health, improvements in social and environmental factors, advances in medicine and therapeutics, and health system performance. Despite dramatic improvements in overall childhood mortality since the 1900s, Black children continue to suffer substantially higher death rates than do White children. Deaths from all causes for Black and White female children ages 1 to 4 years old in 1985 were 71.1 and 40.0 deaths per 100,000 population, respectively, with a Black/White ratio of 1.77, or a 77 percent higher death rate among Black children within this age range. In 1996 the respective death rates for Black and White female children in this age group were 63.7 and 28.5 deaths per 100,000 population, yielding a Black/White mortality ratio of 2.24 and a 124 percent higher death rate for Blacks—reflecting a substantial widening of the gap for death rates among Black and White female children in this age group over the 11-year period. Death rates from all causes in 1985 for Black and White female children ages 5 to 14 years old were 28.6 and 19.5 deaths per 100,000 population, respectively, or a Black/White death ratio of 1.47 and a rate 47 percent higher among Blacks. In 1996, the death rate from all causes for Black and White female children in this age range were 25.9 and 16.4 deaths per 100,000 population, yielding a Black/White mortality or risk ratio of 1.6 and a 58 percent higher death rate for Black female children, reflecting persistent and significant disparities.

For Black and White male children ages 1 to 4 years old, the death rates from all causes in 1985 were 90.1 and 52.8 deaths per 100,000 population respectively, resulting in a Black/White ratio of 1.71 and a 71 percent higher mortality rate for Black male children. In 1996 the rates were 71.4 and 37.1 respectively, a risk ratio of 1.92 and a 92 percent higher death rate for Black male children of this age, reflecting substantial widening of the mortality gap. Black and White male children ages 5 to 14 were noted to have death rates per 100,000 population from all causes of 42.3 and 30.1 (a Black rate 40.5 percent higher than White rate), respectively, in 1985 and 38.1 and 23.2 (a Black rate 64.2 percent higher than White rate), in 1996. These rates indicated death ratios of 1.4 in 1985 and 1.6 in 1996 in Black male children compared to White male children of this age group. Clearly, significant Black/White mortality disparities, and the health status and outcome they represent, persist for all Black children under the age of 14 years old, and they were widening for three out of the four race-gender categories between 1985 and 1996. Black females ages 5 to 14 were the only category to show improvement in the disparity in death rate when compared to Whites of the same age during this period. Wide and persistent disparities in children's health best symbolize and capture the African America's health dilemma, where: "the demands of society require that he be as productive, as resourceful, and as responsible as those who have never had these health experiences.... Whether the black American is to be allowed the sound mind and body to compete in this system is the question that must be answered now."[253] Adult diseases present no brighter picture for African Americans.[254]

### Heart Disease

By far the leading cause of death, accounting for 31.7 percent of total deaths in 1996, was heart disease. It contributed the most to the White male and female advantage in life expectancies compared to Blacks.[255] Despite highly publicized improvements in heart disease mortality, the disparities between the heart disease outcomes of White and Black Americans have increased in recent years. As Michael Horan, director of the Division of Heart and Vascular Diseases at the National Heart, Lung, and Blood Institute (NHLBI), noted about cardiovascular disease (CVD) mortality in Blacks in 1992, "Blacks die of heart failure 2.5 times more frequently than whites and seven times more frequently than Asians."[256] Paralleling the rise in racial disparities in the overall death rates from 1.5 in 1960 to 1.6 in 1995, the 1960 Black/White heart disease death rate ratio was 1.2, rising to 1.5 in 1995. As Richard F. Gillum had documented by the early 1990s, death rates for heart disease were higher for Blacks, especially for males of younger ages, beginning in the 1 to 4 year age old group, and, "[a]t younger ages, rates were higher in Black than White women."[257] The Black/White mortality ratio for all causes of death rose from 1.5 in 1980 to 1.7 in 1995 for Black males. Black male heart disease death rates, which were 49.3 percent higher than White death rates in 1980, rose to 66.5 percent higher than White rates by 1995. For Black females, the Black/White heart disease death rate ratio rose steadily from 1.4 in 1980 to 1.6 in 1995. Black female heart disease death rates, which were 49.4 percent higher than White female heart disease death rates in 1980, became 64.7 percent higher in 1995.

During this era, medical myths about coronary heart disease (CHD) in Blacks were dispelled conclusively for the first time in *The Report of the Secretary's Task Force on Black and Minority Health*. The Secretary's Task Force consensus findings concluded the following:

1. Instead of CHD being uncommon in Blacks, CHD is the leading cause of death in U.S. Blacks;
2. Instead of acute myocardial infarction (AMI) being rare in Blacks, AMI hospitalization rates are high in Blacks with higher case fatality rates than Whites.
3. Despite the myth of angina being rare in Blacks, they have high prevalence rates of angina in the United States.
4. Despite the myth of a White preponderance of CHD compared to Blacks, U.S. CHD mortality and prevalence rates are similar in Black and White males, with Black females having higher CHD mortality and prevalence rates than White females.
5. Despite the myth that Blacks are immune to CHD, they proved to be relatively susceptible in the United States.[258]

Moreover, greater percentages of deaths (presumably of cardiac origin) occurred out of hospital for Blacks compared to Whites. And incomplete morbidity data suggest angina pectoris and chronic CHD excesses in Blacks.

## Hypertension

Gillum's statement, "Hypertension acting in concert with other risk factors determines many patterns of cardiovascular mortality and morbidity,"[259] captures hypertensive disease's unique contribution to U.S. mortality and morbidity, which often relates to, and works in concert with, heart and cerebrovascular diseases. The prevalence of hypertensive disease (HD) and hypertensive heart disease (HHD) as secondary causes of death in 20:1 ratios for the former, and 1:1 ratios with other causes, respectively, speak to the prevalence and importance of these interrelationships. Although there are wide geographic variations in the racial prevalence and incidence of HD and HHD—which for Blacks seem to be between 1.4 to 2 times White rates[260]—a sampling of age-adjusted HD and HHD mortality in the middle of the period indicated that Black death rates related to these causes may be as high as four and five times White death rates for both genders. At the very least, "Comparing black women and men to the total population, you see nearly a twofold difference in death rates,"[261] according to Charles Francis, director of the Department of Medicine at Harlem Hospital Center, speaking at a 1992 NHLBI conference, "Minority Health Issues for an Emerging Majority." Although age-adjusted death rates per 100,000 declined for HD and HHD in each sex and race group between 1979 and 1988—for Black males, HD −13.3 percent, HHD −14.3 percent; for Black females, HD −10.6 percent, HHD −17.4 percent—the percentage declines in Whites were greater: White males, HD −21.8 percent, HHD −23.7 percent; White females HD −23.0 percent, HHD −25.5 percent. Moreover, survey and sampling data during the era indicated higher percentages of Whites with blood pressures controlled by treatment than Blacks.[262]

*Stroke*

The available information on stroke, a constellation of illnesses with wide racial disparities, is also mixed. The prevalence, incidence, and hospitalization rates for stroke, the third leading cause of death, were higher in Blacks than in Whites in recent surveys. Moreover, as Horan of the NHLBI noted, "Blacks die of stroke three times more frequently than whites."[263] The overall mortality rates for Cerebrovascular diseases (strokes) declined 35 percent between 1980 and 1995. However, the long-term decline in stroke mortality rates, which had accelerated in 1973, began slowing after 1980 in contrast with the spectacular 44 percent decline in stroke mortality between 1965 and 1980. The Black/White mortality ratio increased over 15 years from 1.8 (Black death rates 80.3 percent higher than Whites) in 1980 to 1.9 in 1985 and 1990 (respective Black death rates 85.3 percent and 89.8 percent higher than White rates), declining slightly to 1.8 (Black death rates 82.2 percent higher than White rates) by 1995. Further, as Richard F. Gillum noted: "[R]ace ratios were much higher for ill-defined stroke (IDS). . . . This suggests that access to diagnostic services such as CT scanning was poorer for Blacks and did not improve over the decade."[264] The male/female sex ratios for sample subgroups in Blacks (male/female about 1.3 for intracranial hemorrhage [IH], 1.2 for thromboembolic stroke [TES] and IDS) and Whites (male/female, IH 1.3, TES 1.4, IDS 1.4) were similar. Age-adjusted hospital discharge rates for first-listed cerbrovascular disease in the NHDS were 30 percent higher in Blacks, and the "[l]imited published data suggest poorer survivorship after acute stroke in Blacks than Whites,"[265] according to the *Handbook of Black American Health*.[266]

## Cancer

Meanwhile, the disproportionate cancer scourge on the Black community continues. Cancer, the second leading cause of death in the United States, was expected to kill 564,800 Americans in 1998, one of every four of the nation's deaths. It "kills more people annually than AIDS, accidents, and homicide *combined*."[267] In 1996 cancer accounted for the deaths of 469,406 White Americans (23.5 percent of total White deaths) and 60,766 Black American deaths (21.5 percent of total Black deaths). After a more-than-10-year trend of increasing age-adjusted mortality continuing throughout the 1980s, "[b]etween 1991 and 1995 the national cancer death rate fell 2.6 percent."[268] Age-adjusted mortality rates for African Americans—initially lower than Whites, but which began increasing and surpassing Whites from the mid-1950s onwards[269]—demonstrated similar trends, reaching a high point of 182.0 deaths per 100,000 resident population in 1990, which was 38.4 percent higher than the White rate, declining to 171.6 deaths per 100,000 population by 1995, which was 35.1 percent higher than the White rate. Between 1979 and 1990, Ki Moon Bang observed: "Blacks experience[d] 10 percent higher cancer incidence and 30 percent higher mortality than Whites."[270] The American Cancer Society (ACS) noted in 1998 that "[b]etween 1990 and 1994, mortality rates fell 0.3 percent per year for whites and 0.7 percent per year for African Americans."[271] However, the Black/White racial mortality rate ratios, 1.3 in 1980 and increasing to 1.4 in 1990, remained at the higher level in 1995, and the slight drop in cancer mortality in 1996 was not considered statistically significant by the NCHS.

Of all racial or ethnic groups in the United States, African Americans continue to have the highest age-adjusted cancer incidence and mortality rates for all types of cancer. The ACS noted:

> *Overall, African Americans are more likely to develop cancer than whites. In 1994, the incidence rate for African Americans was 454 per 100,000 and for whites, 394 per 100,000. Between 1990 and 1994, cancer incidence rates increased 1.2 percent per year in African Americans and decreased 0.8 percent per year in whites.*[272]

Cancer incidence is at least 50 percent higher in African Americans for multiple myeloma, cancers of the esophagus, cervix (uterus), larynx, prostate, stomach, liver, and pancreas. Additionally, Blacks demonstrate higher incidence rates for cancers of the lung and bronchus, urinary bladder, and leukemia.

Due to the higher age-adjusted mortality rates previously noted, "African Americans are about 30 percent more likely to die of cancer than whites."[273] Blacks have at least a 50 percent greater risk than Whites of dying of multiple myeloma and cancers of the esophagus, cervix (uterus), liver, and pancreas. Much of this differential outcome results from the 5-year relative survival rate for African Americans, which "was 12 percentage points below that of non-minorities (1973–81)"[274] and is now 44 percent compared to 60 percent for Whites—a 16 percent differential—between 1989 and 1993. As Claudia Baquet and Carrie Hunter noted in *Cancer Prevention and Control* (1995): "African Americans experienced substantially higher age-adjusted incidence and mortality rates and lower 5-year survival rates for cancers of the oral cavity and pharynx, esophagus, liver, pancreas, lung and bronchus, cervix uteri, and prostate than their white counterparts."[275] Furthermore, "[A]lthough African American patients exhibited lower overall incidence rates than did whites for cancers of the colon and rectum, breast, and corpus uteri, the mortality rates among African Americans for these diseases were comparable to or exceeded those for whites."[276] As the ACS noted, "Much of this difference in survival can be attributed to African Americans being diagnosed at a later stage of disease."[277] A large proportion of cancers, including lung, prostate, colon and rectum, and female breast, cervical and uterine cancers, are diagnosed more frequently at localized stages in Whites than Blacks. Examining survival trends, Bang emphasizes: "Survival rate is much better in cases of localized cancer than regional cancer."[278] Further, according to the ACS: "Most of these sites represent cancers for which screening tests are available; and early detection and timely treatment could increase survival."[279] Thus, for African Americans, the delay in detection and later stage at diagnosis, often followed by delay and differences in treatment, far override biological/constitutional factors for poor outcomes. As the Secretary's Task Force stated:

> *Much of the scientific literature to date supports a hypothesis that the differences in cancer survival between non-minorities and Blacks are attributable to social or environmental factors rather than inherent genetic or biological deficits. Emerging theory suggests that distribution of resources ... can effect cancer outcome, e.g., survival.*[280]

Although lifestyle factors (e.g., cigarette smoking, alcohol consumption, eating habits), occupational/environmental exposure (e.g., toxin exposure, lead exposure), screening behaviors, genetic/biological/constitutional factors, and cultural values and belief systems regarding health care are important; socio-economic status/resource distribution: "Factors such as a lack of health insurance or transportation can impede access to health care and can lead to late diagnoses and poorer survival,"[281] according to the ACS. Compounding these factors, "Studies have shown that poor and medically underserved populations receive fewer cancer prevention services,"[282] according to George Alexander, past chief, Special Populations Studies Branch of the NCI.[283]

## HIV/AIDS

Threatening to displace cancer as the most significant epidemiological event adversely affecting African American health in the 20th century is HIV/AIDS, the new plague wreaking havoc on the African American community. Like the mythological phoenix rising from the ashes, HIV/AIDS rose to become the nation's eighth leading cause of death (43,115, or 1.9 percent of the total deaths), the ninth leading cause of death in the White population (25,509 or 1.3 percent of White deaths), and the fourth leading cause of death in African Americans (17,139 or 6 percent of Black deaths) between 1981, when the first cases were identified, and 1995. Until 1998, HIV/AIDS was the leading cause of death for all persons 25–44 years of age, when it shifted to the second-leading cause for that age group. Of the nearly 300,000 cases reported to the CDC by 1993, almost one-half died; of the 604,200 adults and adolescents with AIDS in the United States reported by May 1998, 62 percent (375,000) died from the disease. Primarily a sexually transmitted disease (STD) that can also be transmitted in nonsexual ways, HIV/AIDS underwent an epidemiologic shift, aggravated existing health problems in the Black community, and has come to have a devastating and disproportionate impact on African Americans.

The first 100,000 cases of AIDS in the United States were reported to the CDC in the first eight and a half years of the epidemic. Homosexual/bisexual White men with no history of injection drug use (IDU) made up 61 percent of these cases. Of the remaining cases, 20 percent were among female or heterosexual male injection drug users, and 5 percent were attributed to heterosexual transmission. Early in the epidemic the media led the public and the Black community to believe AIDS was primarily a disease of gay White men. Proving themselves an influential and effective force, the relatively affluent White gay community mobilized preventive information campaigns, aggressively sought medical care in the mainstream health system and research centers, and spurred, if not demanded, a national commitment to AIDS research. Benefits accrued from these efforts almost immediately. There was an exponential increase in basic science and biomedical research knowledge about the disease; a host of effective primary, secondary, and tertiary prevention methodologies evolved; and an armamentarium of new drugs, led by AZT and other antiretroviral agents, was developed. These developments almost transformed what had been a fatal epidemic when untreated (from AIDS-defining diagnosis to death, 12 months for Whites and 7 months for Blacks) into a chronic disease for some people fortunate enough to have access to highly active antiretroviral therapy (HAART); certain victims lived a decade or more after diagnosis. Prerequisites for success in such efforts included untrammeled access to the health system (especially by making appropriate adjustments to managed care), being sophisticated and affluent enough to politically influence the health and political establishments, and possessing the financial and political means to purchase the expensive new treatment regimens and drugs. The Black community, already crippled by a legitimate and history-based suspicion of the medical and research establishments fueled by a paranoia regarding pronouncements of Haitian and African origins of HIV/AIDS,[284] had little of these.

The second 100,000 cases, reported in the next two years and two months of the epidemic, highlighted the changing epidemiology of HIV/AIDS in the United States and the racial dimensions of the problem. The driving force behind the disproportionate effect of HIV/AIDS on the Black community during the 1990s is the transmission of the virus by IDU-associated heterosexual activity, including the "number of sex partners, frequency of unprotected sexual contact, prostitution, sex with a prostitute, history of STDs, lack of circumcision, and ulcerative as well as non-ulcerative genital disease."[285] As a result, in the second wave of cases ending in the early 1990s, only 55 percent occurred among homosexual/bisexual men without histories of IDU, 24 percent occurred among females or heterosexual males with IDU behavior, and 7 percent were attributed to heterosexual transmission. The proportion of Blacks with AIDS increased from 27 percent to more than 31 percent, and 31.5 percent of males and 57.5 percent of females with AIDS were Black by 1996. By December 1997, Blacks constituted 36 percent (230,029 cases) of the cases reported (641,086), and approximately one in 50 African American men and one in 160 African American women were part of the 93,000 Blacks living with AIDS.

Upon closer examination of the emerging epidemiological profile of the disease in the Black community, Wayne L. Greaves found that "[a]mong Black men, who account for 26 percent of all AIDS cases in adult men, homosexual contact accounts for 43 percent of the cases and IDU use accounts for 36 percent, and homosexual men who inject drugs account for another 7 percent of cases."[286] This contrasts strongly with the epidemiologic profile of the White community. While the number of AIDS diagnoses among gay and bisexual men has decreased dramatically among White men since 1989, the incidence in Black homosexual men has increased. As the DHHS noted in 1998:

> AIDS cases and new infections related to injecting drug use appear to be increasingly concentrated in minorities; of these cases, almost 75 percent were among minority populations (56 percent black and 20 percent Hispanic). Of cases reported among women and children, more than 75 percent were among racial and ethnic minorities.[287]

Therefore, by 1998: "Racial and ethnic minorities constitute[d] approximately 25 percent of the total U.S. population, yet they account[ed] for nearly 54 percent of all AIDS cases," and "the *number* of new AIDS cases among blacks [was] ... greater than the number of new AIDS case among whites."[288] As the *CDC Update* noted, "In 1997, more African Americans were reported with AIDS than any other racial/ethnic group. Of the total AIDS cases reported that year, 45 percent (27,075) were reported among African Americans, 33 percent (20,197) were reported among whites, and 21 percent (12,466) were reported among Hispanics."[289] This epidemiologic shift was facilitated by coalescing with and aggravating an already extent IDU problem, by exacerbating minority groups' inadequate and inequitable access to quality health care, and by its patterns of infection affecting far more women and children than in earlier White gay paradigms.

America's "dual and unequal" health system and its traditional prejudices against substance abusers, poor persons and MIAs, homosexuals, and racial and ethnic minority groups have coalesced and helped impede effective mobilization to attack the problem—especially in Black communities. The underfunded tiers of the public health subsystem represented by a contracting patchwork of increasingly outmoded, underfunded, understaffed public hospitals; declining numbers of overburdened, understaffed, underfunded CHCs and NHCs; a threatened network of neglected teaching hospitals; and remnants of government-funded health services, community outreach, and research programs in poor communities and their provider institutions have not been up to the demands imposed by the HIV/AIDS epidemic. These are the essential community provider, safety net institutions that large blocs of the Black and MIA populations depend upon for basic health services.

Campaigns, political action, and individually motivated efforts to defeat the provision of clean needles to drug abusers, to press criminal charges against infected mothers, and to deny Black and certain groups of MIAs access to state-of-the-art AIDS therapies are examples of the prejudicial, sometimes racist, medical-social barriers to addressing the crisis. There is also the danger that acceptance of HIV/AIDS as a chronic disease will vitiate attention to what is, in fact, an urgent health issue threatening the viability of the Black community. Thus recognition and reassessment are required of the issues of race, homophobia, and the present configuration of and attitudes within the health system as important factors in the current HIV/AIDS epidemic. Moreover:

> *The current health insurance system must change drastically so that the poorest patient, Black or White, has equal access to the same medical care as those who are wealthy. The health care system needs to provide better social services along with medical care for AIDS patients. Financially strapped urban hospitals and physicians and other health providers caring for poor Black patients must be better remunerated. Health education and AIDS prevention messages need to be more relevant and culturally appropriate.*[290]

Proof that intense education programs, political clout regarding the health agenda, and access to efficacious new treatment (which costs between $10,000 and $12,000 annually) works is evidenced by the 23 percent decline in AIDS death rates, deaths from AIDS decreasing 46.4 percent in 1997 (from 31,130 to 16,685), and AIDS dropping off the top 10 causes of death list for the first time since 1991 (for the White community). Despite fewer deaths, the infection rate of 40,000 per year is holding steady and increasingly involves poor, minority communities—attacking groups much less likely to have access to health care that will pay for the new drugs. Attempting to counteract such systemic and epidemiologic changes requires full-fledged mobilization of the nation, the Black community, and all well-meaning Americans concerned with the public's health. Such a campaign will by necessity include the entire health community, both the public and private sectors, and the Black community's churches, politicians, educational institutions, professionals, and volunteers, to brighten the prognosis of the HIV/AIDS epidemic nationally and within the African American community.[291]

### Diabetes

The Malone-Heckler report focused attention on the alarming excess morbidity and mortality minorities suffered from diabetes and other chronic diseases. Diabetes is the fifth most frequent cause of death due to disease in African Americans and the sixth leading cause of death due to disease in the overall population, reflecting the fact that its prevalence, morbidity, and mortality are at least twice as high among African Americans as in the U.S. White population. Facts reveal that: "[F]rom 1963 to 1985, the rates of known diabetes in the United States doubled for Whites, but tripled for African Americans" and that "African-American males had a lower rate than White males from 1963 to 1973; but, after 1975, there was a crossover such that the rate for Black males became higher than the rate for White males."[292] Moreover, since the Secretary's Task Force report, Black diabetes mellitus death rates have been increasing from 20.1, to 24.8, to 25.3, to 26.8, to 27.4, to 28.5 deaths per 100,000 population in 1985, 1990, 1992, 1993, 1994, and 1995, respectively. And Black/White mortality differentials have increased from 2.3 (133.7 percent higher than White rates), to 2.4 (138.4 percent higher than White rates), to 2.4 (143.6 percent higher than White rates) times the White rates in 1985, 1990, and 1995 respectively. Recently released 1996 final data from the NCHS reveal no significant improvements.[293] The complications of diabetes, such as cardiovascular disease and stroke, diabetic nephropathy and end-stage renal disease (Black ESRD rate is 2.9 times White rate), the highest rates of blindness due to diabetes between the ages of 20 and 74, and lower extremity amputations (Black LEA rates 1.5 to 2.0 times White rates) remain much higher in Blacks.[294] Limited research on minority group factors influencing this disease has been performed, despite the uncertain relationships between personal characteristics such as genetics, age, sex, and history of glucose intolerance and lifestyle factors such as physical activity and obesity that influence the occurrence of, and racial/ethnic variations and differentials in (i.e., these are very important in Latino/Hispanic American and Native American populations), diabetes mellitus. The differential ravages diabetes inflicts on the African American community have been obvious for several decades; however, there appears to be another menace to Black health on the horizon.[295]

### Respiratory Diseases

Chest and/or diseases that affect respiratory function, including the Pneumonia and influenza and Chronic obstructive pulmonary diseases (COPD) categories, were the eighth and ninth leading causes of death in the Black population in 1995. They ranked fourth (COPD) and sixth (Pneumonia and influenza) for the general population in 1996, representing racial variations in the leading cause of death patterns. The Black/White mortality ratio for Pneumonia and influenza (climbing from 1.4 in 1995 to 1.5 in 1996) represented one of the cause of death categories "for which the ratio was large,"[296] according to the NCHS. Moreover, the racial mortality differential for this constellation of diseases, which is responsive to access and therapeutic interventions, has hovered erratically between a Black rate from 44 to 58 percent higher than the White rate for almost two decades, beginning in 1980. For the COPD category—which includes items 490 to 496 of the ninth revision of the International Classification of Diseases (ICD-9), namely bronchitis, emphysema, asthma, and other conditions—the trends for African Americans are also unfavorable, but in different ways. COPD, responsible for 6,667 Black deaths in 1995, was not among the 10 leading causes of death for African Americans in 1980. It was traditionally considered a predominantly "White" category of diseases. Although its age-adjusted mortality rates have continued to rise in the White population from 16.3 deaths per 100,000 population in 1980 to 21.3 deaths per 100,000 in 1995 (a 31 percent rise), it has climbed more rapidly in the Black population from 12.5 deaths per 100,000 population in 1980 to 17.6 deaths per 100,000 population in 1995 (a 41 percent rise). Between 1979 and 1990, "The increase for COPD death rates was 94.5 percent for Black females and 42.5 percent for Black males."[297] During this same period the Black mortality rate for asthma increased by 78.9 percent. Thus a newly emerging major health problem in the Black community began extracting an alarmingly disparate racial toll wherein, by the 1990s: "Mortality rates for asthma in Blacks was 3.4 per 100,000 population compared with 1.2 in Whites,"[298] according to Bang. This represents a 2.8 Black/White mortality differential, which began to display a predilection for children less than six years old as early as the 1970s (NHIS asthma rates for Black children were 36.4 per 1,000 compared to 27.9 per 1,000 for White children), whose effects were later compounded by NHANES I data, which "showed Black children aged 1 to 5 years had more episodes of pneumonia than white children."[299] The continuing rise in COPD and chest disease mortality, especially in Black children, requires more investigation and attention. Disentangling the effects of known risk factors such as age and cigarette smoking from changing fashions in chest disease diagnosis and mounting evidence of Black exposure to environmental allergens and pollutants must begin. If prevention and treatment, along with necessary research, are not forthcoming, another Black/White crossover in another major disease category (COPD) and a further widening of racial disparities in already significant disaggregated health indicators (e.g., asthma, pneumonia and influenza) seem inevitable.[300]

## The Medical Profession: A Waning Influence

### White Professional Complicity and the Loss of Authority and Relevance

White organized medicine entered the 1980s chastened by the Medicare/ Medicaid "defeat" but scrambling to maintain power. AMA stalwart Ernest B. Howard, M.D., observed in 1984:

> [M]edicine has proceeded on two parallel courses over the years. One is clearly academic, clearly medical, clearly focused on the education of the physician. The other is clearly political, governmental, related to the prevention of the socializing or the nationalizing of medicine. The two courses are clearly related to each other.[301]

Blind spots in the White profession's medical-social view and worldview served to undermine its successful pursuit of either course.

Instead of capturing the nation's intergenerational mood—primed by FDR and the Depression, World War II, and the 1960s revolution, enmeshed in a Western cultural synchrony with other developed Western European nations— which assumes several level social playing fields (basic citizenship rights, access to education, health and health care, and humane levels of social security)—the U.S. medical and health establishments sided with rogue South Africa on health matters.[302] For example, the medical profession's almost phobic preoccupation with the government's role in health and health care hobbled its ability to react appropriately to a changing health care environment. As a result, it failed to protect either its own, or its patient's, interests:

> While solidly supporting private medicine and private medical insurance, physicians acknowledge a role for the government in the financing of medical care, though most of them ardently want the government role confined to help for those unable to finance their own care. They argue that mainstream Americans—those who support themselves in a basically private economy—should be served by a basically private medical care system. They believe that a patient should be free to choose among the various forms of medical care that are available; they value their own freedom to choose the type of practice they engage in.[303]

This professional choice, based on contemporary practices, allowed discrimination against patients on the basis of race or class. In spite of reasonable sounding and balanced language, extreme policies that preserved physicians' version of a pluralistic health system often drove the profession into the arms of the

HMO–managed care and hospital industries. Such policies also promoted actions perceived as self-serving and/or ignoring patients' basic medical needs in the name of cost-cutting and profit-taking. White organized medicine ignored several realities: Americans' demand for a national and universal health system since the end of World War II;[304] the flaws, exploitation, abuse, and adverse health consequences associated with racial segregation and race and class discrimination in the nation's health and health system; and the quagmire produced by uncontrolled health care cost inflation.

The U.S. health system and medical profession's integrity and viability are brought into question by supporting policies and practices that are yielding increasing millions of uninsured citizens; perpetuating and sometimes worsening race- and class-based health disparities; producing a decline in overall consumer satisfaction with the health system;[305] increasing the likelihood of the system's failing to provide care for the poor, disadvantaged minorities, and the disabled — populations already being underserved; and threatening the availability of health care for all except privileged Americans in the future. The profession's recent elevation of token, symbolic, conservative African Americans to highly visible, although barely influential, titular positions in several medical and health professions organizations failed to impress most African Americans and other disadvantaged minority Americans and, as expected, yielded few tangible results.[306]

The profession's narrow vision is also reflected in its continued overreliance on science and technology, persistent failure to esteem primary care and human values in the care of patients, failure to address and correct the previously mentioned physician production and distribution problems, and failure to reign in graduate *medical education*. Despite proportional representation's proven improved access and medical-social benefits, the medical profession, in alliance with a conservative and increasingly authoritarian judiciary and political process, is rolling back the production and participation of underrepresented minorities in medicine.[307] Moreover, Dr. Arnold Relman's predictions of ethical conflicts borne of the entrepreneurial drift in the health care system and the profession's participation in such activities have accentuated the lowering of the ethical standards pervading the health system.[308] He warned in 1985: "The AMA's present position has an even more troublesome aspect ... the AMA's statements ignore the damage done to the public trust in the medical profession by even the *appearance* of conflicts of interest"[309] [Dr. Relman's emphasis]. This situation worsened as physicians frequently became investors and shareholders in health provider, management, and supply entities, creating virtually automatic conflicts of interest. Subsequent developments, with numerous instances of dishonesty, professional arrogance, fraud, waste, patient abuse, and incompetence in the medical and health care communities, have borne out his predictions.[310] White organized medicine did little to deter these developments.

Equally, if not more, ominous has been the sweeping aside or routine appropriation of the American medical establishment by commercially oriented

HMO–managed care and governmental forces during the past 20 years. In a contemporaneous *Medical Economics* article, "Why Doctors Will Take Back Health Care," health economist Uwe E. Reinhardt, when queried as to why doctors had been placed in a position where they had to "regain influence" and "retake control of the health-care system," noted, "because physicians were caught off-guard; the managed care revolution rolled over them without their having been prepared for it."[311] White organized medicine sat passively on the sidelines as the imposition of the "market" ethic and "competitive" organizational policies and practices were inexorably implemented. Unproven (in terms of whether they improve quality of care) administrative interventions to limit patient access to services and specialty care were enacted; physicians were coerced and/or forced to adhere to practice guidelines imposed by HMOs and act as "gatekeepers" between patients and specialty and emergency health care services; physicians and patients failed to resist HMO–managed care attempts to influence clinical decision-making with utilization management/review; financial risks were shifted to physicians through capitation and other mechanisms for therapies they ordered for their patients; and physicians were financially rewarded for denying care to patients under their care.[312] Managed care's financial and administrative developments had dramatic, often unanticipated, effects that could be threatening to disadvantaged minority, inner-city, and rural poor populations. Such policies and practices continue to mount as we enter a new millennium.

Another corollary of the organizational changes that affect physician behavior and thus the doctor-patient relationship in the "competitive market" health care environment is the commodification of health care. David Blumenthal observes:

> Society is telling physicians in multiple ways—the trend toward investor ownership of health care organizations and the adoption by those and other organizations of marketing techniques used in other economic sectors—that they should regard health care as a commodity much like many others that are exchanged in the marketplace. The implication is that the practice of medicine is an economic transaction, not a professional calling.[313]

The process is so pervasive and counterintuitive to the profession that it raises the question of whether medicine is being deprofessionalized. Seemingly, in exchange for incomes that continued to rise until the mid-1990s and health policy and system changes they perceived as resonating with their conservative ideology and agenda (e.g., less government involvement, radical individualism, classical competitive markets, rugged individualism regarding social services, maintaining separate race- and class-based social orders), physicians remained relatively silent.

When the window of opportunity for meaningful health reform opened after the Reagan-Bush era and Americans expressed a desire for some type of national universal health system, White organized medicine equivocated, then fought against President Clinton's halting—flawed from justice and equity perspectives—steps toward a universal, although multitiered, system. Physicians have remained detached and figuratively "above the fray," for example, "exempt[ing] themselves from blame for health care inflation,"[314] as Taylor, Leitman, and Edwards noted.

Nevertheless, most physicians have become increasingly dissatisfied with the health system, how it functions, and how they must work within it. Primarily through acts of omission such as these, but also through some acts of commission such as the AMA's summary dismissal of highly respected *JAMA* editor George Lundberg, M.D., for, seemingly, ideological and political reasons, the White American medical profession is losing influence, authority, prestige, public confidence, and the appearance of professional competence at the group or organizational level. AMA membership is also declining in relative terms. Whether the medical profession's immensely valuable social capital and authority can or will be regained remains to be seen.[315]

### African American Physicians' Reaffirmation to Health and Health Care Justice and Equity: New Rivers to Cross

Between the 1980s and early 1990s, Black doctors remained vigilant in their little acknowledged and largely unappreciated oversight of the U.S. health system. They were especially diligent at addressing cutting-edge issues affecting patient care, the health delivery system, and the biomedical education and research infrastructure. Although the carefully orchestrated rhetoric to the contrary intensified, U.S. health system policies moved away from maintaining the doctor-patient relationship, correcting the racial health deficits, attaining the vital goal of proportional representation of underrepresented minorities in the health professions, preserving patients' freedom of choice in choosing their doctors or institutions for care, ensuring universal access to acceptable levels of quality care for all Americans, integration of the health system—including organized medicine—along race and class lines, and protecting individual patients' rights in the health system. Nevertheless, African American physicians clung tenaciously to these previously cherished core values. Despite Black doctors' efforts, the mainstream system continued to evolve in directions that adversely affected their practices, future participation and patients in particular, and the entire health system in general.

Black physicians, health providers, and their allies articulated their positions on such issues as the "Black Health Crisis of the 1980s and 1990s"; health planning, health care cost containment, and health care financing; health care marketing and competition; the adverse impact of the Reagan-Bush administrations' public policies and subsequent health policies on Black health; the effect of managed care on African American patients and practitioners; medical-legal and malpractice reform; their ethical and medical-social concerns; failures by the medical/health education and research infrastructures to keep their promises of equitable minority representation and participation; peer review at the professional, grassroots, and health care legislative levels; and the impending threats to Black doctors, medical schools, and Black hospitals caused by the changing health system structure, financing, and environment. They continued their civil rights–oriented struggle for inclusion as national health policy advisors to presidential administrations (including President Clinton's), Congress, and various components of the USPHS with varying degrees of success. During the 12 years of the Reagan-Bush era and its aftermath, African American health providers maintained their unwavering historical commitment to providing access to high-quality services for all segments of the population, with a special emphasis on the health and health care of African Americans, other underserved groups, and disadvantaged Americans.[316]

As Black doctors and health professionals forged ahead in their struggle, dealing with a matrix of complex issues, they remained acutely aware of the ethical dilemma with which the health system was faced. They recognized that: "Health care for the poor will remain a moral challenge to the architects of health policy and the medical profession."[317] It was clear that their view of restructuring the health system, particularly with the way health care should be financed, created "[s]erious implications for health services, social policy and for the application of ethical and moral principles to a broad range of health and human services."[318] Black doctors remained troubled and vocal about the conflicts between the altruistic ideals of medicine and the financial imperatives of cost containment, the move toward managed care, and the corporate takeover of medicine. Concerns were raised about whether the changing health care environment would further encourage differential treatment of patients based on perceived social worth or financial status.

Black doctors and other culturally competent providers\* knew that "an awareness and assessment of the ethical, social, and economic implications of bedside allocation is necessary to prevent an ethical frenzy for the provider and tragic disillusion for the patient when the escape valve in the health system is finally turned off."[319] Without legal and ethical safeguards and such reasoned reflection, another round of value-laden, scientific racist, racially and ethnically discriminatory alloca-

---

\**Cultural competence* involves the capacity of practitioners, systems, agencies, and institutions to respond appropriately to the unique needs of populations whose cultures are different from that which might be called "dominant" or "mainstream." Becoming culturally competent is a developmental process and involves a continuum that ranges from cultural destructiveness to cultural incapacity, cultural blindness, cultural precompetence, cultural competence, and, finally, cultural proficiency. The culturally competent individual or system values diversity, has the capacity for cultural self-assessment; is conscious of the dynamics inherent when cultures interact, possesses institutionalized cultural knowledge, and has developed adaptations to diversity. *Source*: U.S. Department of Health and Human Services. *Cultural Competence for Evaluators: A Guide for Alcohol and Other Drug Abuse Prevention Practitioners Working with Ethnic/Racial Communities*. Rockville, MD: Office for Substance Abuse Prevention, Alcohol, Drug Abuse, and Mental Health Administration, DHHS Publication No. (ADM)92–1884, 1992.

tion processes would continue. Some Black doctors felt that divarication of the fundamental values of the health professions was inevitable because doctors and other health professionals were being charged with the dual role of serving as clinicians and patient advocates at the same time as they were expected to function efficiently as agents to contain costs.

As third-party payers and government (e.g., Medicare and Medicaid) developed mechanisms to manage, contain, then cut costs, further evidence of the Black health crisis mounted—highlighted by the release of the Malone-Heckler report on Black and minority health in October 1985. African American physicians, who were acutely aware of the crisis portrayed in the report long before its release, rose to the challenge of addressing the various factors contributing to the emergency described therein. They voiced concerns that, despite lofty intentions and substantive revelations, "no governmental programs were instituted nor significant funding by government made for improving the health status of blacks and other minorities"[320] as a result of the Malone-Heckler report. Moreover, Ms. Heckler concluded: "that many of these health problems are related to what she called 'lifestyles and knowledge.' 'Progress,' she said, 'depends more on education and a change in personal behavior than it does on more doctors, more hospitals or more technology.'"[321] This flew in the face of the realities faced by most Black inner-city practitioners and providers. As 1985 NMA president, Dr. Edith Irby Jones, noted about Heckler's new "minority health strategy": "Her implication ... is that if black people would only 'behave,' their health problems would be solved ... as black Americans, we know it is not as simple as all that. Blaming the patient will not cure the ills of America's underserved minorities."[322] Moreover, in spite of the fiction implicit in its almost total reliance on behavioral causation of Black health problems, "no major new programs or funding to change this behavior were suggested in the HHS report."[323] This further exacerbated flaws already embodied in this new and cost-neutral "minority health strategy."

The leadership of the NMA and individual Black doctors also voiced grave concerns about the adverse impact of Reaganomics on health care for the poor and underserved. There was concern for the further widening of the Black/White gap in health indices as a result of the Reagan administration's health policies. For example, one authority on cardiovascular diseases in minorities stated that:

> *the health policies of the Reagan Administration pose a serious threat to the efforts to move from 50 percent hypertension control to an even higher figure and to close the black-white gap in CV mortality. The list of programs slated for the fiscal ax reads like an honor roll in the campaign for hypertension control: Medicaid, community health centers, the "ghetto medicine" Act, National Health Service Corps, etc. The reshaping of health care services according to the perspective of the current administration threatens to undermine one of the most important*

*public health advances since World War II; it is, furthermore, a direct*
*challenge to the most important step toward racial equality taken in*
*medicine in at least as many years.*[324]

Black physicians recognized that lack of health insurance was another major problem limiting access, availability, and quality of health care for African Americans. They also recognized that with escalating health costs and efforts to contain and cut costs, Blacks and the poor would be increasingly pushed out of private hospitals, forced to use emergency rooms, forgo treatment for serious chronic health problems, and experience being "dumped" in greater numbers each year onto struggling, underfunded, deteriorating, public hospitals.

As the "Black Health Crisis" continued to worsen—with increasing maldistribution of health care providers, resources, and facilities; inaccessibility of medical care; continual rising costs of health care; increasing numbers of uninsured; persistent racism and discrimination in the health system; and further fragmentation of the health system, all contributing to the health care "netherworld"—Black doctors found themselves increasingly carrying the burden of being "Disproportionate Health Care Providers."* As frontline providers of care to burgeoning underserved populations—expanding as a result of Reagan-Bush policies—they recognized, quite appropriately and consistent with empirical laws of public health, that poor patients who are sicker require more services. Nevertheless, they, as their primary care providers, received "less reimbursement for similar services than providers of care to the economically advantaged."[325] It became increasingly clear that in spite of the health access and financing progress and successes of the late 1960s and 1970s, the "Black Health Crisis of the 1980s and 1990s" was a crisis for both African American patients and their doctors and other health care providers for the underserved, driven by an engine of public policy.

Because of increasing concern for retrogression in medicine and public health, populations affected by the "Black Health Crisis," and large, growing, blocks of uninsured U.S. citizens and immigrants, the NMA became a strong advocate for a comprehensive national health plan. Thus positions of African American providers were products of empirical deduction and medical ethics–oriented caring, more than a simple continuation of their ideological or "civil rights" traditions. Black physicians and disadvantaged minority health providers also made substantive recommendations for addressing the crisis by including African Americans at the policy level. R. Hester and Jesse B. Barber recognized, "There is a need to fund a major health policy research institute to include experts from historical black colleges and public hospitals, physicians and nurses to engage in research on the major health problems of the poor and disadvantaged"[326] by 1990.

---

*By the season of Clinton health reform, this term had become synonymous with *essential community providers* (ECPs).

As the "Black Health Crisis" continued into the 1990s, Black physicians began to recognize that strategic planning, public health, and health policy flaws were being promulgated in the health system, often under the guise of managed care. In an analysis of the serious health problems affecting African Americans, Barber noted that undergirding the overall situation was the fact that a "basic health issue in 1990 is the racism that underlies health policy and practices just as it did in 1895. Racism in health in 1990 is perhaps a bit more subtle and less direct than it was in 1895, but possibly even more frustrating because we have a much greater capacity to correct some of the problems."[327] Through a disarming panoply of what could be interpreted as dissembling, disingenuous, and confusing policy mechanisms, this health crisis seemed, in many ways, more difficult to reveal, confront, and ameliorate. Despite the health system's inequitable, sometimes brutal past; glaring and growing race- and class-based health disparities; the realities of a health system still largely segregated on the basis of race and class; and the imposition of new policies and events that were worsening the situation, concerns of African American physicians were seldom recognized as valid, and crusading for race and class justice in health and health care in the United States was almost analogous to "punching a cloud."

Nevertheless, African American physicians recognized that the health crisis could be resolved only through efforts to expand health insurance protection or, preferably, establish a national health plan that allowed all Americans equal access to quality medical and health care services; increase health manpower in underserved areas; institute relevant data collection requisite to improve disadvantaged minority health; ensure managed care contracting and oversight with cultural competence goals in mind; implement bias prevention blocking redlining along with Title VI enforcement; make health care a human rights and civil rights issue; increase the number of Black and underserved minority physicians; specifically address the medical conditions accounting for the excess deaths and disparities in health status and outcome with resource allocation based on assessments of need; substantively implement culturally competent HP/DP programs; based on equitable inclusion policies, increase the number of African Americans in federal and state health policy and administrative positions; legally mandate African American inclusion on a proportionate basis in any peer review and quality assurance efforts; and legally mandate provisions against, along with a system of monitoring with the goal of eliminating, all forms of racial discrimination in the U.S. health delivery system.[328]

A bevy of virtually untapped and relevant articles critically analyzing all aspects of the "Black Health Crisis" appeared in the *Journal of the National Medical Association (JNMA)* throughout the 12 years of the Reagan-Bush era and the period that followed. Emanating from a broad cross section of biomedical, health care and health policy authorities and legislators, they ranged from epidemiologic and biostatistical assessments of the crisis to highly sophisticated recommendations on health policy, legislation, and reform strategies to eliminate the crisis, reduce costs without compromising quality, and ultimately provide health care equity for all Americans.

Competitive strategies and efforts to contain cost throughout the 1980s and early 1990s threatened the economic survival of Black physicians and the few remaining Black hospitals. It became increasingly clear that "competition"* under the managed care mantra and prospective payments using diagnosis-related groups (DRGs) implemented in October 1983 were having disproportionately negative effects on Black physicians' practices on the front end, directly, by lowering their incomes from fees and, indirectly, by the cost-driven, illness-avoiding, "peer review" and "quality assurance" activities. Other "Disproportionate Health Care Providers" differentially affected were Black hospitals, public hospitals, and other hospitals with a high case-mix of Black and poor patients (e.g., stressed inner-city and teaching hospitals). As prepaid "competitive" plans such as HMOs and PPOs gained increasing dominance in the health care industry, economic survival of Black practices and other institutions serving Black patients became even more threatened.

The malpractice crisis, with escalating professional liability insurance premiums and a declining patient base (i.e., declining Medicaid roles and more uninsured patients) from a financing perspective secondary to Reagan-Bush cutbacks and "competitive" strategies, further eroded the economic survival of Black doctors. Hester and Barber noted: "Despite the successes of the Medicare prospective payment in lowering national hospital costs in recent years, this new policy has encouraged Black hospital closures, and many inner city public and private hospitals have experienced financial losses."[329] African American physicians articulated their concerns and outrage about escalating costs secondary to administration, artificially inflated pharmaceutical pricing, costly marketing and public relations campaigns, and the all-important profit motive of the managed care organizations (MCOs) and hospitals while the paradox of worsening health care access and quality for the nation's Black and poor populations loomed in the shadows of these phenomena.

Emsley Davis noted:

> Somewhere along the line those who manage many of the nation's hospitals have lost sight of the fact that as a part of the health care system, hospitals should provide the mechanisms to prolong life through the prevention of premature death, to treat the underprivileged, and to minimize incapacitations and illness and thereby promote a high level of wellness rather than generate a profit.[330]

---

*As Evans, Navarro, and others have repeatedly noted, "[t]here is in health care no 'private, competitive market' of the form described in the economics textbooks, anywhere in the world." *Source:* Evans RG. Going for the gold: The redistributive agenda behind market-based health care reform. *Journal of Health Politics, Policy and Law* 1997; 22:21–22; quote p. 21.

Black doctors made numerous recommendations on how to control costs and the need to modify diagnosis-related group (DRG) prospective hospital payments in ways not to penalize those facilities with patients having a disproportionately high disease burden, thereby inevitably consuming more hospital resources, in order to provide more equitable reimbursement for those providers. But such recommendations usually fell on deaf ears at the level of health care power brokers and legislators. By the early 1990s, data verified that Black doctors were losing practices because of inadequate reimbursements by Medicaid, Medicare, and third-party payers. Charles Johnson reported that the Old North State Medical Society in North Carolina surveyed Black physicians in that state to determine if any had lost practices in 1990: "We were astounded to learn that between 30 percent and 40 percent of Afro-American physicians' practices in North Carolina had already been lost, with physicians working for emergency rooms in other locations or for health maintenance organizations at significant reductions in income."[331] Although the sweeping changes in the "competitive" market-driven health care environment of the 1980s and 1990s took its toll on the economic survival of Black physicians, the Black medical profession was no less committed to serving the underserved, advocating health care as a right for all Americans, and developing effective strategies for appropriate reform while ensuring its own survival.[332]

Despite the increasing demand for health care services by Blacks and the poor, there remained a critical shortage of Black and other underserved minority physicians, dentists, nurses, pharmacists, and other providers. The NMA and its membership continued to advocate for improvements in medical and health professions, school enrollments and financial aid for students, recruitment of minority physicians in the specialty and subspecialty postgraduate residency training programs, and recruitment of African American physicians to majority medical school faculty and research positions. In 1990, it was reported that only 1.9 percent of medical school faculty were African Americans, with less than 1.0 percent representation on White medical school faculties. Frierson summed up the medical school enrollment shortfalls:

> [T]he enrollment goal, established in 1970 and endorsed by the National Medical Association, American Association of Medical Colleges, American Medical Association, and the American Hospital Association was 12 percent enrollment for blacks by 1976, this goal has never come close to being reached. The highest enrollment percentage for blacks was just 7.5 percent, and that was only for one year, 1975.[333]

Moreover, Black acceptance rates began to decline after the late 1970s:

> In 1975, the year that the highest percentage of blacks were accepted into medical schools, the black acceptance rate was 43 percent, but it declined to 40 percent in 1980.... By comparison, the acceptance

> *rate for nonminority applicants rose from 35 percent in 1974 to 50 percent in 1983. Thus, a diverging acceptance rate for black and white applicants has occurred.*[334]

These phenomena occurred despite the increased numbers of Black applicants and their improved MCAT scores, both absolutely and comparatively, between 1974 and 1983. Authorities "concluded that medical schools' commitments to affirmative action ha[d] slackened considerably."[335] Throughout the period, the NMA made numerous recommendations for increasing the number of Black doctors; improving health manpower shortages, especially in underserved areas; and increasing disadvantaged minority medical school enrollment.

In the early 1980s the NMA challenged the Report of the Graduate Medical Education National Advisory Committee (GMENAC), which predicted there would be a surplus of between 35,000 and 85,000 physicians by year 2000. Hilliard indicated that the report did not recognize the tremendous underrepresentation of Black physicians, discuss the shortages of physicians in underserved inner-city areas, or acknowledge the need for increased number of minority medical students.[336] Despite the Bakke decision by the Supreme Court, which helped undermine most medical school affirmative action programs, the Black medical profession continued its quest for equity in medical school admissions, postgraduate training, and faculty positions for African Americans throughout the 1980s and 1990s.[337]

Meanwhile, racial discrimination and differential treatment within the medical profession reemerged as a major problem in the 1980s. This differentially affected African American physicians and, thus, their patients. Historical foundations of systematic racial segregation and discrimination; elitism, professional exclusion, and control as represented by the nineteenth-century sectarian wars; more than a century of civil rights struggles to obtain hospital privileges and a modicum of official participation in the professions for Black doctors; passage of the Health Care Quality Improvement Act of 1986 (H.R. 5540);* and the notorious Patrick case,** all laid firm foundations for the subsequent near-complete appropriation and control of the medical profession by

---

*H.R. 5540 was legislation supported by White organized medicine, including the hospital and managed care establishment, granting legal immunity to inquisitor physicians against discrimination, defamation of character, or restraint of trade lawsuits, as they carry out the health establishment's peer review and QA policies. In American medicine, much of this activity has a sordid history of being racially, socially, and politically motivated (e.g., blocking Black doctors from hospital staff appointments and unfairly disciplining them, eliminating competition among doctors, purging "unpopular" or "controversial" doctors from the profession, and enforcing medical establishment political agendas).

**Dr. Patrick, an Oregon surgeon, was abused so blatantly by his peers in a "quality control" audit at his local hospital that for the first time in the nation's history an appellate court upheld a jury verdict wherein he was awarded damages from his inquisitor doctors and the hospital. This forced the Supreme Court, for the first time, to review the physician disciplinary-audit process.

managed care forces by the mid-1990s. NMA-sponsored surveys in the early 1990s revealed that over 95 percent of African American physicians experienced racial discrimination in their practices on a daily basis—which, interestingly, corroborated Bullock and Houston's and Firerson's findings of prejudice, discrimination, and overall negativism in the medical school environment for at least 97 percent of Black medical students.[338] Moreover, White physicians are still making biased clinical decisions based on race and gender in 2001, and policy investigations reveal that much of this activity is having direct and indirect, differential, and adverse effects on Black patients.[339] The plutocratic control imposed by a White peer review system, which intensified during the 1980s—already race- and class-insensitive, autocratic, and unrestrained—augmented by H.R. 5540 and managed care dictates, often under a guise of controlling costs, with uncorrected and institutionalized race- and class-discriminatory patterns built into and remaining in the system, segued easily into the corporate-dominated health system of the 1990s. Serendipity will not solve these problems. As has been previously noted, patients of all persuasions have been the ultimate losers. As African American physicians have pointed out for more than 150 years, race and class issues in the United States health system still remain to be rectified.[340]

Despite the persistent realities of racism, discrimination, and inequities in the health system, there have been rays of hope embodied in the stellar leadership provided by certain African American health professionals during this era. Some of their contributions are well known and acknowledged publically, such as those of Dr. Louis W. Sullivan, the second African American secretary of USDHHS (see Figure 7.5); Dr. Deborah Prothrow-Stith of HSPH, America's "Pied Piper" against violence who successfully applied public health measures to the problem of leading the national effort on violence prevention; Dr. M. Jocelyn Elders, America's first African American Surgeon General; and Dr. David Satcher, the first African American CDC Director, who now serves as Surgeon General. (See Figure 7.6.) Although they are major role models and high-profile personalities, some of their exploits, many of which will provide long-lasting national benefits, are not widely appreciated. For example, Dr. Sullivan's singular efforts in establishing a sorely needed African American medical school and his role in establishing permanent branches of the NIH and NCI to deal with minority health issues are little known to the general public, but will positively affect the nation's health and its health system into this millennium. Dr. Satcher's virtual rescue from closure of Meharry Medical College, America's oldest, largest, African American health professions school upon his assumption of its presidency in the early 1980s, his establishment of the Institute on Health Care for the Poor and Underserved at Meharry, and his unflagging efforts to eliminate minority health and health care disparities may be little appreciated, but will be treated kindly by history.

There was another cadre of Black health professionals who worked, largely behind the scenes, making unprecedented contributions and efforts to secure

**Figure 7.5  Louis W. Sullivan (1933– )**
As founder and president of Morehouse
School of Medicine and in his service as the
second African American Secretary of Health
and Human Services, Sullivan ranks as one of
the nation's premier health leaders.

Reproduced from *The Sphinx* magazine,
Winter, 1989, volume 75, number 4, cover.

**Figure 7.6  David Satcher (1941– )**
His tenure as president of Meharry Medical
College, director of the CDC in Atlanta, and
term as Surgeon General mark Satcher as a
national health and public health leader of
the first rank.

Courtesy of Meharry Medical College,
Black Medical History Archive Collection,
Meharry Medical College Library, Kresge
Learning Resources Center, Nashville,
Tennessee.

health care justice and equity in America. Drs. William Darity, M. Alfred Haynes, Richard Butcher, Hank Foster, Ezra Davidson, Claudia Baquet, Vivian Pinn, John Boyce, Richard Allen Williams, and Herbert Nickens labored tirelessly in the background, furthering the cause of Black and disadvantaged populations' health and health care. Congressman Louis Stokes's Health Braintrust, annual hearings on minority health issues, and CBC-sponsored programs may have saved the Black medical schools and kept Black health on the national agenda. Some of their accomplishments, such as Dr. Darity's achievements in the World Health Organization (WHO) and deanship of the academic School of Public Health at the University of Massachusetts at Amherst, leading public health efforts to improve disadvantaged group health in the world and the nation; Dr. Davidson's presidency, unprecedented for an African American, of the American College of Obstetrics and Gynecology, and significant tenure as NMA board chairman; Dr. Pinn's efforts and leadership in the NMA and her appointment as the first director of the Office of Research on Women's Health (ORWH) at the NIH; Dr. Foster's national crusade against teen pregnancy; and Dr. Butcher's leadership roles as president of the NMA and the Summit Health Coalition to place the "Black Health Crisis" on the national agenda, may have received some publicity, but more often were labors of love and principle—often in silence. Undoubtedly, Dr. Baquet's labors at the NCI, OMH, and the University of Maryland laying a foundation for the battle to conquer cancer in disadvantaged minorities; Dr. Haynes's efforts as a medical school president, Johns Hopkins's School of Public Health faculty member, and NCI leadership official to close disparities in Black health and cancer; Dr. Boyce's unparalleled contribution, often against great odds, to improving urban health, especially in the areas of OB-GYN and womens' health, while attempting to transform a traditional AHC-affiliated, inner-city hospital into a culturally competent facility—Kings County Hospital Center, an oasis in central Brooklyn meeting the needs of a largely African American and Afro-Carribean population; academic cardiologist Dr. Richard Allen Williams's singular efforts as editor and author of *The Textbook of Black-Related Diseases* and founder of the Association of Black Cardiologists (ABC), spearheading a Humane Medicine movement and establishing the Minority Health Institute, all consistently elevated African American health issues to the front rank—making them available for national consideration; and the late Dr. Nickens's tireless efforts at the American Association of Medical Colleges (AAMC) to increase African American entry and representation in American medicine were most often of a low-profile, academic, or policy-making nature, and may not have received the public recognition they deserve. Their brilliant efforts and impact, a tiny minority in a sea of adversity, are proofs of why proportional representation of Blacks and other disadvantaged groups at policy levels are essential. There have been many other health professions "soldiers"—especially on the faculties of the Black medical and health professions schools, on the frontlines in public hospitals, NHCs and CHCs, and in the ranks of the NMA, NDA, and NBNA, especially their presidents—who are too numerous to name here. Nevertheless, for African American and other disadvantaged patients, their presence has made a difference—and they will never be forgotten.[341]

---

## Conclusions: The End Game—from "Crisis" to "Permanent Underclass"?

The "Black Health Crisis" described herein evolved within a complex matrix of factors and events that created a unique health policy milieu requisite for its generation. Politically and for the health system, it was a "crisis" born of broken national promises; crushed African American dreams of equitable, if not equal, health and health care; the thwarting of one aspect of the American dream for working- and middle-class Americans—a human "right" to decent health and care for all; feigned social, health, and public policy awareness by the medical and health establishments; resignation by progressive public policy and health policy makers to perpetuation of a "dual and unequal" health system into the twenty-first century and beyond; virtual abandonment of physicians' patients and professional principles, along with complicity and capitulation by White organized medicine to greed and corporate medicine; deception of the majority public by the medical establishment, academe, certain facets of the media, and the health care political process; and dominance through capitulation of a new and dangerous nihilistic and negative social policy angst, even to the detriment of the nation's children (in both education and health), poisoning the nation's social fabric and environment. Almost inadvertently, by the time of President Clinton's election, the "Black Health Crisis" loomed as one arm of America's "dual health crisis," which will be discussed in the final chapter.

After the exuberant days of the 1960s and early 1970s, when the nation seemed committed to justice and equity in health care for all Americans (including Blacks, for the first time on a legal basis), the ideological profile, public policy, and health policy perspectives on health and health care, and their status and outcome implications, turned 180 degrees. Lee, Benjamin, and Weber recalled historical observations concerning the American character, a major factor shaping health policy:

> Comte de Tocqueville wrote more than 150 years ago: "Americans are proud and loud, daring, and caring. They extol individuality but always pitch in when it comes to helping others.... [T]hey are industrious, hospitable; brash, confident, outspoken and resourceful." While much of de Tocqueville's description remains accurate, we are ... less willing to pitch in when it comes to helping others and we seem less hospitable, particularly to immigrants from Latin America, than in years past.[342]

These character traits of alienation and social self-indulgence are imposed by the majority on African Americans, the Civil Rights Movement and its accomplishments (e.g., affirmative action, ensuring voting rights for all, women's rights, proportional representation), and other disadvantaged groups, to a lesser degree.[343] Moreover, erosion of the country's communitarian traditions, the nation's drift into more extreme rights-centered individualism, and American distrust of government[344] are reflected in "dominance of the private sector in most aspects of American life, including the emphasis placed on support of the private sector in public policy."[345] The retreat from the "creative federalism" of the Lyndon Johnson administration, extending the "traditional federal-state relationship to include direct federal support for local governments, non-profit organizations, and private businesses and corporations to carry out health, education, training, social services, and community development programmes,"[346] led to the conservative New Right, traditional interpretation of federalist beliefs. Thus the Reagan administration shifted responsibility back to the states for the provision of health and welfare policies and programs, while cutting their funding, based on its reading of the Tenth Amendment of the Constitution (i.e., powers not delegated to the U.S. by the Constitution are reserved to the States respectively, or to the people). The harvests of these seasons and events created a ripe garden for the birth of a "health and health care underclass" in America.

More than 20 years of denigrating the government and public service, consigning august institutions and high callings to the categories of special interests "instead of the essential broad framework for the processes of choice and effective decisions in the public interest," rendered the "problems of the mid-1990s . . . more critical than those of the 1960s and 1970s."[347] The powerful influences of pluralism and interest group politics are making health policies and politics increasingly vulnerable to co-option by the corporate and private sectors and unresponsive to the needs of the public or its will.[348] Moreover, the powerful conservative movement that dominates Congress is skillfully applying Lindblom's method of "disjointed incrementalism" to distort and delay attempted moves toward progressive health policies or reform. Incrementalism encourages dilution through "a process of successive approximations of some desired objectives in that what is desired itself continues to change under reconsideration."[349] Lindblom and Walker described the process that is now determining the lion's share of the nation's health policies and programs:

> *Public policies seldom result from a rational process in which problems are precisely identified and then carefully matched with optimal solutions. Most policies emerge, haltingly and piecemeal, from a complicated series of bargains and compromises that reflect the biases, goals, and enhancements of needs of established agencies, professional communities and ambitious political entrepreneurs.*[350]

These findings were fundamentally corroborated by the policy analyses surrounding the defeat of recently attempted health reform by Haynes Johnson, David Broder, Theda Skocpol, and Vicente Navarro.[351] U.S. health policy, in the grip of such a political and policy-making system, and shaped by processes and factors described here, is on a dangerous threshold of total, potentially fatal, detachment from the American public, including the institutionalization of a permanent "health and health care underclass"—a concept distasteful to most Americans.[352]

As liberal reform and expansion of access to the health system was virtually brought to a halt during the Reagan-Bush era, progress in the improvement of major health indicators slowed. For disadvantaged groups such as African Americans, MIAs, and poor or disabled Americans whose health status and outcomes had improved dramatically between 1965 and 1980, improvements in health status and outcomes were minimal and in many areas deteriorated. There were a number of reasons Black health status and outcome stagnated or deteriorated throughout the 1980s.

Between 1984 and 1990 Black males experienced a period of declining longevity, along with the implicit erosion in health status and outcome that represented. This was the first such event clearly documented during the twentieth century. Although there was slow overall improvement, Black/White differences in IMRs diverged over the past 18 years, with more rapid rates of improvement for Whites increasingly surpassing Black rates, a flattening of Black rates in several instances, and increasing racial disparities generally. Besides the evidence of wide, deep, race- and class-based health disparities not only remaining but entrenching themselves between 1980 and 1995 despite the 1960s health reforms, a resignation to, if not outright acceptance of, disparate health outcomes for large blocs of Americans showed signs of becoming institutionalized.

African Americans, the economically disadvantaged, the elderly poor, the disabled, large blocs of children, and, increasingly, part-time, low-wage, service-sector, working Americans make up a large and increasing group of MIAs and public health care sector enrollees. Euphemisms from the dominant mainstream health sector, such as uninsured, underinsured, SES-disadvantaged, "government program" enrollees, "bad debt care" recipients, "self-pay," dependent on the "free care pool," medically uninsurable (e.g., patients with certain serious chronic illnesses such as cancer or AIDS), eligible but uncovered (e.g., for Medicaid coverage), and "too high-risk" (by managed care standards), based on race, class, socioeconomic status, poverty program standards, insurance industry criteria, restructuring of the health delivery system, and managed care guidelines, threaten to wall off a "health and health care underclass." The end result is the same—marginalization or exclusion from the "mainstream," average to high-quality health system. Even the year 2000 goals were "separate and unequal," with lower targets and goals for African Americans[353]—almost as if 380 years of health segregation, discrimination, and disadvantage or some "biological difference" automatically confers illness, lower standards of health, and higher disability rates on particular U.S. populations on a predetermined basis. Furthermore, as far as African Americans are concerned, such "separate and unequal" goals in the United States have always been equated with inadequate levels of concern, finances, and other types of resources applied to ameliorate problems. Health system events and performance between 1980 and 1995 bear this out.

There is another difficult-to-explain health system phenomenon that the authors have encountered. We have found it increasingly difficult to locate and track the operational and disaggregated health data and statistics necessary to document and follow wide, deep, and increasingly disparate race-, class-, and gender-based (when associated with race) health status and outcomes. Therefore, deterioration, stagnation, or improvements in disease-specific conditions by race and gender for Blacks are often difficult to obtain, and thus discern, from standard sources. As a 1999 *Morbidity and Mortality Weekly Report* noted, "Reporting accurate and complete race and ethnicity data in public health surveillance systems provides critical information to target and evaluate public health interventions, particularly for minority populations."[354] Recent CDC surveillance of health data reporting revealed: "Despite increased emphasis on collecting race and ethnicity data in the national health objectives for 2000, no improvement was found for 1994–1997, and reporting completeness for these data continues to be lower than reporting levels for age and sex."[355] Compounding lax reporting, several other factors seem to be at work that tend to isolate and insulate this requisite information from lay or trained health analysts or health policy researchers interested in race- or class-based data and health trends. Government and institutional data collectors, increasingly detached from the clinical realities of the health system,[356] seem to arbitrarily impose shifting and changing criteria and classifications regarding race- and class-related data collection and analysis. This automatically creates inconsistencies and confusion in whatever data and analyses they present over time—obscuring, sometimes preventing, any clear interpretations or revelation of trends in the process. Moreover, virtually no consistent sets of racial health data are presented on a regular, predictable basis (annual reporting would be ideal). For example, there is no year-to-year consistency in presenting disaggregated measurement of health by specific disease causes of death by race and gender for children's age categories. And there is no readily available and variegated menu of racially comparative children's health data, in spite of the fact that disparities in health status and outcomes and their uninsured rates have climbed steadily in the 1990s.[357] Whether the health of Black children, disproportionately affected by such trends, merits public health analyses and policy formulation born of wholesome information sharing seems in question. From a public health perspective, this should not be an issue. Logic dictates that populations faring poorly should be the focus of our attention. The raw data in all areas often seem to be manipulated through analytic methods that obscure the trends of the racial disparities whose weight or public health significance would capture and increase the interests of clinicians or health policy-makers—in effect, sanitizing them before they are presented to the public. Substantial cases could be made for reporting, presentation, or publication bias regarding the analysis and presentation of health data with regard to race; more fundamental flaws of interpretive, conceptual, or detection bias affecting racial data could be entertained, but would be more difficult to argue, much less prove.

Further obscuring the utility of the data from racial or ethnic perspectives, by methods such as the data not being consistently reported from year to year, are the general availability and presentation of analyzed data to the public. For example, differences in recent race-, gender- (when associated with race), and class-based data on children's health, renal disease, pneumonia and influenza, and diabetes mellitus, all of which show many signs of becoming increasingly disparate according to race, are difficult to discern and/or are often unavailable in basic government and foundation documents that circulate at august medical libraries. Aggravating all these problems is the varying response of major scientific journal editors in a recent survey of major scientific journals regarding research on race and ethnicity. Journal editor responses ranged from "disinterest" (21%) to those who were at the early stages of implementing publishing policies and standards regarding racial and ethnic research (24%). Virtually all of the responding editors demonstrated some degree of lack of cultural competence and expressed anxiety at the lack of adequate standards.[358] This circumstance reinforces the general perception in the scientific community that race and ethnicity research lacks rigor in conceptualization, terminology, and analysis. This stereotype is another barrier for the publication and dissemination of this much-needed information in the medical and scientific literature.

What we and other authorities on Black and disadvantaged minority health fear, as health priorities shift based on White population improvements,* is that changing disparities based on race, class, and ethnicity will seemingly no longer merit detailed discussion in the advanced, special, or final reports from NCHS. After the publication of *Health United States and Prevention Profile, 1991*—which was dedicated to the eminent Dr. Joel Kleinman, who guided the production of the publication for more than a decade and excelled at communicating important public health issues through the data—there has been a paucity of systematic socially relevant health data consistently presented on a racial basis. Without this information presented consistently in standard government and foundation publications, access to government and foundation health data—the costs of their collection, analysis, and publication being borne by the public and resting in the public domain—becomes prohibitively expensive, only accessible to subspecialized biostaticians in governmental and institutional settings, and walled off from

---

*Since the White population's IMR and perinatal parameters have improved and have subsequently dropped out of the top 10 leading causes of death for the overall population, less is written and data are harder to obtain in government documents about the florid effects these indices continue to exert on the Black community's health.

broad-based health policy analysis and public view. Moreover, health data presented in terms so technical that neither local, state, or nationally elected officials or policy-makers can comprehend them would be considered largely unaccessible and useless by most Americans.[359]

Indirectly, all these mechanisms combine to lend the impression that in reporting health outcomes, the priority is to emphasize improvements in the health of the White majority—in spite of widening race- and class-based health disparities. If the nation's and *all* the citizen's health needs are to be met in an equitable and rational manner, the president's, Congress's and surgeon general's recent initiatives to eliminate racial, ethnic health disparities must be taken seriously and acted upon in an appropriate manner.[360] Through such actions, the establishment of a permanent "health and health care underclass" in the United States might be avoided.

It is hoped that the reaffirmation of another set of American values will reorient and lead the U.S. health system on another course—toward the elimination of race- and class-based health disparities. Appreciation of fairness, justice, "all men [and women] being created equal," and health care as a human right also resonate strongly in the American character and political culture. Reflecting this more hopeful perspective, Lee, Benjamin, and Weber agree with Shafer that American political culture must also be viewed through the prism of "populism." Although "[e]lements of populism include individualism, voluntarism, religiosity, optimism, achievement, and self-realization," pragmatically: "Populism as an approach to political life is most fundamentally an insistence that mainstream cultural values, the operating assumptions and personal style by which individuals conduct their routine and daily lives, must govern the conduct of national government and national policy making as well."[361] These factors, along with implications created by populism's "little man" versus "big man" mentality help explain why the American public can be anti–big government, anti–big business, and anti–big labor at the same time and also, in some ways, make Americans vulnerable to exploitation by an influential and powerful, often admired, media-controlling, conservative corporate class. Populism rejects the notions of elitism, exclusion, disdain for the common man, and, on occasion, cruelty often being promoted by the entrepreneurial, "market"-based, increasingly corporate-dominated health system. Of the three prominent models or theories of the causes of existing arrangements in U.S. health care: "(a) the pluralist or market perspective; (b) the bureaucratic or planning perspective; and (c) the institutional or class perspective," the first two have remained dominant.[362] As Lee, Benjamin, and Weber noted:

> *While the pluralists hold that the present system is appropriate for our time and society, the bureaucrats see a more rational planned system in which resources are effectively co-ordinated (as opposed to the fragmentation accepted by the pluralists) and more appropriately allocated.*

> *Perceiving the primary obstacle to rational planning and resource alloca-*
> *tion as the professional monopoly of physicians over medical education*
> *and practice, bureaucratic reformers would basically adjust the existing*
> *system to achieve agreed upon goals, such as equity of access and cost*
> *containment.*[363]

It is hoped that employing models and theories that examine the race and class bases of health policies and problems plaguing the U.S. health system, while practicing alternative principals such as the American creed, populism, and egalitarianism, will eventually provide African Americans and other health-disadvantaged groups a level playing field health-wise and the opportunities to develop their full human potential, as was promised in the founding documents and principles of this country.[364]

# Race, Medicine, Health Reform, and the Future

## CHAPTER EIGHT

# Black and Disadvantaged Health, Health Reform, and the Future

## President Clinton's Failed Health Reform

The generalized insecurity of the American citizenry about runaway health care cost inflation and future access to the health system converged to catapult a publicly, but quietly, perceived health "crisis" into a nationally recognized political issue in 1992.[1] In retrospect, elements embodied in a national health system "crisis" elevated the 1991 Wofford senatorial contest in Pennsylvania—an election that hinged on the health care issue—into a heraldic banner flagging a smoldering issue whose time had seemingly come.

### Background: A Perceived "Mainstream" Health Crisis

Components of the mainstream health system "crisis" of 1992 included, but were not limited to:

1. Runaway health care cost inflation, wherein nearly 50 percent of the population reported it was having difficulty paying for health care.
2. A growing insecurity, wherein 60 percent of Americans worried about losing their health care coverage.
3. A health system already consuming 14 percent of the GDP and projected to consume even more.

4. Growing additions to the 37 million Americans with no health insurance and to the 50 million more who were underinsured.
5. A growing insecurity among all Americans, including the middle and upper classes, about future access to basic health services.
6. An increasingly sophisticated public awareness of the United States's mediocre to poor health status and outcomes compared to other developed countries.
7. A generalized perception, based on framing of the problem by pundits and the media, that the "crisis" boiled down simply to concerns about costs and access.

Despite the legitimacy and generalized health system effects highlighted by these issues, from a Black and disadvantaged health population perspective, the mainstream crisis overlaid, oversimplified, and in many ways obscured an older, more ominous, historical, and culturally driven health crisis afflicting African American and other poor populations.[2]

### Reality: A "Dual" Health Crisis in Black/Poor and White

What actually dropped in Bill Clinton's lap during the 1992 campaign was the highly publicized "mainstream crisis" issues noted here, complicated by a "Dual Health Crisis in Black and White." The first group of problems was strongly rooted in dysfunctional health system financing, overreliance on market mechanisms, and refusal to acknowledge health system problems tied to America's class stratification and social arrangements. A second set of problems was dominated by America's unique history-based, hierarchical, structural, and institutional arrangements in the health system; its tradition of inadequate resource allocation to certain sectors of the population, often based on race and moral judgments; the absence of and/or resistance to public health–driven, population-based health system planning; and a flawed medical-social culture regarding race and class. Logically, some type of national "community" approach to both structure and financing is needed to reconcile and resolve such dramatic health system malfunctions and medical-social problems. As the new millennium begins, Americans are discovering that neither group of problems can be ameliorated piecemeal or in isolation—as on a day-to-day basis citizens witness examples and verify repeated explanations of why incrementalism devoid of a national social commitment (such as Social Security, for example) doesn't seem to work.

Built upon history-based foundations of race and class, the "Dual Health Crisis in Black and White" differentially affecting African American and poor populations—if not openly and specifically addressed in terms we have discussed—has the potential to evolve into a permanent "health and health care underclass" in the United States. African Americans, Hispanic/Latino Americans, Native Americans, the disabled, the indigent, other disadvantaged groups, and the working poor (almost 80 percent of the uninsured are working poor Americans or their families) would serve as its foundation. What the authors refer to as the "African American Health Crisis," the oldest major component of the dual health crisis that uniquely and disproportionately affects the Black population (who have displayed the worst health status and outcomes for almost 400 years), serves as the archetype for the disadvantaged and underserved racial and ethnic groups in the U.S. health system. It serves as the flashpoint of the health system's race, class, equity, ethical, medical-social, and cultural competence problems. If the African American problem in the health system is overcome, the system will be well along the road to achieving justice, equity, and equality in health care in America.

Characteristics of the African American Health Crisis include, but are not limited to:

1. Persistent or increasing segregation of the health system along race and class lines, along with an additional and relentless new form of discrimination—often clothed in the guise of "managed care" or health financing, clinical or administrative "sorting" of various groups subjected to outright denial of services, restricted levels of service, and access to low-quality health care.
2. Perpetuation of 382-year-old race- and class-based structural inequalities and inequities in the health system.
3. Continued underrepresentation of African Americans in medicine and the health professions.
4. Continued wide race- and class-based health status, outcome, and utilization disparities, many of which are worsening.
5. A chronic African American insurance crisis wherein approximately 25 percent of African Americans are uninsured (versus 12 percent of Whites), approximately 25 percent are underinsured (versus 15 percent of Whites), and approximately another 25–35 percent depend on stigmatized—some consider inferior—government insurance (Medicaid and/or public aid) for basic health services (versus 6.8 percent of Whites).

Moreover, the African American Health Crisis is fueled by a medical-social culture centuries-old and heavily laden with ideological, intellectual and scientific, and discriminatory race and class problems.[3] There has been a reemerging assumption and projection that poor health status and outcomes for Blacks and the poor are "normal" and acceptable.[4] There is a persistent marginalization of Blacks and the poor at all levels of the U.S. health system—from patients to providers—grounded in America's ideological tradition that the poor and "unworthy" do not deserve decent health care.[5] A corollary set of problems emerges at the professional, research, and health institutional levels.[6]

The mainstream health profession's and health system "blind spot" regarding the effects that segregation and discrimination have on Black and poor patients, and their denial that this presents "real" problems in the health system, exacerbates their intractability.[7] The tradition of the American health system, its professionals, and the health professions research and educational systems to engage in self-serving and elite behavior that relegates most Blacks and the poor to the fringes of health policy along with an inferior subset of city and public hospitals, NHCs and CHCs, health departments, and inner-city ERs virtually renders the potential for amelioration of race- and class-based health and health care disparities moot.

The mix of medical-social, financial, and cultural imperatives driving the health system may help explain the medical and health establishment's virtual refusal to address the problem of unequal representation of the nation's racial and disadvantaged ethnic minorities in the health professions.[8] There is also a persistence, even disturbing resurgence, of the U.S. problem, with scientific racism plaguing the health sciences and research communities.[9] Characteristic of the new forms of racism, the health system changes configurations to meet new needs. Operationally, Blacks get less of whatever is considered more desirable, and of whatever is considered less desirable, they get more. In contrast to the overutilization of Blacks and the poor for medical experimentation three decades ago, as experimental therapies have become desirable, Blacks and disadvantaged minorities are being largely ignored and left out of medical and clinical research. Despite the fact such selection bias generates bad science and undercuts the applicability of any findings to the overall population (because large groups have been excluded at the outset), the practice continues. Perhaps more ominous has been the virtually unassailable documentation beginning in 1999 that racial bias and sexism still adversely affect White physician clinical decision making—an allegation virtually all Black and some socially sensitive White doctors had been making for decades.[10] Simultaneously, from the behavioral sciences, biased reliance upon White culture–based IQ and "aptitude" and "achievement" tests continues to "justify" the existing social order and to hinder disadvantaged racial and ethnic minorities' equal opportunity and advancement. One example is that differential, culture-based test scores are still a major factor buttressing the new move to purge medical schools of African Americans and other disadvantaged minorities. Additionally, a new wave of linking tests and health outcome differences to genes and biological differences accompanies the movement.[11]

Another symptom of the American health system's medical-social pathology is the racially and ethnically divided health professions, with factions often contentious of and conflicting with each other (e.g., the NMA and the AMA). They are often diametrically opposed, ideologically and philosophically, regarding health needs, health care services, and the health rights of minority and disadvantaged populations.[12] Failure to address, and eventually resolve, these race- and class-based health policy, structural, medical-social and cultural problems plaguing the American health system could potentially undermine any possibility of a level playing field in health and health care for African American and other poor populations—eroding at the front end (i.e., before and during birth, by unmet childhood health needs, and system failures leading to almost hidden inferior health status and outcome) the very foundations of American democracy.[13]

---

## A Conscious Choice: Health Reform for the Mainstream and Corporate Interests

The quiet phenomenon that had caught political pundits off guard reaffirmed a traditional law of public health that unmet health care needs are usually silent. In the Democratic upset of the 1992 presidential election,

> *the deterioration in health care, including the increase in the number of Americans who either have insufficient insurance or none at all, was the result of the class aggression carried out by the Reagan and Bush administrations, with the support of the Democratic-controlled Congress, over the past thirteen years. The result—an unprecedented crisis in health care ... led to such an enormous demand for change that health care reform became the second most important issue (after jobs) in the 1992 election.[14]*

Given an opportunity to comprehensively address a problem shared by the majority of Americans, newly elected President Clinton delivered a landmark speech on "Health Security," September 22, 1993. Focusing on the concerns of more privileged, middle-class citizens, never once mentioning the poor, his vision and promises to solve the health system's problems received overwhelmingly positive responses.

A year later, by September 26, 1994, Senate Majority Leader George Mitchell acknowledged the death knell of Clinton health reform.[15] The deficiencies of Clinton's "managed competition" version of health reform and how it was politically mishandled have been well documented.[16] The gravity of health reform failure and the system's virtual abdication in addressing the Dual Health Crisis in Black and White, much less the ongoing African American Health Crisis, are both instructive and disturbing.

First, analyzing such a systemic, historical, and culture-based health system problem from a strictly mainstream health and health care perspective—in terms the medical and health establishment allege are amenable to untried, theoretical, competitive, market based solutions—automatically trumped any successful outcome. Second, the debate and most of the planning and negotiation processes seeking solutions were closed and confined to a cadre of elite, nationally influential White physicians, corporate executives, managed care plan executives, and health policy theoreticians, called the "Jackson Hole group." Third, most of the subsequent government deliberations supervised by the Clinton administration were unrepresentative (they did not include proper or adequate Black, disadvantaged minority, and underserved patient community representation—or at least 30% of the population); secretive (they were largely dominated by government bureaucrats, health industry consultants, and interest group lobbyists); based on flawed and inappropriate ideology (for the equitable distribution of a modern universal social necessity); shaped to advantage interest groups such as the insurance and pharmaceutical industries; and based on a traditionally entrenched set of false health system assumptions and myths, defective analysis, and a set of solutions that, logically, could not work to the advantage of the entire U.S. population.

Substantive input from the African American and disadvantaged patient communities was spearheaded by the Congressional Black Caucus (CBC), the National Medical Association (NMA), and a broad-based, quickly assembled (by necessity) coalition of some 150 African American and progressive community groups, civil rights organizations, professional associations, and social organizations, named "Summit '93: African American Prescription for Health." This consortium was headed by charismatic San Diego physician, and then sitting NMA president, Richard Butcher, M.D. With the assistance of the NMA's energetic new executive director, Rosemary Davis, health policy consultant Ruth Perot, and the NMA staff, support was mobilized to facilitate the effort. These largely community-based groups and ombudsmen for disadvantaged minorities were excluded from the formulation of the Clinton health plan proposal—which was supervised by First Lady Hillary Rodham Clinton and Ira Magaziner, the coordinator of the President's Task Force on Health Care Reform. The "Summit '93" coalition articulated and espoused health policies and recommendations crafted on a part-time, largely voluntary basis by a diverse group of health, health care, and health policy experts drawn from various minority communities, academic health care and legal institutions, and the public health care sector. These policy representatives were usually selected by and convened at the behest of the NMA and the various "Summit '93" participants. Thus, the resulting expert panels and policy groups met and conferred repeatedly, outside the mainstream process at the White House, analyzed the mainstream proposals and plans they had access to, and created policy memos, recommendations, draft legislation, and proposals grounded in the needs and experiences of African American and disadvantaged minority communities.[17] Finally, after several national and highly publicized meetings convened by the CBC, NMA, and "Summit '93," this broad-based and representative group—probably the largest human and civil rights (African Americans have been forced to view health care both as a human and civil right) coalition since the 1960s Civil Rights Movement—was consulted by the Clinton Health Reform Taskforce in the summer of 1993, after the president's health plan had been almost completely formulated. The White House consultation lasted several days, and the minority and disadvantaged consultants— by then named the Minority Health Care Review Group (MHCRG)—were pushed to hurriedly make recommendations. Prophetically, in an uneasy atmosphere of strained conciliation, the final executive session involving Magaziner and the coalition was held in the Indian Treaty Room of the Old Executive Office Building of the White House.

The coalition's primary recommendations, largely crafted by the MHCRG, for a national, universal, unitary, cost-efficient, single-payer health system—which was reaffirmed by the NMA board of trustees under the leadership of Dr. Ezra Davidson, California-based academic physician and past-president of the American College of Obstetrics and Gynecology—were rejected. A few of the MHCRG's "emergency" stop-gap measures were purportedly adopted. These measures were designed to protect and preserve threatened *essential community providers* (e.g., Black and Hispanic/Latino physicians and providers practicing in underserved areas, stressed inner-city hospitals, NHCs, and CHCs) serving underserved minority communities; establish legal protections against racial and class discrimination in the health system; protect and preserve the vital Black medical and health professions schools; establish multicultural and cultural competence guidelines for the health system; and, craft some measures minimizing the Clinton plan's virtually automatic race and class tiering of the health system, all in response to flaws or oversights inherent in the Administration proposal. Even these emergency, last-ditch proposals were rendered moot by the Clinton plan's subsequent defeat.

Thus, the experience of representatives of African American and disadvantaged patients confirmed the overall impression that, as far as health reform was concerned, the "process embraced by the Clinton White House Task Force did not correct basic conceptual, representational, or ideological flaws and inequities."[18] Although unacknowledged, the health and health care fate of African American and other disadvantaged populations for the next generation hung in the balance during this round of health reform.[19]

The significance of the Clinton health reform failure is magnified not only by the African American Health Crisis but also by the fact that there have been only two previous periods of health reform intended to correct health deficits differentially affecting the U.S. Black population. The "First Reconstruction," whose health care measures may have saved the Black population from extinction, lasted from 1865 to 1872. Health care measures were part of the Freedmen's Bureau legislation. During that short period, drastic Black population death rates and numerical decline slowed, then halted; many health status and outcome parameters improved; but, the already underfunded programs were stopped too soon to permanently improve African American health status or outcomes. The "Second Reconstruction," which lasted from 1965 to 1975,* was a result, and a part, of the

---

*Though many consider 1980 the "official" end of the the Civil Rights era, or what could be referred to as a "Second Reconstruction," Haynes' landmark article, "The Gap in Health Status Between Black and White Americans," documented most Black health progress had ceased by 1975. Moreover, there was a cessation of the closure of the racial health gaps that had been evident since 1965.

Black Civil Rights Movement. Virtually every measurable health status, outcome, and utilization parameter improved dramatically. Stagnation occurred in 1975, and relative or absolute deterioration (compared to the White population) set in after 1980. Both of these periods—each lasting a decade or less—failed to correct African Americans' "slave health deficit."[20]

From the perspective of average Americans and disadvantaged groups such as African Americans, the post–Clinton reform health system era, in the throes of runaway cost inflation, social insensitivity, lack of accountability, financing dysfunction, and excess technology, does not bode well. A multilayered, disparate, disorganized "nonsystem," commonly referred to as a "multitiered and unequal" or a "dual and unequal" health system—which some projected would consume up to 17 percent of the GDP by the millennium and 37 percent by 2030—looms in America's future and is projected to leave between 27 and 30 percent of America's workers without health insurance coverage by 2005.[21] Congress seems unwilling to rein in a commercial, increasingly Wall Street–dominated, U.S. managed care model,* health system that seems to be increasingly out of control.

Americans seem, once again, to be expressing anxiety about the future direction the health system is taking. Unless they are intimidated by the malfunctioning health system itself,** another round of demands for health reform may be imminent. There have been several other periods when the majority of Americans favored a health system reform providing some type of national, universal, stable health plan during the twentieth century. The World War I period, the era during the 1930s when Social Security legislation was enacted, and following World War II during President Harry Truman's administration are prominent examples. Prior to the Clinton health reform effort, public opinion favoring such major changes reached a 40-year high.[22] Nevertheless, efforts to reform the health system into a national universal format were thwarted, and the public's interests were not served.

Repeatedly, White organized medicine, the private-influenced regulatory infrastructure, a conservative-dominated Congress, and private and corporate interest groups within the health system have successfully blocked the public's wishes for some type of universal health system. These groups have wielded influence through Congressional lobbying, propagandistic media campaigns, and political PAC money. The strategy has been to work from the "top down,"

---

*The U.S. version of managed care is the only one that incorporates private ownership, entrepreneurialism including expensive media-mediated advertising and marketing, a "market" ideology and administrative ethos, "cut-throat" competition, and autonomy from social or political planning or controls.

**Americans are terrified of losing personal or family health coverage. They are increasingly frightened and burdened by unmet long-term care needs for themselves and their elderly relatives. Economic ruin, or grudging acceptance of substandard quality care, is increasingly being associated with catastrophic or serious chronic illnesses. Complaining individually or collectively (e.g., in the workplace or through labor unions) about this worsening situation is often greeted with threats and intimidation by powerful employers or institutions to cut off even the limited coverage offered.

convincing legislators, medical leaders, and White organized medicine's regulatory infrastructure that such plans were not feasible or were politically unpalatable. As previously noted, propagandistic, deceptive terror tactics alluding to political subversion and "communist takeovers" of the U.S. government were not considered beyond the pale in what has repeatedly amounted to political wars about health care on Capitol Hill. As early as World War I, labor movement actions toward compulsory national health insurance were blocked by insurance and pharmaceutical industry interests. Morris Fishbein's entire term as editor of *JAMA* served as a front line offensive by White organized medicine and the ruling classes to block progressive health legislation from the 1920s to 1950s. There are no obvious signs that the new White organized medical order will discontinue its tradition of battling progressive causes and thwarting the free and open exchange of ideas concerning health and health care.[23]

One tangible health system result of this decades-long deteriorating situation — that only paused temporarily, on a very superficial level, to produce cosmetic changes the health industry felt necessary to defuse the public's perception of a need for substantive health reform* — is that huge blocs of Blacks, Hispanic/Latino Americans, and the poor with already high uninsured and underinsured rates, who also disproportionately contribute to the growing millions of uninsured, are being forced structurally into a contracting, deteriorating, underfunded, overcrowded, understaffed, stigmatized public sector concentrated in the nation's inner cities or into a growing "nether world" health nonsystem, first systematically described by African American physicians during the 1980s and early 1990s. This "nether world" health care system into which the uninsured and some underinsured are driven is largely concentrated at, and emanates from, the nation's ERs. It is inconstant; inconsistent, being dependent on the largesse of the private sector providers; and possesses chimerical, "shell-game" qualities depending on where one is located and how the poor in that geographic area interface with it.[24] Moreover, "nether world" care is extraordinarily inefficient and expensive and imposes the shortfalls of health care neglect on the patient, such as failure to present at early, often treatable, stages of disease when preventive therapies could work; diagnoses at late and terminal stages of many illnesses; and lack of follow-up or continuity of care. Some communities such as Boston have an ever-threatened infrastructure of NHCs and CHCs;[25] others have charity clinics;[26] and many communities, especially in the South and West, have virtually no provisions for the care

---

*As has been documented earlier, after failed health reform in 1994 the corporate-controlled health insurance and managed care industry held premium rate increases in check, often absorbing losses or tolerating flat profit margins. The pharmaceutical industry, threatened with government regulation during early stages of the Clinton health reform, followed suit. By 1998 with the threat of reform over, the financial impact of these cosmetic measures resurfaced as a "crisis." Huge premium and cost increases were implemented by the managed care industry, pharmaceutical costs skyrocketed once more, and health care inflation rates are resuming their pre-reform escalation.

of "nether world" patients or system overflow of uninsured Americans. These are signs of the poor state of the U.S. health "nonsystem" and the lackluster and inappropriate adjustments it has made to a changing sociocultural and political economic milieu.[27]

---

## A Changing World: New Standards

> *Racial discrimination is now less blatant than in previous years.... Some of the gross abuses of human and civil rights have mostly disappeared now, both in the North and the South. But we all know that discrimination lives on beneath the surface.... Unhappily it hits blacks and other minorities where they live and affects when and how they die.*
>
> EDITH IRBY JONES, M.D., NMA PRESIDENT, 1985

Health care, once a privileged commodity of the rich, is now considered a social necessity. Its changed status over the past century is emblematic of why African Americans must obtain justice and equity in health care—if disadvantaged minorities are to be healthy enough to be as competitive as Whites and other groups in the United States. Health status and outcomes comparable to levels in developing and underdeveloped foreign countries will no longer suffice—African Americans and their children must compete with European Americans and their children for their life chances and survival. Virtually everyone agrees that most nineteenth and early twentieth century improvements in health were related to improved sanitation, nutrition, and living conditions. Prior to World War II medical interventions affected certain restricted areas of health such as maternal deaths, infant morality, and vaccinations for prevention of a few diseases. President Franklin Roosevelt, who died from complications of virtually untreated (by today's standards) hypertension, would now be categorized as an "excess death." As late as 1950, when a diagnosis of cancer was a virtual death sentence, Black cancer patients fared as well as, if not better than, White cancer patients. Now that cancer prevention, screening, early detection, and treatments are increasingly effective, African Americans are falling farther behind European Americans in cancer outcomes.

Contemporary findings of Lee, Benjamin, and Weber in the 1990s reaffirm these impressions, attest to the effectiveness of modern health care, and suggest "that both curative measures and clinical preventive services are significant in reducing the burden of illness and prolonging life."[28] Bunker's team reported its findings in 1994 on extending life expectancy, comparing the effects of medical care (clinical curative services as they affected outcomes in colorectal cancer, diabetes mellitus, heart disease, cerebrovascular disease, kidney failure, tuberculosis, and maternal mortality) with clinical preventive services (screening, immunization, hormone replacement for postmenopausal women, and aspirin prophylaxis for heart attack in men over 40): "They observed, 'the current effects of preventive measures on life expectancy (roughly 18–19 months) are less than half as great as the prolongation of life from curative measures (roughly 44–45 months).'"[29] Dr. Samuel Broder noted about cancer therapies in 1992: "[O]ne point that has struck me since being the Director of the NCI is that as technology for prevention, diagnosis and treatment improves, groups that are underserved actually appear to suffer more."[30] There is a growing consensus that as medical care, curative measures, and therapeutic interventions continue to improve, they will become larger determinants of population-based health status and outcomes. Thus, doing without health care will become an even larger social handicap. Cumulative evidence suggests, "American medicine is now devastatingly effective, corrective, preventive, and selective. Doing without health care these days spells doom or defectiveness."[31] Almost 15 years ago, responding to the health milieu generated by the Reagan-Bush era, the lead author expanded the dimensions of the health and health care issue, framing it in broader historical, ethical, and medical-social terms, while posing a question:

> *Is this society to consciously move in unethical directions, to perpetuate a "holocaust in slow motion" on the Negro? Or will it move in humane, just directions to end 367 years of health deprivation, to allow its black citizens to emerge from their dark basement of "third world" health into the brightness of mainstream American medicine? Whether the black American is to be allowed the sound mind and body to compete in this system is the question that must be answered now. This is America's health dilemma.*[32]

This issue is as germane today as it was then.[33]

Since the failed health reform in 1994, continued expansion of a health system driven by market forces, entrepreneurialism, overspecialization, and inefficient utilization of medical technology has undercut illusions of predicted cost savings, forced HMO failures, and triggered more rationing and health care costs inflation.[34] Madison Avenue marketing (a phenomenon largely confined to the U.S. health system) and media manipulation of biomedical science have created a climate of unrealistic expectations and artificial, often specious, demand in the American public. Evidence of the deteriorating health system environment is highlighted by the observation of Surgeon General Dr. David Satcher that of the $1.5 trillion currently being spent on health care, less than 1 percent is expended on prevention. He recommends not only that allocations for HP/DP be increased dramatically—producing what he refers to as a "balanced health system"—but also that the health system feature universal access with an emphasis on children's health. Moreover, adhering to the laws of public health, extra efforts should be targeted at populations that are doing worse, and this could be accomplished without taking anything away from others in the system.[35] If present trends continue—in the absence of reform efforts incorporating features to specifically correct historically rooted race- and class-based health status, outcome, and utilization disparities—African Americans and the disadvantaged will be subjected to virtually insurmountable, institutionalized health disadvantages. In the process, they will become members of a permanent "health and health care underclass."[36]

---

## Flawed Assumptions and Myths

> *The poor ranking of America's black population in the indices of good health is a scandal of such long standing that it has lost the power to shock.... The issue of minority health ... has held a high place on the rhetorical agenda.... Lacking, however, are both the needed financial resources and a willingness to abandon some of the political hallucinations that persist in the politics of minority health improvements.*
> D. S. GREENBERG, *THE LANCET*

Helping drive both failed health reform and the current health system is a flawed set of assumptions and myths that undergird the ideology, deliberations, agenda setting, policy determination, and implementation strategies and practices in the U.S. health system on a recurring basis. Their institutionalization into the "common wisdom" of our health system precludes rational and meaningful reform, undercutting the amelioration of African American health problems. Perhaps the most prominent, and least thought about, myth is *the myth of a U.S. health system.*

The reality is that the U.S. "system" is actually a poorly stitched together nonsystem of autonomous institutions, profit-taking and non-profit (many of which now function like for-profit entities) health provider microsystems and networks, Wall Street profit-taking corporations, government and private agencies all driven by quasi-market rather than public service or public health forces. The operational infrastructure lacks any central planning, and the health system it operates and increasingly owns is multitiered in demographic, financing, and quality characteristics. At the top of the personal health services pyramid is a small, emerging upper tier of largely fee-for-service, freedom of choice, well-financed care reserved for the well-to-do, executive, and corporate class. It is largely financed by tax breaks and medical savings accounts subsidized by the corporations themselves. A privately financed (mainly through payroll deductions, out-of-pocket deductibles and co-payments, and tax subsidies), mainstream, so-called middle-class, HMO-dominated layer of the system serves the largest group of Americans. This shrinking segment (as the middle-class shrinks) is the one under the most public fire for service denials, restricting patient choices, draconian delivery methods (e.g., drive-through deliveries, surgery on the run), and silencing physicians. A growing lower tier of care provided at crumbling public institutions, teaching hospitals, NHCs and CHCs, public and charity clinics, and inner-city and rural hospital ERs is publicly financed. Another rapidly expanding layer doesn't appear on most of the neat graphs and charts in the health policy literature. This previously mentioned "nether world," which along with portions of the mainstream system is assuming more characteristics of a black market health system, is financed almost entirely outside the formal private system. Massachusetts, with one of the few formal statewide programs for indigent care, struggles with the "nether world" health system's existence piecemeal by providing a shrinking "free care pool," while most states simply deny its existence. This expensively and inefficiently delivered, hit-or-miss, often archaic menu of crisis-oriented, often retrospective, cost-shifting dependent, health financing mechanisms and health services, often delivered when patients are in distress or advanced stages of disease, is increasingly being delivered outside formal financing or delivery mechanisms*—further contributing to its "nether world" characteristics. Moreover, this, along with the other lower-tier sectors, is becoming increasingly low-tech and will soon resemble "third world medicine." As more than a million Americans lose their health insurance annually, formal welfare or poverty health care coverage is declining, presently covering less than half the poor who need it. One result is that, much like wealth in America, perhaps as much as 90–95 percent of the resources for the present system are concentrated in the mainstream segment serving the upper 65–70 percent of the population.

As the "market" drives the unregulated nonsystem, the maldistribution of physicians continues unabated with overspecialization and the concentration of medical manpower in affluent urban areas. The pattern, as noted by David Rogers in the 1980s, wherein 5–10 percent of physicians, most of whom are in training, provide care for the lower tiers (now representing 20–40 percent of the patients) of the system is being reinforced. Thus, the least experienced continue to care for the sickest. Destabilization of the nonsystem continues as a result of the souring relationship between health insurance and employment. As the political economy of employment shifts overseas and becomes more dependent on part-time workers, as corporations self-insure, as worker benefit packages are cut, and as the employment market reorganizes to cut the work force, health and health care conditions and considerations will understandably deteriorate. It is disturbing that U.S. hospitals are implementing barter systems with patients[37] in a health care system providing care for the "most advanced" society on earth—a "system" seemingly increasingly unable to provide answers or alternatives to meet America's health or medical-social needs.[38]

Another misrepresentation imposed on Americans is *the myth that there is health planning in the United States.* Reality is that due to the concentrated efforts of the White medical establishment, the dominant political parties and health care

---

*There is little concern with the quality of care delivered outside the financial system. Unless a reportable catastrophe such as a maternal death occurs, quality assurance mechanisms are seldom marshaled to evaluate this informal "level," derogatorily considered by health managers as unavoidable "charity care."

interest groups, there is very little rational, comprehensive or coordinated national health planning in the United States. As we have seen, even federal, state, and regional efforts to solve wasteful duplication of expensive medical technology and to control wasteful excesses in bed capacity have been thwarted. Even efforts to distribute health care to underserved populations flounder. When efforts to defeat regulation are taken up, health care maldistribution and wasteful and expensive inefficiencies due to insurance companies and health financing flaws are often overlooked. Preserving the "market," private enterprise and promoting "competition" are not seen as contributing to waste or systemic inefficiency.[39]

Pervasive and recurrent is *the myth that health care is a commodity and market forces and competition will control costs, produce efficiency, and correct maldistribution of health care.* Internationally renowned health economist Eli Ginzberg reflecting upon 60 years of health policy research stated, "I am worried about the predominance of commercial and market thinking in health care today. As a close student of *The Wealth of Nations,* I know that even Adam Smith did not look to the competitive market as the sole regulator of a modern economy—something that the for-profit health plans have still to learn."[40] Adam Smith, Kenneth Arrow, Victor Fuchs, Henry Aaron, Paul Starr, and Anne Stoline and Jonathan P. Weiner all concur that health care is not a commodity in the classical sense. It is not a material object that can be traded on an exchange. And health systems are not markets, and, thus, cannot be successfully or strictly governed by market and financial forces.[41] Nevertheless, the corporate class, White organized medicine, and large blocs of health system academics attempt to force the paradigm onto the U.S. health system.

On a commonsense and ethical level, whether cut-throat competition is a good, or appropriate, thing in health care is problematic. Reliance on monetary incentives to provide equitable health distribution to poor, often unemployed, medically high-risk populations living in economically depressed areas is unproven, specious, counterintuitive, and fraught with difficulty. Moreover, cut-throat competition automatically means that there will be winners and losers. And as Freidman, Randall, Sardell, Woolhandler and Himmelstein, Andrulis and Carrier, the Sidels, the authors, and others have pointed out, historically and contemporaneously the losers are African American and other disadvantaged minority patients; high-risk patients, such as those with several simultaneous diseases and co-morbidities, serious chronic diseases, cancer, and preexisting conditions; rural patients; socioculturally disadvantaged and lower socioeconomic status patients; and incarcerated, homeless, and socially undesirable patients.[42] Besides inserting new layers of elite, corporate, and administrative "experts," most of whom have no clinical training or experience, between patients and their care and care givers—not being bound by the public utility model of service delivery—private health care corporations can be expected to ignore or marginalize the public health care sector. Thus, public hospitals, health departments, NHCs and

CHCs, migrant health centers, and charity clinics that Blacks and other poor patients have relied upon in the past are being forced to make drastic adjustments or risk being downsized or eliminated. Moreover, seldom are alternative institutions being created to replace them. Due to the unproven efficacy of so-called competitive health systems in the delivery of universal and equitable health care to entire populations, the United States is currently engaged in a massive radical social experiment in quasi-market-based, entrepreneurial, capitalistic health care. Until the major inflation-generating components of the health system are regulated, rational health planning takes place, and the health system's goals and objectives are geared toward serving the public, virtually no equitable or positive results will occur. Cost effectiveness, affordable health care, appropriate manpower distribution, uniformly high-quality health care, simplicity in negotiating the system, and health care security will be the missing ingredients beyond the grasp of the U.S. system.[43]

Also impeding justice and equity in U.S. health care is *the myth that race and class are not major health system problems and that race- and class-based health disparities are primarily financial problems.* Competitive health reform strategists define the mainstream health crisis almost exclusively in financial or access terms. Other than acknowledging the categories of "uninsured" or "underinsured," competitive models ignore the plethora of race and class problems plaguing the health system. Thus, as predicted by previous knowledge about ethical and social distancing and metaracism associated with capitalist transformation and corporatization, U.S. health planners and policy makers virtually ignore the system's race and class problems. In so doing, they ignore the fact the health system's race and class problems are almost four centuries old and the U.S. health system has been discriminatorily structured on those bases since its beginnings. Therefore, the health system's race and class problems have been structured and institutionalized into the U.S. health system at the cultural and institutional levels—it now represents the way our health care system "normally" does business. These facts, understandably, render the system's medical-social, discriminatory structural, and cultural problems extremely difficult to appreciate, confront, and ameliorate. Moreover, as therapeutic and curative medical interventions become more effective, their systematic denial to specific groups on the basis of race or class will be tantamount to undermining these groups' ability to compete and thwarting the American democratic processes.[11]

Pervasive is *the myth that numerical increases in doctors will solve the nation's maldistribution and access problems.* This dangerous oversimplification fails to address several major problems. Over the years it has been proven that overreliance on the market produces dysfunctional incentives and leads to young health professionals overspecializing and concentrating their practices in affluent, largely suburban, predominantly White areas. Such a distribution process automatically creates shortages in our nation's inner-city, rural, and poverty areas. African

Americans and other disadvantaged minorities are disproportionately affected. Data have verified these patterns for over 30 years, and many underserved areas existing in 1970 remain underserved today. As Eli Ginzberg said:

> I pointed out that even a large increase in the number of medical school graduates would have only a marginal effect on providing adequate coverage for these underserved [low-income rural and ghetto areas] populations. It appeared to me then, as it does now, that in the absence of a system of short-term compulsory or liberally compensated voluntary service, recently licensed physicians will do whatever they find necessary to avoid practicing in low-income areas. Expanding the total supply is not the answer to attracting young physicians to areas they would otherwise shun.[45]

Proportional representation in the health professions would serve as a great, almost immediate, remedy to some of these access problems.

Not dependent on social and attitudinal changes toward race and class—which could take decades, even generations—proportional representation in the professions provides immediate measures for relief to underserved minority and poverty areas, as young professionals, fresh out of training, naturally gravitate toward serving their own communities. Waiting on social or spontaneous amelioration of these problems has not been efficacious. African American representation in the medical profession hovers around 3 percent, little more than the 2.5 percent levels attained in 1910, while their proportion of the general population has risen from 10 percent early in the century to 13 percent today. Recently, another Pew Health Professions Commission report has detailed the devastating effect the federal court–led attack on affirmative action is having on the medical profession, further decreasing minority applications, admissions, and enrollment. Nevertheless, the report implores U.S. medical schools to increase their diversity. Perhaps this report will not experience the fate of scores of others and will not fall on deaf ears or be ignored by the White medical establishment.[46]

Most Americans are misinformed and could be considered living in an unreality based on *the myth that rural America's health delivery shortfalls have not reached crisis proportions*. As a result of population redistribution, shifting employment patterns, and impoverishment of the nation's rural areas, these areas constitute health care crisis zones. Moreover, based on a market-controlled health nonsystem absent defined public service goals, most of these areas present few marketable incentives for reestablishing disappearing and deteriorating health infrastructures. This crisis is especially severe in rural areas of the South heavily populated by African Americans who live under virtual third world health situations.[47]

These are just a few of the unsound assumptions and myths bedeviling the U.S. health system and impeding its appropriate reform. These ideas are widely disseminated, are projected as conventional wisdom, and, whether the public is aware of it or not, underlie most health policy agenda setting, selection of alternatives, policy choices, and implementation strategies in the U.S. health system. Whether the medical establishment and health system can escape the stifling effects of these ideas will in large measure determine if America will create a health system that meets the needs of its racially and ethnically diverse multicultural population in the twenty-first century.[48]

## A Universal Health System: What Most Americans Want and the Nation Probably Needs

> [M]ajor reform of our health care financing and delivery systems is
> unavoidable and will need to occur sooner rather than later.... Looking
> at the national scene, I don't think that this country can avoid enacting
> national health insurance coverage for all citizens and legal immigrants.
> —Eli Ginzberg

Variants of single-payer and unitary systems have worked in Japan and Europe for over 40 years. Thus, there is a great deal of objective and pragmatic evidence that single-payer approaches, such as *The American Health Security Act of 1993* H.R. 1200 proposed by Wellstone, Conyers, and others,[49] which was defeated in the last round of major health reform efforts, could meet most U.S. public health, financial, and medical-social needs. This may explain why single-payer approaches have been viewed favorably by authorities such as Rashi Fein, Steffie Woolhandler and David Himmelstein, and Theda Skocpol—all from Harvard; the American Public Health Association; the NMA and CBC; and Henry J. Aaron of the Brookings Institution.[50] These and other experts have catalogued a number of advantages in this approach.

As previously noted, polling data on Americans have repeatedly shown that a significant proportion, between 35 and 73 percent, want some type of national, universal, comprehensive health program. By the end of the Reagan-Bush era in the early 1990s, this rose to over 72 percent. Even if public approval is not a consideration favoring this paradigm, universal, single-payer approaches are not experimental in that they embody tried and tested components currently in use from successful national health programs in Canada, Japan, and Europe.[51] Most universal, single-payer models offer one tier of health despite race, place of employment, illness, or income level. Virtually all are outperforming our system based on health indicators and outcomes. Because of their public accountability, universal and single-payer approaches help rein in the spiraling costs of health care. Single-payer approaches offer the possibility of paying for themselves,[52] after proper tailoring and factoring-in significant cost savings from the elimination of costly administrative overhead, layers of management, and process duplication.[53]

## Conclusions: A Permanent "Health and Health Care Underclass" as We Enter the Twenty-First Century?

This journey through the African American health experience has been a cautionary tale. Whether the U.S. health system is capable of solving America's almost 400-year-old health dilemma regarding its African American population, here described comprehensively and in detail for the first time, raises several questions:

- Will America's racial obsession—heavily framed, influenced, and buttressed by Western science and its roots (embodied in New Right politics, the rejection of affirmative action, and reappearance of overt discrimination)—preclude equitable reform of the health system?
- Can the health care, biomedical, and scientific infrastructures that examined, derogatorily classified, denigrated, exploited and abused, and supplied the rationale for social segregation and discrimination against certain racial and ethnic populations now respond to these groups' plea for fulfillment of their health and health care needs in the new millennium?
- Can American medicine and science undergo the traumatic process of shedding these traditions and burdensome legacies just as its German counterparts are presently struggling to do?
- Will the production of a culturally competent health system, strongly grounded in the objective realities and mutual respect borne of a full awareness of our health system's tortured past and imperfections, become a major priority?
- Will the resultant race and class deficiencies in the health system become disentangled from politically mediated rejection of universality and community good and responsibilities?
- Have the choices of greed, selfishness, personal autonomy, distrust of government, and generalized cynicism, epitomized by the recent rejection of a "universal," albeit inequitable and unequal—"everybody would have had something"—health system, been precise representations of America's mood when it comes to health and health care?

What is really at stake is whether African Americans and other disadvantaged sectors of the U.S. population will be afforded the opportunities for equitable health, absence from deformity, and disability status necessary to compete with mainstream White Americans. While the ongoing pursuit of economic, educational, and social equality are commendable goals—which seemingly will take generations to accomplish—they cannot be held as prerequisites for the attainment and receipt of equitable health and health care. As has been acknowledged in Western Europe since the nineteenth century, without health, none of the others will be possible.[54]

Will issues such as these, augemented by media that have mastered oversimplification and incessant overselling while becoming increasingly cynical as they pander to corporate interests and establishment-funded politicians, ever be addressed? Or will health systems' failure to deal with the "African American Health Crisis," the most recent embodiment of America's ongoing racial health dilemma, be a major marker bringing the viability of the entire U.S. social system into question?

The nation is faced with the possibility of establishing a permanent "health and health care underclass," with Blacks, Hispanic/Latino Americans, and the working poor at its base. The groundwork for such an eventuality already has been laid. A new age of Social Darwinism may be on the horizon, as pundits such as Arthur Jensen, Richard Herrnstein, and Charles Murray recommend that U.S. society virtually write off large segments of certain populations. The health system could emerge as a major mediator of such a policy. History has taught that the seeds of racism, classism, sexism, and disdain for the poor are present in Western scientific culture and the life sciences, and nefarious outcomes have been the result in the past.[55] Is the public's disillusionment with the health system and lack of faith in the government's capacity to solve the nation's social problems emblematic of a democratic form of government at the breaking point?[56] Only time will provide the answers.[57]

# Volume I Contents

# ✕ APPENDIX TWO A

# Documentary Report[*][†]: Medical Establishment Activities Against Progressive Health Legislation, Programs, and Health Delivery Activities

W. Michael Byrd, M.D.

[*]*Source:* Cancer Control Research Unit, Meharry Medical College.
[†]D represents defeated proposals. R represents resistance to proposals.

Sardell D. *The U.S. Experiment in Social Medicine* (continued)

| | | |
|---|---|---|
| D | Health Ins Bill (NY) 1922 | p. 36 |
| D | Health Ins Bill (NY) 1923 | p. 36 |
| D | Health Ins Bill (NY) 1924 | p. 36 |
| D | Health Ins Bill (NY) 1925 | p. 36 |
| D | Health Ins Bill (NY) 1926 | p. 36 |
| D | Health Ins. Bill (NY) 1927 | p. 36 |
| D | Health Ins Bill (NY) 1928 | p. 36 |
| D | Health Ins Bill (NY) 1929 | p. 36 |
| D | Health Ins Bill (NY) 1930 | p. 36 |
| D | Health Ins Bill (NY) 1931 | p. 36 |
| D | Health Ins Bill (NY) 1932 | p. 36 |
| D | Health Ins Bill (NY) 1933 | p. 36 |
| D | Health Ins Bill {NY) 1934 | p. 36 |
| D | Health Ins Bill (NY) 1935 | p. 36 |
| D | Health Ins Bill (NY) 1936 | p. 36 |
| D | Health Ins Bill (NY) 1937 | p. 36 |
| D | Health Ins Bill (NY) 1938 | p. 36 |
| D | Health Ins Bill (NY) 1939 | p. 36 |
| D | Health Ins Bill (NY) 1940 | p. 36 |
| D | Health Ins Bill (NY) 1941 | p. 36 |
| D | Health Ins Bill (NY) 1942 | p. 36 |
| D | Health Ins Bill (NY) 1943 | p. 36 |
| D | Health Ins Bill (NY) 1944 | p. 36 |
| D | Health Ins Bill (NY) 1945 | p. 36 |
| D | Health Ins Bill (NY) 1946 | p. 36 |
| D | Health Ins Bill (NY) 1947 | p. 36 |
| D | Health Ins. Bill (NY) 1948 | p. 36 |
| D | Health Ins. Bill (NY) 1949 | p. 36 |
| D, R | Rockefeller Foundation Committee on Dispensary Development, 1920; | p. 42–43 |
| | Comprehensive Natl. Health Ins. Bills, 1935–1949 | p. 48 |

Bullough B, Bullough VL *Poverty Ethnic Identity and Health Care*

| | | |
|---|---|---|
| D | AALL (American Assoc. for Labor Legislation (20 states) 1914–1920 | p. 181 |
| D | CCMC | p. 182 |
| D | Wagner Bill, 1939 | |
| D | Repeated variations | |
| R | Medicare/Medicaid, 1965 | p. 196 |

Cray B. *In Failing Health*

| | | |
|---|---|---|
| D | Govt. Grants in Aid for Mat. & Inf. Care (Sheppard Towner Act) 1920s | p. 50 |
| D | Renewal Sheppard Towner, 1931 | p. 50 |
| D | Renewal Sheppard Towner, 1932 | p. 50 |
| D | Pepper Bill, 1945 | p. 52 |
| D | P.T.A. Bill, 1948 | p. 52 |
| D | Children's School Care Bill, 1949 | p. 53 |
| R | EMIC – Resisted, 1943–1948 | p. 53–54 |
| D | EMIC – Renewal | p. 53–54 |

Cray B. *In Failing Health* (continued)
| | | |
|---|---|---|
| R | VA Up to 1952 | p. 56–57, 64–65 |
| D | World War I Vet. Act, 1924 | p. 56 |
| R | NCI, Direct Grants for Reg., 1937 | p. 57 |
| | Comm. on Economic Security, 1934 | p. 66 |
| D | Comm. of Economic Security Natl. Health Ins. Plan | p. 67 |
| D | Wagner-Murray-Dingell Bill, 1941 | p. 73 |
| D | Truman Bill, 1949 | p. 82 |
| D | Falk Cohen Plan, 1951 | p. 84 |
| D | Forand Bill, 1957 | p. 87 |
| D | King Anderson, 1960 | p. 94–96 |
| D | Kerr Mills, 1962 | p. 96 |
| D | Pepper Bill, 1949 | p. 119 |
| | Veterans' Health Bill, 1924 (opposed) | p. 54 |
| | Campaign against VA, 1924–1956 | p. 56–57 |

Sidel VS, Sidel R *Reforming Medicine*
| | | |
|---|---|---|
| D | Forand Bill, 1959 | p. 55–56 |
| D | King Anderson, 1960 | p. 57 |

Starr P. *The Social Transformation of Amer. Med.*
| | | |
|---|---|---|
| D | Health Center Movement, 1910 | p. 194 |
| D | Warren Health Plan, CMA killed it | p. 282 |
| D | Biggs Health Centers, 1923 | p. 195–196 |
| D | Sheppard-Towner Act, 1921–1927 | p. 261 |
| D | CCMC, early 1930s | |
| D | Comm. on Economic Security Report, 1935 | p. 260–269 |
| D | Roosevelt's Interdepartmental Committee to Coordinate Health and Welfare Activities Technical Comm. on Med. Care, 1937 | |
| D | Natl. Health Conference, 1938 | |
| D | Wagner-Murray-Dingell Bill, 1943 | p. 280 |
| D. | Truman Plan, 1945 | p. 281–282 |
| D | Ross-Loos Clinic Founders, 1929 – Expelled | p. 304 |
| D | Oklahoma Health Cooperative, 1929 | p. 302 |
| D | AALL (Rubinow Plan), 1917 | |
| D | Social Security – Health Ins. Omitted from 1935 Act | p. 275–277 |
| D | Wagner Bill, 1939 | |
| D | Kerr Mills, 1965 | p. 260–289 |
| R | OEO-CHC Movements | p. 260–289 |
| R | Region Medical Programs – Med. Schools | p. 260–289 |

Beardsley EH. *A History of Neglect*
| | | |
|---|---|---|
| R | Sheppard Towner Act – Prof. fought at state level | p. 137–139 |
| R | Soc. Sec. Cripple Child. Aid | p. 170 |
| | Prof. fight or non-participation | |
| R | LaFollette-Bullwinkle Act, 1938 | p. 172 |
| R | Z. Smith Reynolds Foundation | p. 172 |
| R | Emergency Maternal & Infant Care Program (EMIC) 1940s | p. 174–176 |
| R | Children's Bureau program | p. 175 |
| D | Truman Plan | p. 251 |

Brown RE. *Rockefeller Medicine Men*

| | | |
|---|---|---|
| R | Medicaid | p. 2 |
| R | Medicare | p. 2 |
| D | CCMC (Comm. on Costs of Medical Care), 1927–1931 | p. 197–199 |
| | Succession of Bills defeated | |
| D | AALL (American Assoc. for Labor Legislation) | p. 201 |
| D | Wagner-Murray-Dingell Bills, 1940s (at least 5) | p. 202 |
| R | Medicare/Medicaid | p. 202, 213 |
| D | Dellums Bill | p. 216 |
| D | Kennedy Bill | p. 216 |

Stevens R. *American Medicine in the Public Interest*

| | | |
|---|---|---|
| R | Sheppard Towner, 1921 | p. 142–144 |
| R | Sheppard Towner – Renewal, 1926 | p. 142–144 |
| D | Sheppard Towner – Renewal, 1929 | p. 142–144 |
| D | Attempted reinstatements, 1931 | p. 142–144 |
| D | Attempted reinstatements, 1932 | p. 142–143 |
| D | U.S-House of Rep. Bill (for low income workers), 1938 | p. 193–194 |
| D | Natl. Health Act, 1939 (Wagner Bill) | p. 194 |

*Bibliography*

Numbers RL. *Almost Persuaded: American Physicians and Compulsory Health Insurance, 1912– 1970*. Baltimore: Johns Hopkins University Press, 1978, 64–70, 45–46, 81–82, 107.

Starr P. *The Social Transformation of American* Medicine. New York: Basic Books, Publishers, 1982, 194–196, 260–289, 302–304.

Stevens R. *American Medicine in the Public Interest*. New Haven: Yale University Press, 1971, 142–143, 193–194.

Morais HM. *The History of the Negro in Medicine*. 2d ed. The Association of Negro Life and History. New York: Publishers Company, 1967, 173.

Sidel VW, Sidel R. *Reforming Medicine: Lessons of the Last Quarter* Century. New York: Pantheon, 1984, 55–57.

Beardsley EH. *A History of Neglect: Health Care for Blacks and Mill Workers in the Twentieth-Century South*. Knoxville: The University of Tennessee Press, 1987, 137–139, 170, 172, 174–176, 251.

Brown ER. *Rockefeller Medicine Men: Medicine and Capitalism in America*. Berkeley: University of California Press, 1979, 2, 197, 199, 201, 202, 213, 216.

Bullough B, Bullough VL. *Poverty, Ethnic Identity, and Health Care*. New York: Appleton-Century-Croffs, 1972, 181, 182, 186.

Cray E. *In Failing Health: The Medical Crisis and the A.M.A.* Indianapolis: Bobbs-Merrill, 1970, 50–57, 64–67, 72–75, 82–87, 94–96, 119.

Sardell A. *The U.S. Experiment in Social Medicine: The Community Health Center Program, 1965–1986*. Pittsburgh: The University of Pittsburgh Press, 1988, 26–28, 32, 35–36.

# Summaries of Majority and Minority CCMC Reports*

## CHRONOLOGY

| | | |
|---|---|---|
| | 1912 | Social Insurance Commission of the AALL created. |
| | 1915 | Social Insurance Committee of the AMA established. |
| | 1916 | Publication of AALL Model Bill. |
| | 1917 | AMA House of Delegates endorses compulsory health insurance. |
| | 1920 | AMA House of Delegates condemns compulsory health insurance. |
| | 1921 | Sheppard-Towner Act passed. |
| | 1924 | Veterans' medical care program revised. |
| | 1927 | CCMC established. |
| | 1929 | Sheppard-Towner Act expires. |
| | 1929 | Baylor University Hospital Plan started—origin of Blue Cross. |
| | 1932 | Final Reports of GCMG. |
| Summer, | 1933 | FERA medical relief program begun. |
| June, | 1934 | CES created. |
| June, | 1934 | "Ten Principles" of AMA House of Delegates passed. |
| November, | 1934 | National Conference on Economic Security. |
| January, | 1935 | Final Report of the CES to the President. |
| February, | 1935 | Special Section of the AMA Home of Delegates condemns health insurance. |
| March, | 1935 | Final Report on Medical Care of the CES. |
| | 1935 | Model Bill of AASS released. |
| August, | 1935 | Social Security Act passed by Congress. |
| Summer, | 1935 | Beginning of medical programs of WPA. |
| Autumn, | 1935 | Interdepartmental Committee to Coordinate Health and Welfare Activities created. |

---

*Source: Hirshfeld DS. *The Lost Reform: The Campaign for Compulsory Health Insurance in the United States, 1932 to 1943*. Cambridge, MA: Harvard University Press, 1970, Appendix B.

| | | |
|---|---|---|
| | 1937 | Farm Security Administration takes over and expands medical program of Resettlement Administration. |
| March, | 1937 | Technical Committee on Medical Care of Interdepartmental Committee to Coordinate Health and Welfare Activities created. |
| June, | 1937 | "Ten Principles of Group Hospitalization" of AMA House of Delegates passed. |
| November, | 1937 | Program of Committee of Physicians for the Improvement of Medical Care publicly announced. |
| February, | 1938 | National Health Program publicly released. |
| July, | 1938 | National Health Conference. |
| August, | 1938 | Negotiations between AMA and Interdepartmental Committee. |
| September, | 1938 | Special Sessions of AMA House of Delegates on National Health Program. |
| January, | 1939 | Senator Wagner introduces S. 1620, the National Health Bill. |
| Spring, | 1939 | AMA loses antitrust suit concerning Group Health Association. |
| Spring, | 1939 | National Physicians' Committee for the Extension of Medical Service created. |
| April, | 1939 | Hearings begin on S. 1620. |
| May, | 1989 | AMA House of Delegates condemns S. 1620. |
| May, | 1940 | Senate passes S. 3230, the "Forty Little Hospitals Bill." |
| January, | 1942 | President Roosevelt calls for federal hospitalization insurance. |
| | 1943 | First Wagner-Murray-Dingell Bill proposed. |

## SIX ESSENTIALS OF CCMC MAJORITY

1. The plan must safeguard the quality of medical service and preserve the essential personal relationship between doctor and patient.
2. The plan must provide for the future development of preventive and therapeutic services in all kinds and amounts as will meet the needs of substantially all the people and not merely their present effective demands.
3. It must provide services on financial terms which the people can and will meet, without undue hardship, either through individual or collective resources.
4. There should be a full application of existing knowledge to the prevention of disease, so that all medical practice will be permeated with the concept of prevention. The program must include, therefore, not only medical care of the individual and the family, but also a well-organized and adequately supported public health program.
5. The basic plan should include provisions for assisting and guiding patients in the selection of competent practitioners and suitable facilities for medical care.
6. Adequate and assured payment must be provided to the individuals and agencies which furnish the care.

Abstracted from CCMC *Medical Care for the American People* (Chicago: University of Chicago Press, 1932), p. 38.

## CCMC MAJORITY RECOMMENDATIONS

1. Medical service should be more largely furnished by groups of physicians and related practitioners, so organized as to maintain high standards of care and to retain the personal relationship between doctor and patient.
2. Methods of preventing disease should be more extensively and more effectively applied, as measures both of service and economy; and should be so financed as to minimize the economic deterrents to their extension.
3. The costs of medical care should be distributed over groups of people and over periods of time, through the use of insurance, taxation or both.
4. The facilities for medical care should be coordinated by appropriate agencies on a community basis, with special attention given to the coordination of rural and urban services.
5. The education of physicians and the members of related professions should be extended and made more relevant to modern conditions.

Abstracted from CCMC *Medical Care for the American People* (Chicago: University of Chicago Press, 1932), pp. 109–134.

## CCMC MINORITY RECOMMENDATIONS

1. Government competition in the practice of medicine should be discontinued except for (a) care of the indigent, (b) care of those with diseases best treated in governmental institutions, (c) public health services, (d) medical care for military personnel and those government employees whose occupations prohibit their use of private facilities, (e) care of veterans suffering from *bona fide* service-connected disabilities and diseases, except in the case of tuberculosis and nervous and mental diseases.
2. Expansion of governmental medical care for the indigent should be undertaken with the ultimate objective of relieving the private medical profession of this burden.
3. Community agencies to coordinate medical services are endorsed.
4. United attempts are urged to restore the general practitioner to the central place in medical practice.
5. The corporate practice of medicine, financed through intermediary agencies, is condemned.
6. Careful experiments which are fitted to our present institutions and agencies and which will not interfere with the fundamentals of medical practice are urged.
7. The development by state and county medical societies of plans for supplying medical care are recommended.

Abstracted from CCMC *Medical Care for the American People* (Chicago: University of Chicago Press, 1932), pp. 170–183.

## AMA TEN PRINCIPLES

1. All features of medical service in any method of medical practice should be under the control of the medical profession. No other body or individual is legally or educationally equipped to exercise such control.
2. No third party must be permitted to come between the patient and his physician in any medical relation. All responsibility for the character of medical service must be borne by the profession.
3. Patients must have absolute freedom to choose a legally qualified Doctor of Medicine who will serve them from among all those qualified to practice and who are willing to give service.
4. The method of giving the service must retain a permanent, confidential relation between the patient and the "family physician." This relation must be the fundamental and dominating feature of any system.
5. All medical phases of all institutions involved in the medical service should be under professional control, it being understood that hospital service and medical service should be considered separately. These institutions are but expansions of the equipment of the physician. He is the only one whom the laws of all nations recognize as competent to use them in the delivery of service. The medical profession alone can determine the adequacy and character of such institutions. Their value depends on their operation according to medical standards.
6. However the cost of medical service may be distributed, the immediate cost should be borne by the patient, if able to pay, at the time the service is rendered.
7. Medical service must have no connection with any cash benefits.
8. Any form of medical service should include within its scope all qualified physicians in the locality covered by its operation who wish to give service under the conditions established.
9. Systems for the relief of low income classes should be limited strictly to those below the "comfort level" standard of income.
10. There should be no restrictions by nonmedical groups on treatment or prescribing unless formulated and enforced by the medical profession.

*JAMA*, 102:2199–2201 (1934).

# The Nuremberg Code*

### The Proof as to War Crimes and Crimes against Humanity

Judged by any standard of proof the record clearly shows the commission of war crimes and crimes against humanity substantially as alleged in counts two and three of the indictment. Beginning with the outbreak of World War II criminal medical experiments on non-German nationals, both prisoners of war and civilians, including Jews and "asocial" persons, were carried out on a large scale in Germany and the occupied countries. These experiments were not the isolated and casual acts of individual doctors and scientists working solely on their responsibility, but were the product of coordinated policy-making and planning at high governmental, military, and Nazi Party levels, conducted as an integral part of the total war effort. They were ordered, sanctioned, permitted, or approved by persons in positions of authority who under all principles of law were under the duty to know about these things and to take steps to terminate or prevent them.

### Permissible Medical Experiments

The great weight of the evidence before us is to the effect that certain types of medical experiments on human beings, when kept within reasonably well-defined bounds, conform to the ethics of the medical profession generally. The protagonists of the practice of human experimentation justify their views on the basis that such experiments yield results for the good of society that are unprocurable by other methods or means of study. All agree, however, that certain basic principles must be observed in order to satisfy moral, ethical and legal concepts:

1.  The voluntary consent of the human subject is absolutely essential. This means that the person involved should have legal capacity to give consent; should be so situated as to be able to exercise free power of choice, without the intervention of any element of force, fraud, deceit, duress, over-reaching, or other ulterior form of constraint or coercion; and should have sufficient

---

*Reprinted from Trials of War Criminals before the Nuremberg Military Tribunals under Control Council Law No. 10. vol. 2. Washington DC: U.S. Government Printing Office, 1949), pp. 181–182; Source: Reiser RJ, Dyck AJ, Curran WJ, eds. Ethics in Medicine: Historical Perspectives and Contemporary Concerns. Cambridge, MA: MIT Press, 1977, pp. 272–273.

knowledge and comprehension of the elements of the subject matter involved as to enable him to make an understanding and enlightened decision. This latter element requires that before the acceptance of an affirmative decision by the experimental subject there should be made known to him the nature, duration, and purpose of the experiment; the method and means by which it is to be conducted; all inconveniences and hazards reasonably to be expected; and the effects upon his health or person which may possibly come from his participation in the experiment. The duty and responsibility for ascertaining the quality of the consent rests upon each individual who initiates, directs or engages in the experiment. It is a personal duty and responsibility which may not be delegated to another with impunity.

2.  The experiment should be such as to yield fruitful results for the good of society, unprocurable by other methods or means of study, and not random and unnecessary in nature.

3.  The experiment should be so designed and based on the results of animal experimentation and a knowledge of the natural history of the disease or other problem under study that the anticipated results will justify the performance of the experiment.

4.  The experiment should be so conducted as to avoid all unnecessary physical and mental suffering and injury.

5.  No experiment should be conducted where there is an a priori reason to believe that death or disabling injury will occur; except, perhaps, in those experiments where the experimental physicians also serve as subjects.

6.  The degree of risk to be taken should never exceed that determined by the humanitarian importance of the problem to be solved by the experiment.

7.  Proper preparations should be made and adequate facilities provided to protect the experimental subject against even remote possibilities of injury, disability, or death.

8.  The experiment should be conducted only by scientifically qualified persons. The highest degree of skill and care should be required through all stages of the experiment of those who conduct or engage in the experiment.

9.  During the course of the experiment the human subject should be at liberty to bring the experiment to an end if he has reached the physical or mental state where continuation of the experiment seems to him to be impossible.

10.  During the course of the experiment the scientist in charge must be prepared to terminate the experiment at any stage, if he has probable cause to believe, in the exercise of the good faith, superior skill and careful judgment required of him that a continuation of the experiment is likely to result in injury, disability, or death to the experimental subject.

# Declaration of Helsinki Recommendations Guiding Doctors in Clinical Research*

Declaration I, 18th World Medical Assembly, Helsinki, June 1964
Declaration II, 29th World Medical Assembly, Tokyo, October 1975
Declaration III, 35th World Medical Assembly, Venice, October 1983
Declaration IV, 41st World Medical Assembly, Hong Kong, September 1989

*World Medical Association*
**Declaration of Helsinki I**
**18th World Medical Assembly**
**Helsinki, Finland, June 1964**

It is the mission of the doctor to safeguard the health of the people. His or her knowledge and conscience are dedicated to the fulfillment of this mission.

The Declaration of Geneva of the World Medical Association binds the physician with the words, "The health of my patient will be my first consideration"; and the International Code of Medical Ethics declares that, "Any act or advice which could weaken physical or mental resistance of a human being may be used only in his interest."

Because it is essential that the results of laboratory experiments be applied to human beings to further scientific knowledge and to help suffering humanity, the World Medical Association has prepared the following recommendations as a guide to every physician in clinical research. It must be stressed that the standards as drafted are only a guide to physicians all over the world. Doctors are not relieved from criminal, civil and ethical responsibilities under the laws of their own countries.

---

*Source: Annas GJ, Grodin MA, eds. *The Nazi Doctors and the Nuremberg Code: Human Rights in Human Experimentation*. New York: Oxford University Press, 1992, 331–333.

In the field of clinical research a fundamental distinction must be recognzed between clinical research in which the aim is essentially therapeutic for a patient, and clinical research the essential object of which is purely scientific and without therapeutic value to the person subjected to the research.

### I. Basic Principles

1. Clinical research must conform to the moral and scientific principles that justify medical research, and should be based on laboratory and animal experiments or other scientifically established facts.
2. Clinical research should be conducted only by scientifically qualified persons and under the supervision of a qualified medical man.
3. Clinical research cannot legitimately be carried out unless the importance of the objective is in proportion to the inherent risk to the subject.
4. Every clinical research project should be preceded by careful assessment of inherent risks in comparison to foreseeable benefits to the subject or to others.
5. Special caution should be exercised by the doctor in performing clinical research in which the personality of the subject is liable to be altered by drugs or experimental procedure.

### II. Clinical Research Combined with Professional Care

1. In the treatment of the sick person, the physician must be free to use a new therapeutic measure if in his or her judgment it offers hope of saving life, re-establishing health, or alleviating suffering.

   If at all possible, consistent with patient psychology, the doctor should obtain the patient's freely given consent after the patient has been given a full explanation. In case of legal incapacity consent should also be procured from the legal guardian; in case of physical incapacity the permission of the legal guardian replaces that of the patient.
2. The doctor can combine clinical research with professional care, the objective being the acquisition of new medical knowledge, only to the extent that clinical research is justified by its potential diagnostic or therapeutic value for the patient.

### III. Non-Therapeutic Clinical Research

1. In the purely scientific application of clinical research carried out on a human being it is the duty of the physician to remain the protector of the life and health of that person on whom clinical research is being carried out.
2. The nature, the purpose, and the risk of clinical research must be explained to the subject by the doctor.
3a. Clinical research on a human being cannot be undertaken without his free consent, after he has been fully informed; if he is legally incompetent the consent of the legal guardian should be procured.
3b. The subject of clinical research should be in such a mental, physical, and legal state as to be able to exercise fully his power of choice.
3c. Consent should as a rule be obtained in writing. However, the responsibility

for clinical research always remains with the research worker; it never falls on the subject, even after consent is obtained.

4a. The investigator must respect the right of each individual to safeguard his personal integrity, especially if the subject is in a dependent relationship to the investigator.

4b. At any time during the course of clinical research the subject or his guardian should be free to withdraw permission for research to be continued. The investigator or the investigating team should discontinue the research if in his or their judgment it may, if continued, be harmful to the individual.

# ✕ A Glossary of Commonly Used Managed Care, Health Policy, and Health Reform Terms

***Access***: A measure of an individual's ability to obtain medical services on a timely geographically and financially acceptable basis. Factors determining ease of access include location of health care facilities, transportation, and hours of operation.

***Accountability***: Having to give reasons to other stakeholders (such as employees or regulators who have legitimate interests in what and how a person or an organization behaves) for organizational performance.

***Acute Care***: Medical care of a limited duration, provided in a hospital or outpatient setting, to treat an injury or short-term illness.

***Administrative Costs***: Nonmedical expenditures incurred by the delivery of health care services, including billing, claims processing, marketing, and overhead.

***Administrative Services Only (ASO)***: A contract between an insurance company and a self-funded plan where the insurance company performs administrative services only and does not assume any risk.

***Adverse Selection***: The problem of attracting members who are sicker than the general population (specifically, members who are sicker than was anticipated when the budget for medical costs was developed). Another definition is the process whereby individuals who know they are most at risk of having an insurance claim disproportionately purchase insurance.

***Aid to Families with Dependent Children (AFDC)***: Usually called welfare, this is a joint federal-state program that provides grants to those low-income individuals and their dependent children who meet eligibility criteria.

***Alternate Delivery System (ADS)***: A method of providing health care benefits paying for and different from the usual indemnity approach. An example is the HMO.

***Ambulatory Care***: Care provided to individuals who are not inpatients in a health care institution.

*Ancillary Services*: Supplemental services (including, but not limited to) laboratory, radiology and physical therapy that are provided in conjunction with medical care. Such services are considered standard benefits in other western industrialized countries.

*Any Willing Provider (AWP)*: This is a form of state law that requires an MCO to accept any provider willing to meet the terms and conditions in the MCO's contract, whether the MCO wants or needs that provider or not.

*Average Length of Stay (ALOS)*: The American Hospital Association computes the ALOS by dividing the number of inpatient days by the number of admissions.

*Bad Debt and Free Care*: Hospital bills which are not paid. Free care refers to the bills of those too poor to be expected to pay. Bad debt refers to bills left unpaid by those who reasonably might be expected to pay.

*Balance Billing*: The practice of a provider billing a patient for all charges not paid for by the insurance plan, even if those charges are above the plan's UCR (usual, customary, or reasonable) or are considered medically unnecessary.

*Beneficiary*: Any person, either a subscriber or a dependent, eligible for service under a health plan contract.

*Benefits/Benefit Package*: The services provided (e.g., hospitalization, outpatient care, laboratory tests) to a patient under any given health insurance/HMO plan.

*Capitation*: A fixed rate of payment to cover a specified set of health services. The rate is usually provided on a per month basis.

*Case Management*: An organized program that coordinates individual patient care throughout the entire spectrum of services with the goals of managing utilization of services and providing quality care in the most effective manner.

*Case Mix*: The spectrum of illnesses and the severity in the case-population of any provider.

*Catchment Area*: The geographic area from which an organized health service draws its patients.

*Certificate of Need (CON)*: The requirement that a health care organization obtain permission from an oversight agency before making changes. Generally applies only to facilities or facility-based services.

*Chronic Condition*: A condition that persists over time. Usually used in opposition to an acute or emergent condition.

*Claims*: A bill for health services submitted to a health benefits plan for payment.

*Clinical Trial*: A carefully conducted study of the effectiveness of a new medical drug, device, or treatment. Such trials often rely on "random assignment" and can be "double blind." For a variety of reasons, African Americans are increasingly underrepresented in these studies.

*Closed Panel*: A managed care plan that contracts with physicians on an exclusive basis for services and does not allow those physicians to see patients for another managed care organization. Examples include staff and group model HMOs.

*Coinsurance*: A provision in a member's coverage that limits the amount of coverage by the plan to a certain percentage, commonly 80 percent. Any additional costs are paid by the member out of pocket.

*Commercial Insurance*: Refers to insurance purchased through a for-profit commercial insurance company.

*Community Hospital*: A hospital offering short-term (ALOS less than 30 days) general and other special services, owned by groups other than the federal government.

*Community Rating*: All the people in a population, regardless of their different risk of becoming ill, are charged the same monthly insurance premium.

*Consolidated Omnibus Reconciliation Act (COBRA)*: A portion of this act requires employers to offer the opportunity for terminated employees to purchase continuation of health care coverage under the group's medical plan.

*Copayment*: That portion of a claim or medical expense that a member must pay out of pocket.

*Cost-Sharing*: The share of health expenses that a beneficiary must pay, including the deductibles, co-payments, coinsurance, and extra bill.

*Cost Shifting*: Refers to passing the cost of health care for one population subgroup onto another such group. For example, if the rate one group of health plan enrollees pays for services is less than the actual cost of those services, the difference is made up based on charges higher than cost paid by another group.

*Credentialing*: The most common use of the term refers to obtaining and reviewing the documentation of professional providers. Such documentation includes licensure, certifications, insurance, evidence of malpractice insurance, malpractice history, and so forth.

*Current Procedural Terminology (CPT)*: A listing of descriptive terms and identifying codes for reporting physician services and procedures.

*Custodial Care*: Care provided to an individual primarily to support the basic activities of living; may be medical or nonmedical, but the care is not meant to be curative and is often lifelong; rarely covered by group health insurance.

*Deductible*: The amount of medical expense that must be incurred and paid by an individual before a third party will assume any liability for payment of benefits.

*Defensive Medicine*: Performing or ordering tests or procedures that would not have otherwise been performed, in order to be able to defend against a malpractice claim.

*Deinstitutionalization*: The term applied to the gradual and continuing closure of state mental hospitals that has been under way since the mid-1960s which has resulted in the discharge of tens of thousands of mental patients nationally, and the national inability to provide ongoing inpatient mental health care to many patients who would have previously been institutionalized.

*Dependent*: A health insurance beneficiary covered by virtue of a family relationship with a person having a health plan coverage.

*Diagnosis-Related Group (DRG)*: A statistical system of classifying any inpatient stay into groups for purposes of payment.

*Diminishing Marginal Returns*: An economics concept which says that additional resources devoted to producing any output eventually become less effective and so produce less output. This phenomenon explains "flat of the curve" medicine.

*Direct Teaching Cost Adjustment*: A payment to a teaching hospital made by the Medicare program that covers the actual costs of supporting the teaching function.

*Discounting*: A lower rate of pricing by a provider to a particular HMO or insurance company.

*Disenrollment*: The process of termination of coverage.

*Disproportionate Share Hospital (DSH)*: A hospital that provides a large amount (disproportionate share) of uncompensated care and/or care to Medicaid and low-income Medicare beneficiaries.

*Drug Formulary*: A dynamic, comprehensive, list of drugs designed to direct physicians to prescribe the most cost-effective medications (sometimes referred to as restrictive pharmacy lists).

*Employer Mandate*: The requirement that all employers offer health insurance to their employees–with the employers covering some specified fraction of the cost.

*Employee Retirement Income Security Act of 1974 (ERISA)*: The federal law that sets pension plan requirements. One provision of this Act allows self-funded plans to avoid paying premium taxes, complying with state-mandated benefits, or otherwise complying with state laws and regulations regarding insurance, even when insurance companies and managed care plans that stand risk for medical costs must do so. Some plans have used the Act to deflect medical malpractice lawsuits.

*Encounter*: An outpatient or ambulatory visit by a member to a provider.

*Enrollee*: Individual covered by a health benefit plan.

*Enrollment*: The process by which an individual becomes a subscriber for himself and/or his dependents for coverage in a health plan.

*Entitlements*: Government benefits (e.g., Medicare, Medicaid, Social Security, food stamps) that are provided automatically to all qualified individuals and are therefore part of mandatory spending programs.

*Essential Community Providers (ECPs)*: Comprehensive primary care providers (such as neighborhood and community health centers, departments of health, public hospitals, inner-city "distressed" hospitals, and private physicians) serving in medically underserved areas where a high percentage of their patients fall in the disadvantaged minority or low-income categories.

*Ethics*: A socially determined set of standards of public behavior that do not have the force of law behind them, but for which there is a societal expectation of compliance by each member.

*Exclusive Provider Organization (EPO)*: An EPO is similar to an HMO in that it often uses primary physicians as gatekeepers, often capitates providers, has a limited provider panel, and uses an authorization system, etc. It is referred to as exclusive because the member must remain within the network to receive benefits.

*Experience Rating*: Individuals or groups are charged premiums proportional to their expected level of utilization.

*Fee-for-Service (FFS)*: A method of paying practitioners on a service by service rather than a salaried or capitated basis.

*Flat of the Curve Medicine*: Medical care that produces relatively little or no benefit for the patient as a result of "diminishing marginal returns."

*Fixed Benefit Plan*: A defined benefit (pension) plan.

*For-Profit Hospitals*: Those owned by private corporations that declare dividends or otherwise distribute profits to individuals. Also called *investor-owned*, they are usually short-term general hospitals.

*Gatekeeper*: An informal, though widely used term that refers to a primary care case management model health plan. In this model, all care from providers other than the primary care physician, except for true emergencies, must be authorized by the primary care physician before care is rendered.

*Generic Drugs*: Drugs that are essentially identical to brand name drugs–without the brand name–sold by other manufacturers at lower prices than the original product.

*Global Budget*: Setting the total volume of expenditures in a health care system in advance.

*Graduate Medical Education (sometimes Postgraduate Medical Education)*: Additional training undertaken by physicians beyond medical school. The various training programs are based in hospitals and are accredited by the specialty society for each type of study. Those in such training (e.g., residents) provide patient care under the supervision of senior physicians.

*Group Practice*: The American Medical Association defines group practice as three or more physicians who deliver patient care, make joint use of equipment and personnel, and divide income by a prearranged formula.

*Head Tax*: A tax that does not vary at all with income. Financing health care with insurance premiums is equivalent to a head tax and as such is extremely "regressive."

*Health*: A state of complete physical, mental, and social well-being and not merely the absence of disease or infirmity. [WHO definition]

*Health Care*: Those services provided to individuals or communities by agents of the health services or professions, for the purpose of promoting, maintaining, monitoring, or restoring health. Health care is broader than, and not limited to medical care, which implies therapeutic action by or under the supervision of a physician.

*Health Department*: A unit of state or local government (county or city, generally) that has responsibility primarily for public health services (ranging from infectious disease control to the collection of vital statistics) for a given geographic area. In the modern era, some health departments also provide direct treatment services.

*Health Maintenance Organization (HMO)*: An entity that accepts responsibility and financial risk for providing specified services to a defined population during a defined period of time at a fixed price.

*House Officer or House Staff*: See Residents

*Healthplan Employer Data Information Set (HEDIS)*: HEDIS is an ever-evolving set of data reporting standards for MCOs. HEDIS is designed to provide some standardization in performance reporting for financial, utilization, membership, and clinical data so that employers and others can compare performance among them.

*Home Health Care*: Defined by the National Home and Hospice Care Survey as care provided to individuals and families in their place of residence for promoting, maintaining, or restoring health or for minimizing the effects of disability and illness, including terminal illness.

*Hospice Care*: Defined by the National Home and Hospice Care Survey as a program of palliative and supportive care services providing physical, psychological, social, and spiritual care for dying persons, their families, and other loved ones.

*Indemnity Plan*: Indemnity means the insured patient is paid in the event of a covered loss. Under this plan, subscribers incur a medical expense then submit a claim to the third party. Indemnity plans usually control their potential liabilities by excluding discretionary expenses, setting fixed limits on reimbursements for specific services and overall cost and/or stipulating that the subscriber pay an initial deductible and ongoing share of cost. The expectation of this plan is that cost sharing will limit overall use of services. In the indemnity plan, the physician and hospital have essentially no direct relationship with the indemnity plan and the indemnity plan has no responsibility for the quality of services received by the subscriber.

*Indirect Teaching Cost Adjustment*: A special provision of the Medicare funding system that provides extra money to teaching hospitals for those costs which cannot be directly identified. These sums now [1993] amount to approximately $180,000 per "resident" per year.

*Individual Mandate*: Requirement that all individuals purchase health insurance. This proposal is usually combined with an "employer mandate" and with some scheme for aiding low-income workers and the unemployed with the costs of such coverage.

*Individual or Independent Practice Association (IPA)*: A health maintenance organization that contracts with private physicians who serve HMO enrollees in their offices, generally on a fee-for-services basis.

*Insurer*: Organization that bears the financial risk for the cost of defined categories of services for a defined group of enrollees.

*Integrated Delivery System (IDS)*: A group of health care organizations that collectively provide a full range of health-related services from prevention to complex hospital-based treatment in a coordinated fashion to those using the system.

*Integration, Horizontal*: Affiliations among providers of the same type (e.g., a hospital forming relationships with other hospitals).

*Integration, Vertical*: Affiliations among providers of different types (e.g., a hospital, clinic, and nursing home forming an affiliation).

*Job-Lock*: Inability of individuals to change jobs because they believe they will not be able to get health insurance coverage if they do change.

*Joint Commission for the Accreditation of Healthcare Organizations (JCAHO or Joint Commission)*: A not-for-profit organization that performs accreditation reviews primarily on hospitals, other institutional facilities, and out-patient facilities.

*Long Term Care*: Custodial Care. Typically provided in a Nursing Home.

*Loss Ratio (or Medical Loss Ratio)*: A term used to describe the proportion of payments made for health services actually spent on the provision of health care. A company with a loss ratio of .85, for instance, spends 85 cents of every premium dollar on health care and the remaining 15 cents on administrative costs, including paperwork, marketing, executive salaries, and profits.

*Mainstream*: A term that is often used to describe the "general market," usually refers to a broad population that is primarily White and middle class.

*Major Medical Insurance*: A precursor of "catastrophic coverage," it covers costs above a fairly high minimum (usually covered by conventional health insurance) to a very high maximum. It is intended to cover the costs associated with a truly major ("catastrophic") illness or injury.

*Managed Care Organization (MCO or HMO)*: A generic term applied to a managed care plan. Some prefer it to the term HMO because it encompasses plans that do not conform exactly to the strict definition of an HMO.

*Managed Competition*: This is a theoretical concept of Alain Enthoven, that involves the creation of large groups of insurance purchasers in order to give them the bargaining power needed to create strong incentives for providers to come up with the highest quality service for the lowest possible cost. Minimum benefits packages would be established by Nationals Boards. Tax incentives would be offered to bring consumers and doctors into managed care groups.

*Managed Health Care*: A system of health care delivery that tries to manage the cost of health care, the quality of that health care, and access to that care.

*Mandated Benefits*: Benefits that a health plan is required to provide by law.

*Medicaid (Title XIX)*: Officially titled "Grants to States for Medical Assistance Programs" as established by the Social Security Amendments of 1965 (Public Law 89–97) as amended by Public Law 93–233. This Act provided for Federal Grants to states and was originally intended to provide medical care for the poor. Medicaid is a state administered program as compared to Medicare, which is a federally administered program. More than 3/4 of the funds provided under Medicare have been shifted away from the poor and are today utilized by the nursing home industry to support and subsidize long term care for the elderly (i.e. predominantly middle class White elderly).

*Medical Savings Account*: Accounts similar to individual retirement accounts (IRAs), into which employers and employees can make tax-deferred contributions and from which employees may withdraw funds to pay covered health care expenses.

*Medical Sociology*: The sociology of health and illness.

*Medical Staff*: All the physicians who are allowed to admit patients to a specific hospital. In most hospitals the existing staff decides who else may join. Most staff members derive their income from patients–they are not paid by the hospital.

*Medicare (Title XVIII)*: Health insurance for the aged and disabled as established by the Social Security Amendments of 1965 (Public Law 89–97).

*Medicare Part A*: The portion of the Medicare Program applicable to the reimbursement of hospitals for hospital cost.

*Medicare Part B*: The portion of Medicare which is payable to physicians (or to hospitals for services for hospital based physicians) for the professional component of services the physicians render to Medicare patients.

*Medigap Insurance*: Health insurance policies purchased by individuals covered by Medicare that pay for those expenses that are not covered by Medicare. See Wraparound Plan

*Midlevel Practitioner (MLP)*: Physician's assistants, clinical nurse practitioners, nurse midwives, and the like. Nonphysicians who deliver medical care, generally under the supervision of a physician but for less cost.

*Mixed Model*: A managed care plan that mixes two or more types of delivery system. This has traditionally been used to describe an HMO that has both closed panel and open panel delivery systems.

*Neighborhood or Community Health Center (NHC or CHC)*: Organizations in some cities that provide ambulatory health care in poor neighborhoods. They are financed by a mixture of patient care revenues (predominantly from Medicaid) as well as various grants and subsidies.

*Network Model*: A health plan that contracts with multiple physician groups to deliver health care to members. It is generally limited to large single or multi-specialty groups and is distinguished from group model plans that contract with a single medical group, IPAs that contract through an intermediary, and direct contract model plans that contract with individual physicians in the community.

*Nonprofit*: A term applied to a provider to whom no part of the net earnings accrues or may lawfully accrue to the benefit of any private shareholder or individual; an organization that has received 501-C-3 or 501-C-4 designation by the Internal Revenue Service.

*Nurse Practitioners*: Individuals with special training beyond their RN preparation–typically at the master's level. They function independently although under some supervision by a physician (a very controversial boundary).

*Open Enrollment Period*: The period when an employee may change health plans; usually occurs once per year.

*Office Visit*: A formal face-to-face contact between the physician and the patient in a health center, office, or hospital outpatient department.

*Organization of Economic Cooperation and Development (OECD)*: An international organization that includes all Western European nations, the United States, Canada, New Zealand, Australia, and Japan. Among other functions, the organization collects and publishes many kinds of comparative national statistics including health statistics.

*Outlier*: A provider that is supplying services at either a rate and/or intensity well above or well below the norm.

*Out-of-Pocket Costs*: Direct individual payments for care, including what they pay for "co-insurance" and "deductibles" as well as payments for uncovered services.

*Outpatient Care*: Care offered by a hospital to patients not admitted to the hospital.

*Outpatient or Ambulatory Surgery*: Surgery that is done on an outpatient basis. This means that the patient cannot stay overnight at the institution doing the operation. Such care is offered by hospitals or freestanding centers.

*Payer (sometimes "third-party payer")*: Any individual or organization that pays for health care services–including insurance companies and various government programs like Medicare and Medicaid.

*Peer Review*: Quality assessment of a physician's performance by other physicians, usually within the same geographic area and medical specialty.

*Penetration*: The percentage of total eligibles in a given geographical area that an MCO is able to enroll.

*Personal Health Care Expenditures*: These are outlays for goods and services relating directly to patient care.

*Physician Assistant*: Individual who has completed a training program (inspired in part by the example of medical corpsmen during the Vietnam war). Enrollees have some prior practical experience. Individuals so trained function under the guidance and supervision of physicians.

*Play or Pay*: This type plan gives employers a choice of either providing coverage for employees or paying payroll taxes to cover the cost of publicly provided insurance.

*Point of Service*: A plan where members do not have to choose how to receive services until they need them.

*Practice Guidelines*: Clinical recommendations for patient care.

*Practitioner*: One who practices medicine, and may include physicians, chiropractors, dentists, podiatrists, nurse practitioners, and physician's assistants.

*Pre-admission Review*: Assessment of the clinical justification for a proposed hospital admission.

*Precertification*: A requirement on the part of the admitting physician (and often the hospital) to notify the plan before a member is admitted for inpatient care or an outpatient procedure.

*Preexisting Condition*: Physical and/or mental conditions of the insured person that exist prior to the issuance of his or her policy. These may or may not be covered.

*Preexisting Condition Exclusion*: A provision of a health insurance plan which says that the costs of caring for an illness a subscriber already has will not be paid. The exclusion lasts for a specified period, usually one or two years.

*Preferred Provider Arrangement (PPA)*: Same as a PPO but sometimes used to refer to a somewhat looser type of plan in which the payer (i.e., the employer) makes the arrangement rather than the providers.

*Preferred Provider Organization (PPO)*: A plan that contracts with independent providers at a discount for services. The plan is limited in size and usually has some type of utilization review system associated with it.

*Premium*: An amount paid periodically to purchase health insurance benefits.

*Prevention*: Refers to all efforts to prevent disease from developing–from efforts at encouraging better nutrition and exercise to attempts to diminish drunk driving and teen violence or to improve air pollution.

*Price Negotiation*: Negotiation between a managed care entity and health providers to arrive at a favorable rate, usually at a discount, in exchange for the assurance to the provider of future service provision.

***Primary Care***: Medical practice based on direct contact with the patient without referral from another physician. Such practice is undertaken by doctors trained in various ways including pediatricians, obstetricians, general internists, family physicians, and general practitioners. In addition, many specialists in fact engage in a significant amount of primary care.

***Primary Care Physician (PCP)***: Generally applies to internists, pediatricians, family physicians, and general practitioners and occasionally to obstetrician/gynecologists.

***Prior Approval***: A form of "utilization review" where an insurance company requires a hospital or doctor to get permission from the insurance company before providing care.

***Private Insurance***: Any health insurance policy that is not government financed. It also includes the policies that cover government workers.

***Profile Analysis***: Use of aggregate statistical data on an institution or practitioner to compare practice and use patterns, identify inappropriate practices, or assess other characteristics of practice.

***Profile Monitoring***: A process in which the practice patterns of individual physicians are compared to various norms. The purpose is to identify who uses surgery, tests, or hospitalization especially frequently.

***Proprietary (for-profit) Hospital***: A hospital operated as a normal corporation. Most such hospitals are part of large chains.

***Prospective Payment System (PPS)***: A generic term applied to a reimbursement system that pays prospectively rather than on the basis of charges.

***Provider***: An individual or organization that provides personal health services.

***Public Good***: An economics concept that refers to a good (or service) that affects more than one individual at a time—like air pollution or national defense. The opposite idea is a private (or ordinary) good that benefits only the purchaser.

***Public Health***: Public health is one of the efforts organized by society to protect, promote, and restore the people's health. It is the combination of sciences, skills, and beliefs that is directed to the maintenance and improvement of the health of all the people through collective or social actions. The programs, services, and institutions involved emphasize the prevention of disease and the health needs of the population as a whole. Public health activities change with changing technology and social values, but the goals remain the same: to reduce the amount of disease, premature death, and disease-produced discomfort and disability in the population. Public health is thus a social institution, a discipline, and a practice.

***Public Hospitals***: These are hospitals owned by agencies of federal, state, and local governments. Some are short-term, general public hospitals, while those located in major urban areas are staffed by salaried physicians and manned by residents in training to provide services. The deficits of some, thought not all, public hospitals and systems are paid for from local taxes or federal Medicare and Medicaid "disproportionate share" hospital payments.

*Quality Assurance or Quality Management (QA or QM)*: An organized program to protect or improve quality of care by evaluating medical care, correcting problems, and monitoring corrective actions. Existing quality assurance programs focus primarily on cost containment.

*Overutilization*: Use of a health service or services by an individual user or subpopulation of users that exceeds use norms established by a large population of users.

*Rationing*: Process of limiting the use of all possible health care services. Rationing can be done by price, by waiting lists, or by deciding not to provide certain services.

*Resource Based Relative Value Scale (RBRVS)*: A system for paying doctors instituted by Medicare. Each type of encounter or treatment is assigned a "relative value"–typically a number of points–based on the time, skill, and training required of the doctor. Then the entire fee structure can be adjusted up or down by setting the payment for each point.

*Residents (also called "house officers" or "house staff")*: Individuals who have graduated from medical school (and thus are called "doctor") who have not yet completed their training. Typically residents work in teaching hospitals from one to six years–depending on the specialty–receiving what is called "graduate medical education."

*Risk:* For a health care provider or insurer, the measure of chance of financial loss or the possibility that revenues of the health plan will not be sufficient to cover the expenditures incurred in the delivery of contractual services. For individual patients or population groups, risk is the chance of incurring a given disease or negative health condition.

*Risk Adjustment*: Paying an insurance company or Accountable Health Plan extra for enrolling subscribers who have higher than average health costs.

*Risk-Bonus Arrangements*: Structured evaluation programs and bonus payments based on provider efficiencies in areas such as productivity, medical charting, dependability, after-hours call duty, medical knowledge, management of patient care, management of outside resources, patient relations, staff relations, attitude and leadership, and participation.

*Risk Contract*: A contract between an HMO or CMP [competitive medical plan] and the HCFA to provide services to Medicare beneficiaries under which the health plan receives a fixed monthly payment for enrolled Medicare members, and then must provide all services on an at-risk basis.

*Risk Management*: Process by which a hospital or HMO limits its risk for being sued for malpractice, sometimes also used as a synonym for "risk selection."

*Risk Selection*: Process by which an insurer limits the "risks" it will cover. In health insurance, the process of encouraging sicker individuals not to enroll in your health insurance plan.

*Rural Health Centers*: Health care organizations in rural areas designed to provide comprehensive "outpatient services." They typically employ several physicians plus other kinds of health care workers. They are financed by patient revenues plus various kinds of grant programs.

*Secondary Prevention*: Efforts made by the health care system to prevent disease–or its recurrence–once a patient has an illness.

*Second Opinion*: An opinion about the appropriateness of a proposed treatment provided by a practitioner other than the one making the original recommendation.

*Self Insurance or Self-Funded Plan*: When an organization bears financial risk for hazards (for example: medical cost and property damage) that the organization itself may experience.

*Service Area*: The region in which a health organization provides access to health services.

*Single Payer*: This refers to any plan where health coverage is paid by a single government entity. It is noted for administrative efficiency, universal coverage and comprehensive benefits.

*Sociology*: The study of social life and behavior, especially in relation to social systems, how they work, how they change, the consequences they produce, and their complex relation to people's lives.

*Specialist*: Strictly, any physician who has pursued specialty training beyond the first year of residency. More loosely, those specialists who do not provide "primary care."

*Spend Down*: A requirement under many state Medicaid programs that individuals use up their assets when these are above the level required for eligibility before being able to collect benefits.

*Staff Model*: An HMO that employs providers directly, and those providers see members in the HMO's own facilities.

*Subspecialist*: Strictly, any physician who has gone on to specialized training beyond the training for general surgery, general internal medicine, obstetrics and gynecology, or pediatrics. Within internal medicine, for example, there are many subspecialties such as those in oncology (cancer), nephrology (kidney disease), or cardiology (heart disease).

*Supplemental Security Income (SSI)*: A federal program of income support for those who are disabled.

*Teaching Hospital*: Strictly, any hospital that has any residency program. Since many hospitals have one or two such programs, the distinction is made as to which are major teaching hospitals, i.e., those that have a significant teaching role.

*Third Party Payer*: An organization other than the patient (first party) or health care provider (second party) involved in the financing of personal health services.

An agency which contracts with hospitals and patients to pay for the care of insured patients.

*Tort Reform*: Refers to a variety of proposals to reform malpractice law in particular and more generally the law on all liability for injuries (which is called tort law). These proposals include simplified procedures, limits on awards, limits on attorneys' fees, and, more radically, "no fault" schemes or "enterprise liability."

*Total Quality Management (TQM)*: Originally developed by W. Edward Deming to study systems and processes, identifies sources of error, waste, organizations, and redundancy; uses input and feedback from all staff and patients to understand and make improvements in current procedures.

*Triage*: The process of sorting out requests for services by members into time categories, such as those who need to be seen right away, those who can wait a little while, and those whose problems can be handled with advice over the phone.

*Triple Option*: The offering of an HMO, a PPO, and a traditional insurance plan by one carrier.

*Underutilization*: Use of a health service or services by an individual user or a subpopulation of users that falls below use norms established by a large population of users.

*Underwriting*: This refers to bearing the risk for something (i.e., a policy is underwritten by an insurance company). Another definition refers to the analysis of a group that is done to determine rates or to determine whether the group should be offered coverage at all. A related definition refers to health screening of each individual applicant for insurance and refusing to provide coverage for pre-existing conditions.

*Usual, Customary, or Reasonable (UCR)*: A method of profiling prevailing fees in an area and reimbursing providers on the basis of that profile.

*Utilization Review*: Retrospective review of health care focusing on issues of quality and the elimination of the overuse of medical procedures and services.

*Vertical Integration*: The affiliation of organizations providing different kinds of service, such as hospital care, ambulatory care, long-term care, and social services.

*Volume Performance Standards*: These state the volume of physician services that the managers of a health plan expect to be provided in a given period.

*Voluntary ("nonprofit") Hospitals*: These are community owned (religious groups, nonprofit corporations), nonprofit hospitals whose sole purpose is providing hospital care to the community.

*Workers' Compensation*: A form of social insurance provided through property-casualty insurers, providing medical benefits and replacement of lost wages that result from injuries or illnesses that arise from the workplace. In turn, the employee cannot normally sue the employer unless true negligence exists.

*Wraparound Plan*: Commonly used to refer to insurance or health plan coverage of copays and deductibles that are not covered under a member's base plan. This is often used for Medicare.

## References

American Public Health Association. Managed competition: Wonder drug or snake oil? *The Nation's Health*, March, 1993, 1.

Ammes C, Ammes DS. *Dictionary of Business and Economics*. Revised and Expanded Edition. New York: The Free Press, 1984.

Andrulis DP, Carrier B. *Managed Care in the Inner City: The Uncertain Promise for Providers, Plans, and Communities*. San Francisco: Jossey-Bass, 1999.

Byrd WM, Clayton LA, Randall V, McCoy S, Calliste G. Minority Health Care Review Group: Executive Summary, of report "Recommendations on National Health Care Reform from Providers of Health Care to African American and Other Underserved Populations," submitted to the Clinton Health Reform Task Force by the Congressional Black Caucus Foundation, Washington, D.C., June, 1993.

Byrd WM, Clayton LA, Perot R. Common Terms In the Health Care Reform Debate: A Bibliographed Glossary. Section VI. In: Byrd WM, Clayton LA. *A Guide for Health Care Reform* [unpublished document], Revised Edition. Prepared for the "Grassroots Education Initiative for Health Care Reform," sponsored by the Hoosier State Medical Society, National Medical Association and "Summit '93: Regional Summit on Health Care Reform," Westin Hotel, Indianapolis, Indiana, Saturday, June 18, 1994.

Detels R, Holland WW, McEwen J, Omenn GS, eds. *Oxford Textbook of Public Health*. Three Volumes. Third Edition. New York: Oxford University Press, 1997.

Institute of Medicine. *Controlling Cost and Changing Patient Care? The Role of Utilization Management*. Editors. Bradford H. Gray and Marilyn J. Field. National Academy Press, Washington D.C. 1989.

Johnson AG. *The Blackwell Dictionary of Sociology: A User's Guide to Sociological Language*. Cambridge, Massachusetts: Basil Blackwell Inc., 1995.

Kongstvedt PR. *The Managed Health Care Handbook*. Second Edition. Gaithersburg, Maryland: Aspen Publishers, Inc., 1993.

Kovner AR, Jonas S, eds. *Jonas and Kovner's Health Care Delivery in the United States*. Sixth Edition. New York: Springer Publishing Company, 1999.

Last JM, ed. *A Dictionary of Epidemiology*. Second Edition. New York: Oxford University Press, for the International Epidemiological Association, 1988.

Mullan F, Rivo M, Politzer RM. Doctors, dollars, and determination: Making physician work-force policy. *Health Affairs* (Millwood) 1993 (Suppl.); 12:138–151.

Neumann BR., Suver JD, Zelman WN. *Financial Management, Concepts and Applications for Health Care Providers*. National Health Publishing, Owings Mills, Maryland 1988.

Roberts MJ, Clyde AT. *Your Money or Your Life: The Health Care Crisis Explained*. New York: Main Street Books published by Doubleday, 1993.

U.S. Department of Health and Human Services. *Cultural Competence for Evaluators: A Guide for Alcohol and Other Drug Abuse Prevention Practitioners Working With Ethnic/Racial Communities*. Rockville, Maryland: Office for Substance Abuse and Prevention, Alcohol, Drug Abuse, and Mental Health Administration, DHHS Publication No. (ADM)92–1884, 1992.

Washington HA. Medicine's mainstream overlooks Blacks. *Emerge* 1996 (May, No. 7): 7:22.

Wilson FA, Neuhauser D. *Health Services in the United States*. Second Edition. Cambridge, Massachusetts: Ballinger Publishing Company, 1982.

# ✕ Notes

Note to the reader: Each reference is given in full the first time it appears in a chapter. Thereafter, a shortened form of the reference, including author(s) and abbreviated title, is given for all other citations within the same chapter.

## Preface

1. Blendon RJ, Donelan K. Public opinion and efforts to reform the U.S. health care system: Confronting issues of cost-containment and access to care. *Stanford Law and Policy Review* Fall 1991:146; Summer L, Shapiro I. *Trends in Health Insurance Coverage, 1987 to 1993.* Washington, DC: Center on Budget and Policy Priorities, 1994, pp. 4–6; American Public Health Association. Managed competition: Wonder drug or snake oil? *The Nation's Health* March 1993; 23:1; Blendon RJ, Edwards JN, eds. *System in Crisis: The Case for Health Care Reform* (Vol. 1, *The Future of American Health Care*). New York: Faulkner and Gray, 1991; Stanford University. Health care in America: Armageddon on the horizon? *Stanford Law and Policy Review* Fall 1991; 3:1–260; Lundberg GD. National health care reform: An aura of inevitability is upon us. *Journal of the American Medical Association* 1991; 265.2566–2567.

2. Blendon RJ, Edwards JN, eds. *System in Crisis*; American Public Health Association. Managed competition.

3. Blendon RJ, Edwards JN, eds. *System in Crisis.*

4. Stanford University. Health care in America.

5. Friedman E. The uninsured: From dilemma to crisis. *Journal of the American Medical Association* 1991; 265:2491–2495.

6. Blendon RJ, Edwards JN, eds. *System in Crisis*, American Public Health Association. Managed competition.

7. Starr P. Healthy compromise: Universal coverage and managed competition under a cap. *The American Prospect* Winter 1993; 12:44–52.

8. Johnson H, Broder DS. *The System: The American Way of Politics at the Breaking Point.* Boston: Little, Brown, 1996; Skocpol T. *Boomerang: Health Care Reform and the Turn against Government.* New York: W.W. Norton, 1997.

9. Knox RA. Study sees poor, elderly doing worse in HMO care. *Boston Globe* October 2, 1996:A1, A7; Pear R. Laws won't let H.M.O.s tell doctors what to say. *New York Times* September

17, 1996:A12; Anders G. Who pays the cost of cut-rate heart care? *Wall Street Journal* October 15, 1996:B1, B8; Johannes L. More HMOs order outpatient mastectomies. *Wall Street Journal* November 6, 1996:B1, B8; Kuttner R. Managed-care malpractice. *Boston Globe* November 25, 1996:A15; Broder DS. Candidates skirt the health care issue. *Boston Globe* October 21, 1996:A15. Seger A, et. al. *Boston Sunday Globe*, April 25, 1999: p. C1; Knox RA. HMO's creator urges reform in quality of care. *Boston Sunday Globe*, May 2, 1999: p. A1. Pear R. Insurers ask government to extend health plans. *New York Times*, May 23, 1999, p. A16.

10. Byrd WM, Clayton LA. America's dual health crisis in black and white. Report prepared for the hearings, "Health Care Reform: The African American Agenda," held for the Congressional Black Caucus's Health Brain Trust, 103rd Congress, Special Session, April 13, 1993, Washington, DC; Malone TE, Johnson KW. *Report of the Secretary's Task Force on Black and Minority Health.* Washington, DC: U.S. Department of Health and Human Services, 1986; Byrd WM, Clayton LA. An American health dilemma: A history of blacks in the health system. *Journal of the National Medical Association* 1992; 84:189–200; Feagin JR, Feagin CB. *Racial and Ethnic Relations*, 6th ed. Upper Saddle River, NJ. Prentice Hall, 1999; Byrd WM, Clayton LA. Race, medicine, and health care in the United States: A historical survey, *Journal of the National Medical Association.* In press 2000.

11. Blackwell, A. The impact of health care reform on the African American consumer. Address delivered at "Grassroots Initiative for Health Care Reform," sponsored by Region VI, National Medical Association and "Summit '93: Regional Summit on Health Care Reform," San Francisco, CA, April 30, 1994; Guinier L. *The Tyranny of the Majority: Fundamental Fairness in Representative Democracy.* New York: The Free Press, 1994; Hacker A. *Two Nations: Black and White, Separate, Hostile, Unequal.* New York: Ballantine Books, 1992; expanded and updated edition, 1995.

12. Malone TE, Johnson KW. *Report of the Secretary's Task Force on Black and Minority Health.*

13. Health Policy Advisory Center. The emerging health apartheid in the United States. *Health/PAC Bulletin* 1991; 21:3–4.

14. Byrd WM, Clayton LA. An American health dilemma.

15. Byrd WM, Clayton LA. America's dual health crisis in black and white.

16. Edwards WS. *National Medical Expenditure Survey: Questionnaires and Data Collection Methods for the United States Population.* Rockville, MD: U.S. Department of Health and Human Services, Agency for Health Care Policy and Research, 1989 (DHHS Pub. PHY 89-3440); Cornelius LJ. Limited access to health care continues in minority groups. *National Medical Association News* March/April 1993:1.

17. Byrd WM, Clayton LA. *A Black Health Trilogy* (videotape and 188-page documentary report). Washington, DC: The National Medical Association and the African American Heritage and Education Foundation, 1991.

18. Greenberg DS. Black health: Grim statistics. *The Lancet* 1990; 355:780–781; Thomas VG. Explaining health disparities between African-American and white populations: Where do we go from here? *Journal of the National Medical Association* 1992; 84:837–840.

19. Byrd WM, Clayton LA. An American health dilemma, Charatz-Litt C. A chronicle of racism: The effects of the white medical community on black health. *Journal of the National Medical Association* 1992; 84:717–725.

20. Charatz-Litt C. A chronicle of racism, Byrd WM, Clayton LA. America's dual health crisis in black and white.

21. Cray E. *In Failing Health: The Medical Crisis and the* A.M.A. Indianapolis: Bobbs-Merrill, 1970; Harmer RM. *American Medical Avarice.* New York: Abelard-Schuman, 1975; Tunley R. *The American Health Scandal.* New York: Harper & Row, 1966; Starr P. *The Social Transformation of American Medicine.* New York: Basic Books, 1982; Cobb WM. The black American in medicine. *Journal of the National Medical Association* 1981; 73 (Suppl 1):1183–1244.

22. Komaromy M, Grumbach K, Drake M. The role of black and Hispanic physicians in providing health care for underserved poulations. *New England Journal of Medicine* 1996; 334:1305–1314; Shea S, Fullilove MT. Entry of black and other minority students in US medical schools: Historical perspectives and recent trends. *New England Journal of Medicine* 1985; 313:933–940; Hanft RS, Fishman LE, Evans W. *Blacks and the Health Professions in the 80s: A*

*National Crisis and a Time for Action.* Prepared for the Association of Minority Health Professions Schools. N.P., 1983; Sullivan LW. The status of blacks in medicine. *New England Journal of Medicine* 1983; 309:807–809.

23. Duster T. *Backdoor to Eugenics.* New York: Routledge, 1990; Brandt AM. Racism and research: The case of the Tuskegee Syphilis Study. In: Leavitt JW, Numbers RL, eds. *Sickness and Health in America: Readings in the History of Medicine and Public Health.* Madison. University of Wisconsin Press, 1985, pp. 331–343; Reynolds V, Falger V, Vine I, eds. *The Sociobiology of Ethnocentrism: Evolutionary Dimensions of Xenophobia, Discrimination, Racism and Nationalism.* London: Croom Helm, 1987; Herrnstein RJ, Murray C. *The Bell Curve: Intelligence and Class Structure in American Life.* New York: The Free Press, 1994; Fish JM. Mixed blood. *Psychology Today* November/December 1995; 6(28):55; Byne W. Debate: Is homosexuality biologically influenced? The biological evidence challenged. *Scientific American* May 1994; (270):43, 50; LeVay S, Hamer DH. Debate: Is homosexuality biologically influenced? Evidence for a biological influence in male homosexuality. *Scientific American* May 1994; 5(270):43, 44; Chase A. *The Legacy of Malthus: The Social Costs of the New Scientific Racism.* New York: Knopf, 1980; Nelkin D, Tancredi L. *Dangerous Diagnostics: The Social Power of Biological Information.* New York: Basic Books, 1989; Lewontin RC, Rose S, Kamin LJ. *Not in Our Genes: Biology, Ideology, and Human Nature.* New York: Pantheon Books, 1984.

24. Cobb WM. The black American in medicine; Cobb WM. *The First Negro Medical Society: A History of the Medico-Chirurgical Society of the District of Columbia.* Washington, DC: The Associated Publishers, 1939; Charatz-Litt C. A chronicle of racism; Morais HM. *The History of the Negro in Medicine.* New York: Publishers Company, 1967; Byrd WM, Clayton LA. An American health dilemma, Byrd WM. Inquisition, peer review, and black physician survival. *Journal of the National Medical Association* 1987; 79:1027–1029; Wolinsky H. Healing wounds: Lonnie R. Bristow steps up to head the American Medical Association, one of the nation's premier

## Introduction

1. Schulman KA, Berlin JA, Harless W, Kerner JF, Sistrunk SS, Gersh BJ, et al. The effect of race and sex on physician recommendations for cardiac catheterization. *New England Journal of Medicine* 1999; 340:618–626.

2. Massey DS, Denton NA. *American Apartheid: Segregation and the Making of the Underclass.* Cambridge, MA: Harvard University Press, 1993, 15.

3. Haynes MA. The gap in health status between black and white Americans. 1–30. In: Williams RA, ed. *Textbook of Black-Related Diseases.* New York: McGraw-Hill, 1975, 30; Williams C. *The Destruction of Black Civilization: Great Issues of a Race from 4500 B.C. to 2000 A.D.* Chicago, IL: Third World Press, 1974, 54; Byrd WM. Race, biology, and health care: Reassessing a relationship. *Journal of Health Care for the Poor and Underserved* 1990; 1:278–292; Byrd WM, Clayton LA. An American health dilemma: A history of blacks in the health system. *Journal of the National Medical Association* 1992; 84:189–200; Smith DB. *Health Care Divided: Race and Healing a Nation.* Ann Arbor: University of Michigan Press, 1999; Malone TE, Johnson KW. *Report of the Secretary's Task Force on Black and Minority Health.* Washington, DC: U.S. Department of Health and Human Services, 1986; Kong D. Study: Minorities' health lags. *The Boston Globe* April 23, 1992: 1; Komaromy M, Grumbach K, Drake M. The role of Black and Hispanic physicians in providing health care for underserved populations. *New England Journal of Medicine* 1996; 334:1305–1314; Shea S, Fullilove MT. Entry of black and other minority students in US medical schools: Historical perspectives and recent trends. *New England Journal of Medicine* 1985; 313:933–940; Garrett L. *Betrayal of Trust: The Collapse of Global Public Health.* New York: Hyperion, 2000; Mayberry RM, Mili F, Ofli E. Racial and ethnic differences in access to medical care. *Medical Care Research and Review* 2000; 57(suppl 1):108–145; Clayton LA, Byrd WM. Race: A major health status and outcome variable, 1980–1999. *Journal of the National Medical Association* 2001; 93(suppl):35s–54s; Sheifer SE, Escarce JJ, Schulman KA. Race and sex differences in the management of coronary artery disease. *American Heart Journal* 2000; 139:848–857; Peterson ED, Shaw LK, DeLong ER, Pryor DB, Califf RM, Mark DB. Racial variation in the use of coronary-revascularization procedures: Are the differences real? Do they matter? *New England Journal of*

*Medicine* 1997; 336:480–486; Block SH. Managed care: Minorities and the poor. *Medicine and Health, Rhode Island* 1996; 79:266–268; Cooper-Patrick L, Gallo JJ, Gonzales JJ, Vu HT, Powe NR, Nelson C, et al. Race, gender, and partnership in the patient-physician relationship. *Journal of the American Medical Association* 1999; 282:583–589; Schulman KA et al. The effect of race and sex on physician recommendations for cardiac catheterization; Escarce JJ, Epstein KR, Colby DC, Schwartz JS. Racial differences in the elderly's use of medical procedures and diagnostic tests. *American Journal of Public Health* 1993; 83:948–954; Richardson L. White patients more likely to use AIDS drugs, study says. *New York Times* July 27, 1997: 24; Wenneker MB, Epstein AM. Racial inequalities in the use of procedures for patients with ischemic heart disease in Massachusetts. *Journal of the American Medical Association* 1990; 263:2344–2346; Blustein J, Weitzman BC. Access to hospitals with high-technology cardiac services: How is race important? *American Journal of Public Health* 1995; 85:345–351; Carlisle DM, Leake B, Shapiro MF. Racial and ethnic differences in the use of invasive cardiac procedures among cardiac patients in Los Angeles County, 1986 through 1988. *American Journal of Public Health* 1995; 85:352–356; Braveman P, Egerter S, Edmonston F, Verdon M. Racial/ethnic differences in the likelihood of caesarean delivery. *American Journal of Public Health* 1995; 85:625–630; Krieger N. Analyzing socioeconomic and racial/ethnic patterns in health and health care. *American Journal of Public Health* 1993; 83:1086–1087; Breast cancer deaths decrease—but not among Black women. *The Nation's Health* February, 1995: 24; Byrd WM, Clayton LA. *An American Health Dilemma*. Vol. 1. *A Medical History of African Americans and the Problem of Race: Beginnings to 1900*. New York: Routledge, 2000.

    4. Byrd WM, Clayton LA. *An American Health Dilemma*. Vol. 1.

    5. Banton M, Harwood J. *The Race Concept*. New York: Praeger, 1975, 13.

    6. van den Berghe PL. *Race and Racism: A Comparative Perspective*. New York: Wiley, 1967, 9.

    7. Smedley A. *Race in North America: Origin and Evolution of a Worldview*. 2nd ed. Boulder, CO: Westview Press, 1999, 2.

    8. van den Berghe PL. *Race and Racism*, 9.

    9. van den Berghe PL. *Race and Racism*, 11.

    10. van den Berghe PL. *Race and Racism*, 11.

    11. Levi-Strauss C. Race and History. In: *Race and History*. Paris: United Nations Educational, Scientific and Cultural Organization, 1951, 123–163; Comas J. *Racial Myths*. United Nations Education, Scientific and Cultural Organization. Paris: Unesco, 1958; Reilly K. Racism and color: Colonialism and slavery. In: *The West and the World: A Topical History of Civilization*. New York: Harper & Row, 1980, 355–383; van den Berghe PL. *Race and Racism*; Terry RW. *For Whites Only*. Grand Rapids, MI: William B. Eerdmans, 1970, paperback, rev. ed. 1992; Kovel J. *White Racism: A Psychohistory*. New York: Random House, 1970, reprint ed. 1984; Smedley A. *Race in North America*; Banton M, Harwood J. *The Race Concept*; Byrd WM, Clayton LA. *An American Health Dilemma*. Vol. 1; Barzun J. *From Dawn to Decadence: 500 Years of Western Cultural Life: 1500 to the Present*. New York: HarperCollins, 2000; Stringer C, McKie R. *African Exodus: The Origins of Modern Humanity*. New York: Henry Holt, 1997; Cavalli-Sforza LL, Menozzi P, Piazza A. *The History and Geography of Human Genes*. Princeton, NJ: Princeton University Press, 1994; Cavalli-Sforza LL. *Genes, Peoples, and Languages*. New York: Farrar, Straus and Giroux, 2000; Gossett TF. *Race: The History of an Idea in America*. Dallas, TX: Southern Methodist University Press, 1963. reprint ed. New York: Schocken Books, 1965; Stanton W. *The Leopard's Spots: Scientific Attitudes Toward Race in America, 1815–1859*. Chicago: The University of Chicago Press, 1960; Haller JS. Jr. *Outcasts from Evolution: Scientific Attitudes of Racial Inferiority, 1859–1900*. New York: McGraw-Hill, 1971; Tucker WH. *The Science and Politics of Racial Research*. Urbana, IL: University of Illinois Press, 1994; Reed J. Scientific racism. In: Wilson CR, Ferris W, eds. *Encyclopedia of Southern Culture*. Chapel Hill: The University of North Carolina Press, 1989, 1358–1360; Byrd WM. Race, biology, and health care; Chase A. *The Legacy of Malthus: The Social Costs of the New Scientific Racism*. New York: Knopf, 1980; Milner R. *The Encyclopedia of Evolution: Humanity's Search for its Origins*. New York: Facts on File, 1990; Shipman P. *The Evolution of Racism: Human Differences and the Use and Abuse of Science*. New York: Simon and Schuster, 1994; Banton M, Harwood J. *The Race Concept*; Banton M. *Racial Theories*. Cambridge: Cambridge University Press, 1987; Hubbard R, Wald E. *Exploding the Gene Myth: How Genetic Information Is Produced and Manipulated by Scientists, Physicians, Employers, Insurance Companies, Educators, and Law Enforcers*. Boston: Beacon Press, 1993.

12. Kovel J. *White Racism*, xi.

13. van den Berghe PL. *Race and Racism*; Terry RW. *For Whites Only*; Kovel J. *White Racism*; Reilly K. *The West and the World: A Topical History of Civilization*. New York: Harper & Row, 1980; Smith DB. *Health Care Divided*; Cose E. *Color-Blind: Seeing Beyond Race in a Race-Obsessed World*. New York: HarperCollins, 1997; Kozol J. *Savage Inequalities: Children in America's Schools*. New York: Crown, 1991; Feagin JR, Spikes MP. *Living with Racism: The Black Middle-Class Experience*. Boston: Beacon, 1994; Massey DS, Denton NA. *American Apartheid*; Meyer SG. *As Long as They Don't Move Next Door: Segregation and Racial Conflict in American Neighborhoods*. Lanham, MD: Rowman and Littlefield, 2000; Lemann N. *The Big Test: The Secret History of the American Meritocracy*. New York: Farrar, Straus and Giroux, 1999; Hacker A. *Two Nations: Black and White, Separate, Hostile, Unequal*. New York: Ballantine Books, 1992, 1995; Kaiske BL, Neylan JF, Riggko RR, Danovitch GM, Kahana L, et al. The effect of race on access and outcome in transplantation. *New England Journal of Medicine* 1991; 324:302–307; Norris GMK. Disparities for minorities in transplantation: The challenge to critical care nurses. *Heart and Lung* 1991; 20:419–420; Carlisle DM, Leake B, Shapiro MF. Racial and ethnic differences in the use of invasive cardiac procedures among cardiac patients in Los Angeles County, 1986 through 1988; Wenneker MB, Epstein AM. Racial inequalities in the use of procedures for patients with ischemic heart disease in Massachusetts; Glasgow DG. *The Black Underclass: Poverty, Unemployment, and Entrapment of Ghetto Youth*. London: Jossey-Bass Limited, 1980. paperback ed. New York: Vintage Books, 1981.

14. Montagu A. *Race, Science and Humanity*. New York: Van Nostrand Reinhold Company, 1963; Byrd WM, Clayton LA. *An American Health Dilemma*. Vol. 1; Lewis B. *Race and Slavery in the Middle East: An Historical Enquiry*. New York: Oxford University Press, 1990; Drake SC. *Black Folk Here and There: An Essay in History and Anthropology*. Vol. 2. Los Angeles: Center for Afro-American Studies, University of California, 1990.

15. Stanton W. *The Leopard's Spots*; Haller JS Jr. *Outcasts from Evolution*; Lewis B. *Race and Slavery in the Middle East*; Byrd WM, Clayton LA. *An American Health Dilemma*. Vol. 1; Byrd WM, Clayton LA. Race, medicine, and health care in the United States: A historical survey. *Journal of the National Medical Association* 2001; 93(suppl):11s–34s; Davis DB. *Slavery and Human Progress*. New York: Oxford University Press, 1984; Smedley A. *Race in North America*; Devisse J. *The Image of the Black in Western Art*. Part II. *From the Early Christian Era to the "Age of Discovery."* 1. *From the Demonic Threat to the Incarnation of Sainthood*. Cambridge, MA: The Minil Foundation, distributed by the Harvard University Press, 1979; Barzun J. *From Dawn to Decadence*; Drake S. *Black Folk Here and There*, Vol. 2, 45; Byrd WM. Race, biology, and health care. *Journal of Health Care for the Poor and Underserved* 1990; 1:278–292; Byrd WM, Clayton LA. An American health dilemma.

16. De Tocqueville A. *Democracy in America*. Vol. 2. Ed. JP Mayer. Trans. G Lawrence. New York: Harper & Row, 1966. paperback ed. New York: Harper Perennial, 1988, 530.

17. Higginbotham AL, Jr. *In the Matter of Color: Race and the American Legal Process, The Colonial Period*. New York: Oxford University Press, 1978, 54, 121, 198, 211, 243; Byrd WM, Clayton LA. The "slave health deficit": Racism and health outcomes. *Health/PAC Bulletin* 1991; 21:25–28; Byrd WM, Clayton LA. Race, medicine, and health care in the United States; Fredrickson GM. *The Black Image in the White Mind: The Debate on Afro-American Character and Destiny, 1871–1914*. New York: Harper & Row, 1971. Reprint ed. Middletown, CT: Wesleyan University Press, 1987; Gossett TF. *Race*; Thomas H. *The Slave Trade: The Story of the Atlantic Slave Trade: 1440–1870*. New York: Simon & Schuster, 1997; Byrd WM, Clayton LA. *An American Health Dilemma*. Vol. 1.

18. Davis DB. *The Problem of Slavery in Western Culture*. Ithaca: Cornell University Press, 1966, 49, 66–72, 85, 203; Davis DB. *Slavery and Human Progress*, 3, 14, 23, 25–27; Wasserman HP. *Ethnic Pigmentation: Historical, Psychological, and Clinical Aspects*. New York: American Elsevier, 1974, 17–19; Comas J. *Racial Myths*.

19. Milner R. *The Encyclopedia of Evolution*, 201.

20. Wasserman HP. *Ethnic Pigmentation*, 17–19; Bernal M. *Black Athena: The Afroasiatic Roots of Classical Civilization*. Vol. 1. *The Fabrication of Ancient Greece 1785–1985*. New Brunswick, NJ: Rutgers University Press, 1987, 28, 202, 212; Harris JE. *Africans and Their History*. Rev. ed. New York: New American Library, 1972, 13–16; Devisse J. *The Image of the Black in Western Art*. Part II, 1979, 60, 223 n224; Byrd WM, Clayton LA. *An American Health Dilemma*. Vol. 1.

21. Drake SC. *Black Folk Here and There: An Essay in History and Anthropology*. Two Volumes.

Los Angeles: Center for Afro-American Studies, University of California, 1987, 1990; Goldberg DT. The social formation of racist discourse. In: Goldberg DT, ed. *Anatomy of Racism*. Minneapolis: University of Minnesota Press, 1990, 295–318; Milner R. *The Encyclopedia of Evolution*, 201; Jordan WD. *White Over Black: American Attitudes Toward the Negro, 1550–1812*. New York: W.W. Norton, 1968; Harris JE. *Africans and Their History*, 13–28; Outlaw L. Toward a critical theory of race. In: Goldberg DT, ed. *Anatomy of Racism*. Minneapolis: University of Minnesota Press, 1990, 58–82; Wasserman HP. *Ethnic Pigmentation*, 17–19; Comas J. *Racial Myths*; Byrd WM, Clayton LA. *An American Health Dilemma*. Vol. 1.

22. Finley MI. *Ancient Slavery and Modern Ideology*. New York: Viking Penguin, 1980, 105–106.

23. Lyons AS, Petrucelli RJ. *Medicine: An Illustrated History*, 229; Guthrie D. *A History of Medicine*. Philadelphia: J.B. Lippincott, 1946, 63–64; Majno G. *The Healing Hand: Man and Wound in the Ancient World*. Cambridge, MA: Harvard University Press, 1975, 327–328; Sigerist HE. *The Great Doctors: A Biographical History of Medicine*. New York: W. W. Norton, 1933. Reprint ed. New York: Dover, 1971, 42–50; Finley MI. *Ancient Slavery and Modern Ideology*, 118–119; Gould SJ. Bound by the great chain. In: Gould SJ. *The Flamingo's Smile: Reflections in Natural History*. New York: W. W. Norton, 1985, 281–291; Lovejoy AO. *The Great Chain of Being: A Study of the History of an Idea*. Cambridge, MA: Harvard University Press, 1936. paperback ed. 1964; Patterson O. *Slavery and Social Death: A Comparative Study*. Cambridge, MA: Harvard University Press, 1982, 86–94; Davis DB. *Slavery and Human Progress*, 42; Sanders R. *Lost Tribes and Promised Lands: The Origins of American Racism*. Boston: Little, Brown, 1978; Byrd WM, Clayton LA. *An American Health Dilemma*. Vol. 1.

24. Davis DB. *Slavery and Human Progress*, 42; Devisse J. *The Image of the Black in Western Art*. Part II, 1979, 37–80, 46; Drake SC. *Black Folk Here and There*. Vol. 2, 45; Bynum WF, Browne EJ, Porter R, eds. *The Dictionary of the History of Science*. New York: Macmillan Press, 1981, paperback ed. Princeton, NJ: Princeton University Press, 1985; Byrd WM, Clayton LA. *An American Health Dilemma*. Vol. 1.

25. Devisse J. *The Image of the Black in Western Art*. Part II, 50–57, 52; Lewis B. The African diaspora and the civilization of Islam. 37–56. In: Kilson ML, Rothberg RI, eds. *The African Diaspora: Interpretive Essays*. Cambridge, MA: Harvard University Press, 1976, 49.

26. Davis DB. *Slavery and Human Progress*, 42; Davis DB. *The Problem of Slavery in Western Culture*, 50; Gordon M. *Slavery in the Arab World*. New York: New Amsterdam Books, 1989, 99; Devisse J. *The Image of the Black in Western Art*. Part II, 46, 50–52; Drake SC. *Black Folk Here and There*, Vol. 2, 45.

27. Davis DB. *Slavery and Human Progress*, 30; Sanders R. *Lost Tribes and Promised Lands*, 48–52, 55–58; Davis DB. *The Problem of Slavery in Western Culture*, 50; Lewis B. *Race and Slavery in the Middle East*, 53–61; Gordon M. *Slavery in the Arab World*, 98.

28. Sirasi NG. *Medieval and Early Renaissance Medicine: An Introduction to Knowledge and Practice*. Chicago: University of Chicago Press, 1990; Lyons AS, Petrucelli RJ. *Medicine*; Bender GA. *Great Moments in Medicine*. Detroit: Northwood Institute Press, 1966; Majno G. *The Healing Hand*; Sigerist HE. *The Great Doctors*; Zanca A, ed. *Pharmacy Through the Ages: From the Beginnings to Modern Times*. Parma, Italy: Farmitalia Carlo Erba, 1987.

29. Nuland SB. *Doctors: The Biography of Medicine*. New York: Knopf, 1988; Meadows J. *The Great Scientists*. New York: Oxford University Press, 1987; Lyons AS, Petrucelli RJ. *Medicine*; Luce HR. *Life's Picture History of Western Man*. New York: Time, 1951; Boorstin DJ. *The Discoverers*. New York: Random House, 1983. illustrated ed. New York: Harry N. Abrams, 1991.

30. Stannard DE. *American Holocaust: Columbus and the Conquest of the New World*. New York: Oxford University Press, 1992, 209; Lyons AS, Petrucelli RJ. *Medicine*; Nuland SB. *Doctors*.

31. Jordan WD. *White Over Black*; Drake SC. *Black Folk Here and There*. Vol. 2; Sanders R. *Lost Tribes and Promised Lands*; Byrd WM. Race, biology, and health care; Byrd WM, Clayton LA. The "slave health deficit"; Byrd WM, Clayton LA. *An American Health Dilemma*. Vol. 1.

32. Luce HR. *Life's Picture History of Western Man*; Roberts J. *The Triumph of the West*. Boston: Little, Brown, 1985; Byrd WM, Clayton LA. *A Black Health Trilogy* (video and 188-page report). Washington, DC: The National Medical Association and the African American Heritage and Education Foundation, 1991; Pieterse JN. *White on Black: Images of Africa and Blacks in Western Pop-*

*ular Culture.* New Haven, CT: Yale University Press, 1992, 30–63; Byrd WM, Clayton LA. *An American Health Dilemma.* Vol. 1.

33. Shryock RH. *The Development of Modern Medicine: An Interpretation of the Social and Scientific Factors Involved.* Madison: The University of Wisconsin Press, 1974, 3–16; Guthrie D. *A History of Medicine,* 134–175; Ackerknecht EH. *A Short History of Medicine.* Rev. ed. Baltimore: The Johns Hopkins University Press, 1982, 94–127; Boorstin DJ. The equality of the human species. In: Boorstin DJ. *Hidden History: Exploring our Secret Past.* New York: Harper & Row, 1987. paperback ed. New York: Vintage Books, 1989, 111–123; Davis DB. *The Problem of Slavery in Western Culture,* 454; Wassermann HP. *Ethnic Pigmentation,* 27, 35, 39; Jordan WD. *White Over Black,* 246; Byrd WM. Race, biology, and health care; Gossett TF. *Race;* Byrd WM, Clayton LA. *An American Health Dilemma.* Vol. 1.

34. Jordan WD. *White Over Black,* 158n, 222–223, 227, 230, 236, 246, 505; Drake SC. *Black Folk Here and There,* Vol. 1, 26, 27; Honour H. *The Image of the Black in Western Art.* Part IV. *From the American Revolution to World War I.* 2. *Black Models and White Myths.* Cambridge: Menil Foundation, Inc., Distributed by the Harvard University Press, 1989, 14–20; Davis DB. *The Problem of Slavery in Western Culture,* 454, 455; Shryock RH. *The Development of Modern Medicine,* 3–16; Guthrie D. *A History of Medicine,* 134–175; Ackerknecht EH. *A Short History of Medicine,* 94–127; Pieterse JN. *White on Black,* 30–51; Boorstin DJ. The equality of the human species; Davis DB. *The Problem of Slavery in Western Culture,* 454; Wassermann HP. *Ethnic Pigmentation,* 27, 35, 39; Byrd WM. Race, biology, and health care; Gossett TF. *Race,* 35–37, 69–70; Byrd WM, Clayton LA. *An American Health Dilemma.* Vol. 1.

35. Byrd WM, Clayton LA. *An American Health Dilemma.* Vol. 1; Jordan WD. *White Over Black,* 216–263, 230, 236, 483–511, Smith SS; Jordan WD, ed. *An Essay on the Causes of the Variety of Complexion and Figure in the Human Species.* 1810. Reprint ed., Cambridge, MA: Belknap, 1965; Boorstin DJ. The equality of the human species; Pieterse JN. *White on Black;* Jordan WD. *White Over Black;* Drake SC. *Black Folk Here and There,* Vol. 1; Byrd WM, Clayton LA. Meharry Medical Archive-NMA Slide Collection. Nashville and Boston: Meharry Medical Library, Countway Medical Library of Harvard Medical School, 1991–1999; Haller JS Jr. *Outcasts from Evolution,* 1–14; Magnusson M, ed. *Cambridge Biographical Dictionary.* Cambridge: Cambridge University Press, 1990, 225–226, 900; Marshall PJ, Williams G. *The Great Map of Mankind: Perceptions of New Worlds in the Age of Enlightenment.* Cambridge, MA: Harvard University Press, 1982, 245; Davis DB. *The Problem of Slavery in Western Culture,* 454–455; Mannix DP, Cowley M. *Cargoes: The Atlantic Slave Trade, 1518–1865.* New York: Viking Press, 1962; Pope-Hennessy J. *Sins of the Fathers: A Study of the Atlantic Slave Traders, 1441–1807.* New York: Knopf, 1967. Reprint ed. New York: Capricorn Books, 1969; Gratus J. *The Great White Lie: Slavery, Emancipation, and Changing Racial Attitudes.* New York: Monthly Review Press, 1973; Honour H. *The Image of the Black in Western Art.* Part IV, 13–14; Cohen IB. *Album of Science: From Leonardo to Lavoisier, 1450–1800.* New York: Charles Scribner's Sons, 1980, 228; Gould SJ. *The Mismeasure of Man.* New York: W. W. Norton, 1981, 35; Stanton W. *The Leopard's Spots;* Muir H, ed. *Larousse Dictionary of Scientists.* New York: Larousse, 1994, 83, 321; Nuland SB. *Doctors.*

36. Morais HM. *The History of the Negro in Medicine.* New York: Publishers Company, 1967; Savitt TL. *Medicine and Slavery: The Diseases and Health Care of Blacks in Antebellum Virginia.* Urbana: University of Illinois Press, 1987; Postell WD. *The Health of Slaves on Southern Plantations.* Baton Rouge: Louisiana State University Press. Reprint ed. Gloucester, MA: Peter Smith, 1970; 1951; Horsman R. *Josiah Nott of Mobile: Southerner, Physician, and Racial Theorist.* Baton Rouge: Louisiana State University Press, 1987; Armstrong M. *Fanny Kemble: A Passionate Victorian.* New York: Macmillan, 1938, 220–222; Byrd WM, Clayton LA. *An American Health Dilemma.* Vol. 1; Sheridan RB. *Doctors and Slaves: A Medical and Demographic History of Slavery in the British West Indies, 1680–1834.* Cambridge: Cambridge University Press, 1985.

37. Byrd WM, Clayton LA. The "slave health deficit"; Curry LP. *The Free Black in Urban America, 1800–1850: The Shadow of the Dream.* Chicago: The University of Chicago Press, 1981; Savitt TL. *Medicine and Slavery;* Byrd WM, Clayton LA. An American health dilemma; Wade RC. *Slavery in the Cities: The South 1820–1860.* London: Oxford University Press, 1964; Byrd WM, McHollin M. "Tennessee Black Medical Heritage Tour." A report prepared for the Tennessee Humanities Council for the 1990 Black Medical Heritage Tour, Meharry Medical College Black Medical History Archive, Meharry Medical College, Nashville, Tennessee, Spring, 1991; Byrd WM, Clayton LA. *An American Health Dilemma.* Vol. 1.

38. Drake SC. *Black Folk Here and There*. Vol. 1, 27; Jordan WD. *White Over Black*, 229–234; Pieterse JN. *White on Black*, 40–41; Haller JS Jr. *Outcasts from Evolution*, 6, 10; Honour H. *The Image of the Black in Western Art*. Part IV. *From the American Revolution to World War I*. 2. *Black Models and White Myths*. Cambridge, MA: Menil Foundation, Inc., Distributed by the Harvard University Press, 1989, 13–16, 18–19; Gould SJ. *The Mismeasure of Man*, 33–34, 36–37.

39. Horsman R. *Josiah Nott of Mobile*; Reed J. Scientific racism; Pieterse JN. *White on Black*; Stanton W. *The Leopard's Spots*; Byrd WM, Clayton LA. *An American Health Dilemma*. Vol. 1; Gould SJ. *The Mismeasure of Man*; Burke J. Fit to rule. In: *The Day the Universe Changed*. Boston: Little, Brown, 1985, 239–273; Roberts J. *The Triumph of the West*.

40. Duffy J. States' rights medicine. In: Wilson CR, W Ferris, eds. *Encyclopedia of Southern Culture*. Chapel Hill: The University of North Carolina Press, 1989, 1355–1356; Jones JH. *Bad Blood: The Tuskegee Syphilis Experiment*. New York: The Free Press, 1981; Reed J. Scientific racism; Beardsley EH. *A History of Neglect: Health Care for Blacks and Mill Workers in the Twentieth-Century South*. Knoxville: The University of Tennessee Press, 1987; Byrd WM, Clayton LA. The "slave health deficit"; Byrd WM, Clayton LA. *A Black Health Trilogy*; Byrd WM, Clayton LA. An American health dilemma; Byrd WM, Clayton LA. *An American Health Dilemma*. Vol. 1.

41. Savitt TL. *Medicine and Slavery*; Sheridan RB. *Doctors and Slaves*; Mannix DP, Cowley M. *Cargoes*, 45, 88–89, 116–119, 120, 121, 122; Pope-Hennessy J. *Sins of the Fathers*, 101–102, 106; Gratus J. *The Great White Lie*, 47–48, 50–51, 56, 71, 87, 105, 119, 129, 270–271; Numbers RL, ed. *Medicine in the New World: New Spain, New France, and New England*. Knoxville: The University of Tennessee Press, 1987; Byrd WM, Clayton LA. *A Black Health Trilogy*; Byrd WM, Clayton LA. The "slave health deficit"; Horsman R. *Josiah Nott of Mobile*; Postell WD. *The Health of Slaves on Southern Plantations*; Byrd WM, Clayton LA. *An American Health Dilemma*. Vol. 1.

42. Morais HM. *The History of the Negro in Medicine*, 154; Jackson H. Race and the politics of medicine in nineteenth-century Georgia. In: Blakely RL, Harrington JM, eds. *Bones in the Basement: Postmortem Racism in Nineteenth-Century Medical Training*. Washington, DC: Smithsonian Institution Press, 1997, 184–205; Duffy J. States' rights medicine; Jones JH. *Bad Blood*, 17, 24; Jordan WD. *White Over Black*, 519–521, 530; Savitt TL. *Medicine and Slavery*, 42; Shryock RH. *Medicine in America: Historical Essays*. Baltimore: The Johns Hopkins Press, 1966, 96–97; Savitt TL, Young JH, eds. *Disease and Distinctiveness in the American South*. Knoxville: The University of Tennessee Press, 1988, 128–129, 132; Horsman R. *Josiah Nott of Mobile*, 217; Byrd WM. *Documentary Report: Negro Diseases and Physiological Peculiarities*. Nashville: Cancer Control Research Unit, Meharry Medical College, July 12, 1990. In: Byrd WM, Clayton LA. *A Black Health Trilogy*; Byrd WM, Clayton LA. *An American Health Dilemma*. Vol. 1.

43. Byrd WM, Clayton LA. The "slave health deficit"; Shryrock RH. Medical practice in the Old South. 49–70. In: Shryrock RH. *Medicine in America*; Savitt T. Black health on the plantation: Masters, slaves, and physicians. In: Leavitt JW, Numbers RL, eds. *Sickness and Health in America: Readings in the History of Medicine and Public Health*. Madison: The University of Wisconsin Press, 1985, 313–330; Owens LH. *This Species of Property: Slave Life and Culture in the Old South*. Oxford: Oxford University Press, 1976, 19–49; Savitt TL. Black health on the plantation: Masters, slaves, and physicians. In: Numbers RL, Savitt TL, eds. *Science and Medicine in the Old South*. Baton Rouge: Louisiana State University Press, 1989, 327–355; Byrd WM. Race, biology, and health care; Byrd WM, Clayton LA. *A Black Health Trilogy*; Byrd WM, Clayton LA. An American health dilemma; Byrd WM, Clayton LA. *An American Health Dilemma*. Vol. 1.

44. Morais HM. *The History of the Negro in Medicine*; Savitt TL. *Medicine and Slavery*; Ewbank DC. History of Black mortality and health before 1940. In: Willis DP, ed. *Health Policies and Black Americans*. New Brunswick, NJ: Transaction Publishers, 1989, 100–128; Kiple KF, King VH. *Another Dimension to the Black Diaspora: Diet, Disease, and Racism*. Cambridge, England: Cambridge University Press, 1981; Jackson H. Race and the politics of medicine in nineteenth-century Georgia, 188–195; Farley R. *Growth of the Black Population: A Study of Demographic Trends*. Chicago: Markham, 1970, 1–40; Farley R, Allen WR. *The Color Line and the Quality of Life in America*. New York: Oxford University Press, 1989, 1–31; Byrd WM, Clayton LA. The "slave health deficit"; Postell WD. *The Health of Slaves on Southern Plantations*; Duffy J. States' rights medicine; Byrd WM, Clayton LA. *An American Health Dilemma*. Vol. 1.

45. Savitt TL. The use of blacks for medical experimentation and demonstration in the old south. *Journal of Southern History* 1982; 48:331–348; Jackson H. Race and the politics of medicine

in nineteenth-century Georgia, 194; Savitt TL. *Medicine and Slavery*; Byrd WM, Clayton LA. *An American Health Dilemma*. Vol. 1.

46. Morais HM. *The History of the Negro in Medicine*; Savitt TL. The use of blacks for medical experimentation and demonstration in the old south; Curry LP. *The Free Black in Urban America, 1800–1850*; Savitt TL. *Medicine and Slavery*; Kiple KF, King VH. *Another Dimension to the Black Diaspora*; Postell WD. *The Health of Slaves on Southern Plantations*; Ewbank DC. History of Black mortality and health before 1940; Byrd WM, Clayton LA. *An American Health Dilemma*. Vol. 1.

47. Cobb WM. Alexander Thomas Augusta. *Journal of the National Medical Association* 1952; 44:327–329; Shryock RH. A medical perspective on the civil war. In: Shryock RH. *Medicine in America*, 90–108; Cobb WM. Martin Robison Delany. *Journal of the National Medical Association* 1952; 44:232–238; Barbeau AE, Henri F. *The Unknown Soldiers: Black American Troops in World War I*. Philadelphia: Temple University Press, 1974; Low WA, Clift VA. eds. *Encyclopedia of Black America*. New York: McGraw-Hill. Reprint ed. New York: Da Capo Press, 1981; Morais HM. *The History of the Negro in Medicine*; Ward GC, Burns R, Burns K. *The Civil War*. New York: Knopf, 1990, 253; Ullman V. *Martin R. Delany: The Beginnings of Black Nationalism*. Boston: Beacon, 1971, 283–284; Cornish DT. *The Sable Arm: Negro Troops in the Union Army, 1861–1865*. New York. W. W. Norton, 1966; Mohr CL. *On the Threshold of Freedom: Masters and Slaves in Civil War Georgia*. Athens: The University of Georgia Press, 1986; Bremner RH. *The Public Good: Philanthropy and Welfare in the Civil War Era*. New York: Knopf, 1980.

48. Rosenberg CE. *The Care of Strangers: The Rise of America's Hospital System*. New York: Basic Books, 1987, 40, 178, 301–303; Stevens RA. Times past, times present. In: Long DE, Golden J, eds. *The American General Hospital: Communities and Social Contexts*. Ithaca: Cornell University Press, 1989, 191–206; Dowling HF. *City Hospitals: The Undercare of the Underprivileged*. Cambridge, MA: Harvard University Press, 1982, 12; Jackson H. Race and the politics of medicine in nineteenth-century Georgia, 193–194; Curry LP. *The Free Black in Urban America, 1800–1850*, 136–146; Rosenberg CE. Community and communities: The evolution of the American hospital. In: Long DE, Golden J, eds. *The American General Hospital: Communities and Social Contexts*. Ithaca: Cornell University Press, 1989, 3–17; Savitt TL. The use of blacks for medical experimentation and demonstration in the old south.

49. Curry LP. *The Free Black in Urban America, 1800–1850*; Rosenberg CE. *The Care of Strangers*; Dowling HF. *City Hospitals*; Stevens RA. Times past, times present; Rosenberg CE. Community and communities.

50. Rosenberg CE. *The Care of Strangers*; Vogel MJ. *The Invention of the Modern Hospital: Boston 1870–1930*. Chicago: The University of Chicago Press, 1980; Rosen G, Rosenberg CE, eds. *The Structure of American Medical Practice 1875–1941*. Philadelphia: University of Pennsylvania Press, 1983; Stevens RA. Times past, times present; Rosenberg CE. Community and communities; Novotny A, Smith C. eds. *Images of Healing: A Portfolio of American Medical and Pharmaceutical Practice in the 18th, 19th, and early 20th Centuries*. New York: Macmillan, 1980; Blakely RL, Harrington JM, eds. *Bones in the Basement: Postmortem Racism in Nineteenth-Century Medical Training*. Washington, DC: Smithsonian Institution Press, 1997.

51. Morais HM. *The History of the Negro in Medicine*; Stevens RA. Times past, times present; Gamble VN. Hospitals, Black. In: Salzman J, Smith DL, West C. eds. *Encyclopedia of African-American Culture and History* (5 vols.). New York: Macmillan Library Reference USA, 1996, 1305–1309; Byrd WM, Clayton LA. An American health dilemma; Curry LP. *The Free Black in Urban America, 1800–1850*, 136–146; Rosen G, Rosenberg CE, eds. *The Structure of American Medical Practice 1875–1941*; Rosenberg CE. *The Care of Strangers*; Rosenberg CE. Community and communities; Cobb WM. The Black American in medicine. *Journal of the National Medical Association* 1981; 73(suppl 1):1185–1244; Blakely RL, Harrington JM, eds. *Bones in the Basement*; Savitt TL. The use of blacks for medical experimentation and demonstration in the old south; Byrd WM, Clayton LA. *An American Health Dilemma*. Vol. 1.

52. Starr P. *The Social Transformation of American Medicine*. New York: Basic Books, 1982; Rosen G, Rosenberg CE, eds. *The Structure of American Medical Practice 1875–1941*, 67–68; Byrd WM, Clayton LA. An American health dilemma; Byrd WM. Medical associations. In: Salzman J, Smith DL, West C. eds. *Encyclopedia of African-American Culture and History* (5 vols.). New York: Macmillan Library Reference USA, 1996, 1747–1749; Byrd WM, Clayton LA. *An American Health Dilemma*. Vol. 1; Curtis JL. *Blacks, Medical Schools, and Society*. Ann Arbor: The Univer-

sity of Michigan Press, 1971; Takaki RY. *Iron Cages: Race and Culture in Nineteenth-Century America*. New York: Knopf, 1979; Contee CG. John Sweat Rock, M.D., Esq., 1825–1866. *Journal of the National Medical Association* 1976; 68:237–242.

53. Hutchins RM, ed. *Great Books of the Western World*. Vol. 49. *Darwin. The Origin of Species by Means of Natural Selection*. By Charles Darwin. Chicago: University of Chicago Press, 1952, 1–252; Hutchins RM, ed. *Great Books of the Western World*. Vol. 49. *Darwin. The Descent of Man and Selection in Relation to Sex*. By Charles Darwin. Chicago: University of Chicago Press, 1952, 253–600; Gobineau JA. *The Inequality of Human Races*. Trans. Collins A. London: Heinemann, 1915; Barzun J. *Race: A Study in Modern Superstition*. N.P., 1937. *Race: A Study in Superstition*. Rev. ed. New York: Harper & Row, 1965; Malik K. *The Meaning of Race: Race, History and Culture in Western Society*. New York: New York University Press, 1996; Gossett TF. *Race*; Jones JH. *Bad Blood*; Burke J. Fit to rule; Reed J. Scientific racism; Stanton W. *The Leopard's Spots*; Fredrickson GM. *The Black Image in the White Mind*; Haller JS Jr. *Outcasts from Evolution*; Tucker WH. *The Science and Politics of Racial Research*; Hoffmann FL. *Race Traits and Tendencies of the American Negro*. New York: Publication of the American Economic Association, 1st Series, XI, August 1896; Byrd WM, Clayton LA. *An American Health Dilemma*. Vol. 1.

54. Gould BA. *Investigations in the Military and Anthropological Statistics of American Soldiers*. New York, 1869; Baxter JH. *Statistics, Medical and Anthropological, of the Provost Marshal-General's Bureau, Derived from Records of the Examination for Military Service in the Armies of the United States during the Late War of the Rebellion, of over a Million Recruits, Drafted Men, Substitutes, and Enrolled Men* (2 vols.). Washington, DC: N.P., 1875; Van Everie JH. *White Supremacy and Negro Subordination*. New York, 1868; Hoffman FL. *Race Traits and Tendencies of the American Negro*; Johnson JT. On some of the apparent peculiarities of parturition in the Negro race, with remarks on race pelvis in general. *American Journal of Obstetrics* 1875–1876; 8:88–123; Parker AJ. Simian characteristics in Negro brains. Philadelphia Academy of Natural Sciences. *Proceedings* 1879; 31:339; Parturition of the Negro. *Philadelphia Medical Times* 1885; 16:296; McIntosh J. The future of the Negro race. *Transactions of the South Carolina Medical Association* 1891; 41:186; Tipton F. The Negro problem from a medical point of view. *New York Medical Journal* 1886; 43:570; Byers JW. Diseases of the Southern Negro. *Medical and Surgical Reporter* 1888; 43:735; Sholl EH. The Negro and his death rate. *Alabama Medical and Surgical Age* 1891; 3:340; McGuire H, Lydston GF. Sexual crimes among the Southern Negroes—scientifically considered—an open correspondence between. *Virginia Medical Monthly* 1893; 20:105; Lydston GF. Letter to Dr. McGuire: Sexual crimes among the Southern Negroes scientifically considered. *Virginia Medical Monthly* 1893; 20:118; Dixon WA. The morbid proclivities and retrogressive tendencies in the offspring of mulattoes. American Medical Association, *Journal* 1893; 20:1–2; Miller JF. The effects of emancipation upon the mental and physical health of the Negro in the South. *North Carolina Medical Journal* 1896; 38:285–294; Walton JT. The comparative mortality of the White and Colored races in the South. *Charlotte Medical Journal* 1897; 10:291–294; Bacon CS. The race problem. *Medicine* 1903; 9:338–342; Herrick SS. Comparative vital movement of the White and Colored races in the United States. *New Orleans Medical and Surgical Journal* 1881–1883; 9:678; Kilpatrick AR. An account of the Colored population in Grimes County, Texas. A comparison between their present and former condition. *Richmond and Louisville Medical Journal* 1872; 14:610; Joynes LS. Remarks on the comparative mortality of the White and Colored population of Richmond. *Virginia Medical Monthly* 1875; 5:155. Hodges JA. The effect of freedom upon the physical and psychological development of the Negro. *Richmond Journal of Practice* (June) 1900; 14:170–171; Harris S. The future of the Negro from the standpoint of the southern physician. *Alabama Medical Journal* January 1902; 14:58; Howard WL. The Negro as a distinct ethnic factor in civilization. *Medicine* 1903; 9:424; English WT. The Negro problem from the physician's point of view. *Atlanta Journal-Record of Medicine* October 1903; 5:462–463; Hecht D. Tabes in the Negro. *American Journal of Medical Sciences* 1903; 126:708; McHatton H. The sexual status of the Negro—past and present. *American Journal of Dermatology and Genito-Urinary Diseases* 1906; 10:6–8; Murrell TW. Syphilis in the Negro: Its bearing in the race problem. *American Journal of Dermatology and Genito-Urinary Diseases* 1906; 10;305–306; Murrell TW. Syphilis and the American Negro: A medico-sociologic study. *Journal of the American Medical Association* 1910; 54:846–847; Castration instead of lynching. *Atlanta Journal-Record of Medicine* (October) 1906; 8:457; Fox H. Observations on skin diseases in the Negro. *Journal of Cutaneous Diseases* 1908; 26:109; Hazen HH. Syphilis in the American Negro. *Journal of the American Medical Association* 1914; 63:463; Keller RL. Syphilis

and tuberculosis in the Negro race. *Texas State Journal of Medicine* 1924; 19:498; Jones F. Syphilis in the Negro. *American Journal of Dermatology and Genito-Urinary Diseases* 1906; 10:277–279; Corson ER. Syphilis in the Negro. *American Journal of Dermatology and Genito-Urinary Diseases* 1906; 10:241, 247; Quillian DD. Racial peculiarities as a cause of the prevalence of syphilis in Negroes. *American Journal of Dermatology and Genito-Urinary Diseases* 1906; 10:277–279; Green EM. Psychoses among Negroes—a comparative approach. *Journal of Nervous and Mental Diseases* 1914; 41:703–708; Lynch KM, McInnes BK, McInnes GF. Concerning syphilis in the American Negro. *Southern Medical Journal* 1915; 8:452; Graves ML. Practical remedial measures for the improvement of hygiene conditions of the Negro in the South. *American Journal of Public Health* 1915; 5:212; Zimmerman EL. A comparative study of syphilis in Whites and Negroes. *Archives of Dermatology and Syphilology* 1921; 4:73–74; Belding DL, Hunter IL. The Wassermann test: VI. The influence of race and nationality upon routine Wassermann tests in a maternity hospital. *American Journal of Syphilis* 1925; 126:130; Nicholas F. Some health problems of the Negro. *Journal of Social Hygiene* 1925; 8:281–285; Douglas SW. Difficulties and superstitions encountered in practice among Negroes. *Southern Medical Journal* 1926; 19:736–738; Douglas SW, Miller CJ. Comparative study of certain gynecologic and obstetric conditions as exhibited in the Colored and White races. *American Journal of Obstetrics and Gynecology* 1928; 26:662–663; Walsh G, Stickley C. Arsphenamine poisoning occurring among Negro women. *American Journal of Syphilis and Neurology* 1935; 324–325; Quillian DD. Racial peculiarities as a cause of the prevalence of syphilis in Negroes. *Medical Era* 1911; 20:416; Jones JH. *Bad Blood*; Reed J. Scientific racism; Stanton W. *The Leopard's Spots*; Haller JS Jr. *Outcasts from Evolution*; Shryock RH. *Medicine in America*; Tucker WH. *The Science and Politics of Racial Research*; Haller JS Jr. Haller RM. *The Physician and Sexuality in Victorian America*. N.P.: University of Illinois Press, 1974. Reprint ed. New York: W. W. Norton, 1977, 44–87.

55. Epps HR. The Howard University medical department in the Flexner era: 1910–1929. *Journal of the National Medical Association* 1989; 81:885; Hunt S. The Flexner report and Black academic medicine: An assignment of place. *Journal of the National Medical Association* 1993; 85:151–155; Savitt TL. Abraham Flexner and the Black medical schools. In: Barzansky EM, Gevitz N, eds. *Beyond Flexner: Medical Education in the 20th Century*. New York: Greenwood Press, 1992, 65–81; Roman CV. *Meharry Medical College: A History*. Nashville: Sunday School Publishing Board of the National Baptist Convention, 1934; Mullowney JJ. *America Gives a Chance*. Tampa, FL: The Tribune Press, 1940; Summerville J. *Educating Black Doctors: A History of Meharry Medical College*. University, AL: The University of Alabama Press, 1983; Savitt TL. "A journal of our own": *The Medical and Surgical Observer* at the beginnings of an African-American medical profession in late 19th-century America. *Journal of the National Medical Association* 1996; 88:52–60, 115–122; Williamson J. *The Crucible of Race: Black-White Relations in the American South Since Emancipation*. New York: Oxford University Press, 1984; Byrd WM, Clayton LA. *An American Health Dilemma*. Vol. 1.

56. Cobb WM. *The First Negro Medical Society: A History of the Medical-Chiurgical Society of the District of Columbia*. Washington, DC: The Associated Publishers, 1939, 35; Morais HM. *The History of the Negro in Medicine*, 52–58.

57. Jones JH. *Bad Blood*; Brandt AM. Racism and research: The Case of the Tuskegee Syphilis study. *Hastings Center Report* 1978; 8:21–29; Jones JH. Tuskegee syphilis experiment. 2685–2687. In: Salzman J, Smith DL, West C. eds. *Encyclopedia of African-American Culture and History* (5 vols.). New York: Macmillan Library Reference USA, 1996; Reed J. Scientific racism; Tucker WH. *The Science and Politics of Racial Research*; Byrd WM, Clayton LA. *An American Health Dilemma*. Vol. 1.

58. Morais HM. *The History of the Negro in Medicine*, 174.

59. Savitt TL. Entering a white profession: Black physicians in the new south, 1880–1920. *Bulletin of the History of Medicine* 1987; 61:507–540.

60. Morais HM. *The History of the Negro in Medicine*; Cobb WM. The Black American in medicine. *Journal of the National Medical Association* 1981; 73(suppl 1):1183–1244; Byrd WM, Clayton LA. An American health dilemma; Reynolds PP. Hospitals and civil rights, 1945–1963: *Simkins v. Moses H. Cone Memorial Hospital*. *Annals of Internal Medicine* 1997; 126:898–906; Reynolds PP. The federal government's use of Title VI and Medicare to racially integrate hospitals in the United States, 1963 through 1967. *American Journal of Public Health* 1997; 87:1850–1858; Beardsley EH. *A History of Neglect*.

61. Ewbank DC. History of Black mortality and health before 1940; Du Bois WEB. *Mortality Among Negroes in Cities*. Atlanta: Atlanta University Publications, 1896; Du Bois WEB. *Social and Physical Conditions of Negroes in Cities*. Atlanta: Atlanta University Publications, 1897; Du Bois WEB. *The Health and Physique of the Negro American*. Atlanta: Atlanta University Publications, 1906; Farley R. *Growth of the Black Population*; Farley R, Allen WR. *The Color Line and the Quality of Life in America*; Reuter EB. *The American Race Problem*. Rev. 3rd ed. Revision and Preface by Masuoka J. New York: Thomas Y. Crowell Company, 1970; Amidei NJ, Russell JS. Second class medicine. In: Newman DK, Amidei NJ, Carter BL, Day D, Kruvant WJ, Russell JS, eds. *Protest, Politics, and Prosperity: Black Americans and White Institutions, 1940–75*. New York: Pantheon Books, 1978, 187–235; Byrd WM, Clayton LA. *An American Health Dilemma*. Vol. 1.

62. Rosenberg CE. *The Care of Strangers*; Starr P. *The Social Transformation of American Medicine*; Stevens RA. *In Sickness and in Wealth: American Hospitals in the Twentieth Century*. Baltimore: The Johns Hopkins University Press, 1999; Gamble VN. *Making a Place for Ourselves: The Black Hospital Movement, 1920–1945*. New York: Oxford University Press, 1995; Vogel MJ. *The Invention of the Modern Hospital*.

63. Cobb WM. 1981. The Black American in medicine; Morais HM. *The History of the Negro in Medicine*; Byrd WM. Race, biology, and health care; Byrd WM, Clayton LA. The "slave health deficit"; Byrd WM, Clayton LA. An American health dilemma; Bullough B, Bullough VL. *Poverty, Ethnic Identity, and Health Care*. New York: Appleton-Century-Crofts, 1972; Amidei NJ, Russell JS. Second class medicine; Smith DB. *Health Care Divided*; Byrd WM, Clayton LA. *An American Health Dilemma*. Vol. 1.

64. Summerville J. *Educating Black Doctors*; Ludmerer KM. *Learning to Heal: The Development of American Medical Education*. New York: Basic Books, 1985; Cobb WM. *Medical Care and the Plight of the Negro*. New York: The National Association for the Advancement of Colored People, 1947; Cobb WM. *Progress and Portents for the Negro in Medicine*. New York: The National Association for the Advancement of Colored People, 1948; Morais HM. *The History of the Negro in Medicine*; Byrd WM. Race, biology, and health care; Byrd WM, Clayton LA. The "slave health deficit"; Byrd WM, Clayton LA. An American health dilemma; Amidei NJ, Russell JS. Second class medicine; Byrd WM, Clayton LA. *An American Health Dilemma*. Vol. 1.

65. Rosenberg CE. *The Care of Strangers*; Ludmerer KM. *Learning to Heal*; Dowling HF. *City Hospitals*; Rothstein WG. *American Medical Schools and the Practice of Medicine*. New York: Oxford University Press, 1987.

66. Morais HM. *The History of the Negro in Medicine*; Sidel VW, Sidel R, eds. *Reforming Medicine: Lessons of the Last Quarter Century*. New York: Pantheon Books, 1984; Robert Wood Johnson Foundation. Special Report Number One, The Foundation's Minority Medical Training Programs, "Minority Applicants to Medical School Are Better Qualified Today Than in Mid-70s, Yet Less Likely to be Accepted." Princeton, NJ: Robert Wood Johnson Foundation, 1987.

67. Cobb WM. *The First Negro Medical Society*; Cobb WM. *Medical Care and the Plight of the Negro*; Cobb WM. *Progress and Portents for the Negro in Medicine*; Epps HR. The Howard University medical department in the Flexner era; Summerville J. *Educating Black Doctors*; Hanft RS, Fishman LE, Evans W. *Blacks and the Health Professions in the 80s: A National Crisis and a Time for Action*. Prepared for the Association of Minority Health Professions Schools, N.P., 1983.

68. The American Anti-Slavery Society. *American Slavery As It Is: Testimony of a Thousand Witnesses*. The Anti-Slavery Examiner, 1839 (No. 6), New York: The American Anti-Slavery Society, 1839; Savitt TL. The use of blacks for medical experimentation and demonstration in the old south; Schultz SM. *Body Snatching: The Robbing of Graves for the Education of Physicians*. Jefferson, NC: McFarland, 1992, 39; Byrd WM, Clayton LA. *A Black Health Trilogy*; Blakely RL, Harrington JM, eds. *Bones in the Basement*; Jones JH. *Bad Blood*; Walker HE. *The Negro in the Medical Profession*. Publications of the University of Virginia Phelps-Stokes Fellowship Papers. N.P. University of Virginia, 1949; Kenney JA. Second annual oration on surgery. *Journal of the National Medical Association* 1941; 33:203–214; Lewis JH. Contribution of an unknown Negro to anesthesia. *Journal of the National Medical Association* 1931; 23:23–24; Shryock RH. *The Development of Modern Medicine*; Bullough B, Bullough VL. *Poverty, Ethnic Identity, and Health Care*.

69. Jones JH. Tuskegee syphilis experiment; Strait G, DiIanni D. *The Deadly Deception*. A documentary video segment for *Nova*, Boston, WGBH, 1993; Thomas SB, Quinn SC. Public health then and now: The Tuskegee syphilis study, 1932 to 1972: Implications for HIV education and

AIDS risk education programs in the Black community. *American Journal of Public Health* 1991; 81:1498–1504; Gamble VN. Under the shadow of Tuskegee: African Americans and health care. *American Journal of Public Health* 1997; 87:1773–1778.

70. Gamble VN. Under the shadow of Tuskegee; Brandt AM. Racism and research: The case of the Tuskegee syphilis study. In: Leavitt JW, Numbers RL, eds. *Sickness and Health in America: Readings in the History of Medicine and Public Health.* Madison: The University of Wisconsin Press, 1985, 331–343; Thomas SB, Quinn SC. Public health then and now; Jones JH. *Bad Blood;* Hornblum AM. *Acres of Skin: Human Experiments at Holmesburg Prison: A True Story of Abuse and Exploitation in the Name of Medical Science.* New York: Routledge, 1998; Welsome E. *The Pluto- nium Files: America's Secret Medical Experiments in the Cold War.* New York: The Dial Press, 1999; Byrd WM, Clayton LA. *An American Health Dilemma.* Vol. 1.

71. Lynk MV. *Sixty Years of Medicine, or The Life and Times of Dr. Miles V. Lynk: An Autobi- ography.* Memphis: Twentieth Century Press, 1951; Perry JE. *Forty Cords of Wood: Memoirs of a Medical Doctor.* Jefferson City, MO: Lincoln University Press, 1947; Beardsley EH. *A History of Neglect;* Morais HM. *The History of the Negro in Medicine;* Gamble VN. *Making a Place for Our- selves;* Gamble VN. The Negro hospital renaissance: The Black hospital movement, 1920–1945. In Long DE, Golden J, eds. *The American General Hospital: Communities and Social Contexts.* Ithaca: Cornell University Press, 1989, 82–105; Smith DB. *Health Care Divided.*

72. Du Bois WEB. *Mortality Among Negroes in Cities;* Du Bois WEB. *Social and Physical Con- ditions of Negroes in Cities;* Du Bois WEB. *The Health and Physique of the Negro American;* Poindexter H. Handicaps in the normal growth and development of rural Negro children. *American Journal of Public Health* 1938; 28:1049; Cornely PB. Morbidity and mortality from scarlet fever in the Negro. *American Journal of Public Health* 1939; 29:999–1005; Cornely PB. Observations on the health progress of Negroes in the U.S. during the past two decades. *Southern Medical Journal* 1941; 34:1286; Cornely PB. Trends in public health activities among Negroes in 96 Southern counties during the period 1930–39. *American Journal of Public Health* 1942; 32:1117–1123; Cor- nely PB. Distribution of Negro physicians in the United States in 1942. *Journal of the American Medical Association* 1944; 124:826; Haynes MA. Distribution of black physicians in the United States, 1967. *Journal of the American Medical Association* 1969; 210:93–95; Haynes MA, McGarvey MR. Physicians, hospitals, and patients in the inner city. In: Norman JC, ed. *Medicine in the Ghetto.* New York: Appleton-Century-Crofts, 1969; Haynes MA. The gap in health status between black and white Americans.

73. Bullough B, Bullough VL. *Poverty, Ethnic Identity, and Health Care;* Gamble VN. *Making a Place for Ourselves;* Amidei NJ, Russell JS. Second class medicine; Sidel VW, Sidel R, eds. *Reforming Medicine;* Cray E. *In Failing Health: The Medical Crisis and the A.M.A.* Indianapolis: The Bobbs-Merrill Company, Inc., 1970; Morais HM. *The History of the Negro in Medicine;* Beard- sley EH. *A History of Neglect;* Smith DB. *Health Care Divided;* Byrd WM, Clayton LA. *An Ameri- can Health Dilemma.* Vol. 1.

74. Byrd WM. An American health dilemma. *Journal of the National Medical Association* 1986; 78:1025–1026; Charatz-Litt C. A chronicle of racism: The effects of the White medical commu- nity on black health. *Journal of the National Medical Association* 1992; 84:717–725; Byrd WM, Clayton LA. *A Black Health Trilogy;* Mayberry RM, Mili F, Ofli E. Racial and ethnic differences in access to medical care; Shiefer SE, Escarce JJ, Schulman KA. Race and sex differences in the man- agement of coronary artery disease; Blustein J, Arons RR, Shea S. Sequential events contributing to variations in cardiac revascularization rates. *Medical Care Research and Review* 1995; 33:864–880; Peterson ED, et al. Racial variation in the use of coronary-revascularization procedures; Canto JG, Allison JJ, Kiefe CI, Fincher C, Farmer R, et al. Relation of race and sex to the use of reperfusion therapy in Medicare beneficiaries with acute myocardial infarction. *New England Journal of Med- icine* 2000; 342:1094–1100; Einbinder LC, Schulman KA. The effect of race on the referral process for invasive cardiac procedures. *Medical Care Research and Review* 2000; 57(suppl 1):162–180; Ayanian JZ, Udvarhelyi IS, Gatsonis CA, Pashos CL, Epstein AM. Racial differences in the use of revascularization procedures after coronary angiography. *Journal of the American Medical Associa- tion* 1993; 269:2642–2646; Goldberg KC, Hartz AH, Jacobsen SJ, Krakauer H, Rimm AA. Racial and community factors influencing coronary artery bypass graft surgery rates for all 1986 Medicare patients. *Journal of the American Medical Association* 1992; 267:1473–1477; Ford ES, Cooper RS. Racial/ethnic differences in health care utilization of cardiovascular procedures: A review of the

evidence. *Health Service Research* 1995; 30:237–252; Ball JK, Elixhauser A. Treatment differences between Blacks and Whites with colorectal cancer. *Medical Care* 1996; 34:970–984; Bach PB, Cramer LD, Warren JL, Begg CB. Racial differences in the treatment of early-stage lung cancer. *New England Journal of Medicine* 1999; 341:1198–1205; Guadagnoli E, Ayanian JZ, Gibbons G, McNeil BJ, LoGerfo FW. The influence of race on the use of surgical procedures for treatment of peripheral vascular disease of the lower extremities. *Archives of Surgery* 1995; 130:381–386; Ayanian JZ, Weissman JS, Chasan-Taber S, Epstein AM. Quality of care by race and gender for congestive heart failure and pneumonia. *Medical Care* 1999; 37:1260–1269; Todd KH, Samaroo N, Hoffman JR. Ethnicity as a risk factor for inadequate emergency department analgesia. *Journal of the American Medical Association* 1993; 269:1537–1539; Van Ryan M, Burke J. The effect of patient race and socio-economic status on physicians' perceptions of patients. *Social Science and Medicine* 2000; 50:813–828; Fiscella K, Franks P, Gold MR, Clancy CM. Inequality in quality: Addressing socioeconomic, racial, and ethnic disparities in health care. *Journal of the American Medical Association* 2000; 283:2579–2584; Ayanian JZ. Race, class and the quality of medical care. *Journal of the American Medical Association* 1994; 271:1207–1208; Blustein J, Weitzman BC. Access to hospitals with high-technology cardiac services; Braveman P, Egerter S, Edmonston F, Verdon M. Racial/ethnic differences in the likelihood of caesarean delivery; Breast cancer deaths decrease — but not among Black women, 24; Brennan TA, Hebert LE, Laird NM, et al. Hospital characteristics associated with adverse events and substandard care. *Journal of the American Medical Association* 1991; 266:3265–3269; Brooks DD, Smith DR, Anderson RJ. Medical apartheid, an American perspective. *Journal of the American Medical Association* 1991; 266:2746–2749; Carlisle DM, Leake B, Shapiro MF. Racial and ethnic differences in the use of invasive cardiac procedures among cardiac patients in Los Angeles County, 1986 through 1988; Council on Ethical and Judicial Affairs. Black-White disparities in health care. *Journal of the American Medical Association* 1990; 263:2344–2346; Chu J, Polisor L, Tamimi HK. Quality of care in women with stage-1 cervical cancer. *Western Journal of Medicine* 1982; 137:13–17; Diehr P, Yergan J, Chu J, et al. Treatment modality and quality differences for Black and White breast-cancer patients treated in community hospitals. *Medical Care* 1989; 27:942–958; Eisenberg JM. Sociologic influences on decision making by clinicians. *Annals of Internal Medicine* 1979; 318:158–163; Elixhauser A, Ball JK. Black-White differences in colorectal tumor location in a national sample of hospitals. *Journal of the National Medical Association* 1994; 86:449–458; Escarce JJ et al. Racial differences in the elderly's use of medical procedures and diagnostic tests; Foster HW. Reaching parity for minority medical students: A possibility or a pipe dream? *Journal of the National Medical Association* 1996; 88:17–21; Geiger HJ. Annotation: Racism resurgent—building a bridge to the 19th century. *American Journal of Public Health* 1997; 87:1765–1766; Geiger HJ. Comment: Ethnic cleansing in the groves of academe. *American Journal of Public Health* 1998; 88:1299–1300; Hadley J, Steinberg E, Feder J. Comparison of underinsured and privately insured hospital patients. *Journal of the American Medical Association* 1991; 265:374–379; Kahn KL, Pearson ML, Harrison ER, Desmond KA, Rodgers WH, et al. Health care for Black and poor hospitalized Medicare patients. *Journal of the American Medical Association* 1994; 271:1169–1174; Keil JE, Sutherland SE, Knapp RG, Tyrder HA. Does equal socioeconomic status in Black and White mean equal risk of mortality? *American Journal of Public Health* 1992; 82:1133–1136; Kong D. Study: Minorities' health lags; Krieger N. Analyzing socioeconomic and racial/ethnic patterns in health and health care; Jones JH. *Bad Blood*; McBride D. Inequality in the availability of Black physicians. *New York State Journal of Medicine* 1985; 85:139–142; McBride D. *From TB to AIDS. Epidemics Among Urban Blacks Since 1900.* Albany: State University of New York Press, 1991; McWhorter WP, Moyer WJ. Black-White differences in type of initial breast cancer treatment and implications for survival. *American Journal of Public Health* 1987; 77:1515–1517; Peterson ED, Wright SM, Doley J, Thibault GE. Racial variations in cardiac procedure use and survival following acute myocardial infarction in the Department of Veterans Affairs. *Journal of the American Medical Association* 1994; 271:1175–1180; Rice MF. Inner-city hospital closures/relocations: Race, income status and legal issues. *Social Science and Medicine* 1987; 24:889–896; Schwartz E, Kofie VY, Rivio M, Tuckson RV. Black/White comparisons of deaths preventable by medical intervention: United States and the District of Columbia, 1980–1986. *International Journal of Epidemiology* 1990; 19:591–598; Sorlie P, Rogot E, Anderson R, Johnson NJ, Blacklund E. Black-White mortality differences by family income. *Lancet* 1992; 340:346–350; Washington HA. Medicine's mainstream overlooks Blacks. *Emerge* May 1996; 7:22; Washington HA. Piece of the genetic puzzle is left out. *Emerge* September 1997; 8:30; Wenneker MB, Epstein AM. Racial inequalities in the use of procedures for patients with ischemic heart disease in Massachusetts; Whittle J, Conigliaro J, Good CB, Lofgren RP. Racial differences in the use of invasive cardiovascular procedures in the Department of Veterans Affairs medical system. *New England Journal of Medicine* 1993; 329:621–627; Yergan J, Flood AB, Lo Gerfo JP, Diehr P. Relationship between patient race and the intensity of hospital services. *Medical Care* 1987; 25:592–603; Byrd WM, Clayton LA. *An American Health Dilemma*. Vol. 1.

75. Morais HM. *The History of the Negro in Medicine*; Byrd WM, Clayton LA. An American health dilemma; Smith DB. *Health Care Divided*; Cobb WM. The Black American in medicine; Gamble VN. *Making a Place for Ourselves*; Reynolds PP. Hospitals and civil rights, 1945–1963; Reynolds PP. The federal government's use of Title VI and Medicare to racially integrate hospitals in the United States, 1963 through 1967; Beardsley EH. *A History of Neglect*; Byrd WM, Clayton LA. *An American Health Dilemma*. Vol. 1.

76. Smith DB. *Health Care Divided*; Smith DB. Addressing racial inequities in health care: Civil rights monitoring and report cards. *Journal of Health, Policy and Law* 1998; 23:75–105; Wing KR, Rose MG. Health facilities and the enforcement of civil rights. In: Roemer R, McKray G, eds. *Legal Aspects of Health Policy: Issues and Trends*. Westport, CT: Greenwood Press, 1980; Lief BJ. Legal and administrative barriers to health care. *New York State Journal of Medicine* 1985; 85:126–127; McBride AD. Racial equality in the American health care system: An unfulfilled ideal. *New York State Journal of Medicine* 1985; 85:125; Randall VR. Racist health care: Reforming an unjust health care system to meet the needs of African-Americans. *Health Matrix: Journal of Law-Medicine* Spring 1993; (1):3:127–194, 164, 188–193; Randall VR. Slavery, segregation and racism: Trusting the health care system ain't always easy! An African American perspective on bioethics. *Saint Louis University Public Law Review* 1996; (2); 15:191–235, 211–212; Byrd WM, Clayton LA. "Designing a New Health Care System for the United States." Boston: Harvard School of Public Health, 1992. Photocopy.

77. Haynes MA. The gap in health status between black and white Americans; Byrd WM, Clayton LA. An American health dilemma; Byrd WM, Clayton LA. *A Black Health Trilogy*; Sidel VW, Sidel R, eds. *Reforming Medicine*; Manton KG, Patrick CH, Johnson KW. Health differentials between Blacks and Whites: Recent trends in mortality and morbidity. In: Willis DP, ed. *Health Policies and Black Americans*. New Brunswick, NJ: Transaction Publishers, 1989, 129–199.

78. Shea S, Fullilove MT. Entry of Black and other minority students into US medical schools: Historical perspective and recent trends. *New England Journal of Medicine* 1985; 313:933–940; Odegaard CE. *Minorities in Medicine: From Receptive Passivity to Positive Action 1966–1976*. Josiah Macy Jr. Foundation, 1977; Strelnick H, Younge R. Affirmative action in medicine: Money becomes the admissions criteria of the 1980s. In: Sidel VW, Sidel R, eds. *Reforming Medicine*, 151–175; Sullivan LW. The status of blacks in medicine. *New England Journal of Medicine* 1983; 309:807–809; Hanft RS, Fishman LE, Evans W. *Blacks and the Health Professions in the 80s*; Robert Wood Johnson Foundation. Special Report Number One, The Foundation's Minority Medical Training Programs, "Minority Applicants to Medical School are Better Qualified Today than in Mid 70s, Yet Less Likely to be Accepted."

79. Byrd WM, Clayton LA. *An American Health Dilemma*. Vol. 1; Smith DB. *Health Care Divided*; Haynes MA. The gap in health status between black and white Americans; Clayton LA, Byrd WM. Race: A major health status and outcome variable, 1980–1999. *Journal of the National Medical Association* 2001; 93(suppl):35s–54s; Byrd WM, Clayton LA. An American health dilemma; Hacker A. *Two Nations*.

80. National Center for Health Statistics. *Health United States, 1995*. Hyattsville, MD: Public Health Service, May, 1996; Greenberg DS. Black health: Grim statistics. *The Lancet* 1990; 355:780–781; Livingston IL, ed. *Handbook of Black American Health: The Mosaic of Conditions, Issues, Policies, and Prospects*. Westport, CT: Greenwood Press, 1994; Braithwaite RL, Taylor SE, eds. *Health Issues in the Black Community*. San Francisco: Jossey-Bass Publishers, 1992; Byrd WM, Clayton LA. An American health dilemma; Clayton LA, Byrd WM. Race: A major health status and outcome variable, 1980–1999.

81. Smith DB. *Health Care Divided*; Wilson WJ. *The Declining Significance of Race: Blacks and Changing American Institutions*. Chicago: The University of Chicago Press, 1978; Wilson WJ. *The Truly Disadvantaged: The Inner City, the Underclass, and Public Policy*. Chicago: The University of Chicago Press, 1987; Massey DS, Denton NA. *American Apartheid*; Meyer SG. *As Long as*

636 ■ Notes

*They Don't Move Next Door*; Wilson WJ. *When Work Disappears: The World of the New Urban Poor*. New York: Knopf, 1996; Hacker A. *Two Nations*; Feagin JR. *Racist America: Roots, Current Realities, and Future Reparations*. New York: Routledge, 2000.

82. Jones W, Rice MF. *Health Care Issues in Black America: Policies, Problems, and Prospects*. Westport, CT: Greenwood Press, 1987; Ginzberg E. Improving health care for the poor: Lessons from the 1980s. *Journal of the American Medical Association* 1994; 271:464–467; Lewis S. *Hospital: An Oral History of Cook County Hospital*. New York: The New Press, 1994; Dowling HF. *City Hospitals*; Randall VR. Racist health care; Smith DB. Addressing racial inequities in health care; Smith DB. *Health Care Divided*; Byrd WM, Clayton LA. *An American Health Dilemma*. Vol. 1.

83. Geiger HJ. Comment; Shea S, Fullilove MT. Entry of black and other minority students in US medical schools; Strelnick AH, Massad RJ, Bateman WB, Shepherd SD. Minority students in U.S. medical schools. *New England Journal of Medicine* 1986; 315:67–68; Komaromy M, Grumbach K, Drake M. The role of Black and Hispanic physicians in providing health care for underserved populations; Hanft RS, Fishman LE, Evans W. *Blacks and the Health Professions in the 80s*; Hanft RS, White CC. Constraining the supply of physicians: Effects on black physicians. In: Willis DP, ed. *Health Policies and Black Americans*. New Brunswick, NJ: Transaction Publishers, 1989, 249–269.

84. Dowling HF. *City Hospitals*; Kosa J, Zola IK, eds. *Poverty and Health: A Sociological Analysis*. Rev. ed. Cambridge, MA: Harvard University Press, 1975; Bullough B, Bullough VL. *Poverty, Ethnic Identity, and Health Care*; Byrd WM. Race, biology, and health care; Byrd WM, Clayton LA. An American health dilemma; Clayton LA, Byrd WM. Race: A major health status and outcome variable, 1980–1999; Byrd WM, Clayton LA. *An American Health Dilemma*. Vol. 1.

85. Greenberg DS. Black health; Smith DB. *Health Care Divided*; Smith DB. Addressing racial inequities in health care; Anderson GF, Poullier J-P. Health spending, access, and outcomes: Trends in industrialized countries. *Health Affairs* 1999; 18:178–192; Wilson WJ. *The Truly Disadvantaged*; Massey DS, Denton NA. *American Apartheid*; McCord C, Freeman HP. Excess mortality in Harlem. *New England Journal of Medicine* 1990; 322:173–177; Wilson WJ. *When Work Disappears*; Johnson H, Broder DS. *The System: The American Way of Politics at the Breaking Point*. Boston: Little, Brown, 1996; Skocpol T. *Boomerang: Health Care Reform and the Turn Against Government*. New York: W. W. Norton, 1997; Pear R. Still uninsured, and still a campaign issue. *New York Times* June 25, 2000: 16; Toner R. Gore and Bush health proposals fall short of counterparts' plans 8 years ago. *New York Times* October 15, 2000: 22.

86. Du Bois WEB. *The Souls of Black Folk: Essays and Sketches by W.E. Burghardt Du Bois*. N.P.: Fawcett Publications, 1961. Illustrated ed. New York: Dodd, Mead, and Company, 1979, 10.

87. Reed J. Scientific racism; Kovel J. *White Racism*; Byrd WM, Clayton LA. An American health dilemma; Byrd WM, Clayton LA. *An American Health Dilemma*. Vol. 1; Ryan W. *Blaming the Victim*. New York: Vintage Books, 1971. Rev. ed. New York: Vintage Books, 1976; Katz MB. *In the Shadow of the Poorhouse: A Social History of Welfare in America*. New York: Basic Books, 1986. Rev. ed. 1996; Veatch RM. *A Theory of Medical Ethics*. New York: Basic Books, 1981; Tucker WH. *The Science and Politics of Racial Research*; Harding S, ed. *The "Racial Economy" of Science: Toward a Democratic Future*. Bloomington: Indiana University Press, 1993; Dula A. Toward an African-American perspective on bioethics. *Journal of Health Care for the Poor and Underserved* 1991; 2:259–269; Proctor RN. *Value-Free Science? Purity and Power in Modern Knowledge*. Cambridge, MA: Harvard University Press, 1991; Kragh H. *An Introduction to the Historiography of Science*. Cambridge: Cambridge University Press, 1987. Paperback ed. 1989; Smith DB. *Health Care Divided*; Churchill LR. *Rationing Health Care in America: Perceptions and Principles of Justice*. Notre Dame, IN: University of Notre Dame Press, 1987; Churchill LR. *Self-Interest and Universal Health Care: Why Well-Insured Americans Should Support Coverage for Everyone*. Cambridge, MA: Harvard University Press, 1994; Nisbet R. *Prejudices: A Philosophical Dictionary*. Cambridge, MA: Harvard University Press, 1982; Fuchs VR. *The Future of Health Policy*. Cambridge, MA: Harvard University Press, 1993; Gans HJ. *The War Against the Poor: The Underclass and Antipoverty Policy*. New York: Basic Books, 1995; Charatz-Litt C. A chronicle of racism; Byrd WM. Race, biology, and health care; Washington HA. Of men and mice: Human guinea pigs: Unethical testing targets Blacks and the poor. *Emerge* 1994 October; (1): 6:24; Haller JS Jr. *Outcasts from Evolution*; Gould SJ. *The Mismeasure of Man*; Stanton W. *The Leopard's Spots*; Johnson AG. *The Blackwell Dictionary of Sociology: A User's Guide to Sociological Language*. Cambridge, MA: Basil Blackwell, 1995.

88. Chase A. *The Legacy of Malthus*, xv.

89. Gould SJ. *The Mismeasure of Man*, 35–36; Gould SJ. Racism and recapitulation. In: Gould SJ, *Ever Since Darwin: Reflections in Natural History*. New York: W.W. Norton, 1977, 214–221; Burke J. Fit to rule; Gould SJ. The Hottentot Venus. In: Gould SJ, *The Flamingo's Smile: Reflections in Natural History*. New York: W. W. Norton, 1985, 291–305.

90. Gould SJ. *The Mismeasure of Man*, 42–50, 50–69; Haller JS Jr. *Outcasts from Evolution*, 76, 77, 84–86, 103; Stanton W. *The Leopard's Spots*, 25–35, 40, 41, 42, 99–109, 149, 154; Gould SJ. Flaws in the Victorian veil. In: Gould SJ, *The Panda's Thumb: More Reflections in Natural History*. New York: W. W. Norton, 1980, 169–176.

91. Chase A. *The Legacy of Malthus*, 71, 105–107, 114–115, 136, 517–518; Gould SJ. *The Mismeasure of Man*, 117; Burke J. Fit to rule, 268–271, 271–272; Tucker WH. *The Science and Politics of Racial Research*, 26–28, 33; Fredrickson GM. *The Black Image in the White Mind*, 249–252.

92. Chase A. *The Legacy of Malthus*; Malthus T. *An Essay on the Principle of Population*. Flew A, ed. Penguin Classics. Middlesex, England: Penguin Books Ltd., 1982; Tucker WH. *The Science and Politics of Racial Research*; Gould SJ. *The Mismeasure of Man*; Herrnstein RJ, Murray C. *The Bell Curve: Intelligence and Class Structure in American Life*. New York: The Free Press, 1994; Hoffman FL. *Race Traits and Tendencies of the American Negro*; Grant, M. *The Passing of the Great Race*. New York: Charles Scribner's Sons, 1916. Rev. ed. 1918; Stoddard L. *The Rising Tide of Color Against White World-Supremacy*. New York: Charles Scribner's Sons, 1920; Allen GE. Eugenics comes to America. In: Jacoby R, Glauberman N, eds. *The Bell Curve Debate: History, Documents, Opinions*. New York: Times Books Division of Random House, 1995, 441–475; Fraser S, ed. *The Bell Curve Wars: Race, Intelligence, and the Future of America*. New York: Basic Books, 1995; Guthrie RV. *Even the Rat Was White: A Historical View of Psychology*. 2nd ed. Boston: Allyn and Bacon, 1998; Byrd WM. Race, biology, and health care; Byrd WM, Clayton LA. An American health dilemma; Bynum WF, Browne EJ, Porter R, eds. *The Dictionary of the History of Science*, 333–335; Jones JH. *Bad Blood*; Byrd WM, Clayton LA. *An American Health Dilemma*. Vol. 1.

93. Chase A. *The Legacy of Malthus*, xvi.

94. Chase A. *The Legacy of Malthus*; Reed J. Scientific racism; Smedley A. *Race in North America*; Zuckoff M. An Australian call for justice: For the Olympics, Aborigines camp out to remind the world of a long, enduring legacy of oppression by White colonialists. *Boston Sunday Globe* August 20, 2000: 1; Quindlen A. The problem of the color line. *Newsweek* March 13, 2000: 76; Byrd WM, Clayton LA. *An American Health Dilemma*. Vol. 1; Smith DB. *Health Care Divided*; Tucker WH. *The Science and Politics of Racial Research*; Jones JH. *Bad Blood*; Harding S, ed. *The "Racial Economy" of Science*; Churchill LR. *Rationing Health Care in America*; Dula A. Toward an African-American perspective on bioethics; Proctor RN. *Value-Free Science?*, 109–120, 241–254; Churchill LR. *Self-Interest and Universal Health Care*; Nisbet R. *Prejudices*; Gould SJ. *The Mismeasure of Man*; Haller JS Jr. *Outcasts from Evolution*; Stanton W. *The Leopard's Spots*; Byrd WM, Clayton LA. An American health dilemma; Byrd WM. Race, biology, and health care.

95. Greenberg DS. Black health; Jones JH. *Bad Blood*; Byrd WM, Clayton LA. An American health dilemma; Morais HM. *The History of the Negro in Medicine*; Chase A. *The Legacy of Malthus*; Beardsley EH. *A History of Neglect*; Williams DR. Race, socioeconomic status, and health: The added effects of racism and discrimination. *Annals of the New York Academy of Sciences* 1999: 896:173–188; Van Ryn M, Burke J. The effect of patient race and socio-economic status on physicians' perceptions of patients; Feagin JR, Vera H. *White Racism: The Basics*. New York: Routledge, 1995; Feagin JR. *Racist America*; Feagin JR, Spikes MP. *Living With Racism*; Smedley A. *Race in North America*; Bennett T, Bhopal R. US health journal editors' opinions and policies on research in race, ethnicity, and health. *Journal of the National Medical Association* 1998; 90:401–408; Roberts D. *Killing the Black Body: Race, Reproduction, and the Meaning of Liberty*. New York: Pantheon Books, 1997; Weisbord RG. *Genocide? Birth Control and the Black American*. Westport, CT: Greenwood Press, 1975; Schultz SM. *Body Snatching*; Fineberg KS, Peters JD, Willson JR, Kroll DA. *Obstetrics/Gynecology and the Law*. Ann Arbor, MI: Health Administration Press, 1984; Smith DB. *Health Care Divided*; Dula A. Toward an African-American perspective on bioethics; 2:259–269; Annas GJ, Grodin MA, eds. *The Nazi Doctors and the Nuremberg Code: Human Rights in Human Experimentation*. New York: Oxford University Press, 1992; Proctor RN. *Value-Free Science?*; Chomsky N. *Profit Over People: Neoliberalism and Global Order*. New York: Seven Stories Press, 1999; Kovel J. *White Racism: A Psychohistory*; Van Ausdale D, Feagin JR. *The First R: How Children Learn Race and Racism*. Lanham, MD: Rowman and Littlefield, 2001; Omi M, Winant H. *Racial Formation in the United States: From the 1960s to the 1990s*. 2nd ed. New

York: Routledge, 1994; Lemann N. The structure of success in America. *The Atlantic Monthly* August 1995; (2)276:41; Lemann N. The great sorting: The first mass administrations of a scholastic-aptitude test led with surprising speed to the idea that the nation's leaders would be the people who did well on tests. *The Atlantic Monthly* September 1995; (3)276:84; Lemann N. *The Big Test*; Washington HA. Of men and mice; Washington HA. Henrietta Lacks—An unsung hero. *Emerge* October 1994; (1)6:29; Washington HA. Straightening out *The Bell Curve*: An old IQ argument gets a new airing. *Emerge* January 1995; (3) 6:28; Washington HA. Medicine's mainstream overlooks Blacks; Churchill LR. *Rationing Health Care in America*; Churchill LR. *Self-Interest and Universal Health Care*; Nisbet R. *Prejudices*; Fuchs VR. *The Future of Health Policy*.

96. Annas GJ, Grodin MA, eds. *The Nazi Doctors and the Nuremberg Code*.

97. Allen GE. Eugenics comes to America; Chase A. *The Legacy of Malthus*; Kamin LJ. The pioneers of IQ testing. In: Jacoby R, Glauberman N, eds. *The Bell Curve Debate: History, Documents, Opinions*. New York: Times Books Division of Random House, 1995, 476–509; Proctor RN. *Racial Hygiene: Medicine under the Nazis*. Cambridge, MA: Harvard University Press, 1988; Beardsley EH. *A History of Neglect*; Morais HM. *The History of the Negro in Medicine*; Byrd WM, Clayton LA. An American health dilemma; Gould SJ. *The Mismeasure of Man*; Haller JS Jr. *Outcasts from Evolution*; Stanton W. *The Leopard's Spots*; Cobb WM. *Medical Care and the Plight of the Negro*; Cobb WM. *Progress and Portents for the Negro in Medicine*; Takaki RY. *Iron Cages*; Stannard DE. *American Holocaust*; Lifton RJ. *The Nazi Doctors: Medical Killing and the Psychology of Genocide*. New York: Basic Books, 1986; Arad Y, ed. *The Pictorial History of the Holocaust*. New York: Macmillan, 1990; Smith JD, Nelson KR. *The Sterilization of Carrie Buck*. Far Hills, NJ: New Horizon Press, 1989; Davenport CB. *Heredity in Relation to Eugenics*. New York: Henry Holt and Company, 1911; Weisbord RG. *Genocide?*; Omi M, Winant H. *Racial Formation in the United States*; Williams DR. Race, socioeconomic status, and health; Van Ryn M, Burke J. The effect of patient race and socio-economic status on physicians' perceptions of patients; Feagin JR, Vera H. *White Racism*; Feagin JR. *Racist America*; Feagin JR, Spikes MP. *Living with Racism*; Smedley A. *Race in North America*; Chomsky N. *Profit Over People*; O'Reilly K. *Nixon's Piano: Presidents and Racial Politics from Washington to Clinton*. New York: The Free Press, 1995; Washington HA. Of men and mice; Washington HA. Henrietta Lacks—An unsung hero; Byrd WM, Clayton LA. *An American Health Dilemma*. Vol. 1.

98. Morais HM. *The History of the Negro in Medicine*; Cobb WM. *Medical Care and the Plight of the Negro*; Cobb WM. *Progress and Portents for the Negro in Medicine*; Williams DR. Race, socioeconomic status, and health; Van Ryn M, Burke J. The effect of patient race and socio-economic status on physicians' perceptions of patients; Feagin JR, Vera H. *White Racism*; Feagin JR. *Racist America*; Feagin JR, Spikes MP. *Living with Racism*; Smedley A. *Race in North America*; Reynolds PP. The federal government's use of Title VI and Medicare to racially integrate hospitals in the United States, 1963 through 1967; Gamble VN. Hospitals, Black. In: Salzman J, Smith DL, West C. eds. *American Culture and History* (5 vols.). New York: Macmillan Library Reference USA, 1996, 1305–1309; Gamble VN. Under the shadow of Tuskegee; Gamble VN. *Making a Place for Ourselves*; Bell CC. Impaired Black health professionals: Vulnerabilities and treatment approaches. *Journal of the National Medical Association* 1986; 78:925–930; Geiger HJ. Annotation; Geiger HJ. Comment; O'Bannon LC. Are African-American doctors being locked out? The down side of managed care. *Natl Med Assoc News* Winter 1995; Byrd WM. Inquisition, peer review, and black physician survival. *Journal of the National Medical Association* 1987; 79:1027–1029; Byrd WM, Clayton LA, Kinchen K, Richardson D, Lawrence L, Butcher R, et al. African-American physicians' views on health reform: Preliminary results of a survey. *Journal of the National Medical Association* 1994; 86:93–94; Byrd WM, Clayton LA, Kinchen K, Richardson D, Lawrence L, Butcher R, et al. African-American physicians' views on health reform: Results of a survey. *Journal of the National Medical Association* 1994; 86:191–199; Lavizzo-Mourey R, Clayton LA, Byrd WM, Johnson III G, Richardson D. The perceptions of African-American physicians concerning their treatment by managed care organizations. *Journal of the National Medical Association* 1996; 88:210–214; Byrd WM, Clayton LA. *An American Health Dilemma*. Vol. 1.

99. Byrd WM. Race, biology, and health care; Byrd WM, Clayton LA. An American health dilemma; Smith DB. *Health Care Divided*; Randall VR. Racist health care; Randall VR. Does Clinton's health care reform proposal ensure (e)qual(ity) of health care for ethnic Americans and the poor? *Brooklyn Law Review* Spring 1994; 60:167–237; Randall VR. Slavery, segregation and racism;

Massey DS, Denton NA. *American Apartheid*; Starr P. *The Social Transformation of American Medicine*; Byrd WM, Clayton LA. *An American Health Dilemma*. Vol. 1.

100. Byrd WM. Race, biology, and health care; Byrd WM, Clayton LA. An American health dilemma; Smith DB. *Health Care Divided*; Sigerist HE. *The Great Doctors*, 43–44; Haeger K. *The Illustrated History of Surgery*. New York: Bell Publishing Company, 45–46; Byrd WM, Clayton LA. *An American Health Dilemma*. Vol. 1.

101. Schulman KA et al. The effect of race and sex on physician recommendations for cardiac catheterization.

102. Massey DS, Denton NA. *American Apartheid*, 2, 15.

103. Geiger HJ. Comment, 1299.

104. Kinder DR, Sanders LM. *Divided by Color: Racial Politics and Democratic Ideals*. Chicago. The University of Chicago Press, 1996; Sniderman PM, Piazza T. *The Scar of Race*. Cambridge, MA: The Belknap Press of Harvard University Press, 1993; Sniderman PM, Carmines EG. *Reaching Beyond Race*. Cambridge, MA: Harvard University Press, 1997; Schuman H, Steeh C, Bobo L, Krysan M. *Racial Attitudes in America: Trends and Interpretations*. Rev. ed. Cambridge, MA: Harvard University Press, 1997.

105. Bonnyman GG Jr. Muddled care, managed care. *Health Affairs (Millwood)* 1999; 18:264–265, 264. Review of: Andrulis DP, Carrier B. *Managed Care in the Inner City: The Uncertain Promise for Providers, Plans, and Communities*.

106. Navarro V. *Dangerous to Your Health: Capitalism in Health Care*. New York: Monthly Review Press, 1993; Fuchs VR. *The Future of Health Policy*; Andrulis DP, Carrier B. *Managed Care in the Inner City: The Uncertain Promise for Providers, Plans, and Communities*. San Francisco: Jossey-Bass, 1999; Friedman E. The Human Factor: The Effect of Emerging Models of Competition on Patients and the Public. Presented at the Robert Wood Johnson Foundation/Alpha Center Conference on Rethinking Competition in Health Care, Washington, D.C., January 7–8, 1993; Fein R. Health care reform. *Scientific American*, November, 1992, 46–53; Churchill LR. *Self-Interest and Universal Health Care*; Richardson L. White patients more likely to use AIDS drugs, study says, 24; Myerson AR. When healing collides with the drive for profits. *New York Times* July 27, 1997: 14; Pear R. Investigators say a Medicare option is rife with fraud. *New York Times* July 27, 1997: 1; Hacker A. *Two Nations*; Byrd WM, Clayton LA. The "slave health deficit"; Byrd WM, Clayton LA. An American health dilemma; Clayton LA, Byrd WM. Race: A major health status and outcome variable, 1980–1999; Byrd WM, Clayton LA. Race, medicine, and health care in the United States; Myrdal G. *An American Dilemma: The Negro Problem and Modern Democracy*. New York: Harper & Row, 1944; Wood A. Capitalism. In: Honderich T, ed. *The Oxford Companion to Philosophy*. Oxford: Oxford University Press, 1995, 119–120; *The American Heritage Dictionary of the English Language* Third Edition., s.v. "entrepreneur." *Webster's New Universal Unabridged Dictionary*, s.v. "entrepreneur."

107. Kovel J. *White Racism*, 26, 27.

108. Skocpol T. *Boomerang*; Anderson GF, Poullier J-P. Health spending, access, and outcomes; Starr P. *The Social Transformation of American Medicine*; Wolff EN. *Top Heavy: A Study of the Increasing Inequality of Wealth in America*. New York: The Twentieth Century Fund Press, 1995; Botelho RJ. Overcoming the prejudice against establishing a national health care system. *Archives of Internal Medicine* 1991; 151:863–869; Byrd WM, Clayton LA, McCoy SP, Calliste GJ. Access to health care: Provision by the major health reform proposals, policy memorandum prepared for the Congressional Black Caucus Foundation, March 26, 1994; Greenberg DS. Black health; Myrdal G. *An American Dilemma*; Myrdal G. *Asian Drama: An Inquiry Into the Poverty of Nations* (3 vols.). New York: Pantheon, 1968; Cobb WM. 1981. The Black American in medicine; Morais HM. *The History of the Negro in Medicine*; Byrd WM. An American health dilemma. *Journal of the National Medical Association* 1986; 78:1025–1026; Clayton LA, Byrd WM. Race: A major health status and outcome variable, 1980–1999; Johnson AG. *The Blackwell Dictionary of Sociology*.

## Chapter One

1. Starr P. *The Social Transformation of American Medicine*. New York: Basic Books, 1982; Brinkley A. *The Unfinished Nation: A Concise History of the American People*. New York: Knopf,

1993; Feagin JR. *Racist America: Roots, Current Realities, and Future Reparations.* New York: Routledge, 2000. Brown ER. *Rockefeller Medicine Men: Medicine and Capitalism in America.* Berkeley: University of California Press, 1979; Stevens RA. *American Medicine and the Public Interest.* New Haven, CT: Yale University Press, 1971; Jonas G. *The Circuit Riders: Rockefeller Money and the Rise of Modern Science.* New York: W. W. Norton, 1989; Morais HM. *The History of the Negro in Medicine.* New York: Publishers Company, 1967; Byrd WM, Clayton LA. An American health dilemma: A history of blacks in the health system. *Journal of the National Medical Association* 1992; 84:189–200.

2. Brinkley A. *The Unfinished Nation,* 465.

3. Brinkley A. *The Unfinished Nation;* Zinn H. *A People's History of the United States.* New York: Harper & Row, 1980. Paperback ed. New York: Harper Perennial, 1990; Feagin, JR. *Racist America;* Churchill LR. *Rationing Health Care in America: Perceptions and Principles of Justice.* Notre Dame, IN: University of Notre Dame Press, 1987; Starr P. *The Social Transformation of American Medicine;* Morais HM. *The History of the Negro in Medicine;* Byrd WM, Clayton LA. An American health dilemma; Charatz-Litt C. A chronicle of racism: The effects of the White medical community on Black health. *Journal of the National Medical Association* 1992; 84:717–725; Beardsley EH. *A History of Neglect: Health Care for Blacks and Mill Workers in the Twentieth-Century South.* Knoxville: The University of Tennessee Press, 1987.

4. Brinkley A. *The Unfinished Nation;* Zinn H. *A People's History of the United States;* Frazier EF. *The Negro in the United States.* Rev. ed. New York: Macmillan, 1957; Brawely B. *A Social History of the American Negro: Being a History of the Negro Problem in the United States Including a History and Study of the Republic of Liberia.* New York: Macmillan, 1921. Paperback ed. London: Collier-Macmillan, 1970; Morais HM. *The History of the Negro in Medicine;* Byrd WM, Clayton LA. An American health dilemma; Charatz-Litt C. A chronicle of racism; Beardsley EH. *A History of Neglect,* 11–41.

5. Starr P. *The Social Transformation of American Medicine,* 243–244.

6. Brinkley A. *The Unfinished Nation,* 597.

7. Low WA, Clift VA. eds. *Encyclopedia of Black America.* New York: McGraw-Hill. Reprint ed. New York: Da Capo Press, 1981, 86.

8. Brinkley A. *The Unfinished Nation,* 596.

9. McNeil Jr., DG. Its past on its sleeve, tribe seeks Bonn's apology. *New York Times,* May 31, 1998:3.

10. Brinkley A. *The Unfinished Nation;* O'Reilly K. *Nixon's Piano: Presidents and Racial Politics from Washington to Clinton.* New York: The Free Press, 1995, 63–97; Kennedy DM. *Birth Control in America: The Career of Margaret Sanger.* New Haven, CT: Yale University Press, 1970; Davis AY. *Women, Race and Class.* New York: Random House, 1981. Reprint ed. New York: Vintage Books, 1983, 202–221; Chase A. *The Legacy of Malthus: The Social Costs of the New Scientific Racism.* New York: Knopf, 1980, 71, 105, 517–518; Haller MH. *Eugenics: Hereditarian Attitudes in American Thought.* New Brunswick, NJ: Rutgers University Press, 1963; Takaki RY. *Iron Cages: Race and Culture in Nineteenth-Century America.* New York: Knopf, 1979; McNeil Jr., DG. Its past on its sleeve, tribe seeks Bonn's apology; Chalk F, Jonassohn K. *The History and Sociology of Genocide: Analyses and Case Studies.* New Haven, CT: Yale University Press, 1990, 173–203, 230–248.

11. Brinkley A. *The Unfinished Nation,* 574.

12. Zinn H. *A People's History of the United States,* 339.

13. Brinkley A. *The Unfinished Nation,* 512–652; Sitkoff H. History of the United States. In *The New Grolier Multimedia Encyclopedia,* release 6, MPC Version. Novato, CA: Grolier Electronic Publishing, The Software Toolworks, 1993, 33–41; Racial relationship. *Journal of the National Medical Association* 1918, 10:44–45; O'Reilly K. *Nixon's Piano,* 63–108; Burns, R, Ades, L. *The Way West: The Way the West Was Lost and Won, 1845–1893* (video). For: *The American Experience,* Boston: WGBH Educational Foundation, 1995; Dr. Jackson and the Tulsa, Okla., riots. *Journal of the National Medical Association* 1921, 202–203; Chase A. *The Legacy of Malthus,* 68–360; Morais HM. *The History of the Negro in Medicine,* 67–124; Beardsley EH. *A History of Neglect,* 11–41.

14. Brinkley A. *The Unfinished Nation,* 643.

15. Brinkley A. *The Unfinished Nation,* 628.

16. Dr. Jackson and the Tulsa, Okla., riots; Staples B. Unearthing a riot, *New York Times Magazine,* Dec. 19, 1999, sec. 6:64, 67, 68.

17. Brinkley A. *The Unfinished Nation*, 629.

18. Chase A. *The Legacy of Malthus*, 482.

19. Brinkley A. *The Unfinished Nation*, 512–652; O'Reilly K. *Nixon's Piano*, 63–110; Zinn H. *A People's History of the United States*; Staples B. Unearthing a riot, 6:64; Burke J. *The Day the Universe Changed*. Boston: Little, Brown, 1985, 239–273; Racial relationship; Chase A. *The Legacy of Malthus*, 482, 658, 68–360; Tucker WH. *The Science and Politics of Racial Research*. Urbana, IL: University of Illinois Press, 1994; Kennedy DM. *Birth Control in America*; Reilly PR. *The Surgical Solution: A History of Involuntary Sterilization in the United States*. Baltimore: The Johns Hopkins University Press, 1991; Larson EJ. *Summer for the Gods: The Scopes Trial and America's Continuing Debate over Science and Religion*. Cambridge, MA: Harvard University Press, 1997; Weisbord RG. *Genocide? Birth Control and the Black American*. Westport, CT: Greenwood Press, 1975, Lewis DL. *W.E.B. Du Bois: Biography of a Race, 1868–1919*. New York: Henry Holt, 1993; Brawely B. *A Social History of the American Negro*; Logan RW. *The Negro in American Life and Thought: The Nadir, 1877–1901*. New York: Macmillan, 1954. *The Betrayal of the Negro: From Rutherford B. Hayes to Woodrow Wilson*. Enlarged, rev., Paperback ed. London: Collier-Macmillan, 1965; NMA communications. Minutes of the Richmond meeting of the National Medical Association, 1918. *Journal of the National Medical Association* 1918; 10:128–141; Cannon GE. The Negro medical professon and the United States Army. *Journal of the National Medical Association* 1919; 11:21–28; Cobb WM. John Andrew Kenney, M.D., 1874–1950. *Journal of the National Medical Association* 1950; 42:175–177, 176; Du Bois WEB. Opinion: The Tuskegee hospital. *The Crisis* 1923; 26:106–107; Smith JD, Nelson KR. *The Sterilization of Carrie Buck*. Far Hills, NJ: New Horizon Press, 1989; Davenport CB. *Heredity in Relation to Eugenics*. New York: Henry Holt, 1911; Haller MH. *Eugenics*; Terman LM. *The Measurement of Intelligence*. Boston: Houghton Mifflin, 1916; Terman LM. Feeble-minded children in the public schools of California. *School and Society* 1917; 5:165; Goddard HH. How shall we educate mental defectives? *The Training School Bulletin* 1912; 9:43; Goddard HH. *Human Efficiency and Levels of Intelligence*. Princeton, NJ: Princeton University Press, 1920. Yerkes RM, ed. *Psychological Examining in the United States Army*. Memoir XV. Washington, DC: National Academy of Sciences, 1921; Kevles DJ. *In the Name of Eugenics: Genetics and the Uses of Human Heredity*. Berkeley: University of California Press, 1985; Herrnstein RJ, Murray C. *The Bell Curve: Intelligence and Class Structure in American Life*. New York: The Free Press, 1994.

20. Townsend AM. President's address, Rock City Academy, October 17, 1910. *Journal of the National Medical Association* 1911; 3:33–39; Kenney JA. Second annual oration on surgery. *Journal of the National Medical Association* 1941; 33:203–214; Bullough B, Bullough VL. *Poverty, Ethnic Identity, and Health Care*. New York: Appleton-Century-Crofts, 1972; Roberts D. *Killing the Black Body: Race, Reproduction, and the Meaning of Liberty*. New York: Pantheon Books, 1997; Reilly PR. *The Surgical Solution*; Weisbord RG. *Genocide? Birth Control and the Black American*.

21. Numbers RL. *Almost Persuaded: American Physicians and Compulsory Health Insurance, 1912–1920*. Baltimore: The Johns Hopkins University Press, 1978; Bullough B, Bullough VL. *Poverty, Ethnic Identity, and Health Care*; Reilly PR. *The Surgical Solution*; Beck A. *Beck A. A History of the British Medical Administration of East Africa, 1900–1950*. Cambridge, MA: Harvard University Press, 1970; Saltman RB, ed. *The International Handbook of Health-Care Systems*. New York: Greenwood Press, 1988; Shryock RH. *The Development of Modern Medicine: An Interpretation of the Social and Scientific Factors Involved*. Madison, WI: The University of Wisconsin Press, 1974; Starr P. *The Social Transformation of American Medicine*; Ginzberg E. The monetarization of medical care. *New England Journal of Medicine* 1984; 310:1162–1165; Navarro V. *Dangerous to Your Health: Capitalism in Health Care*. New York: Monthly Review Press, 1993.

22. Starr P. *The Social Transformation of American Medicine*, 235–275; Shryock RH. *Medicine in America: Historical Essays*. Baltimore: The Johns Hopkins Press, 1966, 381–430; Byrd WM, Clayton LA. An American health dilemma; Dula A. Toward an African-American perspective on bioethics. *Journal of Health Care for the Poor and Underserved* 1991; 2:259–269; Myrdal G. *An American Dilemma: The Negro Problem and Modern Democracy*. New York: Harper & Row, 1944; Churchill LR. *Rationing Health Care in America*; Sheridan RB. *Doctors and Slaves: A Medical and Demographic History of Slavery in the British West Indies, 1680–1834*. Cambridge: Cambridge University Press, 1985. Savitt TL. *Medicine and Slavery: The Diseases and Health Care of Blacks in Antebellum Virginia*. Urbana: University of Illinois Press, 1987. Beck A. *A History of the British Medical Administration of East Africa, 1900–1950*, 12–16, 198–210; Saltman RB, ed. *The Interna-*

*tional Handbook of Health-Care Systems*, 230–233; Benatar SR. Medicine and health care in South Africa. *New England Journal of Medicine* 1986; 315:527–532; Patton Jr. A. Howard University and Meharry medical schools in the training of African physicians, 1868–1978. In: Harris JE, ed. *Global Dimension of the African Diaspora*. 2nd ed. Washington, DC: Howard University Press, 1993, 109–124; Byrd WM. Race, biology, and health care: Reassessing a relationship. *Journal of Health Care for the Poor and Underserved* 1990; 1:278–292.

23. Brinkley A. *The Unfinished Nation*, 431–652; Zinn H. *A People's History of the United States*, 167–367; Morais HM. *The History of the Negro in Medicine*; Byrd WM, Clayton LA. The "slave health deficit": Racism and health outcomes. *Health/PAC Bulletin* 1991; 21:25–28; Byrd WM, Clayton LA. An American health dilemma; Kenney JA. Health problems of the Negroes. *Journal of the National Medical Association* 1911; 3:127–135; Kenney JA. The hospital idea essentially altruistic. *Journal of the National Medical Association* 1912; 4:193–199; Kenney JA. Some facts concerning Negro nurse training schools and their graduates. *Journal of the National Medical Association* 1919; 11:53–68; Kenney JA. Hospital symposium: The Negro hospital renaissance. *Journal of the National Medical Association* 1930; 22:109–157; Boyle EM. A comparative physical study of the Negro. *Journal of the National Medical Association* 1912; 4:124–130; Frazier EF. *The Negro in the United States*; Roberts JM. *History of the World*. New York: Knopf, 1976. Rev. rep. ed., *The Penguin History of the World*. London: Penguin Books, 1990; Cobb WM. The Black American in medicine. *Journal of the National Medical Association* 73 1981; 73(suppl 1):1183–1244; Takaki RY. *Iron Cages*, 108–144; Chase A. *The Legacy of Malthus*.

24. Chase A *The Legacy of Malthus*, 48.

25. Starr P. *The Social Transformation of American Medicine*, 237.

26. Starr P. *The Social Transformation of American Medicine*, 180–270; Numbers RL. *Almost Persuaded*; Jonas G. *The Circuit Riders*; Duffy J. *The Sanitarians: A History of American Public Health*. Urbana: University of Illinois Press, 1990; Rosen G. *A History of Public Health*. Expanded ed. Baltimore: The Johns Hopkins University Press, 1993; Zinn H. *A People's History of the United States*; Brinkley A. *The Unfinished Nation*, 462–652; Rosenberg CE. Community and communities: The evolution of the American hospital. In: Long DE, Golden J, eds. *The American General Hospital: Communities and Social Contexts*. Ithaca: Cornell University Press, 1989, 3–17; Ackerknecht EH. *A Short History of Medicine*. Rev. ed. Baltimore: The Johns Hopkins University Press, 1982; Shryock RH. *Medicine in America*; Navarro V. *Dangerous to Your Health*.

27. Perry JE. *Forty Cords of Wood: Memoirs of a Medical Doctor*. Jefferson City, MO: Lincoln University Press, 1947, 244.

28. Kusmer KL *A Ghetto Takes Shape: Black Cleveland, 1870–1930*. Urbana: University of Illinois Press, 1976, 60–61.

29. Farley R, Allen WR. *The Color Line and the Quality of Life in America*. New York: Oxford University Press, 1989, 30.

30. Rosenberg CE. Community and communities, 3–17, quote p. 4.

31. Navarro V. *Dangerous to Your Health*; Starr P. *The Social Transformation of American Medicine*, 180–266; Numbers RL. *Almost Persuaded*; Brown ER. *Rockefeller Medicine Men*; Veatch RM. *A Theory of Medical Ethics*. New York: Basic Books, 1981; Zinn H. *A People's History of the United States*; Brinkley A. *The Unfinished Nation*, 462–652; Rosenberg CE. Community and communities; Kusmer KL. *A Ghetto Takes Shape*, 60–61, 180–182; Bailey EJ. Health care use patterns among Detroit African Americans: 1910–1939. *Journal of the National Medical Association* 1990; 82:721–723; Frazier EF. *The Negro in the United States*, 171–305; Dowling HF. *City Hospitals: The Undercare of the Underprivileged*. Cambridge, MA: Harvard University Press, 1982; Bracey JH, Meier A, Rudwick E, eds. *The Rise of the Ghetto*. Belmont, CA: Wadsworth, 1971; Myrdal G. *An American Dilemma*; Hirsch AR. *Making the Second Ghetto: Race and Housing in Chicago 1940–1960*. Cambridge: Cambridge University Press, 1983, xi–39; Shryock RH. *Medicine in America*; Beardsley EH. *A History of Neglect*, 11–41; Woodson CG. *The Rural Negro*. New York: Russell and Russell, 1930; Johnson CS. *Shadow of the Plantation*. Chicago: University of Chicago Press, 1934.

32. Last JM, ed. *A Dictionary of Epidemiology*. 2nd ed. New York: Oxford University Press, 1988, 57.

33. Tocqueville A de. *Democracy in America*. 2 vols. Ed. JP Mayer, trans. G Lawrence. New York: Harper & Row, 1966. Paperback ed., New York: Harper Perennial, 1988, 530.

34. Starr P. *The Social Transformation of American Medicine*; Stevens RA. *American Medicine and the Public Interest*; Tocqueville A de. *Democracy in America*, 448, 530–532, 636–639; Morais HM. *The History of the Negro in Medicine*; Byrd WM, Clayton LA. *A Black Health Trilogy* (video and 188-page report). Washington, DC: The National Medical Association and the African American Heritage and Education Foundation, 1991; Cobb WM. The Black American in medicine.

35. Starr P. *The Social Transformation of American Medicine*, 180–266; Morais HM. *The History of the Negro in Medicine*; Jonas G. *The Circuit Riders*; Dummett CO. *Afro-Americans in Dentistry: Sequence and Consequence of Events*. N.P.: Clifton O. Dummett, 1978; Lyons AS, Petrucelli RJ. *Medicine: An Illustrated History*. New York: Harry N. Abrams, 1978; Stevens RA. *American Medicine and the Public Interest*; Ackerknecht EH. *A Short History of Medicine*; Navarro V. *Dangerous to Your Health*.

36. Shryock RH. *The Development of Modern Medicine*, 384.

37. Shryock RH. *The Development of Modern Medicine*, 381–402; Ackerknecht EH. *A Short History of Medicine*, 227–240; Bender GA. *Great Moments in Medicine*. Detroit: Northwood Institute Press, 1966.

38. The efficiency of arsphenamines. *Journal of the National Medical Association* 1924; 16:19.

39. Shryock RH. *The Development of Modern Medicine*, 381–402; Ackerknecht EH. *A Short History of Medicine*, 227–240; Bender GA. *Great Moments in Medicine*; The efficiency of arsphenamines; Starr P. *The Social Transformation of American Medicine*; Lyons AS, Petrucelli RJ. *Medicine*.

40. Shryock RH. *The Development of Modern Medicine*, 381–402; Ackerknecht EH. *A Short History of Medicine*, 227–240; Bender GA. *Great Moments in Medicine*; Starr P. *The Social Transformation of American Medicine*.

41. Shryock RH. *The Development of Modern Medicine*, 384.

42. Shryock RH. *Medicine in America*, 385.

43. Bailey EJ. Health care use patterns among Detroit African Americans: 1910–1939, 722.

44. Bailey EJ. Health care use patterns among Detroit African Americans: 1910–1939, 722.

45. Shryock RH. *The Development of Modern Medicine*, 384–430; Ackerknecht EH. *A Short History of Medicine*; Starr P. *The Social Transformation of American Medicine*, 180–266; Zinn H. *A People's History of the United States*; Brinkley A. *The Unfinished Nation*, 462–652; Byrd WM, Clayton LA. *A Black Health Trilogy*; Byrd WM, Clayton LA. An American health dilemma; Bailey EJ. Health care use patterns among Detroit African Americans: 1910–1939; Kusmer KL. *A Ghetto Takes Shape*; Morais HM. *The History of the Negro in Medicine*, 59–125.

46. Gamble VN. *Making a Place for Ourselves: The Black Hospital Movement 1920–1945*. New York: Oxford University Press, 1995, 3, 7.

47. Rosenberg CE. *The Care of Strangers: The Rise of America's Hospital System*. New York: Basic Books, 1987, 237–352; Downing LC. Some points on developing a hospital. *Journal of the National Medical Association* 1919; 11:95–98; Starr P. *The Social Transformation of American Medicine*, 180–266; Vogel MJ. *The Invention of the Modern Hospital: Boston 1870–1930*. Chicago: The University of Chicago Press, 1980; The National Hospital Association. *Journal of the National Medical Association* 1924; 16:48–49; Gamble VN. *The Black Community Hospital: A Historical Perspective*. New York: Garland, 1989; Gamble VN. *Making a Place for Ourselves*; Gamble VN. Hospitals, Black. In Salzman J, Smith DL, West C. eds. *Encyclopedia of African-American Culture and History*. 5 vols. New York: Macmillan Library Reference USA, 1996, 1305–1309; Factors influencing the fate of the Negro hospital. *Journal of the National Medical Association* 1967, 59:217; Bailey EJ. Health care use patterns among Detroit African Americans: 1910–1939.

48. Rosenberg CE. *The Care of Strangers*, 237–352; Starr P. *The Social Transformation of American Medicine*, 180–266; Gamble VN. *Making a Place for Ourselves*; Vogel MJ. *The Invention of the Modern Hospital*; A grave injustice. *Journal of the National Medical Association* 1911; 3:159; New York hospitals. *Journal of the National Medical Association* 1912; 4:143–144.

49. Rosenberg CE. Community and communities, 5.

50. Rosenberg CE. Community and communities, 5.

51. Rosenberg CE. Community and communities, 5.

52. Rosenberg CE. *The Care of Strangers*, 340; Rosenberg CE. Community and communities; Downing LC. Some points on developing a hospital; Roman CV. Fifty years' progress of the Amer-

ican Negro in health and sanitation. *Journal of the National Medical Association* 1917; 9:61–67; Morais HM. *The History of the Negro in Medicine*; Bullough B, Bullough VL. *Poverty, Ethnic Identity, and Health Care*; Ginzberg E. The monetarization of medical care.

53. Rosenberg CE. Community and communities, 8–9.

54. Stevens RA. Times past, times present. In: Long DE, Golden J, eds. *The American General Hospital*, 191–206, quote p. 202.

55. Rosenberg CE. *The Care of Strangers*; Rosenberg CE. Community and communities; Morais HM. *The History of the Negro in Medicine*; Bullough B, Bullough VL. *Poverty, Ethnic Identity, and Health Care*; Stevens RA. Times past, times present; Gamble VN. The Negro hospital renaissance: The Black hospital movement, 1920–1945. In: Long DE, Golden J, eds. *The American General Hospital*, 82–105; Gamble VN. Hospitals, Black; Gamble VN. *Making a Place for Ourselves*, 3–34; Jones PA. Three against the storm: Facing an awesome array of problems, black community hospitals advance toward an uncertain future. *The Crisis* October 1985; 92:35; Travella S. Black hospitals struggle to survive. *Modern Health Care* July 2, 1990, 20–26; Travella S. Black hospitals struggling to survive: Of more than 200 medical centers, only 8 are left. *Health: A Weekly Journal of Medicine, Science and Society, The Washington Post*, September 11, 1990: 12; Ginzberg E. The monetarization of medical care.

56. Kovner AR. *Health Care Delivery in the United States*. 4th ed. New York: Springer, 1990, 355.

57. Gamble VN. The Negro hospital renaissance, 91.

58. Kovner AR. *Health Care Delivery in the United States*, 354–355; Starr P. *The Social Transformation of American Medicine*, 145–179; Stevens RA. *American Medicine and the Public Interest*, 91–92; Gamble VN. *Making a Place for Ourselves*, 35–69; Gamble VN. The Negro hospital renaissance; The National Hospital Association; National Medical Association (Chairman, Green HM). *A More or Less Critical Review of the Hospital Situation Among Negroes in the United States*. Published under the auspices of the National Hospital Association, National Medical Association: N.D.

59. Stoline A, Weiner JP. *The New Medical Marketplace: A Physician's Guide to the Health Care Revolution*. Baltimore: The Johns Hopkins University Press, 1988, 6–46; Starr P. *The Social Transformation of American Medicine*, 145–266; Aaron HJ, Schwartz WB. *The Painful Prescription: Rationing Hospital Care*. Washington, DC: The Brookings Institution, 1984; Menzel PT. *Medical Costs, Moral Choices: A Philosophy of Health Care Economics in America*. New Haven, CT: Yale University Press, 1983; Brown ER. *Rockefeller Medicine Men*; Jonas G. *The Circuit Riders*; Frazier EF. *The Negro in the United States*; Brawely B. *A Social History of the American Negro*; Morais HM. *The History of the Negro in Medicine*, 67–124; Jones JH. *Bad Blood: The Tuskegee Syphilis Experiment*. New York: The Free Press, 1981.

60. Starr P. *The Social Transformation of American Medicine*, 110.

61. Starr P. *The Social Transformation of American Medicine*, 181–266; Haller JS Jr. *American Medicine in Transition 1840–1910*. Urbana, IL: University of Illinois Press, 1981; Morais HM. *The History of the Negro in Medicine*; Rothstein WG. *American Physicians in the 19th Century: From Sects to Science*. Baltimore, MD: The Johns Hopkins University Press, 1972; Byrd WM, Clayton LA. "Designing a New Health Care System for the United States," Boston: Harvard School of Public Health, 1992; Wilson FA, Neuhauser D. *Health Services in the United States*. 2nd ed. Cambridge, MA: Ballinger, 1982.

62. Ludmerer KM. *Learning to Heal: The Development of American Medical Education*. New York: Basic Books, 1985, 191.

63. Hubbard GW. Yesterday, today and tomorrow. *Journal of the National Medical Association* 1909; 1:133–135; Gamble HF. Report on medical education. *Journal of the National Medical Association* 1910; 2:23–29.

64. Ludmerer KM. *Learning to Heal: The Development of American Medical Education*. New York: Basic Books, 1985; Rothstein WG. *American Medical Schools and the Practice of Medicine*. New York: Oxford University Press, 1987; Jonas G. *The Circuit Riders*; Epps HR. The Howard University medical department in the Flexner era: 1910–1929. *Journal of the National Medical Association* 1989; 81:885; Gamble VN. *Making a Place for Ourselves*; Ginzberg E, Dutka AB. *The Financing of Biomedical Research*. Baltimore: The Johns Hopkins University Press, 1989; Savitt TL. The education of Black physicians at Shaw University, 1882–1918. In: Crow J, Hatley FJ, eds. *Black Americans in North Carolina and the South*. Chapel Hill: University of North Carolina Press, 1984,

160–188; Savitt TL. Abraham Flexner and the black medical schools. In: Barzansky EM, Gevitz N, eds. *Flexner and the 1990s: Medical Education in the 20th Century*. N.P., 1989, 23.

65. Brinkley A. *The Unfinished Nation: A Concise History of the American People*. New York: Knopf, 1993, 462–652; Starr P. *The Social Transformation of American Medicine*, 145–266; Zinn H. *A People's History of the United States*; Morais HM. *The History of the Negro in Medicine*; Kenney JA. Some facts concerning Negro nurse training schools and their graduates, 66; Announcement. The John A. Andrew Memorial Hospital, Tuskegee Institute, Alabama. *Journal of the National Medical Association* 1918; 10:xx; Harlan LR, Smock RW, eds. *The Booker T. Washington Papers* (Vol. 9), Urbana: The University of Illinois Press, 1972–1984, 404–405, 415–416; National Medical Association (Chairman, Green HM). *A More or Less Critical Review of the Hospital Situation Among Negroes in the United States*; Gamble VN. *The Black Community Hospital*: A Historical Perspective; Gamble VN. Hospitals, Black; Cobb WM. *Medical Care and the Plight of the Negro*. New York: The National Association for the Advancement of Colored People, 1947.

66. Brown ER. *Rockefeller Medicine Men*, 1.

67. Brown ER. *Rockefeller Medicine Men*, 7.

68. Jonas G. *The Circuit Riders*, 23–24.

69. Brown ER. *Rockefeller Medicine Men*, 10–11.

70. Brown ER. *Rockefeller Medicine Men*; Jonas G. *The Circuit Riders*; Navarro V. *Dangerous to Your Health*; Jacobson TC. *Making Medical Doctors: Science and Medicine at Vanderbilt Since Flexner*. Tuscaloosa: The University of Alabama Press. 1987; Bullough B, Bullough VL. *Poverty, Ethnic Identity, and Health Care*; Byrd WM, Clayton LA. An American health dilemma; Charatz-Litt C. A chronicle of racism; Epps HR. The Howard University medical department in the Flexner era: 1910–1929; Savitt TL. Abraham Flexner and the black medical schools, 65–81; Morais HM. *The History of the Negro in Medicine*; Beardsley EH. *A History of Neglect*, 11–41.

71. Starr P. *The Social Transformation of American Medicine*, 194.

72. Brinkley A. *The Unfinished Nation*, 462–652; Starr P. *The Social Transformation of American Medicine*, 180–266; Rosen G. *The Structure of American Medical Practice 1875–1941*. Philadelphia: University of Pennsylvania Press, 1983; Zinn H. *A People's History of the United States*; Woodson CG. *The Negro Professional Man and the Community*. Washington, DC: The Association for the Study of Negro Life and History, 1934.

73. Starr P. *The Social Transformation of American Medicine*; Stevens RA. *American Medicine and the Public Interest*; Savitt TL. Entering a white profession: Black physicians in the new south, 1880–1920. *Bulletin of the History of Medicine* 1987; 61:507–540; Perry JE. *Forty Cords of Wood*, 138–166; Morais HM. *The History of the Negro in Medicine*; Woodson, CG. *The Negro Professional Man and the Community*; Brown ER. *Rockefeller Medicine Men*; Kaufman M, Galishoff S, Savitt TL, eds. *Dictionary of American Medical Biography*. 2 vols. Westport, CT: Greenwood Press, 1984, 37–38, 541, 806–807.

74. Roberts D. *Killing the Black Body*, 73.

75. Roberts D. *Killing the Black Body*, 59.

76. Roberts D. *Killing the Black Body*, 72.

77. Roberts D. *Killing the Black Body*, 61.

78. Chase A. *The Legacy of Malthus*, 12.

79. Roberts D. *Killing the Black Body*, 59.

80. Roberts D. *Killing the Black Body*, 60.

81. Roberts D. *Killing the Black Body*, 80.

82. Chase A. *The Legacy of Malthus*, 14.

83. Galton F. *Inquiries into Human Faculty*. London: Macmillan, 1883, 24–25.

84. Roberts D. *Killing the Black Body*, 61.

85. Roberts D. *Killing the Black Body*, 56–103.

86. Chase A. *The Legacy of Malthus*, 116–117.

87. Weisbord RG. *Genocide? Birth Control and the Black American*, 32.

88. Roberts D. *Killing the Black Body*, 61.

89. Weisbord RG. *Genocide? Birth Control and the Black American*, 32.

90. Popenoe P, Johnson RH. *Applied Eugenics*. New York: Macmillan, 1918, 284.

91. Popenoe P, Johnson RH. *Applied Eugenics*, 290.

92. Roberts D. *Killing the Black Body*, 67.

93. Tucker WH. *The Science and Politics of Racial Research*, 31.

94. Popenoe P, Johnson RH *Applied Eugenics*, 284–296; Roberts D. *Killing the Black Body*, 22–103; Chase A. *The Legacy of Malthus*; Weisbord RG. *Genocide? Birth Control and the Black American*; Tucker WH. *The Science and Politics of Racial Research*; Kennedy DM. *Birth Control in America*; Davis AY. *Women, Race and Class*; An impending crisis; Errata. *Journal of the National Medical Association* 1910, 2:193–194; Birnie CW. The influence of environment and race on diseases. *Journal of the National Medical Association* 1910; 2:243–251; Kenney JA. Syphillis and the American Negro—A medico-sociologic study. *Journal of the National Medical Association* 1911; 3:115–117; Roman CV. Ethnology. *Journal of the National Medical Association* 1912; 4:352–354; Spingarn AB. The war and venereal diseases among Negroes. *Journal of the National Medical Association* 1919; 11:47–52; Lydston GF. *Diseases of Society*. Philadelphia: Lippincott, 1906; Fineberg KS, et al. *Obstetrics/Gynecology and the Law*. Ann Arbor, MI: Health Administration Press, 1984; Jones JH. *Bad Blood*; Haller MH. *Eugenics*; Kevles DJ. *In the Name of Eugenics*; Birth control. *Journal of the National Medical Asociation* 1917; 9:93–94; Reilly PR. *The Surgical Solution*.

95. Chase A. *The Legacy of Malthus*, 125.

96. Chase A. *The Legacy of Malthus*, 119.

97. Chase A. *The Legacy of Malthus*, 118–137.

98. Proctor RN. *Racial Hygiene: Medicine under the Nazis*. Cambridge, MA: Harvard University Press, 1988, 286.

99. Proctor RN. *Racial Hygiene*, 400, note 11.

100. Chase A. *The Legacy of Malthus*, 116.

101. Chase A. *The Legacy of Malthus*, 116.

102. Chase A. *The Legacy of Malthus*, 117.

103. Chase A. *The Legacy of Malthus*, 300–301.

104. Chase A. *The Legacy of Malthus*, 313.

105. Smith JD, Nelson KR. *The Sterilization of Carrie Buck*, 177.

106. Weisbord RG. *Genocide? Birth Control and the Black American*, 33–34.

107. Chase A. *The Legacy of Malthus*, 126.

108. Weisbord RG. *Genocide? Birth Control and the Black American*, 34.

109. Roberts D. *Killing the Black Body*, 71.

110. Roberts D. *Killing the Black Body*, 71.

111. Allen GE. Eugenics comes to America. In: Jacoby R, Glauberman N, eds. *The Bell Curve Debate: History, Documents, Opinions*. New York: Times Books Division of Random House, 1995, 441–475; Smith JD, Nelson KR. *The Sterilization of Carrie Buck*; Davenport CB. *Heredity in Relation to Eugenics*; Reilly PR. *The Surgical Solution*; Rice TB. *Racial Hygiene—A Practical Discussion of Eugenics and Race Culture*. New York: Macmillan, 1929; Hall PF. *Immigration and its Effects on the United States*. New York: Henry Holt, 1906; Trombley S. "The Lynchburg Story" (video), *Discovery Journal*, July 1994; Chase A. *The Legacy of Malthus*; Weisbord RG. *Genocide? Birth Control and the Black American*, 25–40; Shipman P. *The Evolution of Racism: Human Differences and the Use and Abuse of Science*. New York: Simon and Schuster, 1994, 126–127; Roberts D. *Killing the Black Body*; Proctor RN. *Racial Hygiene*; Larson EJ. *Sex, Race, and Science: Eugenics in the Deep South*. Baltimore: The Johns Hopkins University Press, 1995; Boyle EM. A comparative physical study of the Negro.

112. Reed J. Scientific racism. In: Wilson CR, Ferris W, eds. *Encyclopedia of Southern Culture*. Chapel Hill: The University of North Carolina Press, 1989, 1358–1360.

113. Jones JH. *Bad Blood*, 17.

114. Chalk F, Jonassohn K. *The History and Sociology of Genocide*, 231.

115. Jones JH. *Bad Blood*, 28.

116. Jones JH. *Bad Blood*, 16–29; Chase A. *The Legacy of Malthus*; Reed J. Scientific racism, 1358–1360; Brandt AM. Racism and research: The case of the Tuskegee Syphilis Study. In: Leavitt JW, Numbers RL, eds. *Sickness and Health in America: Readings in the History of Medicine and Public Health*. Madison, WI: The University of Wisconsin Press, 1985, 331–343; Haller JS Jr. *Out-*

*casts from Evolution: Scientific Attitudes of Racial Inferiority, 1859–1900*. New York: McGraw-Hill, 1971; Smith JD, Nelson KR. *The Sterilization of Carrie Buck*; Reilly PR. *The Surgical Solution*; Smith DB. *Health Care Divided: Race and Healing a Nation*. Ann Arbor: The University of Michigan Press, 1999; Morais HM. *The History of the Negro in Medicine*; Byrd WM, Clayton LA. *A Black Health Trilogy*; Bullough B, Bullough VL. *Poverty, Ethnic Identity, and Health Care*; Beecher HK. Ethics and clinical research. *New England Journal of Medicine* 1966; 274:1354–1360; Washington HA. Of men and mice: Human guinea pigs: Unethical testing targets Blacks and the poor. *Emerge* October 1994 (1)(6):24; Duster T. *Backdoor to Eugenics*. New York: Routledge, 1990.

117. Jonas G. *The Circuit Riders*; Stevens RA. *American Medicine and the Public Interest*; Brown ER. *Rockefeller Medicine Men*; Williams AW. Venereal disease. *Journal of the National Medical Association* 1918; 10:183–184; Starr P. *The Social Transformation of American Medicine*; Roman CV. Fifty years' progress of the American Negro in health and sanitation. *Journal of the National Medical Association* 1917; 9:61–67; Byrd WM. Race, biology, and health care; Byrd WM, Clayton LA. An American health dilemma; Morais HM. *The History of the Negro in Medicine*; Tucker WH. *The Science and Politics of Racial Research*; Roberts D. *Killing the Black Body*.

118. Hoffmann FL. *Race Traits and Tendencies of the American Negro*. New York: American Economic Association, 1st Ser., XI, August, 1896.

119. Gilliam EW. The African in the United States. *Popular Science Monthly* 1883; 22:437.

120. Tucker WH. *The Science and Politics of Racial Research*, 33.

121. Tucker WH. *The Science and Politics of Racial Research*, 33.

122. Tucker WH. *The Science and Politics of Racial Research*, 33.

123. Tucker WH. *The Science and Politics of Racial Research*, 30.

124. Tucker WH. *The Science and Politics of Racial Research*, 31.

125. Bacon CS. The race problem. *Medicine* 1903; 9:338, 342.

126. Tucker WH. *The Science and Politics of Racial Research*, 31.

127. Tucker WH. *The Science and Politics of Racial Research*, 32–33.

128. Du Bois WEB *Mortality among Negroes in Cities*. Atlanta: Atlanta University Publications, 1896, 20.

129. Du Bois WEB. *Mortality among Negroes in Cities*, 9.

130. Breeden JO. Science and medicine. In: Wilson CR, Ferris W, eds. *Encyclopedia of Southern Culture*, 1337–1343; Duffy J. States' rights medicine. In: Wilson CR, Ferris W, eds. *Encyclopedia of Southern Culture*, 1337–1343; Reed J. Scientific racism; Hart N. The social and economic environment and human health. In: Detels R. et al., eds. *Oxford Textbook of Public Health*. Vol. 1. *The Scope of Public Health*. 3rd ed. New York: Oxford University Press, 1997, 95–123; Hart N. The social and economic environment and human health. In: Holland WW et al., eds. *Oxford Textbook of Public Health*. Vol. 1. *Influences of Public Health*. 2nd ed. Oxford: Oxford University Press, 1991, 151–195; Hoffmann FL. *Race Traits of the American Negro*; Ewbank DC. History of Black mortality and health before 1940. In: Willis DP, ed. *Health Policies and Black Americans*. New Brunswick, NJ: Transaction Publishers, 1989, 100–12; Roman CV. Ethnology.

131. Du Bois WEB. *The Health and Physique of the Negro American*. Atlanta: Atlanta University Publications, 1906, 5.

132. Farley R, Allen WR. *The Color Line and the Quality of Life in America*, 24.

133. Farley R, Allen WR. *The Color Line and the Quality of Life in America*, 31.

134. Farley R, Allen WR. *The Color Line and the Quality of Life in America*, 30.

135. Ewbank DC. History of Black mortality and health before 1940, 109.

136. Ewbank DC. History of Black mortality and health before 1940; Roman CV. Fifty years' progress of the American Negro in health and sanitation, 65; Farley R. *Growth of the Black Population: A Study of Demographic Trends*. Chicago: Markham, 1970; Farley R, Allen WR. *The Color Line and the Quality of Life in America*; Fredrickson GM. *The Black Image in the White Mind: The Debate on Afro-American Character and Destiny, 1871–1914*. New York: Harper & Row, 1971. Reprint ed. Middletown, CT: Wesleyan University Press, 1987, 249–253; Haller JS Jr. *Outcasts from Evolution*, 60–68; Du Bois WEB. Mortality among Negroes in Cities, 1896; Du Bois WEB. *The Health and Physique of the Negro American*; Byrd WM, Clayton LA. *A Black Health Trilogy*; Morais HM. *The History of the Negro in Medicine*.

137. Ewbank DC. History of Black mortality and health before 1940, 123.

138. Ewbank DC. History of Black mortality and health before 1940; Farley R. *Growth of the Black Population*; Farley R, Allen WR. *The Color Line and the Quality of Life in America*; Leavitt JW, Numbers RL. Sickness and health in America: An Overview. In: Leavitt JW, Numbers RL, eds. *Sickness and Health in America: Readings in the History of Medicine and Public Health*, 3–10; Morais HM. *The History of the Negro in Medicine*.

139. Du Bois WEB. *The Health and Physique of the Negro American*, 80.

140. Ewbank DC. History of Black mortality and health before 1940, 116.

141. Ewbank DC. History of Black mortality and health before 1940; Farley R. *Growth of the Black Population*; Farley R, Allen WR. *The Color Line and the Quality of Life in America*; Du Bois WEB. *The Health and Physique of the Negro American*; Byrd WM, Clayton LA. *A Black Health Trilogy*; Morais HM. *The History of the Negro in Medicine*; Leavitt JW, Numbers RL. Sickness and health in America; Smith DS. Differential mortality in the United States before 1900. *Journal of Interdisciplinary History* 1983; 13:735–759.

142. Du Bois WEB. *The Health and Physique of the Negro American*, 76.

143. Du Bois WEB. *The Health and Physique of the Negro American*, 80, 84.

144. Du Bois WEB. *The Health and Physique of the Negro American*, 88.

145. Ewbank DC. History of Black mortality and health before 1940, 109.

146. Du Bois WEB. *The Health and Physique of the Negro American*, 88.

147. Du Bois WEB. *The Health and Physique of the Negro American*, 88.

148. Ewbank DC. History of Black mortality and health before 1940; Farley R. *Growth of the Black Population*; Farley R, Allen WR. *The Color Line and the Quality of Life in America*; Du Bois WEB. *The Health and Physique of the Negro American*; Byrd WM, Clayton LA. *A Black Health Trilogy*; Morais HM. *The History of the Negro in Medicine*; Boyle EM. A comparative physical study of the Negro; Leavitt JW, Numbers RL. Sickness and health in America.

149. Leavitt JW, Numbers RL. Sickness and health in America, 3.

150. Leavitt JW, Numbers RL. Sickness and health in America, 5.

151. Murrell Thomas W. Syphilis and the American Negro–a medico-sociologic study. *Journal of the National Medical Association* 1910; 54:846.

152. Fields BJ. In: Burns K. *The Civil War*. Pt. 3. *1862—Forever Free*. (9-part video doc.) Washington, DC, Public Broadcasting System, 1990.

153. Jones JH. *Bad Blood*, 23–24.

154. Starr P. *The Social Transformation of American Medicine*; Brown ER. *Rockefeller Medicine Men*; Shryock RH. *The Development of Modern Medicine*; Roman CV. An impending crisis. *Journal of the National Medical Association* 1909; 1:232–236; Frazier EF. *The Negro in the United States*; Myrdal G. *An American Dilemma*; Du Bois WEB. *The Health and Physique of the Negro American*; Boyle EM. Comparative physical study of the Negro. *Journal of the National Medical Association* 1912; 4:124–129; Taylor JM. The Negro and his health problems. *Medical Record* September 21, 1912; Byrd WM, Clayton LA. *A Black Health Trilogy*; Morais HM. *The History of the Negro in Medicine*; Smith DB. *Health Care Divided*; Leavitt JW, Numbers RL. Sickness and health in America; Roman CV. Ethnology; Bowens GJ. President's annual address. *Journal of the National Medical Association* 1917; 9:127–128; Murrell TW. Syphilis and the American Negro—a medico-sociologic study. *Journal of the American Medical Association* 1910; 54:846–847; Roman CV. The venereal situation. *Journal of the National Medical Association* 1919; 11:72; Williams AW. Venereal disease. *Journal of the National Medical Association* 1918; 10:183–184; Dula A. Toward an African-American perspective on bioethics; Churchill LR. *Rationing Health Care in America*; Veatch RM. *A Theory of Medical Ethics*.

155. Scott HC. Annual address. *Journal of the National Medical Association* 1910; 2:96–101, 98.

156. Stevens RA. *American Medicine and the Public Interest*; Starr P. *The Social Transformation of American Medicine*; Morais HM. *The History of the Negro in Medicine*; Rothstein WG. *American Physicians in the 19th Century*; Brown ER. *Rockefeller Medicine Men*; Dula A. Toward an African-American perspective on bioethics; Roberts MJ, Clyde AT. *Your Money or Your Life: The Health Care Crisis Explained*. New York: Doubleday, 1993; Ginzberg E. *The Medical Triangle: Physicians, Politicians, and the Public*. Cambridge, MA: Harvard University Press, 1990; Ginzberg E, Ostow M. *The Road to Reform: The Future of Health Care in America*. New York: The Free Press, 1994.

157. Stevens RA. *American Medicine and the Public Interest*, 59.

158. Stevens RA. *American Medicine and the Public Interest*, 59.

159. Gamble HF. Report of committee on medical education and Negro medical schools. *Journal of the National Medical Association* 1909; 1:257–258; Gamble HF. Report on medical education; Errata: Acknowledged receipt of Bulletin Number Four. *Journal of the National Medical Association* 1910; 2:193–194; Errata. *Journal of the National Medical Association* 1910, 2:306; Items of interest: Item 7. *Journal of the National Medical Association* 1912; 4:96–97; Roman CV. A college education as a requisite preparation for the study of medicine. *Journal of the National Medical Association* 1917; 9:6–8; Needs of Negro medical schools. *Journal of the National Medical Association* 1917; 9:221–223; The passing of Leonard Medical School. *Journal of the National Medical Association* 1918; 10:126; Smith DB. *Health Care Divided*, 14–16.

160. Stevens RA. *American Medicine and the Public Interest*, 180.

161. Stevens RA. *American Medicine and the Public Interest*, 34–171; Starr P. *The Social Transformation of American Medicine*, 79–266; Morais HM. *The History of the Negro in Medicine*, 59–110; Shea S, Fullilove MT. Entry of black and other minority students in US medical schools: Historical perspectives and recent trends. *New England Journal of Medicine* 1985; 313:933–940; Cobb WM. *The First Negro Medical Society: A History of the Medico-Chirurgical Society of the District of Columbia*. Washington, DC: The Associated Publishers, 1939, 2–4; Cobb WM. *Medical Care and the Plight of the Negro*, 17–19; Epps Jr. CH, Johnson DG, Vaughan AL. Black medical pioneers: African-American 'firsts' in academic and organized medicine: part 1. *Journal of the National Medical Association* 1993; 85:629–644; Epps Jr. CH, Johnson DG, Vaughan AL. Black medical pioneers: African-American 'firsts' in academic and organized medicine: part 2. *Journal of the National Medical Association* 1993; 85:703–720; Epps Jr. CH, Johnson DG, Vaughan AL. Black medical pioneers: African-American 'firsts' in academic and organized medicine: part 3. *Journal of the National Medical Association* 1993; 85:777–796; O'Bannion LC. Are African-American doctors being locked out? The down side of managed care. *National Medical Association News* 1995 (Winter), 1.

162. Ludmerer KM. *Learning to Heal*, 245.

163. Ludmerer KM. *Learning to Heal*; Rothstein WG. *American Medical Schools and the Practice of Medicine*; Byrd WM. Race, biology, and health care; Starr P. *The Social Transformation of American Medicine*; Stevens RA. *American Medicine and the Public Interest*, 34–171; Cobb WM. The Black American in medicine; Savitt TL. The education of Black physicians at Shaw University, 1882–1918; Savitt TL. Entering a white profession.

164. Hubbard GW. Yesterday, today and tomorrow; Racial relationship, 44.

165. Stevens RA. *American Medicine and the Public Interest*, 34–171; Brown ER. *Rockefeller Medicine Men*; Rothstein WG. *American Physicians in the 19th Century*; Rothstein WG. *American Medical Schools and the Practice of Medicine*.

166. Stoline A, Weiner JP. *The New Medical Marketplace*, 17.

167. Stoline A, Weiner JP. *The New Medical Marketplace*; Stevens RA. *American Medicine and the Public Interest*, 34–171; Starr P. *The Social Transformation of American Medicine*, 79–266; Needs of Negro medical schools; Hubbard GW. Yesterday, today and tomorrow; Morais HM. *The History of the Negro in Medicine*; Ludmerer KM. *Learning to Heal*.

168. Starr P. *The Social Transformation of American Medicine*, 117.

169. Stevens RA. *American Medicine and the Public Interest*, 63–64.

170. Gamble HF. Report of committee on medical education and Negro medical schools; Gamble HF. Report on medical education.

171. Stevens RA. *American Medicine and the Public Interest*, 64.

172. Stevens RA. *American Medicine and the Public Interest*, 64.

173. Stevens RA. *American Medicine and the Public Interest*, 64.

174. Stevens RA. *American Medicine and the Public Interest*, 34–171; Starr P. *The Social Transformation of American Medicine*, 79–266; Morais HM. *The History of the Negro in Medicine*, 59–110; Ludmerer KM. *Learning to Heal*; Brown ER. *Rockefeller Medicine Men*; Cobb WM. The Black American in medicine; Bullough B, Bullough VL. *Poverty, Ethnic Identity, and Health Care*.

175. Stevens RA. *American Medicine and the Public Interest*, 65.

176. Stevens RA. *American Medicine and the Public Interest*, 34–171; Starr P. *The Social Transformation of American Medicine*, 112–123; Gamble HF. Report of committee on medical educa-

tion and Negro medical schools; Gamble HF. Report on medical education; Needs of Negro medical schools; Morais HM. *The History of the Negro in Medicine*, 59–110; Savitt TL. The education of Black physicians at Shaw University, 1882–1918; Brown ER. *Rockefeller Medicine Men*.

177. Brown ER. *Rockefeller Medicine Men*, 139.

178. Brown ER. *Rockefeller Medicine Men*, 139.

179. Brown ER. *Rockefeller Medicine Men*, 141.

180. Brown ER. *Rockefeller Medicine Men*, 127.

181. Bevan AD. Cooperation in medical education and medical service. *Journal of the American Medical Association* 1928; 90:1173; Brown ER. *Rockefeller Medicine Men*; Jonas G. *The Circuit Riders*; Stevens RA. *American Medicine and the Public Interest*, 34–171.

182. Brown ER. *Rockefeller Medicine Men*, 143.

183. Stevens RA. *American Medicine and the Public Interest*; Brown ER. *Rockefeller Medicine Men*; Starr P. *The Social Transformation of American Medicine*.

184. Brown ER. *Rockefeller Medicine Men*, 144–145.

185. Kaufman M et al. eds. *Dictionary of American Medical Biography*, 251–252; Stevens RA. *American Medicine and the Public Interest*; Brown ER. *Rockefeller Medicine Men*; Starr P. *The Social Transformation of American Medicine*; Flexner A. *Medical Education in the United States and Canada: A Report to the Carnegie Foundation for the Advancement of Teaching*. New York: Carnegie Foundation for the Advancement of Teaching, Bulletin no. 4, 1910.

186. Stoline A, Weiner JP. *The New Medical Marketplace*, 17.

187. Ackerknecht EH. *A Short History of Medicine*; Shryock RH. *The Development of Modern Medicine*; Stoline A, Weiner JP. *The New Medical Marketplace*; Stevens RA. *American Medicine and the Public Interest*; Ludmerer KM. *Learning to Heal*; Smith DB. *Health Care Divided*; Starr P. *The Social Transformation of American Medicine*; Morais HM. *The History of the Negro in Medicine*; Brown ER. *Rockefeller Medicine Men*; Cobb WM. The Black American in medicine; Epps HR. The Howard University medical department in the Flexner era: 1910–1929; Savitt TL. Abraham Flexner and the black medical schools; Hunt S. The Flexner report and Black academic medicine: An assignment of place. *Journal of the National Medical Association* 1993; 85:151–155; Charatz-Litt C. A chronicle of racism; Wolinsky H. Healing wounds: Lonnie R. Bristow steps up to head the American Medical Association, one of the nation's premier—and most rigidly segregated—professional groups. *Emerge* July/August 1994 (July/August, No. 10); Geiger HJ. Annotation: Racism resurgent—building a bridge to the 19th century. *American Journal of Public Health* 1997; 87:1765–1766; Geiger HJ. Comment: Ethnic cleansing in the groves of academe. *American Journal of Public Health* 1998; 88:1299–1300.

188. Brown ER. *Rockefeller Medicine Men*, 145.

189. Ludmerer KM. *Learning to Heal*, 172.

190. Flexner A. "Reminiscences of Dr. Welch," May 16, 1934, File, "William Welch," General Correspondence, Abraham Flexner Papers, Library of Congress; Stevens RA. *American Medicine and the Public Interest*; Brown ER. *Rockefeller Medicine Men*; Starr P. *The Social Transformation of American Medicine*; Ludmerer KM. *Learning to Heal*; Rothstein WG. *American Medical Schools and the Practice of Medicine*.

191. Ludmerer KM. *Learning to Heal*, 174.

192. Brown ER. *Rockefeller Medicine Men*, 145.

193. Stevens RA. *American Medicine and the Public Interest*, 68.

194. Rothstein WG. *American Medical Schools and the Practice of Medicine*, 163.

195. Rothstein WG *American Medical Schools and the Practice of Medicine*, 163.

196. Stevens RA. *American Medicine and the Public Interest*; Brown ER. *Rockefeller Medicine Men*; Starr P. *The Social Transformation of American Medicine*; Ludmerer KM. *Learning to Heal*; Rothstein WG. *American Medical Schools and the Practice of Medicine*; Savitt TL. Abraham Flexner and the Black medical schools. In: Barzansky EM, Gevitz N, eds. *Beyond Flexner: Medical Education in the twentieth Century*. New York: Greenwood Press, 1992, 65–81; Kenney JA. The passing of the Leonard Medical School. *Journal of the National Medical Association* 1918; 10:126; Summerville J. *Educating Black Doctors: A History of Meharry Medical College*. University, Alabama: The University of Alabama Press, 1983.

197. Stevens RA. *American Medicine and the Public Interest*, 68.

198. Stevens RA. *American Medicine and the Public Interest*, 69.

199. Stevens RA. *American Medicine and the Public Interest*; Brown ER. *Rockefeller Medicine Men*; Starr P. *The Social Transformation of American Medicine*; Ludmerer KM. *Learning to Heal*; Rothstein WG. *American Medical Schools and the Practice of Medicine*; Jonas G. *The Circuit Riders*.

200. Brown ER. *Rockefeller Medicine Men*, 153.

201. Ludmerer KM. *Learning to Heal*, 60, 248.

202. Ludmerer KM. *Learning to Heal*, 248.

203. Stevens RA. *American Medicine and the Public Interest*; Savitt TL. The education of Black physicians at Shaw University, 1882–1918; Ludmerer KM. *Learning to Heal*; Brown ER. *Rockefeller Medicine Men*; Wolinsky H. Healing wounds; Shea S, Fullilove MT. Entry of black and other minority students in US medical schools; Walsh MR. *Doctors Wanted No Women Need Apply: Sexual Barriers in the Medical Profession, 1835–1975*. New Haven, CT: Yale University Press, 1977; Geiger HJ. Annotation: Racism resurgent; Geiger HJ. Comment: Ethnic cleansing in the groves of academe.

204. Hunt S. The Flexner report and Black academic medicine.

205. Hunt S. The Flexner report and Black academic medicine, 153.

206. Hunt S. The Flexner report and Black academic medicine, 153.

207. Flexner A. *Medical Education in the United States and Canada*.

208. Hunt S. The Flexner report and Black academic medicine, 153.

209. Hunt S. The Flexner report and Black academic medicine, 153.

210. Flexner A. *Medical Education in the United States and Canada*.

211. Flexner A. *Medical Education in the United States and Canada*.

212. Flexner A. *Medical Education in the United States and Canada*.

213. Flexner A. *Medical Education in the United States and Canada*.

214. Flexner A. *Medical Education in the United States and Canada*.

215. Flexner A. *Medical Education in the United States and Canada*.

216. Hunt S. The Flexner report and Black academic medicine, 155.

217. Hunt S. The Flexner report and Black academic medicine, 153.

218. Brown ER. *Rockefeller Medicine Men*, 149.

219. Flexner A. *Medical Education in the United States and Canada*; Epps HR. The Howard University medical department in the Flexner era: 1910–1929; Hunt S. The Flexner report and Black academic medicine; Savitt TL. Abraham Flexner and the black medical schools; Brown ER. *Rockefeller Medicine Men*; Johnston GS. The Flexner report and the Black medical schools. *Journal of the National Medical Association* 1984; 76:223–225; Kenney JA. Health problems of the Negroes; Barabin JH. President's address: Negro Medical, Dental and Pharmaceutical Association of Arkansas. *Journal of the National Medical Association* 1912; 4:130; Smith DB. *Health Care Divided*, 14–16; Walsh MR. *Doctors Wanted: No Women Need Apply*; Ludmerer KM. *Learning to Heal*; Rothstein WG. *American Medical Schools and the Practice of Medicine*; Summerville J. *Educating Black Doctors*.

220. Ludmerer KM. *Learning to Heal*, 220.

221. Rothstein WG. *American Medical Schools and the Practice of Medicine*, 174.

222. Rothstein WG *American Medical Schools and the Practice of Medicine*, 174–175.

223. Rothstein WG *American Medical Schools and the Practice of Medicine*, 174–175.

224. Rothstein WG. *American Medical Schools and the Practice of Medicine*, 175.

225. Needs of Negro medical schools, 1917; Bullough B, Bullough VL. *Poverty, Ethnic Identity, and Health Care*; Cobb WM. *Medical Care and the Plight of the Negro*; Cobb WM. *Progress and Portents for the Negro in Medicine*. New York: The National Association for the Advancement of Colored People, 1948; Townsend AM. President's address, Rock City Academy, October 17, 1910.

226. Dowling HF. *City Hospitals*; Stevens RA. *American Medicine and the Public Interest*; Brown ER. *Rockefeller Medicine Men*; Starr P. *The Social Transformation of American Medicine*; Ludmerer KM. *Learning to Heal*; Rothstein WG. *American Medical Schools and the Practice of Medicine*; Bullough B, Bullough VL. *Poverty, Ethnic Identity, and Health Care*; Bailey EJ. Health care use patterns among Detroit African Americans, 1910–1939.

227. Stevens RA. *American Medicine and the Public Interest*, 145.

228. Mossell NF. The modern hospital: Its construction, organization and management. *Journal of the National Medical Association* 1909; 1:94–102.

229. Stevens RA. *American Medicine and the Public Interest*; Starr P. *The Social Transformation of American Medicine*; Morais HM. *The History of the Negro in Medicine*; Mossell NF. The modern hospital; Du Bois WEB. *The Health and Physique of the Negro American*; The South and Negro education. *Journal of the National Medical Association* 1919; 11:157–158; Bullock HA. *A History of Negro Education in the South: From 1619 to the Present*. New York: Praeger Publishers, 1967; Kluger R. *Simple Justice: The History of Brown v. Board of Education and Black America's Struggle for Equality*. New York: Knopf, 1976. Paperback ed. New York: Vintage Books, 1977; Mossell NF. The modern hospital; McBride D. *Integrating the City of Medicine: Blacks in Philadelphia Health Care, 1910–1965*. Philadelphia: Temple University Press, 1989. Gamble VN. The Negro hospital renaissance; Gamble VN. Hospitals, Black.

230. Starr P. *The Social Transformation of American Medicine*; Rosenberg CE. *The Care of Strangers*; Stoline A, Weiner JP. *The New Medical Marketplace*; Cobb WM. Robert Fulton Boyd. *Journal of the National Medical Association* 1953; 45: 233–234.

231. Starr P. *The Social Transformation of American Medicine*; Numbers RL. *Almost Persuaded*; Stevens RA. *American Medicine and the Public Interest*; Brinkley A. *The Unfinished Nation*; Zinn H. *A People's History of the United States*; Morais HM. *The History of the Negro in Medicine*; Boyle EM. A comparative physical study of the Negro; Townsend AM. President's address, Rock City Academy, October 17, 1910; Roman CV. Fifty years' progress of the American Negro in health and sanitation; Roman CV. Vitality of the Negroes. *Journal of the National Medical Association* 1910; 2:180–181; Kenney JA. Some facts concerning Negro nurse training schools and their graduates; Kenney JA. Health problems of the Negroes.

232. Starr P. *The Social Transformation of American Medicine*, 258.

233. Stoline A, Weiner JP. *The New Medical Marketplace*, 19.

234. Starr P. *The Social Transformation of American Medicine*, 259.

235. Rosen G. *The Structure of American Medical Practice 1875–1941*, 69.

236. Starr P. *The Social Transformation of American Medicine*, 265.

237. Stevens RA. *American Medicine and the Public Interest*, 186.

238. Editorial. *Journal of the American Medical Association* 1932; 99:2035

239. Stevens RA. *American Medicine and the Public Interest*, 187.

240. Stevens RA. *American Medicine and the Public Interest*, 188.

241. Starr P. *The Social Transformation of American Medicine*; Numbers RL. *Almost Persuaded*; Stevens RA. *American Medicine and the Public Interest*; Morais HM. *The History of the Negro in Medicine*; Rosen G. *The Structure of American Medical Practice 1875–1941*.

242. Starr P. *The Social Transformation of American Medicine*, 184.

243. Starr P. *The Social Transformation of American Medicine*, 185.

244. Starr P. *The Social Transformation of American Medicine*; U.S. Department of Health and Human Services. *Health in America: 1776–1976*. Washington, DC: U.S. Health Resources Administration, DHEW Pub. No. (HRA) 76–616, 1976; Breeden JO. Science and medicine, 1340–1342; Duffy J. *The Sanitarians*; Lyons AS, Petrucelli RJ. *Medicine*; Shryock RH. *The Development of Modern Medicine*, 403–430.

245. Stevens RA. *American Medicine and the Public Interest*, 51; Starr P. *The Social Transformation of American Medicine*, 180–189; Shryock RH. *The Development of Modern Medicine*, 403–430; Byrd WM, Clayton LA. *A Black Health Trilogy*; Stevens RA. *In Sickness and in Wealth: American Hospitals in the Twentieth Century*. Baltimore: The Johns Hopkins University Press, 1999, 48–51, 86–89.

246. Starr P. *The Social Transformation of American Medicine*, 183.

247. Starr P. *The Social Transformation of American Medicine*, 186–187.

248. Starr P. *The Social Transformation of American Medicine*, 187–188.

249. Stevens RA. *In Sickness and in Wealth*, 48–51, 86–89; Stevens RA. *American Medicine and the Public Interest*; Starr P. *The Social Transformation of American Medicine*, 180–89; Shryock RH. *The Development of Modern Medicine*, 403–430; Duffy J. *The Sanitarians*; Rosen G. *The Structure*

*of American Medical Practice 1875–1941*; Byrd WM, Clayton LA. *A Black Health Trilogy*; Beardsley EH. *A History of Neglect*.

250. Chase A *The Legacy of Malthus*; Jones JH. *Bad Blood*; Breeden JO. Science and medicine; Brandt AM. Racism and research, 331–343; Jonas G. *The Circuit Riders*; Tucker WH. *The Science and Politics of Racial Research*; Roberts D. *Killing the Black Body*; Kevles DJ. *In the Name of Eugenics*; Haller MH. *Eugenics*; Degler CN. *In Search of Human Nature: The Decline and Revival of Darwinism in American Social Thought*. New York: Oxford University Press, 1991; Hubbard R, Wald E. *Exploding the Gene Myth: How Genetic Information Is Produced and Manipulated by Scientists, Physicians, Employers, Insurance Companies, Educators, and Law Enforcers*. Boston: Beacon Press, 1993; Gould SJ. *The Mismeasure of Man*. New York: W. W. Norton, 1981; Stanton W. *The Leopard's Spots: Scientific Attitudes Toward Race in America, 1815–1859*. Chicago: The University of Chicago Press, 1960; Lemann N. *The Big Test: The Secret History of the American Meritocracy*. New York: Farrar, Straus and Giroux, 1999; Proctor RN. *Racial Hygiene*; Roman CV. Ethnology; Lemann N. The structure of success in America. *The Atlantic Monthly* August 1995; 2 (276):41; Lemann N. The great sorting: The first mass administrations of a scholastic-aptitude test led with surprising speed to the idea that the nation's leaders would be the people who did well on tests. *The Atlantic Monthly* September 1995, 3 (276):84.

251. Woodson CG. *The Negro Professional Man and the Community*, 26, 27.

252. Brawley B. *A Social History of the American Negro*, 311.

253. Savitt TL. "A journal of our own": *The Medical and Surgical Observer* at the beginnings of an African-American medical profession in late nineteenth-century America. *Journal of the National Medical Association* 1996; 88:52–60, 115–122.

254. Byrd WM. Letters to the editor, "The NMA founding date laid to rest," *Journal of the National Medical Association* 1993; 85:99.

255. Cobb WM. *The First Negro Medical Society*, 1–21; Woodson CG. *The Negro Professional Man and the Community*; Smith DB. *Health Care Divided*, 14–16, 32–95; Gamble VN. *Making a Place for Ourselves*; Factors influencing the fate of the Negro hospital; Summerville J. Formation of a black medical profession in Tennessee, 1880–1920. *Journal of the Tennessee Medical Association* October, 1983; 644–646; First item: Books, lay press, etc. *Journal of the National Medical Association* 1911; 3:192–193, 192; Savitt TL. "A journal of our own"; Morais HM. *The History of the Afro-American in Medicine*. Cornwells Heights, PA: The Publishers Agency, 1978, 52–57; Wilkins JH. History of the Lone Star State Medical, Dental and Pharmaceutical Association. *Journal of the National Medical Association* 1912; 4:87–88; Scott HC. Annual address; Byrd WM, Letters to the editor. "The NMA founding date laid to rest."

256. Our New York meeting. *Journal of the National Medical Association* 1909; 1:33–34; Minutes. *Journal of the National Medical Association* 1909; 1:24–32.

257. Cobb WM. *The First Negro Medical Society*, 4.

258. Cobb WM. *The First Negro Medical Society*, 4.

259. Cobb WM. *The First Negro Medical Society*, 3.

260. Cobb WM. *The First Negro Medical Society*, 1–5; Bullough VL. *The Development of Medicine as a Profession: The Contribution of the Medieval University to Modern Medicine*. New York: Hafner, 1966, 1–5; Morais HM. *The History of the Negro in Medicine*; Perry JE. *Forty Cords of Wood*, 387–410; Minutes. *Journal of the National Medical Association* 1909; 1:24–32.

261. Hubbard GW. Yesterday, today and tomorrow.

262. Roman CV. The deontological orientation of its membership and chief function of a medical society. *Journal of the National Medical Association* 1909; 1:19–23; Kenney JA. Report of the Secretary of the National Medical Association ... August 25, 1908. *Journal of the National Medical Association* 1909; 1:34–35; The John A. Andrew clinical society. *Journal of the National Medical Association* 1919; 11:70–71; Hubbard GW. Yesterday, today and tomorrow; Buckler II. *Daniel Hale Williams: Negro Surgeon*. New York: Pitman Publishing, 1954; Morais HM. *The History of the Negro in Medicine*; Haley JT. Dr. Robert Fulton Boyd. In: *The Afro-American Encyclopedia*. Nashville, TN: Haley and Florida, 1896, 59–62; Cobb WM. Robert Fulton Boyd; Cobb WM. Nathan Francis Mossell, M.D., 1856–1946. *Journal of the National Medical Association* 1954; 46:118–130; Perry JE. *Forty Cords of Wood*; News items. *Journal of the National Medical Association* 1909; 1:102; Townsend AM. President's address, Rock City Academy, October 17, 1910; Kenney JA. Health problems of the Negroes; Savitt TL. Entering a white profession.

263. Organ CH, Kosiba MM, eds. A *Century of Black Surgeons: The U.S.A. Experience*. 2 vols. Norman, OK: Transcript Press, 163.

264. Organ CH, Kosiba MM, eds. *A Century of Black Surgeons*, 163.

265. Haber L. *Black Pioneers of Science and Invention*. San Diego: Harcourt Brace Jovanovich, 1970, 147.

266. Haber L. *Black Pioneers of Science and Invention*, 147.

267. Organ CH, Kosiba MM, eds. *A Century of Black Surgeons*, 172.

268. Savitt TL. Abraham Flexner and the Black medical schools, 81.

269. Morais HM. *The History of the Negro in Medicine*; Haber L. *Black Pioneers of Science and Invention*, 123–151; Organ CH, Kosiba MM, eds. *A Century of Black Surgeons*; Alexander PN. Maynard, Aubre de Lambert (1901– ). In: Salzman J, Smith DL, West C. eds. *Encyclopedia of African-American Culture and History*. 5 vols. New York: Macmillan Library Reference USA, 1996, 1721–1722; Reynolds PP. Hospitals and civil rights, 1945–1963: *Simkins v. Moses H. Cone Memorial Hospital. Annals of Internal Medicine* 1997; 126:898–906; Gamble HF. Report of committee on medical education and Negro medical schools; Gamble HF. Report on medical education; Gamble HF, France JJ, Anderson JC. Report of committee on medical education on colored hospitals. *Journal of the National Medical Association* 1910, 2:283–290; Errata, 1910, 2:306; Needs of Negro medical schools, 1917; Lester JA. The evolution in the standard of medical education. *Journal of the National Medical Association* 1918; 10:10–12; The passing of Leonard Medical School; The South and Negro education; Beardsley EH. *A History of Neglect*; Cornely PB. Observations on the health progress of Negroes in the U.S. during the past two decades. *Southern Medical Journal* 1941; 34:1286.

270. Organ CH, Kosiba MM. eds. *A Century of Black Surgeons*, 202–203.

271. Morais HM. *The History of the Negro in Medicine*, 94–95.

272. Savitt TL. Abraham Flexner and the Black medical schools; Morais HM. *The History of the Negro in Medicine*; Factors influencing the fate of the Negro hospital; Organ CH, Kosiba MM. eds. *A Century of Black Surgeons*; Epps HR. The Howard University medical department in the Flexner era: 1910–1929.

273. Kenney JA. Some facts concerning Negro nurse training schools and their graduates.

274. Hine DC. *Black Women in White: Racial Conflict and Cooperation in the Nursing Profession, 1890–1950*. Bloomington: Indiana University Press, 1989, 9.

275. Hine DC. Nursing. In: Salzman J, Smith DL, West C. eds. *Encyclopedia of African-American Culture and History*. 5 vols. New York: Macmillan Library Reference USA, 1996, 2034, 2034–2036; quote p. 2034.

276. Summerville J. *Educating Black Doctors*, 51.

277. Summerville J. *Educating Black Doctors*, 51.

278. Morais HM. *The History of the Negro in Medicine*, 70–74; Hine DC. *Black Women in White*; Carnegie ME. Black nurses in the United States: 1879–1992. *Journal of the National Black Nurses Association* 1992; 6:13–18; Kenney JA. Some facts concerning Negro nurse training schools and their graduates; Hine DC. Nursing.

279. Roman CV. An impending crisis, 232.

280. Errata, 1910; 2:193–194.

281. Birnie CW. The influence of environment and race on diseases.

282. Roman CV. An impending crisis, 232.

283. Roberts D. *Killing the Black Body*, 63.

284. Chase A. *The Legacy of Malthus*, 231.

285. Guthrie RV. *Even the Rat Was White: A Historical View of Psychology*. 2nd ed. Boston: Allyn & Bacon, 1998, 57.

286. Guthrie RV. *Even the Rat Was White*, 60.

287. Chase A. *The Legacy of Malthus*, 232.

288. Chase A. *The Legacy of Malthus*, 236.

289. Chase A. *The Legacy of Malthus*; Kevles DJ. *In the Name of Eugenics*; Haller MH. *Eugenics*; Tucker WH. *The Science and Politics of Racial Research*; Roberts D. *Killing the Black Body*;

Proctor RN. Nazi biomedical policies. In: Caplan AL, ed. *When Medicine Went Mad: Bioethics and the Holocaust.* Totowa, NJ: Humana Press, 1992, 23–42.

290. Goddard HH. The Binet tests in relation to immigration. *Journal of Psycho-Asthenics* 1913/1914; 18:105.

291. Guthrie RV. *Even the Rat Was White,* 61.

292. Chase A. *The Legacy of Malthus,* 234.

293. Guthrie RV. *Even the Rat Was White,* 62.

294. Guthrie RV. *Even the Rat Was White,* 62.

295. Chase A. *The Legacy of Malthus,* 234.

296. Terman LM. *The Measurement of Intelligence.* Boston: Houghton Mifflin, 1916, 92.

297. Terman LM. *The Measurement of Intelligence,* 92.

298. Chase A. *The Legacy of Malthus,* 235.

299. Chase A. *The Legacy of Malthus,* 242.

300. Guthrie RV. *Even the Rat Was White,* 63.

301. Chase A. *The Legacy of Malthus,* 243.

302. Guthrie RV. *Even the Rat Was White,* 66.

303. Guthrie RV. *Even the Rat Was White,* 66.

304. Chase A. *The Legacy of Malthus,* 251.

305. Chase A. *The Legacy of Malthus,* 262–264.

306. Lemann N. The structure of success in America, 41, 48.

307. Roberts D. *Killing the Black Body,* 63.

308. Roberts D. *Killing the Black Body,* 63.

309. Lemann N. The structure of success in America, 41, 48.

310. Lemann N. The structure of success in America, 41, 49–50.

311. Lemann N. The structure of success in America, 41, 48.

312. Tucker WH. *The Science and Politics of Racial Research,* 77.

313. Roman CV. An impending crisis, 1909, 232.

314. Roman CV. An impending crisis, 1909, 235.

315. Chase A. *The Legacy of Malthus,* 226–360; Guthrie RV. *Even the Rat Was White,* 3–110; Herrnstein RJ, Murray C. *The Bell Curve;* Roberts D. *Killing the Black Body;* Tucker WH. *The Science and Politics of Racial Research,* 1–137; Lemann N. *The Big Test;* Lemann N. The structure of success in America, 41; Lemann N. The great sorting, 84; Goddard HH. *The Kallikak Family: A Study in the Heredity of Feeblemindedness.* New York: Macmillan, 1912; Dugdale RL. *The Jukes: A Study in Crime, Pauperism, and Heredity.* 4th ed. New York: G.P. Putnam's Sons, 1910; Estabrook KA, Davenport CB. *The Nam Family: A Study in Cacogenics.* Cold Spring Harbor, NY: Eugenics Record Office, 1912; Roman CV. An impending crisis; Boyle EM. A comparative physical study of the Negro; Ethnology; Errata, 1910, 2:193–194; The N.M.A.—a review and forecast. *Journal of the National Medical Association* 1910; 2:295–297, 296; Boyle EM. A comparative physical study of the Negro; Kenney JA. Syphilis and the American Negro; Health and disease. *Journal of the National Medical Association* 1912; 4:142–143.

316. Roberts IH. Presidential address to the Old Dominion Medical Society. *Journal of the National Medical Association* 1920; 12:8–10.

317. Roberts IH. Presidential address to the Old Dominion Medical Society.

318. Barbeau AE, Henri F. *The Unknown Soldiers: Black American Troops in World War I.* Philadelphia: Temple University Press, 1974, 37.

319. Cannon GE. The Negro medical profession and the United States Army. *Journal of the National Medical Association* 1919; 11:21–28.

320. Barbeau AE, Henri F. *The Unknown Soldiers,* 41.

321. Barbeau AE, Henri F. *The Unknown Soldiers,* 48.

322. Barbeau AE, Henri F. *The Unknown Soldiers,* 50.

323. Barbeau AE, Henri F. *The Unknown Soldiers,* 41.

324. Barbeau AE, Henri F. *The Unknown Soldiers,* 100.

325. Barbeau AE, Henri F. *The Unknown Soldiers,* 100.

326. Barbeau AE, Henri F. *The Unknown Soldiers*, 53.

327. Morais HM. *The History of the Negro in Medicine*, 113.

328. Perry JE. *Forty Cords of Wood*, 402.

329. Perry JE. *Forty Cords of Wood*, 402.

330. Chase A. *The Legacy of Malthus*; Cannon GE. The Negro medical profession and the United States Army; Barbeau AE, Henri F. *The Unknown Soldiers*; Hine DC. *Black Women in White*, 102–105; Morais HM. *The History of the Negro in Medicine*, 59–130; Gamble VN. *Making a Place for Ourselves*; Cobb WM. John Andrew Kenney, M.D., 1874–1950; Alexander PN. Kenney, John Andrew. In: Salzman J, Smith DL, West C, eds. *Encyclopedia of African-American Culture and History*. 5 vols. New York: Macmillan Library Reference USA, 1996, 1533; National Medical Association communications—the minutes of the executive board. *Journal of the National Medical Association* 1918; 10:138–139; Recognition of the N.M.A. *Journal of the National Medical Association* 1919; 11:75; Requirements for membership in the N.M.A. *Journal of the National Medical Association* 1919; 11:76.

331. Epps HR. The Howard University medical department in the Flexner era: 1910–1929; Savitt TL. Abraham Flexner and the Black medical schools; Du Bois WEB. *Mortality among Negroes in Cities*, 1896; Du Bois WEB. *The Health and Physique of the Negro American*; Needs of Negro medical schools, 1917; Lester JA. The evolution in the standard of medical education; Beardsley EH. *A History of Neglect*; Starr P. *The Social Transformation of American Medicine*; Farley R. *Growth of the Black Population*; Farley R, Allen WR. *The Color Line and the Quality of Life in America*; Ewbank DC. History of Black mortality and health before 1940; Duffy J. *The Sanitarians*.

332. Morais HM. *The History of the Negro in Medicine*, 88.

333. Morais HM. *The History of the Negro in Medicine*, 87.

334. Dowling HF. *City Hospitals*, 107.

335. Dowling HF. *City Hospitals*, 107–108.

336. Dowling HF. *City Hospital*, 108.

337. Commission for the Study of Uncinariasis. *Journal of the National Medical Association* 1910; 2:140–141; Tuberculosis Commission of the National Medical Association. *Journal of the National Medical Association* 1910:2:142; The N.M.A.—a review and forecast; Kenney JA. Health problems of the Negroes; Green HM. Report of the pellagra commission. *Journal of the National Medical Association* 1917; 9:223–227; National medical commissions. *Journal of the National Medical Association* 1918; 10:125; Boyle EM. A comparative physical study of the Negro; Clayton LA, Byrd WM. The African American cancer crisis, part 1: The problem. *Journal of Health Care for the Poor and Underserved* 1993; 4: 83–101; Byrd WM, Clayton LA. The African-American cancer crisis, part II: A prescription. *Journal of Health Care for the Poor and Underserved* 1993; 4:102–116; Kenney JA. Hospital symposium; Gamble VN. *Making a Place for Ourselves*; Needs of Negro medical schools, 1917; The National Hospital Association; National Medical Association (Chairman, Green HM). *A More or Less Critical Review of the Hospital Situation among Negroes in the United States*; Dowling HF. *City Hospitals*, 107–108; Boyd RF. Mercy Hospital. *Journal of the National Medical Association* 1909; 1:43; Mossell NF. The modern hospital; Errata, 1910, 2:133–136; New hospital opened today. *Journal of the National Medical Association* 1911; 3:105–107; Kenney JA. The hospital idea essentially altruistic; The tidewater colored hospital. *Journal of the National Medical Association* 1919; 11:21; Morais HM. *The History of the Negro in Medicine*; Kenney JA. Some facts concerning Negro nurse training schools and their graduates; Downing LC. Some points on developing a hospital; Hine DC. *Black Women in White*; Beardsley EH. *A History of Neglect*; Starr P. *The Social Transformation of American Medicine*; Cannon GE. The Negro medical profession and the United States Army; Roman CV. An impending crisis.

338. Roman CV. An impending crisis, 235.

339. Morais HM. *The History of the Negro in Medicine*; Beardsley EH. *A History of Neglect*. Roman CV. Fifty years' progress of the American Negro in health and sanitation.

## Chapter Two

1. Brinkley A. *The Unfinished Nation: A Concise History of the American People*. New York: Knopf, 1993, 659.

2. Brinkley A. *The Unfinished Nation*, 653–746; Sitkoff H. History of the United States. In: *The New Grolier Multimedia Encyclopedia*. Release 6, MPC Version. Novato, CA: Grolier Electronic Publishing, The Software Toolworks, 1993; Starr P. *The Social Transformation of American Medicine*. New York: Basic Books, 1982.

3. Hamilton DC. Great Depression and the New Deal. In: Salzman J, Smith DL, West C, eds. *Encyclopedia of African-American Culture and History*. 5 Vols. New York: Macmillan Library Reference USA, Simon & Schuster Macmillan, 1996, 1134–1142, quote 1135.

4. Shryock RH. *The Development of Modern Medicine: An Interpretation of the Social and Scientific Factors Involved*. Madison: University of Wisconsin Press, 1974, 414.

5. Hamilton DC. Great Depression and the New Deal. *Encyclopedia of African-American Culture and History*, 1135; Brinkley A. *The Unfinished Nation*, 653–706; Sitkoff H. History of the United States; Shryock RH. *The Development of Modern Medicine*, 413–417; Garrett L. *Betrayal of Trust: The Collapse of Global Public Health*. New York: Hyperion, 2000; Beardsley EH. *A History of Neglect: Health Care for Blacks and Mill Workers in the Twentieth-Century South*. Knoxville: University of Tennessee Press, 1987, 152–155.

6. Brinkley A. *The Unfinished Nation*, 653–706; Sitkoff H. History of the United States; Hirshfield DS. *The Lost Reform: The Campaign for Compulsory Health Insurance in the United States 1932 to 1943*. Cambridge, MA: Harvard University Press, 1970; Garrett L. *Betrayal of Trust*; Starr P. *The Social Transformation of American Medicine*.

7. Brinkley A. *The Unfinished Nation*, 700.

8. Brinkley A. *The Unfinished Nation*, 695.

9. Haynes GE. Lily-white social security. *The Crisis* 1935; 42:85–86.

10. Marable M. *Race, Reform, and Rebellion: The Second Reconstruction in Black America, 1945–1990*. Rev. 2nd ed. Jackson: University Press of Mississippi, 1991, 14.

11. Zinn H. *A People's History of the United States*. New York: Harper & Row, 1980. Paperback ed. New York: Harper Perennial, 1990, 394.

12. Brinkley A. *The Unfinished Nation*, 701.

13. Brinkley A. *The Unfinished Nation*, 660.

14. Hamilton DC. Great Depression and the New Deal, 1134–1142; Brinkley A. *The Unfinished Nation*, 653–706; Sitkoff H. History of the United States; Garrett L. *Betrayal of Trust*, 315; Randolph AP. Why should we march? *Survey Graphic* November 1942; 31:488–489; The march-on-Washington movement. New York *The Amsterdam New York Star-News* June 28, 1941:1; Haynes GE. Lily-white social security; Davis JP. A black inventory of the New Deal. *The Crisis* 1935; 42:154–155; Beardsley EH. *A History of Neglect*, 156–185; O'Reilly K. *Nixon's Piano: Presidents and Racial Politics from Washington to Clinton*. New York: The Free Press, 1995, 109–144; Zinn H. *A People's History of the United States*, 377–397.

15. Brinkley A. *The Unfinished Nation*, 707–722; Sitkoff H. History of the United States; Zinn H. *A People's History of the United States*, 398–415.

16. Brinkley A. *The Unfinished Nation*, 723–746; Marable M. *Race, Reform, and Rebellion*, 13–18; Sitkoff H. History of the United States; Winston H. Jim-Crow army. *Old Jim Crow Has Got To Go!* (pamphlet). New York: New Age Publishers, March, 1941, 9–11; Anonymous. Jim Crow in the army camps. *The Crisis* December 1940; 47:12; Granger LB. Barriers to Negro war employment. *Annals of the American Academy of Political and Social Science*. September 1942; 223:72–80; Hughes L, Meltzer M, Lincoln CE. *A Pictorial History of Black Americans*. Rev. 5th ed. New York: Crown Publishers, 1983, 281–302; Zinn H. *A People's History of the United States*, 398–423; Beardsley EH. *A History of Neglect*, 173–178.

17. Lochard MTP. Negroes and defense. *The Nation* January 1941; 152:14–16; Du Bois WEB. As the crow flies. *The Amsterdam New York Star-News*. March 14, 1942.

18. Zinn H. *A People's History of the United States*, 410.

19. Zinn H. *A People's History of the United States*, 410.

20. Marable M. *Race, Reform, and Rebellion*, 14–15.

## 658 ■ Notes

21. Brinkley A. *The Unfinished Nation*, 723–746; Marable M. *Race, Reform, and Rebellion*, 13–18; Hughes L, Meltzer M, Lincoln CE. *A Pictorial History of Black Americans*, 281–302; Zinn H. *A People's History of the United States*, 398–423; Byrd WM, Clayton LA. *A Black Health Trilogy* (videotape and 188-page documentary report). Washington, DC: National Medical Association and African American Heritage and Education Foundation, 1991; Morais HM. *The History of the Negro in Medicine*. New York: Publishers Company, 1967.

22. Hirshfield DS. *The Lost Reform*, 71.

23. Starr P. *The Social Transformation of American Medicine*; Committee on the Costs of Medical Care. *Medical Care for the American People*. Chicago: University of Chicago Press, 1932; Hirshfield DS. *The Lost Reform*; Garrett L. *Betrayal of Trust*; Morais HM. *The History of the Negro in Medicine*; Stevens RA. *In Sickness and in Wealth: American Hospitals in the Twentieth Century*. 2nd ed. Baltimore: Johns Hopkins University Press, 1999.

24. Cray E. *In Failing Health: The Medical Crisis and the A.M.A.* Indianapolis: Bobbs-Merrill, 1970, 51.

25. Beardsley EH. *A History of Neglect*, 41.

26. Cray E. *In Failing Health*, 50–52; Hirshfield DS. *The Lost Reform*; Stevens RA. *In Sickness and in Wealth*; Morais HM. *The History of the Negro in Medicine*; Beardsley EH. *A History of Neglect*, 11–41.

27. Hirshfield DS. *The Lost Reform*, 44.

28. Brinkley A. *The Unfinished Nation*, 684–686; Starr P. *The Social Transformation of American Medicine*, 266–279; Hirshfield DS. *The Lost Reform*, 42–70; Stevens RA. *American Medicine and the Public Interest*. New Haven, CT: Yale University Press, 1971, 187–188.

29. Starr P. *The Social Transformation of American Medicine*, 269–270.

30. Starr P. *The Social Transformation of American Medicine*, 266–279; Hirshfield DS. *The Lost Reform*, 42–86; Stevens RA. *In Sickness and in Wealth*, 140–170; Hamilton DC. Great Depression and the New Deal; Douglas PH. *Social Security in the United States*. New York: McGraw-Hill, 1936, 100–101; Wilson FA, Neuhauser D. *Health Services in the United States*. 2nd ed. Cambridge, MA: Ballinger Publishing, 1982, 305–306; Cray E. *In Failing Health*, 66–72; Haynes GE. Lilywhite social security; Beardsley EH. *A History of Neglect*, 156–185.

31. Hirshfield DS. *The Lost Reform*, 81.

32. Hirshfield DS. *The Lost Reform*, 82.

33. Cray E. *In Failing Health*, 66.

34. Hirshfield DS. *The Lost Reform*, 83.

35. Brinkley A. *The Unfinished Nation*, 676–706; Hirshfield DS. *The Lost Reform*, 42–86; Cray E. *In Failing Health*, 66–67; Stevens RA. *American Medicine and the Public Interest*, 178–179; Stevens RA. *In Sickness and in Wealth*, 140–170; Beardsley EH. *A History of Neglect*, 156–185.

36. Hirshfield DS. *The Lost Reform*, 86.

37. Brinkley A. *The Unfinished Nation*, 676–706; Hirshfield DS. *The Lost Reform*, 80–86; Cray E. *In Failing Health*, 40–89; Starr P. *The Social Transformation of American Medicine*, 271, 304, 321; Stevens RA. *American Medicine and the Public Interest*, 188–197, 268–289; Stevens RA. *In Sickness and in Wealth*, 140–170.

38. Hirshfield DS. *The Lost Reform*, 87.

39. Hirshfield DS. *The Lost Reform*, 86–99, 169–170; Numbers RL. *Almost Persuaded: American Physicians and Compulsory Health Insurance, 1912–1920*. Baltimore: Johns Hopkins University Press, 1978; Stevens RA. *American Medicine and the Public Interest*, 188–197, 268–289; Starr P. *The Social Transformation of American Medicine*, 270–272, 295–310.

40. Hirshfield DS. *The Lost Reform*, 87.

41. Hirshfield DS. *The Lost Reform*, 89.

42. Hirshfield DS. *The Lost Reform*; 87–89; Stevens RA. *American Medicine and the Public Interest*, 188; Starr P. *The Social Transformation of American Medicine*, 198–289, 301–306, 357; Morais HM. *The History of the Negro in Medicine*.

43. Hirshfield DS. *The Lost Reform*, 90.

44. Hirshfield DS. *The Lost Reform*, 90–91; Starr P. *The Social Transformation of American Medicine*, 198–289, 207–208, 306–307; Cray E. *In Failing Health*, 202–204.

45. Stevens RA. *In Sickness and in Wealth*, 141.

46. Stevens RA. *In Sickness and in Wealth*, 143.

47. Starr P. *The Social Transformation of American Medicine*, 270.

48. Starr P. *The Social Transformation of American Medicine*, 270.

49. Starr P. *The Social Transformation of American Medicine*, 298.

50. Beardsley EH. *A History of Neglect*, 155.

51. Starr P. *The Social Transformation of American Medicine*, 198–301, 295–301; Stevens RA. *In Sickness and in Wealth*; Hirshfield DS. *The Lost Reform*, 91–94; Gamble VN. *Making a Place for Ourselves: The Black Hospital Movement 1920–1945.* New York: Oxford University Press, 1995, 105–130; Stevens RA. *American Medicine and the Public Interest*, 269–272, 426; Cray E. *In Failing Health*, 202–204; Beardsley EH. *A History of Neglect*, 77–127, 152–155, 156–185.

52. Hirshfield DS. *The Lost Reform*, 100.

53. Starr P. *The Social Transformation of American Medicine*, 272.

54. Starr P. *The Social Transformation of American Medicine*, 272.

55. Hirshfield DS. *The Lost Reform*, 94–102; Cray E. *In Failing Health*, 63–74, 113–115, 182–198; Starr P. *The Social Transformation of American Medicine*, 211, 266–306; Rosen G. *The Structure of American Medical Practice 1875–1941.* Philadelphia: University of Pennsylvania Press, 1983; Morais HM. *The History of the Negro in Medicine.*

56. Stevens RA. *American Medicine and the Public Interest*, 268–272; Jacobson TC. *Making Medical Doctors: Science and Medicine at Vanderbilt since Flexner.* Tuscaloosa: University of Alabama Press, 1987, 242–250; Morais HM. *The History of the Negro in Medicine*; Beardsley EH. *A History of Neglect*, 173–178; Byrd WM, Clayton LA. *A Black Health Trilogy*; Hughes L, Meltzer M, Lincoln CE. *A Pictorial History of Black Americans*, 292–299.

57. Jacobson TC. *Making Medical Doctors*, 243.

58. Jacobson TC. *Making Medical Doctors*, 242–250; Morais HM. *The History of the Negro in Medicine*; Kidd F, ed. *Profile of the Negro in American Dentistry*. Washington, DC: Howard University Press, 1979, 57–58; Summerville J. *Educating Black Doctors: A History of Meharry Medical College*. University: University of Alabama Press, 1983, 92.

59. Beardsley EH. *A History of Neglect*, 174.

60. Stevens RA. *American Medicine and the Public Interest*, 268; Garrett L. *Betrayal of Trust*; Morais HM. *The History of the Negro in Medicine*; Beardsley EH. *A History of Neglect*, 156–178; Byrd WM, Clayton LA. *A Black Health Trilogy*; Farley R, Allen WR. *The Color Line and the Quality of Life in America.* New York: Oxford University Press, 1989, 28.

61. Stevens RA. *American Medicine and the Public Interest*, 271.

62. Hirshfield DS. *The Lost Reform*, 161.

63. Stevens RA. *American Medicine and the Public Interest*, 268–272; Morais HM. *The History of the Negro in Medicine*; Hughes L, Meltzer M, Lincoln CE. *A Pictorial History of Black Americans*, 292–299; Byrd WM, Clayton LA. *A Black Health Trilogy*; Hirshfield DS. *The Lost Reform*, 161.

64. Stevens RA. *American Medicine and the Public Interest*, 268; Beardsley EH. *A History of Neglect*, 173–178.

65. Beardsley EH. *A History of Neglect*, 174.

66. Beardsley EH. *A History of Neglect*, 77–185, 174–175; Byrd WM, Clayton LA. *A Black Health Trilogy*; Stevens RA. *American Medicine and the Public Interest*, 268; Hirshfield DS. *The Lost Reform*, 161; Morais HM. *The History of the Negro in Medicine*, 128–130.

67. Reuter EB. *The American Race Problem.* Rev. 3rd ed. New York: Thomas Y. Crowell Company, 1970, 162.

68. Farley R, Allen WR. *The Color Line and the Quality of Life in America*, 16.

69. Farley R, Allen WR. *The Color Line and the Quality of Life in America*, 31.

70. Byrd WM, Clayton LA. *A Black Health Trilogy*; Farley R, Allen WR. *The Color Line and the Quality of Life in America*, 16–33; Morais HM. *The History of the Negro in Medicine*, 111; Byrd WM, Clayton LA. An American health dilemma: A history of blacks in the health system. *Journal of the National Medicial Association* 1992; 84:189–200; Reuter EB. *The American Race Problem*, 154–184.

71. Abelin T. Health promotion. In: Detels R et al., eds. *Oxford Textbook of Public Health*. Vol. 3, *The Practice of Public Health*. 3rd ed. New York: Oxford University Press, 1997, 557–589, quote 576.

72. Farley R, Allen WR. *The Color Line and the Quality of Life in America*, 16–33; Farley R. *Growth of the Black Population: A Study of Demographic Trends*. Chicago: Markham Publishing, 1970; Ewbank DC. History of Black mortality and health before 1940. In: Willis DP, ed. *Health Policies and Black Americans*. New Brunswick, NJ: Transaction Publishers, 1989, 100–128, quote 102; Walker CE. The national health program. *Journal of the National Medical Association* 1938; 30:147–151; Reuter EB. *The American Race Problem*, 154–184; Bousefield MO. An account of physicians of color in the United States. *Bulletin of the History of Medicine* 1945; 17:61–84; Abelin T. Health promotion; World Health Organization. *Global Strategy for Health for All by the Year 2000*. Geneva: WHO, 1981; World Health Organization. *Development of Indicators for Monitoring Progress towards Health for All by the Year 2000*. Geneva: WHO, 1981.

73. Farley R, Allen WR. *The Color Line and the Quality of Life in America*, 25.

74. Farley R, Allen WR. *The Color Line and the Quality of Life in America*, 25.

75. Reuter EB. *The American Race Problem*, 162.

76. Farley R, Allen WR. *The Color Line and the Quality of Life in America*, 25–31; Farley R. *Growth of the Black Population*, 69–75; Hart N. The social and economic environment and human health. In: Holland WW, Detels R, Knox G, eds. *Oxford Textbook of Public Health*. Vol. 1, *Influences of Public Health*. 2nd ed. Oxford: Oxford University Press, 1991, 151–195.

77. Reuter EB. *The American Race Problem*, 182.

78. Farley R, Allen WR. *The Color Line and the Quality of Life in America*, 27.

79. Farley R, Allen WR. *The Color Line and the Quality of Life in America*, 28..

80. Beardsley EH. *A History of Neglect*, 154.

81. Reuter EB. *The American Race Problem*, 166–167.

82. Myrdal G. *An American Dilemma: The Negro Problem and Modern Democracy*. New York: Harper & Row, 1944, 174.

83. Reuter EB. *The American Race Problem*, 182.

84. Farley R, Allen WR. *The Color Line and the Quality of Life in America*, 16–33; Farley R. *Growth of the Black Population*; Ewbank DC. History of Black mortality and health before 1940, 106; Reuter EB. *The American Race Problem*, 158–182; Beardsley EH. *A History of Neglect*, 77–185; Myrdal G. *An American Dilemma*, 167–181; Gamble VN. The Negro hospital renaissance: The Black hospital movement, 1920–1945. In: Long DE, Golden J, eds. *The American General Hospital: Communities and Social Contexts*. Ithaca: Cornell University Press, 1989, 82–105; Hirshfield DS. *The Lost Reform*, 161; Cray E. *In Failing Health*, 60–89, 70.

85. Reuter EB. *The American Race Problem*, 165.

86. Ewbank DC. History of Black mortality and health before 1940, 108.

87. Ewbank DC. History of Black mortality and health before 1940, 114.

88. Ewbank DC. History of Black mortality and health before 1940; Reuter EB. *The American Race Problem*, 165–168; Myrdal G. *An American Dilemma*, 171–175; Morais HM. *The History of the Negro in Medicine*, 122–130; Abelin T. Health promotion, 576–577.

89. Ewbank DC. History of Black mortality and health before 1940, 112.

90. Morais HM. *The History of the Negro in Medicine*, 122.

91. Farley R, Allen WR. *The Color Line and the Quality of Life in America*, 22.

92. Myrdal G. *An American Dilemma*, 175.

93. Ewbank DC. History of Black mortality and health before 1940; Reuter EB. *The American Race Problem*, 158–182; Myrdal G. *An American Dilemma*, 167–181; Morais HM. *The History of the Negro in Medicine*, 122–130; Farley R, Allen WR. *The Color Line and the Quality of Life in America*, 16–23.

94. Morais HM. *The History of the Negro in Medicine*, 125.

95. Morais HM. *The History of the Negro in Medicine*, 124.

96. Morais HM. *The History of the Negro in Medicine*, 125.

97. Myrdal G. *An American Dilemma*, 171–172.

98. Morais HM. *The History of the Negro in Medicine*, 126.

99. Johnson CS. *Shadow of the Plantation.* Chicago: University of Chicago Press, 1934; Woodson CG. *The Rural Negro.* New York: Russell and Russell, 1930; Woodson, CG. *The Negro Professional Man and the Community.* Washington, DC: Association for the Study of Negro Life and History, 1934; Ewbank DC. History of Black mortality and health before 1940; Reuter EB. *The American Race Problem,* 158–182; Myrdal G. *An American Dilemma,* 167–181; Morais HM. *The History of the Negro in Medicine,* 122–130; Cobb WM. *Medical Care and the Plight of the Negro.* New York: National Association for the Advancement of Colored People, 1947; Cobb WM. *Progress and Portents for the Negro in Medicine.* New York: National Association for the Advancement of Colored People, 1948; Kenney JA. Hospital symposium: The Negro hospital renaissance. *Journal of the National Medical Association* 1930; 22:109–157; Dowling HF. *City Hospitals: The Undercare of the Underprivileged.* Cambridge, MA: Harvard University Press, 1982; Beardsley EH. *A History of Neglect,* 77–100, 156–185; Byrd WM. *An American health dilemma*; Summerville J. *Educating Black Doctors*; Hirshfield DS. *The Lost Reform,* 161; Cray E. *In Failing Health,* 60–89, 70.

100. Chase A. *The Legacy of Malthus: The Social Costs of the New Scientific Racism.* New York: Knopf, 1980; Byrd WM, Clayton LA. *An American health dilemma*; Byrd WM. Race, biology, and health care: Reassessing a relationship. *Journal of Health Care for the Poor and Underserved* 1990; 1:278–292; Roberts D. *Killing the Black Body: Race, Reproduction, and the Meaning of Liberty.* New York: Pantheon Books, 1997; Smith DB. *Health Care Divided: Race and Healing a Nation.* Ann Arbor: University of Michigan Press, 1999; Haller MH. *Eugenics: Hereditarian Attitudes in American Thought.* New Brunswick, NJ: Rutgers University Press, 1963; Tucker WH. *The Science and Politics of Racial Research.* Urbana: University of Illinois Press, 1994.

101. Beardsley EH. *A History of Neglect,* 37.

102. Kenney JA. Second annual oration on surgery. *Journal of the National Medical Association* 1941; 33:203–214, 213.

103. Kenney JA. Second annual oration on surgery, 212–213.

104. Jones JH. *Bad Blood: The Tuskegee Syphilis Experiment.* New York: The Free Press, 1981, 93–97, 223–229; Smith, DB. *Health Care Divided*; Jones JH. Tuskegee syphilis experiment. In: Salzman J, Smith DL, West C, eds. *Encyclopedia of African-American Culture and History.* 5 Vols. New York: Macmillan Library Reference USA, Simon and Schuster Macmillan, 1996, 2685–2687; Harmer RM. *American Medical Avarice.* New York: Abelard-Schuman, 1975, 79–93; McGregor DK. *Sexual Surgery and the Origins of Gynecology: J. Marion Sims, His Hospital, and His Patients.* New York: Garland Publishing, 1989; Bullough B, Bullough VL. *Poverty, Ethnic Identity, and Health Care.* New York: Appleton-Century-Crofts, 1972, 11–13, 50–51, 149; Chase A. *The Legacy of Malthus,* 12–23; Kenney JA. Second annual oration on surgery; Ehrenreich B, Ehrenreich J. *The American Health Empire: Power, Profits, and Politics.* New York: Random House, 1970, 13–28, 40–49, 54; Beecher HK. Ethics and clinical research. *New England Journal of Medicine* 1966; 274:1354–1360; Dula A. Toward an African-American perspective on bioethics. *Journal of Health Care for the Poor and Underserved* 1991; 2:259–269; Associated Press. MIT president rues radiation tests. *Fort Worth Star-Telegram* January 9, 1993:A23; Hoversten P. Radiation tests used inmates as guinea pigs. *USA Today* November 21, 1994:A3; Washington HA. Of men and mice: Human guinea pigs: Unethical testing targets Blacks and the poor. *Emerge* October 1994; 1(6):24; Sidel VW, Sidel R, eds. *Reforming Medicine: Lessons of the Last Quarter Century.* New York: Pantheon Books, 1984, 109–110, 116–123; Cray E. *In Failing Health,* 143.

105. Myrdal G. *An American Dilemma*; Morais HM. *The History of the Negro in Medicine,* 122–130; Cobb WM. *Medical Care and the Plight of the Negro*; Cobb WM. *Progress and Portents for the Negro in Medicine*; Byrd WM, Clayton LA. *An American health dilemma.*

106. Hirshfield DS. *The Lost Reform,* 1.

107. Hirshfield DS. *The Lost Reform,* 4.

108. Hirshfield DS. *The Lost Reform,* 1.

109. Hirshfield DS. *The Lost Reform,* 40–41.

110. Hirshfield DS. *The Lost Reform,* 1–41; Starr P. *The Social Transformation of American Medicine,* 235–334; Cray E. *In Failing Health*; Stevens RA. *In Sickness and in Wealth,* 1999, 140–199.

111. Hirshfield DS. *The Lost Reform,* 35.

112. Jones JH. *Bad Blood,* 32.

113. Jones JH. *Bad Blood,* 34.

114. Jones JH. *Bad Blood*, 95.

115. Hirshfield DS. *The Lost Reform*, 34–41; Starr P. *The Social Transformation of American Medicine*, 270–280; Jones JH. *Bad Blood*; Chase A. *The Legacy of Malthus*; Cray E. *In Failing Health*, 60–76; Numbers RL. *Almost Persuaded*.

116. Brinkley A. *The Unfinished Nation*; Hirshfield DS. *The Lost Reform*, 1–41; Numbers RL. *Almost Persuaded*; Cray E. *In Failing Health*, 60–89; Starr P. *The Social Transformation of American Medicine*, 235–257.

117. Cray E. *In Failing Health*, 64.

118. Cray E. *In Failing Health*, 65.

119. Hirshfield DS. *The Lost Reform*, 32.

120. Hirshfield DS. *The Lost Reform*, 32.

121. Fishbein M. Committee on the costs of medical care. *Journal of the American Medical Association* 1932; 99:1950–1952.

122. Fishbein M. Committee on the costs of medical care; Cray E. *In Failing Health*, 65; Campion FD. *The AMA and U.S. Health Policy since 1940*. Chicago: Chicago Review Press, 1984, 117–118; Harmer RM. *American Medical Avarice*, 253.

123. Hirshfield DS. *The Lost Reform*, 31–41, 61–62, app. 3-B; Campion FD. *The AMA and U.S. Health Policy since 1940*, 117–118; Harmer RM. *American Medical Avarice*, 252–253; Starr P. *The Social Transformation of American Medicine*, 261–267; Cray E. *In Failing Health*, 60–89.

124. Hirshfield DS. *The Lost Reform*, 62.

125. Cray E. *In Failing Health*, 68.

126. Hirshfield DS. *The Lost Reform*, 42–70, app. 3-B; Harmer RM. *American Medical Avarice*, 252–259; Cray E. *In Failing Health*, 60–89, 182–190; Starr P. *The Social Transformation of American Medicine*, 257–279.

127. Dummett CO, Dummett LD. *Afro-Americans in Dentistry: Sequence and Consequence of Events*. Published by author, 1978.

128. Cray E. *In Failing Health*, 68.

129. Hirshfield DS. *The Lost Reform*, 80–99; Cray E. *In Failing Health*, 60–89, 184–208; Harmer RM. *American Medical Avarice*, 245–259; Starr P. *The Social Transformation of American Medicine*, 266–310; Dummett CO, Dummett LD. *Afro-Americans in Dentistry*, 31.

130. Hirshfield DS. *The Lost Reform*, 100–134; Starr P. *The Social Transformation of American Medicine*, 266–279; Cray E. *In Failing Health*, 60–89.

131. Hirshfield DS. *The Lost Reform*, 100–165; Cray E. *In Failing Health*, 60–89, 184–190; Harmer RM. *American Medical Avarice*, 9–25, 245–259; Walker CE. The national health program. *Journal of the National Medical Association* 1938; 30:147–153; The achievement session, N.M.A. Hampton—1938. Editorial. *Journal of the National Medical Association* 1938; 30:154; Kenney JA. The national health act of 1939. *Journal of the National Medical Association* 1939; 31:154–160; Dummett CO, Dummett LD. *Afro-Americans in Dentistry*, 29, 34.

132. Cray E. *In Failing Health*, 60–89, 71; Hirshfield DS. *The Lost Reform*, 100–165; Starr P. *The Social Transformation of American Medicine*, 266–310; Harmer RM. *American Medical Avarice*, 9–25.

133. Cray E. *In Failing Health*, 74.

134. Cray E. *In Failing Health*, 60–89, 65, 70–71, 72; Campion FD. *The AMA and U.S. Health Policy since 1940*, 136–137, 142, 144–146 (Rich Report); Hirshfield DS. *The Lost Reform*, 100–165; Harmer RM. *American Medical Avarice*, 9–25, 245–259; Starr P. *The Social Transformation of American Medicine*, 266–310.

135. Woodson CG. *The Negro Professional Man and the Community*, 18–131; Morais HM. *The History of the Negro in Medicine*, 89–130, 100; Smith DB. *Health Care Divided*; Epps HR. The Howard University medical department in the Flexner era: 1910–1929. *Journal of the National Medical Association* 1989; 81:885; Savitt TL. Abraham Flexner and the Black medical schools. In: Barzansky EM, Gevitz N, eds. *Beyond Flexner: Medical Education in the twentieth Century*. New York: Greenwood Press, 1992, 65–81.

136. Myrdal G. *An American Dilemma*, 324.

137. Myrdal G. *An American Dilemma*, 324.

138. Woodson CG. *The Negro Professional Man and the Community*; Cobb WM. The Black American in medicine. *Journal of the National Medical Association* 73(Suppl 1):1183–1244; Morais HM. *The History of the Negro in Medicine*; Byrd WM, Clayton LA. *A Black Health Trilogy*; Byrd WM, Clayton LA. *An American health dilemma*; Myrdal G. *An American Dilemma*; The case against the AMA. *Opportunity* 1939; 17:194; Reynolds PP. Hospitals and civil rights, 1945–1963: *Simkins v. Moses H. Cone Memorial Hospital*. *Annals of Internal Medicine* 1997; 126:898–906.

139. Cobb WM. *Medical Care and the Plight of the Negro*, 14.

140. Morais HM. *The History of the Negro in Medicine*, 89–130, 100; Epps HR. The Howard University medical department in the Flexner era; Cobb WM. *Medical Care and the Plight of the Negro*, 11–14; Cobb WM. *Progress and Portents for the Negro in Medicine*, 18–25, 23; Woodson CG. *The Negro Professional Man and the Community*, 29–131; Beardsley EH. *A History of Neglect*, 77–100, 78; Summerville J. *Educating Black Doctors*, 60–105.

141. Morais HM. *The History of the Negro in Medicine*, 21–34, 59–95; Falk LA. Black abolitionist doctors and healers, 1810–1885. *Bulletin of the History of Medicine* 1980; 54:253–272; Sterling D. *The Making of an Afro-American: Martin Robison Delany, 1812–1885*. Garden City, NY: Doubleday, 1971; Du Bois WEB. *Mortality among Negroes in Cities*. Atlanta: Atlanta University Publications, 1896, 20–24; Beardsley EH. *A History of Neglect*, 82; Errata. *Journal of the National Medical Association* 1910; 2:193–194; Commission for the Study of Uncinariasis. *Journal of the National Medical Association* 1910; 2:140–141; Tuberculosis Commission of the National Medical Association. *Journal of the National Medical Association* 1910; 2:142; Kenney JA. Health problems of the Negroes. *Journal of the National Medical Association* 1911; 3:127–135; Kenney JA. *The Negro in Medicine*. Tuskegee: Tuskegee Institute Press, 1912; Green HM. Report of the pellagra commission. *Journal of the National Medical Association* 1917; 9:223–227; National medical commissions. *Journal of the National Medical Association* 1918; 10:125; Cannon GE. The Negro medical profession and the United States Army. *Journal of the National Medical Association* 1919; 11:21–28; Reynolds PP. Hospitals and civil rights, 1945–1963; Lewis JH. Contribution of an unknown Negro to anesthesia. *Journal of the National Medical Association* 1931; 23:23–24; Lewis JH. *The Biology of the Negro*. Chicago: University of Chicago Press, 1942; Kenney JA. The interracial committee of Montclair, New Jersey: Report of survey of hospital committee. *Journal of the National Medical Association* 1931; 23:97–108; Kenney JA. The relationship between the N.M.A. and the A.M.A. and the federal government. *Journal of the National Medical Association* 1939; 31:150–151; Kenney JA. The National Health Act of 1939. *Journal of the National Medical Association* 1939; 31:154–160; Kenney JA. Senator Wagner says non-governmental hospitals are eligible for support under his bill. Negroes are protected. *Journal of the National Medical Association* 1939; 31:173–177; Kenney JA. Where are we? *Journal of the National Medical Association* 1939; 31:177–178; Kenney JA. Second annual oration on surgery.

142. Beardsley EH. *A History of Neglect*, 98.

143. Reynolds PP. Hospitals and civil rights, 1945–1963, 898.

144. Reynolds PP. Hospitals and civil rights, 1945–1963, 899.

145. Reynolds PP. Hospitals and civil rights, 1945–1963, 899.

146. Morais HM. *The History of the Negro in Medicine*, 89–130; Beardsley EH. *A History of Neglect*, 77–100; Cornely PB. The economics of medical practice and the Negro physician. *Journal of the National Medical Association* 1951; 43:84–92; Reynolds PP. Hospitals and civil rights, 1945–1963; Summerville J. *Educating Black Doctors*; Organ CH, Kosiba MM, eds. *A Century of Black Surgeons: The U.S.A. Experience*. 2 Vols. Norman, OK: Transcript Press, 1987; Venable HP. The history of Homer G. Phillips Hospital. *Journal of the National Medical Association* 1961; 53:542.

147. Beardsley EH. *A History of Neglect*, 96.

148. Morais HM. *The History of the Negro in Medicine*, 39–130; Beardsley EH. *A History of Neglect*, 77–100, 94–100, 152–185; Smith DB. *Health Care Divided* 32–63.

149. Beardsley EH. *A History of Neglect*, 97.

150. Proctor RN. *Racial Hygiene: Medicine under the Nazis*. Cambridge, MA: Harvard University Press, 1988, 286.

151. Beardsley EH. *A History of Neglect*, 96.

152. Morais HM. *The History of the Negro in Medicine*, 89–130; Smith DB. *Health Care*

*Divided*; Byrd WM. Medical associations. In: Salzman J, Smith DL, West C, eds. *Encyclopedia of African-American Culture and History*, 1747–1749; Beardsley EH. *A History of Neglect*, 77–100, 152–185; Cobb WM. *Medical Care and the Plight of the Negro*; Cobb WM. *Progress and Portents for the Negro in Medicine.*

153. Reynolds PP. Hospitals and civil rights, 1945–1963, 900.

154. Beardsley EH. *A History of Neglect*, 158.

155. Dummett CO, Dummett LD. *Afro-Americans in Dentistry*, 34.

156. Morais HM. *The History of the Negro in Medicine*, 89–130, 102; Smith DB. *Health Care Divided*; Beardsley EH. *A History of Neglect*, 77–100, 152–185; Cornely PB. Morbidity and mortality from scarlet fever in the Negro. *American Journal of Public Health* 1939; 29:999–1005; Cornely PB. Observations on the health progress of Negroes in the U.S. during the past two decades. *Southern Medical Journal* 1941; 34:1286; Cornely PB. Trends in public health activities among Negroes in 96 Southern counties during the period 1930–39. *American Journal of Publi Health* 1942; 32:1117–1123; Cornely PB. Distribution of Negro physicians in the United States in 1942. *Journal of the American Medical Association* 1944; 124:826; Cornely PB. Race relations in community health organizations. *American Journal of Public Health* 1946; 36:990; Poindexter H. Handicaps in the normal growth and development of rural Negro children. *American Journal of Public Health* 1938; 28:1049; Du Bois WEB. *Mortality among Negroes in Cities*; Du Bois WEB. *Social and Physical Conditions of Negroes in Cities*. Atlanta: Atlanta University Publications, 1897; Du Bois WEB. *The Health and Physique of the Negro American*. Atlanta: Atlanta University Publications, 1906; U.S. Bureau of the Census. *Negro Population of the United States: 1790–1915* (1918); U.S. Bureau of the Census. *Negroes in the United States 1920–32* (1935); Walker CE. The national health program, 147–153; The achievement session; Kenney JA. The National Health Act of 1939; Cobb WM. Statement in support of National Health Bill, S. 1606, on behalf of the National Association for the Advancement of Colored People. *Journal of the American Medical Association* 1946; 38: 133–137.

157. Morais HM. *The History of the Negro in Medicine*, 89–130; Smith DB. *Health Care Divided*, 32–63; Beardsley EH. *A History of Neglect*, 77–100, 152–185.

158. Organ CH, Kosiba MM. eds. *A Century of Black Surgeons*, 164–166, 197–216, 211–214; Hembree MF. African Civilization Society (AfCS). In: Salzman J, Smith DL, West C, eds. *Encyclopedia of African-American Culture and History*, 59; Wright LT. Factors controlling Negro health. *The Crisis* September 1935; 9: 42; Fox SR. *The Guardian of Boston: William Monroe Trotter*. New York: Atheneum, 1971, 46–64; Gatewood WB. *Aristocrats of Color: The Black Elite, 1880–1920*. Bloomington: Indiana University Press, 1990, 307–309; Thornbrough EL. *T. Thomas Fortune: Militant Journalist*. Chicago: University of Chicago Press, 1972, 105–122; Alexander WG, Miller K. Opens medical clinic. *Journal of the National Medical Association* 1929; 21:80; Rudwick EM. *W. E. B. Du Bois: Propagandist of the Negro Protest*. New York: Atheneum, 1978, 94–95; Cronon ED. *Black Moses: The Story of Marcus Garvey and the Universal Negro Improvement Association*. Madison: University of Wisconsin Press, 1955, 172–174; Haber L. *Black Pioneers of Science and Invention*. San Diego: Harcourt Brace Jovanovich, 1970, 123–150; Morais HM. *The History of the Negro in Medicine*, 114–115; Smith DB. *Health Care Divided*, 32–63; Venable HP. The history of Homer G. Phillips Hospital, 542; Reynolds PP. Hospitals and civil rights, 1945–1963.

159. Beardsley EH. *A History of Neglect*, 90–91, 118–119; Cobb WM. Integration in medicine: A national need. *Journal of the National Medical Association* 1957; 49:4; Smith DB. *Health Care Divided*, 32–63; Haber L. *Black Pioneers of Science and Invention*, 146–148; Alexander E. *Equal Opportunity: No More, No Less* (pamphlet). New York: Executive Committee, Manhattan Medical Society, January 28, 1931; Morais HM. *The History of the Negro in Medicine*, 81, 118–119; Smith, DB. *Health Care Divided*, 32–63; Garvin CH. Post-war planning for "Negro" hospitals. *Journal of the National Medical Association* 1945; 38:28–29; Cobb WM. *Medical Care and the Plight of the Negro.*

160. Cobb WM. *Progress and Portents for the Negro in Medicine*, 18–25; Summerville J. *Educating Black Doctors*, 69–70, 96–97; Morais HM. *The History of the Negro in Medicine*, 91–93; Epps HR. The Howard University medical department in the Flexner era: 1910–1929; Needs of Negro medical schools. *Journal of the National Medical Association* 1917; 9:221–223.

161. Reid IDA. The Negro in the American Economic System. Unpublished manuscript prepared for *An American Dilemma* project. 2 Vols., 1944, Vol. 2, 186–187.

162. Reid IDA. The Negro in the American Economic System, 186–187.

163. Morais HM. *The History of the Negro in Medicine*, 94.

164. Morais HM. *The History of the Negro in Medicine*, 93–100; Reid IDA. The Negro in the American Economic System; Cobb WM. *Medical Care and the Plight of the Negro*, 14–20.

165. Morais HM. *The History of the Negro in Medicine*, 95.

166. Morais HM. *The History of the Negro in Medicine*, 93–100; Cobb WM. *Medical Care and the Plight of the Negro*, 14–20; Summerville J. *Educating Black Doctors*; Organ CH, Kosiba MM, eds. *A Century of Black Surgeons*; Venable HP. The history of Homer G. Phillips Hospital; Ludmerer KM. *Learning to Heal: The Development of American Medical Education*. New York: Basic Books, 1985.

167. Buckler H. *Daniel Hale Williams: Negro Surgeon*. New York: Pitman Publishing, 1954; Morais HM. *The History of the Negro in Medicine*, 93–100, 102–110; Bullock HA. *A History of Negro Education in the South: From 1619 to the Present*. London: Praeger Publishers, 1967. U.S. paperback ed. New York: Praeger Publishers, 1970; Anderson JD. *The Education of Blacks in the South, 1860–1935*. Chapel Hill: University of North Carolina Press, 1988; Cobb WM. *Medical Care and the Plight of the Negro*, 14–20; Stevens RA. *American Medicine and the Public Interest*.

168. Buckler H. *Daniel Hale Williams: Negro Surgeon*; Morais HM. *The History of the Negro in Medicine*, 93–100, 102–110; Cobb WM. *Medical Care and the Plight of the Negro*, 14–20; Stevens RA. *American Medicine and the Public Interest*.

169. Morais HM. *The History of the Negro in Medicine*, 101–102, 122–128; Smith, DB. *Health Care Divided*, 41–44; Beardsley EH. *A History of Neglect*, 114–118; Hine DC. *Black Women in White: Racial Conflict and Cooperation in the Nursing Profession, 1890–1950*. Bloomington: Indiana University Press, 1989; Hine DC. Nursing. In: Salzman J, Smith DL, West C., eds. *Encyclopedia of African-American Culture and History*, 2034–2036; Cobb WM. *Medical Care and the Plight of the Negro*; Summerville J. *Educating Black Doctors*, 31, 50–51, 86–88.

170. Cobb WM. *Progress and Portents for the Negro in Medicine*, 38–42, 51–52; Kidd F., ed. *Profile of the Negro in American Dentistry*, 1–7, 67–79; Dummett CO, Dummett LD. *Afro-Americans in Dentistry*, 29–37; Summerville J. *Educating Black Doctors*, 28–30, 30–31.

171. Morais HM. *The History of the Negro in Medicine*, 122.

172. The case against the AMA. *Opportunity* 1939; 17:194.

173. Morais HM. *The History of the Negro in Medicine*; Beardsley EH. *A History of Neglect*, 77–185; The case against the AMA.

## Chapter Three

1. Brinkley A. *The Unfinished Nation: A Concise History of the American People*. New York: Knopf, 1993, 738–825; Sitkoff H. History of the United States. In: *The New Grolier Multimedia Encyclopedia*. Release 6, MPC Version. Novato, CA: Grolier Electronic Publishing, The Software Toolworks, 1993, 44–56.

2. Brinkley A. *The Unfinished Nation*, 750, 755–759; Sitkoff H. History of the United States, 44–46; Marable M. *Race, Reform, and Rebellion: The Second Reconstruction in Black America, 1945–1990*. Rev. 2nd ed. Jackson: University Press of Mississippi, 1991, 13–39; Branch T. *Parting the Waters: America in the King Years, 1954–63*. New York: Simon & Schuster, 1988, 31.

3. Brinkley A. *The Unfinished Nation*, 747–753; Sitkoff H. History of the United States, 45–46.

4. Massey DS, Denton NA. *American Apartheid: Segregation and the Making of the Underclass*. Cambridge, MA: Harvard University Press, 1993, 51–57.

5. Morais HM. *The History of the Negro in Medicine*. New York: Publishers Company, 1967; Smith DB. *Health Care Divided: Race and Healing a Nation*. Ann Arbor: The University of Michigan Press, 1999, 220; Weaver RC. The health care of our cities. *Journal of the National Medical Association* 1968; 60:42–46; Kellar AZ. High mortality rate for Negroes: Design or accident? *Journal of the National Medical Association* 1968; 60:287–288; Smith EB. Health hazards of the slums. *Journal of the National Medical Association* 1967; 59:141; Washington HA. Alarming new diseases among urban poor. *Emerge* April 1996 (6)(7):22; Sabír NZ. A hazardous existence. *Black Enterprise*

666 ■ Notes

March 1995 (8)(25):30; Flatow I. The Rise of Environmental Justice. Video segment for Earth Keeping, WGBH, Boston, 1993.

6. Brinkley A. The Unfinished Nation, 760–766, 778–793; Sitkoff H. History of the United States, 46–48; Massey DS, Denton NA. American Apartheid; Meyer SG. As Long as They Don't Move Next Door: Segregation and Racial Conflict in American Neighborhoods. Lanham, MD: Rowman and Littlefield, 2000; Cray E. In Failing Health: The Medical Crisis and the A.M.A. Indianapolis: The Bobbs-Merrill Company, 1970; Morais HM. The History of the Negro in Medicine; Lemann N. The Promised Land: The Great Black Migration and How It Changed America. New York: Knopf, 1991; Lambert B. At 50, Levittown contends with legacy of racial bias. New York Times December 28, 1997, 23; Halberstam D. Fear and the dream, part one. Segment of multipart video series The Fifties, 1997, the History Channel; Starr P. The Social Transformation of American Medicine. New York: Basic Books, 1982.

7. Brinkley A. The Unfinished Nation, 763–766.

8. Sitkoff H. History of the United States, 48.

9. Brinkley A. The Unfinished Nation, 760–766, 778–793; Sitkoff H. History of the United States, 46–48; O'Reilly K. Nixon's Piano: Presidents and Racial Politics from Washington to Clinton. New York: The Free Press, 1995; Caldwell C. The Southern captivity of the GOP. The Atlantic Monthly June 1998 (6)(281):55; Starr P. The Social Transformation of American Medicine, 311.

10. Marable M. Race, Reform, and Rebellion, 18.

11. Brinkley A. The Unfinished Nation, 760–766, 771–793; Sitkoff H. History of the United States, 46–48; Marable M. Race, Reform, and Rebellion, 13–60; Halberstam D. Fear and the dream, part one; Halberstam D. Fear and the dream, part two. Segment of multipart video series The Fifties, 1997, The History Channel; O'Reilly K. Nixon's Piano; Du Bois WEB. Social medicine. In: Du Bois WEB. Against Racism: Unpublished Essays, Papers, Addresses, 1887–1961. Aptheker H, ed. Amherst: University of Massachusetts Press, 1985, 265–276; O'Reilly K. Black Americans: The FBI Files. New York: Carroll and Graff Publishers, 1994; Rampersand A. Hughes, Langston. In: Salzman J, Smith DL, West C. eds. Encyclopedia of African-American Culture and History. 5 vols. New York: Macmillan Library Reference USA, Simon and Schuster Macmillan, 1996, 1324–1325; Rampersand A. Robeson, Paul. In: Salzman J, Smith DL, West C. eds. Encyclopedia of African-American Culture and History. 5 vols. New York: Macmillan Library Reference USA, Simon & Schuster Macmillan, 1996, 2346–2348; Marable M. W. E. B. Du Bois: Black Radical Democrat. Boston: Twayne Publishers, 1986; Curley B. W. E. B. Du Bois of Great Barrington. Videotape. A production of PBS member WGBY, Springfield, Massachusetts, sponsored by the Massachusetts Cultural Council, 1992; McCullough D. Paul Robeson: Here I Stand. Video documentary segment of The American Experience, WGBH, Boston, March 1, 1999.

12. Brinkley A. The Unfinished Nation, 785.

13. Brinkley A. The Unfinished Nation, 784–785, 787–791; Hughes L, Meltzer M, Lincoln CE, Spencer JM. A Pictorial History of Black Americans. Rev. 6th ed. New York: Crown Publishers, 1995, 298–329, 350–357; Riggs MT. Color Adjustment. Film strip. San Francisco: The American Film Institute and the California Council for the Humanities, produced in cooperation with KQED, San Francisco, 1991; Turner PA. Ceramic Uncles and Celluloid Mammies: Black Images and Their Influence on Culture. New York: Anchor Books, 1994; Ely MP. The Adventures of Amos 'n' Andy: A Social History of an American Phenomenon. New York: The Free Press, 1991; Jhally S, Lewis J. Enlightened Racism: The Cosby Show, Audiences, and the Myth of the American Dream. Boulder, CO: Westview Press, 1992.

14. Brinkley A. The Unfinished Nation, 785–791, 803–819, 830–833; Sitkoff H. History of the United States, 48–49, 53–55; Marable M. Race, Reform, and Rebellion, 13–60; Halberstam D. The rage within, part six. Segment of multipart video series The Fifties, 1997, the History Channel; Hughes L, Meltzer M, Lincoln CE, Spencer JM. A Pictorial History of Black Americans, 298–329, 350–357; Lemann N. The Promised Land.

15. Harrington M. The Other America: Poverty in the United States. New York: Macmillan, 1962. Paperback ed. Penguin Books, 1963; Hughes L, Meltzer M, Lincoln CE, Spencer JM. A Pictorial History of Black Americans, 293, 302–303; Kluger R. Simple Justice: The History of Brown v. Board of Education and Black America's Struggle for Equality. New York: Knopf, 1976. Paperback ed. New York: Vintage Books, 1977, 234–237, 260–269, 274–278; Weisbrot R. Civil rights movement. In: Salzman J, Smith DL, West C, eds., Encyclopedia of African-American Culture and His-

*tory*, 563–569; Marable M. *Race, Reform, and Rebellion*, 13–41; Sitkoff H. History of the United States, 47; U.S. President's Committee on Civil Rights. *To Secure These Rights*. New York, 1947; Nieman DG. Civil rights and the law. In: Salzman J, Smith DL, West C, eds. *Encyclopedia of African-American Culture and History*, 552–563; Walton Jr H. *Black Politics: A Theoretical and Structural Analysis*. Philadelphia: J.B. Lippincott Company, 1972, 154; McNeil GR. *Groundwork*. Philadelphia: University of Pennsylvania Press, 1983, 200; Weiss NJ. National Urban League. In: Salzman J, Smith DL, West C, eds. *Encyclopedia of African-American Culture and History*, 1963–1965.

16. Reynolds PP. Hospitals and civil rights, 1945–1963: *Simkins v. Moses H. Cone Memorial Hospital. Annals of Internal Medicine* 1997; 126:898–906.

17. McNeil GR. *Groundwork*; Ellwood W. *The Road to* Brown. Videotape. Produced by the University of Virginia and California Newsreel, 1990; Brinkley A. *The Unfinished Nation*, 788–790; Sitkoff H. History of the United States, 48–49; Kluger R. *Simple Justice*, 73–83, 400–424; Weisbrot R. Civil rights movement, 564; Nieman DG. Civil rights and the law, 558; Hughes L, Meltzer M, Lincoln CE, Spencer JM. *A Pictorial History of Black Americans*, 304–311; Reynolds PP. Hospitals and civil rights, 1945–1963.

18. Hughes L, Meltzer M, Lincoln CE, Spencer JM. *A Pictorial History of Black Americans*, 293, 302–303, 306–313; Curry GE. The death that won't die: Memories of Emmett Till 40 years later. *Emerge* July/August 1995; (6)(9).24; Williams J. *Eyes on the Prize: America's Civil Rights Years, 1954–1965*. New York: Viking Penguin, 1987, 1–161; Marable M. *Race, Reform, and Rebellion*, 13–85; O'Reilly K. *Black Americans: The FBI Files*; O'Reilly K. *Nixon's Piano*; Morais HM. *The History of the Negro in Medicine*, 159–188; Weisbrot R. Civil rights movement; Nieman DG. Civil rights and the law, 558.

19. Campion FD. *The AMA and U.S. Health Policy since 1940*. Chicago: Chicago Review Press for the American Medical Association, 1984; Starr P. *The Social Transformation of American Medicine*; Cobb WM. The N.M.A. and civil rights. *Journal of the National Medical Association* 1966; 58:130; Cobb WM. What hath God wrought: Position reversals by the AMA and the AAMC. *Journal of the National Medical Association* 1968; 60:518–521; Byrd WM, Clayton LA. An American health dilemma: A history of blacks in the health system. *Journal of the National Medical Association* 1992; 84:189–200; Byrd WM, Clayton LA. *A Black Health Trilogy*. Videotape and 188-page documentary report. Washington, DC: The National Medical Association and the African American Heritage and Education Foundation, 1991.

20. Brinkley A. *The Unfinished Nation*, 814.

21. Hughes L, Meltzer M, Lincoln CE, Spencer JM. *A Pictorial History of Black Americans*, 309–323; Williams J. *Eyes on the Prize*, 120–249; Marable M. *Race, Reform, and Rebellion*, 61–85; Weisbrot R. Civil rights movement; Branch T. *Parting the Waters*; Brinkley A. *The Unfinished Nation*, 811–819.

22. Williams J. *Eyes on the Prize*, 120–249; Weisbrot R. Civil rights movement; Nieman DG. Civil rights and the law; Marable M. *Race, Reform, and Rebellion*, 61–85; Hughes L, Meltzer M, Lincoln CE, Spencer JM. *A Pictorial History of Black Americans*, 309–323; Branch T. *Parting the Waters*; Branch T. *Pillar of Fire: America in the King Years, 1963–65*. New York: Simon & Schuster, 1998; Brinkley A. *The Unfinished Nation*, 811–819.

23. Morais HM. *The History of the Negro in Medicine*, 130–208; Byrd WM, Clayton LA. An American health dilemma; Byrd WM, Clayton LA. *A Black Health Trilogy*; Manning KR. Health and health care providers. In: Salzman J, Smith DL, West C, eds., *Encyclopedia of African-American Culture and History*, 1247–1255; McBride D. Medical Committee for Human Rights. In: Salzman J, Smith DL, West C, eds. *Encyclopedia of African-American Culture and History*, 1749–1750; Kerner O. *Report of the National Advisory Commission on Civil Disorders*. New York: E.P. Dutton and Company. 1968. Paperback ed. New York: Bantam Books, 1968; Brinkley A. *The Unfinished Nation*, 803–811, 836–839, 847–851.

24. Starr P. *The Social Transformation of American Medicine*, 337–338.

25. Cray E. *In Failing Health*, 25.

26. Brinkley A. *The Unfinished Nation*, 762, 765, 788, 808, 810–811; Cray E. *In Failing Health*, 5–6, 25–39; Bullough B, Bullough VL. *Poverty, Ethnic Identity, and Health Care*. New York: Appleton-Century-Crofts, 1972, 53–54, 79–80; Starr P. *The Social Transformation of American Medicine*, 290–334; Campion FD. *The AMA and U.S. Health Policy since 1940*, 177–252; Lewis S. *Hospital*:

*An Oral History of Cook County Hospital.* New York: The New Press, 1994, 75–82, 85–91, 105–106, 135–138; Dowling HF. *City Hospitals: The Undercare of the Underprivileged.* Cambridge, MA: Harvard University Press, 1982, 151–189; Reynolds PP. Hospitals and civil rights, 1945–1963; Reynolds PP. The federal government's use of Title VI and Medicare to racially integrate hospitals in the United States, 1963 through 1967. *American Journal of Public Health* 1997; 87:1850–1858.

27. Ehrenreich B, Ehrenreich J. *The American Health Empire: Power, Profits, and Politics.* New York: Random House, 1970, 14.

28. Kosa J, Antonovsky A, Zola IK, eds. *Poverty and Health: A Sociological Analysis.* Cambridge, MA: Harvard University Press, 1969, 229.

29. Coleman AH. Title 19 and medical civil rights. *Journal of the National Medical Association* 1966; 58:397.

30. Cray E. *In Failing Health,* 35.

31. Stevens RA. *In Sickness and in Wealth: American Hospitals in the Twentieth Century.* New York: Basic Books, 1989. 2nd ed. Baltimore: Johns Hopkins University Press, 1999, 199–283; Gamble VN. *Making a Place for Ourselves: The Black Hospital Movement 1920–1945.* New York: Oxford University Press, 1995, 182–196; Starr P. *The Social Transformation of American Medicine,* 347–351, 350, 375–377; Cray E. *In Failing Health,* 33–38; Smith DB. *Health Care Divided;* Meyer SG. *As Long as They Don't Move Next Door;* Wilson WJ. *The Truly Disadvantaged: The Inner City, the Underclass, and Public Policy.* Chicago: University of Chicago Press, 1987; Wilson WJ. *When Work Disappears: The World of the New Urban Poor.* New York: Knopf, 1996; Ehrenreich B, Ehrenreich J. *The American Health Empire;* Ginzberg E. *Teaching Hospitals and the Urban Poor.* New Haven, CT: Yale University Press, 2000, 4–5; Ginzberg E. *The Medical Triangle: Physicians, Politicians, and the Public.* Cambridge, MA: Harvard University Press, 1990; Ginzberg E. The monetarization of medical care. *New England Journal of Medicine* 1984; 310:1162–1165; The Hill-Burton program and civil rights. *Journal of the National Medical Association* 1965; 57:59–61; Reynolds PP. Hospitals and civil rights, 1945–1963; Reynolds PP. The federal government's use of Title VI and Medicare to racially integrate hospitals in the United States, 1963 through 1967; Byrd WM, Clayton LA. An American health dilemma; Bullough B, Bullough VL. *Poverty, Ethnic Identity, and Health Care,* 14–59, 149–159; Berry LH. Special health care needs of the disadvantaged. *Journal of the National Medical Association* 1966; 58:72–73; Berry LH. Implementation of new health legislation and its impact upon disadvantaged population groups. *Journal of the National Medical Association* 1966; 58:129; Berry LH. Human rights and regional medical programs. *Journal of the National Medical Association* 1966; 58:387–388; Coleman AH. Title 19 and medical civil rights; Factors influencing the fate of the Negro hospital. *Journal of the National Medical Association* 1967; 59:217; Gamble VN. The Negro hospital renaissance: The Black hospital movement, 1920–1945. In: Long DE, Golden J, eds. *The American General Hospital: Communities and Social Contexts.* Ithaca: Cornell University Press, 1989, 82–105; Travella S. Black hospitals struggle to survive. *Modern Health Care* July 1990 (2):20–26; Travella S. Black hospitals struggling to survive: Of more than 200 medical centers, only 8 are left. *Health: A Weekly Journal of Medicine, Science and Society, The Washington Post,* September 11, 1990:12; Gamble VN. Hospitals, Black. In: Salzman J, Smith DL, West C, eds. *Encyclopedia of African-American Culture and History,* 1305–1309; Dowling HF. *City Hospitals.*

32. Stevens RA. *American Medicine and the Public Interest.* New Haven, CT: Yale University Press, 1971, 350–351.

33. Rothstein WG. *American Medical Schools and the Practice of Medicine.* New York: Oxford University Press, 1987, 233.

34. Ginzberg E, Dutka AB. *The Financing of Biomedical Research.* Baltimore: Johns Hopkins University Press, 1989, 16.

35. Starr P. *The Social Transformation of American Medicine,* 335.

36. Starr P. *The Social Transformation of American Medicine,* 335.

37. Summerville J. *Educating Black Doctors: A History of Meharry Medical College.* University: University of Alabama Press, 1983, 98.

38. Campion FD. *The AMA and U.S. Health Policy since 1940,* 233–252; Ginzberg E. The monetarization of medical care; Ginzberg E, Dutka AB. *The Financing of Biomedical Research,* 83–97; Brown ER. *Rockefeller Medicine Men: Medicine and Capitalism in America.* Berkeley: University of California Press, 1979; Stevens RA. *American Medicine and the Public Interest;* Rothstein

WG. *American Medical Schools and the Practice of Medicine*, 220–255; Starr P. *The Social Transformation of American Medicine*, 338–356; Cray E. *In Failing Health*, 57–59; Cobb WM. The establishment, the Negro and education. *Journal of the National Medical Association* 1968; 60:320–331; Morais HM. *The History of the Negro in Medicine*; Byrd WM, Clayton LA. An American health dilemma; Summerville J. *Educating Black Doctors*, 98–100.

39. Starr P. *The Social Transformation of American Medicine*, 338–356, 347; Cray E. *In Failing Health*, 57–58; U.S. Department of Health and Human Services. *Health in America: 1776–1976*. Washington, DC: U.S. Health Resources Administration, DHEW Pub. No. (HRA) 76–616, 1976; Ginzberg E, Dutka AB. *The Financing of Biomedical Research*.

40. Starr P. *The Social Transformation of American Medicine*, 313.

41. Starr P. *The Social Transformation of American Medicine*, 313.

42. Cray E. *In Failing Health*, 27–29, Starr P. *The Social Transformation of American Medicine*, 290–378, 350–351, 354; Jones J. *American Work: Four Centuries of Black and White Labor*. New York: W. W. Norton, 1998; Smith, DB. *Health Care Divided*; Stoline A, Weiner JP. *The New Medical Marketplace: A Physician's Guide to the Health Care Revolution*. Baltimore: Johns Hopkins University Press, 1988; Campion FD. *The AMA and U.S. Health Policy since 1940*; Hanft RS. National health expenditures, 1950–65. *Social Security Bulletin* 1967, 3–13; Haughton JG. Government's role in health care past, present and future. *Journal of the National Medical Association* 1968; 60:87–91, 89; Bullough B, Bullough VL. *Poverty, Ethnic Identity, and Health Care*, 49, 158–159; Cornely PB. Segregation and discrimination in medical care in the U.S. *American Journal of Public Health* 1956; 46:1074–1081; Cornely PB. Trends in racial integration in hospitals in the United States. *Journal of the National Medical Association* 1957; 49:8–10; Morais HM. *The History of the Negro in Medicine*, 196–198; Reitzes DC. *Negroes and Medicine*. Cambridge, MA: Harvard University Press, 1958; Reynolds PP. Hospitals and civil rights, 1945–1963; Reynolds PP. The federal government's use of Title VI and Medicare to racially integrate hospitals in the United States, 1963 through 1967; Lemann N. *The Promised Land*.

43. Bullough B, Bullough VL. *Poverty, Ethnic Identity, and Health Care*, 49.

44. Starr P. *The Social Transformation of American Medicine*, 320–334, 350–351, 354, 372–373; Bullough B, Bullough VL. *Poverty, Ethnic Identity, and Health Care*, 49–51; Reynolds PP. *Hospitals and civil rights, 1945–1963*; Hart N. The social and economic environment and human health. In: Holland WW, Detels R, Knox G, eds. *Oxford Textbook of Public Health*. Vol. 1, *Influences of Public Health*. 2nd ed. Oxford: Oxford University Press, 1991, 151–195; Lee PR, Benjamin AE. Governmental and legislative control and direction of health services in the United States. In: Holland WW, Detels R, Knox G, eds. *Oxford Textbook of Public Health*. Vol. 1, 217–230; Stevens R. *American Medicine in the Public Interest*. New Haven, CT: Yale University Press, 1971; Smith DB. *Health Care Divided*; Morais HM. *The History of the Negro in Medicine*, 137–188; Ehrenreich B, Ehrenreich J. *The American Health Empire*.

45. Starr P. *The Social Transformation of American Medicine*, 347, 359–363, 360, 368; Cray E. *In Failing Health*, 29–32; Campion FD. *The AMA and U.S. Health Policy since 1940*, 178–180, 177–252; Ginzberg E, Dutka AB. *The Financing of Biomedical Research*; Morais HM. *The History of the Negro in Medicine*, 128–188, 136–140; Smith DB. *Health Care Divided*; Reynolds PP. *Hospitals and civil rights, 1945–1963*; Reynolds PP. The federal government's use of Title VI and Medicare to racially integrate hospitals in the United States, 1963 through 1967; Cobb WM. The Black American in medicine. *Journal of the National Medical Association* 1981; 73 (Suppl 1):1183–1244; Sardell A. *The U.S. Experiment in Social Medicine: The Community Health Center Program, 1956–1986*. Pittsburgh: University of Pittsburgh Press, 1988, 3–48; Brew LE. *Edith: The Story of Edith Irby Jones, M.D.* n.p.: NRT Publishing Company, 1986; Drew CR. Letters to the Editor of J.A.M.A., January 13 and January 30, 1947. *Journal of the National Medical Association* 1947; 39:222–224; Racism rules A.M.A. policies. *Journal of the National Medical Association* 1949; 41:34–35.

46. Starr P. *The Social Transformation of American Medicine*, 363.

47. Starr P. *The Social Transformation of American Medicine*, 335–347; Ehrenreich B, Ehrenreich J. *The American Health Empire*; Cray E. *In Failing Health*, 40–59; Gray BH. *The Profit Motive and Patient Care: The Changing Accountability of Doctors and Hospitals*. Cambridge, MA: Harvard University Press, 1991; Anders G. *Health Against Wealth: HMOs and the Breakdown of Medical Trust*. Boston: Houghton Mifflin, 1996; Wilson FA, Neuhauser D. *Health Services in the*

*United States.* 2nd ed. Cambridge, MA: Ballinger Publishing, 1982, 144–152; Patterson JT. *The Dread Disease: Cancer and Modern American Culture.* Cambridge, MA: Harvard University Press, 1987, 171–200; Reynolds PP. Hospitals and civil rights, 1945–1963; Reynolds PP. The federal government's use of Title VI and Medicare to racially integrate hospitals in the United States, 1963 through 1967.

48. Bullough B, Bullough VL. *Poverty, Ethnic Identity, and Health Care,* 14.

49. Bullough B, Bullough VL. *Poverty, Ethnic Identity, and Health Care,* 50.

50. Bullough B, Bullough VL. *Poverty, Ethnic Identity, and Health Care,* 50.

51. Starr P. *The Social Transformation of American Medicine,* 310–374; Bullough B, Bullough VL. *Poverty, Ethnic Identity, and Health Care,* 1972; Ehrenreich B, Ehrenreich J. *The American Health Empire;* Kosa J, Zola IK, eds. *Poverty and Health: A Sociological Analysis.* Rev. ed. Cambridge, MA: Harvard University Press, 1975; Cray E. *In Failing Health,* 40–59; Cobb WM. The Black American in medicine; Morais HM. *The History of the Negro in Medicine,* 132–188; Reynolds PP. Hospitals and civil rights, 1945–1963; Smith DB. *Health Care Divided;* Reynolds PP. The federal government's use of Title VI and Medicare to racially integrate hospitals in the United States, 1963 through 1967; Wing KR, Rose MG. Health facilities and the enforcement of civil rights. In: Roemer R, McKray G, eds. *Legal Aspects of Health Policy: Issues and Trends.* Westport, CT: Greenwood Press, 1980, 243–267; Rice MF, Jones W. Public policy compliance/enforcement and black American health: Title VI of the civil rights act of 1964. In: Jones Jr W, Rice MF, eds. *Health Care Issues in Black America: Policies, Problems, and Prospects.* New York: Greenwood Press, 1987, 98–115.

52. Ginzberg E. *The Medical Triangle,* 44.

53. Ginzberg E. *The Medical Triangle,* 41–46; Silverman M, Lee PR. *Pills, Profits, and Politics.* Berkeley: University of California Press, 1974, 24–35, App. 2; Starr P. *The Social Transformation of American Medicine,* 280–378; Wilson FA, Neuhauser D. *Health Services in the United States,* 245–256.

54. Jonas S. *Health Care Delivery in the United States.* 3rd ed. New York: Springer, 1986, 125.

55. *The Health Units of Boston,* 1924–1933 and 1934–1944. Boston: Boston Printing Department, 1933, 1945.

56. Kovner AR. *Health Care Delivery in the United States.* 4th ed. New York: Springer, 1990; Dowling HF. *City Hospitals;* Novotny A, Smith C. eds. *Images of Healing: A Portfolio of American Medical and Pharmaceutical Practice in the 18th, 19th, and Early 20th Centuries.* New York: Macmillan, 1980, 30; Geiger HJ. Community health centers: Health care as an instrument of social change. In: Sidel VW, Sidel R, eds. *Reforming Medicine: Lessons of the Last Quarter Century.* New York: Pantheon Books, 1984, 11–32; Rosenberg CE. *The Care of Strangers: The Rise of America's Hospital System.* New York: Basic Books, 1987; Sardell A. *The U.S. Experiment in Social Medicine,* 3–49.

57. Sardell A. *The U.S. Experiment in Social Medicine,* 3–49; Geiger HJ. Community health centers; Last JM, ed. *A Dictionary of Epidemiology.* 2nd ed. New York: Oxford University Press, for the International Epidemiological Association, 1988, 122.

58. Cray E. *In Failing Health,* 37.

59. Cray E. *In Failing Health,* 37; Kovner AR. *Health Care Delivery in the United States.* 4th ed., 82–85; Wilson FA, Neuhauser D. *Health Services in the United States.* Rev. and enlarged 1st ed. Cambridge, MA: Ballinger, 1976, 209–218.

60. Cray E. *In Failing Health,* 43.

61. Cray E. *In Failing Health,* 40–59; Duffy J. *The Sanitarians: A History of American Public Health.* Urbana: University of Illinois Press, 1992; Sardell A. *The U.S. Experiment in Social Medicine,* 3–49; Last JM, ed. *A Dictionary of Epidemiology.* 2nd ed. New York: Oxford University Press, 1988, 107; Sutchfield FD, Keck CW. Concepts and definitions of public health practice. In: Sutchfield FD, Keck CW. *Principles of Public Health Practice.* Albany, NY: Delmar Publishers, 1997, 3–9; Dowling HF. *City Hospitals;* Fee E. History and development of public health. In: Sutchfield FD, Keck CW. *Principles of Public Health Practice,* 10–30.

62. Davis MM, Warner AW. *Dispensaries: Their Management and Development.* New York: Macmillan, 1918, 42.

63. Starr P. *The Social Transformation of American Medicine,* 198, 196.

64. Jonas S. *Health Care Delivery in the United States.* 3rd ed., 145.

65. Ehrenreich B, Ehrenreich J. *The American Health Empire,* 214.

66. Duffy J. *The Sanitarians;* Rosen G. *A History of Public Health.* New York: MD Publications, 1958. Expanded ed. Baltimore: Johns Hopkins University Press, 1993; Starr P. *The Social Transformation of American Medicine,* 180–197; Sardell A. *The U.S. Experiment in Social Medicine,* 3–49; Ginzberg E. *The Medical Triangle;* Ginzberg E. *Teaching Hospitals and the Urban Poor;* Hudson JI, Infeld MD. Ambulatory care reorganization in teaching hospitals. *Journal of Ambulatory Care Management* February 1980; 3:31–50; Fee E. History and development of public health; Dowling HF. *City Hospitals;* Sutchfield FD, Keck CW. Concepts and definitions of public health practice; Ehrenreich B, Ehrenreich J. *The American Health Empire;* Massey DS, Denton NA. *American Apartheid;* Lemann N. *The Promised Land.*

67. Bullough B, Bullough VL. *Poverty, Ethnic Identity, and Health Care,* 14–16.

68. Bennett JT, DiLorenzo TJ. *Unhealthy Charities: Hazardous to Your Health and Wealth.* New York: Basic Books, 1994, x.

69. Wilson FA, Neuhauser D. *Health Services in the United States,* 239–243; Cray E. *In Failing Health,* 27; Bennett JT, DiLorenzo TJ. *Unhealthy Charities;* Starr P. *The Social Transformation of American Medicine,* 342–347; Patterson JT. *The Dread Disease.*

70. Hart N. The social and economic environment and human health. In: Detels R, Holland WW, McEwen J, Omenn GS, eds. *Oxford Textbook of Public Health.* Vol. 1, *The Scope of Public Health.* 3rd ed. New York: Oxford University Press, 1997, 95–123, 108; Hart N. The social and economic environment and human health. In: Holland WW, Detels R, Knox G, eds. *Oxford Textbook of Public Health.* Vol. 1, *Influences of Public Health.* 2nd ed. Oxford: Oxford University Press, 1991, 151–195, 164.

71. Farley R. *Growth of the Black Population: A Study of Demographic Trends.* Chicago: Markham Publishing, 1970, 207–208.

72. Farley R, Allen WR. *The Color Line and the Quality of Life in America.* New York: Oxford University Press, 1989, 35.

73. Hart N. The social and economic environment and human health; Farley R. *Growth of the Black Population,* 69–75, 206–245; Farley R, Allen WR. *The Color Line and the Quality of Life in America,* 32–57.

74. Morais HM. *The History of the Negro in Medicine,* 154.

75. Jaynes GD, Williams RM. eds. *A Common Destiny: Blacks and American Society.* Washington, DC: National Academy Press, 1989, 272.

76. Kluger R. *Simple Justice,* 256–257.

77. Kluger R. *Simple Justice,* 257.

78. Kluger R. *Simple Justice,* 257.

79. Kluger R. *Simple Justice,* 257.

80. Kluger R. *Simple Justice,* 257.

81. U.S. Bureau of the Census. *Historical Statistics of the United States, Colonial Times to 1970, Bicentennial Edition, Parts 1 and 2.* Washington, DC, 1975, 9, 135; Jaynes GD, Williams RM. eds. *A Common Destiny,* 269–328; Morais HM. *The History of the Negro in Medicine,* 154–158; Kluger R. *Simple Justice.*

82. Low WA, Clift VA. eds. *Encyclopedia of Black America.* New York: McGraw-Hill. Reprint ed. New York: Da Capo Press, 1981, 349.

83. Jaynes GD, Williams RM. eds. *A Common Destiny,* 296.

84. Morais HM. *The History of the Negro in Medicine,* 154.

85. Massey DS, Denton NA. *American Apartheid,* 49.

86. Massey DS, Denton NA. *American Apartheid,* 49, 51.

87. Smith DB. *Health Care Divided,* 325.

88. Hart N. The social and economic environment and human health, 96.

89. Hart N. The social and economic environment and human health, 96.

90. Jaynes GD, Williams RM. eds. *A Common Destiny,* 274.

91. Hart N. The social and economic environment and human health; Lee PR, Benjamin AE, Weber MA. Policies and strategies for health in the United States. In: Detels R, Holland WW,

McEwen J, Omenn GS, eds. *Oxford Textbook of Public Health*. Vol. 1, 297–321; Farley R. *Growth of the Black Population*; Farley R, Allen WR. *The Color Line and the Quality of Life in America*, 7–57; Jaynes GD, Williams RM. eds. *A Common Destiny*; Low WA, Clift VA. eds. *Encyclopedia of Black America*; Kluger R. *Simple Justice*; Morais HM. *The History of the Negro in Medicine*; Smith DB. *Health Care Divided*; U.S. Bureau of the Census. *Historical Statistics of the United States, Colonial Times to 1970, Bicentennial Edition, Parts 1 and 2*; Woodson CG. *The Rural Negro*. New York: Russell and Russell, 1930; Johnson CS. *Shadow of the Plantation*. Chicago: University of Chicago Press, 1934; Moynihan DP. *The Negro Family: The Case for National Action*. Washington, DC: Department of Labor, 1965, 47–124; Mare RD, Winship C. Socioeconomic change and the decline of marriage for Blacks and Whites. In: Jencks C, Peterson PE, eds. *The Urban Underclass*. Washington, DC: The Brookings Institution, 1991, 181–188; Massey DS, Denton NA. *American Apartheid*, 1–59; Meyer SG. *As Long as They Don't Move Next Door*; Halberstam D. Fear and the dream, part one; Smith EB. Health hazards of the slums; Kellar AZ. High mortality rate for Negroes; Weaver RC. The health care of our cities.

92. Jaynes GD, Williams RM. eds. *A Common Destiny*, 394.

93. U.S. Bureau of the Census. *Historical Statistics of the United States, Colonial Times to 1970, Bicentennial Edition, Parts 1 and 2*, 44–64, 55, 59; Jaynes GD, Williams RM. eds. *A Common Destiny*, 391–450; Farley R, Allen WR. *The Color Line and the Quality of Life in America*, 33–35; Hart N. The social and economic environment and human health, 151 n. 1; Morais HM. *The History of the Negro in Medicine*, 154–158; Pettigrew TF. *A Profile of the Negro American*. New York: Van Nostrand Reinhold Company, 1964, 72–99.

94. Farley R. *Growth of the Black Population*, 215.

95. Farley R, Allen WR. *The Color Line and the Quality of Life in America*, 51.

96. Cunningham FG, MacDonald PC, Gant NF, Leveno KJ, Gilstrap LC, et al. *Williams Obstetrics*. 18th ed. Stamford, CT: Appleton and Lange, 1997; Rosenbaum S, Layton C, Liu J. *The Health of America's Children*. Washington, DC: Children's Defense Fund, 1991, 8, 14–15, 17; U.S. Bureau of the Census. *Historical Statistics of the United States, Colonial Times to 1970, Bicentennial Edition, Parts 1 and 2*, 44–64, 57; Ewbank DC. History of Black mortality and health before 1940. In: Willis DP, ed. *Health Policies and Black Americans*. New Brunswick, NJ: Transaction Publishers, 1989, 100–128; Farley R, Allen WR. *The Color Line and the Quality of Life in America*, 7–31; Jaynes GD, Williams RM. eds. *A Common Destiny*, 391–450; Farley R. *Growth of the Black Population*, 206–245.

97. Jaynes GD, Williams RM. eds. *A Common Destiny*, 405.

98. Pettigrew TF. *A Profile of the Negro American*, 88.

99. Ewbank DC. History of Black mortality and health before 1940; National Center for Health Statistics. *Prevention Profile. Health United States, 1991*. Hyattsville, MD: Public Health Service, 1992, Table 27, 152–153; Jaynes GD, Williams RM. eds. *A Common Destiny*, 391–450; National Office of Vital Statistics. *Death Rates for Selected Causes by Age, Color, and Sex: United States and Each State, 1949–1951*. Washington, DC: U.S. Government Printing Office, 1959; Pettigrew TF. *A Profile of the Negro American*.

100. Beardsley EH. *A History of Neglect: Health Care for Blacks and Mill Workers in the Twentieth-Century South*. Knoxville: University of Tennessee Press, 1987, 285.

101. Beardsley EH. *A History of Neglect*, 285.

102. Farley R. *Growth of the Black Population*, 222.

103. Jones JH. *Bad Blood: The Tuskegee Syphilis Experiment*. New York: The Free Press, 1981. New and expanded ed. 1993.

104. Farley R. *Growth of the Black Population*, 223.

105. Beardsley EH. *A History of Neglect*, 245–309; Pettigrew TF. *A Profile of the Negro American*, 72–99; Farley R. *Growth of the Black Population*, 206–245; Morais HM. *The History of the Negro in Medicine*, 154–158.

106. Harmer RM. *American Medical Avarice*. New York: Abelard-Schuman, 1975, 11.

107. Starr P. *The Social Transformation of American Medicine*, 352.

108. Gross ML. *The Doctors*. New York: Random House, 1966, 472.

109. Factors influencing the fate of the Negro hospital. *Journal of the National Medical Association* 1967; 59:217.

110. Starr P. *The Social Transformation of American Medicine*, 360.

111. Starr P. *The Social Transformation of American Medicine*, 360.

112. Starr P. *The Social Transformation of American Medicine*, 360.

113. Starr P. *The Social Transformation of American Medicine*, 360.

114. Starr P. *The Social Transformation of American Medicine*, 354.

115. Starr P. *The Social Transformation of American Medicine*, 354.

116. Marable M. *Race, Reform, and Rebellion*, 13–85; Morais HM. *The History of the Negro in Medicine*, 131–188; Cobb WM. The Black American in medicine; Starr P. *The Social Transformation of American Medicine*, 352–378; Ehrenreich B, Ehrenreich J. *The American Health Empire*; Spellman MW. The physician in the Great Society. *Journal of the National Medical Association* 1966; 58:362–367, 365–366; Summerville J. *Educating Black Doctors*; Gross ML. *The Doctors*; Harmer RM. *American Medical Avarice*, 9–23.

117. Campion FD. *The AMA and U.S. Health Policy since 1940*, 153.

118. Campion FD. *The AMA and U.S. Health Policy since 1940*, 153.

119. Hirshfield DS. *The Lost Reform: The Campaign for Compulsory Health Insurance in the United States 1932 to 1943*. Cambridge, MA: A Commonwealth Fund Book, Harvard University Press, 1970; Campion FD. *The AMA and U.S. Health Policy since 1940*, 153–176.

120. Cray E. *In Failing Health*, 73.

121. Campion FD. *The AMA and U.S. Health Policy since 1940*, 138.

122. Cray E. *In Failing Health*, 52.

123. Cray E. *In Failing Health*, 52.

124. Cray E. *In Failing Health*, 52.

125. Numbers RL. *Almost Persuaded: American Physicians and Compulsory Health Insurance, 1912–1920*. Baltimore: Johns Hopkins University Press, 1978; Campion FD. *The AMA and U.S. Health Policy since 1940*, 137–176; Cray E. *In Failing Health*, 52, 73–74; Starr P. *The Social Transformation of American Medicine*, 280–289; Cobb WM. Statement in support of National Health Bill, S. 1606, on behalf of the National Association for the Advancement of Colored People. *Journal of the National Medical Association* 1946; 38:133–137; U.S. Department of Health and Human Services. *Health in America: 1776–1976*; Byrd WM. *Documentary Report: Medical Establishment Activities against Progressive Health Legislation, Programs, and Health Delivery Activities*. Nashville: Cancer Control Research Unit, Meharry Medical College, July 13, 1990. In: Byrd WM, Clayton LA. *A Black Health Trilogy*; Holloman Jr. JLS. Medical leadership. *Journal of the National Medical Association* 1966; 58:377.

126. Campion FD. *The AMA and U.S. Health Policy since 1940*, 154.

127. Cray E. *In Failing Health*, 76.

128. Campion FD. *The AMA and U.S. Health Policy since 1940*, 159.

129. Campion FD. *The AMA and U.S. Health Policy since 1940*, 159.

130. Cray E. *In Failing Health*, 80.

131. Harmer RM. *American Medical Avarice*, 20.

132. Harmer RM. *American Medical Avarice*, 21.

133. Harmer RM. *American Medical Avarice*, 22.

134. Campion FD. *The AMA and U.S. Health Policy since 1940*, 160.

135. Campion FD. *The AMA and U.S. Health Policy since 1940*, 161.

136. Harmer RM. *American Medical Avarice*, 22–23.

137. Cray E. *In Failing Health*, 81.

138. Harmer RM. *American Medical Avarice*, 23.

139. Cray E. *In Failing Health*, 79.

140. Cray E. *In Failing Health*, 80.

141. Starr P. *The Social Transformation of American Medicine*, 285.

142. Means JH. *Doctors, People, and Government*. Boston: Little, Brown, 1953, 152–153.

143. Cray E. *In Failing Health*, 80.

144. Campion FD. *The AMA and U.S. Health Policy since 1940*, 137–176; Harmer RM. *American Medical Avarice*, 9–25, 18–19; Kaufman M, Galishoff S, Savitt TL, eds. *Dictionary of Ameri-*

*can Medical Biography.* 2 Vols. Westport, CT: Greenwood Press, 1984, 248–249; Cray E. *In Failing Health,* 51–94.

145. Cray E. *In Failing Health,* 53.

146. Cray E. *In Failing Health,* 54.

147. Cray E. *In Failing Health,* 83–84.

148. Cray E. *In Failing Health,* 85.

149. Starr P. *The Social Transformation of American Medicine,* 286.

150. Cray E. *In Failing Health,* 56.

151. Campion FD. *The AMA and U.S. Health Policy since 1940,* 56.

152. Starr P. *The Social Transformation of American Medicine,* 368.

153. Starr P. *The Social Transformation of American Medicine,* 368.

154. Starr P. *The Social Transformation of American Medicine,* 368.

155. Campion FD. *The AMA and U.S. Health Policy since 1940,* 137–176, 210; Cray E. *In Failing Health,* 51–94; Starr P. *The Social Transformation of American Medicine,* 363–378.

156. Cray E. *In Failing Health,* 94.

157. Campion FD. *The AMA and U.S. Health Policy since 1940,* 269.

158. Campion FD. *The AMA and U.S. Health Policy since 1940,* 269.

159. Campion FD. *The AMA and U.S. Health Policy since 1940,* 137–176, 210, 269–270; Cray E. *In Failing Health,* 51–109; Starr P. *The Social Transformation of American Medicine,* 363–378.

160. Campion FD. *The AMA and U.S. Health Policy since 1940,* 256.

161. Campion FD. *The AMA and U.S. Health Policy since 1940,* 256.

162. Starr P. *The Social Transformation of American Medicine,* 368.

163. Campion FD. *The AMA and U.S. Health Policy since 1940,* 254–283; Cray E. *In Failing Health,* 60–109; Starr P. *The Social Transformation of American Medicine,* 363–378; Ehrenreich B, Ehrenreich J. *The American Health Empire,* 176–231.

164. Campion FD. *The AMA and U.S. Health Policy since 1940,* 127–231; Cray E. *In Failing Health;* Starr P. *The Social Transformation of American Medicine,* 290–378.

165. Hirshfield DS. *The Lost Reform,* 148.

166. Campion FD. *The AMA and U.S. Health Policy since 1940,* 136.

167. Campion FD. *The AMA and U.S. Health Policy since 1940,* 136.

168. Campion FD. *The AMA and U.S. Health Policy since 1940,* 137.

169. Cray E. *In Failing Health,* 73.

170. Cray E. *In Failing Health,* 73.

171. Cray E. *In Failing Health,* 74.

172. Cray E. *In Failing Health,* 74.

173. Cray E. *In Failing Health,* 74.

174. Cray E. *In Failing Health,* 75.

175. Campion FD. *The AMA and U.S. Health Policy since 1940,* 137.

176. Campion FD. *The AMA and U.S. Health Policy since 1940,* 137; Cray E. *In Failing Health,* 75.

177. Hirshfield DS. *The Lost Reform,* 148–149; Campion FD. *The AMA and U.S. Health Policy since 1940,* 127–231; Cray E. *In Failing Health,* 72–75.

178. Hirshfield DS. *The Lost Reform,* 148–149; Campion FD. *The AMA and U.S. Health Policy since 1940,* 177–252; Cray E. *In Failing Health;* Starr P. *The Social Transformation of American Medicine,* 292–378.

179. Morais HM. *The History of the Negro in Medicine,* 132–137; Cobb WM. The Black American in medicine; New York County Medical Society condemns discrimination. *Journal of the National Medical Association* 1952; 44:149; Manning KR. Health and health care providers. In Selzman J, Smith DL, West C. eds. *Encyclopedia of African-American Culture and History,* 1247–1255; Byrd WM. Medical associations. In: Salzman J, Smith DL, West C. eds. *Encyclopedia of African-American Culture and History,* 1747–1749; Byrd WM, Clayton LA. *A Black Health Trilogy.*

180. Cobb WM. The Black American in medicine, 1226–1227.

181. Beardsley EH. *A History of Neglect*, 246.

182. Beardsley EH. *A History of Neglect*, 245.

183. Beardsley EH. *A History of Neglect*, 247.

184. Beardsley EH. *A History of Neglect*, 247.

185. Beardsley EH. *A History of Neglect*, 247.

186. Reynolds PP. Hospitals and civil rights, 1945–1963, 898.

187. Cornely PB. Segregation and discrimination in medical care in the U.S.; Cornely PB. Trends in racial integration in hospitals in the United States.

188. Reynolds PP. The federal government's use of Title VI and Medicare to racially integrate hospitals in the United States, 1963 through 1967, 1850–1851.

189. Reynolds PP. The federal government's use of Title VI and Medicare to racially integrate hospitals in the United States, 1963 through 1967, 1851.

190. Holloman Jr. JLS. A new horizon: President's inaugural address, National Medical Association. *Journal of the National Medical Association* 1966; 58:371–376, 374–375; Berry LH. Special health care needs of the disadvantaged; Berry LH. Implementation of new health legislation and its impact upon disadvantaged population groups; Swan LF. The exigencies of the American environment, 1967: President's inaugural address, National Medical Association. *Journal of the National Medical Association* 1967; 59:373–377.

191. Morais HM. *The History of the Negro in Medicine*, 149.

192. Morais HM. *The History of the Negro in Medicine*, 148.

193. Morais HM. *The History of the Negro in Medicine*, 153.

194. Reynolds PP. The federal government's use of Title VI and Medicare to racially integrate hospitals in the United States, 1963 through 1967, 1850.

195. Morais HM. *The History of the Negro in Medicine*, 147.

196. Dowling HF. *City Hospitals*, 168.

197. Morais HM. *The History of the Negro in Medicine*, 147.

198. Morais HM. *The History of the Negro in Medicine*, 147.

199. Morais HM. *The History of the Negro in Medicine*, 147.

200. Morais HM. *The History of the Negro in Medicine*, 147.

201. Morais HM. *The History of the Negro in Medicine*, 147.

202. Morais HM. *The History of the Negro in Medicine*, 148.

203. Morais HM. *The History of the Negro in Medicine*, 148.

204. Morais HM. *The History of the Negro in Medicine*, 148.

205. Morais HM. *The History of the Negro in Medicine*, 148.

206. Beardsley EH. *A History of Neglect*, 247.

207. Morais HM. *The History of the Negro in Medicine*, 128–130, 140–153; Smith DB. *Health Care Divided*; Cornely PB. Segregation and discrimination in medical care in the U.S.; Cornely PB. Trends in racial integration in hospitals in the United States; Freedmen's Hospital school of nursing alumni association. *Journal of the National Medical Association* 1966; 58:23; Holloman Jr. JLS. A new horizon; Berry LH. Special health care needs of the disadvantaged; Berry LH. Implementation of new health legislation and its impact upon disadvantaged population groups; Swan LF. The exigencies of the American environment, 1967; Byrd WM, Clayton LA. An American health dilemma; Cobb WM The Black American in medicine; Beardsley EH. *A History of Neglect*, 245–309; Byrd WM, Clayton LA. *A Black Health Trilogy*; Reynolds PP. Hospitals and civil rights, 1945–1963; Reynolds PP. The federal government's use of Title VI and Medicare to racially integrate hospitals in the United States, 1963 through 1967; Dowling HF. *City Hospitals*; National Council of Arts, Sciences and Professions, Southern California Chapter. *A Survey of Discrimination in the Health Field in Los Angeles*. Los Angeles, 1951; Detroit Commission on Community Relations. *Racial Factors in Policy and Practice: Hospital and Bed Utilization, 47 Detroit Area General Hospitals*. Detroit, 1956; Committee to End Discrimination in Chicago Medical Institutions; What Color Are Your Germs? *Journal of the National Medical Association* 1955; 47:264–267; Chicago Urban League Research Department. A Staff Working Paper on Integration in Hospital Appointments and Hospital Care. Report prepared for the workshops of the Second Imhotep National Conference on Hospital Integration, May 23–24, 1958; Cobb WM. *Progress and Portents*

*for the Negro In Medicine.* New York: National Association for the Advancement of Colored People, 1948, 118.

208. Cobb WM. The Black American in medicine, 1226.

209. Rankin-Hill LM, Blakey ML. William Montague Cobb (1904–1990): Obituary. *American Journal of Physical Anthropology* 1993; 92:545–548, quote 548.

210. Rankin-Hill LM, Blakey ML. William Montague Cobb (1904–1990).

211. Rankin-Hill LM, Blakey ML. William Montague Cobb (1904–1990), 548.

212. Beardsley EH. *A History of Neglect,* 249.

213. The N.M.A. and civil rights. *Journal of the National Medical Association* 1966; 58:130; Morais HM. *The History of the Negro in Medicine,* 131–208; Cobb WM. The Black American in medicine; Falk LA. Black abolitionist doctors and healers, 1810–1885. *Bulletin of the History of Medicine* 1980; 54:253–272; Bousfield MO. An account of physicians of color in the United States. *Bulletin of the History of Medicine* 1945; 17:61–84; Dickerson DC. The Black Physician. A paper presented at the Black Health: Historical Perspectives and Current Issues Conference. Department of the History of Medicine, University of Wisconsin-Madison, April 6, 1990; Dr. Kenney resigns. *Journal of the National Medical Association* 1948; 40:221; Rankin-Hill LM, Blakey ML. William Montague Cobb (1904–1990); Manning KR. Health and health care providers; Byrd WM. Medical associations; Byrd WM, Clayton LA. *A Black Health Trilogy.*

214. Alexander PN. Lewis, JH. In: Salzman J, Smith DL, West C. eds. *Encyclopedia of African-American Culture and History,* 1609–1610, quote 1610.

215. Beardsley EH. *A History of Neglect,* 249.

216. Logan RW. Wright, Louis Tompkins. In Logan RW, Winston MR, eds. *Dictionary of American Negro Biography.* New York: W. W. Norton, 1982, 670–671, quote 670.

217. Cobb WM. Statement in support of National Health Bill, S. 1606, on behalf of the National Association for the Advancement of Colored People.

218. Manning KR. Cobb, William Montague. In: Salzman J, Smith DL, West C, eds. *Encyclopedia of African-American Culture and History,* 601–603, quote 602.

219. Kurtz LH. The history of surgery at the District of Columbia General Hospital. *Journal of the National Medical Association* 1997; 89:761–764, 762.

220. Hayden RC. Wright, Louis Tompkins. In: Salzman J, Smith DL, West C, eds. *Encyclopedia of African-American Culture and History,* 2893–2895, quote 2894.

221. Cobb WM. The Black American in medicine, 1187.

222. Morais HM. *The History of the Negro in Medicine,* 143.

223. Reynolds PP. Hospitals and civil rights, 1945–1963; Reynolds PP. The federal government's use of Title VI and Medicare to racially integrate hospitals in the United States, 1963 through 1967; Manning KR. Cobb, William Montague; Lewis JH. *The Biology of the Negro.* Chicago: University of Chicago Press, 1942; Cobb WM. James McCune Smith. *Journal of the National Medical Association* 1952; 44:160–162; Bousfield MO. An account of physicians of color in the United States; Alexander PN. Lewis, Julian Herman; Blakey ML, et al. The W. Montague Cobb Skeletal Collection Curatorial Project. First Report, Howard University; Hayden RC. Wright, Louis Tompkins; Cobb WM. The Black American in medicine; The N.M.A. and civil rights; Cobb WM. *Medical Care and the Plight of the Negro.* New York: National Association for the Advancement of Colored People, 1947; Cobb WM. *Progress and Portents for the Negro in Medicine;* Cobb WM. The Laboratory of Anatomy and Physical Anthropology of Howard University, Washington, DC; Cobb WM. Race and runners. *Journal of Health and Physical Education* 1936; 7:1–9; Cobb WM. Physical anthropology of the American Negro. *American Journal of Physical Anthropology* 1942; 29:113–222; Rankin-Hill LM, Blakey ML. William Montague Cobb (1904–1990); Kurtz LH. The history of surgery at the District of Columbia General Hospital; Morais HM. *The History of the Negro in Medicine,* 131–208.

224. Morais HM. *The History of the Negro in Medicine,* 142.

225. Morais HM. *The History of the Negro in Medicine,* 142.

226. Beardsley EH. *A History of Neglect,* 258.

227. Morais HM. *The History of the Negro in Medicine,* 107–109, 132–151; Beardsley EH. *A History of Neglect,* 258; Cobb WM. Charles Richard Drew, M.D., 1904–1950. *Journal of the National Medical Association* 1950; 42:239–245; Starr D. *Blood: An Epic History of Medicine and Com-*

*merce*. New York: Knopf, 1998. Paperback ed. New York: Quill, 2000, 96–100; Wynes CE. *Charles Richard Drew: The Man and the Myth*. Urbana: University of Illinois Press, 1988; Yancy Sr. AG. The life of Charles R. Drew, M.D., M.D.Sc. and perspectives of a former resident in general surgery. In: Organ CH, Kosiba MM, eds. *A Century of Black Surgeons: The U.S.A. Experience*. 2 Vols. Norman, OK: Transcript Press, 1987, 63–102; Bernard LJ. The Meharry story: Boyd, McMillan, Hale, and Walker. 103–147. In: Organ CH, Kosiba MM, eds. *A Century of Black Surgeons: The U.S.A. Experience*; Hines RH. *The Health Status of Negroes in a Mid-Southern Urban Community*. Parts 1 and 2. Nashville: Meharry Medical College, 1967; The Meharry North Nashville Neighborhood Health Center. *Journal of the National Medical Association* 1967; 59:448; Summerville J. *Educating Black Doctors*; Carter H. He's doing something about the race problem. *Saturday Evening Post* February 23, 1946; 218:30.

228. Beardsley EH. *A History of Neglect*, 251.

229. Beardsley EH. *A History of Neglect*, 249.

230. Beardsley EH. *A History of Neglect*, 249.

231. Morais HM. *The History of the Negro in Medicine*, 259.

232. Cobb WM. The crushing irony of deluxe Jim Crow. *Journal of the National Medical Association* 1952; 44:387.

233. Beardsley EH. *A History of Neglect*, 259.

234. Beardsley EH. *A History of Neglect*, 252, 245–272; Reynolds PP. Hospitals and civil rights, 1945–1963; Reynolds PP. The federal government's use of Title VI and Medicare to racially integrate hospitals in the United States, 1963 through 1967; Alexander PN. Cornely, Paul Bertau. In: Salzman J, Smith DL, West C, eds. *Encyclopedia of African-American Culture and History*, 661; Anderson JD. *The Education of Blacks in the South, 1860–1935*. Chapel Hill: University of North Carolina Press, 1988; Summerville J. *Educating Black Doctors*; Cornely PB. Morbidity and mortality from scarlet fever in the Negro. *American Journal of Public Health* 1939; 29:999–1005; Cornely PB. Observations on the health progress of Negroes in the U.S. during the past two decades. *Southern Medical Journal* 1941; 34:1286; Cornely PB. Trends in public health activities among Negroes in 96 Southern counties during the period 1930–39. *American Journal of Public Health* 1942; 32:1117–1123; Cornely PB. Distribution of Negro physicians in the United States in 1942. *Journal of the American Medical Association* 1944; 124:826; Cornely PB. Race relations in community health organization. *American Journal of Public Health* 1946; 36:990; Cornely PB. Distribution of Negro dentists in the United States. *Journal of the Ameircan Dental Association* 1947; 34:750; Cornely PB. Report of the Health Consultant for Charleston, South Carolina. Community Relations Project of the National Urban League (unpublished, n.d., but c. 1947); Cornely PB. The economics of medical practice and the Negro physician. *Journal of the National Medical Association* 1951; 43:84–92; Cornely PB. Trends in public health activities. *American Journal of Public Health* 1956; 46:117–123; Cornely PB. Segregation and discrimination in medical care in the U.S.; Cornely PB. Trends in racial integration in hospitals in the United States; Carter H. He's doing something about the race problem; N.A.A.C.P. 1965 resolutions on hospitals and health. *Journal of the National Medical Association* 1965; 57:512–513. Integration Battlefront; N.A.A.C.P. Legal Defense and Educational Fund, Inc., cases. *Journal of the National Medical Association* 1965; 57:513–514; Morais HM. *The History of the Negro in Medicine*, 131–208; Cobb WM. The crushing irony of deluxe Jim Crow.

235. Beardsley EH. *A History of Neglect*, 261.

236. Beardsley EH. *A History of Neglect*, 261.

237. Beardsley EH. *A History of Neglect*, 259.

238. Morais HM. *The History of the Negro in Medicine*, 180.

239. Morais HM. *The History of the Negro in Medicine*, 181.

240. Beardsley EH. *A History of Neglect*, 245–272; Smith DB. *Health Care Divided*; Reynolds PP. Hospitals and civil rights, 1945–1963; Reynolds PP. The federal government's use of Title VI and Medicare to racially integrate hospitals in the United States, 1963 through 1967; Russell T. Eaton, Hubert Arthur. In: Salzman J, Smith DL, West C. eds. *Encyclopedia of African-American Culture and History*, 825; Imhotep National Conference on Hospital Integration. The proceedings of the Imhotep national conference on hospital integration. Parts 1–3. *Journal of the National Medical Association* 1957; 49:189–201, 272–273, 429–433; N.A.A.C.P. 1965 resolutions on hospitals and health; N.A.A.C.P. Legal Defense and Educational Fund, Inc., cases; Morais HM. *The History*

*of the Negro in Medicine,* 173–188, App. 7; Gifis SH. *Law Dictionary.* Woodbury, NY: Barron's Educational Series, Inc., 1984, 431–432.

241. Morais HM. *The History of the Negro in Medicine,* 144.

242. Morais HM. *The History of the Negro in Medicine,* 144.

243. Cobb WM. The Black American in medicine, 1199.

244. Cobb WM. The Black American in medicine, 1199.

245. Morais HM. *The History of the Negro in Medicine,* 140–153; Cobb WM. The Black American in medicine, 1190–1199; The N.M.A. and civil rights; Beardsley EH. *A History of Neglect,* 245–272; Reynolds PP. Hospitals and civil rights, 1945–1963; Reynolds PP. The federal government's use of Title VI and Medicare to racially integrate hospitals in the United States, 1963 through 1967; Imhotep National Conference on Hospital Integration. The proceedings of the Imhotep national conference on hospital integration. Parts 1–3; Johnson RP. The minister's welcome. *Journal of the National Medical Association* 1957; 49:55, 57; The Imhotep National Conference on Hospital Integration. *Journal of the National Medical Association* 1957; 49:55–58; Fitzpatrick S, Goodwin MR. *The Guide to Black Washington: Places and Events of Historical and Cultural Significance in the Nation's Capital.* New York: Hippocrene Books, 1990, 20, 39, 41, 199.

246. Morais HM. *The History of the Negro in Medicine,* 159–160.

247. Morais HM. *The History of the Negro in Medicine,* 161.

248. Morais HM. *The History of the Negro in Medicine,* 162.

249. Morais HM. *The History of the Negro in Medicine,* 162.

250. McBride D. Medical Committee for Human Rights, 1749.

251. Morais HM. *The History of the Negro in Medicine,* 168.

252. Marable M. *Race, Reform, and Rebellion,* 13–85; Brinkley A. *The Unfinished Nation,* 747–835; Morais HM. *The History of the Negro in Medicine,* 159–208; Smith DB. *Health Care Divided;* The N.M.A. and civil rights; Cobb WM. What hath God wrought; Beardsley EH. *A History of Neglect,* 245–314; The president-elect (John L.S. Holloman, B.S., M.D.). *Journal of the National Medical Associaiton* 1965; 57:507–508; The National Medical Association's contribution to the Selma-Montgomery march. *Journal of the National Medical Association* 1965; 57:243–244; McBride D. Medical Committee for Human Rights.

253. Morais HM. *The History of the Negro in Medicine,* 173.

254. Morais HM. *The History of the Negro in Medicine,* 174.

255. Morais HM. *The History of the Negro in Medicine,* 168.

256. Morais HM. *The History of the Negro in Medicine,* 173.

257. Morais HM. *The History of the Negro in Medicine,* 157–208; The N.M.A. and civil rights; Cobb WM. What hath God wrought; Eaton HA. Views of North Carolina Negro physicians on medical assistance for the aged. *Journal of the National Medical Association* 1965; 57:166–167; Beardsley EH. *A History of Neglect,* 245–314; The National Medical Association's contribution to the Selma-Montgomery march; McBride D. Medical Committee for Human Rights; Brinkley A. *The Unfinished Nation,* 811–819; Williams J. *Eyes on the Prize,* 196–205, 250–287; Branch T. *Pillar of Fire;* Marable M. *Race, Reform, and Rebellion,* 13–85; Campion FD. *The AMA and U.S. Health Policy since 1940,* 277, 253–283; Clement KW, Cobb WM. National Medical Association testimony on behalf of H.R. 3920, the King-Anderson Bill, before the Committee on Ways and Means, U.S. House of Representatives, January 22, 1964. *Journal of the National Medical Association* 1964; 56:213–221.

258. Beardsley EH. *A History of Neglect,* 245.

259. Beardsley EH. *A History of Neglect,* 251.

260. Morais HM. *The History of the Negro in Medicine,* 134.

261. Morais HM. *The History of the Negro in Medicine,* 134.

262. Reynolds PP. The federal government's use of Title VI and Medicare to racially integrate hospitals in the United States, 1963 through 1967, 1851.

263. Morais HM. *The History of the Negro in Medicine,* 134.

264. North Carolina Society drops final bars. *Journal of the National Medical Association* 1965; 57:512.

265. Beardsley EH. *A History of Neglect,* 252.

266. Morais HM. *The History of the Negro in Medicine*, 135.

267. Morais HM. *The History of the Negro in Medicine*, 135.

268. Morais HM. *The History of the Negro in Medicine*, 136.

269. Beardsley EH. *A History of Neglect*, 253.

270. Beardsley EH. *A History of Neglect*, 253.

271. Beardsley EH. *A History of Neglect*, 253.

272. Cobb WM. The Black American in medicine, 1227.

273. Beardsley EH. *A History of Neglect*, 253.

274. Cobb WM. *Progress and Portents for the Negro In Medicine*, 116.

275. Morais HM. *The History of the Negro in Medicine*, 137.

276. Morais HM. *The History of the Negro in Medicine*, 138.

277. Reynolds PP. The federal government's use of Title VI and Medicare to racially integrate hospitals in the United States, 1963 through 1967, 1851.

278. Cobb WM. The Black American in medicine, 1226.

279. Morais HM. *The History of the Negro in Medicine*, 131–208; Reynolds PP. Hospitals and civil rights, 1945–1963; Beardsley EH. *A History of Neglect*, 245–272; Cobb WM. The establishment, the Negro and education; Cobb WM. NAACP's resolutions on health. *Journal of the National Medical Association* 1953; 45:438–439; Cobb WM. The national health program of the N.A.A.C.P. *Journal of the National Medical Association* 1953; 45:333–339; Cobb WM. The Black American in medicine; Cobb WM. Integration in medicine: A national need. *Journal of the National Medical Association* 1957; 49:4; A significant step by the Southern Medical Association. *Journal of the National Medical Association* 1967; 59:56; Berry LH. Projection of the 1965 position of the NMA with reference to liaison efforts with the AMA to improve the problems of discrimination in medicine. *Journal of the National Medical Association* 1966; 58:148–149; Reynolds PP. Hospitals and civil rights, 1945–1963; Reynolds PP. The federal government's use of Title VI and Medicare to racially integrate hospitals in the United States, 1963 through 1967; Cobb WM. *Medical Care and the Plight of the Negro*; Cobb WM. *Progress and Portents for the Negro in Medicine*; Kluger R. *Simple Justice*, 187–194, 202–204, 213, 258–260; Cobb WM. The Black American in medicine.

280. Cobb WM. The Black American in medicine, 1226–1227.

281. Beardsley EH. *A History of Neglect*, 251.

282. Cobb WM. The Black American in medicine, 1227.

283. Cobb WM. What hath God wrought, 518–519.

284. Morais HM. *The History of the Negro in Medicine*, 137.

285. Campion FD. *The AMA and U.S. Health Policy since 1940*, 57–58, 136–137, 299–300; Cobb WM. The Black American in medicine; Beardsley EH. *A History of Neglect*, 245–272; Morais HM. *The History of the Negro in Medicine*, 131–208; Hine DC. Nursing. In: Salzman J, Smith DL, West C, eds. *Encyclopedia of African-American Culture and History*, 2034–2036.

286. Cornely PB. The economics of medical practice and the Negro physician.

287. Morais HM. *The History of the Negro in Medicine*, 97–208; Holloman Jr. JLS. Medical leadership; Holloman Jr. JLS. An open letter to the vice president. *Journal of the National Medical Association* 1966; 58:472; Holloman Jr. JLS. Cross currents in the flow of medical practice. *Journal of the National Medical Association* 1967; 59:216; Cobb WM. The Black American in medicine; Cobb WM. *Medical Care and the Plight of the Negro*; Cobb WM. *Progress and Portents for the Negro in Medicine*; Cornely PB. The economics of medical practice and the Negro physician; Campion FD. *The AMA and U.S. Health Policy since 1940*, 277–283.

288. Annas GJ, Grodin MA, eds. *The Nazi Doctors and the Nuremberg Code: Human Rights in Human Experimentation*. New York: Oxford University Press, 1992, 201.

289. Annas GJ, Grodin MA, eds. *The Nazi Doctors and the Nuremberg Code*, 6.

290. Annas GJ, Grodin MA, eds. *The Nazi Doctors and the Nuremberg Code*, 201.

291. Proctor RN. Nazi doctors, racial medicine, and human experimentation. In: Annas GJ, Grodin MA, eds. *The Nazi Doctors and the Nuremberg Code*, 17–31, quote 26; Pross C. Nazi doctors, German medicine, and historical truth. In: Annas GJ, Grodin MA, eds. *The Nazi Doctors and the Nuremberg Code*, 32–52, quote 45.

292. Chase A. *The Legacy of Malthus: The Social Costs of the New Scientific Racism.* New York: Knopf, 1980, 108.

293. Pross C. Nazi doctors, German medicine, and historical truth, 38.

294. Proctor RN. Nazi doctors, racial medicine, and human experimentation, 18.

295. Proctor RN. Nazi doctors, racial medicine, and human experimentation, 286.

296. Kater MH. *Doctors under Hitler.* Chapel Hill: University of North Carolina Press, 1989, 114, 177; Müller-Hill B. *Murderous Science: Elimination by Scientific Selection of Jews, Gypsies, and Others in Germany, 1933–1945.* Plainview, NY: Cold Spring Harbor Laboratory Press, 1998, 8; McNeil Jr., DG. Its past on its sleeve, tribe seeks Bonn's apology *New York Times* May 31, 1998; 3.

297. Annas GJ, Grodin MA, eds. *The Nazi Doctors and the Nuremberg Code*, 32.

298. Annas GJ, Grodin MA, eds. *The Nazi Doctors and the Nuremberg Code*, 38.

299. Pross C. Nazi doctors, German medicine, and historical truth, 39.

300. Proctor RN. *Racial Hygiene: Medicine under the Nazis.* Cambridge, MA: Harvard University Press, 1988, 7.

301. Pross C. Nazi doctors, German medicine, and historical truth, 39.

302. Proctor RN. Nazi doctors, racial medicine, and human experimentation, 23.

303. Chase A. *The Legacy of Malthus*, 349.

304. Larson EJ. *Sex, Race, and Science: Eugenics in the Deep South.* Baltimore: Johns Hopkins University Press, 1995, 155.

305. Weisbord RG. *Genocide? Birth Control and the Black American.* Westport, CT: Greenwood Press, 1975, 32.

306. Weisbord RG. *Genocide?* 151.

307. Weisbord RG. *Genocide?* 151.

308. Weisbord RG. *Genocide?* 32.

309. Annas GJ. The Nuremberg Code in U.S. courts: Ethics versus expediency. In: Annas GJ, Grodin MA, eds. *The Nazi Doctors and the Nuremberg Code*, 201–222; Poliakov L. *The Aryan Myth: A History of Racist and Nationalistic Ideas in Europe.* New York: Barnes and Noble Books, 1974; Starr P. *The Social Transformation of American Medicine*; Morais HM. *The History of the Negro in Medicine*; Marable M. *Race, Reform, and Rebellion*; Chase A. *The Legacy of Malthus*; Lifton RJ. *The Nazi Doctors: Medical Killing and the Psychology of Genocide.* New York: Basic Books, 1986; Caplan AL, ed. *When Medicine Went Mad: Bioethics and the Holocaust.* Totowa, NJ: Humana Press, 1992; Aly G, Chroust P, Pross C. *Cleansing the Fatherland: Nazi Medicine and Racial Hygiene.* Baltimore: Johns Hopkins University Press, 1994; Kater MH. *Doctors under Hitler*; Müller-Hill B. *Murderous Science*; Lifton RJ, Eric Markusen. *The Genocidal Mentality: Nazi Holocaust and Nuclear Threat.* New York: Basic Books, 1990; Fredrickson GM. *The Black Image in the White Mind: The Debate on Afro-American Character and Destiny, 1871–1914.* New York: Harper & Row, 1971. Reprint ed. Middletown, CT: Wesleyan University Press, 1987; Gossett TF. *Race: The History of an Idea in America.* Dallas, TX: Southern Methodist University Press, 1963. Reprint ed. New York: Schocken Books, 1965; Washington HA. Of men and mice: Human guinea pigs: Unethical testing targets Blacks and the poor. *Emerge* October 1994 (1)(6):24; Reilly PR. *The Surgical Solution: A History of Involuntary Sterilization in the United States.* Baltimore: Johns Hopkins University Press, 1991; Larson EJ. *Sex, Race, and Science*; Weisbord RG. *Genocide?*

310. Annas GJ. The Nuremberg Code in U.S. courts, 204.

311. Washington HA. Henrietta Lacks—an unsung hero. *Emerge* October 1994 (1)(6):29.

312. Dixon B. *Health, Medicine and the Human Body.* New York: Macmillan, 1986, 211.

313. Washington HA. Henrietta Lacks—an unsung hero.

314. Annas GJ, Grodin MA, eds. *The Nazi Doctors and the Nuremberg Code*; Chase A. *The Legacy of Malthus*; Ryan W. *Blaming the Victim.* New York: Vintage Books, 1971. Revised, updated ed. New York: Vintage Books, 1976, 5–8; Williams DR, Fenton BT. The mental health of African Americans: Findings, questions, and directions. In: Livingston IL, ed. *Handbook of Black American Health: The Mosaic of Conditions, Issues, Policies, and Prospects.* Westport, CT: Greenwood Press, 1994, 253–268; Bullough B, Bullough VL. *Poverty, Ethnic Identity, and Health Care*; Washington HA. Henrietta Lacks—an unsung hero.

315. Jones JH. *Bad Blood*, 91–112.

316. Jones JH. *Bad Blood*, 16–29, 92–94, 106.

317. Jones JH. *Bad Blood*, 94.

318. Jones JH. *Bad Blood*, 92.

319. Jones JH. Tuskegee syphilis experiment. In: Salzman J, Smith DL, West C, eds. *Encyclopedia of African-American Culture and History*, 2685–2687, quote 2687.

320. Jones JH. Tuskegee syphilis experiment, 2687.

321. Jones JH. Tuskegee syphilis experiment, 2687.

322. Final report of the Tuskegee Syphilis Study Ad Hoc Advisory Panel. In: Reiser RJ, Dyck AJ, Curran WJ, eds. *Ethics in Medicine: Historical Perspectives and Contemporary Concerns.* Cambridge, MA: MIT Press, 1977, 316–321, quote 318.

323. Final report of the Tuskegee Syphilis Study Ad Hoc Advisory Panel, 318.

324. Final report of the Tuskegee Syphilis Study Ad Hoc Advisory Panel, 318.

325. Final report of the Tuskegee Syphilis Study Ad Hoc Advisory Panel, 318.

326. Jones JH. *Bad Blood*, 143–147, 172, 197–201, 209.

327. Jones JH. *Bad Blood*, 178.

328. Jones JH. *Bad Blood*, 180.

329. Jones JH. *Bad Blood*, 172.

330. Final report of the Tuskegee Syphilis Study Ad Hoc Advisory Panel. 316–321, 319.

331. Final report of the Tuskegee Syphilis Study Ad Hoc Advisory Panel. 316–321, 319.

332. Jones JH. *Bad Blood*; Jones JH. Tuskegee syphilis experiment; Johnson CS. *Shadow of the Plantation*; Final report of the Tuskegee Syphilis Study Ad Hoc Advisory Panel; Vonderlehr RA, et al. Untreated syphilis in the male Negro. *Venereal Disease Information* 1936; 17:260–265; Wegner OC. Untreated syphilis in Negro male. Hot Springs Seminar, 09–18–50 (from CDC Files); Brandt AM. Racism and research: The case of the Tuskegee syphilis study. In: Leavitt JW, Numbers RL, eds. *Sickness and Health in America: Readings in the History of Medicine and Public Health.* Madison: University of Wisconsin Press, 1985, 331–343; Strait G, DiIanni D. *The Deadly Deception.* Documentary video segment for *Nova*, Boston, WGBH, 1993; Sawyer D. The Tuskegee Study. Videotape segment, *Prime Time Live*, ABC television network, February 6, 1992.

333. Associated Press. MIT president rues radiation tests. *Fort Worth Star-Telegram*, January 9, 1993:A23; Hoverstein P. Radiation tests used inmates as guinea pigs. *USA Today* November 21, 1994:A3; Washington HA. Of men and mice; Annas GJ, Grodin MA, eds. *The Nazi Doctors and the Nuremberg Code*; Areen J, King PA, Goldberg S, Gostin L, Capron AM. *Law, Science and Medicine.* 2nd ed. Westbury, NY: The Foundation Press, 1996. Hornblum AM. *Acres of Skin: Human Experiments at Holmesburg Prison: A True Story of Abuse and Exploitation in the Name of Medical Science.* New York: Routledge, 1998; Welsome E. *The Plutonium Files: America's Secret Medical Experiments in the Cold War.* New York: The Dial Press, 1999.

334. Associated Press. MIT president rues radiation tests. *Fort Worth Star Telegram*, January 9, 1993:A23; Washington HA. Of men and mice; Annas GJ, Grodin MA, eds. *The Nazi Doctors and the Nuremberg Code*; Areen J, King PA, Goldberg S, Gostin L, Capron AM. *Law, Science and Medicine.* 2nd ed. Westbury, NY: The Foundation Press, 1996. Hornblum AM. *Acres of Skin: Human Experiments at Holmesburg Prison: A True Story of Abuse and Exploitation in the Name of Medical Science.* New York: Routledge, 1998; Welsome E. *The Plutonium Files: America's Secret Medical Experiments in the Cold War.* New York: The Dial Press, 1999.

335. Morais HM. *The History of the Negro in Medicine*; Byrd WM, Clayton LA. An American health dilemma; Byrd WM, Clayton LA. *A Black Health Trilogy*; Chase A. *The Legacy of Malthus*; Williams DR, Fenton BT. The mental health of African Americans; Bullough B, Bullough VL. *Poverty, Ethnic Identity, and Health Care*; Washington HA. Henrietta Lacks—an unsung hero; Dixon B. *Health, Medicine and the Human Body*, 174, 211; Washington HA. Of men and mice; Associated Press. MIT president rues radiation tests; Hoversten P. Radiation tests used inmates as guinea pigs; Robinson LS. Dialogue: Curbing a sick practice: Energy Secretary Hazel O'Leary focuses on government accountability in testing. *Emerge* October 1994;(1)(6):20.

## Chapter Four

1. Brinkley A. *The Unfinished Nation: A Concise History of the American People.* New York: Knopf, 1993, 836.

2. Davis K, Schoen C. *Health and the War on Poverty: A Ten-Year Appraisal.* Washington, DC: Brookings Institution, 1978, 1.

3. Brinkley A. *The Unfinished Nation,* 803–912; Alter J. America's Own Holocaust. *Newsweek* December 8, 1997: 61; Kluger R. *Simple Justice: The History of Brown v. Board of Education and Black America's Struggle for Equality.* New York: Knopf, 1976. Paperback ed. New York: Vintage Books, 1977; Hughes L, Meltzer M, Lincoln CE, Spencer JM. *A Pictorial History of Black Americans.* Rev. 6th ed. New York: Crown Publishers, 1995, 293, 302–303, 306–313; Halberstam D. The rage within, part six. Segment of multipart video series *The Fifties,* 1997, History Channel, May 15, 1998; Curry GE. The death that won't die: Memories of Emmett Till 40 years later. *Emerge* July/August 1995 (6)(9):24; Williams J. *Eyes on the Prize: America's Civil Rights Years, 1954–1965.* New York: Viking Penguin Inc., 1987, 1–161; Marable M. *Race, Reform. and Rebellion: The Second Reconstruction in Black America, 1945–1990.* Rev. 2nd ed. Jackson: University Press of Mississippi, 1991, 41–184; Reynolds PP. Hospitals and civil rights, 1945–1963: *Simkins v. Moses H. Cone Memorial Hospital. Annals of Internal Medicine* 1997; 126:898–906; Reynolds PP. The federal government's use of Title VI and Medicare to racially integrate hospitals in the United States, 1963 through 1967. *American Journal of Public Health* 1997; 87:1850–1858; Sitkoff H. History of the United States. In: *The New Grolier Multimedia Encyclopedia.* Release 6, MPC Version. Novato, CA: Grolier Electronic Publishing, Inc., The Software Toolworks, Inc., 1993, 51–57.

4. Marable M. *Race, Reform, and Rebellion,* 100.

5. Hampton H. Stekler P, Shearer J. *Eyes on the Prize II.* Videotape. The Promised Land (1967–1968). Eight-part documentary video produced by Blackside, WGBH Boston, and the Corporation for Public Broadcasting, 1990.

6. Marable M. *Race, Reform, and Rebellion,* 92.

7. Marable M. *Race, Reform, and Rebellion,* 92.

8. O'Reilly K. *Nixon's Piano: Presidents and Racial Politics from Washington to Clinton.* New York: The Free Press, 1995, 256.

9. Marable M. *Race, Reform, and Rebellion,* 92.

10. Marable M. *Race, Reform, and Rebellion,* 94.

11. Marable M. *Race, Reform, and Rebellion,* 94.

12. Brinkley A. *The Unfinished Nation,* 803–912; Sitkoff H. History of the United States, 51–57; Hampton H, DeVinney J, Lacy Jr. MD. *Eyes on the Prize II.* Videotape. The Time Has Come (1964–1966). Eight-part documentary video produced by Blackside, WGBH Boston, and the Corporation for Public Broadcasting, 1990; Hampton H, Bernard S, Pollard S. *Eyes on the Prize II.* Videotape. Two Societies (1965–1968). Eight-part documentary video produced by Blackside, WGBH Boston, and the Corporation for Public Broadcasting, 1990; Hughes L, Meltzer M, Lincoln CE, Spencer JM. *A Pictorial History of Black Americans,* 293, 302–303, 306–313; Lukas JA. *Common Ground: A Turbulent Decade in the Lives of Three American Families.* New York: Knopf, 1985. Paperback ed. New York: Vintage Books, 1986, 406; Clark KB. The essential educational program. *Journal of the National Medical Association* 1966; 58:109; Marable M. *Race, Reform, and Rebellion,* 41–184; O'Reilly K. *Black Americans: The FBI Files.* New York: Carroll and Graff Publishers, 1994; Hampton H, Stekler P, Shearer J. *Eyes on the Prize II.* Videotape. The Promised Land (1967–1968). Eight-part documentary video produced by Blackside, WGBH Boston, and the Corporation for Public Broadcasting, 1990; Hampton H, Rockefeller TK, Ott T, Massiah L. *Eyes on the Prize II.* Videotape. A Nation of Law? (1968–1971). Eight-part documentary video produced by Blackside, WGBH Boston, and the Corporation for Public Broadcasting, 1990; Cleaver E. *Soul on Ice.* New York: McGraw-Hill, 1968; Newton HP. *Revolutionary Suicide.* New York: Harcourt Brace Jovanovich, 1973; Carmichael S, Hamilton CV. *Black Power: The Politics of Liberation in America.* New York: Vintage Books, 1967; Hampton H, Massiah LJ, Rockefeller TK. *Eyes on the Prize II.* Videotape. Power (1966–1968). Eight-part documentary video produced by Blackside, WGBH Boston, and the Corporation for Public Broadcasting, 1990.

13. Marable M. *Race, Reform, and Rebellion,* 105.

14. Marable M. *Race, Reform, and Rebellion,* 104.

15. Marable M. *Race, Reform, and Rebellion*, 103.

16. Brinkley A. *The Unfinished Nation*, 803–912; Hampton H. *Eyes on the Prize*. Videotape. Six-part documentary video produced by Blackside, WGBH Boston, and the Corporation for Public Broadcasting, 1987; Hampton H. *Eyes on the Prize II*. Videotape. Eight-part documentary video produced by Blackside, WGBH Boston, and the Corporation for Public Broadcasting, 1990; Marable M. *Race, Reform, and Rebellion*, 41–184; Williams J. *Eyes on the Prize*, 1–161; Sitkoff H. History of the United States, 54–60; O'Reilly K. *Nixon's Piano*, 239–329.

17. Brinkley A. *The Unfinished Nation*, 867.

18. Brinkley A. *The Unfinished Nation*, 861.

19. Sitkoff H. History of the United States, 59.

20. Brinkley A. *The Unfinished Nation*, 836–871; Sitkoff H. History of the United States, 57–61; Brodie FM. *Richard Nixon The Shaping of His Character*. New York: W. W. Norton, 1981; McCullough D. *Nixon*. Videotape. Three-part documentary video for *The American Experience*, produced by WGBH Boston; Thames Television, WNET/Thirteen, and the Corporation for Public Broadcasting, 1990; Lukas JA. *Common Ground*.

21. Brinkley A. *The Unfinished Nation*, 873.

22. O'Reilly K. *Nixon's Piano*, 334.

23. O'Reilly K. *Nixon's Piano*, 339.

24. O'Reilly K. *Nixon's Piano*, 340.

25. Sitkoff H. History of the United States, 60.

26. Sitkoff H. History of the United States, 60.

27. Brinkley A. *The Unfinished Nation*, 872–881; Sitkoff H. History of the United States, 60–61; O'Reilly K. *Nixon's Piano*, 331–354; Lind M. *Up from Conservatism: Why the Right Is Wrong for America*. New York: The Free Press, 1996, 191–192; Hampton H, Shearer J, Stekler P. *Eyes on the Prize II*. Videotape. The Keys To The Kingdom (1974–1980). Eight-part documentary video produced by Blackside, WGBH Boston, and the Corporation for Public Broadcasting; Lukas JA. *Common Ground*, 608–609; Hampton H, Lacy Jr. MD, DeVinney JA. *Eyes on the Prize II*. Videotape. Back To The Movement (1979–1983). Eight-part documentary video produced by Blackside, Inc., WGBH Boston, and the Corporation for Public Broadcasting, 1990; McCullough D. *Reagan*. Videotape. Two-part documentary video for *The American Experience*, produced by WGBH Boston, and the Corporation for Public Broadcasting, 1998.

28. Ginzberg E. *The Medical Triangle: Physicians, Politicians, and the Public*. Cambridge, MA: Harvard University Press, 1990, 3.

29. Davis K, Schoen C. *Health and the War on Poverty*, vii.

30. Davis K, Schoen C. *Health and the War on Poverty*, vii.

31. Starr P. *The Social Transformation of American Medicine*. New York: Basic Books, 1982, 379.

32. Davis K, Schoen C. *Health and the War on Poverty*, vii.

33. Starr P. *The Social Transformation of American Medicine*, 379.

34. Starr P. *The Social Transformation of American Medicine*, 380.

35. Smith Mueller M, Gibson RM. National health expenditures, fiscal year 1975. *Social Security Bulletin* February 1976; 39(8):17.

36. Campion FD. *The AMA and U.S. Health Policy since 1940*. Chicago: Chicago Review Press for the American Medical Association, 1984, 305.

37. Cray E. *In Failing Health: The Medical Crisis and the A.M.A.* Indianapolis: Bobbs-Merrill Company, 1970, 236.

38. $60-Billion Crisis in Health Care. *Business Week* January 17, 1970: 50–64.

39. It's Time to Operate. *Fortune* January, 1970: 79.

40. Rutstein DD. *Blueprint for Medical Care*. Cambridge, MA: The MIT Press, 1974, xi.

41. Starr P. *The Social Transformation of American Medicine*, 383.

42. Cray E. *In Failing Health*, 136.

43. Starr P. *The Social Transformation of American Medicine*, 363.

44. Davis K, Schoen C. *Health and the War on Poverty*, 18–48.

45. Relman AS. The new medical-industrial complex. *New England Journal of Medicine* 1980; 303:963–970.

46. Berry LH. Special health care needs of the disadvantaged. *Journal of the National Medical Association* 1966; 58:72, 72; Ginzberg E. *The Medical Triangle*; Starr P. *The Social Transformation of American Medicine*, 367–419; Medical costs: Statement of the AFL-CIO executive council. *Journal of the National Medical Association* 1968; 60:527–528; Ginzberg E. The monetarization of medical care. *New England Journal of Medicine* 1984; 310:1162–1165; Cross EB. Federal roles and responsibilities in the organization, delivery and financing of health care. *Journal of the National Medical Association* 1970; 62:353; Holloman Jr. JLS. A call to arms. *Journal of the National Medical Association* 1967; 59:55; Holloman Jr. JLS. Cross currents in the flow of medical practice. *Journal of the National Medical Association* 1967; 59:216; Swan LF. The exigencies of the American environment, 1967: President's inaugural address, National Medical Association. *Journal of the National Medical Association* 1967; 59:373–377; Cray E. *In Failing Health*; Lindorf D. *Marketplace Medicine: The Rise of the For-Profit Hospital Chains*. New York: Bantam Books, 1992; Campion FD. *The AMA and U.S. Health Policy since 1940*, 305–358; Rutstein DD. *Blueprint for Medical Care*; Davis K, Schoen C. *Health and the War on Poverty*; Patterson JT. *The Dread Disease: Cancer and Modern American Culture*. Cambridge, MA: Harvard University Press, 1987; Haynes MA. The gap in health status between black and white Americans. In: Williams RA, ed. *Textbook of Black-Related Diseases*. New York: McGraw-Hill, 1975, 1–30; Davis K. *National Health Insurance: Benefits, Costs and Consequences*. Washington, DC: Brookings Institution, 1975; Haughton JG. Government's role in health care, past, present and future. *Journal of the National Medical Association* 1968; 60:87–91; Relman AS. The new medical-industrial complex; Whol S. *The Medical Industrial Complex*. New York: Harmony Books, 1984.

47. Starr P. *The Social Transformation of American Medicine*, 382.

48. Starr P. *The Social Transformation of American Medicine*, 380.

49. Starr P. *The Social Transformation of American Medicine*, 394.

50. Belkin L. The Ellwoods: But what about quality? *New York Times Magazine* December 8, 1996; 6:68.

51. Starr P. *The Social Transformation of American Medicine*, 406.

52. Starr P. *The Social Transformation of American Medicine*, 406.

53. Starr P. *The Social Transformation of American Medicine*, 406.

54. Ginzberg E. *The Medical Triangle*; Starr P. *The Social Transformation of American Medicine*, 367–419; Swan LF. The exigencies of the American environment, 1967; Holloman Jr. JLS. Cross currents in the flow of medical practice; Holloman Jr. JLS. A call to arms; Cray E. *In Failing Health*; Campion FD. *The AMA and U.S. Health Policy since 1940*, 305–358; Kingdon JW. *Agendas, Alternatives, and Public Policies*. New York: HarperCollins, 1984, 6–9; Belkin L. The Ellwoods; Davis K, Schoen C. *Health and the War on Poverty*; Haynes MA. The gap in health status between black and white Americans; Rutstein DD. *Blueprint for Medical Care*; Davis K. *National Health Insurance*; Haughton JG. Government's role in health care, past, present and future; Woods CB. The neighborhood health center—the concept and the national scene. *Journal of the National Medical Association* 1971; 63:52–57; Kennedy EM. *In Critical Condition: The Crisis in America's Health Care*. New York: Simon & Schuster, 1972.

55. Lander L. *Defective Medicine: Risk, Anger, and the Malpractice Crisis*. New York: Farrar, Straus and Giroux, 1978, 186.

56. Starr P. *The Social Transformation of American Medicine*, 367–419; Cray E. *In Failing Health*; Lander L. *Defective Medicine*, 169–189; Davis K, Schoen C. *Health and the War on Poverty*; Kennedy EM. *In Critical Condition*; Haynes MA. The gap in health status between black and white Americans; Campion FD. *The AMA and U.S. Health Policy since 1940*, 363–421; Haynes MA. The National Medical Association's health program for the inner city. *Journal of the National Medical Association* 1968; 60:420.

57. Campion FD. *The AMA and U.S. Health Policy since 1940*, 277–283; Starr P. *The Social Transformation of American Medicine*, 367–370.

58. New payment plan for Medicare hospital services. *Journal of the National Medical Association* 1968; 60:20.

59. Haughton JG. Government's role in health care, past, present and future, 91.

60. Cordtz D. Change begins in the doctor's office. *Fortune* January 1970: 84.

61. Ginzberg E. *The Medical Triangle*; Veatch RM. *A Theory of Medical Ethics*. New York: Basic Books, 1981, 1–12; Havighurst CC. *Health Care Law and Policy: Readings, Notes, and Questions*. Westbury, NY: The Foundation Press, 1988, 111–112; Campion FD. *The AMA and U.S. Health Policy since 1940*, 277–283, 305–421; Starr P. *The Social Transformation of American Medicine*, 363–419; Patterson JT. *The Dread Disease*, 255–294; Navarro V. *Dangerous to Your Health: Capitalism in Health Care*. New York: Monthly Review Press, 1993; Starr P. *The Social Transformation of American Medicine*, 367–419; Cray E. *In Failing Health*; Lander L. *Defective Medicine*, 169–189; Lindorf D. *Marketplace Medicine*; Burger Jr EJ. *Science at the White House: A Political Liability*. Baltimore: Johns Hopkins University Press, 1980, 25–44; Davis K, Schoen C. *Health and the War on Poverty*; Kennedy EM. *In Critical Condition*; Haynes MA. The gap in health status between black and white Americans; Haynes MA. The National Medical Association's health program for the inner city; Fukuyama F. *Trust: The Social Virtues and the Creation of Prosperity*. New York: The Free Press, 1995.

62. Young Q. The urban hospital: Inequity, high tech, and low performance. In: Sidel VW, Sidel R, eds. *Reforming Medicine: Lessons of the Last Quarter Century*. New York: Pantheon Books, 1984, 33–49, quote 34.

63. Hammonds KE. Blacks and the urban health crisis. *Journal of the National Medical Association* 1974; 66:226–231, quote 228; U.S. Department of Health, Education, and Welfare. *Towards a Comprehensive Health Policy for the 1970s*. Washington, DC: Government Printing Office, 1971.

64. Relman AS. The new medical-industrial complex, 963.

65. Relman AS. The new medical-industrial complex, 964.

66. Ehrenreich B, Ehrenreich J. *The American Health Empire: Power, Profits, and Politics*. New York: Random House, 1970, 114.

67. Relman AS. The new medical-industrial complex, 964.

68. Ginzberg E. *The Medical Triangle*, 5.

69. Roberts RI. Hospitals continue to grow despite federal cutbacks. *Journal of the National Medical Association* 1974; 66:242.

70. Ginzberg E. *The Medical Triangle*, 112.

71. Young Q. The urban hospital, 34–35.

72. Relman AS. The new medical-industrial complex, 968.

73. Gray BH. *The Profit Motive and Patient Care: The Changing Accountability of Doctors and Hospitals*. Cambridge, MA: Harvard University Press, 1991, 8.

74. Gray BH. *The Profit Motive and Patient Care*, 8.

75. Starr P. *The Social Transformation of American Medicine*, 384.

76. Reynolds PP. The federal government's use of Title VI and Medicare to racially integrate hospitals in the United States, 1963 through 1967, 1856.

77. Reynolds PP. The federal government's use of Title VI and Medicare to racially integrate hospitals in the United States, 1963 through 1967, 1856.

78. The Hill-Burton program and civil rights. *Journal of the National Medical Association* 1965; 57:59–61.

79. Hatcher RG. Does Gary, Indiana, reflect the national problem of medicine in the ghetto? In: Norman JC, ed. *Medicine in the Ghetto*. New York: Appleton-Century-Crofts, 1969, 21–31.

80. Relman AS. The new medical-industrial complex; National Center for Health Statistics. *Prevention Profile. Health United States, 1991*. Hyattsville, MD: Public Health Service, 1992, 255; Starr P. *The Social Transformation of American Medicine*, 379–419; Young Q. The urban hospital, 34; Hammonds KE. Blacks and the urban health crisis; U.S. Department of Health, Education, and Welfare. *Towards a Comprehensive Health Policy for the 1970s*; Ginzberg E. *The Medical Triangle*; Roberts RI. Hospitals continue to grow despite federal cutbacks; Phillips CW. The changing concept of a charity hospital. *Journal of the National Medical Association* 1970; 62:303; Gray BH. *The Profit Motive and Patient Care*; Lindorf D. *Marketplace Medicine*; Smith DB. *Health Care Divided: Race and Healing a Nation*. Baltimore: Johns Hopkins University Press, 1999; Ginzberg E. *Teaching Hospitals and the Urban Poor*. New Haven, CT: Yale University Press, 2000; Holloman Jr. JLS. Cross currents in the flow of medical practice; Swan LF. The exigencies of the American environment, 1967; Reynolds PP. The federal government's use of Title VI and Medicare to racially

integrate hospitals in the United States, 1963 through 1967; Hatcher RG. Does Gary, Indiana, reflect the national problem of medicine in the ghetto?; Haynes MA. The National Medical Association's health program for the inner city; The Commonwealth Fund. *Contributing to the Community: The Economic Significance of Academic Health Centers and Their Role in Neighborhood Development*, Report IV. New York: The Commonwealth Fund, 1987.

81. Ginzberg E. *The Medical Triangle*, 35.

82. Reynolds PP. The federal government's use of Title VI and Medicare to racially integrate hospitals in the United States, 1963 through 1967, 1850.

83. Campion FD. *The AMA and U.S. Health Policy since 1940*, 339.

84. Campion FD. *The AMA and U.S. Health Policy since 1940*, 341.

85. Ginzberg E. *The Medical Triangle*; Anders G. *Health against Wealth: HMOs and the Breakdown of Medical Trust*. Boston: Houghton Mifflin, 1996, 16–34; Ginzberg E. *Teaching Hospitals and the Urban Poor*; Reynolds PP. The federal government's use of Title VI and Medicare to racially integrate hospitals in the United States, 1963 through 1967; Hammonds KE. Blacks and the urban health crisis, 228; U.S. Department of Health, Education, and Welfare. *Towards a Comprehensive Health Policy for the 1970s*; Cross EB. Federal roles and responsibilities in the organization, delivery and financing of health care; Berry LH. Special health care needs of the disadvantaged. *Journal of the National Medical Association* 1966; 58:72–73; Berry LH. Implementation of new health legislation and its impact upon disadvantaged population groups. *Journal of the National Medical Association* 1966; 58:129; National Center for Health Statistics. *Prevention Profile*, 274; Campion FD. *The AMA and U.S. Health Policy since 1940*, 334–349; Cray E. *In Failing Health*, 182–199; Starr P. *The Social Transformation of American Medicine*, 367–378; Davis K, Schoen C. *Health and the War on Poverty*; Haynes MA. The gap in health status between black and white Americans; Geiger HJ. Community health centers: Health care as an instrument of social change. In: Sidel VW, Sidel R, eds. *Reforming Medicine: Lessons of the Last Quarter Century*. New York: Pantheon Books, 1984, 11–32.

86. Gray BH. *The Profit Motive and Patient Care*, 13.

87. Campion FD. *The AMA and U.S. Health Policy since 1940*, 353.

88. Campion FD. *The AMA and U.S. Health Policy since 1940*, 353.

89. Menzel PT. *Medical Costs, Moral Choices: A Philosophy of Health Care Economics in America*. New Haven, CT: Yale University Press, 1983, 127.

90. Menzel PT. *Medical Costs, Moral Choices*, 128.

91. Menzel PT. *Medical Costs, Moral Choices*, 128.

92. Menzel PT. *Medical Costs, Moral Choices*, 130.

93. Menzel PT. *Medical Costs, Moral Choices*, 128 n. 5.

94. Ginzberg E. High-tech medicine. In: Ginzberg E. *The Medical Triangle*, 41–53.

95. Brown ER. *Rockefeller Medicine Men: Medicine and Capitalism in America*. Berkeley: University of California Press, 1979, 69.

96. Gray BH. *The Profit Motive and Patient Care*, 113.

97. Gray BH. *The Profit Motive and Patient Care*, 113–114.

98. Gray BH. *The Profit Motive and Patient Care*, 111–112.

99. Ginzberg E. The monetarization of medical care, 1165.

100. Starr P. *The Social Transformation of American Medicine*, 415.

101. Brown ER. Medicare and Medicaid: Band-aids for the old and poor. In: Sidel VW, Sidel R, eds. *Reforming Medicine: Lessons of the Last Quarter Century*. New York: Pantheon Books, 1984, 50–76, quote 50.

102. Davis K, Schoen C. *Health and the War on Poverty*, 18.

103. Byrd WM. Race, biology, and health care: Reassessing a relationship. *Journal of Health Care for the Poor and Underserved* 1990; 1:278–292; Charatz-Litt C. A chronicle of racism: The effects of the White medical community on black health. *Journal of the National Medical Association* 1992; 84:717–725; Smith DB. *Health Care Divided*; Starr P. *The Social Transformation of American Medicine*.

104. Brown ER. Medicare and Medicaid, 61.

105. Menzel PT. *Medical Costs, Moral Choices*, 127 n. 1.

106. Menzel PT. *Medical Costs, Moral Choices*, 127 n. 1.

107. Relman AS. The new medical-industrial complex; Gray BH. *The Profit Motive and Patient Care*; Ginzberg E. *The Medical Triangle*; Menzel PT. *Medical Costs, Moral Choices*; Enthoven AC. Consumer-choice health plan. *New England Journal of Medicine* 1978; 298:650–658, 709–720; Hoffman R, Steuerle E. Tax expenditures for health care. *Office of Tax Analysis Papers*, no. 38, April 1979, U.S. Department of the Treasury; Campion FD. *The AMA and U.S. Health Policy since 1940*, 325–358; Anders G. *Health Against Wealth*, 16–34; Smith DB. *Health Care Divided*; Ginzberg E. *Teaching Hospitals and the Urban Poor*; Ginzberg E. The monetarization of medical care; Cross EB. Federal roles and responsibilities in the organization, delivery and financing of health care; Hammonds KE. Blacks and the urban health crisis, 228; U.S. Department of Health, Education, and Welfare. *Towards a Comprehensive Health Policy for the 1970s*; Rice MF, Jones Jr. W. The uninsured and patient dumping: Recent policy responses in indigent care. *Journal of the National Medical Association* 1991; 83:874–880; Lief BJ. Legal and administrative barriers to health care. *New York State Journal of Medicine* 1985; 85:126–127; Havighurst CC. *Health Care Law and Policy*, 128–145; Areen J, King PA, Goldberg S, Gostin L, Capron AM. *Law, Science and Medicine*. 2nd ed. Westbury, NY: The Foundation Press, 1996, 1216–1223; Byrd WM. *Peer Review: The Perversion of a Process*. Report prepared for the Subcommittee on Civil Rights of the House Committee on the Judiciary. 99th Congress, 2nd Session, 1986; Byrd WM. Inquisition, peer review, and black physician survival. *Journal of the National Medical Association* 1987; 79:1027–1029; Byrd WM. Black medicine under attack. *Urban Medicine* 1987; 2:22; U.S. Bureau of the Census. *Historical Statistics of the United States, Colonial Times to 1970, Bicentennial Edition, Parts 1 and 2*. Washington, DC: U.S. Government Printing Office, 1975, 82; Starr P. *The Social Transformation of American Medicine*, 379–417; Davis K, Schoen C. *Health and the War on Poverty*; Brown ER. *Medicare and Medicaid*.

108. Mullin F. The National Health Service Corps and health personnel innovations: Beyond poorhouse medicine. In: Sidel VW, Sidel R, eds. *Reforming Medicine*, 176–200, quote 178.

109. Huet-Cox R. Medical education: New wine in old wine skins. In: Sidel VW, Sidel R, eds. *Reforming Medicine*, 129–149, quote 136.

110. Mullin F. The National Health Service Corps and health personnel innovations, 183.

111. Hanft RS, White CC. Constraining the supply of physicians: Effects on black physicians. In: Willis DP, ed. *Health Policies and Black Americans*. New Brunswick, NJ: Transaction Publishers, 1989, 249–269, quote 251.

112. McBride D. Inequality in the availability of Black physicians. *New York State Journal of Medicine* 1985; 85:139–142, quote 142.

113. McBride D. Inequality in the availability of Black physicians, 142.

114. Huet-Cox R. Medical education, 146.

115. Strelnick H, Younge R. Affirmative action in medicine: Money becomes the admissions criteria of the 1980s. In: Sidel VW, Sidel R, eds. *Reforming Medicine*, 151–175, quote 158.

116. Campion FD. *The AMA and U.S. Health Policy since 1940*, 326.

117. U.S. Bureau of the Census. *Historical Statistics of the United States, Colonial Times to 1970, Bicentennial Edition, Parts 1 and 2*, 75–76; Starr P. *The Social Transformation of American Medicine*, 399, 406, 379–419; Hanft RS, White CC. Constraining the supply of physicians; Shea S, Fullilove MT. Entry of black and other minority students in US medical schools: Historical perspectives and recent trends. *New England Journal of Medicine* 1985; 313:933–940; Johnson L. The restraint of progress: Declining participation of Blacks and other minorities in medical schools. *New York State Journal of Medicine* 1985; 85:135–136; Wellington JS, Montero P. Equal opportunity programs in American medical schools. *Journal of Medical Education* 1978; 53:633–639; Mullin F. The National Health Service Corps and health personnel innovations; Huet-Cox R. Medical education; McBride D. Inequality in the availability of Black physicians.

118. Wilson FA, Neuhauser D. *Health Services in the United States*. 2nd ed. Cambridge, MA: Ballinger Publishing, 1982, 237.

119. Campion FD. *The AMA and U.S. Health Policy since 1940*, 345.

120. Campion FD. *The AMA and U.S. Health Policy since 1940*, 345–346.

121. Campion FD. *The AMA and U.S. Health Policy since 1940*, 357.

122. Brown ER. *Medicare and Medicaid*, 67.

123. Brown ER. Medicare and Medicaid, 68.

124. Brown ER. Medicare and Medicaid, 68.

125. Wilson FA, Neuhauser D. *Health Services in the United States*; Campion FD. *The AMA and U.S. Health Policy since 1940*, 345–358; Brown ER. Medicare and Medicaid; Davis K, Schoen C. *Health and the War on Poverty*; Starr P. *The Social Transformation of American Medicine*, 367–378; Davis K, Lillie-Blanton M, Lyons B, Mullan F, Powe N, Rowland D. Health care for black Americans: The public sector role. In: Willis DP, ed. *Health Policies and Black Americans*. New Brunswick, NJ: Transaction Publishers, 1989, 213–247.

126. Starr P. *The Social Transformation of American Medicine*, 414.

127. Menzel PT. *Medical Costs, Moral Choices*, 137.

128. Campion FD. *The AMA and U.S. Health Policy since 1940*, 328.

129. Starr P. *The Social Transformation of American Medicine*, 416.

130. Menzel PT. *Medical Costs, Moral Choices*, 137.

131. Starr P. *The Social Transformation of American Medicine*, 416.

132. Starr P. *The Social Transformation of American Medicine*, 379–419; Campion FD. *The AMA and U.S. Health Policy since 1940*, 328, 325–358; Menzel PT. *Medical Costs, Moral Choices*; Ginzberg E. *The Medical Triangle*.

133. Silverman M, Lee PR. *Pills, Profits, and Politics*. Berkeley: University of California Press, 1974, 30.

134. Silverman M, Lee PR. *Pills, Profits, and Politics*, 17.

135. Ehrenreich B, Ehrenreich J. *The American Health Empire*, 102.

136. Ehrenreich B, Ehrenreich J. *The American Health Empire*, 103.

137. Ehrenreich B, Ehrenreich J. *The American Health Empire*, 103–104.

138. Whol S. *The Medical Industrial Complex*, 132.

139. Whol S. *The Medical Industrial Complex*, 134.

140. Silverman M, Lee PR. *Pills, Profits, and Politics*; Ehrenreich B, Ehrenreich J. *The American Health Empire*, 98–108; Whol S. *The Medical Industrial Complex*; Starr P. *The Social Transformation of American Medicine*; Ginzberg E. High-tech medicine and rising health care costs. *Journal of the American Medical Association* 1990; 263:1820–1822; Ginzberg E. High-tech medicine; Foote SB. *Managing the Medical Arms Race: Innovation and Public Policy in the Medical Device Industry*. Berkeley: University of California Press, 1992; Hammonds KE. Blacks and the urban health crisis; Wilson FA, Neuhauser D. *Health Services in the United States*.

141. Ginzberg E, Dutka AB. *The Financing of Biomedical Research*. Baltimore: Johns Hopkins University Press, 1989, 23.

142. Hammonds KE. Blacks and the urban health crisis, 230.

143. Ehrenreich B, Ehrenreich J. *The American Health Empire*, 24.

144. Ehrenreich B, Ehrenreich J. *The American Health Empire*, 24–25.

145. Ehrenreich B, Ehrenreich J. *The American Health Empire*, 25.

146. English JT. New challenges for physicians in the war on poverty. *Journal of the National Medical Association* 1968; 60:38–41, 40–41.

147. English JT. New challenges for physicians in the war on poverty, 40–41.

148. Ehrenreich B, Ehrenreich J. *The American Health Empire*, 25.

149. Ehrenreich B, Ehrenreich J. *The American Health Empire*, 42.

150. Ginzberg E, Dutka AB. *The Financing of Biomedical Research*, 16.

151. Ginzberg E, Dutka AB. *The Financing of Biomedical Research*, 23.

152. Ginzberg E, Dutka AB. *The Financing of Biomedical Research*, 23.

153. Hanft RS, Fishman LE, Evans W. *Blacks and the Health Professions in the 80s: A National Crisis and a Time for Action*. n.p.: Prepared for the Association of Minority Health Professions Schools, 1983, 24.

154. Ginzberg E, Dutka AB. *The Financing of Biomedical Research*, 2.

155. Ginzberg E, Dutka AB. *The Financing of Biomedical Research*, 2.

156. Ginzberg E, Dutka AB. *The Financing of Biomedical Research*, 23–24.

157. Ginzberg E, Dutka AB. *The Financing of Biomedical Research*, 24.

158. Ehrenreich B, Ehrenreich J. *The American Health Empire*, 195.

159. Ginzberg E, Dutka AB. *The Financing of Biomedical Research*, 25.

160. Hanft RS, Fishman LE, Evans W. *Blacks and the Health Professions in the 80s*, 24.

161. Summerville J. *Educating Black Doctors: A History of Meharry Medical College*. University: University of Alabama Press, 1983; Cobb WM. The first hundred years of the Howard University College of Medicine. *Journal of the National Medical Association* 1967; 59:408–420, 412–413, 419; Walker ML. The Morehouse School of Medicine story: A surgical strike! *Journal of the National Medical Association* 1993; 85:395–400.

162. Ginzberg E, Dutka AB. *The Financing of Biomedical Research*, 27.

163. Starr P. *The Social Transformation of American Medicine*, 352–380; Ehrenreich B, Ehrenreich J. *The American Health Empire*; Young Q. The urban hospital; Hammonds KE. Blacks and the urban health crisis, 228; U.S. Department of Health, Education, and Welfare. *Towards a Comprehensive Health Policy for the 1970s*; Berry LH. Special health care needs of the disadvantaged; Berry LH. Implementation of new health legislation and its impact upon disadvantaged population groups; Berry LH. Human rights and regional medical programs. *Journal of the National Medical Association* 1966; 58:387–388; Coleman AH. Title 19 and medical civil rights. *Journal of the National Medical Association* 1966; 58:397; Huet-Cox R. Medical education; Cray E. *In Failing Health*; Cobb WM. The first hundred years of the Howard University College of Medicine; Ginzberg E, Dutka AB. *The Financing of Biomedical Research*; Summerville J. *Educating Black Doctors*; Foote SB. *Managing the Medical Arms Race*; Burger Jr EJ. *Science at the White House*; Walker ML. The Morehouse School of Medicine story: A surgical strike!; The Commonwealth Fund. *Contributing to the Community*.

164. Rutstein DD. *Blueprint for Medical Care*, 1.

165. Geiger HJ. Community health centers, 11.

166. Lemann N. *The Promised Land: The Great Black Migration and How It Changed America*. New York: Knopf, 1991; Hacker A. *Two Nations: Black and White, Separate, Hostile, Unequal*. New York: Ballantine Books, 1992. Expanded and updated ed. 1995; Massey DS, Denton NA. *American Apartheid: Segregation and the Making of the Underclass*. Cambridge, MA: Harvard University Press, 1993; Minerbrook S. Home ownership anchors the middle class: But lending game sink many prospective owners. *Emerge* October 1993 (1)(5):42; Wilson WJ. *The Truly Disadvantaged: The Inner City, the Underclass, and Public Policy*. Chicago: University of Chicago Press, 1987; Wilson WJ. *When Work Disappears: The World of the New Urban Poor*. New York: Knopf, 1996; Smith DB. *Health Care Divided*.

167. Geiger HJ. Community health centers, 12.

168. Geiger HJ. Community health centers, 12.

169. Geiger HJ. Community health centers, 12–13.

170. Geiger HJ. Community health centers, 17.

171. Geiger HJ. Community health centers, 27.

172. Geiger HJ. Community health centers, 29.

173. Geiger HJ. Community health centers, 21.

174. Kovner AR. *Health Care Delivery in the United States*. 4th ed. New York: Springer, 1990, 106–140; Sardell A. *The U.S. Experiment in Social Medicine: The Community Health Center Program, 1956–1986*. Pittsburgh, PA: University of Pittsburgh Press, 1988; Davis K, Schoen C. *Health and the War on Poverty*; Geiger HJ. Community health centers; Woods CB. The neighborhood health center—the concept and the national scene; Carter Jr. LC. Health and the war on poverty. *Journal of the National Medical Association* 1966; 58:173–178; Davis K, Gold M, Makuc D. Access to health care for the poor: Does the gap remain? *Annual Review of Public Health* 1981; 2:159–182; National Center for Health Statistics. *Health Status of the Disadvantaged Chartbook/1990*. Hyattsville, MD: Public Health Service, 1991, 70; Starr P. *The Social Transformation of American Medicine*, 352–363; Morais HM. *The History of the Negro in Medicine*. New York: Publishers Company, 1967; Ehrenreich B, Ehrenreich J. *The American Health Empire*; Huet-Cox R. Medical education; Mullin F. The National Health Service Corps and health personnel innovations; Strelnick H, Younge R. Affirmative action in medicine; Haynes MA, McGarvey MR. Physicians, hospitals, and patients in the inner city. In: Norman JC, ed. *Medicine in the Ghetto*. New York: Appleton-

Century-Crofts, 1969, 117–124; Haynes MA. The gap in health status between black and white Americans.

175. Bennett JT, DiLorenzo TJ. *Unhealthy Charities: Hazardous to Your Health and Wealth.* New York: Basic Books, 1994, 33.

176. Bakal C. *Charity, U.S.A.* New York: Times Books, 1979, 127.

177. Bennett JT, DiLorenzo TJ. *Unhealthy Charities*, 16.

178. Bennett JT, DiLorenzo TJ. *Unhealthy Charities*, 16.

179. Bennett JT, DiLorenzo TJ. *Unhealthy Charities*, 21.

180. Bennett JT, DiLorenzo TJ. *Unhealthy Charities*, 23–24.

181. Bennett JT, DiLorenzo TJ. *Unhealthy Charities*, 24.

182. Etzioni A, Doty P. Profit in not-for-profit corporations: The example of health care. *Political Science Quarterly* 1976; 91:434.

183. Mendelson MA. *Tender Loving Greed.* New York: Knopf, 1974, 196–197.

184. Bennett JT, DiLorenzo TJ. *Unhealthy Charities*, 2.

185. Bennett JT, DiLorenzo TJ. *Unhealthy Charities*, 31; Bakal C. *Charity, U.S.A.*, 127.

186. Ginzberg E, Dutka AB. *The Financing of Biomedical Research*, 10.

187. Bennett JT, DiLorenzo TJ. *Unhealthy Charities*, 43.

188. Bakal C. *Charity, U.S.A.*, 130–131.

189. Bennett JT, DiLorenzo TJ. *Unhealthy Charities*, 23.

190. Bennett JT, DiLorenzo TJ. *Unhealthy Charities*, 44.

191. Wilson FA, Neuhauser D. *Health Services in the United States*, 239–243; U.S. Bureau of the Census. *Historical Statistics of the United States, Colonial Times to 1970, Bicentennial Edition, Parts 1 and 2*, 359; Bennett JT, DiLorenzo TJ. *Unhealthy Charities*; Bakal C. *Charity, U.S.A.*; U.S. General Accounting Office. *A Proposal for Disclosure of Contractual Arrangements between Hospitals and Members of Their Governing Boards and between Hospitals and Their Medical Specialists.* Washington, DC: General Accounting Office, 1975. US GAO publication MWD-75-73; Mendelson MA. *Tender Loving Greed*; Patterson JT. *The Dread Disease*; Smith H. *The Power Game: How Washington Works.* New York: Ballantine Books, 1988; Ginzberg, E. *The Medical Triangle*; Ginzberg E, Dutka AB. *The Financing of Biomedical Research.*

192. Ginzberg E. *The Medical Triangle*, 24.

193. Starr P. *The Social Transformation of American Medicine*, 417.

194. Starr P. *The Social Transformation of American Medicine*, 418.

195. Starr P. *The Social Transformation of American Medicine*, 418; Havighurst CC. Competition in health services: Overview, issues and answers. *Vanderbilt Law Review* May 1981; 34:1115–1178.

196. Starr P. *The Social Transformation of American Medicine*, 419.

197. Brown ER. Medicare and Medicaid, 63.

198. Starr P. *The Social Transformation of American Medicine*, 419.

199. Brinkley A. *The Unfinished Nation*, 803–880; Starr P. *The Social Transformation of American Medicine*, 352–428; Cray E. *In Failing Health*, 40–59; Garrett L. *Betrayal of Trust: The Collapse of Global Public Health.* New York: Hyperion, 2000; Anders G. *Health against Wealth*; Havighurst CC. Competition in health services; Enthoven AC. *Health Plan: The Only Practical Solution to Soaring Health Costs.* Reading, MA: Addison-Wesley, 1980; Enthoven AC. How interested groups have responded to a proposal for economic competition in health services. *American Economic Review* 1980; 70:142–148; Wing KR, Rose MG. Health facilities and the enforcement of civil rights. In: Roemer R, McKray G, eds. *Legal Aspects of Health Policy: Issues and Trends.* Westport, CT: Greenwood Press, 1980, 243–267; Rice MF, Jones W. Public policy compliance/enforcement and black American health: Title VI of the Civil Rights Act of 1964. In: Jones Jr W, Rice MF, eds. *Health Care Issues in Black America: Policies, Problems, and Prospects.* New York: Greenwood Press, 1987, 98–115; Hanft RS, Fishman LE, Evans W. *Blacks and the Health Professions in the 80s*; Hammonds KE. Blacks and the urban health crisis; Ginzberg E. *The Medical Triangle*; Sidel VW, Sidel R, eds. *Reforming Medicine*; Berry LH. Special health care needs of the disadvantaged; Berry LH. Implementation of new health legislation and its impact upon disadvantaged population groups; Morais HM. *The History of the Negro in Medicine*; Savitt TL. Medical education. In: Salz-

man J, Smith DL, West C. eds. *Encyclopedia of African-American Culture and History*. 5 vols. New York: Macmillan Library Reference USA, Simon & Schuster Macmillan, 1996, 1750–1752; The Commonwealth Fund. *Contributing to the Community.*

200. Haynes MA. The gap in health status between black and white Americans.

201. U.S. Department of Health and Human Services. *Health Status of Minorities and Low Income Groups*. Washington, DC: U.S. Government Printing Office, 1985, 19.

202. Last JM. The determinants of health. In: Sutchfield FD, Keck CW. *Principles of Public Health Practice*. Albany, NY: Delmar Publishers, 1997, 31–41, quote 32.

203. René AA. Racial differences in mortality: Blacks and Whites. In: Jones Jr W, Rice MF, eds. *Health Care Issues in Black America: Policies, Problems, and Prospects*. New York: Greenwood Press, 1987, 21–41, quote 21.

204. Haynes MA. The gap in health status between black and white Americans, 2.

205. Wildavsky A. Doing better and feeling worse: The political pathology of health policy. In: Knowles JH, ed. *Doing Better and Feeling Worse: Health in the United States*. New York: W. W. Norton and the American Academy of Arts and Sciences, 1977, 105–123, quote 105.

206. Wildavsky A. Doing better and feeling worse, 105.

207. Davis K, Schoen C. *Health and the War on Poverty*, 30.

208. Morais HM. *The History of the Negro in Medicine*, 50.

209. White HA. *The Freedmen's Bureau in Louisiana*. Baton Rouge: Louisiana State University Press, 1970, 70.

210. Berry LH. Special health care needs of the disadvantaged; Haynes MA. The gap in health status between black and white Americans; Last JM. The determinants of health; Wildavsky A. Doing better and feeling worse; René AA. Racial differences in mortality; Hammonds KE. Blacks and the urban health crisis; U.S. Department of Health and Human Services. *Health Status of Minorities and Low Income Groups*; Keller AZ. High mortality rates for Negroes: Design or accident? *Journal of the National Medical Association* 1968; 60:287–288; Davis K, Schoen C. *Health and the War on Poverty*; Clark KB. The essential educational program; Breeden JO. Science and medicine. In: Wilson CR, Ferris W. eds. *Encyclopedia of Southern Culture*. Chapel Hill: University of North Carolina Press, 1989, 1337–1343; Mohr CL. *On the Threshold of Freedom: Masters and Slaves in Civil War Georgia*. Athens: University of Georgia Press, 1986; Bremner RH. *The Public Good: Philanthropy and Welfare in the Civil War Era*. New York: Knopf, 1980; Morais HM. *The History of the Negro in Medicine*, 39–52; White HA. *The Freedmen's Bureau in Louisiana*; Byrd WM, Clayton LA. An American health dilemma: A history of blacks in the health system. *Journal of the National Medical Association* 1992; 84:189–200; Byrd WM. Race, biology, and health care; Byrd WM, Clayton LA. A *Black Health Trilogy*. Videotape and 188-page documentary report. Washington, DC: The National Medical Association and the African American Heritage and Education Foundation, 1991.

211. Davis K, et al. Health care for Black Americans, esp. 238–241.

212. Byrd WM, Clayton LA. An American health dilemma, 189–192; Byrd WM, Clayton LA. A *Black Health Trilogy*.

213. Morais HM. *The History of the Negro in Medicine*, 131–208; Cobb WM. The Black American in medicine. *Journal of the National Medical Association* 73 (Suppl 1):1183–1244; Reynolds PP. Hospitals and civil rights, 1945–1963; Reynolds PP. The federal government's use of Title VI and Medicare to racially integrate hospitals in the United States, 1963 through 1967; Savitt TL. Medical education; Byrd WM, Clayton LA. An American health dilemma; Marable M. *Race, Reform, and Rebellion*; Beardsley EH. A *History of Neglect: Health Care for Blacks and Mill Workers in the Twentieth-Century South*. Knoxville: University of Tennessee Press, 1987, 245–309; Byrd WM, Clayton LA. A *Black Health Trilogy*; Byrd WM. Race, biology, and health care, 289–292; Davis K, et al. Health care for Black Americans; U.S. Department of Health and Human Services. *Health in America: 1776–1976*. Washington, DC: U.S. Health Resources Administration, DHEW Pub. No. (HRA) 76–616, 1976; Mullin F. The National Health Service Corps and health personnel innovations; Geiger HJ. Community health centers; Davis K, Schoen C. *Health and the War on Poverty*.

214. Hart N. The social and economic environment and human health. In: Detels R, et al. eds.

*Oxford Textbook of Public Health*. Vol. 1 *The Scope of Public Health*. 3rd ed. New York: Oxford University Press, 1997, 95–123, esp. 95 n. 1.

215. Haynes MA. The gap in health status between black and white Americans, 2.

216. Haynes MA. The gap in health status between black and white Americans, 2.

217. U.S. Department of Health and Human Services. *Health Status of Minorities and Low Income Groups*, 19.

218. Haynes MA. The gap in health status between black and white Americans, 3.

219. Haynes MA. The gap in health status between black and white Americans, 4.

220. Clayton LA, Byrd WM. The African American cancer crisis, part 1: The problem. *Journal of Health Care for the Poor and Underserved* 1993; 4: 83–101.

221. Farley R, Allen WR. *The Color Line and the Quality of Life in America*. New York: Oxford University Press, 1989, 41.

222. Davis K, Schoen C. *Health and the War on Poverty*, 33.

223. Davis K, et al. Health care for Black Americans, 215–216.

224. Hart N. The social and economic environment and human health; Haynes MA. The gap in health status between black and white Americans; Davis K, et al. Health care for Black Americans; U.S. Bureau of the Census. *Historical Statistics of the United States, Colonial Times to 1970, Bicentennial Edition, Parts 1 and 2*, 55, 59; National Center for Health Statistics. *Prevention Profile*, 140, 152–153; National Center for Health Statistics. *Health Status of the Disadvantaged Chartbook/1990*, 28; Davis K, Schoen C. *Health and the War on Poverty*; Clayton LA, Byrd WM. The African American cancer crisis, part 1; Byrd WM, Clayton LA. The African-American cancer crisis, part 2: A prescription. *Journal of Health Care for the Poor and Underserved* 1993; 4:102–116; Byrd WM, Clayton LA. An American health dilemma; Farley R, Allen WR. *The Color Line and the Quality of Life in America*, 32–57; Keller AZ. High mortality rates for Negroes.

225. Haynes MA. The gap in health status between black and white Americans, 5.

226. Haynes MA. The gap in health status between black and white Americans, 5.

227. Davis K, Schoen C. *Health and the War on Poverty*, 20.

228. Haynes MA. The gap in health status between black and white Americans, 5.

229. Haynes MA. The gap in health status between black and white Americans, 5.

230. René AA. Racial differences in mortality, 25.

231. René AA. Racial differences in mortality, 24.

232. Children's Defense Fund. *The State of America's Children*. Washington, DC: Children's Defense Fund, 1991, 17; Haynes MA. The gap in health status between black and white Americans, 10.

233. Cunningham, FG, et al. *Williams Obstetrics*. 20th ed. Stamford, CT: Appleton and Lange, 1997, 798.

234. Institute of Medicine. *Health Care in the Context of Civil Rights*. Washington, DC: National Academy Press, 1981.

235. National Center for Health Statistics. *Prevention Profile*, 152–153.

236. René AA. Racial differences in mortality, 30–31.

237. René AA. Racial differences in mortality, 31.

238. Davis K, Schoen C. *Health and the War on Poverty*; Haynes MA. The gap in health status between black and white Americans; Keller AZ. High mortality rates for Negroes; Rosenbaum S, Layton C, Liu J. *The Health of America's Children*. Washington, DC: Children's Defense Fund, 1991, 14–15; René AA. Racial differences in mortality; National Center for Health Statistics. *Prevention Profile*; Cunningham FG, et al. *Williams Obstetrics*; Wildavsky A. Doing better and feeling worse; Illich I. *Medical Nemesis: The Expropriation of Health*. New York: Pantheon Books, 1976. Paperback ed. Toronto: Bantam Books, 1977; Institute of Medicine. *Health Care in the Context of Civil Rights*.

239. Haynes MA. The gap in health status between black and white Americans, 14–15.

240. Haynes MA. The gap in health status between black and white Americans, 15.

241. René AA. Racial differences in mortality, 35.

242. René AA. Racial differences in mortality, 34.

243. René AA. Racial differences in mortality, 34.

244. René AA. Racial differences in mortality, 35.

245. Davis K, et al. Health care for Black Americans, 216.

246. U.S. Department of Health and Human Services. *Health Status of Minorities and Low Income Groups,* 112.

247. Haynes MA. The gap in health status between black and white Americans; René AA. Racial differences in mortality; National Center for Health Statistics. *Prevention Profile*; Davis K, et al. Health care for Black Americans; Keller AZ. High mortality rates for Negroes; U.S. Department of Health and Human Services. *Health Status of Minorities and Low Income Groups.*

248. Henschke UL, et al. Alarming increase of the cancer mortality in the U.S. black population. *Cancer* 1973; 31:763–768; Leffall Jr LD. Cancer mortality in blacks. *CA–A Cancer Journal for Clinicians* 1974; 24:42–46; Leffall Jr LD. The challenge of cancer among black Americans. In: *The Proceedings of the American Cancer Society National Conference on Meeting the Challenge of Cancer Among Black Americans.* New York: American Cancer Society, 1979, 9–14.

249. Henschke UL, et al. Alarming increase of the cancer mortality in the U.S. black population; U.S. Department of Health and Human Services. *Report of the Secretary's Task Force on Black and Minority Health.* Vol. 3, *Cancer.* Washington, DC: U.S. Government Printing Office, January 1986; Baquet CR, et al. *Cancer among Blacks and Other Minorities: Statistical Profiles.* Washington, DC: U.S. Department of Health and Human Services, 1986. NIH Publication No. 86–2785; Clayton LA, Byrd WM. The African American cancer crisis, part 1; Byrd WM, Clayton LA. The African American cancer crisis, part 2; American Cancer Society. *Cancer Facts and Figures for Minority Americans, 1988.* Atlanta: American Cancer Society, 1988.

250. Clayton LA, Byrd WM. The African American cancer crisis, part 1, 86.

251. René AA. Racial differences in mortality, 34.

252. René AA. Racial differences in mortality, 34.

253. René AA. Racial differences in mortality, 35.

254. Axtell LM, Asire A, Myers MH, eds. *Cancer Patient Survival.* Report No. 5 from the Cancer Surveillance, Epidemiology and End Results Program, DHEW Publication No. 77–992. Washington, DC: U.S. Government Printing Office, 1977.

255. Henschke UL, et al. Alarming increase of the cancer mortality in the U.S. black population; Leffall Jr LD. Cancer mortality in blacks; Leffall Jr LD. The challenge of cancer among black Americans; Clayton LA, Byrd WM. The African American cancer crisis, part 1; Byrd WM, Clayton LA. The African American cancer crisis, part 2; Haynes MA, Smedley BD, eds. *The Unequal Burden of Cancer: An Assesment of NIH Research and Programs for Ethnic Minorities and the Medically Underserved.* Washington, DC: National Academy Press, 1999; Keller AZ. High mortality rates for Negroes; Lilienfeld AM, Levin ML, Kessler II. *Cancer in the United States.* Cambridge, MA: Harvard University Press, 1972; Pickle LW, et al. *Atlas of U.S. Cancer Mortality Among Nonwhites: 1950–1980.* Washington, DC: U.S. Government Printing Office, n.d. NIH Publication No. 90–1582; U.S. Department of Health and Human Services. *Health Status of Minorities and Low Income Groups,* 126; René AA. Racial differences in mortality; U.S. Department of Health and Human Services. *Report of the Secretary's Task Force on Black and Minority Health.* Vol. 3, *Cancer;* Baquet CR, et al. *Cancer among Blacks and Other Minorities;* American Cancer Society. *Cancer Facts and Figures for Minority Americans, 1988;* Axtell LM, Asire A, Myers MH, eds. *Cancer Patient Survival;* Jones LA, ed. *Minorities and Cancer.* New York: Springer-Verlag, 1989.

256. U.S. Department of Health and Human Services. *Health Status of Minorities and Low Income Groups,* 140.

257. U.S. Department of Health and Human Services. *Health Status of Minorities and Low Income Groups,* 139.

258. U.S. Department of Health and Human Services. *Health Status of Minorities and Low Income Groups,* 142.

259. U.S. Department of Health and Human Services. *Health Status of Minorities and Low Income Groups,* 145.

260. René AA. Racial differences in mortality; U.S. Department of Health and Human Services. *Health Status of Minorities and Low Income Groups.*

261. U.S. Department of Health and Human Services. *Health Status of Minorities and Low Income Groups,* 93.

262. René AA. Racial differences in mortality, 38.

263. U.S. Department of Health and Human Services. *Health Status of Minorities and Low Income Groups*, 93.

264. René AA. Racial differences in mortality, 38.

265. U.S. Department of Health and Human Services. *Health Status of Minorities and Low Income Groups*, 93.

266. U.S. Department of Health and Human Services. *Health Status of Minorities and Low Income Groups*; René AA. Racial differences in mortality.

267. U.S. Department of Health and Human Services. *Health Status of Minorities and Low Income Groups*, 117.

268. U.S. Department of Health and Human Services. *Health Status of Minorities and Low Income Groups*, 117.

269. U.S. Department of Health and Human Services. *Health Status of Minorities and Low Income Groups*, 118.

270. Davis K, et al. Health care for Black Americans, 216.

271. National Center for Health Statistics. *Health United States, 1995*. Hyattsville, MD: Public Health Service, May, 1996, 110–111.

272. National Center for Health Statistics. *Health United States, 1996–97 and Injury Chartbook*. Hyattsville, MD: Public Health Service, 1997, 111–114.

273. National Center for Health Statistics. *Prevention Profile*, 156–157.

274. U.S. Department of Health and Human Services. *Health Status of Minorities and Low Income Groups*; René AA. Racial differences in mortality; Scott G. Prevalence of chronic conditions of the genitourinary, nervous, endocrine, metabolic and blood-forming systems and of other selected chronic conditions, United States, 1973. *Vital and Health Statistics*. Series 10, No. 109. DHEW Pub. No. (HRA) 77–1536. Washington, DC: U.S. Government Printing Office, March, 1977; Davis K, et al. Health care for Black Americans; National Center for Health Statistics. *Prevention Profile*, 156–157; National Center for Health Statistics. *Health United States, 1995*; National Center for Health Statistics. *Health United States, 1996–97 and Injury Chartbook*, 111–114.

275. U.S. Department of Health and Human Services. *Health Status of Minorities and Low Income Groups*, 189.

276. Haynes MA. The gap in health status between black and white Americans, 16.

277. U.S. Department of Health and Human Services. *Health Status of Minorities and Low Income Groups*, 189.

278. U.S. Department of Health and Human Services. *Health Status of Minorities and Low Income Groups*, 189.

279. U.S. Department of Health and Human Services. *Health Status of Minorities and Low Income Groups*, 189.

280. Haynes MA. The gap in health status between black and white Americans, 16.

281. Haynes MA. The gap in health status between black and white Americans, 16.

282. Haynes MA. The gap in health status between black and white Americans, 17.

283. National Center for Health Statistics. *Edentulous Persons, United States, 1971*. DHEW Pub. No. (HRA) 74–1516. Series 10. Data from the National Health Survey, no. 89. Rockville, MD, June 1974.

284. U.S. Department of Health and Human Services. *Health Status of Minorities and Low Income Groups*; Haynes MA. The gap in health status between black and white Americans; National Center for Health Statistics. *Edentulous Persons, United States, 1971*; Davis K, Schoen C. *Health and the War on Poverty*.

285. René AA. Racial differences in mortality, 40.

286. Lewis B. South Africans await economic control. *Emerge* July/August 1998 (9)(9):76.

287. René AA. Racial differences in mortality, 40.

288. Davis K, et al. Health care for Black Americans; René AA. Racial differences in mortality; Gonella JS, Louis DZ, McCord JJ. The staging concept: An approach to the assessment of outcome of ambulatory care. *Medical Care* 1976; 14:13–21; Haynes MA. The gap in health status between black and white Americans; Last JM. The determinants of health.

289. U.S. Department of Health and Human Services. *Health Status of Minorities and Low Income Groups*, 231.

290. U.S. Department of Health and Human Services. *Health Status of Minorities and Low Income Groups*, 231.

291. U.S. Department of Health and Human Services. *Health Status of Minorities and Low Income Groups*, 232.

292. Haynes MA. The gap in health status between black and white Americans, 19.

293. Davis K, et al. Health care for Black Americans, 217.

294. Davis K, et al. Health care for Black Americans, 217.

295. Haynes MA. The gap in health status between black and white Americans, 20.

296. Haynes MA. The gap in health status between black and white Americans, 20.

297. U.S. Department of Health and Human Services. *Health Status of Minorities and Low Income Groups*, 235.

298. Davis K, et al. Health care for Black Americans, 217.

299. U.S. Department of Health and Human Services. *Health Status of Minorities and Low Income Groups*, 231.

300. Davis K, Schoen C. *Health and the War on Poverty*, 43.

301. U.S. Department of Health and Human Services. *Health Status of Minorities and Low Income Groups*, 183–204, 237.

302. Haynes MA. The gap in health status between black and white Americans, 26.

303. Haynes MA. The gap in health status between black and white Americans, 26.

304. Starr P. *The Social Transformation of American Medicine*, 365.

305. Kieth VM. Long-term care and the Black elderly. In: Jones Jr W, Rice MF, eds. *Health Care Issues in Black America: Policies, Problems, and Prospects*. New York: Greenwood Press, 1987, 173–209, quote 196–197.

306. U.S. Department of Health and Human Services. *Health Status of Minorities and Low Income Groups*; Haynes MA. The gap in health status between black and white Americans; Davis K, et al. Health care for Black Americans; Smith DB. *Health Care Divided*, 191–275; Smith DB. Addressing racial inequities in health care: Civil rights monitoring and report cards. *Journal of Health, Policy, and Law* 1998; 23:75–105; U.S. Department of Health and Human Services. *Health of the Disadvantaged Chartbook II*. DHHS Pub. No. (HRA) 80–633. Hyattsville, MD: U.S. Health Resources Administration, 1980; Children's Defense Fund. *The Health of America's Children*, 9–12; Starr P. *The Social Transformation of American Medicine*; Reynolds PP. Hospitals and civil rights, 1945–1963; Reynolds PP. The federal government's use of Title VI and Medicare to racially integrate hospitals in the United States, 1963 through 1967; Davis K, Schoen C. *Health and the War on Poverty*; Kieth VM. Long-term care and the Black elderly; Institute of Medicine. *Health Care in the Context of Civil Rights*; Wing KR, Rose MG. Health facilities and the enforcement of civil rights.

307. Davis K, Marshall R. Rural health care in the South. Preliminary summary report prepared for presentation at the meeting of the Task Force on Southern Rural Development, Atlanta, October 1975.

308. Davis K, Schoen C. *Health and the War on Poverty*, 76.

309. Davis K, Schoen C. *Health and the War on Poverty*, 76–77.

310. Davis K, Schoen C. *Health and the War on Poverty*, 77.

311. Davis K, Schoen C. *Health and the War on Poverty*, 77.

312. Last JM. The determinants of health; Davis K, Schoen C. *Health and the War on Poverty*; Byrd WM, Clayton LA. An American health dilemma; Byrd WM, Clayton LA. *A Black Health Trilogy*; Davis K, Gold M, Makuc D. Access to health care for the poor; Davis K, et al. Health care for Black Americans; Smith DB. *Health Care Divided*; Smith DB. Addressing racial inequities in health care.

313. Cobb WM. The Black American in medicine; Byrd WM, Clayton LA. An American health dilemma; Byrd WM, Clayton LA. *A Black Health Trilogy*; Reynolds PP. Hospitals and civil rights, 1945–1963; Smith DB. *Health Care Divided*; Smith DB. Addressing racial inequities in health care; Reynolds PP. The federal government's use of Title VI and Medicare to racially integrate hos-

pitals in the United States, 1963 through 1967; Massey DS, Denton NA. *American Apartheid*; Wilson WJ. *The Declining Significance of Race: Blacks and Changing American Institutions*. Chicago: University of Chicago Press, 1978. 2nd ed. Chicago: University of Chicago Press, 1980; Wilson WJ. *The Truly Disadvantaged*; Marable M. *Race, Reform, and Rebellion*; Sniderman PM, Piazza T. *The Scar of Race*. Cambridge, MA: The Belknap Press of Harvard University Press, 1993; Jencks C. *Rethinking Social Policy: Race, Poverty, and the Underclass*. Cambridge, MA: Harvard University Press, 1992; Geiger HJ. Community health centers; Huet-Cox R. Medical education; Young Q. The urban hospital.

## Chapter Five

1. Campion FD. *The AMA and U.S. Health Policy since 1940*. Chicago: Chicago Review Press for the American Medical Association, 1984, 268.

2. Campion FD. *The AMA and U.S. Health Policy since 1940*, 253–286.

3. Campion FD. *The AMA and U.S. Health Policy since 1940*, 285.

4. Campion FD. *The AMA and U.S. Health Policy since 1940*, 280.

5. Starr P. *The Social Transformation of American Medicine*. New York: Basic Books, 1982, 380.

6. Campion FD. *The AMA and U.S. Health Policy since 1940*, 309.

7. Campion FD. *The AMA and U.S. Health Policy since 1940*, 309.

8. Campion FD. *The AMA and U.S. Health Policy since 1940*, 323.

9. Campion FD. *The AMA and U.S. Health Policy since 1940*, 323.

10. Campion FD. *The AMA and U.S. Health Policy since 1940*; Starr P. *The Social Transformation of American Medicine*, 377–419; Harmer RM. *American Medical Avarice*. New York: Abelard-Schuman, 1975, 9–25; Morais HM. *The History of the Negro in Medicine*. New York: Publishers Company, 1967; Clement KW, Cobb WM. National Medical Association testimony on behalf of H.R. 3920, the King-Anderson Bill, before the Committee on Means and Ways, U.S. House of Representatives, January 22, 1964. *Journal of the National Medical Association* 1964; 56:213–221; Reynolds PP. The federal government's use of Title VI and Medicare to racially integrate hospitals in the United States, 1963 through 1967. *American Journal of Public Health* 1997; 87:1850–1858; National Health Insurance Proposals. *Legislative Analysis* No. 19. Washington: American Enterprise Institute, 1974, 37–54; Cray E. *In Failing Health: The Medical Crisis and the A.M.A.* Indianapolis: Bobbs-Merrill, 1970.

11. Starr P. *The Social Transformation of American Medicine*, 400.

12. Campion FD. *The AMA and U.S. Health Policy since 1940*, 328.

13. Campion FD. *The AMA and U.S. Health Policy since 1940*, 340.

14. Starr P. *The Social Transformation of American Medicine*, 401.

15. Starr P. *The Social Transformation of American Medicine*, 402.

16. Starr P. *The Social Transformation of American Medicine*, 402.

17. Starr P. *The Social Transformation of American Medicine*; Campion FD. *The AMA and U.S. Health Policy since 1940*; Byrd WM. *Peer review: The perversion of a process.* Report prepared for the Subcommittee on Civil Rights of the House Committee on the Judiciary, 99th Congress, 2nd Session, 1986; Byrd WM. Inquisition, peer review, and black physician survival. *Journal of the National Medical Association* 1987; 79:1027–1029; Byrd WM. Black medicine under attack. *Urban Medicine* 1987; 2:22.

18. Starr P. *The Social Transformation of American Medicine*, 398.

19. Starr P. *The Social Transformation of American Medicine*, 398.

20. Starr P. *The Social Transformation of American Medicine*, 407.

21. Starr P. *The Social Transformation of American Medicine*, 398.

22. Starr P. *The Social Transformation of American Medicine*; Campion FD. *The AMA and U.S. Health Policy since 1940*; Morais HM. *The History of the Negro in Medicine*.

23. Campion FD. *The AMA and U.S. Health Policy since 1940*, 238.

24. Campion FD. *The AMA and U.S. Health Policy since 1940*, 244.

25. Starr P. *The Social Transformation of American Medicine*, 382.

26. Campion FD. *The AMA and U.S. Health Policy since 1940*, 440.

27. Campion FD. *The AMA and U.S. Health Policy since 1940*, 440–456.

28. Stevens RA. *American Medicine and the Public Interest*. New Haven, CT: Yale University Press, 1971, 231.

29. Campion FD. *The AMA and U.S. Health Policy since 1940*, 465.

30. Campion FD. *The AMA and U.S. Health Policy since 1940*, 465.

31. Campion FD. *The AMA and U.S. Health Policy since 1940*; Stevens RA. *American Medicine and the Public Interest*; Starr P. *The Social Transformation of American Medicine*; Mullin F. The National Health Service Corps and health personnel innovations: Beyond poorhouse medicine. In: Sidel VW, Sidel R, eds. *Reforming Medicine: Lessons of the Last Quarter Century*. New York: Pantheon Books, 1984, 176–200.

32. Savitt TL. Medical education. In: Salzman J, Smith DL, West C, eds. *Encyclopedia of African-American Culture and History*. 5 Vols. New York: Macmillan Library Reference USA, 1996, 1750–1752; quote 1752.

33. Wolinsky H. Healing wounds: Lonnie R. Bristow steps up to head the American Medical Association, one of the nation's premier—and most rigidly segregated—professional groups. *Emerge* July/August 1994; (10)(5):42, 43.

34. Savitt TL. Medical education, 1752.

35. Strelnick H, Younge R. Affirmative action in medicine: Money becomes the admissions criteria of the 1980s. In: Sidel VW, Sidel R, eds. *Reforming Medicine*, 151–175; quote 156.

36. Morais HM. *The History of the Negro in Medicine*; Strelnick H, Younge R. Affirmative action in medicine; Shea S, Fullilove MT. Entry of black and other minority students in U.S. medical schools: Historical perspectives and recent trends. *New England Journal of Medicine* 1985; 313:933–940; Sullivan LW. The status of blacks in medicine. *New England Journal of Medicine* 1983; 309:807–809; Savitt TL. Medical education; Wolinsky H. Healing wounds.

37. Butler BN. Morality or legality: That is the question: We are a nation of laws, and of men. *Journal of the National Medical Association* 1975; 67:242–246; quote 245.

38. Jaynes GD, Williams RM, eds. *A Common Destiny: Blacks and American Society*. Washington, DC: National Academy Press, 1989, 436.

39. McKinney F. Employment implications of a changing health-care system. In: Simms MC, Malveaux JM, eds. *Slipping through the Cracks: The Status of Black Women*. New Brunswick, NJ: Transaction Books, 1986, 199–215; Keith SN, Bell RM, Swanson AG, Williams AP. Effects of affirmative action in medical schools: A study of the class of 1975. *New England Journal of Medicine* 1985; 313:1519–1525; Gray LC. The geographic and functional distribution of black physicians: Some research and policy considerations. *American Journal of Public Health* 1977; 67:519–526; Hanft RS, Fishman LE, White CC. Minorities and the health professions: An update. Draft of August 1985, Association of Minority Health Professions Schools, Washington, DC.

40. Jaynes GD, Williams RM. eds. *A Common Destiny*, 436–437.

41. Berry LH. Opening remarks. *Journal of the National Medical Association* 1966; 58:209, 211.

42. Odegaard CE. *Minorities in Medicine: From Receptive Passivity to Positive Action 1966–1976*. n.p.: Josiah Macy Jr. Foundation, 1977, 90.

43. Robert Wood Johnson Foundation. Special Report Number One, The Foundation's Minority Medical Training Programs. Minority applicants to medical school are better qualified today than in mid-70s, yet less likely to be accepted. Princeton, NJ: Robert Wood Johnson Foundation, 1987, 7.

44. Huet-Cox R. Medical education: New wine in old wine skins. In: Sidel VW, Sidel R, eds. *Reforming Medicine*, 129–149, 147.

45. Holloman Jr. JLS. Medical leadership. *Journal of the National Medical Association* 1966; 58:377, 377–388; Cobb WM. Salute to the N.A.A.C.P.: 100,000 more in 1974. *Journal of the National Medical Association* 1974; 66:249–250; Morais HM. *The History of the Negro in Medicine*; Butler BN. Morality or legality; Jaynes GD, Williams RM. eds. *A Common Destiny*; U.S. Bureau of the Census. *Historical Statistics of the United States, Colonial Times to 1970, Bicentennial Edition, Parts 1 and 2*. Washington, DC: U.S. Government Printing Office, 1975; McKinney F. Employment implications of a changing health-care system; Keith SN, Bell RM, Swanson AG, Williams

AP. Effects of affirmative action in medical schools; Hanft RS, Fishman LE, White CC. Minorities and the health professions; Barber JB. President's inaugural address: Health status of the Black community. *Journal of the National Medical Association* 1979; 71:87–90; Lloyd Jr. SM, Johnson DG. Practice pattern of Black physicians: Results of a survey of Howard University College of Medicine alumni. *Journal of the National Medical Association* 1982; 74:129–141; Gray LC. The geographic and functional distribution of black physicians; Robert Wood Johnson Foundation. Special Report Number One, The Foundation's Minority Medical Training Programs; Cave VG. How far the way: President's retiring address. *Journal of the National Medical Association* 1975; 67:394; U.S. Bureau of the Census. *Statistical Abstract of the United States, 1993*. U.S. Department of Commerce. Washington, DC: U.S. Government Printing Office, 1992; Hammonds KE. Blacks and the urban health crisis. *Journal of the National Medical Association* 1974; 66:226–231; Applewhite HL. Health manpower. *Journal of the National Medical Association* 1974; 66:219–225; Applewhite HL. Blacks in public health. *Journal of the National Medical Association* 1974; 66:505–510; Odegaard CE. *Minorities in Medicine*; Transcription of a presentation by Dr. Leon Johnson Jr., President, National Medical Fellowships, Inc. to the Special Advisory Commission on Minority Enrollment in Medical Schools. Issues in financing minority enrollment, August 1982; Hanft RS, Fishman LE, Evans W. *Blacks and the Health Professions in the 80s: A National Crisis and a Time for Action*. n.p.: Prepared for the Association of Minority Health Professions Schools, 1983; Shea S, Fullilove MT. Entry of black and other minority students in U.S. medical schools; Huet-Cox R. Medical education.

46. Opportunity and new challenge for the N.M.A. *Journal of the National Medical Association* 1966; 58:210–211.

47. Cobb WM. The Black American in medicine. *Journal of the National Medical Association* 1981; 73(Suppl 1):1183–1244; Morais HM. *The History of the Negro in Medicine*; Cobb WM. N.M.A. president's testimony in support of H.R. 6675: "An act to provide a hospital insurance program for the aged under the Social Security Act." *Journal of the National Medical Association* 1965; 57:335–337; The Hill-Burton program and civil rights. *Journal of the National Medical Association* 1965; 57:59–61; The National Medical Association's contribution to the Selma-Montgomery march. *Journal of the National Medical Association* 1965; 57:243–244; Eaton HA. Views of North Carolina Negro physicians on medical assistance for the aged. *Journal of the National Medical Association* 1965; 57:166–167; Holloman Jr. JLS. A call to arms. *Journal of the National Medical Association* 1967; 59:55; Holloman Jr. JLS. Cross currents in the flow of medical practice. *Journal of the National Medical Association* 1967; 59:216; Cobb WM. The establishment, the Negro and education. *Journal of the National Medical Association* 1968; 60:320–331; Campion FD. *The AMA and U.S. Health Policy since 1940*; Smith DB. *Health Care Divided: Race and Healing a Nation*. Ann Arbor: University of Michigan Press, 1999; Reynolds PP. Hospitals and civil rights, 1945–1963: *Simkins v. Moses H. Cone Memorial Hospital. Annals of Internal Medicine* 1997; 126:898–906; Reynolds PP. The federal government's use of Title VI and Medicare to racially integrate hospitals in the United States, 1963 through 1967; Wing KR, Rose MG. Health facilities and the enforcement of civil rights. In: Roemer R, McKray G, eds. *Legal Aspects of Health Policy: Issues and Trends*. Westport, CT: Greenwood Press, 1980, 243–267; Rice MF, Jones Jr. W. Public policy compliance/enforcement and black American health: Title VI of the civil rights act of 1964. In: Jones Jr. W, Rice MF, eds. *Health Care Issues in Black America: Policies, Problems, and Prospects*. New York: Greenwood Press, 1987, 98–115.

48. Cobb WM. The establishment, the Negro and education.

49. Barber JB. President's inaugural address, 89.

50. Barber JB. President's inaugural address, 87.

51. The president and the nation's health. *Journal of the National Medical Association* 1965; 57:156; Campion FD. *The AMA and U.S. Health Policy since 1940*; Huet-Cox R. Medical education; Smith DB. *Health Care Divided*; Johnson LB. Address to the National Medical Association. *Journal of the National Medical Association* 1968; 60:449–454; Jordan VE. An address. *Journal of the National Medical Association* 1980; 72:378–380; Opportunity and new challenge for the N.M.A.; Holloman Jr. JLS. A new horizon: President's inaugural address, National Medical Association. *Journal of the National Medical Association* 1966; 58:371–376; Holloman Jr. JLS. A call to arms; Swan LF. The exigencies of the American environment, 1967: President's inaugural address, National Medical Association. *Journal of the National Medical Association* 1967; 59:373–377; Hos-

pital compliance in Atlanta. *Journal of the National Medical Association* 1966; 58:382–383; Coleman AH. Title 19 and medical civil rights. *Journal of the National Medical Association* 1966; 58:397.

52. Holloman Jr. JLS. Cross currents in the flow of medical practice, 216.

53. Holloman Jr. JLS. Cross currents in the flow of medical practice, 216.

54. Cobb WM. The establishment, the Negro and education, 326–327.

55. Berry LH. Opening remarks.

56. Swan LF. The start of a voyage—not journey's end. *Journal of the National Medical Association* 1968; 60:133.

57. Books Inc. *In Black America*. Los Angeles: Presidential Publishers, 1970, 254.

58. Walden EC. Miles to go: President's inaugural address. *Journal of the National Medical Association* 1971; 63:474, 476.

59. Becker LE. Health maintenance organizations: A Black physician's comments. *Journal of the National Medical Association* 1971; 63:488–491; quote 489.

60. Cobb WM. The Black American in medicine; Byrd WM, Clayton LA. An American health dilemma: A history of blacks in the health system. *Journal of the National Medical Association* 1992; 84:189–200; Charatz-Litt C. A chronicle of racism: The effects of the White medical community on black health. *Journal of the National Medical Association* 1992; 84:717–725; Books Inc. *In Black America*, 253–256; Opportunity and new challenge for the N.M.A; Holloman Jr. JLS. Cross currents in the flow of medical practice; Holloman Jr. JLS. A call to arms; Cobb WM. The establishment, the Negro and education; The establishment turns the Negro's flank: Or, how the "boat" was missed. *Journal of the National Medical Association* 1969; 61:274–275; Campion FD. *The AMA and U.S. Health Policy since 1940*; The National Medical Association Foundation, Inc.: A comprehensive health care program for the inner-city. *Journal of the National Medical Association* 1968; 60:138–141; Appeal for the NMA Foundation: A matter of simple multiplication. *Journal of the National Medical Association* 1968; 60:533; The National Medical Association Foundation, Inc.: The White House release. *Journal of the National Medical Association* 1968; 60:142–143; Washington WE. Problems and paradoxes of the urban crisis. *Journal of the National Medical Association* 1969; 61:1–5; Walden EC. Miles to go; Johnson ET. The delivery of health care in the ghetto. *Journal of the National Medical Association* 1969; 61:263–270; Wood CB. The neighborhood health center—the concept and the national scene. *Journal of the National Medical Association* 1971; 63:52–57; Becker LE. Health maintenance organizations.

61. Haynes MA. The gap in health status between black and white Americans. In: Williams RA, ed. *Textbook of Black-Related Diseases*. New York: McGraw-Hill, 1975, 1–30; Barber JB. Health status of the Black community: President's inaugural address. *Journal of the National Medical Association* 1979; 71:87–90; Thompson VR. Crisis in health care for the poor. *Journal of the National Medical Association* 1980; 72:1037; Alexander LL. Health objectives for the 1980s. *Journal of the National Medical Association* 1980; 72:654–656; Barber JB. Statement of the National Medical Association to the Select Committee on Aging and Congressional Black Caucus Brain Trust on Aging at the hearing on "Needs of the Minority Elderly." *Journal of the National Medical Association* 1979; 71; Barber JB. An open letter to President Carter. *Journal of the National Medical Association* 1978; 70:717–718; Roman Jr. SA. Health policy and the underserved. *Journal of the National Medical Association* 1978; 70:31–35; Jordan Jr. VE. An address; Walden EC. NMA comments on national health insurance. *Journal of the National Medical Association* 1971; 63:503–506; Walden EC. An NMA health insurance program. *Journal of the National Medical Association* 1971; 63:384; Thompson T. Health and social policy issues of significance to Blacks in the "new federalism." *Journal of the National Medical Association* 1973; 65:422; Hammonds KE. Blacks and the urban health crisis; Sampson CC. Death of the Black community hospital: Fact or fiction. *Journal of the National Medical Association* 1974; 66:165; Ryan W. *Blaming the Victim*. New York: Vintage Books, 1971. Revised, updated ed. New York: Vintage Books, 1976; Byrd WM. An American health dilemma. *Journal of the National Medical Association* 1986; 78:1025–1026; U.S. Department of Health and Human Services. *Report of the Secretary's Task Force on Black and Minority Health*. Vol. 1, *Executive Summary*. Washington, DC: U.S. Government Printing Office, August 1985; Shea S, Fullilove MT. Entry of black and other minority students in U.S. medical schools; Robert Wood Johnson Foundation. Special Report Number One, The Foundation's Minority Med-

ical Training Programs; Last JM, ed. *A Dictionary of Epidemiology.* 2nd ed. New York: Oxford University Press, for the International Epidemiological Association, 1988.

62. Walden EC. The biological imperatives. *Journal of the National Medical Association* 1972; 64:262.

63. Brew LE. *Edith: The Story of Edith Irby Jones, M.D.* n.p.: NRT Publishing Company, 1986; Foster HW, Greenwood A. *Make a Difference.* New York: Scribner, 1997; Organ CH, Kosiba MM, eds. *A Century of Black Surgeons: The U.S.A. Experience.* 2 Vols. Norman, OK: Transcript Press, 661–695; Gamble RL. Henry Floyd Gamble, M.D., 1862–1932. *Journal of the National Medical Association* 1972; 64:85–86.

64. Frierson HT. The status of Black students in medical education. *Journal of the National Medical Association* 1988; 80:387–390; quote 387.

65. Cobb WM. The Black American in medicine; Morais HM. *The History of the Negro in Medicine*; Cobb WM. The establishment, the Negro and education; The establishment turns the Negro's flank; Johnson ET. The delivery of health care in the ghetto; Smith DB. *Health Care Divided*; Gamble VN. Hospitals, Black. In: Salzman J, Smith DL, West C, eds. *Encyclopedia of African-American Culture and History.* 5 Vols. New York: Macmillan Library Reference USA, 1996, 1305–1309; Sampson CC. Death of the Black community hospital; Travella S. Black hospitals struggling to survive: Of more than 200 medical centers, only 8 are left. *Health: A Weekly Journal of Medicine, Science and Society, The Washington Post,* September 11, 1990:12; Cannon JA. The last economic alternative for the Black community. *Journal of the National Medical Association* 1972; 64:458–459; Brew LE. *Edith*; Foster HW, Greenwood A. *Make a Difference*; Organ CH, Kosiba MM, eds. *A Century of Black Surgeons*; Gamble RL. Henry Floyd Gamble, M.D., 1862–1932; Dorsey-Young F. Value socialization of Black medical students at the Howard University College of Medicine: A case report. *Journal of the National Medical Association* 1980; 72:247–258; Strayhorn G. Social supports, perceived stress, and health: The Black experience in medical school—a preliminary study. *Journal of the National Medical Association* 1980; 72:869–881; Bullock SC, Houston E. Perceptions of racism by black medical students attending white medical schools. *Journal of the National Medical Association* 1987; 79:601–608; Frierson HT. Black medical students' perceptions of the academic environment and of faculty and peer interactions. *Journal of the National Medical Association* 1987; 79:737–743; Frierson HT. The status of Black students in medical education.

66. Schwarz GE, Lawrence MS. Selected characteristics of the members of the National Medical Association: Preliminary findings. *Journal of the National Medical Association* 1970; 62:1–7; Richard MP. The Negro physician: A study in mobility and status inconsistency. *Journal of the National Medical Association* 1969; 61:278–279; Haynes MA. The distribution of Black physicians in the United States, 1967. *Journal of the National Medical Association* 1969; 61:470–473; Strayhorn G. Social supports, perceived stress, and health; Geertsma RH. A special tutorial for minority medical students: An account of a year's experience. *Journal of Medical Education* 1977; 52:396–403; Dorsey-Young F. Value socialization of Black medical students at the Howard University College of Medicine.

67. Schwarz GE, Lawrence MS. Selected characteristics of the members of the National Medical Association; Richard MP. The Negro physician; Haynes MA. The distribution of Black physicians in the United States, 1967; Organ CH. Equality and excellence. *Journal of the National Medical Association* 1970; 62:347; Organ CH, Kosiba MM, eds. *A Century of Black Surgeons.*

68. Organ CH. Equality and excellence, 347.

69. Hanft RS, Fishman LE, Evans W. *Blacks and the Health Professions in the 80s,* 34.

70. Organ CH. Equality and excellence, 347.

71. Organ CH. Equality and excellence; Organ CH, Kosiba MM, eds. *A Century of Black Surgeons,* 775–809; Hanft RS, Fishman LE, Evans W. *Blacks and the Health Professions in the 80s*; Strayhorn G. Social supports, perceived stress, and health; Geertsma RH. A special tutorial for minority medical students; Dorsey-Young F. Value socialization of Black medical students at the Howard University College of Medicine.

72. Woodson CG. *The Negro Professional Man and the Community.* Washington, DC: The Association for the Study of Negro Life and History, 1934, 122–126.

73. Richard MP. The Negro physician, 279.

74. Richard MP. The Negro physician; Schwarz GE, Lawrence MS. Selected characteristics of

the members of the National Medical Association; Dorsey-Young F. Value socialization of Black medical students at the Howard University College of Medicine.

75. Richard MP. The Negro physician, 279.

76. Richard MP. The Negro physician, 279.

77. Woodson CG. *The Negro Professional Man and the Community*; Frazier EF. *The Negro in the United States*. Rev. ed. New York: The Macmillan Company, 1957; Frazier EF. *Black Bourgeoisie: The Rise of a New Middle Class in the United States*. New York: The Free Press, 1957; paperback ed. New York: Collier Books, 1962; Schwarz GE, Lawrence MS. Selected characteristics of the members of the National Medical Association; Richard MP. The Negro physician; Richard MP. The Negro physician: Babbitt or revolutionary? *Journal of Health and Social Behavior* 1969; 10:265–274; Schwarz GE. An exploratory descriptive study of the National Medical Association. Unpublished master's thesis, University of Iowa, Iowa City, 1969; Richard MP. The Negro physician: A study in mobility and status inconsistency. Unpublished doctoral dissertation, New York University, New York, 1967; Robert Wood Johnson Foundation. Special Report Number One, The Foundation's Minority Medical Training Programs; Cobb WM. The Black American in medicine; Morais HM. *The History of the Negro in Medicine*.

78. Cannon JA. The last economic alternative for the Black community, 458.

79. Swann LF. The inner city oriented physician: His indispensability in federal health programs. *Journal of the National Medical Association* 1967; 59:139..

80. Cannon JA. The last economic alternative for the Black community, 458–459.

81. Rice MF. Hospital viability and closures. *Journal of Health Care for the Poor and Underserved* 1990; 1:103–106; quote 105.

82. Travella S. Black hospitals struggling to survive, 12.

83. Cannon JA. The last economic alternative for the Black community, 459.

84. Cannon JA. The last economic alternative for the Black community, 459.

85. Becker LE. Health maintenance organizations, 490.

86. Washington WE. Problems and paradoxes of the urban crisis; Cannon JA. The last economic alternative for the Black community; Johnson ET. The delivery of health care in the ghetto; Rice MF. Hospital viability and closures; Travella S. Black hospitals struggling to survive; Coleman AH. Title 19 and medical civil rights; Factors influencing the fate of the Negro hospital. *Journal of the National Medical Association* 1967; 59:217; Becker LE. Health maintenance organizations.

87. Epps Jr. CH. The Black practitioner: Challenges of the future. *Journal of the National Medical Association* 1986; 78:365–370; quote 365.

88. Barnwell S, LaMendola WF. A survey and analysis of techniques used in attracting the Black middle-class patient. *Journal of the National Medical Association* 1985; 77:379–384.

89. Byrd WM. Inquisition, peer review, and black physician survival; Shea S, Fullilove MT. Entry of black and other minority students in U.S. medical schools; Strayhorn G. Social supports, perceived stress, and health, 873; Bullock SC, Houston E. Perceptions of racism by Black medical students in predominantly White medical schools. Presented at the 1981 annual meeting of the American Psychiatric Association, New Orleans, May 14, 1981; Geertsma RH. A special tutorial for minority medical students; Earles L. Doctor, what was your major? *Journal of the National Medical Association* 1984; 76:575–576; Jones EI. Closing the health status gap for Blacks and other minorities. *Journal of the National Medical Association* 1985; 78:485–488; Smith PM. The Black physician: An endangered species? *Journal of the National Medical Association* 1984; 76:1178–1181.

90. Jones EI. Closing the health status gap for Blacks and other minorities, 486.

91. Bell CC. Impaired Black health professionals: Vulnerabilities and treatment approaches. *Journal of the National Medical Association* 1986; 78:925–930, 928.

92. Byrd WM. Inquisition, peer review, and black physician survival.

93. Byrd WM. Inquisition, peer review, and black physician survival.

94. Byrd WM. Inquisition, peer review, and black physician survival, 1027; Lone Star State Medical Association. Charges of racial discrimination in Fort Worth, Texas. *Lone Star State Medical Association Newsletter–Region Five* Feb/March 1984.

95. Gilum RF. Federal regulation of medical practice and the Black physician. *Journal of the National Medical Association* 1973; 65:254–255; quote 255.

96. Epps Jr. CH. The Black practitioner; Barnwell S, LaMendola WF. A survey and analysis of techniques used in attracting the Black middle-class patient; Richard MP. The Negro physician; Jones EI. Closing the health status gap for Blacks and other minorities; Strayhorn G. Social supports, perceived stress, and health; Geertsma RH. A special tutorial for minority medical students; Bell CC. Impaired Black health professionals; Gilum RF. Federal regulation of medical practice and the Black physician; Byrd WM. Inquisition, peer review, and black physician survival; Byrd WM. Black medicine under attack; Byrd WM. *Peer Review*.

97. Phillips CW. Cook County Hospital's potential as a leader in urban medical care. *Journal of the National Medical Association* 1972; 64:169–171; Cross EB. Patients are people: A positive concept of health care. *Journal of the National Medical Association* 1972; 64:167–168; Lewis S. *Hospital: An Oral History of Cook County Hospital*. New York: The New Press, 1994; Anderson EA. The Watts health miracle. *Journal of the National Medical Association* 1972; 64:168; Ellis EF, Attswood JC. A concept of delivery of health care. *Journal of the National Medical Association* 1972; 64:189–196; Shepperd JD, Haedka EK. Impact of the consumer on inner city health centers. *Journal of the National Medical Association* 1972; 64:370–371; Kerner O. *Report of the National Advisory Commission on Civil Disorders*. New York: E.P. Dutton and Company, 1968. Paperback ed. New York: Bantam Books, 1968.

## Chapter Six

1. Gamble VN. Under the shadow of Tuskegee: African Americans and health care. *American Journal of Public Health* 1997; 87:1773–1778, quote 1773.

2. Jones JH. *Bad Blood: The Tuskegee Syphilis Experiment*. New York: The Free Press, 1981. New and expanded ed., 1993, 220.

3. Gamble VN. Under the shadow of Tuskegee, 1773.

4. Geiger HJ. Annotation: Racism resurgent–building a bridge to the nineteenth century. *American Journal of Public Health* 1997; 87:1765–1766.

5. Advisory committee on human radiation experiments, final report. In: Areen J, et al. *Law, Science and Medicine*. 2nd ed. Westbury, NY: The Foundation Press, 1996, 1024–1041, quote 1028.

6. Hornblum AM. *Acres of Skin: Human Experiments at Holmesburg Prison: A True Story of Abuse and Exploitation in the Name of Medical Science*. New York: Routledge, 1998, 85.

7. Hornblum AM. *Acres of Skin*, 234.

8. Hornblum AM. *Acres of Skin*, 234.

9. Hornblum AM. *Acres of Skin*, 235.

10. Jones JH. *Bad Blood*, 189.

11. Annas GJ. The Nuremberg Code in U.S. courts: Ethics versus expediency. In: Annas GJ, Grodin MA, eds. *The Nazi Doctors and the Nuremberg Code: Human Rights in Human Experimentation*. New York: Oxford University Press, 1992, 201–222, quote 201.

12. Jones JH. Tuskegee syphilis experiment. In: Salzman J, Smith DL, West C, eds. *Encyclopedia of African-American Culture and History*. 5 vols. New York: Macmillan Library Reference USA, 1996, 2685–2687, quote 2687.

13. Robinson LS. Dialogue: Curbing a sick practice: Energy Secretary Hazel O'Leary focuses on government accountability in testing. *Emerge* October 1994; (1)(6):20; Jones JH. *Bad Blood*; Gamble VN. Under the shadow of Tuskegee; Geiger HJ. Annotation; Hornblum AM. *Acres of Skin*; Coleman AH. Human experimentation. *Journal of the National Medical Association* 1966; 58:147–148; Reich W, ed. *Encyclopedia of Bioethics*. Vol. 4. New York: Free Press, 1978; Audi R, ed. *The Cambridge Dictionary of Philosophy*. Cambridge, England: Cambridge University Press, 1995; Jones JH. Tuskegee syphilis experiment; Dula A. Toward an African-American perspective on bioethics. *Journal of Health Care for the Poor Underserved* 1991; 2:259–269; Chase A. *The Legacy of Malthus: The Social Costs of the New Scientific Racism*. New York: Knopf, 1980; Annas GJ. The Nuremberg Code in U.S. courts; Harmer RM. *American Medical Avarice*. New York: Abelard-Schuman, 1975, 79–93.

14. Jones JH. Tuskegee syphilis experiment, 2687.

15. Chase A. *The Legacy of Malthus*, 17–19.

16. Tucker WH. *The Science and Politics of Racial Research*. Urbana: University of Illinois Press, 1994, 60.

17. Tucker WH. *The Science and Politics of Racial Research*, 60.

18. Pross C. Nazi doctors, German medicine, and historical truth. In: Annas GJ, Grodin MA, eds. *The Nazi Doctors and the Nuremberg Code*; 32–52, quote 33.

19. Jones JH. *Bad Blood*, 10.

20. Jones JH. *Bad Blood*, 11.

21. Jones JH. *Bad Blood*, 10–11.

22. Pernick MS. Eugenics and public health in American history. *American Journal of Public Health* 1997; 87:1767–1772, quote 1770.

23. Jones JH. *Bad Blood*, 14.

24. Jones JH. *Bad Blood*, 13.

25. Annas GJ, Grodin MA, eds. *The Nazi Doctors and the Nuremberg Code*; Proctor RN. *Racial Hygiene: Medicine under the Nazis*. Cambridge, MA: Harvard University Press, 1988; Jones JH. *Bad Blood*; Tucker WH. *The Science and Politics of Racial Research*; Byrd WM. Race, biology, and health care: Reassessing a relationship. *Journal of Health Care for the Poor and Underserved* 1990; 1:278–292; Pernick MS. Eugenics and public health in American history; Roberts D. *Killing the Black Body: Race, Reproduction, and the Meaning of Liberty*. New York: Pantheon Books, 1997; Gamble VN. Under the shadow of Tuskegee; McGregor DK. *Sexual Surgery and the Origins of Gynecology: J. Marion Sims, His Hospital, and His Patients*. New York: Garland Publishing, 1989; Horsman R. *Josiah Nott of Mobile: Southerner, Physician, and Racial Theorist*. Baton Rouge: Louisiana State University Press, 1987; Chase A. *The Legacy of Malthus*; Larson EJ. *Sex, Race, and Science: Eugenics in the Deep South*. Baltimore: Johns Hopkins University Press, 1995.

26. Pernick MS. Eugenics and public health in American history, 1770.

27. Gould SJ. *The Mismeasure of Man*. New York: W. W. Norton, 1981, 20.

28. Gould SJ. Bound by the great chain. In: Gould SJ. *The Flamingo's Smile: Reflections in Natural History*. New York: W. W. Norton, 1985, 281–291, quote 285–286.

29. Tucker WH. *The Science and Politics of Racial Research*, 11.

30. Tucker WH. *The Science and Politics of Racial Research*, 17–18.

31. Gould SJ. *The Mismeasure of Man*, 20.

32. Tucker WH. *The Science and Politics of Racial Research*, 4.

33. Tucker WH. *The Science and Politics of Racial Research*, 83.

34. Brigham CC. A study of American inteligence. In: Jacoby R, Glauberman N, eds. *The Bell Curve Debate: History, Documents, Opinions*. New York: Times Books, 1995, 571–582, quote 573.

35. Gould SJ. *The Mismeasure of Man*, 20.

36. Guthrie RV. *Even the Rat Was White: A Historical View of Psychology*. New York: Harper & Row, 1976; Gould SJ. *The Mismeasure of Man*, 21; Tucker WH. *The Science and Politics of Racial Research*, 2.

37. Guthrie RV. *Even the Rat Was White*, 193–194.

38. Tucker WH. *The Science and Politics of Racial Research*, 2.

39. Gould SJ. *The Mismeasure of Man*, 21.

40. Pernick MS. Eugenics and public health in American history; Gould SJ. *The Mismeasure of Man*; Gould SJ. Bound by the great chain; Tucker WH. *The Science and Politics of Racial Research*; Kamin LJ. The pioneers of IQ testing. In: Jacoby R, Glauberman N, eds. *The Bell Curve Debate*, 476–509; Jacoby R, Glauberman N, eds. *The Bell Curve Debate*; Guthrie RV. *Even the Rat Was White: A Historical View of Psychology*. 2nd ed. Boston: Allyn & Bacon, 1998; Lemann N. *The Big Test: The Secret History of the American Meritocracy*. New York: Farrar, Straus and Giroux, 1999; East EM. *Heredity and Human Affairs*. New York: Charles Scribner's and Sons, 1929; East EM, ed. *Biology in Human Affairs*. New York: McGraw-Hill, 1931; Bingham CC. *A Study of American Intelligence*. Princeton, NJ: Princeton University Press, 1923; Kragh H. *An Introduction to the Historiography of Science*. Cambridge, England: Cambridge University Press, 1987. Paperback ed., 1989.

41. Tucker WH. *The Science and Politics of Racial Research*, 5.

42. Gould SJ. *The Mismeasure of Man*, 21; Tucker WH. *The Science and Politics of Racial Research*, 3.

43. Myrdal G. *An American Dilemma: The Negro Problem and Modern Democracy*. New York: Harper & Row, 1944, 91.

44. Tucker WH. *The Science and Politics of Racial Research*, 138.

45. Tucker WH. *The Science and Politics of Racial Research*, 139.

46. Klineberg O. Race and psychology. In: UNESCO. *The Race Question in Modern Science*. New York: Whiteside, and William Morrow, 1956, 55–84, quote 55.

47. Tucker WH. *The Science and Politics of Racial Research*, 139.

48. Byrd WM. Race, biology, and health care; Gould SJ. *The Mismeasure of Man*; Tucker WH. *The Science and Politics of Racial Research*; Jones JH. *Bad Blood*; Brandt AM. Racism and research: The case of the Tuskegee syphilis study. *Hastings Center Report* 1978; 8:21–29; Reed J. Scientific racism. In: Wilson CR, Ferris W, eds. *Encyclopedia of Southern Culture*. Chapel Hill: University of North Carolina Press, 1989, 1358–1360; UNESCO. *The Race Question in Modern Science*; Montagu A. *Race, Science and Humanity*. New York: Van Nostrand Reinhold, 1963; Myrdal G. *An American Dilemma*; Stanton W. *The Leopard's Spots: Scientific Attitudes toward Race in America, 1815–1859*. Chicago: University of Chicago Press, 1960; Haller Jr. JS. *Outcasts from Evolution: Scientific Attitudes of Racial Inferiority, 1859–1900*. New York: McGraw Hill, 1971; Haller MH. *Eugenics: Hereditarian Attitudes in American Thought*. New Brunswick, NJ: Rutgers University Press, 1963; Guthrie RV. *Even the Rat Was White*. 2nd ed.; Proctor RN. *Racial Hygiene*; Chase A. *The Legacy of Malthus*; Annas GJ, Grodin MA, eds. *The Nazi Doctors and the Nuremberg Code*; Hornblum AM. *Acres of Skin*; Muir H, ed. *Larousse Dictionary of Scientists*. New York: Larousse, 1994.

49. Tucker WH. *The Science and Politics of Racial Research*, 163–164.

50. Tucker WH. *The Science and Politics of Racial Research*, 164.

51. Shipman P. *The Evolution of Racism: Human Differences and the Use and Abuse of Science*. New York: Simon & Schuster, 1994, 199.

52. Tucker WH. *The Science and Politics of Racial Research*, 169–177.

53. Tucker WH. *The Science and Politics of Racial Research*, 176.

54. Tucker WH. *The Science and Politics of Racial Research*; UNESCO. *The Race Question in Modern Science*; Shipman P. *The Evolution of Racism*; Blakey ML. Skull doctors revisited: Intrinsic social and political bias in the history of American physical anthropology. With special reference to the work of Aleš Hrdliĉka. In: Reynolds LT, Lieberman L, eds. *Race and Other Misadventures: Essays in Honor of Ashley Montagu in His Ninetieth Year*. Dix Hills, NY: General Hall Publishers, 1996, 64–95; Chase A. *The Legacy of Malthus*; Coon CS. *The Origin of Races*. New York: Knopf, 1962; Friedman LM. *Crime and Punishment in American History*. New York: Basic Books, 1993; Guthrie RV. *Even the Rat Was White*. 2nd ed.; Sedgwick J. Inside the Pioneer Fund. In: Jacoby R, Glauberman N, eds. *The Bell Curve Debate*, 144–161; Lane C. Tainted sources. In: Jacoby R, Glauberman N, eds. *The Bell Curve Debate*, 125–139; Garrett HE. Four monographs: (1) *How Classroom Desegregtion Will Work*, (2) *Heredity: The Cause of Racial Differences in Intelligence*, (3) *The Relative Intelligence of Whites and Negroes: The Armed Forces Test*, (4) *Breeding Down*. Richmond, VA: The Patrick Henry Press, undated but c. 1959–1967; George WC. *The Biology of the Race Problem: A Study Prepared by Commission of the Governor of Alabama*. Birmingham, AL: State of Alabama, 1962. Reprint ed. Richmond, VA: The Patrick Henry Press, n.d.; Horton EA. *Apes, Men, and Morons*. New York: G.P Putnam's Sons, 1937; Ingle DJ. *Who Should Have Children? An Environmental and Genetic Approach*. Indianapolis: Bobbs-Merrill, 1973; Graves P. *Edward VIII: The Traitor King*. Documentary videotape for *Biography*, Channel Four Television Corporation, 1995; Wenner-Gren, Axel Leonard. In: Magnusson M., ed. *Cambridge Biographical Dictionary*. Cambridge, U.K.: Cambridge University Press, 1990, 1545; Miller A. Professors of hate. In: Jacoby R, Glauberman N, eds. *The Bell Curve Debate*, 162–178; International Association for the Advancement of Ethnology and Eugenics, New York. Reprint series: (1) *The Inheritance of Mental Ability*. Cyril Burt. Reprint No. 11. Reprinted from *American Psychologist*, Vol. XII. No. 1 (January, 1958). (2) *A Review: Klineberg's Chapter on Race and Psychology*. Henry E. Garrett. Reprint No. 1 from *The Mankind Quarterly*, Vol. 1, No. 1 (July, 1960). (3) *The Emergence of Racial Genetics*. Ruggles R. Gates. Reprint No. 6. Reprinted from the *Mankind Quarterly*. Vol. 1, No. 1

(July 1960). (4) *The S.P.S.S.I. and Racial Differences*. Henry E. Garret. Reprint No. 9. Reprinted from *American Psychologist*, Vol. XVII, No. 5 (May, 1962).

55. Kuttner RE. Letter to the editor. *Perspectives in Biology and Medicine* 1968; 11:707.

56. Tucker WH. *The Science and Politics of Racial Research*, 182; Ingle DJ. Racial differences and the future. *Science* 1964; 146:378.

57. Tucker WH. *The Science and Politics of Racial Research*, 184.

58. Chase A. *The Legacy of Malthus*, 481.

59. Tucker WH. *The Science and Politics of Racial Research*, 184–185.

60. Tucker WH. *The Science and Politics of Racial Research*, 185.

61. Chase A. *The Legacy of Malthus*, 481.

62. Tucker WH. *The Science and Politics of Racial Research*, 186.

63. Chase A. *The Legacy of Malthus*, 482.

64. Tucker WH. *The Science and Politics of Racial Research*, 186.

65. Tucker WH. *The Science and Politics of Racial Research*, 186.

66. Tucker WH. *The Science and Politics of Racial Research*, 187.

67. Chase A. *The Legacy of Malthus*, 488.

68. Tucker WH. *The Science and Politics of Racial Research*, 194; Royster V. Editorial. *Wall Street Journal* May 22, 1968: 18.

69. Tucker WH. *The Science and Politics of Racial Research*; Chase A. *The Legacy of Malthus*; Gould SJ. *The Mismeasure of Man*; Jacoby R, Glauberman N, eds. *The Bell Curve Debate*.

70. Jensen AR. Learning abilities in retarded, average, and gifted children. *Merrill-Palmer Quarterly* 1963; 9:123–140; Jensen AR. The culturally disadvantaged: Psychological and educational aspects. *Educational Research* 1967; 10:4–20.

71. Jensen AR. The culturally disadvantaged, 8.

72. Chase A. *The Legacy of Malthus*, 461; Jensen AR. The culturally disadvantaged, 10.

73. Chase A. *The Legacy of Malthus*, 461; Jensen AR. The culturally disadvantaged,10.

74. Lewontin RC, Rose S, Kamin LJ. *Not in Our Genes: Biology, Ideology, and Human Nature*. New York: Pantheon Books, 1984, 19.

75. Lewontin RC, Rose S, Kamin LJ. *Not in Our Genes*, 19.

76. Tucker WH. *The Science and Politics of Racial Research*, 196.

77. Hearnshaw LS. *Cyril Burt, Psychologist*. Ithaca, NY: Cornell University Press, 1979; Gould SJ. *The Mismeasure of Man*, 234–239; Lewontin RC, Rose S, Kamin LJ. *Not in Our Genes*, 101–106, 118, 212; Tucker WH. *The Science and Politics of Racial Research*, 196; Kevles DJ. In: *the Name of Eugenics: Genetics and the Uses of Human Heredity*. Berkeley: University of California Press, 1985, 281.

78. Tucker WH. *The Science and Politics of Racial Research*; Chase A. *The Legacy of Malthus*; Jensen AR. Learning abilities in retarded, average, and gifted children; Jensen AR. The culturally disadvantaged; Eysenck HJ. *The I.Q. Argument: Race, Intelligence, and Education*. New York: The Library Press, 1971; Gould SJ. *The Mismeasure of Man*; Kevles DJ. In: *the Name of Eugenics*; Lewontin RC, Rose S, Kamin LJ. *Not in Our Genes*; Hearnshaw LS. *Cyril Burt, Psychologist*.

79. Tucker WH. *The Science and Politics of Racial Research*, 196; Jensen AR. The culturally disadvantaged, 5–6.

80. Tucker WH. *The Science and Politics of Racial Research*, 196.

81. Tucker WH. *The Science and Politics of Racial Research*, 197.

82. Jensen AR. Social class, race and genetics: Implications for education. *American Educational Research Journal* 1968; 5:1–42, quote 23; Moynihan DP. *The Negro Family*. Washington, DC: Office of Policy, Planning and Research, U.S. Department of Labor, March 1965; DeNeufville R, Conner C. How good are our schools? *American Education* 1966; 2:6.

83. Tucker WH. *The Science and Politics of Racial Research*, 197; Jensen AR. Social class, race and genetics, 30.

84. Tucker WH. *The Science and Politics of Racial Research*, 197; Jensen AR. The culturally disadvantaged and the heredity-environment uncertainty. In: Hellmuth J, ed. *Disadvantaged Child*. Vol. 2. New York: Brunner-Mazel, 1968, 54.

85. Tucker WH. *The Science and Politics of Racial Research*, 197.

86. Tucker WH. *The Science and Politics of Racial Research*, 199.

87. Tucker WH. *The Science and Politics of Racial Research*; Chase A. *The Legacy of Malthus*; Jensen AR. Social class, race and genetics; Jensen AR. The culturally disadvantaged; Jensen AR. The culturally disadvantaged and the heredity-environment uncertainty; Moynihan DP. *The Negro Family*; DeNeufville R, Conner C. How good are our schools?; Jensen AR. How much can we boost IQ and scholastic achievement? *Harvard Educational Review* 1969; 39:1–123; Kevles DJ. In: *the Name of Eugenics*; Shufeldt RW. *America's Greatest Problem: The Negro*. Philadelphia: E. A. Davis, 1915; Gould SJ. *The Mismeasure of Man*.

88. Gould SJ. Jensen's last stand. In: Gould SJ. *An Urchin in the Storm: Essays about Books and Ideas*. New York: W. W. Norton, 1987, 124–144, quote 125.

89. Lewontin RC, Rose S, Kamin LJ. *Not in Our Genes*, 19.

90. Gould SJ. Racist arguments and IQ. In: Gould SJ. *Ever Since Darwin: Reflections in Natural History*. New York: W. W. Norton, 1977, 243–247, quote 244.

91. Chase A. *The Legacy of Malthus*, 470.

92. Chase A. *The Legacy of Malthus*, 470–471.

93. Tucker WH. *The Science and Politics of Racial Research*; Chase A. *The Legacy of Malthus*; Jensen AR. How much can we boost IQ and scholastic achievement?; Gould SJ. Jensen's last stand; Lewontin RC, Rose S, Kamin LJ. *Not in Our Genes*; Gould SJ. Racist arguments and IQ; Can Negroes learn the way Whites do? Findings of a top authority. *U.S. News and World Report* March 10, 1969: 48–51; A scientist's variation on a disturbing racial theme: Psychologist Arthur Jensen believes Black are born with lower IQ's than Whites—and the furor goes on. *Life* June 12, 1970: 65; Born dumb? *Newsweek* March 31, 1969: 84; Jensen AR. *Bias in Mental Testing*. New York: The Free Press, 1979; Guthrie RV. *Even the Rat Was White*. 2nd ed.; Lane C. Tainted sources; Shuey AM. *The Testing of Negro Intelligence*. 2nd ed. New York: Social Science Press, 1966; Bullock HA. *A History of Negro Education in the South: From 1619 to the Present*. New York: Praeger, 1967; Anderson JD. *The Education of Blacks in the South, 1860–1935*. Chapel Hill: University of North Carolina Press, 1988; Jacoby R, Glauberman N, eds. *The Bell Curve Debate*.

94. Jensen AR. How much can we boost IQ and scholastic achievement?, 2.

95. Tucker WH. *The Science and Politics of Racial Research*, 199–200.

96. Tucker WH. *The Science and Politics of Racial Research*, 200.

97. Tucker WH. *The Science and Politics of Racial Research*, 201.

98. Jensen AR. The culturally disadvantaged and the heredity-environment uncertainty, 19.

99. Jensen AR. How much can we boost IQ and scholastic achievement?, 59.

100. Gould SJ. *The Mismeasure of Man*, 24.

101. Gould SJ. Jensen's last stand, 132.

102. Jensen AR. How much can we boost IQ and scholastic achievement?, 6.

103. Chase A. *The Legacy of Malthus*, 232.

104. Jensen AR. How much can we boost IQ and scholastic achievement?, 5–8.

105. Gould SJ. *The Mismeasure of Man*, 24.

106. Jensen AR. How much can we boost IQ and scholastic achievement?, 28, 28–59.

107. Gould SJ. *The Mismeasure of Man*, 24–25.

108. Tucker WH. *The Science and Politics of Racial Research*; Chase A. *The Legacy of Malthus*; Jensen AR. How much can we boost IQ and scholastic achievement?; Gould SJ. *The Mismeasure of Man*; Thorndike EL. *Human Nature and the Social Order*. New York: The Macmillan Company, 1940; Gould SJ. Jensen's last stand.

109. Gould SJ. Jensen's last stand, 132.

110. Gould SJ. Jensen's last stand, 132.

111. Gould SJ. *The Mismeasure of Man*, 238; Burt C. The measurement of intelligence by the Binet tests. *Eugenics Review* 1914; 6:36–50, 140–152, 36.

112. Spearman C. General intelligence objectively defined and measured. *American Journal of Psychology* 1904; 15:201–293.

113. Gould SJ. Jensen's last stand, 133.

114. Gould SJ. Jensen's last stand, 134.

115. Gould SJ. Jensen's last stand, 136.

116. Gould SJ. *The Mismeasure of Man*, 238.

117. Gould SJ. *The Mismeasure of Man*, 268.

118. Gould SJ. Jensen's last stand, 133.

119. Gould SJ. Jensen's last stand, 136.

120. Gould SJ. Jensen's last stand, 136.

121. Thurstone LL. *The Vectors of Mind*. Chicago: University of Chicago Press, 1935.

122. Gould SJ. Jensen's last stand, 137.

123. Gould SJ. Jensen's last stand, 137–138.

124. Gould SJ. Jensen's last stand; Gould SJ. *The Mismeasure of Man*, 234–320; Guthrie RV. *Even the Rat Was White*. 2nd ed.; Spearman C. General intelligence objectively defined and measured; Spearman C, Wynn Jones L. *Human Ability*. London: MacMillan, 1950, Lemann N. The structure of success in America: The untold story of how educational testing became ambition's gateway—and a national obsession. *The Atlantic Monthly* August 1995; (2)(276):41; Lemann N. The great sorting: The first mass administrations of a scholastic-aptitude test led with surprising speed to the idea that the nation's leaders would be the people who did well on tests. *The Atlantic Monthly* September 1995; (3)(276):84; Thurstone LL. *The Vectors of Mind*; Jensen AR. How much can we boost IQ and scholastic achievement?.

125. Hearnshaw LS. *Cyril Burt, Psychologist*.

126. Gould SJ. Jensen's last stand, 125.

127. Gould SJ. Jensen's last stand; Gould SJ. *The Mismeasure of Man*, 317–320; Lewontin RC, Rose S, Kamin LJ. *Not in Our Genes*, 27, 80, 101–106, 118, 127–129; Kevles DJ. In: *the Name of Eugenics*, 281–282.

128. Gould SJ. Jensen's last stand; Hearnshaw LS. *Cyril Burt, Psychologist*; Jensen AR. *Bias in Mental Testing*; Gould SJ. *The Mismeasure of Man*; Lewontin RC, Rose S, Kamin LJ. *Not in Our Genes*; Kevles DJ. In: *the Name of Eugenics*.

129. Jensen AR. How much can we boost IQ and scholastic achievement?, 78.

130. Jensen AR. How much can we boost IQ and scholastic achievement?, 82.

131. Jensen AR. How much can we boost IQ and scholastic achievement?, 82–83.

132. Jensen AR. How much can we boost IQ and scholastic achievement?, 92; Chase A. *The Legacy of Malthus*, 33–43.

133. Reed EW, Reed SC. *Mental Retardation: A Family Study*. Philadelphia: W. B. Saunders and Company, 1965, 2.

134. Chase A. *The Legacy of Malthus*, 42.

135. Tucker WH. *The Science and Politics of Racial Research*; Chase A. *The Legacy of Malthus*; Jensen AR. How much can we boost IQ and scholastic achievement?; Guthrie RV. *Even the Rat Was White*. 2nd ed.; Lemann N. *The Big Test*, 1999, 159–161; Hacker A. *Two Nations: Black and White, Separate, Hostile, Unequal*. New York: Ballantine Books, 1992. Expanded and updated ed. 1995; Massey DS, Denton NA. *American Apartheid: Segregation and the Making of the Underclass*. Cambridge, MA: Harvard University Press, 1993; Robinson LS. Dialogue: Economist David H. Swinton: Inequities of the past block progress. *Emerge* October 1993; (1)(5):18; Swinton DH. The economic status of African Americans: Limited ownership and persistent inequality. In: Tidwell BJ, ed. *The State of Black America 1992*. New York: National Urban League, 1992; Coleman JS, et al. *Equality of Educational Opportunity*. Washington: Government Printing Office, 1966; Wilson WJ. *The Truly Disadvantaged: The Inner City, the Underclass, and Public Policy*. Chicago: University of Chicago Press, 1987; Sniderman PM, Piazza T. *The Scar of Race*. Cambridge, MA: Belknap Press of Harvard University Press, 1993; Reed EW, Reed SC. *Mental Retardation*; Robie TR. Selective sterilization for race culture. In: The Third International Congress of Eugenics. New York, 1932. *A Decade of Progress in Eugenics: Scientific Papers of the Congress*. Baltimore: Williams and Wilkins Company, 1934, 201–209; Sadler LK. Is the abnormal to become normal? In: *A Decade of Progress in Eugenics*, 193–200; Jacoby R, Glauberman N, eds. *The Bell Curve Debate*.

136. Jensen AR. How much can we boost IQ and scholastic achievement?, 111.

137. Washburn SL. The study of race. In: Harding S, ed. *The "Racial Economy" of Science: Toward a Democratic Future*. Bloomington: Indiana University Press, 1993, 128–132.

138. Jensen AR. How much can we boost IQ and scholastic achievement?; Tucker WH. *The Science and Politics of Racial Research*; Chase A. *The Legacy of Malthus*; Washburn SL. The study of

race; Lemann N. *The Big Test*; Bullock HA. *A History of Negro Education in the South*; Anderson JD. *The Education of Blacks in the South, 1860–1935*; Lemann N. The structure of success in America; Lemann N. The great sorting; Lane C. Tainted sources; Harding S. Introduction: Eurocentric scientific illiteracy—a challenge for the world community. In: Harding S, ed. *The "Racial Economy" of Science*, 1–22; Jacoby R, Glauberman N, eds. *The Bell Curve Debate*.

139. Lewontin RC, Rose S, Kamin LJ. *Not in Our Genes*, 19.

140. DeParle J. Daring research or "social science pornography"? *New York Times Magazine* October 9, 1994: Section 6, 48, 49.

141. Herrnstein RJ. IQ. In: Jacoby R, Glauberman N, eds. *The Bell Curve Debate*, 599–616.

142. Chase A. *The Legacy of Malthus*, 488–492.

143. Chase A. *The Legacy of Malthus*; Lewontin RC, Rose S, Kamin LJ. *Not in Our Genes*; Holden C, Herrnstein RJ: The perils of expounding meritocracy. *Science* July 6, 1973: 36–39; Herrnstein R. *I.Q. in the Meritocracy*. Boston: Little, Brown and Company, 1973; Herrnstein RJ, Murray C. *The Bell Curve: Intelligence and Class Structure in American Life*. New York: The Free Press, 1994; Jacoby R, Glauberman N, eds. *The Bell Curve Debate*; Fraser S, ed. *The Bell Curve Wars: Race, Intelligence, and the Future of America*. New York: Basic Books, 1995; DeParle J. Daring research or "social science pornography"?; Tucker WH. *The Science and Politics of Racial Research*.

144. Chase A. *The Legacy of Malthus*, 16.

145. Roberts D. *Killing the Black Body*, 89.

146. Roberts D. *Killing the Black Body*, 89.

147. Roberts D. *Killing the Black Body*, 89–90.

148. Chase A. *The Legacy of Malthus*, 16.

149. Roberts D. *Killing the Black Body*, 89.

150. Weisbord RG. *Genocide? Birth Control and the Black American*. Westport, CT: Greenwood Press, 1975, 139.

151. Friedman LM. *Crime and Punishment in American History*, 338–339.

152. Roberts D. *Killing the Black Body*, 94.

153. Weisbord RG. *Genocide?*, 141–142.

154. Weisbord RG. *Genocide?*, 143.

155. Weisbord RG. *Genocide?*, 145.

156. Weisbord RG. *Genocide?*, 145–146.

157. Weisbord RG. *Genocide?*, 137.

158. Weisbord RG. *Genocide?*, 138.

159. Weisbord RG. *Genocide?*, 140.

160. Chase A. *The Legacy of Malthus*; Allen GE. Eugenics comes to America. In: Jacoby R, Glauberman N, eds. *The Bell Curve Debate*, 441–475; Roberts D. *Killing the Black Body*; Weisbord RG. *Genocide?*; Davis AY. *Women, Race and Class*. New York: Random House, 1981. Reprint ed. New York: Vintage Books, 1983; Laughlin HH. *The Legal Status of Eugenical Sterilization*. Chicago: Psychological Laboratory of the Municipal Court of Chicago, 1929; Laughlin HH. *The Legal and Administrative Aspects of Sterilization: Report of the Committee to Study and to Report on the Best Practical Means of Cutting Off the Defective Germ-Plasm in the American Population*. 2 Vols. Cold Spring Harbor, NY: Eugenics Records Office, 1914; Laughlin HH. *Eugenical Sterilization in the United States*. Chicago: Psychological Laboratory of the Municipal Court of Chicago, 1922; Robinson FC, Robinson SW, Williams LJ. Eugenic sterilization: Medico-legal and sociological aspects. *Journal of the National Medical Association* 1979; 71:593–598; Rodriguez-Trias H. The women's health movement: Women take power. In: Sidel VW, Sidel R, eds. *Reforming Medicine: Lessons of the Last Quarter Century*. New York: Pantheon Books, 1984, 107–126; Pernick MS. Eugenics and public health in American history; *Skinner v. Oklahoma*, 316 U.S. 535 (1942); Student Nonviolent Coordinating Committee. *Genocide in Mississippi* (pamphlet). Atlanta: Student Nonviolent Coordinating Committee, n.d.; Ferster Z. Eliminating the unfit—Is sterilization the answer? *Ohio State Law Journal* 1966; 27:591–633; *People v. Dominguez*, 64 California Rptr. 290 (1967); *In re: Cager et al.*, 251 Maryland 473 (1967); Friedman LM. *Crime and Punishment in American History*; Planned Parenthood et al. challenge Maryland compulsory birth control. *Journal of the National Medical Association* 1968; 60:524–526.

161. Chase A. *The Legacy of Malthus*, 16.

162. Roberts D. *Killing the Black Body*, 93.

163. Roberts D. *Killing the Black Body*, 90.

164. Chase A. *The Legacy of Malthus*, 16.

165. Chase A. *The Legacy of Malthus*, 17.

166. Roberts D. *Killing the Black Body*, 90.

167. Chase A. *The Legacy of Malthus*, 19.

168. Roberts D. *Killing the Black Body*, 91.

169. Weisbord RG. *Genocide?*, 153.

170. Roberts D. *Killing the Black Body*, 91; Weisbord RG. *Genocide?*, 153.

171. Roberts D. *Killing the Black Body*, 91.

172. Roberts D. *Killing the Black Body*, 91.

173. Weisbord RG. *Genocide?*, 153.

174. Roberts D. *Killing the Black Body*, 91.

175. Weisbord RG. *Genocide?*, 155.

176. Weisbord RG. *Genocide?*, 155.

177. Chase A. *The Legacy of Malthus*; Roberts D. *Killing the Black Body*; Weisbord RG. *Genocide?*; Robinson FC, Robinson SW, Williams LJ. Eugenic sterilization; Cobb CM. Students charge BCH's obstetrics unit with "excessive surgery." *Boston Globe* April 29, 1972: 1; Rodriguez-Trias H. The women's health movement; *Relf v. Weinberger*, Civil Action No. 73–1557, and *National Welfare Rights Organization v. Weinberger*, Civil Action No. 74–243, United States Court for the District of Columbia (1974); Eliot JW, Hall RE, Wilson RJ, Houser C. The obstetrician's view. In: Hall RE, ed. *Abortion in a Changing World*. New York: Columbia University Press, 1970, 93; Areen J, King PA, Goldberg S, Gostin L, Capron AM. *Law, Science and Medicine*. 2nd ed. Westbury, NY: The Foundation Press, 1996, 1297–1302.

178. Roberts D. *Killing the Black Body*, 92.

179. Chase A. *The Legacy of Malthus*, 21.

180. Roberts D. *Killing the Black Body*, 92; Corea G. *The Hidden Malpractice: How American Medicine Treats Women as Patients and Professionals*. New York: Morrow, 1973, 180–181.

181. Roberts D. *Killing the Black Body*, 92; Corea G. *The Hidden Malpractice*, 180–181.

182. Roberts D. *Killing the Black Body*; Chase A. *The Legacy of Malthus*; Corea G. *The Hidden Malpractice*; Weisbord RG. *Genocide?*; Smith JD, Nelson KR. *The Sterilization of Carrie Buck*. Far Hills, NJ: New Horizon Press, 1989; Silver MA. Birth control and the private physician. *Family Planning Perspectives* 1972;4:42–46; Reed J. Scientific racism. In: Wilson CR, Ferris W, eds. *Encyclopedia of Southern Culture*. Chapel Hill: University of North Carolina Press, 1989, 1358–1360.

183. Areen J, et al. *Law, Science and Medicine,* 1299 n. 3.

184. Roberts D. *Killing the Black Body*, 92.

185. Roberts D. *Killing the Black Body*, 92.

186. Roberts D. *Killing the Black Body*, 324 n. 149.

187. Weisbord RG. *Genocide?*, 165; Davis AY. *Women, Race and Class*, 217.

188. Roberts D. *Killing the Black Body*, 93.

189. Davis AY. *Women, Race and Class*, 215.

190. Roberts D. *Killing the Black Body*, 93.

191. Roberts D. *Killing the Black Body*, 93.

192. Weisbord RG. *Genocide?*, 167.

193. Weisbord RG. *Genocide?*, 167.

194. Chase A. *The Legacy of Malthus*, 56.

195. Areen J, et al. *Law, Science and Medicine*, 1299 n. 3.

196. Roberts D. *Killing the Black Body*, 94.

197. Roberts D. *Killing the Black Body*, 94.

198. Roberts D. *Killing the Black Body*, 94–95.

199. Roberts D. *Killing the Black Body*, 95.

200. Roberts D. *Killing the Black Body*, 95.

201. Roberts D. *Killing the Black Body*; Davis AY. *Women, Race and Class*, 202–221; Robinson FC, Robinson SW, Williams LJ. Eugenic sterilization; Areen J, et al. *Law, Science and Medicine*, 1297–1302; Hicks N. Sterilization of Black mother of 3 stirs Aiken, S. C. *New York Times* August 1, 1973: 27; *Walker v. Pierce*, 560 F. 2d 609 (4th Cir. 1977); Sterilization charges grow. *Washington Post* July 24, 1973: A12; Weisbord RG. *Genocide?*; Davis AY. *Women, Race and Class*.

202. Davis AY. *Women, Race and Class*, 221.

203. Davis AY. *Women, Race and Class*, 221.

204. Gordon L. *Woman's Body, Woman's Right: Birth Control in America*. New York: Penguin Books, 1976, 157.

205. Rodriguez-Trias H. The women's health movement, 109.

206. Roberts D. *Killing the Black Body*, 96.

207. Roberts D. *Killing the Black Body*, 96.

208. Roberts D. *Killing the Black Body*; Davis AY. *Women, Race and Class*, 202–221; Areen J, et al. *Law, Science and Medicine*, 1297–1302; Weisbord RG. *Genocide?*; Rodriguez-Trias H. The women's health movement; Gordon L. *Woman's Body, Woman's Right*.

209. Hornblum AM. *Acres of Skin*, xvi.

210. Welsome E. *The Plutonium Files: America's Secret Medical Experiments in the Cold War*. New York: The Dial Press, 1999, 434.

211. Welsome E. *The Plutonium Files*, 425, 441.

212. Starr P. *The Social Transformation of American Medicine*. New York: Basic Books, 1982, 3–29; Annas GJ, Grodin MA, eds. *The Nazi Doctors and the Nuremberg Code*.

213. Hornblum AM. *Acres of Skin*, xviii.

214. Hornblum AM. *Acres of Skin*, xvii.

215. Bernard C. Vivisection. In: Reiser RJ, Dyck AJ, Curran WJ, eds. *Ethics in Medicine: Historical Perspectives and Contemporary Concerns*. Cambridge, MA: MIT Press, 1977, 257–259, quote 257.

216. Hornblum AM. *Acres of Skin*; Veatch RM. *Case Studies in Medical Ethics*. Cambridge, MA: Harvard University Press, 1977; Katz J. *Experimentation with Human Beings: The Authority of the Investigator, Subject, Professions, and State in the Human Experimentation Process*. New York: Russell Sage Foundation, 1972; Washington HA. Of men and mice: Human guinea pigs: Unethical testing targets Blacks and the poor. *Emerge* October 1994; (1)(6)6:24.

217. The National Commission for the Protection of Human Subjects of Biomedical and Behavioral Research. Research on the fetus: Report and recommendations. In: Reiser RJ, Dyck AJ, Curran WJ, eds. *Ethics in Medicine*, 450–485, quote 452.

218. Angell M. Editorial responsibility: Protecting human rights by restricting publication of unethical research. In: Annas GJ, Grodin MA, eds. *The Nazi Doctors and the Nuremberg Code*, 276–285, quote 277.

219. Hornblum AM. *Acres of Skin*; Welsome E. *The Plutonium Files*; Beecher HK. Ethics and clinical research. *New England Journal of Medicine* 1966; 274:1354–1360; Katz J. *Experimentation with Human Beings*; Starr P. *The Social Transformation of American Medicine*, 3–29; Lederer SE. *Subjected to Science: Human Experimentation in America before the Second World War*. Baltimore: Johns Hopkins University Press, 1995; Reiser RJ, Dyck AJ, Curran WJ, eds. *Ethics in Medicine*; Veatch RM. *Case Studies in Medical Ethics*; Washington HA. Of men and mice; Annas GJ, Grodin MA, eds. *The Nazi Doctors and the Nuremberg Code*.

220. Hornblum AM. *Acres of Skin*, 76; Lederer SE. *Subjected to Science*, 75–76.

221. Hornblum AM. *Acres of Skin*, 79.

222. Hornblum AM. *Acres of Skin*, 77.

223. Friedman LM. *Crime and Punishment in American History*, 337–338.

224. Hornblum AM. *Acres of Skin*; Jones JH. *Bad Blood*; Lederer SE. *Subjected to Science*; Washington HA. Of men and mice; Friedman LM. *Crime and Punishment in American History*; Foote SB. *Managing the Medical Arms Race: Innovation and Public Policy in the Medical Device Industry*. Berkeley: University of California Press, 1992; Ginzberg E, Dutka AB. *The Financing of Biomedical Research*. Baltimore: Johns Hopkins University Press, 1989; Berger EJ, Jr. *Science at the White House: A Political Liability*. Baltimore: Johns Hopkins University Press, 1980; Marsa L. *Pre-*

*scription for Profits: How the Pharmaceutical Industry Bankrolled the Unholy Marriage between Science and Business.* New York: Scribner, 1997.

225. Hornblum AM. *Acres of Skin*, 85.

226. Hornblum AM. *Acres of Skin*, 85.

227. Rothman DJ. *Strangers at the Bedside.* New York: Basic Books, 1991, 51.

228. Ethics governing the services of prisoners as subjects in medical experiments: Report of a committee appointed by Governor Dwight H. Green of Illinois. *Journal of the American Medical Association* 1948; 136:457.

229. Hornblum AM. *Acres of Skin*, 69.

230. Hornblum AM. *Acres of Skin*, 92.

231. Papa CM, Kligman AM. Stimulation of hair growth by topical application of androgens. *Journal of the American Medical Association* 1965; 191:521; Baldness breakthrough [Editorial]. *Journal of the American Medical Association* 1965; 191.

232. Hornblum AM. *Acres of Skin*; Welsome E. *The Plutonium Files*; Burger Jr. EJ. *Science at the White House*, 45–86; Jones JH. *Bad Blood*; Katz J. *Experimentation with Human Beings*; Washington HA. Of men and mice; Veatch RM. *Case Studies in Medical Ethics*; Annas GJ. The Nuremberg Code in U.S. courts; Beecher HK. Ethics and clinical research.

233. Hornblum AM. *Acres of Skin*, 13, 90, 95, 101, 102, 124, 131; Advisory committee on human radiation experiments, final report. In: Areen J, et al. *Law, Science and Medicine*, 1086–1091, quote 1096; Advisory committee on human radiation experiments, final report, 1029, 1036,1040; Washington HA. Of men and mice, 26, 34; Brown RK, Warwick KM, Albert J, Kabian E. A clinical evaluation of the effects of deodorants and anti-perspirants. *Journal of the National Medical Association* 1966; 58:110–113.

234. Hornblum AM. *Acres of Skin*, 39, 90, 91, 93, 97, 101, 105, 153–155.

235. Hornblum AM. *Acres of Skin*, xix, 36, 51, 94, 95, 102, 124; Harmer RM. *American Medical Avarice*, 89; Advisory committee on human radiation experiments, final report, 1029, 1030, 1031–1032, 1036; *Mink v. University of Chicago*. In: Areen J, King PA, Goldberg S, Gostin L, Capron AM. *Law, Science and Medicine*, 1081–1086, quote 1082; Advisory committee on human radiation experiments, final report; *In re Cincinnati radiation litigation*. In: Areen J, et al. *Law, Science and Medicine*, 546–552, quote 547; Washington HA. Of men and mice, 26, 27, 29, 34, 35.

236. Beecher HK. Ethics and clinical research, 1354.

237. Beecher HK. Ethics and clinical research, 1354.

238. Hornblum AM. *Acres of Skin*; *Mink v. University of Chicago*, 1082; Jones JH. *Bad Blood*; Washington HA. Of men and mice; Harmer RM. *American Medical Avarice*; Rothman DJ. *Strangers at the Bedside*; Ethics governing the services of prisoners as subjects in medical experiments; Veatch RM. *Case Studies in Medical Ethics*; Foote SB. *Managing the Medical Arms Race*; Ginzberg E, Dutka AB. *The Financing of Biomedical Research*; Burger Jr. EJ. *Science at the White House*; Ethics and clinical research; Beecher HK. *Experimentation in Man*. Springfield, IL: Charles C. Thomas, 1962; Katz J. *Experimentation with Human Beings*; Mitford J. *Kind and Unusual Punishment*. New York: Knopf, 1973; Annas GJ, Grodin MA, eds. *The Nazi Doctors and the Nuremberg Code*; Caplan A, ed. *When Medicine Went Mad*. Totowa, NJ: Humana Press, 1992; Welsome E. *The Plutonium Files*; Marsa L. *Prescription for Profits*; Tucker WH. *The Science and Politics of Racial Research*; Gray BH. *Human Subjects in Medical Experimentation*. New York: Wiley, 1975; Robinson LS. Dialogue.

239. Jones JH. Tuskegee syphilis experiment, 2687.

240. National Commission for the Protection of Human Subjects of Biomedical and Behavioral Research. *The Belmont Report: Ethical Principles and Guidelines for the Protection of Human Subjects of Research.* Washington, DC: Department of Health Education and Welfare, 1979.

241. Thomas SB, Quinn SC. Public health then and now: The Tuskegee syphilis study, 1932 to 1972: Implications for HIV education and AIDS risk education programs in the Black community. *American Journal of Public Health* 1991; 81:1498–1504; Jones JH. *Bad Blood*. 220–241; Gamble VN. Under the shadow of Tuskegee.

242. Chase A. *The Legacy of Malthus*, 22.

243. Angell M. Editorial responsibility, 278–279.

244. Washington HA. Of men and mice, 35.

245. Harmer RM. *American Medical Avarice*, 80.

246. Washington HA. Of men and mice, 27.

247. Brooton G. FDA ban on drug tests by U. of P. specialist imperils research program at Holmesburg Prison. *Philadelphia Sunday Bulletin* July 31, 1966: 27; Drug regulation, investigating the investigator. *Time* August 5, 1966: 65.

248. Hornblum AM. *Acres of Skin*, 54.

249. Hornblum AM. *Acres of Skin*, xix–xx.

250. Hornblum AM. *Acres of Skin*, 35.

251. Hornblum AM. *Acres of Skin*, 34–35.

252. Harmer RM. *American Medical Avarice*, 90.

253. Rugaber W. Prison drug and plasma projects leave fatal trail. *New York Times* July 29, 1969: 1.

254. Hornblum AM. *Acres of Skin*, 96.

255. Hornblum AM. *Acres of Skin*, 97.

256. Hornblum AM. *Acres of Skin*, 98–99.

257. Jones JH. *Bad Blood*; Jones JH. Tuskegee syphilis experiment; Reilly PR. *The Surgical Solution: A History of Involuntary Sterilization in the United States*. Baltimore: Johns Hopkins University Press, 1991, 148–165; Thomas SB, Quinn SC. Public health then and now; Lederer SE. *Subjected to Science*; Katz J. *Experimentation with Human Beings*; Areen J, et al. *Law, Science and Medicine*; Coleman AH. Human experimentation; Barber B. The ethics of experimentation with human subjects. In: Reiser RJ, Dyck AJ, Curran WJ, eds. *Ethics in Medicine*, 322–328; Chase A. *The Legacy of Malthus*; Hornblum AM. *Acres of Skin*; Harmer RM. *American Medical Avarice*; Washington HA. Of men and mice; Brooton G. FDA ban on drug tests by U. of P. specialist imperils research program at Holmesburg Prison; Drug regulation, investigating the investigator; Rugaber W. Prison drug and plasma projects leave fatal trail; *Relf v. Weinberger*, 372F. Supp. 1196. 1199 (D.D.C. 1974), on remand sub nom. *Relf v. Matthews*, 403 F. Supp. 1235 (D.D.C. 1975), vacated sub nom. *Relf v. Weinberger*, 565F.2d 722 (D.D.Cir. 1977); Roberts D. *Killing the Black Body*.

258. Curran WJ. Current legal issues in clinical investigation with particular attention to the balance between the rights of the individual and the needs of society. In: Reiser RJ, Dyck AJ, Curran WJ, eds. *Ethics in Medicine*, 296–301, quote 299.

259. Glantz LH. The influence of the Nuremberg Code on U.S. statutes and regulations. In: Annas GJ, Grodin MA, eds. *The Nazi Doctors and the Nuremberg Code*, 183–222, quote 186.

260. Glantz LH. The influence of the Nuremberg Code on U.S. statutes and regulations, 187.

261. Hornblum AM. *Acres of Skin*, 194.

262. Glantz LH. The influence of the Nuremberg Code on U.S. statutes and regulation, 187.

263. Glantz LH. The influence of the Nuremberg Code on U.S. statutes and regulation, 189.

264. Glantz LH. The influence of the Nuremberg Code on U.S. statutes and regulations, 189.

265. Glantz LH. The influence of the Nuremberg Code on U.S. statutes and regulations; Curran W. Governmental regulation of the use of human subjects in medical research: The approach of two federal agencies. *Daedalus: Ethical Aspect of Experimentation with Human Subjects* 1969; 98:542; Curran WJ. Current legal issues in clinical investigation with particular attention to the balance between the rights of the individual and the needs of society; Coleman AH. Human experimentation; National Commission for the Protection of Human Subjects of Biomedical and Behavioral Research. *The Belmont Report*; *Roe v. Wade*, 410 U.S. 113 (1973).

266. Weisbord RG. *Genocide?*; Roberts D. *Killing the Black Body*.

267. Chase A. *The Legacy of Malthus*; Lemann N. *The Big Test*; Lemann N. The structure of success in America; Lemann N. The great sorting.

268. Chase A. *The Legacy of Malthus*, 22.

269. Roberts D. *Killing the Black Body*, 102.

270. MacKenzie DA. *Statistics in Britain, 1865–1930: The Social Construction of Scientific Knowledge*. Edinburgh: Edinburgh University Press, 1981, 18.

271. Roberts D. *Killing the Black Body*, 103.

272. Roberts D. *Killing the Black Body*, 103.

273. Chase A. *The Legacy of Malthus*; Hornblum AM. *Acres of Skin*; Lederer SE. *Subjected to Science*; Roberts D. *Killing the Black Body*; Weisbord RG. *Genocide?*; Tucker WH. *The Science and Politics of Racial Research*; Welsome E. *The Plutonium Files*; Reilly PR. *The Surgical Solution*; Lemann N. *The Big Test*; Allen GE. *Eugenics comes to America*; Kamin LJ. The pioneers of IQ testing; Bond HM. What the army "intelligence" tests measured (1924). In: Jacoby R, Glauberman N, eds. *The Bell Curve Debate*, 583–598; Lemann N. The structure of success in America; Lemann N. The great sorting; Guthrie RV. *Even the Rat Was White*. 2nd ed.; Walker HI. Some reflection on the death of Dr. Martin Luther King—a commentary on White racism. *Journal of the National Medical Association* 1968; 60:396–400; Pinderhughes CA. Pathogenic social structure: A prime target for preventive psychiatric intervention. *Journal of the National Medical Association* 1966; 58:424–429; Proctor RN. *Racial Hygiene*; Proctor RN. Nazi doctors, racial medicine, and human experimentation. In: Annas GJ, Grodin MA, eds. *The Nazi Doctors and the Nuremberg Code*, 17–31; MacKenzie DA. *Statistics in Britain, 1865–1930*.

## Chapter Seven

1. Brinkley A. *The Unfinished Nation: A Concise History of the American People*. New York: Knopf, 1993, 880, 881.

2. Reagan R. *A Time for Choosing: The Speeches of Ronald Reagan, 1961–1982*. Chicago: Regnery Gateway, 1983, 169.

3. O'Reilly K. *Nixon's Piano: Presidents and Racial Politics from Washington to Clinton*. New York: The Free Press, 1995, 359, 361.

4. O'Reilly K. *Nixon's Piano*, 358.

5. Starr P. The new critics of medical care: The politics of therapeutic nihilism. In: Havighurst CC. *Health Care Law and Policy: Readings, Notes, and Questions*. Westbury, NY: The Foundation Press, 1988, 7–16.

6. Davis K. Access to health care: A matter of fairness. In: *Health Care: How to Improve It and Pay for It*. Washington, DC: Center for National Policy, 1985, 45–57, quote 51.

7. Brinkley A. *The Unfinished Nation*, 778–912; Sitkoff H. History of the United States. In: *The New Grolier Multimedia Encyclopedia*. Release 6, MPC Version. Novato, CA: Grolier Electronic Publishing, The Software Toolworks, 1993; O'Reilly K. *Nixon's Piano*; Delaney P. Voting: The new Black power. *New York Times Magazine* November 27, 1983: 35; Lemann N. Taking affirmative action apart. *New York Times Magazine* June 11, 1995: Section 6, 36; Feagin JR. *Racist America: Roots, Current Realities, and Future Reperations*. New York: Routledge, 2000; *Wall Street Journal*, October 22, 1985; Carter III H. *The Reagan Years*. New York: Braziller, 1988; Norman DL. The strange career of the Civil Rights Division's commitment to *Brown*. *Yale Law Journal* May 1984; 93:989; Berry MF. Taming the Civil Rights Commission. *The Nation* February 2, 1985: 106–108; Frye JC, et al. The rise and fall of the United States Commission on Civil Rights. *Harvard Civil Rights–Civil Liberties Law Review* Spring 1987; 22:478–479, Iglehart JK. The administration's assault on domestic spending and the threat to health care programs. *New England Journal of Medicine* 1985; 312:525–528; Iglehart JK. Medical care for the poor—a growing problem. *New England Journal of Medicine* 1985; 313:59–63; Marable M. *Race, Reform, and Rebellion: The Second Reconstruction in Black America, 1945–1990*. Rev. 2nd ed. Jackson: University Press of Mississippi, 1991; Navarro V. *Dangerous to Your Health: Capitalism in Health Care*. New York: Monthly Review Press, 1993; Starr P. The new critics of medical care; Wildavsky A. Doing better and feeling worse: The political pathology of health policy. In: Knowles JH, ed. *Doing Better and Feeling Worse: Health in the United States*. New York: W. W. Norton and the American Academy of Arts and Sciences, 1977, 105–123; Davis K. Access to health care; Stoline A, Weiner JP. *The New Medical Marketplace: A Physician's Guide to the Health Care Revolution*. Baltimore: Johns Hopkins University Press, 1988.

8. Navarro V. *Dangerous to Your Health*, 54.

9. Brinkley A. *The Unfinished Nation*, 882.

10. Brinkley A. *The Unfinished Nation*, 883.

11. Davidson RH, Oleszek WJ. *Congress and Its Members*. 3rd ed. Washington, DC: CQ Press, 1990, 382.

12. Sitkoff H. History of the United States, 60.

13. Wolff EN. *Top Heavy: A Study of the Increasing Inequality of Wealth in America.* New York: The Twentieth Century Fund Press, 1995, 1.

14. Wolff EN. *Top Heavy*, 2.

15. O'Reilly K. *Nixon's Piano*, 364.

16. Wolff EN. *Top Heavy*, 13.

17. Brinkley A. *The Unfinished Nation*, 884.

18. Hacker A. *Two Nations: Black and White, Separate, Hostile, Unequal.* New York: Ballantine Books, 1992. Expanded and updated ed., 1995; Malone TE, Johnson KW. *Report of the Secretary's Task Force on Black and Minority Health.* Washington, DC: U.S. Department of Health and Human Services, 1986; Sitkoff H. History of the United States, 52–53.

19. Sitkoff H. History of the United States, 63.

20. Brinkley A. *The Unfinished Nation*, 778–912; Sitkoff H. History of the United States; Davidson RH, Oleszek WJ. *Congress and Its Members*, 380–382; Wolff EN. *Top Heavy*; Iglehart JK. The administration's assault on domestic spending and the threat to health care programs; Hart N. The social and economic environment and human health. In Detels R, Holland WW, McEwen J, Omenn GS, eds. *Oxford Textbook of Public Health.* Vol. 1, *The Scope of Public Health.* 3rd ed. New York: Oxford University Press, 1997, 95–123, quote 109; Garrett L. *Betrayal of Trust: The Collapse of Global Public Health.* New York: Hyperion, 2000, 390–428; Davis K. Access to health care; Hacker A. *Two Nations*; O'Reilly K. *Nixon's Piano*; Malone TE, Johnson KW. *Report of the Secretary's Task Force on Black and Minority Health*; Navarro V. *Dangerous to Your Health*; Stoline A, Weiner JP. *The New Medical Marketplace*; Marable M. *Race, Reform, and Rebellion.*

21. Brinkley A. *The Unfinished Nation*, 887.

22. Brinkley A. *The Unfinished Nation*, 889.

23. Brinkley A. *The Unfinished Nation*, 890.

24. Brinkley A. *The Unfinished Nation*; Sitkoff H. History of the United States; O'Reilly K. *Nixon's Piano*; Feagin JR. *Racist America*; Marable M. *Race, Reform, and Rebellion.*

25. Brinkley A. *The Unfinished Nation*, 896.

26. Brinkley A. *The Unfinished Nation*; Sitkoff H. History of the United States; Hacker A. *Two Nations*; Wolff EN. *Top Heavy*; Steinberg S. *The Ethnic Myth: Race, Ethnicity, and Class in America.* n.p.: Antheneum Publishers, 1981. Updated and expanded ed. Boston: Beacon Press, 1989; Navarro V. *Dangerous to Your Health*; Guinier L. *The Tyranny of the Majority: Fundamental Fairness in Representative Democracy.* New York: The Free Press, 1994; Lind M. *Up From Conservatism: Why the Right Is Wrong for America.* New York: The Free Press, 1996.

27. Navarro V. *Dangerous to Your Health*, 12.

28. Brinkley A. *The Unfinished Nation*; Sitkoff H. History of the United States; Navarro V. *Dangerous to Your Health*; Skocpol T. *Boomerang: Health Care Reform and the Turn against Government.* New York: W. W. Norton, 1997; Johnson H, Broder DS. *The System: The American Way of Politics at the Breaking Point.* Boston: Little, Brown, 1996.

29. Malone TE, Johnson KW. *Report of the Secretary's Task Force on Black and Minority Health*; Byrd WM. An American health dilemma. *Journal of the National Medical Association* 1986; 78:1025–1026; Kochanek KD, Jeffrey DM, Rosenberg HM. Why did Black life expectancy decline from 1984 through 1989 in the United States? *American Journal of Public Health* 1994; 84:938–944; Institute of Medicine. *Access to Health Care in America.* Washington, DC: National Academy Press, 1993; Moy E, Bartman BA. Physician race and care of minority and medically indigent patients. *Journal of the American Medical Association* 1995; 273:1515–1520.

30. Public Health Service. *Healthy People: Surgeon General's Report on Health Promotion and Disease Prevention.* Washington, DC: U.S. Department of Health and Human Services, 1979; Public Health Service. *Promoting Health/Preventing Disease: Objectives for the Nation.* Washington, DC: U.S. Department of Health and Human Services, 1980; Public Health Service. *The 1990 Health Objectives for the Nation: A Midcourse Review.* Washington, DC: U.S. Department of Health and Human Services, 1986.

31. Fee E. History and development of public health. In: Sutchfield FD, Keck CW. *Principles of Public Health Practice.* Albany, NY: Delmar Publishers, 1997, 10–30, quote 25.

32. Hart N. The social and economic environment and human health, 109.

33. Fee E. History and development of public health, 24.

34. Lee PR, Benjamin AE, Weber MA. Policies and strategies for health in the United States. In: Detels R et al., eds. *Oxford Textbook of Public Health.* Vol. 1, 297–321, quote 300; Institute of Medicine. *The Future of Public Health.* Washington, DC: National Academy Press, 1988.

35. Sutchfield FD, Keck CW. Concepts and definitions of public health practice. In: Sutchfield FD, Keck CW. *Principles of Public Health Practice,* 3–9, quote 4.

36. Sutchfield FD, Keck CW. Concepts and definitions of public health practice, 7.

37. Krieger N, Birn A-E. A vision of social justice as the foundation of public health: Commemorating 150 years of the spirit of 1848. *American Journal of Public Health* 1998; 88:1603–1606, quote 1605.

38. Lee PR, Benjamin AE, Weber MA. Policies and strategies for health in the United States, 301.

39. Ginzberg E, ed. *Regionalization and Health Policy.* Washington, DC: U.S. Government Printing Office, 1977.

40. Kovner AR. *Jonas's Health Care Delivery in the United States.* 5th ed. New York: Springer, 1995; Kovner AR, Jonas S, eds. *Jonas and Kovner's Health Care Delivery in the United States.* 6th ed. New York: Springer, 1999; Sutchfield FD, Keck CW. *Principles of Public Health Practice;* Lee PR, Benjamin AE, Weber MA. Policies and strategies for health in the United States; Garrett L. *Betrayal of Trust;* Krieger N, Birn A-E. A vision of social justice as the foundation of public health; Roberts MJ, Clyde AT. *Your Money or Your Life: The Health Care Crisis Explained.* New York: Main Street Books, 1993; Institute of Medicine. *The Future of Public Health;* Navarro V. *Dangerous to Your Health;* Malone TE, Johnson KW. *Report of the Secretary's Task Force on Black and Minority Health;* Kochanek KD, Jeffrey DM, Rosenberg HM. Why did Black life expectancy decline from 1984 through 1989 in the United States?; Institute of Medicine. *Access to Health Care in America;* Moy E, Bartman BA. Physician race and care of minority and medically indigent patients. *Journal of the American Medical Association* 1995; 273:1515–1520; Starr P. *The Social Transformation of American Medicine.* New York: Basic Books, 1982; Lindorff D. *Marketplace Medicine: The Rise and Fall of the For-Profit Hospital Chains.* New York: Bantam, 1992; Anders G. *Health against Wealth: HMOs and the Breakdown of Medical Trust.* Boston: Houghton Mifflin, 1996; Stevens RA. *In Sickness and in Wealth: American Hospitals in the Twentieth Century.* New York: Basic Books, 1989. 2nd ed. Baltimore: Johns Hopkins University Press, 1999; Gray BH. *The Profit Motive and Patient Care: The Changing Accountability of Doctors and Hospitals.* Cambridge, MA: Harvard University Press, 1991; Whol S. *The Medical Industrial Complex.* New York: Harmony Books, 1984; Ginzberg E, ed. *Regionalization and Health Policy;* Lee PR, Benjamin AE. Governmental and legislative control and direction of health services in the United States. In: Holland WW, Detels R, Knox G, eds. *Oxford Textbook of Public Health.* Vol. 1. *Influences of Public Health.* 2nd ed. Oxford: Oxford University Press, 1991, 217–230.

41. Starr P. *The Social Transformation of American Medicine,* 428.

42. Starr P. *The Social Transformation of American Medicine,* 428–429.

43. Cobb WM. The Black American in medicine. *Journal of the National Medical Association* 1981; 73 (Suppl 1):1183–1244; Byrd WM, Clayton I.A. An American health dilemma: A history of blacks in the health system. *Journal of the National Medical Association* 1992; 84:189–200; Morais HM. *The History of the Negro in Medicine.* New York: Publishers Company, 1967; Byrd WM, Clayton LA. *An American Health Dilemma.* Vol. 1, *A Medical History of African Americans and the Problem of Race.* New York: Routledge, 2000, 199–120; Seiden DJ. Health care ethics. In: Kovner AR. *Jonas's Health Care Delivery in the United States,* 486–531, esp. 502–503.

44. Starr P. *The Social Transformation of American Medicine,* 429; Relman AS. The new medical-industrial complex. *New England Journal of Medicine* 1980; 303:963–970.

45. Navarro V. *Dangerous to Your Health,* 12.

46. Anders G. *Health against Wealth: HMOs and the Breakdown of Medical Trusts.* Boston: Houghton Mifflin, 1996, 60.

47. Anders G. *Health against Wealth,* 60–62.

48. Anders G. *Health against Wealth,* 68.

49. Whol S. *The Medical Industrial Complex.*

50. Starr P. *The Social Transformation of American Medicine,* 429.

51. Starr P. *The Social Transformation of American Medicine*, 429.

52. Gray BH. *The Profit Motive and Patient Care*, 15.

53. Anders G. *Health against Wealth*, 244.

54. Starr P. The new critics of medical care, 16.

55. Navarro V. *Dangerous to Your Health*, 11.

56. Navarro V. *Dangerous to Your Health*, 11.

57. Navarro V. *Dangerous to Your Health*, 11.

58. Woolhandler S, Himmelstein DU. *For Our Patients, Not for Profits: A Call to Action*. Chartbook and slideshow, 1998 ed. Cambridge, MA: Center for National Health Program Studies, 1998.

59. Navarro V. *Dangerous to Your Health*, 20–21.

60. Starr P. *The Social Transformation of American Medicine*; Ehrenreich B, Ehrenreich J. *The American Health Empire: Power, Profits, and Politics*. New York: Random House, 1970, 95–123; Meyers HB. The medical industrial complex. *Fortune* January 1970: 90; Navarro V. *Dangerous to Your Health*; Cobb WM. The Black American in medicine; Byrd WM, Clayton LA. An American health dilemma; Garrett L. *Betrayal of Trust*; Blendon RJ, Benson JM. Editorial: Whatever happened to the profession's concerns about the nation's uninsured? *American Journal of Public Health* 1998; 88:345–346; Blagrove S, Barrett S, Gaston MH. How much can the safety net hold? *Minority Health Today* 2000; 1:39–43; Morais HM. *The History of the Negro in Medicine*; Seiden DJ. Health care ethics; Ginzberg E. *The Medical Triangle: Physicians, Politicians, and the Public*. Cambridge, MA: Harvard University Press, 1990; Relman AS. The new medical-industrial complex; Gray BH. *The Profit Motive and Patient Care*; Whol S. *The Medical Industrial Complex*; Lindorff D. *Marketplace Medicine*; Anders G. *Health against Wealth*; Starr P. The new critics of medical care; Woolhandler S, Himmelstein DU. *For Our Patients, Not for Profits*; Lee PR, Benjamin AE, Weber MA. Policies and strategies for health in the United States.

61. Navarro V. *Dangerous to Your Health*, 12.

62. Navarro V. *Dangerous to Your Health*, 72.

63. Lee PR, Benjamin AE, Weber MA. Policies and strategies for health in the United States, 301.

64. Navarro V. *Dangerous to Your Health*, 71.

65. Navarro V. *Dangerous to Your Health*, 72.

66. Navarro V. *Dangerous to Your Health*, 72.

67. Anders G. *Health against Wealth*, 55–73, 58.

68. Navarro V. *Dangerous to Your Health*, 72–73.

69. Blendon RJ, Donelan K. The public and the future of U.S. health care system reform. In: Blendon RJ, Edwards JN, eds. *System in Crisis: The Case for Health Care Reform*. Vol. 1, *The Future of American Health Care*. New York: Faulkner and Gray, 1991, 173–194, quote 177; Edwards JN, Blendon RJ, Leitman R. The worried middle class. In: Blendon RJ, Hyams TS, eds. *Reforming the System: Containing Health Care Costs in an Era of Universal Coverage*. Vol. 2, *The Future of American Health Care*. New York: Faulkner and Gray, 1991, 61–81; Roberts MJ, Clyde AT. *Your Money or Your Life*, 4; Navarro V. *Dangerous to Your Health*, 50–51.

70. Edwards JN, Blendon RJ, Leitman R. The worried middle class, 61–62.

71. Edwards JN, Blendon RJ, Leitman R. The worried middle class, 62.

72. Cornelius LJ. Ethnic minorities and access to medical care: Where do they stand? *Journal of the Association for Academic Minority Physicians* 1993; 4:16–25, 24.

73. Edwards WS, Berlin M. *National Medical Expenditure Survey: Questionnaires and Data Collection Methods for the Household Survey and the Survey of American Indians and Alaska Natives*. Rockville, MD: U.S. Dept of Health and Human Services, Agency for Health Care Policy and Research, 1980 (DHHS publication PHS 89–3450).

74. Cornelius LJ. Ethnic minorities and access to medical care, 24.

75. Navarro V. *Dangerous to Your Health*, 31–32.

76. Kovner AR. *Jonas's Health Care Delivery in the United States*; Navarro V. *Dangerous to Your Health*; Lee PR, Benjamin AE, Weber MA. Policies and strategies for health in the United States; Roberts MJ, Clyde AT. *Your Money or Your Life*; Woolhandler S, Himmelstein DU. *For Our Patients, Not for Profits*; Blendon RJ, Edwards JN, eds. *System in Crisis: The Case for Health Care*

*Reform.* Vol. 1; Blendon RJ, Hyams TS, eds. *Reforming the System: Containing Health Care Costs in an Era of Universal Coverage.* Vol. 2; Garrett L. *Betrayal of Trust*; Kemper V, Novak V. What's blocking health care reform? *Common Cause Magazine* January/February 1992; (1)(18):8–13; Cornelius LJ. Ethnic minorities and access to medical care; Edwards WS, Berlin M. *National Medical Expenditure Survey*; Gray BH. *The Profit Motive and Patient Care*; Smith H. *The Power Game: How Washington Works.* New York: Random House, 1988. Paperback ed. New York: Ballantine Books, 1989, 215–269; Kingdon JW. *Agendas, Alternatives, and Public Policies.* New York: HarperCollins, 1984, 48–74; Wolpe BC. *Lobbying Congress: How the System Works.* Washington, DC: CQ Press, 1990, 67–83; Davidson RH, Oleszek WJ. *Congress and Its Members*, 281–304; Johnson H, Broder DS. *The System*; Skocpol T. *Boomerang*.

77. Behar R. Singing the Blue Cross blues: The shocking tale of mismanagement and mischief at New York's huge health insurer is far from unique. *Time*, July 12, 1993: 48; Pretzer M. Can this profligate Blue find a way out of the red? *Medical Economics* August 9, 1993: 41.

78. Kovner AR. *Jonas's Health Care Delivery in the United States*, 276.

79. Nobbe G. Feds may abandon the uninsured. *The Medical Herald* May 1998: 1, 50.

80. Pear R. H.M.O.'s using federal law to deflect malpractice lawsuits. *New York Times* November 17, 1996: 24.

81. Kovner AR. *Jonas's Health Care Delivery in the United States.* 5th ed., 277.

82. Kovner AR. *Jonas's Health Care Delivery in the United States.* 5th ed., 276.

83. Starr P. *The Logic of Health Care Reform.* Knoxville, TN: Whittle, 1992, 38–39.

84. Lee PR, Benjamin AE, Weber MA. Policies and strategies for health in the United States, 303.

85. Higgins W. Myths of competitive reform. *Health Care Management Review* 1991; 16:65–72; Navarro V. *Dangerous to Your Health*; Iglehart JK. Health policy report: The struggle to reform Medicare. *New England Journal of Medicine* 1996; 334:1071–1075, esp. 1071–1072.

86. Quinn JB. Is your HMO OK—or not? It's hard to tell, because employers look mostly at price, not the quality of care. *Newsweek* February 10, 1997: 52.

87. Passell P. In medicine, government rises again. *New York Times* December 7, 1997: Section 4, 1; Fineman H. HMOs under the knife: The capital races to crack down on managed care. *Newsweek* July 27, 1998: 21; Kilborn PT. Voters' anger at H.M.O.'s plays as hot political issue. *New York Times* May 17, 1998: 1; McCall T. Profits, not patients, threaten HMOs. *Boston Sunday Globe* August 2, 1998: C4; Kilborn PT. Complaints about H.M.O.'s rise as awareness grows. *New York Times* October 11, 1998: 22; Quinn JB. Is your HMO OK—or not?; Pear R. H.M.O.'s using federal law to deflect malpractice lawsuits; Lasalandra M. Study finds poor, elderly are losing out on HMOs. *Boston Herald* October 2, 1996: 19; Kolata G. AIDS patients slipping through safety net: Soaring costs of drugs strains the budgets of programs and patients. *New York Times* September 15, 1996: 24.

88. Seay E. To their defense: Lawyer Joseph Romano helps clients get health insurers to pay up: What people don't realize is that obtaining health insurance benefits is an adversarial process. *Wall Street Journal* October 23, 1997: R8; Cropper CM. In Texas, a laboratory test on the effects of suing H.M.O.'s. *New York Times* September 13, 1998: Section 3, 1; Fineman H. HMOs under the knife; Weinstein MM. Getting litigious with H.M.O.'s. *New York Times* July 19, 1998: Section 4, 5; States where managed care liability measures were introduced in 1997. *Ob-Gyn News* September 1, 1997: 49; Spragins EE. To sue or not to sue? A wrinkle in federal law makes it harder than ever to win a claim for medical malpractice. *Newsweek* December 9, 1996: 50; Thirty-six states now mandate coverage for extended hospital stays for mothers and newborns. *Medical Economics* September, 1997: 12; Wasserman E. States pushing to extend post-delivery hospital stays. *Fort Worth Star-Telegram* July 9, 1995: Section A, 7; Pear R. H.M.O.'s using federal law to deflect malpractice lawsuits; Nobbe G. Feds may abandon the uninsured. *The Medical Herald*, May, 1998: 1; Steinhauer J. Rebellion in white: Doctors pulling out of H.M.O. systems. *New York Times* January 10, 1999: 1.

89. Pear R. HMOs denying more claims for emergency care. *Fort Worth Star-Telegram* July 9, 1995: Section A, 7; Gottleib M, Eichenwald K. A hospital chain's brass knuckles, and the backlash. *New York Times* May 11, 1997: Section 3, 1; Tomsho R. Some health insurers leave patients to foot excessive copayments: Firms get sizeable discounts from providers but fail to reduce clients' bills.*Wall Street Journal* August 21, 1995: 1; Bumiller E. Life styles of the rich and ailing: In luxury hospital rooms, everything from high tea to fresh goat. *The New York Times* October 19, 1997: 37;

Anders G. HMOs pile up billions in cash, try to decide what to do with it. *Wall Street Journal* December 21, 1994: 1; Bradshear K. As 1 million leave ranks of insured., debate heats up. *New York Times* August 27, 1995: 1; Survey: 60 million experience lapses in health coverage. *Physician's Financial News* January 15, 1995: 2; Pear R. Government lags in steps to widen health coverage: Uninsured at 41 million. *New York Times* August 9, 1998:1; Pear R. More Americans were uninsured in 1998, U.S. says. *New York Times* October 4, 1999: 1; Toner R. Rx Redux: Fevered issue, second opinion. *New York Times* October 10, 1999: Section 4, 1; Kolata G. AIDS patients slipping through safety net; O'Neill G, et al. Public handouts enrich drug makers, scientists: Public research/private profit. *Boston Sunday Globe* April 5, 1998: 1; Meyerson AR. When healing collides with the drive for profits. *New York Times* July 27, 1997:14; O'Neil G, et al. Profit motives doom Worcester hospital: Sale heralds new corporate era for Mass. health care. *Boston Sunday Globe* November 17, 1996: 1; Gottleib M, Eichenwald K, Barbanel J. For the biggest hospital operator, a debate over ties that bind. *New York Times* April 6, 1997: 1; Carey B. Blue Cross will shrink network of pharmacies. *The Tennessean* December 16, 1997: 1; Nobbe G. Feds may abandon the uninsured; Preston J. Hospitals look on charity care as unaffordable option of past: Squeezed by managed care and reduced aid. *New York Times* April 14, 1996: 1; New HMO target: The poor. *Medical Herald* May 1998: 28.

90. Lawlor J. Not ready for Medicare, and uninsured. *New York Times* December 18, 1997: 11; Stein C. Free market straining health-care safety net. *Boston Sunday Globe* April 21, 1996: 1; Herring HB. Who can heal New York? *New York Times* August 20, 1995: 2F; Nobbe G. Feds may abandon the uninsured; Fialka JJ. Demands on New Orleans's "Big Charity" hospital are symptomatic of U.S. health-care problem. *Wall Street Journal* June 22, 1993: A16; Bradshear K. As 1 million leave ranks of insured., debate heats up; Survey: 60 million experience lapses in health coverage; Sack K. Public hospitals around country cut basic service: Some face elimination. *New York Times* August 20, 1995: 1; Public hospitals across nation cutting services under pressure. *Fort Worth Star-Telegram* August 20, 1995: Section A, 4; Preston J. Hospitals look on charity care as unaffordable option of past: Squeezed by managed care and reduced aid. *New York Times* April 14, 1996: 1; Pear R. Big health gap tied to income, is found in U.S. *New York Times* July 8, 1993: A1; Kolata G. AIDS patients slipping through safety net; Houston E. Black hospitals struggle for support. *Emerge* February 1998: 34; Freudenheim M. States shelving ambitious plans on health care: More people uninsured. *New York Times* July 2, 1995, 1; Public hospitals across nation cutting services under pressure; Bernstein N. New York adds hurdle for Medicaid seekers: Home inspections. *New York Times* September 20, 1998: 43.

91. Spragins EE. The numbers racket: An HMO's approval rating may not say much about its quality. *Newsweek* May 5, 1997: 77; Prager K. Neither costs nor care assured under "cost containment." *Medical Tribune* May 2, 1996: 15; Quinn JB. Is your HMO OK—or not?; Pear R. H.M.O.'s using federal law to deflect malpractice lawsuits; Lasalandra M. Study finds poor, elderly are losing out on HMOs, 199.

92. Quinn JB. Fighting for health care: "Patients' rights" can curb unethical plans, but your coverage might still be chopped. *Newsweek* March 30, 1998: 45; Spragins EE. When your HMO says no: How to fight for the treatment you need—and win. *Newsweek* July 28, 1997: 73; Larson E. The soul of an HMO: Managed care is certainly bringing down America's medical costs, but it is also raising the question of whether patients, especially those with severe illnesses, can still trust their doctors. *Time* January 22, 1996: 45; Doctors' HMO deals may shortchange ailing; Seay E. To their defense; Pear R. H.M.O.'s using federal law to deflect malpractice lawsuits; Reibstein L. Nursing-home verdicts: There's guilt all around. *Newsweek* July 27, 1998: 34; Anders G. *Health against Wealth*; Navarro V. *Dangerous to Your Health*; Lindorf D. *Marketplace Medicine*; Kovner AR. *Jonas's Health Care Delivery in the United States*. 5th ed.; Garrett L. *Betrayal of Trust*.

93. Pear R. Big health gap tied to income, is found in U.S.; Lasalandra M. Study finds poor, elderly are losing out on HMOs; Kolata G. AIDS patients slipping through safety net; Johannes L. State probes HMO's denial of some care. *Wall Street Journal* August 16, 1995: T1; Preston J. A hospital worries about "people who fall through the cracks." *New York Times* April 14, 1996: 12; Pear R. Government lags in steps to widen health coverage; Fialka JJ. Demands on New Orleans's "Big Charity" hospital are symptomatic of U.S. health-care problem; Bradshear K. As 1 million leave ranks of insured., debate heats up; 60 million experience lapses in health coverage. *Physician's Financial News* January 15, 1995: 2; Nobbe G. Feds may abandon the uninsured; Sack K. Public hospitals around country cut basic service; Public hospitals across nation cutting services under

pressure; Preston J. Hospitals look on charity care as unaffordable option of past; Houston E. Black hospitals struggle for support; Freudenheim M. States shelving ambitious plans on health care; Pedersen D, Larson E. Too poor to treat: States are balking at paying for pricey AIDS drugs. *Newsweek* July 28, 1997: 60; New HMO target.

94. Kilborn PT. Fitting managed care into emergency rooms. *New York Times* December 28, 1997: 12; Thompson M. Shining a light on abuse: Following a *Time* story, Congress reports that many nursing-home residents are beaten and starved. *Time* August 3, 1998: 42; Bates E. The shame of our nursing homes: Millions for investors, misery for the elderly. *The Nation* March 29, 1999: 11; Kilborn PT. The uninsured find fewer doctors in the house: Managed care has cut doctors' incomes and left them with less time for charity work. *New York Times* August 30, 1998: Section 4, 14; Study links heart attack survival with care by specialists. *Fort Worth Star-Telegram* November 15, 1995: Section A, 3; Pear R. Home-care denial in Medicare cases is ruled improper: Many benefits restored. *New York Times* February 15, 1998: 1; Pham A. Time to pull the plug on managed care? *Boston Sunday Globe* September 19, 1999; Garrett L. *Betrayal of Trust*, 426–430; Nobbe G. Feds may abandon the uninsured.

95. Kong D. Study: Minorities' health lags. *Boston Globe* April 23, 1992: 1; Lasalandra M. Study finds poor, elderly are losing out on HMOs; Kolata G. AIDS patients slipping through safety net; Fein EB. The elderly poor fear health care changes. *New York Times* November 5, 1995: 1; Rimer S. Blacks carry load of care for their elderly. *New York Times* March 15, 1998: 1; Pear R. Government lags in steps to widen health coverage; Bradshear K. As 1 million leave ranks of insured., debate heats up; 60 million experience lapses in health coverage; Racial gap widens in heart disease deaths. *Boston Globe* November 13, 1998: A17; Maccabe T. Elderly may join poor in HMO abuses. *The Medical Tribune* October, 1998: 1; Curry GE. Black America's health crisis: Statistics indicate that while general health of White Americans is improving, the health status of African-Americans is getting worse. *Emerge* July/August 1998; (9)(9):32; Pear R. Big health gap tied to income, is found in U.S.; Sack K. Hard cases at the hospital door. *New York Times* September 17, 1995: 5; Atkins E. Despite progress, the condition of Black health remains critical. *The Detroit News* February 8, 1993: 1A; Quinn JB. Is your HMO OK—or not?; Sontag D, Richardson L. Doctors withhold H.I.V. pill regimen from some. *New York Times* March 2, 1997: 1; Richardson L. White patients more likely to use AIDS drugs, study says: Sharp racial differences in the use of potent medicine. *New York Times* July 27, 1997: 24; New HMO target; Byrd WM, Clayton LA. *An American Health Dilemma*, 14–24.

96. Eichenwald K. He blew the whistle and health giants quaked. *New York Times* October 18, 1998: Section 3, 1; Wallace M. "Cooking the Books." Videotape segment. *60 Minutes*, CBS television network, WBZ, Channel 4, Boston, Massachusetts, December 27, 1998; Hirsh M, Klaidman D. Bad practices: The federal probe of Columbia/HCA is just part of a broad assault on health care fraud. *Newsweek* August 11, 1997: 42; Fein EB. U.S. auditing 5 hospitals in New York: Part of a wider search for Medicare fraud. *New York Times* April 5, 1998: 31; Eichenwald K. A health care giant's secret payments taint a Texas deal. *New York Times* March 29, 1997: 21; Pear R. H.M.O.'s using federal law to deflect malpractice lawsuits; Pear R. Health insurers skirting new law, officials report. *New York Times* August 22, 1999: 1; Pear R. States called lax on tests for lead in poor children: Most flouting 1989 law. *New York Times* August 22, 1999: 1; Finder A. Court says law forbids hospital tease: Ruling deals blow to Guiliani plan. *New York Times* March 31, 1999: A21; Nobbe G. Feds may abandon the uninsured; Pham A. Time to pull the plug on managed care?; Monney M. City eyes selling 3 hospitals. *Daily News* February 23, 1995: 2; Fein EB. Giuliani's plan to lease a hospital is in jeopardy: Coney Island privatization deal is blocked. *New York Times* June 1, 1997: 35; Pear R. Investigators say a Medicare option is rife with fraud. *New York Times* July 27, 1997: 1; Lewin T, Gottlieb M. In hospital sales, an overlooked side effect. *New York Times* April 27, 1997: 1; Bates E. The shame of our nursing homes.

97. Kovner AR. *Jonas's Health Care Delivery in the United States*. 5th ed.; Navarro V. *Dangerous to Your Health*; Roberts MJ, Clyde AT. *Your Money or Your Life*; Behar R. Singing the Blue Cross blues, 48; Pretzer M. Can this profligate Blue find a way out of the red?; Woolhandler S, Himmelstein DU. *For Our Patients, Not for Profits*; Pham A. Time to pull the plug on managed care? 61. Pear R. H.M.O.'s using federal law to deflect malpractice lawsuits; Starr P. *The Logic of Health Care Reform*; Blendon RJ, Edwards JN, eds. *System in Crisis: The Case for Health Care Reform*. Vol.1; Blendon RJ, Hyams TS, eds. *Reforming the System: Containing Health Care Costs in an Era of Uni-*

*versal Coverage*. Vol. 2; Lee PR, Benjamin AE, Weber MA. Policies and strategies for health in the United States. Garrett L. *Betrayal of Trust*.

98. Starr P. *The Logic of Health Care Reform*, 37.

99. Starr P. *The Logic of Health Care Reform*, 37.

100. Enthoven AC. Why managed care has failed to contain health costs. *Health Affairs* Fall 1993; 12:27–43, esp. 29, 28.

101. Ware Jr. JE., et al. Differences in 4-year health outcomes for elderly and poor, chronically ill patients treated in HMO and fee-for-service systems: Results from the Medical Outcomes Study. *Journal of the American Medical Association* 1996; 276:1039–1047; Kochanek KD, Jeffrey DM, Rosenberg HM. Why did Black life expectancy decline from 1984 through 1989 in the United States?; Institute of Medicine. *Access to Health Care in America*; Lindorff D. *Marketplace Medicine*; Woolhandler S, Himmelstein DU. *The National Health Program Chartbook*. Chartbook and slideshow, 1992 ed. Cambridge, MA: Center for National Health Program Studies, 1992; Woolhandler S, Himmelstein DU. *For Our Patients, Not for Profits*; Navarro V. *Dangerous to Your Health*.

102. Knox RA. HMOs' creator urges reform in quality of care. *Boston Sunday Globe* May 2, 1999: A1.

103. Iglehart JK. The American health system: Managed care. *New England Journal of Medicine* 1992; 327:742–747, quote 745.

104. Knox RA. HMOs' creator urges reform in quality of care.

105. Kilborn PT. Analysts expect health premiums to rise sharply. *New York Times* October 19, 1997: 1; Fisher I. H.M.O. premiums rising sharply, stoking debate on managed care. *New York Times* January 11, 1998: 1; Meyer M. Oh no, here we go again: Health-care costs are soaring—and companies are passing the increases along to their workers. *Newsweek* December 14, 1998: 46; Abelson R. For managed care, free-market shock. *New York Times* January 3, 1999: Section 4, 4; Fineman H. HMOs under the knife; Knox RA. HMOs' creator urges reform in quality of care.

106. Starr P. *The Logic of Health Care Reform*; Stoline A, Weiner JP. *The New Medical Marketplace*; Roberts MJ, Clyde AT. *Your Money or Your Life*; Enthoven AC. Why managed care has failed to contain health costs; Higgins W. Myths of competitive reform; Ware Jr. JE, et al. Differences in 4-year health outcomes for elderly and poor, chronically ill patients treated in HMO and fee-for-service systems; Kochanek KD, Jeffrey DM, Rosenberg HM. Why did Black life expectancy decline from 1984 through 1989 in the United States?; Institute of Medicine. *Access to Health Care in America*; Navarro V. *Dangerous to Your Health*; Enthoven AC. *Health Plan: The Only Practical Solution to Soaring Health Costs*. Reading, MA: Addison-Wesley, 1980; Iglehart JK. The American health system; Smith DB. *Health Care Divided: Race and Healing a Nation*. Ann Arbor: University of Michigan Press, 1999; Pham A. Time to pull the plug on managed care?; Skocpol T. *Boomerang*; Blagrove S, Barrett S, Gaston MH. How much can the safety net hold?; Andrulis DP, Carrier B. *Managed Care in the Inner City: The Uncertain Promise for Providers, Plans, and Communities*. San Francisco: Josey-Bass, 1999; Bonnyman GG. Muddled care, managed care. *Health Affairs* 1999; 18:264–265, review of Andrulis DP, Carrier B. *Managed Care in the Inner City*; Lille-Blanton L, Lyons B. Managed care and low-income populations: Recent state experiences. *Health Affairs* 1998; 17:238–247; Carresquillo O, Himmelstein DU. Woolhandler S, Box DH. Can Medicaid managed care provide continuity of care to new Medicaid enrollees? An analysis of tenure on Medicaid. *American Journal of Public Health* 1998; 88:464–466; Ware Jr. JE, et al. Differences in 4-year health outcomes for elderly and poor, chronically ill patients treated in HMO and fee-for-service systems; Blendon RJ, Benson JM. Editorial; Byrd WM, Clayton LA. *Designing a New Health Care System for the United States*. Boston: Harvard School of Public Health, 1992; Wise PH, Pursley DM. Infant mortality as a social mirror. *New England Journal of Medicine* 1992; 326:1558–1560; Garrett L. *Betrayal of Trust*; Woolhandler S, Himmelstein DU. *For Our Patients, Not for Profits*; Knox RA. HMOs' creator urges reform in quality of care.

107. Kovner AR. *Jonas's Health Care Delivery in the United States*, 128.

108. Starr P. *The Social Transformation of American Medicine*; Ginzberg E. The monetarization of medical care. *New England Journal of Medicine* 1984; 310:1162–1165.

109. Roberts MJ, Clyde AT. *Your Money or Your Life*, 60.

110. Iglehart J. U.S. health care system: A look to the 1990s. *Health Affairs* 1985; 3:120–127.

111. Farley DE. *Trends in Hospital Average Length of Stay, Casemix and Discharge Rates, 1980–1985* (Hospital Studies Program, Research Note 11). Washington, DC: U.S. Department of Health and Human Services, 1988.

112. Kovner AR. *Jonas's Health Care Delivery in the United States*. 5th ed., 164.

113. Byrd WM, Clayton LA. *Designing a New Health Care System for the United States*, 19–20; Jones SB, DuVal MK, Lesparre M. Competition or conscience? Mixed-mission dilemmas of the voluntary hospital. *Inquiry* Summer 1987; 24:110–118.

114. Blendon RJ, Edwards JN. Looking back at hospital forecasts. In: Blendon RJ, Edwards JN, eds. *System in Crisis*. Vol. 1, 7–30, quote 11.

115. Kovner AR. *Jonas's Health Care Delivery in the United States*. 5th ed., 168.

116. Kovner AR. *Health Care Delivery in the United States*. 4th ed. New York: Springer, 1990, 148.

117. Kovner AR. *Jonas's Health Care Delivery in the United States*. 5th ed., 168.

118. Kovner AR. *Health Care Delivery in the United States*. 4th ed., 148; Kovner AR. *Jonas's Health Care Delivery in the United States*. 5th ed., 164; Andrulis DP, Carrier B. *Managed Care in the Inner City*, 70–71.

119. Applebome P. Two Nashville hospitals debate a plan to merge. *New York Times* April 30, 1989: 24; Mitchell C. One empty, one full: Nashville hospitals remain miles apart. *Atlanta Journal and Constitution* August 2, 1989: A4; Snyder B. Meharry Ob closing cuts General residents by 40 percent. *Nashville Banner* June 20, 1991: B1; Roberts MJ, Clyde AT. *Your Money or Your Life*, 65–66; Ginzberg E. The destabilization of health care. *New England Journal of Medicine* 1986; 315:757–767; Byrd WM, Clayton LA. *Designing a New Health Care System for the United States*.

120. Friedman E. Public hospitals: Doing what everyone wants done but few others wish to do. *Journal of the American Medical Association* 1987; 257:1437–1444; Friedman E. Demise of Philadelphia General an instructive case; Other cities treat public hospital ills differently. *Journal of the American Medical Association* 1987; 257:1571–1575; Friedman E. Public hospitals often face unmet capital needs, underfunding, uncompensated patient-care costs. *Journal of the American Medical Association* 1987; 257:1698–1701; Friedman E. Problems plaguing public hospitals: Uninsured patient transfers, tight funds, mismanagement, and misperception. *Journal of the American Medical Association* 1987; 257:1850–1857.

121. Kovner AR. *Jonas's Health Care Delivery in the United States*. 5th ed.; Starr P. *The Social Transformation of American Medicine*; Andrulis DP, Carrier. *Managed Care in the Inner City*; Ginzberg E. The monetarization of medical care; Byrd WM, Clayton LA. *Designing a New Health Care System for the United States*; Byrd WM, et al. Minority Health Care Review Group: Executive Summary of report "Recommendations on National Health Care Reform from Providers of Health Care to African Americans and Other Underserved Populations," submitted to the Clinton Health Reform Task Force by the Congressional Black Caucus Foundation, Washington, DC, June, 1993; Blendon RJ, Edwards JN. Looking back at hospital forecasts; Blendon RJ, Hyams TS, eds. *Reforming the System: Containing Health Care Costs in an Era of Universal Coverage*. Vol. 2; Wilson FA, Neuhauser D. *Health Services in the United States*. 2nd ed. Cambridge, MA: Ballinger Publishing, 1982; Kovner AR. *Health Care Delivery in the United States*. 4th ed.; National Center for Health Statistics. *Health United States, 1995*. Hyattsville, MD: Public Health Service, 1996; Stevens RA. *In Sickness and in Wealth*; Roberts MJ, Clyde AT. *Your Money or Your Life*; Blumenthal D, Meyer GS. Academic health centers in a changing environment. *Health Affairs* (Millwood) 1996; 15:200–215; Rice MF. Inner-city hospital closures/relocations: Race, income status and legal issues. *Social Science and Medicine* 1987; 24:889–896; Jones PA. Three against the storm: Facing an awesome array of problems, black community hospitals advance toward an uncertain future. *The Crisis* October 1985; 92:35; Travella S. Black hospitals struggle to survive. *Modern Health Care* July 2, 1990: 20–26; Travella S. Black hospitals struggling to survive: Of more than 200 medical centers, only 8 are left. *Health: A Weekly Journal of Medicine, Science and Society, Washington Post*, September 11, 1990: 12; Friedman E. Public hospitals; Friedman E. Demise of Philadelphia General an instructive case; Friedman E. Public hospitals often face unmet capital needs, underfunding, uncompensated patient-care costs; Friedman E. Problems plaguing public hospitals.

122. Kovner AR. *Jonas's Health Care Delivery in the United States*. 5th ed., 198.

123. Toner R. Critics of G.O.P.'s budget see a nursing home crisis: How to care for the growing number of elderly. *New York Times* November 12, 1995:16.

124. Harrington C, et al. A national long-term care program for the United States: A caring vision. *Journal of the American Medical Association* 1991; 266:3023–3029, quote 3024.

125. Toner R. Critics of G.O.P.'s budget see a nursing home crisis.

126. Consumers Union. Nursing homes: A special investigative report. *Consumer Reports* August 1995; (8)(60):518; Consumers Union. Who pays for the nursing home? *Consumer Reports* September 1995; (9)(60):591; Consumers Union. Nursing homes: What are the alternatives? *Consumer Reports* October 1995; (10)(60):656; Reibstein L. Nursing-home verdicts: There's guilt all around; Bates E. The shame of our nursing homes.

127. Institute of Medicine. *Health Care in the Context of Civil Rights*. Washington, DC: National Academy Press, 1981; Keith VM. Long-term care and the Black elderly. In: Jones Jr W, Rice MF, eds. *Health Care Issues in Black America: Policies, Problems, and Prospects*. New York: Greenwood Press, 1987, 173–209, esp. 196–198; Smith DB. *Health Care Divided*; Kovner AR. *Jonas's Health Care Delivery in the United States*. 5th ed., 199; Kovner AR, Jonas S, eds. *Jonas and Kovner's Health Care Delivery in the United States*. 6th ed. New York: Springer, 1999, 216.

128. Kovner AR. *Jonas's Health Care Delivery in the United States*. 5th ed.; Toner R. Critics of G.O.P.'s budget see a nursing home crisis; Harrington C, et al. A national long-term care program for the United States, 3024; Consumers Union. Nursing homes: A special investigative report; Consumers Union. Who pays for the nursing home?; Consumers Union. Nursing homes: What are the alternatives?; Institute of Medicine. *Health Care in the Context of Civil Rights*; Keith VM. Long-term care and the Black elderly; Woolhandler S, Himmelstein DU. *For Our Patients, Not for Profits*; Smith DB. *Health Care Divided*.

129. Lee PR, Benjamin AE. Governmental and legislative control and direction of health services in the United States, 225.

130. Kovner AR, Jonas S, eds. *Jonas and Kovner's Health Care Delivery in the United States*. 6th ed., 312.

131. Lee PR, Benjamin AE. Governmental and legislative control and direction of health services in the United States, 225.

132. Lee PR, Benjamin AE. Governmental and legislative control and direction of health services in the United States, 225.

133. Starr P. *The Social Transformation of American Medicine*, 417–449; Lee PR, Benjamin AE. Governmental and legislative control and direction of health services in the United States; Lee PR, Benjamin AE, Weber MA. Policies and strategies for health in the United States; Kovner AR. *Jonas's Health Care Delivery in the United States*. 5th ed.; Starr P. *The Logic of Health Care Reform*; Kovner AR, Jonas S, eds. *Jonas and Kovner's Health Care Delivery in the United States*. 6th ed.; Garrett L. *Betrayal of Trust*; Stevens RA. *In Sickness and in Wealth*, 321–350.

134. Evans RG. Going for the gold: The redistributive agenda behind market-based health care reform. *Journal of Health Politics, Policy and Law* 1997; 22:21–22, quote 21.

135. Evans RG. Going for the gold, 21.

136. Evans RG. Going for the gold, 21.

137. Evans RG. Going for the gold, 21.

138. Iglehart JK. Health care report: The struggle to reform Medicare. *New England Journal of Medicine* 1996; 334:1071–1075, quote 1071–1072.

139. Lee PR, Benjamin AE, Weber MA. Policies and strategies for health in the United States; Navarro V. *Dangerous to Your Health*; Garrett L. *Betrayal of Trust*; Kovner AR, Jonas S, eds. *Jonas and Kovner's Health Care Delivery in the United States*. 6th ed., 206–242, 307–337, 401–438.

140. Lee PR, Benjamin AE, Weber MA. Policies and strategies for health in the United States, 299.

141. Lee PR, Benjamin AE, Weber MA. Policies and strategies for health in the United States, 299.

142. Lee PR, Benjamin AE, Weber MA. Policies and strategies for health in the United States, 299.

143. Aaron HJ. *Serious and Unstable Condition: Financing America's Health Care*. Washington, DC: The Brookings Institution, 1991, 37.

144. Woolhandler S, Himmelstein DU. The deteriorating administrative efficiency of the U.S. health care system. *New England Journal of Medicine* 1991; 324:1253–1258.

145. Lee PR, Benjamin AE, Weber MA. Policies and strategies for health in the United States, 304.

146. Keck CW, Sutchfield FD. The future of public health. In: Sutchfield FD, Keck CW. *Principles of Public Health Practice*, 361–372, quote 365–366; Garrett L. *Betrayal of Trust*; Lee PR, Benjamin AE, Weber MA. Policies and strategies for health in the United States, 300; Institute of Medicine, Committee for the Study of the Future of Public Health. *The Future of Public Health*. Washington, DC: National Academy Press, 1988; National Association of County Health Officials. *Blueprint for a Healthy Community: A Guide for Local Health Departments*. Washington, DC: National Association of County Health Officials, 1994; Andrulis DP, Carrier B. *Managed Care in the Inner City*.

147. Lee PR, Benjamin AE, Weber MA. Policies and strategies for health in the United States, 304.

148. Roemer MI. Analysis of a national health system. In: Detels R, Holland WW, McEwen J, Omenn GS, eds. *Oxford Textbook of Public Health*. Vol. 3, *The Practice of Public Health*. 3rd ed. New York: Oxford University Press, 1997, 1539–1551, quote 1543.

149. Lee PR, Benjamin AE, Weber MA. Policies and strategies for health in the United States, 300–301

150. Lee PR, Benjamin AE, Weber MA. Policies and strategies for health in the United States, 301.

151. Lee PR, Benjamin AE, Weber MA. Policies and strategies for health in the United States, 301.

152. Starr P. *The Social Transformation of American Medicine*, 417–449; Lee PR, Benjamin AE. Governmental and legislative control and direction of health services in the United States; Kovner AR. *Jonas's Health Care Delivery in the United States*. 5th ed.; Starr P. *The Logic of Health Care Reform*; Evans RG. Going for the gold; Iglehart JK. Health care report; National Center for Health Statistics. *Prevention Profile. Health United States, 1991*. Hyattsville, MD: Public Health Service, 1992; National Center for Health Statistics. *Health United States, 1995*; Navarro V. *Dangerous to Your Health*; Garrett L. *Betrayal of Trust*; Lee PR, Benjamin AE, Weber MA. Policies and strategies for health in the United States; U.S. Department of Health and Human Services. *For a Healthy Nation: Returns on Investment in Public Health*. Washington, DC: U.S. Government Printing Office, 1995; Drug-resistant TB raises fear of new scourge. *New York Times* October 23, 1997: A13; Food safety system due for an overhaul, committee says. *The Nation's Health* October 1998: 1; Revkin AC. Mosquito virus exposes a hole in the safety net. *New York Times* October 4, 1999: A1; Underwood A. The winged menace. *Newsweek* September 20, 1999: 37; Hayden T. A fair that went foul. *Newsweek*, September 20, 1999, 37; Spoke A. Death came in the water. *U.S. News and World Report* September 20, 1999: 56; Aaron HJ. *Serious and Unstable Condition*; Woolhandler S, Himmelstein DU. The deteriorating administrative efficiency of the U.S. health care system; Sutchfield FD, Keck CW. *Principles of Public Health Practice*; Duffy J. *The Sanitarians: A History of American Public Health*. Urbana. University of Illinois Press, 1992, 294–316; Roemer MI. Analysis of a national health system; Woolhandler S, Himmelstein DU. *For Our Patients, Not for Profits*.

153. Kovner C, Salsberg ES. The health care workforce. In: Kovner AR, Jonas S, eds. *Jonas and Kovner's Health Care Delivery in the United States*. 6th ed., 64–116, quote 65.

154. Kovner C, Salsberg ES. The health care workforce. In: Kovner AR, Jonas S, eds. *Jonas and Kovner's Health Care Delivery in the United States*. 6th ed., 65.

155. Stevens RA. *In Sickness and in Wealth*, 358.

156. Navarro V. *Dangerous to Your Health*, 102–103.

157. Navarro V. *Dangerous to Your Health*, 103.

158. Navarro V. *Dangerous to Your Health*, 104.

159. Kovner AR, Jonas S, eds. *Jonas and Kovner's Health Care Delivery in the United States*. 6th ed.; Navarro V. *Dangerous to Your Health*; Steinberg S. *The Ethnic Myth*; Herman ES, Chomsky N. *Manufacturing Consent: The Political Economy of the Mass Media*. New York: Pantheon Books, 1988; Kovel J. *White Racism: A Psychohistory*. New York: Random House, 1970. Reprint ed. New York: Columbia University Press, 1984; Jones J. *American Work: Four Centuries of Black and White Labor*. New York: W. W. Norton, 1998; Stevens RA. *In Sickness and in Wealth*.

160. Lee PR, Benjamin AE, Weber MA. Policies and strategies for health in the United States, 304.

161. Kovner C, Salsberg ES. The health care workforce. In: Kovner AR, Jonas S, eds. *Jonas and Kovner's Health Care Delivery in the United States*. 6th ed., 84.

162. Woolhandler S, Himmelstein DU. *For Our Patients, Not for Profits*, 97.

163. Kovner C, Salsberg ES. The health care workforce. In: Kovner AR, Jonas S, eds. *Jonas and Kovner's Health Care Delivery in the United States*. 6th ed., 71.

164. Woolhandler S, Himmelstein DU. *For Our Patients, Not for Profits*; Steinhauer J. Rebellion in white.

165. Lee PR, Benjamin AE, Weber MA. Policies and strategies for health in the United States; Council on Graduate Medical Education. *Seventh Report*. Washington, DC: U.S. Department of Health and Human Services, 1995; Kovner AR, Jonas S, eds. *Jonas and Kovner's Health Care Delivery in the United States*. 6th ed.; Lindorff D. *Marketplace Medicine*; Anders G. *Health against Wealth*; Andrulis DP, Carrier B. *Managed Care in the Inner City*; Woolhandler S, Himmelstein DU. The deteriorating administrative efficiency of the U.S. health care system.

166. Kovner C, Salsberg ES. The health care workforce. In: Kovner AR, Jonas S, eds. *Jonas and Kovner's Health Care Delivery in the United States*. 6th ed., 86.

167. Kovner C, Salsberg ES. The health care workforce. In: Kovner AR, Jonas S, eds. *Jonas and Kovner's Health Care Delivery in the United States*. 6th ed., 90.

168. Mullan F, Rivo M, Politzer RM. Doctors, dollars, and determination: Making physician work-force policy. *Health Affairs* 1993; 12(Suppl):138–151.

169. Kovner C, Salsberg ES. The health care workforce. In: Kovner AR, Jonas S, eds. *Jonas and Kovner's Health Care Delivery in the United States*. 6th ed., 106; Inglehart JK. Health Policy Report: The struggle to reform Medicare. *New England Journal of Medicine* 1996; 334:1071–1075.

170. Pew Health Professions Commission, *Critical Challenges: Revitalizing the Health Professions for the Twenty-first Century*. San Francisco: University of California, San Francisco, Center for the Health Professions, 1995.

171. Campbell EG, Weissman JS, Blumenthal D. Relationship between market competition and the activities and attitudes of medical school faculty. *Journal of the American Medical Association* 1997; 278:222–226; Moy E. Relationship between National Institutes of Health research awards to U.S. medical schools and managed care market penetration. *Journal of the American Medical Association* 1997; 278:217–221; Woolhandler S, Himmelstein DU. *For Our Patients, Not for Profits*.

172. Sergent JS. Code blue? Halls of medical learning are worried for their very survival. *The Tennessean* February 1, 1995: 11A.

173. O'Neill G, et al. Public handouts enrich drug makers, scientists, 1.

174. Roemer MI. Analysis of a national health system; Kovner AR, Jonas S, eds. *Jonas and Kovner's Health Care Delivery in the United States*. 6th ed.; Graduate medical education, *Journal of the American Medical Association* 1993; 270:1116–1122, Appendix II; Graduate medical education, *Journal of the American Medical Association* 1996; 276:739, Appendix II, Table 1; Mullan F, Rivo M, Politzer RM. Doctors, dollars, and determination; Iglehart JK. Health policy report; Pew Health Professions Commission, *Critical Challenges*; Rosenthal E. Where it pays not to teach. *New York Times* February 23, 1997: 2; Woolhandler S, Himmelstein DU. *For Our Patients, Not for Profits*; Gordon. Is research being "managed" out of existence? *Boston Sunday Globe* October 13, 1996: D1; Sergent JS. Code blue?; Lee PR, Benjamin AE, Weber MA. Policies and strategies for health in the United States; Navarro V. *Dangerous to Your Health*; O'Neill G, et al. Public handouts enrich drug makers, scientists; Campbell EG, Weissman JS, Blumenthal D. Relationship between market competition and the activities and attitudes of medical school faculty; Moy E. Relationship between National Institutes of Health research awards to U.S. medical schools and managed care market penetration.

175. Lee PR, Benjamin AE, Weber MA. Policies and strategies for health in the United States, 302.

176. Lee PR, Benjamin AE, Weber MA. Policies and strategies for health in the United States, 302.

177. Lee PR, Benjamin AE, Weber MA. Policies and strategies for health in the United States, 302–303.

178. Billings J. Access to health care services. In: Kovner AR, Jonas S, eds. *Jonas and Kovner's Health Care Delivery in the United States.* 6th ed., 401–438, quote 411.

179. Billings J. Access to health care services, 411–412.

180. Lee PR, Benjamin AE, Weber MA. Policies and strategies for health in the United States; Lindorff D. *Marketplace Medicine;* Anders G. *Health against Wealth;* Smith DB. *Health Care Divided;* Garrett L. *Betrayal of Trust;* Andrulis DP, Carrier B. *Managed Care in the Inner City;* American Hospital Association. *Hospital Statistics, 1993–1994 Edition.* Chicago: American Hospital Association, 1993; Kovner AR, Jonas S, eds. *Jonas and Kovner's Health Care Delivery in the United States.* 6th ed.; Taylor D. Stokes, Louis. In: Salzman J, Smith DL, West C, eds. *Encyclopedia of African American Culture and History.* 5 Vols. New York: Macmillan Library Reference, 1996, 2579; Stokes L. Health Care Reform and Its Impact on the African American Community (keynote address). In: *Proceedings: Summit '93: African American Prescription for Health.* National Medical Association and the Black Congressional Caucus Foundation, Washington, DC, May 2, 1993, 11–13; Abelson R. For managed care, free-market shock; Freudenheim M. So far, "Medicare plus choice" is minus most options. *New York Times* October 4, 1998: Section 3, 10; Maccabe T. Elderly may join poor in HMO abuses; Kilborn PT. Oregon falters on a new path to health care. *New York Times* January 3, 1999: 1; Iglehart JK. Health policy report; Lasalandra M. Study finds poor, elderly are losing out on HMOs.

181. Lee PR, Benjamin AE, Weber MA. Policies and strategies for health in the United States, 314.

182. Nobbe G. Feds may abandon the uninsured.

183. U.S. Department of Health and Human Services. *Report of the Secretary's Task Force on Black and Minority Health.* Vol. 1, *Executive Summary.* Washington, DC: U.S. Government Printing Office, August, 1985, ix.

184. U.S. Department of Health and Human Services. *Report of the Secretary's Task Force on Black and Minority Health.* Vol. 1, ix.

185. U.S. Department of Health and Human Services. *Report of the Secretary's Task Force on Black and Minority Health.* Vol. 1, ix.

186. U.S. Department of Health and Human Services. *Report of the Secretary's Task Force on Black and Minority Health.* Vol. 1, 2.

187. Byrd WM. An American health dilemma; Byrd WM, Clayton LA. An American health dilemma.

188. Jaynes GD, Williams RM, eds. *A Common Destiny: Blacks and American Society.* Washington, DC: National Academy Press, 1989, 393.

189. Braithwaite RL, Taylor SE, eds. *Health Issues in the Black Community.* San Francisco: Jossey-Bass Publishers, 1992, 4.

190. Livingston IL, ed. *Handbook of Black American Health: The Mosaic of Conditions, Issues, Policies, and Prospects.* Westport, CT: Greenwood Press, 1994, xxxi–xxxii.

191. Hart N. The social and economic environment and human health, 95; René AA. Racial differences in mortality: Blacks and Whites. In: Jones Jr W, Rice MF, eds. *Health Care Issues in Black America: Policies, Problems, and Prospects.* New York: Greenwood Press, 1987, 21–41, esp. 21, 30.

192. Jaynes GD, Williams RM. eds. *A Common Destiny,* 397.

193. Jaynes GD, Williams RM. eds. *A Common Destiny,* 397.

194. U.S. Department of Health and Human Services. *Report of the Secretary's Task Force on Black and Minority Health.* Vol. 1, 3.

195. Jaynes GD, Williams RM. eds. *A Common Destiny,* 397.

196. Byrd WM. An American health dilemma, 1026.

197. Byrd WM. An American health dilemma, 1026.

198. Braithwaite RL, Taylor SE, eds. *Health Issues in the Black Community,* xiii.

199. Floyd VD. "Too soon, too small, too sick": Black infant mortality. In: Braithwaite RL, Taylor SE, eds. *Health Issues in the Black Community,* 165–167, quote 166.

200. U.S. Department of Health and Human Services. *Healthy People 2000: National Health*

*Promotion and Disease Prevention Objectives* (Summary Report). Washington, DC: U.S. Department of Health and Human Services, Public Health Service, (Publication No. [PHS] 91–50213), 1990.

201. Sullivan LW. Foreword. In: Braithwaite RL, Taylor SE, eds. *Health Issues in the Black Community*, xiii–xv; U.S. Department of Health and Human Services. *Report of the Secretary's Task Force on Black and Minority Health*. Vol. 1; Hart N. The social and economic environment and human health; René AA. Racial differences in mortality; Byrd WM. An American health dilemma; Jaynes GD, Williams RM. eds. *A Common Destiny*; Livingston IL, ed. *Handbook of Black American Health*; Garrett L. *Betrayal of Trust*.

202. Smedley A. *Race in North America: Origin and Evolution of a Worldview*. 2nd ed. Boulder, CO: Westview Press, 1999, 332–333; Bohannan P, Curtin P. *Africa and Africans*. 4th ed. Prospect Heights, IL: Waveland Press, 1995.

203. U.S. health report card shows room for improvement. *The Nation's Health* October 1993; 1, 11.

204. Kumanyika S. Gathering together to close the gap in minority health status: Conference explores the health needs of the nation's emerging majority. In: *Minority Health Issues for an Emerging Majority: Proceedings of the 4th National Forum on Cardiovascular Health, Pulmonary Disorders, and Blood Resources, Washington, D.C., June 26–27, 1992*, by the National Heart, Lung, and Blood Institute (NHLBI), the NHLBI Ad Hoc Committee on Minority Populations, and the National Medical Association, 12; U.S. Bureau of the Census. *Statistical Abstract of the United States, 1998*. 118th ed. U.S. Department of Commerce. Washington, DC: U.S. Government Printing Office, 1998; Baquet CR, Hunter CP. Patterns in minorities and special populations. In: Greenwald P, Kramer BS, Weed DL, eds. *Cancer Prevention and Control*. New York: Marcel Dekker, 1995, 26–36; National Center for Health Statistics. *Prevention Profile. Health United States, 1991*; National Center for Health Statistics. *Health United States, 1995*; National Center for Health Statistics. *Health United States, 1996–97 and Injury Chartbook*. Hyattsville, MD: 1997; National Center for Health Statistics. Advance report of final mortality statistics, 1989. *Monthly Vital Statistics Report* 1992; 40(8)(Suppl 2). Hyattsville, MD: Public Health Service; National Center for Health Statistics. Deaths: Final data for 1996. *National Vital Statistics Reports* 1998; 47(9). Hyattsville, MD: U.S. Department of Health and Human Services; U.S. health report card shows room for improvement. *The Nation's Health* October 1993: 1; U.S. Department of Health and Human Services. *Report of the Secretary's Task Force on Black and Minority Health*. Vol. 1; Jaynes GD, Williams RM. eds. *A Common Destiny*.

205. National Center for Health Statistics. Deaths: Final data for 1996, 16.

206. National Center for Health Statistics. Deaths: Final data for 1996, 5.

207. National Center for Health Statistics. Deaths: Final data for 1996, 5.

208. National Center for Health Statistics. Deaths: Final data for 1996, 5.

209. National Center for Health Statistics. Advance report of final mortality statistics, 1989.

210. National Center for Health Statistics. Advance report of final mortality statistics, 1989.

211. National Center for Health Statistics. Advance report of final mortality statistics, 1989, 8.

212. National Center for Health Statistics. *Health United States, 1998 with Socioeconomic Status and Health Chartbook*. Hyattsville, MD, 1998, 212.

213. National Center for Health Statistics. Deaths: Final data for 1996, 9.

214. National Center for Health Statistics. Deaths: Final data for 1996; U.S. Department of Health and Human Services. *Report of the Secretary's Task Force on Black and Minority Health*. Vol. 1; National Center for Health Statistics. *Health United States, 1996–97 and Injury Chartbook*; National Center for Health Statistics. *Health United States, 1998 with Socioeconomic Status and Health Chartbook*; National Center for Health Statistics. Advance report of final mortality statistics, 1989.

215. Suchindran CM, Koo HP. Demography and public health. In: Detels R, Holland WW, McEwen J, Omenn GS, eds. *Oxford Textbook of Public Health*. Vol. 3, *The Practice of Public Health*. 3rd ed. New York: Oxford University Press, 1997, 829–848, quote 833.

216. Floyd VD. "Too soon, too small, too sick," 165.

217. Singh GK, Yu SM. Infant mortality in the United States: Trends, differentials, and projections, 1950 through 2010. *American Journal of Public Health* 1995; 85:957–964, quote 958.

218. Ewbank DC. History of Black mortality and health before 1940. In: Willis DP, ed. *Health Policies and Black Americans*. New Brunswick, NJ: Transaction Publishers, 1989, 100–128; Reuter EB. *The American Race Problem*. Rev. 3rd ed. New York: Thomas Y. Crowell Company, 1970; Farley R, Allen WR. *The Color Line and the Quality of Life in America*. New York: Oxford University Press, 1989.

219. National Center for Health Statistics. Deaths: Final data for 1996, 13.

220. National Center for Health Statistics. Deaths: Final data for 1996, 13.

221. Ahmed F. Infant mortality and related issues. In: Livingston IL, ed. *Handbook of Black American Health*, 217–231, quote 219.

222. Ahmed F. Infant mortality and related issues, 219.

223. Ahmed F. Infant mortality and related issues, 219.

224. National Center for Health Statistics. Deaths: Final data for 1996, 13.

225. Rosenbaum S, Layton C, Liu J. *The Health of America's Children*. Washington, DC: Children's Defense Fund, 1991, 16.

226. National Center for Health Statistics. Deaths: Final data for 1996, 13.

227. Ahmed F. Infant mortality and related issues, 231.

228. Ahmed F. Infant mortality and related issues, 231.

229. Ahmed F. Infant mortality and related issues, 231.

230. Ahmed F. Infant mortality and related issues, 231.

231. Ahmed F. Infant mortality and related issues, 232.

232. Ahmed F. Infant mortality and related issues, 232.

233. Ahmed F. Infant mortality and related issues, 232.

234. Ahmed F. Infant mortality and related issues, 232.

235. Centers for Disease Control. Concensus set of health status indicators for the general assessment of community health status—United States. *Morbidity and Mortality Weekly Report* 1991; 40;449–451; Floyd VD. "Too soon, too small, too sick"; National Center for Health Statistics. Deaths: Final data for 1996; Singh GK, Yu SM. Infant mortality in the United States; U.S. Bureau of the Census. *Historical Statistics of the United States, Colonial Times to 1970, Bicentennial Edition, Parts 1 and 2*. Washington, DC, 1975; Rosenbaum S, Layton C, Liu J. *The Health of America's Children*; National Center for Health Statistics. *Health United States, 1996–97 and Injury Chartbook*; Ahmed F. Infant mortality and related issues; Lee KS, Paneth N, Gartner LM, Pearlman MR, Gruss L. Neonatal mortality: An analysis of the recent improvements in the United States. *American Journal od Public Health* 1980; 70:15–22; National Commission to Prevent Infant Mortality. *Death before Life: The Tragedy of Infant Mortality* (Appendix). Washington, DC: The report of the National Commission to Prevent Infant Mortality. The Honorable Lawton Chiles, United States Senate, Chairman, 1988; Kaunitz AM. Honing in on maternal deaths. *Contemporary Ob/Gyn* 1984; 24:31–34.

236. Braveman P, Bennett T. *Information for Action: An Advocates Guide to Using Maternal and Child Health Data* (pamphlet). Washington DC: Children's Defense Fund, 1993, 1.

237. Children's Defense Fund. *The State of America's Children Yearbook 1998*. Washington DC: Children's Defense Fund, 1998, 4.

238. Children's Defense Fund. *The State of America's Children Yearbook 1998*, 3.

239. Children's Defense Fund. *The Health of America's Children 1992: Maternal and Child Health Data Book*. Washington DC: Children's Defense Fund, 1992, 24.

240. Children's Defense Fund. *The State of America's Children Yearbook 1998*, 22; U.S. Bureau of the Census. *Statistical Abstract of the United States, 1998*, 127.

241. Children's Defense Fund. *The Health of America's Children 1992*, 19.

242. Children's Defense Fund. *The State of America's Children Yearbook 1998*; Children's Defense Fund. *The Health of America's Children 1992*; U.S. Bureau of the Census. *Statistical Abstract of the United States, 1998*; U.S. Department of Health and Human Services. *Health United States 1998*. Washington, DC: U.S. Government Printing Office, 287.

243. Jones DJ, Roberts VA. Black children: Growth, development and health. In: Livingston IL, ed. *Handbook of Black American Health*, 333–343, quote 335.

244. Rosenstreich DL, et al. The role of cockroach allergy and exposure to cockroach allergen in

causing morbidity among inner-city children with asthma. *New England Journal of Medicine* 1997; 336:1356–1384.

245. National Center for Health Statistics. *Health United States, 1998 with Socioeconomic Status and Health Chartbook*, 82.

246. Jones DJ, Roberts VA. Black children; Children's Defense Fund. *The State of America's Children Yearbook 1998*, 55–56; Children's Defense Fund. *The Health of America's Children 1992: Maternal and Child Health Data Book*; National Center for Health Statistics. *Health United States, 1998 with Socioeconomic Status and Health Chartbook*; Rosenstreich DL, et al. The role of cockroach allergy and exposure to cockroach allergen in causing morbidity among inner-city children with asthma.

247. Reed WL. Lead poisoning: A modern plague among African American children. In: Braithwaite RL, Taylor SE, eds. *Health Issues in the Black Community*, 178–191, quote 182.

248. Reed WL. Lead poisoning, 181.

249. Reed WL. Lead poisoning, 179.

250. Reed WL. Lead poisoning; National Center for Health Statistics. *Health United States, 1998 with Socioeconomic Status and Health Chartbook*; Warren C. *Brush with Death: A Social History of Lead Poisoning*. Baltimore: Johns Hopkins University Press, 2000.

251. Jones DJ, Roberts VA. Black children, 336.

252. Centers for Disease Control. Measles—Los Angeles County, California, 1988. *Morbidity and Mortality Weekly Report* 1989; 38:49; Centers for Disease Control. Update: measles outbreak—Chicago, 1989. *Morbidity and Mortality Weekly Report* 1990; 39:317; Centers for Disease Control. Measles—United States, 1989 and first 20 weeks 1990. *Morbidity and Mortality Weekly Report* 1990; 39:353; Centers for Disease Control. Measles outbreak—New York City, 1990–1991. *Morbidity and Mortality Weekly Report* 1991; 40:305.

253. Byrd WM. An American health dilemma, 1026.

254. René AA. Racial differences in mortality; Jaynes GD, Williams RM. eds. *A Common Destiny*; Centers for Disease Control. Measles outbreak—New York City, 1990–1991; Centers for Disease Control. Update: Measles outbreak—Chicago, 1989; Centers for Disease Control. Measles—United States, 1989 and first 20 weeks 1990; Centers for Disease Control. Measles—Los Angeles County, California, 1988; Centers for Disease Control. Measles vaccination levels among selected groups of preschool-aged children—United States. *Morbidity and Mortality Weekly Report* 1991;40:36–39; Children's Defense Fund. *The State of America's Children Yearbook 1998*; National Center for Health Statistics. *Health United States, 1998 with Socioeconomic Status and Health Chartbook*.

255. National Center for Health Statistics. Deaths: Final data for 1996, 10.

256. Horan M. CVD death rate 50 percent higher among Blacks. In: *Minority Health Issues for an Emerging Majority: Proceedings of the 4th National Forum on Cardiovascular Health, Pulmonary Disorders, and Blood Resources, Washington, DC, June 26–27, 1992*. National Heart, Lung, and Blood Institute (NHLBI), the NHLBI Ad Hoc Committee on Minority Populations, and the National Medical Association, 22.

257. Gillum RF. The epidemiology of cardiovascular diseases: An American overview. In: Livingston IL, ed. *Handbook of Black American Health*, 3–23, quote 5.

258. U.S. Department of Health and Human Services. *Report of the Secretary's Task Force on Black and Minority Health*, Vol. 4, *Cardiovascular and Cerebrovascular Diseases, Part 1*. Washington, DC: U.S. Government Printing Office, 1986, 99.

259. Gillum RF. The epidemiology of cardiovascular diseases, 13.

260. Gillum RF. The epidemiology of cardiovascular diseases, 15–16; U.S. Department of Health and Human Services. *Report of the Secretary's Task Force on Black and Minority Health*. Vol. 4, *Part 1*, 7.

261. Francis C. CVD mortality among Harlem's Black males higher than in third world. In: *Minority Health Issues for an Emerging Majority*, 16.

262. National Center for Health Statistics. Deaths: Final data for 1996; National Center for Health Statistics. *Health United States, 1995*; National Center for Health Statistics. *Health United States, 1996–97 and Injury Chartbook*; Horan M. CVD death rate 50 percent higher among Blacks; René AA. Racial differences in mortality; Gillum RF. The epidemiology of cardiovascular diseases;

U.S. Department of Health and Human Services. *Report of the Secretary's Task Force on Black and Minority Health.* Vol. 4, *Part 1*; Hannan EL, et al. Access to coronary bypass surgery by race/ethnicity and gender among patients who are appropriate for surgery. *Medical Care* 1999; 37:68–77; Weitman S, et al. Gender, racial, and geographic differences in the performance of cardiac diagnostic and therepeutic procedures for hospitalized acute myocardial infarction in four states. *American Journal of Cardiology* 1997; 79:722–726; *Minority Health Issues for an Emerging Majority.*

263. Horan M. CVD death rate 50 percent higher among Blacks, 22.

264. Gillum RF. The epidemiology of cardiovascular diseases, 10.

265. Gillum RF. The epidemiology of cardiovascular diseases, 13.

266. Davis K, Schoen C. *Health and the War on Poverty: A Ten-Year Appraisal.* Washington, DC: Brookings Institution, 1978; National Center for Health Statistics. *Prevention Profile. Health United States, 1991,* National Center for Health Statistics. Deaths: Final data for 1996; National Center for Health Statistics. *Health United States, 1995;* National Center for Health Statistics. *Health United States, 1996–97 and Injury Chartbook;* Gillum RF. The epidemiology of cardiovascular diseases; *Minority Health Issues for an Emerging Majority.*

267. American Cancer Society. *Cancer Facts and Figures—1997.* Atlanta: American Cancer Society, 1997, 18.

268. American Cancer Society. *Cancer Facts and Figures—1998.* Atlanta: American Cancer Society, 1998, 1.

269. Clayton LA, Byrd WM. The African American cancer crisis, part 1: The problem. *Journal of Health Care for the Poor Underserved* 1993; 4: 83–101; Byrd WM, Clayton LA. The African-American cancer crisis, part 2: A prescription. *Journal of Health Care for the Poor Underserved* 1993; 4:102–116; U.S. Department of Health and Human Services. *Report of the Secretary's Task Force on Black and Minority Health.* Vol. 3, *Cancer.* Washington, DC: U.S. Government Printing Office, 1986, 1, 13.

270. Bang KM. Cancer and Black Americans. In: Livingston IL, ed. *Handbook of Black American Health,* 77–93, quote 81.

271. American Cancer Society. *Cancer Facts and Figures—1998,* 18.

272. American Cancer Society. *Cancer Facts and Figures—1998,* 18.

273. American Cancer Society. *Cancer Facts and Figures—1998,* 18.

274. U.S. Department of Health and Human Services. *Report of the Secretary's Task Force on Black and Minority Health.* Vol. 3, *Cancer,* 4.

275. Baquet CR, Hunter CP. Patterns in minorities and special populations, 28.

276. Baquet CR, Hunter CP. Patterns in minorities and special populations, 28.

277. American Cancer Society. *Cancer Facts and Figures—1998,* 18.

278. Bang KM. Cancer and Black Americans, 82–85.

279. American Cancer Society. *Cancer Facts and Figures—1998,* 18.

280. U.S. Department of Health and Human Services. *Report of the Secretary's Task Force on Black and Minority Health.* Vol. 3, *Cancer,* 18.

281. American Cancer Society. *Cancer Facts and Figures—1998,* 18.

282. Alexander GA. Cancer control in special populations: African-Americans, Native Americans, Hispanics, poor and underserved. In: Greenwald P, Kramer BS, Weed DL, eds. *Cancer Prevention and Control,* 371–391, quote 386.

283. American Cancer Society. *Cancer Facts and Figures—1997;* National Center for Health Statistics. Deaths: Final data for 1996; American Cancer Society. *Cancer Facts and Figures—1998;* Baquet CR, Hunter CP. Patterns in minorities and special populations; National Center for Health Statistics. *Health United States, 1996–97 and Injury Chartbook;* U.S. Department of Health and Human Services. *Report of the Secretary's Task Force on Black and Minority Health.* Vol. 3, *Cancer;* Bang KM. Cancer and Black Americans; Clayton LA, Byrd WM. The African American cancer crisis, part 1; Byrd WM, Clayton LA. The African-American cancer crisis, part 2; Alexander GA. Cancer control in special populations.

284. Thomas SB, Quinn SC. Public health then and now: The Tuskegee syphilis study, 1932 to 1972: Implications for HIV education and AIDS risk education programs in the Black community. *American Journal of Public Health* 1991; 81:1498–1504; Gamble VN. Under the shadow of Tuskegee: African Americans and health care. *American Journal of Public Health* 1997;

87:1773–1778; Andrulis DP, Carrier B. *Managed Care in the Inner City*; Greaves WL. AIDS and sexually transmitted diseases. In: Livingston IL, ed. *Handbook of Black American Health*, 157–168; Farmer P. *AIDS and Accusation: Haiti and the Geography of Blame*. Berkeley: University of California Press, 1992; Hooper E. *The River: A Journey to the Souce of HIV and AIDS*. Boston: Little, Brown, 1999; Horowitz LG. *Emerging Viruses: AIDS and Ebola—Nature, Accident, or Intentional?* Sandpint, ID: Tetrahedron, 1996.

285. Greaves WL. AIDS and sexually transmitted diseases, 158.

286. Greaves WL. AIDS and sexually transmitted diseases, 158.

287. "Initiative to Eliminate Racial and Ethnic Disparities in Health: Goal 5—Eliminate disparities in HIV infection." On U.S. Department of Health and Human Services World Wide Web site (updated May 26, 1998; cited February 8, 1999) (database online). Washington, DC, 1.

288. "Initiative to Eliminate Racial and Ethnic Disparities in Health: Goal 5—Eliminate disparities in HIV infection," 1.

289. Centers for Disease Control and Prevention. Critical need to pay attention to HIV prevention for African Americans. *CDC Update* June 1998:1.

290. Greaves WL. AIDS and sexually transmitted diseases, 165.

291. National Center for Health Statistics. *Health United States, 1996–97 and Injury Chartbook*; National Center for Health Statistics. *Health United States, 1994*; "Initiative to Eliminate Racial and Ethnic Disparities in Health: Goal 5—Eliminate disparities in HIV infection"; Centers for Disease Control and Prevention. Young people at risk—Epidemic shifts further toward young women and minorities. *CDC Update* September 1998: 1; Greaves WL. AIDS and sexually transmitted diseases; Thomas SB, Quinn SC. Public health then and now; Smith DB. *Health Care Divided.*; Garrett L. *Betrayal of Trust*; Andrulis DP, Carrier B. *Managed Care in the Inner City*; Gamble VN. Under the shadow of Tuskegee; Farmer P. *AIDS and Accusation*; Centers for Disease Control and Prevention. Critical need to pay attention to HIV prevention for African Americans; Nobbe G. Feds may abandon the uninsured; Sack K. Public hospitals around country cut basic service; Public hospitals across nation cutting services under pressure; Kotelchuck R. Down and out in the "New Calcutta": New York City's health care crisis. *Health/PAC Bulletin* 1989 (Summer); 19:4–11; Kotelchuck R. Preserving integration: Defending the hospital rights of the poor. *Health/PAC Bulletin* Summer 1989; 19:11–14; Richardson L. White patients more likely to use AIDS drugs, study says. *New York Times* July 27, 1997: 24; Sontag D, Richardson L. Doctors withhold H.I.V. pill regimen from some; Gideonse T. AIDS deaths drop, but the plague continues. *Newsweek* October 19, 1998: 72.

292. Tull ES, Makame MH, Roseman J. Diabetes mellitus in the African American population. In: Livingston IL, ed. *Handbook of Black American Health*, 94–109, quote 98.

293. National Center for Health Statistics. *Health United States, 1996–97 and Injury Chartbook*; National Center for Health Statistics. Deaths: Final data for 1996.

294. Murphy FG, Elders MJ. Diabetes and the Black community. In: Braithwaite RL, Taylor SE, eds. *Health Issues in the Black Community*, 121–143, quote 125–126.

295. U.S. Department of Health and Human Services. *Report of the Secretary's Task Force on Black and Minority Health*. Vol. 1; U.S. Department of Health and Human Services. *Report of the Secretary's Task Force on Black and Minority Health*. Vol. 2, *Crosscutting Issues in Minority Health*. Washington, DC: U.S. Government Printing Office, 1985; National Center for Health Statistics. *Health United States, 1996–97 and Injury Chartbook*; National Center for Health Statistics. Deaths: Final data for 1996; Tull ES, Makame MH, Roseman J. Diabetes mellitus in the African American population; Murphy FG, Elders MJ. Diabetes and the Black community.

296. National Center for Health Statistics. Deaths: Final data for 1996, 9.

297. Bang KM. Chronic obstructive pulmonary disease in Blacks. In: Livingston IL, ed. *Handbook of Black American Health*, 110–22, quote 111.

298. Bang KM. Chronic obstructive pulmonary disease in Blacks, 111.

299. Bang KM. Chronic obstructive pulmonary disease in Blacks, 113, 118.

300. National Center for Health Statistics. *Health United States, 1996–97 and Injury Chartbook*; National Center for Health Statistics. Deaths: Final data for 1996; Bang KM. Chronic obstructive pulmonary disease in Blacks.

301. Campion FD. *The AMA and U.S. Health Policy since 1940*. Chicago: Chicago Review Press for the American Medical Association, 1984, 515.

302. Wolinsky H. Healing wounds: Lonnie R. Bristow steps up to head the American Medical Association, one of the nation's premier—and most rigidly segregated—professional groups. *Emerge* July/August 1994; (10)(5):42; Smith PM. NMA opposes World Medical Association meeting in South Africa. *Journal of the National Medical Association* 1985; 77:259–260; Wright CH. Opposition to the World Medical Association assembly in South Africa, 1985. *Journal of the National Medical Association* 1985; 78:541–542.

303. Campion FD. *The AMA and U.S. Health Policy since 1940*, 506.

304. Blendon RJ, Donelan K. The public and the emerging debate over national health insurance. *New England Journal of Medicine* 1990; 323:208–212.

305. Taylor H, Leitman R. Consumers' satisfaction with their health care. In: Blendon RJ, Edwards JN, eds. *System in Crisis: The Case for Health Care Reform*. Vol 1, 75–102; Woolhandler S, Himmelstein DU. *For Our Patients, Not for Profits*.

306. Campion FD. *The AMA and U.S. Health Policy since 1940*; Wolinsky H. Healing wounds; Smith PM. NMA opposes World Medical Association meeting in South Africa; Wright CH. Opposition to the World Medical Association assembly in South Africa, 1985; Blendon RJ, Donelan K. The public and the emerging debate over national health insurance; Taylor H, Leitman R. Consumers' satisfaction with their health care; Smith DB. *Health Care Divided.*; Garrett L. *Betrayal of Trust*; Woolhandler S, Himmelstein DU. *For Our Patients, Not for Profits*; Woolhandler S, Himmelstein DU. *The National Health Program Chartbook*.

307. Washington HA. Political realities hit medical school rolls. *Emerge* March 1998; (5)(9):22; Council on Graduate Medical Education. *Seventh Report*; Kovner AR, Jonas S, eds. *Jonas and Kovner's Health Care Delivery in the United States* 6th ed.; Parker SG. Pew Commission Report: U.S. medical schools urged to increase diversity. *Ob.Gyn. News* March 1, 1999: 36.

308. Relman AS. Dealing with conflicts of interest. *New England Journal of Medicine* 1985; 313:749–751; Relman AS. Practicing medicine in the new business climate. *New England Journal of Medicine* 1987; 316:1150–1151; Bogdanich W. *The Great White Lie: Dishonesty, Waste, and Incompetence in the Medical Community*. New York: Simon & Schuster, 1991; Woolhandler S, Himmelstein DU. *For Our Patients, Not for Profits*.

309. Relman AS. Dealing with conflicts of interest, 751.

310. Illich I. *Medical Nemesis: The Expropriation of Health*. New York: Pantheon Books, 1976. Paperback ed. Toronto: Bantam Books, 1977; Inlander CB, Levin LS, Weiner E. *Medicine on Trial: The Appalling Story of Medical Ineptitude and the Arrogance That Overlooks It*. New York: Pantheon Books and the People's Medical Society, 1988; Hiatt HH. *America's Health in the Balance: Choice or Chance?* New York: Harper & Row, 1987; Konner M. *Medicine at the Crossroads: The Crisis in Health Care*. New York: Pantheon Books, 1993; Woolhandler S, Himmelstein DU. *For Our Patients, Not for Profits*; Woolhandler S, Himmelstein DU. *The National Health Program Chartbook*; Bogdanich W. *The Great White Lie*; Whol S. *The Medical Industrial Complex*.

311. Murata S. Why doctors will take back health care. *Medical Economics* January, 1996: 29, 30.

312. Blumenthal D. Effects of market reforms on doctors and their patients. *Health Affairs* Summer 1996; 15:170–184.

313. Blumenthal D. Effects of market reforms on doctors and their patients, 172.

314. Taylor H, Leitman R, Edwards J. Physicians' response to their changing environment. In: Blendon RJ, Edwards JN, eds. *System in Crisis: The Case for Health Care Reform*. Vol. 1, 149–172, quote 163.

315. Kovner AR, Jonas S, eds. *Jonas and Kovner's Health Care Delivery in the United States*. 6th ed., 64–115, 333–335; Washington HA. Political realities hit medical school rolls; Relman AS. Dealing with conflicts of interest; Relman AS. Practicing medicine in the new business climate; Blumenthal D. Effects of market reforms on doctors and their patients; Illich I. *Medical Nemesis*; Inlander CB, Levin LS, Weiner E. *Medicine on Trial*; Hiatt HH. *America's Health in the Balance*; Konner M. *Medicine at the Crossroads*; Woolhandler S, Himmelstein DU. *For Our Patients, Not for Profits*; Woolhandler S, Himmelstein DU. *The National Health Program Chartbook*; Bogdanich W. *The Great White Lie*; Whol S. *The Medical Industrial Complex*; Taylor H, Leitman R, Edwards J.

Physicians' response to their changing environment, 163; Blendon RJ, Donelan K. The public and the emerging debate over national health insurance; Taylor H, Leitman R. Consumers' satisfaction with their health care; Starr P. *The Social Transformation of American Medicine*, 3–29, 420–449; Byrd WM, Clayton LA. "The American Health Dilemma Continues: An Analysis of the Clinton Health Plan from an African American and Disadvantaged Patient Perspective." Report prepared for the National Medical Association and the Congressional Black Caucus, Harvard School of Public Health, submitted October 27, 1993; Johnson H, Broder DS. *The System*; Lindorff D. *Marketplace Medicine*; Anders G. *Health against Wealth*; Andrulis DP, Carrier B. *Managed Care in the Inner City*; Skocpol T. *Boomerang*.

316. Sampson CC. Health care problems in the 1980s from a Black perspective. *Journal of the National Medical Association* 1984; 76:968; Jones EI. NMA's commitment to quality health care for all. *Journal of the National Medical Association* 1985; 77:987–991; Tuckson R. The Black physician and the challenges of the 1980s. *Journal of the National Medical Association* 1984; 76:977–980. Health care problems in the 1980s from a Black perspective: Part II of a series begun in 1984. *Journal of the National Medical Association* 1984; 76:968; Byrd WM, Clayton LA. "America's Dual Health Crisis in Black and White." Report for hearings on *Health Care Reform: The African American Agenda*. The Congressional Black Caucus's Health Brain Trust, April 13, 1993, Washington, DC; Byrd WM, Clayton LA. *A Black Health Trilogy*, Videotape and 188-page documentary report. Washington, DC: The National Medical Association and the African American Heritage and Education Foundation, 1991; Hilliard RLM. Providing sound and effective health care delivery for all Americans. *Journal of the National Medical Association* 1983; 75:1135–1138; Jones EI. The direct relationship of health status to health care. *Journal of the National Medical Association* 1986; 78:271–272; Byrd WM. An American health dilemma; Keith SN. A legislative agenda for health: 1987 to 1992. *Journal of the National Medical Association* 1987; 79:888; Byrd WM, et al. African-American physicians's views on health reform: Results of a survey. *Journal of the National Medical Association* 1994; 86:191–199; Byrd WM, Clayton LA, McCoy SP, Calliste GJ. "Access to health care: Provision by the major health reform proposals." A policy memorandum prepared for the Congressional Black Caucus Foundation, March 26, 1994; Barber JB. Black Americans in crisis. *Journal of the National Medical Association* 1990; 82:664–666; Hester RD, Barber JB. Health reforms and the Black community. *Journal of the National Medical Association* 1990; 82:291–293; Barber JB. Quality of health care: National Medical Association perspective: Report from the NMA Task Force. *Journal of the National Medical Association* 1991; 83:1113–1116; O'Bannon LC. Are African-American doctors being locked out? The down side of managed care. *National Medical Association News* Winter 1995: 1; Bonnyman GG Jr. Health care and civil rights for a new generation. *Minority Health Today* 2000; 1: 43–45.

317. Prasad N. A systems view of health care for the poor. *Journal of the National Medical Association* 1989; 81:169–178, quote 169.

318. Walker B. Ethics in health services and medical care. *Journal of the National Medical Association* 1989; 81:13–15, quote 13.

319. Elkowitz A. Physicians at the bedside: Thoughts and actions with regard to health care allocation. *Journal of the National Medical Association* 1986; 78:423–426, quote 427.

320. Jones EI. Overcoming challenges to serve. *Journal of the National Medical Association* 1986; 78:806–808, quote 807.

321. Jones EI. Closing the health status gap for Blacks and other minorities. *Journal of the National Medical Association* 1985; 78:485–488, quote 486.

322. Jones EI. Closing the health status gap for Blacks and other minorities, 486.

323. Jones EI. Closing the health status gap for Blacks and other minorities, 486.

324. Cooper R. Cardiovascular mortality among Blacks, hypertension control and the Reagan budget. *Journal of the National Medical Association* 1981; 73:1019–1020, quote 1020.

325. Jones EI. Disproportionate care providers: Lauded or harassed? *Journal of the National Medical Association* 1985; 77:871–872, quote 871.

326. Hester RD, Barber JB. Health reforms and the Black community, 293.

327. Barber JB. Black Americans in crisis, 664.

328. U.S. Department of Health and Human Services. *Cultural Competence for Evaluators: A Guide for Alcohol and Other Drug Abuse Prevention Practitioners Working With Ethnic/Racial Communities*. Rockville, MD: Office for Substance Abuse and Prevention, Alcohol, Drug Abuse,

and Mental Health Administration (DHHS Publication No. [ADM]92–1884), 1992; Malone TE, Johnson KW. *Report of the Secretary's Task Force on Black and Minority Health*; Barber JB. Black Americans in crisis; Thompson VR. Recommendations to the Transition Team for the Reagan Administration. *Journal of the National Medical Association* 1981; 73:393–394; Washington H. Barriers to Black physicians and health care. *Journal of the National Medical Association* 1984; 76:11–12; Starkenburg RJ, Rosner F, Kowal S. Patient "dumping." *Journal of the National Medical Association* 1990; 82:660–662; Bell CC. Statistics on Black populations. *Journal of the National Medical Association* 1982; 74:829–830; Neighbors HW, Jackson JS. Uninsured risk groups in a national survey of Black Americans. *Journal of the National Medical Association* 1986; 78:979–983; Hilliard RLM. The president's inaugural address: Insuring quality health care. *Journal of the National Medical Association* 1983; 75:81–83; Neighbors HW. Ambulatory medical care among adult Black Americans: The hospital emergency room. *Journal of the National Medical Association* 1986; 78:275–282; Barber Jr. JB, Sinnette CH. Presidential politics and minority health. *Journal of the National Medical Association* 1984; 76:969–971. Health care problems in the 1980s from a Black perspective: Part I of a series begun in 1984; 76:968; Cooper R. Is the United States entering a period of retrogression in public health? *Journal of the National Medical Association* 1983; 75:741–744; Peniston RL. Will the National Medical Association support a comprehensive national health plan? *Journal of the National Medical Association* 1989; 81:1027–1029; Pinn-Wiggins VW. The National Medical Association: Furthering the mission. *Journal of the National Medical Association* 1990; 82:793–796; Pinn-Wiggins VW. The National Medical Association and our challenges as we enter the next decade. *Journal of the National Medical Association* 1989; 81:1213–1216; Webb Jr. H. Community health centers: Providing care for urban Blacks. *Journal of the National Medical Association* 1984; 76:1063–1067. Health care problems in the 1980s from a Black perspective: Part IV of a series begun in 1984. *Journal of the National Medical Association* 1984; 76:968; Hester RD, Barber JB. A new research agenda: Incentive payments for urban physicians. *Journal of the National Medical Association* 1984; 76:991–993. Health care problems in the 1980s from a Black perspective: Part III of a series begun in 1984. *Journal of the National Medical Association* 1984; 76:968; Schtzkin A, Cooper R, Green L. Antiracism and the level of health services: A sociomedical hypothesis. *Journal of the National Medical Association* 1984; 76:381–386; Walker Jr. B. Health care in the 1980s. *Journal of the National Medical Association* 1985; 77:601–604; Neighbors HW, Jackson JS. Barriers to medical care among adult Blacks: What happens to the uninsured? *Journal of the National Medical Association* 1987; 79:489–493; Byrd WM. Inquisition, peer review, and Black physician survival. *Journal of the National Medical Association* 1987; 79:1027–1029; Benjamin GC. Quality assurance: Public hospital clinics. *Journal of the National Medical Association* 1989; 81:355; Jones EI. Society's responsibility for health care of the indigent. *Journal of the National Medical Association* 1986; 78:95–96; Rice H. In search of an ethical equilibrium: A new dilemma in health services. *Journal of the National Medical Association* 1986; 78:57–60; Jones EI. Preventing disease and promoting health in the minority community. *Journal of the National Medical Association* 1986; 78:18–20; Staggers FE. President's inaugural address: Black health care. *Journal of the National Medical Association* 1988; 80:1281–1282; Smith DB. *Health Care Divided.*; Andrulis DP, Carrier. *Managed Care in the Inner City.*

329. Hester RD, Barber JB. Health reforms and the Black community, 291.

330. Davis E. Cutting the nation's health care costs. *Journal of the National Medical Association* 1987; 79:953–960, quote 956.

331. Johnson C. The survival of Afro-American physicians in 1990 and beyond: Inaugural address. *Journal of the National Medical Association* 1990; 82:761–765, quote 764.

332. Smith PM. Economic survival for Black physicians. *Journal of the National Medical Association* 1985; 77:17; Davis E. Cutting the nation's health care costs; Johnson C. The survival of the Afro-American physicians in 1990 and beyond; Muñoz E, et al. Race and diagnostic related group prospective hospital payment for medical patients. *Journal of the National Medical Association* 1989; 81:844–848; Muñoz E, et al. Health care financing policy for hospitalized Black patients. *Journal of the National Medical Association* 1988; 80:972–976; Jones EI. Change—threat or opportunity? *Journal of the National Medical Association* 1985; 77:773–774; McDaniel RR. Management and medicine, never the twain shall meet. *Journal of the National Medical Association* 1985; 77:107–112; Keith SN. Prospective payment for hospital costs using diagnosis-related groups: Will cost inflation be reduced? *Journal of the National Medical Association* 1983; 75:609; Prasad N. The health economics cascade of the '80s. *Journal of the National Medical Association* 1988;

80:1165–1166; Earles III LC. President's inaugural address: Priorities. *Journal of the National Medical Association* 1983; 75:1139–1143; Earles III LC. Interview with the Honorable Louis Stokes, Congressman, twenty-first Congressional District of Ohio. *Journal of the National Medical Association* 1984; 76:575–576; Wesley Jr. N, Hester RD. Costs, choice, and competition: Some considerations of alternative delivery systems. *Journal of the National Medical Association* 1984; 76:1079–1084. Health care problems in the 1980s from a Black perspective: Part VI of a series begun in 1984. 76:968; Iglehart VR, Taneja KS. Prospective payment system: Experience of a public hospital. *Journal of the National Medical Association* 1984; 76:765–768; Ruiz DS, Herbert TA. The economics of health care for elderly Blacks. *Journal of the National Medical Association* 1985; 77:365–368; Joyner JE. Future of health care in America: What is the NMA's role? *Journal of the National Medical Association* 1987; 79:1129–1133; Prasad N. The dehiscence of health care. *Journal of the National Medical Association* 1989; 81:931–935; Hilliard RLM. The impact of the new Mediciad (Medi-Cal) changes in California. *Journal of the National Medical Association* 1982; 74:939–940; Rice MF, Winn M. Black health care in America: A political perspective. *Journal of the National Medical Association* 1990; 82:429–437; Joyner JE. Nothing ventured—nothing gained. *Journal of the National Medical Association* 1988; 80:377–378; Davidson AT, Coleman AH. The legal status of physicians on hospital staffs. *Journal of the National Medical Association* 1983; 75:87–88; Davidson AT, Coleman AH. Legal options in securing hospital appointments. *Journal of the National Medical Association* 1983; 75:318–320; Obayuwana AO. The malpractice feud. *Journal of the National Medical Association* 1981; 73:363–370; Sommers PA. Malpractice risk and patient relations. *Journal of the National Medical Association* 1984; 76:953–956; Legislative update: A report of the NMA Legislative Council. *Journal of the National Medical Association* 1986; 78:899–900; Lee IW. The Health Care Financing Administration study of excess mortality in U.S. short-term, acute care hospitals during 1984. *Journal of the National Medical Association* 1988; 80:462–464; Crockett GW. Political action committees: Impact on our political system. *Journal of the National Medical Association* 1986; 78:697–700; Davidson AT, et al. Declaration of a medical practice liability crisis. *Journal of the National Medical Association* 1986; 78:789. NMA Activities; Mazique EC. National medical political action committee. *Journal of the National Medical Association* 1986; 78:138; Barber JB, Tuckson R. Legislative activity at the 1985 NMA convention and selected resolutions. *Journal of the National Medical Association* 1985; 77:839; Waxman H. Legislative forum. *Journal of the National Medical Association* 1985; 77:311, 415, 515–520; Gullattee A, et al. Selected NMA resolutions, 1984 prepared by the legislation council. *Journal of the National Medical Association* 1985; 77:151; Smith PM. The importance of the NMA political action committee (NMPAC). *Journal of the National Medical Association* 1985; 77:75–76; Hester RD, Barber JB. The relative value scale: Reforming physician payment policy. *Journal of the National Medical Association* 1987; 79:1298–1303; Barber J, Hester RD, Tuckson R. Legislative resolutions at the 92nd annual convention of the NMA, 1987. *Journal of the National Medical Association* 1988; 80:207–212; Pinn-Wiggins VW. Testimony before the House of Representatives Committee on Energy and Commerce, Subcommittee on Health and the Environment on HR 3240, the Disadvantaged Minority Health Improvement Act of 1989. *Journal of the National Medical Association* 1990; 82:851–854; Pinn-Wiggins VW. Testimony to the Pepper Commission: The United States Bipartisan Commission on Comprehensive Health Care. *Journal of the National Medical Association* 1990; 82:169–172; Staggers FE. President's inaugural address: Black health care; Smith DB. *Health Care Divided.*; Andrulis DP, Carrier. *Managed Care in the Inner City.*

333. Frierson HT. The status of Black students in medical education. *Journal of the National Medical Association* 1988; 80:387–390, quote 390.

334. Frierson HT. The status of Black students in medical education, 389.

335. Frierson HT. The status of Black students in medical education, 389.

336. Hilliard RLM. Will there be a physician glut or an exaggeration of the present maldistribution of physicians? Another view. *Journal of the National Medical Association* 1983; 75:855–859.

337. Epps Jr. CH. The Black practitioner: Challenges of the future. *Journal of the National Medical Association* 1986; 78:365–370; Sampson CC. Provident Medical Center: Fulfillment of a need. *Journal of the National Medical Association* 1983; 75:665–666; Smith PN. The Black physician: An endangered species? *Journal of the National Medical Association* 1984; 76:1178–1180; Joyner JE. Health and social issues: The National Medical Association's commitment. *Journal of the National Medical Association* 1988; 80:1169–1171; Peniston RL. The disappearance of the Black hospital.

*Journal of the National Medical Association* 1988; 80:849–850; Jones EI. Effects of competition on access to care: Will new trends in competition limit access to health care for Blacks? *Journal of the National Medical Association* 1985; 77:967–968; Stitt Jr. VJ. Health care: Development of data for a marketing approach. *Journal of the National Medical Association* 1985; 77:485–488; Hilliard RLM. Will there be a physician glut or an exaggeration of the present maldistribution of physicians? Another view; Pinn-Wiggins VW. Recognition of the plight of minorities in the educational process and health care system. *Journal of the National Medical Association* 1990; 82:333–335; Smith PM. The importance of maintaining Black institutions. *Journal of the National Medical Association* 1985; 77:175–176; Peniston RL. Institutional imperatives: A clear message from the Association of American Medical Colleges. *Journal of the National Medical Association* 1988; 80:354; Wilson DE. Minorities and the medical profession: A historical perspective and analysis of current and future trends. *Journal of the National Medical Association* 1986; 78:177–180; Pinn-Wiggins VW. The future of medical practice and its impact on minority physicians. *Journal of the National Medical Association* 1990; 82:397–401; Hilliard RLM. Is there a doctor in the house? Budget cut impacts on the shortage of Black physicians. *Journal of the National Medical Association* 1982; 74:1155–1156; Pisano JC, Epps AC. The impact of MCAT intervention efforts on medical student acceptance rates. *Journal of the National Medical Association* 1983; 75:773–777; Watts VG. New government proposals: The effect on minority medical education. *Journal of the National Medical Association* 1983; 75:247–249; Hansen AC. The future of medical education in the United States: The GPEP report. *Journal of the National Medical Association* 1985; 77:775–776; Peniston RL. A racial view of medical education. *Journal of the National Medical Association* 1987; 79:143–145; Satcher D. The Meharry Hubbard and Nashville General Hospital merger proposal statement. *Journal of the National Medical Association* 1990; 82:83–85; Epps AC. National board and the minority medical student. *Journal of the National Medical Association* 1990; 82:161–163; Pinn-Wiggins VW. Diversity in medical education and health care access: After the '80s, what? *Journal of the National Medical Association* 1990; 82:89–92; Peniston RL. Further reflection on a racial view of medical education. *Journal of the National Medical Association* 1990; 82:325; Jones B. Disproportionate health risks in minorities: Does medical education need to change? *Journal of the National Medical Association* 1990; 82:395–396; Davidson AT. The role of the historic Black colleges in the training of Black professionals. *Journal of the National Medical Association* 1983; 75:1019–1022; Sullivan LW. The Morehouse School of Medicine: A state of mind, of mission, and of commitment. *Journal of the National Medical Association* 1983; 75:837–839; Freeman HP, et al. Physician manpower need of the nation: Position paper of the Surgical Section of the National Medical Association. *Journal of the National Medical Association* 1982; 74:617–619; Martinez Jr. C. Physician and health professional manpower. *Journal of the National Medical Association* 1983; 75:545–546; Joyner JE. Health manpower today and future implications. *Journal of the National Medical Association* 1988; 80:717–720; Watts TC, Lecca PJ. Minorities in the health professions: A current perspective. *Journal of the National Medical Association* 1989; 81:1225–1229; Pinn-Wiggins VW. Comments from the National Medical Association concerning a "white paper" on proposed strategies for fulfilling primary care manpower needs. *Journal of the National Medical Association* 1990; 82:245–248.

338. Byrd WM, et al. African-American physicians' views on health reform: Preliminary results of a survey. *Journal of the National Medical Association* 1994; 86:93–94; Byrd WM, et al. African-American physicians' views on health reform: Results of a survey. *Journal of the National Medical Association* 1994; 86:191–199; Bullock SC, Houston E. Perceptions of racism by Black medical students attending White medical schools. *Journal of the National Medical Association* 1987; 79:601–608; Frierson HT. Black medical students' perceptions of the academic environment and of faculty and peer interactions. *Journal of the National Medical Association* 1987; 79:737–743; Frierson HT. The status of Black students in medical education.

339. Schulman KA, et al. The effect of race and sex on physician recommendations for cardiac catheterization. *New England Journal of Medicine* 1999; 340:618–626; Council on Ethical and Judicial Affairs. Black-White disparities in health care. *Journal of the American Medical Association* 1990; 263:2344–2346; Greenberg DS. Black health: Grim statistics. *The Lancet* 1990; 355:780–781; Gaston RS, Ayres I, Dooley LG, Diethelm AG. Racial equity in renal transplantation: The disparate impact of HLA-based allocation. *Journal of the American Medical Association* 1993; 270:1352–1355; Escarce JJ, Epstein KR, Colby DC, Schwartz JS. Racial differences in the elderly's use of medical procedures and diagnostic tests. *American Journal of Public Health* 1993;

83:948–954; Carlisle DM, Leake B, Shapiro MF. Racial and ethnic differences in the use of invasive cardiac procedures among cardiac patients in Los Angeles County, 1986 through 1988. *American Journal of Public Health* 1995; 85:352–356; Wenneker MB, Epstein AM. Racial inequalities in the use of procedures for patients with ischemic health disease in Massachusetts. *Journal of the American Medical Association* 1989; 261:253–257; Schwartz E, Kofie VY, Rivio M, Tuckson RV. Black/White comparisons of deaths preventable by medical intervention: United States and the District of Columbia, 1980–1986. *International Journal of Epidemiology* 1990; 19:591–598; Pappas G, Queen S, Hadden W, Fisher G. The increasing disparity in mortality between socioeconomic groups in the United States, 1960–1986. *New England Journal of Medicine* 1993; 329:103–109; Pappas G. Elucidating the relationships between race, socioeconomic status, and health. *American Journal of Public Health* 1994; 84:892–893; Moy E, Bartman BA. Physician race and care of minority and medically indigent patients; McCord C, Freeman HP. Excess mortality in Harlem. *New England Journal of Medicine* 1990; 322:173–177; Kaiske BL, Neylan JF, Riggko RR, Danovitch GM, et al. The effect of race on access and outcome in transplantation. *New England Journal of Medicine* 1991; 324:302–307; Keil JE, Sutherland SE, Knapp RG, Tyrder HA. Does equal socioeconomic status in Black and White men mean equal risk of mortality? *American Journal of Public Health* 1992; 82:1133–1136; Kahn KL, et al. Health care for Black and poor hospitalized Medicare patients. *Journal of the American Medical Association* 1994; 271:1169–1174; Kahn KL, et al. Health care for Black and poor hospitalized Medicare patients; Brooks DD, Smith DR, Anderson RJ. Medical apartheid, an American perspective. *Journal of the American Medical Association* 1991; 266:2746–2749; Brennan TA, Hebert LE, Laird NM, et al. Hospital characteristics associated with adverse events and substandard care. *Journal of the American Medical Association* 1991; 266:3265–3269; Bergner L. Race, health, and health services. *American Journal of Public Health* 1993; 83:939–941; Bang KM, White JE, Gause BL, Leffall LD. Evaluation of recent trends in cancer mortality and incidence among blacks. *Cancer* 1988; 61:1255–1261.

340. Cobb WM. The Black American in medicine; Byrd WM, Clayton LA. An American health dilemma; Charatz-Litt C. A chronicle of racism: The effects of the White medical community on black health. *Journal of the National Medical Association* 1992; 84:717–725; Harris C. Update on pro harassment. *Medical Tribune*, December 5, 1984, 36; Gans RH. The hospital disciplinary process. *Legal Aspects of Medical Practice*, 1985; 13:1–4; Hairston GE. Interview: Doctor David Satcher. *The Crisis* 1985; 92:38–44; Crittendon D. Black doctors charge bias at area hospitals. *The Detroit News* April 23, 1984; Celis W, Poirot C. Black doctors may sue five hospitals. *Fort Worth Star-Telegram* November 25, 1983; Crittendon D. Doors of his specialty closed to Black surgeon. *The Detroit News* April 23, 1984; *Patrick v. Burget*. 800 F. 2d 1498, 9th Cir, 1986; Lobel M. A hospital privileges battle: The toughest fight of your career. *Generics* Fall 1986; 20–27; Supreme Court may review peer review case. *American Medical News* February 13, 1987; Byrd WM. "Peer review abuse: Medicine's marker of its reemerging racial dilemma." Unpublished document. Tyler, Texas, 1986; Lone Star State Medical Association. Charges of racial discrimination in Fort Worth, Texas. *Lone Star State Medical Association Newsletter–Region Five* Feb/March 1984; 1; Byrd WM. *Peer Review: The Perversion of a Process*. Report prepared for the Subcommittee on Civil Rights of the House Committee on the Judiciary on behalf of the National Medical Association. 99th Congress, 2nd Session, 1986; Byrd WM. Inquisition, peer review, and black physician survival; Hilliard RLM. Increasing NMA membership: A challenge to minority physicians. *Journal of the National Medical Association* 1983; 75:341–344; Byrd WM. Black medicine under attack. *Urban Medicine* 1987; 2:22; Schulman KA, et al. The effect of race and sex on physician recommendations for cardiac catheterization; Byrd WM, et al. African-American physicians' views on health reform: Preliminary results of a survey; Byrd WM, et al. African-American physicians' views on health reform: Results of a survey; Bullock SC, Houston E. Perceptions of racism by black medical students attending white medical schools; Frierson HT. Black medical students' perceptions of the academic environment and of faculty and peer interactions; Frierson HT. The status of Black students in medical education.

341. Sullivan LW. The status of blacks in medicine. *New England Journal of Medicine* 1983; 309:807–809; Walker ML. The Morehouse School of Medicine story: A surgical strike! *Journal of the National Medical Association* 1993; 85:395–400; Haynes MA, Bernard LJ. Drew/Meharry/Morehouse Consortium Cancer Center: An approach to targeted research in minority institutions. *Journal of the National Medical Association* 1991; 84:505–511; Prothrow-Stith D. *Deadly Consequences*. New York: HarperCollins, 1991; Prothrow-Stith D, Spivak H, Sage

RD. Interpersonal violence prevention: A recent public health mandate. In: *The Oxford Textbook of Public Health*. Vol. 3, *The Practice of Public Health*, 1331–1336; Williams RA. *Humane Medicine: A New Paradigm in Medical Education and Healthcare Delivery*. Philadelphia: Lippincott Williams and Wilkins, 1999; Darity WA, Turner CB. Family planning, race consciousness, and fears of genocide. *American Journal of Public Health* 1972; 62:1454; Darity WA. Turner CB. Fears of genocide among African Americans as related to age, sex, and religion. *American Journal of Public Health* 1973; 63:1029; Andrulis DP, Carrier B. *Managed Care in the Inner City*; Robinson LS. Dialogue with Dr. M. Jocelyn Elders: The Surgeon General's controversial remedies. *Emerge* July/August 1994; (10)(5):20; Satcher D. "Black Access to Health Care." Presentation for Black Health: Historical Perspectives and Current Problems Conference, University of Wisconsin Medical School, April 5–7, 1990, Madison, Wisconsin; Baquet CR, et al. *Cancer Among Blacks and Other Minorities: Statistical Profiles*. Washington, DC: U.S. Department of Health and Human Services, 1986 (NIH Publication No. 86–2785); National Institutes of Health. *News and Features* 1997 (Fall), NIH Office of Communications, Bethesda, Maryland, 3; Baquet CR, et al. *Annotated Bibliography of Cancer-Related Literature on Black Populations*. Washington, DC: U.S. Department of Health and Human Services, 1988 (NIH Publication No. 89–3024).

342. Lee PR, Benjamin AE, Weber MA. Policies and strategies for health in the United States, 305–306.

343. Sniderman PM, Piazza T. *The Scar of Race*. Cambridge, MA: The Belknap Press of Harvard University Press, 1993; Simone TM. *About Face: Race in Postmodern America*. Brooklyn, NY: Autonomedia, 1989; Feagin JR, Spikes MP. *Living with Racism: The Black Middle-Class Experience*. Boston: Beacon Press, 1994; Ryan W. *Blaming the Victim*. New York: Vintage Books, 1971. Revised updated ed. New York: Vintage Books, 1976; Steinberg S. *The Ethnic Myth*; Fukuyama F. *Trust: The Social Virtues and the Creation of Prosperity*. New York: The Free Press, 1995.

344. Fukuyama F. *Trust*.

345. Lee PR, Benjamin AE, Weber MA. Policies and strategies for health in the United States, 306.

346. Lee PR, Benjamin AE, Weber MA. Policies and strategies for health in the United States, 307.

347. Lee PR, Benjamin AE, Weber MA. Policies and strategies for health in the United States, 307.

348. Lee PR, Benjamin AE, Weber MA. Policies and strategies for health in the United States; Navarro V. *Dangerous to Your Health*; Johnson H, Broder DS. *The System*; Skocpol T. *Boomerang*; Garrett L. *Betrayal of Trust*.

349. Lee PR, Benjamin AE, Weber MA. Policies and strategies for health in the United States, 309; Lindblom CE. The science of "muddling through." *Public Administration Review* 1959; 10:79–88.

350. Lee PR, Benjamin AE, Weber MA. Policies and strategies for health in the United States, 309; Walker JL. The diffusion of knowledge, policy, communities and agenda setting: The relationship of knowledge and power. In: Tropman JE, Dluhey MJ, Lind RM, eds. *New Strategic Perspectives on Social Policy*. New York: Pergamon Press, 1981.

351. Johnson H, Broder DS. *The System*; Skocpol T. *Boomerang*; Navarro V. *Dangerous to Your Health*.

352. Lind M. *Up From Conservatism*. Steinberg S. *Turning Back: The Retreat from Racial Justice in American Thought and Policy*. Boston: Beacon Press, 1995; Stefanic J, Delgado R. *No Mercy: How Conservative Think Tanks and Foundations Changed America's Social Agenda*. Philadelphia: Temple University Press, 1996; Johnson H, Broder DS. *The System*; Skocpol T. *Boomerang*; Navarro V. *Dangerous to Your Health*; Sniderman PM, Piazza T. *The Scar of Race*; Simone TM. *About Face*; Feagin JR, Spikes MP. *Living with Racism*; Ryan W. *Blaming the Victim*; Steinberg S. *The Ethnic Myth*; Fukuyama F. *Trust*; Garrett L. *Betrayal of Trust*.

353. U.S. Department of Health and Human Services. *The 1990 Health Objectives of the Nation: A Midcourse Review*. Washington, DC: U.S. Department of Health and Human Services, Public Health Service, 1986; U.S. Department of Health and Human Services. *Healthy People 2000*; U.S. Department of Health and Human Services. *Healthy People 2000: Midcourse Review and 1995 Revisions*. Washington, DC: U.S. Department of Health and Human Services, Public Health Service, 1995.

354. Centers for Disease Control. Reporting race and ethnicity data—National Electronic Telecommunication System for surveillance, 1994–1997. *Morbidity and Mortality Weekly Report* 1999; 48:305–311, quote 305.

355. Centers for Disease Control. Reporting race and ethnicity data, 310.

356. Singh GK, Yu SM. Infant mortality in the United States; After noting that the "relatively unfavorable international standing of the United States in terms of infant mortality stems in large part from the substantial racial (Black/White) disparity in infant survival" and assuming this is due to socioeconomic status (which is unproven), this NCHS-led research team then skimps on racial disparity data, "for the sake of brevity" and asks researchers to mail them for information on one of the most important findings in their paper. In spite of a cavalier attitude about presenting this important data, the authors note in the discussion: "despite the impressive reduction in overall infant mortality, the race (Black/White) disparity in infant mortality not only has persisted but has increased over time and, unfortunately, is not expected to diminish in the near future."

357. U.S. Bureau of the Census. *Statistical Abstract of the United States, 1998.*

358. Bennett T, Bhopal R. U.S. health journal editors' opinions and policies on research in race, ethnicity, and health. *Journal of the National Medical Association* 1998; 90:401–408.

359. Centers for Disease Control. Reporting race and ethnicity data; Bennett T, Bhopal R. U.S. health journal editors' opinions and policies on research in race, ethnicity, and health; Ethnicity, race, and culture: guidelines for research, audit, and publication. *British Medical Journal* 1996; 312:1094; McKenzie K, Crowcroft NS. Describing race, ethnicity and culture in medical research. *British Medical Journal* 1996; 312:1054; National Center for Health Statistics. *Prevention Profile. Health United States, 1991.*

360. U.S. Department of Health and Human Services. President Clinton announces new racial and ethnic health disparities initiative. USDHHS: President's Announcement, February 21, 1998; Satcher D. Meeting health challenges and setting priorities: An interview with U.S. Surgeon General, David Satcher, MD, PhD. *Journal of the National Medical Association* 1999; 91:191–192; "Eliminating Racial and Ethnic Disparities in Health: Overview," U.S. Department of Health and Human Services World Wide Web site (updated May 26, 1998; cited May 18, 1999) (data-base online). Washington, DC, pp. 1–6; "Goal 1—Eliminate Disparities in Infant Mortality Rates," U.S. Department of Health and Human Services World Wide Web site, pp. 1–3; "Goal 2—Eliminate Disparities in Cancer Screening and Management," U.S. Department of Health and Human Services World Wide Web site, pp. 1–4; "Goal 3—Eliminate Disparities in Cardiovascular Disease," U.S. Department of Health and Human Services World Wide Web site, pp. 1–3; "Goal 4—Eliminate Disparities in Diabetes," U.S. Department of Health and Human Services World Wide Web site, pp. 1–3; "Goal 5—Eliminate Disparities in HIV Infection/AIDS," U.S. Department of Health and Human Services World Wide Web site, pp. 1–3; "Goal 6—Eliminate Disparities in Child and Adult Immunization Rates," U.S. Department of Health and Human Services World Wide Web site, pp. 1–3; S.1880, *The Health Care Fairness Act of 1999.*

361. Lee PR, Benjamin AE, Weber MA. Policies and strategies for health in the United States, 309; Shafer BE. Exceptionalism in American politics? *Political Science and Politics* 1989; 22:588–594.

362. Lee PR, Benjamin AE, Weber MA. Policies and strategies for health in the United States, 310; Alford RR. *Health Care Politics, Ideological and Interest Group Barriers to Reform.* Chicago: University of Chicago Press, 1975.

363. Lee PR, Benjamin AE, Weber MA. Policies and strategies for health in the United States, 310.

364. U.S. Department of Health and Human Services. President Clinton announces new racial and ethnic health disparities initiative; Satcher D. Meeting health challenges and setting priorities: An interview with U.S. Surgeon General, David Satcher, MD, PhD; "Eliminating Racial and Ethnic Disparities in Health: Overview"; "Goal 1—Eliminate Disparities in Infant Mortality Rates"; "Goal 2—Eliminate Disparities in Cancer Screening and Management"; "Goal 3—Eliminate Disparities in Cardiovascular Disease"; "Goal 4—Eliminate Disparities in Diabete"; "Goal 5—Eliminate Disparities in HIV Infection/AIDS"; "Goal 6—Eliminate Disparities in Child and Adult Immunization Rates"; Lee PR, Benjamin AE, Weber MA. Policies and strategies for health in the United States; Fukuyama F. *Trust*; Sniderman PM, Piazza T. *The Scar of Race*; Simone TM. *About Face*; Feagin JR, Spikes MP. *Living with Racism*; Ryan W. *Blaming the Victim*; Steinberg S. *The*

*Ethnic Myth*; Lindblom CE. *Politics and Markets*. New York: Basic Books, 1977; Lindblom CE. The science of "muddling through"; Walker JL. The diffusion of knowledge, policy, communities and agenda setting; Navarro V. *Dangerous to Your Health*; Johnson H, Broder DS. *The System*; Skocpol T. *Boomerang*; Myrdal G. *An American Dilemma: The Negro Problem and Modern Democracy*. New York: Harper & Row, 1944; Shafer BE. Exceptionalism in American politics?; Alford RR. *Health Care Politics, Ideological and Interest Group Barriers to Reform*; U.S. Department of Health and Human Services. *The 1990 Health Objectives of the Nation: A Midcourse Review*; U.S. Department of Health and Human Services. *Healthy People 2000*; U.S. Department of Health and Human Services. *Healthy People 2000: Midcourse Review and 1995 Revisions*; Last JM, ed. *A Dictionary of Epidemiology*. 2nd ed. New York: Oxford University Press, for the International Epidemiological Association, 1988; Kochanek KD, Jeffrey DM, Rosenberg HM. Why did Black life expectancy decline from 1984 through 1989 in the United States?; Institute of Medicine. *Access to Health Care in America*; U.S. health report card shows room for improvement; Kozak LJ. Underreporting of race in the National Hospital Discharge Survey. *Advance Data from Vital and Health Statistics*, no. 265. Hyattsville, MD: National Center for Health Statistics. 1995; Hoyert DL. Effect on mortality rates of the 1989 change in tabulating race. National Center for Health Statistics. *Vital and Health Statistics* (20)25; 1994; Anderson RN, Rosenberg HM. Age standardization of death rates: Implementation of the year 2000 standard. *National Vital Statistics Reports*, 47(3). Hyattsville, MD: National Center for Health Statistics, 1998; Clinton WJ. Saturday Radio Address. Radio address by the president to the nation, February 21, 1998; U.S. Department of Health and Human Services. New web site links public to HHS initiative to eliminate racial, ethnic health disparities. *HHS News* July 1, 1998; U.S. Department of Health and Human Services. Elimination of racial and ethnic disparities in health: Overview. *USDHHS: Initiative Overview*, October 28, 1998; U.S. Department of Health and Human Services. President Clinton announces new racial and ethnic health disparities initiative.

## Chapter Eight

1. Lundberg GD. National health care reform: An aura of inevitability is upon us. *Journal of the American Medical Association* 1991; 265:2566–2567; Blendon RJ, Edwards JN, eds. *System in Crisis: The Case for Health Care Reform*. Vol. 1, *The Future of American Health Care*. New York: Faulkner and Gray, 1991; American Public Health Association. Managed competition: Wonder drug or snake oil? *The Nation's Health* March 1993; 23:1; Johnson H, Broder DS. *The System: The American Way of Politics at the Breaking Point*. Boston: Little, Brown, 1996; Skocpol T. *Boomerang: Health Care Reform and the Turn against Government*. New York: W. W. Norton, 1997.

2. Lundberg GD. National health care reform; Blendon RJ, Edwards JN, eds. *System in Crisis* (Vol. 1); American Public Health Association. Managed competition; Navarro V. *Dangerous to Your Health: Capitalism in Health Care*. New York: Monthly Review Press, 1993; Johnson H, Broder DS. *The System*; Skocpol T. *Boomerang*; Friedman E. The uninsured: From dilemma to crisis. *Journal of the American Medial Association* 1991; 265:2491–2495; Starr P. Healthy compromise: Universal coverage and managed competition under a cap. *The American Prospect*, Winter 1993; 12:44–52; Stanford University. Health Care in America: Armageddon on the Horizon? *Stanford Law and Policy Review* Fall 1991; 3:1–260; World Health Organization. *World Health Organization Statistics Annuals* (Vols. 1985–1990). Geneva, 1985–1990; Byrd WM, Clayton LA. "America's Dual Health Crisis in Black and White." Report prepared for hearings on *Health Care Reform: The African American Agenda*, held for the Congressional Black Caucus's Health Brain Trust, Congressman Louis Stokes, D-OH, Presiding, 103rd Congress, Special Session, Meeting Room, Cannon House Office Building, Tuesday, April 13, 1993, Washington, DC.

3. Byrd WM, Clayton LA. An American health dilemma: A history of blacks in the health system. *Journal of the National Medical Association* 1992; 84:189–200; Greenberg DS. Black health: Grim statistics. *The Lancet* 1990; 355:780–781; Byrd WM, Clayton LA. *A Black Health Trilogy* (videotape and 188-page documentary report). Washington, DC: The National Medical Association and the African American Heritage and Education Foundation; 1991; Charatz-Litt C. A chronicle of racism: The effects of the white medical community on black health. *Journal of the National Medical Association* 1992; 84:717–725; Byrd WM, Clayton LA. *An American Health*

*Dilemma* (Vol. 1, A *Medical History of African Americans and the Problem of Race: Beginnings to 1900*). New York: Routledge, 2000; Feagin JR. *Racist America*. New York: Routledge, 2000; Feagin JR, Vera H. *White Racism: The Basics*. New York: Routledge, 1995; Van Ausdale D, Feagin JR. *The First R: How Children Learn Race and Racism*. Lanham, MD: Rowman and Littlefield, 2001; Gordon LR. *Her Majesty's Other Children: Sketches of Racism from a Neo-colonial Age*. Lanham, MD: Rowman and Littlefield, 1997; Williams DR. Race, socioeconomic status, and health: The added effects of racism and discrimination. *Annals of the New York Academy of Sciences* 1999; 896:173–188.

4. Greenberg DS. Black health; Thomas VG. Explaining health disparities between African-American and white populations: Where do we go from here? *Journal of the National Medical Association* 1992; 84:837–840.

5. Chase A. *The Legacy of Malthus: The Social Costs of the New Scientific Racism*. New York: Knopf, 1980; Churchill LR. *Rationing Health Care in America: Perceptions and Principles of Justice*. Notre Dame, IN: University of Notre Dame Press, 1987, 79–82; Churchill L. *Self-Interest and Universal Health Care: Why Well-Insured Americans Should Support Coverage for Everyone*. Cambridge, MA: Harvard University Press, 1994, 9; Ryan W. *Blaming the Victim*. New York: Vintage Books, 1971; Revised, updated ed. New York: Vintage Books, 1976; Dowling HF. *City Hospitals: The Undercare of the Underprivileged*. Cambridge, MA: Harvard University Press, 1982; Byrd WM, Clayton LA. An American health dilemma; Charatz-Litt C. A chronicle of racism; Smith DB. *Health Care Divided: Race and Healing a Nation*. Ann Arbor: University of Michigan Press, 1999; Katz MB. *In the Shadow of the Poorhouse: A Social History of Welfare in America*. New York: Basic Books, 1986; revised and updated ed., 1996, ix–113; Byrd WM, Clayton LA. *An American Health Dilemma* (Vol. 1).

6. Byrd WM, Clayton LA. "America's Dual Health Crisis in Black and White"; Navarro V. *Dangerous to Your Health*; Eckholm E, ed. *Solving America's Health-Care Crisis*. New York: Times Books, Random House, 1993, 301–314; Churchill L. *Self-Interest and Universal Health Care*; Skocpol T. *Boomerang*; Byrd WM. Race, biology, and health care: Reassessing a relationship. *Journal of Health Care for the Poor and Underserved* 1990; 1:278–292; Byrd WM, Clayton LA. An American health dilemma; Morais HM. *The History of the Negro in Medicine*. New York: Publishers Company, 1967; Cobb WM. The Black American in medicine. *Journal of the National Medical Association* 1981; 73 (Suppl 1):1183–1244; Smith, DB. *Health Care Divided*; Quinn JB. The invisible uninsured: Congress fiddles while rising numbers of Americans lose their access to medical care. *Newsweek* March 1, 1999: 49; Malone TE, Johnson KW. *Report of the Secretary's Task Force on Black and Minority Health*. Washington, DC: U.S. Department of Health and Human Services, 1986; Health Policy Advisory Center. The emerging health apartheid in the United States. *Health/PAC Bulletin* 1991; 21:3–4; Braithwaite RL, Taylor SE, eds. *Health Issues in the Black Community*. San Francisco: Jossey-Bass, 1992; Livingston IL, ed. *Handbook of Black American Health: The Mosaic of Conditions, Issues, Policies, and Prospects*. Westport, CT: Greenwood Press, 1994; Edwards WS. *National Medical Expenditure Survey: Questionnaires and Data Collection Methods for the United States Population*. Rockville, MD: U.S. Department of Health and Human Services, Agency for Health Care Policy and Research: 1989 (DHHS Pub. PHY 89–3440); Cornelius LJ. Limited access to health care continues in minority groups. *National Medical Association News* March/April, 1993: 1; Byrd WM, Clayton LA. *A Black Health Trilogy*; Elkowitz A. Physicians at the bedside: Thoughts and actions with regard to health care allocation. *Journal of the National Medical Association* 1986; 78:423–427; Schulman KA et al. The effect of race and sex on physician recommendations for cardiac catheterization. *New England Journal of Medicine* 1999; 340:618–626; Charatz-Litt C. A chronicle of racism; Greenberg DS. Black health; Thomas VG. Explaining health disparities between African-American and white populations; Dowling HF. *City Hospitals*; Katz MB. *In the Shadow of the Poorhouse*; Chase A. *The Legacy of Malthus*.

7. Greenberg DS. Black health; Smith DB. *Health Care Divided*; Byrd WM, Clayton LA. *An American Health Dilemma* (Vol. 1); Jones JH. *Bad Blood: The Tuskegee Syphilis Experiment*. New York: The Free Press, 1981, new and expanded ed., 1993; Byrd WM, Clayton LA. An American health dilemma; Byrd WM, Clayton LA. *A Black Health Trilogy*; Charatz-Litt C. A chronicle of racism; Byrd WM, Clayton LA. "America's Dual Health Crisis in Black and White"; Elkowitz A. Physicians at the bedside; Schulman KA et al. The effect of race and sex on physician recommendations for cardiac catheterization.

8. Geiger HJ. Comment: Ethnic cleansing in the groves of academe. *American Journal of Pub-*

*lic Health* 1998; 88:1299–1300; Shea S, Fullilove MT. Entry of black and other minority students in US medical schools: Historical perspectives and recent trends. *New England Journal of Medicine* 1985; 313:933–940; Smith DB. *Health Care Divided*; Byrd WM, Clayton LA. *An American Health Dilemma* (Vol. 1); Kovner AR, Jonas S, eds. *Jonas and Kovner's Health Care Delivery in the United States*. 6th ed. New York: Springer, 1999, 64–115; Hanft RS, Fishman LE, Evans W. *Blacks and the Health Professions in the 80s: A National Crisis and a Time for Action*. N.P.: Prepared for the Association of Minority Health Professions Schools, 1983; Hanft RS, Fishman LE, White CC. "Minorities and the Health Professions: An Update." Draft of August 1985, Association of Minority Health Professions Schools, Washington, DC; Hanft RS, White CC. Constraining the supply of physicians: Effects on black physicians. In: Willis DP, ed. *Health Policies and Black Americans*. Brunswick, NJ: Transaction Publishers, 1989, 249–269; Ukawuilulu JO, Livingston IL. Black health care providers and related professionals: Issues of underrepresentation and change. In: Livingston IL, ed. *Handbook of Black American Health*, 344–360; Washington HA. Political realities hit medical school rolls. *Emerge* March 1998; (5)(9):22.

9. Harding S. Eurocentric scientific illiteracy—a challenge for the world community. In: Harding S, ed. *The "Racial Economy" of Science: Toward a Democratic Future*. Bloomington: Indiana University Press, 1993, 1–22; Geiger HJ. Comment; Geiger HJ. Annotation: Racism resurgent—building a bridge to the 19th century. *American Journal of Public Health* 1997; 87:1765–1766; Chase A. *The Legacy of Malthus*; Duster T. *Backdoor to Eugenics*. New York: Routledge, 1990; Nelkin D, Tancredi L. *Dangerous Diagnostics: The Social Power of Biological Information*. New York: Basic Books, 1989; Lewontin RC, Rose S, Kamin LJ. *Not in Our Genes: Biology, Ideology, and Human Nature*. New York: Pantheon Books, 1984; Reynolds V, Falger V, Vine I, eds. *The Sociobiology of Ethnocentrism: Evolutionary Dimensions of Xenophobia, Discrimination, Racism and Nationalism*. London: Croom Helm, 1987; Washington HA. Genetic research might engineer genocide. *Emerge* March 1994; (6)(5):19; Herrnstein RJ, Murray C. *The Bell Curve: Intelligence and Class Structure in American Life*. New York: The Free Press, 1994; Washington HA. Straightening out *The Bell Curve*: An old IQ argument gets a new airing. *Emerge* January 1995; (3)(6):28.

10. Schulman KA et al. The effect of race and sex on physician recommendations for cardiac catheterization; Elkowitz A. Physicians at the bedside; Dula A. Toward an African-American perspective on bioethics. *Journal of Health Care for the Poor and Underserved* 1991; 2:259–269; Charatz-Litt C. A chronicle of racism; Ayanian JI, Cleary PD, Weissman JS, Epstein AN. The effects of patients' preferences on racial differences in access to renal transplantation. *New England Journal of Medicine* 1999; 341:1661–1669.

11. Washington HA. Medicine's mainstream overlooks Blacks. *Emerge* May 1996; (7)(7):22; Hunter C, et al. Selection factors in clinical trials: Results from the community clinical oncology program physician's patient log. *Cancer Treatment Reports* 1987; 71:559–565; Geiger HJ. Annotation; Geiger HJ. Comment; Hubbard R, Wald E. *Exploding the Gene Myth: How Genetic Information Is Produced and Manipulated by Scientists, Physicians, Employers, Insurance Companies, Educators, and Law Enforcers*. Boston: Beacon Press, 1993; Chase A. *The Legacy of Malthus*; Duster T. *Backdoor to Eugenics*; Lewontin RC, Rose S, Kamin LJ. *Not in Our Genes*; Herrnstein RJ, Murray C. *The Bell Curve*; Washington HA. Straightening out *The Bell Curve*; Lemann N. *The Big Test: The Secret History of the American Meritocracy*. New York: Farrar, Strauss, and Giroux, 1999; Lemann N. The structure of success in America: The untold story of how educational testing became ambition's gateway—and a national obsession. *The Atlantic Monthly* August 1995; (2)(276):41; Lemann N. The great sorting: The first mass administrations of a scholastic-aptitude test led with surprising speed to the idea that the nation's leaders would be the people who did well on tests. *The Atlantic Monthly* September 1995; (3)(276):84; Jacoby R, Blauberman N, eds. *The Bell Curve Debate: History, Documents, Opinions*. New York: Times Books, 1995; Fraser S, ed. *The Bell Curve Wars: Race, Intelligence, and the Future of America*. New York: Basic Books, 1995; DeParle J. Daring research or 'social science pornography'? *New York Times Magazine* October 9, 1994: Section 6, 48; Stringer C, McKie R. *African Exodus: The Origins of Modern Humanity*. London: Jonathan Cape, 1996, first American ed. New York: Henry Holt, 1997.

12. Cobb WM. The Black American in medicine; Charatz-Litt C. A chronicle of racism; Morais HM. *The History of the Negro in Medicine*; Byrd WM, Clayton LA. An American health dilemma; Smith DB. *Health Care Divided*; Byrd WM, Clayton LA. *An American Health Dilemma* (Vol. 1); Byrd WM et al. African-American physicians' views on health reform: Preliminary results

of a survey. *Journal of the National Medical Association* 1994; 86:93–94; Byrd WM et al. African-American physicians' views on health reform: Results of a survey. *Journal of the National Medical Association* 1994; 86:191–199; Byrd WM. Inquisition, peer review, and black physician survival. *Journal of the National Medical Association* 1987; 79:1027–1029; Wolinsky H. Healing wounds: Lonnie R. Bristow steps up to head the American Medical Association, one of the nation's premier—and most rigidly segregated—professional groups. *Emerge* July/August 1994; (10)(5):42; Byrd WM, Clayton LA, McCoy SP, Calliste GJ. Access to health care: Provision by the major health reform proposals. Policy memorandum prepared for the Congressional Black Caucus Foundation, March 26, 1994; Byrd WM, Clayton LA. "The American Health Dilemma Continues: An Analysis of the Clinton Health Plan From An African American and Disadvantaged Patient Perspective." Report prepared for the National Medical Association and the Congressional Black Caucus, Harvard School of Public Health, submitted October 27, 1993.

13. Greenberg DS. Black health; Jones JH. *Bad Blood*; Charatz-Litt C. A chronicle of racism; Byrd WM, Clayton LA. "America's Dual Health Crisis in Black and White"; Navarro V. *Dangerous to Your Health*; Smith DB. *Health Care Divided*; Byrd WM, Clayton LA. *An American Health Dilemma* (Vol. 1); Shea S, Fullilove MT. Entry of black and other minority students in U.S. medical schools; Hanft RS, Fishman LE, Evans W. *Blacks and the Health Professions in the '80s*; Hanft RS, Fishman LE, White CC. "Minorities and the Health Professions"; Hanft RS, White CC. Constraining the supply of physicians; Ukawuilulu JO, Livingston IL. Black health care providers and related professionals; Washington HA. Political realities hit medical school rolls; Hunter C, et al. Selection factors in clinical trials; Washington HA. Medicine's mainstream overlooks Blacks; Anders G. *Health against Wealth: HMOs and the Breakdown of Medical Trust*. Boston: Houghton Mifflin, 1996; Lemann N. *The Big Test*; Guthrie RV. *Even the Rat Was White: A Historical View of Psychology*. 2nd ed. Boston: Allyn and Bacon, 1998; Lemann N. The structure of success in America; Lemann N. The great sorting; Lewontin RC, Rose S, Kamin LJ. *Not in Our Genes*; Stringer C, McKie R. *African Exodus*; Harding S, ed. *The "Racial Economy" of Science*; Jaynes GD, Williams RM, eds. *A Common Destiny: Blacks and American Society*. Washington, DC: National Academy Press, 1989; Byrd WM. An American health dilemma. *Journal of the National Medical Association* 1986; 78:1025–1026.

14. Navarro V. *Dangerous to Your Health*, 12.

15. Hey RP. Last-ditch reform effort fails. *AARP Bulletin* October 1994: 1.

16. Navarro V. *Dangerous to Your Health*; Skocpol T. *Boomerang*; Johnson H, Broder DS. *The System*; Byrd WM, Clayton LA. "The American Health Dilemma Continues."

17. Simms PB. "National Leadership Summit on Health Care Reform: Structure and Administration." Discussion paper for initial board meeting of Summit '93: African American Prescription for Health, Washington, DC, March 29, 1993; Summit '93: African American Prescription for Health. "Summit Policy Paper." Washington Vista Hotel, Washington, DC, May 2–3, 1993; Byrd WM, Clayton LA. CBC analysis and response to "Managed Competition" model health reform (bibliographed version), A health policy memorandum generated for the Congressional Black Caucus, Harvard School of Public Health, Boston, Massachusetts, submitted May 16, 1993; Burchette-Pierce C, et al. Minority Health Care Review Group: Executive Summary. Working paper, National Medical Association/Congressional Black Caucus Foundation, Inc. project on health reform, June 7–9, 1993, Washington, DC; *Summit '93: African American Prescription for Health*. Proceedings of a conference on African American and disadvantaged population health and health-care co-convened by the National Medical Association and the Congressional Black Caucus Foundation, Vista International Hotel, May 2–3, 1993, Washington, DC: National Medical Association and Congressional Black Caucus Foundation, Inc., 1993; Byrd WM, Clayton LA, McCoy SP, Calliste GJ. Access to health care.

18. Byrd WM, Clayton LA. "The American Health Dilemma Continues," 3.

19. Navarro V. *Dangerous to Your Health*; Eckholm E, ed. *Solving America's Health-Care Crisis*, 301–314; Skocpol T. *Boomerang*; Johnson H, Broder DS. *The System*; Byrd WM, Clayton LA. CBC analysis and response to "Managed Competition" model health reform (bibliographed version); Clayton LA, Byrd WM. Report prepared for hearings and submitted into the *Congressional Record* on "Health Care Reform: What Does It Mean to African Americans," held for the Congressional Black Caucus Health Braintrust, 103rd Congress, Congressman Louis Stokes, D-OH, Presiding, Rayburn House Office Building, Room 2175, Washington, DC, September 16, 1993;

Jackson Hole Group (Paul Ellwood, Alain Enthoven, and Lynn Etheredge). *The 21st Century American Health System* (Jackson Hole, WY), 1991–1992 (Series of policy documents); Byrd WM, Clayton LA. "Minority Health Issues for Health Care Reform." Report prepared for hearings on *Minority Health Issues for Health Care Reform*, held for the Senate Human Resources Committee, Senator Edward Kennedy, Massachusetts, Presiding, 103rd Congress, Special Session at Harvard School of Public Health, February 19, 1993, Boston, Massachusetts; Byrd WM, Clayton LA. "America's Dual Health Crisis in Black and White"; Simms PB. "National Leadership Summit on Health Care Reform"; Burchette-Pierce C, et al. Minority Health Care Review Group; *Summit '93*; Byrd WM, Clayton LA, McCoy SP, Calliste GJ. Access to health care; Byrd WM, Clayton LA. "Designing a New Health Care System for the United States," Boston: Harvard School of Public Health, 1992; Byrd WM, Clayton LA. "The American Health Dilemma Continues."

20. Cobb WM. The Black American in medicine; Morais HM. *The History of the Negro in Medicine*; Byrd WM, Clayton LA. An American health dilemma; Byrd WM, Clayton LA. The "slave health deficit": Racism and health outcomes. *Health/PAC Bulletin* 1991; 21:25–28; Byrd WM, Clayton LA. *An American Health Dilemma* (Vol. 1)

21. U.S. Congress, House. *The American Health Security Act of 1993*. 103rd Congress, 1st session, H.R. 1200. *Congressional Record*. March 3, 1993; Blendon RJ, Hyams TS, eds. *Reforming the System: Containing Health Care Costs in an Era of Universal Coverage* (Vol. 2, *The Future of American Health Care*). New York: Faulkner and Gray, 1991; Kronick R, Gilmer T. Explaining the decline in health insurance coverage, 1979–1995. *Health Affairs* 1999; 18(2):30–47.

22. Blendon RJ, Edwards JN, eds. *System in Crisis (Vol. 1)*.

23. Sager A, Socolar D, Ford D, Brand R. More care, at less cost. *Boston Sunday Globe* April 25, 1999: C1; Knox RA. HMO's creator urges reform in quality of care. *Boston Sunday Globe* May 2, 1999: A1; U.S. Congress, House. *The American Health Security Act of 1993*; Blendon RJ, Benson JM. Editorial: Whatever happened to the politicians' concerns about the nation's uninsured? *American Journal of Public Health* 1998; 88:345–346; Blendon RJ, Hyams TS, eds. *Reforming the System* (Vol. 2); Blendon RJ, Edwards JN, eds. *System in Crisis (Vol. 1)*; Kronick R, Gilmer T. Explaining the decline in health insurance coverage, 1979–1995; Cray E. *In Failing Health: The Medical Crisis and the A.M.A.* Indianapolis: Bobbs-Merrill, 1970; Churchill LR. *Self-Interest and Universal Health Care*; Mullen F, Lundberg G. Looking back, looking forward: Straight talk about U.S. medicine. *Health Affairs* 2000; 19:117–123; Lindorf D. *Marketplace Medicine: The Rise of For-Profit Hospital Chains*. New York: Bantam Books, 1992; Anders G. *Health against Wealth*; Califano Jr. JA. *America's Health Care Revolution: Who Lives? Who Dies? Who Pays?* New York: Random House, 1986; Sardell A. *The U.S. Experiment in Social Medicine: The Community Health Center Program, 1956–1986.* Pittsburgh: The University of Pittsburgh Press, 1988; Dickman RL et al. An end to patchwork reform of health care. *New England Journal of Medicine* 1987; 317:1086–1089; Skocpol T. *Boomerang*; Numbers RL. *Almost Persuaded: American Physicians and Compulsory Health Insurance, 1912–1920.* Baltimore: Johns Hopkins University Press, 1978; Campion FD. *The AMA and U.S. Health Policy since 1940.* Chicago: Chicago Review Press for the American Medical Association, 1984; Navarro V. *Dangerous to Your Health*; Johnson H, Broder DS. *The System*.

24. Gressin S et al., eds. Health care in America: Armageddon on the horizon? *Stanford Law and Policy Review* 1991; 3:1–260; Byrd WM, Clayton LA. "Designing a New Health Care System for the United States"; Byrd WM. "Widening Racial Health Disparities: A Continuum." Presentation in Turning Back the Clock: Widening Health Differentials in Urban Areas, sponsored by Medical Care Forum on Bioethics, American Public Health Association, 120th Annual Meeting and Exhibition, Washington, DC, November 9, 1992; Hairston GE, Byrd WM. Medical care in America: A tragic turn for the worst. *The Crisis* October 1985; 92:25; Kotelchuck R. Down and out in the "New Calcutta": New York City's health care crisis. *Health/PAC Bulletin* Summer 1989; 19:4–11; American Medical Association. Caring for the uninsured and the underinsured: A compendium from the specialty journals of the American Medical Association. *Journal of the American Medical Association* 1991; 265(suppl):1–163; Roberts MJ, Clyde AT. *Your Money or Your Life: The Health Care Crisis Explained.* New York: Doubleday, 1993.

25. *The Boston Globe* Dialogues: Health care. Will care be there? Cost, compassion compete for center stage in health reform debate. *Boston Sunday Globe* June 1, 1997: C2; Daniel M. Health center's bankruptcy puts neighborhood care at risk. *Boston Sunday Globe* January 31, 1999: 6.

26. Former "Wild Kingdom" star rounds up medical care for poor: In Appalachia, patients, pets given treatment and compassion. *Boston Sunday Globe* October 18, 1998: A25; Janofsky M. West Virginia pares welfare, but poor remain. *New York Times* March 7, 1999: 14.

27. U.S. Congress, House. *The American Health Security Act of 1993*; Sager A, Socolar D, Ford D, Brand R. More care, at less cost; Knox RA. HMO's creator urges reform in quality of care; Gressin S et al., eds. Health care in America; Byrd WM. "Widening Racial Health Disparities"; History shows trends of African Americans' high mortality rates and poor health care. *National Medical Association News* March/April, 1993; 1; Byrd WM, Clayton LA. "America's Dual Health Crisis in Black and White"; Kotelchuck R. Down and out in the "New Calcutta"; American Medical Association. Caring for the uninsured and the underinsured; Health Policy Advisory Center. The emerging health apartheid in the United States; McKenzie N, Bilofsky E. Shredding the safety net: The dismantling of public programs. *Health/PAC Bulletin* 1991; 21:5–11; Gray BH, Rowe C. Safety-net health plans: A status report. *Health Affairs* 2000; 19:185–193; Kamal RD, Lukan CD, Young GJ. Public hospitals: Privatization and uncompensated care. *Health Affairs* 2000; 19:167–184; Quinn JB. Health plans: Not always safe. *Newsweek* August 14, 2000: 39; Roberts MJ, Clyde AT. *Your Money or Your Life*; Hairston GE, Byrd WM. Medical care in America; Wilson WJ. *The Truly Disadvantaged: The Inner City, the Underclass, and Public Policy*. Chicago: The University of Chicago Press, 1987; Wilson WJ. *When Work Disappears: The World of the New Urban Poor*. New York: Knopf, 1996; Anders G. HMOs pile up billions in cash, try to decide what to do with it. *Wall Street Journal* December 21, 1994: 1; Anders G. Who pays the cost of cut-rate heart care? *Wall Street Journal* October 15, 1996: B1, B8; Abelson R. For managed care, free-market shock. *New York Times* January 3, 1999: Section 4, 4; Eckholm E. While Congress remains silent health care transforms itself. *New York Times* December 18, 1994: 1; Kolata G. AIDS patients slipping through safety net: Soaring costs of drugs strains the budgets of programs and patients. *New York Times* September 15, 1996: 24; Freudenheim M. Consumers across the nation are facing sharp increases in health care costs in 2001. *New York Times* December 10, 2000: 40; Rosenbaum DE. Swallow hard: What if there is no cure for health care's ills? *New York Times* December 10, 2000: Section 4, 1; Kong D. Seeking a safety net. *Boston Sunday Globe* July 16, 2000: H4; Winter G. Cuts in loan program squeeze doctors who work with poor. *New York Times* July 30, 2000: 1.

28. Lee PR, Benjamin AE, Weber MA. Policies and strategies for health in the United States. In: Detels R, Holland WW, McEwen J, Omenn GS, eds. *Oxford Textbook of Public Health* (Vol. 1, *The Scope of Public Health*). 3rd ed. New York: Oxford University Press, 1997, 298.

29. Lee PR, Benjamin AE, Weber MA. Policies and strategies for health in the United States, 297–321; Bunker JP, Frazier HS, Mosteller F. Improving health: Measuring effects of medical care. *Milbank Quarterly* 1994; 2:247.

30. Prevention, early diagnosis seen as keys to controlling breast and cervical cancer. *National Medical Association News* November/December 1992; 1, 2.

31. Byrd WM. An American health dilemma, 1026.

32. Byrd WM. An American health dilemma, 1026.

33. Jones EI. Closing the health status gap for Blacks and other minorities. *Journal of the National Medical Association* 1985; 78:485–488, 485; Hart N. The social and economic environment and human health. In: Detels R, Holland WW, McEwen J, Omenn GS, eds. *Oxford Textbook of Public Health* (Vol. 1), 95–123; Lee PR, Benjamin AE, Weber MA. Policies and strategies for health in the United States; Byrd WM. An American health dilemma; Byrd WM. Race, biology, and health care; Byrd WM, Clayton LA. An American health dilemma; Byrd WM, Clayton LA. *An American Health Dilemma* (Vol. 1); Bunker JP, Frazier HS, Mosteller F. Improving health; Health Policy Advisory Center. The emerging health apartheid in the United States.

34. Lawton RB, Cacciamani J, Clement J, Acquino W. The fall of the house of AHERF: The Allegheny bankruptcy. *Health Affairs* 2000; 19:7–41; McCall T, Gordon S. Profits, not patients, threaten HMOs. *Boston Sunday Globe* August 2, 1998: C4; Abelson R. For managed care, free-market shock; Meyer M. Oh no, here we go again: Health care costs are soaring—and companies are passing the increases along to their workers. *Newsweek* December 14, 1998: 46–47; Kilborn PT. Analysts expect health premiums to rise sharply. *New York Times* October 19, 1997: 1; Fisher I. H.M.O. premiums rising sharply, stoking debate on managed care. *New York Times* January 11, 1998: 1; Smothers R, Drew C. Failed H.M.O. reveals flaws in industry: Lack of oversight is found in managed care's financial dealings. *New York Times* December 27, 1998: 30; Kilborn PT. Oregon falters on a new path to health care: State officials rethink rationing for the poor. *New York Times*

January 3, 1999: 1; Freudenheim M. Consumers across the nation are facing sharp increases in health care costs in 2001; Rosenbaum DE. Swallow hard; Garrett L. *Betrayal of Trust*; Quinn JB. Health plans; Pear R. Government lags in steps to widen health coverage: Uninsured at 41 million. *New York Times* August 9, 1998: 1.

35. Satcher D. "The Settlement: Will the African-American Community Pay the Bill?" Address delivered at Roxbury Community College Media Arts Center, Roxbury, Massachusetts, Monday, April 12, 1999.

36. Abelson R. For managed care, free-market shock; Freudenheim M. Consumers across the nation are facing sharp increases in health care costs in 2001; Rosenbaum DE. Swallow hard; Garrett L. *Betrayal of Trust*; Quinn JB. Health plans; Meyer M. Oh no, here we go again; Kilborn PT. Analysts expect health premiums to rise sharply; Fisher I. H.M.O. premiums rising sharply, stoking debate on managed care; Smothers R, Drew C. Failed H.M.O. reveals flaws in industry; Kilborn PT. Oregon falters on a new path to health care; Pear R. Government lags in steps to widen health coverage; Wright R. The technology time bomb. *The New Republic* 208 (March 29, 1993): 25–30; Kronick R, Gilmer T. Explaining the decline in health insurance coverage, 1979–1995; Ginzberg E. High-tech medicine and rising health care costs. *Journal of the American Medical Association* 1990; 263:1820–1822; Ginzberg E. High-tech medicine. In: Ginzberg E. *The Medical Triangle: Physicians, Politicians, and the Public*. Cambridge, MA: Harvard University Press, 1990, 41–53, Gressin S et al. eds., Health care in America; Blendon RJ, Edwards JN, eds. *System in Crisis (Vol. 1)*; Churchill LR. *Self-Interest and Universal Health Care*; Lindorf D. *Marketplace Medicine*; Anders G. *Health against Wealth*; Lundberg GD. National health care reform.

37. Gold D. Hospital establishes barter system to help underinsured: Contract for care will allow patients to pay off bills. *Boston Sunday Globe* March 15, 1998: C9.

38. Greenberg DS. Black health; Hairston GE, Byrd WM. Medical care in America; American Public Health Association. Managed competition; Fuchs VR. *The Future of Health Policy*. Cambridge, MA: Harvard University Press, 1993; Fuchs VR. *The Health Economy*. Cambridge, MA: Harvard University Press, 1986; Pear R. Insurers ask government to extend health plans. *New York Times* May 23, 1999: 16; Quinn JB. Health plans; Reinhardt U. *Medical Economics* 1996 (January, No. 1); 15:29; Ginzberg E. *The Medical Triangle: Physicians, Politicians, and the Public*; Navarro V. *Dangerous to Your Health*; Roberts MJ, Clyde AT. *Your Money or Your Life*; Wilson WJ. *The Truly Disadvantaged*; Wilson WJ. *When Work Disappears*; Pear R. Government lags in steps to widen health coverage; Kronick R, Gilmer T. Explaining the decline in health insurance coverage, 1979–1995; Rogers DE. Who needs Medicaid? *New England Journal of Medicine* 1982; 307:13–18; Passell P. Benefits dwindle along with wages for the unskilled: Even less for have nots: What was seen as an equalizer has instead contributed to a growing disparity. *New York Times* June 14, 1998: 1; Baquet D, Fritsch J. New York's public hospitals fail, and babies are the victims. *New York Times* March 5, 1995: 1; Toner R. Gore and Bush health proposals fall short of counterparts' plans 8 years ago. *New York Times* October 15, 2000: 22; Andrulis DP, Carrier B. *Managed Care in the Inner City*. San Fransico: Josey-Bass, 1999; Sager A, Socolar D, Ford D, Brand R. More care, at less cost; Knox RA. HMO's creator urges reform in quality of care.

39. Cornely PB. Health planning in the U.S.: Is it a myth? *Journal of the National Medical Association* 1984; 76: 1071–1074; Starr P. *The Social Transformation of American Medicine*. New York: Basic Books, 1982; Brown ER. *Rockefeller Medicine Men: Medicine and Capitalism in America*. Berkeley: University of California Press, 1979; Garrett L. *Betrayal of Trust*; Hairston GE, Byrd WM. Medical care in America; Navarro V. *Dangerous to Your Health*; Woolhandler S, Himmelstein DU. *The National Health Program Chartbook* (chartbook and slideshow, 1992 ed.). Cambridge, MA: Center for National Health Program Studies, 1992; Woolhandler S, Himmelstein DU. *For Our Patients, Not for Profits: A Call to Action* (chartbook and slideshow, 1998 ed.). Cambridge, MA: Center for National Health Program Studies, 1998; Bodenheimer T. Should we abolish the private health insurance industry? *International Journal of Health Services* 1990; 20:199–219; Bogdanich W. *The Great White Lie: Dishonesty, Waste, and Incompetence in the Medical Community*. New York: Simon & Schuster, 1991; Whol S. *The Medical Industrial Complex*. New York: Harmony Books, 1984; Sager A, Socolar D, Ford D, Brand R. More care, at less cost; Kong D. Seeking a safety net; Pear R. Cash to ensure health coverage for poor goes unused. *New York Times* May 21, 2000: 18; Knutson LL. Clinton decries drug markup: Says Medicare losing billions. *Boston Sunday Globe* December 14, 1997: A2; Sidel VW, Sidel R, eds. *Reforming Medicine: Lessons of the Last Quarter*

*Century*. New York: Pantheon Books, 1984; Campion FD. *The AMA and U.S. Health Policy since 1940*; Byrd WM, Clayton LA. *A Black Health Trilogy*.

40. Ginzberg E. A life in health policy. *Health Affairs* 2000; 19: 239–244, 244.

41. Smith A. *The Wealth of Nations*. New York: Modern Library, 1937, 105; Arrow KJ. Uncertainty and the welfare economics of medical care. *The American Economic Review* 1963; 53:941–973; Fuchs VR. *The Health Economy*, 17–31; Aaron HJ. *Serious and Unstable Condition: Financing America's Health Care*. Washington, DC: The Brookings Institution, 1991, 8–37; Stoline A, Weiner JP. *The New Medical Marketplace: A Physician's Guide to the Health Care Revolution*. Baltimore: Johns Hopkins University Press, 1988, 47–53; Starr P. *The Social Transformation of American Medicine*.

42. Friedman E. "The Human Factor: The Effect of Emerging Models of Competition on Patients and the Public." Presented at the Robert Wood Johnson Foundation/Alpha Center Conference on Rethinking Competition in Health Care, Washington, DC, January 7–8, 1993; Byrd WM, Clayton LA. An American health dilemma; California Physicians Alliance. Managed competition versus single-payer health insurance reform: How do they compare? San Francisco: California Physicians Alliance, April 21, 1991; Randall VR. Does Clinton's health care reform proposal ensure (e)qual(ity) of health care for ethnic Americans and the poor? *Brooklyn Law Review* 1994 (Spring, No. 1); 60:167–237; Woolhandler S, Himmelstein DU. *The National Health Program Chartbook*; Woolhandler S, Himmelstein DU. *For Our Patients, Not for Profits*; Andrulis DP, Carrier B. *Managed Care in the Inner City*; Brandon RM, Podhorzer M, Pollak TH. Premiums without benefits: Waste and inefficiency in the commercial health insurance industry. *International Journal of Health Services* 1991; 21:265–283; Fuchs VR. *The Health Economy*; Fuchs VR. *The Future of Health Policy*; Sardell A. *The U.S. Experiment in Social Medicine*; Sidel VW, Sidel R, eds. *Reforming Medicine*.

43. Smith A. *The Wealth of Nations*, 105; Arrow KJ. Uncertainty and the welfare economics of medical care; Fuchs VR. *The Health Economy*, 17–31; Fuchs VR. *The Future of Health Policy*; Aaron HJ. *Serious and Unstable Condition*, 8–37; Andrulis DP, Carrier B. *Managed Care in the Inner City*; Stoline A, Weiner JP. *The New Medical Marketplace*, 47–53; Starr P. *The Social Transformation of American Medicine*; American Public Health Association. Managed competition; Judis JB. Whose managed competition? *The New Republic* 208 (March 29, 1993):20–24; Friedman E. "The Human Factor: The Effect of Emerging Models of Competition on Patients and the Public"; California Physicians Alliance. Managed competition versus single-payer health insurance reform; Randall VR. Does Clinton's health care reform proposal ensure (e)qual(ity) of health care for ethnic Americans and the poor?; Kronick R, Gilmer T. Explaining the decline in health insurance coverage, 1979–1995; Byrd WM, Clayton LA. An American health dilemma; Brandon RM, Podhorzer M, Pollak TH. Premiums without benefits; Sardell A. *The U.S. Experiment in Social Medicine*; Sidel VW, Sidel R, eds. *Reforming Medicine*; Woolhandler S, Himmelstein DU. *The National Health Program Chartbook*; Woolhandler S, Himmelstein DU. *For Our Patients, Not for Profits*; Evans RG. Going for the gold: The redistributive agenda behind market-based health care reform. *Journal of Health Politics, Policy and Law* 1997; 22:21–22; Higgins W. Myths of competitive reform. *Health Care Management Review* 1991; 16:65–72; Navarro V. *Dangerous to Your Health*; Sager A, Socolar D, Ford D, Brand R. More care, at less cost; Knox RA. HMO's creator urges reform in quality of care.

44. Jackson Hole Group (Paul Ellwood, Alain Enthoven, and Lynn Etheredge). *The 21st Century American Health System*; U.S. Congress, House. *Managed Competition Act of 1993*. 103rd Congress, 2d session, H.R. 3222. *Congressional Record*. October 6, 1993; Conyers Jr J. Principles of health care reform: An African-American perspective. *Journal of Health Care for the Poor and Underserved* 1993; 4:1–8; Kovel J. *White Racism: A Psychohistory*. New York: Random House, 1970, Reprint ed. New York: Columbia University Press, 1984; Kongstvedt PR. *The Managed Health Care Handbook*. 2nd ed. Gaithersburg, MD: Aspen Publishers, 1993, 9; Malone TE, Johnson KW. *Report of the Secretary's Task Force on Black and Minority Health*; Greenberg DS. Black health; Pear R. Big health gap tied to income is found in U.S. *New York Times* July 8, 1993: A1; Omi M, Winant H. *Racial Formation in the United States: From the 1960s to the 1990s*. 2nd ed. New York: Routledge, 1994; Feagin JR. *Racist America*; Feagin JR, Vera H. *White Racism*; Van Ausdale D, Feagin JR. *The First R*; Gordon LR. *Her Majesty's Other Children*; Williams DR. Race, socioeconomic status, and health; Cobb WM. The Black American in medicine; Byrd WM, Clayton LA. An American health dilemma; Amidei NJ, Russell JSQ, Newman DK. Second Class Medicine. In: Newman

DK, et al. *Protest, Politics, and Prosperity: Black Americans and White Institutions, 1940–75.* New York: Pantheon Books, 1978, 187–235; Byrd WM. Race, biology, and health care; Charatz-Litt C. A chronicle of racism; Dula A. Toward an African-American perspective on bioethics; Morais HM. *The History of the Negro in Medicine*; Byrd WM. An American health dilemma.

45. Ginzberg E. A life in health policy, 243.

46. Ginzberg E. A life in health policy, 243; Andrulis DP, Carrier B. *Managed Care in the Inner City*; Kovner AR. *Jonas's Health Care Delivery in the United States.* 5th ed. New York: Springer, 1995; Kovner AR, Jonas S, eds. *Jonas and Kovner's Health Care Delivery in the United States.* 6th ed.; King G, Bendel R. A statistical model estimating the number of African American physicians in the United States. *Journal of the National Medical Association* 1995; 84:264–272; Shea S, Fullilove MT. Entry of black and other minority students in US medical schools; Foster HW. Reaching parity for minority medical students: A possibility or a pipe dream? *Journal of the National Medical Association* 1996; 88:17–21; Komaromy M, Grumbach K, Drake M. The role of Black and Hispanic physicians in providing health care for underserved populations. *New England Journal of Medicine* 1996; 334:1305–1314; Parker SG. U.S. medical schools urged to increase diversity. *Ob. Gyn. News* March 1, 1999: 36.

47. Friedman E. "The Human Factor: The Effect of Emerging Models of Competition on Patients and the Public"; Kronick R, Goodman DC, Wennberg J. The marketplace in health care reform: Demographic limitations of managed competition. *New England Journal of Medicine* 1993; 328:148–152; Branche CL. Health care in rural America. *Journal of the National Medical Association* 1991; 83:659; Branche CL. Rural medicine: A formidable challenge. *Journal of the National Medical Association* 1991; 83:1045.

48. Fuchs VR. *The Health Economy*; Fuchs VR. *The Future of Health Policy*; Kingdon JW. *Agendas, Alternatives, and Public Policies.* New York: HarperCollins, 1984; Navarro V. *Dangerous to Your Health*; Byrd WM, Clayton LA. "Designing a New Health Care System for the United States"; Kronick R, Gilmer T. Explaining the decline in health insurance coverage, 1979–1995; Dula A. Toward an African-American perspective on bioethics; Garrett L. *Betrayal of Trust.*

49. U.S. Congress, House. *The American Health Security Act of 1993.*

50. Fein R. Health care reform. *Scientific American* November 1992: 46–53; American Public Health Association. Managed competition; Woolhandler S, Himmelstein DU. *The National Health Program Chartbook*; Woolhandler S, Himmelstein DU. *For Our Patients, Not for Profits*; Skocpol T. *Boomerang*; Byrd WM, Clayton LA. "The American Health Dilemma Continues"; Byrd WM, Clayton LA, McCoy SP, Calliste GJ. Access to health care; Aaron HJ. *Serious and Unstable Condition*; Sager A, Socolar D, Ford D, Brand R. More care, at less cost.

51. White J. Health care reform the international way. *Issues of Science and Technology* Fall 1995; (1)(12):35–42; Himmelstein DU, Woolhandler S. A national health program for the United States: A physicians' proposal. *New England Journal of Medicine* 1989; 320:102–108; U.S. Library of Congress. Congressional Research Service. *Health Care Reform: Single-Payer Approaches.* Washington, DC, March 15, 1993 (CRS Issue Brief 93006); McDermott J. Evaluating health system reform: The case for a single-payer approach. *Journal of the American Medical Association* 1994; 271:782–784; American Public Health Association. Managed competition; Glaser WA. The United States needs a health system like other countries. *Journal of the American Medical Association* 1993; 270:980–984.

52. U.S. Library of Congress. Congressional Research Service. *Health Care Reform*; U.S. Congress, House. *The American Health Security Act of 1993*; Woolhandler S, Himmelstein DU. Free care: A quantitative analysis of health and cost effects of a national health program for the United States. *International Journal of Health Services* 1988; 18:393–399.

53. Ginzberg E. A life in health policy, 244; Sager A, Socolar D, Ford D, Brand R. More care, at less cost; U.S. Congress, House. *The American Health Security Act of 1993*; White J. Health care reform the international way; Fein R. Health care reform; American Public Health Association. Managed competition; Himmelstein DU, Woolhandler S. A national health program for the United States; Woolhandler S, Himmelstein DU. *The National Health Program Chartbook*; Woolhandler S, Himmelstein DU. *For Our Patients, Not for Profits*; Skocpol T. *Boomerang*; Aaron HJ. *Serious and Unstable Condition*; Blendon RJ, Donelan K. The public and the emerging debate over National Health Insurance. *New England Journal of Medicine* 1990; 323:208–212; Blendon RJ, Donelan K. The public and the future of U.S. health care reform. In: Blendon RJ, Edwards JN,

eds. *System in Crisis (Vol. 1)*, 173–194; Conyers Jr J. Twelve principles for national health insurance reform. *Journal of Health Care for the Poor and Underserved* 1992; 2:423–426; U.S. Library of Congress. Congressional Research Service. *Health Care Reform*; McDermott J. Evaluating health system reform; Woolhandler S, Himmelstein DU. Free care; Byrd WM, Clayton LA. "Designing a New Health Care System for the United States."

54. Navarro V. *Dangerous to Your Health*; Byrd WM. An American health dilemma; Byrd WM, Clayton LA. An American health dilemma; Garrett L. *Betrayal of Trust*; Quinn JB. Health plans; Annas GJ, Grodin MA, eds. *The Nazi Doctors and the Nuremberg Code: Human Rights in Human Experimentation*. New York: Oxford University Press, 1992; Byrd WM, Clayton LA. *An American Health Dilemma* (Vol. 1); Smith DB. *Health Care Divided*; Andrulis DP, Carrier B. *Managed Care in the Inner City*.

55. Harding S, ed. *The Racial Economy of Science: Toward a Democratic Future*. Bloomington: Indiana University Press, 1993; Tucker WH. *The Science and Politics of Racial Research*. Urbana: University of Illinois Press, 1994; Gould SJ. *The Mismeasure of Man*. New York: W. W. Norton, 1981; Stanton W. *The Leopard's Spots: Scientific Attitudes toward Race in America, 1815–1859*. Chicago: The University of Chicago Press, 1960; Haller Jr. JS. *Outcasts from Evolution: Scientific Attitudes of Racial Inferiority, 1859–1900*. New York: McGraw Hill, 1971; Caplan AL, ed. *When Science Went Mad: Bioethics and the Holocaust*. Totowa, NJ: Humana Press, 1992; Lederer SE. *Subjected to Science: Human Experimentation in America before the Second World War*. Baltimore: Johns Hopkins University Press, 1995; Kater MH. *Doctors under Hitler*. Chapel Hill: University of North Carolina Press, 1989; Chase A. *The Legacy of Malthus*; Roberts D. *Killing the Black Body: Race, Reproduction, and the Meaning of Liberty*. New York: Pantheon Books, 1997; Aly G, Chroust P, Pross C. *Cleansing the Fatherland: Nazi Medicine and Racial Hygiene*. Baltimore: Johns Hopkins University Press, 1994; Müller-Hill B. *Murderous Science: Elimination by Scientific Selection of Jews, Gypsies, and Others in Germany, 1933–1945*. Plainview, NY: Cold Spring Harbor Laboratory Press, 1998; Hubbard R, Wald E. *Exploding the Gene Myth*; Duster T. *Backdoor to Eugenics*; Kevles DJ. *In the Name of Eugenics: Genetics and the Uses of Human Heredity*. Berkeley: University of California Press, 1985; Horsman R. *Race and Manifest Destiny: The Origins of American Racial Anglo-Saxonism*. Cambridge, MA: Harvard University Press, 1981; Guthrie RV. *Even the Rat Was White*; Lewontin RC, Rose S, Kamin LJ. *Not in Our Genes*.

56. Johnson H, Broder DS. *The System*; Skocpol T. *Boomerang*.

57. Council on Ethical and Judicial Affairs. Black-White disparities in health care. *Journal of the American Medical Association* 1990; 263:2344–2346; Dula A. Toward an African-American perspective on bioethics; Cobb WM. The Black American in medicine; Byrd WM. Race, biology, and health care; Charatz-Litt C. A chronicle of racism; Byrd WM. An American health dilemma; Byrd WM, Clayton LA. An American health dilemma; Cose E. *The Rage of a Privileged Class*. New York: HarperCollins, 1993; Cose E. *Color-Blind: Seeing Beyond Race in a Race-Obsessed World*. New York: HarperCollins, 1997; Lemann N. Taking affirmative action apart. *New York Times Magazine* June 11, 1995: Section 6, 36; Kinder DR, Sanders LM. *Divided by Color: Racial Politics and Democratic Ideals*. Chicago: The University of Chicago Press, 1996; Schuman H, Steeh C, Bobo L, Krysan M. *Racial Attitudes in America: Trends and Interpretations*. rev. ed. Cambridge, MA: Harvard University Press, 1997; Sniderman PM, Piazza T. *The Scar of Race*. Cambridge, MA: The Belknap Press of Harvard University Press, 1993; Sniderman PM, Carmines EG. *Reaching beyond Race*. Cambridge, MA: Harvard University Press, 1997; Annas GJ, Grodin MA, eds. *The Nazi Doctors and the Nuremberg Code*; Katz J. *Experimentation with Human Beings: The Authority of the Investigator, Subject, Professions, and State in the Human Experimentation Process*. New York: Russell Sage Foundation, 1972; Kater MH. *Doctors under Hitler*; Aly G, Chroust P, Pross C. *Cleansing the Fatherland*; Chase A. *The Legacy of Malthus*; Tucker WH. *The Science and Politics of Racial Research*; Proctor RN. *Racial Hygiene: Medicine under the Nazis*. Cambridge, MA: Harvard University Press, 1988; Müller-Hill B. *Murderous Science*; Hubbard R, Wald E. *Exploding the Gene Myth*; Duster T. *Backdoor to Eugenics*; Kevles DJ. *In the Name of Eugenics*; Guthrie RV. *Even the Rat Was White*; Lewontin RC, Rose S, Kamin LJ. *Not in Our Genes*; Gould SJ. *The Mismeasure of Man*; Stanton W. *The Leopard's Spots*; Haller Jr. JS. *Outcasts from Evolution*; Lederer SE. *Subjected to Science*; Roberts D. *Killing the Black Body*; Navarro V. *Dangerous to Your Health*; Johnson H, Broder DS. *The System*; Smith DB. *Health Care Divided*; Skocpol T. *Boomerang*.

# ☀ Select Bibliography

Aaron HJ. *Serious and Unstable Condition: Financing America's Health Care*. Washington, D.C.: The Brookings Institution, 1991.

Aaron HJ, Schwartz WB. *The Painful Prescription: Rationing Hospital Care*. Washington, D.C.: The Brookings Institution, 1984.

Abelin T. Health promotion. 557–589. In: Detels R, Holland WW, McEwen J, Omenn GS, eds. *Oxford Textbook of Public Health*. Volume 3. *The Practice of Public Health*. Third Edition. New York: Oxford University Press, 1997.

Abelson R. For managed care, free-market shock. *The New York Times*, Sunday, January 3, 1999, Section 4, p. 4.

The achievement session, N.M.A. Hampton — 1938. Editorial. *J Natl Med Assoc* 1938; 30:154.

Ackerknecht EH. *A Short History of Medicine*. Revised Edition. Baltimore: The Johns Hopkins University Press, 1982.

Advisory committee on human radiation experiments, final report. 1024–1041. In: Areen J, King PA, Goldberg S, Gostin L, Capron AM. *Law, Science and Medicine*. Second Edition. Westbury, New York: The Foundation Press, Inc., 1996.

Advisory committee on human radiation experiments, final report. 1086–1091. In: Areen J, King PA, Goldberg S, Gostin L, Capron AM. *Law, Science and Medicine*. Second Edition. Westbury, New York: The Foundation Press, Inc., 1996.

Ahmed F. Infant mortality and related issues. 217–235. In: Livingston IL, ed. *Handbook of Black American Health: The Mosaic of Conditions, Issues, Policies, and Prospects*. Westport, Connecticut: Greenwood Press, 1994.

Alexander E. *Equal Opportunity: No More, No Less*, an eight page pamphlet issued by the Executive Committee, Manhattan Medical Society, New York, January 28, 1931.

Alexander GA. Cancer control in special populations: African-Americans, Native Americans, Hispanics, poor and underserved. 371–391. In: Greenwald P, Kramer BS, Weed DL, eds. *Cancer Prevention and Control*. New York: Marcel Dekker, Inc., 1995.

Alexander LL. Health objectives for the 1980s. *J Natl Med Assoc* 1980; 72:654–656. Guest Editorial.

Alexander PN. Cornely, Paul Bertau. 661. In: Salzman J, Smith DL, West C. eds. *Encyclopedia of African-American Culture and History*. 5 Vols. New York: Macmillan Library Reference USA, Simon and Schuster Macmillan, 1996.

Alexander PN. Kenney, John Andrew. 1533. In: Salzman J, Smith DL, West C. eds. *Encyclopedia of African-American Culture and History*. 5 Vols. New York: Macmillan Library Reference USA, Simon and Schuster Macmillan, 1996.

Alexander PN. Lewis, Julian Herman. 1609–1610. In: Salzman J, Smith DL, West C. eds. *Encyclopedia of African-American Culture and History*. 5 Vols. New York: Macmillan Library Reference USA, Simon and Schuster Macmillan, 1996.

Alexander PN. Maynard, Aubre de Lambert (1901– ). 1721–1722. In: Salzman J, Smith DL, West C. eds. *Encyclopedia of African-American Culture and History*. 5 Vols. New York: Macmillan Library Reference USA, Simon and Schuster Macmillan, 1996.

Alford RR. *Health Care Politics, Ideological and Interest Group Barriers to Reform*. Chicago, Illinois: University of Chicago Press, 1975.

# 750 ■ Select Bibliography

Allen GE. Eugenics comes to America. 441–475. In: Jacoby R, Glauberman N, eds. *The Bell Curve Debate: History, Documents, Opinions*. New York: Times Books Division of Random House, Inc., 1995.

Alter J. America's 'Own Holocaust.' *Newsweek*, December 8, 1997, 61.

Aly G, Chroust P, Pross C. *Cleansing the Fatherland: Nazi Medicine and Racial Hygiene*. Baltimore: The Johns Hopkins University Press, 1994.

The American Anti-Slavery Society. *American Slavery As It Is: Testimony of a Thousand Witnesses. The Anti-Slavery Examiner*, 1839 (No. 6), New York: The American Anti-Slavery Society, 1839.

American Cancer Society. *Cancer Facts and Figures for Minority Americans, 1988*. Atlanta: American Cancer Society, 1988.

American Cancer Society. *Cancer Facts and Figures-1997*. Atlanta, Georgia: American Cancer Society, 1997.

American Cancer Society. *Cancer Facts and Figures-1998*. Atlanta, Georgia: American Cancer Society, 1998.

American Medical Association. Caring for the uninsured and the underinsured: A compendium from the specialty journals of the American Medical Association. *JAMA* 1991; 265 (suppl):1–163.

American Public Health Association. Managed competition: Wonder drug or snake oil? *The Nation's Health* 23 (March 1993):1.

Amidei NJ, Russell JS. Second Class Medicine. 187–235. In: Newman DK, Amidei NJ, Carter BL, Day D, Kruvant WJ, Russell JS. *Protest, Politics, and Prosperity: Black Americans and White Institutions, 1940–75*. New York: Pantheon Books, 1978.

Ammer C, Ammer DS. *Dictionary of Business and Economics*. Revised and Expanded Edition. New York: The Free Press, 1984.

Anders G. HMOs pile up billions in cash, try to decide what to do with it. *The Wall Street Journal*, Wednesday, December 21, 1994, p. 1.

Anders G. *Health Against Wealth: HMOs and the Breakdown of Medical Trust*. Boston: Houghton Mifflin Company, 1996.

Anders G. Who pays the cost of cut-rate heart care? *The Wall Street Journal*, October 15, 1996, pp. B1, B8.

Anderson EA. The Watts health miracle. *J Natl Med Assoc* 1972; 64:168. Briefs.

Anderson GF, Poullier J-P. Health spending, access, and outcomes: Trends in industrialized countries. *Health Affairs* (Millwood) 1999; 18:178–192.

Anderson JD. *The Education of Blacks in the South, 1860–1935*. Chapel Hill: The University of North Carolina Press, 1988.

Anderson RN, Rosenberg HM. Age standardization of death rates: Implementation of the year 2000 standard. *National Vital Statistics Reports*; vol. 47 no. 3. Hyattsville, Maryland: National Center for Health Statistics. 1998.

Andrulis DP, Carrier B. *Managed Care in the Inner City: The Uncertain Promise for Providers, Plans, and Communities*. San Francisco: Jossey-Bass, 1999.

Angell M. Editorial responsibility: Protecting human rights by restricting publication of unethical research. 276–285. In: Annas GJ, Grodin MA, eds. *The Nazi Doctors and the Nuremberg Code: Human Rights in Human Experimentation*. New York: Oxford University Press, 1992.

An impending crisis. *J Natl Med Assoc* 1909; 1:232–236.

Annas GJ, Grodin MA, eds. *The Nazi Doctors and the Nuremberg Code: Human Rights in Human Experimentation*. New York: Oxford University Press, 1992.

Annas GJ. The Nuremberg Code in U.S. courts: Ethics versus expediency. 201–222. In: Annas GJ, Grodin MA, eds. *The Nazi Doctors and the Nuremberg Code: Human Rights in Human Experimentation*. New York: Oxford University Press, 1992.

Announcement. The Annual Clinic of the John A. Andrew Memorial Hospital, Tuskegee Institute, Alabama. *J Natl Med Assoc* 1918; 10:43.

Announcement. The John A. Andrew Memorial Hospital, Tuskegee Institute, Alabama. *J Natl Med Assoc* 1918; 10:xx.

Anonymous. Jim Crow in the Army camps. *The Crisis*. 1940 (December); 47:12.

Appeal for the NMA Foundation: A matter of simple multiplication. *J Natl Med Assoc* 1968; 60:533. NMA Activities.

Applebome P. Two Nashville hospitals debate a plan to merge. *The New York Times*, Sunday, April 30, 1989, p. 24.

Applewhite HL. Blacks in public health. *J Natl Med Assoc* 1974; 66:505–510.

Arad Y, ed. *The Pictorial History of the Holocaust*. New York: Macmillan Publishing Company, 1990.

Areen J, King PA, Goldberg S, Gostin L, Capron AM. *Law, Science and Medicine*. Second Edition. Westbury, New York: The Foundation Press, Inc., 1996.

Armstrong M. *Fanny Kemble: A Passionate Victorian*. New York: The Macmillan Company, 1938.

Arrow KJ. Uncertainty and the welfare economics of medical care. *The American Economic Review* 1963; 53:941–973.

Associated Press. MIT president rues radiation tests. *Fort Worth Star-Telegram*, Sunday, January 9, 1993, Section A, p. 23.

Atkins E. Despite progress, the condition of Black health remains critical. *The Detroit News*, Monday, February 8, 1993, p. 1A.

Audi R, ed. *The Cambridge Dictionary of Philosophy*. Cambridge, U.K.: Cambridge University Press, 1995.

Axtell LM, Asire A, Myers MH, eds. "Cancer Patient Survival," Report No. 5 from the Cancer Surveillance, Epidemiology and End Results Program, DHEW Publication No. 77–992. Washington, D.C.: GPO, 1977.

Ayanian JZ, Udvarhelyi IS, Gatsonis CA, Pashos CL, Epstein AM. Racial differences in the use of revascularization procedures after coronary angiography. *JAMA* 1993; 269:2642–2646.

Ayanian JZ. Race, class and the quality of medical care. *JAMA*. 1994; 271:1207–1208.

Ayanian JZ, Cleary PD, Weissman JS, Epstein AM. The effect of patients' preferences on racial differences in access to renal transplantation. *N Engl J Med* 1999; 341:1661–1669.

Ayanian JZ, Weissman JS, Chasan-Taber S, Epstein AM. Quality of care by race and gender for congestive heart failure and pneumonia. *Medical Care* 1999; 37:1260–1269.

Bach PB, Cramer LD, Warren JL, Begg CB. Racial differences in the treatment of early-stage lung cancer. *N Engl J Medicine* 1999; 341:1198–1205.

Bacon CS. The race problem. *Medicine* 1903; 9:338–342.

Bailey EJ. Health care use patterns among Detroit African Americans: 1910–1939. *J Natl Med Assoc* 1990; 82:721–723.

Bakal C. *Charity, U.S.A.*. New York: Times Books, 1979.

Baldness breakthrough, Editorial in *JAMA*, vol.191, no. 7, (February 15, 1965).

Ball JK, Elixhauser A. Treatment differences between Blacks and Whites with colorectal cancer. *Medical Care* 1996; 34:970–984.

Bang KM, White JE, Gause BL, Leffall LD. Evaluation of recent trends in cancer mortality and incidence among blacks. *Cancer* 1988; 61:1255–1261.

Bang KM. Cancer and Black Americans. 77–93. In: Livingston IL, ed. *Handbook of Black American Health: The Mosaic of Conditions, Issues, Policies, and Prospects*. Westport, Connecticut: Greenwood Press, 1994.

Bang KM. Chronic obstructive pulmonary disease in Blacks. 110–122. In: Livingston IL, ed. *Handbook of Black American Health: The Mosaic of Conditions, Issues, Policies, and Prospects*. Westport, Connecticut: Greenwood Press, 1994.

Banton M, Harwood J. *The Race Concept*. New York: Praeger Publishers, 1975.

Banton M. *Racial Theories*. Cambridge: Cambridge University Press, 1987.

Baquet CR, Ringen K, Pollack ES, Young JL, Horm JW, Goeckler R, Simpson NK. *Cancer Among Blacks and Other Minorities: Statistical Profiles*. Washington, D.C.: U.S. Department of Health and Human Services, 1986, NIH Publication No. 86–2785.

Baquet CR, Simpson NK, Bartee DLP, Ringen K, Heinonen JA, Clayton L, King G, Roberson NL, Schatzkin A. *Annotated Bibliography of Cancer-Related Literature on Black Populations*. Washington, D.C.: U.S. Department of Health and Human Services, 1988, NIH Publication No. 89–3024.

Baquet CR, Hunter CP. Patterns in minorities and special populations. 23–36. In: Greenwald P, Kramer BS, Weed DL, eds. *Cancer Prevention and Control*. New York: Marcel Dekker, Inc., 1995.

Baquet D, Fritsch J. New York's public hospitals fail, and babies are the victims. *The New York Times*, Sunday, March 5, 1995, p. 1.

Barabin JH. President's address: Negro Medical, Dental and Pharmaceutical Association of Arkansas. *J Natl Med Assoc* 1912; 4:130.

Barbeau AE, Henri F. *The Unknown Soldiers: Black American Troops in World War I*. Philadelphia: Temple University Press, 1974.

Barber B. The ethics of experimentation with human subjects. 322–328. In: Reiser RJ, Dyck AJ, Curran WJ, eds. *Ethics in Medicine: Historical Perspectives and Contemporary Concerns*. Cambridge, MA: MIT Press, 1977.

Barber JB. Statement of the National Medical Association to the Select Committe on Aging and Congressional Black Caucus Brain Trust on Aging at the hearing on "Needs of the Minority Elderly." *J Natl Med Assoc* 1979; 71:N.P.

Barber JB. President's inaugural address: Health status of the Black community. *J Natl Med Assoc* 1979; 71:87–90.

Barber JB. An open letter to President Carter. *J Natl Med Assoc* 1978; 70:717–718.
Barber Jr. JB, Sinnette CH. Presidential politics and minority health. *J Natl Med Assoc* 1984; 76:969–971. Health care problems in the 1980s from a Black perspective: Part I of a series begun in 1984; 76:968.
Barber JB, Tuckson R. Legislative activity at the 1985 NMA convention and selected resolutions. *J Natl Med Assoc* 1985; 77:839.
Barber JB, Hester RD, Tuckson R. Legislative resolutions at the 92nd annual convention of the NMA, 1987. *J Natl Med Assoc* 1988; 80:207–212. NMA Activities.
Barber JB. Black Americans in crisis. *J Natl Med Assoc* 1990; 82:664–666.
Barber JB. Quality of health care: National Medical Association perspective: Report from the NMA Task Force. *J Natl Med Assoc* 1991; 83:1113–1116.
Barnwell S, LaMendola WF. A survey and analysis of techniques used in attracting the Black middle-class patient. *J Natl Med Assoc* 1985; 77:379–384.
Barzun J. *Race: A Study in Superstition*. New York: Harper and Row, Publishers, 1937, 1965.
Barzun J. *From Dawn to Decadence: 500 Years of Western Cultural Life: 1500 to the Present*. New York: HarperCollins Publishers, 2000.
Bates E. The shame of our nursing homes: Millions for investors, misery for the elderly. *The Nation*, March 29, 1999, 11.
Baxter JH. *Statistics, Medical and Anthropological, of the Provost Marshal-General's Bureau, Derived from Records of the Examination for Military Service in the Armies of the United States during the Late War of the Rebellion, of over a Million Recruits, Drafted Men, Substitutes, and Enrolled Men*. Two Vols. Washington, D.C.: N.P., 1875.
Beardsley EH. *A History of Neglect: Health Care for Blacks and Mill Workers in the Twentieth-Century South*. Knoxville: The University of Tennessee Press, 1987.
Beck A. *A History of the British Medical Administration of East Africa, 1900–1950*. Cambridge, Massachusetts: *A Commonwealth Fund Book* Harvard University Press, 1970.
Becker LE. Health maintenance organizations: A Black physician's comments. *J Natl Med Assoc* 1971; 63:488–491.
Beecher HK. *Experimentation in Man*. Springfield, Illinois: Charles C. Thomas, 1962.
Beecher HK. Ethics and clinical research. *N Engl J Med* 1966; 274:1354–1360.
Behar R. Singing the Blue Cross blues: The shocking tale of mismanagement and mischief at New York's huge health insurer is far from unique. *Time*, July 12, 1993, 48.
Belding DL, Hunter IL. The Wassermann test: VI. The influence of race and nationality upon routine Wassermann tests in a maternity hospital. *American Journal of Syphilis* 1925; 126:130.
Belkin L. The Ellwoods: But what about quality? *The New York Times Magazine*, December 8, 1996, Section 6, 68.
Bell CC. Statistics on Black populations. *J Natl Med Assoc* 1982; 74:829–830. Letters to the Editor.
Bell CC. Impaired Black health professionals: Vulnerabilities and treatment approaches. *J Natl Med Assoc* 1986; 78:925–930.
Benatar SR. Medicine and health care in South Africa. *N Engl J Med* 1986; 315:527–532.
Bender GA. *Great Moments in Medicine*. Detroit: Northwood Institute Press, 1966.
Benjamin GC. Quality assurance: Public hospital clinics. *J Natl Med Assoc* 1989; 81:355.
Bennett JT, DiLorenzo TJ. *Unhealthy Charities: Hazardous to Your Health and Wealth*. New York: Basic Books, 1994.
Bennett T, Bhopal R. US health journal editors' opinions and policies on research in race, ethnicity, and health. *J Natl Med Assoc* 1998; 90:401–408.
Bergner L. Race, health, and health services. *Am J Public Health* 1993; 83:939–941.
Bernal M. *Black Athena: The Afroasiatic Roots of Classical Civilization*. Vol. 1. *The Fabrication of Ancient Greece 1785–1985*. New Brunswick, New Jersey: Rutgers University Press, 1987.
Bernard C. Vivisection. 257–259. In: Reiser RJ, Dyck AJ, Curran WJ, eds. In: *Ethics in Medicine: Historical Perspectives and Contemporary Concerns*. Cambridge, MA: MIT Press, 1977.
Bernstein N. New York adds hurdle for Medicaid seekers: Home inspections. *The New York Times*, Sunday, September 20, 1998, p. 43.
Berry LH. Special health care needs of the disadvantaged. *J Natl Med Assoc* 1966; 58:72–73.
Berry LH. Implementation of new health legislation and its impact upon disadvantaged population groups. *J Natl Med Assoc* 1966; 58:129.
Berry LH. Projection of the 1965 position of the NMA with reference to liaison efforts with the AMA to improve the problems of discrimination in medicine. *J Natl Med Assoc* 1966; 58:148–149.
Berry LH. Opening remarks. *J Natl Med Assoc* 1966; 58:209. President's Column.
Berry LH. Human rights and regional medical programs. *J Natl Med Assoc* 1966; 58:387–388.
Berry MF. Taming the Civil Rights Commission. *The Nation*, February 2, 1985, 106–108.

Bevan AD. Cooperation in medical education and medical service. *JAMA* 1928; 90:1173.

Billings J. Access to health care services. 401–438. In: Kovner AR, Jonas S, eds. *Jonas and Kovner's Health Care Delivery in the United States*. Sixth Edition. New York: Springer Publishing Company, 1999.

Birnie CW. The influence of environment and race on diseases. *J Natl Med Assoc* 1910; 2:243–251.

Birth control. *J Natl Med Assoc* 1917; 9:93–94.

Blagrove S, Barrett S, Gaston MH. How much can the safety net hold? *Minority Health Today* 2000; 1:39–43.

Blakely RL, Harrington JM, eds. *Bones in the Basement: Postmortem Racism in Nineteenth-Century Medical Training*. Washington: Smithsonian Institution Press, 1997.

Blakey ML, et al. (1988) The W. Montague Cobb Skeletal Collection Curatorial Project. First Report, Howard University.

Blakey ML. Skull doctors revisited: Intrinsic social and political bias in the history of American physical anthropology. With special reference to the work of Aleš Hrdlička. 64–95. In: Reynolds LT, Lieberman L, eds. *Race and Other Misadventures: Essays in Honor of Ashley Montagu in His Ninetieth Year*. Dix Hills, New York: General Hall, Inc. Publishers, 1996.

Blendon RJ, Donelan K. The public and the emerging debate over National Health Insurance. *N Engl J Med* 1990; 323:208–212.

Blendon RJ, Donelan K. The public and the future of U.S. health care system reform. 173–194. In: Blendon RJ, Edwards JN, eds. *System in Crisis: The Case for Health Care Reform*. Volume 1. *The Future of American Health Care*. New York: Faulkner and Gray, Inc., 1991.

Blendon RJ, Hyams TS, eds. *Reforming the System: Containing Health Care Costs in an Era of Universal Coverage*. Volume 2. *The Future of American Health Care*. New York: Faulkner and Gray, Inc., 1991.

Blendon RJ, Benson JM. Editorial: Whatever happened to the politicians' concerns about the nation's uninsured? *Amer J Public Health* 1998; 88:345–346.

Block SH. Managed care: Minorities and the poor. *Medicine and Health, Rhode Island* 1996; 79:266–268.

Blumenthal D. Effects of market reforms on doctors and their patients. *Health Affairs* (Millwood) 1996 (Summer); 15:170–184.

Blumenthal D, Meyer GS. Academic health centers in a changing environment. *Health Affairs* (Millwood) 1996; 15:200–215.

Blustein J, Weitzman BC. Access to hospitals with high-technology cardiac services: How is race important? *Am J Public Health* 1995; 85:345–351.

Blustein J, Arons RR, Shea S. Sequential events contributing to variations in cardiac revascularization rates. *Medical Care* 1995; 33:864–880.

Bogdanich W. *The Great White Lie: Dishonesty, Waste, and Incompetence in the Medical Community*. New York: Simon and Schuster, 1991.

Bohannan P, Curtin P. *Africa and Africans*. 4th Edition. Prospect Heights, Illinois: Waveland Press, 1995.

Bond HM. What the Army "intelligence" tests measured (1924). 583–598. In: Jacoby R, Glauberman N, eds. *The Bell Curve Debate: History, Documents, Opinions*. New York: Times Books Division of Random House, Inc., 1995.

Bonnyman GG Jr. Muddled care, managed care. *Health Affairs* (Millwood) 1999; 18:264–265. Review of: Andrulis DP, Carrier B. *Managed Care in the Inner City: The Uncertain Promise for Providers, Plans, and Communities*.

Bonnyman GG Jr. Health care civil rights for a new generation. *Minority Health Today* 2000; 1:43–45.

Books Inc. *In Black America*. Los Angeles: Presidential Publishers, 1970.

Boorstin DJ. *The Discoverers*. New York: Random House, Inc., 1983. Illustrated, Two Volume Edition. New York: Harry N. Abrams, Inc., 1991.

Boorstin DJ. The equality of the human species. 111–123. In: Boorstin DJ. *Hidden History: Exploring our Secret Past*. New York: Harper and Row Publishers, Inc., 1987.

*The Boston Globe* Dialogues: Health Care. Will care be there? Cost, compassion compete for center stage in health reform debate. *The Boston Sunday Globe*, Sunday, June 1, 1997, p. C2.

Bousefield MO. An account of physicians of color in the United States. *Bull Hist Med* 1945; 17:61–84.

Bowens GJ. President's annual address. *J Natl Med Assoc* 1917; 9:127–128.

Boyd RF. Mercy Hospital. *J Natl Med Assoc* 1909; 1:43.

Boyle EM. A comparative physical study of the Negro. *J Natl Med Assoc* 1912; 4:124–130.

Bracey JH, Meier A, Rudwick E, eds. *The Rise of the Ghetto*. Belmont, California: Wadsworth Publishing Company, Inc., 1971.

Bradshear K. As 1 million leave ranks of insured, debate heats up. *The New York Times*, Sunday, August 27, 1995, p. 1.

Braithwaite RL, Taylor SE, eds. *Health Issues in the Black Community*. San Francisco: Jossey-Bass Publishers, 1992.

Branche CL. Health care in rural America. *J Natl Med Assoc* 1991; 83:659.

Branche CL. Rural medicine: A formidable challenge. *J Natl Med Assoc* 1991; 83:1045.

Branch T. *Parting the Waters: America in the King Years, 1954–63*. New York: A Touchstone Book Published by Simon and Schuster Inc., 1988.

Branch T. *Pillar of Fire: America in the King Years, 1963–65*. New York: Simon and Schuster, 1998.

Brandon RM, Podhorzer M, Pollak TH. Premiums without benefits: Waste and inefficiency in the commercial health insurance industry. *International Journal of Health Services* 1991; 21:265–283.

Brandt AM. Racism and Research: The Case of the Tuskegee Syphilis Study. 331–343. In: Leavitt JW, Numbers RL, eds. *Sickness and Health in America: Readings in the History of Medicine and Public Health*. Madison, Wisconsin: The University of Wisconsin Press, 1985.

Braveman P, Bennett T. *Information for Action: An Advocates Guide To Using Maternal and Child Health Data.*, pamphlet. Washington D.C.: Children's Defense Fund, 1993.

Braveman P, Egerter S, Edmonston F, Verdon M. Racial/ethnic differences in the likelihood of caesarean delivery. *Am J Public Health* 1995; 85:625–630.

Brawley B. *A Social History of the American Negro: Being A History of the Negro Problem in the United States Including A History and Study of the Republic of Liberia*. New York: Macmillan Company, 1921. Paperback Edition. London: Collier-Macmillan Ltd., 1970.

Breast cancer deaths decrease—but not among Black women, *The Nation's Health*, February, 1995, 24.

Breeden JO. "Science and Medicine". 1337–1343. In: Wilson CR, Ferris W. eds. *Encyclopedia of Southern Culture*. Chapel Hill: The University of North Carolina Press, 1989.

Bremner RH. *The Public Good: Philanthropy and Welfare in the Civil War Era*. New York: Alfred A. Knopf, 1980.

Brennan TA, Hebert LE, Laird NM, et al. Hospital characteristics associated with adverse events and substandard care. *JAMA* 1991; 266:3265–3269.

Brew LE. *Edith: The Story of Edith Irby Jones, M.D.*. N.P.: NRT Publishing Company, Publishers, 1986.

Brigham CC. *A Study of American Intelligence*. Princeton: Princeton University Press, 1923.

Brigham CC. A study of American intelligence. 571–582. In: Jacoby R, Glauberman N, eds. *The Bell Curve Debate: History, Documents, Opinions*. New York: Times Books Division of Random House, Inc., 1995.

Brinkley A. *The Unfinished Nation: A Concise History of the American People*. New York: Alfred A. Knopf, 1993.

Brodie FM. *Richard Nixon: The Shaping of His Character*. New York: W.W. Norton and Company, 1981.

Brooks DD, Smith DR, Anderson RJ. Medical apartheid, an American perspective. *JAMA* 1991; 266:2746–2749.

Brooton G. FDA ban on drug tests by U. of P. specialist imperils research program at Holmesburg Prison. *Philadelphia Sunday Bulletin*, July 31, 1966, p. 27.

Brown ER. *Rockefeller Medicine Men: Medicine and Capitalism in America*. Berkeley: University of California Press, 1979.

Brown ER. Medicare and Medicaid: Band-aids for the old and poor. 50–76. In: Sidel VW, Sidel R, eds. *Reforming Medicine: Lessons of the Last Quarter Century*. New York: Pantheon Books, 1984.

Brown RK, Warwick KM, Albert J, Kabian E. A clinical evaluation of the effects of deodorants and anti-perspirants. *J Natl Med Assoc* 1966; 58:110–113.

Buckler H. *Daniel Hale Williams: Negro Surgeon*. New York: Pitman Publishing Corporation, 1954.

*Buck v. Bell*, 274 U.S. 200 (1927).

Bullock HA. *A History of Negro Education in the South: From 1619 to the Present*. New York: Praeger Publishers, 1967.

Bullock SC, Houston E. Perceptions of racism by black medical students attending white medical schools. *J Natl Med Assoc* 1987; 79:601–608.

Bullough B, Bullough VL. *Poverty, Ethnic Identity, and Health Care*. New York: Appleton-Century-Crofts, 1972.

Bumiller E. Life styles of the rich and ailing: In luxury hospital rooms, everything from high tea to fresh goat. *The New York Times*, Sunday, October 19, 1997, p. 37.

Bunker JP, Frazier HS, Mosteller F. Improving health: Measuring effects of medical care. *Milbank Quarterly* 1994; 2:247.

Burchette-Pierce C, Clayton LA, Randall VR, Byrd WM, Simms PB, Butcher R, Kong BW, et al.

Minority Health Care Review Group: Executive Summary. Working paper, National Medical Association/Congressional Black Caucus Foundation, Inc. project on health reform, June 7–9, 1993, Washington, D.C.; *Summit '93: African American Prescription for Health*. Proceedings of a conference on African American and disadvantaged population health and healthcare co-convened by the National Medical Association and the Congressional Black Caucus Foundation, Vista International Hotel, May 2–3, 1993. Washington, D.C.: National Medical Association and Congressional Black Caucus Foundation, Inc., 1993.

Burger EJ Jr. *Science at the White House: A Political Liability*. Baltimore: The Johns Hopkins University Press, 1980.

Burke J. Fit to rule. 239–273. In: *The Day the Universe Changed*. Boston: Little, Brown and Company, 1985.

Burns R, Ades L. *The Way West: The Way the West Was Lost and Won, 1845–1893*. A six hour documentary series [videotape] for *The American Experience*, Boston: WGBH Educational Foundation, WGBH, Boston, 1995.

Burt C. The measurement of intelligence by the Binet tests. *Eugenics Review* 1914; 6:36–50, 140–152.

Butler BN. Morality or legality: That is the question: We are a nation of laws, and of men. *J Natl Med Assoc* 1975; 67:242–246.

Byers JW. Diseases of the Southern Negro. *Medical and Surgical Reporter* 1888; 43:735.

Bynum WF, Browne EJ, Porter R, eds. *The Dictionary of the History of Science*. New York: Macmillan Press, 1981. Paperback Edition. Princeton, New Jersey: Princeton University Press, 1985.

Byrd WM. *Peer Review: The Perversion of a Process*. Report prepared for the Subcommittee on Civil Rights of the House Committee on the Judiciary. 99th Congress, 2nd Session, 1986.

Byrd WM. "Peer review abuse: Medicine's marker of its reemerging racial dilemma." (Unpublished document), Tyler, Texas, 1986.

Byrd WM. An American health dilemma. *J Natl Med Assoc* 1986; 78:1025–1026.

Byrd WM. Inquisition, peer review, and black physician survival. *J Natl Med Assoc* 1987; 79:1027–1029.

Byrd WM. Black medicine under attack. *Urban Medicine* 1987; 2:22.

Byrd WM. Race, biology, and health care: Reassessing a relationship. *Journal of Health Care for the Poor and Underserved* 1990; 1:278–292.

Byrd WM. *Documentary Report: Negro Diseases and Physiological Peculiarities*. Nashville: Cancer Control Research Unit, Meharry Medical College, July 13, 1990. In: Byrd WM, Clayton LA. *A Black Health Trilogy* [videotape and 188 page documentary report]. Washington, D.C.: The National Medical Association and the African American Heritage and Education Foundation; 1991.

Byrd WM. *Documentary Report: Medical Establishment Activities Against Progressive Health Legislation, Programs, and Health Delivery Activities*. Nashville: Cancer Control Research Unit, Meharry Medical College, July 13, 1990. In: Byrd WM, Clayton LA. *A Black Health Trilogy* [videotape and 188 page documentary report]. Washington, D.C.: The National Medical Association and the African American Heritage and Education Foundation; 1991.

Byrd WM, Clayton LA. *A Black Health Trilogy* [videotape and 188 page documentary report]. Washington, D.C.: The National Medical Association and the African American Heritage and Education Foundation; 1991.

Byrd WM, Clayton LA. The "slave health deficit": Racism and health outcomes. *Health/PAC Bulletin* 1991; 21:25–28.

Byrd WM. "Widening Racial Health Disparities: A Continuum." A presentation in Turning Back the Clock: Widening Health Differentials in Urban Areas, sponsored by Medical Care Forum on Bioethics, American Public Health Association, 120th Annual Meeting and Exhibition, Washington, D.C., November 9, 1992.

Byrd WM, Clayton LA. Meharry Medical Archive-NMA Slide Collection. Nashville and Boston: Meharry Medical Library, Countway Medical Library of Harvard Medical School, 1991–1999.

Byrd WM, Clayton LA. An American health dilemma: A history of blacks in the health system. *J Natl Med Assoc* 1992; 84:189–200.

Byrd WM, Clayton LA. *Designing a New Health Care System for the United States*, Boston: Harvard School of Public Health, 1992. Photocopy.

Byrd WM. Medical associations. 1747–1749. In: Salzman J, Smith DL, West C. eds. *Encyclopedia of African-American Culture and History*. 5 Vols. New York: Macmillan Library Reference USA, Simon and Schuster Macmillan, 1996.

Byrd WM, Clayton LA. The African-American cancer crisis, part 2: A prescription. *J Health Care Poor Underserved* 1993; 4:102–116.

Byrd WM, Letters to the Editor, "The NMA Founding Date Laid to Rest," *J Natl Med Assoc* 1993; 85:99.

Byrd WM, Clayton LA. "Minority Health Issues for Health Care Reform." Report prepared for hearings on Minority Health Issues for Health Care Reform, held for the Senate Human Resources Committee, Senator Edward Kennedy, Massachusetts, Presiding, 103rd Congress, Special Session at Harvard School of Public Health, February 19, 1993, Boston, Massachusetts.

Byrd WM, Clayton LA. "America's Dual Health Crisis in Black and White." Report prepared for hearings on Health Care Reform: The African American Agenda, held for the Congressional Black Caucus's Health Brain Trust, Congressman Louis Stokes, D-OH, Presiding, 103rd Congress, Special Session, Meeting Room, Cannon House Office Building, Tuesday, April 13, 1993, Washington, D.C.

Byrd WM, Clayton LA. CBC analysis and response to "Managed Competition" model health reform (bibliographed version), a health policy memorandum generated for the Congressional Black Caucus, Harvard School of Public Health, Boston, Massachusetts, submitted May 16, 1993.

Byrd WM, Clayton LA. "The American Health Dilemma Continues: An Analysis of the Clinton Health Plan from an African American and Disadvantaged Patient Perspective." Report prepared for the National Medical Association and the Congressional Black Caucus, Harvard School of Public Health, submitted October 27, 1993.

Byrd WM, Clayton LA, Randall V, McCoy S, Calliste G. Minority Health Care Review Group: Executive Summary, of report "Recommendations on National Health Care Reform from Providers of Health Care to African American and Other Underserved Populations," submitted to the Clinton Health Reform Task Force by the Congressional Black Caucus Foundation, Washington, D.C., June, 1993.

Byrd WM, Clayton LA. Health System Component Analysis: A Health Policy Analytic Tool. A documentary report prepared for Summit 93': Regional Summits on Health Care Reform, Department HPM, Harvard School of Public Health, November, 1993.

Byrd WM, Clayton LA, Kinchen K, Richardson D, Lawrence L, Butcher R, et al. African-American physicians' views on health reform: Preliminary results of a survey. *J Natl Med Assoc* 1994; 86:93–94.

Byrd WM, Clayton LA, Kinchen K, Richardson D, Lawrence L, Butcher R, et al. African-American physicians's views on health reform: Results of a survey. *J Natl Med Assoc* 1994; 86:191–199.

Byrd WM, Clayton LA, McCoy SP, Calliste GJ. "Access to health care: Provision by the major health reform proposals," a policy memorandum prepared for the Congressional Black Caucus Foundation, March 26, 1994.

Byrd WM, Clayton LA, Perot R. Common Terms In the Health Care Reform Debate: A Bibliographed Glossary. Section VI. In: Byrd WM, Clayton LA. *A Guide for Health Care Reform* [unpublished document], Revised Edition. Prepared for the "Grassroots Education Initiative for Health Care Reform," sponsored by the Hoosier State Medical Society, National Medical Association and "Summit '93: Regional Summit on Health Care Reform," Westin Hotel, Indianapolis, Indiana, Saturday, June 18, 1994.

Byrd WM, Clayton LA. *An American Health Dilemma*. Volume 1. *A Medical History of African Americans and the Problem of Race: Beginnings to 1900*. New York: Routledge, 2000.

Byrd WM, Clayton LA. Race, medicine, and health care in the United States: A historical survey. *J Natl Med Assoc* 2001; 93 (suppl 1):11s–34s.

Byrd WM, McHollin M. "Tennessee Black Medical Heritage Tour." A report prepared for the Tennessee Humanities Council for the 1990 Black Medical Heritage Tour, Meharry Medical College Black Medical History Archive, Meharry Medical College, Nashville, Tennessee, Spring, 1991.

In re: Cager et al., 251 Maryland 473 (1967)

Caldwell C. The Southern captivity of the GOP. *The Atlantic Monthly* 1998 (June, No. 6); 281:55.

Califano Jr. JA. *America's Health Care Revolution: Who Lives? Who Dies? Who Pays?* New York: Random House, 1986; Sardell A. *The U.S. Experiment in Social Medicine: The Community Health Center Program, 1956–1986*. Pittsburgh: The University of Pittsburgh Press, 1988.

California Physicians' Alliance. Managed competition versus single-payer health insurance reform: How do they compare? San Francisco: California Physicians' Alliance, April 21, 1991.

Campbell EG, Weissman JS, Blumenthal D. Relationship between market competition and the activities and attitudes of medical school faculty. *JAMA* 1997; 278:222–226.

Campion FD. *The AMA and U.S. Health Policy Since 1940*. Chicago: Chicago Review Press, 1984.

Can Negroes learn the way Whites do? Findings of a top authority. *U.S. News and World Report*, March 10, 1969, 48–51.

Cannon GE. The Negro medical profession and the United States Army. *J Natl Med Assoc* 1919; 11:21–28.

Cannon JA. The last economic alternative for the Black community. *J Natl Med Assoc* 1972; 64:458–459.

Canto JG, Allison JJ, Kiefe CI, Fincher C, Farmer R, et al. Relation of race and sex to the use of reperfusion therapy in Medicare beneficiaries with acute myocardial infarction. *N Engl J Med* 2000; 342:1094–1100.

Caplan AL, ed. *When Medicine Went Mad: Bioethics and the Holocaust.* Totowa, New Jersey: Humana Press, 1992.

Carey B. Blue Cross will shrink network of pharmacies. *The Tennessean*, Tuesday, December 16, 1997, p. 1.

Carlisle DM, Leake B, Shapiro MF. Racial and ethnic differences in the use of invasive cardiac procedures among cardiac patients in Los Angeles County, 1986 through 1988. *Am J Public Health* 1995; 85:352–356.

Carmichael S, Hamilton CV. *Black Power: The Politics of Liberation in America.* New York: Vintage Books, 1967.

Carnegie ME. Black nurses in the United States: 1879–1992. *J Natl Black Nurses Assoc* 1992; 6:13–18.

Carrasquillo O, Himmelstein DU, Woolhandler S, Bor DH. Can Medicaid managed care provide continuity of care to new Medicaid enrollees? An analysis of tenure on Medicaid. *Amer J Public Health* 1998; 88:464–466.

Carter H. He's doing something about the race problem. *Saturday Evening Post*, February 23, 1946, p. 30.

Carter III H. *The Reagan Years.* New York: Braziller, 1988.

Carter Jr. LC. Health and the war on poverty. *J Natl Med Assoc* 1966; 58:173–178.

"The Case Against the AMA," *Opportunity* 1939; 17:194.

Castration instead of lynching. *Atlanta Journal-Record of Medicine* (October) 1906; 8:457.

Cavalli-Sforza LL, Menozzi P, Piazza A. *The History and Geography of Human Genes.* Princeton, New Jersey: Princeton University Press, 1994.

Cavalli-Sforza LL. *Genes, Peoples, and Languages.* New York: North Point Press/Farrar, Straus and Giroux, 2000.

Cave VG. How far the way: President's retiring address. *J Natl Med Assoc* 1975; 67:394.

Celis W, Poirot C. Black doctors may sue five hospitals. *Fort Worth Star-Telegram*, November 25, 1983, p. 27A.

Centers for Disease Control. Measles—Los Angeles County, California, 1988. *MMWR* 1989; 38:49.

Centers for Disease Control. Update: measles outbreak—Chicago, 1989. *MMWR* 1990; 39:317.

Centers for Disease Control. Measles—United States, 1989 and first 20 weeks 1990. *MMWR* 1990; 39:353.

Centers for Disease Control. Measles vaccination levels among selected groups of preschool-aged children—United States. *MMWR* 1991;40:36–39.

Centers for Disease Control. Measles outbreak—New York City, 1990–1991. *MMWR* 1991; 40:305.

Centers for Disease Control. Consensus set of health status indicators for the general assessment of community health status—United States. *MMWR* 1991; 40:449–451.

Centers for Disease Control and Prevention. Critical need to pay attention to HIV prevention for African Americans. *CDC Update*, June, 1998.

Centers for Disease Control and Prevention. Young people at risk—Epidemic shifts further toward young women and minorities. *CDC Update*, September, 1998, 1.

Centers for Disease Control. Reporting race and ethnicity data—National Electronic Telecommunication System for surveillance, 1994–1997. *MMWR* 1999; 48:305–311.

Chalk F, Jonassohn K. *The History and Sociology of Genocide: Analyses and Case Studies.* Published in cooperation with The Montreal Institute for Genocide Studies. New Haven: Yale University Press, 1990.

Charatz-Litt C. A chronicle of racism: The effects of the White medical community on black health. *J Natl Med Assoc* 1992; 84:717–725.

Chase A. *The Legacy of Malthus: The Social Costs of the New Scientific Racism.* New York: Alfred A. Knopf, 1980.

Chasteen ER. *The Case for Compulsory Birth Control.* Englewood Cliffs, New Jersey: Prentice-Hall, 1971.

Chicago Urban League Research Department. "A Staff Working Paper on Integration in Hospital Appointments and Hospital Care." Report prepared for the workshops of the Second Imhotep National Conference on Hospital Integration, May 23–24, 1958.

Children's Defense Fund. *The State of America's Children*. Washington, D.C.: Children's Defense Fund, 1991.

Children's Defense Fund. *The Health of America's Children 1992: Maternal and Child Health Data Book*. Washington D.C.: Children's Defense Fund, 1992.

Children's Defense Fund. *The State of America's Children Yearbook 1998*. Washington D.C.: Children's Defense Fund., 1998.

Chomsky N. *Profit Over People: Neoliberalism and Global Order*. New York: Seven Stories Press, 1999.

Chu J, Polisor L, Tamimi HK. Quality of care in women with stage-1 cervical cancer. *West J Med* 1982; 137:13–17.

Churchill LR. *Rationing Health Care in America: Perceptions and Principles of Justice*. Notre Dame, Indiana: University of Notre Dame Press, 1987.

Churchill LR. *Self-Interest and Universal Health Care: Why Well-Insured Americans Should Support Coverage for Everyone*. Cambridge, Massachusetts: Harvard University Press, 1994.

In re Cincinnati radiation litigation. 546–552. In: Areen J, King PA, Goldberg S, Gostin L, Capron AM. *Law, Science and Medicine*. Second Edition. Westbury, New York: The Foundation Press, Inc., 1996.

Clark KB. The essential educational program. *J Natl Med Assoc* 1966; 58:109.

Clayton LA, Byrd WM. The African American cancer crisis, part 1: The problem. *J Health Care Poor Underserved* 1993; 4: 83–101.

Clayton LA, Byrd WM. Report prepared for hearings and submitted into the *Congressional Record* on "Health Care Reform: What Does It Mean to African Americans," held for the Congressional Black Caucus Health Braintrust, 103rd Congress, Congressman Louis Stokes, D-Ohio, Presiding, Rayburn House Office Building, Room 2175, Washington, D.C., September 16, 1993.

Clayton LA, Byrd WM. Race: A major health status and outcome variable 1980–1999. *J Natl Med Assoc* 2001; 93 (suppl 1):35s–54s.

Cleaver E. *Soul on Ice*. New York: McGraw-Hill, 1968.

Clement KW, Cobb WM. National Medical Association testimony on behalf of H.R. 3920, the King-Anderson Bill, before the Committee on Ways and Means, U.S. House of Representatives, January 22, 1964. *J Natl Med Assoc* 1964; 56:213–221.

Clinton WJ. *Saturday Radio Address*, radio address by the President to the nation, February 21, 1998.

Cobb CM. Students charge BCH's obstetrics unit with "excessive surgery," *Boston Globe*, April 29, 1972, p. 1.

Cobb WM. The Laboratory of Anatomy and Physical Anthropology of Howard University. Washington, D.C., 1936.

Cobb WM. Race and runners. *J Health and Phys Educ* 1936; 7:1–9.

Cobb WM. *The First Negro Medical Society: A History of the Medico-Chirurgical Society of the District of Columbia*. Washington, D.C.: The Associated Publishers, 1939.

Cobb WM. Physical anthropology of the American Negro. *Am J Phys Anthropol* 1942; 29:113–222.

Cobb WM. Statement in support of National Health Bill, S. 1606, on behalf of the National Association for the Advancement of Colored People. *J Natl Med Assoc* 1946; 38: 133–137.

Cobb WM. *Medical Care and the Plight of the Negro*. New York: The National Association for the Advancement of Colored People, 1947.

Cobb WM. *Progress and Portents for the Negro In Medicine*. New York: The National Association for the Advancement of Colored People, 1948.

Cobb WM. John Andrew Kenney, M.D., 1874–1950. *J Natl Med Assoc* 1950; 42:175–177.

Cobb WM. Charles Richard Drew, M.D., 1904–1950. *J Natl Med Assoc* 1950; 42:239–245.

Cobb WM. Martin Robison Delany. *J Natl Med Assoc* 1952; 44:232–238.

Cobb WM. Alexander Thomas Augusta. *J Natl Med Assoc* 1952; 44:327–329.

Cobb WM. The crushing irony of deluxe Jim Crow. *J Natl Med Assoc* 1952; 44:387.

Cobb WM. Robert Fulton Boyd. *J Natl Med Assoc* 1953; 45: 233–234.

Cobb WM. The national health program of the N.A.A.C.P. *J Natl Med Assoc* 1953; 45:333–339.

Cobb WM. NAACP's resolutions on health. *J Natl Med Assoc* 1953; 45:438–439.

Cobb WM. Nathan Francis Mossell, M.D., 1856–1946. *J Natl Med Assoc* 1954; 46:118–130.

Cobb WM. John Andrew Kenney, M.D., 1874–1950. *J Natl Med Assoc* 1956; 48:75.

Cobb WM. Integration in medicine: A national need. *J Natl Med Assoc* 1957; 49:4 (history of the fight against segregated private and VA hospital facilities).

Cobb WM. The first hundred years of the Howard University College of Medicine. *J Natl Med Assoc* 1967; 59:408–420.

Cobb WM. The establishment, the Negro and education. *J Natl Med Assoc* 1968; 60:320–331.

Cobb WM. "What hath God wrought": Position reversals and the AMA and AAMC. *J Natl Med Assoc* 1968; 60:518–521.

Cobb WM. Salute to the N.A.A.C.P.: 100,000 more in 1974. *J Natl Med Assoc* 1974; 66:249–250. Editorials.

Cobb WM. 1981. The Black American in Medicine. *J Natl Med Assoc* 73 (Suppl 1):1183–1244.

Cohen IB. *Album of Science: From Leonardo to Lavoisier, 1450–1800.* New York: Charles Scribner's Sons, 1980.

Coleman AH. Human experimentation. *J Natl Med Assoc* 1966; 58:147–148. Legal Counsel.

Coleman AH. Title 19 and medical civil rights. *J Natl Med Assoc* 1966; 58:397. Legal Counsel.

Coleman JS, et al. *Equality of Educational Opportunity.* Washington: Government Printing Office, 1966.

Comas J. *Racial Myths.* United Nations Education, Scientific and Cultural Organization. The Race Question in Modern Science Series, Paris: Unesco, 1958.

Commission for the Study of Uncinariasis. *J Natl Med Assoc* 1910; 2:140–141.

Committee on the Costs of Medical Care. *Medical Care for the American People.* Chicago: University of Chicago Press, 1932.

Committee To End Discrimination In Chicago Medical Institutions. "What Color Are Your Germs?" *J Natl Med Assoc* 1955; 47: 264–267.

The Commonwealth Fund. *Contributing to the Community: The Economic Significance of Academic Health Centers And Their Role in Neighborhood Development,* Report IV. Report of the task force on academic health centers. New York: The Commonwealth Fund, 1987.

Consumers Union. Nursing homes: A special investigative report. *Consumer Reports* 1995 (August, No. 8); 60:518.

Consumers Union. Who pays for the nursing home? *Consumer Reports* 1995 (September, No. 9); 60:591.

Consumers Union. Nursing homes: What are the alternatives? *Consumer Reports* 1995 (October, No. 10); 60:656.

Contee CG. John Sweat Rock, M.D., Esq., 1825–1866. *J Natl Med Assoc* 1976; 68:237–242.

Conyers Jr. J. Twelve principles for national health insurance reform. *J Health Care Poor and Underserved* 1992; 2:423–426.

Conyers Jr. J. Principles of health care reform: An African-American perspective. *J Health Care Poor and Underserved* 1993; 4:1–8.

Cooper-Patrick L, Gallo JJ, Gonzales JJ, Vu HT, Powe NR, Nelson C, et al. Race, gender, and partnership in the patient-physician relationship. *JAMA* 1999; 282:583–589.

Cooper R. Cardiovascular mortality among Blacks, hypertension control and the Reagan budget. *J Natl Med Assoc* 1981; 73:1019–1020.

Cooper R. Is the United States entering a period of retrogression in public health? *J Natl Med Assoc* 1983; 75:741–744.

Cordtz D. "Change Begins in the Doctor's Office," *Fortune,* January, 1970, 84.

Corea G. *The Hidden Malpractice: How American Medicine Treats Women as Patients and Professionals.* New York: Morrow, 1973.

Cornelius LJ. Limited access to health care continues in minority groups. *National Medical Association News,* March/April, 1993, 1.

Cornelius LJ. Ethnic minorities and access to medical care: Where do they stand? *J Assoc for Academic Minority Physicians* 1993; 4:16–25.

Cornely PB. Morbidity and mortality from scarlet fever in the Negro. *Am J Public Health* 1939; 29:999–1005.

Cornely PB. Observations on the health progress of Negroes in the U.S. during the past two decades. *South Med J* 1941; 34:1286.

Cornely PB. Trends in public health activities among Negroes in 96 Southern counties during the period 1930–39. *Am J Public Health* 1942; 32:1117–1123.

Cornely PB. Distribution of Negro physicians in the United States in 1942. *JAMA* 1944; 124:826.

Cornely PB. Race relations in community health organizations. *Am J Public Health* 1946; 36:990.

Cornely PB. Distribution of Negro dentists in the United States. *JADA* 1947; 34:750.

Cornely PB. "Report of the Health Consultant for Charleston, South Carolina." Community Relations Project of the National Urban League (unpublished, n.d., but c. 1947).

Cornely PB. The economics of medical practice and the Negro physician. *J Natl Med Assoc* 1951; 43:84–92.

Cornely PB. Trends in public health activities. *Am J Public Health* 1956; 46:117–123.

Cornely PB. Segregation and discrimination in medical care in the U.S. *Am J Public Health* 1956; 46:1074–1081.

Cornely PB. Trends in racial integration in hospitals in the United States. *J Natl Med Assoc* 1957; 49:8–10.

Cornish DT. *The Sable Arm: Negro Troops in the Union Army, 1861–1865.* New York: W.W. Norton and Company, Inc., 1966.

Corson ER. Syphilis in the Negro. *American Journal of Dermatology and Genito-Urinary Diseases* 1906; 10:241, 247.

Cose E. *The Rage of a Privileged Class.* New York: HarperCollins Publishers, 1993.

Cose E. *Color-Blind: Seeing Beyond Race in a Race-Obsessed World.* New York: HarperCollins Publishers, 1997.

Council on Ethical and Judicial Affairs. Black-White disparities in health care. *JAMA* 1990; 263:2344–2346.

Council on Graduate Medical Education. *Seventh Report.* Washington, D.C.: U.S. Department of Health and Human Services, 1995.

Cray E. *In Failing Health: The Medical Crisis and the A.M.A.* Indianapolis: The Bobbs-Merrill Company, Inc., 1970.

Crittendon D. Black doctors charge bias at area hospitals. *The Detroit News*, April 23, 1984, p. 1.

Crittendon D. Doors of his specialty closed to Black surgeon. *The Detroit News*, April 23, 1984, p. 1.

Crockett GW. Political action committees: Impact on our political system. *J Natl Med Assoc* 1986; 78:697–700. Legislative Forum.

Cropper CM. In Texas, a laboratory test on the effects of suing H.M.O.'s, *The New York Times*, Sunday, September 13, 1998, Section 3, p. 1.

Cross EB. Federal roles and responsibilities in the organization, delivery and financing of health care. *J Natl Med Assoc* 1970; 62:353.

Cross EB. Patients are people: A positive concept of health care. *J Natl Med Assoc* 1972; 64:167–168. Briefs.

Cunningham FG, MacDonald PC, Gant NF, Leveno KJ, Gilstrap LC, et al. *Williams Obstetrics.* Eighteenth Edition. Stamford, Connecticut: Appleton and Lange, 1997.

Curley B. *W.E.B. Du Bois of Great Barrington*, [videotape] A production of PBS member WGBY, Springfield, Massachusetts, A project sponsored by the Massachusetts Cultural Council, 1992.

Curran W. Governmental regulation of the use of human subjects in medical research: The approach of two federal agencies. *Daedalus: Ethical Aspect of Experimentation with Human Subjects* 1969; 98:542.

Curran WJ. Current legal issues in clinical investigation with particular attention to the balance between the rights of the individual and the needs of society. 296–301. In: Reiser RJ, Dyck AJ, Curran WJ, eds. *Ethics in Medicine: Historical Perspectives and Contemporary Concerns.* Cambridge, MA: MIT Press, 1977.

Curry GE. The death that won't die: Memories of Emmett Till 40 years later. *Emerge* 1995 (July/August, No. 6); 9:24.

Curry GE. Black America's health crisis: Statistics indicate that while general health of White Americans is improving, the health status of African-Americans is getting worse. *Emerge* 1998 (July/August, No. 9); 9:32.

Curry LP. *The Free Black in Urban America, 1800–1850: The Shadow of the Dream.* Chicago: The University of Chicago Press, 1981.

Curtis JL. *Blacks, Medical Schools, and Society.* Ann Arbor: The University of Michigan Press, 1971.

Daniel M. Health center's bankruptcy puts neighborhood care at risk. *The Boston Sunday Globe*, Sunday, January 31, 1999, p. 6.

Darity WA, Turner CB. Family planning, race consciousness, and the fear of race genocide. *Am J Public Health* 1972; 62:1454.

Darity WA, Turner CB. Fears of genocide among Black Americans as related to age, sex, and region. *Am J Public Health* 1973; 63:1029.

Davenport CB. *Heredity in Relation to Eugenics.* New York: Henry Holt and Company, 1911.

Davidson AT, Coleman AH. The legal status of physicians on hospital staffs. *J Natl Med Assoc* 1983; 75:87–88.

Davidson AT, Coleman AH. Legal options in securing hospital appointments. *J Natl Med Assoc* 1983; 75:318–320.

Davidson AT. The role of the historic Black colleges in the training of Black professionals. *J Natl Med Assoc* 1983; 75:1019–1022.

Davidson AT, Freeman HP, Reed EW, Shropshire CN, Yancy Sr. AG. Declaration of a medical practice liability crisis. *J Natl Med Assoc* 1986; 78:789. NMA Activities.

Davidson RH, Oleszek WJ. *Congress and Its Members.* Third Edition. Washington, D.C.: CQ Press, a Division of Congressional Quarterly, Inc., 1990.

Davis AY. *Women, Race and Class.* New York: Random House, Inc., 1981. Reprint Edition. New York: Vintage Books, 1983.

Davis DB. *The Problem of Slavery in Western Culture.* Ithaca: Cornell University Press, 1966.

Davis DB. *Slavery and Human Progress.* New York: Oxford University Press, 1984.

Davis E. Cutting the nation's health care costs. *J Natl Med Assoc* 1987; 79:953–960.

Davis JP. A black inventory of the New Deal. *The Crisis* 1935; 42:154–155.

Davis K. *National Health Insurance: Benefits, Costs and Consequences.* Washington, D.C.: Brookings Institution, 1975.

Davis K, Marshall R. "Rural Health Care in the South," preliminary summary report prepared for presentation at the meeting of the Task Force on Southern Rural Development, Atlanta, October, 1975.

Davis K, Schoen C. *Health and the War on Poverty: A Ten-Year Appraisal.* Washington, D.C.: Brookings Institution, 1978.

Davis K, Gold M, Makuc D. Access to health care for the poor: Does the gap remain? *Annual Review of Public Health* 1981; 2:159–182.

Davis K. Access to health care: A matter of fairness. 45–57. In: *Health Care: How to Improve It and Pay for It.* Washington, D.C.: Center for National Policy, 1985.

Davis K, Lillie-Blanton M, Lyons B, Mullan F, Powe N, Rowland D. Health care for black Americans: The public sector role. 213–247. In: Willis DP, ed. *Health Policies and Black Americans.* New Brunswick, New Jersey: Transaction Publishers, 1989.

Davis MM, Warner AW. *Dispensaries: Their Management and Development.* New York: Macmillan, 1918.

Degler CN. *In Search of Human Nature: The Decline and Revival of Darwinism in American Social Thought.* New York: Oxford University Press, 1991.

Delaney P. Voting: The new Black power. *New York Times Magazine,* November 27, 1983, p. 35.

DeNeufville R, Conner C. How good are our schools? *American Education* 1966; 2:6.

DeParle J. Daring research or 'social science pornography'? *The New York Times Magazine,* October 9, 1994, Section 6, pp. 48, 49.

De Tocqueville A. *Democracy in America.* Two Volumes. Ed. JP Mayer. Trans. G Lawrence. New York: Harper and Row, 1966. Paperback Edition. New York: Harper Perennial, 1988.

Detroit Commission on Community Relations. *Racial Factors in Policy and Practice: Hospital and Bed Utilization, 47 Detroit Area General Hospitals.* Detroit, 1956.

Devisse J. *The Image of the Black in Western Art. Part II. From the Early Christian Era to the "Age of Discovery". 1. From the Demonic Threat to the Incarnation of Sainthood.* Cambridge, Massachusetts: The Minil Foundation, distributed by the Harvard University Press, 1979.

Dickerson DC. "The Black Physician." A paper presented at the "Black Health: Historical Perspectives and Current Issues Conference." Department of the History of Medicine, University of Wisconsin-Madison, April 6, 1990.

Dickman RL, Ford AB, Liebman J, Milligan S, Schorr AL. An end to patchwork reform of health care. *N Engl J Med* 1987; 317:1086–1089.

Diehr P, Yergan J, Chu J, et al. Treatment modality and quality differences for Black and White breast-cancer patients treated in community hospitals. *Med Care* 1989; 27:942–958.

Dixon B. *Health, Medicine and the Human Body.* New York: Macmillan Publishing Company, 1986.

Dixon WA. The morbid proclivities and retrogressive tendencies in the offspring of mulattoes. *American Medical Association, Journal* 1893; 20:1–2.

Doctors' HMO deals may shortchange ailing. *Fort Worth Star-Telegram,* December 21, 1995, Section B, p. 3.

Dorsey-Young F. Value socialization of Black medical students at the Howard University College of Medicine: A case report. *J Natl Med Assoc* 1980; 72:247–258.

Douglas PH. *Social Security in the United States.* New York: McGraw-Hill, 1936.

Douglas SW. Difficulties and superstitions encountered in practice among Negroes. *Southern Medical Journal* 1926; 19:736–738.

Douglas SW, Miller CJ. Comparative study of certain gynecologic and obstetric conditions as exhibited in the Colored and White races. *American Journal of Obstetrics and Gynecology* 1928; 26:662–663.

Dowling HF. *City Hospitals: The Undercare of the Underprivileged.* Cambridge, Massachusetts: Harvard University Press, 1982.

Downing LC. Some points on developing a hospital. *J Natl Med Assoc* 1919; 11:95–98.

Dr. Jackson and the Tulsa, Okla., riots. *J Natl Med Assoc* 1921; 202–203.

Drake SC. *Black Folk Here and There: An Essay in History and Anthropology.* 2 Volumes. Los Angeles: Center for Afro-American Studies, University of California, 1987, 1990.

Drew CR. "Banked Blood: A Study in Blood Preservation." (Ph.D. dissertation, Columbia University, June, 1940.)

Drew CR, *et al.* Report Concerning the Project for Supplying Blood Plasma to England. New York: Blood Transfusion Association, June, 1941.

Drew CR, Scudder J. Studies in blood preservation; fate of cellular elements and prothrombin in citrated blood. *Journal of Laboratory and Clinical Medicine* 1941; 26:1473–1478.

Drew CR. The early recognition and treatment of shock. *Anesthesiology* 1942; 3:176–194.

Drew CR. Letters to the Editor of J.A.M.A., January 13 and January 30, 1947. *J Natl Med Assoc* 1947; 39:222–224.

Drug regulation, investigating the investigator. *Time*, August 5, 1966, p. 65.

Drug-resistant TB raises fear of new scourge. *The New York Times*, Thursday, October 23, 1997, p. A13.

Du Bois WEB. *Mortality Among Negroes in Cities*. Proceeding of the Conference for Investigation of City Problems. Atlanta: Atlanta University Publications, 1896.

Du Bois WEB. *Social and Physical Conditions of Negroes in Cities*. Proceedings of the Second Conference for the Negro City Life. Atlanta: Atlanta University Publications, 1897.

Du Bois WEB. *The Souls of Black Folk: Essays and Sketches by W.E. Burghardt Du Bois*. N.P.: Fawcett Publications, Inc., 1961. Illustrated Edition. New York: Dodd, Mead, and Company, 1979.

Du Bois WEB. *The Health and Physique of the Negro American*. A Social Study Made under the Direction of the Eleventh Atlanta Conference. Atlanta: Atlanta University Publications, 1906.

Du Bois WEB. Opinion: The Tuskegee hospital. *The Crisis* 1923; 26:106–107.

Du Bois WEB. Opinion: Tuskegee and Moton. *The Crisis* 1924; 28:200–202.

Du Bois WEB. Social medicine. 265–276. In: Du Bois WEB. *Against Racism: Unpublished Essays, Papers, Addresses, 1887–1961*. Aptheker H, ed. Amherst: The University of Massachusetts Press, 1985.

Duffy J. States' Rights Medicine. 1355–1356. In: Wilson CR, W Ferris, eds. *Encyclopedia of Southern Culture*. Chapel Hill: The University of North Carolina Press, 1989.

Duffy J. *The Sanitarians: A History of American Public Health*. Urbana: University of Illinois Press, 1990.

Dugdale RL. *The Jukes: A Study in Crime, Pauperism, and Heredity*. 4th Edition. New York: G.P. Putnam's Sons, 1910.

Dula A. Toward an African-American perspective on bioethics. *J Health Care Poor Underserved* 1991; 2:259–269.

Dummett CO. *Afro-Americans in Dentistry: Sequence and Consequence of Events*. N.P.: Clifton O. Dummett, 1978.

Duster T. *Backdoor to Eugenics*. New York: Routledge, 1990.

Earles III LC. President's inaugural address: Priorities. *J Natl Med Assoc* 1983; 75:1139–1143.

Earles L. Doctor, what was your major? *J Natl Med Assoc* 1984; 76:575–576.

East EM. *Heredity and Human Affairs*. New York: Charles Scribner's and Sons, 1929.

East EM, ed. *Biology in Human Affairs*. New York: McGraw-Hill, 1931.

Eaton HA. Views of North Carolina Negro physicians on medical assistance for the aged. *J Natl Med Assoc* 1965; 57:166–167.

Eckholm E, ed. *Solving America's Health-Care Crisis*. New York: Times Books, Random House, 1993, 301–314.

Eckholm E. While Congress remains silent health care transforms itself. *The New York Times*, Sunday, December 18, 1994, p. 1.

Editorial, *JAMA* 1932; 99:2035.

Edwards JN, Blendon RJ, Leitman R. The worried middle class. 61–81. In: Blendon RJ, Hyams TS, eds. *Reforming the System: Containing Health Care Costs in an Era of Universal Coverage*. Volume 2. *The Future of American Health Care*. New York: Faulkner and Gray, Inc., 1991.

Edwards WS, Berlin M. *National Medical Expenditure Survey: Questionnaires and Data Collection Methods for the Household Survey and the Survey of American Indians and Alaska Natives*. Rockville, Md: US Dept of Health and Human Services, Agency for Health Care Policy and Research; 1980. DHHS publication PHS 89–3450.

Edwards WS. *National Medical Expenditure Survey: Questionnaires and Data Collection Methods for the United States Population*. Rockville, Maryland: U.S. Department of Health and Human Services, Agency for Health Care Policy and Research: 1989. DHHS Pub. PHY 89–3440.

The efficiency of arsphenamines. *J Natl Med Assoc* 1924; 16:19.

Ehrenreich B, Ehrenreich J. *The American Health Empire: Power, Profits, and Politics*. New York: Random House, 1970.

Eichenwald K. A health care giant's secret payments taint a Texas deal. *The New York Times*, Saturday, March 29, 1997, p. 21.

Eichenwald K. He blew the whistle and health giants quaked. *The New York Times*, Sunday, October 18, 1998, Section 3, p. 1.

Einbinder LC, Schulman KA. The effect of race on the referral process for invasive cardiac procedures. *Medical Care Research and Review* 2000; 57 (suppl 1):162–180.

Eisenberg JM. Sociologic influences on decision making by clinicians. *Ann Intern Med* 1979; 318:158–163.

"Eliminating Racial and Ethnic Disparities in Health: Overview." in U.S. Department of Health and Human Services World Wide Web site [updated May 26, 1998; cited May 18, 1999][data-base online]. Washington, D.C., pp. 1–6.

Eliot JW, Hall RE, Willson RJ, Houser C. The obstetrician's view. I. 93. In: Hall RE, ed. *Abortion in a Changing World*. New York: Columbia University Press, 1970.

Elixhauser A, Ball JK. Black-White differences in colorectal tumor location in a national sample of hospitals. *J Natl Med Assoc* 1994; 86:449–458.

Elkowitz A. Physicians at the bedside: Thoughts and actions with regard to health care allocation. *J Natl Med Assoc* 1986; 78:423–426.

Ellis EF, Attswood JC. A concept of delivery of health care. *J Natl Med Assoc* 1972; 64:189–196.

Ellwood W. *The Road to Brown* [56 min. videotape], produced by the University of Virginia and California Newsreel, 1990.

Ely MP. *The Adventures of Amos 'n' Andy: A Social History of an American Phenomenon*. New York: The Free Press, 1991.

English JT. New challenges for physicians in the war on poverty. *J Natl Med Assoc* 1968; 60:38–41.

English WT. The Negro problem from the physician's point of view. *Atlanta Journal-Record of Medicine* 1903 (October); 5:462–463.

Enthoven AC. Consumer-choice health plan. *N Engl J Med* 1978; 298:650–658, 709–720.

Enthoven AC. *Health Plan: The Only Practical Solution to Soaring Health Costs*. Reading, Massachusetts: Addison-Wesley, 1980.

Enthoven AC. Why managed care has failed to contain health costs. *Health Affairs* (Millwood) 1993 (Fall); 12:27–43.

Epps AC. National board and the minority medical student. *J Natl Med Assoc* 1990; 82:161–163.

Epps HR. The Howard University medical department in the Flexner era: 1910–1929. *J Natl Med Assoc* 1989; 81:885.

Epps Jr. CH. The Black practitioner: Challenges of the future. *J Natl Med Assoc* 1986; 78:365–370.

Epps Jr. CH, Johnson DG, Vaughan AL. Black medical pioneers: African-American 'firsts' in academic and organized medicine: Part one. *J Natl Med Assoc* 1993; 85:629–644.

Epps Jr. CH, Johnson DG, Vaughan AL. Black medical pioneers: African-American 'firsts' in academic and organized medicine: Part two. *J Natl Med Assoc* 1993; 85:703–720.

Epps Jr. CH, Johnson DG, Vaughan AL. Black medical pioneers: African-American 'firsts' in academic and organized medicine: Part three. *J Natl Med Assoc* 1993; 85:777–796.

Errata. *J Natl Med Assoc* 1910; 2:133–136.

Errata. Acknowledged receipt of Bulletin Number Four. *J Natl Med Assoc* 1910; 2:193–194.

Errata. *J Natl Med Assoc* 1910; 2:306.

Escarce JJ, Epstein KR, Colby DC, Schwartz JS. Racial differences in the elderly's use of medical procedures and diagnostic tests. *Am J Public Health* 1993; 83:948–954.

The establishment turns the Negro's flank: Or, how the "boat" was missed. *J Natl Med Assoc* 1969; 61:274–275. Editorials.

Estabrook KA, Davenport CB. *The Nam Family: A Study in Cacogenics*. Cold Spring Harbor, New York: Eugenics Record Office, 1912.

Ethics governing the services of prisoners as subjects in medical experiments: Report of a committee appointed by Governor Dwight H. Green of Illinois. *JAMA* 1948; 136:457.

Ethnicity, race, and culture: guidelines for research, audit, and publication. *BMJ* 1996; 312:1094.

Ethnology. *J Natl Med Assoc* 1912; 4:352–354.

Etzioni A, Doty P. Profit in not-for-profit corporations: The example of health care. *Political Science Quarterly* 1976; 91:434.

Evans RG. Going for the gold: The redistributive agenda behind market-based health care reform. *Journal of Health Politics, Policy and Law* 1997; 22:21–22.

Ewbank DC. History of Black mortality and health before 1940. 100–128. In: Willis DP, ed. *Health Policies and Black Americans*. New Brunswick, New Jersey: Transaction Publishers, 1989.

Eysenck HJ. *The I.Q. Argument: Race, Intelligence and Education*. New York: The Library Press, 1971.

Factors influencing the fate of the Negro hospital. *J Natl Med Assoc* 1967; 59:217.

Falk LA. Black abolitionist doctors and healers, 1810–1885. *Bulletin of the History of Medicine* 1980; 54:253–272.

Farley DE. *Trends in Hospital Average Length of Stay, Casemix and Discharge Rates, 1980–1985* (Hospital Studies Program, Research Note 11). Washington, D.C.: U.S. Department of Health and Human Services, 1988.

Farley R. *Growth of the Black Population: A Study of Demographic Trends*. Chicago: Markham Publishing Company, 1970.

Farley R, Allen WR. *The Color Line and the Quality of Life in America*. New York: Oxford University Press, 1989.

Farmer P. *AIDS and Accusation: Haiti and the Geography of Blame*. Berkeley: University of California Press, 1992.

Feagin JR, Spikes MP. *Living With Racism: The Black Middle-Class Experience*. Boston: Beacon Press, 1994.

Feagin JR, Vera H. *White Racism: The Basics*. New York: Routledge, 1995.

Feagin JR, Feagin CB. *Racial and Ethnic Relations*. Sixth Edition. Upper Saddle River, New Jersey: Prentice Hall, 1999.

Feagin JR. *Racist America: Roots, Current Realities, and Future Reparations*. New York: Routledge, 2000.

Fee E. History and development of public health. 10–30. In: Sutchfield FD, Keck CW. *Principles of Public Health Practice*. Albany, New York: Delmar Publishers, 1997.

Fein EB. The elderly poor fear health care changes. *The New York Times*, Sunday, November 5, 1995, p. 1.

Fein EB. Giuliani's plan to lease a hospital is in jeopardy: Coney Island privatization deal is blocked. *The New York Times*, Sunday, June 1, 1997, p. 35.

Fein EB. U.S. auditing 5 hospitals in New York: Part of a wider search for Medicare fraud. *The New York Times*, Sunday, April 5, 1998, p. 31.

Fein R. Health care reform. *Scientific American*, November, 1992, 46–53.

Ferster Z. Eliminating the unfit—Is sterilization the answer? *Ohio State Law Journal* 1966; 27:591–633.

Fialka JJ. Demands on New Orleans's 'Big Charity' hospital are symptomatic of U.S. health-care problem. *The Wall Street Journal*, Tuesday, June 22, 1993, p. A16.

Final report of the Tuskegee Syphilis Study Ad Hoc Advisory Panel. 316–321. In: Reiser RJ, Dyck AJ, Curran WJ, eds. *Ethics in Medicine: Historical Perspectives and Contemporary Concerns*. Cambridge, MA: MIT Press, 1977.

Finder A. Court says law forbids hospital lease: Ruling deals a blow to a Giuliani plan. *The New York Times*, Wednesday, March 31, 1999, p. A21.

Fineberg KS, Peters JD, Willson JR, Kroll DA. *Obstetrics/Gynecology and the Law*. Ann Arbor: Health Administration Press, 1984.

Fineman H. HMOs under the knife: The capital races to crack down on managed care. *Newsweek*, July 27, 1998, 21.

Finley MI. *Ancient Slavery and Modern Ideology*. New York: Viking Penguin, Inc., 1980.

First item: Books, lay press, etc. *J Natl Med Assoc* 1911; 3:192–193.

Fiscella K, Franks P, Gold MR, Clancy CM. Inequality in quality: Addressing socioeconomic, racial, and ethnic disparities in health care. *JAMA* 2000; 283:2579–2584.

Fishbein M. Committee on the costs of medical care. *JAMA* 1932; 99:1950–1952.

Fisher I. H.M.O. premiums rising sharply, stoking debate on managed care. *The New York Times*, Sunday, January 11, 1998, p. 1.

Fitzpatrick S, Goodwin MR. *The Guide to Black Washington: Places and Events of Historical and Cultural Significance in the Nation's Capital*. New York: Hippocrene Books, 1990.

Flatow I. *The Rise of Environmental Justice*, video segment in *Earth Keeping*, WGBH, Boston, 1993.

Flexner A. *Medical Education in the United States and Canada: A Report to the Carnegie Foundation for the Advancement of Teaching*. New York: Carnegie Foundation for the Advancement of Teaching, Bulletin no. 4, 1910.

Floyd VD. "Too soon, too small, too sick": Black infant mortality. 165–177. In: Braithwaite RL, Taylor SE, eds. *Health Issues in the Black Community*. San Francisco: Jossey-Bass Publishers, 1992.

Food safety system due for an overhaul, committee says. *The Nation's Health*, October, 1998, p. 1.

Foote SB. *Managing the Medical Arms Race: Innovation and Public Policy in the Medical Device Industry*. Berkeley: University of California Press, 1992.

Former "Wild Kingdom" star rounds up medical care for poor: In Appalachia, patients, pets given treatment and compassion. *The Boston Sunday Globe*, Sunday, October 18, 1998, p. A25.

Foster HW. Reaching parity for minority medical students: A possibility or a pipe dream? *J Natl Med Assoc* 1996; 88:17–21.

Foster HW, Greenwood A. *Make A Difference*. New York: Scribner, 1997.

Fox H. Observations on skin diseases in the Negro. *Journal of Cutaneous Diseases* 1908; 26:109.

Francis C. CVD mortality among Harlem's Black males higher than in third world. In: *Minority Health Issues for an Emerging Majority: Proceedings of the 4th National Forum on Cardiovascular Health, Pulmonary Disorders, and Blood Resources, Washington, D.C., June 26–27, 1992*, by the National Heart, Lung, and Blood Institute (NHLBI), the NHLBI Ad Hoc Committee on Minority Populations, and the National Medical Association.

Fraser S, ed. *The Bell Curve Wars: Race, Intelligence, and the Future of America*. New York: Basic Books, 1995.

Frazier EF. *The Negro in the United States*. Revised Edition. New York: The Macmillan Company, 1957.

Frazier EF. *Black Bourgeoisie; The Rise of a New Middle Class in the United States*. New York: The Free Press, 1957. Paperback Edition. New York: Collier Books, 1962.

Fredrickson GM. *The Black Image in the White Mind: The Debate on Afro-American Character and Destiny, 1871–1914*. New York: Harper and Row Publishers, 1971. Reprint Edition. Middletown, Connecticut: Wesleyan University Press, 1987.

Freeman HP, Bernard L, Matory W, Smith FM, Whittico JJ, Yancy Jr. AG, et al. Physician manpower need of the nation: Position paper of the Surgical Section of the National Medical Association. *J Natl Med Assoc* 1982; 74:617–619.

Freudenheim M. States shelving ambitious plans on health care: More people uninsured. *The New York Times*, Sunday, July 2, 1995, p. 1.

Freudenheim M. Consumers across the nation are facing sharp increases in health care costs in 2001. *The New York Times*, Sunday, December 10, 2000, p. 40.

Friedman E. Public hospitals: Doing what everyone wants done but few others wish to do. *JAMA* 1987; 257:1437–1444.

Friedman E. Demise of Philadelphia General an instructive case; Other cities treat public hospital ills differently. *JAMA* 1987; 257:1571–1575.

Friedman E. Public hospitals often face unmet capital needs, underfunding, uncompensated patient-care costs. *JAMA* 1987; 257:1698–1701.

Friedman E. Problems plaguing public hospitals: Uninsured patient transfers, tight funds, misman-agement, and misperception. *JAMA* 1987; 257:1850–1857.

Friedman E. The uninsured: From dilemma to crisis. *JAMA* 1991; 265:2491–2495.

Friedman E. "The Human Factor: The Effect of Emerging Models of Competition on Patients and the Public." Presented at the Robert Wood Johnson Foundation/Alpha Center Conference on Rethinking Competition in Health Care, Washington, D.C., January 7–8, 1993.

Friedman LM. *Crime and Punishment in American History*. New York: Basic Books, 1993.

Frierson HT. The status of Black students in medical education. *J Natl Med Assoc* 1988; 80:387–390.

Frierson HT. Black medical students' perceptions of the academic environment and of faculty and peer interactions. *J Natl Med Assoc* 1987; 79:737–743.

Frye JC, et al. The rise and fall of the United States Commission on Civil Rights. *Harvard Civil Rights–Civil Liberties Law Review* 1987 (Spring); 22:478–479.

Fuchs VR. *The Health Economy*. Cambridge, Massachusetts: Harvard University Press, 1986.

Fuchs VR. *The Future of Health Policy*. Cambridge, Massachusetts: Harvard University Press, 1993.

Fukuyama F. *Trust: The Social Virtues and the Creation of Prosperity*. New York: The Free Press, 1995.

Galton F. *Inquiries into Human Faculty*. London: Macmillan, 1883.

Gamble HF. Report of committee on medical education and Negro medical schools. *J Natl Med Assoc* 1909; 1:257–258.

Gamble HF. Report on medical education. *J Natl Med Assoc* 1910; 2:23–29.

Gamble HF, France JJ, Anderson JC. Report of committee on medical education on colored hospi-tals. *J Natl Med Assoc* 1910; 2:283–290.

Gamble RL. Henry Floyd Gamble, M.D., 1862–1932. *J Natl Med Assoc* 1972; 64:85–86. Medical History.

Gamble VN. *The Black Community Hospital: A Historical Perspective*. New York: Garland Publishing, 1989.

Gamble VN. The Negro hospital renaissance: The Black hospital movement, 1920–1945. 82–105. In: Long DE, Golden J, eds. *The American General Hospital: Communities and Social Contexts*. Ithaca: Cornell University Press, 1989.

Gamble VN. *Making a Place for Ourselves: The Black Hospital Movement 1920–1945*. New York: Oxford University Press, 1995.

Gamble VN. Hospitals, Black. 1305–1309. In: Salzman J, Smith DL, West C. eds. *Encyclopedia of African-American Culture and History*. 5 Vols. New York: Macmillan Library Reference USA, Simon and Schuster Macmillan, 1996.

Gamble VN. Under the shadow of Tuskegee: African Americans and health care. *Am J Public Health* 1997; 87:1773–1778.

Gans HJ. *The War Against the Poor: The Underclass and Antipoverty Policy*. New York: Basic Books, 1995.

Gans RH. The hospital disciplinary process. *Leg Aspects Med Pract*, 1985; 13:1–4.

Garrett HE. Negro-White differences in mental ability in the United States. *Scientific Monthly* 1947; 65:329–333.

Garrett HE. Four monographs: (1) *How Classroom Desegregation Will Work*, (2) *Heredity: The Cause of Racial Differences in Intelligence*, (3) *The Relative Intelligence of Whites and Negroes: The Armed Forces Tests*, (4) *Breeding Down*. Richmond, Virginia: The Patrick Henry Press, undated but c. 1954–1967.

Garrett L. *Betrayal of Trust: The Collapse of Global Public Health*. New York: Hyperion, 2000.

Garvin CH. Post-war planning for "Negro" hospitals. *J Natl Med Assoc* 1945; 38:28–29.

Gaston RS, Ayres I, Dooley LG, Diethelm AG. Racial equity in renal transplantation: The disparate impact of HLA-based allocation. *JAMA* 1993; 270:1352–1355.

Geertsma RH. A special tutorial for minority medical students: An account of a year's experience. *J Med Educ* 1977; 52:396–403.

Geiger HJ. Community health centers: Health care as an instrument of social change. 11–32. In: Sidel VW, Sidel R, eds. *Reforming Medicine: Lessons of the Last Quarter Century*. New York: Pantheon Books, 1984.

Geiger HJ. Annotation: Racism resurgent–building a bridge to the 19th century. *Am J Public Health* 1997; 87:1765–1766.

Geiger HJ. Comment: Ethnic cleansing in the groves of academe. *Am J Public Health* 1998; 88:1299–1300.

George WC. *The Biology of the Race Problem: A Study Prepared by Commission of the Governor of Alabama*. Birmingham, Alabama: State of Alabama, 1962. Reprint Edition. Richmond, Virginia: The Patrick Henry Press, N.D.

Gideonse T. AIDS deaths drop, but the plague continues. *Newsweek*, October 19, 1998, 72.

Gilliam EW. "The African in the United States." *Popular Science Monthly* 1883; 22:437.

Gillum RF. The epidemiology of cardiovascular diseases: An American overview. 3–23. In: Livingston IL, ed. *Handbook of Black American Health: The Mosaic of Conditions, Issues, Policies, and Prospects*. Westport, Connecticut: Greenwood Press, 1994.

Gillum RF. Federal regulation of medical practice and the Black physician. *J Natl Med Assoc* 1973; 65:254–255. Briefs.

Ginzberg E, ed. *Regionalization and Health Policy*. Washington, D.C.: U.S. Government Printing Office, 1977.

Ginzberg E. The monetarization of medical care. *N Engl J Med* 1984; 310:1162–1165.

Ginzberg E. The destabilization of health care. *N Engl J Med* 1986; 315:757–767.

Ginzberg E, Dutka AB. *The Financing of Biomedical Research*. Baltimore: The Johns Hopkins University Press, 1989.

Ginzberg E. *The Medical Triangle: Physicians, Politicians, and the Public*. Cambridge, Massachusetts: Harvard University Press, 1990.

Ginzberg E. High-tech medicine and rising health care costs. *JAMA* 1990; 263:1820–1822.

Ginzberg E. "High-Tech Medicine." 41–53. In: Ginzberg E. *The Medical Triangle: Physicians, Politicians, and the Public*: Cambridge, Massachusetts: Harvard University Press, 1990.

Ginzberg E, Ostow M. *The Road to Reform: The Future of Health Care in America*. New York: The Free Press, 1994.

Ginzberg E. Improving health care for the poor: Lessons from the 1980s. *JAMA* 1994; 271:464–467.

Ginzberg E. *Teaching Hospitals and the Urban Poor*. New Haven: Yale University Press, 2000.

Ginzberg E. A life in health policy. *Health Affairs* (Millwood) 2000; 19:239–244.

Glantz LH. The influence of the Nuremberg Code on U.S. statutes and regulations. 183–222. In: Annas GJ, Grodin MA, eds. *The Nazi Doctors and the Nuremberg Code: Human Rights in Human Experimentation*. New York: Oxford University Press, 1992.

Glaser WA. The United States needs a health system like other countries. *JAMA* 1993; 270:980–984.

Glasgow DG. *The Black Underclass: Poverty, Unemployment, and Entrapment of Ghetto Youth*. London: Jossey-Bass Limited, 1980. Paperback Edition. New York: Vintage Books, 1981.

"Goal 1—Eliminate Disparities in Infant Mortality Rates." in U.S. Department of Health and Human Services World Wide Web site [updated May 26, 1998; cited May 18, 1999][data-base online]. Washington, D.C., pp. 1–3.

"Goal 2—Eliminate Disparities in Cancer Screening and Management." in U.S. Department of Health and Human Services World Wide Web site [updated May 26, 1998; cited May 18, 1999][data-base online]. Washington, D.C., pp. 1–4.

"Goal 3—Eliminate Disparities in Cardiovascular Disease." in U.S. Department of Health and Human Services World Wide Web site [updated May 26, 1998; cited May 18, 1999][data-base online]. Washington, D.C., pp. 1–3.

"Goal 4—Eliminate Disparities in Diabetes." in U.S. Department of Health and Human Services World Wide Web site [updated May 26, 1998; cited May 18, 1999][data-base online]. Washington, D.C., pp. 1–3.

"Goal 5—Eliminate Disparities in HIV Infection/AIDS." in U.S. Department of Health and Human Services World Wide Web site [updated May 26, 1998; cited May 18, 1999][data-base online]. Washington, D.C., pp. 1–3.

"Goal 6—Eliminate Disparities in Child and Adult Immunization Rates." in U.S. Department of Health and Human Services World Wide Web site [updated May 26, 1998; cited May 18, 1999][data-base online]. Washington, D.C., pp. 1–3.

Goddard HH. *The Kallikak Family: A Study in the Heredity of Feeblemindedness*. New York: Macmillan, 1914.

Goddard HH. How shall we educate mental defectives? *The Training School Bulletin* 1912; 9: 43.

Goddard HH. The Binet tests in relation to immigration. *Journal of Psycho-Asthenics* 1913/1914; 18:105.

Goddard HH. *Human Efficiency and Levels of Intelligence*. Princeton: Princeton University Press, 1920.

Goldberg DT. The social formation of racist discourse. 295–318. In: Goldberg DT, ed. *Anatomy of Racism*. Minneapolis: University of Minnesota Press, 1990.

Gold D. Hospital establishes barter system to help underinsured: Contract for care will allow patients to pay off bills. *The Boston Sunday Globe*, Sunday, March 15, 1998, p. C9.

Gonella JS, Louis DZ, McCord JJ. The staging concept: An approach to the assessment of outcome of ambulatory care. *Medical Care* 1976; 14:13–21.

Gordon L. *Woman's Body, Woman's Right: Birth Control in America*. New York: Penguin Books, 1976.

Gordon LR. *Her Majesty's Other Children: Sketches of Racism from a Neo-colonial Age*. Lanham, Maryland: Rowman and Littlefield Publishers, Inc., 1997.

Gordon S. Is research being 'managed' out of existence. *The Boston Sunday Globe*, October 13, 1996, p. D1.

Gossett TF. *Race: The History of an Idea in America*. Dallas, Texas: Southern Methodist University Press, 1963. Reprint Edition. New York: Schocken Books, 1965.

Gottleib M, Eichenwald K, Barbanel J. For the biggest hospital operator, a debate over ties that bind. *The New York Times*, Sunday, April 6, 1997, p. 1.

Gottleib M, Eichenwald K. A hospital chain's brass knuckles, and the backlash. *The New York Times*, Sunday, May 11, 1997, Section 3, p. 1.

Gobineau JA. *The Inequality of Human Races*. Trans. Collins, A. London: Heinemann, 1915.

Gould BA. *Investigations in the Military and Anthropological Statistics of American Soldiers* (New York, 1869).

Gould SJ. Racism and recapitulation. 214–221. In: Gould SJ. *Ever Since Darwin: Reflections in Natural History*. New York: W.W. Norton, 1977.

Gould SJ. Racist arguments and IQ. 243–247. In: Gould SJ. *Ever Since Darwin: Reflections in Natural History*. New York: W.W. Norton and Company, 1977.

Gould SJ. Flaws in the Victorian veil. 169–176. In: Gould SJ. *The Panda's Thumb: More Reflections in Natural History*. New York: W. W. Norton, 1980.

Gould SJ. *The Mismeasure of Man*. New York: W.W. Norton and Company, 1981.

Gould SJ. Bound by the great chain. 281–290. In: Gould SJ. *The Flamingo's Smile: Reflections in Natural History*. New York: W.W. Norton and Company, 1985.

Gould SJ. The Hottentot Venus. 291–305. In: Gould SJ. *The Flamingo's Smile: Reflections in Natural History*. New York: W.W. Norton and Company, 1985.

Gould SJ. Jensen's last stand. 124–144. In: Gould SJ. *An Urchin In the Storm: Essays about Books and Ideas*. New York: W.W. Norton, 1987.

Graduate medical education, *JAMA* 1993; 270:1116–1122, Appendix II.

Graduate medical education, *JAMA* 1996; 276:739, Appendix II, Table 1.

Granger LB. Barriers to Negro war employment. *Annals of the American Academy of Political and Social Science*. 1942 (September); 223:72–80.

Grant, M. *The Passing of the Great Race*. New York: Charles Scribner's Sons, 1916. Revised, Amplified Edition. 1918.

Gratus J. *The Great White Lie: Slavery, Emancipation, and Changing Racial Attitudes*. New York: Monthly Review Press, 1973.

A grave injustice. *J Natl Med Assoc* 1911; 3:159.

Graves ML, Practical remedial measures for the improvement of hygiene conditions of the Negro in the South. *American Journal of Public Health* 1915; 5:212.

Graves P. *Edward VIII: The Traitor King*. A 93 min. documentary [videotape] for *Biography*, Channel Four Television Corporation, 1995.

Gray BH. *Human Subjects in Medical Experimentation*. New York: Wiley and Sons, 1975.

Gray BH. *The Profit Motive and Patient Care: The Changing Accountability of Doctors and Hospitals*. A Twentieth Century Fund Report. Cambridge, Massachusetts: Harvard University Press, 1991.

Gray BH, Rowe C. Safety-net health plans: A status report. *Health Affairs* (Millwood) 2000; 19:185–193.

Gray LC. The geographic and functional distribution of black physicians: Some research and policy considerations. *American Journal of Public Health* 1977; 67:519–526.

Greaves WL. AIDS and sexually transmitted diseases. 157–168. In: Livingston IL, ed. *Handbook of Black American Health: The Mosaic of Conditions, Issues, Policies, and Prospects*. Westport, Connecticut: Greenwood Press, 1994.

Green EM. Psychoses among Negroes–a comparative approach. *Journal of Nervous and Mental Diseases* 1914; 41:703–708.

Green HM. Report of the pellagra commission. *J Natl Med Assoc* 1917; 9:223–227.

Greenberg DS. Black health: Grim statistics. *The Lancet* 1990; 335:780–781.

Gressin S, Krause JH, Ryzen E, Stern AN, Zemelman C, eds. Health care in America: Armageddon on the horizon? *Stanford Law and Policy Review* 1991; 3:1–260.

Gross ML. *The Doctors*. New York: Random House, 1966.

Guadagnoli E, Ayanian JZ, Gibbons G, McNeil BJ, LoGerfo FW. The influence of race on the use of surgical procedures for treatment of peripheral vascular disease of the lower extremities. *Archives of Surgery* 1995; 130:381–386.

Guinier L. *The Tyranny of the Majority: Fundamental Fairness in Representative Democracy*. New York: The Free Press, 1994.

Gullattee A, Kenney J, Mazique E, Royal F, Staggers F, Tuckson R, et al. Selected NMA resolutions, 1984 prepared by the legislation council. *J Natl Med Assoc* 1985; 77:151. NMA Activities.

Guthrie D. *A History of Medicine*. Philadelphia: J.B. Lippincott Company, 1946.

Guthrie RV. *Even the Rat Was White: A Historical View of Psychology*. New York: Harper and Row Publishers, 1976.

Guthrie RV. *Even the Rat Was White: A Historical View of Psychology*. Second Edition. Boston: Allyn and Bacon, 1998.

Haber L. *Black Pioneers of Science and Invention*. San Diego: Harcourt Brace Jovanovich, Publishers, 1970.

Hacker A. *Two Nations: Black and White, Separate, Hostile, Unequal*. New York: Ballantine Books, 1992. Expanded and Updated Edition. 1995.

Hadley J, Steinberg E, Feder J. Comparison of underinsured and privately insured hospital patients. *JAMA* 1991; 265:374–379.

Hairston GE, Byrd WM. Medical care in America: A tragic turn for the worst. *The Crisis* (October)1985; 92:25.

Hairston GE. Interview: Doctor David Satcher. *The Crisis* 1985; 92:38–44.

Halberstam D. "Fear and the Dream, Part One." Segment of multi-part video series *The Fifties*, 1997, the History Channel, May 11, 1998.

Halberstam D. "Fear and the Dream, Part Two." Segment of multi-part video series *The Fifties*, 1997, the History Channel, May 11, 1998.

Halberstam D. "The Rage Within, Part Six." Segment of multi-part video series *The Fifties*, 1997, the History Channel, May 15, 1998.

Haley JT. Dr. Robert Fulton Boyd. 59–62. In *The Afro-American Encyclopedia*. Nashville, TN: Haley and Florida, 1896.

Hall PF. *Immigration and its Effects on the United States*. New York: Henry Holt and Company, 1906.

Haller Jr. JS. *Outcasts from Evolution: Scientific Attitudes of Racial Inferiority, 1859–1900*. New York: McGraw Hill Book Company, 1971.

Haller Jr. JS, Haller RM. *The Physician and Sexuality in Victorian America.* N.P.: University of Illinois Press, 1974. Reprint Edition. New York: W.W. Norton and Company, 1977.

Haller Jr. JS. *American Medicine in Transition 1840–1910.* Urbana, Illinois: University of Illinois Press, 1981.

Haller MH. *Eugenics: Hereditarian Attitudes in American Thought.* New Brunswick, New Jersey: Rutgers University Press, 1963.

Hamilton DC. Great depression and the new deal. 1134–1142. In: Salzman J, Smith DL, West C, eds. *Encyclopedia of African-American Culture and History.* 5 Vols. New York: Macmillan Library Reference USA, Simon and Schuster Macmillan, 1996.

Hammonds KE. Blacks and the urban health crisis. *J Natl Med Assoc* 1974; 66:226–231.

Hampton H. *Eyes on the Prize.* [videotape]. A six part documentary video produced by Blackside, Inc., WGBH, Boston, and the Corporation for Public Broadcasting, 1987.

Hampton H, DeVinney J, Lacy Jr. MD. *Eyes on the Prize II.* [videotape]. The Time Has Come (1964–1966). An eight part documentary video produced by Blackside, Inc., WGBH, Boston, and the Corporation for Public Broadcasting, 1990.

Hampton H, Bernard S, Pollard S. *Eyes on the Prize II.* [videotape]. Two Societies (1965–1968). An eight part documentary video produced by Blackside, Inc., WGBH, Boston, and the Corporation for Public Broadcasting, 1990.

Hampton H, Massiah LJ, Rockefeller TK. *Eyes on the Prize II.* [videotape]. Power (1966–1968). An eight part documentary video produced by Blackside, Inc., WGBH, Boston, and the Corporation for Public Broadcasting, 1990.

Hampton H, Stekler P, Shearer J. *Eyes on the Prize II.* [videotape]. The Promised Land (1967–1968). An eight part documentary video produced by Blackside, Inc., WGBH, Boston, and the Corporation for Public Broadcasting, 1990.

Hampton H, Rockefeller TK, Ott T, Massiah L. *Eyes on the Prize II.* [videotape]. A Nation of Law? (1968–1971). An eight part documentary video produced by Blackside, Inc., WGBH, Boston, and the Corporation for Public Broadcasting, 1990.

Hampton H, Shearer J, Stekler P. *Eyes on the Prize II.* [videotape]. The Keys To The Kingdom (1974–1980). An eight part documentary video produced by Blackside, Inc., WGBH, Boston, and the Corporation for Public Broadcasting, 1990.

Hampton H, Lacy Jr. MD, DeVinney JA. *Eyes on the Prize II.* [videotape]. Back To The Movement (1979–1983). An eight part documentary video produced by Blackside, Inc., WGBH, Boston, and the Corporation for Public Broadcasting, 1990.

Hanft RS. National health expenditures, 1950–65. *Social Security Bull* 1967, 3–13.

Hanft RS, Fishman LE, Evans W. *Blacks and the Health Professions in the 80s: A National Crisis and a Time for Action.* Prepared for the Association of Minority Health Professions Schools, N.P., 1983.

Hanft RS, Fishman LE, White CC. "Minorities and the Health Professions: An Update." Draft of August 1985, Association of Minority Health Professions Schools, Washington, D.C.

Hanft RS, White CC. Constraining the supply of physicians: Effects on black physicians. 249–269. In: Willis DP, ed. *Health Policies and Black Americans.* Brunswick, New Jersey: Transaction Publishers, 1989.

Hannan EL, Ryn MV, Burke J, Stone D, Kumar D, Arani D, et al. Access to coronary artery bypass surgery by race/ethnicity and gender among patients who are appropriate for surgery. *Medical Care* 1999; 37:68–77.

Hansen AC. The future of medical education in the United States: The GPEP report. *J Natl Med Assoc* 1985; 77:775–776.

Harding S, ed. *The "Racial Economy" of Science: Toward A Democratic Future.* Bloomington: Indiana University Press, 1993.

Harding S. Introduction: Eurocentric scientific illiteracy–a challenge for the world community. 1–22. In: Harding S, ed. *The "Racial Economy" of Science: Toward A Democratic Future.* Bloomington: Indiana University Press, 1993.

Harlan LR, Smock RW, eds. *The Booker T. Washington Papers.* Vol. 9 of 13 vol. set. Urbana: The University of Illinois Press, 1972–1984.

Harmer RM. *American Medical Avarice.* New York: Abelard-Schuman, 1975.

Harrington M. *The Other America: Poverty in the United States.* New York: The Macmillan Company, 1962. Paperback Edition. Penguin Books Inc., 1963.

Hart N. The social and economic environment and human health. 151–195. In: Holland WW, Detels R, Knox G, eds. *Oxford Textbook of Public Health.* Volume 1. *Influences of Public Health.* Second Edition. Oxford: Oxford University Press, 1991.

Harrington C, Cassel C, Carroll LE, Woolhandler S, Himmelstein DU. A national long-term care program for the United States: A caring vision. *JAMA* 1991; 266:3023–3029.

Harris C. Update on pro harassment. *Medical Tribune*, December 5, 1984, p. 36.

Harris JE. *Africans and Their History*. Revised and Updated Edition. New York: New American Library, 1972.

Harris S. The future of the Negro from the standpoint of the southern physician. *Alabama Medical Journal* (January) 1902; 14:58.

Hart N. The social and economic environment and human health. 95–123. In: Detels R, Holland WW, McEwen J, Omenn GS, eds. *Oxford Textbook of Public Health*. Volume 1. *The Scope of Public Health*. Third Edition. New York: Oxford University Press, 1997.

Hatcher RG. Does Gary, Indiana, reflect the national problem of medicine in the ghetto? 21–31. In: Norman JC, ed. *Medicine in the Ghetto*. New York: Appleton-Century-Crofts, 1969.

Haughton JG. Government's role in health care, past, present and future. *J Natl Med Assoc* 1968; 60:87–91.

Havighurst CC. Competition in health services: Overview, issues and answers. *Vanderbilt Law Review* 1981 (May); 34:1115–1178.

Havighurst CC. *Health Care Law and Policy: Readings, Notes, and Questions*. Westbury, New York: The Foundation Press, Inc., 1988.

Hayden RC. Drew, Charles Richard. 802–803. In: Salzman J, Smith DL, West C. eds. *Encyclopedia of African-American Culture and History*. 5 Vols. New York: Macmillan Library Reference USA, Simon and Schuster Macmillan, 1996.

Hayden RC. Wright, Louis Tompkins. 2893–2895. In: Salzman J, Smith DL, West C. eds. *Encyclopedia of African-American Culture and History*. 5 Vols. New York: Macmillan Library Reference USA, Simon and Schuster Macmillan, 1996.

Hayden T. A fair that went foul. *Newsweek*, September 20, 1999, p. 37.

Haynes GE. Lily-white social security. *The Crisis* 1935; 42:85–86.

Haynes MA. The National Medical Association's health program for the inner city. *J Natl Med Assoc* 1968; 60:420.

Haynes MA. The distribution of Black physicians in the United States, 1967. *J Natl Med Assoc* 1969; 61:470–473.

Haynes MA, McGarvey MR. Physicians, hospitals, and patients in the inner city. 117–124. In: Norman JC, ed. *Medicine in the Ghetto*. New York: Appleton-Century-Crofts, 1969.

Haynes MA. The gap in health status between black and white Americans. 1–30. In: Williams RA, ed. *Textbook of Black-Related Diseases*. New York: McGraw-Hill Book Company, 1975.

Haynes MA, Bernard LJ. Drew/Meharry/Morehouse Consortium Cancer Center: An approach to targeted research in minority institutions. *J Natl Med Assoc* 1991; 84:505–511.

Haynes MA, Smedley BD, eds. *The Unequal Burden of Cancer: An Assessment of NIH Research and Programs for Ethnic Minorities and the Medically Underserved*. Washington, D.C.: National Academy Press, 1999.

Hazen HH. Syphilis in the American Negro. *Journal of the American Medical Association* 1914; 63:463.

Health and disease. *J Natl Med Assoc* 1912; 4:142–143.

Health Policy Advisory Center. The emerging health apartheid in the United States. *Health/PAC Bulletin* 1991; 21:3–4.

*The Health Units of Boston*, 1924–1933 and 1934–1944. Boston: Boston Printing Department, 1933 and 1945.

Hearnshaw LS. *Cyril Burt, Psychologist*. Ithaca, New York: Cornell University Press, 1979.

Hecht D. Tabes in the Negro. *American Journal of Medical Sciences* 1903; 126:708.

Henschke UL, Leffall Jr LD, Mason CH, Reinhold AW, Schneider RL, White JE. Alarming increase of the cancer mortality in the U.S. black population. *Cancer* 1973; 31:763–768.

Herman ES, Chomsky N. *Manufacturing Consent: The Political Economy of the Mass Media*. New York: Pantheon Books, 1988.

Herrick SS. Comparative vital movement of the White and Colored races in the United States. *New Orleans Medical and Surgical Journal* 1881–1883; 9:678.

Herring HB. Who can heal New York? *The New York Times*, Sunday, August 20, 1995, p. 2F.

Herrnstein RJ. *I.Q. in the Meritocracy*. Boston: Little, Brown and Company, 1973.

Herrnstein RJ, Murray C. *The Bell Curve: Intelligence and Class Structure in American Life*. New York: The Free Press, 1994.

Herrnstein RJ. IQ. 599–616. In: Jacoby R, Glauberman N, eds. *The Bell Curve Debate: History, Documents, Opinions*. New York: Times Books Division of Random House, Inc., 1995.

Hester RD, Barber JB. A new research agenda: Incentive payments for urban physicians. *J Natl Med*

*Assoc* 1984; 76:991–993. Health care problems in the 1980s from a Black perspective: Part III of a series begun in 1984; 76:968.

Hester RD, Barber JB. The relative value scale: Reforming physician payment policy. *J Natl Med Assoc* 1987; 79:1298–1303. Legislative Forum.

Hester RD, Barber JB. Health reforms and the Black community. *J Natl Med Assoc* 1990; 82:291–293.

Hey RP. Last-ditch reform effort fails. *AARP Bullitin*, October, 1994, 1.

Hiatt HH. *America's Health in the Balance: Choice or Chance?* New York: Harper and Row, Publishers, 1987.

Hicks N. Sterilization of Black mother of 3 stirs Aiken, S.C. *New York Times*, August 1, 1973, p. 27.

Higginbotham AL Jr. *In the Matter of Color: Race and the American Legal Process, The Colonial Period*. New York: Oxford University Press, 1978.

Higgins W. Myths of competitive reform. *Health Care Management Rev* 1991; 16:65–72.

The Hill-Burton program and civil rights. *J Natl Med Assoc* 1965, 57.59–61. Integration Battlefront.

Hilliard RLM. The impact of the new Mediciad (Medi-Cal) changes in California. *J Natl Med Assoc* 1982; 74:939 940. President's Column.

Hilliard RLM. Is there a doctor in the house? Budget cut impacts on the shortage of Black physicians. *J Natl Med Assoc* 1982; 74:1155–1156. President's Column.

Hilliard RLM. The President's inaugural address: Insuring quality health care. *J Natl Med Assoc* 1983; 75:81–83.

Hilliard RLM. Will there be a physician glut or an exaggeration of the present maldistribution of physicians? Another view. *J Natl Med Assoc* 1983; 75:855–859.

Hilliard RLM. Providing sound and effective health care delivery for all Americans. *J Natl Med Assoc* 1983; 75:1135–1138.

Himmelstein DU, Woolhandler S. A national health program for the United States: A physicians' proposal. *N Engl J Med* 1989; 320:102–108.

Hine DC. *Black Women in White: Racial Conflict and Cooperation in the Nursing Profession, 1890–1950*. Bloomington: Indiana University Press, 1989.

Hine DC. Nursing. 2034–2036. In: Salzman J, Smith DL, West C. eds. *Encyclopedia of African-American Culture and History*. 5 Vols. New York: Macmillan Library Reference USA, Simon and Schuster Macmillan, 1996.

Hirsch AR. *Making the Second Ghetto: Race and Housing in Chicago 1940–1960*. Cambridge: Cambridge University Press, 1983, xi–39.

Hirshfield DS. *The Lost Reform: The Campaign for Compulsory Health Insurance in the United States 1932 to 1943*. Cambridge, Massachusetts: A Commonwealth Fund Book, Harvard University Press, 1970.

Hirsh M, Klaidman D. Bad practices: The federal probe of Columbia/HCA is just part of a broad assault on health care fraud. *Newsweek*, August 11, 1997, 42.

History shows trends of African Americans' high mortality rates and poor health care. *National Medical Association News*, March/April, 1993, p. 1.

Hodges JA. The effect of freedom upon the physical and psychological development of the Negro. *Richmond Journal of Practice* (June) 1900; 14:170–171.

Hoffmann FL. *Race Traits and Tendencies of the American Negro*. New York: Publication of the American Economic Association, 1st Ser., XI , August, 1896.

Hoffman R, Steuerle E. "Tax Expenditures for Health Care." *Office of Tax Analysis Papers*, no. 38, April 1979 (U.S. Department of the Treasury).

Holden C, RJ Herrnstein: The perils of expounding meritocracy. *Science*, July 6, 1973, 36–39.

Holloman Jr. JLS. A new horizon: President's inaugural address, National Medical Association. *J Natl Med Assoc* 1966; 58:371–376.

Holloman Jr. JLS. Medical leadership. *J Natl Med Assoc* 1966; 58:377.

Holloman Jr. JLS. An open letter to the vice president. *J Natl Med Assoc* 1966; 58:472.

Holloman Jr. JLS. A call to arms. *J Natl Med Assoc* 1967; 59:55.

Holloman Jr. JLS. Cross currents in the flow of medical practice. *J Natl Med Assoc* 1967; 59:216.

Honour H. *The Image of the Black in Western Art. Part IV. From the American Revolution to World War I. 2. Black Models and White Myths*. Cambridge, Massachusetts: Menil Foundation, Inc., Distributed by Harvard University Press, 1989.

Hooper E. *The River: A Journey to the Source of HIV and AIDS*. Boston: Little, Brown and Company, 1999.

Hooton EA. *Apes, Men, and Morons*. New York: G.P. Putnam's Sons, 1937.

Horan M. CVD death rate 50 percent higher among Blacks. In: *Minority Health Issues for an Emerging Majority: Proceedings of the 4th National Forum on Cardiovascular Health, Pulmonary Disorders, and Blood Resources, Washington, D.C., June 26–27, 1992*, by the National Heart,

Lung, and Blood Institute (NHLBI), the NHLBI Ad Hoc Committee on Minority Populations, and the National Medical Association.

Hornblum AM. *Acres of Skin: Human Experiments at Holmesburg Prison: A True Story of Abuse and Exploitation in the Name of Medical Science*. New York: Routledge, 1998.

Horowitz LG. *Emerging Viruses: AIDS and Ebola — Nature, Accident or Intentional?* Sandpoint, Idaho: Tetrahedron, Inc., 1996.

Horsman R. *Race and Manifest Destiny: The Origins of American Racial Anglo-Saxonism*. Cambridge, Massachusetts: Harvard University Press, 1981.

Horsman R. *Josiah Nott of Mobile: Southerner, Physician, and Racial Theorist*. Baton Rouge: Louisiana State University Press, 1987.

Hospital compliance in Atlanta. *J Natl Med Assoc* 1966; 58:382–383. Integration Battlefront.

Hospital for ex-service men to be at Tuskegee. *J Natl Med Assoc* 1922; 14:208.

Houston E. Black hospitals struggle for support. *Emerge*, February, 1998, 34.

Hoversten P. Radiation tests used inmates as guinea pigs. *USA Today*, Monday, November 21, 1994, 3A.

Howard WL. The Negro as a distinct ethnic factor in civilization. *Medicine* 1903; 9:424.

Hoyert DL. Effect on mortality rates of the 1989 change in tabulating race. National Center for Health Statistics. *Vital and Health Statistics* 1994; 20:25.

Hubbard GW. Yesterday, today and tomorrow. *J Natl Med Assoc* 1909; 1:133–135.

Hubbard R, Wald E. *Exploding the Gene Myth: How Genetic Information Is Produced and Manipulated by Scientists, Physicians, Employers, Insurance Companies, Educators, and Law Enforcers*. Boston: Beacon Press, 1993.

Hudson JI, Infeld MD. Ambulatory care reorganization in teaching hospitals. *Journal of Ambulatory Care Management* (February, No. 3) 1980, 31–50.

Huet-Cox R. Medical education: New wine in old wine skins. 129–149. In: Sidel VW, Sidel R, eds. *Reforming Medicine: Lessons of the Last Quarter Century*. New York: Pantheon Books, 1984.

Hughes L, Meltzer M, Lincoln CE. Rev 5th ed. *A Pictorial History of Blackamericans*. New York: Crown Publishers, Inc., 1983.

Hughes L, Meltzer M, Lincoln CE, Spencer JM. Rev 6th ed. *A Pictorial History of Blackamericans*. New York: Crown Publishers, Inc., 1995.

Hunter C, Frelick RW, Feidman AR, Bavier AR, Dunlap WH, Ford L, Henson D, Macfarlane D, Smart CR, Yancik R, Yates JW. Selection factors in clinical trials: Results from the community clinical oncology program physician's patient log. *Cancer Treatment Reports* 1987; 71:559–565.

Hunt S. The Flexner report and Black academic medicine: An assignment of place. *J Natl Med Assoc* 1993; 85:151–155.

Hutchins RM, ed. *Great Books of the Western World*. Vol. 49. *Darwin. The Origin of Species by Means of Natural Selection*. by Charles Darwin (Chicago: University of Chicago Press, 1952), 1–252.

Hutchins RM, ed. *Great Books of the Western World*. Vol. 49. *Darwin. The Descent of Man and Selection in Relation to Sex*. by Charles Darwin (Chicago: University of Chicago Press, 1952), 253–600.

Iglehart JK. Medical care for the poor–a growing problem. *N Engl J Med* 1985; 313:59–63.

Iglehart JK. U.S. health care system: A look to the 1990s. *Health Affairs* (Millwood) 1985; 3:120–127.

Iglehart JK. The administration's assault on domestic spending and the threat to health care programs. *N Engl J Med* 1985; 312:525–528.

Iglehart JK. The American health system: Managed care. *N Engl J Med* 1992; 327:742–747.

Iglehart JK. Health policy report: The struggle to reform Medicare. *N Engl J Med* 1996; 334:1071–1075.

Iglehart VR, Taneja KS. Prospective payment system: Experience of a public hospital. *J Natl Med Assoc* 1984; 76:765–768.

Illich I. *Medical Nemesis: The Expropriation of Health*. New York: Pantheon Books, Inc., 1976. Paperback Edition. Toronto: Bantam Books, 1977.

The Imhotep National Conference on Hospital Integration. *J Natl Med Assoc* 1957; 49:55–58.

Imhotep National Conference on Hospital Integration. The proceedings of the Imhotep national conference on hospital integration. Parts 1–3. *J Natl Med Assoc* 1957; 49:189–201, 272–273, 429–433.

Ingle DJ. Racial differences and the future. *Science* 1964; 146:378.

Ingle DJ. *Who Should Have Children? An Environmental and Genetic Approach*. Indianapolis: The Bobbs-Merrill Company, 1973.

"Initiative to Eliminate Racial and Ethnic Disparities in Health: Goal 5 — Eliminate disparities in HIV infection." in U.S. Department of Health and Human Services World Wide Web site [updated May 26, 1998; cited February 8, 1999] [data-base online]. Washington, D.C.

Inlander CB, Levin LS, Weiner E. *Medicine on Trial: The Appalling Story of Medical Ineptitude and the Arrogance That Overlooks It.* New York: Pantheon Books and the People's Medical Society, 1988.

Institute of Medicine. *Health Care in the Context of Civil Rights.* Washington, D.C.: National Academy Press, 1981.

Institute of Medicine. *The Future of Public Health.* Washington, D.C.: National Academy Press, 1988.

Institute of Medicine. *Controlling Cost and Changing Patient Care? The Role of Utilization Management.* Editors. Bradford H. Gray and Marilyn J. Field. Washington D.C.: National Academy Press, 1989.

Institute of Medicine. *Access to Health Care in America.* Washington, D.C.: National Academy Press, 1993.

Items of interest: Item 7, Medical School of Shaw University. *J Natl Med Assoc* 1912; 4:96–97.

International Association for the Advancement of Ethnology and Eugenics, New York. Reprint series: (1) *The Inheritance of Mental Ability,* by Cyril Burt. Reprint No. 11. Reprinted from *American Psychologist,* Vol. XII, No. 1 (January, 1958). (2) *A Review: Klineberg's Chapter on Race and Psychology,* by Henry E. Garrett. Reprint from *The Mankind Quarterly,* Vol. 1, No. 1 (July, 1960). (3) *The Emergence of Racial Genetics,* by Ruggles R. Gates. Reprint No. 6. Reprinted from *The Mankind Quarterly,* Vol. 1, No. 1 (July, 1960). (4) *The S.P.S.S.I. and Racial Differences,* by Henry E. Garrett. Reprint No. 9. Reprinted from *American Psychologist,* Vol. XVII, No. 5 (May, 1962).

"It's Time to Operate," *Fortune,* January, 1970, 79.

Jackson H. Race and the politics of medicine in nineteenth-century Georgia. 184–205. In: Blakely RL, Harrington JM, ed. *Bones in the Basement: Postmortem Racism in Nineteenth-Century Medical Training.* Washington: Smithsonian Institution Press, 1997.

Jackson Hole Group (Paul Ellwood, Alain Enthoven, and Lynn Etheredge). *The 21st Century American Health System.* [Jackson Hole, Wyoming] 1991–1992. (Series of policy documents).

Jacobson TC. *Making Medical Doctors: Science and Medicine at Vanderbilt Since Flexner.* Tuscaloosa: The University of Alabama Press. 1987.

Jacoby R, Glauberman N, eds. *The Bell Curve Debate: History, Documents, Opinions.* New York: Times Books Division of Random House, Inc., 1995.

Janofsky M. West Virginia pares welfare, but poor remain. *The New York Times,* Sunday, March 7, 1999, p. 14.

Jaynes GD, Williams RM. eds. *A Common Destiny: Blacks and American Society.* Washington, D.C.: National Academy Press, 1989.

Jensen AR. Learning abilities in retarded, average, and gifted children. *Merrill-Palmer Quarterly* 1963; 9:123–140.

Jensen AR. The culturally disadvantaged: Psychological and educational aspects. *Educational Research* 1967; 10:4–20.

Jensen AR. Social class, race and genetics: Implications for education. *American Educational Research Journal* 1968; 5:1–42.

Jensen AR. The Culturally Disadvantaged and the Heredity-Environment Uncertainty. In: Hellmuth J, ed. *Disadvantaged Child.* Vol. 2. New York: Brunner-Mazel, 1968.

Jensen AR. How much can we boost IQ and scholastic achievement? *Harvard Educational Review* 1969; 39:1–123.

Jensen AR. *Bias in Mental Testing.* New York: Free Press, 1979.

Jhally S, Lewis J. *Enlightened Racism: The Cosby Show, Audiences, and the Myth of the American Dream.* Boulder: Westview Press, 1992.

Johannes L. State probes HMO's denial of some care. *The Wall Street Journal,* Wednesday, August 16, 1995, p. T1.

The John A. Andrew clinical society. *J Natl Med Assoc* 1919; 11:70–71.

Johnson AG. *The Blackwell Dictionary of Sociology: A User's Guide to Sociological Language.* Cambridge, Massachusetts: Basil Blackwell Inc., 1995.

Johnson C. The survival of Afro-American physicians in 1990 and beyond: Inaugural address. *J Natl Med Assoc* 1990; 82:761–765.

Johnson CS. *Shadow of the Plantation.* Chicago: University of Chicago Press, 1934.

Johnson ET. The delivery of health care in the ghetto. *J Natl Med Assoc* 1969; 61:263–270.

Johnson H, Broder DS. *The System: The American Way of Politics at the Breaking Point.* Boston: Little, Brown and Company, 1996.

Johnson JT. On some of the apparent peculiarities of parturition in the Negro race, with remarks on race pelvis in general. *American Journal of Obstetrics* (1875–1876); 8:88–123.

Johnson L. The restraint of progress: Declining participation of Blacks and other minorities in medical schools. *New York State J Med* 1985; 85:135–136.

Johnson LB. Address to the National Medical Association. *J Natl Med Assoc* 1968; 60:449–454.
Johnson RP. The minister's welcome. *J Natl Med Assoc* 1957; 49:55, 57.
Johnston GS. The Flexner report and the Black medical schools. *J Natl Med Assoc* 1984; 76:223–225.
Jonas G. *The Circuit Riders: Rockefeller Money and the Rise of Modern Science.* New York: W.W. Norton and Company, 1989.
Jonas S. *Health Care Delivery in the United States.* Third Edition. New York: Springer, 1986.
Jones B. Disproportionate health risks in minorities: Does medical education need to change? *J Natl Med Assoc* 1990; 82:395–396.
Jones DJ, Roberts VA. Black children: Growth, development and health. 333–343. In: Livingston IL, ed. *Handbook of Black American Health: The Mosaic of Conditions, Issues, Policies, and Prospects.* Westport, Connecticut: Greenwood Press, 1994.
Jones EI. Change—threat or opportunity? *J Natl Med Assoc* 1985; 77:773–774.
Jones EI. NMA's commitment to quality health care for all. *J Natl Med Assoc* 1985; 77:987–991.
Jones EI. Society's responsibility for health care of the indigent. *J Natl Med Assoc* 1986; 78:95–96.
Jones EI. The direct relationship of health status to health care. *J Natl Med Assoc* 1986; 78:271–272.
Jones EI. Closing the health status gap for Blacks and other minorities. *J Natl Med Assoc* 1985; 78:485–488.
Jones EI. Disproportionate care providers: Lauded or harassed? *J Natl Med Assoc* 1985; 77:871–872.
Jones EI. Effects of competition on access to care: Will new trends in competition limit access to health care for Blacks? *J Natl Med Assoc* 1985; 77:967–968.
Jones EI. Preventing disease and promoting health in the minority community. *J Natl Med Assoc* 1986; 78:18–20.
Jones EI. Overcoming challenges to serve. *J Natl Med Assoc* 1986; 78:806–808.
Jones F. Syphilis in the Negro. *American Journal of Dermatology and Genito-Urinary Diseases* 1906; 10:277–279.
Jones J. *American Work: Four Centuries of Black and White Labor.* New York: W.W. Norton and Company, 1998.
Jones JH. *Bad Blood: The Tuskegee Syphilis Experiment.* New York: The Free Press, 1981. New and Expanded Edition, 1993.
Jones JH. Tuskegee syphilis experiment. 2685–2687. In: Salzman J, Smith DL, West C. eds. *Encyclopedia of African-American Culture and History.* 5 Vols. New York: Macmillan Library Reference USA, Simon and Schuster Macmillan, 1996.
Jones LA, ed. *Minorities and Cancer.* New York: Springer-Verlag, 1989.
Jones PA. Three against the storm: Facing an awesome array of problems, black community hospitals advance toward an uncertain future. *The Crisis* (October) 1985; 92:35.
Jones SB, DuVal MK, Lesparre M. Competition or conscience? Mixed-mission dilemmas of the voluntary hospital. *Inquiry* 1987 (Summer); 24:110–118.
Jordan VE. An address. *J Natl Med Assoc* 1980; 72:378–380. NMA Activities.
Jordan WD. *White Over Black: American Attitudes Toward the Negro, 1550–1812.* New York: W.W. Norton and Company, Inc., 1968.
Joyner JE. Future of health care in America: What is the NMA's role? *J Natl Med Assoc* 1987; 79:1129–1133. President's Inaugural Address.
Joyner JE. Nothing ventured—nothing gained. *J Natl Med Assod* 1988; 80:377–378. President's Column.
Joyner JE. Health manpower today and future implications. *J Natl Med Assoc* 1988; 80:717–720.
Joyner JE. Health and social issues: The National Medical Association's commitment. *J Natl Med Assoc* 1988; 80:1169–1171.
Joynes LS. Remarks on the comparative mortality of the White and Colored population of Richmond. *Virginia Medical Monthly* 1875; 5:155.
Judis JB. Whose managed competition? *The New Republic,* 208 (March 29, 1993):20–24.
Kahn KL, Pearson ML, Harrison ER, Desmond KA, Rodgers WH, et al. Health care for Black and poor hospitalized Medicare patients. *JAMA* 1994; 271:1169–1174.
Kaiske BL, Neylan JF, Riggko RR, Danovitch GM, Kahana L, et al. The effect of race on access and outcome in transplantation. *N Engl J Med* 1991; 324:302–307.
Kamal RD, Lukas CV, Young GJ. Public hospitals: Privatization and uncompensated care. *Health Affairs* (Millwood) 2000; 19:167–172.
Kamin LJ. The pioneers of IQ testing. 476–509. In: Jacoby R, Glauberman N, eds. *The Bell Curve Debate: History, Documents, Opinions.* New York: Times Books Division of Random House, Inc., 1995.
Kater MH. *Doctors Under Hitler.* Chapel Hill: The University of North Carolina Press, 1989.

Katz J. *Experimentation with Human Beings: The Authority of the Investigator, Subject, Professions, and State in the Human Experimentation Process.* New York: Russell Sage Foundation, 1972.

Katz MB. *In the Shadow of the Poorhouse: A Social History of Welfare in America.* New York: Basic Books, 1986. Revised and Updated Edition, 1996.

Kaufman M, Galishoff S, Savitt TL, eds. *Dictionary of American Medical Biography.* 2 Vols. Westport, Connecticut: Greenwood Press, 1984.

Kaunitz AM. Honing in on maternal deaths. *Contemp Ob/Gyn* 1984; 24:31–34.

Keck CW, Sutchfield FD. The future of public health. 361–372. In: Sutchfield FD, Keck CW. *Principles of Public Health Practice.* Albany, New York: Delmar Publishers, 1997.

Keil JE, Sutherland SE, Knapp RG, Tyrder HA. Does equal socioeconomic status in Black and White men mean equal risk of mortality? *Am J Public Health* 1992; 82:1133–1136.

Keith SN. Prospective payment for hospital costs using diagnosis-related groups: Will cost inflation be reduced? *J Natl Med Assoc* 1983; 75:609.

Keith SN, Bell RM, Swanson AG, Williams AP. Effects of affirmative action in medical schools: A study of the class of 1975. *N Engl J Med* 1985; 313:1519–1525.

Keith SN. A legislative agenda for health: 1987 to 1992. *J Natl Med Assoc* 1987; 79:888.

Keith VM. Long-term care and the Black elderly. 173–209. In: Jones Jr W, Rice MF, eds. *Health Care Issues in Black America: Policies, Problems, and Prospects.* New York: Greenwood Press, 1987.

Keller AZ. High mortality rate for Negroes: Design or accident? *J Natl Med Assoc* 1968; 60:287–288.

Keller RL. Syphilis and tuberculosis in the Negro race. *Texas State Journal of Medicine* 1924; 19:498.

Kemper V, Novak V. What's blocking health care reform? *Common Cause Magazine* 1992 (January/February/March, No. 1); 18:8–13.

Kennedy EM. *In Critical Condition: The Crisis in America's Health Care.* New York: Simon and Schuster, 1972.

Kennedy DM. *Birth Control in America: The Career of Margaret Sanger.* New Haven: Yale University Press, 1970.

Kenney JA. Report of the Secretary of the National Medical Association...August 25, 1908. *J Natl Med Assoc* 1909; 1:34–35.

Kenney JA. Syphillis and the American Negro—A medico-sociologic study. *J Natl Med Assoc* 1911; 3:115–117.

Kenney JA. Health problems of the Negroes. *J Natl Med Assoc* 1911; 3:127–135.

Kenney JA. *The Negro in Medicine.* Tuskegee: Tuskegee Institute Press, 1912.

Kenney JA. The hospital idea essentially altruistic. *J Natl Med Assoc* 1912; 4:193–199.

Kenney JA. Some facts concerning Negro nurse training schools and their graduates. *J Natl Med Assoc* 1919; 11:53–68.

Kenney JA. The editor afield. *J Natl Med Assoc* 1920; 12:24–27.

Kenney JA. Howard University School of Medicine. *J Natl Med Assoc* 1920; 12:30–31.

Kenney JA. Hospital symposium: The Negro hospital renaissance. *J Natl Med Assoc* 1930; 22:109–157.

Kenney JA. The inter-racial committee of Montclair, New Jersey: Report of survey of hospital committee. *J Natl Med Assoc* 1931; 23:97–108.

Kenney JA. A brief history of the origin of the John A. Andrew Clinics by the founder. *J Natl Med Assoc* 1934; 26:65–68.

Kenney JA. The relationship between the N.M.A. and the A.M.A. and the Federal government. *J Natl Med Assoc* 1939; 31:150–151.

Kenney JA. The national health act of 1939. *J Natl Med Assoc* 1939; 31:154–160.

Kenney JA. Senator Wagner says non-governmental hospitals are eligible for support under his bill. Negroes are protected. *J Natl Med Assoc* 1939; 31:173–177.

Kenney JA. Where are we? *J Natl Med Assoc* 1939; 31:177–178.

Kenney JA. Second annual oration on surgery. *J Natl Med Assoc* 1941; 33:203–214.

Kerner O. *Report of the National Advisory Commission on Civil Disorders.* New York: E.P. Dutton and Company, Inc., 1968. Paperback Edition. New York: Bantam Books Inc., 1968.

Kevles DJ. *In the Name of Eugenics: Genetics and the Uses of Human Heredity.* Berkeley: University of California Press, 1985.

Kidd F, ed. *Profile of the Negro in American Dentistry.* Washington, D.C.: Howard University Press, 1979.

Kieth VM. Long-term care and the Black elderly. 173–209. In: Jones Jr W, Rice MF, eds. *Health Care Issues in Black America: Policies, Problems, and Prospects.* New York: Greenwood Press, 1987.

Kilborn PT. Analysts expect health premiums to rise sharply. *The New York Times,* Sunday, October 19, 1997, p. 1.

Kilborn PT. Fitting managed care into emergency rooms. *The New York Times*, Sunday, December 28, 1997, p. 12.

Kilborn PT. voters' anger at H.M.O.'s plays as hot political issue, *The New York Times*, Sunday, May 17, 1998, p. 1.

Kilborn PT. The uninsured find fewer doctors in the house: Managed care has cut doctors' incomes and left them with less time for charity work. *The New York Times*, Sunday, August 30, 1998, Section 4, p. 14.

Kilborn PT. Complaints about H.M.O.'s rise as awareness grows. *The New York Times*, Sunday, October 11, 1998, p. 22.

Kilborn PT. Oregon falters on a new path to health care: State officials rethink rationing for the poor. *The New York Times*, Sunday, January 3, 1999, p. 1.

Kilpatrick AR. An account of the Colored population in Grimes County, Texas. A comparison between their present and former condition. *Richmond and Louisville Medical Journal* 1872; 14:610.

Kinder DR, Sanders LM. *Divided by Color: Racial Politics and Democratic Ideals*. Chicago: The University of Chicago Press, 1996.

King G, Bendel R. a statistical model estimating the number of African American physicians in the United States. *J Natl Med Assoc* 1995; 84:264–272.

Kingdon JW. *Agendas, Alternatives, and Public Policies*. New York: HarperCollins Publishers, 1984.

Kiple KF, King VH. *Another Dimension to the Black Diaspora: Diet, Disease, and Racism*. Cambridge, England: Cambridge University Press, 1981.

Klineberg O. Race and psychology. 55–84. In: UNESCO. *The Race Question in Modern Science*. New York: Whiteside Inc., and William Morrow and Company, 1956.

Kluger R. *Simple Justice: The History of Brown v. Board of Education and Black America's Struggle for Equality*. New York: Alfred A. Knopf, Inc., 1976. Paperback Edition. New York: Vintage Books, 1977.

Knox RA. HMOs' creator urges reform in quality of care. *The Boston Sunday Globe*, May 2, 1999, p. A1.

Knutson LL. Clinton decries drug markup: Says Medicare losing billions. *The Boston Sunday Globe*, December 14, 1997, p. A2.

Kochanek KD, Jeffrey DM, Rosenberg HM. Why did Black life expectancy decline from 1984 through 1989 in the United States? *Am J Public Health* 1994; 84:938–944.

Kolata G. AIDS patients slipping through safety net: Soaring costs of drugs strains the budgets of programs and patients. *The New York Times*, Sunday, September 15, 1996, p. 24.

Komaromy M, Grumbach K, Drake M. The role of Black and Hispanic physicians in providing health care for underserved populations. *N Engl J Med* 1996; 334:1305–1314.

Kong D. Study: Minorities' health lags. *The Boston Globe*, Thursday, April 23, 1992, p. 1.

Kong D. Seeking a safety net. *The Boston Sunday Globe*, Sunday, July 16, 2000, p. H4.

Kongstvedt PR. *The Managed Health Care Handbook*. Second Edition. Gaithersburg, Maryland: Aspen Publishers, Inc., 1993.

Konner M. *Medicine at the Crossroads: The Crisis in Health Care*. New York: Pantheon Books, 1993.

Kosa J, Antonovsky A, Zola IK, eds. *Poverty and Health: A Sociological Analysis*. Cambridge, Massachusetts: Harvard University Press, 1969.

Kotelchuck R. Down and out in the "New Calcutta": New York City's health care crisis. *Health/PAC Bulletin* 1989 (Summer); 19:4–11.

Kotelchuck R. Preserving integration: Defending the hospital rights of the poor. *Health/PAC Bulletin* 1989 (Summer): 19:11–14.

Kovel J. *White Racism: A Psychohistory*. New York: Random House, 1970. Reprint Edition. New York: Columbia University Press, 1984.

Kovner AR, ed. *Health Care Delivery in the United States*. Fourth Edition. New York: Springer, 1990.

Kovner AR, ed. *Jonas's Health Care Delivery in the United States*. Fifth Edition. New York: Springer Publishing Company, 1995.

Kovner AR, Jonas S, eds. *Jonas and Kovner's Health Care Delivery in the United States*. Sixth Edition. New York: Springer Publishing Company, 1999.

Kovner C, Salsberg ES. The health care workforce. 64–115. In: Kovner AR, Jonas S, eds. *Jonas and Kovner's Health Care Delivery in the United States*. Sixth Edition. New York: Springer Publishing Company, 1999.

Kozak LJ. Underreporting of race in the National Hospital Discharge Survey. *Advance Data from Vital and Health Statistics*; no 265. Hyattsville, Maryland: National Center for Health Statistics. 1995.

Kozol J. *Savage Inequalities: Children in America's Schools*. New York: Crown Publishers, Inc., 1991.

Kragh H. *An Introduction to the Historiography of Science*. Cambridge, England: Cambridge University Press, 1987. Paperback Edition, 1989.

Krieger N. Analyzing socioeconomic and racial/ethnic patterns in health and health care. *Am J Public Health* 1993; 83:1086–1087.

Krieger N, Birn A-E. A vision of social justice as the foundation of public health: Commemorating 150 years of the spirit of 1848. *Am J Public Health* 1998; 88:1603–1606.

Kronick R, Goodman DC, Wennberg J. The marketplace in health care reform: Demographic limitations of managed competition. *N Engl J Med* 1993; 328:148–152.

Kronick R, Gilmer T. Explaining the decline in health insurance coverage, 1979–1995. *Health Aff* 1999; 18(2):30–47.

Kumanyika S. Gathering together to close the gap in minority health status: Conference explores the health needs of the nation's emerging majority. In: *Minority Health Issues for an Emerging Majority: Proceedings of the 4th National Forum on Cardiovascular Health, Pulmonary Disorders, and Blood Resources, Washington, D.C., June 26–27, 1992*, by the National Heart, Lung, and Blood Institute (NHLBI), the NHLBI Ad Hoc Committee on Minority Populations, and the National Medical Association.

Kurtz LH. The history of surgery at the District of Columbia General Hospital. *J Natl Med Assoc* 1997; 89:761–764.

Kusmer KL. *A Ghetto Takes Shape: Black Cleveland, 1870–1930*. Urbana: University of Illinois Press, 1976.

Kuttner RE. Letter to the editor. *Perspectives in Biology and Medicine* 1968; 11:707.

Lambert B. At 50, Levittown contends with legacy of racial bias. *The New York Times*. Sunday, December 28, 1997, 23.

Lander L. *Defective Medicine: Risk, Anger, and the Malpractice Crisis*. New York: Farrar, Straus and Giroux, 1978.

Lane C. Tainted sources. 125–139. In: Jacoby R, Glauberman N, eds. *The Bell Curve Debate: History, Documents, Opinions*. New York: Times Books Division of Random House, Inc., 1995.

Larson E. The soul of an HMO: Managed care is certainly bringing down America's medical costs, but it is also raising the question of whether patients, especially those with severe illnesses, can still trust their doctors. *Time*, January 22, 1996, 45.

Larson EJ. *Sex, Race, and Science: Eugenics in the Deep South*. Baltimore: The Johns Hopkins University Press, 1995.

Larson EJ. *Summer for the Gods: The Scopes Trial and America's Continuing Debate over Science and Religion*. Cambridge, Massachusetts: Harvard University Press, 1997.

Lasalandra M. Study finds poor, elderly are losing out on HMOs. *The Boston Herald*, Wednesday, October 2, 1996, p. 19.

Last JM, ed. *A Dictionary of Epidemiology*. Second Edition. New York: Oxford University Press, for the International Epidemiological Association, 1988.

Last JM. The determinants of health. 31–41. In: Sutchfield FD, Keck CW. *Principles of Public Health Practice*. Albany, New York: Delmar Publishers, 1997.

Laughlin HH. *The Legal and Administrative Aspects of Sterilization: Report of Committee to Study and to Report on the Best Practical Means of Cutting Off the Defective Germ-Plasm in the American Population*. 2 Volumes. Cold Spring Harbor, New York: Eugenics Record Office, 1914.

Laughlin HH. *Eugenical Sterilization in the United States*. Chicago: Psychopathic Laboratory of the Municipal Court of Chicago, 1922.

Laughlin HH. *The Legal Status of Eugenical Sterilization*. Chicago: Psychopathic Laboratory of the Municipal Court of Chicago, 1929.

Lavizzo-Mourey R, Clayton LA, Byrd WM, Johnson III G, Richardson D. The perceptions of African-American physicians concerning their treatment by managed care organizations. *J Natl Med Assoc* 1996; 88:210–214.

Lawlor J. Not ready for Medicare, and uninsured. *The New York Times*, Sunday, December 18, 1997, p. 11.

Lawton RB, Cacciamani J, Clement J, Aquino W. The fall of the house of AHERF: The Allegheny bankruptcy. *Health Affairs* (Millwood) 2000; 19:7–41.

Leavitt JW, Numbers RL. Sickness and Health in America: An Overview. 3–10. In: Leavitt JW, Numbers RL, eds. *Sickness and Health in America: Readings in the History of Medicine and Public Health*. Madison, Wisconsin: The University of Wisconsin Press, 1985.

Lederer SE. *Subjected to Science: Human Experimentation in America before the Second World War*. Baltimore: The Johns Hopkins University Press, 1995.

Lee IW. The Health Care Financing Administration study of excess mortality in US short-term, acute care hospitals during 1984. *J Natl Med Assoc* 1988; 80:462–464. Legislative Column.

Lee KS, Paneth N, Gartner LM, Pearlman MR, Gruss L. Neonatal mortality: An analysis of the recent improvements in the United States. *Amer J Public Health* 1980; 70:15–22.

Lee PR, Benjamin AE. Governmental and legislative control and direction of health services in the United States. 217–230. In: Holland WW, Detels R, Knox G, eds. *Oxford Textbook of Public Health*. Volume 1. *Influences of Public Health*. Second Edition. Oxford: Oxford University Press, 1991.

Lee PR, Benjamin AE, Weber MA. Policies and strategies for health in the United States. 297–321. In: Detels R, Holland WW, McEwen J, Omenn GS, eds. *Oxford Textbook of Public Health*. Volume 1. *The Scope of Public Health*. Third Edition. New York: Oxford University Press, 1997.

Leffall Jr LD. Cancer mortality in blacks. *CA* 1974; 24:42–46.

Leffall Jr LD. The challenge of cancer among black Americans. 9–14. From: the *Proceedings of the American Cancer Society National Conference on Meeting the Challenge of Cancer Among Black Americans*. New York: American Cancer Society, Inc., 1979.

Legislative Update: A Report of the NMA Legislative Council. *J Natl Med Assoc* 1986; 78:899–900.

Lemann N. *The Promised Land: The Great Black Migration and How It Changed America*. New York: Alfred A. Knopf, 1991.

Lemann N. Taking affirmative action apart. *The New York Times Magazine*, June 11, 1995, Section 6, 36.

Lemann N. The structure of success in America. *The Atlantic Monthly* 1995 (August, No. 2); 276:41.

Lemann N. The great sorting: The first mass administrations of a scholastic-aptitude test led with surprising speed to the idea that the nation's leaders would be the people who did well on tests. *The Atlantic Monthly* 1995 (September, No. 3); 276:84.

Lemann N. *The Big Test: The Secret History of the American Meritocracy*. New York: Farrar, Straus and Giroux, 1999.

Lester JA. The evolution in the standard of medical education. *J Natl Med Assoc* 1918; 10:10–12.

Levi-Strauss C. "Race and History." 123–163. In: *Race and History*. Paris: United Nations Educational, Scientific and Cultural Organization, 1951.

Lewin T, Gottlieb M. In hospital sales, an overlooked side effect. *The New York Times*, Sunday, April 27, 1997, p. 1.

Lewis B. The African diaspora and the civilization of Islam. 37–56. In: Kilson ML, Rothberg RI, eds. *The African Diaspora: Interpretive Essays*. Cambridge, Massachusetts: Harvard University Press, 1976.

Lewis B. *Race and Slavery in the Middle East: An Historical Enquiry*. New York: Oxford University Press, 1990.

Lewis B. South Africans await economic control, *Emerge* 1998 (July/August, No. 9); 9:76.

Lewis DL. *W.E.B. Du Bois: Biography of a Race, 1868–1919*. New York: Henry Holt and Company, Inc., 1993.

Lewis JH. Contribution of an unknown Negro to anesthesia. *J Natl Med Assoc* 1931; 23:23–24.

Lewis JH. *The Biology of the Negro*. Chicago: The University of Chicago Press, 1942.

Lewis S. *Hospital: An Oral History of Cook County Hospital*. New York: The New Press, 1994.

Lewontin RC, Rose S, Kamin LJ. *Not In Our Genes: Biology, Ideology, and Human Nature*. New York: Pantheon Books, 1984.

Lief BJ. Legal and administrative barriers to health care. *New York State J Med* 1985; 85:126–127.

Lifton RJ. *The Nazi Doctors: Medical Killing and the Psychology of Genocide*. New York: Basic Books, Inc., Publishers, 1986.

Lifton RJ, Eric Markusen. *The Genocidal Mentality: Nazi Holocaust and Nuclear Threat*. New York: Basic Books, Inc., Publishers, 1990.

Lilienfeld AM, Levin ML, Kessler II. *Cancer in the United States*. Cambridge, Massachusetts: Harvard University Press, 1972.

Lillie-Blanton M, Lyons B. Managed care and low-income populations: Recent state experiences. *Health Affairs* (Millwood) 1998; 17:238–247.

Lind M. *Up From Conservatism: Why the Right is Wrong for America*. New York: The Free Press, 1996.

Lindblom CE. The science of "muddling through." *Public Administration Review* 1959; 10:79–88.

Lindblom CE. *Politics and Markets*. New York: Basic Books, 1977.

Lindorf D. *Marketplace Medicine: The Rise of the For-Profit Hospital Chains*. New York: Bantam Books, 1992.

Livingston IL, ed. *Handbook of Black American Health: The Mosaic of Conditions, Issues, Policies, and Prospects*. Westport, Connecticut: Greenwood Press, 1994.

Lloyd Jr. SM, Johnson DG. Practice pattern of Black physicians: Results of a survey of Howard University College of Medicine alumni. *J Natl Med Assoc* 1982; 74:129–141.

Lobel M. A hospital privileges battle: The toughest fight of your career. *Generics*, Fall, 1986, 20–27.

Logan RW. *The Negro in American Life and Thought: The Nadir, 1877–1901*. New York: Macmillan Publishing Company, 1954. *The Betrayal of the Negro: From Rutherford B. Hayes to Woodrow Wilson*. Enlarged, Revised, Paperback Edition. London: Collier-Macmillan Ltd., 1965.

Logan RW. Drew, Charles Richard. 190–192. In: Logan RW, Winston MR, eds. *Dictionary of American Negro Biography*. New York: W.W. Norton and Company, 1982.

Logan RW. Wright, Louis Tompkins. 670–671. In Logan RW, Winston MR, eds. *Dictionary of American Negro Biography*. New York: W.W. Norton and Company, 1982.

Lone Star State Medical Association. Charges of racial discrimination in Fort Worth, Texas. *Lone Star State Medical Association Newsletter–Region Five*, Feb/March, 1984.

Lovejoy AO. *The Great Chain of Being: A Study of the History of an Idea*. Cambridge, Massachusetts: Harvard University Press, 1936. Reprint Paperback Edition. 1964.

Low WA, Clift VA. eds. *Encyclopedia of Black America*. New York: McGraw-Hill, Inc. Reprint Edition. New York: Da Capo Press, Inc., 1981.

Luce HR. *Life's Picture History of Western Man*. New York: Time Incorporated, 1951.

Ludmerer KM. *Learning to Heal: The Development of American Medical Education*. New York: Basic Books, Inc., Publishers, 1985.

Lukas JA. *Common Ground: A Turbulent Decade in the Lives of Three American Families*. New York: Alfred A. Knopf, 1985. Paperback Edition. New York: Vintage Books, 1986.

Lundberg GD. National health care reform: An aura of inevitability is upon us. *JAMA* 1991; 265:2566–2567.

Lydston GF. Letter to Dr. McGuire: Sexual crimes among the Southern Negroes scientifically considered. *Virginia Medical Monthly* 1893; 20:118.

Lydston GF. *Diseases of Society*. Philadelphia: Lippincott, 1906.

Lynch KM, McInnes BK, McInnes GF. Concerning syphilis in the American Negro. *Southern Medical Journal* 1915; 8:452.

Lynk MV. *Sixty Years of Medicine, or The Life and Times of Dr. Miles V. Lynk: An Autobiography*. Memphis: Twentieth Century Press, 1951.

Lyons AS, Petrucelli RJ. *Medicine: An Illustrated History*. New York: Harry N. Abrams, Inc., Publishers. 1978.

Maccabe T. Elderly may join poor in HMO abuses. *The Medical Tribune*, October, 1998, p. 1.

MacKenzie DA. *Statistics in Britain, 1865–1930: The Social Construction of Scientific Knowledge*. Edinburgh: Edinburgh University Press, 1981.

Magnusson M, ed. *Cambridge Biographical Dictionary*. Cambridge: Cambridge University Press, 1971.

Majno G. *The Healing Hand: Man and Wound in the Ancient World*. Cambridge, Massachusetts: Harvard University Press, 1975.

Malik K. *The Meaning of Race: Race History and Culture in Western Society*. New York: New York University Press, 1996.

Malone TE, Johnson KW. *Report of the Secretary's Task Force on Black and Minority Health*. Washington, D.C.: U.S. Department of Health and Human Services, 1986.

Malthus T. *An Essay on the Principle of Population*. Flew A, ed. Penguin Classics. Middlesex, England: Penguin Books Ltd., 1982.

Manning KR. Cobb, William Montague. 601–603. In: Salzman J, Smith DL, West C. eds. *Encyclopedia of African-American Culture and History*. 5 Vols. New York: Macmillan Library Reference USA, Simon and Schuster Macmillan, 1996.

Manning KR. Health and health care providers. 1247–1255. In: Salzman J, Smith DL, West C. eds. *Encyclopedia of African-American Culture and History*. 5 Vols. New York: Macmillan Library Reference USA, Simon and Schuster Macmillan, 1996.

Mannix DP, Cowley M. *Cargoes: The Atlantic Slave Trade, 1518–1865*. New York: Viking Press, 1962.

Manton KG, Patrick CH, Johnson KW. Health differentials between blacks and whites: Recent trends in mortality and morbidity. 129–199. In: Willis DP, ed. *Health Policies and Black Americans*. New Brunswick, New Jersey: Transaction Publishers, 1989.

Marable M. *W.E.B. Du Bois: Black Radical Democrat*. Boston: Twayne Publishers, A Division of G.K. Hall and Company, 1986.

Marable M. *Race, Reform. and Rebellion: The Second Reconstruction in Black America, 1945–1990*. Revised Second Edition. Jackson: University Press of Mississippi, 1991.

The march-on-Washington movement. New York *The Amsterdam New York Star News*, June 28, 1941, p. 1.

Mare RD, Winship C. Socioeconomic change and the decline of marriage for Blacks and Whites.

175–196. In: Jencks C, Peterson PE, eds. *The Urban Underclass*. Washington, D.C.: The Brookings Institution, 1991, 181–188.

Marsa L. *Prescriptions for Profits: How the Pharmaceutical Industry Bankrolled the Unholy Marriage Between Science and Business*. New York: Scribner, 1997.

Marshall PJ, Williams G. *The Great Map of Mankind: Perceptions of New Worlds in the Age of Enlightenment*. Cambridge, Massachusetts: Harvard University Press, 1982.

Martinez Jr. C. Physician and health professional manpower. *J Natl Med Assoc* 1983; 75:545–546. President's Column.

Massey DS, Denton NA. *American Apartheid: Segregation and the Making of the Underclass*. Cambridge, Massachusetts: Harvard University Press, 1993.

Mayberry RM, Mili F, Ofli E. Racial and ethnic differences in access to medical care. *Medical Care Research and Review* 2000; 57 (suppl 1):108–145.

Mazique EC. National medical political action committee. *J Natl Med Assoc* 1986; 78:138.

McBride AD. Racial equality in the American health care system: An unfulfilled ideal. *New York State J Med* 1985; 85:125.

McBride D. Inequality in the availability of Black physicians. *New York State J Med* 1985; 85:139–142.

McBride D. *Integrating the City of Medicine: Blacks in Philadelphia Health Care, 1910–1965*. Philadelphia: Temple University Press, 1989.

McBride D. *From TB to AIDS. Epidemics Among Urban Blacks Since 1900*. Albany, New York: State University of New York Press, 1991.

McBride D. Medical Committee for Human Rights. 1749–1750. In: Salzman J, Smith DL, West C. eds. *Encyclopedia of African-American Culture and History*. 5 Vols. New York: Macmillan Library Reference USA, Simon and Schuster Macmillan, 1996.

McCall T. Profits, not patients, threaten HMOs. *The Boston Sunday Globe*, Sunday, August 2, 1998, p. C4.

McCord C, Freeman HP. Excess mortality in Harlem. *N Engl J Med* 1990; 322:173–177.

McCullough D. *Nixon*. [videotape]. A three part documentary video for *The American Experience*, produced by WGBH, Boston, Thames Televesion, WNET/Thirteen, and the Corporation for Public Broadcasting, 1990.

McCullough D. *Reagan*. [videotape]. A two part documentary video for *The American Experience*, produced by WGBH, Boston and the Corporation for Public Broadcasting, 1998.

McCullough D. *Paul Robeson: Here I Stand*. Video documentary segment of *The American Experience*, WGBH, Boston, March 1, 1999.

McDaniel RR. Management and medicine, never the twain shall meet. *J Natl Med Assoc* 1985; 77:107–112.

McDermott J. Evaluating health system reform: The case for a single-payer approach. *JAMA* 1994; 271:782–784.

McGregor DK. *Sexual Surgery and the Origins of Gynecology: J. Marion Sims, His Hospital, and His Patients*. New York: Garland Publishing, Inc., 1989.

McGuire H, Lydston GF. Sexual crimes among the Southern Negroes–scientifically considered–an open correspondence between. *Virginia Medical Monthly* 1893; 20:105.

McHatton H. The sexual status of the Negro–past and present. *American Journal of Dermatology and Genito-Urinary Diseases* 1906; 10:6–8.

McIntosh J. The future of the Negro race. *Transactions of the South Carolina Medical Association* 1891; 41:186.

McKenzie K, Crowcroft NS. Describing race, ethnicity and culture in medical research. *BMJ* 1996; 312:1054.

McKenzie N, Bilofsky E. Shredding the safety net: The dismantling of public programs. *Health/PAC Bulletin* 1991; 21:5–11.

McKinney F. Employment implications of a changing health-care system. 199–215. In: Simms MC, Malveaux JM, eds. *Slipping Through the Cracks: The Status of Black Women*. New Brunswick, New Jersey: Transaction Books, 1986.

McNeil GR. *Groundwork*. Philadelphia: University of Pennsylvania Press, 1983.

McNeil Jr., DG. Its past on its sleeve, tribe seeks Bonn's apology, *The New York Times*, Sunday, May 31, 1998, p. 3.

McWhorter WP, Moyer WJ. Black-White differences in type of initial breast cancer treatment and implications for survival. *Am J Public Health* 1987; 77:1515–1517.

Meadows J. *The Great Scientists*. New York: Oxford University Press, 1987.

Means JH. *Doctors, People, and Government*. Boston: Little Brown, 1953.

Medical costs: Statement of the AFL-CIO executive council. *J Natl Med Assoc* 1968; 60:527–528.

Mendelson MA. *Tender Loving Greed.* New York: Alfred A. Knopf, 1974.

Menzel PT. *Medical Costs, Moral Choices: A Philosophy of Health Care Economics in America.* New Haven: Yale University Press, 1983.

Meyer M. Oh no, here we go again: Health-care costs are soaring—and companies are passing the increases along to their workers. *Newsweek,* December 14, 1998, 46.

Meyer SG. *As Long as They Don't Move Next Door: Segregation and Racial Conflict in American Neighborhoods.* Lanham, Maryland: Rowman and Littlefield Publishers, Inc, 2000.

Meyers HB. The medical industrial complex. *Fortune,* January, 1970, 90.

Meyerson AR. When healing collides with the drive for profits. *The New York Times,* Sunday, July 27, 1997, p. 14.

Miller A. Professors of hate. 162–178. In: Jacoby R, Glauberman N, eds. *The Bell Curve Debate: History, Documents, Opinions.* New York: Times Books Division of Random House, Inc., 1995.

Miller JF. The effects of emancipation upon the mental and physical health of the Negro in the South. *North Carolina Medical Journal* 1896; 38:285–294.

Milner R. *The Encyclopedia of Evolution: Humanity's Search for its Origins.* New York: Facts on File, Inc., 1990.

Mink v. University of Chicago. 1081–1086. In: Areen J, King PA, Goldberg S, Gostin L, Capron AM. *Law, Science and Medicine.* Second Edition. Westbury, New York: The Foundation Press, Inc., 1996.

Minutes. *J Natl Med Assoc* 1909; 1:24–32.

Mitchell C. One empty, one full: Nashville hospitals remain miles apart. *The Atlanta Journal and Constitution,* Wednesday, August 2, 1989, p. A-4.

Mitford J. *Kind and Unusual Punishment.* New York: Alfred A. Knopf, 1973.

Mohr CL. *On the Threshold of Freedom: Masters and Slaves in Civil War Georgia.* Athens: The University of Georgia Press, 1986.

Montagu A. *Race, Science and Humanity.* New York: Van Nostrand Reinhold, 1963.

Mooney M. City eyes selling 3 hosps. *Daily News,* Thursday, February 23, 1995, p. 2.

Morais HM. *The History of the Negro in Medicine.* Under auspices of The Association for the Study of Negro Life and History. New York: Publishers Company, Inc., 1967.

Morais HM. *The History of the Afro-American in Medicine.* Cornwells Heights, Pennsylvania: The Publishers Agency, 1978.

Mossell NF. The modern hospital: Its construction, organization and management. *J Natl Med Assoc* 1909; 1:94–102.

Moy E, Bartman BA. Physician race and care of minority and medically indigent patients. *JAMA* 1995; 273:1515–1520.

Moy E. Relationship between National Institutes of Health research awards to US medical schools and managed care market penetration. *JAMA* 1997; 278:217–221.

Moynihan DP. *The Negro Family.* Washington, D.C.: Office of Policy, Planning and Research, U.S. Department of Labor, March, 1965.

Moynihan DP. *The Negro Family: The Case for National Action.* Washington, D.C.: Department of Labor, 1965, 47–124.

Muir H, ed. *Larousse Dictionary of Scientists.* New York: Larousse, 1994.

Mullan F. The National Health Service Corps and health personnel innovations: Beyond poorhouse medicine. 176–200. In: Sidel VW, Sidel R, eds. *Reforming Medicine: Lessons of the Last Quarter Century.* New York: Pantheon Books, 1984.

Mullan F, Rivo M, Politzer RM. Doctors, dollars, and determination: Making physician work-force policy. *Health Affairs* (Millwood) 1993 (Suppl.); 12:138–151.

Mullan F, Lundberg G. Looking back, looking forward: Straight talk about U.S. medicine. *Health Affairs* (Millwood) 2000; 19:117–123.

Müller-Hill B. *Murderous Science: Elimination by Scientific Selection of Jews, Gypsies, and Others in Germany, 1933–1945.* Plainview, New York: Cold Spring Harbor Laboratory Press, 1998.

Mullowney JJ. *America Gives a Chance.* Tampa, Florida: The Tribune Press, 1940.

Muñoz E, Johnson H, Goldstein J, Benacquista T, Mulloy K, Wise L. Health care financing policy for hospitalized Black patients. *J Natl Med Assoc* 1988; 80:972–976.

Muñoz E, Barrios E, Johnson H, Goldstein J, Mulloy K, Chalfin D, Wise L. Race and diagnostic related group prospective hospital payment for medical patients. *J Natl Med Assoc* 1989; 81:844–848.

Murata S. Why doctors will take back health care. *Medical Economics,* January, 1996, pp. 29–30.

Murphy FG, Elders MJ. Diabetes and the Black community. 121–143. In: Braithwaite RL, Taylor SE, eds. *Health Issues in the Black Community.* San Francisco: Jossey-Bass Publishers, 1992.

Murrell TW. Syphilis in the Negro: Its bearing in the race problem. *American Journal of Dermatology and Genito-Urinary Diseases* 1906; 10;305–306.

Murrell TW. Syphilis and the American Negro: A medico-sociologic study. *Journal of the American Medical Association* 1910; 54:846–847.

Myrdal G. *An American Dilemma: The Negro Problem and Modern Democracy.* New York: Harper and Row, Publishers, 1944.

N.A.A.C.P. Legal Defense and Educational Fund, Inc., cases. *J Natl Med Assoc* 1965; 57:513–514. Integration Battlefront.

N.A.A.C.P. 1965 resolutions on hospitals and health. *J Natl Med Assoc* 1965; 57:512–513. Integration Battlefront.

National Association of County Health Officials. *Blueprint for a Healthy Community: A Guide for Local Health Departments.* Washington, D.C.: National Association of County Health Officials, 1994.

National Center for Health Statistics: Edentulous Persons, United States, 1971. DHEW Pub. No. (HRA) 74–1516. Series 10. Data from the National Health Survey; No. 89. Rockville, MD, June 1974.

National Center for Health Statistics. *Health Status of the Disadvantaged Chartbook/1990.* Hyattsville, Maryland: Public Health Service, 1991.

National Center for Health Statistics. *Prevention Profile. Health United States, 1991.* Hyattsville, Maryland: Public Health Service, 1992.

National Center for Health Statistics. Advance report of final mortality statistics, 1989. *Monthly Vital Statistics Report:* 1992; 40(8)(suppl 2). Hyattsville, Maryland: Public Health Service.

National Center for Health Statistics. *Health United States, 1995.* Hyattsville, Maryland: Public Health Service, May, 1996.

National Center for Health Statistics. *Health United States, 1996–97 and Injury Chartbook.* Hyattsville, Maryland: Public Health Service, 1997.

National Center for Health Statistics. Deaths: Final data for 1996. *National Vital Statistics Reports:* 1998; 47(9). Hyattsville, Maryland: U.S. Department of Health and Human Services.

National Center for Health Statistics. *Health United States, 1998 with Socioeconomic Status and Health Chartbook.* Hyattsville, Maryland: 1998.

National Commission for the Protection of Human Subjects of Biomedical and Behavioral Research. *The Belmont Report: Ethical Principles and Guidelines for the Protection of Human Subjects of Research.* Washington, D.C.: Department of Health Education and Welfare, 1979.

National Commission to Prevent Infant Mortality. *Death Before Life: The Tragedy of Infant Mortality.* Appendix. Washington, D.C.: The report of the National Commission to Prevent Infant Mortality. The Honorable Lawton Chiles, United States Senate, Chairman, 1988.

National Council of Arts, Sciences and Professions, Southern California Chapter. *A Survey of Discrimination in the Health Field in Los Angeles.* Los Angeles, 1951.

National Health Insurance Proposals, *Legislative Analysis* No. 19. 37–54. Washington: American Enterprise Institute, 1974.

The National Hospital Association. *J Natl Med Assoc* 1924; 16:48–49.

National Medical Association. Chairman, Green HM. *A More or Less Critical Review of the Hospital Situation Among Negroes in the United States.* N.P. Published under the auspices of the National Hospital Association, National Medical Association. N.D.(circa 1930).

National Medical Association Communications—the minutes of the executive board. *J Natl Med Assoc* 1918; 10:138–139.

The National Medical Association Foundation, Inc.: A comprehensive health care program for the inner-city. *J Natl Med Assoc* 1968; 60:138–141. Special Feature.

The National Medical Association Foundation, Inc.: The White House release. *J Natl Med Assoc* 1968; 60:142–143. Special Feature.

The National Medical Association's contribution to the Selma-Montgomery march. *J Natl Med Assoc* 1965; 57:243–244.

National medical commissions. *J Natl Med Assoc* 1918; 10:125.

National Office of Vital Statistics. *Death Rates for Selected Causes by Age, Color, and Sex: United States and Each State, 1949–1951.* Washington, D.C.: U.S. Government Printing Office, 1959.

The nation...races...Black vacuum. *Time* 1968 (March, 29, No. 13); 91:26.

Navarro V. *Dangerous to Your Health: Capitalism in Health Care.* New York: Monthly Review Press, 1993.

Needs of Negro medical schools. *J Natl Med Assoc* 1917; 9:221–223.

Negro surgeon, world plasma expert, derides Red Cross blood segregation, *Chicago Defender,* September 26, 1942, p. 6.

Neighbors HW. Ambulatory medical care among adult Black Americans: The hospital emergency room. *J Natl Med Assoc* 1986; 78:275–282.

Neighbors HW, Jackson JS. Uninsured risk groups in a national survey of Black Americans. *J Natl Med Assoc* 1986; 78:979–983.

Neighbors HW, Jackson JS. Barriers to medical care among adult Blacks: What happens to the uninsured? *J Natl Med Assoc* 1987; 79:489–493.

Nelkin D, Tancredi L. *Dangerous Diagnostics: The Social Power of Biological Information*. New York: Basic Books, 1989.

Neumann BR., Suver JD, Zelman WN. *Financial Management, Concepts and Applications for Health Care Providers*. National Health Publishing, Owings Mills, Maryland 1988.

New HMO target: The poor. *Medical Herald*, May, 1998, p. 28.

New payment plan for Medicare hospital services. *J Natl Med Assoc* 1968; 60:20.

New York County Medical Society condemns discrimination. *J Natl Med Assoc* 1952; 44:149.

New hospital opened today. *J Natl Med Assoc* 1911; 3:105–107.

News Items. *J Natl Med Assoc* 1909; 1·102.

Newton HP. *Revolutionary Suicide*. New York: Harcourt Brace Jovanovich, Inc., 1973.

New York hospitals. *J Natl Med Assoc* 1912; 4:143–144.

Nicholas F. Some health problems of the Negro. *Journal of Social Hygiene* 1925; 8:281–285.

Nieman DG. Civil rights and the law. 552–563. In: Salzman J, Smith DL, West C. eds. *Encyclopedia of African-American Culture and History*. 5 Vols. New York: Macmillan Library Reference USA, Simon and Schuster Macmillan, 1996.

Nisbet R. *Prejudices: A Philosophical Dictionary*. Cambridge, Massachusetts: Harvard University Press, 1982.

The N.M.A. — A review and forecast. *J Natl Med Assoc* 1910; 2:295–297.

The N.M.A. and civil rights. *J Natl Med Assoc* 1966; 58:130. Editorials.

NMA communications. Minutes of the Richmond meeting of the National Medical Association, 1918. *J Natl Med Assoc* 1918; 10:128–141.

Nobbe G. Feds may abandon the uninsured. *The Medical Herald*, May, 1998, p. 1, 50.

Norman DL. The strange career of the Civil Rights Division's commitment to *Brown. Yale Law Journal* 1984 (May); 93:989.

Norris GMK. Disparities for minorities in transplantation: The challenge to critical care nurses. *Heart and Lung* 1991; 20:419–420.

North Carolina Society drops final bars. *J Natl Med Assoc* 1965; 57:512. Integration Battlefront.

Novotny A, Smith C. eds. *Images of Healing: A Portfolio of American Medical and Pharmaceutical Practice in the 18th, 19th, and early 20th Centuries*. New York: Macmillan Publishing Company, Inc., 1980.

Nuland SB. *Doctors: The Biography of Medicine*. New York: Alfred A. Knopf, 1988.

Numbers RL. *Almost Persuaded: American Physicians and Compulsory Health Insurance, 1912–1920*. Baltimore: The Johns Hopkins University Press, 1978.

O'Bannion LC. Are African-American doctors being locked out? The down side of managed care. *National Medical Association News* 1995 (Winter), 1.

Obayuwana AO. The malpractice feud. *J Natl Med Assoc* 1981; 73:363–370.

Odegaard CE. *Minorities in Medicine: From Receptive Passivity to Positive Action 1966–1976*. Josiah Macy Jr. Foundation, 1977.

Omi M, Winant H. *Racial Formation in the United States: From the 1960s to the 1990s*. Second Edition. New York: Routledge, 1994.

O'Neil G, Zuckoff M, Kong D, Rodriguez C. Profit motives doom Worcester hospital: Sale heralds new corporate era for Mass. health care. *The Boston Sunday Globe*, Sunday, November 17, 1996, p. 1.

O'Neill G, Zuckoff M, Dembner A, Carroll M, Tlumacki J. Public handouts enrich drug makers, scientists: Public research/private profit. *The Boston Sunday Globe*, Sunday, April 5, 1998, p. 1.

Opportunity and new challenge for the N.M.A. *J Natl Med Assoc* 1966; 58:210–211. Editorials.

O'Reilly K. *Black Americans: The FBI Files*. New York: Carroll and Graff Publishers, Inc., 1994.

O'Reilly K. *Nixon's Piano: Presidents and Racial Politics from Washington to Clinton*. New York: The Free Press, 1995.

Organ CH. Equality and excellence. *J Natl Med Assoc* 1970; 62:347.

Organ CH, Kosiba MM, eds. *A Century of Black Surgeons: The U.S.A. Experience*. 2 Vols. Norman, Oklahoma: Transcript Press, 1987.

Our New York Meeting. *J Natl Med Assoc* 1909; 1:33–34.

Outlaw L. Toward a critical theory of race. 58–82. In: Goldberg DT, ed. *Anatomy of Racism*. Minneapolis: University of Minnesota Press, 1990.

Owens LH. *This Species of Property: Slave Life and Culture in the Old South.* Oxford: Oxford University Press, 1976.

Papa CM, Kligman AM. Stimulation of hair growth by topical application of androgens. *JAMA* 1965; 191:521.

Pappas G, Queen S, Hadden W, Fisher G. The increasing disparity in mortality between socioeconomic groups in the United States, 1960–1986. *N Engl J Med* 1993; 329:103–109.

Pappas G. Elucidating the relationships between race, socioeconomic status, and health. *Am J Public Health* 1994; 84:892–893.

Parker AJ. Simian characteristics in Negro brains. Philadelphia Academy of Natural Sciences. *Proceedings* 1879; 31:339.

Parker SG. Pew Commission Report: U.S. medical schools urged to increase diversity. *Ob.Gyn. News,* March 1, 1999, p. 36.

Parturition of the Negro. *Philadelphia Medical Times* 1885; 16:296.

Passell P. In medicine, government rises again. *The New York Times,* Sunday, December 7, 1997, Section 4, p. 1.

Passell P. Benefits dwindle along with wages for the unskilled: Even less for have nots: What was an equalizer has instead contributed to a growing disparity. *The New York Times,* Sunday, June 14, 1998, p. 1.

The passing of Leonard Medical School. *J Natl Med Assoc* 1918; 10:126.

*Patrick v. Burget.* 800 F. 2d 1498, 9th Cir, 1986.

Patterson JT. *The Dread Disease: Cancer and Modern American Culture.* Cambridge, Massachusetts: Harvard University Press, 1987.

Patterson O. *Slavery and Social Death: A Comparative Study.* Cambridge, Massachusetts: Harvard University Press, 1982.

Patton Jr. A. Howard University and Meharry Medical schools in the training of African physicians, 1868–1978. 109–124. In: Harris JE, ed. *Global Dimension of the African Diaspora.* Second Edition. Washington, D.C.: Howard University Press, 1993.

Pear R. Big health gap tied to income, is found in U.S. *The New York Times,* Thursday, July 8, 1993, p. A1.

Pear R. HMOs denying more claims for emergency care. *Fort Worth Star-Telegram,* Sunday, July 9, 1995, Section A, p. 7.

Pear R. H.M.O.'s using federal law to deflect malpractice lawsuits. *The New York Times,* Sunday, November 17, 1996, p. 24.

Pear R. Investigators say a Medicare option is rife with fraud. *The New York Times,* Sunday, July 27, 1997, p. 1.

Pear R. Health insurers skirting new law, officials report. *The New York Times,* Sunday, October 5, 1997, p. 1.

Pear R. Home-care denial in Medicare cases is ruled improper: Many benefits restored. *The New York Times,* Sunday, February 15, 1998, p. 1.

Pear R. Government lags in steps to widen health coverage: Uninsured at 41 million. *The New York Times,* Sunday, August 9, 1998, p. 1.

Pear R. Insurers as government to extend health plans. *The New York Times,* Sunday, May 23, 1999, p. 16.

Pear R. States called lax on tests for lead in poor children: Most flouting 1989 law. *The New York Times,* Sunday, August 22, 1999, p. 1.

Pear R. More Americans were uninsured in 1998, U.S. says, *The New York Times,* Monday, October 4, 1999, p. 1.

Pear R. Cash to ensure health coverage for the poor goes unused. *The New York Times,* Sunday, May 21, 2000, p. 18.

Pear R. Still uninsured, and still a campaign issue. *The New York Times,* Sunday, June 25, 2000, p. 16.

Pedersen D, Larson E. Too poor to treat: States are balking at paying for pricey AIDS drugs. *Newsweek,* July 28, 1997, 60.

Peniston RL. A racial view of medical education. *J Natl Med Assoc* 1987; 79:143–145.

Peniston RL. Institutional imperatives: A clear message from the Association of American Medical Colleges. *J Natl Med Assoc* 1988; 80:354.

Peniston RL. The disappearance of the Black hospital. *J Natl Med Assoc* 1988; 80:849–850.

Peniston RL. Will the National Medical Association support a comprehensive national health plan? *J Natl Med Assoc* 1989; 81:1027–1029.

Peniston RL. Further reflection on a racial view of medical education. *J Natl Med Assoc* 1990; 82:325.

*People v. Dominguez,* 64 California Rptr. 290 (1967).

Pernick MS. Eugenics and public health in American history. *Am J Public Health* 1997; 87:1767–1772.

Perry JE. *Forty Cords of Wood: Memoirs of a Medical Doctor.* Jefferson City, MO: Lincoln University Press, 1947.

Peterson ED, Wright SM, Doley J, Thibault GE. Racial variations in cardiac procedure use and survival following acute myocardial infarction in the Department of Veterans Affairs. *JAMA* 1994; 271:1175–1180.

Peterson ED, Shaw LK, DeLong ER, Pryor DB, Califf RM, Mark DB. Racial variation in the use of coronary-revascularization procedures: Are the differences real? Do they matter? *N Engl J Med* 1997; 336:480–486.

Pettigrew TF. *A Profile of the Negro American.* New York: Van Nostrand Reinhold Company, 1964.

Pew Health Professions Commission, *Critical Challenges: Revitalizing the Health Professions for the Twenty-first Century.* San Francisco: University of California, San Francisco, Center for the Health Professions, 1995.

Pham A. Time for pulling the plug on managed care? *The Boston Sunday Globe,* September 19, 1999, p. C1.

Phillips CW. The changing concept of a charity hospital. *J Natl Med Assoc* 1970; 62:303. Editorials.

Phillips CW. Cook County Hospital's potential as a leader in urban medical care. *J Natl Med Assoc* 1972; 64:169–171. Briefs.

Pickle LW, Mason TJ, Howard N, Hoover R, Fraumeni JF Jr. *Atlas of U.S. Cancer Mortality Among Nonwhites: 1950–1980.* Washington, D.C.: U.S. Govt. Printing Office, N.D. [NIH Publication No. 90–1582].

Pieterse JN. *White on Black: Images of Africa and Blacks in Western Popular Culture.* New Haven: Yale University Press, 1992.

Pinderhughes CA. Pathogenic social structure: A prime target for preventive psychiatric intervention. *J Natl Med Assoc* 1966; 58:424–429.

Pinn-Wiggins VW. Diversity in medical education and health care access: After the '80s, what? *J Natl Med Assoc* 1990; 82:89–92.

Pinn-Wiggins VW. The future of medical practice and its impact on minority physicians. *J Natl Med Assoc* 1990; 82:397–401.

Pinn-Wiggins VW. The National Medical Association and our challenges as we enter the next decade. *J Natl Med Assoc* 1989; 81:1213–1216.

Pinn-Wiggins VW. Testimony to the Pepper Commission: The United States Bipartisan Commission on Comprehensive Health Care. *J Natl Med Assoc* 1990; 82:169–172.

Pinn-Wiggins VW. Comments from the National Medical Association concerning a "white paper" on proposed strategies for fulfilling primary care manpower needs. *J Natl Med Assoc* 1990; 82:245–248.

Pinn-Wiggins VW. Recognition of the plight of minorities in the educational process and health care system. *J Natl Med Assoc* 1990; 82:333–335.

Pinn-Wiggins VW. Testimony before the House of Representatives Committee on Energy and Commerce, Subcommittee on Health and the Environment on HR 3240, the Disadvantaged Minority Health Improvement Act of 1989. *J Natl Med Assoc* 1990; 82:851–854.

Pinn-Wiggins VW. The National Medical Association: Furthering the mission. *J Natl Med Assoc* 1990; 82:793–796. President's Farewell Address.

Pisano JC, Epps AC. The impact of MCAT intervention efforts on medical student acceptance rates. *J Natl Med Assoc* 1983; 75:773–777.

Planned Parenthood et al. challenge Maryland compulsory birth control. *J Natl Med Assoc* 1968; 60:524–526.

Poindexter H. Handicaps in the normal growth and development of rural Negro children. *Am J Public Health* 1938; 28:1049.

Poliakov L. *The Aryan Myth: A History of Racist and Nationalist Ideas in Europe.* New York: Barnes and Noble Books, 1974.

Pope-Hennessy J. *Sins of the Fathers: A Study of the Atlantic Slave Traders, 1441–1807.* New York: Alfred A Knopf, Inc., 1967. Reprint Edition. New York: Capricorn Books, 1969.

Popenoe P, Johnson RH. *Applied Eugenics.* New York:The Macmillan Co., 1918.

Postell WD. *The Health of Slaves on Southern Plantations.* Baton Rouge: Louisiana State University Press, 1951. Reprint Edition. Gloucester, Massachusetts: Peter Smith, 1970.

Prager K. Neither costs nor care assured under 'cost containment'. *Medical Tribune,* May 2, 1996, p. 15.

Prasad N. The health economics cascade of the '80s. *J Natl Med Assoc* 1988; 80:1165–1166.

Prasad N. A systems view of health care for the poor. *J Natl Med Assoc* 1989; 81:169–178.

Prasad N. The dehiscence of health care. *J Natl Med Assoc* 1989; 81:931–935.
The president and the nation's health. *J Natl Med Assoc* 1965; 57:156. Editorials.
The president-elect (John L.S. Holloman, B.S., M.D.). *J Natl Med Assoc* 1965; 57:507–508.
Preston J. Hospitals look on charity care as unaffordable option of past: Squeezed by managed care and reduced aid. *The New York Times*, Sunday, April 14, 1996, p. 1.
Preston J. A hospital worries about 'people who fall through the cracks.' *The New York Times*, Sunday, April 14, 1996, p. 12.
Pretzer M. Can this profligate Blue find a way out of the red? *Medical Economics*, August 9, 1993, 41.
Prevention, early diagnosis seen as keys to controlling breast and cervical cancer. *National Medical Association News*, November/December, 1992, pp. 1, 2.
Proctor RN. *Racial Hygiene: Medicine under the Nazis*. Cambridge, Massachusetts: Harvard University Press, 1988.
Proctor RN. *Value-Free Science? Purity and Power in Modern Knowledge*. Cambridge, Massachusetts: Harvard University Press, 1991.
Proctor RN. Nazi doctors, racial medicine, and human experimentation. 17–31. In: Annas GJ, Grodin MA, eds. *The Nazi Doctors and the Nuremberg Code: Human Rights in Human Experimentation*. New York: Oxford University Press, 1992.
Proctor RN. Nazi biomedical policies. 23–42. In: Caplan AL, ed. *When Medicine Went Mad: Bioethics and the Holocaust*. Totowa, New Jersey: Humana Press, 1992.
Pross C. Nazi doctors, German medicine, and historical truth. 32–52. In: Annas GJ, Grodin MA, eds. *The Nazi Doctors and the Nuremberg Code: Human Rights in Human Experimentation*. New York: Oxford University Press, 1992.
Prothrow-Stith D. *Deadly Consequences*. New York: HarperCollins Publishers, 1991.
Protthrow-Stith D, Spivak H, Sege RD. Interpersonal violence prevention: A recent public health mandate. 1321–1336. In: Detels R, Holland WW, McEwen J, Omenn GS, eds. *Oxford Textbook of Public Health*. Volume 3. *The Practice of Public Health*. Third Edition. New York: Oxford University Press, 1997.
Public Health Service. *Healthy People: Surgeon General's Report on Health Promotion and Disease Prevention*. Washington, D.C.: U.S. Department of Health and Human Services, 1979.
Public Health Service. *Promoting Health/Preventing Disease: Objectives for the Nation*. Washington, D.C.: U.S. Department of Health and Human Services, 1980.
Public Health Service. *The 1990 Health Objectives for the Nation: A Midcourse Review*. Washington, D.C.: U.S. Department of Health and Human Services, 1986.
Public hospitals across nation cutting services under pressure. *Fort Worth Star-Telegram*, Sunday, August 20, 1995, Section A, p. 4.
Quillian DD. Racial peculiarities as a cause of the prevalence of syphilis in Negroes. *American Journal of Dermatology and Genito-Urinary Diseases* 1906; 10:277–279.
Quillian DD. Racial peculiarities as a cause of the prevalence of syphilis in Negroes. *Medical Era* 1911; 20:416.
Quindlen A. The problem of the color line. *Newsweek*, March 13, 2000, 76.
Quinn JB. Is your HMO ok—or not? It's hard to tell, because employers look mostly at price, not the quality of care. *Newsweek*, February 10, 1997, 52.
Quinn JB. Fighting for health care: 'Patients' rights' can curb unethical plans, but your coverage might still be chopped. *Newsweek*, March 30, 1998, 45.
Quinn JB. The invisible uninsured: Congress fiddles while rising numbers of Americans lose their access to medical care. *Newsweek*, March 1, 1999, 49.
Quinn JB. Health plans: Not always safe. *Newsweek*, August 14, 2000, 39.
Racial gap widens in heart disease deaths. *The Boston Globe*, Friday, November 13, 1998, p. A17.
Racial relationship. *J Natl Med Assoc* 1918; 10:44–45.
Racism rules A.M.A. policies. *J Natl Med Assoc* 1949; 41:34–35.
Rampersand A. Hughes, Langston. 1324–1325. In: Salzman J, Smith DL, West C. eds. *Encyclopedia of African-American Culture and History*. 5 Vols. New York: Macmillan Library Reference USA, Simon and Schuster Macmillan, 1996.
Rampersand A. Robeson, Paul. 2346–2348. In: Salzman J, Smith DL, West C. eds. *Encyclopedia of African-American Culture and History*. 5 Vols. New York: Macmillan Library Reference USA, Simon and Schuster Macmillan, 1996.
Randall VR. Racist health care: Reforming an unjust health care system to meet the needs of African-Americans. *Health Matrix: Journal of Law-Medicine* 1993 (Spring, No. 1); 3:127–194.
Randall VR. Does Clinton's health care reform proposal ensure (e)qual(ity) of health care for ethnic Americans and the poor? *Brooklyn Law Review* 1994 (Spring, No. 1); 60:167–237.
Randall VR. Slavery, segregation and racism: Trusting the health care system ain't always easy! An

African American perspective on bioethics. *Saint Louis University Public Law Review* 1996 (No. 2); 15:191–235.

Randolph AP. Why should we march? *Survey Graphic* 1942 (November); 31:488–489.

Rankin-Hill LM, Blakey ML. William Montague Cobb (1904–1990): Obituary. *Am J Phys Anthropology* 1993; 92:545–548.

Reagan R. *A Time for Choosing: The Speeches of Ronald Reagan, 1961–1982*. Chicago: Regnery Gateway, 1983.

Recognition of the N.M.A. *J Natl Med Assoc* 1919; 11:75.

Reed EW, Reed SC. *Mental Retardation: A Family Study*. Philadelphia: W.B. Saunders and Company, 1965.

Reed J. "Scientific Racism." 1358–1360. In Wilson CR, Ferris W, eds. *Encyclopedia of Southern Culture*. Chapel Hill: The University of North Carolina Press, 1989.

Reed WL. Lead poisoning: A modern plague among African American children. 178–191. In: Braithwaite RL, Taylor SE, eds. *Health Issues in the Black Community*. San Francisco: Jossey-Bass Publishers, 1992.

Reibstein L. Nursing-home verdicts: There's guilt all around. *Newsweek*, July 27, 1998, 34.

Reid IDA. "The Negro in the American Economic System," unpublished manuscript prepared for the *An American Dilemma* project, 2 Vols, Vol. 2, 186–187.

Reilly K. Racism and color: Colonialism and slavery. 355–383. In: *The West and the World: A Topical History of Civilization*. New York: Harper and Row, Publishers, 1980.

Reilly K. *The West and the World: A Topical History of Civilization*. New York: Harper and Row, Publishers, 1980.

Reilly PR. *The Surgical Solution: A History of Involuntary Sterilization in the United States*. Baltimore: The Johns Hopkins University Press, 1991.

Reiser RJ, Dyck AJ, Curran WJ, eds. In: *Ethics in Medicine: Historical Perspectives and Contemporary Concerns*. Cambridge, MA: MIT Press, 1977.

Reitzes DC. *Negroes and Medicine*. Cambridge, Massachusetts: Harvard University Press published for the Commonwealth Fund, 1958.

*Relf v. Weinberger*, 372 F.Supp. 1196, 1199 (D.D.C. 1974), on remand sub nom. *Relf v. Mathews*, 403 F.Supp. 1235 (D.D.C. 1975), vacated sub nom. *Relf v. Weinberger*, 565 F.2d 722 (D.C. Cir. 1977).

Relman AS. The new medical-industrial complex. *N Engl J Med* 1980; 303:963–970.

Relman AS. Dealing with conflicts of interest. *N Engl J Med* 1985; 313:749–751.

Relman AS. Practicing medicine in the new business climate. *N Engl J Med* 1987; 316:1150–1151.

René AA. Racial differences in mortality: Blacks and Whites. 21–41. In: Jones Jr W, Rice MF, eds. *Health Care Issues in Black America: Policies, Problems, and Prospects*. New York: Greenwood Press, 1987.

Requirements for membership in the N.M.A. *J Natl Med Assoc* 1919; 11:76.

Reuter EB. *The American Race Problem*. Revised Third Edition. Revision and Preface by Masuoka J. New York: Thomas Y. Crowell Company, 1970.

Revkin A. Mosquito virus exposes a hole in the safety net. *The New York Times*, Monday, October 4, 1999, p. A1.

Reynolds PP. Hospitals and Civil Rights, 1945–1963: *Simkins v. Moses H. Cone Memorial Hospital*. *Annals of Internal Medicine* 1997; 126:898–906.

Reynolds PP. The federal government's use of Title VI and Medicare to racially integrate hospitals in the United States, 1963 through 1967. *Am J Public Health* 1997; 87:1850–1858.

Reynolds V, Falger V, Vine I, eds. *The Sociobiology of Ethnocentrism: Evolutionary Dimensions of Xenophobia, Discrimination, Racism and Nationalism*. London: Croom Helm Ltd., 1987.

Rice H. In search of an ethical equilibrium: A new dilemma in health services. *J Natl Med Assoc* 1986; 78:57–60.

Rice MF, Jones W. Public policy compliance/enforcement and black American health: Title VI of the civil rights act of 1964. 98–115. In: Jones Jr W, Rice MF, eds. *Health Care Issues in Black America: Policies, Problems, and Prospects*. New York: Greenwood Press, 1987.

Rice MF. Inner-city hospital closures/relocations: Race, income status and legal issues. *Soc Sci Med* 1987; 24:889–896.

Rice MF, Winn M. Black health care in America: A political perspective. *J Natl Med Assoc* 1990; 82:429–437.

Rice MF. Hospital viability and closures. *J Health Care for the Poor and Underserved* 1990; 1:103–106.

Rice MF, Jones Jr. W. The uninsured and patient dumping: Recent policy responses in indigent care. *J Natl Med Assoc* 1991; 83:874–880.

Rice TB. *Racial Hygiene—A Practical Discussion of Eugenics and Race Culture.* New York: Macmillan Company, 1929.

Richard MP. The Negro physician: A study in mobility and status inconsistency. Unpublished Doctoral Dissertation, New York University, New York City, New York, 1967.

Richard MP. The Negro physician: Babbitt or revolutionary? *J Health Soc Behav* 1969; 10:265–274.

Richard MP. The Negro physician: A study in mobility and status inconsistency. *J Natl Med Assoc* 1969; 61:278–279.

Richardson L. White patients more likely to use AIDS drugs, study says: Sharp racial differences in the use of potent medicine. *The New York Times,* Sunday, July 27, 1997, p. 24.

Riggs MT. *Color Adjustment.* San Francisco: The American Film Institute and the California Council for the Humanities, produced in cooperation KQED, San Francisco, 1991. Filmstrip.

Rimer S. Blacks carry load of care for their elderly. *The New York Times,* Sunday, March 15, 1998, p. 1.

Roberts D. *Killing the Black Body: Race, Reproduction, and the Meaning of Liberty.* New York: Pantheon Books, 1997.

Roberts IH. Presidential address to the Old Dominion Medical Society. *J Natl Med Assoc* 1920; 12:8–10.

Roberts JM. *The Triumph of the West.* Boston: Little, Brown, and Company, Publishers, 1985.

Roberts JM. *History of the World.* New York: Alfred A. Knopf, 1976. Revised, Reprint, Edition. *The Penguin History of the World.* London: Penguin Books, Ltd., 1990.

Roberts MJ, Clyde AT. *Your Money or Your Life: The Health Care Crisis Explained.* New York: Main Street Books published by Doubleday, 1993.

Roberts RI. Hospitals continue to grow despite federal cutbacks. *J Natl Med Assoc* 1974; 66:242.

Robert Wood Johnson Foundation. Special Report Number One, The Foundation's Minority Medical Training Programs, "Minority Applicants to Medical School are Better Qualified Today than in Mid-70s, Yet Less Likely to be Accepted." Princeton, New Jersey: Robert Wood Johnson Foundation, 1987.

Robie TR. Selective sterilization for race culture. 201–209. In: Third International Congress of Eugenics (New York, 1932). *A Decade of Progress in Eugenics: Scientific Papers of the Congress.* Baltimore: The Williams and Wilkins Company, 1934.

Robinson FC, Robinson SW, Williams LJ. Eugenic sterilization: Medico-legal and sociological aspects. *J Natl Med Assoc* 1979; 71:593–598.

Robinson LS. Dialogue: Economist David H. Swinton: Inequities of the past block progress. *Emerge* 1993 (October, No. 1); 5:18.

Robinson LS. Dialogue with Dr. M. Jocelyn Elders: The Surgeon General's controversial remedies. *Emerge* 1994 (July/August, No. 10); 5:20.

Robinson LS. Dialogue: Curbing a sick practice: Energy Secretary Hazel O'Leary focuses on government accountability in testing. *Emerge* 1994 (October, No. 1); 6:20.

Roemer MI. Analysis of a national health system. 1539–1551. In: Detels R, Holland WW, McEwen J, Omenn GS, eds. *Oxford Textbook of Public Health.* Volume 3. *The Practice of Public Health.* Third Edition. New York: Oxford University Press, 1997.

*Roe v. Wade,* 410 U.S. 113 (1973).

Rogers DE. Who needs Medicaid? *N Engl J Med* 1982; 307:13–18.

Roman CV. The deontological orientation of its membership and chief function of a medical society. *J Natl Med Assoc* 1909; 1:19–23.

Roman CV. Ethnology. *J Natl Med Assoc* 1912; 4:352–354.

Roman CV. A college education as a requisite preparation for the study of medicine. *J Natl Med Assoc* 1917; 9:6–8.

Roman CV. Fifty years' progress of the American Negro in health and sanitation. *J Natl Med Assoc* 1917; 9:61–67.

Roman CV. The venereal situation. *J Natl Med Assoc* 1919; 11:72.

Roman CV. Vitality of the Negroes. *J Natl Med Assoc* 1910; 2:180–181.

Roman CV. *Meharry Medical College: A History.* Nashville: Sunday School Publishing Board of the National Baptist Convention, Inc., 1934.

Roman Jr. SA. Health policy and the underserved. *J Natl Med Assoc* 1978; 70:31–35.

Rosen G. Rosenberg CE, ed. *The Structure of American Medical Practice 1875–1941.* Philadelphia: University of Pennsylvania Press, 1983.

Rosen G. *A History of Public Health.* Expanded Edition. Baltimore: The Johns Hopkins University Press, 1993.

Rosenbaum DE. Swallow hard: What if there is no cure for health care's ills? *The New York Times,* Sunday, December 10, 2000, Section 4, p. 1.

Rosenbaum S, Layton C, Liu J. *The Health of America's Children*. Washington, D.C.: Children's Defense Fund, 1991.

Rosenberg CE. *The Care of Strangers: The Rise of America's Hospital System*. New York: Basic Books, Inc., Publishers, 1987.

Rosenberg CE. Community and communities: The evolution of the American hospital. 3–17. In: Long DE, Golden J, eds. *The American General Hospital: Communities and Social Contexts*. Ithaca: Cornell University Press, 1989.

Rosenthal E. Where it pays not to teach. *The New York Times*, Sunday, February 23, 1997, p. 2.

Rosenstreich DL, Eggleston P, Kattan M, Baker D, Slavin, RG, Gergen P, et al. The role of cockroach allergy and exposure to cockroach allergen in causing morbidity among inner-city children with asthma. *N Engl J Med* 1997; 336:1356–1384.

Rothman DJ. *Strangers at the Bedside*. New York: Basic Books, 1991.

Rothstein WG. *American Physicians in the 19th Century: From Sects to Science*. Baltimore, Maryland: The Johns Hopkins University Press, 1972.

Rothstein WG. *American Medical Schools and the Practice of Medicine*. New York: Oxford University Press, 1987.

Rugaber W. Prison drug and plasma projects leave fatal trail. *The New York Times*, July 29, 1969, p. 1.

Ruiz DS, Herbert TA. The economics of health care for elderly Blacks. *J Natl Med Assoc* 1985; 77:365–368.

Russell T. Eaton, Hubert Arthur. 825. In: Salzman J, Smith DL, West C. eds. *Encyclopedia of African-American Culture and History*. 5 Vols. New York: Macmillan Library Reference USA, Simon and Schuster Macmillan, 1996.

Rutstein DD. *Blueprint for Medical Care*. Cambridge, Massachusetts: The MIT Press, 1974.

Ryan W. *Blaming the Victim*. New York: Vintage Books, 1971. Revised, Updated Edition. New York: Vintage Books, 1976.

S. 1880, *The Health Care Fairness Act of 1999*.

Sabir NZ. A hazardous existence. *Black Enterprise*. (March, No. 8) 1995; 25:30.

Sack K. Public hospitals around country cut basic service: Some face elimination. *The New York Times*, Sunday, August 20, 1995, p. 1.

Sack K. Hard cases at the hospital door. *The New York Times*, Sunday, September 17, 1995, p. 5.

Sadler LK. Is the abnormal to become normal? 193–200. In: Third International Congress of Eugenics (New York, 1932). *A Decade of Progress in Eugenics: Scientific Papers of the Congress*. Baltimore: The Williams and Wilkins Company, 1934.

Sager A, Socolar D, Ford D, Brand R. More care, at less cost. *The Boston Sunday Globe*, Sunday, April 25, 1999, C1.

Saltman RB, ed. *The International Handbook of Health-Care Systems*. New York: Greenwood Press, 1988.

Sampson CC. Death of the Black community hospital: Fact or fiction. *J Natl Med Assoc* 1974; 66:165. Editorials.

Sampson CC. Provident Medical Center: Fulfillment of a need. *J Natl Med Assoc* 1983; 75:665–666.

Sampson CC. Dispelling the myth surrounding Drew's death. *J Natl Med Assoc* 1984; 76:415–416.

Sampson CC. Health care problems in the 1980s from a Black perspective. *J Natl Med Assoc* 1984; 76:968.

Sanders R. *Lost Tribes and Promised Lands: The Origins of American Racism*. Boston: Little, Brown, and Company, Publishers, 1978.

Sardell A. *The U.S. Experiment in Social Medicine: The Community Health Center Program, 1956–1986*. Pittsburgh: The University of Pittsburgh Press, 1988.

Satcher D. The Meharry Hubbard and Nashville General Hospital merger proposal statement. *J Natl Med Assoc* 1990; 82:83–85.

Satcher D. "Black Access to Health Care." Presentation for Black Health: Historical Perspectives and Current Problems Conference, University of Wisconsin Medical School, April 5–7, 1990, Madison, Wisconsin.

Satcher D. "The Settlement: Will the African-American Community Pay the Bill?" Address delivered at Roxbury Community College Media Arts Center, Roxbury, Massachusetts, Monday, April 12, 1999.

Satcher D. Meeting health challenges and setting priorities: An interview with US Surgeon General, David Satcher, MD, PhD. *J Natl Med Assoc* 1999; 91:191–192. Health Tidbits.

Savitt TL. The use of blacks for medical experimentation and demonstration in the old south. *J Southern History* 1982; 48:331–348.

Savitt TL. The education of Black physicians at Shaw University, 1882–1918. 160–188. In Crow

J, Hatley FJ, eds. *Black Americans in North Carolina and the South.* Chapel Hill: University of North Carolina Press, 1984.

Savitt T. Black Health on the Plantation: Masters, Slaves, and Physicians. 313–330. In: Leavitt JW, Numbers RL, eds. *Sickness and Health in America: Readings in the History of Medicine and Public Health.* Madison, Wisconsin: The University of Wisconsin Press, 1985.

Savitt TL. *Medicine and Slavery: The Diseases and Health Care of Blacks in Antebellum Virginia.* Urbana: University of Illinois Press, 1987.

Savitt TL. Entering a white profession: Black physicians in the new south, 1880–1920. *Bulletin of the History of Medicine* 1987; 61:507–540.

Savitt TL, Young JH, eds. *Disease and Distinctiveness in the American South.* Knoxville: The University of Tennessee Press, 1988.

Savitt TL. Abraham Flexner and the black medical schools. 65–81. In: Barzansky EM, Gevitz N, eds. *Beyond Flexner: Medical Education in the 20th Century.* New York: Greenwood Press, 1992.

Savitt TL. Black Health on the Plantation: Masters, Slaves, and Physicians. 327–355. In: Numbers RL, Savitt TL, eds. *Science and Medicine in the Old South.* Baton Rouge: Louisiana State University Press, 1989.

Savitt TL. Medical education. 1750–1752. In: Salzman J, Smith DL, West C. eds. *Encyclopedia of African-American Culture and History.* 5 Vols. New York: Macmillan Library Reference USA, Simon and Schuster Macmillan, 1996.

Savitt TL. 'A journal of our own': *The Medical and Surgical Observer* at the beginnings of an African-American medical profession in late 19th-century America. *J Natl Med Assoc* 1996; 88:52–60, 115–122.

Sawyer D. "The Tuskegee Study." [videotape segment], *Prime Time*, ABC television network, February 6, 1992.

Schtzkin A, Cooper R, Green L. Antiracism and the level of health services: A sociomedical hypothesis. *J Natl Med Assoc* 1984; 76:381–386.

Schulman KA, Berlin JA, Harless W, Kerner JF, Sistrunk SS, Gersh BJ, et al. The effect of race and sex on physician recommendations for cardiac catheterization. *N Engl J Med* 1999; 340:618–626.

Schultz SM. *Body Snatching: The Robbing of Graves for the Education of Physicians.* Jefferson, North Carolina: McFarland and Company, Inc., Publishers, 1992.

Schuman H, Steeh C, Bobo L, Krysan M. *Racial Attitudes in America: Trends and Interpretations.* Revised Edition. Cambridge, Massachusetts: Harvard University Press, 1997.

Schwartz E, Kofie VY, Rivio M, Tuckson RV. Black/White comparisons of deaths preventable by medical intervention: United States and the District of Columbia, 1980–1986. *Int J Epidemiol* 1990; 19:591–598.

Schwarz GE. An Exploratory Descriptive Study of the National Medical Association, Unpublished Master's Thesis, The University of Iowa, Iowa City, 1969.

Schwarz GE, Lawrence MS. Selected characteristics of the members of the National Medical Association: Preliminary findings. *J Natl Med Assoc* 1970; 62:1–7.

A scientist's variation on a disturbing racial theme: Psychologist Arthur Jensen believes Black are born with lower IQ's than Whites–and the furor goes on. *Life*, June 12, 1970, 65.

Scott G. "Prevalence of Chronic Conditions of the Genitourinary, Nervous, Endocrine, Metabolic and Blood-forming Systems and of Other Selected Chronic Conditions, United States, 1973." *Vital and Health Statistics*, Series 10, No. 109. DHEW Pub. No. (HRA) 77–1536. U.S. Government Printing Office, Washington, D.C., March, 1977.

Scott HC. Annual address. *J Natl Med Assoc* 1910; 2:96–101.

Seay E. To their defense: Lawyer Joseph Romano helps clients get health insurers to pay up: What people don't realize is that obtaining health insurance benefits is an adversarial process. *The Wall Street Journal*, Thursday, October 23, 1997, p. R8.

Sedgwick J. Inside the Pioneer Fund. 144–161. In: Jacoby R, Glauberman N, eds. *The Bell Curve Debate: History, Documents, Opinions.* New York: Times Books Division of Random House, Inc., 1995.

Seiden DJ. Health care ethics. 486–531. In: Kovner AR. *Jonas's Health Care Delivery in the United States.* Fifth Edition. New York: Springer Publishing Company, 1995.

Sergent JS. Code blue? Halls of medical learning are worried for their very survival. *The Tennessean*, Wednesday, February 1, 1995, p. 11A.

Shafer BE. Exceptionalism in American politics? *Political Science and Politics* 1989; 22:588–594.

Shea S, Fullilove MT. Entry of black and other minority students in US medical schools: Historical perspectives and recent trends. *N Engl J Med* 1985; 313:933–940.

Sheifer SE, Escarce JJ, Schulman KA. Race and sex differences in the management of coronary artery disease. *Am Heart J* 2000; 139:848–857.

Shepperd JD, Haedka EK. Impact of the consumer on inner city health centers. *J Natl Med Assoc* 1972; 64:370–371. Briefs.

Sheridan RB. *Doctors and Slaves: A Medical and Demographic History of Slavery in the British West Indies, 1680–1834.* Cambridge: Cambridge University Press, 1985.

Shipman P. *The Evolution of Racism: Human Differences and the Use and Abuse of Science.* New York: Simon and Schuster, 1994.

Sholl EH. The Negro and his death rate. *Alabama Medical and Surgical Age* 1891; 3:340.

Shryock RH. *Medicine in America: Historical Essays.* Baltimore: The Johns Hopkins Press, 1966.

Shryock RH. Medical practice in the Old South, 49–70. In: Shryock RH. *Medicine in America: Historical Essays.* Baltimore: The Johns Hopkins Press, 1966.

Shryock RH. A medical perspective on the civil war. 90–108. In: Shryock RH. *Medicine in America: Historical Essays.* Baltimore: The Johns Hopkins Press, 1966.

Shryock RH. *The Development of Modern Medicine: An Interpretation of the Social and Scientific Factors Involved.* Madison, Wisconsin: The University of Wisconsin Press, 1974.

Shucy AM. *The Testing of Negro Intelligence.* Second Edition. New York: Social Science Press, 1966.

Shufeldt RW. *America's Greatest Problem: The Negro.* Philadelphia: F.A. Davis Company, 1915.

Sidel VW, Sidel R, eds. *Reforming Medicine: Lessons of the Last Quarter Century.* New York: Pantheon Books, 1984.

Sigerist HE. *The Great Doctors: A Biographical History of Medicine.* Reprint Edition. New York: Dover Publications, 1971.

A significant step by the Southern Medical Association. *J Natl Med Assoc* 1967; 59:56.

Silver MA. Birth control and the private physician. *Family Planning Perspectives* 1972; 4:42–46.

Silverman M, Lee PR. *Pills, Profits, and Politics.* Berkeley: University of California Press, 1974.

Simms PB. "National Leadership Summit on Health Care Reform: Structure and Administration." Discussion paper for initial board meeting of Summit '93: African American Prescription for Health, Washington, D.C., March 29, 1993.

Singh GK, Yu SM. Infant mortality in the United States: Trends, differentials, and projections, 1950 through 2010. *Am J Public Health* 1995; 85:957–964.

Sirasi NG. *Medieval and Early Renaissance Medicine: An Introduction to Knowledge and Practice.* Chicago: University of Chicago Press, 1990.

Sitkoff H. History of the United States. In: *The New Grolier Multimedia Encyclopedia.* Release 6, MPC Version. Novato, California: Grolier Electronic Publishing, Inc., The Software Toolworks, Inc., 1993.

Sixth annual clinic: John A. Andrew Memorial Hospital, Tuskegee Institute, Alabama. *J Natl Med Assoc* 1917; 9:109–112.

"$60-Billion Crisis in Health Care," *Business Week*, January 17, 1970, 50–64.

*Skinner v. Oklahoma*, 316 U.S. 535 (1942)

Skocpol T. *Boomerang: Health Care Reform and the Turn Against Government.* New York: W.W. Norton and Company, 1997.

Smedley A. *Race in North America: Origin and Evolution of a Worldview.* Second Edition. Boulder, Colorado: Westview Press, 1999.

Smith A. *The Wealth of Nations.* New York: Modern Library, 1937.

Smith DB. Addressing racial inequities in health care: Civil rights monitoring and report cards. *Journal of Health, Policy and Law* 1998; 23:75–105.

Smith DB. *Health Care Divided: Race and Healing a Nation.* Ann Arbor: The University of Michigan Press, 1999.

Smith DS. Differential mortality in the United States before 1900. *Journal of Interdisciplinary History* 1983; 13:735–759.

Smith EB. Health hazards of the slums. *J Natl Med Assoc* 1967; 59:141.

Smith H. *The Power Game: How Washington Works.* New York: Random House, Inc., 1988. Paperback Edition. New York: Ballantine Books, 1989.

Smith JD, Nelson KR. *The Sterilization of Carrie Buck.* Far Hills, New Jersey: New Horizon Press, 1989.

Smith Mueller M, Gibson RM. "National Health Expenditures, Fiscal Year 1975." *Social Security Bulletin*, vol. 39 (February 1976).

Smith PM. The Black physician: An endangered species? *J Natl Med Assoc* 1984; 76:1178–1181.

Smith PM. Economic survival for Black physicians. *J Natl Med Assoc* 1985; 77:17.

Smith PM. The importance of the NMA political action committee (NMPAC). *J Natl Med Assoc* 1985; 77:75–76. President's Column.

Smith PM. The importance of maintaining Black institutions. *J Natl Med Assoc* 1985; 77:175–176. President's Column.

Smith PM. NMA opposes World Medical Association meeting in South Africa. *J Natl Med Assoc* 1985; 77:259–260. President's Column.

Smith SS; Jordan WD, ed. *An Essay on the Causes of the Variety of Complexion and Figure in the Human Species.* 1810. Reprint, Cambridge, Massachusetts: The Belknap Press of Harvard University Press, 1965.

Smothers R, Drew C. Failed H.M.O. reveals flaws in industry: Lack of oversight is found in managed care's financial dealings. *The New York Times,* Sunday, December 27, 1998, p. 30.

Sniderman PM, Piazza T. *The Scar of Race.* Cambridge, Massachusetts: The Belknap Press of Harvard University Press, 1993.

Sniderman PM, Carmines EG. *Reaching Beyond Race.* Cambridge, Massachusetts: Harvard University Press, 1997.

Snyder B. Meharry Ob closing cuts General residents by 40 percent. *Nashville Banner,* Thursday, June 20, 1991, p. B-1.

Sommers PA. Malpractice risk and patient relations. *J Natl Med Assoc* 1984; 76:953–956.

Sontag D, Richardson L. Doctors withhold H.I.V. pill regimen from some. *The New York Times,* Sunday, March 2, 1997, p. 1.

Sorlie P, Rogot E, Anderson R, Johnson NJ, Blacklund E. Black-White mortality differences by family income. *Lancet* 1992; 340:346–350.

The South and Negro education. *J Natl Med Assoc* 1919; 11:157–158.

Spake A. Death came in the water. *U.S. News and World Report,* September 20, 1999, p. 56.

Spearman C. General intelligence objectively defined and measured. *American Journal of Psychology* 1904; 15:201–293.

Spearman C, Wynn Jones L. *Human Ability.* London: MacMillan, 1950.

Spellman MW. The physician in the Great Society. *J Natl Med Assoc* 1966; 58:362–367, 365–366.

Spingarn AB. The war and venereal diseases among Negroes. *J Natl Med Assoc* 1919; 11:47–52.

Spragins EE. To sue or not to sue? A wrinkle in federal law makes it harder than ever to win a claim for medical malpractice. *Newsweek,* December 9, 1996, 50.

Spragins EE. The numbers racket: An HMO's approval rating may not say much about its quality. *Newsweek,* May 5, 1997, 77.

Spragins EE. When your HMO says no: How to fight for the treatment you need—and win. *Newsweek,* July 28, 1997, 73.

Staggers FE. President's inaugural address: Black health care. *J Natl Med Assoc* 1988; 80:1281–1282.

Stanford University. "Health Care In America: Armageddon on the Horizon?" *Stanford Law and Policy Review* (Fall) 1991; 3:1–260.

Stannard DE. *American Holocaust: Columbus and the Conquest of the New World.* New York: Oxford University Press, 1992.

Stanton W. *The Leopard's Spots: Scientific Attitudes Toward Race in America, 1815–1859.* Chicago: The University of Chicago Press, 1960.

Staples B. Unearthing a riot. *The New York Times Magazine,* December 19, 1999, Section 6, p. 64.

Starkenburg RJ, Rosner F, Kowal S. Patient "dumping." *J Natl Med Assoc* 1990; 82:660–662.

Starr D. *Blood: An Epic History of Medicine and Commerce.* New York: Alfred A. Knopf, 1998. Paperback Edition. New York: Quill, 2000.

Starr P. *The Social Transformation of American Medicine.* New York: Basic Books, Inc., Publishers, 1982.

Starr P. The new critics of medical care: The politics of therapeutic nihilism. 7–16. In: Havighurst CC. *Health Care Law and Policy: Readings, Notes, and Questions.* Westbury, New York: The Foundation Press, Inc., 1988.

Starr P. *The Logic of Health Care Reform.* Knoxville, Tennessee: Whittle, 1992.

Starr P. Healthy compromise: Universal coverage and managed competition under a cap. *The American Prospect,* no. 12 (Winter 1993):44–52.

States where managed care liability measures were introduced in 1997. *Ob-Gyn News,* September 1, 1997, p. 49.

Stefancic J, Delgado R. *No Mercy: How Conservative Think Tanks and Foundations Changed America's Social Agenda.* Philadelphia: Temple University Press, 1996.

Stein C. Free market straining health-care safety net. *The Boston Sunday Globe,* Sunday, April 21, 1996, p. 1.

Steinberg S. *The Ethnic Myth: Race, Ethnicity, and Class in America.* N.P.: Antheneum Publishers, 1981. Updated and Expanded Edition. Boston: Beacon Press, 1989.

Steinberg S. *Turning Back: The Retreat from Racial Justice in American Thought and Policy.* Boston: Beacon Press, 1995.

Steinhauer J. Rebellion in white: Doctors pulling out of H.M.O. systems. *The New York Times,* Sunday, January 10, 1999, p. 1.

Sterling D. *The Making of an Afro-American: Martin Robison Delany, 1812–1885.* Garden City, New York: Doubleday and Company, Inc., 1971.

Stevens RA. *American Medicine and the Public Interest.* New Haven: Yale University Press, 1971.

Stevens RA. Times past, times present. 191–206. In: Long DE, Golden J, eds. *The American General Hospital: Communities and Social Contexts.* Ithaca: Cornell University Press, 1989.

Stevens RA. *In Sickness and in Wealth: American Hospitals in the Twentieth Century.* Baltimore: The Johns Hopkins University Press, 1999.

Stitt Jr. VJ. Health care: Development of data for a marketing approach. *J Natl Med Assoc* 1985; 77:485–488.

Stoddard L. *The Rising Tide of Color Against White World-Supremacy.* New York: Charles Scribner's Sons, 1920.

Stokes L. Health Care Reform and Its Impact on the African American Community, keynote address, *Proceedings: Summit '93: African American Prescription for Health,* convened by the National Medical Association and the Congressional Black Caucus Foundation, Inc., Washington, D.C., May 2, 1993, 11–13.

Stoline A, Weiner JP. *The New Medical Marketplace: A Physician's Guide to the Health Care Revolution.* Baltimore: The Johns Hopkins University Press, 1988.

Strait G, DiIanni D. "The Deadly Deception," A documentary video segment for *Nova,* Boston, WGBH, 1993.

Strayhorn G. Social supports, perceived stress, and health: The Black experience in medical school— a preliminary study. *J Natl Med Assoc* 1980; 72:869–881.

Strelnick H, Younge R. Affirmative action in medicine: Money becomes the admissions criteria of the 1980s. 151–175. In: Sidel VW, Sidel R, eds. *Reforming Medicine: Lessons of the Last Quarter Century.* New York: Pantheon Books, 1984.

Strelnick AH, Massad RJ, Bateman WB, Shepherd SD. Minority students in U.S. medical schools. *N Engl J Med* 1986; 315:67–68.

Stringer C, McKie R. *African Exodus: The Origins of Modern Humanity.* London: Jonathan Cape Ltd., 1996. First American Edition. New York: A John Macrae Book, Henry Holt and Company, 1997.

Student Nonviolent Coordinating Committee. *Genocide in Mississippi* (pamphlet). Atlanta: Student Nonviolent Coordinating Committee, N.D.

Study links heart attack survival with care by specialists. *Fort Worth Star-Telegram,* Wednesday, November 15, 1995, Section A, p. 3.

Suchindran CM, Koo HP. Demography and public health. 829–848. In: Detels R, Holland WW, McEwen J, Omenn GS, eds. *Oxford Textbook of Public Health.* Volume 3. *The Practice of Public Health.* Third Edition. New York: Oxford University Press, 1997.

Sullivan LW. The status of blacks in medicine. *N Engl J Med* 1983; 309:807–809.

Sullivan LW. The Morehouse School of Medicine: A state of mind, of mission, and of commitment. *J Natl Med Assoc* 1983; 75:837–839.

Sullivan LW. Foreword. *xiii-xv.* In: Braithwaite RL, Taylor SE, eds. *Health Issues in the Black Community.* San Francisco: Jossey-Bass Publishers, 1992.

Summerville J. Formation of a black medical profession in Tennessee, 1880–1920. *Journal of the Tennessee Medical Association* October, 1983; 644–646.

Summerville J. *Educating Black Doctors: A History of Meharry Medical College.* University, Alabama: The University of Alabama Press, 1983.

Summit '93: African American Prescription for Health. "Summit Policy Paper." Washington Vista Hotel, Washington, D.C., May 2–3, 1993.

Supreme Court may review peer review case. *Am Med News,* February 13, 1987.

Survey: 60 million experience lapses in health coverage. *Physician's Financial News,* January 15, 1995, p. 2.

Sutchfield FD, Keck CW. *Principles of Public Health Practice.* Albany, New York: Delmar Publishers, 1997.

Sutchfield FD, Keck CW. Concepts and definitions of public health practice. 3–9. In: Sutchfield FD, Keck CW. *Principles of Public Health Practice.* Albany, New York: Delmar Publishers, 1997.

Swan LF. The start of a voyage—not journey's end. *J Natl Med Assoc* 1968; 60:133. President's Column.

Swan LF. The exigencies of the American environment, 1967: President's inaugural address, National Medical Association. *J Natl Med Assoc* 1967; 59:373–377.

Swinton DH. The economic status of African Americans: Limited ownership and persistent inequality. In: Tidwell BJ, ed. *The State of Black America 1992*. New York: National Urban League, Inc., 1992.

Taylor D. Stokes, Louis. 2579. In: Salzman J, Smith DL, West C, eds. *Encyclopedia of African-American Culture and History*. 5 Vols. New York: Macmillan Library Reference USA, Simon and Schuster Macmillan, 1996.

Taylor H, Leitman R. Consumers' satisfaction with their health care. 75–102. In: Blendon RJ, Edwards JN, eds. *System in Crisis: The Case for Health Care Reform*. Volume 1. *The Future of American Health Care*. New York: Faulkner and Gray, Inc., 1991.

Taylor H, Leitman R, Edwards J. Physicians' response to their changing environment. 149–172. In: Blendon RJ, Edwards JN, eds. *System in Crisis: The Case for Health Care Reform*. Volume 1. *The Future of American Health Care*. New York: Faulkner and Gray, Inc., 1991.

Taylor JM. The Negro and his health problems. *Medical Record*, September 21, 1912.

Takaki RY. *Iron Cages: Race and Culture in Nineteenth-Century America*. New York: Alfred A. Knopf, 1979.

Terman LM. *The Measurement of Intelligence*. Boston: Houghton Mifflin, 1916.

Terman LM. Feeble-minded children in the public schools of California. *School and Society* 1917; 5: 165.

Terry RW. *For Whites Only*. Grand Rapids, Michigan: William B. Eerdmans, 1970. Paperback, Revised, Reprint Edition. Grand Rapids, Michigan: William B. Eerdmans, 1992.

Thirty-six states now mandate coverage for extended hospital stays for mothers and newborns. *Medical Economics*, September, 1997, p. 12.

Thomas H. *The Slave Trade: The Story of the Atlantic Slave Trade: 1440–1870*. New York: Simon and Schuster, 1997.

Thomas SB, Quinn SC. Public health then and now: The Tuskegee syphilis study, 1932 to 1972: Implications for HIV education and AIDS risk education programs in the Black community. *Am J Public Health* 1991; 81:1498–1504.

Thomas VG. Explaining health disparities between African-American and white populations: Where do we go from here? *J Natl Med Assoc* 1992; 84:837–840.

Thompson M. Shining a light on abuse: Following a *Time* story, Congress reports that many nursing-home residents are beaten and starved. *Time*, August 3, 1998, 42.

Thompson T. Health and social policy issues of significance to Blacks in the "new federalism." *J Natl Med Assoc* 1973; 65:422.

Thompson VR. Crisis in health care for the poor. *J Natl Med Assoc* 1980; 72:1037. President's Column.

Thompson VR. Recommendations to the Transition Team for the Reagan Administration. *J Natl Med Assoc* 1981; 73:393–394.

Thorndike EL. *Human Nature and the Social Order*. New York: The Macmillan Company, 1940.

Thurstone LL. *The Vectors of Mind*. Chicago: University of Chicago Press, 1935.

The tidewater colored hospital. *J Natl Med Assoc* 1919; 11:21.

Tipton F. The Negro problem from a medical point of view. *New York Medical Journal* 1886; 43:570.

Todd KH, Samaroo N, Hoffman JR. Ethnicity as a risk factor for inadequate emergency department analgesia. *JAMA* 1993; 269:1537–1539.

Tomsho R. Some health insurers leave patients to foot excessive copayments: Firms get sizeable discounts from providers but fail to reduce clients' bills. *The Wall Street Journal*, Monday, August 21, 1995, p. 1.

Toner R. Critics of G.O.P.'s budget see a nursing home crisis: How to care for the growing number of elderly. *The New York Times*, Sunday, November 12, 1995, p. 16.

Toner R. Rx redux: fevered issue, second opinion, *The New York Times*, Sunday, October 10, 1999, Section 4, p. 1.

Toner R. Gore and Bush health proposals fall short of counterparts' plans 8 years ago. *The New York Times*, Sunday, October 15, 2000, p. 22.

Townsend AM. President's address, Rock City Academy, October 17, 1910. *J Natl Med Assoc* 1911; 3:33–39.

Transcription of a presentation by Dr. Leon Johnson Jr., President, National Medical Fellowships, Inc. to the Special Advisory Commission on Minority Enrollment in Medical Schools. *Issues in Financing Minority Enrollment*, August, 1982.

Travella S. Black hospitals struggle to survive. *Modern Health Care* 1990 (July 2), 20–26.

Travella S. Black hospitals struggling to survive: Of more than 200 medical centers, only 8 are left. 12. In: *Health: A Weekly Journal of Medicine, Science and Society*, *The Washington Post*, Tuesday, September 11, 1990.

Trombley S. "The Lynchburg Story" [videotape segment], for *Discovery Journal,* hosted by John Palmer, July, 1994.

Tuberculosis Commission of the National Medical Association. *J Natl Med Assoc* 1910; 2:142.

Tucker WH. *The Science and Politics of Racial Research.* Urbana, Illinois: University of Illinois Press, 1994.

Tuckson R. The Black physician and the challenges of the 1980s. *J Natl Med Assoc* 1984; 76:977–980. Health care problems in the 1980s from a Black perspective: Part II of a series begun in 1984; 76:968.

Tull ES, Makame MH, Roseman J. Diabetes mellitus in the African American population. 94–109. In: Livingston IL, ed. *Handbook of Black American Health: The Mosaic of Conditions, Issues, Policies, and Prospects.* Westport, Connecticut: Greenwood Press, 1994.

Turner PA. *Ceramic Uncles and Celluloid Mammies: Black Images and Their Influence on Culture.* New York: Anchor Books, 1994.

U.S. Bureau of the Census. *Historical Statistics of the United States, Colonial Times to 1970, Bicentennial Edition, Parts 1 and 2.* Washington, D.C.: U.S. Government Printing Office, 1975.

U.S. Bureau of the Census. *Negro Population of the United States: 1790–1915* (1918).

U.S. Bureau of the Census. *Negroes in the United States 1920–32* (1935).

U.S. Bureau of the Census. *Statistical Abstract of the United States, 1993.* U.S. Department of Commerce. Washington, D.C.: U.S. Government Printing Office, 1992.

U.S. Bureau of the Census. *Statistical Abstract of the United States, 1998.* (118th edition.) U.S. Department of Commerce. Washington, D.C.: U.S. Government Printing Office, 1998.

U.S. Congress. House. *The American Health Security Act of 1993.* 103rd Congress, 1st session, H.R. 1200. *Congressional Record.* March 3, 1993.

U.S. Congress. House. *Managed Competition Act of 1993.* 103rd Congress. 2d session, H.R. 3222. *Congressional Record.* October 6, 1993.

U.S. Department of Health and Human Services. *Health in America: 1776–1976.* Washington, D.C.: U.S. Health Resources Administration, DHEW Pub. No. (HRA) 76–616, 1976.

U.S. Department of Health and Human Services. *Health Status of Minorities and Low Income Groups.* Washington, D.C.: U.S. Government Printing Office, 1985.

U.S. Department of Health and Human Services. *Report of the Secretary's Task Force on Black and Minority Health.* Vol. 1. *Executive Summary.* Washington, D.C.: U.S. Government Printing Office, August, 1985.

U.S. Department of Health and Human Services. *Report of the Secretary's Task Force on Black and Minority Health.* Vol. 2. *Crosscutting Issues in Minority Health.* Washington, D.C.: U.S. Government Printing Office, August, 1985.

U.S. Department of Health and Human Services. *The 1990 Health Objectives of the Nation: A Midcourse Review.* Washington, D.C.: U.S. Department of Health and Human Services, Public Health Service, November, 1986.

U.S. Department of Health and Human Services. *Report of the Secretary's Task Force on Black and Minority Health.* Vol. 3. *Cancer.* Washington, D.C.: U.S. Government Printing Office, January, 1986.

U.S. Department of Health and Human Services. *Report of the Secretary's Task Force on Black and Minority Health.* Vol. 4. *Cardiovascular and Cerebrovascular Diseases. Part 1.* Washington, D.C.: U.S. Government Printing Office, January, 1986.

U.S. Department of Health and Human Services. *Healthy People 2000: National Health Promotion and Disease Prevention Objectives.* (Summary Report). Washington, D.C.: U.S. Department of Health and Human Services, Public Health Service, Publication No. (PHS) 91–50213, 1990.

U.S. Department of Health and Human Services. *Cultural Competence for Evaluators: A Guide for Alcohol and Other Drug Abuse Prevention Practitioners Working With Ethnic/Racial Communities.* Rockville, Maryland: Office for Substance Abuse and Prevention, Alcohol, Drug Abuse, and Mental Health Administration, DHHS Publication No. (ADM) 92–1884, 1992.

U.S. Department of Health and Human Services. *For A Healthy Nation: Returns on Investment in Public Health.* Washington, D.C.: U.S. Government Printing Office, 1995.

U.S. Department of Health and Human Services. *Healthy People 2000: Midcourse Review and 1995 Revisions.* Washington, D.C.: U.S. Department of Health and Human Services, Public Health Service, 1995.

U.S. Department of Health and Human Services. *Health United States 1998.* U.S. Government Printing Office. Washington, D.C., 1998.

U.S. Department of Health and Human Services. President Clinton announces new racial and ethnic health disparities initiative. *USDHHS: President's Announcement,* February 21, 1998.

U.S. Department of Health and Human Services. New web site links public to HHS initiative to eliminate racial, ethnic health disparities. *HHS News*, Wednesday, July 1, 1998.

U.S. Department of Health and Human Services. Elimination of racial and ethnic disparities in health: Overview. *USDHHS: Initiative Overview*, October 28, 1998.

U.S. Department of Health, Education, and Welfare. *Towards a Comprehensive Health Policy for the 1970s*. Washington, D.C.: Government Printing Office, 1971.

U.S. health report card shows room for improvement. *The Nation's Health*, October, 1993, p. 1.

U.S. Library of Congress. Congressional Research Service. *Health Care Reform: Single-Payer Approaches*. Washington, D.C., March 15, 1993, CRS Issue Brief 93006.

U.S. President's Committee on Civil Rights. *To Secure These Rights*. New York, 1947.

Ukawuilulu JO, Livingston IL. Black health care providers and related professionals: Issues of underrepresentation and change. 344–360. In: Livingston IL, ed. *Handbook of Black American Health: The Mosaic of Conditions, Issues, Policies, and Prospects*. Westport, Connecticut: Greenwood Press, 1994.

Ullman V. *Martin R. Delany: The Beginnings of Black Nationalism*. Boston: Beacon Press, 1971.

Underwood A. The winged menace. *Newsweek*, September 20, 1999, p. 37.

UNESCO. *The Race Question in Modern Science*. New York: Whiteside Inc., and William Morrow and Company, 1956.

Van Ausdale D, Feagin JR. *The First R: How Children Learn Race and Racism*. Lanham, Maryland: Rowman and Littlefield Publishers, Inc., 2001.

Van den Berghe PL. *Race and Racism: A Comparative Perspective*. New York: Wiley, 1967.

Van Everie JH. *White Supremacy and Negro Subordination* (New York, 1868).

Van Ryn M, Burke J. The effect of patient race and socio-economic status on physicians' perceptions of patients. *Social Science and Medicine* 2000; 50:813–828.

Veatch RM. *Case Studies in Medical Ethics*. Cambridge, Massachusetts: Harvard University Press, 1977.

Veatch RM. *A Theory of Medical Ethics*. New York: Basic Books Inc., Publishers, 1981.

Venable HP. The history of Homer G. Phillips Hospital. *J Natl Med Assoc* 1961; 53:542.

Vogel MJ. *The Invention of the Modern Hospital: Boston 1870–1930*. Chicago: The University of Chicago Press, 1980.

Vonderlehr RA, et al. Untreated syphilis in the male Negro. *Venereal Disease Information* 1936; 17:260–265.

Wade RC. *Slavery in the Cities: The South 1820–1860*. London: Oxford University Press, 1964.

Walden EC. An NMA health insurance program. *J Natl Med Assoc* 1971; 63:384. President's Column.

Walden EC. Miles to go: President's inaugural address. *J Natl Med Assoc* 1971; 63:474.

Walden EC. NMA comments on national health insurance. *J Natl Med Assoc* 1971; 63:503–506.

Walden EC. The biological imperatives. *J Natl Med Assoc* 1972; 64:262. President's Column.

Walker B. Ethics in health services and medical care. *J Natl Med Assoc* 1989; 81:13–15.

Walker CE. The national health program. *J Natl Med Assoc* 1938; 30:147–151.

Walker HE. *The Negro in the Medical Profession*. Publications of the University of Virginia Phelps-Stokes Fellowship Papers. N.P.: University of Virginia, 1949.

Walker HI. Some reflection on the death of Dr. Martin Luther King—a commentary on White racism. *J Natl Med Assoc* 1968; 60:396–400.

Walker JL. The diffusion of knowledge, policy, communities and agenda setting: The relationship of knowledge and power. In: Tropman JE, Dluhey MJ, Lind RM, eds. *New Strategic Perspectives on Social Policy*. New York: Pergamon Press, 1981.

Walker Jr. B. Health care in the 1980s. *J Natl Med Assoc* 1985; 77:601–604.

Walker ML. The Morehouse School of Medicine story: A surgical strike! *J Natl Med Assoc* 1993; 85:395–400.

*Walker v. Pierce*, 560 F.2d 609 (4th Cir. 1977).

Wallace M. "Cooking the Books." [videotape segment], *60 Minutes*, CBS television network, WBZ, Channel 4, Boston, Massachusetts, Sunday, December 27, 1998.

Walsh G, Stickley C. Arsphenamine poisoning occurring among Negro women. *American Journal of Syphilis and Neurology* 1935; 324–325.

Walsh MR. *Doctors Wanted No Women Need Apply: Sexual Barriers in the Medical Profession, 1835–1975*. New Haven, Connecticut: Yale University Press, 1977.

Walton H Jr. *Black Politics: A Theoretical and Structural Analysis*. Philadelphia: J.B. Lippincott Company, 1972.

Walton JT. The comparative mortality of the White and Colored races in the South. *Charlotte Medical Journal* 1897; 10:291–294.

Ward GC, Burns R, Burns K. *The Civil War*. New York: Alfred A. Knopf, 1990.

Ware Jr. JE, Bayliss MS, Rogers WH, Kosinski M, Tarlov AR. Differences in 4-year health outcomes for elderly and poor, chronically ill patients treated in HMO and fee-for-service systems: Results from the Medical Outcomes Study. *JAMA* 1996; 276:1039–1047.

Warren C. *Brush with Death: A Social History of Lead Poisoning*. Baltimore: The Johns Hopkins University Press, 2000.

Washburn SL. The study of race. 128–132. In: Harding S, ed. *The "Racial Economy" of Science: Toward A Democratic Future*. Bloomington: Indiana University Press, 1993.

Washington H. Barriers to Black physicians and health care. *J Natl Med Assoc* 1984; 76:11–12.

Washington HA. Genetic research might engineer genocide. *Emerge* 1994 (March, No. 6): 5:19.

Washington HA. Of men and mice: Human guinea pigs: Unethical testing targets Blacks and the poor. *Emerge* 1994 (October, No. 1): 6:24.

Washington HA. Henrietta Lacks—An unsung hero. *Emerge* 1994 (October, No. 1); 6:29.

Washington HA. Straightening out *The Bell Curve*: An old IQ argument gets a new airing. *Emerge* 1995 (January, No. 3): 6:28.

Washington HA. Alarming new diseases among urban poor. *Emerge* 1996 (April, No. 6); 7:22.

Washington HA. Medicine's mainstream overlooks Blacks. *Emerge* 1996 (May, No. 7); 7:22.

Washington HA. Piece of the genetic puzzle is left out. *Emerge* 1997 (September, No. 10); 8:30.

Washington HA. Political realities hit medical school rolls. *Emerge* 1998 (March, No. 5); 9:22.

Washington WE. Problems and paradoxes of the urban crisis. *J Natl Med Assoc* 1969; 61:1–5.

Wasserman E. States pushing to extend post-delivery hospital stays. *Fort Worth Star-Telegram*, Sunday, July 9, 1995, Section A, p. 7.

Wasserman HP. *Ethnic Pigmentation: Historical, Psychological, and Clinical Aspects*. New York: American Elsevier Publishing Company, 1974.

Watts VG. New government proposals: The effect on minority medical education. *J Natl Med Assoc* 1983; 75:247–249.

Watts TC, Lecca PJ. Minorities in the health professions: A current perspective. *J Natl Med Assoc* 1989; 81:1225–1229.

Waxman H. Legislative forum. *J Natl Med Assoc* 1985; 77:311, 415, 515–520.

Weaver RC. The health care of our cities. *J Natl Med Assoc* 1968; 60:42–46.

Webb Jr. H. Community health centers: Providing care for urban Blacks. *J Natl Med Assoc* 1984; 76:1063–1067. Health care problems in the 1980s from a Black perspective: Part IV of a series begun in 1984; 76:968.

Wegner OC. Untreated syphilis in the Negro male. Hot Springs Seminar, 09-18-50 (From CDC files).

Weinstein MM. Getting litigious with H.M.O.'s, *The New York Times*, Sunday, July 19, 1998, Section 4, p. 5.

Weiss NJ. National Urban League. 1963–1965. Salzman J, Smith DL, West C. eds. *Encyclopedia of African-American Culture and History*. 5 Vols. New York: Macmillan Library Reference USA, Simon and Schuster Macmillan, 1996.

Weisbord RG. *Genocide? Birth Control and the Black American*. Westport, Connecticut: Greenwood Press, 1975.

Weisbrot R. Civil rights movement. 563–569. In: Salzman J, Smith DL, West C. eds. *Encyclopedia of African-American Culture and History*. 5 Vols. New York: Macmillan Library Reference USA, Simon and Schuster Macmillan, 1996.

Weitzman S, Cooper L, Chambless L, Rosamond W, Clegg L, Marucci G, et al. Gender, racial and geographic differences in the performance of cardiac diagnostic and therapeutic precedures for hospitalized acute myocardial infarction in four states. *American Journal of Cardiology* 1997; 79:722–726.

Wellington JS, Montero P. Equal opportunity programs in American medical schools. *J Med Educ* 1978; 53:633–639.

Welsome E. *The Plutonium Files: America's Secret Medical Experiments in the Cold War*. New York: The Dial Press, 1999.

Wenneker MB, Epstein AM. Racial inequalities in the use of procedures for patients with ischemic health disease in Massachusetts. *JAMA* 1989; 261:253–257.

Wenner-Gren, Axel Leonard. 1545. In: Magnusson M., ed. *Cambridge Biographical Dictionary*. Cambridge: Cambridge University Press, 1990.

Wesley Jr. N, Hester RD. Costs, choice, and competition: Some considerations of alternative delivery systems. *J Natl Med Assoc* 1984; 76:1079–1084. Health care problems in the 1980s from a Black perspective: Part VI of a series begun in 1984; 76:968.

White HA. *The Freedmen's Bureau in Louisiana*. Baton Rouge: Louisiana State University Press, 1970.

White J. Health care reform the international way. *Issues of Science and Technology* 1995 (Fall, No. 1); 12:35–42.

Whittle J, Conigliaro J, Good CB, Lofgren RP. Racial differences in the use of invasive cardiovascular procedures in the Department of Veterans Affairs Medical System. *N Engl J Med* 1993; 329:621–627.

Whol S. *The Medical Industrial Complex.* New York: Harmony Books, 1984.

WHO (World Health Organization) (1981*a*) *Global strategy for health for all by the year 2000.* WHO, Geneva.

WHO (World Health Organization) (1981*b*) *Development of indicators for monitoring progress towards health for all by the year 2000.* 'Health For All' Series, No. 4. WHO, Geneva.

Wildavsky A. Doing better and feeling worse: The political pathology of health policy. 105–123. In: Knowles JH, ed. *Doing Better and Feeling Worse: Health in the United States.* New York: W.W. Norton and Company and the American Academy of Arts and Sciences, 1977.

Wilkins JH. History of the Lone Star State Medical, Dental and Pharmaceutical Association. *J Natl Med Assoc* 1912; 4:87–88.

Williams AW. Venereal disease. *J Natl Med Assoc* 1918; 10:183–184.

Williams C. *The Destruction of Black Civilization: Great Issues of A Race from 4500 B.C. to 2000 A.D.* Chicago, Illinois: Third World Press, 1974.

Williams DR, Fenton BT. The mental health of African Americans: Findings, questions, and directions. 253–268. In: Livingston IL, ed. *Handbook of Black American Health: The Mosaic of Conditions, Issues, Policies, and* Prospects. Westport, Connecticut: Greenwood Press, 1994.

Williams DR. Race, socioeconomic status, and health: The added effects of racism and discrimination. *Annals of the New York Academy of Sciences* 1999: 896:173–188.

Williams J. *Eyes on the Prize: America's Civil Rights Years, 1954–1965.* New York: Viking Penguin Inc., 1987.

Williamson J. *The Crucible of Race: Black-White Relations in the American South Since Emancipation.* New York: Oxford University Press, 1984.

Williams RA, ed. *Textbook of Black-Related Diseases.* New York: McGraw-Hill Book Company, 1975.

Wilson DE. Minorities and the medical profession: A historical perspective and analysis of current and future trends. *J Natl Med Assoc* 1986; 78:177–180.

Wilson FA, Neuhauser D. *Health Services in the United States.* Second Edition. Cambridge, Massachusetts: Ballinger Publishing Company, 1982.

Wilson WJ. *The Truly Disadvantaged: The Inner City, the Underclass, and Public Policy.* Chicago: The University of Chicago Press, 1987.

Wilson WJ. *When Work Disappears: The World of the New Urban Poor.* New York: Alfred A. Knopf, 1996.

Wing KR, Rose MG. Health facilities and the enforcement of civil rights. 243–267. In: Roemer R, McKray G, eds. *Legal Aspects of Health Policy: Issues and Trends.* Westport, Connecticut: Greenwood Press, 1980.

Winston H. Jim-Crow Army. From a fifteen page pamphlet, *Old Jim Crow Has Got To Go!* New York: New Age Publishers, March, 1941, 9–11.

Winter G. Cuts in loan program squeeze doctors who work with poor. *The New York Times,* Sunday, July 30, 2000, p. 1.

Wise PH, Pursley DM. Infant mortality as a social mirror. *N Engl J Med* 1992; 326:1558–1560.

Wolff EN. *Top Heavy: A Study of the Increasing Inequality of Wealth in America.* New York: The Twentieth Century Fund Press, 1995.

Wolinsky H. Healing wounds: Lonnie R. Bristow steps up to head the American Medical Association, one of the nation's premier—and most rigidly segregated—professional groups. *Emerge* 1994 (July/August, No. 10); 5:42.

Wolpe BC. *Lobbying Congress: How the System Works.* Washington, D.C.: CQ Press, a Division of Congressional Quarterly, Inc., 1990.

Woods CB. The neighborhood health center—the concept and the national scene. *J Natl Med Assoc* 1971; 63:52–57.

Woodson CG. *The Rural Negro.* New York: Russell and Russell, 1930.

Woodson, CG. *The Negro Professional Man and the Community.* Washington, D.C.: The Association for the Study of Negro Life and History, Inc., 1934.

Woolhandler S, Himmelstein DU. Free care: A quantitative analysis of health and cost effects of a national health program for the United States. *Int J Health Serv* 1988; 18:393–399.

Woolhandler S, Himmelstein DU. The deteriorating administrative efficiency of the U.S. health care system. *N Engl J Med* 1991; 324:1253–1258.

Woolhandler S, Himmelstein DU. *The National Health Program Chartbook.* Chartbook and

Slideshow, 1992 Edition. Cambridge, Massachusetts: Center for National Health Program Studies, 1992.

Woolhandler S, Himmelstein DU. *For Our Patients, Not for Profits: A Call to Action.* Chartbook and Slideshow, 1998 Edition. Cambridge, Massachusetts: Center for National Health Program Studies, 1998.

World Health Organization. *World Health Organization Statistics Annuals.* Vols. *1985–1990.* Geneva, 1985–1990.

Wright CH. Opposition to the World Medical Association assembly in South Africa, 1985. *J Natl Med Assoc* 1985; 78:541–542.

Wright R. The technology time bomb. *The New Republic* 208 (March 29, 1993): 25–30.

Wynes CE. *Charles Richard Drew: The Man and the Myth.* Urbana, Illinois: University of Illinois Press, 1988.

Yancy Sr. AG. The life of Charles R. Drew, M D., M.D.Sc., and perspectives of a former resident in general surgery. 63–102. In: Organ CH, Kosiba MM, eds. *A Century of Black Surgeons: The U.S.A. Experience.* 2 Vols. Norman, Oklahoma. Transcript Press, 1987.

Yergan J, Flood AB, Lo Gerfo JP, Diehr P. Relationship between patient race and the intensity of hospital services. *Med Care* 1987; 25:592–603.

Yerkes RM, ed. *Psychological Examining in the United States Army. Memoir XV.* Washington, D.C.: National Academy of Sciences, 1921.

Young Q. The urban hospital: Inequity, high tech, and low performance. 33–49. In: Sidel VW, Sidel R, eds. *Reforming Medicine: Lessons of the Last Quarter Century.* New York: Pantheon Books, 1984.

Zanca A, ed. *Pharmacy Through the Ages: From Beginnings to Modern Times.* Parma, Italy: Farmitalia Carlo Erba, 1987.

Zimmerman EL. A comparative study of syphilis in Whites and Negroes. *Archives of Dermatology and Syphilology* 1921; 4:73–74.

Zinn H. *A People's History of the United States.* New York: Harper and Row Publishers, 1980. Paperback Edition. New York: Harper Perennial, 1990.

Zuckoff M. An Australian call for justice: For the Olympics, Aborigines camp out to remind the world of a long, enduring legacy of oppression by White colonialists. *Boston Sunday Globe*, Sunday, August 20, 2000, p. 1.

# ✕ A Note on Sources

One of the major limiting factors in modern scholarship has been overspecialization. This fragmentation prevents planners from coming to grips with large issues and may be partially responsible for recent U.S. failures in domestic planning, economic planning, and government. It certainly bedevils the current attempts at health policy planning. In response to this challenge, *An American Health Dilemma. Volume I. A Medical History of African Americans and the Problem of Race: Beginnings to 1900* and Volume II. *Race, Medicine, and Health Care in the United States: 1900–2000* have been built upon an eclectic data base. Good sources translate into good results and sound conclusions. Therefore, models, hypotheses, and quantitative pronouncements in this study meet the criteria of being logically consistent and thoroughly grounded in facts. Based on these principles, it is not likely that one will go too far afield. With this in mind, a short overview on sources utilized — including a brief sampling — will reveal the "bloodlines" of these books.

By the utilization of first rate documentation, this study does not intend to be handicapped by requiring specialty-level expertise in order to express oneself, have an opinion, or form conclusions in a particular discipline. Therefore, one of the strengths of this study is the use of information in many fields. A brief survey of the academic terrain we traveled, with some of the books that served as our signposts, follows.

The medical literature was a major source of information for this study. Medical journals such as the *New England Journal of Medicine*, *The Journal of Health Care for the Poor and Underserved*, the *American Journal of Cardiology*, *The Lancet*, the *Journal of the American Medical Association*, the *Journal of the National Medical Association*, the *Annals of Internal Medicine*, the *American Heart Journal*, and many others were freely utilized. Medical textbooks such as *William's Obstetrics*, Richard Allen Williams' *Textbook of Black-Related Diseases*, *Manson's Tropical Diseases*, and *Cancer: Principles and Practice of Oncology* were also sources.

Works from the realm of public health were another resource we tapped. Examples of a few noted references used include *The American Journal of Public Health, Medical Care Research and Review, Social Science and Medicine,* the *International Journal of Health Services,* and the *Oxford Textbook of Public Health.* Harvard School of Public Health professor Deborah Prothrow-Stith's important public health study on violence, *Deadly Consequences*; David Barton Smith's unique *Health Care Divided: Race and Healing a Nation*; and Dade Moeller's contemporary work based on his broad experiences at Harvard, *Environmental Health*, were also utilized.

The sociological literature was a consistent source of useful material. Some of the classical literature in this field we utilized were W.E.B. Du Bois's *The Atlanta University Studies*, Benjamin Brawley's *A Social History of the American Negro*, Gunnar Myrdal's epochal *An American Dilemma*, E. Franklin Frazier's *The Negro Family in the United States*, and Dorothy K. Newman, Nancy J. Amidei, et al.'s *Protest, Politics, and Prosperity: Black Americans and White Institutions, 1940–75*. Some of the modern period works dealing with the problems of today are Michael Harrington's classic *The Other America*, Frances Fox Piven and Richard A. Cloward's *Regulating the Poor*, Stephen Steinberg's *The Ethnic Myth*, William Julius Wilson's *The Truly Disadvantaged* and *When Work Disappears*, Reynolds Farley and Walter R. Allen's *The Color Line and the Quality of Life in America*, Alphonso Pinkney's *The Myth of Black Progress*, and Douglas G. Glasgow's *The Black Underclass*. Recent cutting edge works in the field include Andrew Hackers' *Two Nations: Black and White, Separate, Hostile, Unequal*, Ellis Cose's *The Rage of a Privileged Class* and *Color Blind*, Joe R. Feagin and Melvin Spikes's *Living With Racism: The Black Middle-Class Experience*, Paul M. Sniderman and Thomas Piazza's *The Scar of Race*, Christopher Jencks's *Rethinking Social Policy: Race, Poverty, and the Underclass*, and Douglas A. Massey and Nancy A. Denton's *American Apartheid: Segregation and the Making of the Underclass*. From the young field of medical sociology we utilized Paul Starr's Pulitzer Prize winning *The Social Transformation of American Medicine*, Stanley Whol's *The Medical Industrial Complex*, Edward Beardsley's *A History of Neglect: Health Care for Blacks and Mill Workers in the Twentieth-Century South*, and Rosemary Stevens' *American Medicine and the Public Interest*. The origins and evolution of the American hospital system were explored in Charles Rosenberg's *The Care of Strangers: The Rise of America's Hospital System*, Rosemary Stevens's *In Sickness and in Wealth*, and Morris Vogel's *The Invention of the Modern Hospital*.

Studies from the fields of philosophy and ethics as related to "racial thought" include Michael Banton's *Racial Theories*, Lucius Outlaw's landmark article "Toward a Critical Theory of Race," included in David Theo Goldberg's *Anatomy of Racism*, Cornel West's *Race Matters*, and Timothy Simone's *About Face: Race in Postmodern America*. Reference works in the field such as *The Oxford Companion to Philosophy* and *The Cambridge Dictionary of Philosophy* were freely utilized.

Studies focused on "racial thought" in general and scientific racism in particular were invaluable. Classic works in the field such as Michael Banton and J. Harwood's *The Race Concept*, William Stanton's *The Leopard's Spots: Scientific Attitudes Toward Race in America, 1815–1859*, Winthrop Jordan's *White Over Black: American Attitudes Toward the Negro, 1550–1812*, Thomas F. Gossett's *Race: The History of an Idea in America*, Ronald Sanders' *Lost Tribes and Promised Lands: The Origins of American Racism*, George M. Fredrickson's *The Black Image in the White Mind: The Debate on Afro-American Character and Destiny, 1871–1914*, and John S. Haller, Jr.'s *Outcasts from Evolution: Scientific Attitudes of Racial Inferiority, 1859–1900* were foundations of much of the inquiry. James H. Jones's riveting study about the Tuskegee study, *Bad Blood*, served as a singular source in fields as varied as medical sociology, medical history, racism and discrimination in medicine, and medical ethics. Related works dealing specifically with race and class issues and eugenics such as Charles Benedict Davenport's *Heredity in Relation to Eugenics*, Daniel J. Kevles' *In the Name of Eugenics*, Mark H. Haller's *Eugenics: Hereditarian Attitudes in American Thought*, Robert G. Weisbord's *Genocide? Birth Control and the Black American*, Philip R. Reilly's *The Surgical Solution*, Dorothy Roberts' *Killing the Black Body*, and Troy Duster's *Backdoor to Eugenics* were especially valuable. A few other examples of the contemporaneous outpourings of scholarly literature on scientific racism and "racial thought" utilized in the books deserve mention. Some are Stephen J. Gould's *The Mismeasure of Man*, *Ever Since Darwin: Reflections in Natural History*, *The Panda's Thumb: More Reflections in Natural History*, *The Flamingo's Smile: Reflections in Natural History*, and *An Urchin In the Storm: Essays about Books and Ideas*; Allan Chase's *The Legacy of Malthus: The Social Costs of the New Scientific Racism*; R. C. Lewontin, Steven Rose, and Leon J. Kamin's *Not In Our Genes: Biology, Ideology, and Human Nature*; Pat Shipman's *The Evolution of Racism: Human Differences and the Use and Abuse of Science*; and Reginald Horsman's *Race and Manifest Destiny: The Origins of American Racial Anglo-Saxonism*. Noteworthy examinations of human experimentation, overutilization for scientific and demonstration purposes, and racial research include Jay Katz's classic *Experimentation with Human Beings*, Allen Hornblum's *Acres of Skin*, Robert Blakely and Judith Harrington's *Bones in the Basement: Postmortem Racism in Nineteenth-Century Medical Training*, Eileen Welsome's *The Plutonium Files*, Sue Schultz's *Body Snatching: The Robbing of Graves for the Education of Physicians*, and William H. Tucker's *The Science and Politics of Racial Research*. Investigations into the medical profession's preoccupation and participation in scientific racist, eugenic, and unethical human experimentation included Robert Jay Lifton's *The Nazi Doctors*, Lifton and Markusen's *The Genocidal Mentality*, Bruno Müller-Hill's *Murderous Science: Elimination by Scientific Selection of Jews, Gypsies, and Others in Germany, 1933–1945*, Robert N. Proctor's *Racial Hygiene: Medicine Under the Nazis*, Götz Aly, Peter Chroust, and Christian Pross's *Cleansing the Fatherland: Nazi Medicine and Racial Hygiene*, Michael Kater's *Doctors Under Hitler*, and Arthur L. Caplan's *When Medicine Went Mad*.

From the health policy and management literature we utilized journals such as *Health Affairs*, the *Stanford Law and Policy Review*, *Medical Care*, and the *International Journal of Health Services*. Books in the field such as Dennis Andrulis and Betsy Carrier's *Managed Care in the Inner City*, Robert Blendon's *System in Crisis: The Case for Health Care Reform* and *Reforming the System: Containing Health Care Costs in an Era of Universal Coverage*, George Anders's *Health Against Wealth: HMOs and the Breakdown of Medical Trust*, and Dave Lindorff's *Marketplace Medicine: The Rise of the For-Profit Hospital Chains* served as resources. Landmark references dealing with the recent failed health reform were Haynes Johnson and David Broder's *The System: The American Way of Politics at the Breaking Point* and Theda Skocpol's *Boomerang: Health Care Reform and the Turn Against Government*.

Political science research, especially focusing on the African American and disadvantaged experiences, provided sociocultural insights, understanding, and depth to the work. These include Frantz Fanon's *The Wretched of the Earth*, Harold Cruse's *Plural But Equal*, and Haynes Walton's *The Political Philosophy of Martin Luther King, Jr.*

Historical works served as the bedrock upon which much of the study was conducted. This too was consistent with the basic premises and goals and objectives laid out for this work, striving to perform a history-based structural analysis of the U.S. health system from an African American and disadvantaged patient perspective. Works were culled from the areas of general history, medical history, and the history of science. Some rare primary references utilized were C.V. Roman's classic *Meharry Medical College: A History*, John A. Kenney's rare and significant *The Negro in Medicine*, Julian Lewis's *The Biology of the Negro*, Samuel George Morton's *Crania Americana; or A Comparative View of the Skulls of Various Aboriginal Nations of North and South America to which is prefixed An Essay on the Varieties of the Human Species*, W. Montague Cobb's *The First Negro Medical Society: A History of the Medico-Chirurgical Society of the District of Columbia*, Robley Dunglison's *Human Physiology with Three Hundred and Sixty-Eight Illustrations*, and Josiah Clark Nott and George Gliddon's *Types of Mankind or, Ethnological Researches*. Some eclectic historical references focusing on Blacks and antiquity included the Menil Foundation and Harvard's multivolume *The Image of the Black in Western Art*, St. Clair Drake's *Black Folk Here and There*, and Martin Bernal's *Black Athena*. Ancient historical foundations were provided by Sir Moses Finley's *Ancient Slavery and Modern Ideology*, and Joseph E. Harris's *Africans and Their History*. General historical works that are more readily available are J. Mark Roberts's *The Triumph of the West* and the *History of the World*, Lerone Bennett's *Before the Mayflower*, Ronald Takaki's *Iron Cages*, W.E.B. Du Bois's *The Suppression of the African Slave Trade*, and John Hope Franklin's *From Slavery to Freedom*. They were extremely useful. Works focusing specifically on American history such as Alan Brinkley's *The Unfinished Nation: A Concise History of the American People*, and Howard Zinn's *A Peoples History of the United States* were also necessary to complete the undertaking. Specialized works focusing on African Americans such as Manning Marable's *Race, Reform, and Rebellion: The Second Reconstruction in Black America, 1945–1990* and Nicholas Leamann's *The Promised Land: The Great Black Migration and How It Changed America* were also useful.

General medical historical works that proved useful were Albert S. Lyons and R. Joseph Petrucelli's epochal *Medicine: An Illustrated History*, Douglas Guthrie's *A History of Medicine*, Castiglioni's *A History of Medicine*, Richard Harrison Shryock's *The Development of Modern Medicine: An Interpretation of the Social and Scientific Factors Involved*, Erwin Ackernecht's *A Short History of Medicine*, Jurgen Thorwald's *Science and Secrets of Early Medicine: Egypt, Babylonia, India, China, Mexico, Peru*, W. B. Blanton's *Medicine in Virginia in the Seventeenth Century* and *Medicine in Virginia in the Eighteenth Century*, George A. Bender's *Great Moments in Medicine*, Ronald Numbers's *Medicine in the New World*, Nancy Sirasi's *Medieval and Early Renaissance Medicine*, and Guido Majno's *The Healing Hand*. There were a few medical history works that included significant information about the African American experience in the health system. Some of these include Herbert Morais's *The History of the Negro in Medicine*, Vanessa Northington Gamble's *Making a Place for Ourselves: The Black Hospital Movement, 1920–1945*, Darlene Clark Hine's *Black Women in White: Racial Conflict and Cooperation in the Nursing Profession, 1890–1950*, Harry F. Dowling's *City Hospitals: Undercare of the Underprivileged*, and James Summerville's *Educating Black Doctors*. Other medical history works such as Todd Savitt's classic *Medicine and Slavery: The Diseases and Health Care of Blacks in Antebellum Virginia*, Richard Sheridan's *Doctors and Slaves: A Medical and Demographic History of Slavery in the British West Indies, 1680–1834*, and William Postell's *The Health of Slaves on Southern Plantations*, contained huge amounts of information on Blacks in the health system, and proved to be immensely valuable. The few modern monographs on African American health included Ivor Livingston's *Handbook of Black American Health: The Mosaic of Conditions, Issues, Policies, and Prospects*, Woodrow Jones and Mitchell Rice's *Health Care Issues in Black America*, and Ronald Braithwaite and Sandra Taylor's *Health Issues in the Black Community*.

Historic epidemiologic information about African Americans was culled from works as disparate as Leslie Howard Owen's *This Species of Property: Slave Life and Culture in the Old South*, Philip Curtin's *The Atlantic Slave Trade: A Census*, John W. Blassingame's *The Slave Community* and *Black New Orleans, 1860–1880*, Jack Gratus's *The Great White Lie: Slavery, Emancipation, and Changing Racial Attitudes*, James Pope-Hennessy's *Sins of the Fathers: A Study of the Atlantic Slave Traders, 1441–1807*, and Daniel P. Mannix and Malcolm Cowley's *Black Cargoes: A History of the Atlantic Slave Trade*, and Sir Hugh Thomas's *The Slave Trade*. Epidemiologically oriented works containing more contemporary information such as Oliver Ransford's *Bid the Sickness Cease: Disease in the History of Black Africa*, Reynolds Farley's *Growth of the Black Population*, Edward Byron Reuter's

*The American Race Problem*, Abraham and David Lilienfeld's *Foundations of Epidemiology*, and Charles H. Hennekens and Julie E. Buring's *Epidemiology in Medicine*, were all useful in different ways. Douglas Ewbank's landmark article, "History of Black mortality and health before 1940," in the book edited by D.P. Willis, *Health Policies and Black Americans*, proved especially valuable as a rare source quantitatively evaluating the African American health experience over time. Ewbanks also applied the latest statistical methodology to old data and resurrected some unutilized data bases on the subject.

Health policy monographs provided historical and contemporary perspective regarding the U.S. health system. Works covering earlier periods included Ronald Numbers' *Almost Persuaded: American Physicians and Compulsory Health Insurance, 1912–1920*, E. Richard Brown's *Rockefeller Medicine Men: Medicine and Capitalism in America*, Daniel S. Hirshfield's *The Lost Reform: The Campaign for Compulsory Health Insurance in the United States 1932 to 1943*, Ed Cray's *In Failing Health: The Medical Crisis and the A.M.A*, B. Bullough and Vern L. Bullough's *Poverty, Ethnic Identity, and Health Care*, and Barbara and John Ehrenreich's *The American Health Empire: Power, Profits, and Politics*. More contemporary perspectives were gained by researching Victor and Ruth Sidel's *Reforming Medicine: Lessons of the Last Quarter Century*, Rosemary Stevens' *In Sickness and in Wealth: American Hospitals in the Twentieth Century*, Eli Ginzberg's *The Medical Triangle: Physicians, Politicians, and the Public* and *Teaching Hospitals and the Urban Poor*, and Walt Bogdanich's *The Great White Lie: Dishonesty, Waste, and Incompetence in the Medical Community*. Valuable sources in health policy and economics were Victor Fuch's *The Health Economy* and *The Future of Health Policy*, Henry Aaron's *Serious and Unstable Condition: Financing America's Health Care*, Aaron and Schwartz's *The Painful Prescription: Rationing Hospital Care*, and Vincente Navarro's *Dangerous to Your Health: Capitalism in Health Care*.

Periodicals proved to be particularly useful. Some of the most important newspapers include the *New York Times*, *The Boston Globe*, the *Wall Street Journal*, the *Dallas Morning News*, *The Washington Post*, and the *Detroit News*. Relevant information from magazines such as *The New Republic*, *Emerge*, *The Atlantic Monthly*, *The Crisis*, *Ebony*, *Time*, *U.S. News and World Report*, and *Newsweek* was also used.

Public documents were invaluable. Some of the more prominent ones include *The Report of the Secretary's Task Force on Black and Minority Health*, *The Health Status of Minorities and Low Income Groups*, and issues of *Health United States* from the 1980s to 2000.

Research foundation, community organization, and voluntary health organization documents and reports were useful. Some of the important ones utilized include the American Cancer Society's *Cancer Facts and Figures*, the Children's Defense Fund's *America's Children in Poverty*, the Twentieth Century Fund reports *The Profit Motive and Patient Care: The Changing Accountability of*

*Doctors and Hospitals* and *Top Heavy: A Study of Increasing Inequality of Wealth in America*, the National Research Council's *A Common Destiny: Blacks and American Society*, and the National Urban League's *The State of Black America*.

Psychiatric and behavioral science references proved to be a mother lode of information, especially about the dynamics of prejudice in Western society in general, U.S. society in particular, and in the learned professions. Classic works such as T.W. Adorno, Else Frenkel-Brunswik, Daniel J. Levinson, and R. Nevitt Sanford's *The Authoritarian Personality*, and Gordon Allport's *The Nature of* Prejudice, lived up to their reputations. Some particularly valuable works were Jacques Barzun's *Race: A Study in Superstition*, Pierre van den Berghe's *Race and Racism: A Comparative Perspective*, Joel Kovel's *White Racism: A Psychohistory*, Frances Cress Welsing's *The Isis Papers*, Patricia Turner's *Ceramic Uncles and Celluloid Mammies: Black Images and Their Influence on Culture*, and Robert Terry's revised edition of *For Whites Only*.

Medical ethics works proved to be extremely valuable in lending perspective, condemning past blunders, and proposing health system solutions grounded in medical ethical principles. Some especially useful ones include Robert M. Veatch's *A Theory of Medical Ethics*, Joel Reiser, Arthur J. Dyck, and William J. Curran's *Ethics in Medicine*, George J. Annas and Michael A. Grodin's *The Nazi Doctors and the Nuremberg Code: Human Rights in Human Experimentation*, and Larry Churchill's *Rationing Health Care in America* and *Value-Free Science?*.

An unexpected gold mine of information on African American health and the sociocultural environments producing it proved to be biographical literature. Some of the outstanding sources were J. Edward Perry's *Forty Cords of Wood: Memoirs of a Medical Doctor*, Fawn Brody's *Thomas Jefferson*, Helen Buckler's *Daniel Hale Williams: Negro Surgeon*, and Kenneth Manning's epochal *Ernest Everett Just: Black Apollo of Science*. Deeper insights into the growth of scientific racism and Black and poor patient abuse were also obtained from biographical works such as Reginald Horsman's *Josiah Nott of Mobile: Southerner, Physician, and Racial Theorist*, and Deborah Kuhn McGregor's *Sexual Surgery and the Origins of Gynecology: J. Marion Sims, His Hospital, and His Patients*.

Determining the legal status of African Americans throughout their sojourn in North America, especially in relation to the health system, was critical. Sound legal scholarship with the requisite health-care ramifications was available in A. Leon Higginbotham, Jr.'s classics *In the Matter of Color: Race and the American Legal Process, The Colonial Period* and *Shades of Freedom: Racial Politics and Presumptions of the American Legal Process*; Areen, King, Goldberg, Gostin, and Capron's *Law, Science and Medicine*; Fineberg, Peters, Willson, and Kroll's *Obstetrics/Gynecology and the Law*; and Havighurst's *Health Care Law and Policy: Readings, Notes, and Questions*. Richard Kluger's magisterial *Simple Justice: The History of Brown v. Board of Education and Black America's Struggle for Equality* also proved invaluable in adding legal context to the African American experience.

# ✕ Credits

## 810 ■ Credits

p. 491, Figure 7.2  From P.R. Lee, A.E. Benjamin, M.A. Weber, *Policies and strategies for health in the United States*. In: R. Detels, M.W. Holland, J. McEwan, GS Omenn, eds. *Oxford Textbook of Public Health*, vol. 1: *The Scope of Public Health*. 3ʳᵈ ed. New York: Oxford University Press, 1997.

p. 505, Figure 7.3  From *Jona's Health Care Delivery in the United States*. Fifth Edition. Copyright © 1995. Used by permission from Springer Publishing Company, Inc., New York, 10012.

p. 512, Figure 7.4  From *Dangerous to Your Health: Capitalism in Health Care* by V. Navarro. Copyright © 1993. Reprinted by permission from the Monthly Review Foundation.

p. 558, Figure 7.5  From *The Sphinx* 75, no. 4 (Winter 1989), *cover*. Reprinted with permission from Louis W. Sullivan.

# ⟩⟨ Index